Part 4

Pay, Benefits, Terms and Conditions of Employment

Part 5

Managing Performance

Part 6

Terminating Employment

- Employment at Will with Exceptions

- Just Cause

- Due Process

- Downsizing

Employment Law for Human Resource Practice

Employment Law for Human Resource Practice

FOURTH EDITION

DAVID J. WALSH

Miami University

SOUTH-WESTERN
CENGAGE Learning·

Australia • Brazil • Japan • Korea • Mexico • Singapore • Spain • United Kingdom • United States

SOUTH-WESTERN
CENGAGE Learning

Employment Law for Human Resource Practice, Fourth Edition
David J. Walsh

Vice President of Editorial/Business: Jack W. Calhoun

Editor-in-Chief (or Publisher): Rob Dewey

Senior Acquisition Editor: Vicky True-Baker

Developmental Editor: Ted Knight

Editorial Assistant: Ben Genise

Marketing Manager: Laura-Aurora Stopa

Senior Marketing Communications Manager: Sarah Greber

Senior Media Editor: Kristen Meere

Rights Acquisition Specialist, Text: Amber Hosea

Manufacturing Planner: Kevin Kluck

Production Management and Composition: PreMediaGlobal

Senior Art Director: Michelle Kunkler

Cover Designer: Rokusek Design

Cover Image(s): © Gilmanshin/Shutterstock

For product information and technology assistance, contact us at **Cengage Learning Customer & Sales Support, 1-800-354-9706**

For permission to use material from this text or product, submit all requests online at **www.cengage.com/permissions**. Further permissions questions can be emailed to **permissionrequest@cengage.com**

Library of Congress Control Number: 2012931265

ISBN-13: 978-1-111-97219-6

ISBN-10: 1-111-97219-2

South-Western
5191 Natorp Boulevard
Mason, OH 45040
USA

Cengage Learning products are represented in Canada by Nelson Education, Ltd.

For your course and learning solutions, visit **www.cengage.com**

Purchase any of our products at your local college store or at our preferred online store **www.cengagebrain.com**.

Printed in the United States of America
1 2 3 4 5 6 7 16 15 14 13 12

Brief Contents

Contents

PART 2   The Hiring Process

PART 3   Managing a Diverse Workforce

PART 6   Terminating Employment

Preface

This is a book about employment law—the set of legal requirements that govern the workplace. A distinction is often made between "employment law" and "labor law" (the latter describing laws related to unions and collective bargaining), but I will generally use the term *employment law* to refer to both. This book has two main objectives. The first is to *explain the major issues and rules of employment law*. What things are legal matters? What does the law say about those matters? The second objective is to *explain what employment law means for human resource practice*. What is it that employers should be doing to comply with the law? What is the legal reasoning behind this practical advice?

Special Features of This Text

Unique Employment Life Cycle Approach

This dual purpose of understanding the substance of employment law and its implications for human resource practice accounts for the way this book is organized. The first three chapters provide broad overviews. The remainder of the book traces the steps in the employment process and addresses the particular legal issues associated with them. We start with issues that lead up to hiring and promotion, including recruitment, interviewing, background checks, references, and employment testing. We then turn to a range of issues that arise when a person is on the job, including harassment, reasonable accommodation of disability, compensation, benefits, performance appraisal, and occupational safety and health. The last two chapters of the book deal with issues related to the termination of employment. This structure is intended to highlight the legal issues that managers regularly confront.

> *The employee life cycle approach to this text offers students the ability to understand the employment process, from beginning to end, while considering the legal environment and its implications for business success. Walsh's personnel law book provides a solid foundation for students to successfully navigate the always changing and rarely certain areas of personnel law within an organization.*
> Professor Sarah Sanders Smith, SPHR, Purdue University

> *Of all of the texts that I reviewed, this one has the most practical and usable advice for soon-be-HR practitioners. The life cycle approach is strong and the writing easy to read.*
> Nancy K. Lahmers, JD, The Ohio State University

Practical Focus

This book is full of advice for carrying out human resource activities in a lawful manner. *These guidelines are general principles for sound human resource practice. They cannot be—and do not purport to be—specific legal advice for particular situations that you might encounter. Only a trained legal professional thoroughly familiar with the details of your case can provide the latter.*

> *This text offers a unique human resource perspective of employment law that is typically not afforded attention in other comparable texts.*
> Dr. Kim LaFevor, Athens State University

Clippings This feature consists of brief synopses of recent cases, events, or studies that illustrate the issues dealt with in each chapter. The clippings should pique your interest and begin to show how employment law relates to real things that are happening in the world around us.

> *I love the Clippings features—they are well chosen and give the students a great intro into why what we are covering is relevant to their businesses.*
> *Alexis C. Knapp, Houston Baptist University*

The Changing Workplace This feature adds a forward-looking flavor to the book by highlighting contemporary developments in the workplace, the workforce, and human resource practices that have particular implications for the law. The business world is nothing if not dynamic. Changes in the workplace raise new legal questions and point to the types of legal disputes that we can expect to see more of in the future.

Just the Facts This feature provides facts from some interesting and recent court decisions. Thinking through these cases and arriving at a decision is a great way to test your grasp of legal concepts. In this feature, you are not told the outcomes of the cases; instead, you are given the information needed to make your own determinations ("just the facts"). Use the citations provided to look up the decisions to check your conclusions against the decisions of the courts. Or maybe you can prevail upon your instructor to "spill the beans."

Practical Considerations Employers need to follow many rules to meet their legal obligations to employees. But legal compliance is not entirely cutanddried. Managers have many choices about how to comply with the law, and this feature highlights some of those choices.

Elements of a Claim In any situation that gives rise to a legal dispute, numerous facts might be considered. The facts that we deem most relevant and the order in which we consider them go a long way toward determining the outcome of our deliberations. When judges decide cases, they typically rely on established frameworks that spell out a methodology for deciding those cases. Who has the burden of proof? What must the plaintiff show? What must the defendant show? In what order should certain facts be considered? This feature lays out these frameworks—the "elements" of particular legal claims. Grasping this information gives us real insight into how cases are decided. Judges still exercise considerable discretion and judgment in applying these frameworks, but they make the process of arriving at decisions in legal disputes far more systematic and consistent than it would otherwise be.

Practical Implications of the Law Each chapter in this book contains many suggestions for carrying out human resource activities in a lawful manner. This advice appears in italics to make it stand out from the rest of the text. But the advice should still be considered in the context of the specific legal problems that it aims to help employers avoid. *It is important to know not only what to do but also why those things should be done.*

The law is a basic determinant of human resource practice and one that cannot be ignored. However, the law is best conceived of as providing a "floor," rather than a "ceiling," for human resource practices. It establishes minimum standards of acceptable treatment of employees, but often it is sensible for employers—based on motivational, pragmatic, or ethical considerations—to go well beyond the bare minimum legal requirements. Thus, our purpose in understanding what the law requires is not to identify "loopholes" that can be exploited or to advocate superficial measures that look good on paper but fail to realize the underlying purposes (e.g., equal employment opportunity) of the law. Instead, *this book encourages you to embrace the "spirit"—and not merely the "letter"—of the law. It invites you to consider how to achieve these important social purposes by implementing policies and practices that also make sense given the operational realities of the workplace.*

Practical Advice Summary For easy reference, the practical advice sprinkled liberally throughout chapters is collected at the end of each chapter. This summary can be used as a convenient "checklist" for legal compliance.

Legal Cases

Each chapter contains three or four substantial excerpts from decisions in court cases. One of the things that is unusual (and admirable) about legal decision making is that the decision makers (e.g., judges) set down in writing their rationale for the decisions they make in the cases that are brought before them. This gives us the opportunity to read firsthand accounts of legal disputes, to have the decision makers explain the relevant rules of law, and to see how those principles were applied to the facts of cases. I describe the law and other cases for you as well, but there is nothing like reading cases to get a real feel for the law. Getting comfortable with reading legal cases is a bit like learning a new language. It will take some doing, but with diligent effort and practice, it will pay off in terms of enhanced ability to access and understand the law.

The words in the case excerpts are the same as those you would find if you looked up the cases online or in print. However, to maximize readability, I have shortened the case decisions by focusing on a brief statement of the facts, the legal issue, and (at greatest length) the explanation of the decision maker's rationale. Where part of a sentence is removed, you will see three dots (. . .). Where more than part of a sentence is removed, you will see three stars (* * *). This is to alert you that text has been removed from the full case decision. Legal decisions are replete with numerous footnotes and citations to previous cases that addressed similar questions. In most instances, I have removed the citations and footnotes from the case excerpts. Occasionally, I have included in brackets [ ] a brief explanation of a legal term.

What Is New in This Edition

This edition of *Employment Law for Human Resource Practice* retains the essential structure and focus of the previous editions. Linking a thorough understanding of principles of employment law to advice on how to conduct human resource practice remains the central aim of this book. Consistent with this aim, the book continues to be organized around stages in the employment process, from the formation of an employment relationship through the termination of that relationship. This fourth edition is the product of a thorough, line-by-line revision of the previous edition, aimed at enhancing clarity and ensuring that the material is as current as possible. Users of this text will find a significant number of new case excerpts. Over half of the chapter cases are new to this edition. If, through a lapse in taste or judgment, I have eliminated one of your favorite cases from the previous edition, chances are the case still appears somewhere in this edition, perhaps as a new end-of-chapter question. I have also included many new case problems to puzzle over. My hope is that both students who are reading this book for the first time and instructors who have used previous editions will find it engaging and informative.

Significant Revisions

Here are some highlights of the revised contents of this edition.

- **Chapter 1:** *This chapter includes three new excerpted cases. The issues of limitations periods for filing legal claims and class action lawsuits receive more extensive treatment. The Supreme Court's decision in* Wal-Mart v. Dukes *(certification of class action lawsuits) is among the new chapter cases. The discussion of limitations period includes consideration of the Lilly Ledbetter Fair Pay Act.*

- **Chapter 2:** *This chapter extends and updates the previous edition's discussion of the misclassification of employees as independent contractors. Close attention is also paid to the employment status of unpaid interns. New chapter cases include* Solis v. Laurelbrook Sanitarium and School *(status of student workers).*

- **Chapter 3:** *The centrality of EEO laws to employment law is well reflected in this chapter. All three of the cases excerpted in this chapter are new to this edition. Chapter cases include* Jones v. Oklahoma City Public Schools *and* Hasan v. Foley & Lardner LLC. *There are new or enhanced discussions of the subordinate bias theory, "but for" causation, mixed-motives, the distinction between direct and circumstantial evidence of discrimination, and retaliation.*

- **Chapter 4:** *New to this chapter is a discussion of the problem of labor trafficking. The issue of employers refusing to hire the long-term unemployed is also raised. A new chapter case on preemployment medical inquiries,* Harrison v. Benchmark Electronics Huntsville, *is included.*

- **Chapter 5:** *Coverage of immigration, undocumented workers, and recent changes in the enforcement of immigration laws is expanded and updated. Legal issues surrounding the use of credit reports and credit information receive closer attention. A Fair Credit Reporting Act case,* Burghy v. Dayton Racquet Club, *is one of two new chapter cases.*

- **Chapter 6:** *The coverage of medical exams and the use of medical information in making employment decisions is expanded in this edition.* Brownfield v. City of Yakima, *an ADA case on medical testing, is new to this edition. There is also an expanded discussion of the Genetic Information Nondiscrimination Act (GINA) and consideration of the implications of the Supreme Court's* Ricci *decision for dealing with employment tests that have adverse impact.*

- **Chapter 7:** *There are two new cases in this chapter, including an interesting sex-stereotyping case (*Lewis v. Heartland Inns of America*). The discussion of legal issues surrounding employment interviews is expanded.*

- **Chapter 8:** *A new chapter case,* Lomack v. City of Newark, *is included. There is a new discussion of the affirmative action responsibilities of subcontractors.*

- **Chapter 9:** *Two new cases are excerpted in this chapter. New chapter cases include* EEOC v. Fairbrook Medical Clinic, P.A. *(hostile environment resulting from verbal conduct). Treatment of workplace bullying and racial harassment is expanded.*

- **Chapter 10:** *Two new ADA cases are excerpted in this chapter. The ADA Amendments Act (ADAA) and the EEOC's guidelines interpreting the ADAA are covered in some detail. A new "Changing Workplace" feature focuses on religion in the workplace and discrimination experienced by Muslim employees.*

- **Chapter 11:** *Substantial coverage of the Family and Medical Leave Act is retained and updated. A new FMLA case,* Scobey v. Nucor Steel-Arkansas *(notification of the need for FMLA leave), is included. The repeal of the military's "don't ask, don't tell" policy is discussed.*

- **Chapter 12:** *The discussion of the blurring of work and nonwork time (e.g., employees' use of BlackBerry and other communication devices to check e-mail and perform work from home) and its relationship to compensable time under the FLSA is expanded. A new chapter case,* Whalen v. J.P. Morgan Chase, *takes up the question of whether loan underwriters for a bank are exempt administrative employees.*
- **Chapter 13:** *The Patient Protection and Affordable Care Act is examined in some depth. The discussion of the fiduciary duties of employers with defined contribution benefit plans is updated and expanded.*
- **Chapter 14:** *Two new cases are excerpted in this chapter, including* NLRB v. Whitesell Corp. *(duty to bargain in good faith). There are new or expanded discussions of a number of topics including employee use of social media to discuss employment issues, the "recognition bar," and challenges to the collective bargaining rights of public employees.*
- **Chapter 15:** *Clippings are included of significant, recent workplace safety disasters, including the explosions at the Upper Big Branch mine and BP's Deepwater Horizon oil rig. Discussion of intentional injuries falling outside of workers' compensation coverage is updated and expanded.*
- **Chapter 16:** *A new chapter case on discrimination in performance appraisals,* Senske v. Sybase, *is included. The discussion of the enforceability of training contracts is updated and expanded.*
- **Chapter 17:** *Two new cases are excerpted in this chapter. The privacy of employees' electronic communications receives added attention. New chapter cases include* Hernandez v. Hillsides *(covert video surveillance) and* Stengart v. Loving Care Agency *(privacy of e-mails).*
- **Chapter 18:** *Three new cases, including* Danny v. Laidlaw Transit Services *(public policy exception to employment at will) and* Decotiis v. Whittemore *(speech rights of public employees), are excerpted in this chapter. Whistleblower protection, including under Sarbanes-Oxley and the Dodd-Frank Wall Street Reform and Consumer Protection Act, is given expanded coverage in this edition.*
- **Chapter 19:** *Chapter cases new to this edition include* Collins v. Gee West Seattle *(WARN Act) and* Proudfoot Consulting v. Gordon *(enforceability of non-competition agreements).*

Instructor Resources

Instructor's Manual

www.cengagebrain.com

The Instructor's Manual for this edition of *Employment Law for Human Resource Practice* provides a succinct chapter outline, answers to questions raised in the "Just the Facts" and "Practical Considerations" features, answers to case questions following excerpted cases, answers to end-of-chapter questions, and suggestions for in-class exercises and discussions (including role-plays, practical exercises, and more).

Test Bank

www.cengagebrain.com

The Test Bank questions for this edition not only test student comprehension of key concepts but also focus on business application and ethical implications. The questions have been updated to reflect the new content and cases of the fourth edition and expanded to include hypothetical questions that ask what the student, as a human resources manager, should do in particular situations. Donna J. Cunningham of Valdosta State University edited and updated the Test Bank for the fourth edition.

PowerPoint Slides

www.cengagebrain.com

PowerPoint slides have been created to highlight the key learning objectives in each chapter—including case summaries and hyperlinks to relevant materials. In addition, "Smart Practice" and "What Would You Do?" slides emphasize applying legal concepts to business situations (answers to these questions are provided in "Instructor's Note" slides at the end of the presentation). The PowerPoint slides were prepared by Donna J. Cunningham of Valdosta State University.

Text Companion Web Site

www.cengagebrain.com

The companion Web site for this edition of *Employment Law for Human Resource Practice* has been greatly enhanced to streamline necessary resources. In addition to providing access to the Instructor's Manual, Test Bank, PowerPoint slides, and Court Case Updates, the Web site now offers links to the following: important labor and employment law sites, labor and employment law blogs, legal forms and documents, free legal research sites (comprehensive and circuit-specific), help in the classroom, labor and employment law directories, departments, agencies, associations, and organizations. In addition, a list of recent labor and employment law cases with links to each full case is available.

Court Case Updates

www.cengagebrain.com

South-Western's Court Case Updates provide monthly summaries of the most important legal cases happening around the country.

Westlaw Access

www.westlaw.com

Westlaw, West Group's vast online source of value-added legal and business information, contains more than 15,000 databases of information spanning a variety of jurisdictions, practice areas, and disciplines. Qualified instructors may receive ten complimentary hours of Westlaw for their course (certain restrictions apply; contact your South-Western sales representative for details).

Business Law Digital Video Library

www.cengagebrain.com

This dynamic online video library features more than sixty video clips that spark class discussion and clarify core legal principles, including fourteen videos that address employment law topics (such as employment at will, employment discrimination, and employee privacy). The library is organized into four series:

- *Legal Conflicts in Business* includes specific modern business and e-commerce scenarios.
- *Ask the Instructor* contains straightforward explanations of concepts for student review.
- *Drama of the Law* features classic business scenarios that spark classroom participation.
- *LawFlix* contains clips from many popular films, including Bowfinger, The Money Pit, Midnight Run, and Casino.

Access to the Business Law Digital Video Library is available at no additional charge as an optional package with each new student text. Contact your South-Western sales representative for details.

Business Law Community Web Site

www.cengage.com/community/blaw

Visit South-Western's Community Web site for a wealth of resources to help you deliver the most effective course possible, including our "Great Ideas in Teaching Business Law" section. Our Community Web site offers teaching tips and ideas for making the subject interesting and appealing to your students. Ideas include class presentations, discussion topics, research projects, and more.

Note to the Instructor

Since I have been touting the contents of this book, it is only fair to acknowledge material that is largely omitted. Beyond a glancing blow struck in Chapter 1, this book provides relatively little information about such matters as the legislative process, courtroom procedures, and the historical development of employment laws. These are all worthwhile topics, but they are not emphasized in this book because its focus is the current substance of employment law and the implications for human resource practice. The treatment of labor law in this book does not reach a number of the more specialized issues in this area, but I do attempt to show how labor law continues to be relevant to both unionized and nonunion workplaces. Additionally, while cross-national comparisons can enhance our understanding of U.S. law, a comparative perspective is beyond the scope of this book.

In appreciation of my wife Susan and in memory of our buddy, Baxter the cat.

Acknowledgments

Thanks to the many faculty and students who have used *Employment Law for Human Resource Practice*. I hope that this edition will serve your needs even better. If you are not presently using this book, I hope that you will consider adopting it. Please do not hesitate to contact me regarding any questions you have about the book (and ancillary materials) or suggestions for improvement (walshdj@muohio.edu).

Many thanks also to numerous others at Cengage and its business partners. Being an author provides a small glimpse of the "cast of thousands" who are needed to produce a work of this type.

Finally, I wish to thank and publicly acknowledge the following individuals who provided valuable comments and suggestions that helped shape this edition and previous editions:

FREDERICK R. BRODZINSKI
The City College of New York

LISA A. BURKE
University of Tennessee at Chattanooga

BRUCE W. BYARS
University of North Dakota

TERRY CONRY
Ohio University

DIYA DAS
Bryant University

THOMAS DAYMONT
Temple University

LINDA SUE FICHT
Indiana University, Kokomo

JASON M. HARRIS
Augustana College

MICHAEL A. KATZ
Delaware State University

ALEXIS C. KNAPP
Houston Baptist University

KIM LAFEVOR
Athens State University

NANCY K. LAHMERS
The Ohio State University

SUSAN LUBINSKI
Slippery Rock University

JEANNE M. MACDONALD
Dickinson State University

JAMES F. MORGAN
California State University, Chico

DIANE M. PFADENHAUER
St. Joseph's College

SARAH SANDERS SMITH
Purdue University North Central

VICKI FAIRBANKS TAYLOR
Shippensburg University

CHRISTINE M. WESTPHAL
Suffolk University

PART 1

Introduction to Employment Law

CHAPTER **1**

Overview of Employment Law

The purpose of this first chapter is to present a big picture of the body of law that we will apply to particular human resource practices throughout this book. This chapter contains an overview of employment laws, the rights they confer on employees, and the processes involved in enforcing these laws. Special attention is given to the use of alternatives to litigation to resolve employment disputes.

Heard at the Staff Meeting

Congratulations on your new job as human resources manager! You pour a cup of coffee and settle into your seat to hear the following reports from staff members:

> *"We've lined up some interns from a local college to take the place of vacationing staff members this summer. We won't pay the interns, of course, but hopefully they will be self-starters who can make a real contribution."*
>
> *"One of our employees recently converted to Islam. She says that her faith requires her to wear a hijab [head scarf] when out in public. We informed her that she would not be able to do so because this would violate our dress policy."*
>
> *"A number of our employees are in the Army Reserves. One of them has been deployed to Afghanistan twice and has missed more than two years of work. She will be returning to the United States soon and has indicated that she wants her job back. Her supervisor believes that since her job skills are now out of date and she might be deployed again at any time, it would be best not to reinstate her."*
>
> *"With health insurance being so expensive these days, we're requiring all of our applicants to complete lengthy medical histories, including whether certain diseases run in their families."*

You get up to get another—large—cup of coffee and feel fortunate that you were paying attention during that employment law class you took.

What legal issues emerged during this staff meeting? What should this company be doing differently to better comply with the law? Although you might not encounter this many legal problems in one sitting, employment law pervades virtually every aspect of human resource practice and managers regularly confront employment law questions.

U.S. Employment Law Is a Fragmented Work in Progress

"Just tell me what the law is, and I'll follow it." Were matters only that simple! No single set of employment laws covers all workers in the United States. Instead, the employment

3

law system is a patchwork of federal, state, and local laws. Whether and how laws apply also depend on such things as whether the employees work for the government or in the private sector, whether they have union representation, and the size of their employer. Our principal focus will be on federal laws because these reach most widely across U.S. workplaces and often serve as models for state and local laws. However, we will also mention significant variations in the employment laws of different states.

There is another problem with the idea of just learning the legal rules and adhering to them. Employment law is dynamic. New law is created and old law is reinterpreted continuously. Further, changing workplace practices pose new legal questions. At any point in time, there are "well-settled" legal questions on which there is consensus, other matters that are only partially settled (perhaps because only a few cases have arisen or because courts have issued conflicting decisions), and still other questions that have yet to be considered by the courts and other legal decision makers. Attaining a solid grasp of employment law principles will allow you to make informed judgments in most situations. You must be prepared to tolerate some ambiguity and keep learning, however, as the law of the workplace continues to develop.

Sources of Employment Law

What comes to mind when you think of the law? Judges making decisions in court cases? Congress legislating? The Constitution? All of these are parts of the law in general and employment law in particular. Legal rules governing the workplace are found in the U.S. Constitution and state constitutions, statutes enacted by legislatures, executive orders issued by presidents and governors, regulations created by administrative agencies, and judicially authored common law. All of these pieces of law are regularly interpreted and expanded on by the courts as they are presented with specific legal disputes (cases) to decide. Distinguishing between these basic sources of law is useful because some forms of law are more authoritative than others, apply to particular groups of employees, or provide for different enforcement mechanisms and remedies.

Constitutions

Constitutions are the most basic source of law. **Constitutions** address the relationships between different levels of government (e.g., states and the federal government) and between governments and their citizens. A legal claim based on a constitution must generally assert a violation of someone's constitutional rights by the government (in legal parlance, the element of "state action" must be present). In practical terms, this means that usually only employees of government agencies—and not employees of private corporations—can look to the U.S. Constitution or state constitutions for protection in the workplace. Examples of constitutional protections available to government employees include speech rights, freedom of religion, protection from unreasonable search and seizure, equal protection under the law, and due process rights.

Statutes

In the U.S. democratic system, voters elect representatives to legislative bodies such as the U.S. Congress. These bodies enact laws, or **statutes**, many of which affect the workplace. Among the many important statutes with implications for human resource practice are Title VII of the Civil Rights Act, the National Labor Relations Act, the Equal Pay Act, the Americans with Disabilities Act, the Family and Medical Leave Act, and the Employee Retirement Income Security Act.

Executive Orders

The executive branch of government has the power to issue executive orders that affect the employment practices of government agencies and companies that have contracts to provide goods and services to the government. **Executive orders** function much like statutes, although they reach fewer workplaces and can be overridden by the legislative branch. One important example of an executive order affecting employment is Executive Order (E.O.) 11246, which establishes affirmative action requirements for companies that do business with the federal government.

Regulations, Guidelines, and Administrative Decisions

When Congress enacts a statute, it often creates an agency, or authorizes an existing one, to administer and enforce that law. Legislators do not have the expertise (and sometimes do not have the political will) to fill in all the details necessary to put statutes into practice. For example, Congress mandated in the Occupational Safety and Health Act that employers provide safe workplaces but largely left it to the Occupational Safety and Health Administration (OSHA) to give content to that broad principle by promulgating safety standards governing particular workplace hazards. Formal **regulations** are put in place only after an elaborate set of requirements for public comment and review has been followed. Regulations are entitled to considerable deference from the courts (generally, they will be upheld when challenged), provided that the regulations are viewed as reasonable interpretations of the statutes on which they are based.[1] Agencies also contribute to the law through their decisions in individual cases that are brought before them and the guidance that they provide in complying with laws.

Common Law

Many disputes are resolved through courts interpreting and enforcing the types of law discussed earlier. However, sometimes courts are asked to resolve disputes over matters that have not been objects of legislation or regulation. Over time, courts have recognized certain **common law** claims to remedy harm to people caused by other people or companies. Common law is defined by state courts, but broad similarities exist across states. One branch of common law is the traditional role of the courts in interpreting and enforcing contracts. The other branch is recognition of various **tort** claims for civil wrongs that harm people. Tort claims relevant to employment law include negligence, defamation, invasion of privacy, infliction of emotional distress, and wrongful discharge in violation of public policy.

Substantive Rights Under Employment Laws

Employment laws confer rights on employees and impose corresponding responsibilities on employers. Paradoxically, the starting point for understanding employee rights is a legal doctrine holding that employees do not have any right to be employed or to retain their employment. This doctrine, known as **employment at will**, holds that in the absence of a contract promising employment for a specified duration, the employment relationship can be severed at any time and for any reason not specifically prohibited by law. Statutory and other rights conferred on employees have significantly blunted the force of employment at will. But in the absence of any clear right that employees can assert not to be terminated, employment at will is the default rule that permits employers to terminate employment without needing to have "good" reasons for doing so.

Broadly speaking, employees have the following rights under employment laws.

---

[1]*Chevron U.S.A., Inc. v. National Resources Defense Council*, 467 U.S. 837 (1984).

Nondiscrimination and Equal Employment Opportunity

A central part of employment law is the set of protections for employees against discrimination based on their race, sex, age, and other grounds. The equal protection provisions of the U.S. Constitution (Fourteenth Amendment), Title VII of the Civil Rights Act of 1964, the Age Discrimination in Employment Act, the Equal Pay Act, and the Americans with Disabilities Act are examples of federal laws that prohibit discrimination in employment and express the societal value of equal employment opportunity.

Freedom to Engage in Concerted Activity and Collective Bargaining

Another approach to protecting workers is to provide them with greater leverage in dealing with their employers and negotiating contractual standards of fair treatment. Labor laws exist to protect the rights of employees to join together to form labor unions and attempt to improve their terms and conditions of employment through collective bargaining with their employers. Important federal labor laws include the National Labor Relations Act, the Railway Labor Act, and the Civil Service Reform Act (covering collective bargaining by federal government employees).

Terms and Conditions of Employment That Meet Minimum Standards

Some employment laws protect workers in a more direct fashion by specifying minimum standards of pay, safety, and other aspects of employment. Federal laws exemplifying this approach include the Fair Labor Standards Act (minimum wage and overtime pay requirements), the Occupational Safety and Health Act (workplace safety standards), and the Family and Medical Leave Act (leave policy requirements).

Protection of Fundamental Rights

Some legal challenges to employer practices are based on broader civil liberties and rights. For example, a variety of privacy protections exist, including privacy torts, the Electronic Communications Privacy Act, the Employee Polygraph Protection Act, and the Fair Credit Reporting Act.

Compensation for Certain Types of Harm

Employees can take legal action to recover damages when, for example, they are the victims of employer negligence, are defamed, or have emotional distress inflicted upon them; their employment contract is breached; or they are wrongfully discharged.

In the *Turner v. Memorial Medical Center* case that follows, a terminated employee sues his former employer. Although one might sympathize with the employee under the facts of this case, it is apparent from this decision that employment at will still presents a large hurdle for terminated employees.

This excerpt from *Turner v. Memorial Medical Center* is the first of a number of employment law cases that you will have the opportunity to read in this text. The words are those of the judge who wrote the decision. You would find the same words if you looked up the case—which you can easily do by using an online legal database and searching for either the names of the parties or the citation that appears below the names of the parties. The only difference is that we have shortened the case by selecting only the most essential details and by removing internal citations and footnotes. By seeing the law applied to particular factual circumstances and reading the judges' rationales for their decisions, you will gain a fuller understanding of the law.

Turner v. Memorial Medical Center
911 N.E.2d 369 (Ill. 2009)

OPINION BY JUSTICE FREEMAN:

Plaintiff, Mark Turner, brought a retaliatory discharge action … against defendant, Memorial Medical Center (Memorial). * * * A divided panel of the appellate court upheld the dismissal. We … now affirm the judgment of the appellate court.

I. BACKGROUND

* * * Plaintiff is a trained and licensed respiratory therapist. Beginning in 1983, plaintiff was employed by Memorial, which is a community hospital. During his employment, plaintiff had consistently met legitimate employment expectations, and his employment evaluations consistently indicated excellent work performance.

In September 2006, the Joint Commission on Accreditation of Healthcare Organizations (hereinafter, Joint Commission) performed an on-site survey at Memorial. The Joint Commission is an independent, not-for-profit organization that establishes various health-care standards and evaluates an organization's compliance with those standards and other accreditation requirements. The purpose of the on-site survey was to determine whether Memorial would continue to receive Joint Commission accreditation. Memorial's failure to receive this accreditation would result in the loss of federal Medicare/Medicaid funding.

Memorial uses a computer charting program that allows medical professionals to electronically chart a patient's file. The Joint Commission standard is that such electronic charting be performed immediately after care is provided to a patient. However, Memorial's respiratory therapy department did not require immediate charting. Rather, Memorial required a respiratory therapist to chart patient care merely at some point during his or her shift.

On September 28, 2006, plaintiff was asked to speak with a Joint Commission surveyor. Also present at this meeting was Memorial's vice-president of patient care services. During this meeting, plaintiff truthfully advised the surveyor of the discrepancy between the Joint Commission standard of immediate charting and Memorial's requirement of charting at some point during the shift. Plaintiff further advised the surveyor that Memorial's deviation from the Joint Commission standard was jeopardizing patient safety.

Plaintiff alleged that as a result of his truthful statements to the Joint Commission surveyor, Memorial discharged plaintiff on October 4, 2006. * * *

II. ANALYSIS

* * * In Illinois, "a noncontracted employee is one who serves at the employer's will, and the employer may discharge such an employee for any reason or no reason." However, an exception to this general rule of at-will employment arises where there has been a retaliatory discharge of the employee. This court has recognized a limited and narrow cause of action for the tort of retaliatory discharge. To state a valid retaliatory discharge cause of action, an employee must allege that (1) the employer discharged the employee, (2) in retaliation for the employee's activities, and (3) that the discharge violates a clear mandate of public policy. * * *

[A]n employee has a cause of action for wrongful discharge when the discharge is contrary to a clear mandate of public policy. However, unless an employee at will identifies a "specific" expression of public policy, the employee may be discharged with or without cause. * * *

In the present case, we must determine whether the complaint, on its face, contains sufficient allegations that plaintiff's discharge contravened some clear mandate of public policy. The complaint alleges only two such sources: the Joint Commission standards and the Medical Patient Rights Act. Because plaintiff's complaint fails to set forth a specific public policy, much less a clearly mandated public policy, we conclude that it does not support a cause of action for retaliatory discharge.

* * * The circuit court found that plaintiff "failed to establish the existence of a public policy clearly mandated by a provision of law which is violated when a concern is voiced to a [Joint Commission] surveyor about the time during a given work shift when patient care is charted. No Illinois law or administrative regulation directly requires immediate bedside charting of patient care." … [T]he circuit court further found that Joint Commission "standards are not Illinois law and thus cannot be said to be representative of the public policy of the State of Illinois." * * *

Plaintiff did identify an additional, specific source of his alleged clearly mandated public policy of "patient safety." The complaint alleged that section 3 of the Medical Patient Rights Act "recognizes Illinois public policy establishing '[t]he right of each patient to care consistent with sound nursing and medical practices.'" However, the mere citation of a constitutional or statutory provision in a complaint will not, by itself, be sufficient to state a cause of action for retaliatory discharge. Rather, an employee must show that the discharge violated the public policy that the cited provision clearly mandates.

We do not read section 3 of the Medical Patients Rights Act to establish a clearly mandated public policy of patient safety that was violated by plaintiff's discharge. Section 3(a) of the Act establishes the following rights:

"(a) The right of each patient to care consistent with sound nursing and medical practices, to be informed of the name of the physician responsible for coordinating his or her care, to receive information concerning his or her condition and proposed treatment, to refuse any treatment to the extent permitted by law, and to privacy and confidentiality of records except as otherwise provided by law." It is apparent that, as far as this section addresses medical record preparation at all, it is only concerned with record confidentiality, rather than record timeliness. * * *

We agree ... that the provision of good medical care by hospitals is in the public interest. "It does not follow, however, that all health care employees should be immune from the general at-will employment rule simply because they claim to be reporting on issues that they feel are detrimental to health care." * * *

Adherence to a narrow definition of public policy, as an element of a retaliatory discharge action, maintains the balance among the recognized interests. Employees will be secure in knowing that their jobs are safe if they exercise their rights according to a clear mandate of public policy. Employers will know that they may discharge their at-will employees for any or no reason unless they act contrary to public policy. Finally, the public interest in the furtherance of its public policies, the stability of employment, and the elimination of frivolous lawsuits is maintained.

Based on the narrow scope of a retaliatory discharge action, the general concept of "patient safety," by itself, is simply inadequate to justify finding an exception to the general rule of at-will employment. * * *

CASE QUESTIONS

1. What was the legal issue? What did the court decide?
2. The plaintiff, a long-time employee with "excellent" work performance, was apparently terminated for being truthful about hospital record-keeping practices. Why, then, is the termination not illegal?
3. Do you think that decisions like this make it less likely that healthcare workers will come forward with their concerns about practices that jeopardize patient safety or the quality of their care?
4. Do you agree with the court's decision? Why or why not? How far should courts go in protecting employees from wrongful termination?

When reading cases, it is important to pay attention to how the legal issues are framed. One might be tempted to say that the legal issue in the *Turner* case was whether the hospital had the right to terminate this employee for reporting truthfully about the medical charting practices of the hospital, or more generally, whether the termination was fair. But these statements do not get to the heart of the *legal* issue in this case. Under employment at will, a termination is lawful unless the terminated employee proves that he or she had some specific right not to be terminated under the circumstances. In the *Turner* case, the terminated employee looked to the "tort of retaliatory discharge" (also known as the public policy exception to employment at will) as the basis for his wrongful termination claim. The court's mission was to decide whether the employee's actions were linked to a clear public policy that would be undermined if employees could be fired for acting as this employee did. The court was not deciding whether the termination was wise, necessary, or fair. Not finding a sufficient public policy basis for the wrongful discharge claim, the court dismissed the case. The employee was left without a legal remedy for his termination.

Determining Which Employment Laws Apply

Because U.S. employment law is a patchwork of legal protections that apply to some groups of employees but not others, it is necessary to briefly elaborate on some of the key contextual factors that determine which, if any, employment laws apply in a given situation. You need to consider these factors when presented with situations posing potential legal problems.

Public or Private Sector Employment

The legal environment differs substantially depending on whether **public sector** (i.e., government) employees or **private sector** employees are being considered. Public and private sector does not refer to whether a company trades its stock on the stock market (i.e., publicly traded versus privately held companies), but rather whether the employer is a government agency or a corporation (including private, nonprofit agencies). Public employees make up roughly 15 percent of the workforce. One reason that public employees are a different case has already been mentioned. In general, constitutional protections pertain only to public employees and not to private sector employees. Beyond this, public employees are often covered by state or municipal civil service laws and tenure provisions.

Not all comparisons favor public employees. Public employees are subject to restrictions on their political activities, excluded from coverage under the National Labor Relations Act and the Occupational Safety and Health Act, and limited in their ability to sue for violations of federal law. This last point should be underscored. A series of U.S. Supreme Court decisions has held, based on the Eleventh Amendment and the broad concept of state sovereignty, that state governments cannot be sued by their public employees, whether in state or federal court, for violations of such federal employment laws as the Fair Labor Standards Act and the Americans with Disabilities Act (however, the Court reached the opposite decision regarding certain suits brought under the Family and Medical Leave Act).[2] Thus, even though these federal laws still apply to state government employees, options for enforcement are limited.

Unionized or Nonunion Workplace

When employees opt for union representation and negotiate a collective bargaining agreement with their employer, the employer is contractually committed to live up to the terms of the agreement. In contrast to the vast majority of employees who lack employment contracts, unionized employees have many of their terms and conditions of employment spelled out in enforceable labor agreements. These contractual terms typically go well beyond the minimum requirements of the law (e.g., by providing for daily overtime rather than the weekly overtime required by federal law). Employers in unionized workplaces are also more limited in their ability to make unilateral changes in workplace practices without first negotiating those changes with unions. Discipline or discharge of a unionized employee is contractually limited to situations where the employer can establish "just cause" for the discipline or discharge, which stands in stark contrast to the at-will employment of most nonunion workers.

Employer Size

The legal environment also varies depending on the size of the employer. Size can be variously construed. For purposes of some statutes, including the Fair Labor Standards Act and the National Labor Relations Act, size is measured in financial terms and

---

[2]*Alden v. Maine,* 527 U.S. 706 (1999); *University of Alabama v. Garrett,* 531 U.S. 356 (2001); *Nev. Dep't of Human Res. v. Hibbs,* 538 U.S. 721 (2003).

TABLE 1.1 EMPLOYMENT SIZE OF FIRMS (2008)				
EMPLOYMENT SIZE (NO. OF EMPLOYEES)	**FIRMS**		**EMPLOYEES**	
	(N)	**(%)**	**(N)**	**(%)**
0–4	3,617,764	61.0	6,086,291	5.0
5–9	1,044,065	17.6	6,878,051	5.7
10–19	633,141	10.7	8,497,391	7.0
20–99	526,307	8.9	20,684,691	17.1
100–499	90,386	1.5	17,547,567	14.5
500+	18,469	0.3	61,209,560	50.6
Total	**5,930,132**	**100.0**	**120,903,551**	**99.9**

Source: Adapted from U.S. Census Bureau, *Statistics of U.S. Business*, viewed April 17, 2011 (http://www.census.gov/econ/susb/).

coverage is limited to employers that exceed a minimum level of revenue (e.g., the general minimum for coverage under the FLSA is $500,000). More often, statutes specify a minimum employer size in terms of number of employees. For instance, both Title VII of the Civil Rights Act and the Americans with Disabilities Act limit coverage to companies that have fifteen or more employees, the Age Discrimination in Employment Act applies to employers with twenty or more employees, and the Family and Medical Leave Act applies only to employers with fifty or more employees.

These size limitations are not trivial. Table 1.1 shows that nearly 90 percent of firms in the United States had fewer than twenty employees in 2008. This means that many federal employment laws do not reach the vast majority of U.S. firms. There are two countervailing factors to consider, however. First, although the major federal employment laws do not cover most firms due to their small size, the minority of companies that are covered nonetheless employ most U.S. workers (because each larger company employs many more people). Thus, the approximately 10 percent of all firms that had twenty or more employees in 2008 employed a little over 82 percent of the workforce. The second important factor is that most states have enacted laws that mirror federal employment laws and that apply to smaller workplaces. In Ohio, for example, the Ohio Civil Rights Act covers employees whose employer has four or more employees.[3] Thus, in Ohio, employers with between four and fourteen employees would fall under state law, but not federal law, whereas employers with fifteen or more employees would be subject to both federal law and state law. Only employers with fewer than four employees would not be subject to civil rights statutes.

There is another aspect to the size issue. Counting the number of employees that an employer has is more complex than it first appears. For one thing, employment levels can change rapidly. A smaller company could easily vacillate above and below the minimum number of employees specified in a statute. When must the employer have the requisite number of employees? At the time of the alleged violation? When the claim is filed? Over some longer period of time? Part-time employees present another complication. Should part-time employees be counted the same as full-time employees?

Congress addressed these questions partially in Title VII of the Civil Rights Act of 1964 (parallel language appears in several other employment statutes). An employer is defined as someone "who has fifteen or more employees for each working day in each of twenty or more calendar weeks in the current or preceding calendar year...."[4]

---

[3]O.R.C. Ann. § 4112.01(A) (2) (2011).

[4]42 U.S.C.A. § 2000e(b) (2011).

"Current" calendar year refers to the year in which the alleged discrimination occurred. The Supreme Court has ruled that the proper method for counting employees is the **payroll method**. Under this method, an employee is counted for each full week between when she is hired and when she leaves employment, regardless of the number of hours the employee worked during those weeks.[5]

Geographic Location

Practical Considerations How should employers that operate in different states and cities deal with lack of uniformity in employment laws?

An employee's rights are affected by where he happens to live. Some states and cities go much further than others, and also further than the federal government, in conferring rights on workers. States and cities have become increasingly important as sources of employment laws in recent years. The interrelationship between federal and state laws is a complex legal matter. At the risk of oversimplification, states are free to enact laws pertaining to issues not addressed by federal law. State laws also can match or exceed the protections available under federal laws dealing with the same matters, but they cannot reduce the rights employees have under federal law. Thus, state laws are important not only because they reach smaller workplaces than federal employment laws but also because they sometimes provide employees with rights not available under federal law. Examples of state laws that exceed federal law include higher minimum wages in some states, laws regulating the handling of personnel records, limitations placed on drug and HIV testing, and prohibitions against discrimination based on sexual orientation.

Government Contracts

Federal, state, and local governments sometimes use the contracting process as leverage to get employers to implement desired workplace practices. Employers that contract to do business with the federal government (e.g., defense contractors, construction companies, computer suppliers) and that meet certain other criteria are required to engage in affirmative action as a condition of their contracts. Likewise, both the Drug-Free Workplace Act (requiring that employers take certain actions to stop workplace drug use) and the Rehabilitation Act (prohibiting discrimination against and requiring affirmative action on behalf of disabled persons) apply to private employers based on their contracts with the federal government.

Industry and Occupation

Most employment laws apply to any industry, but some are more narrowly targeted. For example, the Omnibus Transportation Employees Testing Act of 1991 mandates extensive drug (and alcohol) testing, but only for employees in industries regulated by the Department of Transportation (e.g., airlines, railroads, trucking companies). Likewise, employees in the historically dangerous mining industry are not covered under the Occupational Safety and Health Act, but instead under a separate statute, the Mine Safety and Health Act. Agricultural workers, despite their generally poor working conditions, are wholly or partly excluded from the protection of many employment laws, including the National Labor Relations Act, the Fair Labor Standards Act, and state workers' compensation statutes. An important example of an occupation-based distinction is the National Labor Relations Act's exclusion of supervisors and managers.

Historical Development of U.S. Employment Law

Detailing what the law said previously and how it has changed over time is beyond the scope of this book. However, you should have some sense of when employment laws

---

[5] *Walters v. Metropolitan Educational Enterprises, Inc.,* 117 S. Ct. 660 (1997).

FIGURE 1.1 Timeline of Major U.S. Employment Laws

1900	Workers' Compensation (most states between 1911 and 1920)
1920	Railway Labor Act (1926)
	National Labor Relations Act (Wagner Act) (1935)
	Social Security Act (1935)
	Fair Labor Standards Act (1938)
1940	Labor-Management Relations Act (Taft-Hartley Act) (1947)
1960	Equal Pay Act (1963)
	Title VII of the Civil Rights Act (1964)
	Executive Order 11246 (1965)
	Age Discrimination in Employment Act (1967)
1970	Occupational Safety and Health Act (1970)
	Rehabilitation Act (1973)
	Employee Retirement Income Security Act (1974)
	Pregnancy Discrimination Act (1978)
1980	Common Law Wrongful Discharge Claims (majority of states adopted one or more of these from the late 1970s through the 1980s)
	Consolidated Omnibus Budget Reconciliation Act (COBRA) (1985)
	Immigration Reform and Control Act (1986)
	Employee Polygraph Protection Act (1988)
	Worker Adjustment and Retraining Notification Act (1988)
1990	Americans with Disabilities Act (1990)
	Older Workers Benefit Protection Act (1990)
	Civil Rights Act of 1991 (1991)
	Family and Medical Leave Act (1993)
	Uniformed Services Employment and Reemployment Rights Act (1994)
	Health Insurance Portability and Accountability Act (1996)
2000	Pension Protection Act (2006)
	ADA Amendments Act (2008)
	Genetic Information Nondiscrimination Act (2008)
	Patient Protection and Affordable Care Act (2010)

© Cengage Learning 2013.

came into existence. Figure 1.1 is a timeline of major employment laws (ignoring, for the most part, amendments to these laws).

At the turn of the twentieth century, employment law was virtually nonexistent in the United States. The first significant departure from an unregulated workplace was the adoption of state workers' compensation laws to deal with the severe problem of injured workers. A major breakthrough came in the 1930s, when the National Labor Relations Act and the Fair Labor Standards Act were enacted. Employment law took large strides forward in the 1960s with the passage of major antidiscrimination statutes, including Title VII of the Civil Rights Act, the Age Discrimination in Employment Act, and the Equal Pay Act. Common law claims, particularly for wrongful discharge, came into vogue in the late 1970s and throughout the 1980s. Benefits have been the object of a number of employment laws since the 1970s, with health insurance and pensions being at the center of recent legislative efforts.

Legislation does not emerge in a vacuum. Many of our employment laws reflect the work of **social movements**, organized efforts to create needed changes in workplaces and society. The workers' compensation statutes adopted in the early part of the twentieth century were influenced by the progressive movement that addressed the social problems of that time. The National Labor Relations Act was enacted in 1935 during the early part of the New Deal and in the depths of the Depression. The act both reflected and furthered the efforts of ordinary workers and their unions, joined together in the labor movement, to gain some control over their work lives. Likewise, the Civil Rights Act of 1964 was a crowning achievement of the civil rights movement. The civil rights movement had to overcome enormous opposition to obtain legislation protecting the basic civil rights of all people, and the struggle to realize this law's promise continues. Thus, although we will focus on the effects of employment laws on the human resource practices of companies, the major employment laws mean much more than that; they are windows into important periods in our history, express basic societal values, and represent hard-won accomplishments that should not be taken for granted.

The timeline in Figure 1.1 covers more than a century, but most of the laws are clustered in the second half of this period. As a consequence, many interesting legal questions have yet to be resolved by the courts. Is there "too much" employment law now? Certainly, in comparison to the not-so-distant past, the workplace is far more regulated than it used to be. On the other hand, U.S. employers enjoy considerably more freedom to carry out human resource decisions as they see fit than do employers in most of the other major industrialized nations in the world, particularly in Europe.

Procedures for Enforcing Employment Laws

Simply conferring rights on employees is not enough. Means of enforcing those rights must be available when employers do not live up to their legal responsibilities. TV lawyers get cases and emerge victorious in the space of single episodes. In the real world, the process of resolving employment disputes is anything but simple and quick. A wide variety of **enforcement procedures** exist for bringing and resolving claims related to violations of employment laws. The applicable procedure depends on the particular law that forms the basis for the claim. However, it is possible to convey some of the more typical ways in which employment law claims proceed.

What Does an Employee Decide to Do When She Believes That Her Rights Were Violated?

In a few situations, employment laws are enforced by government agencies at their own initiative, such as when OSHA elects to inspect a workplace based on the occurrence of a serious accident or because it operates in a particularly dangerous industry. However, as a general rule, both the courts and government agencies rely on individual employees to come forward with complaints before enforcement actions are undertaken. Thus, the decision of an employee to challenge some action of her employer is a key part of the enforcement process.

Although there are undoubtedly some frivolous claims brought against employers, it is a mistake to assume that most employee complaints are baseless and rooted in opportunism. Contesting one's employer in the legal system is an expensive, protracted, uncertain, and emotionally draining process. Most likely, the cases that are brought are just the tip of the iceberg. Most employees who have their rights violated by their employers do something other than take legal action; they quit, join a union, withhold commitment and discretionary effort, just let it go, or talk it over with the employer and work things out. Ultimately, although no employer can be expected to like it, our system of employment law depends on employees being willing to come forward and assume the burden of taking legal action to both remedy the harm that was done to them as individuals and to uphold public policy.[6]

How Long Does the Employee Have to Bring a Case?

An important feature of any enforcement procedure is the length of time that an aggrieved person has to come forward with a complaint. This is the **limitations period**. Time limits for filing lawsuits or charges with administrative agencies vary. Unfair labor practice charges must be brought to the National Labor Relations Board within six months of their occurrence. In discrimination cases, employees generally have 300 days to file a charge with the EEOC (180 days in states that do not have their own state civil rights agencies), but only 90 days to file suit if the EEOC's efforts to resolve the case conclude unsuccessfully. Wage and hour cases brought under the Fair Labor Standards Act can go back as far as three years. State laws typically allow tort claims to be brought based on events that occurred several years in the past. A major practical consequence is that *employers must be prepared to defend actions taken well in the past by individuals who might no longer work for their companies. The only way to do this is to maintain solid documentation regarding all human resource decisions.*

Employees who fail to bring charges in a timely fashion generally lose their right to pursue legal action. The clock usually starts ticking on the limitations period when the employee receives unequivocal written or oral notice of a decision (e.g., termination), rather than on the effective date of that decision (if these differ). However, if an employee is unaware of her rights because she was actively misled by her employer or the employer failed to meet its legal obligation to post information in the workplace, a court might excuse an untimely filing.[7] This is known as **equitable tolling**. This doctrine is applied sparingly and generally does not shield employees from the consequences of negligent legal representation. Thus, when an employee's religious discrimination lawsuit was filed late due to a clerical error made by her lawyer's office, the employee's suit was dismissed for lack of timeliness.[8] However, when an employee's legal representatives mistakenly filed a timely claim with the wrong federal enforcement agency and the mistake was not corrected until after the limitations period had expired, the employee's case was allowed to proceed. In deciding to apply equitable tolling in this case, the court pointed to the facts that the employee's lawyers had exercised due diligence in pursuing her claim by promptly filing the charge and repeatedly contacting the agency—which, for its part, inexplicably failed to correct the error and merely informed the lawyers that it was still investigating the case.[9]

When applying limitations periods to discrimination cases, courts distinguish between "discrete acts" (such as non-hiring and termination) that occur at particular points in time and acts that recur and have a cumulative impact. Repeated acts of harassment that, over time, create a "hostile environment" are a prime example of the latter. Employees who claim that they were subjected to a hostile environment can challenge all of the harassing acts, even if these go back well beyond the limitations period, provided that at least one incident of harassment occurred during the limitations period.[10] What about pay discrimination in this light? Is it a discrete act in which a decision is made at a particular point in time to pay an employee a discriminatorily low amount? Or is it more like a violation that recurs with each paycheck that is lower than it ought to be if discrimination had not occurred? The Supreme Court had said that it was the

[6]*McKennon v. Nashville Banner Publishing Co.*, 115 S. Ct. 879, 884 (1995).

[7]*Mercado v. The Ritz-Carlton San Juan Hotel, Spa & Casino*, 410 F.3d 41 (1st Cir. 2005).

[8]*Harris v. Boyd Tunica Inc.*, 628 F.3d 237 (5th Cir. 2010).

[9]*Granger v. Aaron's Inc.*, 2011 U.S. App. LEXIS 5995, 10-12 (5th Cir.).

[10]*National Railroad Passenger Corporation v. Morgan*, 536 U.S. 101 (2002).

JUST THE FACTS

An employee of the accounting firm PricewaterhouseCoopers was denied promotion to partner on at least two occasions between 1999 and 2000. The employee believes that the denials were based on his age (he was about 57 at the time). Given that the employee's pay in recent years was lower than it would have been had he been promoted, would an age discrimination claim filed now still be timely?

See *Schuler v. PricewaterhouseCoopers LLP*, 595 F.3d 370 (D.C. Cir. 2010).

---

former,[11] but Congress subsequently enacted the **Lilly Ledbetter Fair Pay Act of 2009**, which established that each discriminatorily low paycheck is a separate violation that starts the limitations period anew.[12] An unlawful employment practice occurs "when an individual is affected by application of a discriminatory compensation decision or other practice, including each time wages [are] … paid."[13]

Can a Lawsuit Be Brought? By Whom?

Most employment laws enable employees to enforce their rights through lawsuits against their employers. The Occupational Safety and Health Act is an exception in this regard. When an employee believes that a safety hazard exists in his workplace, he needs to contact OSHA and get an inspector to come. If the inspector does not agree that there is a problem and the employer is not cited, no course of legal action is available to the employee. Likewise, if the General Counsel of the National Labor Relations Board declines to bring a complaint regarding an alleged unfair labor practice, the employee is out of luck. Suits in discrimination cases can be brought by individuals or the EEOC. However, because the Commission goes to court in only a small percentage of the cases it receives, the burden of taking legal action to enforce antidiscrimination laws falls mainly on individual employees. Finding an attorney willing to take an employment law case, particularly on a contingent fee basis (the attorney incurs most of the cost of litigation with the promise of a substantial share of any award if the litigation is successful), can be difficult. Employment lawyers accept only an estimated 5 percent of the employment discrimination cases brought to them. Lower-wage workers, for whom provable damages are relatively low, are particularly likely to have their cases turned away.[14]

A great deal happens between when a lawsuit is filed and when the case is actually heard in court (if the action proceeds that far). Considerable managerial time is spent responding to requests for records, answering interrogatories (sets of questions), and giving sworn depositions (statements) regarding the facts of the case. If you are involved in making human resource decisions, you can expect to experience this part of the litigation process firsthand. *The best advice is to answer questions truthfully and succinctly and to have documentation to back you up.* Settlement negotiations are likely, both at this point and throughout the course of the litigation. Settlements are a common outcome of litigation.

Employment law cases are brought in both state and federal courts. Where the case will end up depends on such factors as the legal basis for the claim, where the parties to the case

---

[11]*Ledbetter v. Goodyear Tire & Rubber Co.*, 550 U.S. 618 (2007).

[12]Pub. L. No. 111-2, 123 Stat. 5 (2009).

[13]42 U.S.C.S. § 2000e-5 (e) (3) (A) (2011).

[14]Elizabeth Hill. "Due Process at Low Cost: An Empirical Study of Employment Arbitration Under the Auspices of the American Arbitration Association." *Ohio State Journal on Dispute Resolution*, 18 (2003), 777–783.

reside or are incorporated, and the strategic choices of the parties. A case that goes into the federal court system starts at the **district court** (trial court) level. The role of the district court is to establish the facts of the case and to reach a decision about the merits of the employee's claim. However, many cases filed against employers are thrown out (the employer is granted **summary judgment**) because the court determines that even if the allegations of the **plaintiff** (the employee who is suing) are accepted as true, they are not sufficient to support a legal claim. If the case makes it to trial, the plaintiff bears the **burden of proof** to show, generally by a "preponderance (the majority) of the evidence," that his rights were violated. Cases that go to trial are sometimes decided by juries and other times by judges. District court decisions can be appealed by either party to a federal **appeals court** (circuit court). Appeals courts typically accept the facts of cases as given and focus on whether the lower courts properly applied the law in deciding cases. Appeals court decisions can be appealed to the **U.S. Supreme Court**. However, because the Supreme Court exercises its discretion as to which cases it hears (when the court decides to hear a case, it grants **certiorari**), and it hears relatively few cases each year, rarely does the case go that far. Thus, although you will read about many U.S. Supreme Court decisions in this book, these cases are included because they raise important employment law issues and because the Court has decided them authoritatively, not because they are typical cases.

Judges enjoy considerable discretion in deciding cases. However, while courts sometimes change their minds about the law, they have a strong preference for adhering to prior decisions ("precedents")—or at least giving the appearance of doing so. This desire for consistency and stability in the law is sometimes captured by the Latin phrase **stare decisis** ("let the decision stand").

Clippings

A study examining a sample of 1,672 discrimination claims filed in federal court between 1988 and 2003 provides a good picture of typical case outcomes. Overall, about 58 percent of the cases ended in settlements, typically for modest sums but occasionally for much larger amounts. About 37 percent of the cases were dismissed early in the litigation or disposed of prior to any trial through summary judgment for the employer. Only about 6 percent of the cases filed actually went to trial, with the plaintiffs prevailing in a third of these (accounting for 2 percent of the entire sample). The median award to plaintiffs who succeeded at trial was $110,000.

Laura Beth Nielsen, Robert Nelson, and Ryon Lancaster. "Individual Justice or Collective Legal Mobilization? Employment Discrimination Litigation in the Post Civil Rights United States." *Journal of Empirical Legal Studies* 7, 2 (2010), 184–88.

Clippings

Dick's Sporting Goods has agreed to pay nearly $15 million to settle a class action lawsuit brought on behalf of more than 3,500 employees in twenty-three states. The employees claimed that their employer had violated the Fair Labor Standards Act by not paying them for time worked. Payments to individual plaintiffs will range from as little as $100 to $20,000 for the four original named plaintiffs in the case.

Jay-Anne B. Casuga. "Dick's Sporting Goods to Pay $15 Million to Settle 23 Wage and Hour Class Actions." *Daily Labor Report* 22 (February 2, 2011), A-1.

Lawsuits are not limited to claims brought by individual employees. In **class-action lawsuits**, numerous plaintiffs join forces in claiming that their rights were violated in essentially the same manner by their employer. Any award is shared by the class members. Class-action lawsuits are controversial. Plaintiffs' counsel see them as an efficient means for pursuing the claims of many individuals who might not otherwise be able to take legal action, whereas corporate defendants tend to see them as collections of disparate allegations strung together by attorneys seeking to maximize their earnings. Whether multiple employees have claims that are sufficiently similar to justify certification as a "class" is a key determination in these cases. In *Wal-Mart Stores v. Dukes*, the Supreme Court is presented with the question of whether a class-action sex discrimination suit brought on behalf of more than a million current and former employees can go forward. The Court decides only the issue of class standing—and not whether the retailer actually discriminated against any of its female employees—but its decision likely diminishes the ability of employees to effectively challenge the policies and practices of large corporations.

Wal-Mart Stores v. Dukes
2011 U.S. LEXIS 4567

OPINION BY JUSTICE SCALIA:

We are presented with one of the most expansive class actions ever. The District Court and the Court of Appeals approved the certification of a class comprising about one and a half million plaintiffs, current and former female employees of petitioner Wal-Mart who allege that the discretion exercised by their local supervisors over pay and promotion matters violates Title VII by discriminating against women. * * * We consider whether the certification of the plaintiff class was consistent with Federal Rules of Civil Procedure ....

Petitioner Wal-Mart is the Nation's largest private employer. It operates four types of retail stores throughout the country: Discount Stores, Supercenters, Neighborhood Markets, and Sam's Clubs. Those stores are divided into seven nationwide divisions, which in turn comprise 41 regions of 80 to 85 stores apiece. Each store has between 40 and 53 separate departments and 80 to 500 staff positions. In all, Wal-Mart operates approximately 3,400 stores and employs more than one million people.

Pay and promotion decisions at Wal-Mart are generally committed to local managers' broad discretion, which is exercised "in a largely subjective manner."* * * Wal-Mart permits store managers to apply their own subjective criteria when selecting candidates as "support managers," which is the first step on the path to management. Admission to Wal-Mart's management training program, however, does require that a candidate meet certain objective criteria, including an above-average performance rating, at least one year's tenure in the applicant's current position, and a willingness to relocate. But except for those requirements, regional and district managers have discretion to use their own judgment when selecting candidates for management training. Promotion to higher office—e.g., assistant manager, co-manager, or store manager—is similarly at the discretion of the employee's superiors after prescribed objective factors are satisfied.

The named plaintiffs in this lawsuit, representing the 1.5 million members of the certified class, are three current or former Wal-Mart employees who allege that the company discriminated against them on the basis of their sex by denying them equal pay or promotions, in violation of Title VII of the Civil Rights Act of 1964. * * * These plaintiffs, respondents here, do not allege that Wal-Mart has any express corporate policy against the advancement of women. Rather, they claim that their local managers' discretion over pay and promotions is exercised disproportionately in favor of men, leading to an unlawful disparate impact on female employees. And, respondents say, because Wal-Mart is aware of this effect, its refusal to cabin its managers' authority amounts to disparate treatment. * * *

Importantly for our purposes, respondents claim that the discrimination to which they have been subjected is common to all Wal-Mart's female employees. The basic theory of their case is that a strong and uniform "corporate culture" permits bias against women to infect, perhaps subconsciously, the discretionary decisionmaking of each one of Wal-Mart's thousands of managers—thereby making every woman at the company the victim of one common discriminatory practice. Respondents therefore wish to litigate the Title VII claims of all female employees at Wal-Mart's stores in a nationwide class action.

Class certification is governed by Federal Rule of Civil Procedure 23. Under Rule 23(a), the party seeking certification must demonstrate, first, that:

"(1) the class is so numerous that joinder of all members is impracticable,

"(2) there are questions of law or fact common to the class,

"(3) the claims or defenses of the representative parties are typical of the claims or defenses of the class, and

"(4) the representative parties will fairly and adequately protect the interests of the class"

Second, the proposed class must satisfy at least one of the three requirements listed in Rule 23(b). Respondents rely on Rule 23(b)(2), which applies when "the party opposing the class has acted or refused to act on grounds that apply generally to the class, so that final injunctive relief or corresponding declaratory relief is appropriate respecting the class as a whole." * * * [The other two are that individual suits would create a risk of inconsistent or varying decisions and that the common issues are predominant, rendering a class action superior to individual litigation.]

The class action is "an exception to the usual rule that litigation is conducted by and on behalf of the individual named parties only." In order to justify a departure from that rule, "a class representative must be part of the class and 'possess the same interest and suffer the same injury' as the class members." Rule 23(a) ensures that the named plaintiffs are appropriate representatives of the class whose claims they wish to litigate. The Rule's four requirements—numerosity, commonality, typicality, and adequate representation—"effectively 'limit the class claims to those fairly encompassed by the named plaintiff's claims.'"

The crux of this case is commonality—the rule requiring a plaintiff to show that "there are questions of law or fact common to the class." * * * Commonality requires the plaintiff to demonstrate that the class members "have suffered the same injury." This does not mean merely that they have all suffered a violation of the same provision of law. * * * Quite obviously, the mere claim by employees of the same company that they have suffered a Title VII injury … gives no cause to believe that all their claims can productively be litigated at once. Their claims must depend upon a common contention—for example, the assertion of discriminatory bias on the part of the same supervisor. That common contention, moreover, must be of such a nature that it is capable of classwide resolution—which means that determination of its truth or falsity will

resolve an issue that is central to the validity of each one of the claims in one stroke. * * *

In this case, proof of commonality necessarily overlaps with respondents' merits contention that Wal-Mart engages in a pattern or practice of discrimination. That is so because, in resolving an individual's Title VII claim, the crux of the inquiry is "the reason for a particular employment decision." Here respondents wish to sue about literally millions of employment decisions at once. Without some glue holding the alleged reasons for all those decisions together, it will be impossible to say that examination of all the class members' claims for relief will produce a common answer to the crucial question why was I disfavored. * * *

"[S]ignificant proof" that Wal-Mart "operated under a general policy of discrimination" … is entirely absent here. Wal-Mart's announced policy forbids sex discrimination and … the company imposes penalties for denials of equal employment opportunity. The only evidence of a "general policy of discrimination" respondents produced was the testimony of Dr. William Bielby, their sociological expert.… Bielby testified that Wal-Mart has a "strong corporate culture," that makes it "'vulnerable'" to "gender bias." He could not, however, "determine with any specificity how regularly stereotypes play a meaningful role in employment decisions at Wal-Mart. * * * "[W]hether 0.5 percent or 95 percent of the employment decisions at Wal-Mart might be determined by stereotyped thinking" is the essential question on which respondents' theory of commonality depends. If Bielby admittedly has no answer to that question, we can safely disregard what he has to say. It is worlds away from "significant proof" that Wal-Mart "operated under a general policy of discrimination."

The only corporate policy that the plaintiffs' evidence convincingly establishes is Wal-Mart's "policy" of allowing discretion by local supervisors over employment matters. On its face, of course, that is just the opposite of a uniform employment practice that would provide the commonality needed for a class action; it is a policy against having uniform employment practices. It is also a very common and presumptively reasonable way of doing business—one that we have said "should itself raise no inference of discriminatory conduct." To be sure, we have recognized that … giving discretion to lower-level supervisors can be the basis of Title VII liability … since "an employer's undisciplined system of subjective decisionmaking [can have] precisely the same effects as a system pervaded by impermissible intentional discrimination." But the recognition that this type of Title VII claim "can" exist does not lead to the conclusion that every employee in a company using a system of discretion has such a claim in common. * * *

In a company of Wal-Mart's size and geographical scope, it is quite unbelievable that all managers would exercise their discretion in a common way without some common direction. Respondents attempt to make that showing by means of statistical and anecdotal evidence, but their evidence falls well short. * * *

In sum, the members of the class:

held a multitude of different jobs, at different levels of Wal-Mart's hierarchy, for variable lengths of time, in 3,400 stores, sprinkled across 50 states, with a kaleidoscope of supervisors (male and female), subject to a variety of regional policies that all differed .... Some thrived while others did poorly. They have little in common but their sex and this lawsuit. [quoting from the dissenting opinion of Chief Judge Kozinski of the Ninth Circuit Court of Appeals]

* * * We also conclude that respondents' claims for backpay were improperly certified under Federal Rule of Civil Procedure 23(b)(2). * * * We now hold that [claims for monetary relief] may not [be certified under that provision], at least where (as here) the monetary relief is not incidental to the injunctive or declaratory relief [e.g., hiring, reinstatement].

Rule 23(b)(2) allows class treatment when "the party opposing the class has acted or refused to act on grounds that apply generally to the class, so that final injunctive relief or corresponding declaratory relief is appropriate respecting the class as a whole." One possible reading of this provision is that it applies only to requests for such injunctive or declaratory relief and does not authorize the class certification of monetary claims at all. We need not reach that broader question in this case, because we think that, at a minimum, claims for individualized relief (like the backpay at issue here) do not satisfy the Rule. The key to the (b)(2) class is "the indivisible nature of the injunctive or declaratory remedy warranted—the notion that the conduct is such that it can be enjoined or declared unlawful only as to all of the class members or as to none of them." In other words, Rule 23(b)(2) applies only when a single injunction or declaratory judgment would provide relief to each member of the class. * * * [I]t does not authorize class certification when each class member would be entitled to an individualized award of monetary damages.

* * * Wal-Mart is entitled to individualized determinations of each employee's eligibility for backpay. Title VII includes a detailed remedial scheme. If a plaintiff prevails in showing that an employer has discriminated against him in violation of the statute, the court "may enjoin the respondent from engaging in such unlawful employment practice, and order such affirmative action as may be appropriate, [including] reinstatement or hiring of employees, with or without backpay ... or any other equitable relief as the court deems appropriate." But if the employer can show that it took an adverse employment action against an employee for any reason other than discrimination, the court cannot order the "hiring, reinstatement, or promotion of an individual as an employee, or the payment to him of any backpay." We have established a procedure for trying pattern-or-practice cases that gives effect to these statutory requirements. When the plaintiff seeks individual relief such as reinstatement or backpay after establishing a pattern or practice of discrimination, "a district court must usually conduct additional proceedings ... to determine the scope of individual relief." At this phase, the burden of proof will shift to the company, but it will have the right to raise any individual affirmative defenses it may have, and to "demonstrate that the individual applicant was denied an employment opportunity for lawful reasons."

The Court of Appeals believed that it was possible to replace such proceedings with Trial by Formula. A sample set of the class members would be selected, as to whom liability for sex discrimination and the backpay owing as a result would be determined in depositions supervised by a master. The percentage of claims determined to be valid would then be applied to the entire remaining class, and the number of (presumptively) valid claims thus derived would be multiplied by the average backpay award in the sample set to arrive at the entire class recovery—without further individualized proceedings. We disapprove that novel project.... [A] class cannot be certified on the premise that Wal-Mart will not be entitled to litigate its statutory defenses to individual claims. * * *

* * * The judgment of the Court of Appeals is Reversed.

CASE QUESTIONS

1. What was the legal issue in this case? What did the Supreme Court decide?
2. What things must be shown in order to achieve class certification in a class action lawsuit? What did the Court say was lacking in this case?
3. What complications do class action suits present when deciding the damages to which class members are entitled? Why does the Court reject the method proposed by the lower court?
4. What are the practical consequences of this decision for plaintiffs in discrimination and other employment law cases? What would the consequences have been for employers if the court had ruled that the class action could proceed?

Is There an Administrative Prerequisite to a Lawsuit?

Many employment laws require that a charge be filed with an administrative agency (e.g., the Equal Employment Opportunity Commission, the Wage and Hour Division of the Department of Labor) and that the agency be given the chance to resolve the matter before an employee can go to court. In discrimination cases, an employee usually starts by filing a charge with either the EEOC or a state fair employment practice agency. If the EEOC dismisses the case or fails to achieve **conciliation** (a settlement agreement) between the parties, it issues a **right to sue letter** to the employee alleging discrimination. Only then is the employee able to commence a lawsuit. Other types of legal claims, such as breach of contract or negligence, can proceed directly to court.

Must the Employee Exhaust Internal Dispute Resolution Mechanisms Before Proceeding?

If an employer has a complaint or grievance procedure, the employee does not usually have to use the internal procedure before taking the case to an enforcement agency or court. However, this is an area of the law where profound changes are taking place. The Supreme Court has held that an employer may be able to escape liability for harassment engaged in by a supervisor when an employee unreasonably refuses to avail herself of the employer's complaint procedure.[15] An even more fundamental change has been the rise of alternative dispute resolution procedures intended to take the place of lawsuits (see "The Changing Workplace").

THE CHANGING WORKPLACE

Alternative Dispute Resolution Procedures

There is great interest in **alternative dispute resolution (ADR)** procedures in all areas of the law. Alternative dispute resolution procedures are alternatives to going to court to resolve disputes. Enthusiasm for ADR stems from the belief that these procedures are cheaper, quicker, more private, and less damaging to relationships than litigation. There are many different types of ADR. Two of the most frequently used types are mediation and arbitration. In **mediation**, a neutral third party (the mediator) facilitates negotiations between the disputing parties to help them reach an agreement but does not have the authority to decide the dispute or impose a settlement. In **arbitration**, a neutral third party (the arbitrator) functions more like a private judge. Arbitrators hear disputes and render decisions that are almost always final and binding on the parties.

The EEOC encourages the parties to discrimination charges to use mediation. Rather than decide whether there has been a violation of the law, the mediator

(a trained EEOC staff member or contractor) focuses on helping the parties "jointly explore and reconcile their differences." Typically undertaken prior to EEOC investigation of a charge, mediation is voluntary and confidential. If it proves unsuccessful, the case reverts to the typical EEOC enforcement procedure of investigation, conciliation, and possible litigation. The EEOC's mediation program achieved a 72 percent settlement rate, resolving 8,840 discrimination charges in fiscal year 2008.[1] Cases that went through mediation were resolved in an average of 97 days, compared to the average of 200 days consumed by the EEOC investigative process.[2] Employer reluctance to use mediation appears to stem primarily from a belief that the charges lack merit, rather than from lack of awareness or distrust of the process itself.[3]

Arbitration has, for decades, been the principal means of enforcing employee rights under collective bargaining agreements in unionized workplaces. This use of arbitration amounts to establishing, through

---

[15]*Faragher v. City of Boca Raton,* 524 U.S. 775 (1998).

collective bargaining, a private system for resolving disputes about violations of private contractual agreements. What has changed is that many employers are now requiring arbitration agreements as a condition of employment (hence, the term *mandatory* or *employer promulgated* arbitration) and that arbitration is being used to resolve all employment law disputes—not simply contractual ones. To get (or keep) the job, employees have to surrender the ability to go to court to vindicate their rights as employees, and they have to do so prior to any dispute arising.

Precise, current estimates of the extent of ADR use in the workplace are lacking. One study placed the number of nonunion employees covered by arbitration agreements at 6 million in 2002, double the number covered in 1997.[4] A 2008 survey of corporate counsel found that some 25 percent of firms required arbitration agreements with their nonunion employees.[5] Whatever the exact number of arbitration agreements in use, the consensus is that the use of arbitration

agreements has substantially increased over the past decade.[6] But are these agreements that bar employees from going to court enforceable?

[1]U.S. Equal Employment Opportunity Commission. "EEOC Mediation Statistics FY 1999 through FY 2008." Viewed April 17, 2011 (http://archive.eeoc.gov/mediate/mediation_stats.html).
[2]U.S. Equal Employment Opportunity Commission. "Questions and Answers About Mediation." Viewed April 17, 2011 (http://www.eeoc.gov/eeoc/mediation/qanda.cfm).
[3]E. Patrick McDermott, Anita Jose, and Ruth Obar. "An Investigation of the Reasons for the Lack of Employer Participation in the EEOC Mediation Program." Viewed April 17, 2011 (http://www.eeoc.gov/eeoc/mediation/report/study3/index.html).
[4]Elizabeth Hill. "Due Process at Low Cost: An Empirical Study of Employment Arbitration Under the Auspices of the American Arbitration Association." *Ohio State Journal on Dispute Resolution*, 18 (2003), 777, 780.
[5]Charles D. Coleman. "Is Mandatory Arbitration Living Up to Its Expectations? A View from the Employer's Perspective." *ABA Journal of Labor & Employment Law* 25, 2 (2010), 227–239.
[6]Ronald L. Seeber and David B. Lipsky. "The Ascendancy of Employment Arbitrators in US Employment Relations: A New Actor in the American System?" *British Journal of Industrial Relations*, 44, 4 (2006), 733.

Enforceability of Mandatory Arbitration Agreements

It is clear that mandatory arbitration agreements requiring employees to use arbitration rather than the courts as the means of resolving employment law claims are generally enforceable. In a case involving an arbitration agreement between a broker and the New York Stock Exchange, the Supreme Court ruled that the broker would have to use the NYSE's arbitration procedure rather than the courts to pursue an age discrimination claim against his employer. Quoting an earlier case, the Court minimized the differences between arbitration and litigation: "by agreeing to arbitrate a statutory claim, a party does not forgo the substantive rights afforded by the statute; it only submits to their resolution in an arbitral, rather than a judicial, forum."[16] In a subsequent case, the Supreme Court decided that arbitration agreements between employers and employees are covered under the Federal Arbitration Act (FAA) and thus generally enforceable (but not when transportation workers are involved, owing to exclusionary language included in the FAA).[17] The Federal Arbitration Act, enacted by Congress in 1925, requires courts to enforce most written arbitration agreements.

The Court's evident enthusiasm for arbitration does not mean that arbitration agreements will always be enforced. In a case involving a disability discrimination suit brought by the EEOC on behalf of an employee who had signed an arbitration agreement, the Supreme Court decided that the agency's suit was not barred by the agreement and

[16]*Gilmer v. Interstate/Johnson Lane Corporation*, 500 U.S. 20, 26 (1991).
[17]*Circuit City Stores v. Adams*, 121 S. Ct. 1302 (2001).

that it could seek to recover victim-specific remedies, including back pay and reinstatement.[18] Thus, even with a signed arbitration agreement in hand, an employer in a discrimination case is still subject to EEOC proceedings and possibly a lawsuit brought on behalf of an employee by the agency. Another issue is that arbitration provisions in the collective bargaining agreements of unionized employees will not bar litigation over violations of individuals' legal rights unless the contract language "clearly and unmistakably" requires arbitration of both legal and contractual disputes.[19]

There are additional limitations on the enforceability of mandatory arbitration agreements. Fundamentally, arbitration agreements are contracts. Courts decline to enforce contracts when fraud is involved, the contract was entered into under extreme duress, or the contract is unconscionable. Contracts are **unconscionable** when the process of contract formation essentially involves a "take-it-or-leave-it" offer of an agreement drafted by a more powerful party (a "contract of adhesion") and when the contents of the agreement unreasonably favor the more powerful party. Mandatory arbitration agreements have *sometimes* not been enforced by courts (i.e., the employee was allowed to go to court despite the existence of the agreement) on the grounds that they are unconscionable. *Nino v. The Jewelry Exchange* is one such case. Although the plaintiff in this case resides in the Virgin Islands, the analysis and outcome of the case would likely have been the same regardless of where the case was heard.

Nino v. The Jewelry Exchange
609 F.3d 191 (3d Cir. 2010)

OPINION BY CIRCUIT JUDGE FUENTES:

Rajae Nino brought this action against his former employer, alleging that he was discriminated against on account of his gender and national origin.... [T]he employer invoked an arbitration provision in Nino's employment contract and moved the District Court to compel the parties to arbitrate their dispute. Nino opposed the motion, arguing that the arbitration agreement was unconscionable and, therefore, unenforceable.... The District Court concluded that although the arbitration agreement contained unconscionable terms, those provisions could be severed from the contract and the remainder of its terms could be enforced. * * *

In our view, the pervasively one-sided nature of the arbitration agreement's terms demonstrates that the employer did not seek to use arbitration as a legitimate means for dispute resolution. Instead, the employer created a system that was designed to give it an unfair advantage through rules that impermissibly restricted employees' access to arbitration and that gave the employer an undue influence over the selection of the arbitrator. We hold that it is not appropriate, in the face of such pervasive one-sidedness, to sever the unconscionable provisions from the remainder of the arbitration agreement. * * * We will thus reverse the District Court's order compelling the parties to arbitrate.

* * * We have repeatedly recognized that the Federal Arbitration Act ("FAA") establishes a "strong federal policy in favor of the resolution of disputes through arbitration." Under the FAA, arbitration agreements "are enforceable to the same extent as other contracts." "A party to a *valid and enforceable* arbitration agreement is entitled to a stay of federal court proceedings pending arbitration as well as an order compelling such arbitration."

* * * Under Virgin Islands law, "[t]he doctrine of unconscionability involves both 'procedural' and 'substantive' elements." The procedural component of the unconscionability inquiry looks to the "process by which an agreement is reached and the form of an

---

[18]*Equal Employment Opportunity Commission v. Waffle House, Inc.*, 534 U.S. 279 (2002).

[19]*14 Penn Plaza LLC v. Pyett*, 129 S.Ct. 1456 (2009).

agreement, including the use therein of fine print and convoluted or unclear language." We have consistently found that adhesion contracts—that is, contracts prepared by the party with greater bargaining power and presented to the other party "for signature on a take-it-or-leave-it basis"—satisfy the procedural element of the unconscionability analysis. "A contract, however, is 'not unconscionable merely because the parties to it are unequal in bargaining position.'" Instead, a party challenging a contract on unconscionability grounds must also show that the contract is substantively unconscionable by demonstrating that the contract contains "terms unreasonably favorable to the stronger party." * * *

Looking first to the question of procedural unconscionability, we agree with the District Court that Nino had no opportunity to negotiate with DI over the contract's terms, that DI was the stronger contractual party, and that the arbitration agreement is thus procedurally unconscionable. First and most significantly, as the District Court expressly found, DI presented the arbitration agreement to Nino "for signature on a take-it-or-leave-it basis." As Nino explained in his deposition, during his first week at the St. Thomas store, DI's human resources manager provided him with a copy of the company's employment contract and instructed him to "read it and sign it," without affording him any opportunity to negotiate over its terms. * * *

We likewise conclude that the arbitration agreement is substantively unconscionable because it contains terms unreasonably favorable to DI, the stronger party. * * * First, ... the arbitration agreement's provision requiring that an employee file a grievance within five days of the complained-of incident in order to preserve his or her opportunity to arbitrate the dispute is substantively unconscionable. We have twice held in no uncertain terms that a thirty-day filing requirement in an arbitration agreement is substantively unconscionable.... [W]hile "a provision limiting the time to bring a claim or provide notice of such a claim to the defendant is not necessarily unfair or otherwise unconscionable," the time period designated by the agreement must still be reasonable. If a thirty-day filing window is "clearly unreasonable" [as held in a prior case], then the five-day filing requirement imposed by the parties' contract in this case is even more unduly favorable to DI .... Indeed, the filing requirement in Nino's arbitration agreement is particularly unreasonable because it is both inflexible and one-sided. With regard to its inflexibility, the agreement states that its filing requirements "are binding

and may not be waived except by written agreement of both parties." * * * DI's "unfair advantage is only compounded by the fact that [DI itself] is apparently not required to provide detailed and written notice to an employee of any of its own claims within a strictly enforced [five]-day time period." Indeed, the arbitration agreement in this case imposes no notice requirement upon DI whatsoever. * * * The one-sided five-day filing requirement is manifestly unreasonable and is substantively unconscionable under Virgin Islands law.

Nino likewise argues, and the District Court found, that the arbitration agreement's requirement that the parties bear their own attorney's fees, costs, and expenses is substantively unconscionable. We agree. * * * [I]f arbitration is to offer claimants the full scope of remedies available under Title VII, arbitrators in Title VII cases, just like courts, must ... ordinarily grant attorney fees to prevailing claimants rather than be restricted by private contractual language. Provisions in arbitration clauses requiring parties to bear their own attorney's fees, costs, and expenses work to "the disadvantage of an employee needing to obtain legal assistance." * * *

Finally, we turn to the arbitration agreement's provision governing the selection of an arbitrator, which Nino contends is substantively unconscionable. Under the arbitration agreement, ... DI is required to submit a request to the AAA for a panel of four arbitrators. The parties select a single arbitrator from this list according to the following process: From the panel the Employer will strike the first arbitrator for whatever reason is unacceptable to the Employer. The Employee will then be allowed to strike one arbitrator from the remaining names of panel members. This process will continue until there remains one arbitrator who will be the arbitrator for this grievance or the parties can decide on an arbitrator that would be mutually acceptable. Although it is phrased in neutral, procedural terms, the upshot of this provision is that DI is permitted to strike two arbitrators from the four-member AAA panel, whereas the employee is permitted to strike just one.

This provision is "one-sided in the extreme and unreasonably favorable to [DI]." It confers an advantage upon DI for no discernible purpose other than to stack the deck in its favor. Courts of Appeals have not hesitated to conclude that provisions in arbitration agreements that give the employer an unreasonable advantage over the employee in the selection of an arbitrator are unconscionable.... "By agreeing to arbitration in lieu of litigation, the parties agree to trade the procedures and opportunity for review of the courtroom for the simplicity, informality, and expedition of arbitration," but they do not accede to procedures "utterly lacking in the rudiments of even-handedness." * * *

Our final task in addressing Nino's unconscionability challenge to the arbitration agreement is to determine whether the unconscionable terms may be severed from the agreement such that the remainder of its terms may be enforced. * * * [T]wo lines of inquiry are relevant to the question of severability. The first of these is whether the unconscionable aspects "of the employment arbitration agreement constitute[] 'an essential part of the agreed exchange' of promises" between the parties. If the unconscionable aspects of the clause do not comprise an essential aspect of the arbitration agreement as a whole, then the unconscionable provisions may be severed and the remainder of the arbitration agreement enforced. * * * The second consideration for the question of severability ... is whether the unconscionability of the arbitration clause demonstrates "a systematic effort to impose arbitration on an employee, not simply as an alternative to litigation, but as an inferior forum that works to the employer's advantage."

* * * We need not discuss whether the unconscionable provisions of the parties' arbitration agreement comprise an essential aspect of the agreement as a whole, because we conclude that the one-sided nature of the arbitration agreement reveals unmistakably that DI "was not seeking a *bona fide* mechanism for dispute resolution, but rather sought to impose a scheme that it knew or should have known would provide it with an impermissible advantage." The provisions in question do not simply accord an advantage upon DI indirectly or by happenstance. Instead, they are baldly one-sided, with only one discernible purpose—to create advantages for the employer that are not afforded to the employee. Of the four members of the arbitration panel, the agreement permits DI to strike two and the employee to strike just one. The employee is required to give notice to DI of the claims he intends to arbitrate, while DI is under no such obligation to provide any notice to the employee. The employee must file a detailed grievance regarding the matter he seeks to arbitrate within five days of the underlying events or lose the right to go to arbitration altogether, while DI is insulated against the risk of default for any failure to adhere to its own filing deadlines. * * *

We conclude ... that the arbitration agreement is procedurally and substantively unconscionable, and that the pervasively one-sided nature of the agreement forecloses any possibility of severing the unfair provisions from the remainder of the agreement. * * *

CASE QUESTIONS

1. What was the legal issue in this case? What did the Court of Appeals decide?
2. What does it mean for a contract to be "unconscionable"? "Procedurally unconscionable"? "Substantively unconscionable"?
3. What was the evidence that this agreement was procedurally unconscionable? Substantively unconscionable?
4. What does it mean to "sever" illegal terms from a contract? Why did the appeals court decline to do so here?
5. What would you advise this employer to do in light of this decision? Should it redraft the language of the arbitration agreement to deal with the court's objections or drop the whole thing?

Since arbitration agreements are typically executed in a procedurally unconscionable fashion, the question of enforceability usually turns on the contents of these agreements. As in the *Nino* case, one area of particular concern is the procedure for selecting an arbitrator. An essential requirement for a fair arbitration is neutrality. Arrangements that give the employer effective control over who can arbitrate a case or require the use of arbitrators with business ties to the employer are unlikely to be enforced.[20] Courts have also closely scrutinized arbitration agreements that require employees to bear a significant part of the arbitration cost. Although some courts hold that any fee-splitting arrangement is objectionable, most courts look at the facts of the situation and the

[20]*McMullen v. Meijer*, 355 F.3d 485 (6th Cir. 2004); *Rodriguez v. Windermere Real Estate/Wall Street, Inc.*, 2008 Wash. App. LEXIS 214 (Div. One), *review denied*, 164 Wn.2d 1017 (2008).

likelihood that the cost would deter employees from bringing claims.[21] Remedies that are markedly different from those available through litigation (e.g., reinstatement or punitive damages are not allowed) are also problematic.[22] Limitations periods for filing arbitration claims that are shorter than those that would apply to court proceedings have sometimes, but not always, been deemed unconscionable.[23] However, courts also recognize that the relative informality, quickness, and lower cost of arbitration are precisely what makes it attractive and therefore do not require that arbitration mirror the procedures and remedies of litigation. Thus, the Supreme Court has determined that arbitration agreements cannot be found unconscionable simply because they contain language prohibiting "classwide" (i.e., class action) arbitration.[24]

JUST THE FACTS

An employee of a defense contractor alleged that she was raped by coworkers while on assignment in Iraq. The sexual assault took place in the employee's bedroom located in barracks provided by the employer, while she was off-duty. Prior to accepting the assignment, she had signed an agreement to use a dispute resolution process culminating in arbitration for legal claims "related to your employment" including "any and all personal injury claim(s) arising in the workplace." Does the arbitration agreement prevent this employee from suing her employer for allowing the assault to occur?

See, *Jones v. Halliburton Co. d/b/a KBR Kellog Brown & Root*, 583 F.3d 228 (5th Cir. 2009), *cert. denied,* 130 S. Ct. 1756 (2010).

Besides delving into the contents of arbitration agreements, courts have considered what adequate notification entails and whether arbitration "agreements" actually existed. For example, job applicants at Prudential Insurance were directed to sign an application form that referred obliquely to arbitration. The applicants were not told about the arbitration agreement, not given copies of the manual containing the terms of the agreement, and not allowed sufficient time to even read the application form. Under these circumstances, a "knowing" agreement to arbitrate rather than go to court did not exist.[25] Other courts do not set the bar as high but still require, as with any valid contract, that a clear offer be made and accepted. An employee who was handed a booklet describing her employer's *Dispute Resolution Procedure* was not held to the arbitration provisions of that procedure because she never provided any written assent to the policy. "For an arbitration agreement to be binding, it must be an agreement, not merely a company policy. Moreover, pursuant to the FAA, the agreement must be in writing."[26] Likewise, an arbitration agreement that was communicated to employees via e-mail was not enforced when the e-mail message did not clearly alert employees to the legal significance of the new policy and the employer did not ascertain whether employees clicked on links that

---

[21]*Blair v. Scott Specialty Gases*, 283 F.3d 595, 609–10 (3d Cir. 2002); *Morrison v. Circuit City Stores*, 317 F.3d 646 (6th Cir. 2003).

[22]*Ingle v. Circuit City Stores*, 328 F.3d 1165, 1178–79 (9th Cir. 2003), *cert. denied,* 540 U.S. 1160 (2004).

[23]*Clark v. DaimlerChrysler Corp.*, 286 Mich. App. 138 (2005), *appeal denied,* 475 Mich. 875 (2006); *Ingle* at 1175.

[24]*AT&T Mobility LLC v. Concepcion*, 2011 U.S. LEXIS 3367.

[25]*Prudential Ins. Co. of America v. Lai*, 42 F.3d 1299 (9th Cir. 1994).

[26]*Lee v. Red Lobster Inns of America*, 92 Fed. Appxx. 158 at 161 (6th Cir. 2004).

would have taken them to the details of the new policy.[27] Communication via e-mail satisfied the requirement that arbitration agreements be written, but the employer's failure to clearly notify employees regarding the policy's legal effect, to track whether employees accessed the linked details, and to obtain from employees acknowledgment that the materials had been read and understood led the court to conclude that employees had received insufficient notice of the arbitration agreement to be bound by it.

Practical Considerations
Would you advise an employer to use arbitration agreements? Why or why not?

Employers that opt to use arbitration agreements should clearly communicate those agreements to employees in written form and obtain written statements of assent. Employers should provide for a fair arbitration process and avoid the temptation to draft one-sided agreements that place burdens on employees without imposing corresponding limitations on themselves. The agreements should provide employees with a genuine opportunity to vindicate their legal rights and not leave them much worse off than if their day in court been available to them.

Remedies for Violations of Employment Laws

If an employee takes legal action against her employer and is successful, what does she get for her trouble? A partial list of **remedies** available in employment cases includes attorneys' fees, court orders, back pay, front pay, reinstatement, hiring, liquidated damages (awarded for serious, intentional violations in amounts up to twice the actual damages incurred), compensatory damages (a wide range of damages beyond loss of wages, including pain and suffering), and **punitive damages** (intended to punish the employer in cases of serious, intentional violations and to create an example to affect the behavior of others). The EEOC has increasingly sought agreements from defendant employers to have their employment practices overseen by external monitors and to institute wide-ranging diversity programs. Not all remedies are available for every legal claim (nor are all the remedies for which a successful plaintiff is eligible necessarily awarded by the courts). Under the National Labor Relations Act, for example, employees are eligible for "make-whole" remedies, including reinstatement and back pay, but not compensatory and punitive damages. In contrast, common law tort claims can yield monetary damages, but not reinstatement.

JUST THE FACTS

A package handler was awarded $8,000 in compensatory damages and $100,000 in punitive damages for his employer's failure to make reasonable accommodation for his deafness. For more than two years, the employee had unsuccessfully sought to obtain written notes from employee meetings, ASL translation, and/or closed-captioning of meeting content. The manager involved knew of his disability but did not consult company policy, authorize training in ADA compliance for the employee's direct supervisor, or seek assistance from other managers who had accommodated deaf employees. The employer, Federal Express, has an ADA compliance policy that calls for reasonable accommodation. Should punitive damages have been awarded in this case? Is the amount of punitive damages awarded excessive?

See *EEOC v. Federal Express*, 513 F.3d 360 (4th Cir. 2008), *cert. denied*, 129 S. Ct. 343 (2009).

---

[27]*Campbell v. General Dynamics*, 407 F.3d 546 (1st Cir. 2005).

The awarding of punitive damages is of particular concern to employers. Yet, the threat of punitive damages plays an important role in ensuring that employers take their legal responsibilities seriously. In discrimination cases, the relevant standard for awarding punitive damages is whether "the employer has engaged in intentional discrimination and has done so 'with malice or with reckless indifference to the federally protected rights of an aggrieved individual.'"[28] Even when the requisite state of mind is present, employers can still avoid *punitive damage* liability for discriminatory acts by their managers if it can be shown that those acts were contrary to the employer's good faith efforts to comply with the law.[29]

Clippings

A state court jury awarded $10.6 million to a stockbroker at UBS Financial Services who had been sexually harassed and then subjected to retaliation for her complaints. The plaintiff's attorney said that "If you look at all of the rules of the road concerning what a firm is supposed to do when it comes to the employer's responsibility to maintain an atmosphere free of harassment, UBS violated every one of those…. That's why there was a $10 million punitive damages award." Not surprisingly, the parties dispute whether the full amount of this judgment will be allowed under Missouri law.

Christopher Brown, "Missouri Jury Hits UBS Financial With $10.6 Million Sex Harassment Verdict." *Daily Labor Report* 87 (May 5, 2011), A-8.

To keep the issue of damages in perspective, remember that the vast majority of cases never go to trial and that headline-grabbing, multi-figure awards including punitive damages are the exceptions rather than the rule. Even when plaintiffs prevail at trial, judges routinely slash jury awards by half or more. Punitive damages are often capped. The ceiling on combined compensatory and punitive damages in discrimination cases brought under Title VII of the Civil Rights Act is $300,000 (with a lower cap for small employers). However, as the case of the UBS stockbroker (see "Clippings") shows, state laws sometimes allow for more substantial awards to plaintiffs. In any event, while the costs of employment law claims are sometimes overstated, they are well worth avoiding.

The Role of Managers in Legal Compliance

Knowledge of employment law will help you recognize, analyze, and deal effectively with the many employment law issues that you are likely to encounter. It should also enable you to put in place sound policies and practices that prevent many legal problems from arising in the first place. *Managers need to know about employment law in order to institute policies that prevent violations, recognize situations that raise legal concerns, and know when to seek legal advice.* Most often, lawyers get involved after the fact, when legally inadvisable actions have already been taken and organizations are in damage-control mode. *Managers—and particularly human resources managers—have a central role in legal compliance and need to have a solid grasp of employment law.*

Noncompliance with the law is not an option—at least not one that will be entertained in this book. But choices remain about how to go about complying with the law. Should employers aim to do no more than that which is strictly required or should they

Practical Considerations What type of legal compliance strategy would you advise an employer to adopt? Why?

- "Pushing the envelope" in areas of legal uncertainty or erring on the side of caution?
- Doing no more than the minimum required by the law or going well beyond that?
- Responding to legal problems as they arise or proactively investing in policies and practices designed to avoid legal problems?
- Litigating aggressively or attempting to work things out with employees who believe that they have been wronged?

[28]*Kolstad v. American Dental Association*, 527 U.S. 526, 529 (1999).
[29]*Kolstad*, at 545.

take a broader view of their legal obligations? How should issues on which the law is currently uncertain be handled? How proactive should employers be in seeking to avoid legal problems? How far should employers go in settling claims rather than litigating them? These choices can be seen as defining an employer's **legal compliance strategy**.

Key Terms

Constitution, p. 4
statute, p. 4
executive order, p. 5
regulation, p. 5
common law, p. 5
tort, p. 5
employment at will, p. 5
public sector, p. 9
private sector, p. 9
payroll method, p. 11
social movement, p. 13
enforcement procedure, p. 13

limitations period, p. 14
equitable tolling, p. 14
Lilly Ledbetter Fair Pay Act of 2009, p. 15
district court, p. 16
summary judgment, p. 16
plaintiff, p. 16
burden of proof, p. 16
appeals court, p. 16
U.S. Supreme Court, p. 16
certiorari, p. 16
stare decisis, p. 16

class-action lawsuits, p. 17
conciliation, p. 20
right to sue letter, p. 20
alternative dispute resolution (ADR), p. 20
mediation, p. 20
arbitration, p. 20
unconscionable, p. 22
remedy, p. 26
punitive damages, p. 26
legal compliance strategy, p. 28

Chapter Summary

The body of law that governs human resource practice consists of many different pieces, including constitutions, statutes, executive orders, regulations, common law, and court decisions interpreting all of these. Because the applicable legal rules differ, it is important to determine whether the employer in question is in the public sector or private sector, whether the employees are unionized, what the size of the employer is, what the geographic location of the employer is, whether the employer is a government contractor, and what industry and occupation are involved. Most employment laws came into being within the last fifty years. These laws confer on employees rights to be protected from discrimination and to enjoy equal employment opportunity, to form unions and engage in collective bargaining with their employers, to have terms and conditions of employment that meet at least minimum standards, to have basic liberties respected, and to receive compensation for certain types of harm done by their employers. However, the starting point for analyzing employees' rights on the job is employment at will. In the absence of a contract of employment for a specified duration, employment can be terminated at any time and for any reason that is not specifically prohibited by law.

The process by which these important rights are enforced varies, but is rarely quick. Employees make choices about whether to undertake legal action, and

if they do so, they face varying time limits, administrative prerequisites, and court proceedings. Most cases are resolved without going to trial. A significant development is the increased use of arbitration agreements, under which employees must agree to take all employment disputes to arbitration rather than court. These agreements are generally enforceable, but they can be rendered unenforceable by their contents and the way they are presented to employees.

Employees who are successful in contesting violations of their rights potentially are entitled to a variety of remedies. The remedies available depend on the legal basis for and strength of the employee's claim. One particularly significant remedy is punitive damages. In discrimination cases, these are available when an employer has engaged in discriminatory acts with malicious intent or reckless indifference to an employee's federally protected rights. Some cases result in large awards to plaintiffs, but these headline-grabbing cases should not be viewed as the typical outcome of employment litigation.

Legal protections for employees and the number of legal claims being brought by employees have clearly increased. Employment laws serve important purposes and express societal values. Anecdotal accounts of frivolous lawsuits and employee windfalls should not be allowed to obscure the far more complex reality of enforcing fair treatment in the workplace.

Practical Advice Summary

- Managers need to be well versed in employment law and remain up to date in the face of ongoing changes.
- Managers should learn about employment law so they can
  - Institute sound policies that prevent violations.
  - Recognize legal issues when they arise.
  - Know when to seek advice from legal counsel.
- Creating and maintaining good documentation of the reasons for human resource decisions is essential.
- If mandatory arbitration agreements are used, such agreements should
  - Be in writing.
  - Clearly notify employees that they are waiving their right to sue.
  - Obtain evidence of employee acceptance in writing.
- Mandatory arbitration agreements should not
  - Place restrictions on employees without corresponding restrictions being placed on the employer.
  - Unreasonably limit the remedies available to employees.
  - Burden employees with excessive payments for the arbitration.
  - Allow undue employer control over the selection of arbitrators.
  - Be subject to change at any time by the employer.

Chapter Questions

1. Do you think that most employees who take legal action against their employers have valid claims or are looking to "get something for nothing"? What is the basis for your opinion?
2. Would you be inclined to take legal action against your employer if you felt strongly that your legal rights had been violated? Why or why not?
3. The XYZ Company had twelve employees for the first half of 2011. It signed a contract with a major retailer in June 2011 and hired an additional eight employees to handle the extra work. The contract was cancelled in January 2012, and the company laid off the eight new hires. In March 2012, an employee was fired. If the employee believed that the termination was discriminatory, could the employee have brought a case under Title VII of the Civil Rights Act?
4. The City of Chicago administered a civil service exam to be used in hiring firefighters. The results of the exam were announced in January 1996. No discrimination charges were filed within 300 days of the announcement. The city used the same eligibility list to hire firefighters numerous times between 1996 and 2002. Would a charge of discrimination brought long after the test was administered and the results originally announced, but within 300 days of one of the subsequent uses of the list, be timely? Why or why not? (*Lewis v. Chicago*, 130 S. Ct. 2191 [2010]).
5. An employee signed an arbitration agreement when he was hired. The agreement provided that the costs of the arbitration would be split equally between the parties, with the employee payment capped at the amount earned in the employee's highest earnings month during the previous year; remedies could not include either punitive damages or reinstatement; all claims must be brought forth within a year; and depositions were limited to one for each side. The employee was fired and filed a lawsuit. The company went to court to compel arbitration. What should the court decide? Why? (*In re Johnny Luna*, 2004 Tex. App. LEXIS 8241 [1st Dist.]).
6. An employee signed an employment application form that included the following: "I agree that any action or suit against the firm arising out of my employment or termination of employment, including but not limited to claims arising under the state or federal civil rights statutes, must be brought within 180 days of the event giving rise to the claims or be forever barred. I waive any limitations periods to the contrary. I further agree that if I should bring any action or claim arising out of my employment against the firm in which the firm prevails, I will pay to the firm any and all costs incurred by the firm in defense of said claims, including attorney fees...." The quoted provisions were not part of any arbitration agreement. The employee sued the employer under the Family and Medical Leave Act (FMLA).

The normal limitations period for FMLA claims is two years (three for willful violations). The employer argued that the employee was contractually bound to the shorter limitations period and that the court should dismiss the case. What should the court decide? Why? (*Madry v. Gibraltor Nat'l Corp.*, 2011 U.S. Dist. LEXIS 44079 [E.D. Mich.])

7. An employee of a car dealership signed an arbitration agreement. The agreement included a cost sharing provision that would require the employee, who earned about $20,000 per year, to pay a deposit of five days' pay ($400–$500) to take a dispute to arbitration. This deposit had to be paid within ten days of the challenged employment decision. However, the procedure also provided for waivers of the deposit, at the discretion of the General Manager of the dealership. Employees who fully prevailed at arbitration got their deposits refunded, in addition to the company paying the arbitrator's fees and expenses. If any part of the arbitrator's decision was in favor of the employer, costs would be shared equally up to the deposited amount. Does this cost sharing arrangement render the arbitration agreement unenforceable? Why or why not? (*Mazera v. Varsity Ford Mgmt. Servs.*, 565 F.3d 997 [6th Cir. 2009]).

8. At the end of a workplace meeting in which a number of issues were discussed, the company president mentioned that a new arbitration policy was being instituted. A pamphlet outlining the new dispute resolution program was available, but it was not read to employees and not all employees picked it up. Employees who continued to work after the effective date of the new policy were deemed to have accepted it. When an employee told the president that he would not sign, he was told "not to worry about it." Subsequently, a new employee handbook was issued. The handbook included the arbitration program. The handbook also included an acknowledgment form, but the employer did not require or receive signed forms. When a group of employees filed suit for unpaid wages, the employer attempted to compel arbitration of the issue. Should the court enforce the arbitration agreement? Why or why not? (*Moran v. Ceiling Fans Direct*, 239 Fed. Appx. 931 [5th Cir. 2007])

9. What legal issues did you identify in the "staff meeting" discussion that opened the chapter? What should this company be doing differently? What aspects of the situation are you unsure of and would want to learn more about?

CHAPTER 2

The Employment Relationship

Readers of this book most likely have had the experience of being employed, if only during summers or at part-time jobs. You might currently be interviewing for jobs and—it is hoped—receiving offers of employment. Most work gets done through the establishment of employment relationships, but this is not always the case. This chapter delves into the meaning behind the terms **employee** and **employer** and the legal significance of determining whether an employment relationship exists. You might be surprised by how slippery the definitions of *employee* and *employer* turn out to be—and how recent changes in the structure of employment have complicated matters. Full-time employment by a single employer is still the norm, but there are many variations on this theme. These variations can affect the legal rights of people performing work.

THE CHANGING WORKPLACE

Contingent Work and Alternatives to Direct Employment

Employment laws premised on the existence of employment relationships run up against the increasing variety of arrangements under which work is performed. This variety in work arrangements is often captured by the terms **contingent** or **nonstandard work**. In general, these terms are used to contrast full-time, year-round employment with a single employer that is expected to continue indefinitely, with looser (i.e., more flexible or less secure, depending on where you sit) relationships that exist only as long as some particular project or piece of work needs to be done. Continuation of these latter relationships is thus "contingent" on an immediate need for the specific services performed. There is no expectation that the relationships will be ongoing or long-term.

The most expansive definitions of contingent or nonstandard work include all part-time employees (roughly 20 percent of the workforce), on the grounds that they are subject to greater variability in hours. More commonly, contingent work is deemed to include independent contractors (7.4 percent of the workforce), temp workers provided through an agency (0.9 percent), temp workers who are directly hired by companies but not given permanent employee status (2–3 percent), contract company workers (e.g., security guards supplied to a particular company) (6 percent), on-call workers (e.g., substitute teachers) or day laborers (1.8 percent), and other self-employed workers not classified as independent contractors (about 5 percent).[1] Furthermore, contracting relationships with the likes of temporary staffing services, labor contractors, employee leasing services, and subcontractor firms have increasingly taken the place of direct employment by a user firm.[2]

Not everyone is a contingent worker or employed through some type of intermediary. Agency temp workers—often regarded as the quintessential nonstandard workers—comprise only a small portion of the overall workforce. However, workers with contingent and nonstandard arrangements number in the millions, and their ranks have grown over the past few decades. The growth of contingent work and labor contracting has forced the courts to wrestle with whether and how our employment laws apply to such workers. There is concern that work arrangements are being manipulated and mischaracterized by employers for the purpose of evading their legal responsibilities.[3]

_____

[1]U.S. Bureau of Labor Statistics. "Contingent and Alternative Employment Arrangements, February 2005." BLS News Release. Viewed April 17, 2008 (http://www.bls.gov/news.release/conemp.nr0.htm); Susan N. Houseman. "The Policy Implications of Nonstandard Work Arrangements." _Employment Research._ W. E. Upjohn Institute (Fall 1999), 5–7.
[2]Noah D. Zatz. "Working Beyond the Reach or Grasp of Employment Law." In Bernhardt, Boushey, Dresser, and Tilly, eds. _The Gloves-Off Economy: Workplace Standards at the Bottom of America's Labor Market._ Champaign, IL: Labor and Employment Relations Association (2008), 37–42.
[3]Zatz, at 42–50.

The Importance of Determining Whether an Employment Relationship Exists

The first important reason to correctly determine whether someone performing work is actually an employee is because this is required for compliance with tax laws. If someone is an employee, her employer is required to withhold income taxes and to pay the employer's share of Social Security and Medicare taxes. Additional payments must be made to provide workers' compensation and unemployment insurance for employees. A study conducted by the Department of Labor in 2000 found that from 10 to 30 percent of employers audited in a sample of states had misclassified at least some of their employees as independent contractors.[1] A Massachusetts study found that almost 19 percent of employers in the state had misclassified employees as independent contractors between 2001 and 2003.[2] The U.S. Government Accountability Office (GAO) estimated that the government lost $4.7 billion in income taxes in 2006 due to the improper classification of employees as independent contractors.[3] A number of states—including Illinois, Maryland, Delaware, Colorado, and New Jersey—have enacted laws that increase penalties to employers and make misclassification, by itself, illegal. Federal enforcement efforts have lagged, in large part because federal tax law provides a generous "safe harbor" to employers that consistently treat a class of workers as independent contractors.[4]

Clippings

Driven by large budget deficits, the federal and state governments have launched crackdowns on employers that misclassify their employees as independent contractors. This practice has become more common in recent years, especially

_____

[1]Lawrence E. Dubé. "'Misclassification' Cases Draw More Attention as States Take Action, Plaintiffs File Lawsuits." _Daily Labor Report_ 225 (November 25, 2009), C-1.

[2]Diane E. Lewis. "UMass-Harvard Study Finds Thousands of Workers Misclassified." _Boston Globe_ (December 13, 2004), C1.

[3]"House Tax Panels Examine Costs of Workers Misclassified as 'Contractors.'" _Daily Labor Report_ 89 (May 9, 2007), A-1.

[4]Dubé.

> among truck drivers, construction workers, home health aides, and high-tech workers. Through misclassification, employers avoid required tax payments—as well as other legal obligations such as overtime pay—saving some 20 to 30 percent per employee. The federal government is projecting that increased enforcement efforts will add $7 billion to the treasury over ten years. Between late 2007 and early 2010, the state of New York identified more than 31,000 cases of misclassification, yielding $11 million in unpaid taxes and $14.5 million in unpaid wages.
>
> Steven Greenhouse. "A Crackdown on 'Contractors' as a Tax Dodge." *New York Times* (February 8, 2010), A1.

The second important reason to determine whether an employment relationship exists is that most of the laws discussed in this book do not apply in the absence of an employment relationship. Thus, a threshold issue in many employment law cases, highlighted in this chapter, is whether an employment relationship exists. Employee status may also be a prerequisite for a claim of contractual benefits stemming from an employer's policies and benefit programs. Remember also that coverage by employment laws often depends on a firm meeting minimum-size requirements. Because only employees are counted, whether particular individuals are employees can determine whether other individuals who clearly are employees will have legal rights to assert.

> ## *Clippings*
>
> Federal Express has been at the epicenter of the worker misclassification issue in recent years. The company has faced numerous legal challenges to its practice of classifying its package delivery drivers as independent contractors. A federal district court judge in Indiana has been hearing dozens of class action lawsuits brought on behalf of FedEx drivers nationwide in a consolidated legal proceeding. Although the plaintiffs won several victories in other jurisdictions, Federal Express appears to have prevailed in the major battleground of the consolidated lawsuits. The district court judge held that while FedEx exerted considerable control over workloads and delivery times, this did not translate to effective control over the means and methods of performing the work.
>
> Lawrence E. Dubé. "Federal Court Mostly Rules for FedEx Ground in Driver Lawsuits Alleging Misclassification." *Daily Labor Report* 240 (December 15, 2010), AA-1.

The other side of the employment relationship must also be considered. Even when a person doing work is clearly an employee, there can still be questions about the identity of the employer. Complexities in corporate structure and practices, such as leasing employees or obtaining them through temp agencies, can cloud the issue of which entity is liable if employees' rights are violated.

Who Is an Employee?

Ascertaining who is an employee is clearly important, but is it problematic? Don't we know an employee when we see one? And surely Congress and other legislative bodies that write employment laws must have defined the intended beneficiaries of those laws. In Title VII of the Civil Rights Act of 1964, which is typical of other employment laws in this regard, Congress defined an employee as "an individual employed by an employer...."[5] Definitions of this sort are hopelessly circular and fail to provide any criteria for discerning who is an employee.

But perhaps Congress neglected to be more specific because the meaning of *employee* is self-evident. Isn't an employee simply a person who performs work for someone else and receives pay in return? In fact, this commonsense definition goes a long way. However, the definition is insufficient to distinguish between employees and independent contractors because both do work in exchange for pay. Difficulties may also arise in distinguishing employees from temps, interns, students, volunteers, and partners.

Clippings

Coverall North America is a commercial cleaning firm. Franchisees pay a fee to the company, sometimes as much as $30,000, to obtain cleaning jobs. Billing and collection is handled by Coverall, which deducts its fees before remitting the remaining revenue to franchisees. A group of franchisees sued, alleging that they are employees entitled to receive the minimum wage and overtime pay. The company maintains that they are independent contractors. A district court judge has ruled that the company failed to prove that its franchisees were independent contractors. If the ruling holds up, this case and others currently in the courts raise basic questions about the employment status of franchisees.

Richard Gibson. "Franchisees: We're Employees, Not Contractors." *The Wall Street Journal Online* (May 10, 2010). Viewed May 14, 2010 (http://online.wsj.com).

Independent Contractors

Distinguishing between **independent contractors** and employees is the central—and most contentious—issue surrounding employee status. Because both employees and independent contractors perform work in exchange for pay, other factors must be considered to distinguish between them. The **economic realities test** is one approach used by courts to distinguish between employees and independent contractors, particularly in Fair Labor Standards Act (wage and hour) cases. The focus of the economic realities test is on whether the person doing work is in business for herself and not dependent on a particular employer to engage in this line of work. The test includes consideration of the following criteria:

1. Who has the right to control how, when, and where the work is done?
2. Who provides the tools, materials, and other resources needed for the work to be performed?
3. Does the method of payment afford opportunity for profit or loss, depending on how well the work is managed?
4. What is the duration of the working relationship?
5. Does the work require some type of special skill?
6. How integral to the business is the work that is being performed?
7. Overall, how dependent is the person performing the work on the hiring party?

---

[5] 42 U.S.C.S. § 2000e(f) (2011).

A worker would be considered an independent contractor if when performing the work, he controls how, when, and where it is done; provides his own tools, materials, and supplies; is paid a specified sum for the work and has the opportunity to profit by managing the work efficiently; is engaged for short periods of time to complete particular projects; has a distinct, marketable skill; performs work that is not so integral to the hiring party's business that it would be needed on a regular basis in order to be in that business; and provides his services to a number of different hiring parties. Only in rare cases do all of these criteria point to the same conclusion. More often, some facts point to independent contractor status and others to employee status. Courts then have to look at the totality of the evidence to determine the worker's status. It is the hiring party who bears the burden of proving that a person performing work is an independent contractor, and not an employee.

JUST THE FACTS

Stan Freund installed home satellite and entertainment systems for a company that sold these systems. The company scheduled installations, although Mr. Freund could reschedule them. The installer worked on his own but was required to wear a company shirt, follow certain minimum specifications for installations, not perform any additional services for customers without the company's approval, and call the company to confirm that installations had been made and to report any problems. Mr. Freund was paid a set amount per installation. He used his own vehicle and tools. Mr. Freund was free to perform installations for other companies and to hire others to do installations. However, while other installers did accept jobs from other companies, Mr. Freund worked six days a week for this company. Is Mr. Freund an employee with rights under the Fair Labor Standards Act?

See, *Freund v. Hi-Tech Satellite*, 185 Fed. Appx. 782 (11th Cir. 2006).

Use of the economic realities test to determine whether workers are properly treated as independent contractors is illustrated by a case involving welders working on natural gas pipelines.[6] In this case, the court found that the welders were employees entitled to overtime pay for their long hours of work. The welders were scheduled, supervised, and not privy to the blueprints for projects. These facts suggest that the pipeline company retained considerable control over how and when the work was done even though the welders, as skilled craftspersons, were not told how to do their welds. The welders were also paid on an hourly basis, did not do welding for other companies while engaged by this company, performed work that was absolutely essential to the completion of pipelines, and did not have contractor's licenses that would allow them to bid on projects. Other facts were arguably more consistent with the existence of an independent contractor relationship. The welders provided their own welding equipment and trucks, they worked on pipelines for relatively brief periods of time (no more than two months at a time), they moved between different construction companies over the course of the year, and they were skilled craftspersons. But overall, and particularly in the context of construction work that is inherently intermittent, the economic realities test criteria pointed to an employment relationship.

---

[6]*Baker v. Flint Engineering & Construction*, 137 F.3d 1436 (10th Cir. 1998).

In contrast, a cable splicer who was enlisted to help a telecom company recover from Hurricane Katrina was deemed an independent contractor.[7] The man owned a separate business in Delaware but decided to accept an offer to travel to New Orleans to do splicing work. He arrived with his own bucket truck and other necessary equipment. The job lasted three months and was the only work that the splicer ever did for the telecom company. He was paid $68 per hour and received a $50 per diem for his long hours of work. He reported to the same site each day and was then told where to go to fix downed telephone lines. Although other splicers were employees of the telecom company and earned overtime, the court emphasized that this was relatively autonomous work; it took place during a one-time, three-month-long stint; the splicer provided his own equipment; and—despite the hourly wage—realized profits that depended on how well he controlled his own costs and expenses. Ultimately, the court concluded that "[t]he circumstances of [the plaintiff's] employment reflect that he is not economically dependant on the defendants. [The] evidence shows that [the plaintiff] is a sophisticated, intelligent business man who entered into a contractual relationship to perform a specific job for the defendants."[8]

The common law test is another widely used method for determining employee status. The **common law test** considers the following factors:[9]

1. The extent of the hiring party's right to control the manner and means by which the work is done
2. The level of skill required
3. The source of necessary tools and materials
4. The location of the work
5. The duration of the work
6. The extent of the hiring party's right to assign additional projects to the hired party
7. The extent of the hired party's discretion over when and how long to work
8. The method of payment
9. The hired party's role is in hiring and paying assistants
10. The extent to which the work is part of the regular business of the hiring party
11. Whether the hiring party is in business
12. Whether benefits of any kind are provided to the hired party
13. The tax treatment of the hired party

There is considerable overlap between the two tests, but the common law test emphasizes right of control, whereas the economic realities test focuses more on the market for the contractor's services and the question of whether the person performing work is in business for herself. When the **right-of-control** factor is considered, the most relevant issue is whether the hiring party has the authority to control where, when, and how the work gets done, even if that party chooses not to fully exercise its authority or to delegate certain decisions to the person doing the work.

In *Narayan v. EGL, Inc.*, a federal appeals court uses a mixture of the economic realities and common law tests to determine the employment status of drivers at a package delivery firm.

---

[7]*Thibault v. BellSouth Telecommunications*, 612 F.3d 843 (5th Cir. 2010).

[8]*Thibault*, at 849.

[9]*Nationwide Mutual Insurance Co. v. Darden*, 503 U.S. 318, 323–24 (1992).

Narayan v. EGL, Inc.
616 F.3d 895 (9th Cir. 2010)

OPINION BY DISTRICT JUDGE KORMAN:

The California Labor Code ("Labor Code") confers certain benefits on employees that it does not afford independent contractors. * * * This appeal from a judgment of the United States District Court for the Northern District of California granting the motion of an employer for summary judgment... principally presents the issue whether, assuming the existence of an employer-employee relationship in California, the employer may avoid its obligations under the Labor Code by inserting a clause in an employer-drafted pre-printed form contract in which: (1) the employee acknowledges that he is an independent contractor and (2) agrees that the contract would be interpreted in accordance with the laws of another jurisdiction where such an agreement is generally enforceable.

EGL, the employer, is a global transportation, supply chain management and information services company incorporated under the laws of Texas and headquartered in Texas. * * * [The plaintiffs] were residents of California who were engaged to provide freight pick-up and delivery services for EGL in California. All three Drivers signed agreements with EGL for "Leased Equipment and Independent Contractor Services" (the "Agreements"). The Agreements provided that the "intention of the parties is to... create a vendor/vendee relationship between Contractor and [EGL]," and acknowledged that "[n]either Contractor nor any of its employees or agents shall be considered to be employees of EGL." * * *

Notwithstanding the terms of the Agreements, the Drivers filed a complaint in California against EGL... alleging that they were EGL employees.... They sought money damages for unpaid overtime wages, business expenses, meal compensation and unlawful deductions from wages as well as other relief, including statutory penalties.

... EGL moved for summary judgment arguing that, under the terms of the Agreements, the Drivers were not employees. Instead they were independent contractors who were not entitled to the benefits conferred upon employees by the Labor Code. Relying on a choice-of-law clause in the Agreements, the district court held that the law of Texas applied, and that declarations in the Agreements that the Drivers were independent contractors rather than employees, compelled the holding that they were independent

contractors as a matter of law. Moreover, although California does not regard such declarations as controlling, and applies a multi-factor analysis in which the intent of the parties is one of over a dozen and a half factors, the district court held, without undertaking any analysis of the relevant factors, that the result would be the same under California law. Consequently, the district court granted EGL's motion for summary judgment.

I. Choice-of-Law

EGL argues that the choice-of-law clause in the Agreements, which provides that the contracts "shall be interpreted under the laws of the State of Texas," applies to the current dispute. * * * The Drivers' claims involve entitlement to benefits under the California Labor Code. Whether the Drivers are entitled to those benefits depends on whether they are employees of EGL, which in turn depends on the definition that the otherwise governing law—not the parties—gives to the term "employee." While the contracts will likely be used as evidence to prove or disprove the statutory claims, the claims do not arise out of the contract, involve the interpretation of any contract terms, or otherwise require there to be a contract. * * * [H]ere, appellants claims arose under the Labor Code, a California regulatory scheme, and consequently, California law should apply to define the boundaries of liability under that scheme.

II. Propriety of Summary Judgment Under California Law

* * * [U]nder California law, once a plaintiff comes forward with evidence that he provided services for an employer, the employee has established a prima facie case that the relationship was one of employer/employee. * * * Once the employee establishes a prima facie case, the burden shifts to the employer, which may prove, if it can, that the presumed employee was an independent contractor. * * *

The Supreme Court of California has enumerated a number of indicia of an employment relationship, the most important of which is the "right to discharge at will, without cause." [The Court] has endorsed other factors... that may point to an employment relationship:

(a) whether the one performing services is engaged in a distinct occupation or business; (b) the kind of occupation, with reference to whether, in the locality, the work is usually done under the direction of the principal or by a specialist without supervision; (c) the skill required in the particular occupation; (d) whether the principal or the worker supplies the instrumentalities, tools, and the place of work for the person doing the work; (e) the length of time for which the services are to be performed; (f) the method of payment, whether by the time or by the job; (g) whether or not the work is a part of the regular business of the principal; and (h) whether or not the parties believe they are creating the relationship of employer-employee. [The Court has] also approvingly cited five factors adopted by cases in other jurisdictions. These include: (1) the alleged employee's opportunity for profit or loss depending on his managerial skill; (2) the alleged employee's investment in equipment or materials required for his task, or his employment of helpers; (3) whether the service rendered requires a special skill; (4) the degree of permanence of the working relationship; and (5) whether the service rendered is an integral part of the alleged employer's business. * * *

All factors… [are] "logically pertinent to the inherently difficult determination whether a provider of service is an employee or an excluded independent contractor." * * * "We must assess and weigh all of the incidents of the relationship with the understanding that no one factor is decisive, and that it is the rare case where the various factors will point with unanimity in one direction or the other. * * *

The delivery services provided by the EGL drivers were an essential part of the regular business of EGL. Indeed, EGL's instructional video shown to the drivers advises them that "as an [EGL] pickup and delivery driver, you have the key role in the shipping process… * * * You can identify shipments that are potential claims before they are put into our system and you ensure our customers' freight is protected by using proper loading work method techniques." * * * The video goes on to describe the drivers as "our company's largest sales force," because "[t]hrough your interactions with the customer, you communicate [EGL's] commitment to excellence." Indeed, the video acknowledges that "for our company to continue to grow, every [EGL] driver must understand the critical importance of the job they do."

Consequently, EGL's Safety and Compliance Manual and Drivers' Handbook instructed the EGL drivers on… how to conduct themselves when receiving assignments and packages, responding to customer complaints and handling damaged freight. The drivers used EGL-supplied forms, received company memoranda and attended meetings on company policies. The Handbook also provided guidelines on how to communicate with EGL's dispatch, instructing drivers to notify the dispatcher before leaving EGL's facility dock, to contact the dispatcher after each delivery stop to report that the delivery was completed, and to immediately report any traffic delays. Indeed, the EGL drivers were told that "[c]ommunicating with dispatch is the single most important aspect of the services drivers are paid for. It is not enough to get the freight picked up or delivered. To be competitive in today's market, the team must be able to identify at a moment's notice exactly where a shipment is in the course of transit." * * *

Moreover, there was evidence that EGL's drivers were ordered to report to the EGL station at a set time each morning—whether or not packages were available to be delivered. Indeed, one of EGL's dispatchers testified that one of the plaintiff Drivers was subject to disciplinary action for showing up late. Similarly, the record indicates that the drivers had to submit advance notice of vacation days. The plaintiff Drivers also submitted evidence that, although their contracts purportedly gave them the right to pick and choose assignments, in practice, EGL presented them with batches of deliveries that they generally had to accept as an all-or-nothing proposition. In some circumstances, standard operating procedure agreements between EGL and many of its customers determined the manner in which drivers made deliveries. Moreover, the plaintiff Drivers drove exclusively for EGL during their period of employment, and there is at least a material issue of fact as to whether they could have driven for other delivery companies because EGL required them to affix EGL logos to their trucks, which the plaintiff Drivers allege could not practically be covered up.

The record also shows that EGL controlled many other details of their drivers' performance. EGL regulated their drivers' appearance—requiring them to wear EGL-branded shirts, safety boots and an EGL identification card. Although their drivers owned their own trucks or vans as noted above, EGL required that they affix EGL logos to the outside of their vehicles. * * * EGL imposed requirements on their drivers' vehicles—in particular, that they be painted white and less than five years old, although EGL disputes whether these requirements were enforced. * * * EGL's drivers supplied some of the equipment used to deliver packages (e.g., hand trucks, lift gates, etc.), but EGL provided other supplies such as EGL-branded boxes and packing tape to their drivers for package pickups. While EGL's drivers retained the right to employ others to assist in performing their contractual obligations, EGL required all helpers to be approved by it. The same rule applied to passengers. * * * [N]one of the plaintiff Drivers hired helpers to perform their duties for EGL.

Significantly, the contracts signed by the plaintiff Drivers contained automatic renewal clauses and could be terminated by either party upon thirty-days notice or upon breach of the agreement. Such an agreement is a substantial indicator of an at-will employment relationship. Moreover, the occupation that the plaintiff Drivers were engaged in did not require a high level of skill. Drivers were not required to possess any special license beyond a normal driver's license, and no skills beyond the ability to drive.

Finally, the length and indefinite nature of the plaintiff Drivers' tenure with EGL also point toward an employment relationship. Here, the plaintiff Drivers worked at EGL for several years, and their Agreements were automatically renewed. This was not a circumstance where a contractor was hired to perform a specific task for a defined period of time. There was no contemplated end to the service relationship at the time that the plaintiff Drivers began working for EGL. * * *

That the Drivers here had contracts "expressly acknowledging that they were independent contractors" is simply not dispositive under California's test of employment. [Drivers] were paid on a regular basis, although their salary was based on a percentage of each delivery. Nevertheless, the fact that their salary was determined in this way is equally consistent with an employee relationship, particularly where other indicia of employment are present.

Similarly, setting aside evidence that the plaintiff Drivers did not, as a practical matter, determine their own routes, the ability to determine a driving route is "simply a freedom inherent in the nature of the work and not determinitive of the employment relation." "[I]f an employment relationship exists, the fact that a certain amount of freedom is allowed or is inherent in the nature of the work involved does not change the character of the relationship, particularly where the employer has general supervision and control."

Ultimately, under California's multi-faceted test of employment, there existed at the very least sufficient indicia of an employment relationship between the plaintiff Drivers and EGL such that a reasonable jury could find the existence of such a relationship. * * * The judgment of the district court granting EGL's motion for summary judgment is REVERSED and REMANDED.

CASE QUESTIONS

1. What issues did the court consider in this case? What was its decision?
2. What factors did the appeals court consider to determine the employment status of the drivers? How do these compare to the economic realities test? Common law test?
3. How did the appeals court apply these factors to the facts of this case?
4. Why had the district court ruled for the employer? Why does the agreement that the drivers signed not matter?
5. Does the business model of this logistics firm, including an emphasis on teamwork, customer service, and real time tracking of parcels, fit with the use of independent contractors? Why or why not?

Using Independent Contractors

One of the clearest practical implications of the foregoing is that a company cannot establish independent contractor status simply by labeling its workers as contractors. Nor do independent contractor agreements suffice to prove that workers are not employees. The details of working relationships measured against the criteria of the applicable tests of employee status are what matter—not labels, self-perceptions, or signed agreements.

This does not mean that agreements are useless. *Companies using independent contractors should have signed agreements spelling out the terms of these relationships.* Clarifying the nature of relationships at the outset can avert misunderstandings. Agreements also serve to document the nature of the relationship when that relationship is disputed, provided that the agreements are accurate and demonstrate genuine independent contractor status.

In light of the particular importance of right of control as an indicator of employee status, firms have to be prepared to relinquish most of their control over how the work is done if they want to use independent contractors rather than employees. This includes refraining from close supervision of independent contractors, directing or scheduling their activities, providing training, or requiring them to attend staff meetings.

The criteria for distinguishing between employees and independent contractors point to several other things that employers should do (or not do) to establish the independent contractor (IC) status of persons performing work. It is not essential that every one of these requirements be met, but if several cannot be met, that is a good indication that the worker should not be treated as an independent contractor:

- *Require that ICs supply their own tools, materials, and equipment and pay their own business expenses*
- *Require that ICs hire their own assistants*
- *Pay ICs a flat fee for the work performed rather than an hourly or weekly rate*
- *Closely review long-term ICs and do not assign new projects without renewing agreements*
- *Don't have ICs doing the same work that regular employees are doing or work that is central to the business that the company is in*
- *Don't provide benefits to ICs, including paid time off*
- *Make it clear that ICs are free to offer their services to others*

Practical Considerations Try your hand at drafting an independent contractor agreement that a company that sells carpeting might use for its installers. Don't worry about making your agreement sound like legalese. Focus instead on what such an agreement should specify.

Questions about independent contractor status are especially likely to arise in situations where some individuals are performing work as independent contractors alongside others who are doing basically the same job as employees. Alternatively, an employee may be downsized or otherwise leave employment, only to return in the guise of an independent contractor "consultant" performing the same work, but with a different employment status. In general, *employers should avoid using both employees and independent contractors to perform the same work and refrain from bringing former employees back as "consultants" with duties that are little changed from their previous employment.*

Temporary Workers

Another variety of contingent worker is **temporary workers**, or "temps." Legal problems can arise when temp workers, particularly those kept on for long periods of time and doing the same work as regular employees, challenge their exclusion from the benefits available to a company's regular employees.

The story of Microsoft's "permatemps" is a case in point. The tale began in the mid-1980s, when a rapidly expanding Microsoft enlisted the services of numerous programmers and systems analysts, classifying them as independent contractors. These arrangements came to the attention of the IRS and led to enforcement actions against Microsoft. Microsoft settled with the IRS, conceding that its independent contractors were really employees. However, rather than abandon its use of workers that it distinguished from regular, permanent employees, Microsoft increasingly turned to temporary staffing firms to supply such workers. The workers continued to be excluded from valuable benefits available to permanent employees of Microsoft, including the company's "Savings Plus Plan" and "Employee Stock Purchase Plan."

In 1992, a group of temp workers, many of whom had been with Microsoft for more than a year and performed the same work as permanent employees, filed suit, challenging their exclusion from these benefits. The lengthy litigation that followed culminated in a 1997 appeals court ruling against Microsoft.[10] The company was under no legal requirement to provide such benefits to any of its employees, but once it undertook to do so, the common law definition of employee applied and the company was not free to arbitrarily exclude a group of workers that met that definition. The fact that the temps signed agreements stating that they were not regular employees of Microsoft did not alter their status under common law. The 1997 court decision did not completely resolve the dispute, but the "handwriting was on the wall" for Microsoft. In December 2000, the company agreed to pay $97 million to settle the claims of more than 8,000 temp workers it employed between 1987 and 2000.[11] Microsoft continues to use large numbers of contract workers, although it now stipulates that its agency temps can work for no longer than a year at a time and cannot be rehired for a substantial period thereafter. Tensions between the company and its temp workers continue to surface periodically.[12]

Employers must not arbitrarily exclude some workers from benefits of employment by designating them as temps when they are employed on a long-term basis, do the same work as regular employees, and meet other legal criteria for establishing employee status.

Students and Interns

Not all of the issues surrounding who is an employee involve contingent workers. If work is performed for educational institutions and serves, at least partly, an educational purpose, are persons performing such work employees, students, or both? The National Labor Relations Board concluded in a 2004 decision involving Brown University that graduate student research and teaching assistants at private universities "are primarily students and have a primarily educational, not economic, relationship with their university."[13] In so deciding, the NLRB implicitly treated employee status as an either/or proposition (i.e., one is either an employee or a student, but not simultaneously both). However, it appears that the NLRB is rethinking this matter. The Board has stated that there are "compelling reasons" to reconsider the employment status of university graduate assistants and remanded a case raising that issue.[14] The *Brown University* decision was somewhat at odds with an earlier decision in which the NLRB had found medical interns and residents to be employees with the right to unionize and engage in collective bargaining with hospitals.,[15] Furthermore, while a decision under tax law does not compel the same conclusion under employment laws, the Supreme Court has recently determined that it is proper for the IRS to treat medical residents who work more than forty hours per week as hospital employees.[16]

What about the employment status of students in a boarding school vocational program who perform substantial amounts of work for a nonprofit organization? *Solis v. Laurelbrook Sanitarium and School* considers this issue.

---

[10]*Vizcaino v. Microsoft,* 120 F.3d 1006 (9th Cir. 1997), *cert. denied,* 118 S. Ct. 899 (1998).

[11]Steven Greenhouse. "Temp Workers at Microsoft Win Lawsuit." *New York Times* (December 13, 2000), C-1.

[12]Benjamin J. Romano. "Microsoft work force includes about 80,000 vendors, temps." *Seattle Times* (March 4, 2009); "Microsoft contract workers protest pay cuts." *Seattle Times* (March 2, 2009), viewed May 24, 2011 (http://seattletimes.nwsource.com).

[13]*Brown University,* 342 NLRB No. 42, at 5 (2004).

[14]*New York University,* 356 NLRB No. 7, at 1 (2010).

[15]*Boston Medical Center,* 330 NLRB No. 30 (1999).

[16]*Mayo Foundation for Medical Education & Research v. United States,* 131 S. Ct. 704 (2011).

Solis v. Laurelbrook Sanitarium and School
2011 U.S. App. LEXIS 8585 (6th Cir.)

OPINION BY DISTRICT JUDGE MURPHY:

Acting on a tip from a concerned citizen, the Wage and Hour Division of the U.S. Department of Labor commenced an investigation into potential child labor violations committed by Laurelbrook Sanitarium and School, Inc. ("Laurelbrook"). After concluding that Laurelbrook had violated the child labor provisions of the Fair Labor Standards Act of 1938, Department of Labor Secretary Hilda Solis ("Secretary") filed suit in federal court seeking prospective injunctive relief against future violations…. [T]he district court denied the Secretary's request … on the ground that Laurelbrook students are not "employees" for purposes of the FLSA, thus rendering the Act's prohibitions on child labor inapplicable to Laurelbrook's operations. We AFFIRM.

* * * Founded in 1950 by a group of Seventh-Day Adventists, Laurelbrook is a non-profit corporation located in Dayton, Tennessee. Laurelbrook follows the philosophy … that children are to receive an education with a practical training component. In conformity with its beliefs, Laurelbrook operates a boarding school for students in grades nine through twelve, an elementary school for children of staff members, and a 50-bed intermediate-care nursing home that assists in the students' practical training (the Sanitarium). The school has been approved and accredited by the Tennessee Department of Education since the 1970s.

Students in Laurelbrook's boarding school learn in both academic and practical settings, spending four hours of each school day in the classroom and four hours learning practical skills. * * * The Sanitarium is an integral part of Laurelbrook's vocational training program. As part of their training, students are assigned to the Sanitarium's kitchen and housekeeping departments. Students sixteen and older may participate in the CNA program, which is approved by the State of Tennessee licensing authority. Students who receive their CNA certification may then be assigned to the Sanitarium to provide medical assistance to patients.

Many of Laurelbrook's practical training courses (16 of 25) are approved by the Tennessee Department of Education for transfer credit. Several others are approved as "special courses," meaning a transferee school can accept the courses at its discretion. Students learn to use tools associated with specific trades, and the learning experience is similar to that received in vocational training courses at public schools. * * * Students do not receive wages for duties they perform. They are not entitled to a job with Laurelbrook upon graduation, and are expected to move on after graduation.

The issue before us is whether the district court erred in concluding that students at Laurelbrook are not employees under the FLSA. There is no settled test for determining whether a student is an employee for purposes of the FLSA. The district court applied what the parties characterize as a "primary benefit test" and considered which party (school or student) receives the primary benefit of the work the student performs. We must address two questions to decide this appeal: 1) whether the district court used the correct legal standard; and 2) whether the district court properly applied the correct standard. We answer both in the affirmative.

* * * We must first determine the specific test to apply in assessing whether employment is present in a training or learning situation. Both sides propose different tests, which we now consider. Laurelbrook's proposed test is categorical, rather than fact-based. It contends that its status as an accredited vocational school should conclusively resolve this litigation in its favor …. * * * According to Laurelbrook, there is no need to analyze whether its students are employees because no vocational school students can be employees under the FLSA.

* * * [C]oncluding that students are not employees simply because they are students at a vocational school … bypasses any real consideration of the economic realities of the relationship and is antithetical to settled jurisprudence calling for consideration of the totality of the circumstances of each case. Indeed, courts have in the past determined that students in vocational training programs were nevertheless employees under the FLSA. * * *

The Secretary urges the application of a six-factor test created by the WHD [Wage & Hour Division] to distinguish between employees and trainees. * * * If all of the following criteria apply, the trainees or students are not employees within the meaning of the Act:

(1) the training, even though it includes actual operation of the facilities of the employer, is similar

to that which would be given in a vocational school;(2) the training is for the benefit of the trainees or students; (3) the trainees or students do not displace regular employees, but work under their close observation; (4) the employer that provides the training derives no immediate advantage from the activities of the trainees or students, and on occasion his operations may actually be impeded; (5) the trainees or students are not necessarily entitled to a job at the conclusion of the training period; and (6) the employer and the trainees or students understand that the trainees or students are not entitled to wages for the time spent in training.

* * * Courts differ on whether the WHD's test is entitled to controlling weight in determining employee status in a training context. Some courts have said that the test is entitled to "substantial deference." Others have rejected it altogether. Still others strike a balance and consider the factors as relevant but not dispositive to the inquiry. We find the WHD's test to be a poor method for determining employee status in a training or educational setting. For starters, it is overly rigid and inconsistent with a totality-of-the-circumstances approach, where no one factor (or the absence of one factor) controls. * * * Furthermore, the … ultimate inquiry in a learning or training situation is whether the employee is the primary beneficiary of the work performed. While the Secretary's six factors may be helpful in guiding that inquiry, the Secretary's test on the whole is not. [Instead], [w]e find that a primary benefit test provides a helpful framework for discerning employee status in learning or training situations. * * * Factors such as whether the relationship displaces paid employees and whether there is educational value derived from the relationship are relevant considerations that can guide the inquiry. Additional factors that bear on the inquiry should also be considered insofar as they shed light on which party primarily benefits from the relationship. * * *

[W]e consider the second question: whether the district court properly applied the primary benefit test. * * * In applying the primary benefit test, the district court recognized that students' activities at Laurelbrook contribute to Laurelbrook's maintenance, thereby benefitting Laurelbrook's operations. Laurelbrook receives payment for services it provides to patients at the Sanitarium; some of these services are performed by students at no cost to Laurelbrook. Hours worked by students in the Sanitarium also contribute to the Sanitarium's satisfaction of its licensing requirements. Laurelbrook sells flowers and produce

grown at Laurelbrook with student help. The proceeds from these sales go directly to Laurelbrook's operations. As part of a course on collision repair, students assist in repairing cars for the public. Beneficiaries of these services pay Laurelbrook directly and the money is recycled back into school programs. Laurelbrook also earns revenue from the sale of wood pallets the students help build.

The value of these benefits to Laurelbrook, however, is offset in various ways. The district court found that Laurelbrook students do not displace compensated workers, and instructors must spend extra time supervising the students at the expense of performing productive work. Specifically, the court found that Laurelbrook is sufficiently staffed such that if the students did not perform work at the Sanitarium, the staff members could continue to provide the same services there without interruption. * * *

On the other side of the ledger are the tangible and intangible benefits that accrue to the students. * * * Students are provided with hands-on training comparable to training provided in public school vocational courses, allowing them to be competitive in various vocations upon graduation. Students learn to operate tools normally used in the trades they are learning, while being supervised by instructors. Students engage in courses of study that have been considered and approved of by the state accrediting agency. In short, the educational aspect of the instruction at Laurelbrook is sound….

Significant, too, are the intangible benefits students receive at Laurelbrook. As the district court found, receiving a well-rounded education—one that includes hands-on, practical training—is a tenet of the Seventh-Day Adventist Church. Laurelbrook provides students with the opportunity to obtain such an education in an environment consistent with their beliefs. The district court found that the vocational training portion of the education teaches students about responsibility and the dignity of manual labor. Parents testified to the benefits their children received from the program, stating that the students learn the importance of working hard and seeing a task through to completion. * * * Service in the Sanitarium engenders sensitivity and respect for the elderly and infirm. Laurelbrook alumni testified that the leadership skills and work ethic developed at Laurelbrook have proved highly valuable in their future endeavors. Employers also testified that Laurelbrook alumni have a strong work ethic, leadership skills, and other practical skills that graduates of other vocational programs lack.

After considering all of the evidence, the district court found that there is benefit to Laurelbrook's operations from the students' activities, but the primary benefit of the program runs to the students. We find no error in the district court's application of the primary benefit test. * * *

CASE QUESTIONS

1. What issues did the court consider in this case? What did the court decide?

2. Why was the employment status of the students of Laurelbrook School in question?

3. What two tests of employment status were proposed by the parties to this litigation? What test did the court choose?

4. Why did the court conclude that the students are not employees? Do you agree? Why or why not?

5. Does this case hold any implications for determining the employment status of students with unpaid internships at corporations?

Clippings

Landing an internship is increasingly seen as a necessary part of a college education. However, perhaps as many as half of all internships are unpaid. Do these unpaid internships violate wage and hour laws? Nancy J. Leppink, acting director of the Department of Labor's Wage and Hour Division, has stated that "If you're a for-profit employer or you want to pursue an internship with a for-profit employer, there aren't going to be many circumstances where you can have an internship and not be paid and still be in compliance with the law." State wage and hour officials have also begun to focus on the illegal use of internships as a source of free labor. Enforcement of the law is complicated by students' realization that they need practical experience and their reluctance to file complaints about prospective future employers.

Steven Greenhouse. "Looking for Experience, Providing Free Labor." *New York Times* (April 3, 2010), B1.

The *Laurelbrook Sanitarium and School* case, insofar as it involves a nonprofit entity and students performing work for another arm of the same religious/educational organization, presents a somewhat different situation than a college student's unpaid internship with a for-profit corporation. But the case does suggest that courts will not necessarily subscribe to a rigid application of the Department of Labor's six criteria for distinguishing internships from employment and that the question of which party benefits most from the arrangement will be central. Proceeding from the general proposition that "internships in the 'for-profit' private sector will most often be viewed as employment," the DOL has stated that *in order for an unpaid internship to be lawful, a college should oversee the internship and provide academic credit; the internship should provide the intern with general skills that could be used in multiple job settings; the intern should not perform the work of the business on a regular basis; the business should not be dependent on the work of the intern; the intern should not be used as a substitute for regular employees or to bolster staffing; the intern should receive close supervision; the intern's experience should be more like job shadowing than holding a job; the internship should be for a fixed, relatively brief, duration agreed upon at the outset of the relationship; and the internship should not generally be used as a trial period in anticipation of eventual hiring.*[17] California has recently provided new guidance as to when internships must be paid in that state.[18] The guidance, in the form of an opinion letter, incorporates the DOL's six criteria approach but looks at the totality of the circumstances, rather than requiring strict compliance with each criterion. The California approach allows for immediate benefit to the employer to be offset by costs of providing close supervision and training and for interns to occasionally perform work done by regular employees, provided that this would not result in the displacement of regular employees. Striking the right balance between encouraging beneficial, career-enhancing educational opportunities and not permitting interns to be exploited as a source of free labor is tricky.

Volunteers

Disputes occasionally arise regarding whether someone performing work is an employee or a **volunteer**. At first blush, disputes of this kind seem unlikely to occur because the element of payment (or expectation of payment) for services that lies at the core of an employment relationship is usually absent in volunteer work. However, in a case that went to the Supreme Court, a nonprofit agency serving addicts and the homeless also ran several commercial businesses to raise its operating funds. The businesses were staffed by the agency's clients ("associates"), who received food, clothing, shelter, and medical care, but not cash wages. Despite the fact that many of the clients testified that they regarded themselves as volunteers and that payment was in noncash forms, the Supreme Court agreed with the lower courts that the clients were, in fact, employees entitled to the minimum wage. The Court concluded that, as a matter of economic reality, the "associates" often worked for long periods of time and were dependent on the agency for food, clothing, housing, and medical care. That the expected compensation took noncash forms was irrelevant.[19] A subsequent appeals court decision held that benefits received by volunteers must amount to "significant remuneration" rather than "inconsequential incidents of an otherwise gratuitous relationship" to conclude that there is an employment relationship.[20]

The nonprofit Seattle Opera ran into problems with its "auxiliary choristers." The opera maintained a pool of individuals with singing ability that could be called on if the number of regular choristers and alternates available for a production was not sufficient. Auxiliary choristers could decline a production without consequence, but if they agreed to perform, they had to follow the opera's rules and show up consistently at rehearsals and performances. They received a flat sum of $214 for each production. The opera claimed that this was reimbursement for transportation expenses rather than wages. The issue of whether the auxiliary choristers were employees or volunteers arose because a union that represents other opera employees sought to negotiate on behalf of the auxiliary choristers, and the opera refused. The case hinged primarily on whether the nominal payment could be viewed as substantial remuneration for work performed. In light of the fact that the amount had no clear relationship to transportation costs incurred, the court agreed with the National Labor Relations Board in concluding

---

[17] U.S. Department of Labor, Wage & Hour Division. "Internship Programs under the Fair Labor Standards Act." Fact Sheet #71 (April 2010), viewed May 23, 2011 (http://www.dol.gov).

[18] California Department of Industrial Relations, Division of Labor Standards Enforcement. Opinion Letter Re: Educational Internship Program. (April 7, 2010).

[19] *Tony and Susan Alamo Foundation v. Secretary of Labor*, 471 U.S. 290 (1985).

[20] *Haavistola v. Community Fire Co. of Rising Sun, Inc.*, 6 F.3d 211, at 222 (4th Cir. 1993).

that the auxiliary choristers were employees who received payment in exchange for performing work controlled by the opera.[21]

In a case involving police officers (referred to as "nonpaid regulars") who performed occasional police work without pay for a small town in Texas, the court decided that the officers were volunteers rather than employees.[22] The primary motive for performing this service was that under Texas law, the officers needed to have their police commissions maintained by a law enforcement agency to keep their licenses. The court applied the Department of Labor's regulation defining a volunteer as "[a]n individual who performs hours of service for a public agency for civic, charitable, or humanitarian reasons, without promise, expectation or receipt of compensation for services rendered ..."[23] to the police officers. However, the court declined to scrutinize the motives of individuals and based its decision instead on the inherently civic nature of police work and the absence of significant remuneration. That the officers benefited by maintaining their licenses and gaining experience was not sufficient to render them employees.

Do these cases involving nonprofit and governmental agencies have any bearing on the use of "volunteers" by for-profit firms? America Online (AOL) provides an interesting case in point. AOL used large numbers of individuals ("community leaders") to monitor activities in its many chat rooms and bulletin boards. Some of the community leaders also performed administrative tasks such as verifying charges and checking for copyright infringement. The monitors received free or discounted subscriptions to AOL and other items. In return, they followed rules established by AOL, were assigned to "shifts," worked a minimum of four hours each week (sometimes considerably more), were trained, and completed paperwork. Suits have been filed alleging that chat room monitors were employees and that AOL failed to pay them the minimum wage and maintain proper wage and hour records. AOL contends that they were volunteers. In one of several suits brought against AOL, the court denied the company's motion to dismiss the class action on the grounds that the community leaders were not employees.[24] The court found that an expectation of compensation could be discerned from the significant benefits received and from the fact that service as a "volunteer" was often a prerequisite to obtaining paid employment with AOL. The court also found material issues of fact in dispute regarding whether the services rendered were integral to the business and provided direct economic benefit to AOL. Finally, the court rejected the argument that because the community leaders derived personal enjoyment from many of the activities in which they engaged, they should be viewed as volunteers: "the FLSA does not require that an employee cannot enjoy any part of their job to be entitled to compensation."[25]

Partners

Partners, officers, board members, and major shareholders generally are not employees. Such individuals personify the business and function as principals rather than agents.[26] However, it is the nature of the individual's relationship to the organization—not the individual's title—that matters. Thus, in an age discrimination suit brought by "partners" at the law firm of Sidley, Austin, Brown, and Wood, the EEOC rejected the firm's

---

[21]*Seattle Opera v. National Labor Relations Board*, 292 F.3d 757 (D.C. Cir. 2002).

[22]*Cleveland v. City of Elmendorf, Texas*, 388 F.3d 522 (5th Cir. 2004).

[23]29 C.F.R. 553.101(a) (2011).

[24]*Hallissey, et al. v. America Online*, 2006 U.S. Dist. LEXIS 12964 (S.D.N.Y.).

[25]*Hallissey* at 40.

[26]*Smith v. Castaways Family Diner*, 453 F.3d 971, 978 (7th Cir. 2006).

JUST THE FACTS

A full-time safety and security assistant at a public school also coached the high school golf team. His coaching duties included supervising tryouts, coaching players during tournaments, conducting daily practices, transporting team members to matches, scheduling matches, communicating with parents, handling the team's finances, and fundraising. In all, the coach spent an estimated 300 to 450 hours per year on his coaching activities, in addition to his full-time employment with the school district. For his services as coach, he received a "stipend" of a little over $2,000 per year, reimbursement for travel and other expenses, and paid administrative leave for coaching activities that occurred during school hours. He was paid separately and on an hourly basis for his work as a safety and security assistant. His continued employment was not predicated on his also agreeing to coach. He sought overtime pay for weeks in which the combination of his school duties and coaching required him to work more than 40 hours. The school contended that in his capacity as a golf coach, he was a volunteer with no entitlement to overtime pay. Was the coach an employee or volunteer with respect to his coaching activities?

See, *Purdham v. Fairfax County School Board*, 2011 U.S. App. LEXIS 4644 (4th Cir.).

---

argument that, as partners, the lawyers were not covered by the ADEA. The EEOC contended that most of these "partners" had no influence over the workings of the firm and were not given the opportunity to vote on such matters as promotions to partnership, removal from partnership, division of profits, and the composition of the management committee. In the settlement agreement, the firm acknowledged that the former partners were, in fact, employees covered by the ADEA.[27]

The EEOC uses the following criteria to distinguish between employees and **partners**:[28]

1. Whether the organization can hire or fire the individual or set rules and regulations controlling the individual's work
2. Whether and to what extent the organization supervises the individual's work
3. Whether the individual reports to someone higher in the organization
4. Whether and to what extent the individual is able to influence the organization
5. Whether the parties intend for the individual to be an employee or a partner as expressed in written agreements or contracts
6. Whether the individual shares in the profits, losses, and liabilities of the organization

The dominant theme expressed in these criteria is the extent to which the individual acts autonomously and participates in the management of the organization. The Supreme Court approved the use of these criteria in a case involving the status of physician–shareholders who simultaneously worked for a medical clinic and served as its board of directors.[29] The issue arose because determining the employment status of the physicians was necessary to determine whether the clinic met the minimum size

---

[27]Michael Bologna. "EEOC Reaches $27.5 Million Settlement in Age-Bias Suit Against Sidley Austin." *Daily Labor Report* 194 (October 9, 2007), A-12.

[28]Equal Employment Opportunity Commission. *Compliance Manual.* "Section 2: Threshold Issues," 2-III A., 1. d.

[29]*Clackamas Gastroenterology Associates v. Wells*, 538 U.S. 440 (2003).

requirements for a suit by another employee under the Americans with Disabilities Act. Applying the criteria to the facts of the case, it was consistent with partner status that the physicians ran the clinic, shared in its profits, and were personally liable for malpractice claims. On the other hand, the fact that the physicians received salaries, reported to a personnel manager, and were required to comply with clinic rules suggested employee status. The Supreme Court remanded the case for further consideration of these issues.

In a case in which a court determined that a partner was not an employee, the plaintiff was one of only four general partners, exercised substantial control over allocation of the firm's profits, could be removed only by unanimous vote of the other partners, shared in the firm's profits, attended partnership meetings, had access to private financial information, and served as trustee of the firm's 401(k) account.[30] Lacking employee status, his retaliation claim under Title VII was dismissed. Even where true partnerships are involved, persons seeking to become partners can still bring claims based on the rights of employees if there is discrimination in the process of promoting employees to partner.[31]

Other Issues Concerning Employee Status

Managers and supervisors, despite being part of management, are generally considered employees and have the same rights under most employment laws as other employees. (The National Labor Relations Act is a significant exception.)

As for undocumented workers (noncitizens who cannot establish their legal right to work in the United States), the general policy of federal agencies is to enforce employment laws without inquiring into the immigration status of workers.[32] Thus, undocumented workers are treated the same as other employees and allowed to pursue their legal claims. However, the remedies to which they are entitled might be affected by their immigration status. An employee whose rights under the National Labor Relations Act were violated admitted during a hearing that he was a Mexican citizen and was in the United States illegally.[33] The Court held that it would contradict national immigration policy to allow undocumented workers who are working illegally to be awarded back pay. Thus, the NLRB could issue a cease and desist order based on the violation of this worker's rights but not award him back pay.

In a subsequent case, an undocumented worker filed a claim for unpaid wages. The employer apparently reported him to federal authorities, who took the employee into custody. In considering the employee's Fair Labor Standards Act claim, the court distinguished pay for work already performed from back pay based on prospective earnings lost due to an employer's illegal act. Although the Supreme Court had ruled out back pay awards to employees in the country illegally, the lower court determined that the purposes of the Fair Labor Standards Act are best served by not allowing employers to get away with cheating undocumented workers out of pay for work already performed.[34] Likewise, state courts have generally held that undocumented workers are entitled to workers' compensation benefits when they are hurt on the job. In one such case, the Georgia Court of Appeals stated that "[i]n as much as the goal of the IRCA [Immigration Reform and Control Act—the federal law prohibiting employment of

---

[30]*Solon v. Kaplan*, 398 F.3d 629 (7th Cir. 2005).

[31]*Hishon v. King & Spalding*, 467 U.S. 69 (1984).

[32]*Patel v. Quality Inn South*, 846 F.2d 700 (11th Cir. 1988), *cert. denied*, 489 U.S. 1011 (1989).

[33]*Hoffman Plastic Compounds, Inc. v. National Labor Relations Board*, 122 S. Ct. 1275 (2002).

[34]*Singh v. Jutla*, 214 F.Supp 2d 1056 (N.D. Cal. 2002).

undocumented workers] is to reduce the incentives for employers to hire illegal aliens, that goal would be subverted by allowing employers to avoid workers' compensation liability for work-related injuries to those employees since such would provide employers with a financial incentive to hire illegal aliens."[35]

Who Is the Employer?

Even when it is agreed that an individual performing work is, in fact, an employee, questions sometimes arise concerning the identity of the employer. This is important because employer status generally determines who will be held liable (legally responsible for and required to provide any award or damages) if an employee's rights are violated. We will consider three aspects of this issue. First, to what extent is an employer liable for the actions of its employees? Second, what parts of far-flung corporate structures are sufficiently interrelated to constitute single employers? Third, under what circumstances can firms be deemed joint employers of the same employees?

Agency

As a general rule, employers are legally responsible for the actions of their employees. When an employer confers the authority to make or significantly influence employment decisions on supervisors and other managers, the employer is liable if those employees use that authority to make employment decisions in ways that violate the law. The argument that the employer was not aware of the employee's actions or that the employee's actions were contrary to company policy will not save an employer from liability (although it might avert the imposition of *punitive damages*). *Employers need to carefully select, train, monitor, and review the actions of their employees, especially those responsible for human resource decisions.*

There are bounds to the responsibility of employers for the actions of their agents. Employer liability is usually limited to employee actions taken within the scope of their employment. Actions are within the **scope of employment** to the extent that they relate to the kind of work the employee was hired to perform, take place substantially within the workplace and during work hours, and serve (at least partially) the interests of the employer. Harmful employee actions taken outside the scope of employment might still form the basis for employer liability if the employer intended the harm to occur, was negligent or reckless in allowing it to occur, impermissibly delegated an employer duty or if the employee's harmful actions were aided by the existence of apparent or actual authority conferred by the employer.[36]

In some circumstances, a supervisor or manager can be held individually liable for violating an employee's rights, but this is generally in addition to rather than in lieu of employer liability.

Single, Integrated Enterprise

The organizational structures of corporations are complex. An intricate network of relations exists between parent companies, subsidiaries, merger and alliance partners, and other entities. In light of all these overlapping, connected, and embedded organizational units, what exactly is the employing organization? The EEOC uses the following criteria

---

[35]*Continental Pet Technologies v. Palacias*, 604 S.E.2d 627 (Ga. App. 2004), *cert. denied*, 546 U.S. 825 (2005).

[36]*Restatement of the Law (Second) Agency* §§ 219, 228 (1958).

to determine whether two or more ostensibly separate entities should be considered parts of an **integrated enterprise**:[37]

1. Degree of interrelation between the operations
2. Degree to which the entities share common management
3. Degree to which there is centralized control of human resource and labor relations policies
4. Degree of common ownership or financial control over the entities

The element of centralized control over human resource and labor relations policy is usually given the greatest weight. Indicators of centralized control include the existence of a single corporate human resources department or another unit with authority to develop personnel policy, maintenance of personnel records in a single location, common screening and testing of applicants for employment, and the same individuals making employment decisions for the involved entities.

In one relevant case, U-Haul International attempted to argue that it was not liable for sex discrimination engaged in by employees of the U-Haul Company of Maine. The court identified numerous grounds for concluding that the two entities were closely intertwined: U-Haul International owns the Maine subsidiary in its entirety; the two companies share three directors; U-Haul International receives revenues from the subsidiary's transactions, as well as daily revenue reports; it establishes equipment rental rates for the subsidiary; and it provides legal, marketing, accounting, and training services to the subsidiary. In the key area of integration in human resource policies, it was shown that there was an interchange of personnel between the two entities and that U-Haul International established wage scales, pay dates, and benefit plans. It also had to approve any deviations from established pay practices and the rehiring of former employees. Employees were directed to present complaints regarding discrimination and other matters to the U-Haul International's human resources department. All of this was more than enough to demonstrate that human resource policymaking was centralized and that U-Haul International and its Maine subsidiary were an integrated enterprise for purposes of complying with antidiscrimination laws.[38]

In another relevant case, the court considered whether a cleaning company and its subsidiary constituted an integrated enterprise.[39] The general reluctance of courts to find a parent company to be the employer of employees hired by one of its subsidiaries was acknowledged, but the court nonetheless concluded that "the evidence of common ownership and management of ABMI [parent] and ABMK [subsidiary]; ABMI's involvement, pursuant to the Service Agreement, in several areas of ABMK's operations; and ABMI's public representations of centralized corporate control of labor and human resources, demonstrate ABMI is the appellants' employer for purposes of the integrated enterprise test."[40] The decision highlighted the centralized character of the human resource function: ABMI purchased ABMK's workers' compensation insurance, obtained licenses for sexual harassment videos, drafted certain forms such as performance evaluations, negotiated the contract for a harassment hotline, supported investigations of discrimination complaints, provided an online human resources manual, established a complaint procedure, delivered sexual harassment and diversity training to ABMK managers, administered benefit plans, and oversaw safety and health practices.

---

[37]Equal Employment Opportunity Commission. *Compliance Manual.* "Section 2: Threshold Issues," 2-III B, iii (a).

[38]*Romano v. U-Haul International, U-Haul Co. of Maine, Inc.*, 233 F.3d 655, 667–68 (1st Cir. 2000), *cert. denied*, 534 U.S. 815 (2001).

[39]*Sandoval v. American Building Maintenance Industries*, 578 F.3d 787 (8th Cir. 2009).

[40]*Sandoval*, at 795–96.

Finding that a single, integrated enterprise exists affects not only the pockets that will be dipped into if liability is established but also the size of the employer. An entity that has too few employees to be covered by a certain law might find that it is part of a larger integrated enterprise with enough employees to fall within the coverage of the statute. For example, an employee of a small company sued her employer for pregnancy discrimination. The company had fewer than fifteen employees, but she was allowed to proceed with her Title VII suit because she presented sufficient evidence that her employer was part of an integrated enterprise with another corporate entity that took care of its human resources and other functions.[41]

Joint Employers

Sometimes companies are linked not because they are parts of the same organization, but because they maintain employment relationships with the same employees. **Joint employers** share in the liability for violation of an employee's rights. One circumstance under which joint employment is sometimes found to exist is when a company producing a good or service contracts with another company to provide part of that good or service. In *Zheng v. Liberty Apparel* Co., the court discusses the criteria used to determine whether a manufacturer of apparel was a joint employer of garment workers whose services had been obtained through small contractors. In this Fair Labor Standards Act case, the "economic reality" of the relationship between the workers and the alleged employer must again be examined. However, the question here is not whether the garment workers were employees, but whether they were jointly employed by the manufacturer and contract firms.

Zheng v. Liberty Apparel Co.
355 F.3d 61 (2d Cir. 2003)

OPINION BY CIRCUIT JUDGE CABRANES:

This case asks us to decide whether garment manufacturers who hired contractors to stitch and finish pieces of clothing were "joint employers" within the meaning of the Fair Labor Standards Act of 1938 ("FLSA") and New York law. Plaintiffs, garment workers in New York City who were directly employed by the contractors, claim that the manufacturers were their joint employers because they worked predominantly on the manufacturers' garments, they performed a line-job that was integral to the production of the manufacturer's product, and their work was frequently and directly supervised by the manufacturers' agents. The manufacturers respond that the contractors, who, among other things, hired and paid plaintiffs to assemble clothing for numerous manufacturers, were plaintiffs' sole employers. * * * The United States District

Court for the Southern District of New York … granted the manufacturers' motion, and held that the manufacturers could not be held liable for violations of the FLSA or its New York statutory analogues. * * * We conclude that the District Court erred … [and remand the case to the lower court]. * * *

Plaintiffs-Appellants are 26 non-English-speaking adult garment workers who worked in a factory … in New York's Chinatown. They brought this action against both (1) their immediate employers, six contractors doing business at 103 Broadway ("Contractor Corporations") … and (2) Liberty Apparel Company, Inc. ("Liberty"). Because the Contractor Defendants either could not be located or have ceased doing business, plaintiffs have voluntarily dismissed their claims against those defendants with prejudice. Accordingly, plaintiffs now seek damages only from the Liberty Defendants. * * *

---

[41]*Smith v. K&F Industries, Inc. and Loral Space & Communications*, 190 F. Supp. 2d 643 (S.D.N.Y. 2002).

From March 1997 through April 1999, Liberty entered into agreements with the Contractor Corporations under which the Contractor Corporations would assemble garments to meet Liberty's specifications. During that time period, Liberty utilized as many as thirty to forty assemblers, including the Contractor Corporations. Liberty did not seek out assemblers; instead, assemblers came to Liberty's warehouse looking for assembly work. In order to obtain such work, a prospective assembler was required by Liberty to sign a form agreement.

Plaintiffs claim that approximately 70–75% of their work during the time period at issue was for Liberty. They explain that they knew they were working for Liberty based on both the labels that were sewn into the garments and the specific lot numbers that came with the garments. Liberty's co-owner, Albert Nigri, asserts that the percentage of the Contractor Corporations' work performed for Liberty was closer to 10–15%. He derives that figure from individual plaintiffs' handwritten notes and records.

The parties do not dispute that Liberty employed people to monitor Liberty's garments while they were being assembled. However, the parties dispute the extent to which Liberty oversaw the assembly process. Various plaintiffs presented affidavits to the District Court stating that two Liberty representatives—a man named Ah Sen and "a Taiwanese woman"—visited the factory approximately two to four times a week for up to three hours a day, and exhorted the plaintiffs to work harder and faster. In their affidavits, these plaintiffs claim further that, when they finished working on garments, Liberty representatives—as opposed to employees of the Contractor Corporations—inspected their work and gave instructions directly to the workers if corrections needed to be made. One of the plaintiffs also asserts that she informed the "Taiwanese woman" that the workers were not being paid for their work at the factory.

Albert Nigri, on the other hand, avers that Liberty's quality control person made brief visits to assemblers' factories and was instructed to speak only with Lai Huen Yam, a co-owner of the Contractor Corporations, or with his wife. Furthermore, Nigri asserts in his affidavit that Liberty representatives were expected to spend just thirty minutes at each of the assemblers' work sites. Finally, Nigri states that Liberty did not employ two quality control persons simultaneously; did not employ a quality control person during some

of the relevant time period; and did not employ a man as a quality control person. * * *

Liberty Defendants moved for summary judgment on all claims against them on the ground that plaintiffs were not their employees. * * * The District Court determined that Liberty Defendants were not joint employers under the FLSA because, based on the plaintiffs' own admissions, these defendants did not (1) hire and fire the plaintiffs, (2) supervise and control their work schedules or conditions of employment, (3) determine the rate and method of payment, or (4) maintain employment records. * * *

The regulations promulgated under the FLSA expressly recognize that a worker may be employed by more than one entity at the same time. In the present case, it is undisputed that the Contractor Defendants, who are no longer parties to this suit, employed plaintiffs. The issue is whether the Liberty Defendants also employed them. * * *

We conclude … that the District Court erred when, based *exclusively* on the four factors …, it determined that the Liberty Defendants were not, as a matter of law, joint employers under the FLSA. In our view, the broad language of the FLSA … demands that a district court look beyond an entity's formal right to control the physical performance of another's work before declaring that the entity is not an employer under the FLSA. * * * Accordingly, the District Court's judgment in favor of the Liberty Defendants must be vacated. * * *

On remand, the District Court must determine whether the Liberty Defendants should be deemed to have been the plaintiffs' joint employer. * * * The factors we find pertinent in these circumstances, listed in no particular order, are (1) whether Liberty's premises and equipment were used for the plaintiffs' work; (2) whether the Contractor Corporations had a business that could or did shift as a unit from one putative joint employer to another; (3) the extent to which plaintiffs performed a discrete line-job that was integral to Liberty's process of production; (4) whether responsibility under the contracts could pass from one subcontractor to another without material changes; (5) the degree to which the Liberty Defendants or their agents supervised plaintiffs' work; and (6) whether plaintiffs worked exclusively or predominantly for the Liberty Defendants. * * *

The first factor—namely, whether a putative joint employer's premises and equipment are used by its putative joint employees—is relevant because the shared use of premises and equipment may support the inference that a putative joint employer has functional control over the plaintiffs' work. Similarly, the second factor—namely, whether the putative joint employees are part of a business organization that shifts as a unit from one putative joint employer to another—is relevant because a subcontractor that seeks business from a variety of contractors is less likely to be part of a subterfuge arrangement than a subcontractor that serves a single client. Although neither shared premises nor the absence of a broad client base is anything close to a perfect proxy for joint employment (because they are both perfectly consistent with a legitimate subcontracting relationship) the fact finder can use these readily verifiable facts as a starting point in uncovering the economic realities of a business relationship.

The other factors we have pointed out are less straightforward. [The third factor is] the extent to which plaintiffs performed a line-job that is integral to the putative joint employer's process of production. Interpreted broadly, this factor could be said to be implicated in every subcontracting relationship, because all subcontractors perform a function that a general contractor deems "integral" to a product or a service. However, we do not interpret the factor quite so broadly. * * * [W]e are mindful of the substantial and valuable place that outsourcing, along with the subcontracting relationships that follow from outsourcing, have come to occupy in the American economy. We are also mindful that manufacturers, and especially manufacturers of relatively sophisticated products that require multiple components, may choose to outsource the production of some of those components in order to increase efficiency. Accordingly, we resist the temptation to say that any work on a so-called production line—no matter what product is being manufactured—should attract heightened scrutiny. Instead, in determining the weight and degree of factor (3), we believe that both industry custom and historical practice should be consulted. Industry custom may be relevant because, insofar as the practice of using subcontractors to complete a particular task is widespread, it is unlikely to be a mere subterfuge to avoid complying with labor laws. * * *

The fourth factor ... is whether responsibility under the contracts could pass from one subcontractor to another without material changes. * * * [T]his factor weighs in favor of a determination of joint employment when employees are tied to an entity ... rather than to an ostensible direct employer.... In such

circumstances, it is difficult not to draw the inference that a subterfuge arrangement exists. Where, on the other hand, employees work for an entity (the purported joint employer) only to the extent that their direct employer is hired by that entity, this factor does not in any way support the determination that a joint employment relationship exists.

The fifth factor listed above—namely, the degree to which the defendants supervise the plaintiffs' work—also requires some comment, as it too can be misinterpreted to encompass run-of-the-mill subcontracting relationships. * * * [E]xtensive supervision weighs in favor of joint employment only if it demonstrates effective control of the terms and conditions of the plaintiff's employment. By contrast, supervision with respect to contractual warranties of quality and time of delivery has no bearing on the joint employment inquiry, as such supervision is perfectly consistent with a typical, legitimate subcontracting arrangement.

Finally, [it must be] considered whether the purported joint employees worked exclusively or predominantly for the putative joint employer. In describing that factor, we use the words "exclusively or predominantly" on purpose. * * * In those situations, the joint employer may *de facto* become responsible, among other things, for the amount workers are paid and for their schedules, which are traditional indicia of employment. On the other hand, where a subcontractor performs merely a majority of its work for a single customer, there is no sound basis on which to infer that the customer has assumed the prerogatives of an employer.

In sum, by looking beyond a defendant's formal control over the physical performance of a plaintiff's work, the "economic reality" test—which has been distilled into a nonexclusive and overlapping set of factors—gives content to the broad language [defining employee] in the statute. However, by limiting FLSA liability to cases in which defendants, based on the totality of the circumstances, function as employers of the plaintiffs rather than mere business partners of plaintiffs' direct employer, the test also ensures that the statute is not interpreted to subsume typical outsourcing relationships. The "economic reality" test, therefore, is intended to expose outsourcing relationships that lack a substantial economic purpose, but it is manifestly not intended to bring normal, strategically oriented contracting schemes within the ambit of the FLSA. * * *

CASE QUESTIONS

1. What was the legal issue in this case? What did the Appeals Court decide?
2. What criteria had the district court applied to determine whether the manufacturers were employers of the garment workers? What additional criteria does the Appeals Court say must be

applied? How do these criteria help determine whether an employment relationship exists?
3. From the facts presented, how would you decide the case?
4. What are the practical implications of this case? For workers who are victims of unscrupulous contractors? For firms that subcontract or otherwise outsource parts of their operations?

Questions of joint employment frequently arise in agriculture, where farm labor contractors (FLCs) are used extensively to provide farmers with seasonal labor. These arrangements raise questions about who is legally responsible for the often substandard conditions under which farmworkers toil. In one such case, a farm was found to be the joint employer of farmworkers harvesting cucumbers and shared liability for a host of employment law violations with the farm labor contractor.[42] The court emphasized the indirect control exerted by the farm; although the FLC chose employees and was responsible for the picking operation, the farm controlled the harvest schedule, had a representative present during picking who inspected the work for quality, and influenced the pay level of the pickers. Additionally, the harvesting occurred on land leased by the farm, and picking the cucumbers was an integral part of its business. A case involving employees recruited by a farm labor contractor to plant seedlings for a paper company had the

JUST THE FACTS

Luann Lepkowski is one of about two hundred employees of Telatron Marketing, a company that provides "customer relationship management services" to corporate clients nationwide. Since early 2006, Ms. Lepkowski has been assigned to work exclusively on the Bank of America account. The computer, software programs, and databases that she uses in performing this work are owned and supplied by Bank of America. The operators identify themselves as representatives of the bank when dealing with customers. The bank provides training on bank products and procedures to Ms. Lepkowski and the other operators. The bank oversees day-to-day operations by monitoring phone calls to ensure that their procedures are being followed.

Ms. Lepkowski works in a call center owned by Telatron. She was hired and is paid and scheduled by Telatron, which also maintains her personnel records.

Ms. Lepkowski and the other operators brought a class action lawsuit against both Telatron and the Bank of America, alleging improper compensation. Is the Bank of America a joint employer of these call center workers?

See, *Lepkowski v. Telatron Marketing Group and Bank of America Corp.*, 2011 U.S. Dist. LEXIS 9388 (W.D. Pa.).

---

[42]*Torres-Lopez v. May*, 111 F.3d 633 (9th Cir. 1997).

opposite outcome.[43] Although the planters worked on the paper company's forestland and performed the type of repetitive, less-skilled tasks conducive to economic dependence, they were not directly controlled or supervised by personnel from the paper company (the presence of company personnel at the work site for the purpose of ensuring compliance with contract specifications was deemed not sufficient to show control); decisions about pay, hiring, and firing were made by the FLC; the duration of the relationship between the planters and the paper company was usually only a matter of several weeks; the hand-planting of seeds was not integral to the paper company's business, as the paper company purchased most of the timber it needed and could use machines to plant; and the paper company did not keep records on the employees, deal with taxes, or engage in any of the other activities common for employers. Under these circumstances, the court concluded that the paper company was not a joint employer of the planters.

Joint employment is also an issue when employers use temporary staffing firms. Arrangements between temporary staffing firms and client firms vary considerably, but the temp agency usually assumes a number of the client company's human resource functions, including initial hiring of the temps, assignment, some general training, payroll administration, and arrangement of workers' compensation coverage. Under these circumstances, a temp agency is most often considered an employer of its temps. Thus, a temp agency's argument that it was not an employer was unavailing when the agency was solely responsible for hiring temps, controlling assignments to employers, establishing work schedules, giving instructions about appropriate dress and work habits, determining the rate and method of payment, maintaining time sheets, and issuing paychecks.[44] The court also pointed to the agency's own promotional materials, in which it promised to handle for client companies "'all the burdensome paperwork, bookkeeping, record keeping, payroll costs, and government reporting'" as further confirmation of the staffing agency's status as employer. However, in another case, the role of the temp staffing firm was so minimal that only the client company was deemed an employer.[45] The client company "leased" its entire workforce from the staffing company. It was concluded that the client company was the employer because, among other things, it assigned workers to jobs and supervised their work; it did most of the hiring and firing of workers; it provided workers with equipment, materials, and transportation; and it set pay rates and hours of work. Although the staffing firm performed payroll administration duties, handled job applications, conducted drug tests, and provided some safety training, it exerted no direct control over the workers and was indifferent to how they performed their jobs. Thus, the leasing agreement notwithstanding, the client company was the sole employer. As the employer, it was financially responsible for providing workers' compensation coverage.

A client company might also be deemed a joint employer of employees it procures through a temporary staffing firm. In one such case, the client firm responded to employee complaints by deciding to obtain all part-time and temporary employees through temporary staffing firms rather than hire them directly. If the client firm thought that this maneuver would absolve it of any legal responsibilities to these employees, it was wrong. The temp agency hired all the former employees of the client firm that would accept the new arrangement, and the client firm continued to manage those employees in the same manner as before. It exerted substantial control, including requesting and receiving the assignment of particular employees, arranging for particular employees to work consecutive days at the client firm, training and supervising the employees, determining work hours, and supplying time cards. The client firm was

---

[43]*Martinez-Mendoza v. Champion International Corp.*, 340 F.3d 1200 (2003).

[44]*Baystate Alternative Staffing v. Herman*, 163 F.3d 668 (1st Cir. 1998).

[45]*Sonners, Inc. v. Department of Labor & Industries*, 3 P.3d 756 (Wash. App. 2000), *review denied*, 2000 Wash. LEXIS 856.

Practical Considerations How should companies that use temp workers supplied by temp agencies deal with those workers if performance problems emerge? If temp workers complain about inequitable treatment? If temp workers request leave under the Family and Medical Leave Act?

found to be a joint employer sharing liability with the temp agency for violations of the National Labor Relations Act.[46]

The message is clear. *Employers cannot assume simply because they obtain workers from temporary staffing agencies or use the services of employees from contract firms that they are free of legal obligations to those workers.* The degree of control exerted over the workers is again a key factor. *The only way not to be deemed an employer (singly or jointly) is to avoid acting like an employer. Actions such as closely supervising, training, setting pay rates for, disciplining, and selecting individual temps for hire or fire should be avoided if an employer does not want to risk being deemed a joint employer of its temps.*

Like much legal advice, this is easier said than done. Carolyn Koenig, Vice President of Human Resources at MasterCard International, a company with a workforce that is more than 20 percent contingent workers, has observed:

> *You always have to be very conscious of that [the distinction between temps and employees].... You don't want to direct their work or treat them like an employee, but at the same time, you want to treat them like a person and keep them motivated. It takes a lot of manager awareness and savvy to walk the line appropriately.*[47]

The notion of auditioning temps for possible hire as permanent employees also runs into problems. No doubt this is an effective way to screen employees and the prospect of being hired as regular employees makes temps more motivated. But if conversion to regular employee status is a standard practice, a client company is again more likely to be viewed as an employer of its temps.

A joint employer cannot afford to be indifferent to the treatment of an employee by his other employer(s). For example, if managers at a temporary staffing agency learn that one of their temps is being harassed at a client firm, the temp agency has to take whatever actions it can to stop the harassment.[48] It will not do for them to say that this is the client firm's problem or that the temp should work things out with the client firm. *Joint employers must not participate in the violation of an employee's rights by another employer of that employee or fail to take appropriate actions to stop violations of their employee's rights by another employer.*

Key Terms

employee, p. 31
employer, p. 31
contingent (nonstandard) work, p. 31
independent contractor, p. 34

economic realities test, p. 34
common law test, p. 36
right-of-control, p. 36
temporary worker, p. 40
volunteer, p. 45

partner, p. 47
scope of employment, p. 49
integrated enterprise, p. 50
joint employers, p. 51

Chapter Summary

Most of the laws discussed in this book apply only if an employment relationship exists. Yet, work is sometimes performed for pay outside of traditional employer–employee relationships. Distinguishing between independent contractors and employees is the central issue in determining who is an employee. Courts use a variety of criteria to make this distinction. These criteria are combined into the economic realities and common law tests of

---

[46]*NLRB v. Western Temporary Services and the Classic Company,* 821 F.2d 1258 (7th Cir. 1987).

[47]Linda Micco. "Employment in the 21st Century: Technology, Outsourcing, Contingent Work." *Daily Labor Report* 1 (January 3, 2000), C-1.

[48]Equal Employment Opportunity Commission. "Enforcement Guidance: Application of EEO Laws to Contingent Workers Placed by Temporary Employment Agencies and Other Staffing Firms." No. 915.002 (December 3, 1997).

employee status. The economic realities test used to determine coverage under the Fair Labor Standards Act focuses on whether the worker is in business for himself and there is a market for the worker's services. Although all the tests consider the issue of right of control over how, when, and where the work is done, this criterion is emphasized most heavily in the common law test. Misclassification of employees as independent contractors—with attendant loss of tax revenues and employee rights—is a fairly widespread practice that has drawn increased attention from government officials.

Questions about employee status also arise in other contexts, although the criteria for distinguishing employees from these other statuses are not as well established. When temps are used to perform the same work as permanent employees and do so over a substantial period of time, employers run the risk that the temps will be considered employees under the common law definition and eligible for benefits available to other employees. Volunteers can be construed as employees if they receive significant remuneration for their services, even if the payment is not in cash. Students and interns who perform work might also be deemed employees, particularly if they are not the primary beneficiaries of the arrangements. Criteria for distinguishing employees from partners center on the degree to which individuals act autonomously and participate in managing organizations. Undocumented workers in the United States illegally are considered employees with rights under employment laws, but they are subject to limitations on the individual remedies they can receive for violations of their rights.

On the other side of the employment relationship, the identity of the employer is not always clear. Employers are generally responsible for the actions of their agents that occur within the scope of employment. When supervisors and managers make human resource decisions that violate the rights of employees, liability typically rests with the employing firm rather than the individual actors. Organizational entities that are presented as separate might be deemed parts of single, integrated enterprises. Entities are sufficiently integrated to warrant their treatment as the same employer when they have closely interrelated operations, shared management, centralized human resource and labor relations policies, and shared financial ownership or control. An employee can have more than a single employer, and thus, more than one firm can be responsible for violations of that employee's rights. Possibilities for joint employment abound as firms increasingly contract with other firms for labor. Joint employment is particularly likely when temporary staffing agencies provide workers to client firms that then closely manage the temps.

Practical Advice Summary

- The status of each person performing work for a company has to be determined using the appropriate legal criteria. Simply labeling workers "independent contractors," "interns," or "partners" does not establish their employment status.
- Independent contractor agreements should be used, but they matter only insofar as they document actual independent contractor relationships.
- Employers that want to use independent contractors (ICs) must be prepared to relinquish most of their control over how the work is done, including refraining from
  — Closely supervising ICs.
  — Directing or scheduling ICs' activities.
  — Providing ICs with training.
  — Requiring or expecting ICs to attend staff meetings.
- Employers that want to use independent contractors also should be prepared to do at least most of the following:
  — Require that ICs supply their own tools, materials, and equipment and pay their own business expenses

  — Require that ICs hire their own assistants
  — Pay ICs a flat fee for the work performed rather than an hourly or weekly rate
  — Closely review the status of long-term ICs
  — Make it clear that ICs are free to offer their services to others
  — Not assign new projects without renewing agreements
  — Not have ICs doing the same work that regular employees are doing or work that is central to the business that the company is in
  — Not provide benefits to ICs, including paid time off

Employers should generally avoid:
- changing the status of workers from employees to contingent workers
- having independent contractors and employees perform the same work
- rehiring former employees to do their former jobs as independent contractors

Interns used by for-profit firms should generally be paid for their services.

Unpaid internships should be offered only if:

- a college oversees the internship and provides academic credit
- the internship provides the intern with general skills useful in multiple job settings
- the intern does not perform the work of the business on a regular basis
- the business does not depend on the work of the intern
- the intern does not substitute for regular employees
- the intern receives close supervision
- the intern's experience is more like job shadowing than holding a job

- the internship is for a fixed, relatively brief, duration agreed on at the outset
- the internship is not used as a trial period in anticipation of eventual hiring

Companies that use workers supplied by temporary staffing agencies must avoid acting like employers if they desire to avoid liability for the mistreatment of temps. This includes refraining from

— Closely supervising temps.
— Providing training.
— Setting pay rates.
— Selecting individual temps for hire or fire.
— Regularly offering permanent employment to temps.

Chapter Questions

1. A company sells health insurance policies. The company has a large sales force comprised of independent contractors. Some of its sales agents, usually after a significant period of service, are promoted to the position of "sales leader." Sales leaders agree to remain as independent contractors when they are promoted. Sales leaders do little selling of policies; instead, their main responsibilities are recruiting, training, and managing sales agents. The income of sales leaders is mainly derived from overwrite commissions on their subordinates' sales. The company retains control over the hiring, firing, assignment, and promotion of sales agents. The company determines sales leaders' territories and does not permit them to sell other insurance products or operate other businesses. Sales leads are distributed by the company and sales leaders are prohibited from purchasing leads from outside sources. Sales leaders set their own hours and conduct their day-to-day activities largely free from supervision. Attendance at company meetings and training sessions is generally considered optional for sales leaders. Sales leaders receive no benefits and the company does not withhold any of their pay for tax purposes. Several sales leaders sued for overtime pay under the Fair Labor Standards Act. Are the sales leaders employees or independent contractors? (*Hopkins v. Cornerstone America*, 545 F.3d 338 [5th Cir. 2008], *cert. denied*, 2009 U.S. LEXIS 2005)

2. Taxi drivers for the Yellow Cab Company sign independent contractor agreements with the company from whom they lease cabs for a daily fee. With a few exceptions, drivers are free to drive any routes and to work as many hours as they choose. Drivers' payment consists of the fares taken in minus the leasing fee and other expenses. Rates for cab rides are set by the company. Drivers are required to use meters, to meet certain appearance requirements, to have their radios on and respond to a dispatcher, to avoid profanity, and to adhere to a variety of other rules of conduct. Drivers who violate rules are subject to suspension. Drivers are required to obtain oil changes and maintenance work from the cab company and to buy gas from it. The cab company provides drivers with insurance and business cards. When one of the Yellow Cab Company's drivers was murdered on the job, his estate sought to obtain workers' compensation death benefits. The cab company claimed that the estate had no entitlement to those benefits because the deceased was an independent contractor. What should the court decide? (*Nelson v. Yellow Cab* Co., 564 S.E.2d 110 [S.C. 2002])

3. An attorney and member of the New York Bar Association became actively involved with international environmental issues. She proposed and developed a program and then presented it under the auspices of the association. She engaged in other efforts, including creating a new bar association committee on international environmental law, making presentations, and participating at the first United Nations Conference on Environment and Development. In return, the association provided her with work space, clerical support, publicity, and reimbursement for

out-of-pocket expenses. The attorney experienced harassment by a bar association official and sued. Was she a volunteer or an employee? (*York v. Association of the Bar of the City of New York,* 286 F.3d 122 [2d Cir. 2002])

4. A musician regularly played the French horn for a nonprofit corporation that provides free classical music concerts to inner-city public schools and other disadvantaged groups. The musicians are all professionals. They are union members and are paid on a per-concert basis at union scale. Each year, the musicians are contacted to determine if they will agree to play the series of concerts that has been scheduled. Musicians are free to perform elsewhere and can opt out of particular concerts if they provide prior notice and arrange an acceptable substitute. However, to remain a "regular" who is invited to play at most or all of the group's concerts, musicians must "accept the vast majority of the work." The corporation does not withhold income or Social Security taxes. No benefits or paid leave are provided except for contributions to the pension fund administered by the musician's union. The French horn player sued for disability discrimination when she was not offered work after being absent to recover from injuries. The corporation says that she was an independent contractor and not covered by the ADA. What should the court decide? (*Lerohl v. Friends of Minnesota Sinfonia,* 322 F.3d 486 [8th Cir. 2003])

5. A surgeon worked as part of the medical staff at a hospital. The surgeon leased his own office space, scheduled his own operating room time, employed and paid his own office staff, billed patients directly, received no benefits, and did not receive tax documents (W-2 or 1099) from the hospital. The doctor performed all of his surgeries at this hospital and could use its nurses and other staff to assist in the treatment of patients. Medical staff membership required the doctor to follow medical staff bylaws, keep medical records, attend an orientation program, participate in continuing education programs, and agree to take calls from the emergency room. After the doctor was diagnosed with and treated for bipolar disorder, he was reinstated with numerous conditions. These included submitting to close review of all of his surgical cases, meeting periodically with a monitoring physician, and providing extensive personal and medical

information. When the surgeon subsequently had an acute manic episode while performing open heart surgery, his medical staff privileges were rescinded. He sued for disability discrimination, and the hospital argued that he was an independent contractor. What should the court decide? (*Wojewski v. Rapid City Regional Hospital,* 450 F.3d 338 [8th Cir. 2006])

6. A waitress at a diner sued for sexual harassment. The employer argued that it had fewer than fifteen employees and was thus not subject to Title VII. Whether the diner had the requisite number of employees depended on whether the two managers in charge of the diner were "employees." The diner is owned by a woman who is the sole proprietor. However, she has delegated virtually all responsibility for the operation of the restaurant to these two managers. Without the owner's input, the managers decide whom to hire and fire, work schedules, work rules, and all of the other operational decisions of the restaurant. The two managers do not have ownership interests in the restaurant (although one is married to the sole proprietor) or hold positions as board members (there is no board). Should the two managers be counted as employees? (*Castaways Family Diner,* 453 F.3d 971 [7th Cir. 2006])

7. A farm labor contractor recruited and hired workers to detassel and remove unwanted corn plants in the fields of the Remington Seed Company. Detasseling is necessary for the growing of hybrid plants and must be performed several times during a season. The workers were paid by the labor contractor. They took instructions from the labor contractor but also followed Remington's work rules. Remington had supervisors in the fields to inspect work and determine when jobs needed to be redone. The labor contractor had no clients other than Remington Seed. Remington advanced several payments to the contractor so that the workers could be paid and covered by workers' compensation insurance. Tools and portable toilets were supplied by Remington. The workers brought suit under the Fair Labor Standards Act against both the labor contractor and Remington Seed Company. Is Remington a joint employer liable for violations of these workers' rights? (See *Reyes v. Remington Hybrid Seed Company,* 495 F.3d 403 [7th Cir. 2007]).

8. Should student-athletes be considered employees of the universities they attend? Why or why not? (*See* Taylor Branch. "The Shame of College Sports." *Atlantic* (October 2011), 81-110).

9. What are the consequences of denying back pay and other individual remedies to undocumented workers? Justice Breyer, dissenting from the majority opinion in *Hoffman Plastic Compounds, Inc. v. NLRB*, writes that denying the NLRB the power to award back pay "lowers the cost to the employer of an initial labor law violation…. It thereby increases the employer's incentive to find and to hire illegal-alien employees." Does denying remedies to undocumented workers reinforce or undermine national immigration policies?

10. Commenting on the increasingly widespread use of labor contractors by large companies, attorney Della Bahan claimed, "These companies are pretending they're not the employer. The contractor is willing to work people seven days a week, not pay payroll taxes, not pay worker's comp taxes. The companies don't want to do that for themselves, but they're willing to look the other way when their contractors do it." Do you agree? To what extent should companies be held responsible for the employment practices of companies with which they contract? (Steven Greenhouse. "Middlemen in the Low-Wage Economy." *New York Times* [December 28, 2003], WK10)

11. Legally, it makes a great deal of difference whether someone performing work is an employee or an independent contractor. But *should* it make a difference? What is the justification for excluding independent contractors from the protection of antidiscrimination and other laws? (Danielle Tarantolo. "From Employment to Contract: Section 1981 and Antidiscrimination Law for the Independent Contractor Workforce," 116 *Yale Law Journal* 170 [2006], 202–04).

CHAPTER 3

Overview of Employment Discrimination

This chapter delves into the concept of employment discrimination, the various types of discrimination, and the methods used in deciding discrimination cases. Because discrimination is a concern in virtually all areas of human resource practice, the material in this chapter is essential background for understanding cases and issues discussed throughout this entire book.

The Continuing Reality of Employment Discrimination

Many things have changed for the better since the 1960s, when our nation's primary antidiscrimination law, the Civil Rights Act of 1964, was enacted. We have made some progress in combating discrimination in the workplace and making equal employment opportunity a reality, but the job is by no means finished. Rooting out the contemporary manifestations of discrimination may prove even more difficult than confronting the overt exclusion and segregation characteristic of earlier years.

THE CHANGING WORKPLACE

The Contemporary Face of Discrimination

Employment discrimination is a continuing reality, but its nature has shifted in accordance with changes in the workplace and societal attitudes. Overt exclusion and segregation still occur but are less common now. As women and persons of color have entered the workforce in record numbers and begun to attain positions in occupations and industries from which they were largely absent in the past, other forms of discrimination have loomed large. These include harassment, obstacles to advancement, pay inequities, retaliation, and discrimination against caregivers.

As a form of discrimination, harassment is calculated to impress upon its victims that they are not respected, much less welcomed, in the workplace. Employees subjected to harassment are made uncom-fortable, find it more difficult to do their jobs well, and frequently quit in disgust. Sexual harassment is especially prevalent, but harassment based on other protected class characteristics, including race and national origin, is also frequently encountered.

Discrimination also increasingly takes the form of blocked access to better jobs.[1] In this regard, there has been extensive discussion of the **glass ceiling** problem, in which "invisible, artificial, and attitudinal barriers" conspire to limit the access of women and persons of color to higher-level positions.[2] Opportunities for training, development, and meaningful job assignments are especially critical at a time when employees are expected to construct their own career paths.[3] Likewise, the more that promotions, pay, and other important decisions are linked to performance, the more important it is that performance appraisals provide accurate, unbiased assessments. Yet, performance appraisals, at their best, require considerable subjective judgment. This leaves a large door open for bias or the perception of bias.[4] Getting ahead also depends heavily on one's "connections." Opportunities for informal mentoring, learning about the availability of jobs, and coming to the attention of those higher up in organizations all rest on social relationships. That race, sex, or other characteristics of people can affect social relationships on the job—and, by extension, employment opportunities—seems beyond question. Ferreting out discrimination when it lies beneath lukewarm performance appraisals, fewer high-profile assignments, or subjective judgments that others would better "fit" positions is extremely difficult.

As employees become aware of their rights and increasingly inclined to contest discriminatory practices, retaliation claims have become more common. Employers frequently compound initial instances of discrimination with the added infraction of punishing employees who complain about discrimination or help other employees obtain their civil rights. In 2010, fully 36.3 percent of EEOC charges included an allegation of retaliation. This was more than double the level of retaliation charges made in 1992.[5] Attorney Joseph Beachboard goes so far as to say, "Retaliation is really the No. 1 risk for employers today."[6]

Finally, discrimination related to the caregiving responsibilities of employees has become a prominent issue. Employers often assume that persons with caregiving responsibilities—including the parents of young children, but also persons who care for the needs of elderly parents and family members with disabilities—will not be able to devote themselves fully to their jobs. Discrimination has occurred to the extent that stereotypes about caregivers of different sexes or other protected class characteristics underlie employment decisions.[7]

---

[1]Anne Lawton. "The Meritocracy Myth and the Illusion of Equal Employment Opportunity." *Minnesota Law Review* 85 (December 2000), 605–12.
[2]U.S. Department of Labor, Office of Federal Contract Compliance Programs. "Glass Ceiling Initiative: Are There Cracks in the Ceiling?" (1997).
[3]Katherine V. W. Stone. *From Widgets to Digits: Employment Regulation for the Changing Workplace.* (New York: Cambridge University Press, 2004).
[4]Susan Bisom-Rapp. "Bulletproofing the Workplace: Symbol and Substance in Employment Discrimination Law Practice." *Florida State University Law Review* 26 (Summer 1999), 1012–18.
[5]Equal Employment Opportunity Commission. "Charge Statistics FY 1992 Through FY 1996" (historical data). Viewed August 15, 2008; "Charge Statistics FY1997 Through FY 2010." Viewed May 26, 2011 (http://www.eeoc.gov/).
[6]Cari Tuna. "Employer Retaliation Claims Rise." *The Wall Street Journal Online* (October 5, 2009).
[7]Equal Employment Opportunity Commission. "Enforcement Guidance: Unlawful Disparate Treatment of Workers with Caregiving Responsibilities." No. 915.002 (May 23, 2007).

Discrimination is inherently difficult to prove. Indeed, much of this chapter is devoted to explaining the methods that courts use to decide these complex cases. One indication that discrimination has not yet been eradicated is found in markedly different employment outcomes such as higher unemployment rates; concentration in lower-level jobs; and pay disparities across different races, sexes, and national origin groups. Unequal labor market outcomes need not have discrimination as their cause, but they are consistent with the presence of discrimination.

A second type of evidence for the continuing reality of discrimination comes from the large numbers of discrimination cases heard by administrative agencies and courts. The number of discrimination charges filed with the EEOC varies from year to year, but it has generally been at least 80,000 per year. Charge filing has increased sharply since 2008, with a record 99,922 charges filed in 2010.[1] Federal court cases alleging discrimination have increased substantially and now number more than 20,000 per year.[2] State civil rights agencies and courts handle an additional, and probably significant, number of

---

[1]U.S. Equal Employment Opportunity Commission. "Charge Statistics FY1997 Through FY 2010." Viewed May 26, 2011 (http://www.eeoc.gov/).

[2]Hoyt N. Wheeler, Brian S. Klaas, and Douglas M. Mahony. *Workplace Justice without Unions* (W. E. Upjohn Institute for Employment Research, 2004), 18.

cases each year. Not every case presents a valid claim, and indeed, the majority of cases do not conclude with a finding of discrimination. But despite plaintiffs' heavy burden in proving discrimination, courts and agencies decide in thousands of cases each year that discrimination has occurred.

Third, field, laboratory, and survey studies of employment discrimination also find discrimination to be real and pervasive. For example, researchers conducted an experiment to gauge the extent of discrimination against African American job applicants. Responding to newspaper listings for entry-level jobs, the researchers sent resumes that were matched in terms of experience, education, and skills but differed in terms of the "applicants'" names. Applicants with "white-sounding" names (e.g., Kristen, Laurie) received 50 percent more call-backs for interviews than did applicants with "black-sounding" names (e.g., Lakisha, Tamika), despite equal qualifications.[3] When the researchers varied applicant credentials, high-quality candidates with African American names were at an even greater disadvantage relative to high-quality candidates with "white-sounding" names.[4] Another study using a similar methodology found that job applicants with names common among Arab and South Asian persons were less likely to receive responses from temporary staffing agencies in California than were applicants whose names did not suggest these backgrounds.[5] Survey data also suggest that the experience of discrimination is far from uncommon. A 2005 Gallup poll found that 31 percent of Asian respondents, 26 percent of African American respondents, 18 percent of Latino respondents, and 12 percent of white respondents had experienced some form of bias during the previous twelve months.[6] Twenty-two percent of female respondents reported having experienced discrimination, compared to 9 percent of males. Perceived bias was especially likely in promotion and compensation decisions.

The Concept of Employment Discrimination

Numerous laws exist that aim to advance the goal of equal employment opportunity by prohibiting discrimination. Major federal antidiscrimination statutes include Title VII of the Civil Rights Act of 1964, the Equal Pay Act, the Age Discrimination in Employment Act, the Pregnancy Discrimination Act, and the Americans with Disabilities Act. The U.S. Constitution, particularly the Fourteenth Amendment's promise of equal protection under the law, also can be used to combat employment discrimination. Executive Order 11246 makes nondiscrimination a requirement for contractors and subcontractors doing work for the federal government. States and cities have their own antidiscrimination laws that mirror and sometimes extend federal protections. Clearly, laws prohibiting discrimination comprise a large and absolutely central part of employment law. But what is discrimination?

Employment **discrimination** can be defined as the limitation or denial of employment opportunity based on or related to the protected class characteristics of persons. This definition, although broad to subsume the different types of discrimination discussed in the following text, conveys some important aspects of employment discrimination. The element of limitation or denial of employment opportunities (also referred to

---

[3]Marianne Bertrand and Sendhil Mullainathan. "Are Emily and Greg More Employable than Lakisha and Jamal?" *American Economic Review* 94 (September 2004), 992.

[4]Bertrand and Mullainathan, 1001.

[5]Larry Swisher. "Temporary Job Agencies' Resume Responses Show Discrimination by Ethnicity." *Daily Labor Report* 195 (October 8, 2004), A-12.

[6]"Study Finds Nine Percent of Workers Experienced Illegal Bias in Last 12 Months." *Daily Labor Report* 236 (December 9, 2005), A-7.

as "adverse employment actions") indicates that it is not prejudice alone that subjects employers to liability, but the effects of bias on employment decisions. However, in one variety of discrimination case—retaliation—the acts that subject an employer to liability are not limited to those that directly affect employment. Thus, the comments immediately below do not apply to retaliation cases. The concept of an **adverse employment action** is elastic enough to encompass harassment that does not directly alter a person's employment status, but makes it more difficult to perform well and stay on the job. On the other hand, minor differences in treatment, stray insensitive comments, or instances of exclusion by coworkers from after-work socializing would not, by themselves, have sufficient impact on employment opportunities to be grounds for discrimination claims. Unwanted transfers and job assignments constitute a gray area. In one case, the involuntary transfer of an employee after she informed her employer that she was pregnant was found to be an adverse employment action.[7] There was evidence, including the fact that existing employees avoided applying for the position, to support the conclusion that the new position was objectively worse and effectively a demotion. In contrast, a court rejected the sex discrimination claim of a former CIA agent who said that her forced reassignment to a remote and more dangerous location in a Latin American country was a discriminatory act. In the court's view, she was unable to show that having entered an inherently dangerous line of work, the reassignment had a "significant detrimental effect" on her terms and conditions of employment.[8]

JUST THE FACTS

The Presidential Rank Award is the highest recognition given to career employees serving in the federal government. This prestigious award is accompanied by a substantial bonus of up to 35 percent of the employee's pay. Employees must be nominated and recommended by their supervisors. Not all nominees receive the award. An African American executive in the Department of Housing and Urban Development sued, based on his belief that race was a factor in his not being recommended by his supervisor for the award. Was the executive subjected to an adverse employment action?

See, *Douglas v. Preston*, 559 F.3d 549 (D.C. Cir. 2009).

Embedded in this definition of discrimination is the idea that it is a relative concept. Unequal treatment and outcomes can be discerned only by comparing what happens to some individuals with what happens to other individuals in a workplace. In contrast to other laws that establish specific minimum standards that employers must meet, U.S. antidiscrimination laws require consistent, evenhanded treatment of employees. But unequal and unfair treatment of individuals is still not sufficient to establish the existence of discrimination. To have discrimination, the unfair treatment must be based on or related to the **protected class** characteristics of persons. Society deems certain characteristics of people, such as race, sex, and age, impermissible grounds for making employment decisions. Linking employment decisions to protected class characteristics is prohibited, whereas unequal treatment based on other

---

[7]*Equal Employment Opportunity Commission v. SBC Communications*, 2005 U.S. Dist. LEXIS 6667, at 5 (N.D. Tex.).

[8]*Peary v. Goss*, 365 F.Supp.2d 713, 724–25 (E.D. Va. 2005), *affirmed*, 180 Fed. Appx. 476 (4th Cir. 2006).

types of distinctions (e.g., personality, personal friendships) generally does not provide the basis for a discrimination claim.

Protected Classes

Not all distinctions between people—and not even all those things that have no bearing on a person's ability to do a job—are protected class characteristics. To be sure, protected class characteristics are things that we generally regard as having little or no relationship to the ability to do a job. However, protected class characteristics also are fundamentally objectionable as grounds for making employment decisions. One reason that they are objectionable is that most protected class characteristics are either immutable (unchangeable) or not readily altered. For example, a person cannot change his race and should not have to change or hide his religion just to suit the preferences of an employer. A second reason that some characteristics are particularly objectionable as grounds for making employment decisions is that they relate to long-standing forms of hatred and prejudice, including racism, sexism, nationalism, and ageism.

The following is a list of protected classes under federal antidiscrimination statutes:

- Race, color (Title VII, Civil Rights Act, 42 U.S.C. § 1981)
- Sex (Title VII, Civil Rights Act, Equal Pay Act)
- National origin (Title VII, Civil Rights Act, 42 U.S.C. § 1981, Immigration Reform and Control Act)
- Religion (Title VII, Civil Rights Act)
- Citizenship—Citizens or legal aliens (Immigration Reform and Control Act)
- Age—40 and over (Age Discrimination in Employment Act)
- Disability—"Qualified individual with a disability" (Americans with Disabilities Act, Rehabilitation Act)
- Pregnancy—Pregnancy, childbirth, and related medical conditions (Pregnancy Discrimination Act)
- Military service (Uniformed Services Employment and Reemployment Rights Act)
- Genetic information (Genetic Information Nondiscrimination Act)

Other protected classes are recognized under the laws of some states and cities, but not under federal law. A few examples are marital status, sexual orientation, gender identity, and tobacco use.

Notice that some antidiscrimination statutes limit the definition of protected class to a particular group that is most likely to be the object of discrimination. For example, the Age Discrimination in Employment Act protects persons who are 40 years of age and older but does not prohibit denial of employment opportunity because someone under 40 is deemed to be "too young." In contrast, the protected class of race under Title VII includes *any* race. Although it is less likely that whites will be subjected to employment discrimination, discrimination against whites is clearly prohibited by Title VII. For example, there was a case in which three employees were charged by their employer with stealing cargo. Two of the employees were white and were discharged for the offense. The third employee was black and was not discharged. The Supreme Court held that "While Santa Fe [the employer] may decide that participation in a theft of cargo may render an employee unqualified for employment, this criterion must be 'applied, alike to members of all races,' and Title VII is violated if, as petitioners alleged, it was not."[9]

---

[9]*McDonald v. Santa Fe Transportation Co.*, 427 U.S. 273, 283 (1976).

Types of Discrimination

Discrimination can be further distinguished into four "types" or legal theories: disparate treatment, adverse impact (also known as disparate impact), failure to reasonably accommodate, and retaliation.

Disparate treatment is unequal treatment based on one or more protected class characteristics that results in the limitation or denial of employment opportunity. As the term implies, there is disparity or inequality in how employees are treated, and the difference in treatment is due to the employee's race, sex, or other protected class characteristic. The key element of disparate treatment is **discriminatory intent.** The meaning of intent in this context is that the decision maker based her decision, in whole or part, on a protected class characteristic of the affected employee. It is not necessary that the decision maker understood her actions to be unlawful or desired to harm anyone.

Suppose an employer believes that tall people make better managers because they are able to command more respect from the employees who report to them. What would happen if that employer required its managers to be at least six feet tall? Very likely, many more women than men would lose the opportunity to be managers (because considerably more men than women are at least six feet tall). Asians and Latinos might also be disadvantaged by this height requirement. But would it be discrimination? If the employer is really selecting managers based on height and not rejecting qualified women who are over six feet tall, it cannot be said that there is disparate treatment. Yet, it is still troubling that women are being disproportionately excluded from these management jobs on this dubious basis.

In fact, this height requirement would most likely be discriminatory because it creates adverse impact. **Adverse impact** (also known as disparate impact) is the disproportionate limitation or denial of employment opportunity for some protected class group that results from the use of a "neutral" requirement or practice that cannot be adequately justified. In adverse impact cases, the focus is on **discriminatory effects** rather than discriminatory intent. In our example, the neutral requirement is the height standard. It does not exclude all women, but it can be expected to exclude substantially more women than men. The employer believes that height is related to managerial ability, but unless the employer is able to present substantial evidence that this connection exists, the employer is guilty of discrimination.

Antidiscrimination laws call for reasonable accommodation of employees under two circumstances: for qualified disabled persons who need such accommodations and for employees whose religious beliefs and practices come into conflict with their employers' requirements. An employer discriminates through **failure to reasonably accommodate** by failing to remove obstacles to employment for persons whose disabilities or religious beliefs require such flexibility and when doing so would not impose "undue hardship" on the employer. For example, if an employee needs a day off for religious observance, the employer has a legal obligation to attempt to accommodate this need, such as by allowing the employee to switch days with another employee. If the employer simply takes a hard line and disciplines the employee for failing to show up, the employer is guilty of discrimination.

Retaliation can be defined as punishing employees for seeking to obtain their rights under antidiscrimination laws or assisting others in doing so. Although retaliation resembles disparate treatment, the decision to disadvantage an employee is based not on protected class per se, but rather on the employee's actions. For example, an employee might experience harassment by her coworkers and file a charge with the EEOC. Following the charge filing, she is discharged for being a "complainer." Under these circumstances, the woman would have a strong claim of retaliation. The retaliation claim would be in addition to, and its outcome independent of, the harassment charge.

Clippings

Automaker Chrysler has agreed to pay $60,000 to settle a retaliation lawsuit brought by the EEOC on behalf of two female employees who had spoken out against sex discrimination. One of the women had been given a less favorable job assignment. When she and a coworker questioned the plant manager about the move, he claimed that they were disrupting the workforce with their complaints about discrimination and threatened to discipline or fire them. Both women were subjected to closed-door meetings with the plant manager during which the manager pounded on the table, yelled, and demanded that they sign statements disavowing their discrimination complaints. John Hendrickson, EEOC regional attorney in Chicago, observed that "this case is a message to employers who act to

> silence complaints of discrimination: this 'nip it in the bud' approach is a losing strategy…. The proper and legal way for management to 'nip it in the bud' is to solve the discrimination situation, not punish the complainants."
>
> U.S. Equal Employment Opportunity Commission. "Chrysler to Pay $60,000 Under Decree Ending EEOC Retaliation Lawsuit." (May 25, 2011), viewed May 26, 2011 (http://www.eeoc.gov/).

In deciding whether discrimination has occurred, the "first cut" is to ask whether an employee has been subjected to an adverse employment action and whether any link is apparent between that action and the protected class characteristics of the employee. If the case appears to raise an issue of discrimination, the next task is to identify the theory (or sometimes theories) of discrimination that best fits the facts of the case. If the employer has allegedly based an employment decision on the protected class characteristics of the person, we have a disparate treatment case. If employment decisions are based on something other than protected class but the result is that some protected class group is substantially disadvantaged, we have an adverse impact case. If an employer is not willing to alter requirements and procedures on behalf of disabled persons and employees with religious conflicts, this may be evidence of a failure to reasonably accommodate. Finally, if punitive measures are taken against an employee who has attempted to enforce his or a coworker's civil rights, retaliation is indicated. Distinguishing between types of discrimination is important because each type of case is analyzed and decided in a different manner. In the following section, we will look more closely at how disparate treatment, adverse impact, and retaliation cases are decided. In-depth discussion of failure to reasonably accommodate appears in Chapter 10.

The discussion to this point also suggests some basic practical advice on how to avoid discrimination. The fundamental implication of disparate treatment is that *employers must not make employment decisions based on the protected class characteristics of their employees.* As with most things in the law, there are a few exceptions to this rule, but this basic guideline goes a long way. More generally, *employers that strive to be fair and to treat like situations alike regardless of the protected class characteristics of the employees involved will be far less likely to discriminate.* The general strategy for avoiding adverse impact is for employers to *closely scrutinize factors used in making employment decisions for their potential to exclude protected class groups and for evidence of their job-relatedness.* Although employers need to exhibit consistency and evenhanded treatment, they also *need to be flexible in accommodating the particular needs of disabled employees and employees whose religious practices conflict with workplace requirements.* Requests for flexibility cannot be ignored or dismissed simply because the requested measures would be a departure from the norm. Finally, *employers need to exercise particular care in taking adverse actions against employees who have filed charges or spoken out about discrimination.* Such employees do not become "untouchable" by virtue of their actions, but having solid reasons for any adverse actions taken under these circumstances is essential.

Disparate Treatment: A Closer Look

The crux of a disparate treatment case is an allegation that an employment decision was intentionally discriminatory in the sense of being based on protected class. However, there are variations on this theme. We need to again draw some distinctions, this time between different types of disparate treatment cases because not all disparate treatment cases are analyzed and decided in the same manner. Types of disparate treatment cases include facially discriminatory policies or practices, reverse discrimination, pretext, mixed motives, pattern or practice, and harassment.

Types of Disparate Treatment Cases

Facially Discriminatory Policy or Practice   In cases involving **facially discriminatory policies or practices**, the employer readily admits to using protected class as a basis for making employment decisions but insists that there is a sound business reason for doing so. For example, early in its history, Southwest Airlines had a policy of hiring only women as flight attendants. Establishing a protected class requirement of this sort is "facially discriminatory." The only way that an employer can prevail in such cases is by showing that the required protected class characteristic is a **bona fide occupational qualification (BFOQ)** for the job in question. Southwest argued that both its marketing strategy and customer preference dictated that they use only female flight attendants. The BFOQ defense is narrow, however, and the court found that Southwest failed to establish a BFOQ because men can also do the job of flight attendant.[10] Facially discriminatory policies or practices and the BFOQ defense are discussed further in Chapter 7.

Reverse Discrimination   In a sense, this term is a misnomer because protected classes such as race and sex include any race and either sex. However, a scenario found in many **reverse discrimination** cases is that an employer with an affirmative action plan hires a woman or person of color. A white male believes that he should have received the employment opportunity instead and sues. The employer does not deny that race or sex played some part in the hiring, but contends that the decision was made in accordance with a lawful affirmative action plan. The case hinges on whether the particular use of affirmative action was legally permissible. Thus, at least when affirmative action plans are involved, these cases take a different course than other disparate treatment cases. Legal challenges to affirmative action are discussed in Chapter 8.

Pretext   A more complex—and common—scenario occurs when an employee is denied an employment opportunity (e.g., not promoted) and the employee believes that the decision was influenced by the employer's consideration of a protected class characteristic (say, being female), whereas the employer contends that the decision was based on some lawful factor other than the woman's sex (e.g., that other candidates were more qualified). **Pretext** cases are so named because if the employee's allegations are true, the employer's stated reason is a cover-up for the true discriminatory motive. As you can imagine, sorting out these conflicting claims about why an employment decision was made is no simple task.

Mixed Motives   The underlying premise of pretext cases is that employment decisions are made *either* for discriminatory or lawful reasons. Yet, because more than one motive can account for a given decision, it is logically possible for an employer to base an employment decision on *both* discriminatory and lawful grounds. For example, in one well-known case,[11] a woman was denied promotion to partner at an accounting firm. The statements of the partners who made the decision clearly indicated that she was being judged differently because she was a woman. Yet, there was also evidence that she had problems relating to staff members and that this was another reason that she did not get promoted. In

---

[10] *Wilson v. Southwest Airlines*, 517 F. Supp. 292 (N.D. Tex. 1981).

[11] *Price Waterhouse v. Hopkins*, 490 U.S. 228 (1989).

mixed motives cases such as this, where strong evidence exists of both discriminatory and lawful motives affecting an employment decision (and not just conflicting claims as in a pretext case), the employer is guilty of discrimination. However, the plaintiff's award will be minimized if the employer can prove that the same decision would have been made absent the discriminatory motive (in other words, that the lawful motive was strong enough by itself to produce the same result).[12] The Supreme Court has clarified that the evidence relied on to demonstrate that a discriminatory motive played a part in an employment decision, justifying a mixed motives analysis, can be either direct or circumstantial.[13] The Court has also made it clear that a mixed motives analysis is not permitted in age discrimination cases brought under the ADEA.[14] Instead, the plaintiff must show that age was the "but-for" cause (i.e., the same decision would not have been made had the employer not considered the plaintiff's age) of the challenged adverse employment action, rather than just a contributing factor. An appeals court has said that the same is true for disability discrimination cases brought under the ADA.[15]

Pattern or Practice   Although many disparate treatment cases involve single plaintiffs, the concept of intentional discrimination is not limited to challenges of individual employment decisions. Sometimes intentional discrimination is more systematic and affects numerous employees. Employer policies that have the effect of segregating certain groups into lower-paid and less-desirable jobs or limiting the advancement of such persons are often at the center of pattern or practice claims. In **pattern or practice** cases, the plaintiffs marshal statistical data showing the systematic effects of an employer's discrimination and evidence of intentional discrimination against individuals in the larger affected group.

Harassment   Harassment is a form of disparate treatment because the victim of harassment is subjected to inferior working conditions because of her sex, race, or other protected class characteristic. Chapter 9 provides a detailed discussion of harassment. Here, the key point is that harassment is a form of discrimination rather than some entirely separate type of legal claim.

Analyzing Pretext Cases

Pretext cases, in which the employer's motive in making an employment decision is disputed, present a difficult problem. Proof of discriminatory intent is essential. Yet, although the plaintiff bears the burden of proving that discrimination has occurred, the defendant knows the most about why a particular decision was made. The defendant also has an incentive not to be entirely forthcoming if, in fact, the decision was tainted by consideration of an employee's protected class characteristics.

In *McDonnell Douglas v. Green*, the Supreme Court provided a method for deciding pretext cases.[16] This landmark case arose shortly after passage of the Civil Rights Act of 1964. The plaintiff Green was an African American who had worked for the aerospace company as a mechanic and laboratory technician until he was laid off due to a business downturn. When the company advertised openings for mechanics about a year later, Green applied for a position. McDonnell Douglas refused to rehire Green because of his involvement in an illegal "stall-in" outside the plant. To protest perceived racist

---

[12]Title VII, Civil Rights Act of 1964, 42 U.S.C.S. § 2000e-5(g)(2)(B) (2011).

[13]*Desert Palace v. Costa,* 123 S. Ct. 2148 (2003).

[14]*Gross v. FBL Financial Services,* 129 S. Ct. 2343 (2009).

[15]*Serwatka v. Rockwell Automation,* 2010 U.S. App. LEXIS 948 (7th Cir.).

[16]*McDonnell Douglas v. Green,* 411 U.S. 792 (1973).

ELEMENTS OF A CLAIM

Disparate Treatment—Pretext

I. Plaintiff must establish a "prima facie" case of disparate treatment by showing

  a) The protected class characteristic(s) of the plaintiff relevant to the case.
  b) That the employment opportunity was applied for.
  c) That the employment opportunity was available.
  d) That the plaintiff was qualified for the employment opportunity.
  e) That the plaintiff was denied the employment opportunity.
  f) That the employer continued to consider candidates for the employment opportunity or selected someone with contrasting protected class characteristics.

II. If the plaintiff successfully establishes a prima facie case, the employer is required to "produce" evidence of a lawful motive for the employment decision.

III. If the employer successfully produces such a motive, the plaintiff has the opportunity to rebut the employer's claims by

  a) Providing evidence that sheds doubt on the credibility of the employer's claimed motive and/or
  b) Providing other evidence that supports the claim that a discriminatory motive is the most likely explanation for the employer's decision.

The plaintiff bears the ultimate burden of proving that the employer intentionally discriminated.

© Cengage Learning 2013.

---

hiring practices of the company, Green and other employees had stalled their cars and blocked traffic at the time of the morning shift change. Green sued, alleging that the real reason he was not rehired was his race (and his civil rights protest activities). The approach that the Supreme Court provided for sorting out these difficult cases (*"McDonnell Douglas" analysis*), which it has refined over the years, is outlined in the following "Elements of a Claim" feature.

Prima Facie Case of Disparate Treatment The elements of a claim in a pretext case begin with a **prima facie case**. This is a showing by the plaintiff that discrimination is a plausible explanation for an adverse employment action. A plaintiff who cannot establish a prima facie case is out of luck. On the other hand, the plaintiff who establishes a prima facie case does not "win" anything. It simply means that there is sufficient likelihood of discrimination to warrant further inquiry. The Court recognized that the employer has most of the relevant information about the motivation behind an employment decision. Thus, the bar was set relatively low for the plaintiff to establish a prima facie case. Yet, this device also incorporates a degree of deference to the autonomy of employers. An employer will not be required to account for an employment decision unless the plaintiff can first provide the court reason to believe that discrimination might have occurred.

It is important to appreciate how the prima facie case allows a plaintiff to create an inference that discrimination has occurred without having to provide compelling and difficult to come by evidence of the employer's state of mind. The main thing that the prima facie case accomplishes is the elimination of some of the most common nondiscriminatory reasons for denial of an employment opportunity, thereby rendering discrimination a more plausible explanation. There is nothing surprising about an employee not getting a job if he never applied for it, if he sought employment when none was available, if he did not meet the basic qualifications required of all candidates, or if he did not give the employer sufficient time to make a decision. In establishing a prima facie case, the plaintiff is ruling out these other mundane reasons. If, on top of this, the employer continues to seek candidates or hires someone whose protected class characteristics contrast with the plaintiff's (e.g., the plaintiff is black and the person hired is white), discrimination begins to look like a real possibility. Alternatively, if the person chosen for an employment opportunity is the same race or sex as the plaintiff, this is usually a strong indication that race or sex was not a relevant factor; the reason must be something more particular to the individual. An important exception is when both the person selected and the person rejected are over 40 years of age (and thus both are within the protected class for ADEA suits). In this instance, the plaintiff is still able to establish a prima facie case of age discrimination as long as the person selected is "substantially" younger than the plaintiff.[17]

In *McDonnell Douglas*, the plaintiff was able to establish a prima facie case by showing that he was an African American, that McDonnell Douglas was hiring mechanics, that he was qualified to work as a mechanic and had performed well in his previous stint with the company, that he was refused employment, and that the company continued to seek applicants to fill mechanic positions.

Courts are somewhat flexible in how they apply these criteria. Failure to apply might not be fatal to the plaintiff's case if the employer placed unreasonable obstacles in the way of the person desiring to apply. Lack of stated qualifications will not defeat a claim when the person hired also lacks those qualifications.[18] Likewise, if the applicant is strung along and continuously told that the decision has not yet been made, the plaintiff will be deemed to have been denied employment. Hiring someone of the same race or sex as the person passed over might not be fatal to the plaintiff's case if, for example, the hiring occurred *after* discrimination charges were filed or if a significant period of time elapsed between the decisions or if different decision makers were involved.[19] Also, although this statement of the requirements for a prima facie case is oriented toward hiring decisions, courts have modified these requirements to better fit other employment decisions, such as terminations (see Chapter 18).

The requirement of identifying the protected class characteristic(s) relevant to the case is usually easily met by the plaintiff. If, for example, a plaintiff is claiming national origin discrimination, his national origin must be shown. A notable exception is the difficulty plaintiffs have in showing that they are "qualified individuals with a disability," entitled to protection against disability discrimination. A discrimination claim may allege discrimination on the basis of more than a single protected class and on some combination of protected classes (e.g., discrimination against African American males). Although the Supreme Court referred in *McDonnell Douglas* to the plaintiff showing "that he belongs to a racial minority"[20] rather than identifying protected class in general, that wording reflected the particular facts of the case. But courts sometimes require an additional showing by nonminority applicants, such as someone of another race making the

---

[17]*O'Connor v. Consolidated Coin Caterers Corp.*, 517 U.S. 308 (1996).

[18]*Scheidemantle v. Slippery Rock University*, 470 F.3d 535 (3d Cir. 2006).

[19]*Miles v. Dell*, 429 F.3d 480 (4th Cir. 2005).

[20]*McDonnell Douglas*, at 802.

employment decision, to establish a prima facie case.[21] As one court stated, nonminority plaintiffs must show "that background circumstances support the suspicion that the defendant is that unusual employer who discriminates against the majority."[22] Plaintiffs might also be required to establish that the employer was aware of the relevant protected class characteristic. Not all protected class characteristics are readily discernible (e.g., religion, disability), and not all employment decisions are made by personnel who have had direct contact with the affected applicant or employee. It is difficult to argue that an adverse employment action was based on a protected class characteristic when no evidence exists that the decision maker was aware of that characteristic. This issue has arisen in a number of cases in which employees alleging pregnancy discrimination were not yet visibly pregnant.[23] Likewise, an employee's age discrimination complaint failed because she was not able to show that the decision maker knew that she was significantly older than another employee who took over her duties.[24]

Articulation of a Lawful Motive

If a prima facie case is shown, the employer must "produce" evidence of a lawful, nondiscriminatory motive. Because the employer is maintaining that no discrimination occurred, the employer should be able to articulate why the plaintiff was denied an employment opportunity. This is not a heavy burden, and the court does not weigh the truthfulness of the employer's claims at this stage of the inquiry. However, the explanation still needs to be reasonably specific and not obviously contrived. In *McDonnell Douglas*, the employer's claim that it refused to rehire Green because of his participation in an illegal action detrimental to the company met the company's burden to produce a nondiscriminatory motive. In contrast, an employer failed to do so when it simply asserted that the plaintiff was "not sufficiently suited" for the position, without giving any further justification or elaboration.[25] The very real prospect of having to defend against discrimination charges underscores the fact that *employers should maintain good documentation and be prepared to explain the nondiscriminatory reasons for particular employment decisions.*

Evidence of Pretext and/or Discriminatory Motive

If the employer meets its burden of articulating a lawful, nondiscriminatory motive, the case does not end. The plaintiff still has the opportunity to present additional evidence of discrimination in two ways. First, the plaintiff can try to show that the employer's stated reason, although sufficient as a response to the prima facie case, is ultimately not credible (i.e., it is pretext). Second, the plaintiff can try to amass additional evidence of the employer's discriminatory motive.

An employer's explanation for an employment decision is pretext if (1) it has no basis in fact (e.g., the true reason for not hiring the plaintiff could not be poor interview performance because no interview was conducted) or (2) it has a basis in fact but was not actually a motivating factor (e.g., the plaintiff did poorly on his interview, but the decision maker did not bother to get information from the recruiter about the interview before rejecting the plaintiff) or (3) it was a factor but one insufficient to motivate the decision (e.g., the employer regularly hires people despite poor interviews).[26] An

---

[21]*Notari v. Denver Water Department*, 971 F.2d 585 (10th Cir. 1992).

[22]*Murray v. Thistledown Racing Club, Inc.*, 770 F.2d 63, 67 (6th Cir. 1985).

[23]*Prebilich-Holland v. Gaylord Entertainment Company*, 297 F.3d 438 (6th Cir. 2002).

[24]*Woodman v. WWOR-TV*, 411 F.3d 69 (2d Cir. 2005).

[25]*Patrick v. Ridge*, 394 F.3d 311 (5th Cir. 2004).

[26]*Carberry v. Monarch Marking Systems, Inc.*, 2002 U.S. App. LEXIS 2462, at 6 (6th Cir.); but see also *Forrester v. Rauland-Borg Corp.*, 453 F.3d 416 (7th Cir. 2006) arguing that the insufficient motivation alternative for showing pretext is either redundant or erroneous.

employer's claim that it had rejected a pregnant, African American candidate because another candidate had superior qualifications was clearly pretext because the candidate had been rejected before any other candidates had even applied.[27] Likewise, an employer's shifting explanations for why it did not promote a 56-year-old candidate led a court to conclude that they were pretext for age discrimination.[28] The employer had responded to the candidate's EEOC charge by saying that she was not promoted due to poor performance in her current job. However, at trial, the employer argued that she lacked relevant experience, rather than that her performance was deficient. Furthermore, the candidate was the only one who had the three years of recruiting experience "required" for the position and her managerial experience—which the employer said she lacked—was actually greater than that of the successful (34-year-old) candidate.

Explanations for employment decisions are pretext if they are lies or cover-ups for discrimination. When decisions are made for reasons that are "mistaken, ill considered, or foolish, so long as [the employer] honestly believed those reasons, pretext has not been shown."[29] The function of courts in discrimination cases is not to decide whether the employer made the "correct" employment decision, but rather whether the decision was motivated by discrimination. When an employer offers multiple reasons for an employment decision, plaintiffs are generally required to rebut all of those reasons.[30] It is usually not sufficient to throw cold water on just a part of the employer's rationale unless the reasons are intertwined with one another or some claims are so obviously pretext that they cast doubt on the employer's overall credibility.

Most often, plaintiffs in discrimination cases lack "smoking gun" evidence. Their employers usually know better than to verbalize or put in writing statements that unequivocally express a discriminatory motive. But sometimes this happens. There was **direct evidence** of discrimination when individuals involved in a casino's decision not to hire a well-qualified African American poker dealer said that "they hired who they wanted to hire and were not going to hire a black person unless there were extenuating circumstances," "good old white boys don't want blacks touching their cards in their face," and "maybe I've been told not to hire too many blacks in the poker room."[31] Likewise, the statement by a supervisor to two coworkers of a 63-year-old property manager that he wanted to "replace her with a young chippie with big tits" was found to be direct evidence of motivation to discriminate based on age.[32] No further inquiry into the existence of a discriminatory motive is needed in these cases because the employers have made it clear that their employment decisions were based on protected class. Direct evidence is most likely to be found where the written or spoken statement is clear, comes from someone involved with making the adverse employment decision, refers specifically to the individual denied the employment opportunity, and is expressed close in time to when the employment decision was made.

Most evidence of discriminatory motive is circumstantial. **Circumstantial evidence** hints at the possibility of discrimination, but by itself it is not sufficient to compel that conclusion. It includes the likes of statements made by company officials suggesting bias (but not sufficiently specific to constitute direct evidence), information about prior mistreatment of the plaintiff or other employees, the employer's track record in complying with antidiscrimination laws, and possibly statistics showing a pattern of discriminatory

[27]*EEOC v. JP Morgan Chase Bank N.A.*, 2010 U.S. Dist. LEXIS 105237 (W.D. Wis.).

[28]*Jones v. National American University*, 608 F.3d 1039 (8th Cir. 2010).

[29]*Millbrook v. IBP, Inc.*, 280 F.3d 1169, 1175 (7th Cir. 2002).

[30]*Crawford v. City of Fairburn*, 482 F.3d 1305 (11th Cir. 2007), *cert. denied*, 128 S. Ct. 495 (2007).

[31]*Jones v. Robinson Property Group*, 427 F.3d 987, 993 (5th Cir. 2005).

[32]*Glanzman v. Metropolitan Management Corp.*, 391 F.3d 506, 510 (3d Cir. 2004).

> ## JUST THE FACTS
>
> An African American employee sought promotion to a vacant shift manager position. There were two available positions and both went to white employees. At the time, the employee had been with Tyson for thirteen years and had worked his way up to "superintendent," the position just below shift manager in the plant hierarchy. One of the men given the shift manager jobs was a shift manager at another plant who was persuaded to transfer. The other had been working at another plant for less than two years, came to this plant as a "maintenance supervisor," and three months later was promoted to shift manager. There had never been an African American manager or shift manager in the history of this plant. On two occasions shortly before he was turned down for promotion, the plant manager had used the word "boy" in addressing the African American employee ("Boy, you better get going"; "Hey, boy"). The main reason cited by the plant manager for his promotion decision was that he wanted shift managers who had not been in a managerial position in the plant while it had struggled over the past two years. Is this discrimination? Why or why not?
>
> See, *Ash v. Tyson Foods*, 392 Fed. Appx. 817 (11th Cir. 2010).

effects. Evidence of discriminatory motive can be wide-ranging and circumstantial, but "stray remarks" by individuals not involved with or having influence over challenged employment decisions are not likely to be persuasive. However, in an age discrimination case brought against Google, the California Supreme Court criticized the tendency of federal courts to dismiss remarks as "stray."[33] During the employee's brief tenure at Google, derisive, arguably age-related comments were regularly made by high-level managers and coworkers. The employee was told that his ideas were "obsolete" and "too old to matter"; he was described as "slow," "fuzzy," "sluggish," "lethargic," and "lack[ing] energy"; and he was called "old man," an "old guy," and an "old fuddy-duddy." He was also told that he was terminated because he lacked a "cultural fit" with Google's youth-oriented corporate culture. The Court rejected Google's vociferous arguments that the comments should be dismissed as stray remarks not probative of discrimination because they were ambiguous, not directly related to the termination, and (at least in some instances) made by non-decision makers. Instead, the Court said that the appeals court acted properly in considering this evidence as part of the totality of evidence in the case. Plaintiffs also sometimes seek to introduce the testimony of other employees who have experienced or heard of discrimination in the company that did not involve the plaintiff's own supervisors or work area. The Supreme Court has said that the answer to the question of whether such evidence would be admissible is "maybe."[34] The decision to admit such evidence is case-specific and depends on how closely related the evidence is to the plaintiff's circumstances and legal claims.

What about a situation in which there is evidence of a discriminatory motive on the part of a supervisor or other manager, but not on the part of the HR manager or other individual who actually makes the employment decision? Insofar as intent is a necessary element of a disparate treatment claim, is the requisite discriminatory motivation present in such cases? This is an important issue since it is common for decisions, particularly terminations,

---

[33] *Reid v. Google*, 2010 Cal. LEXIS 7544.

[34] *Sprint/United Management Co. v. Mendelsohn*, 128 S. Ct. 1140 (2008).

to be made or at least approved by higher-level managers not well-acquainted with the employee in question. In a case involving a hospital technician who was a member of the Army Reserve,[35] the technician's supervisors expressed their views that his military service was placing a strain on the department and was a "waste of taxpayers' money." They made it clear that they wanted to get rid of the reservist. The supervisors imposed a requirement that the employee not leave his work area without first contacting a supervisor and then wrote him up for allegedly having done so. The vice president of human resources terminated the technician on the basis of the supervisor's report and a review of his personnel file. The technician's grievance was denied without any consideration of his claim that the supervisors' actions had been discriminatorily motivated. The Supreme Court held that "if a supervisor performs an act motivated by antimilitary animus that is *intended* by the supervisor to cause an adverse employment action, and if that act is a proximate cause of the ultimate employment action, then the employer is liable under the USERRA."[36] The employee did not have to show, as the hospital had contended, that the termination decision was the product of "blind reliance" on the supervisors' claims. Nor was it sufficient to avoid liability that the vice president for HR had engaged in a brief investigation of her own before the termination. The precise boundaries of this **subordinate bias** (or "cat's paw") **theory** are not yet clear. Nor is it absolutely certain that the same logic applies to discrimination cases brought under other laws, although that is likely. For now, this recent Supreme Court ruling underscores that *employers should closely review employment decisions and recommendations made by lower-level managers.*

Comparative evidence, in which the employer is shown to have treated the plaintiff worse than another employee under the same circumstances, with the only difference being that the other employee was of a different race or sex, is especially powerful. Such evidence simultaneously addresses pretext (e.g., If the plaintiff's actions really warranted termination, why didn't the company also terminate another employee who acted in the same manner?) and discriminatory motive (e.g., if two employees acted in the same manner and differed only in their race, the plaintiff's race is a likely reason for why she was treated more harshly). But the employees being compared must be truly "similarly situated" for comparisons of their treatment to have this force. The plaintiff in the *McDonnell Douglas* case was unable to show that employees of other races had engaged in activities comparable to the stall-in and had been retained or rehired. Lacking this and any other strong evidence of a discriminatory motive, Green ultimately lost his case on remand.[37] The importance of comparative evidence underscores the fact that *a general strategy for eliminating disparate treatment is to establish policies rather than make decisions ad hoc and to enforce those policies in a consistent manner.* Consistency does not mean rigidity; nor does it preclude consideration of legitimate factors that might make one case different from another. But the basic principle remains: treat like cases alike regardless of the protected class characteristics of the people involved.

What if pretext is shown but the plaintiff has little or no additional evidence of a discriminatory motive? The Supreme Court has held that a plaintiff can prevail based on a prima facie case and strong showing of pretext, even though further evidence of a discriminatory motive is absent.[38] The Court's reasoning is worth quoting at length:

> *[T]he trier of fact [judge or jury] can reasonably infer from the falsity of the explanation that the employer is dissembling to cover up a discriminatory purpose. Such an*

---

[35]*Staub v. Proctor Hospital*, 131 S. Ct. 1186 (2011).

[36]*Staub*, at 1194.

[37]*Green v. McDonnell Douglas*, 528 F.2d 1102 (8th Cir. 1976).

[38]*Reeves v. Sanderson Plumbing*, 530 U.S. 133 (2000).

Practical Considerations In light of the way in which disparate treatment cases are decided, why is it important that employers document the reasons for their employment decisions? Develop and consistently adhere to policies? Carefully monitor and review decisions, particularly terminations? Train supervisors?

inference is consistent with the general principle of evidence law that the fact finder is entitled to consider a party's dishonesty about a material fact as "affirmative evidence of guilt." Moreover, once the employer's justification has been eliminated, discrimination may well be the most likely alternative explanation, especially since the employer is in the best position to put forth the actual reason for its decision. Thus, a plaintiff's prima facie case, combined with sufficient evidence to find that the employer's asserted justification is false, may permit the trier of fact to conclude that the employer unlawfully discriminated.[39]

There is some murkiness in the Court's position that a prima facie case in addition to a showing of pretext *permits* but does not require finding for the plaintiff. But the decision generally reinforces the notion that narrowing the inquiry to the truthfulness of the employer's stated motive is the key to making disparate treatment cases based largely on circumstantial evidence tractable.

The *Jones v. Oklahoma City Public Schools* case that follows illustrates both the importance of a showing of pretext in disparate treatment cases and a distinctive aspect of age discrimination claims.

Jones v. Oklahoma City Public Schools
617 F.3d 1273 (10th Cir. 2010)

OPINION BY CIRCUIT JUDGE LUCERO:

Judy F. Jones appeals from the district court's grant of summary judgment in favor of her employer, Oklahoma City Public Schools ("OKC"), dismissing her claim of discrimination in violation of the Age Discrimination in Employment Act ("ADEA"). Although the district court found that Jones produced sufficient evidence to establish a prima facie case of discrimination and submitted evidence to show that OKC's proffered explanations for her demotion were pretextual, the court granted summary judgment to OKC on the ground that no reasonable juror could find that OKC had committed age discrimination. Because we conclude that the district court engaged in a "pretext plus" analysis in rendering its decision, we reverse.

Jones began working for OKC as a teacher in 1969. She then served as a principal of an elementary school for approximately fifteen years. In 2002, Jones was promoted to Executive Director of Curriculum and Instruction. * * * In July 2006, Linda Brown became OKC's interim superintendent [sic]. Brown altered OKC protocol such that Jones reported first to Manny Soto and later to Linda Toure, two of OKC's five executive directors in charge of schools and support services. Over the course of the next year, both Soto and Toure asked Jones when she was going to retire. On one occasion, Brown also questioned Jones about her retirement plans.

OKC eventually hired John Porter as its permanent superintendant in spring 2007. * * * After reviewing the district's organizational chart, Porter determined that OKC's executive team should be reorganized. In particular, he decided that Jones' position could be eliminated and its duties absorbed by other directors. * * * Porter directed Michael Shanahan, OKC's senior human resources officer, to notify Jones that her position would be eliminated and she would be reassigned as an elementary school principal. * * * Shanahan communicated Porter's orders and informed Jones that her salary would stay the same for the ensuing school year only. Jones asked Shanahan who made the decision to demote her, and Shanahan responded that it was Brown and Porter. Shanahan subsequently stated that four other executive directors were involved in the reassignment decision. Scott Randall, OKC's senior finance officer, later told Jones that she was the only director the administration had "gone after." Randall also stated that if Porter was transferring Jones for financial or budgetary reasons, Porter would have "run" it by him.

---

[39]*Reeves*, at 147–48.

After her reassignment and during her first year of employment as an elementary school principal, Jones retained her previous salary level. Her vacation benefits, however, were affected immediately. After Jones completed her first year as principal, her salary was decreased by approximately $17,000. This pay cut had the effect of reducing her retirement benefits. Jones' daily pay rate was also reduced by roughly five dollars per day.

One month after Jones' reassignment, Porter decided to create a new OKC executive position, Executive Director of Teaching and Learning. The job description and responsibilities for this position were quite similar to those of Jones' former position of Executive Director of Curriculum and Instruction. * * * OKC filled this new position with an individual who was forty-seven years of age. At the time of Jones' reassignment, she was nearly sixty years old.

In May 2008, Jones filed suit in the District Court for the Western District of Oklahoma alleging OKC violated the ADEA when it demoted her to the position of elementary school principal. * * * Before reaching the merits of parties' arguments, we must first determine whether the Supreme Court's holding in *Gross v. FBL Financial Services, Inc.* [a 2009 decision], decided after the district court issued its summary judgment order, affects our analysis on appeal. * * * The ADEA, like other anti-discrimination statutes, includes a causation requirement. It prohibits employers from "discriminat[ing] against any individual with respect to his compensation, terms, conditions, or privileges of employment, *because of* such individual's age." The statute, however, does not define the phrase "because of," and before *Gross*, it was unclear which causal standard applied. *Gross* clarified that the ADEA requires "but-for" causation. Consequently, to succeed on a claim of age discrimination, a plaintiff must prove by a preponderance of the evidence that her employer would not have taken the challenged action but for the plaintiff's age. OKC argues that in mandating but-for causation, *Gross* established that "age must have been the only factor" in the employer's decision-making process. We disagree. * * * [A]n employer may be held liable under the ADEA if other factors contributed to its taking an adverse action, as long as "age was the factor that made a difference."

* * * [W]e must now address the issue of whether Jones demonstrated a prima facie case of age discrimination. To prove a prima facie case of age discrimination, a plaintiff must show: "1) she is a member of the class protected by the [ADEA]; 2) she suffered an adverse employment action; 3) she was qualified for the position at issue; and 4) she was treated less favorably than others not in the protected class." The parties do not dispute that Jones demonstrated she was a member of the class protected by the ADEA, that she was qualified for her former position, and that she was treated less favorably than others not in the protected class. OKC argues, however, that Jones did not suffer an adverse employment action because she remained employed in a position with similar responsibilities and received a daily pay rate that was "almost exactly the same" as her per diem rate as an executive director. * * * Under the facts of this case, the district court correctly determined that Jones suffered an adverse employment action. Jones' reassignment letter specifically stated that her salary level would remain the same for the ensuing school year only, and Jones suffered a $17,000 decrease in salary the following year. Her vacation benefits were reduced immediately upon reassignment, and her retirement benefits were reduced the following year. Although OKC argues that Jones did not experience a demotion, she certainly lost professional prestige and fell to a lower position in the district's organizational hierarchy. * * * All told, the record in this case conclusively shows that Jones suffered an adverse employment action and proved a prima facie case of age discrimination.

We thus consider the ultimate question of whether OKC was entitled to summary judgment. * * * In *Reeves* [*v. Sanderson Plumbing*], the Supreme Court rejected the so-called "pretext plus" standard that required plaintiffs using the *McDonnell Douglas* framework to both show pretext and produce "additional evidence of discrimination" in order to avoid summary judgment. *Reeves* expressly held that "a plaintiff's prima facie case [of discrimination], combined with sufficient evidence to find that the employer's asserted justification is false, may permit the trier of fact to conclude that the employer unlawfully discriminated."

* * * A plaintiff produces sufficient evidence of pretext when she shows "such weaknesses, implausibilities, inconsistencies, incoherencies, or contradictions in the employer's proffered legitimate reasons for its action that a reasonable factfinder could rationally find them unworthy of credence and hence infer that

the employer did not act for the asserted non-discriminatory reasons." * * * OKC proffered two legitimate reasons for Jones' reassignment: Porter's desire to undertake a reorganization of OKC's executive team in a revenue-neutral fashion and his belief that Jones' former position contained only narrow duties that could be absorbed by other directors. With respect to Porter's first goal, Jones produced evidence that her former position stayed on the books for the 2007–2008 fiscal year and that staff in her department remained employed in the same positions after her transfer. Further, Randall told Jones that if her transfer was actually motivated by budgetary reasons, Porter would have "run" it by him. * * *

Second, Jones presented evidence that a new position, Executive Director of Teaching and Learning, was created shortly after her transfer…. [T]his position's job responsibilities were strikingly similar to those of Jones' former position as Executive Director of Curriculum and Instruction. Although OKC argues that the new position entailed more responsibility, it also admits that the position reabsorbed many of the same duties of Jones' former position and was filled by someone thirteen years Jones' junior. Together, this evidence was sufficient to satisfy *McDonnell Douglas's* third step, and the district court's grant of summary judgment was therefore improper.

… [W]e recognize that *Reeves* carved out a narrow exception to our general rule against a "pretext plus" requirement. * * * But the *Reeves* exception does not apply here. In reasoning that Jones generated only a weak question of fact regarding whether OKC's proffered reasons were pretextual, the district court improperly favored OKC's version of the facts. * * * However, the district court was required to view the facts in the light most favorable to Jones. Accordingly,

it should have credited Shanahan's statement that four other directors were involved in the decision to reassign Jones. Properly considered at the summary judgment stage, Jones' evidence of discrimination therefore included age-related comments by three executive directors, all involved in the reassignment decision. Finally, even if we were to assume that Jones "created only a weak issue of fact as to whether [OKC's] reason was untrue," the corollary "abundant and uncontroverted independent evidence that no discrimination had occurred" did not exist in this record.

Rather than properly applying *Reeves*, the district court erroneously held Jones to the discredited "pretext plus" standard. The court faulted Jones for not presenting "additional evidence" that age was a determining factor in her reassignment. But after showing that OKC's reasons for her transfer were pretextual, Jones was under no obligation to provide additional evidence of age discrimination. Accordingly, … we **REVERSE** the district court's grant of summary judgment and **REMAND** for further proceedings.

CASE QUESTIONS

1. What was the legal issue in this case? What did the court decide?
2. How is the plaintiff able to establish a prima facie case of disparate treatment?
3. What reasons did the employer offer for its decision to reassign the employee? What is the evidence that these might be pretext?
4. What does the court mean when it refers to a "pretext-plus standard"? How did the district court err in applying this standard?
5. What does it mean for age to be a "but-for" cause? Do you think that Jones will be able to prove age discrimination at trial? Why or why not?

It is important to remember that while many discrimination cases focus on evidence of pretext, this is just one means of getting at the ultimate question of whether discrimination has occurred. When there is sufficient evidence of a discriminatory motive, whether that evidence is "direct" or circumstantial, plaintiffs can prevail without showing pretext—at least under Title VII and other antidiscrimination laws that permit a mixed motives analysis. Thus, while the indirect approach of the *McDonnell Douglas* analysis remains the predominant method used in disparate treatment cases, a more direct approach is also available to plaintiffs. *Hasan v. Foley & Lardner LLP* illustrates this direct approach, as the plaintiff presents a "mosaic" of circumstantial evidence sufficient to establish a discriminatory motive.

Hasan v. Foley & Lardner LLP
552 F.3d 520 (7th Cir. 2008)

OPINION BY CIRCUIT JUDGE RIPPLE:

Zafar Hasan, a Muslim of Indian descent and a former associate at the law firm Foley & Lardner ("Foley"), brought this action claiming that Foley had terminated his employment after the terrorist attacks of September 11, 2001, because of his religion, race, national origin and color. The district court granted Foley's motion for summary judgment. Mr. Hasan now appeals. For the reasons set forth in this opinion, we reverse the judgment of the district court and remand the case for further proceedings.

* * * Foley invited Mr. Hasan to join the Business Law Department in its Chicago office in October 2000. At first, Foley was pleased with Mr. Hasan's performance. In a June 2001 evaluation, department chair Edwin Mason and partner Robert Vechiola described Mr. Hasan's performance: "Zafar has a great attitude and is eager to learn. He has good business sense and a great deal of maturity for his age." The partners also noted, though, that Mr. Hasan needed to pay more attention to detail, develop his substantive skills and submit more polished work to his supervisors. Six months later, a group of four partners evaluated Mr. Hasan's work for the period between March 15 and September 15, 2001. The partners praised Mr. Hasan as "a hard worker" with a "great attitude" and commented that he managed clients and co-workers exceptionally well. Although the partners repeated their criticisms of Mr. Hasan's drafting skills, efficiency and attention to detail, all of the partners agreed that he was "on track for advancement" and generally exceeded or met the firm's expectations. Mr. Hasan was assigned to work on a large transaction for Foley's client, GMAC, and maintained high billable hours through the late summer of 2001. * * *

Mr. Hasan and Foley agree that matters changed after the terrorist attacks of September 11, 2001. On the day of the attacks, another Foley attorney heard George Simon, a partner on the firm's Management and Compensation Committees, opine that "those people don't belong here ... they should kick them all out." The other attorney understood Mr. Simon to be talking about Muslims. Mr. Hasan responded to the events of September 11 by publishing articles and appearing on television to publicize his view of Islam as a peaceful religion. According to Mr. Hasan, when he posted copies of some of his articles on his office door, Foley partner Doug Hagerman warned him to be "careful" and "not to upset any sacred cows." Hagerman asked, "Are you sure you want to have those [articles] up here?"

* * * After September 11, Mr. Hasan's billable hours began to drop precipitously, while the average hours of other associates in his department increased. * * * Most of the department's associates were assigned to work on a second large project for GMAC, called "MINT." Mr. Hasan was not asked to work on MINT, even though he had requested more work. In fact, even when GMAC representatives asked Mr. Hasan to perform more work for them, Foley did not assign Mr. Hasan to the MINT project. Foley maintains that, although the MINT project occupied many associates, the Business Law Department lacked work generally and, consequently, it assigned what little work there was to its best associates and that Mr. Hasan did not fall into that category.

Mr. Hasan's May 2002 evaluation was less positive than his previous evaluations. His supervising partners stated that Mr. Hasan's technical skills were behind his class level. Partners also criticized Mr. Hasan's efficiency, observing that he billed more time than should have been necessary to complete projects. Mr. Hasan's evaluators did praise his intelligence, confidence and advocacy skills, but they warned Mr. Hasan that he would be "outplaced" if his performance did not improve by September. According to Mr. Hasan, Foley later revised the evaluation, adding that Mr. Hasan had failed to exercise tact with a client in December 2000, some eighteen months earlier. The firm also retracted its threat of "outplacement." Instead, it stated that it would simply place a warning in Mr. Hasan's file and evaluate his progress again in September.

Six partners evaluated Mr. Hasan's work in his next review. Most of the partners agreed that Mr. Hasan's work met or exceeded firm expectations. Peter Schaafsma, with whom Mr. Hasan had worked the most, reported that Mr. Hasan was "one of his corporate 'go to guys'" and was "a joy to work with." Todd Pfister, for whom Mr. Hasan had done little work, was not as positive: "For various reasons, a number of partners seem to have lost confidence in Zafar. As a result, his workload has diminished substantially and he is falling farther behind in his professional development." Pfister concluded that the firm needed to "address this situation promptly." A third partner, Robert Vechiola, mentioned Mr. Hasan's low hours but noted that Mr. Hasan was willing "to do anything to improve his hours, including relocating to another office and/or working with other departments." After Schaafsma submitted his glowing evaluation of Mr. Hasan's work, Mason (the department chair) told him that his praise was inconsistent with the other partners' assessments and asked him to explain his review. In his deposition, Schaafsma stated that he was surprised that other partners had given Mr. Hasan negative reviews and believed that Mason was trying to convince him to retract his praise for Mr. Hasan's work.

* * * [I]n October 2002, Mason chaired a meeting to evaluate the department's associates.... Simon (the partner who made the "kicking out" comment on September 11) criticized Mr. Hasan's performance, even though Simon never had worked with Mr. Hasan. Ultimately the partners decided to terminate Mr. Hasan's employment.... Vechiola described the meeting as a "... pile-on" and reported that, after Simon criticized Mr. Hasan, the rest of the partners joined in. Mr. Hasan says that Vechiola told him that it was "too bad that [Simon] and those guys took out their religious dispute in Israel on you and had you fired." Vechiola, however, does not recall having made that statement. * * *

Mason then e-mailed the firm's nationwide managing partner, Stan Jaspan, to tell him that he planned to fire Mr. Hasan. He noted that the decision was not unanimous and that he had "further background information" that he wanted to tell Jaspan by phone. Mason admitted at his deposition that the "background information" that he wanted to convey to Jaspan was the fact that Mr. Hasan was a Muslim. Mason explained that he told Jaspan that Mr. Hasan was a Muslim because he was concerned that Mr. Hasan "could potentially bring a claim" against the firm.

Although Jaspan gave Mason permission to fire Mr. Hasan, the firm held back. In November 2002, Jaspan and another lawyer, Joseph Tyson, began searching for a job for Mr. Hasan at one of Foley's other offices. Tyson stated in his deposition that the search was unusual given that the firm already had decided to terminate Mr. Hasan's employment. On November 22, Tyson e-mailed Jaspan to tell him that he had had no luck finding a job in another Foley office for "the well educated Muslim in Chicago." * * * Mason

informed Mr. Hasan in early December that Foley was terminating his employment because of "deficiencies in performance" and "a perception that he was behind the level of where he should be" professionally. * * * Foley permitted Mr. Hasan to remain at the firm for six months following his termination. Mr. Hasan ultimately left his employment with Foley on June 13, 2003.

During the time Mr. Hasan worked at Foley, the Business Law Department employed two other Muslim associates. Foley placed one of those associates on probation in May 2002 and then transferred her to the firm's litigation group in 2003. Foley terminated the other Muslim associate's employment shortly after Mr. Hasan left the firm. Foley notes that another Muslim lawyer has worked at the firm since 1996 and became a partner in 2006, but ... [he] was not in the Business Law Department.

About two weeks after Mr. Hasan left the firm, two Foley partners circulated a memo to the entire Chicago office in which they boasted that the firm's "financial picture is strong" and that "profits per equity partner" for 2002 exceeded the prior year's profits by twenty-five percent. According to one partner, Foley did not terminate any other attorneys between 2001 and July of 2003 for economic reasons. * * * In the fall of 2002, the Business Law Department hired new associates from Foley's summer associate class to begin work in 2003.

Mr. Hasan timely filed a charge of discrimination with the Equal Employment Opportunity Commission ("EEOC"). He alleged that Foley had fired him because he is Muslim, a South Asian of Indian origin and has "brown and olive" skin. * * * The district court granted Foley's motion for summary judgment; it concluded that Mr. Hasan had failed to create a "convincing mosaic" of direct or circumstantial evidence that could permit a jury to conclude that Foley intentionally discriminated against him. * * *

* * * Mr. Hasan elected to proceed under the so-called "direct" method of proving discrimination. Despite its name, proof of discrimination under the direct method "is not limited to near-admissions by the employer that its decisions were based on a proscribed criterion." Rather, an employee also can provide circumstantial evidence "which suggests discrimination albeit through a longer chain of inferences." The key to the direct method of proof is that the evidence, whether direct or circumstantial, "'points directly' to a discriminatory reason for the employer's action." There are three categories of

circumstantial evidence, each of which can establish discrimination under the direct approach. Mr. Hasan primarily relies on the first category, which includes "suspicious timing, ambiguous oral or written statements, or behavior toward or comments directed at other employees in the protected group." Some of Mr. Hasan's evidence is also relevant to pretext.... * * * Mr. Hasan submits that the facts in the record, while possibly weak proof of discrimination individually, together would allow a jury to infer that Foley terminated his employment because he is Muslim and of Indian descent. Those facts include Simon's anti-Muslim comments, Hagerman's advice, Mason's warning to Jaspan about Mr. Hasan's religion, the suspicious timing of the downturn in his hours and evaluations following September 11, one partner's testimony that Foley fired no other associates for economic reasons and did well financially in 2001 and 2002, the Business Law Department's treatment of its other Muslim associates and Foley's shifting justifications for firing Mr. Hasan.

Addressing the evidence Mr. Hasan put forward, the district court concluded that Simon's comment that Muslims should be "kicked out" was not valid circumstantial evidence of discrimination because Simon was not Mr. Hasan's direct supervisor. * * * [D]erogatory remarks are relevant if they are made by someone who provided input into the adverse employment decision. The record shows that Simon attended the meeting at which the partners decided to fire Mr. Hasan and that he participated in that decision. That others were also involved in making that decision does not make Simon's participation irrelevant. There is also evidence in the record that Simon's criticisms at that meeting incited anti-Muslim and racially charged commentary from other partners. * * * [T]he record would allow the rational inference that Simon not only participated in the decision to fire Mr. Hasan but also may have instigated it.

The district court also concluded that Simon's comment could not be evidence of discriminatory intent because he expressed his anti-Muslim sentiments on September 11, 2001, a year before Mr. Hasan was fired. The recency of discriminatory comments, together with who made the comments and how extreme those comments were, is relevant to whether they help to build a total picture of discrimination. But the district court may not view recency alone as the decisive factor. Moreover, Simon and Hagerman made their comments around the time that the Business Law Department began to steer work away from

Mr. Hasan, which was a factor upon which they ultimately relied to fire him.

The district court also believed that the fact that Mr. Hasan's hours fell after September 11 did not, on its own, raise any suspicions. Suspicious timing is, however, relevant to whether an employer's conduct was discriminatory. * * * Mr. Hasan's post-September 11 decrease in hours alone may not carry much meaning, but it gains substantial significance in the context of (1) partners' anti-Muslim comments, (2) their refusal to give him work even when he asked for it, (3) Mr. Hasan's good relationship with the department's primary client, (4) Mr. Hasan's previous positive performance reviews and (5) the fact that other associates had sufficient work and even increased their hours on average during the relevant period.

The district court next interpreted Mason's e-mail and phone call to Jaspan regarding Mr. Hasan's religion as evidence that the firm paid attention to equal employment laws. A jury could infer, however, that Mason wanted to talk to Jaspan without leaving a written record precisely because he was worried that Foley had fired Mr. Hasan unlawfully. Such an inference is particularly strengthened by the anti-Muslim comments in the record. This is exactly the type of ambiguous fact, susceptible to competing interpretations, that should be evaluated by a fact-finder.

The district court also held that Mr. Hasan's evidence regarding Foley's treatment of other Muslims in the Business Law Department was irrelevant to his discrimination argument. Our precedents establish, however, that "behavior toward or comments directed at other employees in the protected group" is one type of circumstantial evidence that can support an inference of discrimination. The Supreme Court also has held that this kind of "me too" evidence can be relevant to a discrimination claim. * * * Rather than dismiss this evidence as irrelevant per se, the district court should have analyzed whether, if proven, the fact that Foley fired or transferred all other Muslim associates from its Business Law Department would be a relevant component of the "mosaic" of evidence.

Foley submits that its treatment of other associates matters only if Mr. Hasan can show that the firm gave preferential treatment to similarly situated non-Muslim employees. Mr. Hasan cannot prevail, Foley contends, because he has not produced any evidence regarding similarly situated employees. This argument confuses the direct method of proving employment discrimination with the indirect method. It is true that, under the indirect method of proof, a plaintiff must produce evidence of how the employer treats similarly situated employees. But the direct method of proof imposes no such constraints. In fact, one reason a plaintiff might select the direct method of proof rather than the indirect is that, as Mr. Hasan's attorney explained at oral argument, there simply are no similarly situated employees.

* * * Finally, the record, viewed in the light most favorable to Mr. Hasan, supports neither of Foley's purported reasons for firing Mr. Hasan. Foley initially claimed that it fired Mr. Hasan for poor performance. With the exception of Schaafsma, who is no longer at the firm, Mr. Hasan's supervising partners all testified at their depositions that, at the time Mr. Hasan was fired, his work was uniformly unacceptable. However, after Foley located Mr. Hasan's work evaluations [the firm originally claimed that the evaluations had been destroyed], which were mostly positive, the firm changed its tune, maintaining that it actually fired Mr. Hasan not because his work was unacceptable but because it only had enough work to keep the best associates in the department occupied. Moreover, Mason's attempt to convince Schaafsma to retract his praise for Mr. Hasan's work permits an inference that the Business Law Department intended to sabotage Mr. Hasan's evaluations. * * * Issues of material fact cannot be resolved on summary judgment. The firm cannot, therefore, avoid trial by claiming that its real reason for firing Mr. Hasan was his supposed poor performance, when there is an issue of material fact as to whether this proffered reason is merely a pretext.

A reasonable jury could also find that Foley's alternative explanation—that it fired Mr. Hasan because the firm did not have enough work for all the associates in the Business Law Department—is pretextual as well. * * * [T]he internal firm-wide memo claimed that Foley's economic performance in 2001–2002 was strong, while Foley now contends that the firm was in a downward spiral that required it to jettison Mr. Hasan. A jury could reasonably infer from these facts that Foley partners directed work towards other, non-Muslim associates in the Business Law Department in order to use Mr. Hasan's lack of work as a pretext to fire him. Similarly, it is unclear from the record why Foley hired new associates into its Business Law Department immediately after firing Mr. Hasan. It is possible that the firm lacked work for midlevel associates with Mr. Hasan's skill set and instead needed attorneys with different experience or training. A jury could also conclude, however, that the Business Law Department hired new associates because it actually had plenty of work. * * *

Putting together these items of circumstantial evidence, a reasonable jury could conclude that Foley terminated Mr. Hasan's employment because he is Muslim and of Indian descent. That "mosaic" of evidence, together with the unresolved questions of fact, is sufficient under the direct method of proof for Mr. Hasan to survive summary judgment on his discrimination claims. * * *

CASE QUESTIONS

1. What was the legal issue in this case? What did the court decide?
2. What reasons does the law firm offer for the termination?
3. What is the evidence of a discriminatory motive in this case? In your view, how strong is that evidence?
4. Suppose that this case had been argued under the "indirect method" (*McDonnell Douglas* analysis) instead of the "direct method." What difference, if any, would this have made in the analysis and outcome of this case?
5. What should the law firm have done differently?

Adverse Impact: A Closer Look

In adverse impact cases, the plaintiff does not argue that the basis for an employment decision is something other than what the employer claims. Nor does the plaintiff assert that the decision is based on protected class. Instead, the contention is that some "neutral" (not protected class) requirement poses an unnecessary obstacle to employment opportunity, one that harms some protected class group much more than others. The discriminatory *effects* of the employer's requirements and policies, rather than the employer's intent, are at the core of an adverse impact claim.

In an important early case, the Supreme Court was called on to decide whether an employer's requirements for initial hiring and transfers were discriminatory.[40] The employer (Duke Power) had, like many other employers prior to passage of the Civil Rights Act of 1964, openly discriminated against African Americans. African Americans were hired, but only for low-paying, strenuous positions within the company's Labor Department. Immediately after Title VII went into effect, Duke Power instituted a high school diploma requirement for transfers from the Labor Department to other jobs within the company. Obtaining a passing score on two standardized aptitude tests (with the cutoff for passing geared to the median score for high school graduates) was added as an additional requirement and later offered as a substitute for the high school diploma. The context is critical here. Although employers routinely establish educational and testing requirements for positions and a high school diploma does not sound like an imposing requirement to contemporary ears, the practical effect of these requirements was to lock into place the prior segregation of African Americans into the worst jobs at Duke Power. This is because in the 1960s in North Carolina, whites were nearly three times as likely as African Americans to have obtained a high school diploma. Only one of the African Americans working for Duke Power at the time of the case had a high school diploma. Although many whites (in fact, the majority of the population) also had not graduated from high school, the diploma requirement disproportionately limited the employment opportunities of blacks. The offer to substitute the test for the diploma requirement was an empty gesture. Setting the cutoff score at the median level for high school graduates (meaning the level at which only half of high school graduates would be expected to pass) meant that the tests were actually a more stringent requirement than the high school diploma.

The Supreme Court was thus presented with a case in which an employer's selection criteria disadvantaged African Americans, but there was no evidence that the requirements were instituted for the purpose of discriminating on the basis of race. Citing the broad purpose of Title VII to promote equal employment opportunity, the Court ruled that discrimination in the form of adverse impact, no less than disparate treatment, violates the law: "Under the Act, practices, procedures, or tests neutral on their face, and even neutral in terms of intent, cannot be maintained if they operate to 'freeze' the status quo of prior discriminatory employment practices."[41] Critical to the Court's decision was that Duke Power had not sought to determine that a high school diploma or a passing score on the aptitude tests was meaningfully related to ability to perform jobs at the company. In fact, there was evidence to the contrary. White employees without high school diplomas who were hired before the high school diploma requirement was put into effect and allowed to stay on the job performed satisfactorily and obtained promotions. How necessary, then, was a high school diploma for these jobs? In the Court's words, "The touchstone is business necessity. If an employment practice which operates to exclude Negroes [the term most commonly used for African Americans at the time of this decision] cannot be shown to be related to job performance, the practice is prohibited."[42]

For several decades that followed, the precedent established by the Supreme Court's decision in this landmark case, *Griggs v. Duke Power*, was the legal basis for adverse impact claims. In 1991, Title VII of the Civil Rights Act was amended to specifically cover adverse impact claims.[43]

---

[40]*Griggs v. Duke Power*, 401 U.S. 424 (1971).

[41]*Griggs*, at 430.

[42]*Griggs*, at 431.

[43]*Title VII of the Civil Rights Act of* 1964, 42 U.S.C.S. § 2000e-2(k) (2011).

```
ELEMENTS OF A CLAIM
```

Adverse Impact

I. Plaintiff must establish a "prima facie" case of adverse impact by showing that

    a) A "neutral" employment requirement or practice has the effect of disproportionately limiting the employment opportunities of a protected class group (e.g., women, Latinos) of which the plaintiff is a part.

    b) The difference in outcomes across protected class groups is large enough that it is unlikely to exist by chance.

II. If the plaintiff successfully establishes a prima facie case, the employer must prove that the challenged employment requirement or practice is "job related and consistent with business necessity."

    In age discrimination cases, the employer must defend use of the challenged employment requirement or practice by showing that it is a "reasonable factor other than age."

III. If the employer successfully defends the requirement or practice, the plaintiff can still prevail by showing that a feasible alternative exists that would have less discriminatory impact and the employer nonetheless refuses to adopt it (but not in age discrimination cases).

© Cengage Learning 2013.

Analyzing Adverse Impact Cases

Because the plaintiff in an adverse impact case is claiming that some neutral requirement or practice has discriminatory effects, the plaintiff generally has to point to a specific requirement or practice as the culprit. An exception is where the plaintiff is unable to do so because multiple factors are involved in making the employment decision (such as a hiring process with numerous tests and interviews) and the scoring and relative weight of each factor is unclear. In such cases, the bundle of related practices can be challenged as one. **Neutral requirement** or practice refers to anything other than protected class characteristics used as grounds for making employment decisions. To produce adverse impact, a requirement or practice has to fall more heavily on some protected class group than others. The example given earlier was of a minimum height requirement that, if set high enough, would eliminate from consideration some men, but a much larger proportion of women due to the fact that women are, on average, shorter than men. In *Griggs*, the neutral requirements were the high school diploma and the specified level of performance on the intelligence and aptitude tests. These requirements were causally linked to discriminatory effects because of the extremely low rate of high school completion among African Americans in North Carolina at that time.

Examples of neutral requirements or practices that have *sometimes* been shown to have adverse impact include the following:

- A variety of written employment tests
- Height and weight requirements
- Language requirements
- Physical strength tests
- Military service, type of discharge
- Limitation of employment based on arrests and convictions
- Educational requirements

Note that this is not an exhaustive listing, and none of these are discriminatory in every situation.

How "disproportionate" does the limitation of employment opportunity have to be to have a prima facie case? Adverse impact cases most often involve extensive statistical analyses.[44] We are going to sidestep this complexity for now and simply say that the plaintiff has to present the court with evidence that any differences in outcomes across protected class groups are large and consistent enough that they are highly unlikely to have occurred simply by chance. The burden on plaintiffs to produce convincing evidence of adverse impact is a heavy one. Even with expert testimony and evidence that female employees were significantly less likely to receive overtime work and pay, a court rejected an adverse impact challenge to Boeing's system of allocating overtime because the statistical evidence was not sufficiently fine-grained to rule out the possibility that sex differences in overtime worked were attributable to differences in eligibility for overtime under the collective bargaining agreement rather than unguided managerial discretion.[45]

If the plaintiff fails to establish a prima facie case of adverse impact, the employer is not required to defend the challenged requirement or practice. On the other hand, if a prima facie case is established, the employer bears a relatively heavy burden in showing that the challenged requirement or practice is **job-related** and **consistent with business necessity**. When an employment test is involved, the employer usually must produce statistical evidence that the test is a good measure of ability to do a job. In other circumstances, a more general showing that the requirement is related to safety or efficiency may suffice. "Job related" is not synonymous with "consistent with business necessity." A requirement (e.g., strength) might be related to the ability to perform a job, but the amount of strength required or the particular means used to assess strength might not be consistent with business necessity.

This is another instance in which ADEA claims are handled somewhat differently than cases brought under other laws. In age-based adverse impact claims, the employer has the burden of showing that the challenged requirement or practice is a **reasonable factor other than age**.[46] This is a more lenient standard for employers to meet than "job related and consistent with business necessity." Considerations relevant to determining whether a factor other than age is "reasonable" include whether it comports with common business practices, the extent to which it is related to a specified business goal, the extent to which the factor is applied fairly and accurately, the extent of the adverse impact created by its use, and whether other options were available and considered.[47] However, the latter does not mean that an employer has any obligation to use less discriminatory measures as long as the requirement or practice is a reasonable factor other than age.[48] Thus, employers need to be prepared to defend requirements or practices whose use results in disproportionate outcomes across protected class groups. *Employers should not adopt employment practices without first meaningfully examining their potential discriminatory effects and the evidence supporting their job-relatedness.*

If an employer shows that a challenged practice is job-related and consistent with business necessity, then even though that practice produces unequal outcomes for different protected class groups, it is still legal. However, plaintiffs get one last crack at

---

[44]*Stagi v. National Railroad Passenger Corp.*, 391 Fed. Appx. 133 (3d Cir. 2010).

[45]*Carpenter v. The Boeing Co.*, 2006 U.S. App. LEXIS 20138 (10th Cir.).

[46]*Meacham v. Knolls Atomic Power Lab.*, 128 S. Ct. 2395 (2008).

[47]75 Fed. Reg. 7218 (February 18, 2010) (notice of proposed rulemaking).

[48]*Smith v. City of Jackson*, 125 S. Ct. 1536, 1546 (2005).

winning in adverse impact cases if they can show that there is a feasible alternative practice that would produce more equal outcomes, but which the employer declines to use (but not in ADEA cases).

Retaliation: A Closer Look

In retaliation cases, an employee is disadvantaged due to having engaged in protected activity related to civil rights in employment. If civil rights laws are to be more than a hollow pretense, protecting persons who act to uphold their rights or help others do so is absolutely essential.

Analyzing Retaliation Cases

As with other types of discrimination cases, there is a structured approach that courts use to decide retaliation cases. This method is similar to how disparate treatment cases are analyzed, but here the focus is on mistreatment stemming from an employee's protected activity, rather than because of an employee's protected class characteristic(s).

To have a retaliation claim, an employee must first have engaged in "protected activity." The two broad classes of protected activity are participation and opposition. **Participation** refers to involvement in the enforcement of an antidiscrimination law, such as by filing a charge, bringing a lawsuit, giving testimony, and assisting in the investigation of a discrimination charge. Being named as a potential witness in a coworker's discrimination charge has also been deemed participation.[49] **Opposition** refers to resisting or speaking out against discrimination apart from participating in formal

---

ELEMENTS OF A CLAIM

Retaliation

I. Plaintiff must establish a "prima facie" case of retaliation by showing that

   a) The plaintiff engaged in protected activity (i.e., participated in enforcement procedures or otherwise used reasonable means to oppose discrimination).

   b) The plaintiff was subjected to a materially adverse action.

   c) There is a causal link between engaging in the protected activity and the materially adverse action taken by the employer.

II. If the plaintiff successfully establishes a prima facie case, the employer has the opportunity to produce evidence of a lawful, non-retaliatory motive for the adverse action.

III. If the employer articulates a lawful, non-retaliatory motive, the plaintiff has the opportunity to rebut the employer's claims by

   a) Providing evidence that sheds doubt on the credibility of the employer's claimed motive and/or

   b) Providing other evidence that supports the claim that retaliation is the most likely explanation for the adverse action.

© Cengage Learning 2013.

---

[49]*EEOC v. Creative Networks*, 2010 U.S. Dist. LEXIS 9508 (D. Ariz.).

enforcement procedures. Examples of opposition are complaining about discrimination to supervisors or company officials, contacting civil rights and other organizations, speaking with or writing letters to the media, raising concerns with political representatives, circulating petitions, refusing to carry out an order to discriminate, and picketing. Participation and opposition are protected even when they are undertaken to uphold the civil rights of other employees whose protected class characteristics differ from those of the employee subjected to retaliation.[50]

In general, protection against retaliation does not hinge on the correctness of an employee's perceptions of discrimination. However, protection of employees who engage in opposition is more equivocal than protection of employees who formally participate in the enforcement process. The employee who opposes alleged discrimination must have a reasonable, good faith belief that the employer's policies are unlawful. In a relevant case, the Supreme Court decided that an employee was not protected from retaliation for complaining to her boss about a verbal exchange between two male supervisors that occurred in her presence.[51] Two male employees, reviewing the psychological report in a job applicant's file, came across a statement that the applicant had once made to a coworker: "I hear making love to you is like making love to the Grand Canyon." The comment was read aloud and prompted laughter from the male employees, although the female employee took objection. The Court concluded that no reasonable person could have believed that this exchange, by itself, constituted an unlawful, hostile environment. Hence, she was not protected for making the complaint, even if it was the cause of her termination.

The manner of opposition also matters. Employees who oppose their employer's discriminatory practices cannot engage in illegal activities, trespass, disrupt the work of others, disparage the company's product, or release confidential documents and still expect to be protected against retaliation.

Complaints about discrimination are sometimes made in response to inquiries from an employer, rather than initiated by an employee. Must opposition be consistent and initiated by an employee in order to be protected? The Supreme Court has held that an employee who reported harassment in response to an HR manager's questions during an investigation had engaged in protected opposition.[52] The *Collazo v. Bristol-Myers Squibb Manufacturing* case that follows builds on this precedent.

To establish a prima facie case of retaliation, the plaintiff must also show that a **materially adverse action** was taken. Note that this term does not specifically refer to employment opportunity. That the range of retaliatory acts is broader than the adverse employment actions that can be the subject of other discrimination claims was made clear by the Supreme Court in a case involving a railroad worker who had her job assignment changed and was subjected to a lengthy suspension after she complained about sex discrimination.[53] Even though the job reassignment did not affect her pay and benefits, the change from forklift duty to more physically demanding and lower-status track laborer tasks was clearly undesirable. Likewise, although the thirty-seven-day suspension was ultimately rescinded and the employee was provided with back pay, she was forced to endure a protracted period of time without an income and uncertainty as to whether or when she would be able to go back to work. Thus, both of the actions were "materially adverse" even though her employment opportunities were not fundamentally altered.

Practical Considerations Retaliation claims are ever more common. The urge to "get back at" employees who complain about discriminatory treatment is apparently difficult to resist. What should employers do to lessen the occurrence of retaliation?

---

[50]*Moore v. City of Philadelphia*, 461 F.3d 331, 342 (3d Cir. 2006).

[51]*Clark County School District v. Breeden*, 532 U.S. 268 (2001).

[52]*Crawford v. Metropolitan Government of Nashville & Davidson County*, 555 U.S. 271 (2009).

[53]*Burlington Northern and Santa Fe Railway v. White*, 126 S. Ct. 2405 (2006).

Collazo v. Bristol-Myers Squibb Manufacturing
617 F.3d 39 (1st Cir. 2010)

OPINION BY CIRCUIT JUDGE LIPEZ:

Luis R. Collazo ... brought this action against Collazo's former employer, Bristol-Myers Squibb Manufacturing, Inc. (Bristol-Myers), alleging ... that Bristol-Myers terminated him ... in retaliation for his opposition to the sexual harassment of another Bristol-Myers employee, in violation of Title VII and Puerto Rico law. The district court granted summary judgment to Bristol-Myers on all claims.

Our analysis of Collazo's Title VII claim requires us to apply the Supreme Court's recent decision in *Crawford v. Metropolitan Government of Nashville & Davidson County, Tenn.*, which addressed the scope of conduct protected by the opposition clause of Title VII's antiretaliation provision. Applying *Crawford*, we conclude that Collazo's repeated efforts to assist a fellow employee in filing and pursuing her sexual harassment complaint with the company's Human Resources Department (Human Resources) qualify as protected opposition to the complained-of harassment. We also conclude that Collazo has established genuine issues of material fact on the other elements of his Title VII retaliation claim.

In 1995, Collazo was hired by Bristol-Myers, a pharmaceutical manufacturer, as a scientist at its plant in Barceloneta, Puerto Rico. Several years later, he assumed a management-level position, Senior Process Scientist I. * * * Beginning in April 2002, Collazo's immediate supervisor was Carlos Lopez, the Director of Technical Services for Bristol-Myers' plants in both Barceloneta and Humacao.

On February 10, 2003, Diana Hiraldo, one of the scientists under Collazo's supervision, approached him and told him that she felt sexually harassed by Acevedo, another scientist in her group. * * * Collazo spoke to Acevedo individually about Hiraldo's complaints of sexual harassment. Acevedo apologized for criticizing her work performance, but stated that he preferred to speak with his immediate supervisor about Hiraldo's other allegations. At Hiraldo's request, Collazo then arranged a meeting with Edgardo Garcia, a Human Resources Specialist, and accompanied Hiraldo to the meeting. Hiraldo explained her concerns to Garcia and received information on how to initiate a grievance. After Hiraldo left, Collazo noted to Garcia that this was a "serious case, a serious case where this girl alleges that she is being sexually harassed by this guy." At Garcia's suggestion, Collazo then emailed Lopez to inform him of Hiraldo's complaint and the steps taken to address it.

Two days later, on February 12, Hiraldo approached Collazo to express concern that Human Resources had not yet taken action on her sexual harassment complaint. Collazo again accompanied her to meet with Garcia, and Hiraldo explained the basis for her complaint in more detail. On February 20, Hiraldo came to Collazo to request another meeting with Garcia. Collazo could not find Garcia, but left him a voicemail message stating that he needed to speak with Garcia about Hiraldo's sexual harassment case.

On February 21, in response to a voicemail message, Collazo reported to Human Resources. Lopez and Human Resources Director Viviana Vilanova met briefly with Collazo, and Lopez informed him that he was being terminated because of communication and performance issues and a company reorganization. Shocked, Collazo did not ask for a further explanation of the reasons for his termination. * * *

Title VII provides that "[i]t shall be an unlawful employment practice for an employer to discriminate against any of his employees ... because [the employee] has opposed any practice made an unlawful employment practice by [Title VII], or because he has made a charge, testified, assisted, or participated in any manner in an investigation, proceeding, or hearing under [Title VII]."

To make out a prima facie case of retaliation, ... the plaintiff must prove that (1) he or she engaged in protected activity under Title VII, (2) he or she suffered an adverse employment action, and (3) the adverse employment action was causally connected to the protected activity. Once the plaintiff establishes a prima facie case of retaliation, the burden shifts to the defendant to articulate a legitimate, non-retaliatory reason for its employment decision. If the defendant meets its burden of production, "the burden shifts back to [the plaintiff] to show that the proffered legitimate reason is in fact a pretext and that the job action was the result of the defendant's retaliatory animus."

1. PRIMA FACIE CASE

Bristol-Myers argues that Collazo has not established a prima facie case of retaliation because (a) Collazo did not engage in protected activity and (b) there was no causal connection between Collazo's alleged protected conduct and his termination. We address each issue in turn.

a. Protected Activity

Collazo relies primarily on the opposition clause …. The Supreme Court recently addressed the scope of the opposition clause in *Crawford*. * * * [T]he Court held that a plaintiff who did not *initiate* a complaint about sexual harassment nevertheless engaged in protected conduct under the opposition clause. In response to questions posed to her during an internal investigation, the plaintiff described various instances of sexually harassing behavior by another employee. The Court held that plaintiff's responses to employer questioning could reasonably be seen as resistant or antagonistic to the sexually harassing treatment …. The Court rejected the Sixth Circuit's view that the opposition clause required an employee to engage in "active, consistent 'opposing' activities" and to instigate or initiate a complaint.

A reasonable jury could well find that Collazo "opposed" Acevedo's treatment of Hiraldo. On February 10, after Hiraldo complained to Collazo that she felt sexually harassed by Acevedo, Collazo spoke to Acevedo individually about Hiraldo's sexual harassment complaints and elicited a limited apology. On Hiraldo's request, Collazo then arranged a meeting with Garcia in Human Resources and accompanied her to meet with Garcia so that she could explain her concerns and receive information on how to initiate the grievance process. Afterward, Collazo noted to Garcia that this was a "serious case" of alleged sexual harassment and he apprised Lopez of Hiraldo's complaints. On February 12, after Hiraldo told him that Human Resources had not yet acted on her complaint, Collazo accompanied Hiraldo to meet with Garcia a second time. On February 20, faced with continued inaction from Human Resources, Collazo requested a third meeting with Garcia to discuss Hiraldo's case. This third meeting never occurred, however, because Collazo was terminated on February 21. A jury could reasonably view Collazo's persistent efforts to help Hiraldo initiate her sexual harassment complaint and urge Human Resources to act upon that complaint as resistant or antagonistic to the complained-of conduct.

Relying on *Crawford*, Bristol-Myers argues that Collazo did not "oppose" any discriminatory conduct because he "did not utter words" during the meetings with Garcia but instead "simply listened to Hiraldo." However, in addition to accompanying Hiraldo to meet with Garcia, Collazo discussed her complaints with Garcia, Lopez, and Acevedo himself. Moreover, nothing in *Crawford* or Title VII's antiretaliation provision suggests that employees engage in protected conduct only when they *verbally* communicate their opposition to unlawful employment practices. On the contrary, *Crawford* recognized that an employee can oppose unlawful employment practices by his or her conduct. * * * By repeatedly accompanying Hiraldo to Human Resources to file and pursue her sexual harassment complaint, Collazo effectively and purposefully communicated his opposition to Acevedo's treatment of Hiraldo.

Bristol-Myers further contends that even if Collazo "opposed" Acevedo's treatment of Hiraldo, Collazo did not engage in protected activity because the challenged conduct was not "made an unlawful employment practice by [Title VII]." Bristol-Myers points to evidence that in the month after Collazo's termination, Human Resources Director Vilanova initiated an internal investigation into Hiraldo's sexual harassment claim…. * * * Vilanova concluded that Acevedo had not engaged in conduct amounting to sexual harassment. To establish participation in a protected activity under the opposition clause, however, the plaintiff need not show that the conditions he or she opposed "actually amounted to a violation of Title VII." Instead, the plaintiff must demonstrate only that he or she had "a good faith, reasonable belief that the underlying challenged actions" were unlawful. * * * Based on the evidence of Hiraldo's complaints and Collazo's own observations, a jury could find that it was not unreasonable for Collazo to believe that Acevedo's conduct amounted to sexual harassment. Hiraldo complained to Collazo that she felt sexually harassed by Acevedo, noting that he frequently called her, followed her, and criticized her professional work, and that his behavior made her husband feel uncomfortable. In addition, Collazo had observed that Acevedo regularly called Hiraldo, stared at her "all the time," "undress[ed] her with his eyes," and had made a sexually suggestive comment in her presence. This is not a case in which the challenged conduct amounted to a single, mild incident or offhand comment, such that no reasonable person could have believed that this conduct violated Title VII.

Finally, Bristol-Myers contends that Collazo's conduct was not protected because it was done "in furtherance of his supervisory responsibilities." * * * We assume, without deciding ... that to engage in protected conduct under Title VII's retaliation provision, an employee must step outside his ordinary employment role of representing the company and take action adverse to the company. Even assuming that these requirements apply, we conclude that Collazo has put forth sufficient evidence to support a jury finding that they were satisfied in this case. Collazo was not a personnel manager warning his company of potential harassment claims against it; instead, he was a Senior Process Scientist assisting a subordinate employee in filing a sexual harassment complaint. By supporting Hiraldo in lodging and pursuing her sexual harassment complaint with Human Resources, Collazo "stepp[ed] outside" his normal employment role as a Senior Process Scientist and took "action adverse to the company." Bristol-Myers asserts that Collazo acted in compliance with the company's equal employment policies and therefore his conduct was "in furtherance of his supervisory responsibilities" and was not protected. However, an employer cannot be permitted to avoid liability for retaliation under Title VII simply by crafting equal employment policies that require its employees to report unlawful employment practices.

b. Causal Connection

Bristol-Myers also contends that Collazo has failed to establish the third element of his prima facie case, a causal connection between his protected conduct and termination. However, Collazo has produced evidence that he was terminated on February 21, shortly after his efforts to assist Hiraldo in filing and pursuing her sexual harassment complaint on February 10, February 12, and February 20. This showing of temporal proximity is sufficient to establish a prima facie case of causation.

2. PRETEXT

Bristol-Myers maintains that Collazo's termination resulted from the combination of two legitimate factors: a corporate reorganization that required the elimination of Collazo's position, and perceived deficiencies in Collazo's job performance that made him unqualified to fill a different position in the company. * * * An employer may, of course, exercise its business judgment to eliminate positions as part of a company reorganization or reduction in force, even if the individuals in those positions have engaged in protected activity or are members of protected groups. However, an employer may not use "reorganization" or "layoff" as a convenient excuse for terminating an employee on a discriminatory or retaliatory basis.

... Collazo has submitted evidence from which a reasonable jury could conclude that the purported company reorganization was not the real reason for his termination. Collazo does not dispute that he received emails from Lopez in late January and early February announcing upcoming "reorganizational initiatives" and "administrative changes." However, although those messages detailed ongoing organizational changes, none of them mentioned the possibility that Collazo's position would be eliminated. Bristol-Myers has not produced any other documents discussing the planned reorganization; indeed, Human Resources Director Vilanova testified that she had not seen *any* documents discussing the reorganization. Although Collazo occupied a management-level position and reported directly to Lopez, the Director of Technical Services for both the Humacao and Barceloneta plants, Collazo received no advance notice that Bristol-Myers was considering eliminating his position as part of the reorganization. Moreover, of the dozen or more employees affected by the reorganization in Barceloneta and Humacao, Collazo was the only employee who was terminated. No other positions at the Barceloneta or Humacao plants were eliminated as a result of the reorganization. Although Collazo's position of Senior Process Scientist I was eliminated at the Barceloneta plant, the Senior Process Scientist I position at the Humacao plant, which was occupied by an employee with several years less seniority than Collazo, was not affected by the reorganization. In addition, other employees in Collazo's department were transferred to a different job site or given changes in job responsibilities as part of the reorganization, but Collazo was not offered the opportunity to transfer to a different site or position.

Bristol-Myers appears to acknowledge that when it implemented the reorganization, it could have transferred Collazo to a different location or position rather than terminating him. However, it contends that management rejected these alternatives because of perceived problems with Collazo's work performance. In particular, Bristol-Myers contends that management determined that deficiencies in Collazo's recent performance made him unqualified to occupy the newly created Associate Director position. Lopez, Collazo's immediate supervisor from April 2002 until his termination, testified that as of late 2002 and early 2003, he perceived problems with Collazo's communication and leadership skills and had discussed his concerns with Vilanova and other supervisors. Lopez further stated that he drafted a performance improvement plan for Collazo in December 2002 and January 2003, but had not yet finalized the plan at the time of Collazo's termination. * * *

Although Bristol-Myers' Human Resources Policy Manual sets forth a detailed four-step progressive discipline policy, Collazo did not receive any verbal or written warnings in the months leading up to his termination. Lopez admitted that at the time of Collazo's termination, Lopez had not given Collazo any counseling pursuant to the progressive discipline policy and, importantly, had not yet given the PIP to Collazo. Lopez stated in deposition that he did not counsel Collazo under the progressive discipline policy because his performance problems were of such "serious magnitude" that Lopez preferred to wait until he had developed a detailed PIP. However, before Lopez had completed the PIP or otherwise communicated his concerns to Collazo, Collazo was terminated. Lopez further admitted that as of January 13, 2003, the date of the draft PIP, he did not believe that Collazo's performance warranted termination. Moreover, Collazo has produced evidence that his job performance at Bristol-Myers was exemplary. His most recent written performance evaluation, dated August 1, 2001, was overwhelmingly positive. * * * In addition, around 2000–2001, Collazo received several "President's Awards" for outstanding contributions to particular scientific projects, each of which was accompanied by a monetary prize. Finally, on two occasions in 2002, Bristol-Myers' parent company awarded Collazo with stock options, which are given to managerial employees based on their performance.

* * * A jury could reasonably conclude, based on the particularly close temporal connection between Collazo's protected conduct and his termination and the deficiencies in Bristol-Myers' articulated reorganization and performance rationales, that Collazo was terminated because of his protected conduct.

CASE QUESTIONS

1. What were the legal issues in this case? What did the court decide?
2. In what protected activity did the plaintiff engage? Why did the court reject the employer's claims that the employee's actions did not constitute protected activity?
3. What explanations did the employer offer for the termination? What was the evidence that these explanations were pretext?
4. Do you think that the plaintiff was retaliated against? Why or why not?

The reason for giving this broader reading to retaliatory conduct is partly because of different language used in the relevant sections of Title VII, but also because of differences in the underlying purposes of the law's protections against substantive discrimination and retaliation. Discriminatory limitation or denial of employment opportunity is the basic evil that the law tries to remedy. In contrast, protection against retaliation is needed to achieve this basic purpose of the law by ensuring that employers do not interfere with employees' efforts to obtain their rights. The latter objective cannot be realized "by focusing only upon employer actions and harm that concern employment and the workplace."[54] However, while the concept of a materially adverse action is broad and expressly reaches retaliatory conduct that extends beyond the workplace, it is not unbounded. The harmful act must still be *materially* adverse. That is, it must be severe enough that it would likely have "dissuaded a reasonable worker from making or supporting a charge of discrimination." "[N]ormally, petty slights, minor annoyances, and simple lack of good manners will not create such deterrence."[55] Thus, in a subsequent case, actions that included a delay in providing job training, a two-week assignment to a less desirable department, temporary omission from an "on-call" list, removal of an

[54]*Burlington Northern*, at 2412.

[55]*Burlington Northern*, at 2415.

informal job title, and an unfulfilled threat to alter work schedules were judged to be not materially adverse.[56]

The final element of a prima facie case of retaliation is evidence of a causal link between engagement in protected activity and the occurrence of a materially adverse action. A causal link is usually demonstrated by showing that the employer knew about the employee's protected activity and the materially adverse action closely coincided with the employee's protected activity. An employee who was terminated one day after managers learned that he had filed an EEOC charge was permitted to go to trial on his retaliation claim.[57] Even though the employer cited a number of infractions, including absenteeism, that it said warranted the termination, the combination of the extreme proximity of the termination to the charge filing and shifting explanations for the termination were sufficient to preclude summary judgment for the employer. The element of timing is critical in retaliation cases. As one court has put it, "If a lengthy period of time elapses between the plaintiff's complaint and her adverse employment action, the inference of causation is weakened."[58] A lag of more than a few months is problematic and a gap of more than a year is almost always fatal to an employee's retaliation claim.[59]

JUST THE FACTS

A female employee filed a sex discrimination charge with the EEOC. Three weeks after the employer had been notified of the charge, the woman's fiancée—who worked for the same company—was terminated. There was no evidence that the fiancée had been involved in any way with the filing of the charge. Assuming it could be proven that the termination was in retaliation for the charge filing, would the *fiancée* have a retaliation claim? Both the female employee and the fiancée? Neither party?

See, *Thompson v. North American Stainless*, 131 S. Ct. 863 (2011).

If a prima facie case of retaliation is established, the case proceeds essentially like a pretext case. The employer must articulate a nonretaliatory reason for the decision. If the employer can do so, the plaintiff can still prevail by showing that it is more likely that the employment decision was motivated by the employer's desire to retaliate. An employee of a company doing contract work for NASA was terminated after he communicated a subordinate's sexual harassment complaint about a higher-level manager to the HR manager and later supported her harassment charge in statements made to state agency investigators. Although the employer claimed that the termination was due to poor performance and insubordination, the timing of the termination (less than a month after speaking to investigators), discussions among upper-level managers about firing him for supporting the "bogus" claim, and a statement by the manager who fired him that it would have "made a hell of a difference" if he had gone to him with the complaint rather than to the HR manager all pointed to a retaliatory motive.[60]

Retaliation looks bad. Juries are rightly suspicious of the "coincidence" that termination or other harm befalls an individual on the heels of a discrimination complaint. As

---

[56]*Ahern v. Shinseki*, 629 F.3d 49 (1st Cir. 2010).

[57]*Pantoja v. American NTN Bearing Manufacturing Corp.*, 495 F.3d 840 (7th Cir. 2007).

[58]*Hall v. Eastman Chemical*, 2005 U.S. App. LEXIS 4987, at 8 (6th Cir.).

[59]*Tyler v. University of Arkansas Board of Trustees*, 628 F.3d 980, 986 (8th Cir. 2011).

[60]*Kubicko v. Ogden Logistics Services*, 181 F.3d 544 (4th Cir. 1999).

one lawyer has put it, "Retaliation resonates with the jury. They may not believe the employer terminated someone because they are black, but they will believe they terminated someone because they rocked the boat."[61]

Key Terms

glass ceiling, p. 61

discrimination, p. 63

adverse employment action, p. 64

protected class, p. 64

disparate treatment, p. 66

discriminatory intent, p. 66

adverse impact, p. 67

discriminatory effects, p. 67

failure to reasonably
  accommodate, p. 67

retaliation, p. 67

facially discriminatory policies or
  practice, p. 69

bona fide occupational
  qualification (BFOQ), p. 69

reverse discrimination, p. 69

pretext, p. 69

mixed motives, p. 69

pattern or practice (of
  discrimination), p. 70

prima facie case, p. 71

direct evidence, p. 74

circumstantial evidence, p. 74

subordinate bias theory, p. 76

neutral requirement, p. 85

job-related consistent with
  business necessity, p. 86

reasonable factor other than
  age, p. 86

participation, p. 87

opposition, p. 87

materially adverse action, p. 88

Chapter Summary

Despite real progress, employment discrimination continues to be a serious problem. Contemporary discrimination is expressed less often through outright exclusion and segregation (although these still exist) and more often through harassment, blocked access to advancement, pay inequities, retaliation, and discrimination against caregivers.

Discrimination can be broadly defined as the limitation or denial of employment opportunity based on or related to the protected class characteristics of persons. Bias and unfairness are the essential nature of discrimination; however, only when unfairness is based on or related to protected class does it constitute discrimination. Protected classes include race, sex, national origin, and religion. These are characteristics of people that typically have nothing to do with the ability to perform work, are not readily altered, and are ethically objectionable as grounds for deciding who gets employment opportunities.

It is important to distinguish between different types or legal theories of discrimination. How courts decide whether discrimination has occurred depends on the type of alleged discrimination. Disparate treatment is unequal treatment that is based on protected class and results in an adverse employment action. The employer's intent or motivation in making the employment decision is key. Distinct varieties of disparate treatment cases include facially discriminatory policies, reverse discrimination, pretext, mixed motives, pattern

or practice, and harassment. Proving discriminatory intent or motivation can be difficult. The method for analyzing pretext cases requires a plaintiff to establish an initial presumption that discrimination has occurred largely by ruling out common nondiscriminatory motives (the prima facie case), requires the defendant to focus the inquiry by articulating a lawful nondiscriminatory motive, and then requires the plaintiff to show that discrimination was the most likely reason because the employer's stated motive is not believable and/or there is other evidence of discrimination. In mixed motives cases, the evidence (either direct or circumstantial) of a discriminatory motive is sufficiently strong to conclude that the challenged employment decision was, at least partly, affected by consideration of the plaintiff's protected class characteristic. In such cases (at least under Title VII), the employer has violated the law. The remedies for which the employer will be liable depend on whether the employer can prove that it would have made the same decision regardless of the discriminatory motive.

Another type of discrimination is adverse (or disparate) impact, which occurs when a "neutral" requirement or practice results in the disproportionate limitation or denial of employment opportunity for some protected class group and is not "job-related and consistent with business necessity." Neutral employment practices with the potential to produce adverse impact include written employment tests, size

---

[61]Richard A. Oppel Jr. "Retaliation Lawsuits: A Treacherous Slope." *New York Times* (September 29, 1999), C 8.

and physical strength requirements, and educational credential requirements. The focus in adverse impact cases is on discriminatory effects that cannot be justified. Plaintiffs must show, usually through statistics, that some employment requirement or practice affects one protected class group more detrimentally than others. If this showing can be made, the employer must defend its use by showing it to be job-related and consistent with business necessity. In age discrimination cases, the neutral requirement or practice must be shown to be a "reasonable factor other than age."

Two other major types of discrimination are failure to reasonably accommodate and retaliation. An employer discriminates when it fails to be flexible in meeting the needs of disabled employees and those whose religious beliefs and practices come into conflict with workplace requirements. Retaliation occurs when an employee who asserts her rights under the law is subjected to a materially adverse action for doing so. Employees enjoy considerable protection when participating in the enforcement process for antidiscrimination laws or otherwise opposing the discriminatory practices of an employer.

Practical Advice Summary

- Employers should
  - Be concerned about avoiding discrimination in all employment decisions.
  - Refrain from making employment decisions based in whole or in part on the protected class characteristics of employees.
  - Have policies and be consistent in how they are enforced.
  - Closely scrutinize employment requirements and practices for their potential to disadvantage protected class groups and for evidence of their job relatedness and business necessity.
  - Be flexible in accommodating the particular needs of disabled employees and employees whose religious practices conflict with workplace requirements.
  - Exercise particular care in making decisions regarding employees who have filed charges or spoken out about discrimination.
  - Not punish employees for participating in enforcement procedures or otherwise opposing discrimination.
  - Maintain good documentation and be prepared to explain the nondiscriminatory reasons for why particular employment decisions were made.
  - Closely review employment decisions and recommendations made by lower-level managers.

Chapter Questions

1. An African American who was a senior executive in a federal government agency brought a race discrimination complaint based on allegations that his white supervisor meddled in and undermined his managerial authority. Among the acts he objected to were the supervisor's overriding his decision regarding the hiring of clerical staff (although the supervisor reversed her own decision two days later), removing employees from his division without consulting him, hiring a job candidate over his objection, failing to appoint him as acting director for a day while she was gone, and refusing to authorize discipline against one of the manager's subordinates in a case of possible theft. However, the executive did not lose his job or suffer a pay cut. Assuming it could be shown that the supervisor's acts were racially motivated, did they constitute adverse employment actions? (*Patterson v. Johnson,* 505 F.3d 1296 [D.C. Cir. 2007])

2. A woman worked as a laborer at a manufacturing plant. She had recently given birth to a child whom she was breastfeeding. Over a two-week period after she returned to work from parental leave, the woman took unauthorized breaks (about fifteen minutes each) to pump breast milk. Employees in the plant take bathroom breaks throughout the day, although none that long and not on any schedule. The woman was ordered to stop taking the breaks and then fired for "failure to follow directions" when she continued to take them. She sued. What should the court decide? Why? (*Allen v. totes/Isotoner,* 123 Ohio St. 3d 216 [2009])

3. A fifty-three-year old director of an assisted living facility was terminated. Top managers

regularly made statements such as Silver Oak should be a "youth oriented company," there was "no room for dead wood," Silver Oak was a "young company" that "enjoy[s] hiring energetic people," the company was "missing the boat by not hiring more younger, vibrant people," and that employees "should start looking over applications better and try to consider hiring younger people." On several occasions, the director was pressed to discipline and terminate older employees, which she refused to do. Following her refusal, she was disciplined and placed on indefinite probation for allegedly admitting a patient without permission and terminating an employee without having another administrator present. However, the director claims that she did receive permission to admit the patient and that the administrator who would have been present for the termination told her she did not want to attend. The director was eventually terminated. She had been on an approved medical leave for several weeks. Her supervisor told her that he wanted her to call in every day while she was on medical leave. She did not do that. She was initially told that she was terminated for failing to call in each day, but the list of reasons for termination was subsequently expanded, with different administrators citing different reasons. The terminated director sued. What should the court decide? Why? (*Baker v. Silver Oak Senior Living Management Co.*, 581 F.3d 684 [8th Cir. 2009])

4. A female crane operator was told it was company policy that crane operators urinate over the side of their cranes rather than stop work to take bathroom breaks. Management justified the policy by saying that there was a shortage of staff and that it was necessary for the cranes to operate continuously in that area of the plant. Shifts for crane operators were typically twelve hours. There was evidence that the same policy was applied to male crane operators and that they routinely urinated over the side or back of their cranes in lieu of bathroom breaks. The employer offered the woman some alternative jobs, but none were crane operator positions. She quit. Does the female crane operator have a valid sex discrimination claim? (*Johnson v. AK Steel*, 2008 U.S. Dist. LEXIS 41573 [S.D. Ohio])

5. A waitress was told that the restaurant she worked at needed more servers. She told her 67-year-old friend, who had forty years of experience and was interested in the job. When the waitress told the assistant manager about her friend, she was told that the restaurant did not want her. The 67-year-old applied anyway. When the waitress asked about the status of her friend's application, she was told by the restaurant manager that "we had all these young people in here and he didn't know if [the 67-year-old] would fit into the harmony." The 67-year-old eventually came in for an "orientation," which ended abruptly after the manager said that he had other business to deal with. The 67-year-old made repeated attempts to call back for her work schedule, but her calls were not returned. On another occasion, the manager answered but then placed her on hold until she hung up after twenty minutes. The restaurant maintains that the 67-year-old had been scheduled for work but was terminated for abandoning her job when she did not show up for the shift. What should the court decide? Why? (*EEOC v. International House of Pancakes*, 411 F. Supp. 2d 709 [E.D. Mich. 2006])

6. A female attorney was an associate at a law firm. Soon after she began working at the firm, the managing partner learned that she had a young child. The partner said that he was upset because she had not said anything about the child when she interviewed. The attorney believed that the partner started treating her worse than he treated male associates, using very harsh language toward her, talking about "the commitment differential between men and women," and telling her a story about how incredulous he was when a female partner who had been on maternity leave asked about achieving partnership. Fearing discrimination against women with children, the attorney raised her concerns with a number of people in the firm, including partners in another office of the firm. When it got back to the partners in her office, they were incensed that she had gone outside the office to complain. Partners talked about how the attorney had "caused a problem for" and "embarrassed" the office by complaining to another office. Later that year discussion occurred about what to do regarding the attorney's "situation." A decision was made to withhold the attorney's annual pay increase pending the results of her performance evaluations. When a number of the evaluations came

back negative, the attorney was terminated. All of the negative evaluations were from partners in her own office, while partners from another office gave her positive reviews. She sued. What should the court decide? Why? (*Gallina v. Mintz Levin,* 123 Fed. Appx. 558 [4th Cir. 2005])

7. A manager at an airport rental car station e-mailed a regional manager with allegations of sexual harassment by her immediate supervisor. Although bypassing the immediate supervisor was allowed for under the company's harassment policy, the regional manager testified that he was not happy that she had not dealt directly with her immediate supervisor. The regional manager also said that he liked employees to joke around and that the complaint would "put a muzzle on interaction" between employees. Twenty-eight days after the e-mail was sent, the regional manager and supervisor met with the employee and terminated her. The regional manager testified that he had actually made the termination decision sooner, some fifteen days after the e-mail. The employee was told that her termination was due to a downturn in business following 9/11 and her status as the least senior manager at the location. The employee's requests for a lateral transfer to one of several open positions in other cities was rejected on the grounds that, under company policy, employees with disciplinary warnings in their files were not eligible for transfer. However, although this policy existed, it was regarded as discretionary and not consistently followed. Although it was undisputed that 9/11 had greatly reduced business, this employee was the only manager in the Midwest region who was laid off. When her former position became open a year later, the woman applied for the position but received no response. She sued. What should the court decide? Why? (*Wallace v. DTG Operations,* 563 F.3d 357 [8th Cir. 2009])

8. A hospital appointed a male as acting director of the chaplain staff. During the search for a full-time director, an HR manager solicited the opinions of the staff. A female, part-time chaplain was critical of the acting director, who was a candidate for the full-time position. She expressed concerns about his public speaking ability and his being a "good ole boy." The acting director got the job and the female chaplain continued to convey her concerns about him to an HR manager. Her comments increasingly questioned the director's ability to relate well to female staff. This eventually led to an investigation of whether the director was creating a hostile environment for female staff. The female chaplain reluctantly agreed to be interviewed by the investigator. She reiterated some of her claims about his being a "good ole boy" and holding sexist attitudes. The investigator concluded that there was no evidence of harassment. However, the HR manager was concerned about the nature of the female chaplain's comments. She was initially suspended for thirty days to have time to think over whether she could work with the director and then terminated. The female chaplain sued. What should the court decide? Why? (*Hatmaker v. Memorial Medical Center,* 619 F.3d 741 [7th Cir. 2010], *cert. denied,* 131 S. Ct. 1603 [2011])

9. Look at the examples of neutral requirements or practices that are listed in the chapter. Why is each of these a "good candidate" for an adverse impact claim? How are they linked to protected class?

10. Should other protected classes be recognized under the law? If so, which ones? What is it about these groups that calls for protected class status?

11. How likely is it that *you* might be discriminated against in the workplace? Why do you think this?

PART **2**

The Hiring Process

CHAPTER 4

Recruitment, Applications, and Interviews

Recruitment

To establish an employment relationship, there must be one or more ways in which an employer communicates information about the availability of an employment opportunity and persons interested in pursuing the opportunity make their interest known to the employer. The many **recruitment** methods include want ads placed in newspapers or professional publications, Internet job postings, help-wanted signs placed in storefronts, employment agencies, executive search firms, union hiring halls, job fairs, college placement offices, referrals from state employment services, and word of mouth. Preliminary information about candidates is typically recorded on application forms or resumes. One or more screening interviews are likely. Recruitment includes not only identification of viable job candidates but also efforts undertaken to attract candidates and make it more likely that, if selected, they will accept job offers. Thus, recruitment entails both eliciting information from job candidates and providing information to "sell them" on the job and organization. The focus of this chapter is on external recruiting rather than on internal searches used to fill promotional positions. Discrimination is the fundamental legal concern surrounding these activities. However, other legal issues also arise, including compliance with visa requirements, breach of contract, and fraud.

Discrimination in Recruitment

Recruitment methods create the applicant pools from which employees are ultimately selected. Thus, they are vital to the cause of equal employment opportunity. Unless an employer's recruiting efforts reach a broad spectrum of the available workforce (or at least do not exclude some protected class groups much more than others) and successfully convey the employer's sincere desire that all qualified candidates apply, the most careful and unbiased selection process still will not result in equal employment opportunity.

Although recruitment is critical to equal employment opportunity, showing discrimination in recruitment is particularly complex. After all, it is difficult enough for an employee to discern whether she has been discriminated against after she applies for a job. How does a prospective employee challenge practices that keep her from learning about the existence of an employment opportunity in the first place? Not surprisingly, relatively few cases focus on challenges to recruitment practices, and most of these are initiated by the EEOC on behalf of employees. Since discriminatory recruitment practices affect many potential applicants, statistical evidence usually lies at the center of such cases. One court has commented on the difficulty of interpreting statistical evidence of discriminatory recruitment:

> *[D]iscrimination affects the applicant pool in a way that makes the discrimination harder to detect. The discriminating employer induces qualified blacks not to apply, and these*

nonapplicants—victims of discrimination as much as the nonhired applicants—will make the employer's hiring look "better than it is." An applicant pool is biased against finding discrimination if potential applicants know or suspect that the employer is discriminating.[1]

What is the court saying? If we look only at selection rates and hiring decisions, we might miss the fact that relatively few women or persons of color have come forward to be considered for employment. One reason an employer's applicant pool might lack diversity is because the methods used to communicate the availability of employment opportunities reach only a restricted and homogenous portion of the qualified, available workforce. Alternatively, if an employer is known or reputed to be hostile to hiring women or persons of color, those job seekers might not want to waste their time by applying.

Because recruitment procedures affect the composition of the applicant pool, in order to obtain statistical evidence of discrimination, it is necessary to compare the applicant pool of a particular employer to the group of persons in the labor market who might have become applicants had they known of the employment opportunity. The most informative comparison is not with the population as a whole (which, after all, includes retirees, children, and others not in the labor force), nor with the overall labor force (which includes many people without the necessary skills or credentials for the particular job), but instead with persons in the **relevant labor market**. That is, the employer's applicant pool should be compared to the protected class composition of people who are qualified for the type of work in question and reside within a reasonable recruitment area.[2] The fact that fewer women than men apply for jobs as electrical engineers at an engineering firm does not necessarily mean that there is anything wrong with the firm's recruiting methods, because men are more likely to do this type of work and have the relevant qualifications. But if the applicant pool contains a much smaller percentage of women than the percentage of women in the area workforce who are qualified and work as electrical engineers, that would be evidence of discrimination in recruitment. The geographic scope of the relevant labor market (e.g., local, regional, national) depends on the importance of the job, the availability of people with the needed skills, and the customary hiring practices in the industry. A less refined comparison with the general population or workforce is acceptable when the job in question calls for general skills that most people would possess. The EEOC has collaborated with other government agencies to create a database from the census that provides reasonably detailed information on surrounding labor markets for use by employers and in discrimination cases.[3]

Recruitment Methods

We turn now to particular recruitment methods, including want ads, employment agencies, and word of mouth. All are used by employers, and none are inherently discriminatory. However, each has the potential to be an instrument of discrimination. In light of this, *it is preferable that employers use multiple recruitment methods.* This helps to compensate for the potential exclusionary effects of any single method. Equal employment opportunity is enhanced when employers *disseminate information about employment opportunities as broadly as is feasible*, limited by a reasonable understanding of the geographic extent of the labor market and cost considerations in light of the importance of the position.

Want Ads and Job Announcements   A typical early step in the recruitment process is to produce documents that announce the availability of a job, describe the job and its

[1]*Mister v. Illinois Central Railroad,* 832 F.2d 1427, 1436 (7th Cir. 1987), *cert. denied,* 485 U.S. 1035 (1988).

[2]*Hazelwood School District v. United States,* 433 U.S. 299, 308 (1977).

[3]U.S. Census Bureau. "Census 2000 EEO Data Tool." (http://www.census.gov/eeo2000/).

requirements, and tell prospective applicants what they must do to apply. These documents are then printed in newspapers or professional magazines, posted on bulletin boards, put on the Internet, or otherwise made available for inspection. Title VII of the Civil Rights Act of 1964 is explicit about employers' obligation in producing such materials:

> *It shall be an unlawful practice for an employer ... to print or publish or cause to be printed or published any notice or advertisement related to employment ... indicating any preference, limitation, specification, or discrimination, based on race, color, religion, sex, or national origin....*[4]

Other discrimination laws contain similar prohibitions. The clear requirement is that *the wording of want ads and other types of job announcements must be neutral.* A **neutral message** does not express or imply a preference for some protected class group over another. Sex-linked job titles are not neutral. An employer who advertises for a "waitress" is signaling that it expects to hire a woman and is discouraging males from applying. Terms such as *young people and recent college grad* imply a preference for persons under 40 and tend to discourage applications from older workers. However, courts will consider whether such terms articulate requirements for particular positions or merely suggest groups of people who might be interested in employment.[5]

The content of want ads and job announcements is one matter; where they are published or posted is another. Employers are free to publish neutrally worded ads in publications that are targeted toward particular protected class groups (e.g., a foreign language newspaper). However, if that is all the employer does to get the word out about an employment opportunity, it is likely to produce discriminatory effects. Thus, *employers using narrowly targeted outlets should use these in conjunction with other media that reach a broader spectrum of employees.*

Employers with affirmative action plans often include in job announcements language to the effect that applications from women and minorities are especially encouraged. Such statements, although not required, do not violate the neutrality principle. They are intended to address the reluctance that women and persons of color might have to pursue employment opportunities, given the history of employment discrimination against members of these groups. They also signal that employers are aware of their legal responsibilities and do not intend to discriminate.

Finally, although we have assumed that the employer has produced and disseminated a job announcement of some kind, this is not a foregone conclusion. Employers are under no specific legal requirement to do so, but when information is orally conveyed to a select few and denied everyone else, the hiring process looks very suspect. Failure to post job information and make it available to broader audiences is a common complaint in discrimination cases. For example, in a case successfully challenging the *Boston Herald*'s practices in hiring pressroom workers, the plaintiffs pointed to the paper's failure to post job announcements in the workplace and to advertise vacancies to the public.[6] Thus, implicit in all the foregoing is that *employers should create written job announcements and disseminate them.*

Employment Agencies   Employees are sometimes recruited and hired through employment agencies. These agencies are covered by antidiscrimination laws and are expressly prohibited from discriminating against employees in referrals or in any other

---

[4]42 U.S.C.S. § 2000e-3(b) (2011).

[5]*Hodgson v. Approved Personnel Service, Inc.*, 529 F.2d 760 (4th Cir. 1975).

[6]*Gaines et al. v. Boston Herald*, 998 F. Supp 91, 106 (D. Mass. 1998).

manner.[7] The difficulty here is that employment agencies are businesses. Businesses do well when they make their customers happy. Employment agencies sometimes cater to the actual or perceived discriminatory preferences of their customers. When employment agencies do so, they violate the law. Employers that make such requests of employment agencies are also violating the law. *Employers must not request that employment agencies refer only employees with particular protected class characteristics, nor should they attempt to obtain through employment agencies information about protected class characteristics of referrals that it would be improper for them to obtain directly.*

Clippings

Area Temps Inc., an employment agency in Cleveland, has settled an EEOC suit alleging that the firm engaged in discriminatory recruiting practices. The EEOC charged that the firm failed to refer applicants for temporary employment based on their race, sex, age, and national origin; classified its applicants and employees according to their protected class characteristics; complied with clients' discriminatory preferences in making referrals; and retaliated against employees who challenged its discriminatory practices. An interesting feature of the settlement agreement is that it calls for five unannounced tests of the agency's referral practices conducted by a nonprofit firm that will pose as a customer looking for temp workers.

Kevin P. McGowan. "EEOC, Staffing Firm Settle for $650,000 Suit Charging Unlawful Bias in Job Referrals." *Daily Labor Report* 144 (July 28, 2010), A-8.

In a case involving two employment agencies,[8] the EEOC found evidence that the agencies were using a coding system to convey information about the protected class characteristics of prospective referrals and the discriminatory preferences of client employers. For example, "FLOOR 40" was the code used to designate persons over 40 years of age. "TALK TO ADAM" was one of the codes designating that the employer preferred or required male employees. The EEOC went to court to stop the agencies from erasing the coding data from their computers, after being informed by a former employee that she had been instructed to destroy the evidence in anticipation of an investigation. There were also allegations that one of the agencies had received, and honored, a request from IBM Japan that only Japanese employees be referred. Regarding its own internal hiring practices, there were charges that a supervisor at one of the agencies refused to hire an African American as a receptionist because she was "afraid of them" and thought "they were scarey [*sic*]." It is telling that the supervisor attempted to justify the discrimination by pointing out that if one of the company's many Japanese clients "saw a black face" at the office, the agency would lose the company's business. However, the discriminatory preferences of a customer or client are not a defense against discrimination charges.

Nepotism and Word-of-Mouth Hiring **Nepotism** refers to favoritism toward family members and other relatives. Civil service laws typically prohibit nepotism in the hiring practices of government agencies because it is contrary to the principle that jobs should be awarded on the basis of merit. Large private sector companies often have policies discouraging nepotism. On the other hand, nepotism is probably common among smaller private employers and in certain occupations. Because relatives are most often

---

[7] 42 U.S.C.S. § 2000e-2(b) (2011).

[8] *EEOC v. Recruit U.S.A. and Interplace/Transworld Recruit, Inc.*, 939 F.2d 746 (9th Cir. 1991).

of the same race or national origin, nepotism results in hiring people who are similar in certain protected class characteristics to the people who already work in the company. In one relevant case, a policy of nepotism in hiring schoolteachers (civil service laws either did not exist in this case or were ignored) resulted in the virtual exclusion of African Americans. Teaching positions were posted in each school but not advertised to the public. Relatives of school employees were more likely to learn about the availability of jobs and were preferred in the selection process. Finding against the school district on an adverse impact claim, the court stated, "Nepotism is not per se violative of Title VII. Given an already integrated work force, nepotism might have no impact on the racial composition of that work force. * * * However, when the work force is predominantly white, nepotism and similar practices which operate to exclude outsiders may discriminate against minorities as effectively as any intentionally discriminatory policy."[9]

Word-of-mouth recruiting is often allied with nepotism and has similar potential to result in discrimination. In word of mouth, employers depend on current employees to spread the word about jobs to their friends, family members, and other associates. To be sure, networks of contacts are frequently the key to success in the labor market. From an employer's perspective, word of mouth is essentially costless. It can also be effective because current employees are able to provide realistic job previews to prospective employees and they are unlikely to approach persons whom they think are unsuitable, lest the employer blame them for bad referrals. Again, the threat to equal employment opportunity stems from the fact that people tend to associate with others who are like them, especially in terms of race. If an employer's workforce is racially diverse, current employees referring persons of their own race is not a problem because persons of all races will still be referred. But if the employer's current workforce is racially homogenous, heavy reliance on word-of-mouth recruiting will reproduce a racially skewed workforce.

JUST THE FACTS

Wal-Mart has relied heavily on a word-of-mouth approach to hire new truck drivers. Rather than advertise for applicants, current drivers are asked to distribute "1-800 cards" to people they think might be potential applicants. Those people then call Wal-Mart headquarters. If they meet minimum qualifications, their names are relayed to local transportation offices. Committees composed of current drivers are used to screen these applicants and to conduct initial interviews. Wal-Mart policy specifies that each screening committee be "50% diverse," but many committees have no African American representation. Subsequent interviews are conducted by HR and general managers. Candidates are selected by managers according to their own personal criteria. From January 2000 through September 2005, African Americans comprised 4–6 percent of Wal-Mart drivers. Of the 4,135 drivers hired during this period, 8.4 percent were African American. African Americans were 10.2 percent of the applicants for employment as truck drivers at Wal-Mart during this period. Approximately 15 percent of U.S. truck drivers are African Americans. Are Wal-Mart's recruiting and hiring practices for truck drivers racially discriminatory?

See, *Nelson v. Wal-Mart Stores*, 2009 U.S. Dist. LEXIS 3707 (E.D. Ark.).

The discriminatory potential of word-of-mouth recruiting is clear. However, the case law in this area is limited and not entirely consistent. A federal appeals court found that

---

[9]*Thomas v. Washington County School Board*, 915 F.2d 922, 925 (4th Cir. 1990).

a union that required new members to be "sponsored" by existing members (who were all white) discriminated by creating adverse impact.[10] But another appeals court found a small employer's use of word of mouth not to be discriminatory despite strong statistical evidence of a skewed applicant pool.[11] The rationale in the latter case was that there was insufficient evidence of discriminatory intent and that the employer's passive reliance on word of mouth was not an "employment practice" suitable for adverse impact analysis. Although the courts are not entirely of one mind, a sensible conclusion is that *employers should not rely solely on nepotism and word of mouth, especially when their workforces are already homogenous in terms of race and national origin.*

Clippings

On February 16, 2011, the EEOC held a public hearing addressing concerns that some employers are using current employment status as a screening tool and declining to hire persons who had lost their jobs. Although the extent of this practice is unknown and employer organizations suggest that it is not widely used, testimony was presented that advertisements have been published in fields as varied as electrical engineering, restaurant management, and mortgage underwriting specifying that only currently employed applicants would be considered. Since employment status is not a protected class characteristic, legal concerns center on the potential for adverse impact. Unemployment rates and average durations of unemployment vary across protected class groups and tend to be higher for persons of color, older workers, and disabled persons. The job relatedness and business necessity of such a policy is questionable, as it was noted that "[a] blanket reliance on current employment serves as a poor proxy for successful job performance."

U.S. Equal Employment Opportunity Commission. "Out of Work? Out of Luck." (February 16, 2011), viewed June 4, 2011 (http://www.eeoc.gov/).

Recruiting Foreign Nationals for U.S. Employment In an increasingly global economy, the production of goods and services is often outsourced to other countries. Alternatively, and subject to complex immigration laws,[12] foreign nationals (citizens of other countries) sometimes come to the United States to perform work. Professional sports teams are not the only U.S. employers looking to recruit foreign nationals. Our dependence on people from other countries to fill positions in the sciences and engineering is a source of concern.[13] Many seasonal resort areas rely heavily on temporary labor from other countries.[14] The immigration laws that govern the use of foreign nationals attempt to gain the benefits of this source of labor to the U.S. economy while limiting adverse effects on U.S. workers and exploitation of foreign nationals. Many question whether we have succeeded on any of these counts.

Visa Programs Foreign nationals who do not have permanent resident status (i.e., have a green card) must obtain **visas** that will permit them to work in the United States.

---

[10]*EEOC v. Steamship Clerks Union*, 48 F.3d 594 (1st Cir. 1995), *cert. denied*, 516 U.S. 814 (1995).

[11]*EEOC v. Consolidated Service Systems*, 989 F.2d 233 (7th Cir. 1993).

[12]Immigration and Nationality Act, 8 U.S.C.S. §§ 1101, *et seq.* (2011). American Competitiveness in the 21st Century Act, P.L. 106-313 (2000); H-1B Visa Reform Act, Pub. L. No. 108-447 (2004).

[13]James Glanz. "Study Warns of Lack of Scientists as Visa Applications Drop." *New York Times* (November 20, 2003), A-24.

[14]Denny Lee. "Fewer Visas, Fewer Resort Workers." *New York Times* (June 10, 2005), D-1.

Many **visa classifications** serve this purpose. Among the most relevant are H-1 visas for persons of distinguished merit and ability, H-2 visas for temporary workers (including agricultural "guest workers"), L-1 visas for intracompany transfers (allowing the transfer of high-level employees from foreign subsidiaries or branches of the same company), and TN visas for highly skilled employees from Canada and Mexico. Students from other countries are typically here under the F-1 visa classification (for students) or the J-1 classification (for exchange visitors). The latter two statuses allow people to be employed to receive practical training related to their course of study, although employer sponsorship and conversion to another visa classification is required to continue in longer-term employment.

H-1B visas are granted to persons in "specialty occupations" that require a bachelor's or higher degree in that field. Typical occupations for recipients of these visas include systems analysts, engineers, architects, and accountants. An H-1B visa limits the employee's stay to six years, regardless of the number of employers for which he has worked. Readmission to the United States in the same or another classification can occur only after the employee remains outside the United States for at least a year. The number of H-1B visas granted each year has fluctuated, but they are currently capped at about 65,000 (not including an additional 20,000 visas set aside for advanced degree holders). The H-1B visa is controversial. Employers argue that the number of these visas must be increased if U.S. companies are to stay competitive in scientific and technical endeavors. A study by the National Foundation for American Policy suggests that for each H-1B position requested, companies add an average of five additional positions for American workers.[15] Critics of the H-1B visa program question the methodology of this study. They argue that there is no real shortage of skilled workers in the United States and that employers simply want to drive wages down.[16] A report issued by the Economic Policy Institute concludes that rather than complement the U.S. workforce, the H-1B (and L-1) visa programs are displacing U.S. workers.[17] It is interesting to note that the heaviest users of H-1B visa holders are companies, many of them Indian-owned, that specialize in the outsourcing of technical work. Under this scenario, foreign nationals come to the United States to learn the needs and specifications of client companies as a prelude to the outsourcing of that work.[18]

Clippings

A computer consulting company based in Pittsburgh (iGate Mastech Inc.) agreed to pay $45,000 to settle charges of discrimination against U.S. citizens in its recruiting and hiring practices. The company had placed thirty job announcements for computer programmers, each specifying the company's preference for H-1B visa holders. By excluding U.S. citizens and permanent residents in this manner, the company discriminated on the basis of citizenship status.

"Computer Consultant Settles DOJ Claims of Bias Against Hiring American Citizens." *Daily Labor Report* 87 (May 6, 2008), A-1.

---

[15]"Tech Companies Add Five U.S. Workers for Each H-1B Visa Sought, Study Says." *Daily Labor Report* 48 (March 12, 2008), A-9.

[16]"H-1B Visa Program Is Misused to Import Cheap Labor, Analysis of Wage Data Concludes." *Daily Labor Report* 3 (January 5, 2006), A-5.

[17]Ron Hira. *The H-1B and L-1 Visa Programs: Out of Control.* Economic Policy Institute (October 2010).

[18]Julia Preston. "Outsourcers Are Criticized on Visa Use." *New York Times* (April 1, 2011), A20.

Employers wanting to hire foreign nationals with H-1B visas must first file Labor Condition Application (LCA) forms with the Department of Labor (DOL) for each occupation in which foreign nationals will be employed. Employers must attest that they will pay their H-1B visa holders at least the local prevailing wage or the employer's actual wage, whichever is greater; offer benefits on the same basis as for their U.S. workers; provide working conditions that will not adversely affect those of other workers similarly employed; not use H-1B visa holders to perform work during a strike or lockout; and provide prior notice to existing employees and any union representatives of the intent to use H-1B visa holders. A mortgage company was held liable for over $600,000 in back pay and civil penalties for failing to pay at least the prevailing wage.[19] The company had stated on its LCAs that the H-1B visa holders would be paid between $40,000 and $50,000; instead, they were paid around $18,000. It was also shown that the jobs actually being performed by the visa holders differed from the occupations indicated on their LCAs. There are additional requirements for **H-1B dependent employers**. In general, these are employers for whom H-1B visa holders make up 15 percent or more of their total workforces. H-1B dependent employers must attest that they have not displaced U.S. workers by hiring H-1B visa holders. Specifically, H-1B dependent employers must certify that they have not and will not lay off any Americans in the same job category during the ninety days before and after filing a petition. They must also attempt to recruit U.S. workers and attest that the qualifications of H-1B hires are better than those of any American applicants.

Problems sometimes arise when employers who are sponsoring H-1B visa holders decide that they want to temporarily lay off those employees. For example, a technology firm was required by the DOL to pay a computer engineer more than a year's worth of back pay because, in the face of a slowdown in work, it had allowed him to go on leave at reduced pay rather than terminate his employment.[20] The Immigration and Nationality Act contains a "no benching" provision that requires payment in accordance with the amount stipulated on the Labor Condition Application even for periods of time where the employee might be not productive due to a lack of work. Only a bona fide termination of employment would have relieved the employer of that obligation. Employers who want to terminate H-1B visa holders prior to the end of their contracts must notify the U.S. Citizenship and Immigration Services and may have to pay to return them to their home countries.

H-2 visas are for foreign nationals who come to the United States to perform work on a temporary or seasonal basis. H-2A visas are for temporary workers in agriculture or logging. H-2B visas are for temporary workers in other industries (not including nurses). All H-2 visas must be accompanied by a showing that there are too few U.S. workers available, willing, and able to perform the work in question and that use of foreign nationals will not adversely affect the wages and working conditions of U.S. workers. In practice, this means that employers have to be able to show that they conducted job searches seeking to recruit U.S. workers. H-2A visas for temporary agricultural workers carry many additional stipulations, including an employment contract (which must be provided prior to departure from the home country to protect against abuse by recruiters), reimbursement for travel costs, free housing, and a minimum number of work hours. Importantly, the DOL establishes "adverse-effect wage rates" for H-2A visa holders. These are minimum rates that employers are required to pay and that are set

---

[19]"New Jersey Mortgage Company Must Pay $513,000 to 14 H-1B Workers, DOL ALJ Says." *Daily Labor Report* 57 (March 24, 2006), A-1.

[20]"Firm Didn't Show 'Bona Fide' Termination; ARB Says Employer Owes Pay to H-1B Worker." *Daily Labor Report* 238 (December 11, 2008), A-1.

at levels calculated to avoid adverse effects on the wages of U.S. workers in the same job categories. The relatively far-reaching requirements attached to the lawful use of H-2A visa holders have prompted many farm employers to look elsewhere for labor. In 2009, more than 86,000 foreign nationals were brought to the United States to perform agricultural work under this program.[21] This number pales in comparison to the million or so farm workers needed in the United States, with much of the difference made up by undocumented (illegal) immigrants.

L-1 visas, designed to allow multinational companies to temporarily transfer staff from foreign facilities or subsidiaries to operations in the United States, have also come under increased scrutiny. These visas are attractive to employers because their number is not capped and they carry fewer restrictions than H-1B visas. For example, there is no requirement that L-1 visa holders be paid at least the prevailing rate. Companies using L-1 visa holders must station those employees at the companies' own facilities and retain ultimate supervisory authority over them, rather than contract them out to other employers.[22]

Employers who recruit nonimmigrant foreign nationals to perform work in the United States must be prepared to comply with the numerous and varying requirements attached to the different visa classifications, to monitor the duration of their workers' employment, and to file the necessary petitions and paperwork.

Clippings

Welders from Vietnam were lured by television ads promising several years of work in the United States that would pay $15 per hour, with overtime. The arrangement was brokered by two Vietnamese companies with ties to their government. Welders paid fees of between $6,500 and $15,000 to be recruited for this work. Many mortgaged homes and borrowed heavily from relatives to raise the money. What they encountered when they arrived in the United States was "a form of indentured servitude." The American company that arranged for their travel and housing charged high prices for crowded, dirty living quarters; van transportation to and from work; and welding equipment. It took their passports away, kept the men isolated, and threatened them with arrest and deportation if they left their building. The work ended after only eight months, leaving the men saddled with large debts. A group of fifty Vietnamese welders are attempting to take legal action against both the U.S. and Vietnamese companies involved.

James C. McKinley Jr. "In Debt, Far from Home and Claiming Servitude." *New York Times* (May 13, 2011), A15.

Labor Trafficking   Sometimes the recruiting of persons from other countries to perform work in the United States takes the disturbing forms of labor trafficking, forced labor, and indentured servitude. **Labor trafficking** can be defined as the "recruitment, harboring, transportation, provision, or obtaining of a person" for the purpose of

---

[21]Julia Preston. "New Guest-Worker Rules Seek to Increase Wages." *New York Times* (February 12, 2010), A22.

[22]"DHS to Require Employers to Retain Authority over Certain Foreign Transferees." *Daily Labor Report* 121 (June 24, 2005), A-1.

obtaining his or her labor or services, "through the use of force, fraud, or coercion" and that subjects the person "to involuntary servitude, peonage, debt bondage, or slavery."[23] Situations like those encountered by the Vietnamese welders (see "Clippings") are less rare than we would like to think. The U.S. Department of Justice opened for investigation 278 cases of suspected labor trafficking between January 2008 and June 2010.[24] In the aftermath of Hurricane Katrina, Signal International brought in 500 skilled metal workers from India to repair offshore oil rigs. The workers paid large sums of money to recruiters. They came to the United States with H-2B visas for temporary guest workers and were told that the visas would be converted to green cards allowing them to remain in the United States indefinitely. The promises of the recruiters were not fulfilled. Instead, the workers were subjected to segregation, exorbitant charges for substandard housing and food, harassment, and retaliation.[25] The EEOC has commenced a national origin discrimination lawsuit on their behalf.[26] The EEOC is also pursuing legal action against Global Horizons, a farm labor contractor that has repeatedly come to the attention of the authorities for violations of the rights of workers it recruits from other countries. Indeed, an administrative law judge in the Department of Labor, which had undertaken its own enforcement actions against Global Horizons, recently ordered the company to pay $347,000 in penalties and back wages to agricultural guest workers from Thailand.[27] After having exacted large recruitment fees from the workers to obtain work on farms in Hawaii, Global Horizons failed to pay the employees their correct hourly rate for all hours worked, made impermissible deductions from their pay, failed to pay workers' transportation costs as required by law, and retaliated against workers who complained. The EEOC lawsuit against Global Horizons alleges that the workers were lured with false promises, had their passports taken away, were forced to live in "vermin-ridden housing," were not allowed to leave the farms on which they worked, and were subjected to harassment and physical assaults.[28]

The common elements in these situations of labor trafficking are recruitment with false promises, indebtedness, isolation, dependence on the employer, and severe mistreatment. Undocumented workers who illegally enter the United States are especially vulnerable to this type of exploitation, but many of these cases also involve workers brought in legally under work visa programs.[29] Cases brought against the employers and recruiters who are parties to these arrangements are complex, often involving multiple claims of fraud (see the discussion of recruiting fraud later in this chapter), breach of contract, discrimination, violations of immigration law, and criminal charges against actors both in the United States and elsewhere. Labor trafficking is a subset of human trafficking that also includes sex trafficking. The latter is far more common than labor trafficking in the United States and is much more likely to involve U.S. citizens.[30]

---

[23]U.S. Department of Justice, Bureau of Justice Statistics. *Characteristics of Suspected Human Trafficking Incidents, 2008–2010.* (April 2011), 2.

[24]U.S. Department of Justice, at 3.

[25]Julia Preston. "Suit Points to Guest Worker Program Flaws." *New York Times* (February 2, 2010), A12.

[26]U.S. Equal Employment Opportunity Commission. "EEOC Combats Labor Trafficking, Severe Abuse and Discrimination in Lawsuits Filed Today." (April 20, 2011) Viewed May 26, 2011 (http://www.eeoc.gov/).

[27]Gayle Cinquegrani. "ALJ Orders Global Horizons to Pay $347,000, Debars It from H-2A Program for Three Years." *Daily Labor Report* 98 (May 20, 2011), A-5.

[28]"EEOC Combats Labor Trafficking."

[29]Kevin P. McGowan. "EEOC Hears Testimony on Agency's Role in Fighting Human Trafficking, Forced Labor." *Daily Labor Report* 12 (January 19, 2011), C-1.

[30]U.S. Department of Justice, at 1.

THE CHANGING WORKPLACE

Day Laborers

Recruiting takes its most elemental form in the hiring of day laborers. It is estimated that every day in the United States, more than 100,000 persons seeking work gather in the parking lots of home supply stores, on street corners, or at day labor centers to await potential employers.[1] Day laborers are typically employed by homeowners or construction contractors to perform such tasks as painting, landscaping, installing drywall, and roofing. Day laborers are most often paid in cash and records of their employment are typically nonexistent. Many day laborers are relegated to finding work in this manner because they are undocumented immigrants ineligible to work in the United States (see Chapter 5). At the same time, they perform useful services and are frequently mistreated by employers.

A 2005 study of day laborers based on interviews with 2,660 workers at 264 hiring sites in twenty states found that 49 percent reported having not been paid for work performed during the past two months, 44 percent said that they did not receive any breaks during the workday, 73 percent said that they had been placed in hazardous working conditions, 20 percent reported having suffered injuries serious enough to require medical attention while working, and 28 percent said that their employers had insulted them. About three-quarters of the day laborers interviewed said that they gathered at day labor sites five days a week or more. On average, they found work about three or four days per week.[2] A smaller but more recent study of day laborers in New Jersey paints much the same picture.[3] Of the day laborers surveyed, 48 percent reported at least one instance over the previous year where they were not paid at all for work they had performed and 54 percent said that they had been paid less than promised on one or more occasions. Overtime pay was almost never provided. Injuries on the job and lack of safety equipment were also common.

The visible presence of day laborers has often been associated with tensions in communities. Store owners, shoppers, and others complain that day laborers block sidewalks, trespass on property, obstruct traffic, and litter. For their part, 9 percent of the day laborers surveyed in 2005 reported having been arrested while awaiting work, 11 percent had received citations from the police, 37 percent had been chased away, 19 percent had been insulted by merchants, and 15 percent had been denied access to stores to use bathrooms or make purchases.[4] Cities have responded in different ways to the presence of day laborers. Some have turned to increased policing and legal restrictions to impede the gathering and hiring of day laborers. However, there are constitutional limits on the ability of localities to enact measures targeting day laborers.[5] The Maryland Attorney General has issued an opinion holding that a Gaithersburg, Maryland, law prohibiting anyone from seeking work or hiring workers on city streets, sidewalks, and parking areas is unconstitutional.[6] The City of Danbury, Connecticut, paid $400,000 to settle a suit brought by eight day laborers who claimed that their arrest in 2006 was racial profiling.[7] A Danbury police officer had posed as a contractor and drove a van to an area where day laborers congregated, offered work to the men, and then hauled them off to be arrested. A Redondo Beach city ordinance prohibiting the act of standing in a street or highway and soliciting employment, business, or contributions from motor vehicle occupants was struck down because it restricted speech and was not narrowly tailored. The ordinance restricted more speech than necessary (e.g., it could even be applied to children selling lemonade on the sidewalk in front of their house or offering to wash the cars of passing motorists), while less restrictive means of achieving the government's legitimate goal of traffic safety were available.[8]

Another approach entirely is to form day laborer centers that regulate and structure the hiring of day laborers. These centers often require employers and day laborers to register. Shelter, bathroom facilities, water, and sometimes even English lessons are provided for the laborers awaiting work. Some centers also establish minimum hourly pay rates.

---

[1]Steven Greenhouse. "Broad Survey of Day Laborers Finds High Level of Injuries and Pay Violations." *New York Times* (January 22, 2006), 17.

[2]Greenhouse, 17.

[3]Immigrants' Rights/International Human Rights Clinic. *All Work and No Pay: Day Laborers, Wage Theft, and Workplace Justice in New Jersey.* Seton Hall University School of Law, Center for Social Justice (January 2011), 2.

[4]Greenhouse, 17.

[5]*Lopez v. Cave Creek*, 559 F. Supp. 2d 1030 (D. Ariz. 2008) (anti-solicitation ordinance violated First Amendment speech rights).

[6]"Maryland Attorney General Says Law Banning Hiring Workers on Streets Is Unconstitutional." *Daily Labor Report* 45 (March 7, 2008), A 6.

[7]Sam Dolnick. "Connecticut City Settles Suit in Arrests of Day Laborers." *New York Times* (March 10, 2011), A 24.

[8]*Comite de Jornaleros de Redondo Beach v. Redondo Beach*, 2011 U.S. App. LEXIS 19212 (9th Cir.).

Applications and Interviews
Application Process

By and large, employers are free to decide whether applications will be accepted from anyone (applications need not be accepted if there are no current or anticipated employment opportunities), what must be done to apply (e.g., Will a resume suffice or only a completed application form?), how long applications will be accepted, and how long submitted applications will remain valid. The main guideline here is to avoid disparate treatment. *Establish an application policy and adhere to it consistently. The application process should be the same for everyone seeking the same job.* There should not be, as there was in one case, different application forms for people applying for the same positions (with friends and relatives of current employees receiving lengthier "insider" applications).[31] Additionally, *if applications are being accepted, no individuals wanting to apply should be discouraged from doing so.* Certainly, candidates should be informed about the requirements of jobs, but even candidates who do not at first glance appear promising should be allowed to apply and have their applications treated in the same manner as other applications.

Application forms and any other records produced in the hiring process must be kept at least a year from when a hiring decision is made. If a discrimination charge is filed, the relevant records must be retained until there has been final disposition of the charge. Records related to people hired must be retained throughout their employment and for at least a year thereafter.[32] Employers are also required to maintain records regarding the protected class characteristics of applicants for such purposes as tracking progress in affirmative action and determining whether selection devices (e.g., employment tests) have adverse impact. The need to retain information on applicants raises the question of what exactly makes someone an "applicant." The federal government's definition of **applicant** is broad, including any person who indicates an interest in being considered for an employment opportunity. This interest might be expressed by completing an application form or through other means, depending on the employer's policy. A person who voluntarily withdraws, formally or informally, at any stage of the selection process is no longer an applicant.[33] The widespread use of the Internet to search for jobs has prompted employer concerns about having to obtain and maintain information on large numbers of applicants. Arguably, the low cost and ease of applying for jobs electronically encourages more casual inquiries, many of which may come from unqualified individuals or in the absence of position openings. On the other hand, employer-initiated efforts to identify candidates from existing databases might result in hiring decisions being made without any applicants having expressly indicated their interest in employment with this employer. With regard to record keeping by federal government contractors with affirmative action plans, an **Internet applicant** is an individual who expresses interest in employment via the Internet or other electronic data technology, is considered by the contractor for employment in a particular position, possesses the basic qualifications for the position, and does not remove himself or herself from consideration.[34] However, because federal enforcement agencies have not been able to agree on a

Practical Considerations What type of application policy would you favor? Should nonselected candidates be considered for future positions of the same type? If so, for how long? Should former employees be considered for rehiring?

---

[31]*Gaines,* 107.

[32]29 C.F.R. § 1602.14 (2011).

[33]44 F.R.11996, 11998 (March 2, 1979).

[34]41 C.F.R. § 60-1.3 (1) (2011).

single definition, this narrower definition of *Internet applicant* is used only for affirmative action purposes.[35]

In *EEOC v. Target Corp.*, the potential legal consequences of failing to retain recruitment records and afford all candidates equal opportunity to participate in the recruitment process are made clear.

EEOC v. Target Corp.
2006 U.S. App. LEXIS 21483 (7th Cir.)

OPINION BY CIRCUIT JUDGE CUDAHY:

* * * The EEOC charged that Target violated Title VII of the Civil Rights Act of 1964 by engaging in race discrimination against African-American applicants for managerial positions. The EEOC also alleged that Target violated the Act when it failed to make and preserve records relevant to the determination whether unlawful employment practices had been, or were being, committed. * * * [T]he district court ... dismissed the action. The EEOC now appeals. We reverse and remand for further proceedings.

Target Corporation is headquartered in Minneapolis, Minnesota. One of its retail divisions is Target, a discount chain of more than 1,100 stores nationwide. * * * This case involves District 110 [which] is made up of ... stores in the Madison, Milwaukee, and Waukesha, Wisconsin metropolitan areas. Each district is managed by a District Team Leader, and each store is managed by a Store Team Leader (STL), who is assisted by Executive Team Leaders (ETLs). Each ETL is responsible for a different area of store operation. * * *

This case involves a group of individuals who claim that they were not hired in Target's ETL hiring process because of their race. * * * The claims of Kalisha White, Ralpheal Edgeston and Cherise Brown-Easley involve their contact with STL Matthew Armiger. Before February of 2001, District 110 had a district recruiter. When the district recruiter position was eliminated, STL Richard Walters, who was temporarily assigned recruiting duties, asked fellow STL Armiger for help with those duties. At that time, Armiger was managing a newly-opened and short-staffed Target store in New Berlin, Wisconsin. Walters and Armiger initially shared the recruiting duties equally, but later Armiger's duties were scaled back. Armiger testified

that he believed his recruiting duties were secondary to his management of the store.

1. Kalisha White

Kalisha White, an African-American who attended Marquette University, emailed Target her resume for an ETL position on February 20, 2001, while she was still a student at Marquette. White's resume indicated that she was a member of Alpha Kappa Alpha, an African-American sorority. Armiger e-mailed White and asked her to call to set up an interview. White called at least twice, but each time she spoke with Armiger he said he was too busy to schedule an interview.

White became suspicious of Armiger and decided to conduct an experiment to determine if he had discriminated against her because of her race. Thus, on May 9, 2001, she submitted a resume to Armiger under a fictitious name, "Sarah Brucker." White used her own telephone number, and gave Brucker a Brookfield, Wisconsin, address. She believed the address was located in a predominantly Caucasian neighborhood. Armiger testified that White had a stronger resume than Brucker because White was pursuing an MBA degree, while Brucker was not. On May 10, 2001, Armiger emailed and called Brucker, asking her to return his call. White had a Caucasian acquaintance call Armiger and pretend to be Sarah Brucker. Armiger scheduled an interview with Brucker during their conversation. White testified that she called Armiger soon after Brucker's conversation with him, but he said that he was too busy to schedule an interview with her.

2. Ralpheal Edgeston

Ralpheal Edgeston received an email from Armiger on March 2, 2001, in which Armiger asked her to call and

---

[35]U.S. Equal Employment Opportunity Commission. "Transcript of Commission Meeting on March 17, 2008 on Renewal of UGESP Authorization under the Paperwork Reduction Act." Viewed June 7, 2011 (http://www.eeoc.gov/).

schedule an interview. Edgeston, an African-American student at Marquette University, had submitted her resume to Target for an ETL position at a multicultural job fair held at the University of Wisconsin–Milwaukee in the previous month. Edgeston's resume indicated that one of her college majors was African-American studies and, like Kalisha White's resume, that she was a member of the Alpha Kappa Alpha sorority, which Armiger testified to knowing was an African-American sorority. Additionally, her resume listed that she was a member of the National Association for the Advancement of Colored People (NAACP). Edgeston called Armiger and scheduled a phone interview for March 4, 2001; however, Armiger did not call Edgeston at the appointed time and did not return her calls after that date. Target never scheduled another interview with Edgeston.

3. Cherise Brown-Easley

Class member Cherise Brown-Easley, an African-American, also submitted her resume to Target at the University of Wisconsin–Milwaukee multicultural job fair in February 2001. Brown-Easley's resume indicated that she was a member of the "Metropolitan Alliance of Black School Educators." Brown-Easley received an email from Armiger requesting that she call Armiger to schedule an interview. She called Armiger and scheduled an interview for March 4, 2001. Armiger did not contact Brown-Easley at the appointed time. Instead, Brown-Easley called Armiger a half hour after the interview time, and after being informed that he had left for the day, she left a message for him. The following day, she left another message for Armiger, but she never heard back from him.

During the week that Armiger failed to contact Edgeston and Brown-Easley, he was scheduled to interview nine ETL applicants. In addition to Edgeston and Brown-Easley, Armiger also failed to contact two Caucasian applicants. However, Target later interviewed at least one of the two Caucasian applicants, but Edgeston and Brown-Easley were never interviewed. Armiger testified that he did not know the race of White, Edgeston, or Brown-Easley during the recruiting process. Armiger could not recall reviewing White or Brown-Easley's resumes. He also claimed he did not study Edgeston's resume closely enough to determine her race.

D. TARGET'S RECORD RETENTION

Also at issue in this appeal is Target's practice of employment record retention. * * * Armiger admitted to throwing out the resumes of applicants he deemed unqualified, including those of White, Edgeston and Brown-Easley, rather than retaining them as required by law and by Target's document retention policy. Armiger claims he threw out the resumes to protect the applicants' privacy.

In an effort to comply with the EEOC's document retention requirement, Target currently uses Brass Ring, a nationwide employment recruitment website, to store applicant documents, including: copies of applicants' resumes, applicants' … test results and completed … interview forms. Target recruiters who receive the resumes submit them to Brass Ring and make copies of the resumes of the candidates they plan to interview. * * * Target also has several policies to ensure that job applications and related documents are retained for the required time. Target uses its corporate intranet and email messages to share its record retention policies with STLs. The human resource managers meet biannually to audit each Target store, to conduct training and to remind employees of the record retention policy. The human resource managers instruct on-campus recruiters to retain all resumes, applications and interview guides and notes, and to route the documents to the national headquarters. Finally, the ETL for Team Relations is responsible for ensuring that the record keeping policy is being followed at each Target store.

The success of Target's record retention program through Brass Ring has been disputed. There is some indication that all employees are not following the program. As discussed above, STL Armiger threw out resumes that he should have retained. Additionally, … [an] administrative assistant testified in June of 2003 that she does not send applicant documents to Brass Ring, but instead she retains them herself for the required time. * * * While Target's policy does not include a provision to ensure that relevant documents are retained from the time a discrimination charge is filed until that case is fully concluded, Target claims to address this requirement on a case by case basis, notifying employees to retain documents when a charge arises. * * *

A. RECORD RETENTION

Under Title VII, employers are required to "make and keep such records relevant to the determinations of whether unlawful employment practices have been or are being committed." The EEOC's record keeping regulations require that employers retain applications and other documents related to hiring for one year. Additionally, if a charge of discrimination has been filed, an employer is required to retain all relevant personnel records until the final disposition of the charge. * * *

While we agree that Target has put forth evidence that it has revised its record retention policies in an effort to comply with Title VII, we do not agree that such changes ensure "on [their] face" that Target will not commit further violations. The reforms chosen do not address the particular problems that allowed violations to occur. Individual recruiters and administrative personnel destroyed records that were supposed to be retained because they did not know that they must retain them. * * *

Nothing in Target's new record keeping policy clearly prevents bad faith destruction of resumes or other employment application documents. Target's new policy involves reiterating its procedures for retaining documents to its store managers and recruiters and outsourcing the physical storage of employment documents. Similar to Target's document retention polices prior to 2001, Target depends greatly on the diligence of the company's recruiters and its managerial personnel to ensure that resumes, applications and interview guides are retained because these personnel must forward the original documents to Brass Ring. Target has not claimed that it has adopted a system of penalties for failure to forward documents or in any other way provided new incentives to ensure compliance with the EEOC's record keeping requirements.

Because these genuine issues of fact bear on whether Target's new record retention policy is sufficient to prevent future violations of federal law, Target's motion for summary judgment on this issue should not have been granted. * * *

B. TITLE VII DISPARATE TREATMENT CLAIMS

* * * The parties do not dispute that the EEOC established a prima facie case of disparate treatment.... * * * [T]he district court [found] that Target presented a legitimate, nondiscriminatory reason to explain why White, Edgeston and Brown-Easley were not interviewed for ETL positions. Store Team Leader Matthew Armiger's burdensome workload … caused him to fail in several of his recruitment duties, including failure to conduct interviews when they were scheduled. The EEOC did not contest this finding; therefore step two of the *McDonnell Douglas* test is satisfied and the burden shifts back to the EEOC.

In step three of the McDonnell Douglas test, a plaintiff must show that the defendant's nondiscriminatory reason for rejecting the applicant is a pretext meant to hide a discriminatory motive. * * * [W]e find that the EEOC did present sufficient evidence to establish a genuine issue of material fact as to whether Target's reason for not interviewing White, Edgeston and Brown-Easley

was a pretext for race discrimination. First, Target argued that Armiger could not have discriminated against White, Edgeston and Brown-Easley because he did not know their race. However, * * * [t]he EEOC showed that each applicant's resume contained information that suggested she might be African-American. White's resume indicated that she was a member of Alpha Kappa Alpha sorority, and Armiger testified that he knew this to be an African-American sorority. Edgeston's resume showed that she also was a member of Alpha Kappa Alpha sorority, that she majored in African-American studies, that she wrote a paper titled The African-American Response to School Choice in Milwaukee and that she was a member of the NAACP. Finally, Brown-Easley's resume indicated that she was a member of the "Metropolitan Alliance of Black School Educators." Armiger testified that he typically looked at sorority involvement and extracurricular activities when he reviewed resumes, and that he reviewed White and Edgeston's resumes. In addition, Armiger was in charge of recruiting at University of Wisconsin–Milwaukee, and Edgeston and Brown-Easley's resumes were collected from a multi-cultural career fair at that school.

Additionally, Armiger claims that he failed to interview White because he was "too busy" with his management duties when she called. He claims that he often told applicants that he was too busy to speak to them if they called while he was on the sales floor, and that he did not keep a record of who called. However, fifteen minutes after White called Armiger, Armiger took a call from the fictitious Caucasian applicant, "Sarah Brucker," and scheduled an interview with her. "Brucker" was less qualified than White because White was pursuing an MBA degree but "Brucker" was not, and Armiger recalled seeing in White's resume that she was pursuing this MBA. These facts support a reasonable inference that Armiger's busy schedule was (a) not his actual motivation; or (b) an insufficient reason for failing to interview White, Edgeston and Brown-Easley. * * *

Target claims that Armiger would not have had White's resume in front of him when she called to set up an interview and he said he was too busy to do so, and he therefore would not have known her race. However, the EEOC presented expert testimony indicating that some people can determine a speaker's race based on his or her voice or name. Dr. Thomas Purnell, a linguistics professor, researched racially affiliated dialects and telephone filtered speech. Purnell had White, Edgeston and Brown-Easley read statements to him over the telephone that were similar to those they made to Armiger. He testified that the three women were discernible as African-American. Dr. Marianne Bertrand, an economics professor, testified that some corporate recruiters can identify a person's race based on his or her name. Bertrand's study compared job applicants with Caucasian names, such as Sarah, versus applicants with African-American names, such as Lakisha. Bertrand noted that White's first name, Kalisha, is very similar to the name Lakisha that was used in her study. The expert testimony of Purnell and Bertrand might persuade a reasonable fact finder that, at the time of the phone calls, Armiger at least suspected that White was African-American and that "Brucker" was Caucasian. * * *

This expert evidence likewise could lead a fact finder to conclude that Armiger knew Edgeston and Brown-Easley's race because each of these applicants left at least one message for Armiger after he failed to call at their scheduled interview time. Armiger had set up interviews for March 4 and 6, 2001. He was supposed to interview nine ETL candidates over those two days, including Edgeston and Brown-Easley. * * * The Caucasian candidate was interviewed later by another Target official. Edgeston and Brown-Easley were never interviewed. * * * [A] reasonable fact finder could conclude that contrary to Target's assertion and Armiger's testimony, Armiger did know the race of the applicants at the time he chose not to interview them.

Finally, Target also argues that if Armiger had intended to discriminate against Edgeston and Brown-Easley he would not have contacted them to set up an interview, and that because Armiger did set up the interview it makes sense to assume that he would not miss it for a discriminatory reason. The EEOC claims that Armiger did not choose to interview Edgeston and Brown-Easley, but instead only followed up on the recommendations of his predecessor and of career fair recruiters. This Court need not address the contours of each side's logic on this point any further than to conclude that there is a dispute over when and with how much care Armiger reviewed Edgeston and Brown-Easley's resumes and who actually decided to interview the individuals. * * * [T]he EEOC has presented a genuine issue of fact as to whether Armiger was truly the decision-maker that elected to interview Edgeston and Brown-Easley.

[W]e conclude that there is a genuine issue of material fact as to whether Target's proffered reason that Armiger was too busy to interview White, Edgeston and Brown-Easley was a pretext for discriminatory action based on race. Therefore, summary judgment was improper for these applicants' individual claims. * * *

CASE QUESTIONS

1. What were the legal issues in this case? What did the appeals court decide?
2. What are the obligations of an employer regarding the retention of records related to recruiting? What problems does the court identify with Target's record-retention practices?
3. What is the evidence that the store team leader Armiger was aware of the race of the applicants? That race was a factor in the applicants not receiving interviews?
4. What changes would you recommend to Target's recruiting and hiring practices? What should the role of store managers be?

Practical Considerations What, if any, legal obligation do employers have to reasonably accommodate disabled job applicants during the recruitment process? What types of modifications to the recruiting process might be called for?

In December 2007, the EEOC and Target entered into a consent decree that ended the litigation. Target agreed to pay $510,000 to the plaintiffs, revise its document retention policies, train supervisors in legal compliance, and report on hiring decisions. John Rowe, director of the EEOC's Chicago District Office, commented that the case was "noteworthy for its ruling that the trial court could admit into evidence expert testimony to the effect that the employer may have racially identified the applicants as African American on the basis of their names or accents heard during telephone conversations."[36]

Preemployment Inquiries

To avoid discrimination in hiring, it is essential that employers not ask questions whose answers reveal the protected class characteristics of job candidates. Questions on application

---

[36]EEOC. "Target Corp. to Pay $510,000 for Race Discrimination." (December 10, 2007) Viewed April 30, 2008 (http://www.eeoc.gov/).

forms, during interviews, or in the course of informal chatting with job candidates can end up divulging information about employees that may taint the hiring process. What kinds of questions or inquiries are we talking about? Inadvisable **preemployment inquiries** fall into four general categories.

First, *employers should not directly inquire about protected class characteristics.* If, for example, an application form asks the applicant to check *male* or *female* or *Mr.* or *Mrs./Ms.*, these are direct inquiries about the protected class of sex. Similarly, asking candidates what their age is, where they were born (national origin), or whether they have a disability all constitute direct inquiries into protected class characteristics. This information should not be sought prior to hiring because it can, consciously or not, affect employment decisions and result in disparate treatment. *Information that is needed for other purposes (such as age for participation in a pension plan) can be obtained following the decision to hire (but still kept separate from an employee's regular personnel file).*

Employers who want to track the protected class characteristics of their applicants for affirmative action purposes can do so by providing a voluntary reporting mechanism that is separate from the application form or other materials used in hiring. Also, as Figure 4.1 illustrates, there are often lawful alternatives to inadvisable preemployment inquiries that provide necessary information without crossing the line into questions about protected class. For example, rather than ask for a candidate's age, the employer can ask whether she is at least 18 years of age (which is necessary to perform certain jobs and does not discriminate against persons over 40). Similarly, rather than ask whether a job candidate is a U.S. citizen, it is preferable to ask whether, if hired, he will be able to verify his eligibility to work in the United States. This helps prevent discrimination against those noncitizens who have the legal right to work in the United States (e.g., because they hold green cards).

Second, and slightly less obvious, *employers should not indirectly inquire about the protected class characteristics of job candidates.* Examples of indirect inquiries include asking for an applicant's date of graduation from high school (age), asking for a listing

FIGURE 4.1 Inadvisable Preemployment Inquiries

Inadvisable	Alternative
What is your date of birth?	Are you at least 18 years of age?
Are you a U.S. citizen?	After being hired, will you be able to document your eligibility for work in the United States?
Do you have any health problems that would affect your employment?	Conduct a medical exam following a conditional offer of employment or ask the candidate to demonstrate how a particular job-related task would be performed.
Are you available to work on weekends?	Are you available to work on weekends? We will make an effort to accommodate religious practices.
Have you ever been arrested or convicted of any crime?	Have you ever been convicted of a crime? Answering yes will not automatically disqualify you, but you must provide details about the conviction.
Please list all organizations to which you belong.	Please list all professional associations and other work-related organizations to which you belong.
What was your maiden name?	Please list all names that you have used.
How many children do you have?	If number of dependents must be known for benefit plan participation, this information can be obtained after hire.

of all organizational memberships (race, religion, national origin, etc.), and asking whether the candidate has ever filed a workers' compensation claim for a workplace injury (disability). Again, the concern is with getting information about protected class, leading to disparate treatment. If the employer wants to know *whether* someone has graduated from high school, that is what should be asked, rather than *when* the person graduated. Similarly, questions about professional or work-related organizational affiliations are appropriate, whereas inquiries about all organizational affiliations are not.

Third, *employers should avoid questions about requirements or criteria that are not uniformly applied to job candidates.* This is particularly an issue with respect to sex. Questions about marital status, child-rearing plans, and child-care arrangements and the answers to those questions are sometimes treated differently depending on whether the candidate is a man or a woman. Applying different selection criteria to different protected class groups is again disparate treatment. Additionally, in those states where marital status is a protected class under state law, questions about marital status would be direct inquiries about protected class. Employers with concerns about these matters should clearly explain the requirements of positions and ask all employees if they anticipate any difficulty in meeting them.

Fourth, *employers should avoid questions about requirements that have a high probability of producing adverse impact.* These are requirements that are likely to screen out some protected class groups more than others and for which there is no strong evidence of job relatedness. Examples include questions about prior arrests, type of military discharge, and height and weight.

Notice that we have *not* said that employers must only ask questions about things that are job-related. Although this is a good idea, the law does not require it. The law requires employers to refrain from asking questions eliciting information that could be used to discriminate. For the most part, intrusive or irrelevant inquiries do not subject employers to liability.

JUST THE FACTS

A female manager interviewed for a newly created management position. The male vice president who interviewed her asked whether she had any children, what her child-care responsibilities were, and how her family felt about the weekly commute that she made between her home in New York and the company headquarters in Virginia. He asked "how her husband handled the fact that she was away from home so much, not caring for the family." Her response that the family members "all helped each other" and that they had a "successful family" was met with skepticism by the vice president. The woman was passed over for the job, and a male was hired instead. She was told that one of the reasons for the decision was that the male employee had grown-up children and was able to make a "committed move" to Virginia. Subsequently, it was suggested on several occasions that the woman accept a lower-level position in New York to be closer to her family. About a year later, her position was selected for elimination in a restructuring. Was this sex discrimination?

See, *Lettieri v. Equant,* 478 F.3d 640 (4th Cir. 2007).

Is an employer breaking the law if he asks questions relating to protected class but does not use that information in making hiring decisions? The answer to this question becomes a bit complicated, so let's return to a basic point. Refraining from inadvisable preemployment inquiries is a device for lessening the influence of protected class characteristics on employment decisions. The device is rather limited, however, because an employer who wants to discriminate can glean much information about protected class (e.g., by viewing candidates at interviews, by looking at the length of a person's work history, or by drawing inferences from a person's name) without ever asking a question. Nevertheless, refraining from such inquiries diminishes the chances that knowledge of protected class characteristics will taint employment decisions. This is especially important in the early part of the recruitment and hiring process when candidates have not yet had the opportunity to have their credentials closely evaluated.

Although the EEOC strongly discourages employers from making such preemployment inquiries, most federal antidiscrimination laws (with the notable exception of the ADA) do not explicitly prohibit them, and the EEOC will not find reasonable cause of discrimination solely on this basis. On the other hand, many state antidiscrimination laws do expressly prohibit such inquiries. In either case, however, asking questions about protected class is most likely to have legal repercussions when someone is actually denied an employment opportunity. Asking these questions not only makes a job candidate suspicious of an employer's motives and more likely to challenge a rejection, but it also provides evidence that the employer was aware of the candidate's protected class characteristics and interested enough to ask about them. Thus, preemployment inquiries constitute evidence of discriminatory intent in disparate treatment cases.

Practical Considerations How should job candidates respond when confronted with inadvisable preemployment inquiries?

Medical Inquiries Prior to a Conditional Offer of Employment The Americans with Disabilities Act (ADA) differs from other federal antidiscrimination laws in directly prohibiting preemployment inquiries that might reveal the existence, nature, or severity of an applicant's disability.[37] Congress recognized the particular importance of this provision in the context of disability discrimination. Otherwise, it would be all too easy for the fact of an applicant's disability to overwhelm consideration of her qualifications. But does this prohibition also protect employees who are not disabled? *Harrison v. Benchmark Electronics Huntsville* addresses this question.

Harrison v. Benchmark Electronics Huntsville
593 F.3d 1206 (11th Cir. 2010)

OPINION BY CIRCUIT JUDGE SILER:

John Harrison sued Benchmark Electronics Huntsville, Inc. ("BEHI"), alleging … that BEHI engaged in an improper medical inquiry, in violation of the Americans with Disabilities Act of 1990 ("ADA"). The district court granted summary judgment in favor BEHI…. We reverse.

In November 2005, Aerotek, a company that places temporary workers at BEHI, assigned Harrison to work at BEHI. Harrison worked as a "debug tech," and his responsibilities included identifying problems with, repairing, and testing electronic boards. Although he suffers from epilepsy and takes barbiturates to control his condition, the Equal Employment Opportunity

---

[37] 42 U.S.C.S. § 12112 (d)(2)(A) (2011).

Commission ("EEOC") determined that he did not have a disability as defined under the ADA.

At the time Harrison commenced his temporary position at BEHI, the company had a practice of screening temporary employees for potential permanent employment. If a supervisor believed that a temporary employee would meet BEHI's needs, he would invite that employee to submit an application for employment and complete the necessary drug testing and background check. * * * On May 19, 2006, Harrison submitted an application for permanent employment, at the request of his supervisor, Don Anthony. Along with his application, he consented to a drug test. * * * In July 2006, Lena Williams, employed in BEHI's human resources department, was notified that Harrison's test had come back positive and was awaiting review by a Medical Review Officer ("MRO"). She called Anthony and asked him to "send [Harrison] her way." She stated that she did not tell Anthony about the positive drug screen at any time, because she had a duty to keep such information confidential. * * *

Regardless of how he found out about the drug test results, Anthony informed Harrison that he had tested positive for barbiturates. Harrison responded by claiming to have a prescription, which Anthony instructed him to retrieve. Anthony then called the MRO and passed the phone to Harrison, who answered a series of questions about the medication. The MRO asked him how long he had been disabled, what medication he took, and how long he had taken it. He replied that he had epilepsy since he was two years old, he took barbiturates to control it, and he stated the amount of his dosage. Anthony did not ask any questions, but he remained in the room during this colloquy and heard Harrison's responses to the MRO's questions.

On July 19, 2006, the MRO reported to Williams that Harrison's drug test had been cleared. By this time, Williams had also received clearance to hire Harrison, information she passed on to Anthony. However, Anthony told human resources not to prepare an offer letter for Harrison. Anthony then asked Aerotek not to return Harrison to BEHI. On August 18, 2006, Aerotek informed Harrison that he would not be returning to BEHI, because he had a performance and attitude problem, and because he had been accused of threatening Anthony. He was fired from Aerotek that same day.

Through the course of the litigation, Anthony has asserted three reasons to support his decision not to hire Harrison: (1) he was too busy preparing for a company-wide audit to extend the offer; (2) Harrison had made threats against him; and (3) several employees had expressed concern to him about Harrison's competence. Anthony maintains that, in light of these concerns, he simply needed more time to evaluate Harrison. * * *

On May 3, 2007, Harrison sued BEHI in the United States District Court for the Northern District of Alabama. He alleged various violations of the ADA: namely, that (1) BEHI engaged in an improper medical inquiry, (2) he was not hired due to a perceived disability, and (3) he was terminated due to a perceived disability. * * * The district court granted BEHI's motion, as to both the preemployment medical inquiry and perceived disability claims. * * * Because Harrison "tested positive for barbiturates," the court held that BEHI was then authorized to ask Harrison whether he "had a legitimate use for such medication."

Before addressing the merits of Harrison's appeal, we must first examine whether he, a non-disabled individual, can state a private cause of action for a prohibited medical inquiry in violation of [the ADA]. * * * Harrison urges us to join our sister circuits who are unanimous in recognizing a private cause of action irrespective of the plaintiff's disability status.... In the pre-offer stage, which is at issue in this case, "a covered entity shall not conduct a medical examination or make inquiries of a job applicant as to whether such applicant is an individual with a disability or as to the nature or severity of such disability." * * * [T]he statutory language at issue in this case ... does not predicate suit under the statute on an applicant's disability status. In contrast to the ADA's general prohibition of disability discrimination ... which refers only to "qualified individuals with disabilities," [the preemployment medical examinations and inquiries section of the ADA] refers broadly to "applicants." An "applicant" is "[a] person who submits a formal application to do something or for a position, especially as part of recruitment or selection process; a candidate."

* * * [The language in the ADA prohibiting preemployment medical inquiries] does not limit coverage to applicants who are also "qualified individuals with disabilities," and we do not infer such a restriction. * * * Congress sought to prevent employers from using preemployment medical inquiries "to exclude applicants with disabilities—particularly those with so-called hidden disabilities such as epilepsy, diabetes, emotional illness, heart disease, and cancer-before their ability to perform the job was even evaluated." The legislative history ... indicates that "Congress wished to curtail all questioning that would serve to identify and exclude persons with disabilities from

consideration for employment...." Allowing non-disabled applicants to sue will enhance and enforce Congress's prohibition. Moreover, a contrary reading would vitiate [the ADA's] effectiveness: "It makes little sense to require an [applicant] to demonstrate that he has a disability to prevent his [potential] employer from inquiring as to whether or not he has [one]."

* * * Thus, we now explicitly recognize that a plaintiff has a private right of action under [the section of the ADA prohibiting preemployment medical inquiries], irrespective of his disability status.

* * * Consistent with Congress's intent, the regulations adopted under the ADA by the EEOC provide that an employer may make "preemployment inquiries into the ability of an applicant to perform job-related functions, and/or may ask an applicant to describe or to demonstrate how, with or without reasonable accommodation, the applicant will be able to perform the job related functions." The regulations clarify that while it is appropriate for an employer to inquire into an applicant's ability to perform job-related functions, it is illegal for him to make targeted disability-related inquiries. The EEOC has defined "disability-related" questions as those "likely to elicit information about a disability." On the other hand, "if there are many possible answers to a question and only some of those answers would contain disability-related information, the question is not 'disability-related.'"

In addition to allowing inquiries directed at an applicant's ability to perform job-related functions, the ADA recognizes an exemption for drug tests. ("... a test to determine the illegal use of drugs shall not be considered a medical examination."). Employers may also ask follow-up questions in response to a positive drug test.... ("*[I]f* an applicant tests positive for illegal drug use ... the employer may validate the test results by asking about lawful drug use or possible explanations for the positive result other than the illegal use of drugs. [For example,] the employer may lawfully ask questions such as, 'What medications have you taken that might have resulted in this positive test result? Are you taking this medication under a lawful prescription?'"). However, the regulations, coupled with the EEOC's guidelines, make clear that disability-related questions are still prohibited. * * *

While the district court correctly concluded that employers may conduct follow-up questioning in response to a positive drug test, it failed to acknowledge any limits on this type of questioning. * * * Harrison testified that Anthony told him his drug test was positive, that he disclosed his prescription, that he was then

taken to Anthony's office where he answered questions about his medication, and that Anthony remained in the room during this interview. Anthony denied ever knowing that Harrison suffered from epilepsy, and he acknowledged that it would be improper for him to be present during the MRO interview. Although BEHI was permitted to ask follow-up questions to ensure that Harrison's positive drug test was due to a lawful prescription, a jury may find that these questions exceeded the scope of the likely-to-elicit standard, and that Anthony's presence in the room violated the ADA, especially considering the conflict between Harrison's testimony—that to answer the MRO's questions he was forced to disclose the fact and extent of his epilepsy—and Anthony's—that he never knew Harrison suffered from the condition. A reasonable jury could infer that Anthony's presence in the room was an intentional attempt *likely to elicit* information about a disability in violation of the ADA's prohibition against preemployment medical inquiries. * * *

Finally, BEHI obliquely argues that even assuming an improper medical inquiry, Harrison cannot present evidence of damages sufficient to overcome summary judgment. * * * [O]ur sister circuits require that a non-disabled plaintiff at least show some damages ... caused by a [an impermissible medical inquiry]. We agree. * * * Harrison has presented sufficient evidence for a reasonable jury to find that he suffered damages—namely, that he was not hired as a permanent employee of BEHI because of his responses to allegedly unlawful questions. * * * [A] reasonable jury could infer that Anthony did base his decision not to hire Harrison on information gleaned from an improper medical inquiry. "[I]t may be that, at trial [BEHI] will be able convincingly to show that its proffered reason[s] [were] bona fide. In that case it will prevail." We merely hold that summary judgment cannot be supported at this time; we must, therefore, reverse and remand.

CASE QUESTIONS

1. What were the legal issues in this case? What did the court decide? Why?
2. Would the purpose of prohibiting preemployment medical inquiries be defeated if the court had ruled that this requirement applied only to disabled job candidates?
3. What medical inquiries were made in this case? Why might they have violated the ADA?
4. What should an employer do to verify whether a positive drug test result was caused by a lawful prescription drug?

Employers must refrain from seeking medical information from all applicants, disabled or not. **Medical inquiries** include questions about disabilities, medical and psychological conditions, medical histories, medications taken, and workers' compensation claims filed. However, an employer who is concerned about a job candidate's ability to do a job is permitted to ask that candidate to demonstrate how he would do the job. Furthermore, the prohibition on medical inquiries applies only to preemployment inquiries. An employer who extends a "conditional offer of employment" to a job candidate (meaning that the person will be hired provided that the results of a medical exam are satisfactory) can make any type of medical inquiry or perform any type of medical exam at that point—provided that all persons hired to perform the same type of work are subjected to the same inquiries or exams. Thus, *employers who desire medical information from job candidates should seek that information only after job candidates have been conditionally offered employment based on their other qualifications.* However, such information still cannot be used to discriminate against qualified disabled persons who can perform the main parts of jobs (the "essential functions") with or without reasonable accommodation.

Statements by Employers

Recruitment entails not only extracting information from job candidates but also providing information and attempting to persuade candidates to accept job offers. These statements by employers can have legal consequences. Employers might be tempted to downplay negative information that would scare away prospective employees or make promises regarding the expected duration of employment, promotions, or pay raises when trying to entice desired candidates to take jobs. Later, when circumstances change and the honeymoon period is over, misrepresentations and unfulfilled promises can give rise to a number of different legal claims, including **fraud**, negligent misrepresentation, and breach of contract.

ELEMENTS OF A CLAIM

Fraud

1. A false representation of a material fact was made to another person.
2. The party making the statement knew that it was false at the time that it was made (or had reckless disregard for the truth).
3. The party making the statement intended the other person to rely on the false representation and to act or refrain from acting in a certain way.
4. The other person was, in fact, induced to act or refrain from acting.
5. The other person was harmed by reliance on the false representation.

© Cengage Learning 2013.

A successful fraud claim occurred when a medical practice specializing in coronary care sought to recruit a renowned specialist. Assurances were given that the specialist would be allowed to become an equal partner in the firm within a short period of time. These assurances were critical to the specialist's decision to accept the position. However, the practice was reorganized shortly thereafter and the opportunity to become an equal partner did not materialize. A state appeals court affirmed the lower court in finding that the doctor had been fraudulently induced to accept the position and remanded the case for consideration of punitive damages in light of the egregious conduct of the practice's partners.[38]

In **negligent misrepresentation** cases, the second element of a fraud claim—intent to falsify or reckless disregard for the truth—need not be shown. Instead, it is sufficient for the plaintiff to establish that the employer should have known about the falsity of its statement. Misrepresentations that provide the basis for fraud and negligent misrepresentation cases are not limited to outright lies. Silence can constitute misrepresentation when an employer selectively omits material facts with the intent of creating a false impression or fails to correct a previous misrepresentation after becoming aware of its falsity. In the context of recruiting, "material" facts are those that would affect a person's decision to accept or not accept a job.

Stewart v. Jackson & Nash provides a good example of a successful fraud claim that arises in the context of an attorney being "wooed" away from one law firm to another. Pay particular attention to how the court distinguishes between fraud and breach of contract claims.

Stewart v. Jackson & Nash
976 F.2d 86 (2d Cir 1992)

OPINION BY CIRCUIT JUDGE WALKER:

Victoria A. Stewart appeals from a ... Judgment of the United States District Court for the Southern District of New York.... We ... hold that she ... state[s] a claim for fraudulent inducement. * * *

Stewart ... is an attorney.... Prior to October 1988, she was employed in the environmental law department of the New York law firm of Phillips, Nizer, Benjamin, Krim & Ballon. Ronald Herzog, a partner in the firm of Jackson & Nash, ... contacted Stewart while at Phillips, Nizer regarding the possibility of employment with his firm. Herzog allegedly "represented to Stewart that Jackson had recently secured a large environmental law client, that Jackson was in the process of establishing an environmental law department, and that Stewart would head the environmental law department, and be expected to service the firm's substantial existing environmental law client." Stewart asserts that, in reliance on these representations, she resigned her position with Phillips, Nizer in October 1988 and the following month began work at Jackson & Nash.

Upon her arrival, Stewart alleges that Jackson & Nash put her to work primarily on general litigation matters. When she inquired about the promised environmental work, Herzog repeatedly assured her that it would be forthcoming and "also consistently advised [her] that she would be promoted to a position as head of Jackson's environmental law department." The major environmental law client and substantial environmental case work, however, never materialized. Finally, in May 1990, a Jackson & Nash partner allegedly informed Stewart that "Jackson had never 'really' had this 'type' of work, nor had [it], in fact, secured an environmental law client." Jackson & Nash dismissed Stewart on December 31, 1990. Jackson & Nash, in its affidavit in support of the motion to dismiss, asserts that it engaged in a year-long effort to acquire environmental work but concedes that it failed to achieve this end.

Count I of Stewart's complaint ... alleges that Jackson & Nash fraudulently induced her to enter into and remain in its employ. Stewart asserts that she took the position with the firm in reliance on its knowing misrepresentations, as outlined above. She claims that her "career objective—continuing to specialize in environmental law—was thwarted and grossly undermined during her employment with Jackson," and that she suffered "loss of professional opportunity, loss of professional reputation," and damage to her "career growth and potential." Count II alleges negligent misrepresentation. * * *

---

[38]*Mkparu v. Ohio Heart Care, Inc.*, 740 N.E.2d 293 (1999).

The district court found that Stewart's fraud claim arose from her termination from the firm and dismissed Count I on the authority of *Murphy v. American Home Prod. Corp. Murphy* held that because at-will employees "may be freely terminated … at any time for any reason or even for no reason," they can neither challenge their termination in a contract action nor "bootstrap" themselves around this bar by alleging that the firing was in some way tortious. Following *Murphy*, the court concluded that Stewart, an at-will employee, could not state a fraud claim based on facts arising out of her termination.

We find *Murphy* distinguishable. In *Murphy*, the plaintiff, an at-will employee of the defendant, claimed that he had been fired in a tortious manner. He alleged that his firing "'was deliberately and viciously insulting, was designed to and did embarrass and humiliate plaintiff and was intended to and did cause plaintiff severe mental and emotional distress thereby damaging plaintiff.'" These tort allegations, springing as they do directly from the termination itself, are a transparent attempt to restate the forbidden contractual challenge in the guise of tort. Stewart's alleged injuries, on the other hand, commenced well before her termination and were, in several important respects, unrelated to it. According to the complaint, Jackson & Nash's misrepresentations caused Stewart, a budding environmental lawyer, to leave a firm with an environmental practice and spend two years at one in which she was largely unable to work in her chosen specialty. The resulting damage to her career development was independent of her later termination from Jackson & Nash and began while she was still at the firm. As stated in her complaint, Stewart's "career objective—continuing to specialize in environmental law—was thwarted and grossly undermined *during* her employment with Jackson." (Emphasis added). Although *Murphy* precludes an award of damages for injuries caused by her termination, it does not prevent her from recovering for injuries that resulted from her reliance on the defendants' false statements.

Appellees Jackson & Nash urge a second ground for dismissal of Count I. They contend that Stewart's alleged injuries, both pre-termination and termination related, result in substance from broken contractual promises regarding the terms and conditions of her employment. Such broken promises, they contend, cannot support a fraud claim because "the fraudulent breach of a contract does not give rise to an action for fraud. Thus, where the only fraud charged relates to a breach of the contract and not to its inducement or making, no action for fraud is alleged." Appellees' argument boils down to an assertion that Stewart's claim is nothing more than a contract action, which, since it is based on an oral agreement, is not enforceable under New York's Statute of Frauds. Stewart contends that the firm's misrepresentations are actionable under a theory of fraud in the inducement. She correctly points out that under New York law "it is elementary that where a contract or transaction was induced by false representations, the representations and the contract are distinct and separable…. Thus, fraud in the inducement of a written contract is not merged therein so as to preclude an action for fraud."

Stewart alleges four misrepresentations: (1) "Jackson had recently secured a large environmental law client"; (2) "Jackson was in the process of establishing an environmental law department"; (3) "Stewart would head the environmental law department"; and (4) "[Stewart would] be expected to service the firm's substantial existing environmental law client."

As to representations (1) and (2), we find dispositive the New York Court of Appeals' distinction between a prospective business partner's "promissory statements as to what will be done in the future," which give rise only to a breach of contract claim, and his or her false "'representations of present fact,'" which give rise to a separable claim of fraudulent inducement. In the case of *Coolite Corp. v. American Cyanamid Co*, for example, defendant Cyanamid, a manufacturer of light sticks, represented to Coolite that it had fully tested its product and had developed a means of correcting the product's defects. Coolite, allegedly in reliance on these statements, contracted to become the exclusive distributor of the light sticks. Coolite later found the product not to be of merchantable quality and sued for fraudulent misrepresentation. The Appellate Division let the fraud claim stand on the grounds that "Cyanamid's representations … were representations of fact and not merely promises of future action."

In this case Jackson & Nash's declarations that it "had recently secured a large environmental law client" and "was in the process of establishing an environmental law department" were not future promises but representations of present fact. Under *Coolite*, these representations support a claim for fraudulent inducement, which is distinct and separable from any contract action. * * *

[R]egarding representation (3), [Stewart] asserts that Jackson & Nash informed her that she "would be promoted to a position as head of Jackson's environmental law department … [although], upon information and belief, *at the time Jackson made the aforesaid representations to Stewart, it knew that it did not intend to make her the head of its environmental law department.*" (Emphasis added). While representation (3) appears, initially, to be a future promise (Stewart would be made head of the department), the New York Court of Appeals has explained that

> *while mere promissory statements as to what will be done in the future are not actionable, … it is settled that, if a promise was actually made with a preconceived and undisclosed intention of not performing it, it constitutes a misrepresentation of material existing fact upon which an action … [based on fraudulent inducement] may be predicated.*

Stewart's assertion that Jackson & Nash, at the time it made the promise, "knew that it did not intend" to fulfill it, makes representation (3) an allegation of present fact which gives rise to a claim of fraudulent inducement.

To the extent that representation (4)'s pledge that Stewart would "be expected to service the firm's substantial existing environmental law client" goes beyond representation (1)'s statement of the existence of an environmental law client, it is a future promise and would not be actionable.

In sum, we hold that representation (1) is a representation of present fact and that (2), and (3) included both elements of present fact and future promise. To the extent the representations were of present fact, they are actionable under a theory of fraudulent inducement. * * *

We hold that Count I of Stewart's complaint, alleging fraudulent inducement, survives Jackson & Nash's motion to dismiss.

CASE QUESTIONS

1. What was the legal issue in this case? What did the court decide?
2. How are the elements of a fraud claim satisfied in this case?
3. How does the court distinguish between fraud and breach of contract? Why would the law firm prefer to characterize Stewart's claim as a claim for breach of contract?
4. Why do you think that Herzog made these statements to Stewart?

Breach of contract is sometimes claimed simultaneously with fraud, but as *Stewart* shows, the two are distinct. For one thing, intentional misrepresentation is an essential element of fraud claims, whereas breach of contract is established by a failure to live up to binding promises, regardless of intent. Second, fraud claims usually involve false statements made about current or preexisting facts, whereas breach of contract claims involve promises made about future terms and conditions of employment. An important exception, applicable to Stewart's case, is where the party making promises about future conditions is aware of the falsity of those promises at the time they are made.

Employers should refrain from making promises to job candidates as inducements to accept jobs unless they are willing to live up to those promises. Likewise, employers cannot mislead job candidates by misrepresenting facts that would reasonably be relied on in deciding whether to accept a position. Employers cannot get so caught up in the recruitment process that they promise more than they can ultimately deliver or, worse, more than they know that they will be able to deliver. *Nor should interviewers comment on a job candidate's prospects of being hired.* Candidates who are subsequently not hired after having been led to believe that an offer would be forthcoming are likely to feel that they have been wronged.

JUST THE FACTS

An employee was approached by a "headhunter" who informed her that a direct competitor of her current employer was "very interested" in hiring her. The headhunter cited the details of an attractive compensation package that the rival firm intended to offer. Her supervisor heard of the impending job offer, and the employee confirmed the information. The CEO initially told the supervisor to terminate the employee but then reconsidered after learning that the employee had never signed a noncompetition agreement that would limit her ability to work for a competing firm. Saying to the supervisor that "I guess we have to pay the ransom," the CEO proceeded to renegotiate her compensation. In the course of these negotiations, the employee was told that based on projected revenues for the upcoming year, the employee should not have any problem achieving her full bonus for the year. At the time that these negotiations were occurring, the company was operating with a negative cash flow and was experiencing numerous financial problems. The employee accepted the new compensation package and signed the requisite noncompetition agreement. Several weeks later the company announced a restructuring plan that eliminated the employee's position. Does the employee have an actionable fraud claim?

See, *Sweeney v. MARC Global*, 2008 U.S. Dist. LEXIS 11490 (W.D.N.C.).

False Statements by Employees

Employers are not the only ones who have to watch what they say. There are potential legal consequences for applicants who provide prospective employers with false information or omit important facts in hopes of enhancing their chances of getting hired. First, in cases where employers have to defend their decisions not to hire (such as in discrimination claims), courts regard refusal to hire due to falsification or omission as a legitimate, nondiscriminatory reason. This is particularly true when the employer has a consistently enforced policy to this effect, the employer notifies employees of it (usually on the application form), and the falsification or omission is material rather than trivial. Likewise, employers who discover a falsification or an omission after a person has already been hired and discharge that person will generally be able to defend any wrongful discharge claim that arises out of the termination. Thus, *employers should have a policy requiring that job candidates provide complete and truthful information and specifying that the penalty for failing to do so will be either refusal to hire or termination if the falsification or omission is discovered post-hiring. As with any genuine policy, this policy needs to be consistently enforced and made known to job candidates.*

Cases involving **after-acquired evidence** show that there is another consequence to employee falsifications and omissions during the hiring process. The consequence is that the legal remedies available to employees in suits against their employers may be limited due to their prior misbehavior. For example, suppose that a job candidate falsely claims to have a college degree. The employer does not discover the falsification at the time and hires the woman. Subsequently, she suffers harassment on the job and is forced to quit. She files a sex discrimination suit. In preparing to defend itself, the company goes over all of its records pertaining to this employee, including her application form. They become suspicious of her statements about her educational credentials, and during the discovery process leading up to litigation, she is forced to admit that she fabricated the information. Pursuant to company policy, she is then officially terminated for providing false information on her application. Thus, the employer "acquired" evidence of previous wrongdoing (falsification on her application form), but only after the employee was discriminated against and filed suit.

Should the prior wrongdoing of the employee negate her ability to sue the employer? After all, had the employer known about the false information she submitted, it might not have hired her in the first place (either because she would have been viewed as unqualified or because of a policy against falsification). The Supreme Court has held that employees do not lose their ability to bring suit simply because they do not have entirely clean hands.[39] Lawsuits serve not only to remedy harm to individual plaintiffs but also to uphold public policy. However, if the employer can show that it would not have hired her had it been aware of the falsification, her remedies (such as back pay) will generally be limited to the point in time when the wrongdoing was discovered, and reinstatement will not be ordered.

Not all instances of alleged falsification of an application will be treated as after-acquired evidence cases. For example, a woman was fired after becoming pregnant, and the jury concluded that the employer discriminated based on pregnancy. The employer argued that any damages should be limited because the woman had failed to list several previous jobs on her resume, including one from which she had been fired. The court rejected the employer's argument because it was unclear whether she had actually been fired from any previous job; the omissions were on her resume rather than the company's application form; the application form did not even ask for a job history; and, perhaps most importantly, there was no evidence that the company had ever fired or not hired anyone for falsification of a resume.[40] Put differently, this employer's attempt to limit its damages by invoking the after-acquired evidence doctrine failed because it could not prove that there was falsification, that any falsification that might have occurred related to material facts (If the information was so important to a hiring decision, why was there nothing about it on the application?), and that it had a bona fide policy of firing or refusing to hire persons found to have falsified their resumes.

Key Terms

recruitment, p. 101
relevant labor market, p. 102
neutral message, p. 103
nepotism, p. 104
word-of-mouth recruiting, p. 105
visa, p. 106
visa classification, p. 107

H-1B visa, p. 107
H-1B dependent employer, p. 108
H-2 visa, p. 108
L-1 visa, p. 109
labor trafficking, p. 109
applicant, p. 112
Internet applicant, p. 112

preemployment inquiry, p. 117
medical inquiry, p. 122
fraud, p. 122
negligent misrepresentation, p. 123
breach of contract, p. 125
after-acquired evidence, p. 126

Chapter Summary

The many ways in which employers recruit applicants are vital to the cause of equal employment opportunity. If recruitment methods reach some protected class groups more than others or fail to convey a genuine desire that all interested and qualified candidates apply, equal employment opportunity is doomed from the start. People have to know that jobs are available before they can apply for them, and they have to believe that applying will not be a waste of their time. Recruitment methods affect hiring decisions by determining the composition of applicant pools. Thus, to ascertain whether there is discrimination in

---

[39]*McKennon v. Nashville Banner Publishing Co.,* 115 S. Ct. 879 (1995).

[40]*Sheehan v. Donlen Corp.,* 173 F.3d 1039 (7th Cir. 1999).

recruitment, a comparison must be made between the protected class composition of the applicant pool and the group of persons with the necessary skills in the relevant labor market. Nepotism and word-of-mouth recruiting are especially likely to produce discriminatory effects because they tend to replicate existing workforces, particularly in terms of race.

Employers wanting to recruit nonimmigrant foreign nationals to work in the United States need to deal with a variety of visa classifications, including H-1B visas for persons of distinguished merit and ability, H-2 visas for temporary workers, L-1 visas for intracompany transfers, and TN visas for highly skilled employees from Mexico and Canada. The use of foreign nationals is subject to numerous requirements related to the number of visas available, the types of jobs that can be performed, payment for services, termination of employment, and the duration of employment. There is increased concern in recent years regarding labor trafficking, in which persons from other countries are enticed by the false promises of recruiters to come to the United States at great expense, only to be exploited and denied basic freedoms.

Employers seek to obtain much information from applicants through application forms, interviews, and other means. However, obtaining information about the protected class characteristics of job candidates is inadvisable and can lead to discrimination. Although the inquiries themselves generally do not violate federal law, they may violate state laws and they provide evidence of discriminatory intent. The Americans with Disabilities Act (ADA) is unusual among federal laws in containing an express prohibition against preemployment medical inquiries prior to a job candidate receiving a conditional offer of employment. This prohibition applies regardless of whether the job candidate is disabled.

Employers also make statements to prospective employees. These statements can lead to claims of fraud, negligent misrepresentation, or breach of contract. Fraud occurs in the recruitment and hiring process when an employer knowingly misrepresents a fact that is important to the job candidate deciding to take a job, the employer intends for the job candidate to rely on the false information, the job candidate reasonably relies on that information, and the job candidate is damaged by the misrepresentation. In negligent misrepresentation, it is sufficient to show that the employer should have known of the misrepresentation, even if actual knowledge or reckless disregard for the truth cannot be established. Breach of contract arises out of unfulfilled promises that are made regarding future terms and conditions of employment and is distinct from any fraud that may have induced an employee to enter into a contractual relationship.

False statements by employees also have consequences. Courts have consistently upheld employers who have policies that they will refuse to hire or will terminate employees who have falsified or omitted information used to make hiring decisions. When evidence of a falsification or an omission surfaces after an employee has commenced legal action against an employer, this "after-acquired evidence" will likely limit any remedies awarded to the employee but will not cause a suit to be dismissed.

Practical Advice Summary

- When recruiting, employers should
  - Use multiple recruitment methods rather than rely solely on one way of getting the word out about employment opportunities.
  - Disseminate information about employment opportunities as broadly as is feasible given the nature of the position and the labor market.
  - Create written job announcements.
  - Ensure that the wording of want ads and other types of job announcements is neutral and does not express any preference or requirement based on protected class.
- When recruiting, employers should not
  - Request that employment agencies refer employees with particular protected class characteristics.
  - Attempt to obtain information about the protected class characteristics of referrals from employment agencies.
  - Rely heavily on nepotism and word of mouth to recruit employees, particularly where the existing workforce is relatively homogenous in terms of race or national origin.
- When using foreign nationals with H-1B visas to perform work in the United States, employers should
  - Adhere to the terms and conditions of employment provided for in LCA forms.
  - Ensure that they are not employed continuously in the United States for more than six years.
  - Not lay visa holders off or reduce their pay.

— Notify immigration authorities when the employment of visa holders is terminated before the end of their contracts.

— Not use visa holders to displace or adversely affect the working conditions of U.S. workers.

- Establish an application policy and adhere to it consistently. The policy should specify the following:
  — Whether applications will be accepted
  — What must be done to complete the application process and be considered an applicant
  — How long applications will be accepted
  — How long submitted applications will remain valid
- If applications are being accepted, no individual wanting to apply should be discouraged from submitting an application.
- Be prepared to accommodate disabled persons by providing
  — Assistance in completing application forms.
  — Alternative means of communicating the information in job announcements.
  — Accessible interview sites.
- Application forms should
  — Be signed by applicants and dated.
  — Be retained for at least one year from when the decision not to hire was made (for applicants who are not hired).
  — Be kept for the duration of employment and at least a year thereafter (for applicants who are hired).
  — Be kept until there has been a final disposition in cases where a discrimination charge has been filed.
- Whether on application forms, during interviews, or otherwise, employers should refrain from asking questions
  — Directly or indirectly related to protected class characteristics of job candidates.
  — About requirements or criteria not uniformly applied to job candidates.
  — About requirements or criteria likely to produce adverse impact.
- Requests for medical information of any type should be made only after a conditional offer of employment has been extended to a job candidate.
- Refrain from making promises about future terms and conditions of employment intended to induce job candidates to take jobs unless those promises will be kept.
- Be careful not to present false or misleading information that a job candidate would reasonably rely on in accepting a job. This includes creating a false impression by selectively omitting important facts or failing to correct known prior misrepresentations.
- Have and enforce a clear policy requiring that job candidates provide complete and truthful information, with the penalty for failing to do so being non-hire or termination.

Chapter Questions

1. Over a five-year period, an upscale restaurant hired 108 food servers, all of whom were men. Of the hundreds of applicants during this time, only about 3 percent were women. Charges were filed with the EEOC. For the next five years, women constituted 22 percent of applicants and 21.7 percent of persons hired. In both periods, food servers were recruited and hired through a "roll call" procedure. Applicants were expected to be familiar with this procedure and to report to the restaurant on a particular weekend in October to be interviewed. The restaurant did not post or advertise job openings. However, the court found that there was general knowledge of the roll call procedure among local food servers. Interviews were conducted by a male maitre d', who selected candidates based on his assessment of their appearance, articulation, attitude, and experience. After the EEOC charges were filed, this procedure was modified to substitute a panel of managers for the maitre d' and a test that involved the lifting of a loaded serving tray. The percentage of applicants at other area restaurants who were female ranged between 30 and 42 percent. According to Census data, approximately 32 percent of table servers who resided in the same city as the restaurant and had earnings comparable to the food servers at the restaurant were female. Unable to obtain a conciliation agreement, the EEOC sued the restaurant. What should the court decide? Why? (*EEOC v. Joe's Stone Crab*, 220 F.3d 1263 [11th Cir. 2000], *cert. denied*, 539 U.S. 941 [2006])

2. A truck driver sought employment with a company that hauls new cars. Truckers working for this company had to make expensive investments in tractor trailers. Before accepting employment, the truck driver was told that jobs were assigned to truckers without regard to seniority. He was also given a figure for the average monthly gross

income of the company's truckers over the past few months. Both of these were true at the time. However, the company was simultaneously involved in negotiations with the truck drivers' union to change to a job assignment system based on seniority, a change that would necessarily reduce the income of new drivers. The company was pushing for this change and the manager with whom the prospective truck driver was dealing knew about the proposal. About two months after the truck driver took a job with the company, the new seniority-based system was put into effect. As a new employee, he received very few assignments and his income sunk far below what he had been told company drivers were making. The driver resigned and sued. What should the court decide? Why? (*Varnum v. Nu-Car Carriers*, 804 F.2d 638 [11th Cir. 1986])

3. A veteran with a disability applied for a job as an EEOC investigator. Federal government hiring rules allow for the noncompetitive appointment of veterans with service-connected disabilities of 30 percent or more. Candidates seeking consideration on a noncompetitive basis are required to submit documentation verifying their eligibility. Accordingly, the applicant submitted several documents attesting to his disability. The applicant was reviewed for a noncompetitive appointment, but not selected. The agency cited the applicant's failure to satisfactorily meet one of its established hiring criteria—ability to communicate in writing—as the basis for the rejection. This judgment was based on the many typographical errors, run-on sentences, and fragments found on his application. The applicant sued under the ADA. What should the court decide? Why? (*Bennett v. Dominguez,* 196 Fed. Appx. 785 [11th Cir. 2006])

4. A 55-year-old woman applied online for a financial analyst position and other jobs with an employer. The woman had a master's degree in accounting and an MBA in finance, in addition to fifteen years of experience in fields including financial analysis. She was not interviewed or hired for any of these positions. The application form that she completed asked applicants to indicate "the year you started working professionally." The manager responsible for reviewing applications said that she was not aware of the applicant's age at the time that her applications were reviewed. The employer cited lack of current or relevant experience, the superior qualifications of other candidates, and some positions that were not filled at all as reasons for not hiring her. The woman sued. What should the court decide? Why? (*Smiarowski v. Philip* Morris USA, 2005 U.S. Dist. LEXIS 13299 [S.D.N.Y.], *cert. denied*, 2007 U.S. LEXIS 7546)

5. A French citizen received an H-1B visa for a job in the United States in 1995. She changed jobs in 1996, receiving a new H-1B visa. She worked until 1998, when she attended graduate school under an F-1 student visa. While a student, she completed a four-month internship with a company that ultimately offered her a position. Her formal offer letter stated that the company "will sponsor you for your H-1B visa. When you start work we will begin the process of submitting the documentation necessary for you to obtain your H-1B visa." Both parties believed that the visa would be in effect through 2005. It was subsequently discovered that the visa would expire in 2003. A plan to transfer the employee to the company's Dublin office for a year and possibly bring her back thereafter was proposed but not put into effect because the employee insisted on receiving a statement of the employer's intent in writing. The employee ceased working for the company when her visa expired. Was the employer negligent or otherwise in violation of some legal obligation to the visa holder? Why or why not? (*Lucas v. NCR,* 2005 U.S. Dist. LEXIS 5571 [D. DC])

6. A citizen of India was hired to work in the United States as a computer analyst at a salary of $42,000 per year. He received an H-1B visa and came to the United States. On his arrival, he was informed that he would be employed as a gas station cashier and paid at less than the minimum wage. The employee worked for a period of time and then sued. What should the court decide? Why? (*Chopra v. U.S. Professionals,* 2005 Tenn. App. LEXIS 62)

7. Five communities in New Jersey consolidated their fire departments to create a regional fire department. Applicants for entry-level firefighter positions were required to reside in one of the five communities at the time at which they took the statewide civil service test to be considered for employment. Only two of the department's 302 firefighters were African American. Within the member communities, 3.4 percent of the population is African American, compared to 15.8 percent of the population within a ten-mile radius.

Within the tri-county area surrounding these five communities, 37.4 percent of full-time, protective service workers are African American. The regional fire department asserts that the residency requirement is justifiable because it means that firefighters are more familiar with buildings and streets, response times for emergency call-ins are shorter, and (because the communities are heavily Latino) it increases the number of Spanish-speaking firefighters. However, the residency requirement only pertains to an applicant's residence at the time that the exam is taken. Currently employed firefighters are allowed to live wherever they wish and about two-thirds actually reside outside of the five community area. Does this residency requirement create adverse impact against African Americans? Why or why not? (*NAACP v. North Hudson Regional Fire & Rescue*, 742 F. Supp. 2d 501 [D.N.J. 2010])

8. To the extent it occurs, what do you think about the practice of not hiring unemployed persons? Is it lawful? A sensible human resource practice?

9. In your judgment, is there a need for foreign nationals to perform work in the United States? Do existing laws regulating the employment of nonimmigrant foreign nationals in the United States strike the right balance between employers' desire to tap this source of labor and protecting the interests of U.S. workers?

10. Are day laborers a "problem"? What, if any, approach should be adopted for dealing with day laborers?

11. An employer uses the following application form. What questions would you advise this employer not to ask on the application form? Why?

Name _____ Sex _____

Address _____ Date of Birth _____

City _____ State _____ ZIP _____

Are you a U.S. citizen? _____

Place of birth _____

In case of emergency, who should be notified?

_____

Are you single? _____ married? _____
separated? _____ divorced? _____

Number of dependents _____

Do you hold a valid driver's license? _____

Have you ever been employed by this company before? _____ When? _____

Are you a U.S. veteran? _____ Years of service? _____

Type of discharge? _____

Have you ever filed a workers' compensation claim or been injured on the job? _____

Have you ever been convicted of a crime? _____

List all prior employment, including dates of employment, reason for leaving, address and phone number of employer, and supervisor.

I understand that any misrepresentation or omission of material facts will result in nonhire or termination of employment without notice or recourse.

Signature _____ Date _____

CHAPTER 5

Background Checks, References, and Verifying Employment Eligibility

Identifying promising candidates is just the beginning of the hiring process. Employers typically conduct or arrange for background checks on candidates, solicit and provide employment references, and verify eligibility to work in the United States. These activities pose a number of legal concerns, including negligence, defamation, discrimination, and compliance with the Fair Credit Reporting Act and the Immigration Reform and Control Act.

Background Checks

Background checks are used to verify information provided by candidates and to determine whether any disqualifying factors exist. These checks might entail contacting references; verifying past employment and military service; confirming that necessary degrees, licenses, or other credentials are possessed; checking driving records; checking for criminal convictions; examining credit reports; and even inspecting candidates' online personas on social networking and other sites. A basic motive for conducting background checks is the potential liability of employers for the harmful acts of the people they hire.

Employer Responsibility for Employee Wrongdoing

The common law doctrine of **respondeat superior** ("let the master answer") makes employers directly liable for harm to others that occurs when employees act within the scope of their employment. Employees are deemed to be acting within the **scope of employment** when their actions relate to the kind of work that they were hired to perform; take place substantially within the workplace during work hours; and serve, at least partially, the interests of the employer.[1] For example, if while stocking shelves a stock clerk drops an item and injures a shopper, the employer is clearly liable for the customer's injury (although the employer's insurance might cover the costs). Likewise, an employee of an automobile dealer was acting within the scope of employment when, on a public road, he stopped the driver of a truck that the dealership was seeking to repossess and fired shots into the tires of the vehicle. Even though the employee's acts were criminal in nature, the court deemed them within the scope of employment, and the dealership was liable under respondeat superior. In reaching this conclusion, the court emphasized that the employee's sole motive for the confrontation was to repossess the truck on behalf of the dealership. Additionally, the owner of the dealership was aware

---

[1]*Restatement of the Law (Second) of Agency* § 228 (1) (1958).

that the employee was attempting to repossess the truck, that there had been previous unsuccessful attempts to take back the truck, and that the driver of the truck had threatened other employees who had attempted to repossess the vehicle.[2] In contrast, two drivers of an armored car became enraged at a motorist, repeatedly attempted to run his car off the road, aimed a sawed-off shotgun at the motorist, and threatened to "blow off" his head. Even though the drivers were on duty in the employer's truck and brandished weapons provided by the employer, their actions were judged to be outside the scope of employment. Citing the "unprovoked, unusual, and outrageous" nature of their actions, the court further explained: "We cannot consider the actions of [the drivers] to be 'of the kind' they were employed to perform. [The drivers] were not acting to protect the cargo entrusted to them during this incident—rather, personal animus motivated their actions."[3]

JUST THE FACTS

A 24-year-old woman was working as a photographer covering an event known as the "Porn Star Costume Ball." The event was held at a Sacramento hotel. A fire department captain allowed firefighters to attend, to drive their fire trucks there, and to use the occasion to "pick up" women. The captain also attended the event. At least some of the firefighters in attendance were on duty. A number of the firefighters present were drinking alcohol. The woman was asked to take pictures of the firefighters. While she was in the truck taking pictures, she was sexually assaulted by two firefighters, at least one of whom was duty at the time of the assault. This was not the first time that firefighters had been permitted to take fire trucks to bars and parties. Does the city have respondeat superior liability for the harmful acts of these firefighters?

See, *M.P. v. City of Sacramento*, 177 Cal. App. 4th 121 (3d App. Dist. 2009), *review denied*, 2009 Cal. LEXIS 11669.

Negligent Hiring

The legal concept of **negligence** is based on the idea that people sometimes have a duty to other people to exercise reasonable care in carrying out certain activities. When that duty is not met and this failure is a proximate (relatively direct) cause of harm to others, the party that failed to live up to its responsibilities may be found negligent. It is not necessary to show that the negligent party intended for anyone to be harmed. Employers can be found negligent with respect to a wide range of human resource activities, including hiring, retention, supervision, and training. Our focus in this chapter is on the concept of **negligent hiring**. The significance of negligent hiring is that it extends the liability of employers for harm caused by their employees beyond actions undertaken within the scope of employment (the subject of respondeat superior claims) to harmful actions that lie outside the scope of employment, but for which the careless hiring of an unfit employee set the stage. If, under the circumstances, an employer fails to meet its duty to conduct an adequate background check and hires an unfit employee who

---

[2]*Patterson v. Blair*, 172 S.W.3d 361, 371–72 (Ky. 2005).

[3]*Jordon v. Western Distributing Company*, 2005 U.S. App. LEXIS 7566, at 8 (4th Cir.).

ELEMENTS OF A CLAIM

Negligent Hiring

To establish that negligent hiring has occurred, a plaintiff must show the following:

1. A standard of conduct or duty to others exists with respect to an employer taking reasonable steps to avoid hiring unfit employees. The extent of any such duty is based on:

    a) Foreseeability of harm to others if an unfit person is hired for a particular job.

    b) Knowledge of unfitness that the employer had or should have had if proper hiring procedures were used.

    c) Public policy.

2. The employer fails to exercise the proper degree of care and hires an unfit employee.

3. A coworker or another third party is harmed or injured by the unfit employee.

4. The employer's failure to exercise the proper degree of care in hiring is the proximate cause of the harm or injury that occurred.

© Cengage Learning 2013.

---

uses his or her position to inflict harm on others, that employer may be liable for negligent hiring.

Negligent hiring cases often hinge on the first element—whether the employer had a duty to do more to screen out an unfit employee. No single standard is applicable in all cases for how careful an employer's background check must be or whether a background check must be conducted at all. Instead, the degree of care that an employer must exercise in hiring depends on the following factors: public policy, foreseeability, and knowledge.

Some industries and occupations have specific legal requirements for screening employees. For example, criminal background checks are mandatory for entities that hire child-care workers.[4] A child-care facility that fails to meet this specific legal requirement, with the failure resulting in the hiring of an unfit employee who harms others, would certainly be negligent in hiring. Even when the law does not specify a particular screening procedure, courts sometimes look to **public policy** as an indication that a particular type of employment is sensitive and calls for greater care in hiring. For example, in a case involving an employer's failure to check the criminal history of a truck driver, the court gave considerable weight to the fact that trucking is a highly regulated industry and one in which employers have an obligation not to entrust unfit persons with large, potentially lethal vehicles.[5] In the absence of an industry requirement or standard, a contractual obligation (as in a contract between a screening company and an employer) can be the source of a duty to conduct a background check.[6]

---

[4]*National Child Protection Act of 1993*, 42 U.S.C.S. § 5119 (2011).

[5]*Malorney v. B&L Motor Freight*, 496 N.E.2d 1086 (Ill. App. 1986).

[6]*Rucshner v. ADT Security Systems*, 204 P.3d 271, 279 (Wash. App. 2009), *review denied*, 217 P.3d 336 (2009).

Clippings

A study conducted by the Inspector General of the Department of Health and Human Services based on FBI records found that 92 percent of nursing facilities employed one or more persons with criminal convictions. Overall, 5 percent of all nursing home employees had at least one criminal conviction. Most of the convictions were property or drug-related, but convictions for assault and other crimes against persons were also found. Background check requirements differ across states, with ten states requiring both FBI and state records checks, thirty-three states requiring just state records checks, and the remaining states lacking any requirements. Senator Kohl (D-Wisc.) said that "[t]he current system of background checks is haphazard, inconsistent and full of gaping holes in many states. Predators can easily evade detection during the hiring process, securing jobs that allow them to assault, abuse and steal from defenseless elders."

Robert Pear. "Study Finds Criminal Pasts of Nursing Home Workers." *New York Times* (March 3, 2011), A19.

For most jobs, public policy concerns do not enter the picture. Instead, the degree of care that an employer must exercise in hiring depends heavily on **foreseeability**. Employers are not expected to be omniscient in anticipating bad things that employees might do. Instead, the question is whether a "reasonable person" of average intelligence would be able to foresee that hiring an unfit person for this particular position would render injury or harm to others likely. Foreseeability thus stems primarily from the nature of the position into which an employee is being hired. The more sensitive the position and the greater the foreseeability of harm, the more extensive the background check that should occur. Characteristics of jobs that create greater foreseeability include contact with children, older persons, the mentally ill, and other vulnerable segments of the public; jobs involving personal care and medical treatment; relatively unsupervised work; positions entailing responsibility for security and/or the use of firearms; transportation work; and jobs affording substantial access to the homes and personal possessions of others.

The foreseeability of an employee's harmful act is at the center of the court's decision in the *D.D.N. v. FACE* case that follows.

D.D.N. v. FACE
2010 Minn. App. Unpub. LEXIS 244; *review denied,* 2010 Minn. LEXIS 324.

OPINION BY JUDGE STONEBURNER:

Appellant music-festival organizers appeal from a judgment awarding damages to respondent on her claim that a sexual assault by appellant's employee was directly caused by appellant's negligent-hiring practices. Appellant asserts that it had no duty to respondent and that the district court erred by failing to summarily dismiss respondent's claim. We affirm.

Appellant FACE, Festivals and Concert Events, produces an annual country-music festival held in Detroit Lakes, Minnesota, that draws thousands of patrons, many of whom camp at the venue. In 2006, respondent D.D.N. was sexually assaulted at her campsite at the festival by Eric Fanning, who had been employed by FACE to work at the festival. Fanning pleaded guilty to third-degree criminal sexual conduct.

* * * The facts about Fanning's history, hiring, and assault are not in dispute. Fanning has a 1994 conviction of first-degree sexual assault committed in Colorado in 1993. Before he moved to Minnesota in

February or March of 2006, Fanning was in a hospital in Colorado for drug addiction. He had been fired from three or four jobs and was unemployed and homeless when he was hired by FACE in 2006.

Fanning, like many FACE temporary employees, filled out an on-line application for employment at the 2006 WE Fest. Fanning falsely identified the VA Medical Center in St. Cloud as his address. He did not identify anyone as a reference and described himself as self-employed. Fanning cannot recall if he was interviewed by telephone before he was hired or whether he was informed by e-mail or letter that he had been hired as second-shift "camping staff: front" to admit people into the campground, exchange tickets for wristbands, assist campers, answer questions, and give directions. Fanning was permitted to camp and was given wristbands that gave him access to all parts of the festival and a T-shirt that identified him as festival staff. His employment by FACE lasted 32 hours and ended on the evening of the last day of the festival. He assaulted D.D.N. sometime before 7:00 p.m. that evening.

FACE's 2006 employment director for the festival, Marilyn Sue Holt, along with two assistants, hired approximately 1,400 people for the 2006 festival, mostly through the internet. Applicants were asked to provide their name, address, age, social security number, prior employment history, and what job they were interested in. People who had not previously worked at a festival were subject to a telephone interview, but FACE had no criteria regarding what information should be obtained from an applicant in the interview, and there were no established questions. * * * There was no requirement to ask an applicant about criminal or employment history or references. There were no reference or criminal-history checks. Holt stated that applicants were hired if they "sound like good people" on the telephone. * * *

FACE's awareness of the vulnerability of its female festival patrons at the time it hired Fanning is also undisputed. Holt testified in her deposition that music and drinking are two of the main attractions of the festival and that FACE knew that festival patrons became vulnerable to being victimized due to alcohol consumption. Holt agreed that some individuals, including rapists, would not be good candidates to work at the festival and stated that exposing patrons to individuals with such backgrounds was a "big concern." She considered it common sense not to put a man with that type of background in an environment where he could take advantage of a vulnerable person under the influence of alcohol. She acknowledged that

knowing whether an applicant had a criminal conviction would have been important information.

D.D.N.'s complaint alleged that FACE had a "duty to make sure its employees ... were fit to perform the jobs they were hired for and not to hire convicted felons (sexual offenders) in positions of authority such as acting in the capacity of security personnel" and had a "duty to make sure it did a reasonable background check on its security personnel as such individuals would foreseeably come into contact with festival-goers who had conflicts and also members of the opposite sex who were under the influence of alcohol."

In its motion for summary judgment, FACE argued that there was no evidence supporting the allegation that Fanning was hired to provide security or at any time worked security at the festival, and that there is no "bright line" legal duty to perform criminal background checks for the temporary job of "camping staff front" for which Fanning was hired. FACE argued that there was no evidence that it failed to make a sufficient inquiry into Fanning's fitness for the job for which he was hired and that it had no duty to perform a criminal background check for that position. * * *

At trial, the district court instructed the jury, in relevant part, that "an employer is negligent in hiring an employee if the employer knew or should have known, at the time of hiring, that the employee posed a threat of physical injury to others because of the circumstance[s] of the employment" and that "the test for determining liability [for negligent hiring] is whether or not the employer exercised reasonable care in hiring the employee given the totality of the circumstances." The jury found that FACE was negligent in hiring Fanning and that such negligence was a direct cause of D.D.N's harm.

* * * An employer's liability for hiring is predicated on the negligence of an employer in placing a person with known propensities, or propensities which should have been discovered by reasonable investigation, in an employment position in which, because of the circumstances of the employment, it should have been foreseeable that the hired individual posed a threat of injury to others. * * *

In *Ponticas* [an earlier Minnesota negligent hiring case], the supreme court concluded that because the tenant-victim of a sexual assault by an apartment manager met her assailant as a direct result of his employment and the employer-owner-operator of the apartment complex received a benefit from employing the manager, the employer owed the tenants a duty to exercise reasonable care in hiring a resident manager.

"The scope of the duty was commensurate with the risks of the situation." FACE relies on *Ponticas* to argue that because Fanning's duties did not constitute a high risk of injury to a foreseeable victim, his hiring required only "slight care." But this argument conflates the legal question of the existence of a duty with the fact question of whether a legal duty was breached.

FACE also relies on *Yunker v. Honeywell, Inc.*, affirming, in part, summary judgment to an employer on a claim of negligent hiring because the employer did not owe or breach a duty to the victim at the time of hiring. In that case, Honeywell re-employed a former employee, Randy Landin, after he was released from prison for the strangulation death of a former co-worker at Honeywell. After rehire, Landin began to harass a co-worker who had spurned his romantic interest. The co-worker sought assistance from Honeywell and requested a transfer. The day before the co-worker found a death threat scratched on her locker door was the last day Landin came to work. He formally resigned from employment ten days later. Eight days after he resigned from his employment, Landin shot the co-worker to death on her driveway. He was convicted of first-degree murder.

* * * Honeywell, for purposes of summary judgment, stipulated that it failed to exercise reasonable care in hiring and supervision, but argued that it owed no legal duty to the victim. Honeywell noted that, unlike the employer in *Ponticas*, who provided a dangerous resident apartment manager with a passkey to tenant's apartments, Honeywell's employment of Landin did not enable him to commit the act of violence against his co-worker, which occurred at her home. This court found merit in that argument, citing cases from other jurisdictions defining an employer's duty of reasonable care as largely dependent on the type of responsibilities associated with the particular job. *Yunker* held that Honeywell did not owe a duty to the victim at the time of Landin's hire because Landin "was employed as a maintenance worker whose job responsibilities entailed no exposure to the general public and required only limited contact with coemployees," and the ultimate victim "was not a reasonably foreseeable victim at the time Landin was hired." FACE argues that Fanning's employment, likewise, did not implicate any duty to festival attendees including D.D.N.

But the deposition testimony … demonstrate[s] that FACE was hyperaware of and concerned about the vulnerability of its female patrons and the risk of sexual assault at the festival. Fanning's duties put him in contact with everyone who camped in the campground where he worked; his access to the campsites was unlimited. Fanning had access to campers, their driver's licenses, and knowledge about where and with whom each camper was camped. Plainly, Fanning's employment put him in contact with the general public, including the vulnerable female patrons about whom FACE was concerned. Fanning's criminal history, employment history, and falsification of address, which were discoverable with minimal inquiry, were acknowledged by Holt to make him ineligible for employment by FACE.

We conclude that Fanning's circumstances are more similar to those of the facts in *Ponticas* than to those of the facts in *Yunker* and that the district court did not err in rejecting FACE's argument that, as a matter of law, it had no duty to D.D.N. with regard to hiring festival-campground employees. * * *

FACE argues that the "burdensome" best-hiring practices urged by D.D.N. in this case would have deprived Fanning of work to which he was entitled and raises "the problem of disparate impact and/or disparate treatment of protected classes of people." FACE argues that because "people with criminal histories are frequently minorities, [minorities] are the ones most likely to be adversely affected by" the standards urged by D.D.N.'s expert witness. FACE argues that for these public policy reasons "there should be no duty." We find no merit in this argument. FACE's argument relies in part on its mischaracterization of the duty owed as a duty to perform a criminal-background check. But, as the district court's summary-judgment memorandum implicitly stated, and the jury instructions explicitly stated, FACE's duty was to use reasonable care under the circumstances. We cannot conclude that imposition of such a duty is inconsistent with public policy.

CASE QUESTIONS

1. What was the legal issue in this case? What did the court decide?
2. How are the elements of a negligent hiring case satisfied in this case?
3. Given the nature of the job, what type of background check should have been performed? Are there other things that this employer could or should have done to avoid harm to its customers?
4. Does the court turn the professed concern of FACE staff for the safety of campers against the employer? If so, is that fair?
5. Do you agree with the court's decision? Why or why not?

Foreseeability of harm is a slippery concept and court decisions are not entirely consistent. In a case involving a furniture store delivery person who assaulted a woman to whom he had delivered furniture, the court rejected the employer's argument that there was little foreseeability because the job involved only "incidental contact" with customers and did not provide the employee with a key or other means of direct access to the apartment. The court focused instead on how the position carried with it "indicia of authority" (e.g., uniform, delivery papers) that led customers to open their doors and readily permit entrance to delivery persons.[7] In another case, an employee hired to go door-to-door selling home security systems raped the teenage daughter of a woman to whom he had spoken about purchasing a system. The woman had declined to do so, but as the employee was leaving the teenage daughter called out from her bedroom window and said that her mother had been rude. This led to a conversation, numerous telephone calls from the employee, and (two months later) a break-in during which the assault was perpetrated. The court found evidence of foreseeability of harm in the basic fact that the employee was hired for a job that entailed extensive contact with the public and going around to peoples' homes. Although these efforts were directed toward adult home-owners, it was inevitable that they would place the employee in contact with other family members.[8] Likewise, in the *D.D.N.* case, the court discerned foreseeability of harm in the fact that the employee's position as a member of the festival staff—temporary and low-level as the job was—put the employee in potential contact with all campers, gave him unfettered access to the entire camp grounds, and provided him with knowledge of the locations and companions of campers. In particular, the position gave him access to vulnerable female patrons whom the festival organizers recognized as being at substantial risk for sexual assault.

In a case involving the abduction and murder of a woman by an employee with a history of violent sexual offenses, the court concluded that there was not sufficient foreseeability of harm.[9] The man was hired to oversee the janitorial work of other employees and given a van to use for this purpose. Because the victim was not an employee, client, or customer, she "was not within the class of persons that would render defendant's conduct negligent, and the risk of harm to her was not foreseeable."[10] Nor did the fact that the company van was used in the commission of the crime render it foreseeable, since the employee was not carrying out job duties when he encountered the woman and "mere facilitation" was not sufficient to make the harm foreseeable. Courts sometimes recast the issue of foreseeability in terms of whether a "special relationship" exists between the employer and the person harmed. A special relationship exists when, among other things, the meeting in which harm occurred was a direct consequence of employment and the employer would have received some benefit, if only indirect, from the meeting had the harmful act not occurred. In one case using this approach, an employee was hired to deliver pizza coupons door-to-door. The employee had a criminal record of sexual assault that the employer failed to detect. In the course of distributing coupons, the employee happened upon a female college student waiting at a bus stop, explained that he was working for the pizza company, and convinced her to accept a ride with him. The employee then abducted and raped the woman. Despite the fact that the employee

---

[7]*Tallahassee Furniture Company v. Harrison,* 583 So. 2d 744, at 752 (Fla. App. 1991), *review denied,* 595 So. 2d 558 (Fla. 1992).

[8]*Rucshner,* at 281.

[9]*Wilberger v. Creative Building Maintenance,* 2009 U.S. Dist. LEXIS 52636, *affirmed,* 2010 U.S. App. LEXIS (9th Cir. 2010).

[10]*Wilberger,* at 9.

was on the job at the time of the meeting and invoked the name of his employer to gain her trust, the court concluded that because the woman was not a customer or in some other special relationship to the employer, the company had no legal obligation to do more to protect her from an unfit employee.[11]

Knowledge refers in this context to the fact that the employer was aware, or should have been if proper screening procedures had been followed, that the person hired was unfit. Thus, in contrast to foreseeability, which focuses on the position, knowledge pertains to those characteristics of the person being hired that render him unfit. Importantly, if an employee is hired without an adequate background check and that person proceeds to harm others, the employer still will not be liable for negligent hiring if information indicating unfitness was not available to be found (e.g., the employee had no prior criminal convictions). In *D.D.N.*, the primary evidence of unfitness that should have been discovered through an adequate background check was a prior conviction for sexual assault, although his multiple terminations from previous jobs would also be distinct "red flags." The evidence of unfitness must bear a relationship to the nature of the position and the type of harm that occurred to constitute "knowledge." Likewise, the evidence of unfitness must be relatively specific. Because high-aggression personality is not the equivalent of "violent," an employer that hired a salesperson despite results of a preemployment psychological test that placed the salesperson in a "high-aggression" category was not liable when that salesperson got into a fight with a motorist.[12] In contrast, when an employer had firsthand knowledge of an employee's violent tendencies because it fired him for threatening to assault a supervisor, its decision to rehire the employee (who said that he would file discrimination charges otherwise) resulted in a finding of negligent hiring when the rehired employee assaulted a coworker.[13]

Although the crux of most negligent hiring cases is whether the employer was obligated to do a more thorough background check, plaintiffs must also show that their employers failed to live up to their duties and that these failures were proximate causes of harm. Foreseeability and **proximity** are clearly related; foreseeability pertains to whether harm could be anticipated before the fact, and proximity involves the connection between events as they actually unfolded. A court found that there was not sufficient proximity to establish negligence in the case of an apartment building porter who sexually abused an infant. In reaching this conclusion, the court noted that the abuse occurred twenty-seven years after the employee's manslaughter conviction and eighteen years after he was hired, the child's mother was a friend of the employee and named him the child's godfather, and the mother allowed the employee to have unsupervised visits with the infant. These facts "severed the causal nexus" between any negligence in hiring the porter and harm to the infant.[14] In contrast, a furniture company was liable for negligently hiring a delivery person even though the assault occurred three months after a delivery had been made and the woman allowed the man into the apartment after he asked to use the bathroom. However, the delivery person was in uniform, had returned to the apartment on the pretext that a receipt was needed related to the earlier delivery, and the woman recognized and allowed him in due to the prior delivery.[15]

---

[11]*Poe v. Domino's Pizza*, 139 F.3d 617 (8th Cir. 1998).

[12]*Thatcher v. Brennan*, 657 F. Supp. 6, 12 (S.D. Miss. 1986), *affirmed*, 816 F.2d 675 (5th Cir. 1987).

[13]*Tecumseh Products Co. v. Rigdon*, 250 Ga. App. 739 (2001).

[14]*Ford v. Gildin*, 1994 N.Y. App. Div. LEXIS 5634, at 5.

[15]*Tallahassee Furniture*, at 756.

JUST THE FACTS

A man was hired as a team leader at a fast food restaurant and shortly thereafter made a night manager. The man had two felony convictions in Indiana related to the delivery of crack cocaine. These convictions occurred nine years prior to his hiring. The drug convictions were not discovered when the man was hired because the restaurant, for cost reasons, decided to limit the check of criminal records to one county only (a wider search including Indiana would have cost $35, rather than the $11 they paid for the single county search). The manager conspired with another person to rob his own store and split the proceeds. On the evening of the robbery, he devised an excuse to leave the store before the money in the registers had been put in the safe. The store was left in the hands of a mentally disabled employee who had worked there for fourteen years. The schemers did not anticipate that this employee would put the money from the registers away in the safe. When the other robber entered the store through the drive-in window and found the registers empty, he ordered the employee to open the safe. After the employee repeatedly said that he didn't have the combination to the safe, the robber shot and killed him. The manager's role in the robbery came to light shortly thereafter. Is the restaurant liable for negligently hiring an unfit manager? Why or why not?

See, *Barton v. Whataburger*, 276 S.W.3d 456 (Tex. App. 2008), *review denied*, 2010 Tex. LEXIS 360.

Conducting Background Checks: General Advice   The foregoing discussion of negligent hiring holds some general implications for background checks. *Depending on the circumstances, an adequate background check might include verifying current and previous residences; contacting references; verifying past employment and military service; verifying the possession of degrees, licenses, and other credentials; checking driving and criminal records; examining Internet sites and postings; and examining credit reports. Although none of these measures are legally required in all cases, employers should at minimum follow their own established background check procedures.* If an unfit employee is hired and harms someone, it becomes difficult to explain why the employer did not at least follow its own policies, which were presumably crafted in recognition of the dangers inherent in hiring unfit employees. *Employers should be especially wary of last-minute, rushed hiring decisions* because standard hiring procedures are likely to give way to expediency. Background checks are likely to be fruitless if carried out in a perfunctory, pro forma manner. Instead, a concerted effort to get at the truth is needed. *It is critical that inconsistencies and gaps in information provided by applicants be detected and confronted.* If these gaps and inconsistencies cannot be cleared up in interviews and through corroboration by other sources, hiring should not occur.

Because foreseeability is a key element of negligence claims, *background checks should be more extensive in hiring for those positions in which there is greater chance that unfit employees could do serious harm to others.* Jobs that present high foreseeability of harm (e.g., installers, delivery persons, medical aides) are not necessarily those regarded by employers as important. Since knowledge means that the employer knew or should have known that the person hired was unfit, *it is important for employers to document all efforts at obtaining information on job candidates, even when those efforts are not successful* (e.g., references did not respond or were uninformative). Under these circumstances, it is more difficult to argue that an employer should have known about disqualifying information. Also, *if an employer asks about something that is important and about which the applicant is apt to lie (e.g., criminal background), it is important to attempt to corroborate applicants' answers. If, despite the inadvisability of doing so, an employer opts to hire a needed employee prior to completing a background check, the employer should still finish the background check—but only if willing to use the information of unfitness that is discovered as a basis for terminating the employee.* Otherwise, the employer is left with actual knowledge of unfitness and even greater vulnerability to a negligent hiring or retention claim.

Privacy Rights and Background Checks

Negligent hiring claims are premised on employers not doing enough to screen out unfit employees. But is it is possible for employers to do too much and delve so deeply into the backgrounds of applicants as to invade their privacy? A fuller discussion of the privacy rights of job candidates and employees will be deferred until later (see Chapters 6 and 17). However, in a recent case involving NASA contract employees, the Supreme Court left open the possibility that employees enjoy a constitutional right to informational privacy when being subjected to background checks by government agencies.[16] The contract employees—scientists, engineers, and administrative personnel—were, in the aftermath of 9/11, subjected to the extensive background checks required of federal employees. They specifically objected to detailed questions about prior drug treatment and broad, open-ended inquiries into their fitness for service directed to former employers, landlords, neighbors, and other sources. The Court assumed without explicitly deciding that a constitutional right to privacy exists in the context of background checks but found that the challenged inquiries were reasonable and served legitimate government security and employment interests. Furthermore, the government was not required to show the necessity of its inquiries or that the questions were no more intrusive than necessary.[17] Thus, any constitutional limits on invasive background checks—which would only apply when it is the government, and not private employers, doing the questioning—are not likely to be very stringent.

Another interesting privacy-related question is whether employers have the right to require applicants to provide them with passwords and other means of access to Internet and social media sites that contain background information on those candidates. Anecdotally, this appears to be a growing practice. Legislation has thus far been proposed in one state to make this illegal, but that legislation did not become law.[18]

We turn now to issues surrounding particular aspects of background checks: criminal records, credit reports, and references.

Criminal Records

One of the clearest indications that a prospective employee might be unfit for a position is a history of criminal activity. Failing to check for a criminal record is probably the surest route to negligent hiring. However, legal issues affect both access to information about criminal histories and use of that information. Conviction information is not always readily available and should not be used to exclude all persons with criminal

---

[16]*National Aeronautics and Space Administration v. Nelson*, 131 S. Ct. 746 (2011).

[17]*Nelson*, at 760–61.

[18]Donald G. Aplin. "Bill to Bar Social Media Password Demands by Maryland Employers Dies in 2011 Session." *Daily Labor Report* 79 (April 25, 2011), A-6.

histories from hire. To put this issue in proper perspective, it is important to realize that the number of people in the United States who have been convicted of crimes is quite large. The United States imprisons far more people than any other country in the world. With 5 percent of the world's population, the United States has nearly 25 percent of the world's prisoners.[19] In 2006, an estimated 2.4 million people were in federal and state prisons. Some 5 million people were on probation or parole. This translates to nearly one in every thirty-one adults in the United States having been incarcerated or otherwise under the supervision of the criminal justice system in 2006.[20] About 700,000 persons are released from jail each year.[21] The number of people who have had brushes with the law at some point in their lives—including indiscretions while attending college—is much higher. An estimated 65 million people in the United States, or about a quarter of all adults, have some type of criminal history.[22] At the same time, the vast majority (over 90 percent) of employers conduct criminal background checks for at least some of their positions. Thus, policies limiting employment based on criminal histories stand to affect significant numbers of people.

Clippings

Ayanna Spikes is looking for a job. She studied psychology and finished at the University of California at Berkeley in 2010. Since then, she has been turned down for more than a dozen jobs. While her predicament is hardly unique in a tough job market, her past may be getting in the way of landing a job. Fourteen years ago, at the age of 24, Ms. Spikes was convicted of robbing a video store. She spent eight months in prison and the experience set her life on a different course. She has had a clean record since, but despite her commendable efforts to obtain an education, Ms. Spikes finds herself among a large number of Americans whose criminal histories are impeding their ability to obtain employment.

Erica Goode. "Criminal Past Makes a Job Search Even Harder." *New York Times* (April 29, 2011), A17.

It is important to distinguish between **arrests** and **convictions**. Individuals who are arrested ("picked up" by the police and taken to the police station with the intent of being charged with crimes) are often released without actually being charged. They might be picked up for questioning due to proximity to a crime, mistaken identity, or any of a number of other reasons. Even if charged, a grand jury might decline to indict or the government might be unable to prove its case. Our system of law operates on the presumption that persons accused of crimes are innocent until proven guilty. Thus, an arrest cannot be presumed to say anything valid about a person's character or fitness.

---

[19]Adam Liptak. "Inmate Count in U.S. Dwarfs Other Nations'." *New York Times* (April 28, 2008), A 1.

[20]Solomon Moore. "Justice Dept. Numbers Show Prison Trends." *New York Times* (December 6, 2007), A 16.

[21]Kevin P. McGowan. "EEOC Weighs Guidance on Employers' Use of Criminal Records in Employment Decisions." *Daily Labor Report* 225 (November 21, 2008), A 6.

[22]Derrick Cain. "Many Employers Screen Applicants for Criminal Records, Report Says." *Daily Labor Report* 56 (March 23, 2011), A 2.

On the other hand, a conviction for a crime, following either a trial or a guilty plea, is stronger evidence of lack of fitness. However, crimes differ greatly in severity. **Felonies** are more serious crimes for which imprisonment of more than a year in a state or federal prison may be imposed. **Misdemeanors** are less serious criminal offenses for which fines and/or imprisonment of up to one year, usually in a county facility, may be imposed. Police, prosecutors, and judges all exercise considerable discretion in enforcing criminal laws. Thus, criminal records reflect the judgments of these actors as well as the behaviors of individuals.

Conviction records, unless sealed or "expunged" (removed from the person's record) by a court, are public records and theoretically accessible. However, state laws sometimes limit access to this information and allow people to apply for jobs without revealing their criminal histories. Law enforcement agencies do not routinely make their comprehensive national databases available to employers. Retrieving information about convictions is not as simple as just logging on to the Internet. Decentralized court systems and record keeping mean that a search for conviction records in the area that the job candidate currently resides will not unearth convictions that occurred in other states (or, for that matter, other countries). People with unsavory pasts tend to change their names, move around a lot, and do other things that confound tracking their records. Many employers avoid dealing directly with these problems by relying on the services of background checking companies or private investigators. But whoever assumes the responsibility of checking for criminal convictions, *the comprehensiveness of the search is an important factor. A search limited to a single state might not yield the relevant information.*

To the extent that good information about criminal history can be obtained, what should employers do with it? If the information indicates unfitness for positions where there is foreseeability of harm to others, both the threat of negligent hiring suits and basic ethics clearly dictate that unfit candidates should not be hired. However, problems arise when employers overreact to this legitimate concern by seeking to exclude anyone with a prior criminal conviction (or worse, who has been arrested). There have been successful legal challenges to such policies based on their potential to create adverse impact. How does this work? Under federal law, not having been arrested or convicted for a crime is a neutral requirement rather than a protected class characteristic (assuming that criminal histories are treated the same, regardless of the applicant's race). However, this neutral requirement is likely to exclude persons of color at a much higher rate than whites. African Americans and Latinos are far more likely to be both arrested and convicted of crimes. Statistics show, for example, that African Americans are nearly six times more likely to be incarcerated than whites.[23] This racial disparity in incarceration rates is even more stark for young African American males, who are seven to eight times more likely to be imprisoned than young white males.[24] Hispanics are incarcerated at nearly twice the rate of non-Hispanic whites. While racial disparities in incarceration rates differ markedly across states,[25] the general effect of relying on criminal histories is to screen out African Americans and Latinos at much higher rates than other races and national origins. Thus, a prima facie case of adverse impact is likely.

---

[23]Marc Mauer and Ryan S. King. *Uneven Justice: State Rates of Incarceration by Race and Ethnicity.* Washington, DC: The Sentencing Project (July 2007), 3.

[24]McGowan. "EEOC Weighs Guidance."

[25]Mauer and King, 11.

Is the absence of prior arrests or convictions a defensible requirement? Recall that even sharply disproportionate outcomes can be defended in adverse impact claims when the neutral requirements that produce them are "job-related and consistent with business necessity." The job-relatedness of prior arrests is difficult to argue for most jobs (law enforcement jobs perhaps excepted) because it is unclear whether arrests mean anything about a person's prior behavior or character.[26] EEOC guidelines say that employers "will seldom be able to justify making broad general inquiries about an employee's or applicant's arrests" and that employers using arrest information must "evaluate whether the arrest record reflects the applicant's conduct."[27] Convictions have a stronger claim to job-relatedness and business necessity, but the EEOC and some courts have held that rather than simply slam the door of employment opportunity shut on anyone who has a prior conviction, employers need to consider how serious the offense is, what its relationship is to the job in question, and how long ago the offense occurred.[28] However, this does not preclude the adoption of policies denying employment to all persons who have committed specified types of offenses, provided that it can be shown that such policies distinguish between applicants who pose an unacceptable level of risk and those that do not.[29] *Thus, employers should generally not use information related to prior arrests in making hiring decisions. Information about prior convictions can and often should be used. However, employers should not exclude all persons with prior criminal convictions. Employers should consider the seriousness of the offense, its relationship to the job in question, and its recency. Policies must be drawn narrowly enough to distinguish persons who pose genuine risk from those who do not.*

Practical Considerations What policy would you recommend an employer adopt regarding use of criminal history in hiring decisions? Why? Would the policy differ according to the type of job in question? If so, how?

Credit Reports

Most often, when people think about credit reports, they have in mind information that is gathered about their creditworthiness and used by financial institutions in deciding whether to make loans or offer credit cards. However, credit reports are also used by employers in making hiring decisions. And the legal definition of what constitutes a credit report is very broad, extending well beyond purely financial information.

Fair Credit Reporting Act

The **Fair Credit Reporting Act (FCRA)**[30] is the major federal law regulating the gathering, sharing, and use of information by employers and consumer reporting agencies. It distinguishes two types of credit reports: consumer reports and investigative reports. The FCRA defines a **consumer credit report** as

any written, oral or other communication of any information by a consumer reporting agency bearing on a consumer's credit worthiness, credit standing, credit capacity, character, general reputation, personal characteristics, or mode of living which is

[26]*Gregory v. Litton Systems*, 316 F. Supp. 401 (C.D. Cal. 1970), *affirmed.*, 472 F.2d 631 (9th Cir. 1972).

[27]U.S. Equal Employment Opportunity Commission. "Policy Guidance on the Consideration of Arrest Records in Employment Decisions under Title VII of the Civil Rights Act of 1964." No. 915.061 (September 7, 1990).

[28]*Green v. Missouri Pacific Railroad*, 523 F.2d 1290, at 1298 (8th Cir. 1975).

[29]*El v. Southeastern Pennsylvania Transportation Authority*, 479 F.3d 232, 245 (3d Cir. 2007).

[30]15 U.S.C.S. § 1681 et seq. (2011).

expected to be used or collected in whole or part for the purpose of serving as a factor in establishing the consumer's eligibility for ... employment purposes.[31]

An **investigative report** contains similar information but is also based on personal interviews with friends, neighbors, or other associates. Notice that although these reports may contain financial information such as bankruptcy filings, repayment of loans, and credit scores, they can go far beyond financial matters to reach all other aspects of background checks, including contacting references and examining conviction records. To implicate the FCRA, the information must be obtained from a **consumer reporting agency**. This term is also broadly defined and includes any entity that regularly gathers or evaluates information on consumers to furnish reports to third parties. The term clearly encompasses companies that perform background checks for employers.

Studies have shown that credit reports are frequently rife with errors and inconsistencies.[32] The FCRA is a response to the problem of inaccurate information being gathered and sold about people, resulting in their being denied jobs, mortgages, and other opportunities. It has many detailed provisions. One important requirement is that *a prospective employer must disclose to a job applicant that a credit report will be obtained and receive the applicant's authorization to do so.* The consent form must be solely for this purpose; a statement on an application form will not suffice. Proof of consent is then forwarded to the consumer reporting agency with the request for information. Although the background check cannot proceed without the employee's consent, an employer does not have to consider for employment someone who declines to authorize gathering and sharing of information about him. It also appears that "blanket authorizations," permitting an employer to obtain an employee's credit report again in the future should the need arise, are permissible under the FCRA.[33]

If, based *in any part* on information from a consumer credit report, an employer intends to take an **adverse action** (such as not hiring or promoting) against a job applicant or an employee, the *employer must first provide the individual with a "pre-adverse action disclosure."* The disclosure is to include a copy of the individual's consumer credit report and a statement of his rights under the FCRA. The purpose of this requirement is to provide individuals with notice that negative information about them exists and to afford them the opportunity to address possible inaccuracies. However, employers are under no obligation to reconsider a candidate, even if erroneous information is subsequently corrected by the consumer reporting agency. Furthermore, the FCRA does not cite any specific period of time that must elapse before an adverse action can be finalized. A court concluded that while the statutory language requires that the two notices not be simultaneous, an employer did not violate the FCRA by waiting only fourteen days before issuing a final decision.[34] *After taking an adverse action based on a consumer credit report, an "adverse action notice" must be provided.*

In *Burghy v. Dayton Racquet Club*, the court considers both the adequacy of the employer's disclosure that a credit report would be obtained for employment use and whether the proper procedures for carrying out adverse actions based on the contents of a credit report were followed.

---

[31]15 U.S.C.S. § 1681a(d)(1) (2011).

[32]Kelly Gallagher. "Rethinking the Fair Credit Reporting Act: When Requesting Credit Reports for 'Employment Purposes' Goes Too Far." 91 *Iowa Law Review* 1593, 1598 (July 2006).

[33]*Kelchner v. Sycamore Manor Health Center*, 2005 U.S. App. LEXIS 3697, at 8 (3d Cir.).

[34]*Johnson v. ADP Screening and Selection Services*, 2011 U.S. Dist. LEXIS 18361 (D. Minn.).

Burghy v. Dayton Racquet Club
695 F. Supp. 2d 689 (S.D. Ohio 2010)

OPINION BY DISTRICT JUDGE RICE:

This action arises out of events that occurred between January 15 and January 23, 2008. Plaintiff, Mandy Burghy, was an employee of the Dayton Racquet Club ("Dayton Racquet Club"), an athletic and social club.... * * * Burghy began working in the accounting department of the Dayton Racquet Club, and remained there for seven years. As an Accounting Assistant for Dayton Racquet Club, Burghy handled tasks related to accounts receivable, accounts payable, billing, bill reconciliation, check processing, credit card payment processing and other duties. The Dayton Racquet Club requires all employees engaged in various "critical positions" to occasionally submit to certain investigations of their personal or criminal history in order to ensure that they remain eligible for employment. * * * [A]ll accounting employees were required to submit to a credit history check as part of their continued employment. On January 15, 2008, Plaintiff signed a disclosure form purporting to authorize the Dayton Racquet Club to obtain her credit history report as part of her continued employment in the accounting department.

* * * The next day, January 16, 2008, Burghy was called in for a meeting with Kevin Round, the general manager at Dayton Racquet Club, and Bruce Stricker, her immediate supervisor in the accounting department. The meeting was called to discuss the results of the credit check that had been performed and how it might affect Burghy's employment going forward. The credit check had revealed various adverse items, with the cumulative result being that Burghy apparently did not meet the minimum criteria that Dayton Racquet Club had set for her position. Although exactly what transpired during the meeting is a matter of disagreement between the parties, it is undisputed that, at the conclusion of the meeting, Burghy was told to go home, and that she would never again report for work as an accounting assistant at the Dayton Racquet Club. Also on January 16, Dayton Racquet Club generated a letter that was mailed to Burghy, and which she received shortly thereafter. The letter indicated that the information in Burghy's credit report might, or might not, affect her employment status going forward, and that no final decision had yet been reached.

Enclosed with the letter was a copy of the report on her credit background that had been discussed in the meeting that same day. On January 23, 2008, Dayton Racquet Club sent a second letter to Burghy, indicating that her services were no longer needed and that she was terminated. The letter indicated that information contained in the recent credit report contributed to the decision to terminate her. * * *

The Fair Credit Reporting Act, which gives rise to the majority of Plaintiff's claims, is a federal law enacted to set standards for the reporting of credit information and to protect consumers from inaccurate disclosures of credit information and other abuses. * * * It is permissible for an employer to procure a credit report for employment purposes. * * *

Consumer reports may address topics broader than an individual's credit history; for example, consumer reports may uncover criminal records. Herein, however, both parties are concerned only with the credit information contained in Burghy's report of January 15, and the terms "consumer report" and "credit report" are used interchangeably by the Court.

On March 14, 2008, Plaintiff filed her Complaint against Dayton Racquet Club and its parent company ... asserting [two primary] causes of action [under the FCRA]: (1) Failing to provide a clear and conspicuous disclosure that Plaintiff's credit report would be obtained for employment purposes ...; (2) Taking adverse action against Plaintiff before providing her with a copy of her credit report.... * * *

One protection the FCRA affords consumers is its requirement that employers seeking to obtain a consumer report on a current or potential employee disclose that such a report "may be obtained for employment purposes." "A person may not procure a consumer report, or cause a consumer report to be procured, for employment purposes with respect to any consumer, unless: (i) A *clear and conspicuous* disclosure has been made in writing to the consumer at any time before the report is procured or caused to be procured, in a document that consists solely of the disclosure, that a consumer report may be obtained for employment purposes[.]" * * *

... [T]he statute, unfortunately, does not define "clear and conspicuous".... * * * [O]ther Circuits have looked for guidance from decisions under the

Uniform Commercial Code ("UCC") and the Truth in Lending Act ("TILA"), both of which invoke the same "clear and conspicuous" language. The Court finds their reasons for doing so persuasive: [W]e believe it is appropriate to draw upon the wealth of UCC and TILA case law in determining the meaning of "clear and conspicuous" under the FCRA. The UCC defines conspicuous as "so written, displayed, or presented that a reasonable person against [whom] it is to operate ought to have noticed it." When evaluating a disclaimer of warranty against this standard, we have looked to how many times a customer was made aware of the notice, whether the notice was on the front or back of the document in question, whether the language of the notice was emphasized in some way (such as by bolding the text or by employing all capitals) and whether the notice was set off from the rest of the document so as to draw attention to it.

Plaintiff does not argue that the language of the disclosure was poorly drafted, overly technical, or otherwise incomprehensible. Rather, Plaintiff's argument is that "[a] reasonable person would not have noticed that a consumer report would be obtained for employment purposes." Thus, the issue the Court must address is whether or not the disclosure was sufficiently conspicuous, not whether it was clear. * * *

An examination of the disclosure form indicates that it is conspicuous as to the fact that a consumer report could be used for employment purposes. In the center of the only page of the document are three bullet points that present the background check requirements for various positions at Dayton Racquet Club. The third bullet point provides as follows:

"*Accounting/financial*, General Manager, General Manager in Training, and certain Society and Owner's Club *positions*, as well as solo independent contractors performing similar functions/services, *require credit history checks*, and I understand credit-reporting agencies, credit/bankruptcy litigation, and credit reports may also be included." * * * Although the words that comprise the bullet points are in the same color and size as the rest of the document, the question is whether there is "something about the way that the notice is presented … such that the consumer's attention will be drawn to it." The bullet points serve exactly this function. * * * Anyone who reads the bullet points will realize the background checks mentioned are for employment purposes.

* * * The FCRA does demand that the revelation that a consumer report may be obtained for employment purposes be made "in a document that consists solely of [that] disclosure." * * * The Act specifically states that the language *authorizing* the employer to obtain a consumer report … may be included alongside the language *disclosing* that such a report may be used for employment purposes…. Including the explanatory language alongside the disclosure language is logical, given their relationship, and the Court cannot conclude that the presence of the former renders the latter inconspicuous.

* * * In sum, the disclosure presented to Plaintiff in this case is unlike those that have been found inconspicuous under the FCRA and similar laws. Herein, the disclosure was on the front side of a one-page document, and not concealed on the back; it employed reasonably sized type throughout; it used bullet points to call attention to the disclosures, and, indeed, it appears that Plaintiff was actually aware of the employment-related function of the consumer reports.

Plaintiff [also] argues that Defendants violated [the section of the FCRA] which provides that: "[I]n using a consumer report for employment purposes, before taking any adverse action based in whole or in part on the report, the person intending to take such adverse action shall provide to the consumer to whom the report relates: (i) a copy of the report; and (ii) a description in writing of the rights of the consumer."

It is undisputed that Dayton Racquet Club provided Burghy with a copy of her credit report and a description of her rights. The only issue is whether it did so *before* taking adverse action against her. * * * Both parties agree that on January 15, Plaintiff signed the disclosure form purporting to authorize Dayton Racquet Club to retrieve her credit report, and that on January 16, Plaintiff was summoned at work for a meeting with her supervisors, Kevin Round and Bruce Stricker. A copy of Plaintiff's credit report and an accompanying letter were generated on January 16, mailed, and Plaintiff received them soon after. The letter that arrived on or about Friday, January 18, contained the following paragraph regarding the potential effect of Plaintiff's consumer report on her continued employment: "Although a final decision has not been reached at this time, we wanted to advise you that we have received your report and it may, or may not, affect our decision making process. We will contact you again when our deliberations are complete." On or about January 23, Plaintiff received another letter, this one stating: "We regret to inform you that we no longer require your services at DAYTON RACQUET CLUB INC [sic] Our decision, in part, is the result of reviewing information contained in your personal and/or service file, your consumer report and other criteria."

Defendants contend the sequence and content of these two letters demonstrate that Burghy was not terminated until after she had received a copy of her consumer report and the statement of her rights under the FCRA.... Plaintiff contends that she was actually fired earlier, in the meeting with her supervisors and before either letter had arrived. The relevant disagreement can thus be condensed to this question: Was Plaintiff fired on January 23, by letter, or on January 16, in the meeting with her supervisors? If the former, as Dayton Racquet Club argues, then adverse action was undeniably withheld until after Plaintiff was provided with a copy of her credit report. If the latter, as Plaintiff argues, then the adverse action took place before Plaintiff received the copy to which she was entitled under the FCRA. Viewing all evidence in the light most favorable to Plaintiff and drawing all reasonable inferences therefrom, the Court concludes that a genuine issue of material fact exists as to this question.

... Defendants draw a distinction between "[a]ctually taking an adverse action" and "situations in which the employer has developed a mere intention to take adverse action at some future time *but has not yet actually acted*." Phrased another way, Defendants' argument seems to be that an employer cannot violate the FCRA by forming a mere intention to take an adverse action; rather, it is only once the adverse action has actually taken place that [the FCRA's requirements are] triggered. Thus, if during the meeting on January 16, Defendants did nothing more than inform Plaintiff that her consumer report revealed unfavorable information that *might* force her from her job, they had not yet taken an adverse action against her and their failure to provide her a copy of her report at that time did not violate the FCRA. * * *

In *Obabueki* [an earlier FCRA case], the district court considered the case of a plaintiff who received a provisional job offer from IBM, and subsequently had that offer revoked when his consumer report revealed an undisclosed criminal conviction. Like Dayton Racquet Club, IBM also sent two letters: The first indicated that it intended to revoke Obabueki's provisional job offer and included a copy of the consumer report that revealed his prior conviction, and the second indicated that the job offer had been formally revoked. A period of five days elapsed between the mailing of the first and second letters. The plaintiff argued that IBM took adverse action against him with the first letter, while IBM countered that the first letter merely signaled its intention to withdraw his offer of employment at some later date. Obabueki also pointed to facts that tended to prove that IBM had already completed its internal decision-making process when it sent the first letter, and that no additional inquiry was conducted in the five days leading up to the second letter. The district court agreed with IBM that the adverse action took place when the job offer was actually revoked, and not when the internal decision to revoke the job offer was made or the first letter sent:

> *Holding that an employee may suffer adverse action as a result of an internal decision by the employer is akin to finding that a party's summary judgment motion is denied before the Opinion is composed and issued, following discussion between the judge and his law clerk. The absurdity of such a result is evident. Moreover, the statute expressly allows for the formation of an intent to take adverse action before complying with [its procedures], as it states that "the person intending to take" adverse action must provide the report and description of rights. After all, how can an employer send an intent letter without having first formed the requisite intent?*

Farmers Insurance [another FCRA case] similarly concluded that a group of insurance customers experienced adverse action only when their rates were actually billed at a higher premium, and not when they received a letter indicating that their insurance rates would increase at some future date.

Obabueki and *Farmers Insurance* arguably stand for the proposition that an *internal* decision cannot be the measuring point of an adverse action under the FCRA. Rather, an adverse action occurs when the decision is carried out, when it is communicated or actually takes effect, and an actor has until that time to take the necessary steps to comply with the FCRA's requirements. Though plausible, Dayton Racquet Club's reliance on this contention is unavailing, because Burghy's argument as to when adverse action was taken against her is decidedly less abstract. Here, the Plaintiff does not seek to hold her employer liable for an internal decision or preliminary discussions of her employment status. She contends, simply, that she was fired on January 16, in the meeting with her supervisors, and that this adverse action occurred before she received a copy of her credit report or statement of rights under the FCRA.

* * * Consistent with its position that Plaintiff had not yet been terminated, the Defendants argue, Mr. Round's promise "that he was going to further discuss this situation with other individuals at ClubCorp" meant that no final decision to take adverse action had been made, and that Mr. Round would prevail upon his superiors to allow him to prevent Plaintiff's termination. This interpretation does not provide a full picture of Plaintiff's deposition testimony, as she characterizes the situation thusly: "[Kevin Round said] [t]hat he was going to speak with some people in California about me, *about maybe getting my position back.* Because I was calling to see if they had any luck *trying to get my job back* or anything," "[a]nd when he went down there, he found out there was nothing that could be done *about me getting my position back.*" Thus, Plaintiff has insisted throughout that she was told that she was terminated in the meeting on January 16. Both parties agree that Kevin Round had indicated he would speak with his superiors at ClubCorp, but Plaintiff understood that it was with the goal of getting her position back, while Defendants contend it was to find a way around the otherwise unavoidable need to terminate her position at some future time.

The divergent interpretations of events in the relevant time frame reveal a genuine factual dispute. A jury that believed Plaintiff's recitation of the events from January 15 to January 23, especially her account of what transpired in the meeting of January 16, would be entitled to find in her favor.

* * * The Defendant's Motion is overruled only as it relates to Plaintiff's second claim, that Dayton Racquet Club took adverse action against her before providing her with a copy of her consumer report and a statement of her rights under the FCRA.... This is the only matter that remains to be resolved at trial.

CASE QUESTIONS

1. What are the legal issues in this case? What did the court decide?
2. What does the FCRA require regarding disclosure and authorization for obtaining a credit report? Why did the court conclude that this employer's disclosure was in compliance with the FCRA?
3. When does an adverse action occur under the FCRA? What must an employer do before taking an adverse action based on the contents of a credit report? Why was there a "genuine issue of material fact" as to whether the employer took the required actions in this case?
4. The details of the plaintiff's finances are not divulged in the judge's decision. But even if her credit score was very low, why should that result in termination from a job that she had performed for seven years? Does it make sense to base decisions about hiring or retention on an applicant's or employee's finances and credit standing?

The FCRA places responsibilities on both users of consumer information (e.g., employers) and consumer reporting agencies. A basic responsibility of the latter is to "follow reasonable procedures to ensure maximum possible accuracy of the information concerning the individual about whom the report relates."[35] A consumer reporting agency was denied summary judgment when it, through an array of subcontractors, reported that an applicant had a prior felony conviction for third-degree assault. Although the applicant had indeed been convicted of third-degree assault, that offense is a misdemeanor rather than a felony. The misleading report, in conjunction with a failure to establish reasonable procedures to guide the information gatherers, was enough to show noncompliance with the FCRA.[36] The act also requires that stale information be excluded from consumer reports. Reporting agencies are prohibited from including information relating to civil suits, civil judgments, arrests, paid tax liens, accounts placed for collection, and "any other adverse item of information" when it dates back more than seven years. Information about prior Chapter 11 bankruptcy proceedings can date back no more than ten years. However, these limitations on the inclusion of dated

---

[35]15 U.S.C.S. § 1681e (b) (2011).

[36]*Dalton v. Capital Associated Industries*, 257 F.3d 409 (4th Cir. 2001).

information in consumer reports do not apply if the job for which a candidate is being considered pays more than $75,000 a year. Importantly, "records of convictions of crimes" are explicitly excluded, allowing conviction information (as opposed to arrests) to go back further than seven years.[37]

Clippings

Maryland is now the fifth state to limit the use of an individual's credit history for hiring or other employment decisions, following Hawaii, Illinois, Oregon, and Washington. Similar legislation has been introduced in many other states. The Maryland law exempts certain employers, including financial institutions. The law allows credit information to be obtained only after an offer of employment has been extended and a showing is made by the employer that the information is "substantially job related."

Donald G. Aplin. "Maryland Becomes Fifth State to Restrict Employer Use of Credit History Information." *Daily Labor Report* 78 (April 22, 2011), A-2.

The Fair Credit Reporting Act regulates how employers must go about obtaining credit information when third-party sources are involved, but it does not limit the use of such information. At a time when more Americans are encountering severe economic difficulties, including home foreclosures and extended bouts of unemployment, concern has grown about the use of information on individuals' financial status to make hiring and other employment decisions. Some states have enacted laws prohibiting or limiting the use of such information by employers (see "Clippings"). The EEOC has taken a keen interest in the potential discriminatory effects of employer reliance on credit information and commenced lawsuits against several employers who engage in this practice.[38] The underlying legal theory is that the use of credit history is likely to have an adverse impact on persons of color.[39] At the same time, there appears to be little evidence linking credit history to job performance, including propensity to engage in theft or fraud.[40] While there is currently a dearth of case law on this topic, a reasonable conclusion is that *employers should carefully consider whether to use credit histories in making employment decisions and refrain from doing so if there is not a strong business rationale.* We can be more certain that plaintiffs who are not hired because they had previously filed for bankruptcy will not be able to invoke the protection of federal bankruptcy laws. Even though the bankruptcy code contains language making it illegal for a private sector employer to "terminate the employment of, or discriminate with respect to employment against" persons who have filed for bankruptcy protection,[41] courts have uniformly interpreted this provision as prohibiting only the termination of such employees, and not refusal to hire them.[42]

---

[37]15 U.S.C.S. § 1681c (a) (5) (2011).

[38]Kevin P. McGowan. "EEOC Class Suit Against Kaplan Education Alleges Race Bias in Use of Credit Histories." *Daily Labor Report* 245 (December 22, 2010), A-2.

[39]Susan R. Hobbs. "House Panel Explores Discriminatory Use of Credit Checks in Employment Decisions." *Daily Labor Report* 184 (September 23, 2010), A-16.

[40]Andrew Martin. "As a Hiring Filter, Credit Checks Draw Questions." *New York Times* (April 10, 2010), B1.

[41]11 U.S.C.S. § 525(b) (2011).

[42]*Myers v. Toojay's Management Corp.*, 2011 U.S. App. LEXIS 9947 (5th Cir.); *Rea v. Federated Investors*, 627 F.3d 937 (3d Cir. 2010).

References

Failure to check references—particularly recent ones that possess information regarding wrongdoing by an employee at a previous job—can be evidence of negligence in hiring.[43] But it is *former employers* asked for information about their former employees that have the most to worry about regarding references. The principal legal concern is that former employers will be sued for defaming their former employees. Other worries are that former employers may be viewed as retaliating against their former employees or being negligent in providing misleadingly positive referrals.

Defamation

Defamation claims can arise anytime that a person makes a statement about another person, but here the focus here is on references provided by former employers. The term is being used here in the broad sense of any information that a former employer provides to a prospective new employer; the former employer need not be specifically designated by the former employee as a "reference." The gist of a defamation claim is that false statements that reflect badly on a person are communicated to others, which results in damage to the person's reputation. Defamatory statements are not merely harsh or negative; they must be substantially false. As such, it behooves employers responding to requests for references to *ensure that the information provided is as accurate and objective as possible. Among other things, this means basing responses to requests for information on inspection of documents rather than memory, confining statements to known facts rather than speculation or impressions, and having requests dealt with by designated persons who are accustomed to writing letters of reference and familiar with accessing information regarding former employees.*

ELEMENTS OF A CLAIM

Defamation

To prevail in a defamation claim, the plaintiff must show that:

1. A statement is made that purports to be "factual" in nature.
2. The statement is false or substantially false.
3. The statement challenges the integrity, character, or ability of the plaintiff.
4. The statement is "published" (communicated) either orally (slander) or in writing (libel).
5. There is harm to the reputation of the plaintiff.

Statements that are defamatory still will not subject an employer to liability if those statements were privileged. Qualified privilege can be lost if any of the following are true:

1. There was malicious intent to harm the person's reputation.
2. The statement was made with reckless disregard for the truth.
3. Publication of the statement was overly broad.

© Cengage Learning 2013.

---

[43]*Interim Healthcare of Fort Wayne, Inc. v. Moyer*, 746 N.E.2d 429 (Ind. App. 2001), *transfer denied*, 761 N.E.2d 425 (Ind. 2001).

Defenses to Defamation Claims: Consent and Qualified Privilege Although truthfulness is an absolute defense to a defamation claim, employers do not want to be in the position of defending the accuracy of all their statements. Other defenses are also available to employers that obviate this problem. One is **consent**. If a former employee consents to her former employer providing a reference, statements that might otherwise be defamatory will not subject the former employer to liability. Thus, it makes sense for a former employer *to require that any request for a reference be accompanied by a written "release of information" form that is signed by the former employee and that grants permission to communicate information about the employee.* This precludes off-the-cuff responses to telephone inquiries about former employees (which is also desirable from the standpoint of accuracy), but does not impose an unreasonable burden on other employers seeking references. In anticipation of this requirement, most prospective employers ask applicants to sign releases of information on their applications. Although requiring release forms is definitely a good idea, there is a legitimate question as to whether this constitutes informed consent on the part of former employees because they do not know what their former employers will say. A means of gaining more fully informed consent is for employers to *negotiate with employees prior to their leaving employment and to mutually agree on a letter of reference.* Clearly, this will not work in all cases. When the employee's departure is acrimonious, it might not be possible to agree on the contents of the letter. And some employers might be concerned that their statements could be used against them in a wrongful termination case.

A second and more basic defense against defamation claims is that the statements made, even if otherwise defamatory, were "privileged." The law recognizes that communication between employers about prospective employees serves important social purposes. It also recognizes that if employers have to worry about the strict accuracy of everything they say about former employees, this will choke off the flow of necessary information. Thus, former employers providing references are shielded from defamation claims by **qualified privilege**. This privilege or immunity from liability is conditional rather than absolute. In general, qualified privilege can be lost if false statements are made with **malice** (i.e., intent to harm a person's reputation) or **reckless disregard for the truth** or if the statements receive **overly broad publication**.

Sigal Construction v. Stanbury focuses on whether the employer's statements were made under circumstances that caused the loss of this employer's qualified privilege to defame.

Sigal Construction v. Stanbury
586 A.2d 1204 (D.C. App. 1991)

OPINION BY ASSOCIATE JUDGE FERREN:

In this defamation case, a jury awarded appellee, Kenneth S. Stanbury, $370,440 against his former employer, appellant Sigal Construction Corporation. The jury found that a Sigal project manager, Paul Littman, had slandered Stanbury while giving an employment reference to another construction company after Sigal had terminated Stanbury's employment. * * * Sigal appeals. * * * We affirm.

Stanbury worked as a project manager for Sigal from May 1984 to June 1985. According to Sigal's personnel manager, Pamela Heiber, Sigal terminated Stanbury's employment because he "was not doing his job correctly." Sigal, however, told Stanbury he was let go for "lack of work or reduction in work." According to Heiber, "we felt sympathy for Ken because of his age in life" (he was 63 when Sigal terminated his employment). Stanbury contacted Ray Stevens, a previous employer and Regional Manager at Daniel Construction, to find out whether any work was available. Some time later, Stevens called Stanbury about employment as a project manager on the Pentagon City project. Stanbury was eventually offered the job, subject to approval by the owner of the project, Lincoln Properties.

William Janes, a Lincoln Properties general partner, had responsibility for investigating Stanbury's employment references. Janes called David Orr, a former Sigal project executive, who suggested that Janes contact Paul Littman, a current Sigal project executive. Janes did so, and Littman later memorialized the conversation:

[Janes] claimed David [Orr] had told him not to hire Ken [Stanbury] and asked me what I thought. I told him.

1. Ken seemed detail oriented to the point of losing sight of the big picture.
2. He had a lot of knowledge and experience on big jobs.
3. With a large staff might be a very competent P.M. [project manager].
4. Obviously he no longer worked for us and that might say enough.

At trial, Littman acknowledged and Stanbury confirmed that Littman had made these statements without having supervised, evaluated, read an evaluation of, or even worked with Stanbury (other than seeing Stanbury in the halls at the office). According to them both, their contact was entirely casual. More specifically, Stanbury testified without contradiction that he had talked to Littman only once during Stanbury's fourteen months with Sigal, and that this conversation was a general discussion about Stanbury's previous job. According to Littman, in evaluating Stanbury for Janes he relied entirely on the "general impression [he] had developed" from "hearing people talk about [Stanbury's] work at the job," perhaps at "casual luncheons" or "project executive meetings" or "over a beer on a Friday afternoon." Littman did nothing to verify the second-hand knowledge he had acquired about Stanbury. At trial, he could recall no facts or work-related incidents that would support the impressions he reported to Janes. When asked where his information about one of Stanbury's projects came from, Littman testified that "there aren't any real specific instances I can point to. I think it was a general opinion I had just developed in the year or two [Stanbury] had been there." * * *

* * * Sigal does not contest, on appeal, either that the statements were false or were negligently made. Sigal does contend, however—and Stanbury does not dispute—that Littman's negligent statements were subject to a "qualified privilege." According to the Virginia Supreme court:

A communication, made in good faith, on a subject matter in which the person communicating has an interest, or owes a duty, legal, moral, or social, is qualifiedly privileged if made to a person having a corresponding interest or duty.

* * * Once the privilege applies, the plaintiff has the burden of proving the defendant has abused, and thus lost, it. To defeat the privilege, a plaintiff must prove the defendant acted with "common law malice." Such malice implies a greater level of ill will than the mindset reflected by mere negligence. In this jurisdiction, we have equated common law malice with "bad faith." In Virginia the common law malice formulation, which the trial court used for its instruction, includes "bad faith" but is more comprehensive.[1]

* * * There was sufficient evidence at trial, viewed in the light most favorable to Stanbury, from which a reasonable jury could find by clear and convincing evidence that Littman and Sigal had abused the qualified privilege under Virginia law by acting with "such gross indifference or recklessness as to amount to wanton and willful disregard of the rights of" Stanbury. Littman testified, and Stanbury's testimony confirmed, that Littman had never supervised, worked with, evaluated, or read an evaluation of Stanbury. Moreover, Littman testified that he had not received information from anyone in particular, let alone anyone who had had a work-related relationship with Stanbury. Littman's sources for his statements to Janes were observations in the company's halls and general office contacts with unnamed third parties, perhaps at "casual lunches" or "project executive meetings" or "over beer on a Friday afternoon." But he could recall none of the conversations or otherwise provide any concrete support for his statements, whether first-hand information or hearsay. Littman admitted that he had no facts to support any of his statements to Janes and that he had never sought to verify the information before giving his evaluation. Littman also testified that he knew Janes wanted to speak with someone who had "interacted" with Stanbury at Sigal, and

yet Littman further testified that he did not tell Janes he had never done so. Nor did Littman tell Janes the altogether vague sources of his statements. * * *

In sustaining the conclusion that Sigal (through Littman) abused the qualified privilege, we do not mean to imply that employers are at serious risk when providing employment references in the normal course of business. Nor are we suggesting that employers, when providing such references, may not rely on information from the employee's co-workers, even when hearsay. Our analysis here is limited to an office gossip situation where the recommender (1) has conveyed information which cannot be traced to anyone with personal knowledge of the employee whose reputation is at stake, (2) has not qualified his statements by disclosing the nebulous source of his information, and (3) has led the prospective employer to believe he has worked on a project with the employee and thus has first-hand information.

Cases holding there was no abuse of the qualified privilege are easily distinguishable. This is not a case, for example, where an employee's supervisor, who has worked directly with the employee, provides a negative reference based on personal experience. Nor is this a case where the reference is based on a careful, thorough investigation, or on the employee's own admission.... * * *

On this record, therefore, the jury could find wanton, willful, or reckless conduct that amounted to abuse of the qualified privilege.

CASE QUESTIONS

1. What was the legal issue in this case? What did the court decide?
2. How are the elements of a defamation claim satisfied in this case?
3. Why was the company not shielded by "qualified privilege" in this case?
4. What should this employer have done differently?

_____

[1]The qualified privilege may be overcome by showing the defendant acted:

1. With actual malice; … or
2. … [He or she] used language which was intemperate or disproportionate in strength and violence to the occasion and which was unnecessarily defamatory to the plaintiff; or
3. Not in good faith and without an honest belief in their truth; or
4. Deliberately adopted a method of speaking the alleged words which gave unnecessary publicity to such words; or
5. … purposely arranged to speak the alleged words in the presence of a person or persons who were wholly uninterested in the matter and who had no right to be present and who in the natural course of things would not have been present; or
6. For the purpose of gratifying some sinister or corrupt motive such as hatred, revenge, personal spite, ill will, or desire to injure the plaintiff; or
7. With such gross indifference or recklessness as to amount to a wanton and willful disregard of the rights of plaintiff....

Qualified privilege shields communications only with others who have a legitimate need for that information. One way to avoid overly broad publication is to *verify the identity of any party seeking information about former employees by requiring that requests for references be made in writing on the prospective employer's letterhead.* The same measures that aid an employer in producing accurate and objective letters of reference should more than suffice to avoid reckless disregard for the truth. As the *Sigal Construction* case shows, *it is critical to have a substantive, preferably documentary, basis for references.* Malicious intent is less likely to be inferred if employers *refrain from drawing conclusions about whether former employees should be hired.* A statement that someone should not be hired can sound (especially in court) as though a grudge is motivating the speaker.

Negligent Referral

What if references are provided, but they are misleading and fail to include evidence of unfitness known to the former employer? Concern over possible defamation claims or simply the desire to get rid of problem employees might prompt some employers to gloss over negative information and provide overly positive references that misrepresent former employees to prospective new employers. Can an employer be sued for negligence in referring an unfit employee who harms others in his new job? In a number of states, the answer is yes. In one instructive case,[44] disciplinary action was initiated against a corrections officer who was accused of engaging in improper sexual conduct with female inmates. Shortly before his disciplinary hearing, the officer chose to resign. Within days of the officer resigning under a cloud of suspicion, his former supervisors at the prison agreed to write a letter of recommendation for him. The letter was effusive in its praise of the former employee and omitted any mention of the incidents that led to his resignation. When a mental health facility that was considering hiring the former officer called the prison, the former employee was again heartily recommended. Within a month of being hired at the mental health facility, the former officer sexually harassed and assaulted a female patient. The court decided that while the prison could lawfully have declined to provide any information about the former employee, once they undertook the task of doing so, they had a duty to not misrepresent the former employee by withholding material, negative information about him. The duty was owed to both prospective employers and to third-parties (such as the female patient) foreseeably harmed by the unfit former employee.

To the extent that negligent referral (misrepresentation) is recognized as a legal claim, *employers that choose to respond to requests for information about former employees should not do so in a selective and misleading manner that conceals evidence of unfitness*—at least when referring people for jobs that pose foreseeable harm to others.

JUST THE FACTS

An anesthesiologist addicted to pain killers worked for an anesthesiology practice that treated patients at a hospital. After several incidents, the doctor was terminated for reporting to work impaired and putting "our patients at significant risk." Within two months of his termination for on-the-job drug use, two other doctors in the anesthesiology practice wrote letters of reference for the doctor. The letters stated that the doctor was "an excellent clinician" and would "be an asset to any anesthesia service." The letters made no mention of his drug use, performance problems, or termination. The hospital that was considering the doctor for employment also contacted the hospital he had worked at, with a request for credentialing information that included specific questions about disciplinary actions, judgment, and signs of behavior problems. At the same time this request was made, the hospital had similar requests regarding thirteen other former doctors and replied in full to all of these. However, regarding this doctor, the hospital did not respond to the specific questions and instead sent only a brief statement confirming the doctor's dates of employment and job title. The doctor was hired, and after several uneventful months on his new job, he began using Demerol again. Impaired by his drug use, the doctor's improper administration of anesthesia led to a patient who had come in for a routine elective procedure being left in a permanent vegetative state. The hospital at which this incident occurred sued both the former hospital and the anesthesiology practice based on their failure to disclose the problems with the doctor. What should the court decide regarding the first hospital? The anesthesiology practice? Why?

See, *Kadlec Medical Center v. Lakeview Anesthesia Associates,* 2008 U.S. App. LEXIS 10267 (5th Cir.).

---

[44]*Davis v. The Board of County Commissioners of Doña Ana County,* 987 P.2d 1172 (N.M. App. 1999).

Practical Considerations In light of the many legal concerns surrounding references, should employers provide substantive references on former employees? Or only verification of job title and dates of employment?

At least one more significant legal concern exists regarding references—retaliation. In one such case, an employee was fired and filed a charge of race discrimination against his former employer. While his case was being investigated by the EEOC, the employee applied for a job with another company. The company asked his former employer for a reference. The former employer provided a damaging reference, which the employee alleged was done in retaliation for his discrimination charge. The U.S. Supreme Court decided that the former employee could sue his former employer for retaliation under these circumstances.[45] *When former employees have legal action pending against an employer, particular care should be taken to ensure that any references provided are no more negative than the facts warrant and do not urge that a candidate not be hired.*

Verifying Employment Eligibility

Many people come to the United States from other countries to work. Employers are responsible for verifying that all persons hired have the legal right to work here. Immigration has long shaped the U.S. workforce, but the Immigration Reform and Control Act of 1986 and more recent developments have moved the workplace to the front lines in the government's efforts to curtail illegal immigration.

THE CHANGING WORKPLACE

Immigration and the U.S. Workforce

As of mid-2011, the U.S. population stood at approximately 312 million.[1] The nation's workforce numbered about 154 million in 2010. Approximately 25 million of those workers—15.8 percent of the U.S. workforce—were foreign-born.[2] Immigration has had a profound effect on the U.S. population. It is estimated that immigration will account for 82 percent of the increase in the nation's population between now and 2050. Foreign-born people are expected to comprise over 15 percent of the U.S. population by 2050—and fully 23 percent of the nation's workforce.[3] If these projections hold, the immigrant share of the population and workforce will exceed the previous high-water marks reached during the waves of mass immigration in the second half of the nineteenth century. Mexico is by far the largest single source of immigrants, but substantial numbers of immigrants also come from Southeast Asia, China, and other countries in Central and South America. However, while many immigrants are Latino or "Hispanic," about 60 percent of Latinos residing in the United States were born in this country.[4] The states with the largest numbers of immigrants continue to be California, New York, Texas, Florida, New Jersey, and Illinois. However, over the past decade, many other states have seen significant increases in their immigrant populations.[5]

Immigrants who are not citizens of this country are sometimes referred to as "aliens." Some noncitizens have the legal right to work in the United States. Noncitizens who are eligible to work in the United States are referred to as **legal aliens**, whereas those not eligible to work in the United States are termed **illegal aliens** (or unauthorized or undocumented workers). Persons from other countries who possess unexpired work visas (such as the H-1B visa discussed in the previous chapter) are entitled to work in the United States. Likewise, noncitizens with permanent resident alien status (holders of "green cards") are eligible to work in the United States. Citizens, whether born in the United States or naturalized, are eligible to work in the United States. Despite policies intended to discourage illegal immigration, the number of illegal aliens in the United States in 2010 was estimated to be 11.2 million.

---

[45]*Robinson v. Shell Oil Co.*, 117 S. Ct. 843 (1997).

About 8 million undocumented workers were in the workforce in 2010, constituting roughly 5 percent of the total U.S. workforce.[6]

Undocumented workers are particularly likely to occupy such jobs as drywall installers, meat and poultry plant workers, dishwashers, farm workers, and janitors. The effects of illegal immigration continue to be hotly debated. Certainly, undocumented workers provide a valuable source of labor and frequently pay taxes for programs (e.g., Social Security) and services they will never receive. Employers in industries such as agriculture claim that immigrants are needed because native-born workers will not take these jobs. Others contend that there are actually few occupations in which immigrants are a majority and that if employers offered more attractive pay, benefits, and working conditions, they would not have any problem filling positions with native-born workers.[7] While the magnitude of the impact is disputed, it is generally agreed that the presence of undocumented workers negatively affects the wages and job opportunities of those at the bottom of the labor force, particularly native-born workers without high school diplomas.[8]

---

[1]U.S. Census Bureau (http://www.census.gov).
[2]Larry Swisher. "Size of Foreign-Born Workforce Grew in 2010 for First Time Since Recession." *Daily Labor Report* 103 (May 27, 2011), D-1.
[3]Sam Roberts. "Study Foresees the Fall of an Immigration Record That Has Lasted a Century." *New York Times* (February 12, 2008), A11.
[4]Roberts.
[5]Julia Preston. "U.S. Immigrant Population Is Highest Since the 1920's." *New York Times* (November 29, 2007), A15.
[6]Julia Preston. "11.2 Million Illegal Immigrants in U.S. in 2010 Report Says; No Change From 09." *New York Times* (February 2, 2011), A15.
[7]John M. Broder. "Immigrants and the Economics of Hard Work." *New York Times* (April 2, 2006), Wk3.
[8]Fawn Johnson. "Low-Skilled Workers Bear Brunt of Immigrant Influx, Researchers Agree." *Daily Labor Report* 194 (October 6, 2006), C-1.

The Immigration Reform and Control Act

The **Immigration Reform and Control Act (IRCA)** has two main requirements. First, *all employers are prohibited from knowingly hiring or retaining on the job unauthorized aliens.*[46] Second, *employers with four or more employees are prohibited from discriminating in hiring or termination decisions on the basis of national origin and citizenship.*[47] This protection against discrimination applies only to citizens and legal immigrants. It does not conflict with the requirement that employers screen out undocumented workers. Nor does this requirement prohibit employers from preferring U.S. citizens for employment when two individuals are equally qualified. Nondiscrimination provisions were included in this law because Congress did not want employers to respond to IRCA by excluding all "foreigners."

To avoid hiring or retaining persons ineligible to work in the United States, employers need to do a number of things. The following procedures apply only to people hired, and not to all applicants. *Within three days after a newly hired employee begins work, his employer must verify his eligibility to work in the United States. This must be done for all newly hired workers, and not simply those whose employment eligibility is questioned. This verification is accomplished by viewing documents establishing eligibility to work and recording the types of documents viewed on an Employment Eligibility Verification ("I-9") form provided by the federal government's Office of Citizenship and Immigration Services.* Documents can establish identity, eligibility to work, or both. Documents typically used for these purposes include a Social Security card, a driver's license, a birth certificate, a U.S. passport, a resident alien registration card, and an unexpired employment authorization document. A full list of acceptable documents can be found on the back of the I-9 form. Other than certified copies of birth certificates, *only original documents should be*

---

[46]8 U.S.C.S. § 1324a(a)(1), (2) (2011).
[47]8 U.S.C.S. § 1324b(a)(1) (2011).

accepted. Employers are permitted but not required to make copies of documents provided by newly hired employees. Employers are not required to further investigate the authenticity of documents, provided that these "reasonably appear on their face to be genuine." Retaining copies of the documents presented can help prove that the decision to accept them was reasonable. *I-9 forms and any copies of documents must be kept separate from employees' personnel files and retained for three years from the date of hire or one year after employment is terminated, whichever is longer.* Thus, the minimum period of time that these forms must be kept is three years. Employment for more than two years extends this period.

Until quite recently, enforcement of the Immigration Reform and Control Act was lax. Fake documents were readily available, employers presented with such documents had all of the cover they needed to hire illegal workers without fear of punishment, and government enforcement actions were infrequent and carried minimal sanctions for employers.[48] Enforcement of IRCA increased substantially around 2006. Initially, this entailed highly publicized raids on workplaces in which undocumented workers (and occasionally others eligible to work) were rounded up for mass deportation.[49] More recently, the federal government has shifted to a strategy of conducting large numbers of audits of employers' records. Employers are then forced to terminate undocumented workers, although the workers are not necessarily deported. The employers themselves are increasingly subject to fines and criminal prosecution.[50]

Clippings

The two owners of the Chuy's Mesquite Broiler chain of Mexican restaurants are facing charges of tax fraud and harboring illegal aliens that could result in lengthy jail sentences. An April 20, 2011, raid on fourteen of the chain's restaurants resulted in some deportations and detentions of workers, but netted primarily documents. Prosecutors contend that the owners knowingly employed illegal aliens, kept dual books, and evaded taxes on the wages of the undocumented workers. The indictment alleges that when a customer complained about the restaurant's use of illegal workers, the owner told one of the workers that "I need to hide you in the kitchen."

Julia Preston. "A Crackdown on Employing Illegal Workers." *New York Times* (May 30, 2011), A1.

Another facet of the new immigration enforcement environment has been an effort to encourage and/or require employers to use government databases to verify identity and employment eligibility. "E-Verify" is the current version of a voluntary program under which employers can electronically verify the eligibility of employees to work in the United States. Given a choice about whether to do so, employers have not flocked

---

[48]Eduardo Porter. "The Search for Illegal Immigrants Stops at the Workplace." *New York Times* (March 5, 2006), Bu3.

[49]Steven Greenhouse. "Immigrant Crackdown Upends a Slaughterhouse's Work Force." *New York Times* (October 12, 2007), A1; Amber McKinney. "U.S. Citizens File Claims Against DHS, ICE for Alleged Illegal Detention during Raid." *Daily Labor Report* 84 (May 1, 2008), A-1.

[50]Julia Preston. "Illegal Workers Swept from Jobs in 'Silent Raids.'" *New York Times* (July 10, 2010), A1; Ralph Lindeman. "New I-9 Enforcement Plan Shows Statistical Results, but Raises Questions." *Daily Labor Report* 7 (January 11, 2011), B-1.

Practical Considerations What should employers do to make it less likely that an audit of their I-9s will reveal problems? Would you recommend that employers who are not legally required to do so voluntarily participate in the E-Verify program? Why or why not?

to use E-Verify.[51] However, an executive order (E.O. 12989) issued in 2008 made participation in the program mandatory for federal government contractors[52] and the government's authority to issue that order has been upheld.[53] Additionally, a number of states have enacted laws requiring the use of E-Verify. While the trend appears to be in the direction of requiring employers to do more than just look at the documents presented by applicants, electronic verification is not a panacea. Electronic verification through government databases poses significant costs and administrative burdens on government agencies, is subject to errors and outdated information in databases that could result in erroneous denial of employment, and does not prevent identity fraud or misuse by employers.[54] One estimate is that, because the system cannot confirm whether applicants are presenting their own documentation or stolen information, E-Verify might be failing to detect as many as one out of every two undocumented workers.[55]

While immigration has traditionally fallen exclusively within the domain of the federal government, states and cities are increasingly acting to fill the void left by the absence of a workable national immigration policy. In some cases, this has involved aggressive attempts by local law enforcement officials to use more general laws (e.g., regarding identity theft, housing occupancy limits) to crack down on people who might be illegal immigrants.[56] However, in many cases, legislation directly addressing immigration issues has been proposed and enacted. The authority of state and local governments to legislate regarding immigration issues has been challenged, with various outcomes.[57] However, in the most authoritative statement thus far on whether state immigration laws are "preempted" by the federal Immigration Reform and Control Act, the Supreme Court upheld an Arizona law that permits the state to revoke the business licenses of companies that knowingly hire illegal workers and that requires all employers in the state to use E-Verify.[58] According to the Court, the sanction of revoking business licenses fell under a clause within IRCA that permits states to establish "licensing and similar laws" without fear of preemption. The Court also held that requiring use of E-Verify did not conflict with the basic public policy articulated through the IRCA, even though federal law does not go as far. While this decision does not mean that all state laws addressing immigration will be upheld, it does raise questions about whether we will have a single, consistent national immigration policy in the future or whether employers will be subjected "to a patchwork of enforcement schemes."[59]

Ultimately, the immigration issue requires a comprehensive national approach. Illegal immigration is a complex issue that does not yield to facile solutions such as building bigger fences. A workable law needs to accommodate security needs, concerns of citizens about effects on their communities, the needs of employers for labor, and the dignity of the workers themselves. The reality of many millions of undocumented persons already

[51]U.S. Government Accountability Office (GAO). *Employment Verification: Challenges Exist in Implementing a Mandatory Electronic Employment Verification System.* GAO-08-895T (June 10, 2008), 3.

[52]Amber McKinney. "President Bush Signs Executive Order Requiring Federal Contractors Use E-Verify." *Daily Labor Report* 111 (June 10, 2008), A-1.

[53]*Chamber of Commerce of the United States v. Napolitano*, 648 F. Supp. 2d 726 (D. Md. 2009).

[54]U.S. Government Accountability Office (GAO). *Employment Verification: Agencies Have Improved E-Verify, but Significant Challenges Remain.* GAO-11-522T (April 14, 2011), 4–5.

[55]Louise Radnofsky and Miriam Jordon. "Illegal Workers Slip by System." *The Wall Street Journal* (February 25, 2010) (http://online.wsj.com/).

[56]Julia Preston. "Sheriff Defies Transgressors by Billboard and by Blog." *New York Times* (July 31, 2006), A-15.

[57]Julia Preston. "In Reversal, Courts Uphold Local Immigration Laws." *New York Times* (February 10, 2008), 16.

[58]*Chamber of Commerce of the United States of America v. Whiting*, 2011 U.S. LEXIS 4018.

[59]*Chamber of Commerce*, at 100.

in the United States and enmeshed in communities, families, and workplaces must be dealt with in a humane, sensible manner consistent with our values. The only safe prediction is that whatever framework is devised will not be the last word on immigration and the workplace.

Key Terms

background check, p. 133
respondeat superior, p. 133
scope of employment, p. 133
negligence, p. 134
negligent hiring, p. 134
public policy, p. 135
foreseeability, p. 136
knowledge, p. 140
proximity, p. 140
arrest, p. 143

convictions, p. 143
felony, p. 144
misdemeanors, p. 144
Fair Credit Reporting Act (FCRA), p. 145
consumer credit report, p. 145
investigative report, p. 146
consumer reporting agency, p. 146
adverse action, p. 146
defamation, p. 152

consent, p. 153
qualified privilege, p. 153
malice, p. 153
reckless disregard for the truth, p. 153
overly broad publication, p. 153
legal alien, p. 157
illegal alien, p. 157
Immigration Reform and Control Act (IRCA), p. 158

Chapter Summary

Compelling legal (and ethical) reasons exist for employers' concerns about hiring unfit employees. If an employee inadvertently harms someone in the course of doing his job, his employer is generally liable for that harm under the doctrine of respondeat superior. But the responsibility of employers for harmful actions of their employees does not end with actions that are taken within the scope of employment. Negligent hiring claims hold an employer liable for harmful actions that take place outside the scope of employment, but for which inadequate screening procedures set the stage. More exactly, an employer is liable for negligent hiring when the employer fails to exercise the level of care in screening out unfit employees that a reasonable person would have used under the circumstances and the hiring of an unfit person was the proximate cause of harm to some third party.

No single standard exists for how thorough background checks must be and what employers must do to avoid breaching their duty. Instead, courts look to a combination of public policy, foreseeability, and knowledge to determine the extent of an employer's duty to screen out unfit employees. Foreseeability refers to the likelihood of harm to others if an unfit person is hired for the position in question. The greater the potential harm, the more extensive the background check should be. Knowledge refers to the extent to which the employer knew or should have known of the unfitness of the person hired if a proper background check had been done. Employers will not be held liable for failing to do an adequate

background check when the evidence of unfitness that a background check would uncover does not exist.

Background checks typically include efforts to obtain information from former employers. The legal issues surrounding references primarily affect the former employers asked to provide information. Employers providing references that are false and damaging to the reputations of former employees may be liable for defamation. However, references (or other communications) that would otherwise be defamatory will not subject an employer to liability if the former employee consented to have information released or if qualified privilege was not lost. Qualified privilege is the legal presumption that employers will be immune from liability for engaging in the socially useful act of conveying information about former employees to others with legitimate need to have that information. This immunity is conditional on the absence of malicious intent to harm the former employee's reputation, reckless disregard for the truth, or overly broad communication of the false and damaging information. Former employers providing references must also be concerned about suits for retaliation against former employees who have filed discrimination charges and for negligent referral. The latter occurs when a reference is provided, the reference is misleading because it conceals the former employee's unfitness, another employer relies on the reference to hire the unfit employee, and that employee proceeds to harm someone in his new job when it was foreseeable that such harm could occur.

A record of criminal convictions is a key indicator of unfitness for many jobs. Employers seeking to check for criminal records may find that they are constrained by state laws that limit access to this information and/or its use. Heavy reliance on criminal records to screen out unfit employees may also produce adverse impact discrimination. Information about arrests can rarely be used legally, whereas convictions can be taken into account provided that the severity of the offense, its relationship to the job in question, and its recency are considered.

Consumer credit reports or investigative reports that are compiled by credit reporting agencies and sold to employers are regulated by the Fair Credit Reporting Act (FCRA). Credit reports can contain information about character and lifestyle and are not limited to financial dealings. The FCRA holds many requirements for both employers and consumer reporting agencies. These include the requirement that employers obtain the consent of employees or applicants before seeking to obtain credit reports and provisions for prior and concurrent notice when denial of an employment opportunity (an adverse action) is based in any part on the contents of a credit report. The FCRA establishes a set of procedures that must be used to lawfully obtain and base employment decisions on credit reports; however, this law does not tell employers that they cannot use this source of information. States have shown increasing interest in limiting the use of credit histories in employment. Antidiscrimination laws also potentially limit the use of credit histories for employment decisions to the extent that their use results in adverse impact.

Whatever else employers do in terms of background checks, they are legally required to verify the employment eligibility of all persons they hire. Persons eligible for employment in the United States include U.S. citizens and legal aliens. The Immigration Reform and Control Act (IRCA) prohibits employers from knowingly hiring or retaining illegal or unauthorized aliens. The law also protects legal aliens by prohibiting discrimination in hiring and firing on the basis of national origin or citizenship. Immigrants, both those with proper documentation and those without, continue to come to the United States in large numbers and are projected to make up a large part of the growth in the population and workforce over the coming decades. The enforcement of immigration laws is a contentious issue and is currently in the forefront of public debate. Consensus on the need for a different approach has not been matched by agreement on how to mesh security concerns, employers' need for labor, citizens' concerns about their communities, and the reality of massive numbers of undocumented workers and their families.

Practical Advice Summary

- Depending on the circumstances, an adequate background check might include
  — Contacting references.
  — Verifying places of residence.
  — Verifying past employment and military service.
  — Verifying possession of degrees, licenses, and other credentials.
  — Checking criminal and driving records.
  — Examining credit reports.
  — Accessing Internet sites and postings.
- Background checks must be more extensive when hiring for positions in which unfit employees could do serious harm to others.
- At minimum, an employer should always follow its own established background check procedures and avoid last-minute, rushed hiring decisions that require deviation from normal procedures.
- Inconsistencies and gaps in information provided by applicants should
  — Be detected and confronted.
  — Result in nonhire if they cannot be satisfactorily explained.
- In conducting background checks, employers should
  — Document all efforts to obtain information on job candidates, even when those efforts are not successful.
  — Attempt to corroborate answers, and not merely ask applicants, about important matters such as criminal convictions.
- If, despite the inadvisability of doing so, an employer opts to hire a needed employee prior to completing a background check, the employer should still complete the background check—but only if the employer is willing to use any evidence of unfitness discovered (or application falsification) as a basis for terminating the employee.
- To make references as accurate and objective as possible
  — Base them on inspection of documents rather than memory alone.

— Confine comments to known facts rather than speculation or impressions.

— Centralize the provision of references by assigning them to designated persons thoroughly familiar with procedures for researching and writing letters of reference.

- Former employers should
  — Require that requests for references be accompanied by written release forms signed by former employees.

  — Attempt to reach an agreement with departing employees regarding the content of letters of reference.

  — Verify the identities of persons seeking information about former employees by requiring that requests be made on company letterhead.

  — Refrain from drawing conclusions about whether former employees should be hired by other prospective employers.

- If former employers respond to requests for references at all, then they must do so in a manner that does not mislead by concealing the unfitness of former employees.

- Employers should generally not use information about prior arrests in making hiring decisions.

- Before denying employment based on a criminal conviction, employers should consider the seriousness, job-relatedness, and recency of the offense.

- Employers that rely on other companies or individuals to perform background checks should
  — Ascertain and agree on the comprehensiveness of those searches.

  — Get written consent to obtain a consumer credit report and do so on a separate form containing no other information (i.e., not an application form).

  — Provide a pre–adverse action disclosure if the employer intends to deny an employment opportunity based in whole or in part on a consumer credit report.

  — Provide an adverse action notice if an employment opportunity is denied based in whole or in part on the contents of a consumer credit report.

- Employers should carefully consider whether to use credit histories in making employment decisions and refrain from doing so if there is not a strong business rationale.

- Employers must not knowingly hire or retain employees who are unauthorized aliens.

- Employers must not discriminate on the basis of national origin or citizenship in carrying out their responsibility not to hire unauthorized aliens.

- When hiring new employees, employers must
  — Verify the employment eligibility of newly hired employees within three days after they begin work.

  — View documents (e.g., birth certificate, driver's license, resident alien registration card) to establish identity and eligibility to work in the United States.

  — Record the documents examined on I-9 forms.

- Employers can and should make copies of the original documents examined.

- I-9 forms should be
  — Kept separate from employees' personnel files.

  — Retained for three years or one year after employment is terminated, whichever is longer.

Chapter Questions

1. A passenger on a flight was greeted by a flight attendant whom he had never met and was told that she liked his smile and that "he would be her #1." During the flight, the flight attendant hit the passenger on the head with her open hand several times to initiate a conversation. The passenger moved to another seat to get away from the flight attendant. The flight attendant subsequently poured water on his lap. She proceeded to place stickers labeled "fragile" on the passenger's arm, cheeks, and crotch. The flight attendant forcibly attempted to kiss the passenger on the lips. She also rubbed her tongue along the rim of a beer can before handing it to the passenger. After the plane landed, the flight attendant grabbed the passenger and kissed his lips in an effort to get "one last kiss" while he was standing in line waiting for a rental car. The passenger sued the airline. What should the court decide? Why? (*Twardy v. Northwest Airlines*, 2001 U.S. Dist. LEXIS 2112 [N.D.Ill.])

2. A 15-year-old from a residential facility for troubled teens was traveling on a Greyhound bus. The driver of the bus conversed with the young woman during the trip. At a stop where the driver was scheduled to go off duty for eight hours of rest, as required by law, the driver told the young woman that she would have to come

to his motel room to obtain a pass enabling her to re-board the bus. In the room provided to the driver by the bus line, the young woman was sexually assaulted. The driver eventually pled guilty to sexual imposition and was sentenced to prison. The driver had been hired five years earlier. He had denied any criminal history on his application form. In fact, he had been convicted of criminal sexual conduct with a minor in 1980. Greyhound's criminal background check covered the years of 1987–1997 and did not discover the earlier conviction. A suit was brought against the company on behalf of the young woman. What should the court decide? Why? (*Cromp v. Greyhound Lines*, 2003 U.S. Dist. LEXIS 22921 [D.N.D.])

3. A patient alleged that she was raped by a mental health assistant at a residential treatment facility. Prior to the rape, the assistant had administered medication to incapacitate the woman. Before hiring the employee, the facility had used a private investigation company to investigate his background. The firm found no record of criminal activity when it conducted a seven-year criminal record search in two counties where the employee had lived and worked. However, the screening firm reported that it was unable to locate high school enrollment records for him, that he had misrepresented the reason he had been fired from a previous job (the real reason was poor attendance), and that his prior employment at two businesses listed on his resume could not be confirmed. One of these was a facility at which the employee claimed to have acquired the personal care experience that was deemed critical to his being hired as a mental health assistant. The employee was not interviewed prior to being hired. No attempt was made to require the employee to clear up any of the discrepancies found in the background check. What should the court decide? Why? (*Munroe v. Universal Health Services*, 596 S.E.2d 604 [Ga. 2004])

4. A woman backing her car out of a parking space was confronted by a tow truck driver. The emergency lights were flashing on the tow truck and the driver was in uniform. He screamed at the woman to get out of the car and when she did, he threw her to the ground and stole her car. At the time of the incident, the driver was not attempting to repossess the car or responding to a call for services. There was drug paraphernalia left in the tow truck, suggesting that he had been using cocaine. The driver had a lengthy criminal history of multiple arrests and convictions for property-related crimes, including grand theft of a motor vehicle. Is the tow truck company liable for the assault and theft perpetrated by one of its drivers? Why or why not? (*Magill v. Bartlett Towing*, 2010 Fla. App. LEXIS 7671)

5. Gail Davis worked as an executive assistant to Motown legend Diana Ross. After about a year, the woman voluntarily resigned. About a year later, Diana Ross wrote and distributed the following letter:

    To Whom It May Concern:

    The following people are no longer in my employment.

    [list of former employees including Gail Davis]

    If I let an employee go, it's because either their work or their personal habits are not acceptable to me. I do not recommend these people. In fact, if you hear from these people, and they use my name as a reference, I wish to be contacted.

    Gail Davis had not used Ms. Ross as a reference, nor had any employer requested information from Ms. Ross about Gail Davis. Ms. Davis sued Ms. Ross. What should the court decide? Why? (*Davis v. Ross*, 754 F.2d 80 [2d Cir. 1985])

6. A truck driver applied for a job. The prospective employer contacted former employers, including another trucking company that had terminated the applicant's employment two years ago. The report from the previous employer indicated that the applicant had been arrested while he worked for them and that he had tested positive for drugs. The office worker who completed the report based on personnel records later acknowledged that the statement about the positive drug test was a "mistake on her part." Regarding the arrest, the company had received several reports that the driver had been involved in an altercation with another driver at a truck stop and put the information in his personnel file. However, there is no official record of an arrest and no proof that it ever happened. The applicant was not hired and sued his former employer for defamation. What should the court decide? Why? (*Black v. Usher Transport*, 2011 U.S. Dist. LEXIS 32775 [S.D.Ohio])

7. A man was hired to drive a bus transporting persons with physical and mental disabilities. The hiring was conditional on the successful completion of a criminal background check. The transportation company's subcontract prohibited the hiring of drivers who, among other offenses, had any felony or misdemeanor conviction for a "crime of moral turpitude" or "violence against any person(s)." When it was discovered that the man had been convicted of second-degree murder, his employment was terminated. The sole reason for the termination was the man's criminal record. The conviction stemmed from a gang-related fight that took place more than forty years earlier, when the man was 15 years old. He claimed not to have been the triggerman in the shooting. Consistent with this claim, other individuals were also convicted of the murder. Other than this offense, his record was clean. The man sued the transportation company over the termination. What should the court decide? Why? (*El v. Southeastern Pennsylvania Transportation Authority*, 479 F.3d 232 [3d Cir. 2007])

8. An employee was hired as a service technician by a telecommunications company to perform unsupervised in-home installations and repairs. On his application, he indicated that he had never been convicted of a felony or misdemeanor. It was discovered in a criminal background check conducted about three months later that the man had been arrested in 1982 for attempted murder and found not guilty by reason of insanity. He had been committed to a state psychiatric hospital for two and a half years and spent an additional six months in another mental health facility. Although the man's immediate supervisor recommended that he be retained because he had been performing well, he was terminated. The reason given for the termination was that he had falsified his application. However, comments were also made by various managers that the man had an "emotional dysfunction" that might cause him to engage in this type of behavior on the job; that he might "go off" on a customer; and that due to the time he had spent in a "mental ward," the company could not risk retaining him. The terminated employee sued. What should the court decide? Why? (*Josephs v. Pacific Bell*, 443 F.3d 1050 [9th Cir. 2006])

9. A school janitor was reprimanded for inappropriate verbal conduct toward students. He was subsequently arrested and charged with several counts of child molestation (not involving students). The charges were dropped in exchange for an agreement that the employee would resign. However, the employee was subsequently rehired by the same school district as a substitute bus driver. When he applied for a full-time custodian position at another school district, the school superintendent provided a very positive letter of recommendation. The letter made no reference to the reprimands or criminal charges. When the new employer later learned of the molestation charges, it terminated the custodian for making false statements on his employment application and sued the first school district for negligent misrepresentation of the former employee's record. What should the court decide? Why? (*Richland School District v. Mabton School District*, 45 P.3d 580 [Wash. App. 2002])

10. What do you think about employers using the Internet to check into the online postings and personas of job candidates? Does this practice pose any legal concerns? Ethical concerns?

11. Should employers concern themselves with the credit histories of applicants? Current employees? Only for jobs with significant financial responsibility? If someone has a "bad" credit history or low credit score, what does that tell us about him or her?

12. Immigration policy is controversial. What should U.S. immigration policy look like? What is the best way to deal with illegal immigration?

CHAPTER **6**

Employment Tests

Employers use a bewildering variety of employment tests to make hiring and promotion decisions. Employment tests are also used to ascertain fitness to continue on the job. This chapter considers the legal implications of testing procedures, including drug tests, medical examinations, genetic tests, polygraphs, honesty tests, psychological tests, intelligence and skill tests, and physical fitness tests. Some of these tests are intended to identify disqualifying characteristics (e.g., use of illegal drugs, lack of truthfulness), whereas others focus on measuring the extent to which desirable characteristics (e.g., intelligence, strength) are present. The overriding legal concern with employment tests is discrimination, but invasion of privacy and other claims can also arise.

Drug Tests

Many employers require employees or job candidates to provide urine, blood, saliva, or hair samples that are sent to laboratories and tested for substances indicating use of illegal drugs. **Drug testing** occurs under a variety of circumstances. Tests are given prior to hiring, in conjunction with periodic medical exams, for verification that employees who have been through drug rehabilitation programs are staying "clean," on observations of aberrant behaviors that create **reasonable suspicion** of drug use, after on-the-job accidents, and at random times. In **random drug testing**, a specified percentage of the workforce is selected for periodic drug testing without prior notice and absent individualized suspicion of drug use. If proper procedures are used, a drug test can determine with reasonable certainty whether specified illegal substances are in a person's system. However, it cannot determine how those substances were ingested, what quantity of drugs was taken, and whether the tested individual is currently impaired.

A large national survey of workers conducted in 2002–2003 showed that 14 percent of respondents had used one or more illegal substance during the past twelve months.[1] Marijuana was, by far, the illegal drug of choice. A much smaller percentage of respondents (3.1 percent) reported having used illegal drugs during or just before work hours.[2] However, drug use need not occur in the workplace to produce a positive drug test result (meaning that there is evidence of drug use). In 2007, an estimated 3.8 percent of drug

---

[1] Michael R. Frone. "Prevalence and Distribution of Illicit Drug Use in the Workforce and in the Workplace: Findings and Implications from a U.S. National Survey." *Journal of Applied Psychology* 91, 4 (2006), 861.

[2] Frone, 863.

tests came back positive. There has been a distinct downward trend in the percentage of drug tests failed since 1988, when 13.6 percent of tests came back positive.[3]

What if a job candidate or an employee does not want to be drug tested? Does she have any legal right to refuse drug testing without suffering adverse employment consequences? The general answer is no, with some exceptions. Drug testing is an issue that highlights the fragmented nature of U.S. employment law, as the legal rights of employees vary considerably according to whether they work for the government, are unionized, or live in a state that has chosen to regulate drug testing.

One source of legal limitations on drug testing is state drug testing laws. About half of all states have laws that deal with drug testing.[4] Some of these laws require the drug testing of certain types of employees or under certain circumstances (e.g., post-accident testing), and no state prohibits all drug testing of employees. Random drug testing is subject to the most stringent limitations. Laws in about ten states prohibit random testing outright or limit it to the occupants of safety-sensitive jobs. Thus, *employers should be especially careful in deciding whether to use random testing, particularly for employees who are not in safety-sensitive jobs.*

Another consideration affecting all forms of drug testing except prehire screening is that when employees are represented by a labor union, employers are generally required under the National Labor Relations Act (see Chapter 14) to negotiate with the union about whether there will be drug testing and what the details of the program will entail. This is because the union is the legal representative of the employees (but not job applicants) and drug testing is a "mandatory topic of bargaining" that, if raised by either party, must be negotiated over (but not necessarily agreed on). Thus, *unionized employers cannot unilaterally implement drug testing programs affecting current employees without first negotiating about them with the employees' unions.*

Perhaps the most significant limitation on drug testing is found in the U.S. Constitution and state constitutions. Public employees challenging the drug testing programs of public employers have argued that it is unconstitutional because it violates the **Fourth Amendment** of the U.S. Constitution (and similar language in state constitutions), which protects against **unreasonable search and seizure**. The Supreme Court has consistently held that drug testing, in which employees are required to submit bodily fluids and have those fluids examined for the presence of illegal substances, constitutes a "search."[5] Thus, public employers have had to defend the reasonableness of such searches. Drug testing precipitated by an employer's observations of aberrant behavior is certainly reasonable and constitutional. Drug testing when reasonable suspicion is lacking will be upheld if the government shows a "special need" for the testing that outweighs employees' right to privacy. In a case involving the post-accident testing of railroad employees, a history of accidents involving railroad employees under the influence of drugs provided the special need.[6] The Supreme Court also upheld the testing of U.S. Customs employees who carry firearms or are involved in the interdiction of illegal contraband (including narcotics) as a requirement for promotion. Although there was no known or even suspected problem of drug use among customs agents, their position on the front line in the war against drugs was sufficient to overcome their limited privacy interests in being free

---

[3]"Drug Tests as a Window on Workers." *New York Times* (March 16, 2008), Bu2.

[4]Fred S. Steingold. *The Employer's Legal Handbook*, 8th ed. (Berkeley, CA: Nolo, 2007), pp. 275–84. This source provides a useful summary of state drug testing laws and is the basis for other statements in this chapter about these laws, unless otherwise noted.

[5]*Skinner v. Railway Labor Executives Ass'n*, 489 U.S. 602, 617 (1989).

[6]*Skinner*, at 606–07.

from drug testing.[7] Attempts to apply drug testing to the entire workforces of public agencies without regard to their particular functions have been struck down as unconstitutional.[8] Likewise, vague claims about drugs being a problem in our society and employees potentially having contact with children were not sufficient to justify the drug testing of library pages.[9]

Testing on a random basis is arguably the most intrusive form of drug testing, as it is not suspicion-based or precipitated by any action on the part of the employee. The U.S. Supreme Court has not squarely addressed the issue of random testing in a workplace setting, although it has upheld random drug testing of high school athletes and students participating in after-school programs.[10] A federal appeals court upheld the constitutionality of a random drug testing program applied to probation and parole officers and other employees working in the Michigan criminal justice and mental health systems.[11] However, several state supreme courts have distinguished random testing from other forms of drug testing and found it to be unconstitutional.[12]

Public employers must be prepared to defend the reasonableness of their drug testing programs. The surest way to do this is to focus on safety-sensitive jobs and emphasize testing on reasonable suspicion. To establish reasonable suspicion, supervisors must be well trained at identifying signs of impairment.

JUST THE FACTS

In 2007, the New York City Police Department (NYPD) adopted a new policy regarding breathalyzer testing of officers who have used their firearms. The policy applies whenever any officer "on or off duty, is involved in a firearms discharge within New York City which results in injury to or death of a person." The policy requires that, immediately following the incident, a "portable breathalyzer test" be administered to the police officer in a private setting. If the test yields a reading of blood-alcohol level of 0.08 or greater—the legal limit for driving an automobile in New York State—the officer in question must be taken to an Internal Affairs Bureau testing facility where he or she will be given a second test on a more accurate "Intoxilyzer" machine. The police officers' union challenged the constitutionality of this policy. Does this alcohol testing violate the Fourth Amendment rights of officers?

See, *Lynch v. New York City*, 589 F.3d 94 (2d Cir. 2009), *cert. denied*, 2010 U.S. LEXIS 8217.

Some employers are not only permitted but also legally required to drug test. Laws in a number of states mandate drug testing if employers wish to qualify for discounts on

---

[7]*National Treasury Employees Union v. Von Raab*, 489 U.S. 656 (1989).

[8]*Bolden v. SEPTA*, 953 F.2d 807 (3d Cir. 1991), *cert. denied*, 504 U.S. 943 (1992); *National Treasury Employees Union v. Watkins*, 722 F. Supp. 766 (D.DC 1989).

[9]*Lanier v. City of Woodburn*, 518 F.3d 1147 (9th Cir. 2008).

[10]*Veronia School District 47J v. Acton*, 515 U.S. 646 (1995) (student athletes); *Bd. of Education of Indep. Sch. Dist. No. 92 v. Earls*, 536 U.S. 822 (2002) (after-school programs).

[11]*UAW, Local 1600 v. Winters*, 385 F.3d 1003 (6th Cir. 2004), *cert. denied, Int'l Union, UAW v. Fink*, 544 U.S. 1017 (2005).

[12]*Anchorage Police Department Employees Association v. Municipality of Anchorage*, 24 P.3d 547, at 558 (Alaska 2001); *Petersen v. City of Mesa*, 83 P.3d 35 (Ariz. 2004), *cert. denied*, 125 S. Ct. 51 (2004).

their workers' compensation premiums. However, the most general statutory requirement for drug testing is found in the **Omnibus Transportation Employee Testing Act** of 1991.[13] This federal law requires drug (and alcohol) testing of employees in transportation-related occupations, including airline, railroad, trucking, and public transport workers. The statute calls for testing under a variety of circumstances, including before being hired and on a random basis; specifies the procedures to be used; requires that employees testing positive be suspended or dismissed; and provides for the establishment of rehabilitation programs.

Drug Testing Procedures

Legal questions surround not only whether drug testing can be done but also in what manner it is performed. One source of legal requirements for drug testing procedures is state drug testing laws. Some of the more common procedural requirements found in these state laws are the following:

1. Employees must be provided with written notice that testing is required.
2. Employees must be provided with copies of the employer's substance abuse and drug testing policy.
3. Employers must use licensed laboratories to analyze samples.
4. Employers must perform confirmatory tests if requested or allow employees access to samples to have their own tests done.
5. Employees must be given test results in writing.
6. Employees who test positive must be given the opportunity to explain the result.
7. Samples must be collected with due regard for employee privacy.

The Department of Transportation's (DOT) regulations[14] for drug testing under the Omnibus Transportation Employee Testing Act set out exacting procedures, including steps to balance privacy in producing the sample with safeguards against adulteration of the sample, use of tamperproof custody seals on specimen containers, documentation of the **chain of custody** (the parties who handle the sample), testing by an independent lab, **confirmatory tests** (second, more sophisticated tests) used when initial screening tests come back positive, use of a qualified **medical review officer** to interpret the results and communicate them to the department, and opportunity for the tested employee to explain possible reasons for a positive result (e.g., other legal medications taken). However, the Omnibus Transportation Employees Testing Act does not provide individual employees with the right to sue for improper drug testing procedures and it appears to supersede state drug testing laws that would otherwise allow employees to sue over improperly conducted drug tests.[15] Additionally, the constitutionality of a DOT regulation requiring that transportation workers who previously tested positive and are subject to return-to-duty and follow-up drug tests be directly observed while producing their urine samples has been upheld.[16] While acknowledging the intrusiveness of this requirement, the court found that it was reasonable because of the proliferation of elaborate mechanisms for cheating on drug tests, the greater probability that persons who had previously tested positive would resort to such means, and the lesser expectation of privacy that exists in the pervasively regulated transportation industry.

Nor does it appear that courts will seriously entertain negligence suits against employers for slipshod testing. However, negligence claims against laboratories conducting drug

[13]49 U.S.C.S. §§ 45101 *et seq.* (2011).

[14]49 C.F.R. Part 40 (2011).

[15]*Williams v. United Parcel Service*, 2008 U.S. App. LEXIS 11875 (10th Cir.).

[16]*BNSF Railway Co. v. U.S. Department of Transportation*, 566 F.3d 200 (D.C. Cir. 2009).

tests might be another matter. In a case involving a flight attendant, a laboratory was found negligent for a faulty drug testing procedure.[17] The flight attendant was fired by Delta Airlines after the laboratory concluded that her urine sample had showed signs of "substitution" (it was not sufficiently heavier than water and had too little creatinine) and thus did not allow for a valid test of whether drugs had been used. The procedure used to determine whether adulteration or substitution of a sample has occurred is sensitive to such factors as sex, body size, water intake, and diet. The lab failed to adequately account for these in reaching its finding. The lab's errors were characterized by the court as being "at the simple end of the spectrum, to the point of being crude."[18] Although Delta did not bear liability, it rehired the flight attendant with back pay, suspended its policy of discharging employees based on this "validity test" of samples, and terminated its contract with the laboratory.[19]

State laws requiring that employers provide employees with copies of their substance abuse policies dovetail with the federal **Drug-Free Workplace Act (DFWA)** of 1988.[20] This law applies to companies that have contracts to provide goods or services to the federal government. The DFWA is silent on the subject of drug testing. Instead, it requires that covered employers develop and communicate policies prohibiting drug use, possession, sale, or distribution in the workplace; inform employees about the dangers of drug abuse and options available for drug counseling and treatment; establish penalties for drug abuse violations; and report to the funding agency any convictions relating to drug use or sale in the workplace.

Although no single set of legal requirements exists for how drug tests must be done and the chances of employers being held liable for sloppy drug testing procedures are remote, prudence and the desire not to unfairly deprive individuals of employment suggest that *employers should have policies notifying employees if they are subject to drug testing and, if so, the circumstances under which testing will occur, the procedures used, and the consequences of testing positive. Sound drug testing procedures include the use of confirmatory tests to verify positive results, careful labeling of specimens and documentation of the chain of custody, respect for the privacy of individuals producing specimens, use of reputable labs and monitoring of their performance, use of a medical review officer to interpret results, and opportunity for employees to provide alternative explanations for positive results.*

Use of Drug Test Results

Are there any limitations on how the results of drug tests are used? Courts are reluctant to protect at-will employees from termination based on drug tests, even if the tests were conducted improperly. Disparate treatment claims are possible if the drug test results of otherwise similarly situated employees lead to one employee being terminated and the other given more lenient treatment based on his protected class characteristics. However, adverse impact claims citing drug testing as the neutral requirement appear doomed to fail under Title VII because "a rule barring the employment of an individual who currently and knowingly uses or possesses a controlled substance ... shall be considered an unlawful employment practice ... *only if such rule is adopted or applied with an intent to discriminate* ... [italics added for emphasis]."[21] Employers that discharge unionized

---

[17]*Ishikawa v. Delta Airlines*, 343 F.3d 1129 (9th Cir. 2003).

[18]*Ishikawa*, at 1131.

[19]"Jury Awards Delta Flight Attendant $400,000 for Drug Laboratory Negligence." *Daily Labor Report* 135 (July 16, 2001), A-11.

[20]41 U.S.C.S. § 8102 (2011).

[21]42 U.S.C.S. § 2000e-2(k)(3) (2011).

employees for positive drug tests *sometimes* find that their decisions are overturned by arbitrators because the testing was not done in conformance with contractual requirements or because mitigating factors called for employees to be given second chances. Even with public policy strongly favoring elimination of illegal drug use, courts have generally upheld the decisions of arbitrators to reinstate unionized employees testing positive.[22]

Drug test results are sensitive information. Divulging such information to parties that do not have a legitimate need to know can violate the privacy rights of applicants or employees and violate confidentiality requirements of state drug testing laws. *Employers should treat drug test results as confidential.* False statements about drug test results can be highly damaging to individuals' reputations and thus are fertile ground for defamation suits. A positive drug test cannot support statements such as the tested employee is "a drug addict" or "came into work high on drugs." The test simply indicates the presence of an illegal substance and nothing more. The need to ensure that drug testing results are accurately stated and handled confidentially is another reason for using a medical review officer.

Employers can salvage valuable human resources by allowing employees who test positive to keep their jobs while they get help from substance abuse programs. Many employers provide employee assistance programs (EAPs) to help employees with substance abuse and other problems and give them second chances; however, after an employee who is addicted to illegal drugs has been allowed to undergo treatment in a rehabilitation program or has successfully completed such a program, that employee is protected by the Americans with Disabilities Act (ADA). *Employers must not decide to terminate, fail to promote, or otherwise discriminate against an employee who has undergone treatment for drug addiction and is no longer using illegal drugs.* The ADA does not, however, prohibit an employer from establishing a "one-strike" rule under which employees who test positive for illegal drugs are never again considered for employment.[23] Such a rule excludes all candidates who test positive for any reason and not simply those who are addicted to drugs. Furthermore, while the rule might tend to have adverse impact against disabled persons, the plaintiffs failed to show that recovered drug addicts were disproportionately excluded from the employer's workforce.

Practical Considerations Would you advise an employer that operates retail clothing stores to drug test? If so, under what circumstances? Using what procedures? What should be done regarding applicants or employees who test positive?

Medical Examinations

A **medical examination** is any "procedure or test that seeks information about an individual's impairments or health."[24] The distinction between medical exams and other tests that broadly relate to health is not always clear. For example, a psychological exam might or might not be a medical exam depending on whether the test is designed to reveal a mental impairment or merely to assess personality traits. A court considered the status of a psychological exam used by Rent-A-Center to select management trainees. The test incorporated questions from the Minnesota Multiphasic Personality Inventory (MMPI). Even though the test was not scored by a psychologist, the court concluded that:

> *Because it is designed, at least in part, to reveal mental illness and has the effect of hurting the employment prospects of one with a mental disability, we think the MMPI is best categorized as a medical examination. And even though the MMPI was only a*

---

[22]*Eastern Associated Coal Corp. v. Mine Workers*, 531 U.S. 57 (2000); *Int'l Union v. Michigan Mechanical Services*, 247 Fed. Appx. 649 (6th Cir. 2007).

[23]*Lopez v. Pacific Maritime Association*, 636 F.3d 1197 (9th Cir. 2011).

[24]U.S. Equal Employment Opportunity Commission. *Enforcement Guidance: Disability-Related Inquiries and Medical Examinations of Employees under the ADA.* (July 27, 2000).

TABLE 6.1 EXAMPLES OF TESTS THAT ARE AND ARE NOT CONSIDERED MEDICAL EXAMINATIONS

MEDICAL EXAMINATION	NOT A MEDICAL EXAMINATION
Test to check for use of alcohol	Drug test limited to a search for use of illegal drugs
Blood pressure screening	Physical fitness/agility test
HIV test	Polygraph exam
Genetic test	Honesty test
Psychological test used to diagnose mental illness	Psychological test assessing personality in the normal range
Vision test analyzed by an ophthalmologist or optometrist	Vision test for ability to read or recognize objects
Diagnostic procedure (e.g., MRI) or medical check-up	Demonstrations of ability to perform specific job tasks

© Cengage Learning 2013.

part (albeit a significant part) of a battery of tests administered to employees looking to advance, its use, we conclude, violated the ADA.[25]

Relevant factors in determining whether tests are medical exams include if they are administered and/or interpreted by health care professionals, are designed to reveal physical or mental impairment, are invasive, measure physiological responses to performing a task rather than task performance itself, are given in a medical setting, and require the use of medical equipment.[26] All of these factors need not be present.

Table 6.1 provides examples of tests that are and are not considered medical exams. The significance of this distinction is that medical exams are subject to a number of limitations under the ADA.

Medical Examinations and the ADA

The ADA governs whether medical exams can be conducted, what types of exams can be performed, and to what uses the information gleaned from medical exams can be put. These rules are outlined in Table 6.2.

TABLE 6.2 REQUIREMENTS FOR MEDICAL EXAMINATIONS UNDER THE ADA*

	PRE-OFFER	AFTER CONDITIONAL OFFER	POST-HIRE
Can exam occur?	No	Yes	Yes
What type of exam?	NA	Unrestricted	(1) Job-related and consistent with business necessity or (2) voluntary
Can results be used to deny employment to a disabled person?	NA	Only if (1) cannot perform essential functions of the job even with reasonable accommodation or (2) is a "direct threat" to self or others	

* This table lists requirements under the ADA only. Additional restrictions are imposed by the Genetic Information Nondiscrimination Act on medical exams and inquiries that would reveal genetic information.

---

[25]*Karraker v. Rent-A-Center*, 411 F.3d 831, 837 (7th Cir. 2005), *vacated and remanded on other grounds in* 492 F.3d 896 (7th Cir. 2007).

[26]EEOC. *Enforcement Guidance: Disability Related Inquiries.*

The ADA's requirements differ depending on the stage in the employment process at which medical testing is desired. *Prior to making a conditional offer of employment, employers are prohibited from requiring that applicants submit to medical exams.* But this does not mean that employers must make hiring decisions deprived of information about the health of job candidates. After an employer has considered all of the relevant nonmedical qualifications of a candidate, arrived at a tentative hiring decision, and extended a **conditional offer of employment**, the employer is free to require a medical exam to verify that the person is physically and mentally capable of performing the job. The offer of employment is thus "conditional" upon satisfactory results from the medical exam. Note that this sequencing makes it clear that any subsequent rejection of the candidate was based on his or her health status. Thus, *medical exams, if used, should be the last tests performed and the last information considered prior to finalizing hiring decisions.* Additionally, *individuals cannot be required to take medical exams unless the exams are given to all other persons hired into the same job category.* People who are disabled or "look disabled" cannot be singled out for medical examination.

JUST THE FACTS

An airline was in a hurry to hire flight attendants. After conducting interviews, it issued conditional offers of employment contingent on successful completion of background checks and medical exams. The background checks would be completed later, but the medical exams were conducted immediately on-site by the airline's medical department. The medical exams included blood tests that revealed the HIV-positive status of the candidates. They had not revealed their HIV status when asked to complete medical history questionnaires as part of their medical exams. The airline said that it was rescinding its conditional job offers due to the job candidates' failure to disclose the information. The rejected job candidates sued under the ADA. What should the court decide?

See, *Leonel v. American Airlines*, 400 F.3d 702 (9th Cir. 2005).

The ADA does not limit the scope of medical exams conducted following conditional offers of employment (the Genetic Information Nondiscrimination Act, discussed below, does place certain limits on such exams, however). In contrast, *medical exams of current employees are limited to those that are job-related and consistent with business necessity or are voluntary.* Since employers have ongoing evidence about the job performance of their current employees, that information—and not medical exam results—should be the primary basis for employment decisions. Medical exams are job-related and consistent with business necessity when employers have reasonable belief that individuals may be unable to perform their jobs due to their medical conditions or that they may pose a direct threat to their own safety or that of others. In some occupations (e.g., pilots), periodic exams or health monitoring may be job-related and required by law. A medical exam can also be required to document the existence of a disability that necessitates an accommodation. Finally, the law also allows for medical exams of current employees when these are truly voluntary, such as if an employee chooses to use an employer-sponsored blood pressure screening or other wellness program.

> ## *Clippings*
>
> Sue Bates was fired from a job that she held for twenty-two years at Dura Automotive Systems in Lawrenceburg, Tennessee. Her offense was testing positive for the painkiller hydrocodone. The drug, a narcotic, was prescribed by her doctor to help relieve severe back pain and other symptoms. Concerned about possible safety hazards posed by lawful prescription drugs, the company had broadened its drug testing to include a search for legal substances with sedative effects. Suits alleging violations of the ADA have been filed by the EEOC and individual employees. The case has important practical and legal implications insofar as the use of powerful prescription drugs for a variety of conditions has grown substantially and disabled employees are especially likely to take such drugs.
>
> Katie Zezema and Abby Goodnough. "Employers' Tests for Drugs May Catch Prescriptions, Too." *New York Times* (October 25, 2010), A1.

The case of the auto plant workers (see "Clippings") terminated for using prescription drugs (although the company also disputes the grounds for termination) has produced several court decisions, although not yet a final outcome.[27] While some of the original claims have been dismissed, the crux of the remaining case is that the drug tests constitute medical exams of current employees that are permissible only if they are job-related and consistent with business necessity. It is important to note that drug tests—when restricted to searches for illegal substances—are *not* medical exams because the current use of illegal drugs, even if due to an addiction, is excluded from the definition of disability under the ADA. Thus, such exams do not have the potential to reveal information about a disability. However, if, as in this case, the scope of drug testing is expanded to include prescription drugs taken for medical conditions that might be disabling, the test constitutes a medical exam. ADA regulations allow for employers that drug test to ask about prescription drug use, but only after a positive drug test result and as a means of clarifying the reason for testing positive.[28] While denying summary judgment and setting the stage for a trial, the district court left open the possibility that this medical exam was defensible under the ADA:

> *Dura has brought forth evidence that the Facility is a somewhat dangerous place to work, had significant, drug-related safety issues and that Dura attempted to screen out only those drugs that, it believed, could cause impairment. In light of that evidence [and] the fact that workplace safety is a "business necessity," ... the court cannot say, as a matter of law, that Dura's policy was not "consistent with business necessity." This is a question for the jury.[29]*

In *Brownfield v. City of Yakima*, the court must decide whether requiring a "fitness for duty" exam of a police officer who was exhibiting unusual behavior violated the ADA.

---

[27]*Bates v. Dura Automotive Systems*, 2011 U.S. Dist. LEXIS 33996 (M.D. Tenn.); 625 F.3d 283 (6th Cir. 2010) (interlocutory appeal).

[28]U.S. Equal Employment Opportunity Commission. *ADA Enforcement Guidance: Preemployment Disability-Related Questions and Medical Examinations.* (October 10, 1995).

[29]*Bates v. Dura Automotive Systems*, 2011 U.S. Dist. LEXIS 33996 (M.D. Tenn.); 625 F.3d 283 (6th Cir. 2010) (interlocutory appeal).

Brownfield v. City of Yakima
612 F.3d 1140 (9th Cir. 2010)

OPINION BY CIRCUIT JUDGE LUCERO:

Oscar J. Brownfield appeals the district court's grant of summary judgment in favor of the City of Yakima on his ... Americans with Disabilities Act ("ADA") [claim].... We hold that the City did not violate Brownfield's rights under the ADA by requiring a fitness for duty exam ("FFDE") after he repeatedly exhibited emotionally volatile behavior while serving as a police officer.... * * *

Brownfield began working as a police officer for the City of Yakima Police Department ("YPD") in November 1999. Approximately one year later, he suffered a ... head injury in an off-duty car accident. After recovering from symptoms including reduced self-awareness, Brownfield returned to full duty in July 2001. He received positive performance evaluations and was awarded several commendations over the next three years.

In June 2004, Brownfield complained to his superior, Sergeant Amos, about Officer Dejournette, Brownfield's community service partner for Police Athletic League ("PAL") and Drug Abuse Resistance Education ("DARE") matters. In an interoffice memo titled "Unethical work practices," Brownfield wrote that Dejournette neglected his duties with respect to the DARE program to work on fraud matters, forcing Brownfield to complete tasks assigned to Dejournette. * * * The memo further took issue with Dejournette's use of comp time and overtime. In particular, Brownfield was disturbed that Dejournette was given twenty hours in "time owed" because Lt. Merryman, another superior, requested Brownfield "spend more hours on the development of PAL, but ha[d] never offered [him] time owed as a reward." * * *

Over the next year, Brownfield compiled notes on Dejournette's perceived shortcomings. These notes detail Dejournette's failure to complete reimbursement requests, grant applications, and time sheets in a punctual manner, his continued use of overtime and comp time, and his generally "lackadaisical approach to PAL duties." In May 2005, after Merryman reprimanded Brownfield for failing to schedule an event, Brownfield forwarded his notes to YPD Chief Sam Granato. Shortly after forwarding his notes, Brownfield composed a second email to Granato complaining that Dejournette closed the PAL facility early for illegitimate reasons.

On May 11, 2005, Brownfield, Merryman, and Amos met to discuss Brownfield's problems with Dejournette. Midway through the meeting, Brownfield used an expletive in stating that he needed to talk to a union representative. Despite an order from Merryman to remain in the room, Brownfield stood up and left. When Amos found Brownfield speaking to another officer, Brownfield swore at him and demanded he leave the room. Brownfield was temporarily suspended for insubordination as a result of this incident. He later explained that he had expected to meet with Granato and was concerned that the meeting included Merryman, who was the subject of some of his complaints. Brownfield stated that he was "consumed" with anger and fear, and that he recognized that he needed to take a break.

In September 2005, four incidents occurred that, together with the above-described confrontation, led the YPD to refer Brownfield for an FFDE. First, Brownfield engaged in a disruptive argument with another officer during muster. A sergeant reported that when Brownfield learned that YPD was investigating him—but not the other officer—he became visibly upset, was swearing, and was "just not really speaking full sentences."

Second, Brownfield reported that he felt "himself losing control" during a traffic stop. According to a YPD sergeant, Brownfield reported that a young child riding in a vehicle he pulled over began taunting him during the stop. Brownfield became upset, his legs began shaking, and he "wasn't sure what he was going to do." Brownfield calmed down when a backup officer arrived. Third, the YPD received a domestic violence call from Brownfield's estranged wife, Leticia. Leticia reported that she and Brownfield began arguing when she stopped at his apartment to see their children. As she was backing out of a doorway, Brownfield allegedly struck her by slamming the door. Brownfield disputed this version of events, and no charges were filed. Finally, a YPD officer reported that Brownfield made several statements that caused him concern. The officer told a YPD captain that Brownfield made comments such as "It's not important anyway," "I'm not sure if it's worth it," and "It doesn't matter how this ends." After hearing this report, Captain Copeland placed Brownfield on administrative leave and ordered him to undergo an FFDE.

Dr. Decker conducted the FFDE on October 19, 2005. She diagnosed Brownfield as suffering from "Mood Disorder due to a General Medical Condition with mixed features," which manifested itself in "poor judgment, emotional volatility, and irritability" and which could be related to Brownfield's 2000 head injury. Dr. Decker concluded that Brownfield was unfit for police duty and that his disability was permanent. * * *

In May 2006, the City informed Brownfield that it would hold a pre-termination hearing with respect to his employment with the YPD. In response, Brownfield emailed a YPD captain reiterating his complaints about Dejournette and insinuating that Dejournette may have stolen PAL funds. Brownfield advised: "I don't think it would be a good choice for the chief to fire me prior to the independent audit, but that's just me."

Prior to the hearing, Brownfield obtained a second opinion from a Dr. Mar. Dr. Mar agreed with Dr. Decker that Brownfield was unfit for duty due to his "emotional, cognitive, behavioral, and physical problems." However, Dr. Mar believed that Brownfield's problems might be amenable to treatment. The City continued Brownfield's pre-termination hearing pending treatment and further evaluation by Dr. Mar and Dr. Decker. In December 2006, Dr. Mar reported that Brownfield was progressing well and would be able to return to duty at an unspecified date with continued treatment. Brownfield refused to return to Dr. Decker, leading YPD to order an FFDE with another doctor, Dr. Ekemo. Brownfield attended an initial exam in February 2007, and Dr. Ekemo scheduled a second visit with Brownfield to complete his evaluation. However, Brownfield refused to attend the follow-up session.

The City informed Brownfield that he would likely be terminated unless he cooperated in the FFDE, but Brownfield again refused. A pre-termination hearing was held on March 19, 2007. City Manager Richard Zais determined that Brownfield was insubordinate and unfit for duty. Brownfield was terminated on April 10, 2007. * * *

Brownfield alleges that the City violated the ADA by requiring him to submit to the FFDEs. [A]n employer may not require a medical examination to determine whether an employee is disabled "unless such examination or inquiry is shown to be job-related

and consistent with business necessity." In interpreting the "business necessity" standard in another ADA context, we have cautioned that it "is quite high, and is not to be confused with mere expediency." * * *

Although this circuit has yet to address whether an employer may preemptively require a medical examination, other courts have answered in the affirmative. [T]he Eleventh Circuit considered the legality of an FFDE for a police officer who displayed "unusually defensive and antagonistic behavior towards his coworkers and supervisors," but whose job performance was otherwise satisfactory. Recognizing that "[p]olice departments place armed officers in positions where they can do tremendous harm if they act irrationally," the court held that the ADA does not "require a police department to forego a fitness for duty examination to wait until a perceived threat becomes real or questionable behavior results in injuries." Several district courts have reached similar conclusions. In [one of these decisions], the court noted that an employer could subject itself to liability for negligent hiring or retention by turning a blind eye toward an employee's erratic behavior. It held that, "[a]s a matter of law, a school board's psychological examination of an employee is both job-related and consistent with a business necessity if that employee exhibits even mild signs of paranoid or agitated behavior that causes the school administration to question the employee's ability to perform essential job duties." Similarly, in [another relevant decision], the court condoned a psychiatric examination of an elementary school custodian. Focusing on the employee's daily interactions with school-aged children, the court ruled that "a psychiatric examination is job-related and consistent with business necessity in any case where an elementary school employee exhibits paranoid or agitated behavior that causes the school administration to be concerned about the personal safety of those in contact with the employee."

We agree with these courts that prophylactic psychological examinations can sometimes satisfy the business necessity standard, particularly when the employer is engaged in dangerous work. However, we must be keen to guard against the potential for employer abuse of such exams. [The ADA] prohibits employers from using medical exams as a pretext to harass employees or to fish for non-work-related medical issues and the attendant "unwanted exposure of the employee's disability and the stigma it may carry."

We reiterate that the business necessity standard "is quite high, and is not to be confused with mere expediency." Nevertheless, we hold that the business necessity standard may be met even before an employee's work performance declines if the employer is faced with significant evidence that could cause a reasonable person to inquire as to whether an employee is still capable of performing his job. An employee's behavior cannot be merely annoying or inefficient to justify an examination; rather, there must be genuine reason to doubt whether that employee can perform job-related functions. As the "reasonable person" language suggests, this test is objective. The employer bears the burden of demonstrating business necessity.

We agree with the district court that the City had an objective, legitimate basis to doubt Brownfield's ability to perform the duties of a police officer. Undisputed facts show that Brownfield exhibited highly emotional responses on numerous occasions in 2005, four occurring in a single month immediately prior to his referral: He swore at a superior after abruptly leaving a meeting despite a direct order to the contrary; he engaged in a loud argument with a coworker and became extremely angry when he learned the incident was being investigated; he reported that his legs began shaking and he felt himself losing control during a traffic stop; his wife called police to report a domestic altercation with Brownfield; and he made several comments to a coworker such as "It doesn't matter how this ends."

Brownfield attempts to explain away each incident by providing background facts suggesting his reactions were entirely reasonable and by challenging the third-party reports as factually inaccurate, but he does not dispute that he reacted as described or that the third-party reports were made to the YPD. Although a minor argument with a coworker or isolated instances of lost temper would likely fall short of establishing business necessity, Brownfield's repeated volatile responses are of a different character. Moreover, our consideration of the FFDEs' legitimacy is heavily colored by the nature of Brownfield's employment. Police officers are likely to encounter extremely stressful and dangerous situations during the course of their work. When a police department has good reason to doubt an officer's ability to respond to these situations in an appropriate manner, an FFDE is consistent with the ADA. Reasonable cause to question Brownfield's ability to serve as a police officer was present here.

CASE QUESTIONS

1. What was the legal issue in this case? What did the court decide?
2. On what basis does the court decide that the fitness for duty exams were allowed under the ADA?
3. This decision focuses on the medical exams, but what about the termination? Is there any argument to be made that his termination violates the ADA?
4. How much does this decision rest on the particular context of police work? What if the facts were similar but the employee was a waiter at a restaurant? A stock clerk at a warehouse?

Regardless of whether a medical exam is conducted after a conditional offer of employment or during employment, the results of the exam cannot be used to deny an employment opportunity to a disabled person unless that person is unable to perform the "essential functions" of the job or poses a "direct threat" to himself or others, even with some "reasonable accommodation" that the employer could make. Fuller explanation of these concepts will have to await the discussion in Chapter 10. For now, we can say that *only if an employee's disability does not allow him to perform the core parts of a job, even with some help, is an employer justified in denying an employment opportunity to that individual.* An employer cannot simply conclude from a medical exam that an employee is disabled and exclude him on that basis.

However, if a medical exam conducted at the proper time uncovers information about a medical condition that does not meet the legal definition of a disability, the ADA does not preclude use of that information to deny an employment opportunity. In one such case, seventy-two applicants were rejected for entry-level manufacturing jobs on the basis of "nerve conduction tests."[30] The accuracy of these tests is disputed, but they are intended to identify persons susceptible to developing carpal tunnel syndrome (a condition increasingly seen among workers performing repetitive tasks and one that can have debilitating effects on hands, wrists, and arms). The applicants challenged their rejection based on this type of medical exam as a violation of the ADA. However, the employees were unable to show that they were either currently disabled or regarded by the employer as disabled. Thus, they were not protected under the ADA. The outcome of this case notwithstanding, employers are skating on thin ice when they exclude individuals because of their potential to later develop disabling conditions. This is shown by another ADA case in which a job candidate's offer of employment was withdrawn after it was found that he had several prior workplace injuries for which he had received workers' compensation. The court upheld a jury's finding that the man was denied the job based on "unsubstantiated speculation about future risks from a perceived disability."[31] Denial of employment opportunity based on the potential to develop medical problems in the future also risks violation of the recently enacted Genetic Information Nondiscrimination Act.

Genetic Tests   Medical exams also include **genetic tests** aimed at assessing the predisposition of persons to develop medical conditions or pass them on to offspring. Knowledge regarding the genetic makeup of humans and the genetic basis of diseases has been rapidly accumulating. Genetic testing promises medical benefits but also lends itself to misuse, particularly in the hands of employers and insurers.

THE CHANGING WORKPLACE

Genetic Testing and Employment

Genetic information about employees can be obtained through low-tech means such as compiling family medical histories, indirectly through exams and lab tests, and directly through new methods for testing DNA and other genetic material. Genetic testing can take the form of **genetic screening** of job candidates for desirable or undesirable genetic traits and **genetic monitoring** to spot adverse changes in the genetic material of employees exposed to hazardous substances. When used for screening purposes, genetic information can identify individuals who have diseases that are not yet manifest, who are genetically disposed toward developing conditions in the future, or who are at greater risk of having children with inherited conditions. However, relatively few diseases have known and direct genetic links. The genetic predisposition to develop a disease interacts with numerous other environmental and behavioral factors to determine whether a particular disease actually develops. There is no certainty that it will.

Genetic testing raises troubling questions because it permits employers to delve even deeper into the health status of employees and to potentially exclude persons based not only on conditions that they have but also on conditions that they or their children *might someday have*. Until recently, the legal status of genetic testing was murky. Inquiries or tests aimed at obtaining genetic information clearly fall within the ADA's restrictions on medical exams. But use of the information from a properly conducted genetic test to deny employment does not clearly run afoul of the ADA unless the employee is currently disabled or regarded as such by the employer. A number of states have chosen to regulate genetic testing. Some of

---

[30]*EEOC v. Rockwell International*, 243 F.3d 1012 (7th Cir. 2001).

[31]*Garrison v. Baker Hughes Oilfield Operations, Inc.*, 287 F.3d 955 (10th Cir. 2002).

these laws are narrow, pertaining only to particular gene-linked conditions (e.g., sickle cell anemia) or to particular methods of gathering genetic information. A few states (e.g., New Jersey, Wisconsin)[1] broadly prohibit subjecting employees to genetic tests and using genetic information to make employment decisions. The U.S. Constitution also places limits on genetic testing. In an instructive case, a government laboratory was covertly testing employees for, among other things, the sickle cell trait. An appeals court found that the testing was invasive and lacked sufficient consent, raising a valid constitutional issue.[2] The lab settled the case.

The **Genetic Information Nondiscrimination Act of 2008** (GINA) extends broad protection against discrimination on the basis of genetic information in both health insurance and employment to all employees covered by Title VII of the Civil Rights Act.[3] The EEOC has developed an extensive set of regulations for compliance with GINA,[4] but there will still be many questions for the courts to decide in the future regarding this important new federal law.

[1]N.J. Stat. Ann. § 10:5–12; Wis. Stat. § 111.372.
[2]*Norman-Bloodsaw v. Lawrence Berkeley Laboratory*, 135 F.3d 1260 (9th Cir. 1998).
[3]110 P.L. 233; 122 Stat. 881 (2008).
[4]29 C.F.R. Part 1635 (2011).

Clippings

Pamela Fink saw both of her sisters develop breast cancer. This prompted her to undergo genetic testing that confirmed that she was indeed predisposed to contracting breast cancer herself. She then made the wrenching decision to have a preventative double mastectomy. She informed her employer about her situation. When she returned from leave after having the surgery, she was given fewer responsibilities, demoted, and eventually terminated. She filed a charge with the EEOC, alleging that her termination was based on the genetic information shared with her employer. As early cases like Ms. Fink's wend their way through the legal system, we will get a better idea about the impact of the Genetic Information Nondiscrimination Act.

Steven Greenhouse. "Ex-Worker Says Her Firing Was Based on Genetic Test." *New York Times* (May 1, 2010), A12.

GINA covers employers with fifteen or more employees and applies to both employment decisions and health insurance. Provisions of the law relevant to the latter are discussed in Chapter 13. Concerning employment, *employers must generally refrain from requesting, requiring, purchasing, or otherwise acquiring genetic information regarding applicants and employees.* Genetic information includes information from genetic tests of an employee or family member, family medical history, requests for genetic services by an employee or family member, and genetic information about a fetus.[32] Note that information about what diseases or other medical conditions "run in the family"—i.e., family medical history—is considered genetic information. However, information about conditions (e.g., cancer) or traits (e.g., left-handedness) already manifested by employees, even though these conditions or traits might have significant genetic components, does not fall within the protections of GINA. There are some narrow exceptions to the

[32]29 C.F.R. § 1635.3 (c) (2011).

prohibition on acquiring genetic information including isolated cases of inadvertent disclosure of genetic information by employees (the so-called water cooler exception), health or genetic services (including wellness programs) provided on a voluntary basis, disclosures of relatives' medical conditions to document requests for medical leave, genetic information derived from public sources such as newspapers, and genetic monitoring (for adverse health effects due to occupational exposures) that is legally required or voluntarily provided.[33] One of the circumstances under which employers are especially apt to run afoul of GINA is in making requests for medical information to health care providers. The EEOC has suggested language for making such requests that, if used, provides employers with a "safe harbor." The language references GINA, explains the meaning of genetic information, and then expressly states "To comply with this law, we are asking that you not provide any genetic information when responding to this request for medical information."[34] *Employers should use the EEOC's suggested language when making requests for medical information from health care providers.* To the limited extent that employers can lawfully possess genetic information, this information is subject to the same confidentiality requirements that the ADA imposes on medical information of all types, including confidential handling and maintaining the information in files separate from employees' personnel files.

Genetic information is medical information and genetic tests are a specific type of medical exam. Thus, the ADA's limitations on medical exams and inquiries and on the use of medical information apply to genetic information. But GINA goes further in limiting the acquisition and use of this particular type of medical information. Thus, while the scope of medical exams administered following a conditional offer of employment is not restricted by the ADA, GINA requires that *such exams must not include the taking of a family medical history or other forms of genetic information gathering.* Another difference between GINA and the ADA is that while the latter permits employers to gather medical information on current employees if it is job-related and consistent with business necessity, GINA allows for genetic information to be collected only under the limited circumstances noted above. Lastly, while the ADA allows employers to use the results of lawful medical exams/inquiries to deny employment opportunities to nondisabled persons or to disabled persons not able to perform the essential functions of their jobs, GINA completely prohibits the use of genetic information in making employment decisions.[35] *Employers must never use genetic information for making decisions about employment opportunities.*

Polygraphs and Honesty Tests

Honesty is a highly desirable quality in employees and people in general. Not surprisingly, employers would like to know whether job candidates' representations are credible and whether they can be trusted if hired. A number of tests purport to be able to do so, including polygraphs and voice stress analyzers. A **polygraph** does not "detect lies," but instead it measures changes in physiological responses, including respiration, blood pressure, and perspiration (galvanic skin response). Voice stress analyzers focus on changes in vocal patterns. Telling lies is thought to be stressful, prompting physiological responses or vocal patterns different from baseline readings established by first asking simple neutral questions (e.g., What is your name?). Polygraphers administer exams

Practical Considerations To improve employee health and lower insurance costs, many employers have turned to wellness programs. These programs typically entail an extensive baseline assessment of current health status and incentives for participation. What should employers do to make sure that their wellness programs comply with the ADA and GINA?

---

[33]29 C.F.R. § 1635.8 (b) (2011).

[34]29 C.F.R. § 1635.8 (b)(1)(i)(B) (2011).

[35]U.S. Equal Employment Opportunity Commission. "Questions and Answers for Small Businesses: EEOC Final Rule on Title II of the Genetic Information Nondiscrimination Act of 2008." Viewed February 28, 2011 (http://www.eeoc.gov/).

and combine their own observations of tested individuals, the physiological indicators, attempts to elicit admissions from persons tested, and more than a little intuition to determine whether there is "significant deception" or "no significant deception." Individuals can thus be rejected either because it is concluded that they are engaging in significant deception or because they confess to something serious during polygraph exams.

Concerns have been raised about the accuracy of these tests, intimidation tactics used by polygraphers, and invasive questions. Prior to passage of the **Employee Polygraph Protection Act (EPPA)**,[36] preemployment polygraphs were widely used. The law is now clear: *Private sector employers must not request or require that applicants submit to polygraphs or other mechanical or electrical truth-determining devices (including voice stress analyzers).* There is a limited exception for private sector employers producing or dispensing controlled substances (narcotics) or providing "heavy" security services (e.g., guarding nuclear plants, water supplies). Importantly, government agencies, including law enforcement and security agencies, are still free to polygraph both applicants and employees.

Although the EPPA negates the use of polygraphs in hiring, the law allows polygraphs to be used by private sector employers in conjunction with investigations of employee theft or other serious wrongdoing—subject to many procedural requirements (see Chapter 17). To fill the void left by the polygraph, many employers have turned to paper-and-pencil **honesty tests**, also known as integrity tests. Although the use of these tests is controversial, they are not regulated by the EPPA.

Scored Tests of Ability

The aforementioned tests are intended to screen out candidates with undesirable traits. Employers also use a variety of tests to assess desired characteristics such as intelligence, aptitude, specific job skills or knowledge, work-related attitudes, personality traits, strength, and physical fitness. These tests are typically scored in some fashion, and persons who score better, or at least above a specified cutoff point, get hired. The main concern is that the tests not be discriminatory.

Frequently, scored tests of ability are developed by consultants or testing companies that sell the rights to use the tests to employers, score the tests, and interpret the results. However, this does not absolve employers from responsibility for the tests and from taking reasonable steps to ensure their legality. But what should employers look for? In brief, employers need to pay attention to the wording of test items, the effects of tests on different protected class groups, evidence that tests are job-related and consistent with business necessity, the appropriateness of scoring methods and cutoff levels, and accommodation of disabled test takers.

Examining Test Items

Many employment tests are given on paper or online and contain numerous items (questions) for candidates to answer. *Test items should be examined to see if they relate to protected class characteristics, and tests containing such items should not be used.* In an instructive case, the parent company of Target stores used a psychological test devised by a testing company to screen applicants for store security guard jobs. The test contained many items requiring applicants to divulge the extent to which they held various religious beliefs:

"My soul sometimes leaves my body."

"I believe in the second coming of Christ."

---

[36]29 U.S.C.S. §§ 2001–2009 (2011).

"I go to church almost every week."

"I believe there is a God."

Other test questions pertained to sexual orientation and behavior:

"I have been in trouble one or more times because of my sex behavior."

"I am very strongly attracted by members of my own sex."

"I have never indulged in any unusual sex practices."[37]

These questions not only constituted preemployment inquiries about protected class (in California, where this case arose, sexual orientation is a protected class) but also were scored by the testing company. Thus, some answers to these questions were deemed more desirable than others, and the manner in which an applicant responded affected her ability to be hired. On a variety of grounds, including discrimination based on religion and sexual orientation, the court granted the plaintiffs a court order to stop the testing. The employer eventually settled with the class of plaintiffs for over $2 million.

It does not take a great deal of technical sophistication to examine test questions and to red-flag those that pertain to protected class or are otherwise inappropriate. The latter category includes questions that presume the sex of the test taker or that are premised on religious or cultural beliefs that would be more familiar to some protected class groups than others. Tests that contain such items simply should not be used.

Clippings

Like many large cities, New York City has had problems with its civil service exams, especially those used in hiring firefighters. In a diverse city where African Americans and Latinos each comprise about 27 percent of the population, only about 3 percent of firefighters were African Americans and 6 percent were Latinos in 2009. A suit brought by the Department of Justice challenging the civil service exams given in 1999 and 2002 resulted in rulings that the city discriminated under both adverse impact and pattern or practice theories. In ruling on the latter, District Judge Nicholas G. Garaufis said that the exclusion of persons of color from firefighter jobs was not a "one-time mistake or the product of benign neglect." Instead, "it was part of a pattern, practice and policy of intentional discrimination against black applicants that has deep historical antecedents and uniquely disabling effects."

Diane Cardwell. "Judge Finds Racial Bias in Recruiting by Fire Dept." *New York Times* (July 23, 2009), A24; Al Baker. "Judge Finds 'Intentional Discrimination' Against Blacks in Fire Dept. Hiring." *New York Times* (January 14, 2010), A27.

Examining Test Results

An overriding legal concern with scored tests is that they can produce adverse impact discrimination. Although the tests are neutral requirements (assuming that the same tests are given to all candidates for the same jobs and that they do not contain the types of items mentioned earlier), they may nonetheless have discriminatory effects.

---

[37]*Saroka v. Dayton Hudson Corp.*, 1 Cal. Rptr. 2d 77, 79-80 (Cal. App. 1991), *rev. dismissed*, 862 P.2d 148 (Cal. 1993).

Discriminatory effects of employment tests are best seen by examining **applicant flow data**. Applicant flow data compare the protected class composition of an applicant pool to that of the group of people who pass the test and are successful (or at least still in the running) in obtaining an employment opportunity. The underlying premise is that although individuals vary widely in their abilities, overall, people of different races, sexes, national origins, or other protected classes are equally capable of doing most jobs. Thus, we would expect that if tests actually measure ability to do a job, men and women or whites and blacks should experience similar rates of success in passing the tests and obtaining employment opportunities. If, instead, men pass the test at a much higher rate than women or whites pass the test more often than blacks, this indicates that something about the test is producing discriminatory effects.

How different must test outcomes be to conclude that discriminatory effects (or "disproportionate selection") are occurring? One simple guideline is the EEOC's **four-fifths rule**.[38] The rule says that if the **selection rate**—the percentage of applicants who pass the test and are hired or continue to be considered for employment—for one race or sex or other protected class group is less than 80 percent (4/5) of the selection rate for the race or sex or other protected class group that was most successful at passing the test, this is evidence of discriminatory effects. For example, suppose that one hundred male applicants are given a test assessing the personality trait of conscientiousness and that fifty of these male applicants pass the test. If eighty female applicants take the same test and sixty pass it, there is evidence supporting a prima facie case of adverse impact against men. The selection (pass) rate for males is 50 percent (50/100), while the selection rate for females is 75 percent (60/80). Thus, males are only two-thirds as successful as females in passing this test (0.50/0.75 = 0.666), which is less than the required four-fifths or 0.80. It is important to note that the relevant comparison is between selection *rates* and not *absolute numbers* of persons hired.

The four-fifths rule is a useful "rule of thumb" and is given some deference by the courts, but it does not always suffice. It can be misleading when the number of applicants, and thus the number of test takers on which selection rates are based, is small. In one such case, pass rates for whites and African Americans on a promotional test for firefighters violated the four-fifths rule, but because the number of candidates taking the exam each year was so small (three to seven), there was not a prima facie case.[39] In another case, selection rates on a promotional exam satisfied the four-fifths rule (74.6/89.5 = 0.83), but other statistical methods showed that the difference in mean test scores between white and African American test takers was still far larger than would be expected by chance.[40] The plaintiffs were thus able to establish a prima facie case. When cases go to court, expert witnesses are typically called on to present more sophisticated statistical analyses. The precise techniques used vary, depending on such factors as the number of groups compared and the sample size, but they share the aim of showing that any differences in selection rates or scores for protected class groups are "statistically significant." This means that the obtained results are highly unlikely to occur by chance. "Highly unlikely" is usually translated as an outcome that would be expected to occur no more than five out of one hundred times (i.e., a p-value of 0.05 or less) if there were not a true difference in selection rates or scores.

Thus, *employers need to monitor and maintain records of the effects of testing procedures on different protected class groups. The four-fifths rule should be applied to selection*

---

[38]29 C.F.R. § 1607.4 (D) (2011).

[39]*Mems v. City of St. Paul, Dept. of Fire and Safety Services*, 224 F.3d 735, 740 (8th Cir. 2000), *cert. denied*, 540 U.S. 1106 (2004).

[40]*Isabel v. City of Memphis*, 404 F.3d 404 (6th Cir. 2005).

rates generated from applicant flow data to identify possible discriminatory effects. Tests with discriminatory effects should not continue to be used unless strong evidence of test validity exists and less discriminatory alternatives are not available.

It is important that potential adverse impact and the defensibility of tests be considered at the point when tests are being designed or purchased. Fixing problems after a test has been given is problematic. In a case involving a civil service exam used to make fire department promotions, the Supreme Court ruled that the city of New Haven discriminated in violation of Title VII.[41] The city, which had a history of problems with lack of diversity in its fire department, particularly at the higher ranks, decided to discard the results of the civil service exam because given the number of positions available and their position on the eligibility list, no African Americans would have been promoted. Rather than face a likely adverse impact suit, the city opted to promote no one. This action led to disparate treatment lawsuits by white and Latino candidates who accused the city of intentionally discriminating against them. The Supreme Court essentially agreed, holding that discarding the results of an already-administered test because the outcome disfavored African Americans was disparate treatment that could only be justified if the city could show that there was a "strong basis in evidence" that it would otherwise have been liable for adverse impact.[42] A "strong basis in evidence" exists not simply because plaintiffs can establish a prima facie case that a challenged test produces discriminatory effects, but only if use of the test is not defensible. Employers do not have to use the same exams again in the future, but tossing out exam results and declaring "do-overs" will generally not be the way to go.

Establishing That Tests Are Job-Related and Consistent with Business Necessity

So what makes a test defensible? A test can be successfully defended—despite its discriminatory effects—if the employer can show that the test is **job-related** and **consistent with business necessity** (or that it is a "reasonable factor other than age"). An employer has a legitimate interest in selecting people with the ability to perform jobs well. If more men than women are suited to some jobs (or vice versa), discrepant test results might reflect this fact. But employers bear the burden of proving the job relatedness of tests that create adverse impact. In *EEOC v. Dial Corp.*, the employer is unable to successfully defend its use of a physical strength test.

EEOC v. Dial Corp.
469 F.3d 735 (8th Cir. 2006)

OPINION BY CIRCUIT JUDGE MURPHY:

The Equal Employment Opportunity Commission (EEOC) brought this sex discrimination action against The Dial Corporation under Title VII of the Civil Rights Act of 1964 on behalf of a number of women who had applied for work but were not hired. * * * [T]he district court concluded that Dial's

use of a preemployment strength test had an unlawful disparate impact on female applicants … * * * We … affirm.

Dial is an international company with a plant located in Fort Madison, Iowa that produces canned meats. Entry level employees at the plant are assigned to the sausage packing area where workers daily lift

---

[41] *Ricci v. DeStefano*, 129 S. Ct. 2658 (2009).

[42] *Ricci*, at 2676.

and carry up to 18,000 pounds of sausage, walking the equivalent of four miles in the process. They are required to carry approximately 35 pounds of sausage at a time and must lift and load the sausage to heights between 30 and 60 inches above the floor. Employees who worked in the sausage packing area experienced a disproportionate number of injuries as compared to the rest of the workers in the plant.

Dial implemented several measures to reduce the injury rate starting in late 1996. These included an ergonomic job rotation, institution of a team approach, lowering the height of machines to decrease lifting pressure for the employees, and conducting periodic safety audits. In 2000 Dial also instituted a strength test used to evaluate potential employees, called the Work Tolerance Screen (WTS). In this test job applicants were asked to carry a 35 pound bar between two frames, approximately 30 and 60 inches off the floor, and to lift and load the bar onto these frames. The applicants were told to work at their "own pace" for seven minutes. An occupational therapist watched the process, documented how many lifts each applicant completed, and recorded her own comments about each candidate's performance. Starting in 2001, the plant nurse, Martha Lutenegger, also watched and documented the process. From the inception of the test, Lutenegger reviewed the test forms and had the ultimate hiring authority.

For many years women and men had worked together in the sausage packing area doing the same job. Forty six percent of the new hires were women in the three years before the WTS was introduced, but the number of women hires dropped to fifteen percent after the test was implemented. During this time period the test was the only change in the company's hiring practices. The percentage of women who passed the test decreased almost each year the test was given, with only eight percent of the women applicants passing in 2002. The overall percentage of women who passed was thirty eight percent while the men's passage rate was ninety seven percent. While overall injuries and strength related injuries among sausage workers declined consistently after 2000 when the test was implemented, the downward trend in injuries had begun in 1998 after the company had instituted measures to reduce injuries. * * *

A jury trial was held in August 2004, and EEOC and Dial offered testimony by competing experts. EEOC presented an expert on industrial organization who testified that the WTS was significantly more difficult than the actual job workers performed at the plant. He explained that although workers did 1.25 lifts per minute on average and rested between lifts, applicants who took the WTS performed 6 lifts per minute on average, usually without any breaks. He also testified that in two of the three years before Dial had implemented the WTS, the women's injury rate had been lower than that of the male workers. * * *

Dial presented an expert in work physiology, who testified that in his opinion the WTS effectively tested skills which were representative of the actual job, and an industrial and organizational psychologist, who testified that the WTS measured the requirements of the job and that the decrease in injuries could be attributed to the test. Dial also called plant nurse Martha Lutenegger who testified that although she and other Dial managers knew the WTS was screening out more women than men, the decrease in injuries warranted its continued use. * * *

The district court … found that the WTS had had a discriminatory effect, that Dial had not demonstrated that the WTS was a business necessity or shown either content or criterion validity, and that Dial had not effectively controlled for other variables which may have caused the decline in injuries, including other safety measures that Dial had implemented starting in 1996. * * *

Statistical disparities are significant if the difference between the expected number and the observed number is greater than two or three standard deviations. Here, the disparity between hiring of men and women showed nearly ten standard deviations. The percentage of women who passed the WTS declined with each implementation of the test. Despite knowing about the statistical difference, Dial continued to use the WTS. Dial argues that EEOC's statistics are inapplicable because men and women are not similarly situated and have profound physiological differences. There was evidence, however, that women and men worked the same job together for many years before the WTS was instituted. * * *

In a disparate impact case, once the plaintiff establishes a prima facie case the employer must show the practice at issue is "related to safe and efficient job performance and is consistent with business necessity." An employer using the business necessity defense must prove that the practice was related to the specific job and the required skills and physical requirements of the position. Although a validity study of an employment test can be sufficient to prove business necessity, it is not necessary if the employer demonstrates the procedure is sufficiently related to safe and efficient job performance. If the employer demonstrates business necessity, the plaintiff can still prevail by showing there is a less discriminatory alternative.

Dial contends the WTS was shown by its experts to have both content and criterion validity. Under EEOC guidelines, "A content validity study should consist of data showing that the content of the selection procedure is representative of important aspects of performance on the job for which the candidates are to be evaluated." Dial's physiology expert testified that the WTS was highly representative of the actions required by the job, and Dial claims that his testimony was not rebutted by EEOC, which had no physiology witness. The district court was persuaded by EEOC's expert in industrial organization and his testimony "that a crucial aspect of the WTS is more difficult than the sausage making jobs themselves" and that the average applicant had to perform four times as many lifts as current employees and had no rest breaks. There was also evidence that in a testing environment where hiring is contingent upon test performance, applicants tend to work as fast as possible during the test in order to outperform the competition.

Dial argues the WTS was criterion valid because both overall injuries and strength related injuries decreased dramatically following the implementation of the WTS. The EEOC guidelines establish that criterion validity can be shown by "empirical data demonstrating that the selection procedure is predictive of or significantly correlated with important elements of job performance." Although Dial claims

that the decrease in injuries shows that the WTS enabled it to predict which applicants could safely handle the strenuous nature of the work, the sausage plant injuries started decreasing before the WTS was implemented. Moreover, the injury rate for women employees was lower than that for men in two of the three years before Dial implemented the WTS. The evidence did not require the district court to find that the decrease in injuries resulted from the implementation of the WTS instead of the other safety mechanisms Dial started to put in place in 1996. * * *

Since Dial failed to demonstrate that the WTS was a business necessity, however, EEOC never was required to show the absence of a nondiscriminatory alternative. Part of the employer's burden to establish business necessity is to demonstrate the need for the challenged procedure, and the court found that Dial had not shown that its other safety measures "could not produce the same results." We conclude that the district court findings in its disparate impact analysis were not clearly erroneous, and we see no legal error in its conclusions on liability. * * *

CASE QUESTIONS

1. What was the legal issue in this case? What did the court decide?
2. What is the evidence that use of the strength test disadvantaged women?
3. What is "content validity"? What is "criterion validity"? How did the employer attempt to show the validity of the strength test? Why was the court not convinced?
4. What should Dial do at this point?
5. Do you agree with the court's decision? Why or why not?

It is incumbent upon employers to have evidence of the **validity** of a test that is producing discriminatory effects. In the most general terms, the validity of a measurement device or test refers to whether it actually measures what it purports to measure. Because employment tests are designed to help employers select people who will perform their jobs well, the validity of an employment test rests on how well it predicts future job performance. Does the test help employers make good selection decisions by measuring job-related criteria, or does it impose a needless obstacle?

There are two primary ways to establish the validity of employment tests. The first is **content validation**. A test has content validity to the extent that it requires the performance of the same behaviors and skills as the job in question. A classic example of a content-valid testing procedure is use of a word processing test (e.g., speed, accuracy) to assess candidates for a secretarial job. The test is clearly representative of behaviors and skills that are central to the job. A legal limitation on content validation is that it cannot be used to validate tests of intelligence, personality, or other intangible traits. However, tests of job-specific knowledge or skills can be validated in this manner. Another problem is that the tests assume that candidates already possess and can display the desired skills. But many jobs can be learned relatively quickly. Testing procedures that screen out people who would be capable of performing the job following minimal amounts of on-the-job training and practice are not job-related and consistent with business necessity. *Thus, employers should use content-valid tests as much as possible, but not to assess intangible characteristics such as intelligence and not for tasks that could readily be learned on the job.*

The state of California was able to successfully defend its California Basic Education Skills Test (CBEST) against an adverse impact claim by showing the test's content validity.[43] A passing score on the test is required to be employed as a public schoolteacher, administrator, librarian, or counselor. It was undisputed that pass rates—and, hence, access to education jobs—differed substantially by race and national origin. The test was passed by 73.4 percent of non-Latino whites, 53 percent of Asian Americans, 49.4 percent of Latinos, and 37.7 percent of African Americans.[44] These pass rates failed to meet the four-fifths rule and established a prima facie case of adverse impact. The state was nonetheless able to establish that the test was valid. More specifically, the state showed that the test measures specific abilities (reading, writing, and math skills); a job analysis incorporating the input of many current educators was performed and showed these skills to be central to education jobs; and the test was developed and content-validated consistent with professional standards. In contrast, a court ruled against the New York City Board of Education in a similar adverse impact challenge to one of its requirements for teacher certification—a passing score on the Liberal Arts and Sciences Test (LAST).[45] The Board of Education failed to produce adequate evidence of the content validity of the test. It was not enough to simply rely on the judgments of education professionals. It was necessary to show that a suitable study of the job had been conducted, reasonable competence was used in construction of the test, the content of the test and the job are related, the content of the test is representative of the overall job, and a scoring system allows selection of candidates who are likely to be better performers.[46] Because the district court erred in not requiring the Board of Education to show these things, the case was remanded.

The second primary strategy for validating employment tests is **criterion validation**. *Criterion* refers here to a measure of job performance. The essential project in criterion validation is to demonstrate a statistical association between performance on a test and performance on the job. Criterion validation studies can be "predictive" or "concurrent." In a predictive study, the test is given to applicants, scored, but not used to make hiring decisions (instead, the employer uses other information at its disposal). Six months or a year later, when measures of job performance are available, these are compared to the test results to determine if people who scored higher on the test also tended to be better employees. Conducting a predictive study takes time

---

[43]*Association of Mexican American Educators v. California*, 231 F.3d 572 (9th Cir. 2000).

[44]*Association of Mexican American Educators v. California*, 937 F. Supp. 1397 (N.D. Cal. 1996).

[45]*Gulino v. New York State Education Department*, 460 F.3d 361 (2d Cir. 2006), *cert. denied*, 554 U.S. 917 (2008).

[46]*Gulino*, at 384–85.

because an adequate number of job candidates must be tested and hired and a significant period of time must elapse before performance ratings are available. A concurrent study avoids these problems, but at the expense of having a less representative sample. In a concurrent study, the test that an employer wants to adopt is given to existing employees—a handy sample, but one not necessarily representative of job applicants. Performance measures for those employees are available or can be devised for the validation study. Evidence of validity again comes from showing a statistical association between test scores and job performance ratings. A typical measure of association is the *correlation coefficient*. Correlation coefficients range between –1.0 and +1.0. A positive correlation means that people who score higher on employment tests also tend to be rated more highly for job performance.

The evidence needed to establish the validity (and hence job-relatedness) of a scored employment test comes from a **validation study**. In an early Title VII case, the Supreme Court provided guidance on the requirements for an adequate validation study.[47] The employer conceded that the tests of nonverbal intelligence and general verbal facility that it was using had racially discriminatory effects, but claimed that it had conducted a validation study and found the test to be valid. The Supreme Court scrutinized the methodology of the "validation study" and found it to be inadequate to meet the employer's burden of defending the test as being job-related and consistent with business necessity. Major failings of the company's validation study included no performance of any meaningful study (job analysis) of the jobs for which the test was being used; a focus on employees in jobs near the top of the wage progression rather than on the entry-level positions for which the tests were used; nonsignificant correlations between test performance and job performance for five out of eight job lines; an absence of African Americans in the sample of employees used to validate the test; and unguided, highly subjective assessments of job performance by company supervisors. The Court also observed that "It cannot escape notice that Albemarle's study was conducted by plant officials, without neutral, on-the-scene oversight, at a time when this litigation was about to come to trial."[48] Thus, the Supreme Court sent a strong message to employers that evidence from a credible and methodologically sound validation study would be required to defend testing procedures that have discriminatory effects. Such evidence is best obtained prior to adoption of a test rather than under the gun of pending litigation.

In addition to the Supreme Court's guidance, the EEOC's *Uniform Guidelines on Employee Selection Procedures*[49] and the American Psychological Association's standards are used to judge the adequacy of validation studies. Without getting bogged down in the intricacies of validation studies, a few basic, practical implications for employers can be stated. First, although the law does not strictly require that all tests be validated, a validation study is usually necessary to defend a test that has discriminatory effects. Thus, *it makes sense for employers to have evidence of the validity of all their selection procedures, but particularly scored tests.* Rather than wait to be sued, *employers should undertake validity studies before they put tests into use.* Evidence of validity is specific to jobs or classes of jobs. *Assertions that a test is valid should always be followed with this question: valid for what jobs?* The basic purpose of a validation study—to establish the job-relatedness of a test—presupposes that the party conducting the validation study has detailed knowledge of the job(s) for which the test will be used. Thus, *an adequate validation study should proceed from a thorough **job analysis** in which the tasks of a job and the knowledge, skills, abilities, and other characteristics needed to perform the job are detailed.*

---

[47] *Albemarle Paper Co. v. Moody*, 422 U.S. 405 (1975).

[48] *Albemarle*, at 433 (note 32).

[49] 29 C.F.R. Part 1607 (2011).

Other key aspects of validation studies that should be examined and on which testing companies or consultants should be closely questioned include the following:

- *How large is the sample size?* Small sample sizes render statistics suspect and make it more difficult to perform separate analyses for different protected class groups.
- *Does the validation study include a mixture of races and both male and female candidates?* It is important to assess the effects of tests and their capability to predict performance on diverse samples that are representative of the people who will actually be taking the tests.
- *How good is the assessment of job performance?* Job performance ratings are often "the weakest link" in criterion validation studies. Are raters given clear performance criteria? If there is more than one rater of job performance, to what extent do their ratings agree?
- *How strong is the evidence of validity?* Validity coefficients can be assessed for both their magnitude and statistical significance. Some courts have adopted the guideline that correlation coefficients must be at least 0.3 to be sufficient evidence of validity. Coefficients of any magnitude are not informative unless they are also statistically significant (meaning that the true correlation between test scores and job performance in the population of applicants is highly unlikely to be zero).
- *How current is the evidence of validity?* Jobs change and previously validated tests may no longer be sufficiently related to redesigned jobs.

Finally, *employers should consider whether there are feasible alternatives to tests that have discriminatory effects, even if those tests are job-related.* A plaintiff can prevail in an adverse impact case by showing that a less discriminatory alternative test is available that the employer refuses to adopt (but not under the ADEA).

Determining Appropriate Cutoff Levels for Test Scores

For tests to be used in selection decisions, they must be scored in some fashion (even if only pass/fail). Typically, **cutoff scores** are established for tests so that scores below the cutoff are deemed "failing" and disqualify candidates from further consideration. If the employer cares about the degree of the tested-for characteristic possessed—and not merely whether a minimally sufficient level of the characteristic is present—test takers with passing scores can be ranked and candidates with the highest scores chosen. One consideration in treating test scores is that *employers must not "adjust the scores of, use different cutoff scores for, or otherwise alter the results of employment-related tests on the basis of race, color, religion, sex, or national origin."*[50] This prohibition of what has been termed **race norming**, although it is not specific to race, means that employers cannot establish separate minimum standards based on protected class or obscure the existence of different standards by altering scores (e.g., by creating separate percentile scores for whites and persons of color).

Clearly, the results of a test are affected by what the employer determines to be a passing score. If a test is job-related, are there any legal limitations on how high employers can "set the bar" in terms of cutoff scores? *Lanning v. SEPTA* deals with the cutoff score used in a physical fitness test given to transit officers. Physical fitness tests tend to disfavor women (as well as older workers and the disabled), yet some level of physical fitness is clearly a legitimate requirement for jobs such as police officers and firefighters. This case was litigated for years, and the following case excerpt includes material from the court's 1999 decision (*Lanning* [I]) and its final determination in 2002 (*Lanning* [II]).

---

[50]42 U.S.C.S. § 2000e-2(l) (2011).

Lanning v. SEPTA (I)
181 F.3d 478 (3d Cir. 1999), *cert. denied*, 528 U.S. 1131 (2000)

OPINION BY CIRCUIT JUDGE MANSMANN:

In this appeal, we must determine the appropriate legal standard to apply when evaluating an employer's business justification in an action challenging an employer's cutoff score on an employment screening exam as discriminatory under a disparate impact theory of liability. We hold today that under the Civil Rights Act of 1991, a discriminatory cutoff score on an entry level employment examination must be shown to measure the minimum qualifications necessary for successful performance of the job in question in order to survive a disparate impact challenge. Because we find that the District Court did not apply this standard in evaluating the employer's business justification for its discriminatory cutoff score in this case, we will reverse the District Court's judgment and remand for reconsideration under this standard. * * *

SEPTA is a regional mass transit authority that operates principally in Philadelphia, Pennsylvania. * * * In 1991, SEPTA hired Dr. Paul Davis to develop an appropriate physical fitness test for its police officers. Ultimately, Dr. Davis recommended a 1.5 mile run within 12 minutes. Dr. Davis explained that completion of this run would require that an officer possess an aerobic capacity of 42.5 mL/kg/min, the aerobic capacity that Dr. Davis determined would be necessary to perform the job of SEPTA transit officer. * * * Dr. Davis understood that SEPTA officers would not be required to run 1.5 miles within 12 minutes in the course of their duties, but he nevertheless recommended this test as an accurate measure of the aerobic capacity necessary to perform the job of SEPTA transit police officer. Based upon Dr. Davis' recommendation, SEPTA adopted a physical fitness screening test for its applicants which included a 1.5 mile run within 12 minutes. Beginning in 1991, the 1.5 mile run was administered as the first component of the physical fitness test; if an applicant failed to run 1.5 miles in 12 minutes, the applicant would be disqualified from employment as a SEPTA transit officer.

It is undisputed that for the years 1991, 1993, and 1996, an average of only 12% of women applicants passed SEPTA's 1.5 mile run in comparison to the almost 60% of male applicants who passed. For the years 1993 and 1996, the time period in question in this litigation, the pass rate for women was 6.7% compared to a 55.6% pass rate for men. * * * SEPTA concedes that its 1.5 mile run has a disparate impact on women. * * *

In conjunction with the implementation of its physical fitness screening test, SEPTA also began testing incumbent officers for aerobic capacity in 1991. * * * [S]ignificant percentages of incumbent officers of all ranks have failed SEPTA's physical fitness test. By 1996, however, 86% of incumbent officers reached SEPTA's physical fitness standards. * * * SEPTA has promoted incumbent officers who have failed some or all of the components of the physical fitness test. * * * In addition, due to a clerical error, SEPTA hired a female officer in 1991 who failed the 1.5 mile run. This officer has subsequently been "decorated" by SEPTA and has been nominated repeatedly for awards.... * * *

Under Title VII's disparate impact theory of liability, plaintiffs establish a prima facie case of disparate impact by demonstrating that application of a facially neutral standard has resulted in a significantly discriminatory hiring pattern. Once the plaintiffs have established a prima facie case, the burden shifts to the employer to show that the employment practice is "job related for the position in question and consistent with business necessity...." Should the employer meet this burden, the plaintiffs may still prevail if they can show that an alternative employment practice has a less disparate impact and would also serve the employer's legitimate business interest. * * *

The laudable mission begun by the Court in *Griggs* was the eradication of discrimination through the application of practices fair in form but discriminatory in practice by eliminating unnecessary barriers to employment opportunities. In the context of a hiring exam with a cutoff score shown to have a discriminatory effect, the standard that best effectuates this mission is implicit in the Court's application of the business necessity doctrine to the employer in *Griggs*, i.e., that a discriminatory cutoff score is impermissible unless shown to measure the minimum qualifications necessary for successful performance of the job in question. Only this standard can effectuate the mission begun by the Court in *Griggs;* only by requiring employers to demonstrate that their discriminatory cutoff score measures the minimum qualifications necessary for successful performance of the job in question can we be certain to eliminate the use of excessive cutoff scores that have a disparate impact on minorities as a method of imposing unnecessary barriers to employment opportunities. * * *

Our conclusion that the Act incorporates this standard is further supported by the business necessity language adopted by the Act. Congress chose the terms "job related for the position in question" and "consistent with business necessity." Judicial application of a standard focusing solely on whether the qualities measured by an entry level exam bear some relationship to the job in question would impermissibly write out the business necessity prong of the Act's chosen standard. With respect to a discriminatory cutoff score, the business necessity prong must be read to demand an inquiry into whether the score reflects the minimum qualifications necessary to perform successfully the job in question. See also EEOC Guidelines (noting that cutoff scores should "be set so as to be reasonable and consistent with normal expectations of acceptable proficiency within the work force."). * * *

[T]he [business necessity] standard itself takes public safety into consideration. If, for example, SEPTA can show on remand that the inability of a SEPTA transit officer to meet a certain aerobic level would significantly jeopardize public safety, this showing would be relevant to determine if that level is necessary for the successful performance of the job. Clearly a SEPTA officer who poses a significant risk to public safety could not be considered to be performing his job successfully. * * *

The District Court's application of its understanding of business necessity to SEPTA's business justification further illustrates that the District Court did not apply the correct legal standard. As an initial matter, the District Court seemed to conclude that Dr. Davis' expertise alone is sufficient to justify the 42.5 mL/kg/min aerobic capacity cutoff measured by the 1.5 mile run. This conclusion ... alone is insufficient to validate an employer's discriminatory practices. More fundamentally, however, nowhere in its extensive opinion did the District Court consider whether Dr. Davis' 42.5 mL/kg/min cutoff reflects the minimum aerobic capacity necessary to perform successfully the job of SEPTA transit police officer. * * *

Instead, the District Court upheld this cutoff because it was "readily justifiable." The validation studies of SEPTA's experts upon which the District Court relied to support this conclusion demonstrate the extent to which this standard is insufficient under the Act. The general import of these studies is that the higher an officer's aerobic capacity, the better the officer is able to perform the job. Setting aside the validity of these studies, this conclusion alone does not validate Dr. Davis' 42.5 mL/kg/min cutoff under the Act's business necessity standard. At best, these studies show that aerobic capacity is related to the job of SEPTA transit officer. A study showing that "more is better," however, has no bearing on the appropriate cutoff to reflect the minimal qualifications necessary to perform successfully the job in question. * * *

Under the District Court's understanding of business necessity, which requires only that a cutoff score be "readily justifiable," SEPTA, as well as any other employer whose jobs entail any level of physical capability, could employ an unnecessarily high cutoff score on its physical abilities entrance exam in an effort to exclude virtually all women by justifying this facially neutral yet discriminatory practice on the theory that more is better. This result contravenes *Griggs* and demonstrates why, under *Griggs,* a discriminatory cutoff score must be shown to measure the minimum qualifications necessary to perform successfully the job in question. * * *

Lanning v. SEPTA (II)
308 F.3d 286 (3d Cir. 2002)

OPINION BY CIRCUIT JUDGE BARRY:

* * * [W]e assess the sole issue we caused to be resolved on remand: whether or not SEPTA has proven that its 42.5 mL/kg/min aerobic capacity standard measures the minimum qualifications necessary for the successful performance of the job of SEPTA transit police officers. The District Court concluded that the answer was "yes," and that any lesser standard "would result in officers … who were a danger to themselves, other officers, and the public at large, [and] unable to effectively fight and deter crime." * * *

Neither the District Court nor the parties have explicitly defined the key phrase "minimum qualifications necessary," but a definition is implicit in the parties' respective arguments and the District Court's acceptance of that of SEPTA. SEPTA argued that the run test measures the "minimum qualifications necessary" because the relevant studies indicate that individuals who fail the test will be much less likely to successfully execute critical policing tasks. For example, the District Court credited a study that evaluated the correlation between a successful run time and performance on 12 job standards. The study found that individuals who passed the run test had a success rate on the job standards ranging from 70% to 90%. The success rate of the individuals who failed the run test ranged from 5% to 20%. The District Court found that such a low rate of success was unacceptable for employees who are regularly called upon to protect the public. In so doing, the District Court implicitly defined "minimum qualifications necessary" as meaning "likely to be able to do the job."

Plaintiffs argued, however, that within the group that failed the run test, significant numbers of individuals would still be able to perform at least certain critical job tasks. They argued that as long as some of those failing the run test can do the job, the standard cannot be classified as a "minimum." In essence, plaintiffs proposed that the phrase "minimum qualifications necessary" means "some chance of being able to do the job." Under this logic, even if those failing the test had a 1% chance of successfully completing critical job tasks, the test would be too stringent.

We are not saying, as our distinguished brother in dissent suggests we are saying, that "more is better." While, of course, a higher aerobic capacity will translate into better field performance—at least as to many job tasks which entail physical capability—to set an unnecessarily high cutoff score would contravene *Griggs*. It would clearly be unreasonable to require SEPTA applicants to score so highly on the run test that their predicted rate of success be 100%. It is perfectly reasonable, however, to demand a chance of success that is better than 5% to 20%. In sum, SEPTA transit police officers and the public they serve should not be required to engage in high-stakes gambling when it comes to public safety and law enforcement. SEPTA has demonstrated that the cutoff score it established measures the minimum qualifications necessary for successful performance as a SEPTA officer. * * *

One final note. While it is undisputed that SEPTA's 1.5 mile run test has a disparate impact on women, it is also undisputed that, in addition to those women who could pass the test without training, nearly all the women who trained were able to pass after only a moderate amount of training. It is not, we think, unreasonable to expect that women—and men—who wish to become SEPTA transit officers, and are committed to dealing with issues of public safety on a day-to-day basis, would take this necessary step. * * *

The judgment of the District Court will be affirmed.

CASE QUESTIONS

1. What was the legal issue in this case? What did the court decide?
2. What is the evidence of discriminatory effects in this case?
3. What distinction is the court drawing between "job relatedness" and "business necessity"? What is the evidence that SEPTA's aerobic capacity test is both job-related and consistent with business necessity?
4. Because physical fitness is clearly related to doing the job of transit officer, why shouldn't SEPTA be free to set high standards and hire only the most physically fit?

Not all courts concur with the Third Circuit's relatively stringent approach to establishing business necessity—that cutoff scores with discriminatory effects must be shown to measure no more than the *minimum* qualifications needed to successfully perform the job. Certainly, a showing by plaintiffs that some individuals with lower scores are able to perform a job successfully is not sufficient to establish that a particular cutoff score lacks business necessity when most persons with the lower score cannot perform the job successfully. As a basic principle, the EEOC maintains that *when cutoffs are used, they should be "reasonable and consistent with normal expectations of acceptable proficiency."* [51] Additionally, requirements for one job must not be set unduly high based on the idea that persons hired will then be qualified to move on to other jobs. *Unless progression to higher-level jobs occurs with relative certainty and within a relatively brief period of time, employers should not establish the requirements for lower-level jobs with higher-level jobs in mind.*[52] This does not preclude employers from hiring management trainees and starting them out learning basic production tasks.

JUST THE FACTS

The U.S. Forest Service employs "smokejumpers" whose job it is to parachute into remote areas of national forests to fight fires. Smokejumpers must pass an annual physical fitness test that includes finishing a 1.5 mile run in 11 minutes or less. Ronnie Rucker passed the test and worked as a smokejumper each year from 1973 through 2004. In 2005, at the age of 51, Rucker was unable to pass the running portion of the test despite making ten tries at it. Following the failed test and before Rucker could be removed from his position, he was in a plane crash on the job. Although injured, Rucker helped rescue other occupants of the plane. He subsequently received a medal of heroism for his efforts in the plane crash. In 2006, Rucker returned from medical leave and was again required to take the physical fitness test. He took the test three times and in his best effort completed the run in 11 minutes and 3 seconds. He was deemed to have failed the test and his employment was terminated. Between 2002 and 2005, test takers under age 40 completed the run in an average of 9 minutes and 25 seconds, while those over 40 averaged 10 minutes and 18 seconds. Does Rucker have a valid adverse impact claim?

See, *Rucker v. Vilsack*, 2009 U.S. Dist. LEXIS 42517 (D. Ore.).

Practical Considerations
Physical fitness and strength tests are likely to create adverse impact against women, as well as older workers and those with disabilities. What should employers do to minimize adverse impact when hiring for jobs that have genuine strength and physical fitness requirements?

The "banding" of test scores can diminish the discriminatory effects of tests without compromising the principle of selecting the most able candidates. In **banding**, test scores are treated as estimates of tested-for characteristics (e.g., verbal ability, intelligence). Because estimates contain errors from various sources, test scores are treated differently from one another only if the gap between them is sufficiently wide that the different scores are likely to reflect real differences in the tested-for characteristics. Selecting from within bands of test scores (e.g., 82 through 86) that are not statistically different from one another, rather than treating an 89 as necessarily better than an 88, allows employers more discretion in hiring without ignoring real differences in candidates' abilities. Courts have upheld the

---

[51]29 C.F.R. § 1607.5(H) (2011).
[52]29 C.F.R. § 1607.5(I) (2011).

practice of banding test scores,[53] although the method used for banding should be established before the test is given and not amount to an ad hoc adjustment of results because they are unfavorable to some protected class group.[54]

> ## *Clippings*
>
> Getting into a good law school is tough. It usually requires performing very well on the Law School Admission Test (LSAT). There are typically a dozen or more questions on this exam for which test takers are strongly encouraged to draw out written diagrams as part of their answers. This creates particular problems for blind law students. One of these students, Angelo Binno, has joined forces with attorney Richard Bernstein (who is also blind) to sue the American Bar Association (ABA). They allege that the LSAT violates the Americans with Disabilities Act. The ABA contends that accommodations are made for test takers with disabilities, although the receipt of an accommodation is noted along with test scores and ever-more ratings conscious schools are reluctant to consider admitting students with lower LSAT scores.
>
> Quinn Klinefelter. "Blind Would-Be Law Student Says Test Discriminates." NPR Morning Edition (June 15, 2011) Viewed June 16, 2011 (http://www.npr.org/).

Accommodating Disabled Persons in Testing

The legal responsibility to accommodate disabled persons begins prehire and includes testing procedures. However, unless the need for accommodation is obvious (e.g., a visually impaired person comes in with a guide dog), *an employer is not responsible for providing accommodation unless requested by a disabled job candidate.* For this to be possible, *candidates should be informed in advance about the types of employment tests used.* An exception to the general rule prohibiting preemployment inquiries regarding disability is that *employers can require job candidates to document their need for accommodation in the application and testing process.* Accommodations might include substituting written tests for oral tests (or vice versa), using large-print test forms, providing sign language interpreters, allowing extra time for test completion, allowing breaks or rest periods during long tests, providing alternative testing locations with fewer distractions, or substituting for testing requirements (e.g., by more extensive interviews). Persons with disabilities that limit their vision, hearing, use of hands, concentration, or reading ability are particularly likely to need accommodation in testing.

Key Terms

drug testing, p. 167
reasonable suspicion, p. 167
random drug testing, p. 167
Fourth
   Amendment, p. 168
unreasonable search and
   seizure, p. 168

Omnibus Transportation Employee
   Testing Act, p. 170
chain of custody, p. 170
confirmatory tests, p. 170
medical review officer, p. 170
Drug-Free Workplace
   Act (DFWA), p. 171

medical examination, p. 172
conditional offer of
   employment, p. 174
genetic tests, p. 179
genetic screening, p. 179
genetic monitoring, p. 179

---

[53]*Officers for Justice v. City and County of San Francisco*, 979 F.2d 721 (9th Cir. 1992), *cert. denied*, 507 U.S. 1004 (1993).

[54]*Ricci*, at 2680.

Chapter Summary

Drug testing has proven to be relatively impervious to legal challenge. The primary legal limitations on drug testing stem from state drug testing laws and the U.S. Constitution's protection (for public employees only) against "unreasonable searches or seizures" (Fourth Amendment). Random testing for positions that are not safety-sensitive is the form of drug testing most vulnerable to challenge. State drug testing laws and the Omnibus Transportation Employees Testing Act contain various requirements for drug testing procedures. Overall, employers are not held to a high standard in their drug testing procedures, and employees are unlikely to be successful in suits against their employers for negligent drug testing. The Omnibus Transportation Employee Testing Act requires the drug (and alcohol) testing of millions of transportation employees and specifies procedural guidelines for those tests. The Drug-Free Workplace Act does not mandate drug testing, but instead requires that employers that have contracts with the federal government adopt and communicate policies prohibiting drug use or sale in the workplace.

Medical exams—including HIV tests and genetic tests—are regulated by the ADA. The ADA prohibits medical exams prior to a conditional offer of employment. Exams given following a conditional offer of employment can be wide-ranging provided that they do not delve into genetic information, whereas exams given to current employees must be job-related and consistent with business necessity or voluntary. The results of medical exams cannot be used to exclude qualified disabled persons. Genetic testing includes both genetic screening of candidates for positions and genetic monitoring of current employees for the effects of exposure to hazardous substances. State laws and the U.S. Constitution have provided some protection to employees against the misuse of genetic testing. The Genetic Information Nondiscrimination Act tightly restricts the acquisition of genetic information—including family medical histories—and prohibits using genetic information to make employment decisions.

A major concern with employment tests—particularly scored tests that measure abilities such as intelligence, skill, aptitude, personality, and physical fitness—is adverse impact discrimination. The discriminatory effects of tests are assessed by examining applicant flow data and comparing selection rates for different protected class groups. According to the four-fifths rule, if the selection rate for applicants of one race or sex is less than eighty percent of the selection rate for the race or sex enjoying the highest selection rate, that is a preliminary indication of adverse impact. When plaintiffs challenging employment tests are able to establish a prima facie case of adverse impact, employers must defend those tests as being job-related and consistent with business necessity. Validation studies are generally required to establish job relatedness. A content validation strategy defends a test by showing that the test entails the performance of behaviors and skills that closely mirror important aspects of the job itself. A criterion validation strategy defends a test by demonstrating a statistical association between performance on the test and performance on the job. The adequacy of validation studies hinges on such factors as whether a proper job analysis was performed, whether the job for which the test was validated is the same as the job for which the test is used, on what number of test takers the study is based, how closely the persons in the study mirror the people likely to be taking the test, how well job performance is measured, and whether the magnitude and statistical significance of the validity coefficient are sufficient. If a test has discriminatory effects, cutoff scores in excess of the minimum level needed to perform the job may not be defensible since they are not consistent with business necessity. Even with sufficient evidence that a test is job-related and consistent with business necessity, adverse impact will still be found if a feasible alternative testing procedure exists that has less discriminatory impact.

Practical Advice Summary

- Of the various circumstances for drug testing, employers should be especially careful about random testing of employees that do not hold safety-sensitive positions.
- Unionized employers must negotiate with employees' unions over drug testing that affects current employees.
- Public employers must be prepared to defend the reasonableness of drug testing. Reasonableness is easiest to demonstrate when drug testing programs
  — Focus on safety-sensitive jobs
  — Emphasize testing upon reasonable suspicion
- Supervisors should be well trained at identifying signs of drug use and impairment.
- Employers should have drug testing policies notifying employees of the
  — Circumstances under which testing will occur
  — Procedures that will be used
  — Consequences of testing positive
- Procedurally sound drug testing programs provide for the following:
  — Confirmatory tests to verify positive results
  — Careful labeling of specimens and documentation of the chain of custody
  — Respect for the privacy of individuals in gathering specimens
  — Use of reputable labs and monitoring of their performance
  — Use of a medical review officer to interpret results
  — Opportunity for employees to provide alternative explanations for positive results
  — Information about medications taken to be sought only after positive drug test results occur
  — Handling of drug test results as sensitive and confidential information
- Employers must not terminate or otherwise discriminate against employees who are in drug treatment programs or have completed rehabilitation and are no longer using illegal drugs.
- Employers that use medical exams must
  — Not conduct or require medical exams of job candidates prior to extending conditional offers of employment.
  — Not conduct or require medical exams of job candidates until all other nonmedical aspects of the hiring process have been carried out.
  — Require that all persons hired into the same job categories, rather than selected individuals, submit to exams.
  — Not conduct or require medical exams of current employees unless the exams are either job-related and consistent with business necessity or voluntary.
  — Not exclude disabled persons from employment based on medical exam results unless those persons are unable to perform the essential functions of their jobs or pose a direct threat to the health or safety of themselves or others.
  — Keep medical information (including genetic information) confidential and store it separate from personnel files.
- Employers must generally refrain from requesting, requiring, purchasing, or otherwise acquiring genetic information on applicants and employees.
- Employers should use the EEOC's suggested language when making requests for medical information from health care providers.
- Employers must not use genetic information in making employment decisions.
- Private sector employers must not require or suggest that job candidates submit to polygraphs or other similar devices at any point in the hiring process.
- Employers that use employment tests should
  — Examine test questions to determine whether they pertain to protected class characteristics and refrain from using tests that contain such questions.
  — Examine test results by comparing selection rates for different race, sex, and national origin groups in accordance with the four-fifths rule.
  — Discontinue further use of tests having discriminatory effects unless strong evidence of validity exists.
  — Not discard results of already-administered exams unless there is a strong basis in evidence of adverse impact liability.
  — Have evidence of job relatedness (validity) for all tests, but particularly for tests that have discriminatory effects.
  — Investigate whether feasible alternative testing procedures with less discriminatory effect are available and, if so, use them.

- Content-valid tests should be used to the extent feasible, but
  - Not to assess intangible characteristics.
  - Not for tasks that could readily be learned on the job.
- Criterion validation studies conducted by consultants or testing companies should be assessed by determining whether
  - The test is validated for the type of job in question.
  - A proper job analysis was conducted.
  - The sample size was sufficiently large.
  - The sample was representative of the people who actually took the test, particularly in terms of protected class characteristics.
  - The effects of the test on particular protected class groups were analyzed.
  - Job performance was measured in a reasonable way.
  - The validity coefficient is sufficiently large and statistically significant.
  - The job has been changed since the validation study was conducted.
- Employers must not use different scoring methods for different protected class groups.
- Employers should not establish cutoff scores for tests
  - That exceed the levels needed to hire employees capable of performing jobs with the normal degree of proficiency.
  - That are higher than necessary in anticipation of possible future positions unless promotion to those positions is relatively quick and certain.
- Candidates should be informed in advance of required employment tests.
- When made aware that accommodation is needed, employers must reasonably accommodate disabled persons in the testing process.

Chapter Questions

1. A state mental health department adopted a policy calling for the random drug testing of all of its employees. Three employees objected to the policy and sought a court order declaring it unconstitutional as applied to them. The employees held the positions of Psychiatric Assistant II and Office Support Assistants. The department claimed that the policy was justified because of its belief that illegal drugs were being used by some department personnel and because each employee serves as a caregiver and role model with respect to patients. The evidence regarding illegal drug use concerned employees at residential facilities for mentally retarded patients. The plaintiffs did not work at these facilities. Administrators were unable to cite specific individuals or incidents, but they testified that they had been informed by staff and family members that drug use by employees at these facilities was occurring. The department also claimed that the need for its staff to act as role models applied to all positions as well as to both in-patient and outpatient treatment. What should the court decide? Why? (*Jakubowicz v. Dittemore*, 2006 U.S. Dist. LEXIS 68639 [W.D. Mo.])

2. A truck driver was subjected to a random drug test and tested positive for marijuana use. After a confirmatory test verified the initial result, the driver was terminated. He denied having ever used marijuana. The driver passed a hair follicle test performed by an independent laboratory eighty-four days after the employer's urine test. The hair follicle test is aimed at identifying persons who persistently use drugs over time. The driver also pointed to problems with the employer's drug testing procedures. Specifically, the drug test was administered by a supervisor despite the availability of nonsupervisory employees, the container had been removed from the sealed kit before the driver arrived to be tested, the driver was not instructed to wash his hands at the proper times, access to the collection site for the specimen was not restricted, and the collection container was not kept in full view of the driver during the time between when the specimen was produced and the container was sealed. Did the employer fail to comply with the drug testing procedures required by the Department of Transportation? If so, was it negligent in how it conducted the drug testing? Why or why not? (*Mission Petroleum Carriers v. Solomon*, 106 S.W.3d 705 [Tex. 2003])

3. A company's drug testing policy allowed for drug testing of employees whose on-the-job behavior indicated the possible influence of illegal drugs or alcohol. An African American employee became involved in an argument with two other

employees who he accused of not helping him lift heavy objects. The argument subsided without further incident, but the next day one of the employees involved in the dispute and another coworker complained to a manager about the African American employee's behavior. They alleged that he had been uncooperative and unresponsive throughout the previous day. Based on this report of "uncharacteristic behavior" as well as rumors that the employee had previously used drugs in the workplace, the company ordered a drug test. The employee tested positive and was terminated. Previously, the same manager did not order a drug or alcohol test for a white employee who had shown up to work visibly intoxicated. Instead, the employee was issued a warning for "questionable usage." The manager attributed the difference to his (mistaken) belief that a test for alcohol would not have revealed anything, given the two days that had elapsed before he learned of the incident. Did this employer discriminate in drug testing the African American employee? Terminating him? (*Keys v. Foamex*, 2008 U.S. App. LEXIS 3310 [7th Cir.])

4. An employee of a paper mill took medical leave to have knee surgery. She was required to undergo a "physical capacity evaluation" (PCE) before being reinstated to her position. The PCE takes two days to complete and is administered by a licensed occupational therapist. The evaluation has numerous components, some of which are taking a personal medical history; recording medications used; measuring height, weight, blood pressure, and pulse; assessing range of motion; measuring lifting ability and grip strength; monitoring performance on a "job simulation task" that required lifting and pouring five-gallon buckets filled with forty-five pounds of sand; and measuring heart rate during a treadmill test. Based on the PCE, it was determined that she was not fit to return to her former position. Since there were no other positions available for which she was qualified, the woman was terminated. Did the employer violate the ADA? Why or why not? (*Indergard v. Georgia-Pacific*, 582 F.3d 1049 [9th Cir. 2009]).

5. A timber company used a "physical performance test" to assess candidates for entry-level positions handling lumber and cutting wood. The test was developed by industrial psychologists. In its original version, the test consisted of a "board pull ergometer" (pulling thirty- to seventy-pound weights for specified durations to assess strength), a step test (stepping up and down on an eleven-inch bench for six minutes), and a visual inspection of "gross body coordination." Additionally, applicants' heart rates were measured during the step test to measure endurance. Applicants whose heart rates exceeded a specified level were stopped and deemed to have failed the test. The revised test consisted solely of a "weight stack" (total weight of forty pounds). For the three years that the original test was in effect, 70.2 percent of male applicants and 29.8 percent of the female applicants passed the test. Of female applicants, 24 percent failed because they were stopped due to an excessive heart rate, compared to 3.2 percent of male applicants. With the revised test, 66.9 percent of males passed and 25.8 percent of females passed. A criterion validation study was conducted for both tests, showing statistically significant correlations between test and job performance. Females rejected for employment sued. What should the court decide? Why? (*Equal Employment Opportunity Commission v. Simpson Timber Company*, 1992 U.S. Dist. LEXIS 5829 [W.D. Wash.])

6. The city of Erie, Pennsylvania, used a physical agility test for hiring entry-level police officers. The test underwent various modifications over time, but it basically consisted of running a 220-yard obstacle course and performing specified numbers of push-ups and sit-ups (thirteen of each in the most recent iteration of the test). Candidates passed the test by completing all of the required activities within 90–95 seconds. The test was developed by police department personnel without the input of experts in exercise physiology or industrial and organizational (I/O) psychology. During its development, the test was given to nineteen volunteers from among the existing police force. All were deemed to be performing their jobs well. The average levels of their performance on the test were used in establishing cutoffs. From 1996–2002, 71 percent of male candidates passed the physical agility test, compared to 12.9 percent of female candidates. Pass rates for individual years ranged from 54 percent to 85 percent for males and from 4 percent to 30 percent for females. At the start of litigation, about 4 percent of Erie's police force was female. Can this physical agility test survive

an adverse impact challenge? (*United States of America v. City of Erie, Pennsylvania*, 411 F. Supp. 2d 524 [W.D. Pa. 2005])

7. In the *Siroka* case involving the personality test that had questions relating to religion and sexual orientation, the company claimed that it had evidence of the test's validity for hiring store security officers. Specifically, the company had given the test to eighteen of its most successful store security officers, and they had done well on it. Comment on the adequacy of this "validation study."

8. Staffing experts widely regard tests of general cognitive ability to be the best predictors of success at a wide range of jobs. What are the legal implications of relying on such tests?

9. Jobs are being transformed. Employers are increasingly focusing on processes rather than individual jobs. More work is being done in teams, with team members expected to be capable of taking on each other's functions. What are implications of this for validating tests or other selection criteria? Has it become more difficult to determine what is "job-related?"

CHAPTER **7**

Hiring and Promotion Decisions

This chapter rounds out our discussion of the legal issues involved in selecting employees for initial hire or promotion by considering the legal implications of facially discriminatory requirements, appearance standards (e.g., weight), and subjective criteria (e.g., impressions from interviews). Sex-stereotyping and discrimination against caregivers are also discussed. After a selection decision is made, the process through which employment is offered and accepted requires careful attention. Discrimination claims increasingly center on obstacles to advancement. Thus, legal concerns surrounding promotion decisions are highlighted.

Criteria for Hiring and Promotion Decisions

Facially Discriminatory Policies/Practices: BFOQ Defense

Employers that base employment decisions, including hiring and promotion, on protected class characteristics are engaging in disparate treatment. When they do so overtly and argue that it is necessary to limit a particular type of employment to people with specific protected class characteristics, this type of disparate treatment is termed a **facially discriminatory** policy or practice. An important, but limited, defense is available to employers that adopt facially discriminatory requirements. If an employer can show that a particular *protected class characteristic* (e.g., being male) is a **bona fide occupational qualification (BFOQ)** for the job in question, the facially discriminatory requirement is legal. Thus, we should amend our earlier advice for avoiding disparate treatment by saying that *employers must not establish protected class requirements for jobs, except in rare instances where those protected class requirements are BFOQs for the jobs in question.*

Title VII of the Civil Rights Act, in language that is mirrored in the Age Discrimination in Employment Act, defines the BFOQ defense as follows:

> [I]t shall not be an unlawful employment practice for an employer to hire and employ ... on the basis of his religion, sex, or national origin in those certain instances where religion, sex, or national origin is a bona fide occupational qualification reasonably necessary to the normal operation of that particular business or enterprise....[1]

Notice that the Title VII protected classes of race and color are omitted. Because racial discrimination was the central problem that motivated passage of the Civil Rights Act, Congress was unwilling to allow for any circumstances in which employment

---

[1]42 U.S.C.S. § 2000e-2(e)(1) (2011).

opportunity could be strictly limited on the basis of race or color. Thus, the BFOQ defense is not available for policies that facially discriminate on the basis of race or color, and *employers must not establish racial requirements for jobs*.

Although the term *reasonably necessary* might not sound overly exacting, the EEOC and courts have made it clear that this is a narrow exception to the general rule prohibiting disparate treatment. It is important to distinguish between adverse impact cases in which *neutral requirements* (e.g., employment tests) must be job-related and consistent with business necessity and disparate treatment cases involving facially discriminatory policies in which *specifications based on protected class* (e.g., "We want to hire only female table servers because that is what our customers want") must be bona fide occupational qualifications. These terms apply in different contexts and are *not* synonymous. A neutral requirement with discriminatory effects can be defended as being job-related and consistent with business necessity if it tends to be associated with job performance and appears reasonable given the nature of the business. In contrast, defense of a facially discriminatory policy requires the employer to show that only, or virtually only, people with the specified protected class characteristic can do the job and that the job, as it is currently configured, is integral to the operation of the business. In other words, hiring people without the specified protected class characteristic would not lead simply to lower job performance, but would ultimately undermine the business.

> ## *Clippings*
>
> The EEOC has sued the Houston branch of the security firm Guardsmark for sex discrimination. The suit alleges that when certain clients expressed their desire to not have female security guards assigned to their premises, Guardsmark reassigned the female guards. The new assignments frequently paid less and required a longer commute. It is the position of the EEOC that Guardsmark cannot establish a BFOQ based on customer preference for male security guards.
>
> U.S. Equal Employment Opportunity Commission. "Texas Branch of National Security Company Sued by EEOC for Sex Discrimination." Press Release (September 22, 2009) Viewed June 22, 2011 (http://www.eeoc.gov/).

Practical Considerations It is often said that one of the benefits of a diverse workforce is that employees will be able to better relate to diverse customers. Should employers make hiring decisions or assign work with the aim of matching the protected class characteristics of employees and customers? If not, what should employers do?

Arguments for BFOQs based on the discriminatory preferences of customers, coworkers, or clients are usually unsuccessful. Otherwise, employers could shirk their responsibilities by blaming others: "I would really like to hire a woman as vice president, but our senior managers are old-fashioned and would not be comfortable dealing with her." This would leave a gaping hole in antidiscrimination laws. An appeals court rejected a company's claim that being male was a BFOQ for the position of vice president of international operations for a petrochemical manufacturer.[2] The company's stated concerns—that Latin American clients would refuse to deal with a woman holding that position and that a woman would be unable to conduct business from hotel rooms—were insufficient to establish a BFOQ. In a racial harassment case in which a nursing home excluded an African American nurse's aide from working with residents based on those residents' expressed desire to be served only by white aides, the court observed that "Title VII forbids employers from using race as a BFOQ," but also went on to show that there is nothing unique about the health care setting that would require a facility to accede to

---

[2]*Fernandez v. Wynn Oil* Co., 653 F.2d 1273 (9th Cir. 1981).

such discriminatory demands.[3] The desire of some of Guardsmark's customers to be assigned male security guards (see "Clippings") is unlikely to justify a BFOQ, since women can clearly perform the job of security guard and do not undermine the business of a security firm.

Grounds for Recognizing BFOQs So when is a BFOQ recognized? The courts have recognized three general grounds for establishing BFOQs: authenticity, public safety, and privacy. The classic example of **authenticity**, or genuineness, is a director casting a movie and limiting a female role to female actors. Authenticity also applies where sex or sex appeal is the essence of the job and business. Owners of clubs featuring topless dancers need not consider males for those jobs. The more difficult cases involve jobs that contain both sex-linked and sex-neutral aspects. A BFOQ will be recognized only if the sex-linked aspects clearly predominate.[4] Hooters restaurants hired only women for jobs as table servers, bartenders, and hosts. A company attorney defended this practice: "Being female is a bona fide occupational qualification. We don't believe the position is simple food service. It's a multidimensional job. We think of Hooters Girls as something closer to the Dallas Cowgirls than to a waitress whose only job is to serve food."[5] In 1997, Hooters agreed to pay $3.75 million to settle a class-action sex discrimination suit brought by males denied employment. The company agreed to open all host positions and some bartender and server positions to men. However, the settlement was a compromise and allowed the restaurant to maintain a "modified Hooters Girl" position, open only to women who would be garbed in Hooters Girl uniforms.[6]

The second basis for establishing a BFOQ is **public safety**. When hiring or assigning employees with particular protected class characteristics is necessary to protect the safety of others, facially discriminatory requirements are legally defensible. The Supreme Court held that Alabama could hire only males for certain prison jobs because conditions in the prisons were so bad that there was a real prospect of violent sexual offenders attacking female guards and prison riots ensuing.[7] Importantly, the Court's rationale was based on potential harm to others, not on a paternalistic impulse to protect individual females from accepting potentially dangerous employment. A public safety BFOQ was not established where an employer's "fetal protection policy" excluded fertile women from jobs that involved exposure to lead.[8] Concerns about the safety of a potential fetus, even if within the realm of "public" safety, were deemed to be not sufficiently related to job performance and the essence of the business to warrant a BFOQ. Although the ADEA generally prohibits mandatory retirement and other maximum age requirements, public safety concerns sometimes allow employers to consider only younger people for jobs. A BFOQ based on public safety was upheld for an inner-city bus company that limited new hires to people under 40.[9] Courts are relatively receptive to BFOQs for age requirements based on public safety, but before excluding older people from safety sensitive jobs, *employers must establish that the risks posed by older employees are substantial and that*

---

[3]*Chaney v. Plainfield Healthcare Center*, 612 F.3d 908, 913–15 (7th Cir. 2010).

[4]*Wilson v. Southwest Airlines*, 517 F. Supp. 292, at 301 (N.D. Tex. 1981).

[5]"Food Chain Charged with Bias for Hiring Only Females for 'Hooters Girls' Waitstaff." *Daily Labor Report* 248 (December 30, 1993), D-11.

[6]Nadya Aswad. "Hooters Chain Agrees to Pay $3.75 Million to Settle Bias Claims by Male Job Applicants." *Daily Labor Report* 190 (October 1, 1997), D-32.

[7]*Dothard v. Rawlinson*, 433 U.S. 321 (1977).

[8]*International Union, UAW v. Johnson Controls*, 499 U.S. 187 (1991).

[9]*Usery v. Tamiami Trail Tours*, 531 F.2d 224 (5th Cir. 1976).

more individualized means (e.g., regular medical exams) of identifying people who might pose risks are not feasible.

The third basis for a BFOQ is customer **privacy**. This primarily relates to requirements for employees of a particular sex. One BFOQ case with a privacy basis concerned a psychiatric facility's rule that at least one person of each sex be available on each shift.[10] The rationale for the rule was that many of the hospital's adolescent clients had been victims of sexual abuse and might be willing to speak only with counselors of a specific sex. The court agreed that scheduling shifts based on sex was facially discriminatory, but held that the sex requirement was a BFOQ due to its close relationship to the therapeutic mission of the hospital. Privacy-based BFOQs have also been recognized in cases involving delivery nurses,[11] custodians,[12] and correctional officers assigned to certain female residential facilities.[13]

A number of BFOQ cases involve the staffing of correctional facilities. *Breiner v. Nevada Department of Corrections* provides a good example of the difficulties involved in applying antidiscrimination law to this setting.

Breiner v. Nevada Department of Corrections
610 F.3d 1202 (9th Cir. 2010)

OPINION BY CIRCUIT JUDGE BERZON:

The Nevada Department of Corrections (NDOC) hires only female correctional lieutenants at a women's prison. The district court granted summary judgment upholding NDOC's discriminatory employment policy, concluding that the policy imposed only a "de minimis" restriction on male prison employees' promotional opportunities and, alternatively, that the policy falls within Title VII's exception permitting sex discrimination in jobs for which sex is a bona fide occupational qualification. We reverse as to both holdings.

In September 2003, NDOC's Inspector General learned that a female inmate at the Southern Nevada Women's Correctional Facility (SNWCF) had been impregnated by a male guard. At the time, SNWCF was operated by a private company, Corrections Corporation of America (CCA). * * * In the course of the investigation, the Inspector General ... discovered that SNWCF had become "an uninhibited sexual environment." He noted "frequent instances of inappropriate staff/inmate interaction," "flirtatious activities between staff and inmates," and "widespread knowledge" of "long-term inmate/inmate sexual relationships." In exchange for sex, prison staff "routinely introduce[d] ... contraband into the institution, including alcohol, narcotics, cosmetics, [and] jewelry." * * *

In the wake of the Inspector General's report, which ignited "very high profile" media coverage, CCA announced that it was terminating its contract to operate SNWCF. NDOC resumed control of the facility and, according to Crawford, faced intense political pressure to "mitigate the number of newspaper articles" and to "assure the State of Nevada that we would not be embarrassed like this again." To achieve this goal, Crawford decided to restaff the facility so that seventy percent of the front line staff at SNWCF would be women. Crawford also decided to hire only women in SNWCF's three correctional lieutenant positions. The correctional lieutenants are shift supervisors and are the senior employees on duty seventy-five percent of the time. Correctional lieutenants report to wardens or deputy wardens and are responsible for

---

[10]*Healey v. Southwood Psychiatric Hospital*, 78 F.3d 128 (3d Cir. 1996).

[11]*EEOC v. Mercy Health Center*, 1982 U.S. Dist. LEXIS 12256 (W.D. Ok.).

[12]*Norwood v. Dale Maintenance Systems*, 590 F. Supp. 1410 (N.D. Ill. 1984).

[13]*Everson v. Michigan Department of Corrections*, 391 F.3d 737, 756–759 (6th Cir. 2004) (in addition to security and public safety rationales).

supervising the prison's day-to-day operations, including directing the work of subordinate staff, inspecting the facility and reporting infractions, and monitoring inmates' activities and movement through the facility. There is one correctional lieutenant assigned to SWNCF per shift. Although the correctional lieutenant posting specified that "only female applicants will be accepted for these positions," several males applied for the positions, which were eventually filled by three women.

The ... plaintiffs, all male Nevada correctional officers, * * * filed suit alleging that the state's decision to limit the correctional lieutenant positions to women violated Title VII's prohibition on sex discrimination in employment.

A. THE "DE MINIMIS" THEORY

NDOC asserts that the three SNWCF positions were the only correctional lieutenant promotions in the NDOC system as a whole restricted to women applicants and that twenty-nine out of thirty-seven correctional lieutenant positions filled over a four year period went to men. Relying on these statistics, NDOC maintains that the concededly discriminatory policy of excluding men from the SNWCF correctional lieutenant positions had only a "de minimis" impact on the plaintiffs and so did not violate Title VII with regard to them. This conclusion reflects a fundamental misunderstanding of the basic precepts of Title VII and is not supported by our case law.

It is beyond dispute that the denial of a single promotion opportunity such as the one here at issue is actionable under Title VII. * * * Further, Title VII is offended when an individual suffers discrimination with respect to a particular adverse employment decision, even if others of the same protected group are not similarly disadvantaged. "A racially balanced work force cannot immunize an employer from liability for specific acts of discrimination." * * * Title VII protects the ability to pursue one's own career goals without being discriminated against on the basis of race or sex, even if others of the same race or sex were not subject to disadvantage.

In holding otherwise, the district court relied on Robino v. Iranon. Robino concerned prison officials' decision to assign only female guards to six "posts" in a women's prison—those from which the guard could observe inmates in the shower—to "accommodate the privacy interests of the female inmates and reduce the risk of sexual conduct between [guards] and

inmates." The plaintiffs in Robino were current male guards complaining that female guards—individuals holding the same position—were to a limited degree given different job assignments within the same job category. * * * Thus, the restriction in Robino was "de minimis" not, as the district court thought, because a small proportion of positions were affected, but because "male [guards had] not suffered any tangible job detriment beyond a reduced ability to select their preferred watches."

Robino's premise, then, was necessarily that a minor impact on job assignments was too minimal to be actionable. This very limited concept has no application to NDOC's policy. An employer's "fail[ure] or refus[al] to hire" on the basis of sex is, without limitation, actionable under Title VII. NDOC's refusal to hire men in the correctional lieutenant positions therefore violates Title VII unless NDOC can demonstrate that gender is a BFOQ for the positions. NDOC cannot meet that burden, as we now explain.

B. GENDER AS A BONA FIDE OCCUPATIONAL QUALIFICATION

* * * [T]he BFOQ is an "extremely narrow exception to the general prohibition of discrimination on the basis of sex" that may be invoked "only when the essence of the business operation would be undermined" by hiring individuals of both sexes. To justify discrimination under the BFOQ exception, an employer must prove by a preponderance of the evidence: 1) that the job qualification justifying the discrimination is reasonably necessary to the essence of its business; and 2) that [sex] is a legitimate proxy for the qualification because (a) it has a substantial basis for believing that all or nearly all [men] lack the qualification, or ... (b) it is impossible or highly impractical ... to insure by individual testing that its employees will have the necessary qualifications for the job.

NDOC has not explicitly articulated the "job qualification" for correctional lieutenants for which it claims sex is a legitimate proxy. * * * Glen Whorton, the director of NDOC from 2005 to 2007, declared that "the employment of male correctional lieutenants at SNWCF would create a real risk ... if female inmates were sexually assaulted, abused by male correctional lieutenants and/or male ... subordinates and such abuse was kept silent by the male correctional lieutenants ... because they were protecting themselves and/or their ... subordinates ('code of silence')." * * * Female correctional lieutenants, according to Whorton, "are more inclined to monitor and discipline the wrongful conduct of correctional subordinates and to take steps of prevention with respect to female inmates as their very nature, womanhood, is more conducive to dealing with the complexities and differences of female inmates." * * * Crawford [the current director of the NDOC] also testified that she wanted correctional lieutenants who "understand[ ] management of women. I think that women do have an innate ability to manage women. * * * I just believe [women] are more patient. They're probably more maternal …. they have an instinct and an innate ability to discern what is real and what isn't …. the female officers were able to better discern, you know, what's really happening here."

[I]t appears that NDOC administrators sought to "reduce the number of male correctional employees being compromised by female inmates," and that they believed the gender restriction on shift supervisors would accomplish this because (1) male correctional lieutenants are likely to condone sexual abuse by their male subordinates; (2) male correctional lieutenants are themselves likely to sexually abuse female inmates; and (3) female correctional lieutenants possess an "instinct" that renders them less susceptible to manipulation by inmates and therefore better equipped to fill the correctional lieutenant role.

The first theory fails because NDOC has not shown that "all or nearly all" men would tolerate sexual abuse by male guards, or that it is "impossible or highly impractical" to assess applicants individually for this qualification. As to the second theory, there is no "basis in fact" for believing that individuals in the correctional lieutenant role are particularly likely to sexually abuse inmates. The third theory—and, to a significant degree, the first two—relies on the kind of unproven and invidious stereotype that Congress sought to eliminate from employment decisions when it enacted Title VII.

We begin our analysis by surveying the decisions applying the BFOQ exception in the prison context. Dothard, the only Supreme Court case on the subject, concerned a "peculiarly inhospitable" maximum security prison for men where conditions were so atrocious as to be "constitutionally intolerable," and "a substantial portion of the inmate population [was] composed of sex offenders mixed at random with other prisoners." In the context of this extreme environment,

the Supreme Court upheld a regulation prohibiting women from working in "positions requiring continual close physical proximity to inmates," finding "[m]ore [ ] at stake … than an individual woman's decision to weigh and accept the risks" of working in "a prison system where violence is the order of the day." * * * "The likelihood that inmates would assault a woman because she was a woman would pose a real threat to … the basic control of the penitentiary."

* * * Appellate courts, including this court, have followed Dothard in requiring prison administrators to identify a concrete, logical basis for concluding that gender restrictions are "reasonably necessary." In Everson v. Michigan Department of Corrections, the Sixth Circuit upheld a gender restriction imposed by the Michigan Department of Corrections (MDOC) to eradicate "rampant sexual abuse of female prisoners." MDOC had "pledged … to minimize access to secluded areas and one-on-one contact between male staff and female inmates" pursuant to settlement of two lawsuits, one brought by the United States Department of Justice, alleging that the failure to protect female inmates from ongoing sexual abuse violated their constitutional rights. To effectuate the settlement agreements, MDOC employed only female guards in the housing units of women's prisons. MDOC data showed that most allegations of sexual abuse, and all of the sustained allegations, involved male employees, and that sexual abuse occurred most frequently in the housing units. This data, the court held, "established that the exclusion of male [guards] will decrease the likelihood of sexual abuse."

In Henry v. Milwaukee County, a juvenile detention center decided to staff each housing "pod" with at least one guard of the same sex as the juveniles housed on that pod, to achieve a "direct role model/mentoring form of supervision." During the day, one of the two guards on each male "pod" could be female, but the sole night shift slot on each pod had to be staffed by a man. The Seventh Circuit accepted the administrator's "professional judgment" that same-gender mentoring was "necessary to achieve the [facility's] mission of rehabilitation." Yet, the court found no factual support for the administrator's conclusion that the program's effectiveness required same-sex staff at all times, including on the night shift, when the juvenile inmates were sleeping.

In Robino, we held that even had the gender-based restriction on assignments been actionable under Title VII, it fell within the BFOQ exception.

The prison, based on "a study conducted by a specially appointed task force in compliance with an EEOC settlement agreement," designated as female only those posts that "require[d] the [guard] on duty to observe the inmates in the showers and toilet areas ... or provide[d] unsupervised access to the inmates." Because "a person's interest in not being viewed unclothed by members of the opposite sex survives incarceration," we held that protecting inmate privacy and preventing sexual misconduct warranted the restriction.

These cases illustrate that, even in the unique context of prison employment, administrators seeking to justify a BFOQ must show "a high correlation between sex and ability to perform job functions." * * * Applying this "high correlation" requirement, NDOC's first rationale for restricting the supervisory correctional lieutenant positions to women cannot suffice. Crawford's testimony suggests that because the supervisors employed by CCA were male and had failed to prevent sexual abuse, NDOC was entitled to conclude that men as a class were incapable of adequately supervising front line staff in female prisons.... CCA's acknowledged leadership failure falls far short of providing "a factual basis for believing that all or substantially all [men] would be unable to safely and effectively perform the duties of the job," or that it would be "impossible or highly impracticable to determine job fitness"—here, the ability to enforce workplace rules prohibiting sexual misconduct—"on an individualized basis." * * *

NDOC's second rationale fares no better. There is no evidence indicating that any correctional lieutenant at SNWCF had sexual relationships with an inmate. * * * In fact, the one substantiated case of sexual abuse Crawford mentioned was the front line guard who impregnated an inmate, yet NDOC continues to employ men in thirty percent of these positions. When asked why the complete prohibition on the hiring of men was limited to correctional lieutenants, Crawford stated, "We did not want to go globally on this. We wanted to be specifically, what can we do to bring this thing under control ... ? And it was the recommendation that we just look at ... not the line level, but the supervisor level." This explanation falls short of the "reasoned decision-making process, based on available information and experience," that can support a BFOQ.

Even if there were a factual basis to believe that any correctional lieutenant sexually abused any

inmate, there is no basis to presume that sexual abuse, by correctional lieutenants or by guards with their supervisors' tacit permission, would continue after the state resumed control over the prison. CCA's lax oversight provided male correctional lieutenants "the opportunity not to take action against male correctional subordinates that sexually abused female inmates." That opportunity cannot be presumed to exist after the wholesale change of SNWCF's leadership, designed precisely to cure wholesale management defects going well beyond the sexual abuse issue.

To hold otherwise would be to absolve NDOC from their fundamental responsibility to supervise their staff, from wardens to front-line guards. In Dothard, the inmates' violent behavior, which prison administrators could not directly control, rendered the gender restriction reasonably necessary. Neither Dothard nor any of the cases on which NDOC relies support finding a BFOQ based on the bald assertion that it would be "impossible ... to ensure that any given male correctional lieutenant will take action to prevent and stop sexual misconduct." Where, as here, the problem is employee behavior, prison administrators have multiple resources, including background checks, prompt investigation of suspected misconduct, and severe discipline for infractions, to ensure compliance with institutional rules. NDOC has not demonstrated that these alternative approaches—including the Inspector General's suggestion of enhanced training for both supervisors and front-line guards—are not viable.

Disturbingly, in suggesting that all men are inherently apt to sexually abuse, or condone sexual abuse of, female inmates, NDOC relies on entirely specious gender stereotypes that have no place in a workplace governed by Title VII. NDOC's third theory, that women are "maternal," "patient," and understand other women, fails for the same reason. To credit NDOC's unsupported generalization that women "have an instinct and an innate ability to discern ... what's real and what isn't" and so are immune to manipulation by female inmates would violate "the Congressional purpose to eliminate subjective assumptions and traditional stereotyped conceptions regarding the ... ability of women to do particular work." * * * A BFOQ can be established only by "objective, verifiable requirements [that] concern job-related skills and aptitudes." Though the professional judgment of prison administrators is entitled to deference, "[t]he refusal to hire a [man] because of [his] sex based on assumptions of the comparative employment characteristics of [men] in general" will not support a BFOQ. * * *

Restricting employment opportunity on the basis of gender can be justified by the need to counter uncontrollably violent inmate behavior, as in Dothard. But this case concerns the behavior of employees, not inmates. Precluding men from serving in supervisory positions in women's prisons is not a substitute for effective leadership and enforcement of workplace rules. * * *

CASE QUESTIONS

1. What were the legal issues in this case? What did the court decide?
2. Why did the court reject the NDOC's "de minimis" argument?
3. What criteria for establishing a BFOQ are discussed in this case?
4. Why was the NDOC's BFOQ defense not successful? How is this case different from other corrections cases in which the BFOQ defense was established?
5. Do you agree with the court's decision? Why or why not?

Except when clear authenticity, public safety, or privacy interests are at stake, employers should not impose protected class requirements for employment based on the demands or needs of customers or coworkers. Overall, the best advice regarding BFOQs is that *even when suitability for a job is associated with protected class characteristics, employers should seek more individualized means of assessing suitability rather than rely on protected class as a convenient proxy.* For example, if being knowledgeable about contemporary music is a requirement of a job, the employer should directly assess that knowledge rather than limit hiring to young people on the assumption that older people are not conversant on the subject. Finally, because some state antidiscrimination laws require that BFOQs be certified by the state fair employment practice agency before being put into use, *employers might be required to convince state fair employment practice agencies that BFOQs are warranted before putting them into effect.*

JUST THE FACTS

A hospital had the following policy: "All pregnant personnel must immediately report pregnancy status to the director.... The pregnant personnel shall not partake in any fluoroscopy or portable procedures during her term. This will ensure safety and protection." Fluoroscopy involves high-intensity radiation, and the procedure is carried out by a medical team that includes a cardiologist, registered nurse, and radiology or cardiovascular technologist. The EEOC sued the hospital based on the policy and its effect on two female employees who were reassigned to work in other areas of the hospital during their pregnancies.

See, *EEOC v. Catholic Healthcare West*, 530 F. Supp. 2d 1096 (C.D. Cal. 2008).

"Sex-Plus" Cases

A less obvious form of facially discriminatory policy or practice occurs when neutral criteria are applied to some protected class groups but not others. In an important Supreme Court case, the employer refused to employ women with children under age 5.[14] The company did not concern itself with the ages of the children of male employees. Even though the majority of the company's employees were women and the policy excluded only some women, it was deemed facially discriminatory because it was applied to and limited the employment opportunities of women only. The employer would have to establish a BFOQ to defend not hiring women with young children—an unlikely prospect. Although circumstances may call for sex-specific requirements or policies, the general rule is that *employers must not establish requirements that apply to some protected class groups but not others.* These cases are labeled **sex-plus** because they most often involve differential requirements based on sex, but the issue is really "protected class–plus." Thus, an employer's policy of requiring that candidates for a promotional position who were over 40 years of age submit to EKG exams, while younger candidates were not usually required to do so, was facially discriminatory. A BFOQ could not be established because of the fairly minimal public safety dimensions of the job and because it was possible to require EKG testing on a more individualized basis than age.[15]

Weight and Appearance

Getting ahead in the workplace is like entering a beauty contest. Well, not exactly, but research has shown that physical appearance has a pervasive effect on employment outcomes. People judged better looking are more likely to get hired, to be promoted, and even to be paid more.[16] One aspect of appearance that can affect treatment in the workplace is weight. Research suggests that discrimination on the basis of weight is common and that such bias is particularly detrimental to women. Males are apparently given more slack and have to put on considerably more weight than women before experiencing similar mistreatment.[17] A heavier-than-average woman described her experience when she was a candidate for a grant-writing job. Her phone interview went well, but after she was invited for an in-person interview, everything changed:

> As soon as I shook the interviewer's hand, I knew she would not hire me.... She gave me a look of utter disdain, and made a big deal about whether we should take the stairs or ride the elevator to the room where we were going to talk. During the actual interview, she would not even look at me and kept looking to the side.[18]

Mistreatment of this kind is as common as it is unkind, but what are the legal implications of considering weight in hiring decisions?

Except for a very few jurisdictions (e.g., Michigan, the cities of San Francisco and Santa Cruz), weight is not a protected class. However, employers that discriminate against people because they are "too heavy" might be discriminating on the basis of disability. For example, a hospital for the mentally retarded declined to rehire a 5'2", 320-pound woman as an attendant despite her prior good work record.[19] The woman argued that her obesity led the hospital to regard her as disabled and deny employment on that basis even though she could do the job. The hospital's arguments that obesity should not be considered a disabling condition because it is mutable (capable of being

[14]*Phillips v. Martin Marietta Corp.*, 400 U.S. 542 (1971).

[15]*Epter v. New York City Transit Authority*, 127 F. Supp. 2d 384 (E.D.N.Y. 2001).

[16]Daniel S. Hamermesh and Jeff E. Biddle. "Beauty and the Labor Market." *American Economic Review* 84 (December 1994), 1174–94.

[17]R. M. Puhl, T. Andreyeva, and K. D. Brownell. "Perceptions of Weight Discrimination: Prevalence and Comparison to Race and Gender Discrimination in America." *International Journal of Obesity* 32.6 (2008), 992–1000.

[18]Harriet Brown. "For Obese People, Prejudice in Plain Sight." *New York Times* (March 16, 2010), D6.

[19]*Cook v. State of Rhode Island, Dept. of MHRH*, 10 F.3d 17 (1st Cir. 1993).

altered) and voluntarily incurred, even if supportable, did not impress the appeals court, which ruled on the employee's behalf. But overall, courts have been reluctant to conclude that being overweight is a disability. Any chance of protection under disability discrimination laws depends on the individual being not merely overweight, but "morbidly obese" (more than twice the normal body weight or 100 pounds over normal body weight for a person of that height). Second, courts have usually required that a physiological basis for the obesity (or serious medical problems stemming from it) be shown. Thus, the ADA claim of a dock worker who weighed as much as 450 pounds failed because no evidence was produced that his morbid obesity had a physiological basis.[20] However, recent changes to the ADA have broadened the definition of disability and this *might* facilitate claims of disability discrimination by obese people.[21] Should an employer discriminate against someone deemed "underweight," disability discrimination could be claimed if the person was anorexic or had some other disabling condition (e.g., cancer, AIDS) as the cause of the person's thinness.

What about the merely "chubby"? Is there any legal protection for people disadvantaged by weight that is more within the normal range of variation? Employer policies or practices that place differentially burdensome weight requirements on men and women have been found to constitute sex-plus discrimination. Weight standards for flight attendants at United Airlines were successfully challenged on this basis.[22] The airline had weight limits for both male and female flight attendants, but the limits for males were based on the assumption of a large body frame, whereas the limits for women were based on the assumption of a medium frame. Consequently, female flight attendants were required to weigh between 14 and 25 pounds less than male peers of the same age and height. United was unable to defend its facially discriminatory weight requirements by showing that it was reasonably necessary to its business that female flight attendants be disproportionally thinner than male flight attendants.

Challenges to weight criteria on sex-plus grounds are not limited to formal policies. A highly qualified 270-pound woman was turned down for a sales representative position. She was allegedly told by several managers that because this was an outside sales position involving direct contact with customers, she needed to lose weight to get promoted. The court agreed that her allegations raised a question of sex-plus discrimination, but her case failed because she was unable to point to men in sales positions whose excess weight was not objected to by the company.[23]

Clippings

Resorts Hotel & Casino in Atlantic City fired fifteen of its most senior cocktail servers and replaced them with much younger workers. The women, all over 50 years of age, had been asked to model "flapper costumes." Pictures were taken of them in the costumes. The casino's new owners determined that the women did not fit the casino's "Roaring Twenties" theme of being a place for "fun, excitement, and a one-of-a-kind experience." The hotel's spokesperson said that "Every day, we present a show to our guests that all of our employees are part of...." Attorney Gloria Allred, who is representing the women in their age discrimination suit, said

---

[20]*EEOC v. Watkins Motor Lines*, 463 F.3d 436 (6th Cir. 2006).

[21]*Lowe v. American Eurocopter*, 2010 U.S. Dist. LEXIS 133343, 25 (N.D. Miss.).

[22]*Frank v. United Airlines*, 216 F.3d 845 (9th Cir. 2000), *cert. denied*, 121 S. Ct. 1247 (2001).

[23]*Marks v. National Communications Association*, 72 F. Supp. 2d 322 (S.D.N.Y. 1999).

> that the hotel's arguments about the employee's being actors in a show were part of a futile attempt to invoke the BFOQ defense. She concluded that "It is clear that the cocktail servers are serving drinks, not performing."
>
> Suzette Parmley. "Casinos Trying to Fend Off Suits from Fired Cocktail Servers." *The Philadelphia Inquirer* (June 6, 2011), A1.

Employers impose many types of appearance and grooming requirements. Different rules are often established for men and women relating to such matters as hair length, facial hair, jewelry, and the wearing of dresses. Are such policies discriminatory? A newspaper refused to hire a man for a copy layout artist job because his hair was too long. The newspaper did not have any requirements for the hair length of women. The appeals court distinguished this situation from other sex-plus cases because the neutral requirement paired with sex in this case was not a fundamental right (e.g., having children, getting married) and was not based on an immutable characteristic (i.e., the applicant could get a haircut). Thus, in the court's view, "a hiring policy that distinguishes on … grooming codes or length of hair is related more closely to the employer's choice of how to run his business than to equality of employment opportunity."[24] The court also endorsed the alternative rationale that no differential standard based on sex existed because both sexes were simply being asked to meet generally accepted standards of appearance. Judicial disinclination to get involved in disputes over employers' appearance requirements can readily be discerned in the case law, but courts also employ the logic of sex-plus claims and ask whether differential requirements are truly more burdensome to people of one sex. And increasingly, courts examine whether appearance requirements are rooted in demeaning sexual stereotypes.

JUST THE FACTS

A female bartender had worked at Harrah's Casino for twenty years. During that time, her job performance had consistently been rated as excellent. A "Beverage Department Image Transformation" program was implemented. Under the program, all beverage servers were to be "well-groomed, appealing to the eye, firm, and body toned." Female beverage servers were required to wear stockings, use colored nail polish, and wear their hair "teased, curled, or styled." Additionally, women were required to wear makeup. Male beverage servers were prohibited from wearing makeup or colored nail polish and required to maintain short haircuts and trimmed fingernails. The female bartender specifically objected to the makeup requirement. She tried wearing makeup on the job once previously, but she found that it made her feel like a sexual object and that it was more difficult to deal with unruly guests. Based on her refusal to comply with the makeup requirement, she was terminated. What should the court decide?

See, *Jespersen v. Harrah's*, 444 F.3d 1104 (9th Cir. 2006).

---

[24] *Willingham v. Macon Telegraph Publishing* Co., 507 F.2d 1084, 1091 (5th Cir. 1975).

Sex-Stereotyping

Although courts have generally not been receptive to claims based on differential appearance standards for men and women, requirements that are markedly different and that impose sex-stereotypical standards are sometimes a different story. In one case, a retailer required female salesclerks to wear maternal-looking smocks, while male sales-clerks wore business attire. The court concluded that these disparate standards reinforced stereotypes about women and were discriminatory.[25] Dress requirements that subject women to harassment have also been judged discriminatory.[26] The U.S. Supreme Court made an important statement about **sex-stereotyping** in a case involving a woman denied partnership at an accounting firm.[27] The comments of partners who participated in the decision process made it clear that they saw her as not sufficiently "feminine." Partners criticized her for using profanity, being "macho," "overcompensat[ing] for being a woman," and being "a somewhat masculine hard-nosed manager." When informed that she was denied partnership, the woman was also told that she should "walk more femi-ninely, talk more femininely, dress more femininely, wear makeup, have her hair styled, and wear jewelry." The Court stated the following:

> [W]e are beyond the day when an employer could evaluate employees by assuming or insisting that they matched the stereotype associated with their group.... "Congress intended to strike at the entire spectrum of disparate treatment of men and women, resulting from sex stereotypes." An employer who objects to aggressiveness in women but whose positions require this trait places women in an intolerable and impermissible Catch-22; out of a job if they behave aggressively and out of a job if they don't. Title VII lifts women out of this bind.[28]

Sex stereotypes can also affect men. A restaurant employee who was continually har-assed because he was viewed by coworkers as effeminate had grounds for a sex discrimi-nation claim.[29] An even more sweeping application of sex-stereotyping is found in the case of a transsexual firefighter diagnosed with gender identity disorder. The firefighter began to adopt a more feminine appearance, leading to negative comments from cowor-kers, efforts by managers to force him to quit, and his subsequent suspension. The court said that the crux of the case was the firefighter's gender-nonconforming behavior and appearance. Regardless of the transsexual label, discrimination against an individual because he or she does not conform to stereotypes about how people assigned a particu-lar sex at birth should act and dress violates Title VII.[30] However, courts have been far from unanimous in holding that the sex-stereotyping theory reaches transsexual or trans-gender persons. In one relevant case, an employee in the process of transitioning from male to female was terminated for noncompliance with her employer's dress and groom-ing policy.[31] Over time, the employee started wearing clear nail polish, trimming her eye-brows, using mascara, and wearing her hair longer and in a feminine style. These changes conflicted with the store's policy requiring male employees to have short hair, to refrain from wearing jewelry that required piercing, and to maintain "a conservative, socially acceptable general appearance." The court concluded that while it "may disagree

Practical Considerations Are workplace appearance and grooming policies necessary? If so, what policy would you recommend with regard to office work-ers who have some contact with clients/customers? To what extent should the policy differentiate between male and female employees?

[25] *O'Donnell v. Burlington Coat Factory Warehouse,* 656 F. Supp. 263, 266 (S.D. Ohio 1987).

[26] EEOC v. *Sage Realty Corp.,* 507 F. Supp. 599 (S.D.N.Y. 1981).

[27] *Price Waterhouse v. Hopkins,* 490 U.S. 228 (1989).

[28] *Price Waterhouse v. Hopkins,* 490 U.S. 228 (1989).

[29] *Sanchez v. Azteca Restaurant Enterprises,* 256 F.3d 864 (9th Cir. 2001).

[30] *Smith v. City of Salem, Ohio,* 378 F.3d 566 (6th Cir. 2004).

[31] *Creed v. Family Express Corp.,* 2009 U.S. Dist. LEXIS 237 (N.D. Ind.).

with Family Express that a male-to-female transsexual's intent to present herself according to her gender identity should be considered a violation of its dress code and grooming policy, ... [there is] too little evidence to permit an inference that Family Express didn't actually terminate Ms. Creed for this legally permissible reason."[32]

In *Lewis v. Heartland Inns of America*, the court finds evidence of discrimination in the sex-stereotypical expectations of a manager regarding an employee's appearance.

Lewis v. Heartland Inns of America
591 F.3d 1033 (8th Cir. 2010)

OPINION BY CIRCUIT JUDGE MURPHY:

Alleging that she lost a job she had done well, solely because of unlawful sex stereotyping, Brenna Lewis brought this action for sex discrimination and retaliation against her former employer Heartland Inns of America…. The district court granted summary judgment to Heartland. We reverse and remand.

* * * Heartland Inns operates a group of hotels, primarily in Iowa. Brenna Lewis began work for Heartland in July 2005…. She started as the night auditor at Heartland's Waterloo Crossroads location; at that job she worked at the front desk from 11:00 p.m. to 7:00 a.m. There were also two other shifts for "guest service representatives": the A shift from 7:00 a.m. to 3:00 p.m. and the B shift from 3:00 p.m. to 11:00 p.m. Lewis' manager at Waterloo Crossroads, Linda Gowdy, testified that Lewis "did her job well" and that she had requested a pay raise for her. Heartland recorded two merit based pay raises for Lewis. The record also indicates that Gowdy received a customer comment praising Lewis.

On or about December 7, 2006, Lewis began working various part time front desk shifts at Heartland Inns located near Des Moines, including at Ankeny and Altoona. At both locations she was valued by her direct supervisors. Her manager at the Altoona hotel, Jennifer Headington, testified that Lewis "made a good impression[.]" She offered her a full time night auditor position after receiving telephone permission from Barbara Cullinan, Heartland's Director of Operations. Lori Stifel, Lewis' manager at the Ankeny hotel, testified in her deposition that Lewis did a "great job" in Ankeny, "fit into the [front desk] position really well" and was well liked by customers. Stifel received permission over the phone from Cullinan on December 15

to offer Lewis a full time A shift position. Neither Headington nor Stifel conducted an interview of Lewis before extending their offers, and the record does not reflect that Cullinan ever told them a subsequent interview would be necessary. Lewis accepted the offer for the A shift at Ankeny and began training with her predecessor, Morgan Hammer. At the end of December 2006 Lewis took over the job.

Lewis' positive experience at Heartland changed only after Barbara Cullinan saw her working at the Ankeny desk. * * * She had approved the hiring of Lewis for the Ankeny A shift after receiving Stifel's positive recommendation. After seeing Lewis, however, Cullinan told Stifel that she was not sure Lewis was a "good fit" for the front desk. Cullinan called Stifel a few days later and again raised the subject of Lewis' appearance. Lewis describes her own appearance as "slightly more masculine," and Stifel has characterized it as "an Ellen DeGeneres kind of look." Lewis prefers to wear loose fitting clothing, including men's button down shirts and slacks. She avoids makeup and wore her hair short at the time. Lewis has been mistaken for a male and referred to as "tomboyish."

Cullinan told Stifel that Heartland "took two steps back" when Lewis replaced Morgan Hammer who has been described as dressing in a more stereotypical feminine manner. As Cullinan expressed it, Lewis lacked the "Midwestern girl look." Cullinan was heard to boast about the appearance of women staff members and had indicated that Heartland staff should be "pretty," a quality she considered especially important for women working at the front desk. Cullinan also had advised a hotel manager not to hire a particular applicant because she was not pretty enough. The front desk job description in Heartland's personnel manual

---

[32] *Creed*, at 28.

does not mention appearance. It states only that a guest service representative "[c]reates a warm, inviting atmosphere" and performs tasks such as relaying information and receiving reservations.

… Cullinan ordered Stifel to move Lewis back to the overnight shift. Stifel refused because Lewis had been doing "a phenomenal job at the front desk[.]" The following week, on January 9, 2007, Cullinan insisted that Lori Stifel resign. Around this time, Heartland informed its general managers that hiring for the front desk position would require a second interview. Video equipment was also purchased to enable Cullinan or Kristi Nosbisch, Heartland's Human Resource Director, to see an applicant before extending any offer. * * *

Cullinan met with Brenna Lewis on January 23, 2007. At this point Lewis had held the front desk job for nearly a month after Cullinan's initial approval of her hire for the position. The record contains no evidence of any customer dissatisfaction with Lewis or her service. Nevertheless, Cullinan told Lewis at the meeting that she would need a second interview in order to "confirm/endorse" her A shift position. Lewis was aware from Lori Stifel of what had been said about her appearance, and she protested that other staff members had not been required to have second interviews for the job. Lewis told Cullinan that she believed a second interview was being required only because she lacked the "Midwestern girl look." She questioned whether the interview was lawful, and she cried throughout the meeting.

Cullinan wanted to know who had told Lewis about the comment and asked whether it was Lori Stifel. Thereafter Cullinan talked about the need for new managers when revenue is down like in Ankeny, where Stifel was the manager. Lewis responded that recent policy changes by Heartland, including bans on smoking and on pets, might explain the loss in revenue. Cullinan then encouraged Lewis to share more of her views about the new policies and took notes on what she said. Three days later, Lewis was fired.

Lewis does not challenge Heartland's official dress code, which imposes comparable standards of professional appearance on male and female staff members, and her termination letter did not cite any violation of its dress code. The theory of her case is that the evidence shows Heartland enforced a de facto requirement that a female employee conform to gender stereotypes in order to work the A shift. There was no such requirement in the company's written policies. In its termination letter to Lewis, Heartland asserted that she had "thwart[ed] the proposed interview procedure" and exhibited "host[ility] toward Heartland's most recent policies[.]" * * * Lewis asserts that Heartland terminated her for not conforming to sex stereotypes and contends that this conduct violated Title VII of the Civil Rights Act and the Iowa Civil Rights Act.

* * * Among the authorities relied on by Lewis is Price Waterhouse v. Hopkins, where the Supreme Court decided that sex stereotyping can violate Title VII when it influences employment decisions. * * * In Price Waterhouse, where a female senior manager was denied partnership, partners involved in their decision had referred to her as "'macho'" and in need of "'a course at charm school[.]'" She was advised that to become a partner she should "'walk more femininely, talk more femininely, dress more femininely, wear make-up, have her hair styled, and wear jewelry.'" Such stereotypical attitudes violate Title VII if they lead to an adverse employment decision. * * * Like the plaintiff in Price Waterhouse, Lewis alleges that her employer found her unsuited for her job not because of her qualifications or her performance on the job, but because her appearance did not comport with its preferred feminine stereotype.

Other circuits have upheld Title VII claims based on sex stereotyping subsequent to Price Waterhouse. * * * The Sixth Circuit's Smith case concerned a fire fighter who was born male but subsequently came to identify as a woman. When he began "to express a more feminine appearance" at work, he was told by colleagues that he was not "masculine enough[.]" His superiors then "devise[d] a plan" to terminate him, including an order that he submit to multiple psychological evaluations. If he did not consent, "they could terminate Smith's employment on the ground of insubordination." Lewis similarly alleges that Heartland imposed a second interview and then used her objection to it against her when its real reason for terminating her was because she lacked the "Midwestern girl look" and was not pretty enough to satisfy Cullinan. As the Sixth Circuit concluded in Smith, an adverse employment decision based on "gender nonconforming behavior and appearance" is impermissible under Price Waterhouse. Likewise, in Chadwick, the First Circuit found a decisionmaker's explanation why the plaintiff had not received a promotion evidence that the decision was motivated by an illegal sex stereotype that women would prioritize child care responsibilities over paid employment (with four young children she had "'too much on her plate'"). The Second Circuit similarly concluded in Back that the statement that a mother who received tenure "'would not show the same level of commitment [she] had shown because [she] had little ones at home'" showed discriminatory intent in the tenure decision. The Seventh Circuit found remarks characterizing conduct of a woman employee as "'you're being a blond[e] again today'" probative of sex discrimination.... * * *

The district court recognized that sex stereotyping comments may be evidence of discrimination. The focus of its decision was the mistaken view that a Title VII plaintiff must produce evidence that she was treated differently than similarly situated males. Our court has explicitly rejected that premise. * * * Courts "consistently emphasize[] that the ultimate issue is the reasons for *the individual plaintiff's* treatment, not the relative treatment of different *groups* within the workplace." * * * Comparative evidence is certainly not the "exclusive means by which a plaintiff may establish an inference of discrimination." * * * The Supreme Court has stated that "[t]he critical issue" in a sex discrimination case is "whether members of one sex are exposed to disadvantageous terms or conditions of employment to which members of the other sex are not exposed." * * * "[A]n employer who discriminates against women because, for instance, they do not wear dresses or makeup, is engaging in sex discrimination *because the discrimination would not occur but for the victim's sex.*" * * * Lewis need only offer evidence that *she* was discriminated against because of her sex. The question is whether Cullinan's requirements that Lewis be "pretty" and have the "Midwestern girl look" were because she is a woman. A reasonable factfinder could find that they were since the terms by their nature apply only to women.

We recognize that "[r]emarks at work that are based on sex stereotypes do not inevitably prove that gender played a part in a particular employment decision. The plaintiff must show that the employer actually relied on her gender in making its decision." Lewis met this burden at the summary judgment stage. * * * Cullinan was a primary decisionmaker with authority to hire and fire employees. While several individuals also took part in the decision to terminate Lewis, they relied on Cullinan's description of her January 23, 2007 conversation with Lewis.

Cullinan consistently indicated that female front desk workers must be "pretty," and she criticized Lewis' lack of the "Midwestern girl look" in the same conversation in which she ordered Stifel to move Lewis back to the night audit. Cullinan authorized Stifel to hire Lewis over the phone, but demanded a "confirm/endorse" interview once she saw Lewis' "tomboyish" appearance. * * *

Evidence that Heartland's reason for the termination were pretextual include the fact that Lewis had a history of good performance at Heartland. She had no prior disciplinary record and had received two merit based pay raises. The two individuals who supervised her during the majority of her employment at Heartland both stated that they had no problem with her appearance, and at least one customer had never seen customer service like that Lewis had provided. * * * [A] reasonable factfinder could disbelieve Heartland's proffered reason for terminating Lewis. Heartland asserts that it fired Lewis because of the January 23 meeting when Cullinan informed her that she would need to submit to a second interview. Lewis and Cullinan, the only two individuals in the room, portray the encounter in starkly different terms. On summary judgment we must construe the conversation in the light most favorable to Lewis, however. Lewis denies that she expressed hostility to Heartland's policies or spoke in a disrespectful way or took an argumentative stance or refused to participate in a second interview. It is also relevant that the meeting occurred after Cullinan had given Stifel the understanding that "[Lewis'] appearance ... was not what [she] wanted on the front desk" and after Stifel had shared that discussion with Lewis.

Shortly after Cullinan's conversation with Stifel about Lewis' appearance, Heartland procured video equipment so that Cullinan or Nosbisch could inspect a front desk applicant's look before any hiring. Heartland's termination letter to Lewis only relied on the January 23 meeting she had with Cullinan. Only later did Heartland allege poor job performance would justify her termination. Lewis asserts further that Heartland did not follow its own written termination procedure, which includes assessing the employee's previous disciplinary record (Lewis had none) and conducting an investigation before making the termination decision. Kristi Nosbisch, Heartland's equal employment officer responsible for directing investigations of employment discrimination, knew that Lewis had complained that Cullinan's requirements were illegal, but she nonetheless relied on Cullinan's account of their meeting without asking Lewis for her own.

* * * We turn next to Lewis' retaliation claim. * * * Lewis went into the January 23 meeting with Cullinan after learning about the "Midwestern girl look" comment. Lewis had already held her job for nearly a month and understood that other transferred employees in her situation had not been required to submit to a second interview. She observed Cullinan grow defensive after she asked her about the "Midwestern girl look" comment. Heartland argues that its official policy dictated a second interview, but Lewis has raised a genuine fact issue about whether Heartland imposed second interviews in similar circumstances before January 2007 and whether Heartland began doing so in relation to Cullinan's interaction with Lewis. Heartland suggests that Lewis' comments during the January 23 meeting did not actually oppose any unlawful practice. Cullinan testified, however, that Lewis had "emphatically stated that she thought it was illegal for us to ask her to interview, and illegal for us to schedule her to another shift" and that Lewis said she thought the interview demand was because of her appearance. These statements cannot reasonably be characterized as anything other than opposition to illegal action.

No one questions that Lewis was subjected to an adverse employment action, and there is ample record evidence to support a causal nexus between that and Lewis' protests at the January 23 meeting. Lewis received the termination notice a mere three days after the disputed conversation, and Heartland cited her objection to the second interview in her termination notice. The evidence of pretext already discussed applies with equal force in evaluating whether Lewis has made out a prima facie retaliation claim.

CASE QUESTIONS

1. What were the legal issues in this case? What did the court decide?
2. What was the evidence of sex-stereotyping in this case?
3. Is this also a sex-plus case? Why or why not?
4. In a dissenting opinion, one of the judges who heard this case wrote that "[a]pparently, the majority would hold that an employer violates Title VII if it declines to hire a female cheerleader because she is not pretty enough, or a male fashion model because he is not handsome enough...." Do you agree? Was this case correctly decided? Why or why not?
5. What, if any, appearance policy would you recommend for a hotel?

The influence of appearance on employment decisions is perhaps inevitable. For some jobs, appearance is job-related. Certainly, employers can establish appearance and grooming requirements that are the same for all employees; however, appearance is very closely intertwined with protected class. How will older people fare in workplace beauty contests? Pregnant women? People whose religious beliefs dictate a particular mode of appearance or dress? *When grooming or appearance standards are needed, employers should ensure that requirements for men and women are not widely different, more burdensome on one sex, based on stereotypes, or likely to result in harassment. Appearance policies must also be flexible enough to allow for exceptions to accommodate religious practices of employees* (see Chapter 10).

Discrimination Against Caregivers   Although many sex-stereotyping cases have involved issues of appearance, the concept is broader in its reach. The EEOC has highlighted the issue of discrimination against caregivers.[33] "Caregiver" is not a protected class characteristic, but there are many ways in which existing discrimination laws can be used to challenge employer practices that disadvantage caregivers. Besides childcare, caregiving also includes the likes of caring for an ill or disabled parent or

---

[33]U.S. Equal Employment Opportunity Commission. "Enforcement Guidance: Unlawful Disparate Treatment of Workers with Caregiving Responsibilities." No. 915.002 (May 23, 2007).

spouse. Stereotypes about caregivers can detrimentally affect both male and female employees. Female caregivers may be perceived as less committed to and competent at their jobs, regardless of the actual impact of caregiving responsibilities on their work. Males, on the other hand, may be regarded as ineffectual caregivers and denied leaves or other benefits routinely granted to women. Employers that premise employment decisions on stereotypes of how sex and caregiving responsibilities interact are engaging in disparate treatment.[34] It is not necessary in such cases to show that similarly situated persons of the opposite sex were treated more favorably. However, the law does not go so far as to require employers to be supportive of employees with weighty caregiving responsibilities and it does not alleviate the basic problem that *it is* often difficult for caregivers to give their full attention to both their jobs and the needs of others in their care.

Subjective Criteria

Employment decisions, especially when choosing from among a group of qualified candidates, often rest on subjective judgments. Appearance is often one of these subjective, "in the eye of the beholder" criteria, but there are many others. Does this person seem motivated? Will he be a good "team player"? Is there the right "chemistry" with this person? Does she have a good personality? Is this person a "good fit" with the work group or organization? And at the most elemental level, do we like this person? Impressions about these and other matters are gleaned from interviews, snatches of conversation over lunch, and who knows what else. No bright line exists between "objective" and "subjective" selection criteria—most assessments of job candidates involve elements of both. However, with more **subjective criteria**, the standards and means of assessing candidates are not uniform and clearly specified. Judgments about candidates are likely to vary among decision makers, who might be hard-pressed to explain the basis for those judgments. Subjective criteria rely heavily on intuition and "gut" feelings, rather than systematic observation and measurement.

Subjective hiring criteria are ubiquitous. Do they present any legal issues? One way to view them is as neutral requirements that might have discriminatory effects. In a case involving a woman who was passed over for promotion four times on the basis of interviews conducted by lower-level managers given little guidance on hiring criteria, the Supreme Court held that subjective assessments of this sort—no less than scored tests—can be challenged for their adverse impact.[35] However, the Court also held that proof of a subjective assessment being job-related and consistent with business necessity does not require a formal validation study. Instead, the focus is on how reasonable the subjective criteria are in light of the job and whether more objective means of assessment were available but not used. An adverse impact claim based on interviews conducted by an airline was allowed to go to trial. The plaintiff showed that the pass rate for female candidates interviewed for pilot positions (27.9%) was only about 60 percent of the pass rate for male candidates (46.6%). This difference in pass rates linked to a specific employment practice was sufficient to establish a prima facie case of adverse impact.[36]

Subjective hiring criteria also raise concerns about disparate treatment. An employer that desires to exclude African Americans might claim that an African American job

[34]*Back v. Hasting on Hudson Union Free School District*, 365 F.3d 107 (2d Cir. 2004); *Chadwick v. Wellpoint*, 561 F.3d 38 (1st Cir. 2009).

[35]*Watson v. Fort Worth Bank & Trust*, 487 U.S. 977 (1988).

[36]*Bullington v. United Air Lines*, 186 F.3d 1301 (10th Cir. 1999), *overruled on other grounds, AMTRAK v. Morgan*, 536 U.S. 101 (2002).

THE CHANGING WORKPLACE

Subjective Criteria and "Fit" as Considerations in Hiring

In a service economy, employers increasingly emphasize the **soft skills** of candidates, even for entry-level jobs. Employers assess the motivational, interpersonal, and communication skills of applicants. The means of assessing these skills are usually subjective—primarily impressions gleaned from interviews. Some argue that the increased emphasis on soft skills is a factor in the labor market difficulties of minorities, whom employers view as lacking in these areas. And, in fact, a study of the labor market experiences of inner-city blacks and Latinos found, as have other studies, that informal, subjective hiring criteria result in fewer blacks and Latinos being hired.[1] In a different setting—the selection of musicians by orchestras—a study found that the chances of women being selected to play in orchestras increased when the manner of conducting auditions was changed so that judges could no longer see the musician (and thus his or her sex) during auditions.[2] Apparently, subjective judgments about the quality of musicianship displayed in auditions are substantially affected by knowledge of the auditioning musician's sex. Increased use of subjective criteria clearly has implications for equal employment opportunity.

Employers want employees who are a good **"fit."** Traditionally, this has meant fit with the job, meaning that the candidate has the knowledge, skills, abilities, and other characteristics (e.g., motivation) to perform a particular job well. By requiring employers in adverse impact cases to defend their hiring criteria as "job related and consistent with business necessity," the law incorporates the traditional emphasis on fit with a particular job. However, the concept of "fit" has expanded to include the likes of person-organization fit (degree of congruence between the values of the candidate and the norms and values of the organization), person-vocation fit (match between the candidate's personality and interests and the requirements of a particular career), and person-team fit (extent to which the candidate's personality or skills match or complement those of other work group members).[3]

Assessing the latter types of "fit" is certainly trickier and more subjective than measuring job skills. Methods for assessing whether prospective employees share the values or culture of an organization exist, but they are less developed and less studied for validity than tests of job skills or aptitude. Consider the following description of a "test" given to candidates for employment at Southwest Airlines to ascertain their fit with the airline's distinctive culture.

> Southwest uses a novel approach to measure selflessness, a key value of their culture. Interviewers ask a group of applicants to prepare a five-minute presentation about themselves. During the presentations, Southwest's interviewers watch the audience as well as the speakers. What are they looking for in the audience? They want to determine which applicants are using the time to prepare for their own presentations and which are enthusiastically cheering and providing support for the presenters. Interviewers consider the cheering, supportive applicants a better fit with Southwest's culture than the fastidious applicants who continue to prepare up until their presentations.[4]

The validity of such tests (and whether validity can be established with reference to an organization's culture rather than specific jobs) is unclear. A more basic concern is that the desire to hire people who "fit" comfortably with an organization's culture might be at odds with the value of diversity, in which the aim is to find people who contribute new and different dimensions to an organization. Hiring for cultural fit and hiring for diversity are not necessarily mutually exclusive,[5] but the potential negative implications of maintaining strong cultures for opening up employment opportunity seem quite real.

---

[1]Philip Moss and Chris Tilly. *Stories Employers Tell: Race, Skill, and Hiring in America.* (New York: Russell Sage Foundation, 2001).

[2]Claudia Goldin and Cecilia Rouse. "Orchestrating Impartiality: The Impact of 'Blind' Auditions on Female Musicians." *American Economic Review* 90 (September 2000), 715–41.

[3]Anthony R. Wheeler et al., "'The Elusive Criterion of Fit' Revisited: Toward an Integrative Theory of Multidimensional Fit." Pp. 265–304 in Joseph J. Martocchio, ed., *Research in Personnel and Human Resources Management,* Vol. 24. (Oxford, UK: Elsevier, 2005).

[4]Mark L. Lengnick-Hall. "Recruitment and Selections: Hiring for the Job or the Organization?" Chapter 13 in Ellen Ernst Kossek and Richard N. Block, eds., *Managing Human Resources in the 21st Century: From Core Concepts to Strategic Choice* (Cincinnati, OH: South-Western College Publishing, 2000), pp. 13–16.

[5]Gary N. Powell. "The Simultaneous Pursuit of Person-Organization Fit and Diversity." *Organizational Dynamics* (Winter 1998), 50–61.

candidate "just wasn't a good fit with the organization" or "didn't have a good attitude" to justify rejection. Or an employer might, without being fully aware of it, react negatively to a candidate because of her protected class characteristics. The candidate might then be judged as less likable or motivated. Clearly, subjective assessments are conducive to disparate treatment and cannot be accepted at face value by the courts. At the same time, they are inevitable and to some degree necessary. It is not the role of courts to second-guess all employment decisions, but if protection against disparate treatment is to have any real meaning, it is necessary for courts to delve into whether an employer's impressions were the true reasons behind its decision or whether they were more likely pretext. The "beauty" of a candidate is in the eye of the prospective employer; the role of the courts is to "evaluate truthfulness, not beauty."[37]

In distinguishing between legitimate subjective judgments and those affected by discriminatory bias, courts do not rely on an employer's subjective judgment that a candidate is unqualified for a position to find that a plaintiff lacks a prima facie case of disparate treatment. While it is necessary that the plaintiff show that he or she is qualified for the position sought, it is only the minimum stated, objective qualifications (e.g., diploma, years of experience, license) that are relevant. The employer can still advance its subjective judgment that the candidate was unqualified as its lawful motive for denying a job to the plaintiff, but then the plaintiff has the opportunity to show it is not believable that the employer truly regarded the candidate as unqualified. Thus, in an age discrimination case, an employer's claim that the plaintiff was judged not to have "substantial sales experience" (the employer did not establish a specific experience requirement and judge candidates against that) did not render him unqualified for purposes of establishing a prima facie case. The employer's claim that he was not promoted due to lack of experience was then shown to be pretext because the candidate had more sales and industry experience than each of the three much younger workers promoted over him, the employer offered inconsistent explanations for its decision, and a comment about "get[ting] rid of all of the old people" was made by a person involved in the decision.[38] Likewise, an air carrier that demoted a female pilot due to her allegedly poor communication and interpersonal skills was not successful in arguing that she lacked a prima facie case.[39] Even though these "crew resource management" (CRM) skills are essential for pilots, their assessment required "a subjective evaluation of the pilot's attitude, manner, tone, and other similar traits."[40] Given the opportunity to show pretext, the female pilot was able to establish that different individuals rated her CRM skills very differently and that male pilots judged to be lacking in important job skills were routinely given remedial training, while the female pilot received no such training.

Subjective criteria stand up less well than more objective criteria to claims of pretext. To both lessen the chance of discrimination occurring and to better defend against any charges that nonetheless arise, *employers are well-advised to use objective criteria whenever it is feasible to do so.* But this does not mean that subjective criteria can or should be completely avoided. In a case where two clearly qualified candidates were contesting for a position and the decision ultimately rested on the judgment of the decision makers as to who would make the best agency director, the ability to cite specific aspects of the successful candidate's experiences (e.g., his long military service) that led to the hiring decision resulted in a finding for the defendant county.[41] Likewise, an association was

---

[37]*Medina v. Ramsey Steel Co.*, 238 F.3d 674, 681–82 (5th Cir. 2001).

[38]*Medina*, at 682.

[39]*Nicholson v. Hyannis Air Service*, 2009 U.S. App. LEXIS 20020 (9th Cir.).

[40]*Nicholson*, at 13.

[41]*Champ v. Calhoun County Emergency Management Agency*, 226 Fed. Appx. 908 (11th Cir. 2007).

able to successfully defend its reliance on the organization president's subjective judgment that incompatibility in working styles necessitated the termination of his assistant.[42] The assistant came to be viewed by the president as "rigid and unable to address problems before they affected him," rather than as the "strategic" and "proactive" individual desired. The court acknowledged the subjectivity of perceived incompatibility in working styles, but since "a dysfunctional working relationship is a legitimate ground for dismissal of an assistant" and the plaintiff was not able to show that the president's perception was not genuine, her discrimination claim failed.[43]

Interviews

Interviews are an almost universal aspect of hiring and promotion processes. While the degree of subjectivity involved in assessing candidates via interviews varies, it tends to be high. Contrary to the urging of staffing experts, many employers persist in conducting largely unstructured interviews in which the questions asked—and even more so, the criteria used to assess interview performance—are left to interviewer whim.[44] A systematic, structured interview process has both legal and practical benefits for employers. In a case in which the employer cited poor interview performance as its reason for rejecting a candidate, the court ruled for the employer and observed that

> [w]hile there is certainly a level of subjectivity in any interview-based selection process, [the plaintiff] provides no evidence that the interviewers used their discretion as a means for unlawful discrimination. The panelists asked every applicant the same three questions and then ranked the candidates based on their responses. [The plaintiff] never discredits the City's explanation that she was not ranked highly … because she did not answer the questions completely.[45]

The ability to cite specific grounds for judgments about interview performance is critical. A candidate turned down for promotion to a management position, partly on the basis of his "poor" interview that demonstrated lack of "aggressiveness," did not prevail in his age discrimination suit.[46] The court noted the importance of subjective assessments in selecting managers and professionals and held that "[a] subjective reason is a legally sufficient, legitimate nondiscriminatory reason if the defendant articulates a clear and reasonably specific factual basis upon which it based its subjective opinion."[47] In a sex discrimination case challenging an interview panel's recommendations, a court pointed to the mixed-sex composition of the panel, the fact that all candidates were asked the same questions, and the scoring of applicant's responses as relevant factors in ruling for the employer.[48]

The scoring of interviews does not, by itself, render them objective and nondiscriminatory. In *Dunlap v. Tennessee Valley Authority*, an employer's purported reliance on interview scores was not sufficient to defend against a discrimination claim.

---

[42]*Vatel v. Alliance of Automobile Manufacturers*, 627 F.3d 1245 (D.C. Cir. 2011).

[43]*Vatel*, at 1248.

[44]Herbert G. Heneman III and Timothy A. Judge. *Staffing Organizations*, 6th ed. (Burr Ridge, IL: McGraw-Hill/Irwin, 2009), 451.

[45]*Santana v. City and County of Denver*, 488 F.3d 860, 866 (10th Cir. 2007).

[46]*Chapman v. AI Transport*, 229 F.3d 1012 (11th Cir. 2000).

[47]*Chapman*, at 1034.

[48]*Maxwell v. Springer*, 2008 U.S. App. LEXIS 8177 (3d Cir.).

Dunlap v. Tennessee Valley Authority
519 F.3d 626 (6th Cir. 2008)

OPINION BY CIRCUIT JUDGE MARTIN:

David Dunlap brought suit under Title VII of the Civil Rights Act of 1964, alleging racial discrimination by the Tennessee Valley Authority. The district court found that Dunlap had been subjected to discrimination under both disparate treatment and disparate impact analyses, concluding that the TVA's subjective hiring processes permitted racial bias against both Dunlap and other black job applicants. * * * We find that although the district court was correct in finding disparate treatment, the proof was insufficient for a finding of disparate impact. * * *

David Dunlap is a fifty-two year-old black man who has worked as a boilermaker for twenty years, including nearly fifteen years' experience as a boilermaker foreman responsible for a crew of boilermakers. Most of Dunlap's experience has been with TVA facilities located across Tennessee through contract or temporary work with his union. Dunlap asserts that he has tried to gain employment with the TVA since the 1970s, but had never been offered a job, or even an interview. For the boilermaker position at issue, Dunlap submitted his resume and application before the application deadline. His materials specified his work with TVA facilities, his boilermaker training (through the TVA's own training program), his supervisory experience, and his 27,000 hours of experience in the field.

Of the twenty-one people interviewed for the ten positions available, all were referred by the local boilermaker union as being qualified for the job, including Dunlap. The selection committee at the Cumberland facility, where the job openings were located, was comprised of five white officials and one black official. Participants were asked a combination of technical questions, developed by committee members with boilermaker experience, and non-technical questions, developed by other management and human resources employees. Sometime before the interviews began, the selection committee determined that the interview would account for seventy percent of an applicant's final score and technical expertise would account for thirty percent. After each interview, the committee reviewed the individual score sheets as a group in an effort to even out the scores. This "score-balancing"

caused the final scores to vary widely from the initial scores, even on basic, objective questions such as an applicant's safety record or attendance history. For example, when Dunlap reported that his attendance record was excellent with only a few days off for family illness, he received a score of 3.7. In contrast, when two white applicants gave essentially the same answer, they received a 4.2 and a 5.5. For Dunlap's perfect safety record, he received a 4, while another applicant who had had two accidents in eleven years received a score of 6. Dunlap alleges that although these are the most egregious examples of bias, the entire interview was similarly infected.

After the interviews, the twenty-one applicants were ranked in order of most to least qualified. The selection committee then divided the applicants into three groups: outstanding, well-qualified, and qualified. The ten applicants in the "outstanding" category were all chosen for jobs. Dunlap's scores placed him in fourteenth place. Of the ten people chosen, one was William Parchman, an African-American veteran with thirty years of experience as a boilermaker. Parchman provided testimony that he too had a history of being rejected for jobs at the TVA, and received the boilermaker position at issue after filing a complaint with the Equal Employment Opportunity Commission (EEOC).

Dunlap alleges that the combined weight of his more than twenty years of technical and supervisory experience made him a more qualified applicant than some of the other applicants who were hired, some of whom had only minimal supervisory experience or poorer safety records. Dunlap's score on the technical part of the application equaled that of five of the selected candidates, yet he scored much lower on the interview and was thus not selected. He alleges that the interview process was biased from the beginning to select less qualified candidates, some with family affiliations to the committee members, by hiding racial preferences. * * *

1) DISPARATE IMPACT

The disparate impact theory requires a plaintiff to demonstrate that a facially neutral employment practice falls more harshly on one group than another and that the practice is not justified by business necessity. Under this theory, proof of discriminatory intent is not required. * * *

A prima facie case is established when: (1) the plaintiff identifies a specific employment practice to be challenged; and (2) through relevant statistical analysis proves that the challenged practice has an adverse impact on a protected group. * * * Dunlap did not present evidence that the practices used in his interview were ever used for other hiring decisions, so no statistical proof can show that a protected group was adversely impacted. We therefore conclude that Dunlap challenged only the process used in his own interview, and the district court clearly erred in finding a prima facie case of disparate impact.

2) DISPARATE TREATMENT

The disparate treatment doctrine … requires a plaintiff to demonstrate that an employer has treated some people less favorably than others because of their race, color, religion, sex or national origin. * * * (1) [T]he plaintiff must establish a prima facie case of racial discrimination; (2) the employer must articulate some legitimate, nondiscriminatory reason for its actions; and (3) the plaintiff must prove that the stated reason was in fact pretextual. Under a disparate treatment theory, "proof of discriminatory motive is critical. However, in some cases it may be inferred from the mere fact of differences in treatment." Proof of discriminatory motive may also be inferred from the falsity of the employer's explanation for the treatment. * * *

To rebut a prima facie case, a defendant must articulate a legitimate nondiscriminatory reason for the plaintiff's rejection. In this case, TVA presented the selection matrix used during Dunlap's interview, and showed that his interview scores did not place his final scores into the top ten. The burden then shifted back to Dunlap to prove that the matrix process was pretext for discrimination. * * * The district court found that Dunlap successfully showed pretext by demonstrating that his matrix score was manipulated to keep him out of the top ten applicants. Evidence before the district court showed that the assigned weight given to the interview was changed by the questioners to favor a more subjective process, interview questions were not objectively evaluated, and scores were altered to produce a racially biased result. * * *

First, the selection committee determined that the interview would account for seventy percent of an applicant's final score, and technical expertise would account for thirty percent, therefore transferring the bulk of the final score from an objective measurement (merit and experience) towards a subjective measurement (communication skills). The TVA's "Principles and Practices" on filling vacant positions, however, mandate that "merit and efficiency form the basis for selection of job candidates," stating that "education, training, experience, ability and previous work performance serve as a basis for appraisal of merit and efficiency."

During the interview, the scores varied widely even on seemingly objective questions. Dunlap reported that his attendance record was excellent with only a few days off for family illness and received a score of 3.7. In contrast, when two white applicants gave essentially the same answer, they received a 4.2 and a 5.5. For Dunlap's perfect safety record, he received a 4, while another applicant who had had two accidents in eleven years received a score of 6. Points were also awarded for politeness in answering the first interview question, with an extra half-point awarded for answering "yes, ma'am."

After the interview, the "score balancing" process seems to have been manipulated, again in contravention of TVA policy. The district court found that some of the score sheets were changed as many as seventy times, and there is no evidence of legitimate reasons to support such revisions. An email from the human resources director of the Cumberland plant explicitly states that interviewers should not award points for being a "diversity candidate," so there is no argument that TVA manipulated scores to ensure diversity. (If anything, evidence that a manager may have "talked [with the team] about who was a diversity candidate" supports an argument that TVA manipulated scores to select one, and only one, diversity candidate.) Furthermore, the email emphasizes, "it is really important up front before your interviews start[] to have a definition of what 'Outstanding,' 'Well-Qualified,' and 'Qualified' is. This needs to be documented and dated before the interview process starts." The district court found, however, that the interviewers placed candidates into these categories after the interviews were finished and after the candidates had been ranked, ensuring that the number of "outstanding" applicants equaled exactly the number of job openings. Because of these irregularities, the hiring matrix score offered by TVA as a legitimate reason for Dunlap's rejection cannot be relied upon.

Finally, the district court evaluated the credibility of TVA's witnesses, a determination to which we afford vast deference. Most notably, the court evaluated the credibility of Rosanne Sietins, TVA's Human Resources representative on the selection committee, and Leonard Hancock, the Cumberland plant manager who had final authority on hiring at the plant and oversaw Dunlap's interview process. The court concluded that discrimination motivated the committee's decision-making, and we do not find clear error in that determination.

Once a proffered reason is found to be pretextual, a court may infer the ultimate fact of intentional discrimination. Here, there was ample evidence supporting the district court's finding of pretext, including the contravention of TVA rules on conducting interviews and measuring candidate merit, and the ultimate manipulation of the matrix scores. Considering all of the evidence, the district court found that TVA used the selection process "to mask [TVA's] preferential hiring process" and "to select one black applicant that would satisfy the TVA central management." Therefore the district court's finding of intentional discrimination was not clearly erroneous. * * *

[W]e AFFIRM on the disparate treatment claim, REVERSE on the disparate impact claim, and AFFIRM the court's award of damages and fees.

CASE QUESTIONS

1. What were the legal issues in this case? What did the appeals court decide?
2. Why did the plaintiff's disparate (adverse) impact claim fail?
3. Why did the plaintiff's disparate treatment claim succeed? What was the evidence that the employer's reliance on interview scores was a pretext for race discrimination?
4. Do you agree with the decision? Why or why not?
5. What should the TVA have done differently with regard to interviewing and selecting candidates for these jobs?

The ease with which bias can taint the interview process makes it advisable for employers to *use multiple interviewers, preferably differing in race and sex. Employers should give substantial weight to impressions drawn from interviews only if they are specific and clearly grounded in statements or actions of job candidates. Interviews should be made as standard as possible by using structured interviews and scoring them according to preestablished criteria.* If impressions are going to be formed in this manner, then everyone should at least be given the same "test." Verbatim written notes from interviews are not required, but the absence of any documentation produced at the time of an interview makes it exceedingly difficult to provide specifics in a deposition a year or two later. *Maintain written documentation of interviews, particularly observations relied on in making decisions about candidates.*

Offering and Accepting Employment

Employment can be offered in writing or verbally. To clearly state what is being offered and accepted, *employers (with legal help) should put employment offers in writing.* The offer letter should include the salary or wage associated with the position and the start date. Because it is usually in the interest of employers for employment to be "at will" (i.e., the relationship can be terminated at any time for any lawful reason), *the offer of employment should specify whether employment at will is being offered (and explain in simple language what that means).* The employment offer might reference an employee handbook or other materials as authoritative sources about the terms of the employment relationship. In any event, *the offer should clearly specify what is included in the terms of employment and that no further commitments have been made. If an offer of employment is conditional (e.g., upon a medical exam or upon acceptance of the offer within a specified period), the condition(s) should be clearly stated.*

What if an employer offers a job, the candidate accepts, and then the employer withdraws the offer prior to the start of employment? Might people whose accepted offers of employment are revoked have grounds for legal challenges? One possible claim is fraud (or negligent misrepresentation). However, unless the employer withdrawing an offer knew or should have known at the time the offer was made that the job would not materialize, a successful fraud claim is unlikely. What about breach of contract? Most new hires are employed at will. Courts treat employment-at-will relationships as contractual, but a contract to employ at will amounts to nothing more than a promise to pay a specified wage for work actually performed. Because either party remains free to terminate the employment relationship at any time, there is no breach of contract if a person is hired but not given the chance to commence employment. As one court put it, "It would be absurd to require an employer, which had changed its mind after an offer had been made, to actually employ the applicant for one hour or one day so that the employee could then be discharged."[49] However, a stronger legal claim is available in this situation. Courts recognize claims for **promissory estoppel** in situations where injustice would otherwise occur because a person has reasonably relied to his detriment on the promises of another. The basis for the claim is not a contract but rather the harm that occurs from reasonably relying on another's promises that there would be a contractual relationship.

Practical Considerations What can an employer do to avoid the situation of making and then withdrawing an offer of employment?

ELEMENTS OF A CLAIM

Promissory Estoppel

1. One party makes an unambiguous promise to another.
2. The party that receives the promise acts in reasonable reliance upon it.
3. Reliance on the promise is expected and foreseeable by the party making the promise.
4. The party to whom the promise is made is harmed by reliance on it.

© Cengage Learning 2013.

Applied to the withdrawal of a job offer, it could be argued that the employer's job offer is an unambiguous promise to employ, the new hire reasonably relies on the promise by doing such things as relocating and turning down alternative job offers, the employer should reasonably expect that newly hired people would act in this manner, and these reasonable actions cause harm (e.g., loss of the other job, a now burdensome lease on an apartment). Some courts have accepted this view. For example, the Supreme Court of Nebraska found that a doctor whose job offer was rescinded after she had quit her previous job, was provided with uniforms for her new job, and was already given the schedule for her first week of work had a valid claim for promissory estoppel.[50] A Minnesota state court recognized a promissory estoppel claim in the case of a newly hired person who, on the first day of employment, "went through a hostile re-interview process that led to his immediate termination."[51] On the other hand, many courts have refused to protect employees under these circumstances. The rationale is that an offer of employment at will is not really an unambiguous promise

---

[49] *Sartin v. Mazur,* 375 S.E.2d 741, at 743 (Va. 1989).

[50] *Goff-Hamel v. Obstetricians & Gynecologists,* P.C., 588 N.W.2d 798 (Neb. 1999).

[51] *Gorham v. Benson Optical,* 539 N.W.2d 798, at 801 (Minn. App. 1995).

because employment can be terminated at any time. Alternatively, courts have maintained that it is not reasonable to rely on the essentially empty promise of employment at will. One court, in rejecting a promissory estoppel claim, conceded "the apparent harshness of [its] ruling, the result of which is that an employee who resigns one job for another does so at his peril," but maintained that any other outcome would contradict employment at will.[52]

Obstacles to Advancement on the Job

The problem of discrimination does not end with getting in the door. Women and people of color sometimes experience **segregation** into less desirable jobs and face numerous obstacles to advancement in their careers.

Clippings

Donna Kassman, a former senior manager at the accounting firm KPMG, has filed a sex discrimination suit alleging widespread discriminatory practices impeding the advancement of women in the firm. Ms. Kassman claims that she was stuck in the same position from 1999 until she was forced to resign in 2010. After being told that she was next in line for a managing director position, the job was given to a male with inferior qualifications. She was removed from consideration due to complaints from male colleagues that she was "too direct" and "unapproachable." Ms. Kassman also alleges that the firm uses a highly subjective compensation system to underpay women, that female employees are subjected to harassment, and that women who have children are pressured to accept a "reduced schedule" under which they are paid less while still expected to do the same amount of work as full-time employees. KPMG says that it "is recognized as a leader for its strong commitment to supporting women in the workplace" and that it is tied for the highest percentage of female partners among the "big four" accounting firms. Ms. Kassman's legal team counters that KPMG is one of the industry's "worst offenders" for sex discrimination and cites its own figures. While 50 percent of nonmanagement employees at KPMG are women, only 18 percent of KPMG employees promoted to partner are female (compared to the industry average of 23 percent). Thirty-five percent of the employees promoted to senior management positions at KPMG are women, compared to the industry average of 44 percent.

Elliot T. Dube. "Suit Alleges Major Audit Firm Restricts Career Path Movement of Female Managers." *Daily Labor Report* 106 (June 2, 2011), A-9.

Promotions

Much of the information in this and preceding chapters applies equally to both initial hiring and promotion, but some additional facets of promotion cases deserve mention. First, there are lines of progression in work organizations such that promotions usually occur out of particular positions. Thus, if the effect of initial hiring decisions is to segregate some groups into dead-end jobs from which promotions are not typically made, that will also manifest itself in future promotional decisions. In a case involving Home

---

[52]*White v. Roche Biomedical Laboratories,* 807 F. Supp. 1212, at 1220 (D.S.C. 1992), *affirmed,* 998 F.2d 1011 (4th Cir. 1993).

Depot,[53] stereotypes about what jobs were suitable for women led to the channeling of women into clerk positions and away from merchandising department manager and store manager trainee jobs, which were springboards for becoming store managers. For example, a female applicant with prior experience hauling lumber and working as an office manager for a lumber processing plant was told that "girls don't work in the lumber department" and hired as a cashier instead.[54] A class of female plaintiffs successfully challenged both the store's initial hiring and its promotion decisions.

The process for making promotions is often far more informal and covert than that used for initial hiring decisions. Potential candidates for promotions might not learn about the existence of these employment opportunities until after the fact—when the "winner" is announced. The Home Depot case described the extremely informal promotion process then in place at the retailer:

> *There are no written guidelines for making decisions about promotions to department supervisor positions, and the company does not provide training to Store Managers and Assistant Managers on how to select employees for promotions.... Promotion opportunities in existing stores are not posted, and there is no formal procedure for making vacancies known or requesting a promotion. In making decisions about promotion to department supervisor, there is no requirement that the person under consideration meet any minimum rating on recent performance evaluations, or that written performance reviews are consulted at all in making the decision. Nor is there any requirement to record the reasons why an employee is or is not selected for a promotion.*[55]

Another distinctive aspect of promotions is that employers have a great deal to do with determining which individuals possess the qualifications needed for promotion. In contrast to initial hiring decisions, where job candidates have developed their qualifications in schools and at work for other employers, promotional candidates acquire many of their qualifications through their employer's training and development programs, job assignments, and mentoring. Because not all employees have equal access to these qualification-enhancing opportunities, promotions are, to some extent, "self-fulfilling prophecies." This is intensified by the flattening of corporate structures in recent years, leaving behind fewer promotional opportunities. Companies increasingly attempt to identify high-potential personnel, both managerial and technical, who need to be retained and developed. These judgments, sometimes spelled out in formal succession plans, are then reflected in who is prepared and selected for promotion. In a sex discrimination case involving a male employee who was denied a promotion to the position of Vice President for Compensation, the court accepted the company's argument that the position was seen as providing a less experienced female employee who was being groomed for Senior Vice President of Human Resources with experience that she would need. The court observed that since the employer "determined that it would be best served by using the compensation position to groom and develop one of its existing vice presidents," there was no violation of Title VII.[56]

Candidates for promotion are usually highly qualified. They are also frequently known to one another. Thus, questions about whether the employer has selected the most qualified candidate are especially likely to arise in promotion decisions. Once

---

[53]*Butler v. Home Depot*, 1997 U.S. Dist. LEXIS 16296 (N.D. Cal.).

[54]*Butler*, at 26 (footnote n14).

[55]*Butler v. Home Depot*, 1997 U.S. Dist. LEXIS 16296 (N.D. Cal.).

[56]*Dodge v. Lincoln National Life Insurance Co.*, 2006 U.S. Dist. LEXIS 44955 (N.D. Ind.).

again, the issue is whether an employer's claim that it promoted the candidate it regarded as most qualified is credible or is more likely pretext. In a case involving alleged racial discrimination in making promotions to shift manager positions at a poultry plant, the Supreme Court rejected as "unhelpful and imprecise" an appeals court's view that "Pretext can be established through comparing qualifications only when the disparity in qualifications is so apparent as virtually to jump off the page and slap you in the face."[57] While the Court unfortunately declined to specify exactly what the proper standard would be, in general, it can be said that the differences in qualifications have to be large enough that no reasonable employer could have regarded the selected candidate as more qualified. It is not enough for the plaintiff to merely question the employer's judgment or point to minor differences in qualifications.

Finally, subjective criteria tend to be relied on even more heavily in promotion decisions. In a suit against Costco, the plaintiff's attorneys argued as follows: "Without a system, 'what you have is default mode.'"" Default mode is subjective decision making by a virtually all male managerial apparatus' with gender stereotyping and unconscious bias."[58] "Social framework analysis," which provides the intellectual underpinnings for the attorneys' statement, was not treated kindly in the Supreme Court's Wal-Mart class

---

JUST THE FACTS

An African American woman worked for an employer for seventeen years, rising to the position of Operations Manager. She consistently received satisfactory evaluations and was told by her supervisor that she had the potential to progress in the company and do well in upper management. However, she was also placed on a developmental plan to improve some professional deficiencies, was criticized for weak communication skills, and had some attendance and punctuality issues. The woman applied for a promotion to senior operations manager but was not selected. The next year another senior operations manager position became available. Contrary to company policy, the position was not posted this time. Instead, it was simply announced that a white, female coworker had been promoted. The coworker was highly regarded by her peers, had very good performance evaluations, and had significant relevant experience. However, she did not have a four-year degree, even though the job requisition form stated that a four-year college degree was required for the position. The African American woman did have a four-year degree. The supervisor who made the hiring decision relied on a statement in the job description that substantial experience could substitute for the lack of a degree. Ultimately, the hiring decision was made by the supervisor based on her firsthand knowledge of the current operations managers. The supervisor testified that she "did not consider" the African American woman to be a candidate for the position. The African American employee sued, alleging race discrimination.

See, *Springer v. Convergys Customer Management*, 509 F.3d 1344 (11th Cir. 2007)

---

[57]*Ash v. Tyson Foods*, 546 U.S. 454, 457 (2006).

[58]Joyce E. Cutler. "Suit Charges Costco with Bias in Promoting Women as Managers." *Daily Labor Report* 159 (August 18, 2004), A-10.

action decision,[59] but the essential insight that an unguided, subjective decision-making process provides greater opportunity for discrimination seems beyond cavil.

What are some practical implications for promotional decisions, apart from those that pertain to all hiring? The "fix" for inequities in advancement starts with initial hiring decisions. *Employers must avoid segregating women and people of color into "dead-end" positions that offer little prospect of advancement.* Discrimination in promotions is less likely when a formal application process is used for promotional positions. *Employers should establish formal application procedures for promotions, communicate the availability of promotional opportunities, and facilitate applications from all interested employees. Developmental opportunities should be extended as widely as possible, and particular care should be taken in designating individuals as "high-potential" or "fast-track" employees.*

Glass Ceilings

Obstacles to advancement into high-level management and professional positions have received particular attention.[60] The U.S. Department of Labor defines **glass ceilings** as "those artificial barriers based on attitudinal or organizational bias that prevent qualified individuals from advancing in their organization into upper management positions."[61] *Glass ceiling* is not a legal term or claim, but it succinctly captures the experiences of many highly qualified women and people of color. Such circumstances have prompted lawsuits alleging a pattern or practice of discrimination and other claims.

The glass-ceiling phenomenon can be seen in the legal profession itself. Although people of color have been attending law school in significant numbers and account for about 23 percent of law school graduates, they make up about 13 percent of all associates at law firms and 6 percent of partners. About 48 percent of law school graduates are women, compared to about a third of associates at law firms and about 19 percent of partners.[62] Reasons cited for the difficulties encountered by women in achieving partner status include subjective performance evaluations, women being held to higher performance standards, assumptions about the inability of female attorneys with children to be sufficiently committed to their careers, and negative reactions to women who exhibit aggressiveness and ambition.[63]

Advancing to higher-level positions in elite institutions is a rugged, competitive process. Lack of advancement does not necessarily reflect the workings of unfair, discriminatory obstacles. To the extent that such obstacles exist, the measures needed to deal with them go beyond the general advice for promotions. *Employers should closely monitor the career progress of women and people of color.* Evidence of a disproportionate lack of advancement should prompt a wide-ranging self-analysis. *Employers should examine the protected class composition of positions from which promotions are made and the manner in which key projects and other developmental opportunities are assigned.* Because many promotions rest on previous positions and project assignments, it is important that women and people of color get into "the pipeline" and have access to important positions and developmental experiences. *Employers should provide management*

---

[59]*Wal-Mart Stores v. Dukes*, 2011 U.S. LEXIS 4567, 27–29.

[60]e.g., U.S. Equal Employment Opportunity Commission. *Glass Ceilings: The Status of Women as Officials and Managers* (March 2004).

[61]U.S. Department of Labor, Office of Federal Contract Compliance Programs. "Glass Ceiling Initiative: Are There Cracks in the Ceiling?" (Washington, DC: U.S. Government Printing Office, 1997).

[62]"Proportions of Women, Minorities Rise Slightly at Law Firms, Despite Downturn." *Daily Labor Report* 205 (October 27, 2009), A-6.

[63]Kevin P. McGowan. "Female Lawyers Face Persistent Barriers in Advancement at Law Firms, ABA Told." *Daily Labor Report* 61 (April 2, 2009), C-2.

development programs, assistance in career planning, and mentoring. Mentors provide less senior managers and professionals with the benefit of their experience, coaching on career choices, and visibility and advocacy in higher organizational circles. Other important steps involve *removing impediments to performance, including harassment and aspects of an organization's culture that might be hostile to protected class groups (e.g., heavy emphasis on off-the-job socializing). Turnover patterns should be carefully examined, as they might indicate frustration with lack of advancement or responses to harassment. Flexibility in considering less traditional career paths and backgrounds in promotional candidates opens up opportunities and increases the numbers of qualified women and people of color in the pipeline.* A more diverse pool of qualified external candidates for management positions might be obtained by considering people who have proven their leadership ability in nonprofit organizations, public administration, universities, and the military.

Key Terms

facially discriminatory, p. 201
bona fide occupational
    qualification (BFOQ), p. 201
authenticity, p. 203
public safety, p. 203

privacy, p. 204
sex-plus, p. 209
sex-stereotyping, p. 212
subjective criteria, p. 217
soft skills, p. 218

fit, p. 218
promissory estoppel, p. 224
segregation, p. 225
glass ceilings, p. 228

Chapter Summary

Employers sometimes contend that occupants of jobs must have certain protected class characteristics (most often, a specified sex or age group). Such requirements are facially discriminatory and can be defended only if employers can show that the protected class requirements are bona fide occupational qualifications (BFOQs). The BFOQ defense is narrow. A BFOQ cannot be established for racial requirements. For the BFOQ defense to be valid, an employer has to show that all, or virtually all, the people without the specified protected class characteristic cannot do the job or that protected class must be used as a proxy because a more individualized assessment of ability to do the job cannot be made. To establish a BFOQ, particular protected class characteristics must be shown as being necessary to perform the job, and the job, with its current requirements, must be integral to the nature of the business. The preferences of customers, coworkers, or clients rarely justify BFOQs. However, BFOQs may be recognized where certain protected class characteristics are needed for authenticity, public safety, or privacy.

Pairing protected class requirements with neutral requirements (e.g., no women with children under school age will be hired) is also facially discriminatory and can be defended only by a BFOQ. Because sex is the protected class most often involved in these cases,

placing requirements on one protected class group that are not placed on others is often referred to as "sex-plus" discrimination. When the neutral requirements differentially applied to men and women involve appearance and grooming rather than fundamental rights such as childbearing and marriage, the law is murkier. Courts have generally allowed employers to establish different grooming and appearance requirements for men and women, provided that the differences are not too great. However, appearance requirements that are much more burdensome on one sex than the other will not be allowed. Courts have also applied the theory of sex-stereotyping to appearance and other requirements. It is discrimination for an employer to base employment decisions on employees' failure to conform to demeaning sex-stereotypes or, alternatively, on the assumption that employees will conform to such stereotypes. Importantly, this includes employers disadvantaging women with young children on the assumption that their caregiving responsibilities will necessarily diminish their job performance.

Hiring and promotion decisions often involve making judgments about such matters as candidates' motivation, leadership ability, interpersonal skills, and likeability. Ratings of interview performance also tend to be quite subjective. Subjective criteria can be challenged under both adverse impact and disparate treatment theories. In pretext cases, a claim that a candidate is not qualified based on a subjective judgment will not defeat a prima facie case when the candidate meets other objective criteria. The key issue in these cases is not whether the employer's impressions about a candidate were correct, but rather whether it is believable that the employer viewed the candidate in this way and decided accordingly. To the extent that employers are increasingly concerned with the soft skills of employees and their ability to fit in with organizational cultures and work teams, subjective criteria loom even larger and stand to affect hiring decisions at all levels.

After deciding whom to hire, an employer offers employment and the selected candidate indicates whether the offer is accepted. Withdrawal of an accepted job offer is certainly detrimental to a job candidate, but there is not always a legal remedy available in such situations. Courts sometimes use the doctrine of promissory estoppel to provide relief to job candidates who have had job offers rescinded. Promissory estoppel claims are recognized where an unambiguous promise is made, a party reasonably relies on the promise to her detriment, and such reliance was foreseeable.

Promotions have some features that distinguish them from initial hirings and that have direct implications for equal employment opportunity. Promotions are affected by prior hiring decisions that determine who is positioned for promotion. To a considerable extent, employers predetermine the outcomes of promotion decisions by the manner in which they allocate developmental opportunities and draw up succession plans. Promotion processes tend to be more informal than initial hirings, with positions often not posted and applications not taken. Lastly, the problems presented by subjective criteria tend to be magnified in promotions, where all of the candidates are likely to be highly qualified and the choice often comes down to intangibles.

The term *glass ceiling* is used to convey the existence of obstacles that impede the advancement of women and people of color into high-level management and professional positions. Key barriers include insufficient access to developmental opportunities, exclusion from social networks, lack of advocates in higher management, biased criteria (e.g., availability for socializing after work hours), and exclusionary corporate cultures.

Practical Advice Summary

- Employers must not specify protected class requirements for jobs unless BFOQs can be established for those requirements based on the need for
  — Authenticity.
  — Public safety.
  — Privacy.
- Employers must not specify racial requirements for jobs.
- Rather than use protected class characteristics to identify people with desired abilities, employers should find more individualized means of assessing job-related abilities.
- Employers must not exclude older employees from safety-sensitive jobs based on assumptions about health status unless
  — There is evidence that older employees pose greater risk.
  — It is not feasible to adequately assess the health of individuals.
- Employers should generally refrain from matching employees with customers or clients based on protected class characteristics and, instead, consider alternative indicators of ability to relate to customers, including
  — Interpersonal skills.
  — Cultural sensitivity.
  — Language skills.
  — Prior experience.
- Depending on state law, BFOQs might have to be certified by state fair employment agencies before they can be put into use.
- Employers must not establish requirements that apply to one protected class group but not others.
- Grooming or appearance requirements should not be
  — Widely different for men and women.
  — More burdensome for people of one sex.
  — Based on stereotypes.
  — Likely to result in harassment.
- Interviews and other subjective aspects of the hiring process should be made as standard as possible, such as using structured interviews and scoring them according to preestablished criteria.

- Multiple interviewers should generally be used, preferably including people who differ in race and sex.
- Written documentation of interviews should be maintained, particularly those observations relied on in making decisions about candidates.
- Employers should give substantial weight to impressions from interviews and other subjective assessments only if they are specific and clearly grounded in statements or actions of job candidates.
- Whenever possible, employers should use objective means instead of subjective measures to assess job candidates.
- Employment offers should
  — Be put in writing with the help of legal counsel.
  — State clearly and unequivocally that employment is "at will" if that is the type of employment relationship desired.
  — Clearly specify the terms of employment and the fact that no other commitments have been made.
  — State any conditions attached to the offer (e.g., successful completion of a medical exam).
- Employers should not renege on promises to hire employees when it is reasonable for employees to rely on those promises and they would be harmed by doing so.
- Employers should establish a formal procedure to apply for promotions, communicate the availability of promotional opportunities, and facilitate applications from all interested employees.
- Employers must avoid segregating women and people of color into "dead-end" positions that offer little prospect of advancement.
- Employers should closely monitor the career progress of women and people of color.
- When there is evidence of blocked advancement for some protected class group(s), employers should closely scrutinize the following:
  — The protected class composition of positions from which promotions are made
  — The manner in which key projects and other developmental opportunities are assigned
  — The availability of mentoring
  — The existence of harassment and other impediments to performance
  — The selection criteria and process used in promotions
  — Aspects of the organization's culture that are hostile to protected class groups
  — Turnover patterns
- To remove obstacles to attaining high-level positions, employers should
  — Provide management development programs, career planning assistance, and mentoring.
  — Be open to less traditional career paths and backgrounds for promotional candidates.

Chapter Questions

1. Ninety-five percent of the customers of a weight-loss center are women. Counselors at the center sell the weight-loss program, interact with customers, provide instruction on diet programs, counsel customers about their individual weight problems, and monitor the progress of customers in losing weight. The latter includes taking measurements of size and body fat using a tape measure and calipers, respectively. The measurements involve considerable physical contact with customers and are sometimes taken on bare skin. Arguing that many customers would be uncomfortable and embarrassed having men take their measurements and talk with them about their weight problems, the center hires only women as counselors. Two previous attempts to use male counselors were judged to have been unsuccessful. A male, denied employment as a counselor at the weight center, sues. What should the court decide? Why? (*EEOC v. HI 40 Corp.*, 953 F. Supp. 301 [W.D. Mo. 1996])

2. After a regional sales director had her first child in 2005, she questioned her boss about whether it was necessary to attend every out-of-town conference held by the company. The conferences typically lasted five days. There were originally five conferences per year and this increased to at least ten. In her view, the conferences involved mainly social and recreational activities. She was told that attendance was necessary for team-building and other organizational purposes. When she had a second child in late 2006, she again pressed the issue of the conferences, telling her supervisor that she had great difficulty arranging childcare while she was gone. She was given an ultimatum by her supervisor that she either commit to attending all future conferences or look for another position in the company that

did not require travel. The sales director did neither and was terminated. She sued, alleging that she, unlike any of the other sales directors, had been required to commit to attending the conferences because she was a mother with two young children. What should the court decide? Why? (*Feinerman v. T-Mobile USA*, 2010 U.S. Dist. LEXIS 7007 [S.D.N.Y.])

3. An applicant who had been in the military for twenty-five years, including in Special Forces units, received the unanimous recommendation of the selection committee and was offered a job with the Library of Congress. Over lunch after accepting the position, "David" informed the hiring manager that she was transgender and that she planned to start work as "Diane." She would be transitioning from male to female and would have sexual reassignment surgery in the future. The hiring manager's initial reaction was to say "Why in the world would you want to do that?" She later said "Well, you've given me a lot to think about. I'll be in touch." By phone on the next day, the hiring manager informed "Diane" that "I've determined that you are not a good fit, not what we want." A male with lower interview scores was hired instead. The library cited concerns about possible problems obtaining a security clearance (which was needed for this position and which he had while in the military), possible lack of trustworthiness, the distraction that transitioning might cause, and possible lack of acceptance by congresspersons and military sources. Did the employer discriminate in withdrawing the offer? Why or why not? (*Schroer v. Billington*, 577 F. Supp.2d 293 [D.D.C. 2008]).

4. A company that sold playground equipment established a new, unwritten dress code. All employees were expected to purchase and wear khaki pants. Male employees were expected to purchase and wear denim shirts with the company logo. Female employees were required to purchase and wear a navy blazer over a polo shirt. The policy was intended to "create a more professional image" of sales employees. However, comments were also made that the reason for requiring blazers for women was to "cover up their boobs and [bottoms]." It was also stated by the individual charged with developing the policy that "women should wear blazers because

this is a man's world and to keep up with men, women have to be one up on them." A female employee resisted the new policy and stated on a number of occasions that she could not afford to purchase the required blazers. After reporting to work wearing the denim shirt with company logo and khaki pants and stating that she did not intend to wear the blazer, the woman was terminated. After the termination, the dress code policy was put into writing. The terminated employee sued. What should the court decide? Why? (*Rohaly v. Rainbow Playground Depot*, 2006 Wash. App. LEXIS 1917 [App. Ct., Div. One])

5. A woman with four children (6-year-old triplets and an 11-year-old) was passed over for promotion in favor of another women with two children (a 10-year-old and a 15-year-old). One of the three supervisors who made the promotion decision stated that "It was nothing you did or didn't do. It was just that you're going to school, you have the kids, and you just have a lot on your plate right now." The supervisor also said that she and the other supervisors agreed that they would feel "overwhelmed" in the same circumstances. When one of the supervisors was first informed that the woman had triplets, she responded, "Oh my—I did not know that you had triplets…. Bless you!" After the woman answered a question during her interview about how she would handle a subordinate who failed to finish an assigned task on time, one of the supervisors responded, "You are a mother … would you let your kids off the hook that easy … ?" The woman sued, advancing a sex-stereotyping theory. What should the court decide? Why? (*Chadwick v. Wellpoint, Inc.*, 561 F.3d 38 [1st Cir. 2009])

6. A 350-pound man interviewed for a job as a sales counselor for a weight-loss center. He was told by the interviewer that he was the "most qualified" applicant but that the regional manager had concerns about his weight. He was later informed that he would not be hired now because the company is "image conscious" and his weight would "send the wrong message." He was told to reapply for employment after losing seventy pounds. The man sued. What should the court decide? Why? (*Goodman v. L.A. Weight Loss Centers*, 2005 U.S. Dist. LEXIS 1455 [E.D. Pa.])

7. A woman applied for a part-time position in human resources. At the time she applied, she was working part-time for a benefits consulting company and received the same benefits as full-time employees. During interviews and negotiations with the prospective employer, the woman was repeatedly told that she would receive the same benefits as the company's full-time employees. The letter of offer listed specific benefits, including life insurance, disability, and accidental death and dismemberment, to which she would be entitled after a thirty-day waiting period. The letter also stated that she should "review the Employee Handbook for further information" and that the company retained the "right to change benefit programs at any time." Immediately upon taking the job and receiving a copy of the employee handbook, the woman was dismayed to find that she would not be entitled to the full range of benefits received by full-time employees. Specifically, she would not receive life, AD&D, or long-term disability insurance. The woman complained to the director of human resources about having been misled regarding her benefits and was terminated three days after starting on the job. The HR director claimed that she was being terminated due to a confrontational personality and lack of a good fit with the culture of the company. She sued. What should the court decide? Why? (*Timpe v. WATG Holdings*, 2008 U.S. Dist. LEXIS 45562 [D. Haw.])

8. An African American employee sought promotion to a chemist position with supervisory responsibilities. Promotions were based on the results of "certification" (based on education and work experience) and an interview. Because of his extensive experience, the African American employee received a score of 89 on the certification. The second-ranked candidate scored 28 points lower. A panel of three (all white people) interviewed the five candidates deemed qualified after the certification process. Interviews were scored, and a candidate's score was the average score given by the three interviewers. The highest score on the interview was a 52, and the African American employee ranked third with a score of 48. The interviewers attributed the lower score to the employee not clearly explaining how his skills would be used on the job and how he planned to move the county's environmental programs forward. The white male who scored highest on the interview was promoted, despite the fact that he had scored 34 points lower in the certification stage. The company has an informal policy of hiring from within for promotional positions, although it did not always do so. The African American employee sued. What should the court decide? Why? (*Obi v. Anne Arundel County, Maryland*, 142 F. Supp. 2d 655 [D. Md. 2001], *affirmed*, 2002 U.S. App. LEXIS 2716 [4th Cir.])

9. A woman with twenty-eight years of experience was "an exemplary employee who had been nationally recognized for her planning work." She applied for the promotional position of Plan Formulation Specialist. The selection panel chose a much younger and less experienced candidate. The promotion took place when the employer had expressed concern about its aging workforce. The employer had created an "Emerging Leaders Program" to identify and develop individuals with "leadership potential." The candidate chosen was in this program. Candidates were first scored and ranked according to their experience and qualifications. The woman was ranked as tied for second place (out of six candidates) even though she would have been alone in second place twenty points above the next highest candidate if the employer had simply summed the scores of the panelists. Instead, the ranking was done by "consensus" of the panelists. Interviews were then conducted. The selection panel determined that interview performance would be weighed equally with the pre-interview assessment of qualifications. Each interviewee was asked the same questions, and each interview lasted from fifteen to thirty minutes. The notes and scores from the interviews were not retained. However, panelists testified that the woman did not perform well on the interview, that she had been "curt and blunt" during the interview, and that she appeared not to be making an effort to answer the questions. The woman said that she had given short answers because she didn't think the questions were germane to the position. When all was said and done, the woman was ranked fourth among the candidates and did not get the promotion. She sued for age discrimination. What should the court decide? Why?

(*Hollaway v. Secretary of Army*, 203 Fed. Appx. 563 [5th Cir. 2006])

10. To what extent are caregivers discriminated against in the workplace? Do existing laws go far enough to protect caregivers? Why or why not?

11. Do you think that the glass ceiling phenomenon is primarily a pipeline problem that will disappear over time as women and people of color acquire the relevant experiences, or is it rooted more deeply in organizational cultures and practices hostile to the advancement of women and minorities? Why do you say that?

PART 3

Managing a Diverse Workforce

CHAPTER 8

Affirmative Action

Managers know that important financial and operational outcomes require close attention and planning. Managers are taught to *be proactive* and not to wait until losses or consumer complaints mount before taking action to improve profitability, efficiency, and quality. It is important to have a clear sense of desired outcomes (goals), a strategy for attaining those outcomes, and ways to measure whether progress is being made.

Equal employment opportunity is another important outcome. Rather than simply refrain from discrimination and react to employee grievances or lawsuits, employers can take initiative in studying their workforces, identifying problem areas, devising reasonable measures to enhance equal employment opportunity, setting goals for improvement, and tracking progress. In short, employers can take affirmative action.

Affirmative action has been defined as "those actions appropriate to overcome the effects of past or present practices, policies, or other barriers to equal employment opportunity."[1] To qualify as affirmative action, such efforts must be undertaken pursuant to formal affirmative action plans. The particular focus of affirmative action is improving the employment opportunities of groups that, historically, have been victims of discrimination: women, African Americans, Latinos, Native Americans, Asians, Pacific Islanders, disabled persons, and certain veterans. This chapter considers the situations in which affirmative action is required, circumstances affecting the legality of affirmative action, and the nature of affirmative action plans. The chapter concludes with some thoughts on the relationship between affirmative action and diversity initiatives.

Affirmative action is clearly controversial. Attitudes toward affirmative action are complex and often passionate. The Pew Research Center has tracked attitudes on racial issues through national surveys conducted over the past few decades. A majority of Americans (62 percent) believe that racial discrimination persists and is not a rare event.[2] Interestingly, 70 percent of Americans were in favor of "affirmative action programs to help blacks, women, and other minorities get

---

[1]29 C.F.R. § 1608.1(c) (2011).

[2]The Pew Research Center. *Trends in Political Values and Core Attitudes: 1987–2007.* (March 22, 2007), 39.

better jobs and education" in 2007, up from 58 percent in 1995.[3] However, support for using "preferential treatment" to achieve affirmative action goals is considerably lower (31 percent of respondents endorsed preferences in 2009).[4] Also, while there has been some convergence in the views of white and black Americans, there remain sizable gaps in attitudes—particularly regarding affirmative action and preferences—along race lines.[5]

When Is Affirmative Action Required?

Affirmative action is required of most companies that have contracts to sell goods or services to the federal government. Many states also have affirmative action requirements for contractors. Besides government contracting, the only other time that employers are required to engage in affirmative action is when a discrimination suit results in a settlement or court order that includes affirmative action as a remedy. Otherwise, employers can determine whether they want to have affirmative action plans. Many employers, in fact, choose to adopt voluntary affirmative action plans.

Government Contractors

Companies that contract to do business with the federal government are covered by **Executive Order 11246**.[6] This executive order requires companies with contracts worth at least $10,000 to *have a nondiscrimination clause included in their contracts and abide by its terms.* Importantly, *the same clause must be included in the contracts of subcontractors, and they are also bound by its terms.* In its most relevant part, the **nondiscrimination clause** reads as follows:

> *During the performance of this contract, the contractor agrees as follows: (1) The contractor will not discriminate against any employee or applicant for employment because of race, color, religion, sex, or national origin. The contractor will take affirmative action to ensure that applicants are employed, and that employees are treated during their employment, without regard to their race, color, religion, sex, or national origin. Such action shall include, but not be limited to the following: employment, upgrading, demotion, or transfer; recruitment or recruitment advertising; layoff or termination; rates of pay or other forms of compensation; and selection for training, including apprenticeship. The contractor agrees to post in conspicuous places, available to employees and applicants for employment, notices to be provided by the contracting officer setting forth the provisions of this nondiscrimination clause.[7]*

The nondiscrimination clause also refers to contractors taking affirmative action. Under E.O. 11246, *contractors and subcontractors that have at least fifty employees and contracts worth at least $50,000 must develop written affirmative action plans and submit them to the OFCCP* (within 120 days of the contract commencing). A preapproved affirmative action plan is required for large contracts (in excess of $1 million). Compliance with E.O. 11246 and other laws requiring affirmative action by contractors is monitored by the **Office of Federal Contract Compliance Programs (OFCCP)**.

---

[3]Pew Research Center (2007), at 40.

[4]The Pew Research Center. "Public Backs Affirmative Action, but Not Minority Preferences." (June 2, 2009) (http://www.pewresearch.org/pubs/).

[5]The Pew Research Center (2007), at 41, 43.

[6]30 Fed. Reg. 12319 (September 28, 1965).

[7]Executive Order 11246, part II, subpart B, § 202(1).

Federal contractors and subcontractors are numerous and include many of the nation's major corporations. The underlying rationale is that if public funds are being expended, it is legitimate for the government to require that contractors' employment practices support public policy in favor of equal employment opportunity. However, *all establishments within contracting corporations—and not only facilities that actually perform contract work—are required to comply with E.O. 11246.* Questions sometimes arise as to which entities are subcontractors with affirmative action responsibilities under E.O. 11246. The University of Pittsburgh Medical Center–Braddock was no doubt surprised when it was contacted by the OFCCP to schedule a compliance review. The medical center did not have a contract with the federal government. However, it did have a contract with a health maintenance organization (HMO), which, in turn, had contracted with the federal government to provide medical care to federal government employees. Even though the medical center's contract with the HMO said nothing about affirmative action responsibilities (apparently, the required nondiscrimination clause was omitted), the fact that the medical center was providing services necessary to fulfilling the HMO's government contract was enough to legally establish subcontractor status. Lacking an affirmative action plan and documentation of its affirmative action efforts, the medical center was in violation of E.O. 11246.[8]

Because most contractors are already covered by Title VII of the Civil Rights Act, isn't it redundant to incorporate nondiscrimination language in contracts? Executive Order 11246 reinforces federal antidiscrimination laws by providing additional sanctions and enforcement mechanisms. Under E.O. 11246, the federal government can suspend, cancel, or terminate the contracts of noncomplying contractors and bar companies from bidding on future projects. These sanctions are rarely invoked, but they provide another strong incentive for employers to pay attention to equal employment opportunity. The OFCCP collects considerable workforce data from employers, conducts compliance reviews, and can initiate suits without needing individual plaintiffs to come forth. The agency focuses on systemic violations—particularly in initial hiring, but also promotions and compensation—that might otherwise be difficult to document and pursue. In these ways, the OFCCP bolsters the enforcement of antidiscrimination laws.

Clippings

The Office of Federal Contract Compliance Programs reached a $1.65 million settlement with a meatpacking company in Green Bay, Wisconsin. The company, Green Bay Dressed Beef, is a large provider of beef products to the U.S. military, as well as to school lunch programs. A scheduled compliance review uncovered evidence that the company had violated E.O. 11246 by discriminating against some 970 female applicants who had sought positions as general laborers in 2006 and 2007.

The OFCCP has launched a complaint against another meatpacking company, Tyson Fresh Meats, alleging that it systematically rejected hundreds of female job applicants at its plant in Joslin, Illinois. The agency is requesting that strong measures be taken against the company, including a permanent injunction against violation of E.O. 11246, cancellation of Tyson's government contracts, and debarment from bidding on any future contracts until this matter is resolved.

---

[8]Jon Zimring and Cheryl B. Bryson. "U.S. Government Contractor/Subcontractor Status: The Danger of Continued Complacency." *Daily Labor Report* 74 (April 20, 2010), I-1.

> OFCCP Director Patricia A. Shiu said about this case that "Taxpayer dollars must never be used to discriminate. In our efforts to uncover workplace discrimination, OFCCP will utilize a host of remedies, including debarment, to protect workers, promote diversity and enforce the law."
>
> "OFCCP, Meat Firm Settle for $1.65 Million Claim of Bias against Female Applicants." *Daily Labor Report* 23 (February 3, 2011), A-1.
>
> Michael Bologna. "OFCCP Alleges Sex Discrimination in Hiring against Division of Tyson Foods." *Daily Labor Report* 183 (September 22, 2010), A-4.

Federal contractors also have affirmative action responsibilities under the Rehabilitation Act of 1973.[9] *Contractors or subcontractors with federal contracts worth more than $10,000 are required to take affirmative action to employ qualified individuals with disabilities. Contractors or subcontractors with at least fifty employees and contracts worth at least $50,000 are responsible for preparing and maintaining affirmative action plans.* These plans are less detailed than affirmative action plans required under E.O. 11246 and do not include the establishment of specific goals and timetables. Instead, the focus is on broadening recruitment efforts to reach qualified disabled persons and systematically reviewing workplace policies and practices to identify and remove barriers to the employment of disabled persons.

One other federal law that contains affirmative action requirements for contractors is the Vietnam Era Veteran's Readjustment Assistance Act of 1974 (VEVRAA).[10] The law, as amended, requires that *employers with federal contracts or subcontracts worth more than $100,000 provide equal employment opportunity and affirmative action on behalf of covered veterans.* VEVRAA was originally enacted to address the problems of veterans returning from the Vietnam War, but the law now reaches a much broader group. VEVRAA covers veterans with service-connected disabilities, "campaign veterans" who served on active duty during wars or other military campaigns, armed forces service medal veterans, and veterans discharged from the military within the previous three years.[11] In the past, the affirmative action requirements of the law were fairly minimal, primarily involving the listing of all employment openings (except top management jobs) in places where covered military veterans could easily access them (typically state employment services). But in light of the increasing number of veterans now returning from military conflicts and having problems finding jobs, the OFCCP intends to institute a new set of more stringent requirements for contractors. These include establishing annual hiring benchmarks for protected veterans, collecting data on the availability and utilization of protected veterans, and using more types of outreach and recruiting.[12]

Settlements and Court Orders

Affirmative action is one of the remedies available to courts in discrimination cases. When discrimination has been pervasive and deeply entrenched in an organization, simply punishing the offending employer might not be enough. Affirmative action might be needed to prevent future violations and to undo the damage (e.g., a hostile organizational climate, a dearth of women and persons of color in positions that lead to promotion) that has been

---

[9]29 U.S.C. § 793 (2011).

[10]38 U.S.C.S. § 4212 (2011).

[11]38 U.S.C.S. § 4212 (3)(A) (i–iv) (2011).

[12]76 Fed. Reg. 23358 (April 26, 2011).

done. Affirmative action that arises out of legal proceedings can be imposed either as a remedy following a determination by a court that an employer has engaged in a serious pattern or practice of intentional discrimination or as part of a judicially approved settlement between the parties. The latter is called a **consent decree**. Affirmative action that arises out of legal proceedings is the most far-reaching in the use of preferences.

Court-imposed affirmative action is not common in the private sector, but many of the nation's police and fire departments operate, or have done so in the past, under the terms of consent decrees mandating affirmative action on behalf of women and persons of color. The Boston Police Department's experience is typical in this regard.[13] The department was sued in the early 1970s for discriminatory recruiting and hiring practices. At that time, African Americans comprised about 16.3 percent of Boston's population but only 3.6 percent of its police force. The litigation was settled, and the city entered into a consent decree that called for affirmative action in hiring to achieve "parity" between the percentages of blacks and Latinos hired as entry-level police officers and the city's population. The decree remained in place for thirty years. Over that time, the percentage of entry-level police officers who were people of color grew to about 38 percent, which was roughly the same as the minority share of Boston's population. Consent decrees are not intended to remain in place into perpetuity. When the goals of the affirmative action plan are achieved, as they were by the Boston Police Department, the municipality is relieved of its obligation to comply with the consent decree.

Absent a government contract or a court order, employers are generally free to choose whether to engage in affirmative action. However, to say that affirmative action is voluntary is not to say that employers are free to do whatever they want under the banner of affirmative action. The legal guidelines for affirmative action plans are stringent and appear to be shifting in the direction of closer judicial scrutiny.

Distinguishing Legal Affirmative Action from Reverse Discrimination

Affirmative action often takes the form of good employment practices, such as identifying and encouraging more diverse applicants, posting all employment opportunities, eliminating selection criteria that impose unnecessary barriers to employment, and offering extensive development and mentoring opportunities. Measures such as these do not leave anyone worse off and raise no issue of discrimination. Under E.O. 11246, contractors are limited to these measures and required to "make selections in a nondiscriminatory manner. Placement goals do not provide the contractor with a justification to extend a preference to any individual … on the basis of that person's race, color, religion, sex, or national origin."[14]

The difficulty with these affirmative action measures is that they are not effective without strong commitment from employers (something that might be in short supply in organizations that have been in the habit of discriminating) and any improvements they yield are likely to be gradual. Employers sometimes go further and apply a **preference** for women or persons of color in hiring or promotion decisions to achieve affirmative action goals. In such cases, the protected class characteristics of applicants or employees are considered in making employment decisions, and the outcomes of those decisions might differ from what they would have been in the absence of affirmative action. The use of affirmative action to accord preferences for women and people of color is the most controversial and legally problematic issue.

---

[13]*Deleo v. City of Boston*, 2004 U.S. Dist. LEXIS 24034 (D. Mass.).

[14]41 C.F.R. § 60-2.16(e)(2) (2011).

Practical Considerations What should an employer that has decided to implement an affirmative action program do to maximize support for the program and minimize resentment or backlash?

In **reverse discrimination** cases, an employee alleges disparate treatment, believing that he was passed over for an employment opportunity because an employer with an affirmative action plan considered the protected class characteristics of applicants and chose a woman or person of color instead. In these cases, the employer has, in fact, taken protected class into account (which is not to say that it was the only factor considered) but argues that doing so was permissible because of its affirmative action plan. The question then is whether this use of affirmative action was discriminatory. In reaching an answer, courts will consider both the justification for the affirmative action plan and the reasonableness of the particular measures used to implement it.

Although affirmative action sometimes goes beyond instituting good practices to include the extension of preferences based on race or sex, *affirmative action is not a matter of establishing rigid quotas, "checking boxes," or reserving employment opportunities solely for persons with the desired protected class characteristics regardless of their qualifications.* Loaded terms such as *quota system* obscure the reality of affirmative action and make it impossible to engage in objective analysis of the legal issues. The legal question surrounding affirmative action is not whether quotas are legal; the answer to that question is plainly no. Instead, we are confronted with the question of to what extent, if at all, protected class characteristics can be taken into account in making employment decisions for the purpose of undoing the effects of discrimination on women and persons of color.

Before we look at some of the case law on the legality of affirmative action, a few other caveats are in order. Cases are brought under both Title VII and the U.S. Constitution (the equal protection provisions of the Fifth and Fourteenth Amendments), and the extent to which these bodies of law impose different requirements is not entirely clear. Likewise, affirmative action has been challenged in the context of not only employment but also education (admissions decisions of universities) and public contracting (preferences for minority-owned businesses in the awarding of contracts). Cases considering the legality of affirmative action in education and public contracting are often treated as directly relevant to affirmative action in employment, but drawing distinctions between these settings is possible. Finally, the law in this area is dynamic and has shifted in the direction of greater restriction of the use of preferences in affirmative action programs.

The Legality of Affirmative Action under Title VII

Johnson v. Transportation Agency is an important Supreme Court decision addressing a legal challenge to a voluntary affirmative action plan under Title VII.

Johnson v. Transportation Agency, Santa Clara County
480 U.S. 616 (1987)

OPINION BY JUSTICE BRENNAN:

Respondent, Transportation Agency of Santa Clara County, California, unilaterally promulgated an Affirmative Action Plan applicable, inter alia [among other things], to promotions of employees. In selecting applicants for the promotional position of road dispatcher, the Agency, pursuant to the Plan, passed over petitioner Paul Johnson, a male employee, and

promoted a female employee applicant, Diane Joyce. The question for decision is whether in making the promotion the Agency impermissibly took into account the sex of the applicants in violation of Title VII of the Civil Rights Act of 1964. * * *

In December 1978, Santa Clara ... adopted an affirmative action plan for the County Transportation Agency. * * * [T]he Agency Plan provides that, in making promotions to positions within a traditionally segregated job classification in which women have been significantly underrepresented, the Agency is authorized to consider as one factor the sex of a qualified applicant.

In reviewing the composition of its work force, the Agency noted in its Plan that women were represented in numbers far less than their proportion of the County labor force in both the Agency as a whole and in five of seven job categories. Specifically, while women constituted 36.4% of the area labor market, they composed only 22.4% of Agency employees. Furthermore, women working at the Agency were concentrated largely in EEOC job categories traditionally held by women…. As for the job classification relevant to this case, none of the 238 Skilled Craft Worker positions was held by a woman. * * *

On December 12, 1979, the Agency announced a vacancy for the promotional position of road dispatcher. * * * Nine of the applicants, including Joyce and Johnson, were deemed qualified for the job, and were interviewed by a two-person board. Seven of the applicants scored above 70 on this interview, which meant that they were certified as eligible for selection by the appointing authority. The scores awarded ranged from 70 to 80. Johnson was tied for second with a score of 75, while Joyce ranked next with a score of 73. A second interview was conducted by three Agency supervisors, who ultimately recommended that Johnson be promoted. Prior to the second interview, Joyce had contacted the County's Affirmative Action Office because she feared that her application might not receive disinterested review [due to prior disagreements with two of the interviewers]. The Office in turn contacted the Agency's Affirmative Action Coordinator. * * * The Coordinator recommended to the Director of the Agency, James Graebner, that Joyce be promoted. * * * Graebner, authorized to choose any of the seven persons deemed eligible, thus had the benefit of suggestions by the second interview panel and by the Agency Coordinator in arriving at his decision. After deliberation, Graebner concluded that the promotion should be given to Joyce. * * *

The assessment of the legality of the Agency Plan must be guided by our decision in *Weber*. In that case, the Court addressed the question whether the employer violated Title VII by adopting a voluntary affirmative action plan designed to "eliminate manifest racial imbalances in traditionally segregated job categories." The respondent employee in that case

challenged the employer's denial of his application for a position in a newly established craft training program, contending that the employer's selection process impermissibly took into account the race of the applicants. The selection process was guided by an affirmative action plan, which provided that 50% of the new trainees were to be black until the percentage of black skilled craft workers in the employer's plant approximated the percentage of blacks in the local labor force. Adoption of the plan had been prompted by the fact that only 5 of 273, or 1.83%, of skilled craft workers at the plant were black, even though the work force in the area was approximately 39% black. Because of the historical exclusion of blacks from craft positions, the employer regarded its former policy of hiring trained outsiders as inadequate to redress the imbalance in its work force.

We upheld the employer's decision to select less senior black applicants over the white respondent, for we found that taking race into account was consistent with Title VII's objective of "[breaking] down old patterns of racial segregation and hierarchy." As we stated:

> It would be ironic indeed if a law triggered by a Nation's concern over centuries of racial injustice and intended to improve the lot of those who had "been excluded from the American dream for so long" constituted the first legislative prohibition of all voluntary, private, race-conscious efforts to abolish traditional patterns of racial segregation and hierarchy.

We noted that the plan did not "unnecessarily trammel the interests of the white employees," since it did not require "the discharge of white workers and their replacement with new black hirees." Nor did the plan create "an absolute bar to the advancement of white employees," since half of those trained in the new program were to be white. Finally, we observed that the plan was a temporary measure, not designed to maintain racial balance, but to "eliminate a manifest racial imbalance." As JUSTICE BLACKMUN's concurrence made clear, Weber held that an employer seeking to justify the adoption of a plan need not point to its own prior discriminatory practices, nor even to evidence of an "arguable violation" on its part. Rather, it need point only to a "conspicuous … imbalance in traditionally segregated job categories." Our decision was grounded in the recognition that voluntary employer action can play a crucial role in furthering Title VII's purpose of eliminating the effects of discrimination in the workplace, and that Title VII should not be read to thwart such efforts. * * *

In reviewing the employment decision at issue in this case, * * * [t]he first issue is therefore whether consideration of the sex of applicants for Skilled Craft jobs was justified by the existence of a "manifest imbalance" that reflected underrepresentation of women in "traditionally segregated job categories." In determining whether an imbalance exists that would justify taking sex or race into account, a comparison of the percentage of minorities or women in the employer's work force with the percentage in the area labor market or general population is appropriate in analyzing jobs that require no special expertise. Where a job requires special training, however, the comparison should be with those in the labor force who possess the relevant qualifications. * * * If a plan failed to take distinctions in qualifications into account in providing guidance for actual employment decisions, it would dictate mere blind hiring by the numbers, for it would hold supervisors to "achievement of a particular percentage of minority employment or membership … regardless of circumstances such as economic conditions or the number of available qualified minority applicants…."

The Agency's Plan emphatically did not authorize such blind hiring. It expressly directed that numerous factors be taken into account in making hiring decisions, including specifically the qualifications of female applicants for particular jobs. Thus, despite the fact that no precise short-term goal was yet in place for the Skilled Craft category in mid-1980, the Agency's management nevertheless had been clearly instructed that they were not to hire solely by reference to statistics. The fact that only the long-term goal had been established for this category posed no danger that personnel decisions would be made by reflexive adherence to a numerical standard.

Furthermore, in considering the candidates for the road dispatcher position in 1980, the Agency hardly needed to rely on a refined short-term goal to realize that it had a significant problem of underrepresentation that required attention. Given the obvious imbalance in the Skilled Craft category, and given the Agency's commitment to eliminating such imbalances, it was plainly not unreasonable for the Agency to determine that it was appropriate to consider as one factor the sex of Ms. Joyce in making its decision. The promotion of Joyce thus satisfies the first requirement enunciated in *Weber*, since it was undertaken to further an affirmative action plan designed to eliminate Agency work force imbalances in traditionally segregated job categories.

We next consider whether the Agency Plan unnecessarily trammeled the rights of male employees or created an absolute bar to their advancement. * * * [T]he Plan sets aside no positions for women. The Plan expressly states that "[the] 'goals' established for each Division should not be construed as 'quotas' that must be met." Rather, the Plan merely authorizes that consideration be given to affirmative action concerns when evaluating qualified applicants. As the Agency Director testified, the sex of Joyce was but one of numerous factors he took into account in arriving at his decision. * * * [T]he Agency Plan requires women to compete with all other qualified applicants. No persons are automatically excluded from consideration; all are able to have their qualifications weighed against those of other applicants.

In addition, petitioner had no absolute entitlement to the road dispatcher position. Seven of the applicants were classified as qualified and eligible, and the Agency Director was authorized to promote any of the seven. Thus, denial of the promotion unsettled no legitimate, firmly rooted expectation on the part of petitioner. Furthermore, while petitioner in this case was denied a promotion, he retained his employment with the Agency, at the same salary and with the same seniority, and remained eligible for other promotions.

Finally, the Agency's Plan was intended to attain a balanced work force, not to maintain one. * * * The Agency acknowledged the difficulties that it would confront in remedying the imbalance in its work force, and it anticipated only gradual increases in the representation of minorities and women. It is thus unsurprising that the Plan contains no explicit end date, for the Agency's flexible, case-by-case approach was not expected to yield success in a brief period of time. Express assurance that a program is only temporary may be necessary if the program actually sets aside positions according to specific numbers. * * *

We therefore hold that the Agency appropriately took into account as one factor the sex of Diane Joyce in determining that she should be promoted to the road dispatcher position. The decision to do so was made pursuant to an affirmative action plan that represents a moderate, flexible, case-by-case approach to effecting a gradual improvement in the representation of minorities and women in the Agency's work force. Such a plan is fully consistent with Title VII, for it embodies the contribution that voluntary employer action can make in eliminating the vestiges of discrimination in the workplace. Accordingly, the judgment of the Court of Appeals is [a]ffirmed.

CASE QUESTIONS

1. What was the legal issue in this case? What did the Supreme Court decide?

2. What does this case reveal about the conditions under which affirmative action is legal?
3. What evidence did the county have of the need for affirmative action?
4. Why does the Court conclude that the measures used to implement the county's affirmative action plan do not unduly burden white males such as Johnson?
5. Do you agree with this decision? Why or why not?

Johnson points to some basic requirements for affirmative action plans under Title VII. First, the only reason that Santa Clara County was able to defend its consideration of candidates' sex in the promotion decision was that it did, in fact, have an affirmative action plan. Absent a formal, written affirmative action plan, it would not have worked for the county to claim that it was just trying to help women or that it was committed to diversity. Thus, an *employer that wants to consider protected class characteristics when making employment decisions to enhance the employment of women and persons of color can do so only if a formal affirmative action plan is in place.*

The case also makes it clear that *affirmative action must be remedial in nature to be legal.* Although it is not necessary under Title VII to establish that the employer has discriminated prior to instituting affirmative action, the plan must address a "manifest imbalance" in the protected class composition of the employer's workforce.[15] Put differently, the plan must be designed to remedy the "underutilization" of women and people of color. *Affirmative action cannot be used to maintain the racial or gender balance of an employer's workforce; it can only be used to remedy the underutilization of women and people of color in particular jobs. Affirmative action is a temporary measure that must not continue after the identified underutilization has been eliminated.* Although the failure to cite a specific expiration date was not fatal in *Johnson*, the case suggests that plans calling for more aggressive use of preferences require clearer evidence of their temporary nature.

The Court upheld the use of affirmative action in *Johnson* not only because of the clear underutilization of women in skilled crafts, but also because the means used to pursue affirmative action goals were moderate and not unduly burdensome on males. Specifically, the plan did not establish quotas (i.e., rigid requirements such as a specified number or percentage of new hires that must be women) or set aside positions only for women. Nor did the plan result in the hiring of unqualified persons. Instead, sex was considered among many other factors, and the female candidate selected was judged to be only slightly less qualified through the agency's interview process. *Employers engaging in affirmative action must refrain from establishing quotas, setting aside positions, or hiring unqualified candidates.* Additionally, *affirmative action cannot be invoked as a basis for disciplinary or layoff decisions.* Even though downsizing might undermine gains in minority and female employment, the heavy burden of losing employment falls on specific individuals and "unnecessarily trammels [interferes with] the interests" of whites and males.[16]

---

[15]*United Steelworkers v. Weber*, 443 U.S. 193, 208 (1979).

[16]*Wygant v. Jackson Board of Education*, 476 U.S. 267, 274 (1986).

JUST THE FACTS

Under financial duress, a school district was forced to lay off teachers. The business department of the high school had two female teachers equal in seniority and performance. One of the teachers was African American, and the other was white. Unable to resort to its usual procedure of conducting layoffs in reverse order of seniority and concerned that the business department would be left without any African American faculty, the district invoked its affirmative action plan to retain the African American teacher and lay off her white colleague. Overall, the percentage of African American faculty in the school district exceeded the percentage in the surrounding labor market. However, the district pointed to the effect that laying off the African American teacher would have at the department level and to the need for a highly diverse faculty to serve as role models for a student body that included a high percentage of African American students. The white teacher who was laid off sued.

See, *Taxman v. Board of Education of the Township of Piscataway*, 91 F.3d 1547 (3d Cir. 1996), *cert. dismissed*, 118 S. Ct. 595 (1997).

The Legality of Affirmative Action under the U.S. Constitution

Even though it concerned a government agency, *Johnson* was argued as a Title VII case. However, challenges to the use of preferences by public employers and to court-imposed affirmative action plans often allege violations of the U.S. Constitution. In constitutional cases, courts subject the use of racial preferences in affirmative action plans to **strict scrutiny**—the most stringent form of judicial review of government actions.[17] To survive a constitutional challenge to an affirmative action plan that uses racial preferences, a public employer must show that the plan serves a **compelling governmental interest** and that the measures employed are **narrowly tailored**. Put differently, the plan must serve a very important public purpose and harm the interests of nonpreferred persons no more than absolutely necessary.

One *compelling governmental interest* is remedying the effects of prior discrimination by a particular public employer. Statistical disparities showing underutilization do not suffice as a *constitutional* justification for affirmative action, absent evidence that the public employer's discriminatory acts produced those disparities.[18] A public employer that engages in affirmative action pursuant to a valid court order issued after a finding of discrimination would have a compelling interest in complying with the terms of that order. Whether compliance with a consent decree is a compelling governmental interest is less certain, since a decree is a settlement agreement entered into prior to a definitive ruling, but "the heightened judicial oversight inherent in a properly entered decree" helps ensure that it is serving to remedy prior discrimination.[19] Courts scrutinize whether consent decrees actually require the specific actions taken in their name and whether they have already outlived their usefulness at the

---

[17] *Adarand Constructors v. Pena*, 515 U.S. 200, 227 (1995).

[18] *City of Richmond v. J.A. Croson Co.*, 488 U.S. 469, 504–505 (1989).

[19] *Rutherford v. City of Cleveland*, 179 Fed. Appx. 366, 375 (6th Cir. 2006); *Martinez v. City of St. Louis*, 539 F.3d 857, 861 (2008).

time those actions were taken. For example, the Indianapolis Police Department's attempt to justify the use of preferences in making promotions based on a consent decree failed because the decree did not reach promotions (instead, the decree stated that "[p]romotions shall be based upon relevant standards and criteria *which will be applied without regard to race or color.*")[20]

Compelling governmental interests that might justify racial classifications are not strictly limited to the remedying of past discrimination. In two cases involving student admissions to the University of Michigan, the Supreme Court endorsed the view that a nonremedial purpose—student body diversity—can be a compelling governmental interest that justifies the use of race in university admissions.[21] Diversity, understood broadly to include many factors other than race, is central to the mission and purpose of a public university, particularly a law school. However, this reasoning did not extend to public school districts that adopted student assignment plans to ensure that schools were racially balanced.[22] The districts did not have histories of legal segregation or operate under court orders to desegregate their schools. The diversity rationale accepted for the University of Michigan law school did not apply in this case, in part because the school assignments considered only race as an aspect of diversity. But the Supreme Court also stressed that its rationale for finding student body diversity to be a compelling governmental interest in the University of Michigan cases "rested upon considerations *unique to institutions of higher education.*"[23]

To be constitutional, racial preferences must also be *narrowly tailored*. This requirement is more likely to be met if racial preferences are not applied to layoffs or disciplinary actions,[24] they are no more burdensome than absolutely necessary, race-neutral methods were tried and proved inadequate,[25] they do not amount to rigid quotas, and their use is temporary and flexible.[26] In the University of Michigan cases, the affirmative action program used in selecting students for the law school was upheld as constitutional, while the program used for selecting undergraduates was struck down. The difference was that the law school's efforts to attain a "critical mass" of student body diversity through a highly individualized assessment that considered multiple forms of diversity were deemed "narrowly tailored," whereas the undergraduate admission program that automatically awarded sizable bonuses based on race and ethnicity in a largely quantitative selection process was not sufficiently narrowly tailored.

Thus, although considerable overlap exists between the requirements for private employers under Title VII and public employers under the Constitution, the latter requirements are more stringent. Also, public employers in several states are prohibited outright from extending preferences in public employment, education, and contracting based on race and other protected class characteristics (see "Clippings"). The Supreme Court's decisions in the University of Michigan cases remain significant as statements of the law, but their practical effect has been undone by Michigan voters who passed a ballot initiative outlawing affirmative action—at least to the extent that it

[20]*Finch v. Peterson*, 622 F.3d 725, 729 (7th Cir. 2010).

[21]*Grutter v. Bollinger*, 539 U.S. 306 (2003); *Gratz v. Bollinger*, 539 U.S. 244 (2003).

[22]*Parents Involved in Community Schools v. Seattle School District No. 1*, 127 S. Ct. 2738 (2007).

[23]*Parents Involved*, at 2754 (italics added for emphasis).

[24]*Wygant*.

[25]*Croson*.

[26]*United States v. Paradise*, 480 U.S. 149 (1987).

involves preferences. Attempts to use the courts to strike these laws down have been unsuccessful.[27]

Clippings

Arizona voters approved a ballot initiative ("Proposition 107") in the November 2010 general election that prohibits the state and city governments from giving preferential treatment based on race, sex, color, ethnicity, or national origin. It applies to public employment, education, and contracting. The law is similar to measures previously adopted in California, Michigan, Nebraska, and Washington. A similar ballot initiative in Colorado was rejected by voters.

William H. Carlile. "Arizona Governor Signs Proclamation Implementing Preferential Treatment Ban." *Daily Labor Report* 240 (December 15, 2010), A-7.

While the Supreme Court has identified diversity as a "compelling governmental interest," courts have generally not extended this holding from the context of higher education to public employment.[28] In *Lomack v. City of Newark*, a public employer's diversity rationale falls far short of the mark.

Lomack v. City of Newark
463 F.3d 303 (3d Cir. 2006)

OPINION BY CIRCUIT JUDGE BARRY:

On July 1, 2002, Sharpe James, newly re-elected as Mayor of Newark, New Jersey, issued a "mandate" in his inaugural speech that, "to improve morale," all single-race fire companies in the Newark Fire Department would be eliminated. The racial composition of each of the 108 fire companies was thereafter examined, and dozens of firefighters were involuntarily transferred to different companies solely on the basis of their race. * * *

It is important at the outset to note what this case is not about. This case is not about whether diverse workplaces are desirable. It is not disputed that they are. Neither is this case about a remedy for unlawful past discrimination because, again, it is not disputed that there was no unlawful discrimination in the past. And this case is not about whether the numbers of

minority firefighters being hired are satisfying long-range hiring goals. Rather, this case is about whether the City of Newark may employ a race-based transfer and assignment policy when any racial imbalance in the 108 fire companies is not the result of past intentional discrimination by the City. We hold that it may not and, accordingly, will reverse the District Court's entry of judgment for the defendants.

In 1977, the United States filed a complaint against the State of New Jersey, several New Jersey officials, the City of Newark, and eleven other New Jersey cities alleging "a pattern or practice of discrimination" in the hiring and promotion of minority firefighters. A Consent Decree resolving the United States' claims was approved and entered by the District Court in 1980. * * * Fifteen years passed, and in 1995, the Newark City Council hired Samuel Rosenfarb, a certified public accountant, to "determine [statistical] compliance with

---

[27]*Coalition to Defend Affirmative Action v. Granholm*, 473 F.3d 237 (6th Cir. 2006); *Coral Construction v. City and County of San Francisco*, 235 P.3d 947 (Cal. 2010).

[28]A notable exception is *Petit v. City of Chicago*, 352 F.3d 1111 (7th Cir. 2003), *cert. denied*, 541 U.S. 1074 (2004).

[the 1980] consent decree." Rosenfarb reported his findings to the Council in a December 1995 report, which indicated that 68.8% of the Fire Department's uniformed employees were white, 24% were black, and 6.9% were Hispanic. He also reported that of 195 promotions granted between 1980 and 1994, 168 were given to white employees, twenty-four to black employees and three to Hispanic employees. In conducting his analysis, Rosenfarb noticed that "the [companies] were significantly homogenous either black or white." His report noted that 81 of the 108 companies "had a majority of white personnel with 30 being comprised entirely of white personnel. Fifteen of the [companies] were predominantly black.... Only one ... had a majority of hispanics. The remaining eleven [companies] did not contain a majority of any one group."

The City took no action with respect to the existence of single-race fire companies for another seven years. Then, in July 2002, Mayor James, apparently out of the blue, ordered that all fire houses, i.e., companies, in the Newark Fire Department be integrated "to improve morale" and "to honor a court order to make our Fire Department the mirror of the City of Newark...." * * * [After an initial attempt that was rejected because it did not meet the mayor's goal] Wallace [the fire chief] proposed an alternative transfer list that would achieve 100% diversity. * * * Thirty-four firefighters who were involuntarily transferred or denied requests to transfer due to the new policy, together with the Newark Firefighters Union and the Newark Fire Officers Union, brought this action ... challenging the constitutionality of the policy under the *Equal Protection Clause*; Title VII of the Civil Rights Act of 1964, and the New Jersey Civil Rights Act. Following a bench trial, the District Court dismissed their claims and entered judgment for defendants. This timely appeal followed.

* * * Because the diversity policy is a race-based classification, it must pass strict scrutiny: it must be narrowly tailored to achieve a compelling state interest. * * * The City argues that it has three somewhat interwoven compelling interests in implementing the diversity policy. First, it argues that it has a compelling interest in eliminating *de facto* segregation in the Fire Department. Second, it contends that there is a compelling interest in securing the "educational, sociological and job performance" benefits of diverse fire companies. Finally, it argues that the policy is required by the 1980 Consent Decree, compliance with which constitutes a compelling interest. As we have already suggested, we are not persuaded by these arguments. We will address each in turn.

1. REMEDYING PAST DISCRIMINATION

It is well settled that a government has a compelling interest in remedying its own past discrimination. Accordingly, it may employ racial classifications to cure racial imbalances—but only if it can prove that it engaged in prior intentional discrimination or was a "passive participant" in a third party's discrimination. "[R]ace-based preferences cannot be justified by reference to past 'societal' discrimination in which the municipality played no material role." * * * The City does not even suggest that it participated, directly or passively, in any form of discrimination; indeed, it concedes that it neither intentionally discriminated against minority firefighters with respect to assignments or transfers, nor intentionally segregated firefighters into racially homogeneous companies. Moreover, the City concedes that single race fire companies resulted, not from "Fire Department management," but from the "tendency on the part of management to allow people to work where they choose to work," and to accommodate their desire to work in the neighborhoods where they live. Accordingly, the remedial justification for the use of racial classifications is wholly inapplicable here, and the District Court's finding to the contrary is clearly erroneous.* * *

2. EDUCATIONAL AND SOCIOLOGICAL BENEFITS OF DIVERSE FIRE COMPANIES

In *Grutter v. Bollinger* [the University of Michigan law school case], the Supreme Court clarified that non-remedial goals may also justify race-based classifications in certain circumstances. Specifically, the *Grutter* Court held—quite narrowly—that the "educational benefits" of a diverse student body are a sufficiently compelling interest to justify race-based enhancements of minority students' applications to law school. The City argues that it has a compelling interest in integrating its fire companies because "integration in the workplace is no less important than in an educational setting." Specifically, it contends that "integration in fire companies leads to greater camaraderie between coworkers, acceptance and consideration for people of varying backgrounds, sharing of information and study support. It also promotes tolerance and mutual respect among colleagues." The District Court agreed, as do we, but went on to find that the "educational, sociological, and job-performance enhancements" supported, if not by themselves compelled, the diversity policy. With that, we disagree.

Initially we note that the under-inclusiveness of the diversity policy, specifically its failure to consider gender, other ethnic groups, age, or socio-economic class, seems to belie Newark's claim that "educational benefits" were its actual purpose. It bears mention, as well, that neither Mayor James nor the Fire Department officials called upon to implement the diversity policy referred to "educational benefits" or anything akin thereto as a reason for the policy. By accepting educational benefits as an interest compelling the policy, however, the District Court, at least implicitly, found that that was the City's "actual purpose," or at least one of its purposes.

We need not resolve whether or not the District Court's finding was clearly erroneous, because even if the alleged "educational benefits" were an "actual purpose," they do not constitute a compelling interest in the circumstances presented by this case. While *Grutter* established that educational benefits are compelling *in a law school context*, we do not find its holding applicable in the firefighting context. The "relevant difference" between a law school and a fire department is their respective missions. The mission of a school is to educate students, "prepar[e] students for work and citizenship," and cultivate future leaders. The *Grutter* Court found, based on extensive testimony and other evidence, that a "critical mass" of diverse students was necessary for the University of Michigan Law School to effectively achieve this mission. But *Grutter* does not stand for the proposition that the educational benefits of diversity are *always* a compelling interest, regardless of the context. Rather, it stands for the narrow premise that the educational benefits of diversity can be a compelling interest to an institution whose mission is to educate.

The Fire Department's mission is not to educate. Its mission is "the control, fighting and extinguishment of any conflagration which occurs within the city limits." Accordingly, *Grutter*'s holding regarding a compelling interest in the educational benefits of diversity is unavailing here. And, we note, the City does not argue that diversity within individual fire companies is in any other way necessary, or even beneficial, to the Fire Department's mission of fighting fires, *i.e.*, that the Department has an operational need for diverse fire companies, and we do not read the City's assertions of increased "camaraderie," "acceptance," and "tolerance" as making such an argument. * * * In sum, we conclude that the benefits of diversity, as set forth by the City, are not a compelling interest that justifies its diversity policy.

3. COMPLIANCE WITH THE 1980 CONSENT DECREE

The City also argues that compliance with the 1980 Consent Decree constitutes a compelling interest. This, too, is unavailing. Compliance with a consent decree may certainly be a compelling interest, but only if the decree *mandates* the race-based policy at issue.... The Consent Decree says nothing about the diversity policy at issue here, much less does it *require* the City to engage in that policy. The Decree establishes policies and benchmarks for the hiring and promotion of minority firefighters, with the only language even arguably relevant here found in one paragraph of the twelve-page Decree where the defendants were prohibited from making unlawfully discriminatory assignments. Reading a complete diversity requirement into that prohibition, however, ... would stretch that language beyond its logical or intended limits. * * *

We conclude this opinion as we began, by reiterating what this case is not about. It is not about remedying intentional discrimination in the Newark Fire Department. It is not about improving the Department's ability to extinguish fires. It is not about whether diverse work places are good for employees or for society or whether long-range hiring goals are being met. This case is about whether Newark can "create[] a rainbow" in each of the 108 companies solely by means of a racial classification. We hold that it cannot. Racial balancing, and that is what this is, simply cannot be achieved by means of a racial classification without running afoul of the *Equal Protection Clause of the Constitution*. Accordingly, we will reverse the order of the District Court, and remand for further proceedings consistent with this opinion.

CASE QUESTIONS

1. What was the legal issue in this case? What did the court decide?
2. Why was a compelling governmental interest lacking in this case?
3. If this case had been argued solely under Title VII rather than the Constitution, would the analysis and outcome have been any different? Why or why not?
4. Should the Supreme Court's holding that a diverse student body is a compelling governmental interest for universities be extended to public employment? Why or why not?
5. Do you agree with the court's decision in this case? Why or why not?

Legal battles over affirmative action have most often involved public employers and their practices for hiring and promoting persons to highly sought-after civil service jobs, particularly positions in police and fire departments. Blatant discrimination against women and people of color by these entities led to numerous lawsuits in the 1960s and 1970s. These lawsuits, in turn, produced court orders and consent decrees, requiring strong affirmative action to undo the legacy of discrimination. Challenges to the continuation of these affirmative action plans have also been numerous. *Dean v. City of Shreveport* is one such case.

Dean v. City of Shreveport
438 F.3d 448 (5th Cir. 2006)

OPINION BY CIRCUIT JUDGE DEMOSS:

Appellants are white males who were denied employment after applying to become City firefighters. At the time Appellants applied, the City used a hiring process that placed applicants into separate lists according to race and sex. The City created its race-conscious hiring process in an attempt to comply with a 1980 consent decree drafted to end discriminatory hiring practices in the City's fire department and to remedy the effects of past discrimination. Appellants challenge both the decree and the hiring process.

In 1977, the U.S. Department of Justice ("DOJ") filed a lawsuit against the City alleging its fire department used racially and sexually discriminatory hiring practices. To settle the lawsuit, the City signed a proposed consent decree providing a plan to end then current discriminatory practices and remedy the effects of past discrimination. * * * [T]he decree sets forth a long-term goal that the City achieve—subject to the availability of qualified applicants—the same proportions of blacks and women in its fire department "as blacks and women bear to the appropriate work force in the particular jurisdiction." * * * The decree also requires the City to adopt an interim hiring goal of filling at least fifty percent of all firefighter vacancies with qualified black applicants and at least fifteen percent with qualified female applicants. The interim goal remains in effect until the long-term goal is achieved and maintained for one year.

The decree itself does not mandate any particular hiring process for meeting its goals. Therefore, the City formed its own process. Phase one requires all firefighter applicants to take the Civil Service Exam. To pass, an applicant needs a score of at least seventy-five.

Points are then added to the scores of applicants with prior emergency medical or paramedic training or military service. When the final numerical scores are calculated, the applicants are separated into three lists: a white male list, a black male list, and a female list. Each list is ranked by exam score from highest to lowest. * * * [S]tarting with the highest exam score on each list, the City selects approximately twice as many applicants as vacant spots to proceed to phase two of the hiring process. Of those selected to proceed, fifty percent of the males are white and fifty percent are black. Every female who receives a seventy-five on the exam usually proceeds to phase two because of the extremely low number of female applicants. * * *

Dean, an unsuccessful white male applicant, sued the City … alleging the decree and the hiring process violate the Equal Protection Clause of the Fourteenth Amendment. * * * In October 2004, the magistrate judge denied Dean's motion for summary judgment and granted the City's, dismissing all claims against the City. This timely appeal followed. * * *

It is well settled that the government has a compelling interest in remedying its own past discrimination. However, a general assertion of past societal discrimination is insufficient. Rather, the government must justify its action with a showing of past discrimination by the governmental unit seeking to use the race-conscious remedy. * * *

The district court concluded that the City made an adequate showing of past discrimination. We agree. Prior to 1974, the City's fire department had never hired a black employee. In 1974, after it was sued by black applicants alleging racially discriminatory hiring practices, the City hired three black firefighters. After the lawsuit was settled, the City hired no black employees in 1975, just one black firefighter in 1976, and no black employees in 1977. In 1977, another lawsuit was brought against the City, this time by the DOJ, alleging racially and sexually discriminatory hiring practices. In the time between the 1977 lawsuit and the 1980 decree, the City hired only six additional black firefighters. Thus, when the decree was entered to settle the DOJ lawsuit, only 10 of the City's 270 firefighters were black. At that time, blacks accounted for approximately forty percent of the general population in the City of Shreveport. Further, the City now admits it systematically excluded all black applicants prior to 1974 and hired the few it did between 1974 and 1980 in response to pending lawsuits. * * *

We recognize that the relevant comparison when determining whether discrimination existed is between the number of black firefighters in the City's fire department and the "number of [blacks] qualified to undertake the particular task," not the number of blacks in the general population. We are also aware that the City has not presented a precise calculation of how many black applicants were qualified to become firefighters in the years leading up to the 1980 decree. Nevertheless, we find it inconceivable that the number of qualified blacks was … "zero." In most cases, a governmental unit's failure to provide statistical data comparing the number of minorities in its work force with the number of minorities qualified to undertake the particular task, rather than the number of minorities in the general population, will prove fatal to an attempt to show past discrimination. But in rare cases, the statistical disparity may be so great between a particular work force and the general population that, along with other overwhelming evidence, it may provide us with an adequate basis to conclude no genuine factual issue remains regarding the existence of past discrimination.

This is such a case. In addition to the fact that the City hired no black employees prior to 1974 and only 10 black firefighters as of 1980, the overwhelming evidence shows that (1) the City now admits that for over 100 years it systematically excluded all minorities from its fire department; (2) the City has been sued numerous times for racial and sexual discrimination; and (3) Appellants have failed to offer any alternative explanation, expert or otherwise, for the gross statistical disparity. Therefore, the district court properly concluded that the City had a compelling interest in 1980 to enter into the decree and implement a race-conscious hiring process.

The City argues that this conclusion ends our compelling interest inquiry. We disagree. In addition to showing past discrimination, the City must also convince us that when Appellants were denied employment between 2000 and 2002, lingering effects of past discrimination still necessitated a race-conscious remedy. * * * On remand, the City must properly define a "qualified applicant." It must then provide reliable statistical data showing the percentages of blacks in its work force and in its qualified labor pool between 2000 and 2002. Only when the district court has this information can it properly decide whether a sufficient disparity still existed.* * * Although this alone requires us to reverse the district court's judgment and remand the case for further factual development, we will also review the court's narrow tailoring analysis.

2. NARROW TAILORING

The Supreme Court has focused on the following factors ("Paradise factors") when reviewing a race-conscious remedy to ensure it is narrowly tailored: the necessity of the particular relief and the efficacy of alternative remedies; the flexibility and duration of the relief, including the availability of waiver provisions; the relationship between the numerical goal of the relief and the relevant labor market; and the impact of the relief on the rights of third parties. * * *

a. Necessity of the Particular Relief and Efficacy of Alternative Remedies

The district court concluded that the decree's interim hiring goal and the City's hiring process were necessary remedies. The court also decided that alternative remedies would have been insufficient to remedy past discrimination. * * * The court reasoned that "the absolute lack of black or female firefighters prior to the institution of [the 1973] litigation, followed by a lapse in minority hiring until … the [1980] consent decree," made strong remedial measures necessary. This may have been true in 1980. However, these events alone do not illustrate whether strong measures were still necessary when Appellants were denied employment. On remand, the City must show that the decree and hiring process were necessary when Appellants were denied employment between 2000 and 2002 * * * [and] that race-neutral or less intrusive remedies would have been insufficient between 2000 and 2002.

In addition, the record is currently too inconsistent to determine what alternative remedies, if any, the City has already attempted and whether those or any others will suffice. For example, one alternative to race-conscious hiring is increased recruiting efforts targeting minorities. * * * When asked whether the City's recruiting policy is adequately geared towards attracting minorities, Chief Cochran admitted, "the City has never done any kind of self-evaluation to see if its recruiting efforts are appropriate for recruiting minorities and women." Thus, the efficacy of alternative measures remains a genuine issue of material fact that must be resolved on remand.

b. Flexibility and Duration

The district court found the decree and the hiring process adequately flexible. The court also decided that their long duration did not preclude finding the remedies narrowly tailored. The primary question when analyzing a remedy's flexibility is whether its requirements may be waived. If they may, the remedy is adequately flexible. * * * While the decree does not allow the goals to be waived, it does specify that they are "subject to the availability of qualified applicants."

Despite this explicit exception, Appellants argue that the decree and hiring policy require a rigid fifty percent racial quota. The City, relying on the waiver provision, insists both are flexible. The City also points out that since 1980, it has hired less than fifty percent black employees in all but two hiring classes. We agree with the district court that the remedies are adequately flexible. We do so because the remedies here, as far as their flexibility is concerned, parallel the flexibility of the remedy in Paradise. In that case, the Alabama Department of Public Safety was required to award half of all state trooper promotions to black employees. However, the requirement was contingent on the availability of qualified candidates. This alone satisfied the flexibility requirement. Like the remedy in Paradise, the remedies here are contingent on the availability of qualified applicants and are therefore adequately flexible. * * *

c. Relationship Between the Numerical Goal and the Relevant Labor Market

* * * The long-term numerical goal of a race-conscious remedy must be closely tied to the relevant labor market. * * * Until we know the numerical goal of the decree and the relevant labor market, the relationship between the numerical goal and the relevant labor market remains a genuine issue of material fact to be resolved on remand.

d. Impact of the Relief on Third Parties

The final Paradise factor ensures a remedy does "not impose an unacceptable burden on innocent third parties." The district court found the impact on third parties "not overly significant" in this case. * * * First, remedies requiring nonminorities to be fired impose a severe, and possibly unacceptable, burden on third parties. Hiring preferences are less burdensome. Second, remedies allowing unqualified minorities to be hired are likely not narrowly tailored. Third, remedies merely postponing a benefit to third parties are less burdensome than ones permanently denying a benefit. We agree with the district court that the impact on nonminorities is not significant enough to make the decree and hiring policy unconstitutional per se. * * *

APPELLANTS' TITLE VII CLAIM

Appellants also argue that the City's hiring process violates Title VII. * * * [B]y separating applicants' Civil Service Exam scores by race, the City in effect uses different cutoff scores on the basis of race. We agree…. * * * [This] decision … will stand even if on remand the district court finds that the hiring process passes scrutiny under the Equal Protection Clause [i.e., is constitutional]. * * *

The City [claims] … that the hiring process does not violate the statute because "every applicant, black or white, has to score at least a seventy-five to pass the Civil Service Exam." This conclusion is incomplete, however, because it focuses only on the initial portion of phase one of the City's hiring process instead of on the entire process. The City is correct that all applicants are subject to the same initial requirement at phase one—a score of at least seventy-five on the Civil Service Exam. * * * Later in the process the City again uses the exam scores to choose which applicants will proceed to phase two of the hiring process. The City separates applicants' exam scores by race and sex and selects the same number of blacks and whites to proceed, starting with the highest exam score on each segregated list. This method of selection between phase one and phase two violates the plain language of [Title VII] because it has the practical effect of requiring different cutoff scores, based solely on race and sex, for continuing further in the hiring process. * * *

CASE QUESTIONS

1. What are the legal issues in this case? What did the court decide?

2. In light of the lengthy history of blatant discrimination against African Americans by the city and its fire department, why is there a question as to whether there is a compelling governmental (state) interest in following the affirmative action requirements set out in the consent decree? How can the city prove that there continues to be a compelling governmental interest in race-conscious hiring?

3. If it is shown on remand that the city's hiring of African Americans has increased substantially since inception of the consent decree in 1980 and that the fire department has closed some, but not all, of the gap between the racial composition of its workforce and the percentage of qualified African Americans in the surrounding area, would that be evidence that there is no longer a compelling governmental interest at stake or does it simply demonstrate the efficacy and continued necessity of the affirmative action plan that has been in place?

4. What factors do courts consider to determine if a particular method of affirmative action is "narrowly tailored"? What observations does the court make about whether Shreveport's affirmative action plan is narrowly tailored?

5. Why does the court conclude that, regardless of the constitutional issues, the city has violated Title VII?

6. If the courts ultimately rule against the city, what should it do instead?

Ingredients of Affirmative Action Plans

What do affirmative action plans look like? The EEOC guidelines state that voluntary affirmative action plans must contain three basic elements: a reasonable self-analysis, a reasonable basis for concluding that action is appropriate, and reasonable action.[29] DOL regulations implementing E.O. 11246 contain more detailed requirements for contractors' affirmative action plans,[30] as outlined in Figure 8.1. Because most of the requirements for affirmative action plans under E.O. 11246 fall within the EEOC's three broad categories, they are used to organize the following discussion of the contents of affirmative action plans.

FIGURE 8.1 Required Contents for Affirmative Action Plans Under E.O. 11246

I. Quantitative analyses of the workforce
  A. Organizational profile
  B. Job group analysis
  C. Protected-class composition of job group incumbents
  D. Availability of qualified women and people of color
  E. Comparison of job group incumbents with available, qualified workforce

II. Identification of problem areas
  A. Problems in minority or female utilization or distribution (e.g., glass ceilings)
  B. Personnel activities (e.g., applicant flows, promotions, turnover)
  C. Compensation systems—gender or racial disparities
  D. Selection, recruitment, and referral procedures

III. Placement goals
IV. Action-oriented programs
V. Designation of responsibility for implementation
VI. Procedures for periodic internal audits of progress in meeting goals

---

[29]29 C.F.R. § 1608.4 (2011).
[30]41 C.F.R. § 60-2.10(b) (2011).

Reasonable Self-Analysis

The EEOC guidelines state that the "objective of a self-analysis is to determine whether employment practices do, or tend to, exclude, disadvantage, restrict, or result in adverse impact or disparate treatment of previously excluded or restricted groups or leave uncorrected the effects of prior discrimination, and if so, to determine why."[31] Although the EEOC does not mandate any particular form of **self-analysis**, the requirements for federal contractors with affirmative action plans under E.O. 11246—including an organizational profile, job group analysis, documentation of the protected class characteristics of incumbents, and identification of problem areas—provide a concrete model for a thorough self-analysis. In general, this analysis is done at the level of individual establishments or workplaces. Contractors with multiple workplaces must create affirmative action plans for each location, rather than rely on company-wide plans. However, the OFCCP sometimes permits the use of "functional affirmative action programs" that cover an entire business function (e.g., sales, R&D) or line of business within a company.[32]

An **organizational profile** portrays the staffing patterns in an organization. DOL regulations allow contractors to provide this information in the form of either an *organizational display or a workforce analysis*. An **organizational display** (like an organizational chart) depicts the organizational structure of a company, including the units within it and the relationship of each unit to other units in the organization. *For each unit*, information must be provided on the demographics of the supervisor, the total number of males and females, and the total number of males and females broken down by race and ethnicity (African American, Latino, Asians/Pacific Islanders, Native Americans/ Alaska Natives).

The alternative approach, a **workforce analysis**, requires that individual job titles be listed for each department or other organizational unit in order of pay level. Separate lines of progression in an organizational unit need to be identified. Then, *for each job title*, the same demographic information is provided as stated for the organizational display. The organizational profile is especially helpful in identifying patterns of segregation in an organization, whereby women or persons of color are concentrated within a few units or job titles.

Because skill levels and the available labor force differ substantially across jobs, relatively refined data should be used. Gross portraits of whole organizations or units are not sufficient. Yet, at the same time, dealing with large numbers of individual job titles, some of which might be closely related, becomes unwieldy. In a **job group analysis**, the individual job titles in a contractor's workforce are combined into a more parsimonious set of job groups. The criteria for performing a job group analysis are similarity in job content, pay level, and opportunities for advancement. Contractors with fewer than 150 employees are permitted to use a standard set of job groups established by the EEOC: officials and managers, professionals, technicians, sales, office and clerical, craft workers (skilled), operatives (semiskilled), laborers (unskilled), and service workers.

The forgoing analyses document protected class characteristics of an employer's workforce and the location of women and minorities within the organization. The **identification of problem areas** makes the self-analysis more dynamic by examining flows into and out of positions and the organization. It attempts to get at the question

Practical Considerations To analyze their workforces and determine if affirmative action is needed, employers must document the protected class characteristics of their employees. How can this be accomplished in an effective and legal manner?

---

[31]29 C.F.R. § 1608.4(a) (2011).

[32]41 C.F.R. § 60-2.1(d)(4) (2011); "OFCCP Issues New Directive to Resume Functional Affirmative Action Programs." *Daily Labor Report* 124 (June 28, 2011), AA-1.

of why an employer's workforce looks the way it does. The identification of problem areas is wide-ranging, touching on all aspects of human resource practice, including compensation.

Reasonable Basis for Affirmative Action

A key concept in determining whether a reasonable basis exists for affirmative action is **underutilization**. Underutilization exists when the percentage of women or persons of color in one or more of an employer's job groups is lower than the percentage of women or persons of color with the necessary skills for that type of employment. Under DOL regulations, contractors need to compare the demographics of their existing workforce with the availability of women and minorities for each of their job groups. When the percentage of women or persons of color in a particular job group is less than would be expected based on their availability, the contractor is required to establish a placement goal. Availability is determined by considering two main factors: "the percentage of minorities or women with requisite skills in the reasonable recruitment area" and "the percentage of minorities or women among those promotable, transferable, and trainable within the contractor's organization."[33] The reasonable recruitment area is the geographical area in which the contractor typically recruits or could reasonably do so for the jobs in question. "Trainable" or "promotable" refers to persons who could, with training that the employer could reasonably provide, be rendered qualified within the plan year. The point is simply that *employers embarking on affirmative action need to analyze underutilization by carefully considering the availability of qualified women and persons of color, both in the external labor market and within their organization, and compare availability to current utilization.*

Where does all this information about availability come from? Data for determining the availability of trainable and promotable persons come from an employer's own records, the analysis of which is facilitated if the employer maintains an inventory of employee skills. Data for determining the availability of women and persons of color in the reasonable recruitment area are derived mainly from the census but might also include information from state employment services, colleges, or other training institutions. The data used for determining availability need to be as current and as closely matched to the job group and geographic area in question as possible.

How large does the discrepancy between availability and current utilization have to be to conclude underutilization exists? There is no single, precise answer. The Supreme Court has consistently referred to the need for evidence of a "manifest imbalance" to justify affirmative action, but the degree of underutilization need not be so large as to violate the four-fifths rule. Nor is it necessary, at least for private employers under Title VII, to show that the underutilization of women and persons of color is the result of discrimination. The basic premise is that absent discriminatory practices in the past or present, the percentage of women and persons of color working in jobs should roughly match the percentage of women and persons of color available in the relevant labor market. The more that availability and utilization diverge, the more need there is to take actions to extend equal employment opportunity. Thus, *it is not necessary that the problematic employment practices be severe enough to violate Title VII or that employers admit to violating the law to have a **reasonable basis** for affirmative action.* The point of the self-analysis is to encourage employers to fix problems before they become more severe—and possibly objects of litigation.

---

[33]41 C.F.R. § 60-2.14(c) (2011).

Reasonable Affirmative Actions

If underutilization of women and persons of color exists, what affirmative actions are warranted? One thing that **reasonable actions** include is identifying **goals** for improvement in the utilization of women and minorities and **timetables** for achieving those goals. The EEOC guidelines counsel that goals should take into account the effects of past discrimination, the need for prompt improvement, the availability of qualified or qualifiable candidates, and the number of employment opportunities likely to be available (e.g., based on anticipated growth, turnover). In essence, the more severe the problem of underutilization and the more opportunity there is to remedy it, the more ambitious an employer's goals should be. DOL regulations require that federal government contractors establish placement goals for all job groups for which evidence exists of underutilization of women or people of color. The goals set by contractors must be at least equal to the availability of women and minorities for the job groups in question. Unless there are substantial differences in utilization rates for particular minority groups or for men and women within minority groups, contractors are generally required to establish a single goal for minority placement in each job group where underutilization is noted.

DOL regulations stress that goals serve as "objectives or targets" reasonably attainable through **good faith effort**. There is more than a semantic difference between *goals* and *quotas*. Contractors' "[p]lacement goals may not be rigid and inflexible quotas, which must be met, nor are they to be considered as either a ceiling or a floor for the employment of particular groups. Quotas are expressly forbidden."[34] No doubt it can be difficult for managers, who are accustomed to being evaluated according to attainment of quantitative sales or financial goals, to treat placement goals in a serious but flexible manner. In one reverse discrimination case, a university dean refused to hire a male as a professor in the psychology department, despite the department's strong support for the candidate. The dean's statements betrayed a fundamental misunderstanding of the nature of affirmative action goals: "[T]he hiring goals for the [psychology department] is [*sic*] 61.8 percent women and 9.8 percent minorities…. Thus, the department needs 3.23 women to reach its target…. We cannot send two male candidates forward, given the targets in the department."[35] The court ruled against the university and mused, "[H]ow it was going to appoint 23/100 of a woman Ross [the dean] did not explain." *Employers with affirmative action plans should establish goals as benchmarks against which improvement in the use of underutilized women or persons of color can be measured. A sincere good faith effort to improve the utilization of women and persons of color is called for, not mindless adherence to numerical goals.*

At its best, affirmative action involves a creative effort to solve problems and to go beyond the minimum requirements of the law in extending equal employment opportunity. No finite set of measures constitutes reasonable affirmative actions. The measures that are instituted should correspond to the particular problems identified through self-analysis. Figure 8.2 provides examples of reasonable affirmative actions that do not entail the use of preferences in hiring or promotion. *Employers should make the most of these improvements in human resource practices before considering the use of preferences to achieve affirmative action goals.* Retaining the valuable services of women and people of color is just as important as hiring a diverse group of new employees. *Employers should be concerned about higher turnover among women and people of color. Affirmative action should also be directed at this problem, particularly by eliminating obstacles to advancement and fostering a more welcoming and inclusive organizational climate.*

---

[34] 41 C.F.R. § 60-2.16(e)(1) (2011).

[35] *Hill v. Ross*, 183 F.3d 586, 588–89 (7th Cir. 1999).

FIGURE 8.2 Examples of Reasonable Affirmative Actions

Recruitment	• Communicate the availability of jobs widely. • Develop relationships with religious organizations, community development groups, schools, and cultural organizations that can refer qualified people of color. • Adjust the geographic scope of recruiting. • Use internships and summer jobs to identify qualified women and people of color. • Work with training institutions, such as by providing scholarships, to diversify the pool of persons with needed skills. • Establish or maintain facilities in communities with substantial minority populations.
Selection Procedures	• Validate all scored employment tests. • Eliminate or find alternatives for tests and other requirements that disproportionately screen out women or people of color. • Lean toward a compensatory approach in evaluating candidates (considering multiple criteria in a portfolio fashion, where weaknesses in one area can be offset by strengths in another) rather than strict cutoff levels or multiple hurdles. • "Band" test scores and select from within bands rather than simply choosing the highest score. • Offer assistance to candidates in preparing for tests that tend to screen out women or minorities. • Use multiple well-trained interviewers to conduct structured interviews. • Limit reliance on highly subjective criteria.
Training and Development	• Provide extensive skills training and development opportunities for employees. • Fund tuition costs for employees to upgrade their skills. • Redesign jobs to better prepare employees to move on to other jobs in the organization. • Provide or arrange for English language and literacy courses. • Maintain inventories of employees' skills and work experiences. • Provide formal mentoring and career planning assistance for employees.
Organizational Climate	• Actively enforce antidiscrimination and harassment policies. • Institute work-life programs and do not penalize employees who use them. • Sponsor company social and recreational events that do not exclude women and people of color. • Use inclusive language in reports, memos, and other documents. • Facilitate support groups for women and people of color. • Offer diversity training and programs.

© Cengage Learning 2013.

Effects of Affirmative Action

Some reasons for opposition to affirmative action, such as the view that race or sex should never be considered in employment decisions regardless of the purpose, are more philosophical than empirical. However, other grounds, such as the argument that affirmative action results in the hiring of unqualified persons, are based on assumptions about its effects. One of the most comprehensive studies[36] of the effects of affirmative action surveyed 3,200 employers and looked at differences between firms that did not use affirmative action, those that used it for recruiting only, and those that used it for both recruiting and hiring. Among the major findings were the following:

- Firms using affirmative action used a wider variety of recruitment mechanisms, particularly those likely to reach minority applicants (e.g., community agencies).
- Firms using affirmative action engaged in more intensive screening of applicants, but were also less likely to screen out candidates based on criminal background or lengthy prior unemployment.
- Firms using affirmative action recruited and hired somewhat more women and people of color, with women being the clearest beneficiaries.
- Firms using affirmative action in recruiting generally hired people with comparable educational credentials compared to firms without affirmative action. Firms using affirmative action in hiring hired workers with somewhat lower educational credentials.
- Overall, job performance levels for women and people of color in firms using affirmative action were equal to, and for some groups exceeded, the typical job performance level of employees in those firms.
- Greater investment in training by firms using affirmative action appears to counteract any lower educational credentials of persons hired.

Practical Considerations It is often recommended that managers be evaluated and rewarded in significant part on the basis of their commitment to diversity. Is this a good idea? If so, how should this be done?

The overall picture of affirmative action's effects emerging from this study and others is reasonably positive and does not comport with the view that affirmative action has a negative impact on the quality of the workforce. Perhaps this is because there are usually more qualified candidates than jobs and thus, given the opportunity and perhaps some training, people who seem slightly less qualified on paper can still do a good job. Nor should it be assumed—given the prevalence of discrimination, sloppy screening, organizational politics, favoritism, the limitations of available selection devices, and the idiosyncrasies of hiring decision makers engaging in subjective assessments—that, in the absence of affirmative action, the most able person necessarily gets the job.

Diversity and Affirmative Action

Affirmative action overlaps with the broader and increasingly pervasive notion of valuing **diversity** in the workplace. But a shift in semantics and underlying rationales does not obviate the legal issues that surround affirmative action programs. Indeed, these issues might be further complicated by murkiness in diversity programs about the role that protected class considerations play in the making of employment decisions—and how far employers can go in showing their commitment to diversity.

---

[36]Harry J. Holzer and David Neumark. "What Does Affirmative Action Do?" *Industrial and Labor Relations Review* 53 (January 2000), 240–71.

THE CHANGING WORKPLACE

Diversity in the Workplace

The need to pay attention to workplace diversity is quite real. In workplaces where employees are more likely than ever to come into contact with coworkers and customers who are different in some important ways from themselves, learning how to peacefully and productively coexist—or better yet, to value and benefit from each other's distinctive cultures and contributions—is imperative. Diversity programs are aimed at encouraging awareness and appreciation of human and cultural differences, becoming more adept at interacting with others not like us, learning to avoid stereotyping and bias, and creating workplaces that are truly inclusive. While diversity is generally understood to incorporate forms of difference beyond those that are protected class characteristics, the likes of race and sex remain central to diversity initiatives.

Diversity is an attractive concept for many reasons, including its positive tone asserting that a wide range of differences should be valued (as opposed to merely tolerated or assimilated into the ways of a dominant group), its emphasis on the inclusion of everyone, and the notion that diversity is an asset to organizational performance. In contrast, affirmative action has a negative connotation for many people. It is portrayed as being obsessed with head counts and helping women and people of color at the expense of whites and males. This view of affirmative action certainly does not capture its potential nor, to a considerable extent, actual practice. But in whatever ways diversity initiatives differ from or go beyond engaging in affirmative action, diversity is not a legal term. Except in the context of college admissions, valuing diversity has carried little weight as a defense to discrimination charges.

A widely cited analysis of workplace diversity distinguishes between three approaches, or "paradigms," for managing diversity: discrimination-and-fairness; access-and-legitimacy; and learning-and-effectiveness.[1] *The discrimination-and-fairness* approach to diversity is oriented toward legal concerns. This paradigm has been criticized for paying too much attention to getting people in the door and too little to making good use of their diverse talents and perspectives. However, for women and minorities to meaningfully contribute in organizations, it remains necessary for them to get hired, advance to higher levels, and be retained. Further, they must be present in more than token numbers if their unique voices are to be heard and heeded. Equal employment opportunity laws focus precisely on those differences (e.g., race, sex, national origin) that are primary sources of identity and distinct perspectives in the workplace. The *access-and-legitimacy* paradigm treats diversity as a means of accessing increasingly diverse and global markets. The legal constraints on this strategy are very real. If employers are not careful, the aim of matching employees to markets can result in facially discriminatory job assignments and segregation. The *learning-and-effectiveness* approach is multicultural in nature and views maximizing the distinctive contributions of a diverse workforce as essential to organizational effectiveness. Legal issues arise here as well because protection from harassment, reasonable accommodation, and other legal responsibilities of employers affect the ability of women, people of color, and the disabled to fully contribute. In short, one does not avoid grappling with legal issues simply by invoking diversity as a value.

There are consequences to emphasizing the utility of workforce diversity to employers rather than the considerations of social justice that have traditionally served as the basic rationale for affirmative action. The primary motivation for employer actions becomes organizational performance rather than legal compliance. The types of diversity that are relevant expand beyond those that constitute protected classes under the law. Edelman and her colleagues have observed that:

> Diversity rhetoric, which tends to equate differences based on geography or taste in sports or dress style with differences based on race or sex, offers a conception of equal employment opportunity that is quite different from that embodied in the statutory language of Title VII or other civil rights laws. Diversity rhetoric replaced the legal vision of diversity, which is grounded in moral efforts to right historical wrongs, with a manage-

rial vision of diversity, which is grounded in the notion that organizations must adapt to their environments in order to profit.[2]

If obtaining the benefits of diversity is the primary issue, it can be argued that there are many forms of diversity, and protected class characteristics such as race do not necessarily occupy a privileged place among forms of difference.[3] If, on the other hand, social justice is the fundamental issue, eradicating the corrosive effects of past and current discrimination still dictates special concern for women and people of color.

---

[1]David A. Thomas and Robin J. Ely. "Making Differences Matter: A New Paradigm for Managing Diversity." *Harvard Business Review* (September–October 1996), 79–90.
[2]Lauren B. Edelman, Sally Riggs Fuller, and Iona Mara-Drita. "Diversity Rhetoric and the Managerialization of Law." *American Journal of Sociology* 106, 6 (May 2001), 1626.
[3]*Johnson v. Board of Regents of the University of Georgia*, 263 F.3d 1234, at 1253 (11th Cir. 2001).

© Cengage Learning 2013.

Cases in which diversity efforts—not specifically grounded in affirmative action plans—lead to reverse discrimination claims are likely to become increasingly common. In one such case,[37] a jury verdict holding a group of defendants liable for discriminating against white males in making promotions to the rank of police captain was upheld. The court took note of the fact that the commissioners had evaluated the police chief on his ability to foster diversity and that this was the only aspect of the chief's performance with which the commissioners consistently expressed satisfaction. A consent decree governing affirmative action in initial hiring but not promotions was in place at the beginning of the chief's tenure. The court found that while decision makers "embraced a view of increasing diversity," there was "no policy, no set parameters and no means of assessing how race should be weighed with other promotional criteria."[38] Declaring that the court had "never approved such a loose and indeed effectively standardless approach, the court concluded that [a] race-conscious promotion system with no identifiable standards to narrowly tailor it to the specific, identifiable, compelling needs of the municipal department cannot pass constitutional scrutiny."[39] Likewise, the New Orleans district attorney was found liable for reverse discrimination stemming from events that transpired after he took office.[40] On the new DA's arrival, non-attorney staff members were required to submit to an interview process to retain their jobs. The outcome of this process was that within 72 days of taking office, the racial composition of the non-attorney staff had changed from 77 whites and 56 African Americans to 27 whites and 130 African Americans. 53 white employees were terminated, along with one Latino and two African Americans. The DA claimed that the termination decisions were made on a variety of grounds other than race, including the desire to have political supporters in his office. The DA's transition team had created a "cultural diversity report," which stated that within 100 days of taking office, the racial composition of the DA's office should be made more reflective of the surrounding population. Based on the strong statistical evidence of discrimination and the existence of the report, the court ruled for the plaintiffs.

---

[37]*Alexander v. City of Milwaukee*, 474 F.3d 437 (7th Cir. 2007).

[38]*Alexander*, at 445.

[39]*Alexander*, at 446.

[40]*Decorte v. Jordon*, 497 F.3d 433 (5th Cir. 2007).

JUST THE FACTS

An employee sought promotion to a managerial position. The position was announced both internally and externally. The stated qualifications included a graduate business degree and five to seven years of sourcing-related experience. The employee received the highest score on a panel interview. Shortly thereafter and before the position was filled, the employer received an inquiry from an African American woman. The HR department determined that the woman was qualified even though she did not have at least five years of sourcing experience. She was added to the applicant pool. From the manager charged with making the hiring decision, the woman received a score on the interview that was two points lower than the score of the employee. Nonetheless, the woman was hired. A member of the interview panel subsequently told the employee that although his interview had gone well, he believed that the hiring manager "had a diversity issue" because she was a member of the company's Workforce Diversity Program and it would have looked bad if she had hired all whites for positions reporting to her. The manager denied basing the decision on race and cited a number of qualities and experiences that she said made the African American woman hired the best candidate.

See, *Reilly v. TXU Corp.*, 2008 U.S. App. LEXIS 5657 (5th Cir.).

Diversity programs might also generate retaliation claims. An employee who became actively involved with his employer's new diversity program alleged that this involvement was one of the reasons that evaluations of his performance were downgraded and it was suggested that he pursue other career paths.[41] The court permitted his retaliation (and disparate treatment) claims to go to trial. It should not be surprising that participation in diversity programs sometimes elicits criticism of an employer's civil rights practices. Such statements can be construed as protected "opposition" and become the basis for retaliation claims if the employees are subsequently subjected to materially adverse actions. *Employers with diversity programs should be aware that the goal of valuing diversity does not justify actions that would otherwise be discriminatory and refrain from any such actions.*

Key Terms

affirmative action, p. 237
Executive Order 11246, p. 238
nondiscrimination clause, p. 238
Office of Federal Contract Compliance Programs (OFCCP), p. 238
consent decree, p. 241
preference, p. 241
reverse discrimination, p. 242

strict scrutiny, p. 246
compelling governmental interest, p. 246
narrowly tailored, p. 246
self-analysis, p. 255
organizational profile, p. 255
organizational display, p. 255
workforce analysis, p. 255
job group analysis, p. 255

identification of problem areas, p. 255
underutilization, p. 256
reasonable basis, p. 256
reasonable action, p. 257
goal, p. 257
timetable, p. 257
good faith effort, p. 257
diversity, p. 259

---

[41]*Garrett v. Hewlett-Packard*, 305 F.3d 1210 (10th Cir. 2002).

Chapter Summary

Affirmative action is a systematic program aimed at overcoming the effects of prior or continuing discrimination and removing barriers to equal employment opportunity. Ad hoc decisions to favor particular groups are not affirmative action. Rigid quota systems are not affirmative action. Because affirmative action aims to overcome the lingering effects of discrimination, it is used only on behalf of groups that have historically been victimized by discrimination: women, African Americans, Latinos, Asians, Pacific Islanders, Native Americans, disabled persons, and certain veterans.

The two situations in which employers are required to engage in affirmative action are when they have contracts to provide goods or services to the federal (and in many cases, state) government and when a lawsuit results in either a consent decree or a court order specifying affirmative action as a remedy for discrimination. Otherwise, employers decide whether to adopt affirmative action programs. Affirmative action on behalf of women and minorities by federal contractors is governed by E.O. 11246. Enforcement of E.O. 11246 and other nondiscrimination and affirmative action requirements for federal contractors is carried out by the Office of Federal Contract Compliance Programs (OFCCP). Less far-reaching affirmative action requirements also arise under the Rehabilitation Act (for qualified disabled persons) and the Vietnam Era Veterans Readjustment Assistance Act (for "protected veterans").

Much affirmative action focuses on modifying employers' recruiting, selection, training, development, and other human resource practices to facilitate the identification, hiring, advancement, and retention of qualified women and persons of color. Affirmative action plans created in compliance with E.O. 11246 are limited to such measures. Some affirmative action plans go further and use preferences based on protected class when hiring and promotion decisions are made, such as by using race as a tiebreaker between relatively equal candidates or as a plus factor. Preferences are sometimes challenged as reverse discrimination. Under Title VII, employers must show that their affirmative action plans were adopted to correct "manifest imbalances" in their workforces and that the measures used to accomplish this do not unnecessarily infringe on whites or males. Evidence of a manifest imbalance in Title VII cases typically comes from an analysis of underutilization in which, for each major job group, the percentages of qualified women and minorities available in the surrounding workforce are compared to the percentages of women and minorities currently used by an employer.

The affirmative action plans of public employers are sometimes challenged on constitutional grounds as violating the equal protection provisions of the U.S. Constitution. Government agencies seeking to defend the use of racial preferences must show that their affirmative action plans serve a "compelling governmental interest" and that the measures used are "narrowly tailored" to achieve this important purpose with the least possible harm to non-preferred groups. Evidence of prior discrimination by the public employer is most often required to justify affirmative action, although the Supreme Court has also recognized student body diversity as a compelling governmental interest in the context of higher education. Several states have enacted legislation prohibiting the use of preferences in public employment, education, and contracting. Overall, the law has shifted in the direction of greater restriction of the use of preferences in affirmative action plans.

Under EEOC guidelines, an affirmative action plan must include a reasonable self-study to document the protected class composition of an employer's workforce and its human resource practices; evidence of a reasonable basis for engaging in affirmative action, including an analysis of underutilization; and reasonable actions that will be taken to correct problems and improve the utilization of women and minorities. There are more extensive requirements for affirmative action plans under E.O. 11246, including quantitative analyses of the contractor's workforce, identification of problem areas, placement goals for each job group evidencing underutilization, action-oriented programs, delegation of responsibility for implementation, and procedures for periodic audits of progress in goal attainment.

The concept of managing diversity is a popular way of thinking about the employment and utilization of women, people of color, and other groups. The contribution of diversity to organizational effectiveness provides employers with additional incentive—beyond the need for legal compliance—to attend to the presence and experiences of diverse persons in their organizations. However, diversity is not a legal concept and the motive of valuing diversity does not exempt an employer's actions from legal requirements or scrutiny. The business case for diversity should not be confused with or obscure the social justice concerns, rooted in the lengthy history of discrimination against African Americans and other protected classes, that provide the fundamental basis for affirmative action.

Practical Advice Summary

- Federal contractors and subcontractors with contracts worth at least $10,000 must
  - Have a nondiscrimination clause in their contracts and abide by its terms.
  - Take affirmative action to employ qualified persons with disabilities.
- Federal contractors and subcontractors with at least fifty employees and contracts worth at least $50,000 must
  - Develop written affirmative action plans addressing employment of women and minorities and submit them to the OFCCP within 120 days of their contracts commencing.
  - Develop and maintain affirmative action plans for the employment of qualified disabled persons.
- Federal contractors and subcontractors with contracts worth more than $100,000 must
  - Provide equal employment opportunity and affirmative action on behalf of protected veterans.
  - List all employment openings, other than top management jobs, with state employment services.
- Employers wanting to engage in affirmative action must have valid, written affirmative action plans in place.
- Employers engaging in voluntary affirmative action should
  - Maximize the use of improvements in recruitment, selection, training, development, and organizational climate before considering hiring and promotion preferences.
  - Pay particular attention to retaining and advancing women and persons of color already employed.
- Affirmative action should

- Not be undertaken until the employer has determined that there is underutilization of women or persons of color.
  - Be temporary and discontinued after the identified underutilization has been eliminated.
  - Not include the establishment of quotas, set-asides of positions for women or minorities, or the hiring of unqualified candidates to meet affirmative action goals.
  - Never be used as a basis for making discipline and termination decisions.
- Public employers must
  - Be able to show that any racial preferences are needed to undo prior discrimination by the employer.
  - Be able to show that effective race-neutral alternatives are not available and the particular affirmative actions taken are flexible, time-limited, and no more burdensome than necessary.
- All affirmative action plans should include
  - Results of a reasonable self-study.
  - Analysis of underutilization establishing the basis for affirmative action.
  - Reasonable actions to improve the utilization of women and persons of color.
- Affirmative action plans of government contractors must include
  - Quantitative analyses of current and available workforces.
  - Identification of problem areas, placement goals, and timetables for all job groups showing underutilization.
  - Action-oriented programs to improve utilization.
- Employers with diversity initiatives or programs should be aware that the goal of valuing diversity does not justify actions that would otherwise be discriminatory and refrain from any such actions.

Chapter Questions

1. A white male applicant took a test for a job at General Motors, which has an affirmative action plan that includes a Pre-Apprentice Program (PAP). Minority applicants can participate in this program, and bonus points are added to their test scores. Two minority applicants who initially scored lower than the white applicant participated in the PAP, received the bonus points, and were hired. The white applicant was rejected and

sued. What should the court decide? Why? (*Garnet v. GM Corp.*, 2001 U.S. App. LEXIS 20942 [6th Cir. 2001], *cert. denied*, 535 U.S. 929 [2002])

2. A city fire department has a voluntary affirmative action program. It is not disputed that the department had previously discriminated against women and that only 1 percent of fire department employees were female at the time the plan

was adopted in 1984. The plan established a "long-term" goal of 36 percent female utilization based on the proportion of women in the population (52 percent) but reduced by a third to account for the fact that many women would not have the interest or ability to be firefighters. By 1997, 11.6 percent of firefighters were female. The applicant pool that year was 22 percent female, and 27 percent of the persons hired were female. The department gives preferences to women in hiring by allowing all women who pass the written test to be included in the applicant pool (for males, there is a lottery due to the large number of applicants) and by treating female gender as a plus in making final hiring decisions. A group of males, unsuccessful in obtaining jobs as firefighters, sued. What should the court decide? Why? (*Danskine v. Miami Dade Fire Department,* 253 F.3d 1288 [11th Cir. 2001])

3. A county fire department, undergoing reorganization due to budget shortfalls, eliminated four training captain positions and replaced them with three lieutenant-level training instructor positions. The plaintiff, a white male, was one of the displaced training captains. He applied for one of the new positions and exceeded the stated qualifications. Interviews were conducted by three people who were not firefighters or trainers and who had not been given copies of the job description. Two of the interviewers were known to be proponents of affirmative action. The stated policy was to consider interview results as only one factor in hiring. The plaintiff was rejected. One of those hired was a minority person who did not meet the minimum qualifications. The county had an affirmative action plan but claimed that its decision was based (in conflict with its stated policy) solely on the results of the interview. The rejected candidate sued. What should the court decide? Why? (*Bass v. Board of County Commissioners,* 256 F.3d 1095 [11th Cir. 2001])

4. The Omaha Fire Department had an affirmative action plan that provided for the following regarding promotions: The percentage of African Americans currently in promotional positions was compared against the percentage available within the department. If there was evidence of underutilization of African Americans in any promotional position, hiring goals were set. The goals reflected the number of African Americans who would have to be promoted to eliminate the underutilization, rounded off so that numbers with fractions lower than 1/2 (e.g., 2.3) were rounded down and numbers with fractions above 1/2 (e.g., 2.7) were rounded up. For job categories with underutilization, the personnel director was required to deviate from the usual procedure of referring the top scorers on the civil service eligibility list and refer additional minority candidates. Hiring decisions were made by the fire chief, who, in addition to other factors, took race into account. A white candidate for the position of battalion chief was passed over for promotion in favor of an African American candidate lower on the eligibility list. The chief said that numerous factors were considered in making this promotion, including the fact that only one out of twenty-eight battalion chiefs was African American. The white candidate sued. What should the court decide? Why? (*Kohlbek v. City of Omaha, Nebraska,* 447 F.3d 552 [8th Cir. 2006])

5. A white systems engineer with supervisory responsibilities was terminated. This was the first discipline he had ever received. His problems stemmed from the incarceration of one of his employees, an African American, for a dispute with the employee's girlfriend. After a convoluted series of events, the supervisor was fired for allegedly having been dishonest with other managers about when he became aware that this employee had been jailed. The employee was subsequently replaced by two employees, one of them an African American who had previously physically threatened the supervisor without any disciplinary consequences. About a decade earlier, the company had settled a discrimination suit for $38 million, entered into a consent decree, and agreed to take affirmative action. The consent decree had expired about four years before these events. There was evidence that another employee that the supervisor had managed had violated rules three times, costing the company thousands of dollars, but the supervisor was told not to discipline him because that would "stir up the pot" and "create controversy." In the investigation that led to the supervisor's termination, the investigating manager never interviewed the supervisor himself. The supervisor sued. What should the court decide? Why?

(*Mastro v. Potomac Electric Power Co.*, 447 F.3d 843 [D.C. Cir. 2006], *cert. denied*, 127 S. Ct. 1140 [2007])

6. A female manager who denied a promotion to a male employee had said a few months earlier "that's what we need [around here], a little more diversity." The statement had been made in response to her learning that an African American female had been hired. All three candidates (the plaintiff, another male, and a female) had the experience of having been temporarily assigned in the past to the position in question, Manager of Vehicle Maintenance. The two male candidates were judged to have extensive technical backgrounds but to be lacking in managerial skills. The manager defended the hiring of the female candidate by saying that although her experience in the vehicle maintenance area was limited, she had extensive managerial background. However, both the successful female and the rejected male candidate had a total of thirteen years of managerial experience. The manager also found that the female candidate performed better in her interview. At the time of the promotion, the female employee was in a lower pay grade than the male plaintiff. What should the court decide? Why? (*Plumb v. Potter,* 212 Fed. Appx. 472 [6th Cir. 2007])

7. What are some arguments in favor of affirmative action? Against it? What is your own view of affirmative action? Why? Does your view differ depending on the measures used to achieve affirmative action goals?

8. How important is diversity as a goal in university admissions? If you think that it is important, how should universities go about selecting applicants to ensure sufficient diversity?

CHAPTER **9**

Harassment

Harassment is a major obstacle to realizing equal employment opportunity. Harassment can intimidate and isolate employees, keep them from doing their best work, result in physical or psychological harm, and ultimately drive its victims from the workplace. Employers are clearly on notice that harassment will no longer be tolerated. Eliminating harassment is among the most pressing legal concerns facing employers today.

Although sexual harassment claims are the most common type—and most of the law discussed in this chapter centers on sexual harassment—harassment also affects other protected classes. Racial harassment is a long-standing and still prevalent problem. Employees also experience and seek legal protection from harassment based on their national origin, age, disabilities, and religious beliefs. There are differences in the particular ways that harassment is manifested, but the fundamental nature of harassment—and employer liability for it—are the same regardless of the protected class involved.

Harassment as a Form of Discrimination

Harassment is a form of discrimination. There is some variation in how courts articulate the elements of a harassment claim, but in broad terms, plaintiffs must show that the mistreatment was discriminatory, harmful, unwelcome, and attributable to their employer. The following sections of this chapter consider each of these elements in turn.

ELEMENTS OF A CLAIM

Harassment

Plaintiffs must show that

1. They were subjected to harassment based on a protected class characteristic.
2. The harassment resulted in a tangible employment action or was sufficiently severe or pervasive to alter working conditions and create a hostile environment.
3. The harassment was unwelcome.
4. There is a basis for attributing liability to the employer.

© Cengage Learning 2013.

"Because of Sex"

Legal challenges to harassment come under general antidiscrimination laws, such as Title VII of the Civil Rights Act, rather than laws specifically designed to prohibit harassment. However, just as the mere fact that an employee was terminated does not result in a finding of disparate treatment if the plaintiff cannot establish that the termination was based on a protected class characteristic, plaintiffs in harassment cases must ultimately show that they were subjected to harassment because of a protected class characteristic. In sexual harassment cases, a showing must be made that the plaintiff was subjected to harassment because of his or her sex. Both men and women are protected from harassment. In 2010, 16.4 percent of harassment charges filed with the EEOC were brought by males.[1] But regardless of their sex, plaintiffs must show that they were "exposed to disadvantageous terms or conditions of employment to which members of the other sex are not exposed."[2] In other words, someone of the opposite sex would not have been subjected to harassment or any such harassment would have differed markedly in nature.

Establishing the discriminatory motivation behind harassment can be difficult. Consider **same-sex harassment** cases, in which the harasser and the person harassed are of the same sex. While sexual attraction is not the only—or even the primary—reason that employees are singled out for harassment, judges often have difficulty concluding that heterosexual harassers choose to harass people of the same sex *based on their sex.* The Supreme Court decided the case of a male employee who worked as part of an all-male crew on an oil platform in the Gulf of Mexico.[3] The employee experienced severe harassment at the hands of male coworkers, including physical assaults of a sexual nature and threats of rape. The Court ruled that same-sex harassment cases can be brought under Title VII, but the plaintiffs are still responsible for showing that the harassment is **"because of sex."** This can be done by showing that the harasser is homosexual and motivated by sexual desire for people of the same sex; the victim is harassed in such sex-specific and derogatory terms that it is clear the harasser is motivated by general hostility to the presence of people of the same sex in the workplace; or the harasser in a mixed-sex workplace treated people differently based on their sex.[4]

Although the Supreme Court's decision left the door open for same-sex harassment suits, plaintiffs in subsequent cases have had great difficulty squeezing through that opening. In one relevant case, a male welder was regularly touched in private areas by his male supervisor; stalked; and subjected to the ridicule of coworkers, who called him the supervisor's "girlfriend." An appeals court reversed a jury verdict in the employee's favor on the grounds that although this was a case of "gross, vulgar, male horseplay in a male workplace," the conduct was not motivated by general hostility to men in the workplace.[5] In a comment that reveals much about prevailing judicial views of same-sex harassment, the court opined that if it upheld the verdict in this case, "what's next—towel snapping in the locker room?" Plaintiffs have had more luck in cases in which there is evidence that the harasser is gay or lesbian. In one such case,

[1]U.S. Equal Employment Opportunity Commission. "Sexual Harassment Charges EEOC & FEPA's Combined: FY 1997–FY 2010." Viewed July 1, 2011 (http://www.eeoc.gov/eeoc/statistics/).

[2]*Oncale v. Sundowner Offshore Services,* 523 U.S. 75, 80 (1998).

[3]*Oncale.*

[4]*Oncale,* at 80–81.

[5]*EEOC v. Harbert-Yeargin, Inc.,* 266 F.3d 498, 522 (6th Cir. 2001).

the plaintiff's evidence that the harasser said he was jealous of the plaintiff's girlfriend, touched the plaintiff in a sexual manner, and made sexual advances to another male employee was sufficient to show that the plaintiff was subjected to harassment because he was a man.[6]

The three methods offered by the Supreme Court for establishing that same-sex harassment is "because of sex" is not an exhaustive listing. Some courts have also used the theory of *sex-stereotyping* to find evidence of a discriminatory motive in same-sex harassment cases. For example, a male hotel waiter was subjected to severe harassment by his male coworkers over a two-year period. Actions by the coworkers, including whistling and blowing kisses at the employee and calling him "sweetheart" and "doll," strongly suggested that the harassment was prompted by the coworkers' judgments that the employee was not sufficiently masculine.[7] But it is critical in such cases that the issue is nonconformance with sex roles rather than sexual orientation. If harassment is deemed to be based on the latter, courts will rule against the plaintiffs (at least under Title VII).[8]

What happens if a harasser subjects both men and women to harassment? Courts often conclude in these cases involving "equal opportunity harassers" that because both men and women are victimized, the harassment does not disadvantage members of one sex relative to the other. Hence, it is not discriminatory treatment based on sex. In a case involving a Wal-Mart supervisor, the plaintiff's claim was denied primarily because the harasser "was just an indiscriminately vulgar and offensive supervisor, obnoxious to men and women alike."[9] However, courts have sometimes found discrimination to exist where equal opportunity harassers harassed men and women in different, sex-specific ways.[10] For example, when the executive director of a union was highly abusive to both male and female staff, the court permitted the case to go to trial because incidents involving male employees were less frequent, were less confrontational, took less time to resolve, and had less severe effects.[11] The requirements of discrimination law may also be met where, although members of both sexes are affected by harassment, one sex is more likely to be subjected to harassment than the other. When a woman charged that her employer, a psychiatric hospital, failed to protect her from sexual harassment in the form of sexual assault by a client, the court concluded that while assaults occurred against both male and female staff, the victims of such assaults were disproportionately female.[12] Thus, the woman had a viable harassment claim under Title VII.

Questions about whether harassment was because of sex also arise when there is evidence of the harasser's personal animus toward the plaintiff. For example, a court concluded that the harassment of a female employee by a supervisor who repeatedly said that he wanted to have sex with her teenage daughter, though "deplorable," was based on the supervisor's dislike for her husband rather than the employee's sex.[13] Thus, there was no violation of Title VII. Likewise, when a woman ended a romantic

---

[6]*LaDay v. Catalyst Technology,* 302 F.3d 474, 480–81 (5th Cir. 2002).

[7]*Rene v. MGM Grand Hotel,* 305 F.3d 1061 (9th Cir. 2002), *cert. denied,* 538 U.S. 922 (2003).

[8]*Hamm v. Weyauwega Milk Products,* 332 F.3d 1058 (7th Cir. 2003).

[9]*Lack v. Wal-Mart,* 240 F.3d 255, 262 (4th Cir. 2001).

[10]*Steiner v. Showboat Operating Co.,* 25 F.3d 1459 (9th Cir. 1994), *cert. denied,* 513 U.S. 1082 (1995).

[11]*EEOC v. National Education Association, Alaska,* 422 F.3d 840 (9th Cir. 2005).

[12]*Turnbull v. Topeka State Hospital,* 255 F.3d 1238, at 1244 (10th Cir. 2001), *cert. denied,* 535 U.S. 970 (2002).

[13]*Rizzo v. Sheahan,* 266 F.3d 705, 708 (7th Cir. 2001).

relationship with her male supervisor over his objections and began to receive poor performance appraisals, the court held that any harassment was the result of the relationship gone sour, not because of her sex.[14] Harassment such as continuous sexual banter or graffiti that is not directed at anyone in particular and to which both male and female employees are subjected can also present problems for plaintiffs. In one such case, the court stressed that both male and female employees were subjected to the same conditions and concluded that "[a] dually offensive sexual atmosphere in the workplace, no matter how offensive, is not unlawful discrimination unless one gender is treated differently than the other."[15] However, in another case featuring a working environment infused with harassment, the court concluded that the requisite discriminatory motivation was present because "the depiction of women in the offensive jokes and graphics was uniformly sexually demeaning and communicated the message that women as a group were available for sexual exploitation by men."[16] Likewise, when a shipping company's office featured a daily torrent of profanity, including sexually explicit radio programming, the court ruled for the female plaintiff, noting that:

> If the environment ... just involved a generally vulgar workplace whose indiscriminate insults and sexually-laden conversation did not focus on the gender of the victim, we would face a very different case. However, a substantial portion of the words and conduct ... may reasonably be read as gender-specific, derogatory, and humiliating. This evidence ... is sufficient to afford the inference that the offending conduct was based on the sex of the employee.[17]

Other civil claims and criminal charges (e.g., infliction of emotional distress, assault, battery, rape) can be brought to bear in some harassment cases. But current legal protections against harassment do not reach the full range of "bullying" and abuse that occurs in the workplace.

THE CHANGING WORKPLACE

Workplace Bullying

Not all mistreatment and abuse of employees falls within the ambit of harassment and the protection afforded by discrimination laws. Discussion has increasingly turned to the phenomenon of "workplace bullying" and whether new laws are needed to deal with it. **Workplace bullying** has been defined as "repeated interpersonal mistreatment that is sufficiently severe as to harm a targeted person's health or economic status."[1] A national survey of private sector employees conducted in 1999 found that 33 percent of respondents reported having been verbally abused at work in the past year, including calling people names, provoking arguments, shouting, swearing, threatening, and intimidating.[2] Of the respondents, 5 percent said that they had been physically assaulted at work in the past year, including pushing, grabbing, slapping, kicking, hitting, raping or attempting to rape, and threatening to use or using weapons. A 2007 study by the research firm Zogby International found that 37 percent of American workers said that they had

---

[14]*Pipkins v. City of Temple Terrace, Florida*, 267 F.3d 1197 (11th Cir. 2001).

[15]*Ellett v. Big Red Keno*, 2000 U.S. App. LEXIS 17583, at 2-3 (8th Cir.).

[16]*Petrosino v. Bell Atlantic*, 385 F.3d 210, 222 (2d Cir. 2004).

[17]*Reeves v. C.H. Robinson Worldwide*, 594 F.3d 798, 811 (11th Cir. 2010).

experienced bullying on the job.[3] Research suggests that the "bullies" are often bosses and that women frequently bully other women.[4] Bullying appears to be especially common in healthcare settings, with doctors and supervisors directing this conduct toward nurses and technicians. Bullying takes a heavy toll on its victims, leading to increased use of sick time, stress-related illnesses, depression, and anxiety.[5]

Workplace bullying is not a legal claim recognized by U.S. courts. But a 2008 Indiana case, in which the plaintiff prevailed on an assault charge, is often cited as an example of a successful lawsuit challenging workplace bullying.[6] In this case, a doctor at a hospital became enraged at a male perfusionist (operator of a heart-lung machine during surgeries) who had reported the doctor's mistreatment of other perfusionists to the hospital administration. The doctor charged at the perfusionist, with his fists clenched, eyes bulging, and veins popping—all the while swearing and screaming. The perfusionist was backed up against a wall, cringing, and awaiting the inevitable blows. Amazingly, the doctor stopped before striking the employee, informed him that he was "history," and stalked off. Since "[a]ssault is effectuated when one acts intending to cause an imminent apprehension of a harmful or offensive contact with another person," no physical contact or "battery" is required.[7] The Indiana Supreme Court upheld the jury's award of $325,000 for the assault on the perfusionist (the jury had also rejected an intentional infliction of emotional distress claim) and agreed with the trial court that allowing expert witness testimony regarding workplace bullying was not prejudicial.

This Indiana case notwithstanding, victims of bullying often lack a legal remedy. David Yamada, a legal scholar who has written widely about workplace bullying, goes so far as to say that "workplace bullying remains the most legally neglected form of worker mistreatment despite our amalgam of employment protections."[8] Harassment claims based on bullying conduct are often not successful because the mistreatment is seen as not related to sex (because bullies and victims are often the same sex) or other protected class characteristics, as trivial "horseplay," as personally motivated grudges, or simply as the actions of "tough" bosses. Tort claims (e.g., assault, infliction of emotional distress) can address some of the more severe instances of workplace bullying, but they provide unwieldy mechanisms, at best, for dealing with the problem. Occupational safety and health laws theoretically provide another avenue of legal protection, but in practice, they not been applied to workplace bullying.[9] Thus, a number of scholars and employee advocates have concluded that new laws prohibiting abusive bullying behavior—*regardless of whether it is directed at others because of their protected class characteristics*—are needed to effectively deal with this problem. A model Healthy Workplace Bill has been drafted. The bill prohibits subjecting an employee to an "abusive work environment." Such an environment "exists when the defendant, acting with malice, subjects an employee to abusive conduct so severe that it causes tangible harm to the employee."[10] Versions of the Healthy Workplace Bill have been introduced in twenty-one states since 2003 and were under active consideration in eleven states as of May 2011.[11] However, despite the evident appeal of anti-bullying legislation, no state has yet enacted such a law. Finding the appropriate balance between meaningful protection from bullying and creation of a "general civility code" is no doubt difficult.[12]

---

[1] Gary Namie and Ruth Namie. "Workplace Bullying: How to Address America's Silent Epidemic." *Employee Rights & Employment Policy Journal* 8 (2004), 315.

[2] National Center on Addiction and Substance Abuse. *Report of the United States Postal Commission on a Safe and Secure Workplace.* New York: Columbia University (August 2000), 3.

[3] Tara Parker-Pope. "When the Bully Sits in the Next Cubicle." *New York Times* (March 25, 2008), D5.

[4] Namie and Namie, 325.

[5] Parker-Pope.

[6] *Raess v. Doescher*, 883 N.E.2d 790 (Ind. 2008).

[7] *Raess*, at 794.

[8] David C. Yamada. "As Workplace Bullying Enters the Mainstream of American Employment Relations, Will Law and Public Policy Follow?" *Perspectives on Work* 14 (Summer 2010/Winter 2011), 19.

[9] David C. Yamada. "Workplace Bullying and American Employment Law: A Ten-Year Progress Report and Assessment." *Comparative Labor Law & Policy Journal* 32 (Fall 2010), 259.

[10] Yamada, at 262.

[11] The Healthy Workplace Campaign. "The Healthy Workplace Bill." Viewed July 9, 2011 (http://www.healthyworkplacebill.org/).

[12] *Oncale v. Sundowner Offshore Services*, 523 U.S. 75, 81 (1998).

Recognizing Harassment
What Behaviors Constitute Harassment?

Now that it is clear that not all harassment can be linked to protected class in the manner required to prove discrimination, we need to step back and consider more carefully the kinds of behaviors that constitute harassment. The EEOC has defined sexual harassment as follows:

> Unwelcome sexual advances, requests for sexual favors, and other verbal or physical conduct of a sexual nature … when (1) submission to such conduct is made either explicitly or implicitly a term or condition of an individual's employment, (2) submission to or rejection of such conduct by an individual is used as the basis for employment decisions affecting such individual, or (3) such conduct has the purpose or effect of unreasonably interfering with an individual's work performance or creating an intimidating, hostile, or offensive working environment.[18]

A distinction can be drawn between harassment that results in tangible employment actions (1 and 2 in the preceding extract) and harassment that alters working conditions by subjecting employees to hostile environments but does not directly affect tangible employment outcomes (3). This distinction is important because the criteria for finding employers liable differ depending on which of these two types of harassment has occurred.

Harassment That Results in Tangible Employment Actions

Harassment sometimes results in significant changes in the employment status of individuals. The classic example is where a manager tells an employee that he wants to receive sexual favors from her and that she should comply or her career will suffer. The employee resists the sexual advance and is demoted or fired shortly thereafter. Under these circumstances, the employee's response to harassment has had a tangible effect on her employment opportunities and the woman would have a strong harassment claim. **Harassment that results in tangible employment actions** often involves a sexual advance or demand for sexual favors that can be "traded" for some employment outcome (this is why the term *quid pro quo* is sometimes still used to describe these cases). While these cases most often involve employees disadvantaged because they have rejected advances, some courts have held that the prohibited linking of tangible employment opportunities to harassment also occurs when employees submit to unwelcome advances in order to obtain employment opportunities (e.g., to get a raise) or to maintain existing opportunities (e.g., to keep one's job).[19] In a tangible employment action claim, the harasser must possess sufficient authority to influence or determine employment outcomes (or at least be reasonably perceived as having such authority). However, if a supervisor threatens an employment consequence but does not take any action when the employee refuses his or her sexual advance, there is no tangible employment action (although there might still be a hostile environment).[20]

---

[18]29 C.F.R. § 1604.11(a) (2011).

[19]*Jin v. Metropolitan Life Insurance Co.*, 310 F.3d 84 (2d Cir. 2002); *Holly D. v. California Institute of Technology*, 339 F.3d 1158 (9th Cir. 2003).

[20]*Burlington Industries v. Ellerth*, 524 U.S. 742 (1998).

> ## *Clippings*
>
> Dominion Correctional Services, a private prison company, has settled a sexual harassment and retaliation suit brought by the EEOC on behalf of twenty-one former employees. Much of the harassment took the form of male managers coercing female employees to perform sex acts as the price for keeping their jobs. Male employees also regularly commented on women's bodies, touched women inappropriately, openly viewed pornography in the workplace, and told sexual jokes. Female employees who spoke out were marked for retaliation. In one particularly egregious incident, a female officer who complained about harassment by a male officer was placed in an isolated area of the prison and then raped by that same officer. An EEOC official commented that "This case illustrates the continuing struggle women face in jobs traditionally held by men. The misuse of management power is especially troubling."
>
> U.S. Equal Employment Opportunity Commission. "Private Prison Pays $1.3 Million to Settle Sexual Harassment, Retaliation Claims for Class of Women." Press Release (October 13, 2009) (http://www.eeoc.gov/).

For a tangible employment action claim to succeed, it is critical that the plaintiff show that the tangible employment action is causally linked to her rejection of or submission to harassment. Courts do not require evidence that the harasser made the connection between submission to harassment and a subsequent employment decision explicit, but the mere fact that a tangible employment action coincides in time with the occurrence of an advance is not enough. Thus, an employee's tangible employment action harassment claim failed when she was denied a promotion after being told by her supervisor who had been harassing her that she "needed to do more things" and that she "already knew" what those things were. The supervisor's statements might have been veiled proposals to exchange sex for a promotion, but there was no evidence that the denial of promotion was based on her failure to comply rather than on the employer's stated reasons that she had a history of attendance problems and needed more time to develop in her current position.[21]

What about a situation in which an employee is subjected to severe harassment and quits her job to escape the situation? A resignation under circumstances where a reasonable person would feel compelled to quit is termed a "constructive discharge" (see Chapter 18) and is treated by the courts as a termination rather than a voluntary quit. If an employee is forced to quit due to harassment, that loss of employment is clearly tangible in terms of having a significant effect on employment status. Yet, a quit is not the same as a termination in the sense of being an official act that might prompt managerial review. The Supreme Court has determined that a constructive discharge will be deemed a tangible employment action only if an official act such as a demotion or pay cut prompts the quit. The logic of this decision is closely tied to the rationale for distinguishing between tangible employment action and other harassment cases when attributing liability to employers: "[A]n official act reflected in company records ... shows 'beyond question' that the supervisor has used his managerial or controlling position to the employee's disadvantage."[22]

---

[21]*Frederick v. Sprint/United Management*, 246 F.3d 1305, 1312 (11th Cir. 2001).

[22]*Pennsylvania State Police v. Suders*, 542 U.S. 129, 148 (2004).

Hostile Environment Harassment

Most often, harassment does not directly alter employment status. Instead, it imposes inferior working conditions that make it harder for an employee to perform well or remain on the job. A **hostile environment** can result from a wide range of verbal conduct, including insults, epithets, tasteless jokes, profanity, and requests for sexual favors; physical conduct, including touching, exposure, staring, stalking, sexual assault, and rape; and displays of images, including pictures, posters, e-mails, Web sites, and pornography. Hostile environments can be created not only by managers and supervisors but also by coworkers and third parties (e.g., customers and clients).

JUST THE FACTS

A female mechanic worked at a truck assembly plant. Women made up less than 10 percent of the workforce at the plant. On one occasion, the woman found a tampon hanging from the key ring of a truck to which she was assigned. On another occasion, a picture of a nude woman appeared on the screensaver of a PC when the woman logged into the system. A number of male employees had pictures of scantily clad women taped to the tops of their company-issued toolboxes where they were readily visible to the woman and anyone else. An employee brought in copies of calendars with sexually provocative pictures and placed them at various locations throughout the plant. Repeated complaints to management resulted in the removal of some offensive materials, but no disciplinary actions were ever taken. The woman was involuntarily reassigned to a position involving mostly janitorial work. She sued for harassment. What should the court decide? Why?

See, *Hoyle v. Freightliner*, 2011 U.S. App. LEXIS 6628 (4th Cir.).

While sexual harassment claims frequently entail words, conduct, or images of a blatantly sexual nature, it is important to realize that sexual harassment can also take other, not explicitly sexual, forms. The key issue is again whether an employee is subjected to unwelcome, offensive treatment because of his or her sex. There need not be sexual conduct involved. Thus, the EEOC's definition of sexual harassment cited above should not be taken too literally. In one example of a successful sexual harassment claim unrelated to sexual conduct, an employee was able to show a hostile environment based on evidence that her supervisor altered her work hours with the knowledge that doing so would adversely affect her hypoglycemia, frequently stood at her desk and stared angrily at her, startled her by pounding on her desk with his fist, criticized her work unfairly, and yelled at her in front of coworkers.[23] A female school custodian's allegations that officials unfairly questioned her abilities and those of women in general, plotted to give her job to a male custodian, increased her duties in an attempt to force her to quit, withheld necessary assistance, instructed male custodians not to help female custodians, hid the tools needed to do the job, and made other discriminatory remarks were sufficient to state a sexual harassment claim. Although the challenged acts were not sexual in nature and not highly severe when viewed individually, they disadvantaged the only female in

---

[23]*Marrero v. Goya of Puerto Rico*, 304 F.3d 7 (1st Cir. 2002).

the workplace, imposed inferior working conditions on her, and made it more difficult for the woman to perform her job.[24] Likewise, two years of making repeated comments and questions about the type of underwear being worn by a female employee, interfering with her while she was treating patients, throwing her food away, and removing items from her desk were sufficient to state a claim of sexual harassment. The court observed that "there is no legal requirement that hostile acts be overtly sex- or gender-specific in content, whether marked by language, by sex or gender stereotypes, or by sexual overtures."[25]

"Severe or Pervasive"   The law does not mandate that employees be treated in ways that are "nice" or even "civil." However, employees have the right to not be forced to endure hostile environments based on their protected class characteristics. But how "hostile" must the workplace become before the law is violated? The basic standard is that a hostile environment must be sufficiently **severe or pervasive** to be actionable.[26] Severity gets at the degree of harm posed by particular acts and pervasiveness addresses the frequency and regularity of harassment. Victims of harassment need not suffer psychological harm, although evidence of any such harm is relevant to a hostile environment claim. Conduct that is "physically threatening or humiliating" or that "unreasonably interferes with an employee's work performance" reaches the threshold of a legally actionable hostile environment sooner than "mere offensive utterance[s]."[27] But there is no simple, bright-line test for distinguishing conduct that is merely offensive from a legally actionable hostile environment. A trade-off exists between severity and pervasiveness, such that conduct that is more severe need not happen often (once is enough for a sexual assault), whereas less severe conduct (e.g., insults) must occur more frequently or over a long period of time to constitute a hostile environment.[28] In the landmark Supreme Court case *Meritor v. Vinson*,[29] the harasser's conduct was both severe and pervasive: A bank vice president raped the plaintiff several times, in addition to following her into the bathroom, fondling her, and repeatedly pressing her to have sex—behavior that went on for several years. Similarly, the executive director of a community services agency asked a female employee whether she knew what a "sexual perpetrator" was, explained in graphic detail how rape is committed, and told her "how easy it is to rape a woman." The director also came into her office, closed the door, and stood uncomfortably close, ignoring requests that he move away. Presented with these and other allegations, the court concluded that "if proven, they establish that plaintiff was required to endure an environment that 'objectively' was *severely and pervasively* hostile."[30]

Other successful hostile environment claims have involved actions that, viewed individually, were less severe, but in their totality they were sufficiently severe or pervasive to be harassment. An employee whose sexual advances were rebuffed embarked on a campaign of staring at the woman who spurned him. The employee would park his forklift near her work area and stare at her for minutes at a time. This occurred several times each day and lasted for months. The court concluded that she had a valid hostile

---

[24]*Haugerud v. Amery School District,* 259 F.3d 678 (7th Cir. 2001).

[25]*Rosario v. Department of the Army,* 607 F.3d 242, 248 (1st Cir. 2010) [quoting *EEOC v. NEA Alaska*].

[26]*Harris v. Forklift Systems,* 510 U.S. 17 (1993).

[27]*Harris,* at 23.

[28]*Ellison v. Brady,* 924 F.2d 872, 878 (9th Cir. 1991).

[29]*Meritor v. Vinson,* 477 U.S. 57 (1986).

[30]*Gregory v. Daly & Community Action Agency of Greene Country,* 243 F.3d 687, 692 (2d Cir. 2001).

environment claim.[31] In another case permitted to go to trial, a female employee was forced to endure three months of sharing a cramped office with a male supervisor who repeatedly stared at her in a sexual way, pulled his chair next to hers so that their legs touched, came so close to her that she could feel his breath, obstructed her efforts to leave the office, and smirked at her when she expressed discomfort.[32] An African American employee was allowed to proceed to trial on a hostile environment claim based entirely on verbal conduct. The employee alleged a pattern of supervisors using vile racial epithets to refer to him and other African American employees. On a daily basis, supervisors used the term *boy* to refer to African American, but not white, employees. The plaintiff testified that these terms were "'just the way they speak to you at BFI, like you are less than nothing.'"[33]

In *EEOC v. Fairbrook Medical Clinic, P.A.,* the court must decide whether the verbal harassment of an employee was sufficiently severe or pervasive to constitute a hostile environment.

EEOC v. Fairbrook Medical Clinic, P.A.
609 F.3d 320 (4th Cir. 2010)

OPINION BY CIRCUIT JUDGE WILKINSON:

The Equal Employment Opportunity Commission brought this suit on behalf of Dr. Deborah Waechter against her former employer, Fairbrook Medical Clinic. The agency alleges that Dr. John Kessel, the sole owner of the clinic, subjected Waechter to a hostile work environment because of her sex in violation of Title VII of the Civil Rights Act of 1964. The district court held that Kessel's conduct was not sufficiently severe or pervasive to constitute a hostile work environment. * * * [W]e conclude that the EEOC has presented an issue of triable fact and accordingly reverse.

Dr. Deborah Waechter graduated from medical school in 1999 and completed her residency in 2002. In December of 2002, she accepted a position as a physician at Fairbrook Medical Clinic, a family medicine practice in Hickory, North Carolina. * * * Dr. John Kessel … served as Waechter's immediate supervisor during her entire tenure at the clinic. By Kessel's own estimation, Waechter was an excellent physician. Within a few years of working at Fairbrook, she had between three and four hundred regular patients.

Waechter alleges that Kessel sexually harassed her while she worked at Fairbrook. According to her, the incidents of harassment became so frequent and distressing that she decided to leave the clinic for other employment in early 2006. * * * The first incident occurred a few weeks after Waechter started working at Fairbook. In January of 2003, Kessel showed her an x-ray of his hip for the supposed purpose of revealing a hip abnormality that he had suffered since adolescence. In the x-ray, a shadowy image of his penis was highly visible. After describing his hip condition, Kessel pointed to the image of his penis and called it "Mr. Happy." This comment left Waechter "speechless" and uncomfortable. According to Waechter, Kessel showed this x-ray to other people in the clinic "at least 25 to 30 times," mostly around the time that he had surgery to correct the abnormality. * * *

The next incident occurred in February of 2003. During a staff meeting, Kessel stated that he "was very glad that his wife had had a c-section with their triplets because she still had a nice, tight p**sy." Although Waechter was not present at the meeting, employees who were in attendance later reported the incident to her. On a few occasions, Kessel directly discussed his sex life with Waechter…. When Waechter said that she did not feel comfortable discussing the

---

[31] *Birschstein v. New United Motor Manufacturing, Inc.,* 92 Cal. App. 4th 994 (2001).

[32] *Vera v. McHugh,* 622 F.3d 17 (1st Cir. 2010).

[33] *White v. BFI Waste Services,* 375 F.3d 288, 297 (4th Cir. 2004).

topic, Kessel said "Well, you're just like one of the guys," to which she replied "No, I'm not."

In March of 2003, Kessel approached Waechter to talk about her attire. Kessel reported that a male patient had remarked that Kessel "sure had hired a lady physician with a nice set of breasts." He then instructed Waechter to be "aware … of [her] breasts and dress appropriately." When Waechter asked what the patient had been referring to, Kessel responded that the patient had probably been able to see her nipples through her blouse. Waechter replied that she tried to maintain a professional appearance and did not dress in a manner that would show her nipples.

At some point, Kessel invited Waechter to look at some photographs from his recent vacation to the Caribbean. Waechter agreed, expecting to see innocuous images of beaches or scuba diving. She was shocked, however, to discover a picture of Kessel, his wife, and a few other couples in which the men were wearing Speedos and the women were topless. * * * In the fall of 2004, Kessel was receiving physical therapy in an examination room in the vicinity of Waechter's work station. He opened the door, emerged from the room without a shirt, and called out, "Hey Deborah, don't you want to come in here?" Waechter refused and went about her business.

In March of 2005, Waechter traveled with her daughter to visit her husband in Washington, D.C., where he was doing an internship. While Waechter was gone, Kessel treated one of her regular patients. According to the patient, Kessel said that Waechter was away on vacation and was "probably screwing around so she can have another baby." At the end of the visit, he told the patient, "You can follow up with Dr. Waechter when she returns from screwing." When Waechter returned, the patient informed her of Kessel's remarks. Waechter was "absolutely infuriated" and confronted Kessel. She told him that she considered it very "inappropriate and unprofessional" to speak that way about a colleague, especially in front of a patient. Kessel adamantly denied making the remarks but did not attempt to explain why the patient would have made them up.

Waechter also recalls hearing Kessel tell "dirty jokes" about "two or three times a month" during her time at Fairbrook. * * * According to Waechter, Kessel also made demeaning comments about female drug representatives in front of her. On one such occasion, a female drug representative was walking down the hall with her back turned to Kessel. Kessel looked to Waechter and said, "Doesn't she look great for having had three kids? I sure would like a piece of that." He then gestured as if he were grabbing the representative's buttocks. * * * Other employees similarly report that Kessel joked about sex and made demeaning comments about women. Joseph Sigmon recalls that Kessel frequently talked about "oral sex" and "women's breasts" and occasionally used terms like "slut" and "c**t" to refer to female staff and patients at the clinic. According to Sigmon, Kessel made sexually offensive remarks to "[a]nybody, anytime," whether male or female. He further stated that Kessel delighted in being a "shock jock" and watching women react to his obscene comments. * * *

Kessel's comments to Waechter became much more personal after she became pregnant with her second child. By October of 2005, Waechter was in her ninth month of pregnancy. On two or three occasions that month, Kessel told her "how big [her] breasts were getting and how fat [she] was getting." When Waechter complained that these comments were inappropriate, Kessel responded, "Well[,] you know I'm a breast man. I like breasts." * * * When Waechter returned from maternity leave in December of 2005, Kessel's comments about her breasts became more frequent. On her first day back at work, for instance, Kessel spotted her arriving in the parking lot and said, "You sure have slimmed down, except in your breasts." At that time, Waechter was still nursing her child at home and would pump breast milk in her office, usually during her lunch breaks. On several occasions, Kessel asked her when "[she] was going to let him help [her] pump [her] breasts." Other times, he inquired if she "had a better sexual libido while [she] was pumping" and opined that she "was probably a wild thing in bed." * * * Waechter estimates that Kessel made these comments "at least once or twice per week" from her return in December of 2005 through January of 2006. By January, Waechter found Kessel's behavior "very distressing" and concluded that Fairbrook was no longer "a good working environment for [her]." Accordingly, she began to consider other employment.

* * * The "last straw" for Waechter happened on February 13, 2006. At that time, Waechter was involved in a contract dispute with a hospital called Frye Regional Medical Center that had loaned her money in 2002 so that she could relocate to Hickory, North Carolina. Kessel was paying her legal fees in the matter…. On the day in question, Kessel approached

Waechter at the clinic and said, "You owe me big for helping you with the Frye thing." He then asked, "Are you going to let me help you pump [your breasts]?" Waechter called his comments "ridiculous" and said that they "needed to stop." She explained that, while she appreciated his help with the Frye matter, she "didn't think that he needed to tell [her] that [she] owed him something, especially of a sexual nature." That was the last time that Kessel made an inappropriate comment to her.

On February 17, 2006, Waechter tendered her resignation. In a letter to Kessel, she thanked him for the opportunity to practice medicine at Fairbrook and announced that she would be taking a position at another practice. * * * Nowhere in the letter did she complain about Kessel's behavior. According to Waechter, she declined to do so primarily because she wanted to keep working at Fairbrook until her new job became available in order to provide continuous support for her family. * * *

"[A] plaintiff may establish a violation of Title VII by proving that discrimination based on sex has created a hostile or abusive work environment." To make out such a claim, a plaintiff must show that "the offending conduct (1) was unwelcome, (2) was based on her sex, (3) was sufficiently severe or pervasive to alter the conditions of her employment and create an abusive work environment, and (4) was imputable to her employer."

* * * Fairbrook does not dispute that Waechter found Kessel's conduct to be unwelcome. It does contend, however, that it is entitled to judgment as a matter of law on each of the other three elements of the EEOC's hostile work environment claim. * * * First, Fairbrook contends that Kessel did not make offensive comments to Waechter because of her sex. Instead, it argues that Kessel was a generally crude person who made vulgar comments to men and women alike. This contention is easily dismissed. Although Kessel made offensive remarks in front of both male and female audiences, his use of "sex-specific and derogatory terms" indicates that he intended to demean women.... Kessel used terms like "c**t" and "slut" to refer to women at the clinic and talked about female body parts, including his own wife's, in graphic terms. Moreover, several of his remarks involved "explicit or implicit proposals of sexual activity," that a reasonable jury could infer "would not have been made to someone of the same sex." For instance, Kessel asked Waechter if she had a better libido while she was pumping her breasts, opined that she was probably a "wild thing" in bed, and requested to view and pump her breasts. Based on the nature of these remarks, we think that a jury could conclude that Kessel's comments were based on sex and that their intimate nature was intended to make women in his employ feel acutely embarrassed and uncomfortable. Kessel's delight in being a "shock jock" does nothing to dispel the impression.

The main dispute in this case centers on whether Kessel's conduct was sufficiently severe or pervasive to create a hostile work environment. * * * There is no "mathematically precise test" for determining if an environment is objectively hostile or abusive. Instead, the "objective severity of harassment should be judged from the perspective of a reasonable person in the plaintiff's position, considering 'all the circumstances.'" These circumstances include "the frequency of the discriminatory conduct; its severity; whether it is physically threatening or humiliating, or a mere offensive utterance; and whether it unreasonably interferes with an employee's work performance." This inquiry also "requires careful consideration of the social context in which particular behavior occurs and is experienced by its target." Conduct which is considered normal and appropriate in one setting may be deemed abusive or hostile in another.

Fairbrook's principal argument is that Kessel's conduct, when viewed in its social context, was not severe; instead, it was merely the sort of crude behavior that is not actionable under Title VII. Specifically, it points out that the conduct occurred in a medical clinic where employees dealt with human bodies every day. In this environment, it was not uncommon for both patients and employees to tell off-color jokes to ease the tensions in otherwise awkward situations. * * * If this case were merely about the crude or vulgar commentary which is an unfortunate feature of some workplaces, then Fairbrook would be correct to assert that the EEOC has no claim. Title VII, after all, is not "a general civility code." "[W]hile no one condones boorishness, there is a line between what can justifiably be called sexual harassment and what is merely crude behavior." Activities like simple teasing, offhand comments, and off-color jokes, while often regrettable, do not cross the line into actionable misconduct. * * *

This case involves more than general crudity, however. Waechter's allegations, if proven, show that Kessel targeted her with highly personalized comments designed to demean and humiliate her. In some cases, the remarks seemed intended to ridicule her in the eyes of patients and drug representatives. We have previously recognized that there is a difference between "generalized" statements that pollute the work environment and "personal gender-based remarks" that single out individuals for ridicule. Common experience teaches that the latter have a greater impact on their listeners and thus are more severe forms of harassment.

In this case, many of Kessel's comments ventured into highly personal territory. While Waechter was pregnant, he frequently commented about the size of her breasts. After she gave birth, he asked to see her breasts and to pump them, stated that he wanted to lick up her breast milk, inquired about the status of her libido, and opined that she was probably a "wild thing" in bed. The impact of these comments may have been aggravated by the fact that Kessel had previously made comments to Waechter about his genitals and those of his wife. When assessing the severity of Kessel's conduct, a jury could give significant weight to the intensely personal nature of this interaction.

The fact that this interaction took place at a medical clinic need not negate its severity, as Fairbrook contends. It is true that employees at Fairbrook had clinical duties which are not part of other professions, and it is likewise accurate that some employees, including Waechter, occasionally made off-color remarks. But a plaintiff's claim is not defeated solely because she engages in some crude behavior. As Fairbrook acknowledges, most of the jokes at the clinic were told in fun, and there is no evidence that employees or patients routinely subjected each other to the sort of intensely personal and demeaning remarks that Kessel allegedly directed at Waechter. A jury could thus find that a reasonable person in Waechter's position might tolerate run-of-the-mill jokes and even make some herself while still finding Kessel's unique brand of invective to be hostile or abusive.

Moreover, we decline to accept the argument that a medical setting, because it deals with human anatomy, is somehow liberated from professional norms. * * * Furthermore, a jury might conclude that the environment at the clinic actually enhanced the severity of the harassment rather than negating it. When evaluating the context in which harassment takes place, we have often focused on the "disparity in power between the harasser and the victim." * * * Here, a jury could likewise conclude that severity of Kessel's conduct was exacerbated by the fact that he was not only Waech-

ter's immediate supervisor, but also the sole owner of Fairbrook. Unlike one of Waechter's fellow employees, Kessel had significant authority over her on a day-to-day basis and the ability to influence the rest of her career.

Fairbrook raises several additional arguments about why Kessel's conduct was not sufficiently severe or pervasive. First, it contends that Kessel's conduct was not particularly frequent. We think, however, that a jury could find that the harassment was at least a regular occurrence. Waechter identified a number of specific incidents that occurred over a three year period, estimated that she heard Kessel tell foul jokes two or three times each month, and recalled him displaying an image of his penis twenty-five to thirty times and referring to it as "Mr. Happy" on five to ten of these occasions. More importantly, Waechter testified that the frequency of Kessel's conduct escalated after she returned from maternity leave. By her estimation, he made comments about her breasts at least once or twice a week from December of 2005 through January of 2006. By that point, a reasonable person in her position may well have concluded that the harassment had become a persistent feature of her work environment. Thus, this is simply not a case involving only a handful of isolated and thus non-actionable incidents.

Second, Fairbook argues that Kessel's conduct was not sufficiently severe because it did not cause Waechter to miss work due to stress or otherwise adversely affect her job performance. These factors, while relevant, are not decisive here. "Title VII comes into play before the harassing conduct leads to a nervous breakdown." The fact that a plaintiff continued to work under difficult conditions is to her credit, not the harasser's. * * * The critical inquiry "'is not whether work has been impaired, but whether working conditions have been discriminatorily altered.'" Here, a jury could conclude that Kessel altered Waechter's working conditions by, among other things, bombarding her with graphic and highly personalized comments about intimate features of his and her anatomy. That Waechter may have stuck it out until a new job became available does not, without more, defeat the EEOC's claim.

Third, Fairbrook contends that there is no evidence of any inappropriate touching, physical threats, sexual advances, or propositions that would tend to make Kessel's conduct severe or pervasive. This is not entirely correct. While there is no indication that Kessel touched Waechter inappropriately or threatened her with force, there is evidence that he, at least implicitly, proposed that they engage in sexual activity. In February of 2006, for example, Kessel said that Waechter owed him "big" for his help in the Frye matter and asked if she would let him pump her breasts. A reasonable jury could conclude that he was suggesting that they engage in sexual activity, especially given that he had previously inquired about the status of her libido and had opined that she was probably a "wild thing" in bed. But even if a jury concluded that such comments were merely intended to humiliate Waechter on the basis of gender, it could nonetheless find that her environment was hostile. "A work environment consumed by remarks that intimidate, ridicule, and maliciously demean the status of women can create an environment that is as hostile as an environment that contains unwanted sexual advances." * * *

For the reasons above, we conclude that the EEOC has raised a triable issue with respect to each element of its hostile work environment claim. Accordingly, we reverse the district court's grant of summary judgment and remand for trial.

CASE QUESTIONS

1. What were the legal issues in this case? What did the court decide?
2. Why isn't this a case of an "equal opportunity harasser"?
3. Why does the court conclude that a jury could reasonably find that the harassment was sufficiently severe or pervasive to constitute a hostile environment?
4. Should the fact that the doctor stayed on the job until she found a better one and continued to perform well have any bearing on this case? Why or why not?
5. Do you agree with the court's decision in this case? Why or why not?

Challenges to hostile environments based on race are also quite common. In one recent case, two African American employees were allowed to go to trial based on evidence of a racially hostile environment that included spoken racial slurs and epithets, offensive graffiti, threats of violence, refusals of coworkers to work alongside the employees, false reports of safety violations, and displays of Confederate flags.[34] A component of racially hostile environments that has appeared with disturbing frequency in recent years is the display of hangman's nooses. African Americans and other people of color have been confronted in the workplace with this vicious symbol of a racially segregated past [35] Harking back to the lynching of African Americans that extended well into the twentieth century and took the lives of thousands,[36] there is nothing innocent or remotely humorous about such displays. *Employers that do not respond to these odious displays with the strongest disciplinary measures are not living up to their responsibilities.*

Clippings

A trucking company in North Carolina has been sued by the EEOC for racial harassment. For more than a year, African American employees of A.C. Widenhouse were regularly subjected to racial slurs and derogatory comments. It is alleged that a coworker approached an African American employee with a noose and said "This is for you. Do you want to hang from the family tree?" EEOC

---

[34]*Watson v. CEVA Logistics U.S.*, 619 F.3d 936 (8th Cir. 2010).

[35]Sana Siwolop. "Nooses, Symbols of Race Hatred, at Center of Workplace Lawsuits." *New York Times* (July 10, 2000), A1.

[36]Mark Potok et al. "The Geography of Hate." *New York Times* (November 25, 2007), Wk11.

Regional Attorney Lynette A. Barnes commented that "Cases like this remind us that, sadly, in the 21st century, racial harassment still exists in workplaces across America…. The display of nooses is especially cruel and unacceptable."

U.S. Equal Employment Opportunity Commission. "A.C. Widenhouse Sued by EEOC for Racial Harassment." Press Release (June 22, 2011) (http://www.eeoc.gov/).

When Are Harassing Behaviors Unwelcome?

Individuals can view the same situations very differently. Verbal and physical conduct that would otherwise constitute egregious harassment might be entirely welcomed when engaged in by two employees who are lovers or even just friends who routinely tease each other. Although the principal focus in harassment cases is on the "objective" existence of harassment viewed through the eyes of the hypothetical reasonable person, plaintiffs also must show that they subjectively perceived their treatment as **unwelcome** harassment. Harassing conduct is unwelcome when the person complaining of the conduct did not solicit or provoke it and that person regarded the conduct as offensive and unwanted (at the time it occurred).[37]

A circumstance that can cause the unwelcomeness of conduct to be questioned is when an employee fails to tell the harasser and/or the employer that the conduct is offensive or waits a long time before reporting the conduct. Victims of harassment are not always required to confront their harassers (sometimes they are well advised not to do so). Nor must they always report harassment to their employer to establish that the conduct is unwelcome (establishing employer *liability* for harassment is a separate matter that is discussed later). Some contemporaneous indication of unwelcomeness, even if nonverbal (e.g., appearing disgusted at the harasser's statements, taking obvious steps to avoid the harasser), however, is important to the plaintiff's case. Another problematic situation occurs when a prior romantic relationship goes sour and a party that no longer desires to maintain the relationship continues to be pursued by the other party. It is particularly important in these cases that the person who no longer desires romantic attention clearly notify the other person of this and act accordingly.

Employers seeking to defend harassment claims also sometimes argue that any harassment was not unwelcome because the "victim" provoked or actively participated in the harassment. An employee's own salty language, flirting, pranks, and even sexually provocative dress and appearance[38] can provide indications that the individual was an active participant in, rather than a victim of, harassment. However, an employer was unsuccessful in arguing that a woman's previous conviction on prostitution charges for operating a brothel negated her harassment claim against the owner of the company for which she now worked.[39] The employer claimed that the woman could not have found the owner's sexual advances offensive and unwelcome because she had "engaged in much more sexually inappropriate behavior" in the past. The court pointed out that the criminal conviction had been fourteen years earlier and that there was no evidence of her engaging in sexually provocative behavior at her current workplace. Thus, there was "no basis for concluding that her illegal conduct at that time has any bearing on her

---

[37]U.S. Equal Employment Opportunity Commission. "Policy Guidance on Current Issues of Sexual Harassment." No. N-915-050 (March 19, 1990).

[38]*Meritor*, at 61.

[39]*Terry v. 7700 Enterprises, LLC*, 2010 U.S. Dist. LEXIS 136707 (N.D. Okla.).

subjective evaluation of [the owner's] conduct years later."[40] Likewise, in a case involving a woman who had posed nude in a "biker" magazine, the court concluded:

> *The plaintiff's choice to pose for a nude magazine outside work hours is not material to the issue of whether plaintiff found her employer's work-related conduct offensive. This is not a case where [the plaintiff] posed in provocative and suggestive ways at work. Her private life, regardless how reprehensible the trier of fact might find it to be, did not provide lawful acquiescence to unwanted sexual advances at her work place by her employer.[41]*

What about men who are harassed by women? It is often assumed that men—at least heterosexuals—are more likely to welcome such attention than are women. But in the case of an airport worker who was relentlessly pursued for sex by his female, married coworker, the court said:

> *It cannot be assumed that because a man receives sexual advances from a woman that those advances are welcome. * * * [T]hat is a stereotype … it does not matter to welcomeness whether other men might have welcomed [the coworker's] sexual propositions.[42]*

The court then went on to note the substantial evidence that the woman's advances were not welcomed, including the psychological distress that it caused, the lack of any current or prior sexual relationship between them, the man's recent widowhood, his religious beliefs concerning sex with a married person, and most basically, his clear and unequivocal statements to the woman that he was not interested.

Lastly, an employee's voluntary or consensual participation in sexual activity is not necessarily fatal to her harassment claim. The fact that a plaintiff had consensual sex with her harasser some forty or fifty times over a period of several years did not negate her hostile environment claim when she was able to credibly claim that she did so out of fear of losing her job. The Supreme Court explained that "the fact that sex-related conduct was 'voluntary,' in the sense that the complainant was not forced to participate against her will, is not a defense to a sexual harassment suit brought under Title VII. The gravamen [core requirement] of any sexual harassment claim is that the alleged sexual advances were 'unwelcome.'"[43] Welcomeness and voluntariness are distinct matters.

Liability for Harassment

The grounds for attributing liability to employers for harassment differ depending on the type of harassment (i.e., whether the harassment results in a tangible employment action) and the organizational position of the harasser (i.e., top official, manager, nonsupervisory employee). Table 9.1 outlines the differing standards for employer liability based on these two factors.

Harassment by Top Officials, Managers, and Supervisors

When harassment is engaged in by someone whose position allows him or her to speak and act for the company—for example, an owner, a president, a partner, or a corporate officer—the company is vicariously liable for the harassment. This is true regardless of

---

[40]*Terry*, at 15.

[41]*Burns v. McGregor Electronic Industries, Inc.*, 989 F.2d 959, 963 (8th Cir. 1993).

[42]*EEOC v. Prospect Airport Services*, 621 F.3d 991, 997 (9th Cir. 2010).

[43]*Meritor*, at 68.

TABLE 9.1 EMPLOYER LIABILITY FOR HARASSMENT

POSITION OF HARASSER	TYPE OF HARASSMENT	
	TANGIBLE EMPLOYMENT ACTION	NO TANGIBLE EMPLOYMENT ACTION (HOSTILE ENVIRONMENT)
Top officials	Vicarious liability	Vicarious liability
Managers, supervisors	Vicarious liability	Vicarious liability subject to affirmative defense
Nonsupervisory employees, third parties	N/A	Negligence standard for liability

© Cengage Learning 2013.

the type of harassment. **Vicarious liability** means that if the illegal act(s) (in this case, harassment) occurred, legal responsibility for damages is unconditionally placed with the employing organization. The organization cannot avoid liability by showing that the harassment was contrary to its policies or in spite of its best efforts at prevention.

Clippings

A former sales associate at American Apparel has filed a sexual harassment suit, alleging that when she went to the home of the company's founder and CEO Dov Charney to discuss reemployment, he had something very different in mind. This suit, joined by several other women, is the second suit filed within a month alleging harassment by Mr. Charney. The CEO has also been the object of at least four prior harassment suits, all of which were settled or dismissed. American Apparel is known for its sexually provocative marketing. Mr. Charney is said to hold business meetings in his bedroom and has admitted to having sexual relationships with his employees.

Laura M. Holson. "Chief of American Apparel Faces 2nd Harassment Suit." *New York Times* (March 24, 2011), B2.

Vicarious liability is the norm in discrimination cases. If a manager discriminates against older workers when deciding whom to lay off, the company is liable for that discrimination, regardless of whether owners or top managers were aware of the practice or encouraged it in any way. In harassment cases, the general rule of vicarious liability for discrimination is adhered to when the harassment results in a tangible employment action. If a manager or supervisor uses the decision-making authority that has been conferred on him to try to exact sexual favors and then makes employment decisions accordingly, the employer is vicariously liable. Even though the supervisor or manager is likely acting outside of the scope of his employment in doing so, he is still an agent of the employer and aided in carrying out the harassment by being given the authority to make employment decisions.

Clippings

A jury awarded over $1.5 million to three female former employees in a sexual harassment and retaliation suit brought by the EEOC. Punitive damages alone were in excess of $1 million. Two male managers at Mid-American Specialties, an office supply company, engaged in severe harassment including exposing themselves, touching female employees, and demanding that women participate in a "smooching club" to receive the sales leads they needed to earn their commissions. When female employees resisted these advances and complained, they were fired. During the two years over which the harassment occurred, the company had no sexual harassment policy, no procedure for reporting harassment, and no training regarding harassment. At trial, company officials testified that they did not believe that such measures were necessary. The HR manager testified that she did not even know the definition of harassment.

U.S. Equal Employment Opportunity Commission. "Jury Awards over $1.5 Million in EEOC Sexual Harassment and Retaliation Case against Mid-American Specialties." Press Release (March 4, 2011) (http://www.eeoc.gov/).

Often, managers or supervisors engage in harassment that does not result in tangible employment actions. In such cases, employers can avoid vicarious liability by establishing *both* "prongs" of the following **affirmative defense**:

1. The employer exercised reasonable care to prevent and correct promptly any harassment.
2. The plaintiff unreasonably failed to take advantage of any preventive or corrective opportunities provided by the employer or to avoid harm otherwise.[44]

Whether "reasonable care" to prevent harassment was exercised depends first and foremost on the existence of a sound **harassment policy** and **complaint procedure**. Absent a legally adequate policy prohibiting harassment and identifying a set of actors to whom harassment complaints can be made, an employer will almost certainly be unable to establish the affirmative defense. Reasonable care must be taken not only to prevent harassment but also to promptly correct any harassment that nonetheless occurs. In general, employers need to show that they acted promptly in responding to employee complaints, conducted effective investigations, and took steps reasonably calculated to remedy harassment and prevent future incidents. In a case involving lifeguards subjected to a hostile environment by their supervisors, the Supreme Court concluded that the city could not establish the first prong of the affirmative defense because it had completely overlooked beach employees when it distributed its harassment policy, it made no efforts to monitor the supervisors, and it did not provide the employees with a clear alternative to complaining to the same supervisors that were perpetrating the harassment.[45] The importance of not only having a policy, but disseminating it to employees, was underscored in a case involving a school teacher who was sexually assaulted by her male supervisor. Rejecting the employer's effort to invoke the affirmative defense, the court stated that "An employer's failure to show that it had 'established and *disseminated* an anti-discrimination policy, complete with a *known* complaint procedure' can prevent it from successfully claiming the [affirmative] defense."[46]

---

[44]*Faragher v. City of Boca Raton,* 524 U.S. 775, 807 (1998); *Ellerth,* at 765.

[45]*Faragher,* at 808–09.

[46]*Agusty-Reyes v. Department of Education of the Commonwealth of Puerto Rico,* 601 F.3d 45, 55 (1st Cir. 2010).

JUST THE FACTS

A female employee worked as an administrative assistant. The "warehouse lead" was a male who for several months made repeated sexual advances and propositions to pay her for various sex acts. The woman complained to her immediate supervisor shortly after the offensive conduct began. The supervisor said that he would talk to the warehouse lead, but the advances and propositions continued for two more months until the employee threatened to inform the warehouse lead's wife about his actions. A month later, the branch manager asked the woman about the situation and she described what had been going on. The branch manager then contacted the VP for human resources and the executive team. An outside firm was hired to investigate and the warehouse lead was suspended pending the outcome of the investigation. The investigators concluded that the woman had been sexually harassed. The company's harassment policy, which the woman received when she started work, says that "Any employee who believes that he or she is being harassed in violation of this policy or who becomes aware of harassment of a co-worker is expected to immediately bring the matter to the attention of the human resources department or a member of the executive team." Should this employer be held liable for the sexual harassment that occurred?

See, *Peoples v. Marjack Co.*, 2010 U.S. Dist. LEXIS 19996 (D. Md.).

Employers have often been successful in establishing the affirmative defense. A female sales representative's hostile environment claim failed, in part, because the company had taken reasonable care to prevent and correct harassment. Specifically, the employer had a written policy prohibiting harassment, the policy was published in the employee handbook and reinforced by an annual letter sent to all employees, training was provided to both supervisors and employees, her complaint was responded to promptly, the offending supervisor was immediately placed on administrative leave and later fired, a thorough investigation was launched, and multiple interviews were conducted with the involved parties.[47] Another employer was lauded for its "more than reasonable attempts" to correct harassment, including launching a prompt investigation, terminating an employee for breaching the confidentiality of the investigation, rearranging the plaintiff's schedule to minimize the chances of working alone with the offending supervisor, issuing a three-page warning letter to the supervisor threatening termination if he attempted to retaliate, requiring the supervisor to attend anti-harassment training and evaluations, and sending a letter to the plaintiff thanking her for coming forward, informing her of the steps taken, and reminding her to report any further harassment.[48] In another affirmative defense case, the employer responded to an employee's allegations of harassment by a manager at a Christmas party by conducting a prompt investigation, suspending the manager pending the outcome of the investigation, and terminating the manager six days later.[49] The court said that the

---

[47]*Walton v. Johnson & Johnson Services, Inc.*, 347 F.3d 1272 (11th Cir. 2003), *cert. denied*, 541 U.S. 959 (2004).

[48]*Roby v. CWI*, 579 F.3d 779, 786 (7th Cir. 2009).

[49]*Collette v. Stein-Mart*, 2005 U.S. App. LEXIS 2093 (6th Cir.).

employer's actions "epitomized how a responsible employer should act when confronted with an allegation of employment discrimination."[50]

To prevail using the affirmative defense, employers must not only take the necessary preventative and corrective measures but also show that their employees unreasonably failed to take advantage of these measures. The most common, but not the only, reason for finding that an employee has acted unreasonably is a delay in reporting harassment. Courts have clearly placed the burden on employees experiencing harassment to come forward quickly and to use their employers' established reporting mechanisms. A campus police officer who waited seven months to use the university's formal complaint procedure, during which time she had attempted to resolve the harassment problem informally, was deemed to have acted unreasonably.[51] Likewise, in a case involving an employee of a federal government agency, the court ruled for the employer because the employee had waited about five months before making a formal complaint.[52] The employee had earlier posted a copy of the harassment policy on her door as a warning to the harasser and had confided in a friend of hers who held a management position in the agency. But the court took the view that the report to her friend, who did not have responsibility for handling EEO complaints, was insufficient and the harasser's threat that she would not be believed if she tried to report him did not justify her delay in reporting.

Hardage v. CBS is an interesting example of a harassment case in which an employer successfully invoked the affirmative defense. Note the emphasis that the court places on the plaintiff's failure to promptly and clearly report the harassment he was experiencing.

Hardage v. CBS
2006 U.S. App. LEXIS 3017 (9th Cir.)

OPINION BY CIRCUIT JUDGE WALLACE:

The district court entered summary judgment dismissing Hardage's sexual harassment ... claims against CBS Broadcasting.... The district court concluded that CBS was entitled to assert an affirmative defense to liability. * * * [W]e affirm.

Hardage * * * was promoted to Local Sales Manager in February of 2000.... [He was] supervised by Patty Dean, the General Sales Manager, who was in turn supervised by defendant Sparks, the station's General Manager. * * * Hardage ... alleges that during Sparks' visits to the Seattle office, she repeatedly flirted with him and made inappropriate comments—such as "you need somebody that's older and more stable that can take care of you." Leo Elbert, another employee at KSTW, stated that Sparks would "camp out" in Hardage's office, kick back in his chair with her feet on his desk, and smile and giggle in a flirtatious manner. Hardage asserts that he never flirted with Sparks, but that he is a "flirtatious person by nature" and that there was "playful banter from the gitgo" with Sparks, some of which he concedes could have been perceived as mutually flirtatious. He has also stated that he referred to Sparks as "Sparkalicious," "Baskin Robbins 32nd Flavor" and "Driving Ms. Sparky." He also agreed in his deposition that his love life in general was "definitely" part of the "watercooler talk" and "a big topic of conversation around the office."

---

[50]*Collette,* at 23.

[51]*Gawley v. Indiana University,* 2001 U.S. App. LEXIS 27353 (7th Cir.).

[52]*Taylor v. Solis,* 571 F.3d 1313 (D.C. Cir. 2009).

In addition to the charged workplace harassment, Hardage alleges more serious harassment on five occasions outside of the office. First, … Hardage, Sparks, Dean, Dean's husband, and a few others attended a brunch…. Hardage believes that he might have been the person who invited Sparks to the event. The group consumed alcoholic beverages and eventually relocated to a sports bar. Hardage drove Sparks in her car. After a few more drinks, Sparks allegedly asked Hardage if her hands were pretty, and then put her foot on an air hockey table while Hardage was playing and asked if he thought she had cute feet. Later, while Hardage was on a skateboard game, Sparks allegedly got up on the skateboard behind him, put her arms around his waist and told him that he had a "cute ass."

After the sports bar, the group went to [a] restaurant for dinner and continued drinking alcoholic beverages. Sparks sat across the table from Hardage and allegedly took off her shoe, slid under the table, and put her foot in Hardage's crotch. At the end of the dinner, many people commented that Sparks was too drunk to drive home, and Sparks asked if she could stay at Hardage's apartment for the night. Hardage declined her request and, according to one witness, Sparks became "livid" and "stormed off" to drive herself home.

The second incident of harassment … occurred two days [later] when Sparks called Hardage and invited him to [a] restaurant for drinks after work. At the restaurant, she allegedly told Hardage she had not been able to sleep and "was having orgasms in her sleep." She asked Hardage if he felt the same way about her; Hardage replied that he did not want to damage his career by having a relationship and wanted to go no further than friendship. Hardage asserts that Sparks responded with a snide comment along the lines of, "Don't forget who got you to where you are."

Third, … Hardage and Sparks were both traveling to Texas to visit their respective families. Sparks arranged her travel plans so that she and Hardage sat next to each other on the same flight. Hardage alleges that Sparks took off her shoe and started rubbing her foot on his leg. After he asked her to stop, she began rubbing his back "in a kind of a weird manner." Sparks later referred to Hardage as her boyfriend as she was ordering drinks from a flight attendant, and as they were consuming their drinks, she grabbed his hand and made explicit sexual advances. Hardage contends that she offered him oral sex and told him that one experience of sexual intercourse with her would be life-altering for him. Hardage told her that nothing physical would happen between them.

The fourth incident of alleged harassment occurred … when Hardage and Sparks took some of KSTW's clients to a baseball game. This is the only alleged instance of harassment outside the workplace that occurred during a work-related event. Hardage and Sparks sat next to each other, and Sparks began rubbing his leg with her foot. Hardage responded, "Kathy, cut it out, you know, we got clients sitting next to us, it's inappropriate." Later, Sparks allegedly took off her rain poncho, put it over Hardage's lap and reached under it for Hardage's crotch. Hardage states he elbowed her hand away and told her to stop.

After the game, Hardage invited Sparks to join him for drinks with his friends at [a] bar. Sparks allegedly glared at Hardage while he greeted his friends, including several women, and shouted, "Who haven't you f—ed in here?" Hardage states he pointed to one woman and responded jokingly, "I haven't f—ed anybody in here, you know, but hopefully she's next." Sparks became very upset, asked to be taken back to her car, and shouted obscenities to Hardage. One witness, Leo Elbert, has stated that Sparks told Hardage, "Don't f—ing talk to me. You're finished."

The day after [this] incident, Hardage complained to Dean and told her that "last night, things went way too far" and that Sparks had lost her temper. However, Hardage has stated that he did not tell her "specifics about sexual contact" and never told Dean that Sparks had touched him in an inappropriate way, nor did he share any details of the harassment with anyone else at work. Hardage also testified that Dean later suggested something "to the effect of … 'Why don't you just do it and get it over with. It may put her in a better mood.'" However, … Dean promptly contacted Ray Rajewski, an executive vice president, who in turn called Hardage to let him know that he would be contacted by Paul Falcone, a representative from the company's human resources department. Falcone called Hardage the same day of Hardage's complaint and arranged to meet with him in person the following week.

During their subsequent meeting—which occurred while Hardage drove Falcone to the airport—he did not give Falcone details about the harassment; indeed, he "didn't share any of the so-called gory details with anybody." Instead, he gave Falcone "just the broad statement … that [Sparks] had made … unwanted sexual advances that were denied," that he was uncomfortable with the situation, and that Sparks had lost her temper and was "jeopardizing … the success of the team." Hardage did not tell Falcone about any of the alleged physical contact or groping by Sparks.

It is also undisputed that although Falcone offered to talk to Sparks and treat Hardage's complaint as an anonymous complaint, Hardage insisted on handling the situation by himself. Hardage explained in his deposition that he did not think the complaint could be handled truly anonymously, because Sparks would know the source, and that he "prided himself in handling [his] own business affairs." Approximately two weeks after their meeting, Falcone called Hardage to follow up, and Hardage informed Falcone that nothing new had happened and that he still did not want Falcone to intervene. * * *

An employer is vicariously liable "for an actionable hostile environment created by a supervisor with immediate (or successively higher) authority over the employee." However, the Supreme Court has established an affirmative defense to vicarious liability:

* * * The defense comprises two necessary elements: (a) that the employer exercised reasonable care to prevent and correct promptly any sexually harassing behavior, and (b) that the plaintiff employee unreasonably failed to take advantage of any preventive or corrective opportunities provided by the employer or to avoid harm otherwise.... No affirmative defense is available, however, when the supervisor's harassment culminates in a tangible employment action.... Thus, even if we assume that Hardage was sexually harassed, CBS can avoid liability if it can show that (1) it took no "tangible employment action" against Hardage, (2) it exercised reasonable care to prevent and correct harassment, and (3) Hardage unreasonably failed to take advantage of preventive or corrective opportunities.

A "tangible employment action constitutes a significant change in employment status, such as hiring, firing, failing to promote, reassignment with significantly different responsibilities, or a decision causing a significant change in benefits." A tangible employment action "requires an official act of the enterprise, a company act," and "in most cases inflicts direct economic harm." While employed at KSTW-TV, Hardage never experienced any decrease in compensation, hours, title, duties or benefits. He contends, however, that he was constructively discharged as a result of a hostile work environment, and this constructive discharge constitutes a tangible employment action. He cites the sexual harassment by Sparks as well as allegedly retaliatory actions—namely, the adverse performance memoranda he received, Sparks'

snide remarks, and [a] memorandum warning Hardage that his performance would be reevaluated after a thirty-day period. He contends that after "enduring the severe and pervasive harassment ... and retaliation," he "finally came to the conclusion that CBS would not take his complaints seriously" and saw "no way out" but to resign. He also argues he was constructively discharged by being placed on "the same kind of probation under which [he] had seen other employees consistently lose their jobs."

These arguments miss the mark. [In] a constructive discharge claim, a plaintiff "must show there are triable issues of fact as to whether a reasonable person in [his] position would have felt that [he] was forced to quit because of intolerable and discriminatory working conditions." Hardage concedes that the last time Sparks made inappropriate sexual advances or comments was in March of 2001, yet he did not resign until five months later, on August 31, 2001. As a result, even if Sparks' sexual harassment created a hostile work environment, such harassment ceased well in advance of Hardage's resignation. Nor do the allegedly retaliatory actions taken against Hardage amount to a constructive discharge. CBS has proffered legitimate, non-retaliatory reasons for the adverse performance memoranda, which were addressed to both Hardage and [another manager]. * * * [E]ven if we consider the memoranda as tangible employment actions in and of themselves, rather than as components of a constructive discharge, they do not bar CBS from asserting the [affirmative] defense. * * *

In order to assert the [affirmative] defense successfully, CBS must have "exercised reasonable care to prevent and correct promptly any sexually harassing behavior." * * * [I]t is undisputed that CBS has an anti-harassment policy, with which Hardage had familiarity. As a supervisor, he was responsible for reporting sexual harassment to the human resources department, and he understood that sexual harassment was prohibited. Thus, CBS fulfilled its duty to take preventive measures as a matter of law by adopting and promoting awareness of its anti-harassment policy.

In addition, however, CBS must have taken steps to correct Hardage's particular situation promptly. After Hardage complained to Dean in October 2000, Dean immediately contacted Rajewski, who in turn notified Falcone. Falcone called Hardage the same day he made his complaint, and shortly thereafter, they met in Seattle. At their meeting, Falcone discussed Hardage's options. Hardage asserted that he wanted to "handle it by himself." Approximately two weeks later, Falcone followed up with Hardage by telephone, and Hardage indicated that he still did not want Falcone to intervene. This would appear to end any debate on this issue, but Hardage makes two arguments as to why there is a triable factual dispute regarding this requirement.

First, he emphasizes Falcone's "inexplicable" failure to investigate his complaint or discipline Sparks…. "[N]otice of … sexually harassing conduct triggers an employer's duty to take prompt corrective action that is 'reasonably calculated to end the harassment.'" The reasonableness of the remedy depends on its ability to: (1) 'stop harassment by the person who engaged in harassment;' and (2) 'persuade potential harassers to refrain from unlawful conduct.'" Although an "investigation is a key step," we "consider the overall picture" to determine whether the employer's response was appropriate.

To be sure, CBS's anti-harassment policy states that "following a complaint, a thorough investigation will be made" and the "matter will be handled in the strictest of confidence." Hardage was convinced, however, that there was "absolutely no way that [his complaint] could be handled anonymously," and he therefore told Falcone he wanted to handle the situation by himself. Indeed, he stated that when Sparks later mentioned the words "sexual harassment" to him, he "felt like [his] trust had been possibly violated by corporate … leaking information, because [he had] stated [he] wanted to handle the case on [his] own."

In addition, although Hardage did put CBS on notice of Sparks' "unwanted sexual advances," he did not tell Falcone the "gory details" or apprise Dean of the "specifics about sexual contact." Instead, he was vague about the extent and nature of Sparks' advances. Thus, even if a more thorough investigation and disciplinary measures for the harasser could in some circumstances be essential in spite of a harassed employee's request to handle the situation, there can be no such duty in this case. Dean's alleged comment to Hardage that "Why don't you just do it and get it over with. It may put her in a better mood" is certainly troubling. However, it cannot singularly serve to transform CBS's response into an unreasonable one, nor can it erase the legal significance of his specific request not to investigate his admittedly minimal and vague complaint. Considering the "overall picture," CBS's response was both prompt and reasonable as a matter of law.

There may be circumstances where an employer's "remedial obligation kicks in," regardless of the employee's stated wishes. In other words, the mere fact that the employee tells the employer not to take any remedial action may not always relieve that employer of the obligation to do so. Here, however, it is uncontested that Hardage did not want Falcone to take further action, and that Hardage's wishes were not insincere or uninformed. Moreover, Hardage did not disclose to Falcone the details of the harassment, so Falcone had no way to know of its severity.

Alternatively, Hardage contends there is a triable factual dispute as to whether CBS was on notice prior to his complaint to Dean in October of 2000. He alleges that he made "numerous complaints" to Dean and repeatedly told her he did not want to be left alone with Sparks. Yet when counsel for CBS asked Hardage during his deposition to state every time he could recall speaking to Dean about Sparks' behavior, Hardage … could not remember the dates or what he told Dean about why he did not want to attend the events. Hardage recalled that he may have told Dean he did not want to be alone with Sparks—which Hardage asserts was "an ongoing joke"—but such a statement would hardly have given Dean notice of ongoing sexual harassment. * * *

Hardage also argues that CBS was on notice of the harassment because Dean personally observed some of Sparks' harassing behavior. Yet, Hardage has stated that Dean also witnessed "some flirtation," and he concedes that the mutual "banter" between Sparks and him could have been perceived as flirtatious. Taken in context, Dean did not unreasonably fail to report the incident to CBS management, thereby triggering CBS's duty to remedy the situation promptly. In addition, Hardage suggests Dean "had the opportunity to observe the harassment on a daily basis in the workplace." However, … [because] Hardage worked in Seattle and Sparks worked in Tacoma … Dean had limited opportunities to observe Hardage and Sparks together. Furthermore, given Hardage's playful names for Sparks…, his repeated invitations to Sparks to socialize with him outside of work, and his failure to inform Dean that Sparks' flirtations were unwelcome harassment, Dean did not unreasonably fail to report any flirtatious behavior by Sparks when she was visiting the Seattle office.

We now turn to the … [second] requirement: that Hardage unreasonably failed to take advantage of preventive or corrective opportunities. As a local sales manager in charge of supervising approximately ten employees, Hardage was well aware of CBS's antiharassment policy and the procedure for initiating a complaint. Indeed, he testified he understood that "all actual sexual harassment in [his] workplace [was] dealt with in a serious manner." He contends that he "informally and formally reported the harassment on several occasions," and therefore he did not unreasonably fail to make use of remedial and preventive opportunities.

Yet, although Hardage contends the harassment commenced in April 2000, his first complaint to Dean that he has identified with specificity was in October 2000—approximately half a year later. While proof that an employee failed to fulfill the ... obligation of reasonable care to avoid harm is not limited to showing any unreasonable failure to use any complaint procedure provided by the employer, a demonstration of such failure will normally suffice to satisfy the employer's burden under [this] element of the defense." In addition to waiting half a year to make a complaint, when Hardage finally made his complaint he specifically asked the company not to investigate it. By specifically requesting the company not make use of its remedial and preventative procedures, Hardage unreasonably failed to make use of CBS's antiharassment policies and procedures. * * *

CASE QUESTIONS

1. What were the legal issues in this case? What did the court decide?
2. What tangible employment actions does Hardage allege? Why does the court not agree?
3. Was Hardage subjected to a hostile environment? Were Sparks' actions toward him "unwelcome"? Does it matter that most of the incidents occurred outside of the workplace? Why or why not?
4. What did the employer do to prevent and promptly correct any harassment? Do you think that the company did enough in this case to meet its legal obligations? Why or why not?
5. Why do you suppose that Hardage acted as he did (i.e., continuing to socialize with Sparks, waiting months to complain, not supplying all of the "gory details," saying that he preferred to deal with the matter on his own)? Was he unreasonable in failing to take advantage of the employer's preventive and corrective mechanisms?

Harassment by Coworkers or Third Parties

Employees or third parties (e.g., clients, customers) without the authority to make or influence employment decisions are effectively precluded from engaging in harassment that results in tangible employment actions. However, coworkers and third parties are quite capable of creating hostile environments for other employees. Employer liability for hostile environment harassment by coworkers and third parties rests on whether the employer was negligent in not protecting the employee from harassment. Specifically, the employer is liable under the **negligence standard** for harassment by coworkers and third parties where the *plaintiff* can establish *both* of the following:

1. The employer knew or should have known about the harassment.
2. The employer failed to take prompt and appropriate action to stop the harassment.

Considerable overlap exists between this negligence standard and the affirmative defense, but here it is the plaintiff that must prove these things. The first element establishes that the employer had actual or "constructive" knowledge of the harassment; that is, the employer knew of the harassment or should have known, given its prevalence or visibility. A timely and specific complaint to the employer is the simplest way to establish employer knowledge, but employers cannot use the "ostrich defense" (sticking their heads in the sand) to ignore blatant harassment even in the absence of specific complaints.[53] When a supervisor asked an employee about possible harassment, the employee became upset and said "I can't talk about it." The supervisor's response of

---

[53]*Robinson v. Jacksonville Shipyards, Inc.,* 760 F. Supp. 1486, 1530 (M.D. Fla. 1991).

"That's good because I don't want to know what happened" was the type of willful ignorance that does not shield an employer from liability.[54] However, it is important that the actual or constructive knowledge of harassment rests with someone in a management position charged with at least general responsibility for doing something about it. An employee's reports of harassment to two team leaders in a team manufacturing environment were not sufficient to impute knowledge to the employer because the team leaders were not management-level employees.[55]

Clippings

Fleming's Prime Steakhouse in Scottsdale, Arizona, has settled a sexual harassment suit brought by the EEOC on behalf of male employees at the restaurant. The male head chef allegedly took liberties with his male subordinates, pinching and touching their private parts, groping them from behind, and even finding novel uses for kitchen utensils. There was evidence that several managers were aware of the situation but chose to ignore it. EEOC Regional Attorney Mary Jo O'Neill said that "The key lesson we want people to take from this case [is that] employers must protect their employees from sexual harassment. This means doing a meaningful internal investigation designed to find the truth and not designed to merely cover tracks. Also, employers must immediately stop further sexual harassment from occurring. Here, not only did Fleming's not fire the harasser, they let him continue the harassment for more than a year and a half before allowing him to resign."

U.S. Equal Employment Opportunity Commission. "Flemings Pays $248,750 to Three Men in EEOC Same-Sex Sexual Harassment Lawsuit." Press Release (December 7, 2010) (http://www.eeoc.gov/).

Practical Considerations Under what circumstances is termination of a harasser the appropriate remedy?

Actual or constructive knowledge of harassment triggers a legal obligation to take prompt actions reasonably calculated to stop the harassment. In *EEOC v. Xerxes Corp.*, the court must decide whether, at different points in time, the employer's response to reported harassment was legally sufficient.

EEOC v. Xerxes Corp.
639 F.3d 658 (4th Cir. 2011)

OPINION BY CHIEF JUDGE TRAXLER:

This appeal arises from an action brought by the Equal Employment Opportunity Commission ("EEOC") on behalf of Albert Bernard Pearson [and] Keith Wilson, African-American employees of Xerxes Corporation ("Xerxes"), alleging a hostile work environment on the basis of race, in violation of Title VII of the Civil Rights Act of 1964. The district court granted summary judgment for Xerxes. We affirm in part, vacate in part, and remand.

Xerxes is a fiberglass tank manufacturer based in Minneapolis, Minnesota. Pearson [and] Wilson ...

---

[54]*Duch v. Jakubek*, 588 F.3d 757, 765 (2d Cir. 2009).

[55]*Huston v. Procter & Gamble Paper Products*, 568 F.3d 100 (3d Cir. 2009).

worked as assemblers at Xerxes' plant in Williamsport, Maryland. Bob Shifflett was their shift supervisor. He reported to plant superintendent Greg Carty, who reported to plant manager Wayne Green.

At all times, Xerxes had in place a comprehensive Corporate Compliance Program and Program Guide, prohibiting discrimination and harassment in the plant. Plant employees were instructed to report any violations to their "supervisor, Plant Manager, ... or a member of Xerxes' Compliance Committee." * * * In addition, as of at least January 9, 2006, Xerxes also had in place a separate anti-harassment policy, which prohibited "Sexual, Racial and Other Objectionable Conduct or Unlawful Harassment." The policy provided specific examples of prohibited conduct and, among other directions, instructed plant employees to *Immediately* Report The Incident To Your Supervisor *And* Plant Manager." All employees received copies of Xerxes' antiharassment policies and were trained in them at the time of hire. Refresher training was conducted annually. Xerxes and its nonsupervisory employees were also subject to a Collective Bargaining Agreement (the "CBA") between Xerxes and the United Automobile, Aerospace and Agricultural Implement Workers of America, Local No. 171 (the "Union"). The CBA prohibited "unlawful discrimination against employees on account of race, color, creed, national origin, religion, sex, sexual orientation, pregnancy, marital status, age, disability, or Union affiliation, or any other legally protected class status." * * * The Union president testified that Xerxes took "a strong stance against discrimination," and "seem[ed] to respond very quickly whenever there [were] allegations" of discrimination.

Bernard Pearson ... testified that from June 2005 until February 2006, his coworkers subjected him to repeated racial slurs and pranks in the plant. He testified that Amber Gatrell used the word "n*****" in his presence on repeated occasions and referred to him as "Boy." He testified that Floyd Myers called him "Boy" and "black Polack," and called a white woman a "n***** lover." He also testified that unknown coworkers occasionally played pranks on him, such as turning the lights off in the bathroom and throwing wet paper towels at him, placing gel on the doorknob in the bathroom so that he could not open the door, tampering with his toolbox lock, and hiding his toolbox. Pearson testified that he reported these incidents to Shifflett as they occurred, but that Shifflett did nothing until February 2006. He did not complain to any other members of management.

Keith Wilson ... alleges that he was first subjected to racial harassment by his coworkers in November 2005. He testified that on two or three occasions someone stole or threw away his and Pearson's lunches. He also complained that Tammy Smith called him by racially-tinged names, including "Buckwheat," "Benson," and "Yellow Boy." Wilson testified that he reported the incidents to Shifflett as they occurred, but did not complain to any other management employee because the Union representative told him he had to report them to his direct supervisor first.

On February 3, 2006, however, two related incidents involving Gatrell and Myers were reported to Shifflett and to Green. Wilson testified that while he was working with Gatrell, she said to him, "Boy you don't lay up no manway like that." Wilson reported the incident to Shifflett and told Shifflett that "where I come from ... boy is another name for the N word." Shifflett memorialized the complaint and his response in writing.... * * * "I told [Wilson] and [Pearson] that no they don't have to listen to this and that it would be dealt with right away. I went to [Gatrell] and told her that I think the best thing to do is go to [Wilson] and say to him that if he took [o]ffense about her saying boy to him that she was sorry. The next day [Gatrell] talked to [Wilson] and [Pearson] in the parking lot and told [Wilson] just what I said to." * * * Later that same evening, Myers exchanged words with Pearson and Wilson in the lunchroom and "said something like, yeah, Boy, well I'll see you outside." Myers also admitted using the term "boy" during the exchange, but claimed that he did not intend it to be racially offensive. After Green met with Myers about the incident, Myers apologized to Pearson and Wilson. Green also held a meeting with the shift employees to review Xerxes' anti-harassment policies. Green reminded the employees that racial harassment, including race-based comments, was prohibited and warned that future misconduct would result in disciplinary action.

After February 2006, Wilson reported no further incidents of racial harassment until June 2007. In May 2006, however, Pearson complained to Shifflett that two different coworkers had referred to music being played in the plant as "jungle music" and "n***** music." Shifflett told Pearson that he should report the incidents to Carty. Carty, in turn, met with Pearson and the Union representative. At the meeting, Pearson also told Carty about the problems he had experienced with Gatrell and Myers, and told Carty that he "wanted it to stop." Carty told Pearson not to say anything to anyone and that he would take care of it.

When Green learned of Pearson's complaint, he notified Xerxes' corporate office and Ronald Bachmeier, the EEO coordinator, traveled to the plant to investigate. According to Bachmeier: "While at the plant, I conducted a comprehensive investigation into Mr. Pearson's allegations. I interviewed Mr. Pearson as well as more than 15 other employees. Interviewees either denied Mr. Pearson's allegations, explained that Mr. Pearson had taken their remarks out of context, indicated that they did not mean their remarks to be racially offensive, or had since apologized for those remarks, and explained that Mr. Pearson had himself engaged in interaction with other employees using profanity and the racially offensive term." * * *

At the conclusion of the investigation, the following actions were taken by Xerxes. Myers and Gatrell were each issued two-day unpaid suspensions from work and required to attend refresher training in the anti-harassment policies. They were also "placed on a final warning" that Xerxes "w[ould] terminate [their] employment if [it was] ever determine[d] that [they] engaged, directly or indirectly, in hostile, offensive, or otherwise unlawful conduct toward any Xerxes employee." * * * Bachmeier determined that coworker Brian Bradley "had referred to certain music as 'jungle music,'" but that he "had not made the remark with intent to disparage any employee's race," and had apologized to Pearson and another employee. Bradley was issued a "Written Disciplinary Warning" and also required to attend refresher training. * * * He was also warned that future misconduct would "subject[ ] [him] to further discipline, up to and including the termination of [his] employment." … Bachmeier also learned that coworker Tammy Smith "had used the term 'Buckwheat,' in the context of a conversation with another African-American employee," but determined that her use of the name was related to a television show and that she had "credibly denied that she intended the remark to be in any way racially derogatory." … Smith was provided a "verbal counseling remind[ing] [her] of her obligation to comply with Xerxes … policies," and required to attend refresher training. Smith was also warned that violations of the harassment policies would result in appropriate disciplinary action in the future.

Finally, Bachmeier conducted refresher training of *all* employees regarding Xerxes' EEO and anti-harassment policies. * * * In a separate session, Bachmeier retrained the supervisory personnel as well, including "their responsibilities with respect to the promotion of a work environment in which all employees are treated lawfully, with dignity and respect." Pearson was provided a memorandum summarizing Xerxes' investigation and response to his complaint, and thanking him for coming forward. Pearson withdrew his [discrimination charge under Maryland law] and there were no further reports of harassment at the Xerxes plant until April 2007, nearly a full year later.

On April 10, 2007, Pearson found a 4″ × 4″ piece of fiberglass in his locker with the following message on it: "KKK plans could result in death, serious personal injury, NIGGA BENARd." Pearson reported the incident to the Union representative and Green, and Xerxes promptly began an investigation. * * * Unfortunately, Pearson could not identify the culprit, nor name any particular suspect. Xerxes was also unable to determine who was responsible. On April 20, 2007, Green reported the incident to the local Sheriff's Office. Three days later, Green held a plant meeting with all employees. At this meeting, Green warned the employees that the act was inappropriate and unacceptable, that Xerxes had requested a full police investigation, and that anyone with information about the incident was expected to come forward. The employees were advised that Xerxes "would take immediate and appropriate discipline, which in all likelihood, would result in termination" should Xerxes or the police find the person responsible for the act, and that Xerxes would encourage criminal prosecution if available. * * * The Sheriff's Office was unable to determine who was responsible and advised Pearson to report any further incidents.

* * * On June 11, 2007, Wilson discovered a small, stick-figure drawing depicting a person hanging by a noose and the phrase "IH IH MY N*****." Several days later, Wilson reported the incident to Shifflett, who made a copy of the drawing and notified Green. * * * Green met with Wilson, reported the incident to the Sheriffs' Office, and notified the corporate office. When Mike Zais, Xerxes' EEO Coordinator at that time, learned of the incident, he also traveled to the plant to investigate and interview employees. Unfortunately, the person responsible for this incident was also never identified. * * *

To survive summary judgment on a claim of a racially hostile work environment, the EEOC "must demonstrate that a reasonable jury could find [the] harassment (1) unwelcome; (2) based on race; and (3) sufficiently severe or pervasive to alter the conditions of employment and create an abusive atmosphere." In addition, the EEOC must present "sufficient evidence of a fourth element: that there is some basis for imposing liability" for the harassment on the employer.

Where an employee has been harassed by a coworker, "the employer may be liable in negligence [under the fourth element] if it knew or should have known about the harassment and failed to take effective action to stop it." "Once the employer has notice, then it must respond with remedial action reasonably calculated to end the harassment." "The institution and enforcement of [an anti-harassment] policy, in conjunction with an adequate complaint procedure, aid the employer in establishing that it has exercised reasonable care to prevent discrimination." "However, the mere promulgation of an anti-harassment policy, no matter how well-conceived, will not suffice to show the requisite level of care where the employer has administered the policy in bad faith or has rendered it ineffectual by acting unreasonably."

In this case it is undisputed that Xerxes' anti-harassment policies "provide[d] reasonable procedures for victims to register complaints." Thus, for purposes of the fourth element, we need only inquire as to whether the EEOC presented sufficient evidence to demonstrate that Xerxes' responses to the complaints made under its policies were not reasonably calculated to end the harassment and, therefore, that liability for the harassment may be imputed to it.

There is no "exhaustive list" or "particular combination" of remedial measures or steps that an employer need employ to insulate itself from liability. Among other things, we have considered the promptness of the employer's investigation when complaints are made, whether offending employees were counseled or disciplined for their actions, and whether the employer's response was actually effective. However, the mere fact that harassment reoccurs in the workplace, either by the same offender or different offenders, does not, *ipso facto*, allow a jury to conclude that an employer's response was not reasonably calculated to end the harassment. * * * "A remedial action that effectively stops the harassment will be deemed adequate as a matter of law. On the other hand, it is possible that an action that proves to be ineffective in stopping the harassment may nevertheless be found reasonably calculated to prevent future harassment and therefore adequate … as a matter of law." In such cases, [courts] consider the timeliness of the plaintiff's complaint, whether the employer unduly delayed, and whether the response was proportional to the seriousness and frequency of the harassment....

By way of example, responses that have been held reasonable have often included prompt investigation of the allegations, proactive solicitation of complaints, scheduling changes and transfers, oral or written warnings to refrain from harassing conduct, reprimands, and warnings that future misconduct could result in progressive discipline, including suspension and termination.

The employer is, of course, obliged to respond to any repeat conduct; and whether the next employer response is reasonable may very well depend upon whether the employer progressively stiffens its discipline, or vainly hopes that no response, or the same response as before, will be effective. Repeat conduct may show the unreasonableness of prior responses. * * * [A]n employer is not required to terminate a [particular] perpetrator except where termination is the only response that would be reasonably calculated to end the harassment.

We begin with the district court's grant of summary judgment on the hostile work environment claims advanced by the EEOC on behalf of Pearson and Wilson. The EEOC contends that the district court erred in granting summary judgment to Xerxes as to these claims because a reasonable jury could find (1) that Xerxes was placed on actual notice of racial harassment by coworkers of Pearson in June 2005 and of Wilson in November 2005, when they first complained to Shifflett, respectively; (2) that Xerxes failed to respond to their complaints at all until February 2006; and (3) that Xerxes failed to respond to their complaints thereafter with remedial action reasonably calculated to end the harassment.

… [W]e conclude that a genuine issue of material fact exists as to whether Xerxes had notice of the alleged racial slurs and pranks in the workplace prior to February 2006, but failed to respond with any remedial action. Pearson and Wilson each testified that prior to February 2006, they were subjected to the repeated use of racial slurs by Gatrell and Myers, as well as to various pranks by unknown coworkers that they believed were racially motivated. * * * If the facts are as asserted by Pearson and Wilson, they would constitute racial harassment sufficient to "alter the conditions of employment and create an abusive atmosphere." The men also testified that they first reported this harassment to Shifflett in June 2005 and November 2005, respectively, and continued as the incidents occurred thereafter, up to and including the complaints they made on February 3, 2006 about Gatrell and Myers. However, Xerxes did nothing in response to their complaints until February 2006. * * * As the direct supervisor of Pearson and Wilson, ... Shifflett was specifically designated [under the "Corporate Compliance Program" then in effect] as an appropriate person to receive such complaints. * * * [W]e hold that a reasonable juror could find that the complaints by Pearson and Wilson to Shifflett prior to February 2006 were sufficient to place Xerxes on actual notice of the racial slurs and pranks in the plant and that Xerxes' response was unreasonable. * * *

With regard to the incidents of racial harassment that were reported on February 3, 2006 and beyond, however, we hold that Xerxes' response to each reported incident was reasonably calculated to end the harassment and, therefore, reasonable as a matter of law. Accordingly, we affirm the district court's award of summary judgment for the alleged racial harassment as to this time period.

As of February 2006, Xerxes had in place extensive anti-harassment policies consistent with Title VII that directed plant employees to immediately report any racial harassment to their supervisor *and* the plant manager. The employees were assured that their complaints would be promptly investigated and that appropriate remedial action would be taken. On February 3, 2006, when Shifflett and Green were made aware of the incident involving Gatrell and Myers, Xerxes' response was prompt and proportional to the seriousness of the offense. Gatrell and Myers were individually counseled and they apologized. In addition, Green held a meeting with the shift employees to review Xerxes' anti-harassment policies and warn that future misconduct would result in disciplinary action. The fact that formal disciplinary action, such as suspension or termination, was not taken against Gatrell and Myers at that time is an insufficient basis for concluding that Xerxes' response was unreasonable. * * * While Myers and Gatrell were disciplined for their prior conduct in July 2006, there is no evidence that either of them engaged in acts of racial harassment after February 3, 2006.

In May 2006, Pearson complained to Shifflett and Carty about *other* coworkers using racially-offensive terms to describe music being played in the plant. Pearson also told Carty about his previous problems with Myers and Gatrell, and told Carty that he wanted the racial slurs to stop. When Green learned of Pearson's complaint, he notified the corporate office, and an escalated response ensued. Bachmeier immediately traveled to the plant to conduct a formal investigation and employee interviews. At the conclusion of the

investigation, Xerxes imposed written disciplinary action upon Myers and Gatrell, including two-day unpaid suspensions from work, and issued a final, written warning that any future violations of the anti-harassment policies would result in their termination. Bradley received a written disciplinary warning for his use of a racially-offensive term to describe music, and he was advised that he faced possible termination for future violations as well. Tammy Smith was verbally counseled for her use of a racial nickname during her conversation with another African-American employee, presumably Wilson. In addition, Bachmeier conducted refresher training of all supervisory and nonsupervisory employees in their respective obligations under Xerxes' anti-harassment policies.

In sum, Xerxes' response to the complaints of racial harassment in 2006, taken in consultation with the Union representatives for the victims *and* the accused, was prompt, proportional to the seriousness and frequency of the various offenses, and employed "increasingly progressive measures to address the harassment" that had occurred in the workplace. * * * It was not only "reasonably calculated to end the harassment" as a matter of law, it was actually effective. There were no reported incidents of racial slurs for over two years, and no incidents of pranks for nearly a year thereafter.

In April and June 2007, Pearson and Wilson each found an anonymous, racially-charged message in his locker. The messages were unquestionably abhorrent. However, they were of a much different character than the racial slurs and pranks that had been the subject of the complaints the previous year. There was no reason to believe that the employees disciplined in 2006 were involved in the incidents in 2007. And the EEOC failed to present any evidence that the two incidents occurred because the disciplinary action and training implemented in response to the 2006 complaints were inadequate.

Xerxes' response to these new incidents was also prompt and reasonably calculated to put a stop to any further such activity in the workplace. Indeed, we can think of nothing further that Xerxes could have done to convey to the perpetrators how seriously Xerxes viewed these incidents and how aggressively it would pursue disciplinary action if it succeeded in identifying the culprits. In addition to conducting internal investigations, Xerxes reported the incidents to the local Sheriff's Office. Green held a plant-wide meeting and notified all employees (which would, of course, have included the perpetrators if they were employees) that law enforcement had been notified and a full investigation requested. The employees were advised that anyone with information was "*expect[ed]* to come forward," and they were warned that the perpetrators, if identified, would face probable termination and possible criminal prosecution. * * *

Finally, the EEOC claims that, despite this demonstrable effectiveness, a reasonable jury could find that Xerxes' responses in 2006 and 2007 were unreasonable based upon Pearson's testimony that he was subjected to two isolated racial slurs in August 2007, and Wilson's testimony that he was subjected to a single racial slur in August 2008.

Pearson testified that in August 2007, coworker Sam Crone referred to African-American women as "nappy headed hos," and Tammy Smith told him that he looked like "Curious George" as he was climbing a ladder. Pearson did not, however, report these alleged incidents to Xerxes at the time and he resigned a few months later. Accordingly, Xerxes was given no opportunity to investigate the complaints or respond appropriately. Wilson testified that, in August 2008, after this lawsuit was filed, Tammy Smith said to him, "I hope this does not offend you, but I'm not trying to be nobody's white n*****," as she was cleaning up a work area. Wilson claims that he reported the comment to Shifflett, but does not claim that he reported it to Green or any other management employee as he had been instructed. * * * When Green investigated the claim, he was unable to corroborate it. * * *

The EEOC makes much of these alleged, albeit isolated, racial remarks, particularly the unreported and uncorroborated accusations against Smith, as evidence from which a jury could reasonably conclude that Xerxes' previous disciplinary action against her and the others was unreasonable. We disagree.

As an initial premise, we note that "an employer *cannot* be expected to correct harassment unless the employee makes a concerted effort to inform the employer that a problem exists" under its reasonable procedures. * * * Here, both Pearson and Wilson inexplicably failed to avail themselves of Xerxes' available procedures to report these additional instances of racial slurs in the workplace, procedures of which they were undeniably aware and had effectively used in the past. Even if the alleged racial slurs by Smith had been properly reported, however, this would be an insufficient basis upon which to conclude that Xerxes' discipline of Smith or the others in 2006 was too light to be reasonable. * * * The standard "in no way requires an employer to dispense with fair procedures

for those accused or to discharge every alleged harasser. And a good faith investigation of alleged harassment may satisfy the … standard, even if the investigation turns up no evidence of harassment. Such an employer may avoid liability even if a jury later concludes that in fact harassment occurred." This principle finds particular significance in this case, where Xerxes bore responsibility to investigate its employees' complaints of racial harassment by their coworkers *and* an obligation to fairly investigate and only discipline offending coworkers, including Smith, in a manner consistent with the protections the Union afforded to all nonsupervisory employees in the workplace. * * *

In the end, the crux of the EEOC's claim … is … that … Xerxes' response to the reports of harassment in the workplace was not "reasonably calculated to end the harassment," because subsequent incidents of harassment, albeit isolated and temporally distant, occurred. This, however, is but a variation of strict liability, which employers do not bear for claims of coworker harassment. "While employers can and should be required to adopt reasonable policies aimed at preventing illegal conduct and to take reasonable measures to enforce these policies, they cannot be held to a standard under which they are liable for any and all inappropriate conduct of their employees." "Employers cannot be saddled with the insurmountable task of conforming all employee conduct at all times to the dictates of Title VII, irrespective of their knowledge of such conduct or the remedial measures taken in response to such conduct." So long as the employer's response to each known incident of coworker harassment is reasonably prompt, and the employer takes remedial measures that are reasonably calculated to end the harassment, liability may not be imputed to the employer as a matter of law. * * *

CASE QUESTIONS

1. What was the legal issue in this case? What did the court decide?
2. Why did the court find the employer's response insufficient prior to February 2006, but sufficient thereafter?
3. What, if any, other measures could this employer have taken?
4. What are the implications of absolving an employer from liability even though it has failed to correct a hostile environment?
5. Do you agree with the decision in this case? Why or why not?

Employers have less control over third parties but still must use available means to protect employees from harassment by clients, customers, and contractors. A psychiatric hospital that failed to protect staff from a known problem of sexual assaults by clients—such as by placing treatment rooms in visible areas and providing self-defense training—was found liable for harassment.[56] Likewise, a female table server was subjected to sexually offensive comments from a group of customers. When she complained to the restaurant manager and requested that someone else be assigned to the table, she was told to go back and take care of her customers. The harassment subsequently escalated, with one of the customers pulling her hair, grabbing her breast, and placing his mouth on her breast. The employer was liable because the manager had a significant degree of control over the working environment and instead chose to acquiesce in the harassment.[57]

Eliminating Harassment

Employers have a clear legal obligation to protect employees from harassment. Harassment polices and complaint procedures, responses to reports of harassment, investigations, and remedies for harassment all require close attention.[58]

Harassment Policies and Complaint Procedures

Employers should establish, communicate, and enforce policies prohibiting harassment. Although failure to adopt a policy is not, by itself, a violation of the law, a policy is basic to preventing harassment. Employers will generally not be able to show that reasonable care to prevent harassment was exercised and establish the affirmative defense in the absence of a formal policy. *Harassment policies should include the following:*

* A strong prohibition of harassment, applying to all managers and employees
* A clear explanation of the meaning of prohibited harassment
* A clear and accessible procedure for reporting harassment
* A requirement that employees with knowledge of harassment report it to the appropriate people
* Assurance of protection against retaliation for reporting harassment or providing information to investigators
* Promise of confidentiality in handling harassment complaints to the extent that an effective investigation permits
* A process for handling complaints and investigating them promptly and thoroughly
* Assurance that appropriate corrective action will be taken if it is determined that harassment has occurred
* Disciplinary actions to which harassers are subject
* Assurance that the rights of people accused of harassment will also be respected

Real policies have more than a "paper existence"; they must be communicated, reiterated, adhered to, and enforced. *Harassment policies should be included in employee handbooks, posted in visible areas, discussed when orienting new employees, and made the subject of training.*

An adequate *policy must unequivocally inform all employees that harassment is prohibited by company policy and the law and will not be tolerated.* Concrete examples of

---

[56]*Turnbull,* at 1245.

[57]*Lockard v. Pizza Hut,* 162 F.3d 1062 (10th Cir. 1998).

[58]This section draws heavily on U.S. Equal Employment Opportunity Commission, *Enforcement Guidance: Vicarious Employer Liability for Unlawful Harassment by Supervisors.* No. 915.002 (June 18, 1999).

harassment can be helpful, provided it is made clear that no listing of harassing conduct is exhaustive. Given the high incidence of harassment in settings removed from the principal workplace—for example, conferences, conventions, sales meetings, and company parties—the scope of the policy and examples given should include harassment in such settings. *Employees should be alerted that harassment based on other protected class characteristics, such as race and national origin, is also prohibited by company policy and is illegal.*

Employees must be told how to report harassment. *There should be multiple accessible parties to whom harassment can be reported. Under no circumstances should an employee be required to report harassment to a supervisor or manager who is the alleged harasser.*[59] A college's harassment policy was found to be legally inadequate for requiring that complaints not made to supervisors be brought to the director of personnel and for not giving the campus police a role in handling off-hours complaints.[60] The director was located elsewhere and, in any event, was not accessible to employees working at night or on weekends. Complaint procedures must take into account the dispersed, 24/7 nature of many workplaces. Rather than assume that all harassment complaints can wait until the administratively convenient time and place, *complaint procedures should specifically provide for reports during all hours of operation.*

Harassment policies should require that supervisors and managers with knowledge of harassment, however gained, report it to the appropriate people designated to handle investigations. In the case of the college mentioned previously, the court was also critical of the distinction drawn in the policy between "formal" and "informal" complaints, with supervisors not being obligated to act on or pass along "informal" complaints. Courts do not always go this far,[61] but employers who do not act on information about possible harassment are clearly risking a finding that they failed to exercise reasonable care to correct harassment or were negligent.

It is vital that harassment policies provide strong and credible assurances that people reporting harassment will be protected from retaliation. Employees subjected to harassment are often doubly victimized: first by the harassment and then by retaliation for complaining. A complaint process cannot be effective if employees have reason to fear its use. In a particularly egregious case,[62] bad things happened to a police officer who filed an internal complaint of harassment against her former supervisor. Transferred to a new precinct, the officer had her work scrutinized more vigilantly than other officers, was subjected to repeated shift and work assignment changes, was transferred to undesirable work locations, had baseless disciplinary charges brought against her, was required to undergo psychological exams, and on at least one occasion was ordered to go on patrol without proper equipment. The retaliation apparently continued even after the woman quit the force. She was subsequently arrested for a traffic violation, brought to her former precinct, detained for twenty-seven hours, strip-searched, given a Breathalyzer test (despite the absence of any indication that she was under the influence of alcohol or concealing anything on her person), and told that the precinct did not "need commotion by a woman like you." A jury believed that the woman was retaliated against (among other claims) and awarded her $1.25 million.

Practical Considerations Try drafting a harassment policy for an employer. How does your policy compare to the policy of the employer that you work for or school that you attend?

---

[59]*Meritor*, at 72–73.

[60]*Wilson v. Tulsa Junior College*, 164 F.3d 534 (10th Cir. 1998).

[61]See, e.g., *Madray v. Publix Supermarkets*, 208 F.3d 1290 (2000), *cert. denied*, 531 U.S. 926 (2000).

[62]*Gonzalez v. Police Commissioner Bratton*, 147 F. Supp. 2d 180 (S.D.N.Y. 2001), *affirmed*, 2002 U.S. App. LEXIS 21521 (2d Cir.).

Responding to Reports of Harassment

The employer's response to reports of harassment is critical. *Employers must respond promptly and in a manner reasonably calculated to stop and correct any harassment.* A complaint of harassment is not something to be placed on the "back burner." Courts can be tough on employers that do not respond promptly to complaints of harassment. In one case, a woman being harassed by a coworker complained on several instances to the individual designated to receive complaints under the company's harassment policy, only to have the complaints laughed off and to be told that the coworker is such a "ladies man." Even though the manager who failed to act was terminated after a higher-level manager became aware of the situation and steps were then taken to end the harassment, the four-month delay in acting raised "a question of material fact whether defendant's response was sufficiently prompt."[63] The promptness and adequacy of an employer's response is assessed in light of the seriousness of the alleged harassment. In a case involving harassment that resulted in criminal charges against the harasser, the court found the employer's response not to be sufficiently timely when the employer delayed the start of its investigation to later the same day.[64] *Once informed of possible harassment, employers should look into the matter despite any misgivings that the employee has about going forward with a complaint.* Although courts sometimes, as in the *Hardage* case, overlook employers' failure to act when employees insist that they will handle the matter themselves, the better course of action is to commence an investigation. This is because the employer has been made aware of possible harassment and has a legal responsibility to protect employees from harassment. Reluctance to report harassment or press the issue, particularly when the harasser is a supervisor or another higher-up, is to be expected. Solid assurances of discreet handling of information and protection from retaliation are particularly important in cases with reluctant complainants. For larger employers, it should be possible to establish mechanisms for employees to receive information about harassment anonymously before deciding whether to make reports to their employers.

In an egregious case of failure to adequately respond to repeated complaints of harassment, supervisors ignored verbal abuse that occurred in their presence, responded to complaints about comments by male employees regarding the imagined sexual activities of a female employee by saying that the comments "could be considered a compliment," failed to comply with the company's sexual harassment policy by passing harassment complaints on to the HR manager, failed to administer any meaningful discipline to employees who engaged in harassment, and openly laughed about incidents of harassment they observed. Nor was the HR manager above reproach. He avoided investigating complaints, laughed at the harasser's comments during a disciplinary meeting, discussed the details of an employee's harassment complaint in a public work area where all her coworkers could hear, and failed to discipline harassers while allowing the plaintiff who was experiencing stress from harassment to be disciplined for excessive use of sick time. The HR manager was also quoted as saying, "This is a mill-type environment. If she doesn't like it here, she can go get a job somewhere else."[65] The court concluded that "[f]ailure to engage in adequate investigation—not once, but on multiple occasions—coupled with conduct intended to embarrass and ultimately drive the plaintiff out of the company, is

---

[63]*Prindle v. TNT Logistics,* 331 F. Supp. 2d 739 (W.D. Wis. 2004).

[64]*Wilson,* at 543.

[65]*Parker v. General Extrusions,* 491 F.3d 596, 601 (6th Cir. 2007).

legally sufficient to fulfill the 'malice or reckless disregard' standard," justifying the award of punitive damages to the plaintiff.[66]

Investigating Reports of Harassment In a case that focused on the adequacy of an employer's response to an employee's harassment complaint, the court observed:

> *The most significant immediate measure an employer can take in response to a sexual harassment complaint is to launch a prompt investigation to determine whether the complaint is justified.... By opening a sexual harassment investigation, the employer puts all employees on notice that it takes such allegations seriously and will not tolerate harassment in the workplace. An investigation is a warning, not by words but by action. [H]owever, ... the "fact of investigation alone" is not enough. An investigation that is rigged to reach a pre-determined conclusion or otherwise conducted in bad faith will not satisfy the employer's remedial obligation.[67]*

A police department's **investigation** of a sexual harassment complaint was held to be inadequate when the investigators failed to interview the alleged harasser promptly, gave him time to concoct an elaborate defense, accepted the alleged harasser's claims as true without making any effort to verify them, failed to interview a witness whose account was known to be favorable to the complainant, and discounted evidence favorable to the complainant.[68] Similarly, an employer's grudging investigation, conducted only after repeated complaints and concluded without interviewing an eyewitness to a serious incident of harassment or consulting with the complaining employee, was inadequate to meet the employer's legal responsibility.[69] In contrast, an investigation that took three to four months to complete and in which the investigator apparently failed to interview several coworkers with material information was judged to be sufficient. The court held, "Where, as here, the employer takes prompt steps to stop the harassment, liability cannot be premised on perceived inadequacies in the investigation."[70] Thus, although employers are not held to a very high standard in investigating harassment complaints—particularly if they do not use the lack of definitive evidence as an excuse for doing nothing—*it is important that investigations be free of bias, that all pertinent witnesses be interviewed, that complainants be kept informed, and that evidence be weighed fairly.* Another basic requirement for a fair investigation is that the *investigator(s) should not be under the supervision or control of any of the involved parties.*

Questions that investigators should pose to employees complaining of harassment include the following:

1. To obtain a detailed description of what has happened: Who harassed you? What exactly did the person(s) do? When did it happen? Is it still happening? Where did it occur? How often did it occur?
2. To determine whether the conduct was unwelcome: How did you react? What did you say to the harasser(s) or coworker(s) at the time of the harassment?
3. To determine the effects of the harassment: How did the harassment affect you? Has there been any effect on your employment status?

---

[66]*Parker,* at 604.

[67]*Swenson v. Potter,* 271 F.3d 1184, 1193 (9th Cir. 2001).

[68]*Fuller v. City of Oakland,* 47 F.3d 1523, at 1529 (9th Cir. 1995).

[69]*Hathaway v. Runyon,* 132 F.3d 1214 (8th Cir. 1997).

[70]*Swenson,* at 1198.

Practical Considerations Should employers attempt to prevent harassment by restricting romantic relationships between employees? If so, what should such a policy entail?

4. To ascertain whether someone else has relevant information: Was anyone present when the harassment occurred? Did you tell anyone about the harassment? If so, when? Did you see anyone else nearby when the harassment occurred? Do you know of anyone else who might have been harassed by this person?
5. To determine whether other evidence is available: Do you have any notes, e-mails, pictures, and so on that relate to the harassment?
6. To determine the complainant's preferred outcome: How would you like to see this situation resolved?

Questions that should be asked of people accused of harassment include the following:

1. What is your response to each of the allegations?
2. Are there any reasons why the complainant might make false allegations?
3. Is there any reason to believe that the conduct was welcomed by the complainant?
4. Are there any other people with relevant information?
5. Do you have any other evidence related to the alleged incidents?

Investigators need to remain neutral and resist any pressure from the parties to draw conclusions before all the evidence is gathered. Discretion, but not absolute confidentiality, should be promised. An effective investigation necessarily means that others will become aware of the allegations, *but information should be strictly limited to those with a legitimate need to know.* Allegations of harassment can be highly damaging. If they are false and indiscriminately "published," the wrongly accused employee can have a defamation claim. *Employers need to take harassment complaints seriously but must balance this against respect for the rights of the accused.* This is not always an easy balance to maintain. Some employers include specific warnings against false claims in their harassment policies. Although knowingly false allegations of harassment, to whatever extent they may occur, are clearly reprehensible, the most likely effect of such policy language is to further chill the reporting of harassment. Thus, such statements are best omitted from harassment policies.[71]

JUST THE FACTS

A male employee was accused by a female coworker of "harassing and stalking her." The employee's boss told him that he would be terminated unless he resigned first. The boss had not conducted an investigation, but he was fearful that the female employee would sue and he felt that terminating the male employee would avert a lawsuit. He also told the male employee that "you probably did what she said you did because you're male and nobody would believe you anyway." The male employee resigned. Does he have any legal claim against his former employer?

See, *Sassaman v. Gamache*, 566 F.3d 307 (2d Cir. 2009).

Remedies for Harassment   *Employers should take initial, temporary measures on being presented with harassment complaints and then long-term remedial measures based on the outcomes of investigations.* The thrust of the initial measures is to separate the

---

[71]Anne Lawton. "The Emperor's New Clothes: How the Academy Deals with Sexual Harassment." *Yale Journal of Law and Feminism* 11, 1 (1999), 75–154.

parties and prevent harassment, if any, from continuing. Transfers, reassignments, leaves of absence, and closer supervision of the parties are among the possible initial measures. The employer might also offer to refer the complaining employee to an EAP program or another source of counseling. Particular care is required in responding to harassment claims that involve credible allegations of sexual assault or rape. Despite the fact that an employer immediately suspended and later discharged an employee who sexually assaulted a coworker, a court faulted the employer's initial response because the victim was not allowed to call the police and was not given time off to obtain a protective order.[72]

Wrongdoing discovered through investigation need not be so severe as to establish a legal finding of harassment to justify employer action. The hope is that corrective measures will stop offensive conduct before it deteriorates into illegal harassment. *The discipline or other* **remedies** *used should correspond to the severity of the harassment and be reasonably calculated to end it.* In some cases, discharging harassers is necessary. However, *terminations for harassment need to be conducted in the same careful manner as all other terminations and fully take account of any legal protections that might be available to the discharged employee.* A university breached the due process and contractual rights of a professor when, without following the procedure for terminating tenured faculty specified in the university policy manual, it terminated him for sexually harassing a graduate student.[73] Another court has cautioned employers against overzealousness:

> *Where an employee is not punished even though there is strong evidence that he is guilty of harassment, such failure can embolden him to continue the misconduct and encourage others to misbehave. But where the proof of harassment is weak and disputed, ... the employer need not take formal disciplinary action simply to prove that it is serious about stopping sexual harassment in the workplace.*[74]

Transfers or reassignments can also be used as longer-term measures. Although a transfer is often the most expedient way to deal with harassment, victims of harassment should not be made to bear the burden of being transferred to less desirable locations or positions. *In general, the alleged harasser, not the victim of harassment, should be transferred or reassigned.* If the harasser is transferred, employers should provide for sufficient monitoring to ensure that harassment is not simply being transplanted to new surroundings.

Harassment does not necessarily cease when complaints are made and employers take action. *Employers should closely monitor the effectiveness of their efforts to remedy harassment. Measures taken at one point in time may be legally sufficient, but if they are not effective in ending harassment, stronger measures may be required.* For example, an employer responded to complaints of harassment by suspending the offending employee and issuing a strong warning. However, the employer did not follow through on its requirement that the employee undergo counseling and, when the harassment resumed, on its threat to terminate for future incidents. In the court's view, responding to continued harassment by decreasing sanctions was a negligent response that only served to embolden the harasser.[75] Likewise, an employer failed in its duty to protect employees from racial harassment when a "serial harasser" was allowed to continue on the job with only a few oral warnings and no real investigation into his activities. Racist graffiti

---

[72]*Becker v. Ulster County,* 167 F. Supp. 2d 549, 555 (N.D.N.Y. 2001).

[73]*Chan v. Miami University,* 652 N.E.2d 644 (Ohio 1995).

[74]*Swenson v. Potter,* 271 F.3d 1184, 1193 (9th Cir. 2001).

[75]*Engel v. Rapid City School District,* 506 F.3d 1118 (8th Cir. 2007).

was a long-standing problem at this plant that had received only a tepid response from the employer. The harasser's eventual termination for unrelated reasons did not satisfy the employer's legal obligations to its employees.[76]

Adequate remedial measures not only stop harassment but also seek to undo the damage it causes. In tangible employment action cases, this might mean providing reinstatement, promotion, or some other employment opportunity lost due to harassment. In other cases, correction might mean restoration of leave that was used because of harassment or an apology from the harasser.

Key Terms

harassment, p. 267
same-sex harassment, p. 268
"because of sex," p. 268
workplace bullying, p. 270
harassment that results in tangible employment action, p. 272

hostile environment, p. 274
"severe or pervasive," p. 275
unwelcome, p. 281
vicarious liability, p. 283
affirmative defense, p. 284
harassment policy, p. 284

complaint procedure, p. 284
negligence standard, p. 290
investigation, p. 300
remedy, p. 302

Chapter Summary

Harassment is a form of discrimination. While sexual harassment is especially common, mistreatment based on race, national origin, disability, age, or other protected class characteristics can also give rise to harassment claims. Sexual harassment has been defined as unwelcome sexual advances, requests for sexual favors, and other verbal or physical conduct of a sexual nature. However, conduct that is not explicitly sexual but that imposes inferior working conditions on an employee because of his or her sex also constitutes sexual harassment. The basic elements of a sexual harassment claim are that the harassment (1) was because of sex, (2) resulted in a tangible employment action or was sufficiently severe or pervasive to create a hostile environment, and (3) was unwelcome. It is also necessary to show that (4) there is basis for holding the employer liable for the harassment.

Showing the discriminatory motivation behind sexual harassment is sometimes problematic, as in same-sex harassment (e.g., male-male) cases, when a harasser mistreats both males and females ("equal-opportunity harasser"), when there is evidence of personal animus behind the harassment, when the harassment takes the form of sexually charged surroundings affecting all of the employees in a workplace, and when the content of harassment is not explicitly sexual. Discussions of workplace bullying and proposals for legislation to counter it have arisen out of the inability of harassment claims to reach the full range of abusive treatment of employees.

Harassment resulting in tangible employment actions is perpetrated by a manager or someone else with the authority to influence employment decisions. That individual makes submission to or rejection of sexual advances a basis for employment decisions. In contrast, hostile environment harassment does not directly affect employment status but imposes discriminatory, inferior working conditions on its victims. Hostile environments can be created by managers or supervisors but also by coworkers, clients, and customers. For a hostile environment to exist, the harassment must be sufficiently severe or pervasive such that a reasonable person would find it difficult to do the job and/or experience the working conditions as intimidating and abusive. It is not necessary that the harassment inflict psychological harm. Instances of harassment that are severe need not occur frequently to be legally actionable, whereas conduct that is less severe might still constitute harassment if it is frequent and pervasive.

Determining whether harassment occurred rests primarily on the objective characteristics of situations as viewed by the reasonable person. However, the subjective experiences of people alleging harassment are relevant to showing that the harassing conduct was unwelcome. Harassment is unwelcome when the affected employee did not solicit or provoke it and, instead, regarded the conduct as unwanted and offensive. Examination of the conduct of the employee

---

[76]*Armstrong v. Whirlpool Corp.*, 2010 U.S. Dist. LEXIS 93069 (M.D. Tenn.).

alleging harassment is generally limited to those actions taken in the workplace and directed toward the alleged harasser. Conduct off the job or toward other people is generally not relevant to determining whether an employee welcomed harassing conduct. Submission to a sexual advance can be unwelcome even though it was consensual or voluntary.

Employer liability for harassment depends on the organizational position of the harasser and the type of harassment. The employer is vicariously liable for all harassment by top officials, regardless of the type. Vicarious liability means that if harassment can be proven, the employing organization is unconditionally liable for it. Employers are also vicariously liable for harassment by managers or supervisors that results in tangible employment actions. Liability for hostile environment harassment by managers and supervisors is vicarious but subject to an affirmative defense. The employer can avoid liability if it shows that it exercised reasonable care to prevent and promptly correct harassment and that the employee unreasonably failed to take advantage of these preventive or corrective opportunities. Liability for hostile environment harassment by coworkers and third parties is based on negligence. The employer is liable if the plaintiff can show that the employer knew or should have known of the harassment and failed to take prompt and appropriate action to stop it.

Practical Advice Summary

- Employers are strongly advised to establish, communicate, and enforce policies prohibiting harassment.
- Harassment policies should
  - Apply to all officials, managers, and employees.
  - Clearly explain the meaning of and strongly prohibit harassment.
  - Provide a clear and accessible complaint procedure.
  - Protect employees against retaliation for reporting harassment.
  - Promise careful handling of information but not absolute confidentiality.
  - Specify how complaints will be handled and investigated.
  - Promise that appropriate corrective action will be taken and outline potential discipline for those who violate the policy.
  - Provide assurance that the rights of people accused of harassment will be respected.
  - Be adequately disseminated, such as by providing employees with copies of policies and training in their use.
  - Explicitly apply to conduct in settings such as conventions, business travel, and company parties.
  - Specify that harassment based on any protected class characteristic, and not only sexual harassment, is prohibited.
- Complaint procedures should
  - Provide employees with multiple accessible parties to whom reports of harassment can be made.
  - Not require that harassment be reported to the alleged harasser.
  - Require that all employees with knowledge of harassment, but especially supervisors and low-level managers, report it to people able to take corrective action.
- Employers must respond to reports of harassment
  - Promptly and in a manner reasonably calculated to end the harassment.
  - By commencing an investigation even if the complaining employee asks the employer not to act.
- Investigators should
  - Be free of bias.
  - Interview all pertinent witnesses.
  - Weigh evidence fairly.
  - Avoid drawing conclusions prematurely.
  - Keep complainants apprised of the progress of the investigation.
  - Never be under the supervision or control of an involved party.
- In responding to harassment complaints, employers should
  - Be careful not to be overzealous or assume guilt before the facts are in.
  - Adopt temporary measures, such as granting leaves of absence or transfers, on being presented with serious allegations of harassment.
  - Institute permanent measures if, following completion of investigations, they are warranted.
  - Take corrective action if there is evidence of offensive conduct even if that conduct does not amount to a legal violation.
- In remedying harassment
  - The extent of any discipline imposed against the harasser should correspond to the severity of the harassment.

— Terminations or other discipline imposed against harassers must be conducted in the same careful manner as any other terminations or disciplinary actions.

— Transfers or reassignments should not leave the victim of harassment worse off or permit the harasser to continue harassment in a new setting.

- If investigations of harassment are inconclusive, employers should continue to closely monitor treatment of the complaining employees.
- Employers should maintain records of harassment charges and their disposition.

Chapter Questions

1. A female who worked in a supermarket bakery complained of mistreatment by a female coworker. The coworker smacked the employee's buttocks on at least six occasions, molded dough into shapes resembling genitalia and shoved them into the employee's face, pushed the employee up against a wall and held her there for ten to fifteen seconds while she demonstrated how she would conduct a rape, and showed the employee Barbie dolls that the coworker had placed in sexual positions. Besides this conduct directed at the employee, the coworker also regularly told dirty jokes, baked sexually explicit cakes, struck other male and female employees on the buttocks, and engaged in simulated sex acts with both male and female employees. The woman's complaints about the coworker were ignored by managers. She sued for sexual harassment. What should the court decide? Why? (*Smith v. Hy-Vee*, 622 F.3d 904 [8th Cir. 2010])

2. Over a period of about twelve months, a female employee at a car dealership was subjected to four incidents of unwanted touching. On the first three occasions, a manager of the dealership sat down next to her during business meetings at the dealership, placed his hand on her knee, slid his hand under her skirt, and moved his hand up and down her thigh. On the fourth occasion, the manager did the same thing, but the setting was a restaurant where employees had gone for a reception following the funeral of one of the firm's owners. The employee complained to several managers and was told to keep a record of the incidents, but no other action was taken. The employee sued. What should the court decide? Why? (*Parrish v. Sollecito*, 249 F. Supp.2d 342 [S.D.N.Y. 2003])

3. A single mother who suffered from depression was transferred to an office assistant position at a university. The transfer entailed a six-month probationary period. A professor at the university was her supervisor. During the probationary period, the professor sometimes leered at the woman, made sexual comments, and showed her a pornographic Web site. When the woman told the professor that she was not interested, he eventually ceased the activity. The professor also criticized her work and threatened to extend her probationary period. Two months after her probationary period had ended, the woman received a performance appraisal that she viewed as being unjustifiably negative. She believed that the criticism of her work was related to her failure to respond positively to the professor's sexual overtures and that the way to avoid criticism and keep her job was to go along with him. Shortly thereafter, the professor requested sex from the woman and she complied. The two had sex in the workplace on numerous occasions over the next year. After unsuccessfully attempting to transfer to another position, the woman filed a harassment charge. The university immediately initiated an investigation and placed the woman on paid administrative leave to separate her from the professor. The investigators initially found insufficient evidence of harassment but recommended that the woman be transferred to a different position with a female faculty member as her supervisor. Later, when the woman provided certain physical evidence that she had been withholding, university officials confronted the professor and he resigned. What should the court decide? Why? (*Holly D. v. California Institute of Technology*, 339 F.3d 1158 [9th Cir. 2003])

4. A woman hired as a prison librarian complained about harassment by a supervisor from another agency that operated at the prison. The behavior that was the subject of her complaint, some of which was witnessed by other employees, occurred about four times a week from the time that she was hired in July 2000 to October 2001.

Her complaints about the supervisor included making comments to another male supervisor that the woman should be "spanked" every day; making insistent compliments about her appearance and "how attractive" she was; staring at her breasts during conversations; measuring her skirt for the purported purpose of determining whether it complied with the prison's dress code; and repeatedly remarking that if he had such an attractive wife, he would never allow her to work in a prison around so many inmates. Allegedly for safety reasons, the supervisor had a security camera installed in the librarian's office, permitting him to observe her as she worked at her desk. Right after the objectionable conduct began, the librarian complained to her immediate supervisor, who said that "boys will be boys" and took no action. She did not file a formal complaint. She believed that she was ineligible to file a formal complaint during her first year of employment due to her probationary status. After she had been on the job for more than a year, she complained to another manager and an internal investigation was undertaken at that point. The woman sued. What should the court decide? Why? (*Singleton v. Department of Correctional Education,* 2004 U.S. App. LEXIS 24059 [4th Cir.])

5. A convenience store cashier was subjected to the following behavior by a coworker over a period of eight to nine weeks: throwing objects at her; sneaking up behind her and touching her; smacking her buttocks; discussing his sex life, inability to sleep, and need for a girlfriend; commenting that the woman looked "hot" in her uniform and would look good as a "biker chick"; commenting on his sexual desire for female customers; referring to women as dumb and stupid; and standing over the woman as she counted her register and calling her a "dumb blonde" if she made a mistake. The woman complained to managers. They responded by changing her to the third shift, which she did not like. The coworker would then hang around after his shift to see her. Eventually, she was told by the manager that it was not possible to always schedule the two employees for different shifts. A manager spoke to the coworker about his behavior, but there was no investigation or review of store videotapes. Another female coworker had complained to managers about the coworker's

behavior six months earlier but did not go into detail because she was embarrassed. The cashier sued. What should the court decide? Why? (*Speedway America v. Dupont,* 933 So. 2d 75 [Fla. Dist. Ct. App. 2006])

6. The married owner of a company touched and kissed a female salesperson at work, made comments about oral sex, and suggested that they be alone together. A few months later the woman began making hotel arrangements and meeting the owner in hotel rooms. The two had sex approximately ten times during their relationship. The woman testified that she believed that she had to have sex with the owner to keep her job. She admitted that the owner never explicitly threatened her with loss of her job if she did not go to hotels with him. After about a year, the woman decided that she couldn't take it anymore and told him that she would not continue with the affair. At that point, the owner told her that she would be fired if she stopped seeing him. The owner then informed his wife (the co-owner of the business) about the affair, and the salesperson was fired. She sued. What should the court decide? Why? (*Miles v. DDF, Inc.* 2004 Minn. App. LEXIS 524, *review denied,* 2004 Minn. LEXIS 409)

7. A 17-year-old female supermarket employee was being severely harassed by a coworker. Twice she complained about the harassment to her fiancé, who also worked at the supermarket. Twice the fiancé reported the harassment to the store manager. Both times the manager informed him that under company policy, the woman had to report the harassment herself and make the report directly to the human resources (HR) department. The woman did not make the report to the HR department and later sued. What should the court decide? Why? (*Varner v. National Super Markets,* 94 F.3d 1209 [8th Cir. 1996], *cert. denied,* 519 U.S. 1110 [1997])

8. A woman was hired as parks maintenance foreperson. She was the first female to occupy this position. Other employees questioned her competence and decisions on a daily basis, were insubordinate, called her names such as "bitch," spread rumors about her relationships with other employees and alleged sexual promiscuity, made daily comments about her appearance and clothing, slipped a note addressed to "superbitch" under her door, keyed her personal and work

vehicles, and evaluated her more harshly than other probationary employees. Following her complaint to city officials, the woman had her door glued shut on three occasions, had her shift changed, and faced numerous allegations of wrongdoing. The city's HR department handled her complaint and concluded that she was a victim of harassment. The HR department held a two-hour training session on the harassment and discrimination policy for Parks Department employees, had numerous meetings with supervisors and employees about the city's policy, provided personal counseling and other assistance to the woman, transferred an employee, disciplined a manager and two supervisors, and terminated a seasonal employee. However, the HR department concluded that "despite all of these actions, selected supervisory personnel and hourly employees are increasingly directing harassing comments and initiating extremely negative rumors towards [the woman]." The woman sues. What should the court decide? Why? (*Nievaard v. City of Ann Arbor*, 2005 U.S. App. LEXIS 3690 [6th Cir.])

9. A female police dispatcher worked the evening shift. During her shift, a police sergeant who had supervisory authority over her entered the room and "cupped, touched, and brushed against" the dispatcher's breast. When she objected to being touched, he said, "Oh, stop it. You have a hole in your shirt." When she looked down, the sergeant said, "Stop looking at your tits." The sergeant then said, "If I was the chief, your uniform would be panties and a tank top." Subsequently during the shift, the sergeant sat down next to the dispatcher and "played with and twirled her hair." The sergeant also told the dispatcher that she had "a really sexy voice on radio. You kind of turn me on." As the sergeant prepared to leave, he hugged the dispatcher and another female employee. All of these events occurred over a period of about an hour. Later in the same shift, the dispatcher reported the sergeant's behavior to the highest ranking person on duty. That individual met with the dispatcher before her shift was completed. The police department had a harassment policy in place, and within days of the sergeant's actions, an investigation was conducted by the internal affairs unit. After several hearings, the supervisor ended up being transferred to another facility and demoted to corporal. The dispatcher

sued. What should the court decide? Why? (*McCurdy v Arkansas State Police*, 375 F.3d 762 [8th Cir. 2004])

10. A flight attendant worked a flight from New York to Rome. Staying in a motel room provided by the airline, she accepted an invitation from a male flight attendant on the same crew to come to his hotel room for some wine. After drinking some wine, she lost consciousness. She believes she was repeatedly raped by the coworker and that he had drugged her wine. She reported the rape to her employer a few weeks later. While her report was being investigated, another flight attendant came forward and wrote a memo to the airline stating that she, too, had been invited by the coworker to have a glass of wine, passed out, and was raped. The airline had previously received reports from two other flight attendants, the earliest of which was five years before the incident in question, of rapes by the same coworker under virtually identical circumstances. The airline also had received a formal complaint from a flight attendant who, after having refused the male flight attendant's invitation to dinner, was subjected to highly abusive and threatening behavior—some of which occurred in front of passengers. Her report to the airline included his statement to her that he was using illegal steroids. None of these other reports were acted on by the airline. The investigation of the Rome incident led to suspension of the male flight attendant. With termination pending, he resigned. Is the airline liable for sexual harassment of the flight attendant? Why or why not? (*Ferris v. Delta Air Lines*, 277 F.3d 128 [2d Cir. 2001])

11. The female head of the physical therapy department at a medical clinic encountered problems with a male chiropractor who also worked at the clinic. The chiropractor regularly put his arm around and touched the woman. She initially tried to avoid contact with him. She was told by a nurse at the clinic that she should "get used to it … that's just the way he is." Following an incident in which the chiropractor kissed her on the forehead, she complained to the one of the clinic's managers. It was decided that the woman should draft a letter to the chiropractor clearly informing him that it was not okay to touch or kiss her and that she did not want him to do so again. The letter was read and approved by the manager. The woman presented the letter to the

chiropractor and he apologized to her. About a month later, the woman heard reports from several patients regarding inappropriate touching and kissing by the chiropractor. She reported this information to the manager. A couple of months later, the chiropractor resumed touching the woman, including an incident in which he felt her breasts. This information was reported to the manager and to the clinic's owner. For the first time, clinic managers talked with the chiropractor about these complaints. They asked him to sign a statement acknowledging that he had engaged in "acts of sexual impropriety and familiarity," but he refused to do so. He also rejected a recommendation that he undergo psychological counseling. The chiropractor did attend one sexual harassment training session, but he declined to return for follow-up training. During this period of time, the chiropractor did not touch the woman but acted aggressively toward her (e.g., blocking access to a doorway) and was the object of a complaint from another patient. Eventually, the woman was told that the chiropractor would be terminated within forty-five days. This period elapsed, the chiropractor remained on the job, and the woman was not given any further information about the situation. She quit and sued. What should the court decide? Why? (*Sheriff v. Midwest Health Partners P.C.*, 619 F.3d 923 [8th Cir. 2010])

12. In light of workplace bullying and the difficulties plaintiffs face in same-sex harassment cases, would it be better to have laws prohibiting unwelcome, offensive treatment regardless of whether the motive behind the treatment is discriminatory? Why or why not?

13. Do courts give sufficient weight to the obstacles that might make employees reluctant to report harassment? Why do you say that? (See Anne Lawton. "Between Scylla and Charybdis: The Perils of Reporting Sexual Harassment." *University of Pennsylvania Journal of Labor & Employment Law* 9 [Spring 2007], 603–655)

14. In what ways do the standards used to attribute liability for harassment to employers differ depending on whether the harassers are managers or coworkers? Is it appreciably easier for plaintiffs to establish liability under the affirmative defense? (See David J. Walsh. "Small Change: An Empirical Analysis of the Effect of Supreme Court Precedents on Federal Appeals Court Decisions in Sexual Harassment Cases, 1993–2005." *Berkeley Journal of Employment and Labor Law* 30, 2 [2009], 461–525)

CHAPTER 10

Reasonably Accommodating Disability and Religion

Protection against discrimination means little to disabled persons if workplaces remain full of barriers—sometimes physical obstacles, such as the absence of wheelchair accessibility, but more often inflexible policies and practices—that effectively preclude employment. Likewise, employers with requirements (such as schedules, job duties, and appearance standards) that conflict with the sincere religious beliefs and practices of employees place those persons in the untenable position of choosing between their jobs and their faiths. In mandating reasonable accommodation of disability and religion, the law requires employers to be more flexible and supportive than they might otherwise be, provided that any accommodations are reasonable and do not impose undue hardship.

The obligation to reasonably accommodate is unique to the protected classes of disability and religion. However, the legal basis and nature of this obligation differ depending on whether disability or religion is involved. Thus, the two forms of accommodation are discussed separately in this chapter. The obligation to reasonably accommodate disabled persons is more extensive than the requirement to accommodate religion. Yet, at the same time, it is more difficult for employees to establish entitlement to reasonable accommodation for their disabilities than for their religious beliefs and practices.

Reasonable Accommodation of Disability

The obligation of employers to reasonably accommodate disability arises under two similar laws: the **Americans with Disabilities Act (ADA)** (Title I)[1] and the **Rehabilitation Act**.[2] The ADA was explicitly modeled after the Rehabilitation Act, which covers federal government agencies and federal contractors. We will focus on the ADA because of its broader coverage (private sector employers with at least fifteen employees, state and local governments). The ADA protects "qualified individuals" from discrimination "on the basis of disability." Thus, we have to delve into the meaning of *disability* and *qualified* to understand who is entitled to accommodation (and nondiscrimination). Substantial amendments to the ADA—aimed at ensuring a

---

[1]42 U.S.C.S. §§ 12101–12213 (2011).

[2]29 U.S.C.S. §§ 701–796i (2011).

"broad scope of protection"—were recently enacted.[3] But an essential premise of the ADA remains unchanged: People can have disabilities and still be capable of work, particularly if flexibility and support are available to them. Although some legal definitions of disability (such as that used to determine eligibility for Social Security disability payments) are based on the inability to engage in gainful employment, the view of disabled persons under federal antidiscrimination laws is very different.

ELEMENTS OF A CLAIM

Failure to Reasonably Accommodate Disability

The plaintiff must establish that:

1. He or she has a **disability**—a physical or mental impairment that substantially limits the performance of one or more major life activities
2. He or she is **qualified** for the job in question
   a. meets all of the neutral, job-related requirements for the position; and
   b. is able to perform the essential functions of the job with or without reasonable accommodation; and
   c. is not a **direct threat** to his or her own health and safety or that of others—normally, it is the employer that must establish that the employee *is* a direct threat, but the burden shifts to the plaintiff for jobs with significant public safety implications
3. The employee's need for accommodation was made known, or should have been known, to the employer
4. One or more accommodations exist that are **reasonable** and that the employer did not provide

If the plaintiff can establish the above, the employer will be liable unless it can show that the proposed accommodation(s), although reasonable in general, would pose an **undue hardship**—"significant difficulty or expense"—given the employer's resources and operational requirements.

© Cengage Learning 2013.

Disability

The definition of **disability** under the ADA includes the following:

• A physical or mental impairment that substantially limits one or more major life activities
• A record of such an impairment
• Being regarded as having such an impairment

An employee is protected under the ADA if she meets any of the three criteria. There is also protection for nondisabled persons who are discriminated against

---

[3]ADA Amendments Act of 2008, P.L. 110-325 [S. 3406].

because of their association with disabled persons.[4] Although the definition of disability under the ADA appears broad, plaintiffs have encountered great difficulty in getting past this threshold issue. Prior to enactment of the **ADA Amendments Act** (ADAA), courts applied the law in a parsimonious fashion and found many plaintiffs to not be disabled despite their epilepsy,[5] diabetes,[6] depression,[7] and a host of other conditions that laypersons typically view as disabilities. In amending the ADA, Congress declared that the definition of disability under the ADA "shall be construed in favor of broad coverage of individuals under this Act."[8] Congress also said that—contrary to prior experience under the ADA—"the primary object of attention in cases brought under the ADA should be whether entities covered under the ADA have complied with their obligations ... [while] the question of whether an individual's impairment is a disability ... should not demand extensive analysis."[9] The EEOC has issued a set of guidelines for interpreting and implementing the ADA Amendments Act.[10] But these changes to the ADA did not apply retroactively to cases that arose before the effective date of the legislation (January 1, 2009). There have not yet been a sufficient number of cases, particularly appellate court decisions, applying the new law to say with certainty just how much coverage under the ADA has been expanded.

Actual Disability   The first prong of the ADA's definition of disability refers to persons who are currently disabled. Both **physical** and **mental impairments** are incorporated into the definition of disability. It is critical to realize that not all serious health problems meet the legal definition of disability. The definition of disability is based on an individualized assessment of the effects of health problems on a person's functioning, rather than on diagnostic labels. However, while the ADA calls for individualized assessment and does not list specific impairments that are considered disabilities, the EEOC has identified the following impairments that should easily qualify as disabilities:

> *deafness, blindness, intellectual disability (mental retardation), partially or completely missing limbs, mobility impairments requiring use of a wheelchair, autism, cancer, cerebral palsy, diabetes, epilepsy, HIV infection, multiple sclerosis, muscular dystrophy, major depressive disorder, bipolar disorder, post-traumatic stress disorder, obsessive-compulsive disorder, and schizophrenia.*[11]

This list is not exhaustive and many other types of impairments can be disabilities. Certain conditions or behaviors are expressly *excluded* from the definition of disability (e.g., transsexualism, pedophilia, exhibitionism, and pyromania). Significantly, persons who are current users of illegal drugs, regardless of whether they suffer from drug addiction, are not considered disabled under the ADA. However, persons who are undergoing or have completed rehabilitation for drug addiction and are not currently using illegal drugs are protected by the ADA.

Practical Considerations Under the ADA, how should employers deal with alcoholic employees?

---

[4] 42 U.S.C.S. § 12112 (b)(4) (2011).

[5] See, e.g., *Carlson v. Liberty Mutual Insurance*, 237 Fed. Appx. 446 (11th Cir. 2007).

[6] See, e.g., *Orr v. Wal-Mart*, 297 F.3d 720 (8th Cir. 2002), *cert. denied*, 541 U.S. 1070 (2004).

[7] See, e.g., *Cassimy v. Board of Education*, 461 F.3d 932 (7th Cir. 2006).

[8] P.L. 110-325 § 4(4)(A) (2008).

[9] P.L. 110-325 § 2(b)(5) (2008).

[10] 76 Fed. Reg. No. 58 (March 25, 2011), 16978–17017.

[11] 29 C.F.R. § 1630.2(j)(3)(iii) (2011).

JUST THE FACTS

An employee worked as a "highway maintainer" on a bridge crew. His tasks included bridge work but also operating and repairing maintenance vehicles, directing traffic, and cutting grass. He informed his employer that he had a fear of heights and had occasional difficulty working high up in an unsecured environment. His problem was informally accommodated by trading off work assignments with coworkers, a common practice among the members of the bridge crew. On one occasion, he experienced a panic attack while attempting to change light bulbs on a bridge over the Mississippi River. He was immediately placed on sick leave and diagnosed with acrophobia—a fear of heights. He requested a return to work with the accommodation that he not be required to work at heights in excess of twenty feet. Despite statements from two independent psychiatrists that he was fit to return to work if not required to work at heights, his employer declined to reinstate him to the bridge crew or any other position. The employee sued for failure to reasonably accommodate. Is this a disabled employee with a right to receive the requested accommodation?

See, *Miller v. Illinois Department of Transportation*, 2011 U.S. App. LEXIS 9534 (7th Cir.).

To be considered a disability, a physical or mental impairment must substantially limit an individual in the performance of one or more **major life activities**. Major life activities include, but are not necessarily limited to, caring for oneself, performing manual tasks, seeing, hearing, eating, sleeping, walking, standing, sitting, reaching, lifting, bending, speaking, breathing, learning, reading, concentrating, thinking, communicating, interacting with others, and working. Additionally, the term *major life activities* includes the operation of "major bodily functions," such as the immune system; normal cell growth; and digestive, bowel, bladder, neurological, brain, respiratory, circulatory, endocrine, and reproductive functions.[12]

The third piece to the definition of an actual disability is that the individual must be **substantially limited** in the performance of a major life activity. While this means that not all impairments will constitute disabilities, an impairment need not completely prevent or even "significantly restrict" the performance of a major life activity to be a disability. The central issue is whether, compared to most people in the general population, the individual's impairment substantially limits the conditions, manner, or amount of time it takes to perform a major life activity.[13] The focus is on *how* tasks are performed, rather than the outcomes that the individual manages to achieve. Disabilities are most often chronic (lasting many months or years rather than days or weeks) or expected to have a long-term impact on functioning, rather than acute injuries. However, a condition that is episodic (e.g., flares up unexpectedly) or in remission still constitutes a disability if it would substantially limit a major life activity *when active*.[14] In a case involving an employee who had undergone surgery for renal cancer a year earlier and was currently in remission, the court applied the ADAA and concluded that the employee was disabled because his condition would substantially limit a major life activity when active.[15] Renal

---

[12]29 C.F.R. § 1630.2 (i)(1) (2011).

[13]29 C.F.R. § 1630.2 (j)(1)(ii) (2011).

[14]29 C.F.R. § 1630.2 (j)(1)(vii) (2011).

[15]*Hoffman v. Carefirst of Fort Wayne*, 2010 U.S. Dist. LEXIS 90879 (N.D. Ind.).

cancer has a high rate of recurrence and is often fatal when it comes back. Importantly, the determination of whether an impairment is substantially limiting must be made "without regard to the ameliorative effects of mitigating measures."[16] What does this mean? Disabled persons often utilize a variety of means to help them deal with their disabilities. These include the likes of medications, prosthetic devices, hearing aids and cochlear implants, mobility devices, oxygen therapy equipment, and learned behavioral adaptations. The assessment of whether an impairment is substantially limiting must be based on the nature of the underlying condition rather than on how well the person is able to cope despite her condition. But if mitigating measures exacerbate an employee's disability (such as by the adverse side effects of medication), those adverse effects must be considered. "Mitigating measures" do not include "ordinary eyeglasses or contact lenses" intended to fully correct visual acuity. A person whose vision is poor when not wearing glasses would not be considered disabled if the glasses largely correct his vision.

While the question of whether an employee has a disability often arises because of a need for reasonable accommodation, it is also germane to disparate treatment cases brought under the ADA. In *Horgan v. Simmons*, an HIV-positive employee alleges disability discrimination and the court applies the ADA Amendments Act to readily conclude that the employee is disabled.

Horgan v. Simmons
2010 U.S. Dist. LEXIS 36915 (N.D. Ill.)

OPINION BY DISTRICT JUDGE CASTILLO:

Kenneth Horgan ("Plaintiff") brings this action alleging employment discrimination … against Timothy Simmons ("Simmons") and Morgan Services, Inc. ("Morgan"). Plaintiff claims that Defendants unlawfully terminated him because of his disability and impermissibly inquired as to his disability under the Americans with Disabilities Act ("ADA"). * * *

Plaintiff has been diagnosed as HIV positive for the past ten years, but kept his status confidential, disclosing his medical condition only to his close friends. In February 2001, he began working for Morgan, a linen and uniform rental services company, as a sales manager in Los Angeles. In January 2008, Defendants promoted him to General Manager of the Chicago facility. Plaintiff claims that his HIV positive status never interfered with his ability to perform the essential functions of his job and that he "has always met or exceeded Morgan's legitimate expectations." Specifically, in 2009, Plaintiff claims he brought in a lucrative account with the company's "biggest customer in the country."

Simmons is Morgan's president and was Plaintiff's supervisor in Chicago. On July 15, 2009, Plaintiff alleges that Simmons asked to meet with him for what Simmons termed a "social visit." During their visit, Plaintiff alleges that Simmons "told plaintiff that he was really worried about him." When Plaintiff responded by discussing his work performance, Plaintiff claims that Simmons cut him off saying "this is not about results." Plaintiff alleges that Simmons then "demanded" to know what was going on with him, telling Plaintiff that "if there was something medical going on, [he] needed to know." Plaintiff insisted that there was nothing that affected his ability to work. However, Plaintiff claims that Simmons "continued to insist there was something physical or mental that was affecting [Plaintiff]." Plaintiff claims he was "compelled to tell Simmons that he was HIV positive," but he assured Simmons that his status did not affect his ability to do his job.

Plaintiff alleges that Simmons then asked him about his prognosis. Plaintiff responded that "he had been HIV positive for a long time and that the condition was under control and that his T-cell count was over 300." Next, Plaintiff alleges that Simmons asked "what would happen if his T-cell count went below 200," and Plaintiff replied that he would then have AIDS. After urging Plaintiff to inform his family about his condition, Plaintiff alleges that Simmons asked him "how he

---

[16] 29 C.F.R. § 1630.2 (j)(1)(vi) (2011).

could ever perform his job with his HIV positive condition and how he could continue to work with a terminal illness." Additionally, Plaintiff claims that Simmons told him "that a General Manager needs to be respected by the employees and have the ability to lead," and indicated that he "did not know how [Plaintiff] could lead if the employees knew about his condition."

Simmons allegedly ended the meeting by telling Plaintiff that he needed "to recover" and that he should "go on vacation" and "leave the plant immediately." Simmons then told Plaintiff that he would discuss the situation with Morgan's owner. The next day, Plaintiff alleges that he received a copy of an email sent to all general managers and corporate staff indicating that "effective immediately" Plaintiff was "no longer a member of Morgan []."

The ADA makes it unlawful for an employer to "discriminate against a qualified individual on the basis of disability in regard to … terms, conditions, and privileges of employment." "To prevail on an ADA claim, the plaintiff must show (1) he is disabled; (2) he is qualified to perform the essential function[s] of the job with or without accommodation; and (3) he suffered an adverse employment action because of his disability." The ADA defines "disability," with respect to an individual, as: (1) "a physical or mental impairment that substantially limits one or more major life activities of such individual"; (2) "a record of such an impairment"; or (3) "being regarded as having such an impairment." Plaintiff alleges that he was terminated on the basis of his disability: being HIV positive. Although Defendants acknowledge that being HIV positive is a physical impairment, they argue that Plaintiff has not pled "a limitation of a major life activity," and thus fails to state a claim of disability under the ADA.

Effective January 1, 2009, Congress amended the ADA to "[reinstate] a broad scope of protection." * * * Although the ADAAA [ADA Amendments Act] left the ADA's three-category definition of "disability" intact, significant changes were made to how these categories were interpreted. * * * As relevant to this case, the ADAAA clarified that the operation of "major bodily functions," including "functions of the immune system," constitute major life activities under the ADA's first definition of disability. In addition, "an impairment that is episodic or in remission is a disability if it would substantially limit a major life activity when active." * * * Noting that courts had "created an

inappropriately high level of limitation," the ADAAA states that "it is the intent of Congress that the primary object of attention in cases brought under the ADA should be whether entities covered under the ADA have complied with their obligations …" Therefore, the "question of whether an individual's impairment is a disability under the ADA should not demand extensive analysis."

Defendants claim that even with the additional language of the ADAAA, Plaintiff fails to plead a disability sufficient to state an actionable ADA claim. This Court disagrees…. [I]t is certainly plausible—particularly, under the amended ADA—that Plaintiff's HIV positive status substantially limits a major life activity: the function of his immune system. Such a conclusion is consistent with the EEOC's proposed [and since finalized] regulations to implement the ADAAA which lists HIV as an impairment that will consistently meet the definition of disability. * * * Defendants' motion to dismiss Plaintiff's first claim is therefore denied.

Plaintiff [also] alleges that the questions posed by Simmons on July 15, 2009, "constituted prohibited inquires [sic.] in violation of the ADA." The ADA prohibits "inquiries of an employee as to whether [an] employee is an individual with a disability or as to the nature or severity of the disability, unless such examination or inquiry is shown to be job-related and consistent with business necessity." Here, Plaintiff alleges that Simmons demanded to know whether "something medical [was] going on" and "continued to insist there was something physical or mental that was affecting [Plaintiff]." Plaintiff claims that based on this questioning, he was "compelled to tell Simmons that he was HIV positive." Further, Simmons allegedly asked Plaintiff about his prognosis and what would happen if his T-cell count fell below 200. Such questioning constitutes an inquiry as to whether Plaintiff had a disability and the nature and severity of the disability, and is thus prohibited by the ADA. Nevertheless, Defendants argue that after Plaintiff disclosed his HIV positive status, they were "entitled to ask questions about the stage to which the virus had progressed because it related to [Plaintiff's] possible fitness to work both presently and in the future," and that such questioning was "job-related and consistent with business necessity." Again, Plaintiff alleges that he was "compelled to tell Simmons that he was HIV positive," and disclosed this information only after an impermissible inquiry under the ADA. Further, Plaintiff's allegation that he repeatedly insisted that nothing (including his HIV status) affected his ability to perform his duties directly rebuts Defendants' assertion that the questioning was necessary to discern whether Plaintiff could "cope with the demands and responsibilities of his job." Thus, Plaintiff has sufficiently pled a claim for an impermissible inquiry under the ADA and Defendants' motion to dismiss on this basis is denied.

CASE QUESTIONS

1. What were the legal issues in this case? What did the court decide?

2. On what basis does the court conclude that this employee is disabled? If the court had not found him to have an actual disability, would he have been able to successfully argue that he was "regarded as" having a disability?

3. Why was the employer's questioning of this employee illegal? If, as it appears, the termination was based on the employee's disability, is there any way the employer could defend its actions?

4. Why do you think the company president acted as he did?

Record of a Disability   Employees are sometimes discriminated against not because they are currently disabled (or in addition to that), but because of a prior disability. This might be due to the stigma associated with the condition (e.g., drug addiction, mental illness) or fears that the condition will recur. Sometimes people are misclassified (e.g., as learning disabled) and the record of an erroneous diagnosis stays with them. Persons who have a **record of disability**, whether due to their medical history or misclassification, are protected.

Perceived Disability   Persons who are erroneously **regarded as being disabled** are also protected by the ADA. Many stereotypes, fears, and misconceptions exist regarding people with disabilities. People might be regarded as disabled because of unfounded rumors or, as is more often the case, because conditions they have are assumed to be much more limiting than they really are. This prong of the definition of disability is satisfied by showing that the plaintiff was subjected to discrimination "because of an actual or perceived physical or mental impairment whether or not the impairment substantially limits or is perceived to substantially limit, a major life activity."[17] The impairment must not be transitory (an actual or expected duration of less than six months) and minor. In one relevant case, the commanding officers of a police officer suffering from depression wrongly believed that the officer could not hold any job where firearms were present, although the actual restriction imposed by the employee's doctors was only that the police officer not carry a weapon.[18] Likewise, an electrician who suffered from loss of balance and vertigo following a stroke was regarded as disabled when he was demoted to a janitorial job on the erroneous belief that he could not work around live electrical current under any circumstances.[19] *It is important for managers to have a clear understanding of any medical restrictions placed on their employees before making decisions about their suitability for employment opportunities.* People who are regarded as disabled are protected from discrimination on this basis, but unlike those with an actual disability or a record of a disability, they are *not* legally entitled to receive reasonable accommodation.[20]

---

[17] 29 C.F.R. § 1630.2 (l)(1) (2011).

[18] *Willams v. Philadelphia Housing Authority,* 380 F.3d 751, 766-67 (3d Cir. 2004), *cert. denied,* 125 S. Ct. 1725 (2005).

[19] *Justice v. Crown Cork and Seal,* 527 F.3d 1080 (10th Cir. 2008).

[20] 29 C.F.R. § 1630.2 (o)(4) (2011).

"Qualified Individual with a Disability"   To be protected under the ADA, individuals must be not only disabled but also **qualified**. A qualified individual with a disability satisfies the skill, education, experience, and other job-related requirements for the job held or sought and is able, with or without reasonable accommodation, to perform the essential functions of that job.[21] However, an individual who can perform the essential functions of a job but whose condition is such that she poses a "direct threat" to the health and safety of herself or others—a threat that cannot be eliminated by reasonable accommodation—is not considered qualified.

Able to Perform the Essential Functions of the Job   Jobs consist of bundles of tasks. Some of those tasks are central to why the job exists; others are more peripheral. For example, word processing, filing, and answering phones are essential functions for many clerical workers, but going out to get coffee for others or lifting boxes of copier paper are probably marginal functions. Under the ADA, *a disabled person's ability to perform a job must be judged only in relation to the essential functions of the job in question; inability to perform marginal functions cannot be the basis for adverse employment decisions.* Thus, *it is important that employers determine the essential functions of jobs.* The basic criteria for identifying **essential functions** are as follows:

- The position exists to perform this function.
- Few other employees are available to perform this function.
- The function is highly specialized.

Evidence of essential functions includes the employer's own judgment, written job descriptions, documentation of the amount of time spent performing particular functions, analyses of the consequences of not requiring position occupants to perform the functions, job duties listed in collective bargaining agreements, and statements based on the work experience of job occupants. Tasks that are performed infrequently are less likely to be considered essential, but this is not always the case. A physician's assistant who worked at a prison was unsuccessful in arguing that completion of a physical safety training course was not an essential function of her job. Even though she had worked for the corrections department for eight years before the training requirement was instituted and emergency situations involving attacks by inmates were rare, the court concluded that the employer was free to change job requirements and that the potentially severe consequences of inability to deal with such situations, infrequent as they were, justified treating the training as an essential function of her job. Since her arthritis and fibromyalgia made it impossible to do the physical activities that the training called for, and no reasonable accommodation was proposed that would permit her to perform this essential function, she was not "qualified" and the prison could lawfully terminate her employment.[22]

The ADA does not require that employers perform job analyses (systematic studies of jobs to document the major tasks involved and the knowledge, skill, abilities, and other traits needed for successful job performance) or have job descriptions. However, the importance of documenting essential functions for compliance with the ADA provides employers with a clear reason to carefully study jobs and document them in up-to-date job descriptions. *Job descriptions should distinguish essential functions from marginal functions and specifically state all essential job functions.* An employer that rejects a disabled job candidate because he is unable to perform some function that was not important enough to warrant mention in a job description is in an unenviable legal position. Additionally, *job descriptions, and employers deciding whether disabled persons can*

---

[21]29 C.F.R. § 1630.2(m) (2011).

[22]*Hennagir v. Utah Department of Corrections*, 587 F.3d 1255 (10th Cir. 2009).

perform the essential functions of jobs, should focus on what needs to be accomplished rather than on how tasks are accomplished. Disabled persons are often able to devise alternative ways of doing things. Absent important safety or productivity concerns that dictate adherence to a particular method, employers should be open to different means for producing the same outcomes. Finally, when *assessing the ability of disabled persons to perform the essential functions of jobs, employers must consider not only whether these individuals can do so unaided but also whether they can do so with any reasonable accommodations that could be provided without undue hardship.*

Meets Job-Related Qualification Standards   To be "qualified," disabled persons must meet the same requirements for education, skill, experience, and background that apply to all other job candidates and employees. However, *if a requirement screens out (or tends to screen out) an individual with a disability or a class of such persons, the employer must be prepared to prove that the requirement is job-related and consistent with business necessity.* Only those requirements that relate to ability to perform the essential functions of a job are "consistent with business necessity." Thus, possession of a valid driver's license—a qualification not available to some disabled persons due to the nature of their conditions—is a lawful requirement only if driving is an essential function of the specific position.[23] The U.S. Marshals Service was able to establish the job relatedness and business necessity of its prohibition against the use of hearing aids during preemployment medical exams that include hearing tests. The ban came after a careful study of the job of court security officer. A number of hearing-related essential functions were identified, including comprehending speech over the radio and under other difficult circumstances, hearing sounds requiring investigation, and pinpointing the source of sounds. The facts that hearing aids can malfunction, break, or come loose made it a business necessity for court security officers to be able to perform their jobs relying on unaided hearing.[24]

Not a Direct Threat   In contrast to standards that apply generally to all employees, employers sometimes identify individuals as unfit for employment because their disabilities present a direct threat to safety and health. Such individuals can perform the essential functions of the jobs in question but, for reasons such as the contagious nature of their conditions (e.g., food handlers with hepatitis) or the episodic and unpredictable character of their symptoms (e.g., some persons with epilepsy or mental illness), pose a substantial risk of harm. An employee who had worked in oil refineries for years and who sought employment at a Chevron refinery was rejected due to a liver condition that might be worsened by contact with toxic chemicals. The Supreme Court ruled for the employer, holding that substantial risk to an employee's own safety or health, as well as that of coworkers and customers, falls within the meaning of "direct threat."[25] However, to establish that a person's disability constitutes a **direct threat**, the employer must show that the employee *currently poses a specific risk of significant harm.* This judgment must be made on the basis of *objective medical evidence,* not on stereotypes or fears. Although inability to evacuate during an emergency might render an employee a direct threat to her own safety and health in some settings, DuPont was unable to convince a jury and an appellate court that the threat posed by a lab clerk with severe scoliosis was sufficiently specific and imminent.[26] An employer was also able to successfully argue that a disabled person posed a direct threat when the employee, on medical leave

---

[23]"Employer May Require Driver's License Only if Driving Is Essential, EEOC Says." *Daily Labor Report* 153 (August 9, 2006), A-3.

[24]*Allmond v. Akal Security,* 558 F.3d 1312 (11th Cir. 2009), *cert. denied,* 2010 U.S. LEXIS 742.

[25]*Chevron U.S.A., Inc. v. Echazabal,* 536 U.S. 73 (2002).

[26]*EEOC v. E.I. DuPont de Nemours & Co.,* 480 F.3d 724, 731 (5th Cir. 2007).

for a psychiatric disability, expressed in graphic terms (to a doctor) her desire to kill her supervisor.[27] Threats to safety or health need not be as certain if the potential consequences are severe. A diabetic chlorine-finishing operator at a chemical plant experienced occasional diabetic seizures. The court concluded that, despite the relatively low frequency of seizures, his condition made him a direct threat because of the potentially catastrophic consequences of a chlorine spill.[28] Although the employer usually bears the burden of proving that an employee's disability poses a direct threat, that burden may shift to plaintiffs to show that they will not endanger others in cases involving jobs with public safety functions.[29]

Clippings

A jury awarded a large verdict to a disabled sales manager whom AutoZone failed to reasonably accommodate. The sales manager suffered from permanent back and neck injuries. His condition was exacerbated by engaging in certain physical activities, particularly mopping the floors of his store. He requested to not be assigned the task of mopping floors and provided AutoZone with medical documentation of his need for this accommodation. The new management at his store flatly refused his request and required him to continue mopping. This caused further injury, which led to his taking medical leave and to his eventual termination. The EEOC was able to present convincing evidence that the sales manager could perform all of the essential functions of his job and that mopping floors was a nonessential function that should have been reassigned to other employees.

U.S. Equal Employment Opportunity Commission. "EEOC Obtains $600,000 Verdict Against AutoZone for Failure to Accommodate Disabled Employee." Press Release (June 6, 2011) (http://www.eeoc.gov/).

Practical Considerations What reasonable accommodations would be most appropriate for persons with psychiatric disabilities?

Reasonable Accommodation

The extra flexibility and support to which qualified individuals with disabilities are entitled serve the following purposes: ensuring equal employment opportunity by enabling full participation in the hiring process (e.g., providing additional time on an employment test for an applicant with a learning disability); enabling performance of the essential functions of jobs (e.g., providing voice recognition software for a visually impaired employee); and allowing equal enjoyment of the benefits and privileges of employment (e.g., installing a ramp that affords an employee in a wheelchair access to the staff dining facility). Examples of **reasonable accommodation** specifically mentioned in the ADA include the following:

- Making facilities accessible to and usable by disabled persons (e.g., removing physical barriers such as narrow aisles, deep carpeting that hinders wheelchair use)
- Restructuring jobs (e.g., redistributing marginal functions, allowing tasks to be performed in alternative ways)
- Devising part-time or modified work schedules (e.g., flexible start times, liberal medical leave policies)

---

[27]*Collins v. Blue Cross Blue Shield of Michigan,* 579 N.W.2d 435 (Mich. Ct. App. 1998), *appeal denied,* 590 N.W.2d 571 (Mich. 1999).

[28]*Hutton v. Elf Atochem North America,* 273 F.3d 884 (9th Cir. 2001).

[29]*McKenzie v. Benton,* 388 F.3d 1342 (10th Cir. 2004), *cert. denied,* 125 S. Ct. 2294 (2005).

- Acquiring or modifying equipment or devices (e.g., telephone amplifier, voice recognition software, telephone headset)
- Adjusting or modifying exams, training materials, and policies (e.g., providing training materials in large print, allowing guide dogs in the workplace, altering emergency evacuation procedures)
- Providing qualified readers or interpreters (e.g., sign language interpreters)
- Reassigning disabled individuals to vacant positions (e.g., lateral transfer to an open job)

JUST THE FACTS

A schoolteacher was successful at teaching kindergarten for five years. She requested to teach first grade and was then reassigned to a classroom that had no exterior windows. She told the school principal that she suffered from seasonal affective disorder, a form of depression. She made numerous requests to be moved to a classroom with natural light, but the school refused to do so. She also presented the school district with a letter from her psychologist stating that her depression was being exacerbated by the lack of natural light. Another teacher who had been assigned to a classroom with exterior windows had offered to switch rooms. There was also one vacant room with exterior windows, but this room was being reserved for the possible addition of another class section. The woman's health deteriorated. She suffered from significant inability to concentrate, organize her thoughts, retrieve words, make decisions, and focus on the needs of her students. She also experienced racing thoughts, panic attacks, uncontrollable crying, inability to eat, and thoughts of suicide. She went on medical leave. Eventually, she quit and went to work elsewhere. Did this employer fail to reasonably accommodate this employee?

See, *Ekstrand v. School District of Somerset*, 583 F.3d 972 (7th Cir. 2009).

The Process of Reasonably Accommodating Disability

Not all disabled employees require accommodation. When accommodation is called for, employers are not left to their own devices. Many governmental and nongovernmental agencies can provide advice and assistance to employers seeking to accommodate disabled employees. Disabled employees are usually the best sources of information regarding what their needs are and what will work for them. *Employers that become aware of a disabled employee's need for reasonable accommodation should engage in an **interactive process** aimed at identifying an appropriate and mutually agreeable accommodation.*

Disabled employees should be involved early and continuously in the process of identifying and choosing accommodations. The EEOC has suggested a simple methodology for this interactive process. First, *the job in question should be examined and its essential functions determined. Second, the individual with a disability should be consulted to determine his specific physical or mental abilities and limitations.* Third, *together with the disabled individual, potential accommodations should be identified and assessed.* Fourth, *an accommodation that serves the needs of the employee and employer should be selected.*

What matters is a good faith effort by the employer to engage in the interactive process to identify possible accommodations. A court pointed to a deficient interactive process that included an administrator's knee-jerk response that accommodation would not be made, a delay of four months in meeting to discuss the requested accommodation, an eventual meeting attending by unprepared administrators, and ambiguous communications about what, if anything, would be done, in allowing a teacher's failure to reasonably accommodate claim to go forward.[30] There is no specific number of meetings that must occur. An employee claimed that his employer failed to properly engage in the interactive process by meeting with him only once and not including his attorney and vocational counselor in the meeting. Although the presence of others with relevant expertise might be helpful, there is no legal requirement to this effect. And a single meeting was sufficient in this case because the employee had the opportunity to propose an accommodation and was told that if he thought of other possibilities to let his boss know; in addition, a number of meetings occurred among managers to discuss whether the employee could be accommodated.[31] Indeed, most courts have held that a failure to engage in the interactive process does not, by itself, violate the ADA if a reasonable accommodation is nonetheless offered or no such accommodation is possible.[32] But whatever the legal merits of this view, it is not advisable in practice to forgo the interactive process. After all, how does an employer determine that no accommodation is possible apart from a dialogue with the employee whose needs are at issue?

In general, disabled employees or applicants are responsible for making employers aware of their need for reasonable accommodation. Such notification need not be in writing, nor is it necessary for the employee or applicant to say the magic words *reasonable accommodation* or *ADA*. The individual just needs to indicate problems with doing a job or complying with other employment requirements and link this difficulty to a serious health problem. Thus, *it is critical that managers listen carefully to employees and recognize when an accommodation is being requested.* Also, where the need for accommodation is obvious because the individual's disability is visible and his difficulty performing essential functions of his job apparent, the employer should initiate a discussion regarding accommodation.

The obligation of employers to reasonably accommodate qualified disabled persons is ongoing. Whether an employee requests accommodation when hired or has received other accommodations in the past does not matter. Due to the nature of disabilities, persons who were not previously disabled may be so now, and impairments may improve or worsen over time. Nor can employers arbitrarily decide that they have accommodated employees long enough and discontinue accommodation. An employee who had been accommodated with a part-time schedule for more than ten years had a valid ADA claim when his employer discontinued this accommodation and fired him.[33] Likewise, promotion of a disabled employee to a supervisory position did not give her employer license to simply drop a work-hours restriction that had been granted to the employee in her prior position, particularly when her request for the alternative accommodation of reducing her work hours by permitting her to delegate some tasks was also not honored.[34]

When presented with requests for accommodation, *employers should acknowledge receipt of the requests and act on them as quickly as possible.* If a disability was previously unknown to an employer, the law allows the employer to require documentation of the need for accommodation. The primary source of such information should be the

---

[30]*Lowe v. Independent School District No. 1 of Logan County,* 363 Fed. Appx. 548 (10th Cir. 2010).

[31]*Ammons v. Aramark Uniform Services,* 368 F.3d 809 (7th Cir. 2004).

[32]*McBride v. BIC Consumer Products Manufacturing,* 583 F.3d 92 (2d Cir. 2009).

[33]*Larson v. Seagate Technology, Inc.,* 2001 U.S. Dist. LEXIS 20489 (D. Minn.).

[34]*Smith v. Henderson,* 376 F.3d 529 (6th Cir. 2004).

employee's own health care provider. *Inquiries from employers to health care providers should be restricted to information needed to document the need for accommodations (rather than open-ended excursions into the health status of employees) and should focus on the functional limitations imposed by disabilities.* If the information provided is inadequate to assess the need for accommodation, employers can require employees to be seen by another health professional, at the employer's expense. Although employers can legitimately seek documentation, care should be taken to prevent requests for help that could easily be granted from deteriorating into bureaucratic exercises or power struggles.

Many employers have policies to guide managers in responding to requests for reasonable accommodation. Under E.O. 13164, agencies of the federal government are required to implement formal policies to facilitate reasonable accommodation.[35] *Reasonable accommodation policies should address the manner in which the reasonable accommodation process is initiated, requirements for medical information to document the need for accommodation, the process for identifying reasonable accommodations, and the choice and notification of the outcome. Employers must document all aspects of the accommodation process.* Some larger employers have ADA coordinators or standing committees (including managers, employees, and/or union representatives) that evaluate requests for accommodation. Although accommodations might appear to be "special treatment" and prompt questions from coworkers, *employers are obligated under the ADA to keep medical information about employees confidential, and that principle applies to divulging the reasons for reasonable accommodation as well.*

What Makes an Accommodation Reasonable?

Under the ADA, employers are required to make "reasonable" accommodation unless doing so would impose undue hardship. Most often, the interactive process results in a mutually acceptable accommodation. But in cases where an employer's capability to provide a reasonable accommodation is disputed, the exact meaning of the terms *reasonable* and *undue hardship* becomes important. The ADA does not define reasonable accommodation beyond providing examples. Case law and EEOC guidance[36] suggest a number of criteria for the reasonableness of proposed accommodations. Most of these are stated negatively—as bounds to how far employers must go. Employers remain free to *exceed* minimum legal requirements in meeting the needs of employees. The following are criteria for determining the reasonableness of a proposed accommodation:

- Is effective (i.e., removes or sufficiently reduces the barrier to employment opportunity)
- Does not need to be the employee's preferred option
- Does not include provision of items that are primarily for personal use (e.g., eyeglasses)
- Does not need to be as far-reaching as accommodations made previously if these exceeded legal requirements
- Does not need to render working conditions strictly equal to those of other employees; effective removal of barriers is sufficient
- Does not require creating a new position or making a promotion
- Does not require providing paid leave not available to other employees

---

[35]U.S. Equal Employment Opportunity Commission. "Policy Guidance on Executive Order 13164: Establishing Procedures to Facilitate the Provision of Reasonable Accommodation." No. 915.003 (October 20, 2000).

[36]U.S. Equal Employment Opportunity Commission. "Revised Enforcement Guidance: Reasonable Accommodation and Undue Hardship under the Americans with Disabilities Act" (Updated October 2002). Viewed August 23, 2008 (http://www.eeoc.gov/).

- Does not require eliminating essential functions from a job or lowering production standards
- Does not require excusing or refraining from disciplining misconduct related to a disability
- Does not usually require making exceptions to established seniority rules

In *EEOC v. UPS Supply Chain Solutions*, the court considers whether this employer failed to reasonably accommodate a deaf employee.

EEOC v. UPS Supply Chain Solutions
620 F.3d 1103 (9th Cir. 2010)

OPINION BY DISTRICT JUDGE TUNHEIM:

The Equal Employment Opportunity Commission ("EEOC") filed suit under the Americans with Disabilities Act ("ADA") alleging that UPS Supply Chain Solution ("UPS") failed to provide reasonable accommodations for Mauricio Centeno's deafness because UPS did not provide him with a sign language interpreter for certain staff meetings, disciplinary sessions, and training. The district court granted summary judgment to UPS on all claims. * * * We find that there are genuine issues of material fact as to whether UPS unlawfully discriminated against Centeno by failing to make reasonable accommodations. We therefore reverse and remand.

Mauricio Centeno has been deaf since birth and his first and primary language is American Sign Language ("ASL"). ASL is a visual, three-dimensional, non-linear language, and its grammar and syntax differ from the grammar and syntax of English and other spoken languages. In many cases, there is no one-to-one correspondence between signs in ASL and words in the English language. Centeno reads and writes in English at the fourth or fifth grade level. Centeno's supervisors were aware that Centeno was not able to read written English very well no later than 2002.

From 2001 until 2009, Centeno worked as a junior clerk in the accounts payable division of the accounting department at a UPS facility in Gardena, California. The parties do not dispute that Centeno was able to complete his job duties without the assistance of an ASL interpreter. The dispute centers on whether UPS provided Centeno with reasonable accommodations for certain benefits and privileges of employment that did not affect his ability to complete his job duties. Those benefits include weekly meetings, job training, and understanding the company's sexual harassment policy.

A. MEETINGS

From 2002 until December 2007, the accounting department, which includes the accounts payable division and the accounts receivable division also, held weekly meetings. Beginning in May 2004, the accounts payable division held separate monthly meetings. Centeno's supervisors expected him to attend the weekly and monthly meetings.

Jenny Chan was Centeno's direct supervisor, and Gertraud Schulz was Chan's manager and supervisor. * * * [W]eekly meetings typically took more than thirty minutes, and some meetings took more than an hour. In advance of the meetings, Schulz sent out a written agenda, typically consisting of "three, four, five one line descriptions of topics" to be covered. Topics included changes to employee benefits, quarterly earnings, vacation and holiday scheduling, new human resources rules, safety regulations, time-reporting, a charitable fundraising drive, an employee opinion survey, the company's code of business conduct, computer virus scans, referral bonuses, and possible reorganizations and reductions in force. At these meetings, employees had the opportunity to make general announcements. Some meetings included group discussions.

* * * The primary accommodation that UPS provided to Centeno at these meetings took the form of notes in the English language. When Chan presented at a meeting, she provided Centeno with information by email and with typewritten notes that she created after the meeting. She based these notes on her memory of what was said in the meeting and on any handwritten notes she took during the meeting. During her presentations, however, Chan wrote down only the main point of what she was saying, and she did not always write down the questions and answers from the meeting.

Centeno testified that he "felt frustrated" with the system of Chan emailing him her notes after the meetings. When Chan emailed Centeno her meeting notes, sometimes Centeno went to her and wrote notes telling her that he did not understand what Chan had written. Centeno also "did not like getting the notes after the meeting because [he] did not get the information at the same time as everyone else in the accounting department. [He] did not get a chance to ask questions or give [his] ideas with everyone else." Centeno "asked many times to have an ASL interpreter to sign for [him] at meetings." * * *

During Centeno's September 2004 performance evaluation, after UPS had denied Centeno's initial requests for an ASL interpreter, Centeno requested that UPS provide him with a contemporaneous record of the meetings. UPS implemented this accommodation in October 2004 by arranging for an employee to sit next to Centeno and write out notes of what was happening during the meeting so that Centeno could read them. One employee who was enlisted to take notes in Chan's place complained to Chan that it was "so much to write." Once this contemporaneous note-taking system was in place, Chan stopped regularly providing Centeno with written meeting summaries after the meetings. According to Centeno, this note-taking system "did not work very well. They could not write out everything. They would write just short little words and keep telling me to wait. I could not really understand what was going on." * * *

In 2005, UPS occasionally provided Centeno with an ASL interpreter for the monthly meetings, and starting in July 2006, UPS provided an interpreter for each monthly meeting. * * * On April 25, 2005, Centeno emailed Chan and Schulz to inform them that he would not attend that week's meetings because there would be no interpreter. Someone from UPS's human resources department filled out a "Pittsburgh form" to create a formal record of Centeno's refusal to attend the meetings. In handwriting underneath this typewritten text is the word "insubordination." * * * [H]e stopped attending weekly meetings after April 2005. Schulz testified that even though she regarded the meetings as mandatory, she was told that if Centeno "doesn't come it's okay."

B. JOB TRAINING

In Centeno's 2001, 2002, and 2003 performance reviews, Centeno's supervisors identified a goal of improving Centeno's skills in using the Excel spreadsheet program.* * * In April 2005, Chan reminded Centeno of this goal. Centeno replied that he had tried to use the on-line training program for Excel, but could not read it. * * * UPS set December 31, 2007, as the deadline for Centeno to complete the Excel course. In September 2007, UPS for the first time provided an ASL interpreter to assist Centeno with Excel training.

C. DISCIPLINE AND THE ANTI-HARASSMENT POLICY

* * * In late April 2005, Centeno had an incident with co-workers in the lunchroom. Some of his co-workers were banging on the table, and Centeno told them to stop. He became angry, "said an inappropriate word and made an inappropriate gesture," and left. On May 9, 2005, Centeno had a meeting with Cheryl Nishimura, a supervisor in the human resources department, to discuss the incident. Nishimura provided an ASL interpreter "to be sure that Mr. Centeno understood [Nishimura] and [Nishimura] understood Mr. Centeno." Centeno apologized and acknowledged that he had used inappropriate language and an obscene gesture.

On May 11, 2005, in a meeting without an ASL interpreter, Chan and Nishimura gave Centeno a written warning about his behavior in the lunchroom. Nishimura's manager "said that it was appropriate to type out the explanation and that an interpreter didn't need to be present" for the meeting with Chan. During the meeting …, Centeno wrote a note indicating that he did not understand the written warning. Nishimura and Chan instructed Centeno to underline the words he did not understand. Among the words he underlined were "inappropriate," "forbidden," "conduct" and "termination." According to Nishimura, "[t]hen we wrote notes and brought a dictionary to explain the meaning of words [Centeno] did not understand."

Centeno … "acknowledg[ed] receipt of a copy of this Written Warning," but he testified that he did not understand the warning. * * * On May 16, 2005, Centeno indicated that he wanted to meet with human resources about the written warning because he did not understand it. * * * On May 19, 2005, Centeno met with Nishimura and Chan, with an ASL interpreter present, "to clarify any issues about the discipline—specific to [Centeno's] understanding about the discipline." Centeno confirmed, through the interpreter, that he understood.

On September 6, 2005, Schulz emailed Centeno to let him know about a Harassment Awareness Quotient Questionnaire and UPS's Professional Conduct and Anti-Harassment Policy. Schulz instructed Centeno to complete the Questionnaire, and then to "sign off and date the Professional Conduct and Anti-Harassment policy." Centeno underlined many words in the Anti-Harassment Policy that he could not understand, and he informed Chan that he did not understand them. * * * Chan directed Centeno to use a dictionary to look up the words he did not understand in the Policy and on the Questionnaire. UPS did not provide Centeno with an interpreter to translate those documents.

* * * The district court granted UPS's motion for summary judgment, concluding that UPS "undertook the interactive process with Centeno, and provided a variety of accommodations that effectively enabled Centeno to perform the functions of his job and that gave him access to the privileges and benefits of his employment." The court found that providing "note-writing, agendas, and summaries in connection with the weekly meetings discharged [UPS]'s duty under the ADA as a matter of law." The court further found that "[t]here is no evidence that Centeno missed out on any significant privileges or benefits-related information due to [UPS]'s failure to provide him with an ASL interpreter for any meetings." With respect to the Anti-Harassment Policy, the court found that "[t]here is no evidence that these materials were training, or that they related to Centeno's job functions or to the privileges or benefits of his employment." The Court found that there was no evidence that Centeno "tried to use the dictionary but it was ineffective."

* * * The ADA prohibits discrimination "against a qualified individual on the basis of disability in regard to … job training [] and other terms, conditions, and privileges of employment." The parties agree that Centeno is a qualified individual and that the focus of his claim is on the "privileges of [his] employment." "[T]he ADA says that 'discrimination' includes an employer's *not making reasonable accommodations* to the known physical or mental limitations of an otherwise qualified … employee, *unless* [the employer] can demonstrate that the accommodation would impose an *undue hardship* on the operation of [its] business.'" UPS does not argue … that Centeno's proposed accommodations would impose an undue hardship. * * * UPS's argument on appeal is that it reasonably accommodated Centeno because its modifications were effective.

EEOC regulations define the term reasonable accommodation to include "[m]odifications or adjustments that enable a covered entity's employee with a disability to enjoy equal benefits and privileges of employment as are enjoyed by its other similarly situated employees without disabilities." "An *ineffective* 'modification' or 'adjustment' will not *accommodate* a disabled individual's limitations." * * * "[O]nce an employee requests an accommodation …, the employer must engage in an interactive process with the employee to determine the appropriate reasonable accommodation." * * * "An employer is not obligated to provide an employee the accommodation he requests or prefers, the employer need only provide some reasonable accommodation." * * * "[T]he duty to accommodate is a continuing duty that is not exhausted by one effort." "[T]he employer's obligation to engage in the interactive process … continues when the employee asks for a different accommodation or where the employer is aware that the initial accommodation is failing and further accommodation is needed." * * *

UPS concedes that understanding and participating in mandatory departmental meetings are "benefits and privileges of employment," even when those meetings have no bearing on an employee's job performance. * * * [T]here is a genuine issue of fact regarding whether the agendas, contemporaneous notes, and written summaries contained information sufficient to enable a person reading those documents to enjoy the same benefits and privileges of attending and participating in the weekly meetings as other employees. These meetings, which lasted up to one hour, had agendas that contained only cursory information about the topics to be covered. The contemporaneous notes also contained limited information. Centeno testified that when Chan took contemporaneous notes, she "wasn't writing what was going on in the meeting" and that her writing "was kind of limited." Centeno further explained … that, regardless of who took notes, "[t]hey would write just short little words and keep telling me to wait. I could not really understand what was going on." Centeno also testified that during meetings he did not have an opportunity to express his questions because he did not have an ASL interpreter. * * * [T]here is a genuine issue of material fact regarding whether these modifications, viewed as a whole, would allow a deaf employee, even one who was fluent in written English, to enjoy the benefits and privileges of attending and participating in the departmental meetings. This is especially true in light of Centeno's limited proficiency in written English.

Second, we conclude that there is an issue of fact regarding whether UPS was aware or should have been aware that the modifications were ineffective.... As UPS notes, the ADA does not require an employer to be clairvoyant regarding the effectiveness of a modification. But * * *, a reasonable trier of fact could conclude that Centeno asked for a different modification and that UPS was aware or should have been aware that the modifications it was offering were ineffective.... UPS was aware of Centeno's limited proficiency in written English. * * * Moreover, there is a genuine issue of fact regarding whether UPS was aware or should have been aware that the modifications for the weekly meetings, which relied on Centeno's capacity to understand written English, were ineffective. Centeno complained in writing that Chan's contemporaneous notes were "not enough for me" and that "ASL is better for me get more understand." Centeno testified that he told Chan that he did not understand her handwritten notes. Centeno also testified that he told Chan that he did not understand some of the summaries Chan emailed to him. Centeno persisted in requesting an interpreter for the weekly meetings until he stopped attending. In March 2007, after Centeno continued to complain about UPS's failure to provide an interpreter for the weekly meetings, he met with Chan and a human resources representative and informed them that "he does not understand or comprehend some written communication."

* * * Evidence in the record suggests that in determining whether to provide an ASL interpreter for weekly meetings, UPS did not consider the nature of the information being communicated in a particular meeting or the length of the meeting, but instead relied on relatively arbitrary considerations. Schulz testified that she decided to approve an interpreter for the monthly meetings but not for the weekly meetings because she "felt once a month was sufficient." A trier of fact could conclude that UPS refused to provide an interpreter for regular meetings that were less than two hours long because there was a two-hour minimum charge for ASL interpreter services. If UPS failed to consider whether the circumstances of a weekly meeting necessitated the use of an ASL

interpreter, then the trier of fact could find that UPS failed to engage in the interactive process in good faith.

In summary, an employer has discretion to choose among effective modifications, and need not provide the employee with the accommodation he or she requests or prefers, but an employer cannot satisfy its obligations under the ADA by providing an ineffective modification. * * *

The ADA prohibits employers from discriminating against individuals "in regard to ... job training." The record demonstrates that as early as April 2005, when Chan reminded Centeno of the goal of improving his skills by taking Excel training, Centeno informed Chan that he could not use the on-line training program because he could not read it. Yet Centeno's performance reviews continued to list "Excel knowledge" under Centeno's development plan. UPS waited for more than two years to provide Centeno with an ASL interpreter for Excel training. "The interactive process requires communication and good-faith exploration of possible accommodations between employers and individual employees, and *neither side can delay ... the process.*" With respect to the Excel training, there is a genuine issue of material fact regarding whether UPS acted in good faith in the interactive process and whether UPS delayed providing Centeno with the accommodation he needed in order to receive the training.

There is [also] a genuine issue of material fact regarding whether UPS's modifications were effective in ensuring that Centeno understood the company's Anti-Harassment Policy. During the May 11, 2005 disciplinary meeting with Chan and Nishimura, Centeno consulted an English-language dictionary in an effort to understand his written warning about the lunchroom incident. Soon after this meeting, Centeno notified Chan, Schulz, and Nishimura in writing that he did not understand the warning. * * * In response to Centeno's notification, UPS set up a meeting with an ASL interpreter present to clarify Centeno's "understanding about the discipline." Four months later, when Centeno reviewed the Anti-Harassment Policy and Questionnaire, he informed Schulz and Chan that he did not understand many of the words in the Policy and more than half of the questions in the Questionnaire. * * * In response, Chan did not provide an interpreter, but instead directed Centeno to use an English-language dictionary to look up the words he did not understand. * * * [A] reasonable trier of fact could conclude that as of September 2005, UPS was aware or should have been aware that Centeno needed an ASL interpreter to understand the Anti-Harassment Policy. Even if Centeno did not expressly request an interpreter to understand the Policy, a reasonable trier of fact could conclude that UPS was aware or should have been aware that the modification it offered—consulting an English-language dictionary—was not effective.

* * * [W]e reverse the district court's summary judgment and remand for further proceedings. * * *

CASE QUESTIONS

1. What was the legal issue in this case? What did the court decide?

2. What things did UPS do for this employee? Why does the court nonetheless allow the employee's failure to reasonably accommodate claim to go forward?

3. Why does UPS not argue that providing the ASL interpreter would be an undue hardship?

4. Is the issue in this case deafness or literacy? Are these connected?

5. Do you agree with the court's decision? Why or why not?

As the UPS case illustrates, accommodations must be effective in removing or at least substantially lessening obstacles to full participation in the workplace. When there is more than one accommodation available, *employers should lean toward adopting the accommodations preferred by disabled employees.* After all, the accommodations are intended to meet their needs. *However, the accommodation selected need not be the one preferred by the employee, so long as it is effective.*

While employers are under no obligation to create new positions for, promote, or displace ("bump") other employees to accommodate disabled employees, reassignment to a vacant position is a reasonable accommodation. However, *reassignment to a vacant position should be considered only if the individual cannot be accommodated in her present job.* Reassignment is "plan B" if it proves to not be possible to provide accommodations that will enable employees to perform the essential functions of their current jobs. There is some ambiguity surrounding the meaning of "vacant," but at least one court has held that a position is not vacant if it is currently staffed by temporary workers. Only if the status of the position is such that "it would be available for a similarly-situated non-disabled employee to apply for and obtain" can the position be deemed "vacant."[37] Courts differ in their views of how far employers must go regarding reassignments or transfers. Some courts (and the EEOC) maintain that if a vacant position exists for which a disabled employee who can no longer perform his previous job is qualified, then the employer must give the position to the disabled employee as a reasonable accommodation—even if a more qualified, nondisabled candidate is available.[38] Other courts say that employers are free to follow their own neutral policies governing reassignments—including hiring the person deemed most qualified—and need only consider the disabled employee to meet their legal obligations.[39] The Supreme Court has not yet squarely addressed this question, but it has ruled on whether exceptions must be made to policies basing job assignments on seniority.[40] A disabled airline employee asked to retain his position in the face of bids from more senior employees for his job. Citing its seniority policy, the airline refused to make an exception to accommodate the disabled

[37]*Duvall v. Georgia-Pacific Consumer Products*, 607 F.3d 1255, 1263 (10th Cir. 2010).

[38]*Smith v. Midland Brake*, 180 F.3d 1154 (10th Cir. 1999).

[39]*EEOC v. Humiston-Keeling*, 227 F.3d 1024 (7th Cir. 2000).

[40]*U.S. Airways v. Barnett*, 535 U.S. 391 (2002).

employee. Displaced from the one job that he could perform, the disabled employee was terminated. The Supreme Court ruled that the advantages of a seniority system are sufficiently important that, in the usual case, requiring employers to make exceptions for disabled employees would not be "reasonable." However, a plaintiff might still be able to show the existence of "special circumstances"—such as a seniority system that already provides for numerous exceptions or whose rules are frequently changed—that would overcome the presumption that requiring the employer to bend seniority rules to accommodate a disabled person is not reasonable.

JUST THE FACTS

An employee worked for Wal-Mart as a dry-grocery order filler. After suffering a permanent injury to her right hand and arm, the employee was no longer able to perform the order-filler job. She requested reassignment to a vacant router position. Despite the fact that a router position for which she was qualified existed, Wal-Mart insisted that she would have to apply for the position and compete for it with other applicants. Another applicant deemed more qualified was hired for the router position. The disabled woman was eventually placed in a janitorial position with a much lower rate of pay. Did Wal-Mart fail to reasonably accommodate this disabled employee?

See, *Huber v. Wal-Mart Stores,* 486 F.3d 480 (8th Cir. 2007), *cert. dismissed,* 128 S. Ct. 1116 (2008).

Another significant form of reasonable accommodation is job redesign. However, it is important to note that while functions not essential to jobs must be eliminated if they cannot be performed by disabled employees, employers are not required to eliminate essential functions from jobs. Thus, a court reporter's request to work exclusively in a court reporter control room rather than live courtrooms as an accommodation for her severe incontinence was deemed not reasonable because in-court reporting was an essential function of her job.[41] Likewise, an assistant restaurant manager's request to delegate manual tasks to other employees as an accommodation for her severe shoulder injury was found to be not reasonable.[42] The court rejected her argument that the only essential functions of her job were to oversee the restaurant's operations and to supervise employees. The operation of the restaurant required the active involvement of assistant managers in preparing food and serving customers, tasks that were frequently engaged in and reflected in her job description. In addition to performing the essential functions of jobs, with or without reasonable accommodation, disabled persons are required to meet the same performance and conduct standards as other employees. Employers are not required to reasonably accommodate disabled employees by permitting substandard performance and misconduct, even if these performance problems are the results of employees' disabilities.[43] Such incidents might initiate the interactive process to determine whether accommodation is in order, but provided that the performance standards and

---

[41] *Gratzl v. Office of the Chief Judges,* 601 F.3d 674 (7th Cir. 2010).

[42] *Richardson v. Friendly Ice Cream,* 594 F.3d 69 (1st Cir. 2010).

[43] U.S. Equal Employment Opportunity Commission. *The Americans with Disabilities Act: Applying Performance and Conduct Standards to Employees with Disabilities.* Viewed October 11, 2008 (http://www.eeoc.gov/).

conduct rules are job related and consistent with business necessity, failings need not be overlooked or excused.

> ## Clippings
>
> Telecommunications company Verizon will pay millions to settle a lawsuit brought by the EEOC on behalf of hundreds of its disabled employees. The EEOC had charged that the company violated the ADA by failing to reasonably accommodate employees who needed medical leave for their disabilities. Under Verizon's "no fault" attendance plan, the employees were disciplined or fired for excessive absences, rather than accommodated by making exceptions for needed medical leave. An EEOC official observed that "[t]his settlement demonstrates the need for employers to have attendance policies which take into account the need for paid or unpaid leave as a reasonable accommodation for employees with disabilities."
>
> U.S. Equal Employment Opportunity Commission. "Verizon to Pay $20 Million to Settle Nationwide EEOC Disability Suit." Press Release (July 6, 2011) (http://www.eeoc.gov/).

Many disabilities wax and wane in severity. Periods of leave under circumstances different from, or in durations longer than, the leave normally available to employees can be reasonable accommodations that permit disabled employees to maintain employment while dealing with the varying effects of their disabilities. But the question of how far employers must go in modifying their leave and attendance policies to accommodate the needs of disabled employees is a matter of considerable discussion and debate.[44] Employers are not required to provide *paid* leave to disabled employees that is not available to all employees, but how much leave must be given before it is concluded that the leave is no longer a reasonable accommodation? How many times must leave be provided anew or extended? There are currently no simple answers to these questions, but the main message to employers is to be flexible. Employers like Verizon (see "Clippings") with rigid leave and attendance policies are likely to run afoul of the ADA (and, as we will see in Chapter 11, the Family and Medical Leave Act as well). Employers that are willing to go beyond their established policies and make exceptions on a case-by-case basis to accommodate disabled employees are likely to be okay. An employer does not have to wait indefinitely for the return of a disabled employee from leave, so the failure of an employee to provide even an estimate of when she would be back at work was fatal to her ADA claim.[45] But the mere fact that an employee does not specify an exact date of return or needs one or more extensions does not render the leave indefinite. The key issue is whether there is any reasonable prospect of the disabled employee being able to return to work.[46]

When Does an Accommodation Impose Undue Hardship?

The reasonableness of an accommodation is distinct from whether that accommodation would impose undue hardship on a particular employer. An employer can refuse an otherwise reasonable accommodation if the employer can show that providing it would

---

[44]U.S. Equal Employment Opportunity Commission. "Experts Give EEOC Range of Views on Leave as a Reasonable Accommodation." Press Release (June 8, 2011) (http://www.eeoc.gov/).

[45]*Peyton v. Fred's Stores of Arkansas*, 561 F.3d 900 (8th Cir. 2009), *cert. denied*, 2009 U.S. LEXIS 6148.

[46]Peter J. Petesch. "EEOC Moves toward Guidance Addressing Leave as a Reasonable Accommodation under the ADA." *Daily Labor Report* 121 (June 23, 2011), I-1.

impose "significant difficulty or expense" in relation to the size of the company, its resources, and the nature of its operations. In general, larger employers are required to go further in accommodating disabled employees than are smaller employers. Accommodations imposing **undue hardship** are those that are unduly costly, extensive, substantial, or disruptive or that would require fundamental alteration of the nature or operation of the business.

Many accommodations are inexpensive. The Job Accommodation Network puts the typical cost of an accommodation at $600, but also claims that over half of all accommodations (e.g., schedule changes, job redesign) do not impose any direct cost on employers.[47] Congress, in enacting the ADA, expected that employers would incur some cost and difficulty in opening up their workplaces to disabled persons. Employers claiming undue hardship must produce evidence of significant difficulty or expense and cannot rely on mere speculation about potential costs or problems. *One way to convincingly show undue hardship is to try out an accommodation and document the cost and any operational problems.* (In the process, the employer might learn that providing the accommodation is not such a big deal after all.) A variety of tax breaks and grants are available to assist employers with the costs of accommodating disabled workers. *An employer that cannot meet the cost of a proposed accommodation, even considering external funding, should offer the disabled employee the option of paying for the portion of the cost that is beyond the employer's means.*

Reasonable Accommodation of Religion

Under Title VII, *employers are required to reasonably accommodate religion, unless doing so would impose undue hardship.* The essential nature of this requirement, including engaging in an interactive process with the employee or applicant and being flexible when administering policies, is much the same as that for accommodating a disability. However, courts have interpreted the requirement to reasonably accommodate religion as being much more limited than the responsibility to accommodate disability.

Religion

Religion is not only membership in or affiliation with a particular church, congregation, or denomination. Title VII defines **religion** to encompass

> *all aspects of religious observance and practice, as well as belief, unless an employer demonstrates that he is unable to reasonably accommodate to an employee's or prospective employee's religious observance or practice without undue hardship on the conduct of the employer's business.*[48]

Thus, unlike other protected classes, religion is not only something that a person "is" (e.g., a Jew, a Muslim) but also something that is expressed through words and deeds. This behavioral aspect of religion sometimes requires accommodation.

What makes a belief or practice "religious" as opposed to "philosophical," "political," or "ideological"? The EEOC treats as religious "moral and ethical beliefs as to what is right and wrong which are sincerely held with the strength of religious views."[49] Courts have struggled to distinguish between the secular and the religious. Belief in a particular

---

[47]Job Accommodation Network. *Workplace Accommodations: Low Cost, High Impact.* Fact Sheet Series (updated September 1, 2010), 3.

[48]42 U.S.C.A. § 2000e(j) (2011).

[49]29 C.F.R. § 1605.1 (2011).

god or deity is not a necessary element of religion. In fact, atheism and agnosticism are forms of religious belief.[50] To be considered religious, however, courts generally require that such beliefs or practices perform a function in the individual's life comparable to that of traditional religions. The espoused religion does not have to be popular, well known, or even organized. An individual's own sincere beliefs about what his religion requires, even when these go beyond the formal teachings and requirements of his religion, are still aspects of religious belief and practice that potentially require accommodation.

A court considered whether veganism is a religious creed. A job offer at a pharmaceutical warehouse was withdrawn when a candidate who is a strict vegan refused to be immunized for mumps (the vaccine for mumps is grown in chicken embryos). The candidate refused to be immunized because his vegan beliefs dictated that it is immoral to kill or exploit animals, whether for food, clothing, vaccines, or any other purpose. The court concluded that veganism is not a religious creed within the meaning of the California antidiscrimination statute in question, but rather "a personal philosophy, albeit shared by many others, and a way of life."[51] The court based its decision on the fact that the statutory definition of religious creed is narrower than the EEOC's broad concept, but also on criteria distilled from other court cases. Those criteria emphasize that religions address fundamental questions about human existence; entail comprehensive belief systems rather than isolated precepts; and often display formal and external signs such as leaders, ceremonies, and holidays. Veganism's claim to status as a religious practice failed because it was seen as not addressing ultimate questions of meaning, being narrowly focused on the single issue of the treatment of animals, and lacking the symbols and ceremonies typical of religion.

THE CHANGING WORKPLACE

Religion in the Workplace

The vast majority of Americans profess to believe in a God[1] and identify with a religion.[2] Christian denominations, which are many and varied, are the most popular (about 76 percent of adults indicated this religious affiliation in 2008). A substantial number of U.S. adults (about 15 percent in 2008) identify with no religion, although such individuals do not necessarily view themselves as being atheist or agnostic. The remainder of the adult population either identify with one of a wide range of other faiths (e.g., Jewish, Muslim, Hindu, Wiccan) or decline to answer questions about their religious affiliations. While religious beliefs are often formed early and fervently held, there is a surprising amount of fluidity in religious affiliations. A 2007 survey of U.S. adults found that more than a quarter had abandoned the religious affiliation they had during their childhood.[3]

That employees come to the workplace with religious beliefs and affiliations is not anything new. But the range of religious persuasions found in many workplaces and the desire of employees to openly display and adhere to their religious beliefs in the workplace is arguably greater than in the past. To some degree, this has been encouraged by employers through the creation of religiously based affinity groups.[4] But the potential for clashes between employers' policies and employees' religious practices, and between employees with different religious views, is quite real. Schedules, appearance requirements, and job tasks all potentially conflict with employees' religious beliefs

---

[50]*EEOC v. Townley Engineering & Manufacturing Co.*, 859 F.2d 610 (9th Cir. 1988), *cert. denied*, 489 U.S. 1077 (1989).

[51]*Friedman v. Southern California Permanente Medical Group*, 102 Cal. App. 4th 39, 70 (2d App. Dist. 2002); *cert. denied*, 538 U.S. 1033 (2003).

and practices. The zeal with which some employees communicate about and display their religious beliefs can easily grate on other employees who view this as harassment. Relative to other protected classes, religious discrimination charges account for only a small portion of the EEOC's caseload (3.8 percent of EEOC charges filed in 2010), but the number of cases appears to be growing (up from 2.1 percent of EEOC charges in 1997).[5]

One aspect of religious discrimination that is of particular concern to the EEOC at this time is discrimination against Muslims. A lingering effect of the events of September 11, 2001, has been extreme resentment in some quarters against Muslims. Mary Jo O'Neill, regional attorney at the EEOC's Phoenix office, said (in 2010) "There's a level of hatred and animosity that is shocking, ... I've never seen such antipathy toward Muslim workers."[6] Although Muslims are only a very small portion of the U.S. population (less than 1 percent of U.S. adults in 2008), they were involved in nearly a quarter of all of the religious discrimination charges brought to the EEOC in 2009.[7] Many of these cases involve challenges to dress and appearance policies that do not permit the wearing of a hijab (head scarf) or other religious garb.[8] Clashes over prayer breaks have also been common.[9]

[1] The Pew Research Center. "Not All Nonbelievers Call Themselves Atheists." (April 2, 2009) (http://www.pewforum.org/).
[2] U.S. Bureau of the Census. *Statistical Abstract of the United States.* 130th Ed. (2009) (based on the 2008 American Religious Identification Survey).
[3] Neela Banerjee. "A Fluid Religious Life Is Seen in U.S., with Switches Common." *New York Times* (February 26, 2008), A1.
[4] Kathryn A. Cañas and Harris Sondak. *Opportunities and Challenges of Workplace Diversity.* Upper Saddle River, NJ: Pearson Prentice Hall (2008), 144–45.
[5] U.S. Equal Employment Opportunity Commission. "Charge Statistics FY 1997 through FY 2010." Viewed July 16, 2011 (http://www.eeoc.gov/)
[6] Steven Greenhouse. "Muslims and Rising Tensions." *New York Times* (September 24, 2010), B1.
[7] Greenhouse.
[8] Bernard J. Pazanowski. "Hijabs, Burqas, Khimars and Beards: Avoiding Religious Discrimination Suits." *Daily Labor Report* 110 (June 10, 2010), C-1.
[9] Mark Wolski. "EEOC, Poultry Processor Settle Bias Lawsuit over Muslim Prayer Breaks." *Daily Labor Report* 219 (November 13, 2008), A-9.

A religious belief also must be "sincerely held" to be protected. The tendency of the courts is to accept plaintiffs' assertions about their religious beliefs, at least absent behavior starkly inconsistent with the alleged religious practice. As a general rule, *employers should accept the sincerity of employees' stated religious beliefs and practices and focus on whether it is possible to reasonably accommodate them without undue hardship.* However, in a case involving an employee who claimed religious objections to paying union dues, the union's efforts to verify the sincerity of his beliefs did not violate Title VII.[52] Both the National Labor Relations Act and Title VII require labor unions to allow employees whose sincerely held religious beliefs dictate that they not belong to or financially support unions to contribute an equivalent sum to charity. Suspicious because the employee had worked for years without raising any objection and was being provided with information by an organization hostile to unions, the union required that he provide some independent confirmation of the sincerity of his stated beliefs. The court stressed the limited extent to which employers can inquire into the sincerity of employees' beliefs but held that the union's actions were not illegal. Likewise, while permitting her claim to go to trial, the court noted that the fact that a woman who was suing a retailer over its policy of having clerks wear "sexy, form-fitting" outfits that allegedly conflicted with her religious beliefs, showed up for a deposition wearing a form-fitting shirt would be relevant to determining whether her beliefs were sincere.[53]

[52]*Bushhouse v. Local Union 2209, UAW,* 164 F. Supp. 2d 1066 (N.D. Ind. 2001).
[53]*EEOC v. Abercrombie & Fitch Stores,* 2009 U.S. Dist. LEXIS 99589, at 9 (E.D. Mo.).

ELEMENTS OF A CLAIM

Failure to Reasonably Accommodate Religion

An applicant or employee can establish a **prima facie case of failure to reasonably accommodate religion** by showing the following:

- The existence of a sincere religious belief or practice that conflicts with an employment requirement
- The employer was informed of the conflicting belief or practice
- The employee or applicant suffered an adverse employment outcome due to adhering to the religious belief or practice

If a prima facie case is established, the employer must show one of the following:

- A reasonable accommodation was offered but not accepted
- No reasonable accommodation without undue hardship was available

Inability to establish one of these circumstances will result in a finding that the employer violated Title VII by failing to reasonably accommodate religion.

© Cengage Learning 2013.

Failure to Reasonably Accommodate Religion

Religious beliefs and practices can clash with workplace requirements under a variety of circumstances. One of the most common is when an employee's work schedule conflicts with a Sabbath, a holy day, or another religious observance. Likewise, religious practices regarding the wearing of particular clothing, facial hair, or symbols sometimes run up against employers' grooming, uniform, and appearance requirements. Sometimes the tasks required of employees conflict with religious beliefs. Examples include a Pentecostal nurse's refusal to assist in occasional abortions,[54] an evangelical Christian counselor's refusal to counsel clients who were homosexual or living together outside of marriage,[55] a Muslim ham-processing plant employee's refusal to touch pork,[56] and a Catholic pharmacist's refusal to speak even briefly to customers regarding contraception.[57] Employers are also frequently asked to accommodate employees by allowing them to decorate office space with religious items and by providing special meals at company events.[58] *Maintaining policies that are flexible (e.g., a fixed number of days off that can be used for different reasons) may prevent conflicts from arising in the first place.*

Practical Considerations What are some ways of handling conflicts involving work schedules and religious obligations?

Clippings

The EEOC has sued Abercrombie & Fitch—again—over its dress code and appearance policies. In 2005, the company paid $40 million to settle the claims of a

---

[54]*Shelton v. University of Medicine & Dentistry of New Jersey*, 223 F.3d 220 (3d Cir. 2000).

[55]*Bruff v. North Mississippi Health Services, Inc.*, 244 F.3d 495 (5th Cir. 2001), *cert. denied*, 122 S. Ct 348 (2001).

[56]*Al-Jabery v. Conagra Foods*, 2007 U.S. Dist. LEXIS 79080 (D. Neb.).

[57]*Noesen v. Medical Staffing Network*, 232 Fed. Appx. 581 (7th Cir. 2007).

[58]"Religious Discrimination: Survey Finds Employers Have Greater Need to Accommodate Diverse Needs of Employees." *Daily Labor Report* 127 (July 3, 2001), A-6.

class of plaintiffs disadvantaged by hiring and job assignment decisions based on candidates' perceived fit with an "All-American look" desired by the retailer. In the current case, the EEOC alleges that an 18-year-old Muslim woman was rejected for a job stocking merchandise because she wore a hijab. In so doing, the retailer failed to reasonably accommodate her religious practices by making an exception to its dress code that prohibits head coverings. An EEOC attorney commented that "this retailer that targets a youth market is sending the message that you cannot aspire to their 'All-American' brand if you wear a head covering to comply with your faith."

U.S. Equal Employment Opportunity Commission. "Abercrombie & Fitch Sued for Religious Discrimination." Press Release (September 1, 2010) (http://www.eeoc.gov/).

Employers are not expected to be aware of the religious affiliations and practices of their employees. To be entitled to accommodation, employees must inform their employers regarding the presence of conflicts between their religious practices and workplace requirements—and do so before disciplinary action is taken. In one relevant case,[59] an employee with evangelical Christian beliefs was terminated for mailing upsetting letters to other employees' homes. The letters all conveyed the basic sentiment that the employees were sinners who needed to repent. The court agreed that her letters were religiously motivated and that she was punished for doing what she believed her religion required (again, it is not necessary that others of the same faith feel compelled to act in the same manner). However, she was unable to establish a prima facie case of failure to reasonably accommodate religion because she did not notify the employer before the fact of the conflict arising out of her need to send the letters. Although employees are responsible for making conflicts with their religion known, *employers should listen carefully to employees and be prepared to consider accommodation when alerted to the fact that an employee is having problems complying with a policy or another workplace requirement for reasons related to her religion.*

The final element of a prima facie case of failure to reasonably accommodate is a showing that the employee was subjected to an adverse employment decision (e.g., suspension, demotion, termination) due to following his beliefs. Most courts appear to require actual loss of employment opportunity, not merely the threat. Thus, in a case involving a hospital clerk whose work schedule conflicted with her Sabbath, the hospital was not liable for failing to accommodate her because she suffered no actual adverse employment consequences. Perhaps fearing discipline or termination, the woman had continued to work the assigned hours that made it impossible to observe her Sabbath. The court observed that "Plaintiff's failure to insist upon strict adherence to these beliefs, even at the cost of negative job consequences, effectively absolved her employer of the responsibility to reasonably accommodate her beliefs."[60]

When presented with timely requests for accommodation of sincere religious beliefs or practices, *employers must take requests for reasonable accommodation seriously and make good faith efforts to identify reasonable accommodations that do not impose undue hardship.* Although a good faith effort to find an accommodation might come up empty, employers are in a better position if some accommodation is offered rather than none. As with disability, *a reasonable accommodation of religion need not be the employee's preferred accommodation,*[61] *but providing the employee's preference should be the first inclination.* An accommodation of religion can be "reasonable" even if it does not completely

---

[59]*Chalmers v. Tulon Company of Richmond*, 101 F.3d 1012 (4th Cir. 1996).

[60]*Stone v. West*, 133 F. Supp. 2d 972, 986 (E.D. Mich. 2001).

[61]*Ansonia Board of Education v. Philbrook*, 479 U.S. 60 (1986).

JUST THE FACTS

In 2007, Oregon enacted a law providing legal recognition to same-sex relationships as domestic partnerships. An employee in a county clerk's office asked to be excused from having to register same-sex couples because of her religious belief that homosexuality is a sin. The county clerk initially said that it would not be a problem, provided that another clerk was available at the time to register same-sex couples. But a day later, the county clerk changed her mind and said that the woman must perform the registrations. Without further discussion of her proposed accommodation, the woman was informed that it would be an undue hardship to exempt her from this job requirement. The county offered to discuss a transfer to any other positions that might arise. However, no positions were available at the time and none were ever offered. Shortly thereafter, the woman was terminated when she refused to initial a memo affirming that she would perform the disputed registrations. In the two years following her departure, there were thirty-seven same-sex domestic partner registrations. Twenty-six of these registrations were processed by two clerks, while the remaining eleven registrations were processed by three other clerks. Did the county fail to reasonably accommodate this employee? Why or why not?

See, *Slater v. Douglas County*, 743 F. Supp.2d 1188 (D. Ore 2010).

eliminate a religious conflict.[62] Employees who reject reasonable accommodations offered to them are out of luck. The courts also expect that employees will cooperate in the reasonable accommodation process. Thus, the claim of a nurse who refused to assist in abortions failed because she rejected a transfer to the newborn unit and did not work with the hospital to locate an alternative position.[63]

How far must employers go in accommodating religion? The measures that must be taken to accommodate religion are not extensive. The Supreme Court has characterized the obligation to accommodate religion as "de minimis."[64] In contrast to the ADA's requirement that reasonable accommodations be made absent "significant expense or difficulty," employers need not incur more than minimal expense or operational problems in accommodating religion. In a case involving an employee seeking a work schedule accommodation to allow observance of a Sabbath, the Court concluded that the employer was not required to bear the cost of paying other employees a premium to accept his shift, nor to place the burden of accommodation onto other employees by changing seniority rules or forcing them to work the shift.[65] Likewise, the postal service did not have to exempt a letter carrier from working on Saturdays to accommodate his faith because doing so would have violated the collective bargaining agreement's shift provisions.[66] The alternative of scheduling the employee for Saturday work but allowing him to use earned or unpaid leave for the time would still impose undue hardship

[62]*EEOC v. Firestone Fibers & Textiles Co.*, 515 F.3d 307, 313-15 (4th Cir. 2008).

[63]*Shelton*, at 228.

[64]*TWA v. Hardison*, 432 U.S. 63, 84 (1977).

[65]*Hardison*, at 77–81.

[66]*Harrell v. Donahue*, 638 F.3d 975 (8th Cir. 2011).

because it would shift the burden of working Saturdays to coworkers, many of whom had more seniority. However, an employer violated Title VII by firing an employee who had refused to complete his delivery route because working past sundown on a Friday would go against his religious beliefs.[67] The employee was able to show that with little or no cost and without violating a collective bargaining agreement, the employer could have accommodated his practice by splitting his load more evenly with other drivers. Likewise, an airline's policy prohibiting customer service agents from voluntarily swapping shifts with coworkers during a ninety-day probationary period effectively denied those employees the opportunity to be reasonably accommodated.[68]

Clashes between religious beliefs and job duties can be especially difficult to accommodate. A Catholic pharmacist who refused to have anything to do with contraceptives—to the point that he would simply walk away from customers asking questions about contraception or put them on hold without summoning coworkers to help out—was unsuccessful in his failure to accommodate claim.[69] Even though the store permitted him not to handle contraceptives and prescriptions for them, his desire to be entirely free of customer contact responsibilities so as to avoid any possible inquiries regarding contraceptives would have imposed undue hardship on his employer. Likewise, it would have been an undue hardship for an employer to accommodate an employee who is a member of a sect that believes it violates the Second Commandment to either pose for or carry photographs.[70] The photograph was required as part of the federal government's employee identification procedures (which were strengthened after the employee was originally hired) for port employees. None of the employee's suggested accommodations, including using non-photo forms of ID or biometric identification, would have satisfied the employer's legal obligations.

Accommodating employees' religious beliefs by making exceptions to dress and appearance requirements is often required. The Washington, DC, transit system settled a suit brought by the Department of Justice based on its failure to accommodate the religious practices of a bus driver applicant by permitting her to wear a skirt, rather than the required pants.[71] The EEOC was permitted to proceed to trial in the case of four Muslim applicants for hotel housekeepers jobs who were denied interviews after they refused a request to remove their hijabs.[72] However, safety concerns (e.g., the need to be clean shaven to wear a respirator), effects on coworkers or the public, or the nature of the job might render granting exceptions to grooming and appearance policies an undue hardship. Courts have generally ruled against plaintiffs seeking exceptions to the grooming and uniform requirements of police departments[73] and prisons.[74] In these cases, the courts have emphasized the importance of adhering to authority, presenting a religiously neutral image, and maintaining security as reasons why permitting the wearing of religious garb would be an undue hardship.

In *Cloutier v. Costco,* the court must decide whether it would impose undue hardship on this retailer to make an exception to its appearance policy.

---

[67]*Sturgill v. United Parcel Service,* 512 F.3d 1024 (8th Cir. 2008).

[68]Kevin P. McGowan. "EEOC, Airline Reach $130,000 Settlement of Suit Challenging No Shift Swap Policy." *Daily Labor Report* 246 (December 29, 2009), A-1.

[69]*Noesen.*

[70]*Cherry v. Sunoco,* 2009 U.S. Dist. LEXIS 72755 (E.D. Pa.).

[71]Laura D. Francis. "Justice Department, Metro Settle Lawsuit on Failure to Offer Religious Accommodation." *Daily Labor Report* 24 (February 9, 2009), A-5.

[72]*EEOC v. White Lodging Services,* 2010 U.S. Dist. LEXIS 32492 (W.D. Ky.).

[73]*Webb v. Philadelphia,* 562 F.3d 256 (3d Cir. 2009).

[74]*EEOC v. GEO Group,* 616 F.3d 265 (3d Cir. 2010).

Cloutier v. Costco
390 F. 3d 126 (1st Cir. 2004), *cert. denied,* 2005 U.S. LEXIS 4923

OPINION BY CIRCUIT JUDGE LIPEZ:

Kimberly Cloutier alleges that her employer, Costco Wholesale Corp. (Costco), failed to offer her a reasonable accommodation after she alerted it to a conflict between the "no facial jewelry" provision of its dress code and her religious practice as a member of the Church of Body Modification. She argues that this failure amounts to religious discrimination…. The district court granted summary judgment for Costco, concluding that Costco reasonably accommodated Cloutier by offering to reinstate her if she either covered her facial piercing with a band-aid or replaced it with a clear retainer. We affirm the grant of summary judgment, but on a different basis. We hold that Costco had no duty to accommodate Cloutier because it could not do so without undue hardship.

* * * Kimberly Cloutier began working at Costco's West Springfield, Massachusetts store in July 1997. Before her first day of work, Cloutier received a copy of the Costco employment agreement, which included the employee dress code. When she was hired, Cloutier had multiple earrings and four tattoos, but no facial piercings. * * * In 1998, Costco revised its dress code to prohibit food handlers, including deli employees, from wearing any jewelry. Cloutier's supervisor instructed her to remove her earrings pursuant to the revised code, but Cloutier refused. Instead, she requested to transfer to a front-end position where she would be permitted to continue wearing her jewelry. Cloutier did not indicate at the time that her insistence on wearing her earrings was based on a religious or spiritual belief. Costco approved Cloutier's transfer back to a front-end position in June 1998, and promoted her to cashier soon thereafter. Over the ensuing two years, she engaged in various forms of body modification including facial piercing and cutting. Although these practices were meaningful to Cloutier, they were not motivated by a religious belief. In March 2001, Costco further revised its dress code to prohibit all facial jewelry, aside from earrings, and disseminated the modified code to its employees. Cloutier did not challenge the dress code or seek an accommodation, but rather continued uneventfully to wear her eyebrow piercing for several months. Costco began enforcing its no-facial-jewelry policy in June 2001. On June 25, 2001, front-end supervisors Todd Cunningham and Michele Callaghan informed Cloutier and another employee, Jennifer Theriaque, that they would have to remove their facial piercings. Cloutier and Theriaque did not comply, returning to work the following day still wearing their piercings. When Callaghan reiterated the no-facial-jewelry policy, Cloutier indicated for the first time that she was a member of the Church of Body Modification (CBM), and that her eyebrow piercing was part of her religion.

The CBM was established in 1999 and counts approximately 1000 members who participate in such practices as piercing, tattooing, branding, cutting, and body manipulation. Among the goals espoused in the CBM's mission statement are for its members to "grow as individuals through body modification and its teachings," to "promote growth in mind, body and spirit," and to be "confident role models in learning, teaching, and displaying body modification." The church's website, apparently its primary mode for reaching its adherents, did not state that members' body modifications had to be visible at all times or that temporarily removing body modifications would violate a religious tenet. Still, Cloutier interprets the call to be a confident role model as requiring that her piercings be visible at all times and precluding her from removing or covering her facial jewelry. She does not extend this reasoning to the tattoos on her upper arms, which were covered at work by her shirt.

After reviewing information that Cloutier provided from the CBM website, Callaghan's supervisor, Andrew Mulik, instructed Cloutier and Theriaque to remove their facial jewelry. They refused. * * * Although Cloutier learned during the week of July 2, 2001 that Theriaque had returned to work with retainers, she chose to wait for her EEOC complaint to be resolved rather than following suit. During the week of July 7, 2001, Cloutier inquired of her superiors whether she could use vacation time to cover her absences and was told that she had been suspended. The following week, on July 14, Cloutier received notice in the mail that she had been terminated for her unexcused absences resulting from noncompliance with the dress code. She claims that this was her first notice that Costco had decided not to grant her request for an accommodation that would reconcile the dress code with her religious requirement of displaying her facial jewelry at all times.

The parties remained in contact after Cloutier's termination through the EEOC mediation process. During a meeting on August 10, 2001, Costco offered to let Cloutier return to work wearing either plastic retainers or a Band-Aid over her jewelry (the same accommodation that Cloutier had suggested prior to her termination). Shevchuk repeated the offer in a letter dated August 29, 2001, asking Cloutier to respond by September 6, 2001. Although there is some dispute as to whether Cloutier attempted to respond to Costco's offer before the deadline, she now maintains that neither of the proffered accommodations would be adequate because the CBM's tenets, as she interprets them, require her to display all of her facial piercings at all times. Replacing her eyebrow piercing with a plastic retainer or covering it with a Band-Aid would thus contradict her religious convictions. Cloutier asserts that the only reasonable accommodation would be to excuse her from Costco's dress code, allowing her to wear her facial jewelry to work. Costco responds that this accommodation would interfere with its ability to maintain a professional appearance and would thereby create an undue hardship for its business. * * *

On appeal, Cloutier vigorously asserts that her insistence on displaying all her facial jewelry at all times is the result of a sincerely held religious belief. Determining whether a belief is religious is "more often than not a difficult and delicate task," one to which the courts are ill-suited. Fortunately, as the district court noted, there is no need for us to delve into this thorny question in the present case. Even assuming, arguendo, that Cloutier established her prima facie case, the facts here do not support a finding of impermissible religious discrimination. * * * We find dispositive that the only accommodation Cloutier considers reasonable, a blanket exemption from the no-facial-jewelry policy, would impose an undue hardship on Costco. In such a situation, an employer has no obligation to offer an accommodation before taking an adverse employment action. * * *

Cloutier was terminated on July 14, 2001. She maintains that Costco did not extend any offer of accommodation until August 10, 2001, approximately one month later, during a meeting that was part of the EEOC mediation process. * * * Courts in at least two of our sister circuits have ruled that an accommodation offered after an adverse employment action does not shield an employer from liability under Title VII.

Courts have also acknowledged that the opposite rule, treating as reasonable a post-termination offer extended during the EEOC mediation process, would "encourage the making of such offers, thus furthering [Title VII's] important statutory policy favoring voluntary reconciliation." Yet, as the Tenth Circuit has noted, this rule would also leave employers' conduct "virtually unregulated" when conflicts first arise. As a consequence, "Title VII would provide employees no protection until after the fact, an important consideration given the impact a suspension, termination, or rejection may have on an individual's life." * * * We have yet to consider this question directly and decline to do so here.... Our affirmance rests instead on an alternative ground advanced by Costco—namely, that the only accommodation Cloutier considers reasonable would impose an undue hardship on Costco. * * *

An accommodation constitutes an "undue hardship" if it would impose more than a de minimis cost on the employer. This calculus applies both to economic costs, such as lost business or having to hire additional employees to accommodate a Sabbath observer, and to non-economic costs, such as compromising the integrity of a seniority system. Cloutier argues that Costco has not met its burden of demonstrating that her requested accommodation would impose an undue hardship. She asserts that she did not receive complaints about her facial piercings and that the piercings did not affect her job performance. Hence, she contends that any hardship Costco posits is merely hypothetical and therefore not sufficient to excuse it from accommodating her religious practice under Title VII. Courts are "somewhat skeptical of hypothetical hardships that an employer thinks might be caused by an accommodation that never has been put into practice." "Nevertheless, it is possible for an employer to prove undue hardship without actually having undertaken any of the possible accommodations...." It can do so by "examining the specific hardships imposed by specific accommodation proposals." Here, Costco has only one proposal to evaluate (allowing Cloutier to wear and display her body jewelry as she demands) and has determined that it would constitute an undue hardship.

* * * It is axiomatic that, for better or for worse, employees reflect on their employers. This is particularly true of employees who regularly interact with customers, as Cloutier did in her cashier position. Even if Cloutier did not personally receive any complaints

about her appearance, her facial jewelry influenced Costco's public image and, in Costco's calculation, detracted from its professionalism. Costco is far from unique in adopting personal appearance standards to promote and protect its image. * * *

Courts have long recognized the importance of personal appearance regulations, even in the face of Title VII challenges. * * * Courts considering Title VII religious discrimination claims have also upheld dress code policies that, like Costco's, are designed to appeal to customer preference or to promote a professional public image. The majority of religious discrimination cases in this arena appear to involve policies regulating facial hair. But we are not the first court to consider a religious discrimination claim involving jewelry. In *Daniels v. City of Arlington*, 246 F.3d 500 (5th Cir. 2001), a former police officer claimed that his dismissal for wearing a gold cross pin on his uniform in violation of the police department's no-pin policy violated Title VII. The only reasonable accommodation that Daniels cited was to exempt him from the no-pin policy. The Fifth Circuit granted summary judgment for the police department, concluding that "the only accommodation Daniels proposes is unreasonable and an undue hardship for the city as a matter of law." * * * The assessment of what constitutes an undue hardship may be somewhat different for a private employer than for a police department. Still, we are faced with the similar situation of an employee who will accept no accommodation short of an outright exemption from a neutral dress code. Granting such an exemption would be an undue hardship because it would adversely affect the employer's public image. Costco has made a determination that facial piercings, aside from earrings, detract from the "neat, clean and professional image" that it aims to cultivate. Such a business determination is within its discretion. * * *

Cloutier argues that regardless of the reasons for the dress code, permitting her to display her facial jewelry would not be an undue hardship because Costco already overlooks other violations of its policy. In support of her position, she cites affidavits from two Costco employees identifying co-workers who "were allowed to wear facial piercings … and were not disciplined." Costco responds that any employees who displayed facial jewelry did so without its permission or knowledge, noting that constant monitoring is impossible in a facility with several hundred employees. * * * [T]here is an important distinction between an employee who displays facial jewelry unnoticed in violation of the dress code and one who does so under an exemption from the dress code. In the first scenario, Costco can instruct an employee to remove facial jewelry as soon as it becomes aware of a violation. In the second scenario, Costco forfeits its ability to mandate compliance and thus loses control over its public image. That loss, as we have discussed, would constitute an undue hardship.

CASE QUESTIONS

1. What is the legal issue in this case? What did the court decide?
2. In your view, is Cloutier able to establish a prima facie case of failure to reasonably accommodate? Does she show the existence of a sincere religious belief or practice that conflicts with the employer's appearance requirements?
3. Comment on the *process* of reasonable accommodation in this case. How might Costco have handled the process better? Cloutier?
4. Should courts consider accommodations offered after an adverse employment action has been taken in determining whether an employer failed to offer a reasonable accommodation? Explain.
5. Does Costco meet its burden of showing that no accommodation is acceptable to Cloutier that it could provide without undue hardship? Under the logic of this decision, would employers ever have to make exceptions to established dress and appearance codes to accommodate religious practice?

When it comes to reasonably accommodating religion, the following is advisable:[75] *To deal with scheduling conflicts, employers should allow and facilitate private swaps between employees; allow employees to use available personal time; permit flexible schedules; provide "floating holidays"; and within normal job assignment procedures, explore the possibility of lateral transfers that might lessen conflicts. Exceptions should be made to grooming and appearance requirements unless doing so would impose*

---

[75]U.S. Equal Employment Opportunity Commission. "Best Practices for Eradicating Religious Discrimination in the Workplace." (no date) Viewed August 12, 2008 (http://www.eeoc.gov/).

undue hardship. Note that the accommodation that might be required is making an exception to rather than eliminating the underlying policy. The possibility of meshing appearance requirements with religious practices (e.g., wearing religious garb in the company's colors) should also be investigated. *Conflicts arising from objectionable job duties might require employers to provide assistance in arranging transfers to alternative positions.*

Religious Advocacy and Religious Harassment

Employees sometimes convey their religious beliefs to others in the workplace. Often, the aim is to interest coworkers or customers in a particular religion. Such **religious advocacy** or "proselytizing" puts employers in a difficult position. On the one hand, it is part of the proselytizing employee's religious beliefs and practices, potentially requiring accommodation. At the same time, employers are obligated to protect employees from **religious harassment**. The religious advocacy of one employee can be the hostile environment—based on unwelcome, pervasive religious communications—of others. In one illuminating case, a Catholic woman made a solemn vow to wear a large button graphically depicting an aborted fetus during all of her waking hours, until abortion was no more. This disturbed a number of her coworkers and created an uproar in the workplace. The employer and the court accepted her button wearing as a sincere religious practice. The employer offered three accommodations to the employee: (1) wear the button when in her own cubicle, but remove it when circulating throughout the office; (2) wear a smaller, less graphic button; or (3) wear the same button at all times, but conceal it in some manner (e.g., by wearing a sweater) when outside her cubicle. The employee rejected all three proposals. The court held that one of the proposed accommodations, the third one, allowed her to keep her vow and was thus a reasonable accommodation. Because the woman turned it down, her termination was legal.[76] Notice that although coworker preferences generally do not justify employment decisions based on protected class, the nature of the religious practice involved here and the employer's simultaneous obligation to prevent religious harassment made consideration of coworker sentiments necessary. The religious advocacy was also interfering with employees' ability to work, as opposed to just prompting a few complaints.

In another significant case, an employee who described himself as a "devout Christian" objected to a series of posters displayed by Hewlett-Packard as part of its workplace diversity campaign.[77] The employee particularly objected to what he saw as the company's approval of homosexual activities that his faith instructed him were sinful. The employee responded by posting two biblical passages condemning homosexuality. The quotes from the Bible were visible to coworkers, customers, and other passersby. The employee admitted that the quotes were intentionally "hurtful" toward gays and lesbians to prompt them to repent. Numerous meetings were held with the employee. When the employee continued to refuse to remove the posted material, he was terminated. Regarding the employee's failure-to-accommodate claim, the court expressed "doubt that the doctrines to which [the employee] professes allegiance compel any employee to engage in either expressive or physical activity designed to hurt or harass one's fellow employees," but decided that accommodating the employee would impose undue hardship in any event. The employee indicated that the only acceptable arrangements were for the company to allow him to continue to post the biblical verses or for the company to

---

[76]*Wilson v. U.S. West Communications*, 58 F.3d 1337 (8th Cir. 1995).

[77]*Peterson v. Hewlett-Packard*, 358 F.3d 599 (9th Cir. 2004).

remove its "gay posters," in which case he would reciprocate by removing the biblical verses. The court concluded:

> *[The] first proposed accommodation would have compelled Hewlett-Packard to permit an employee to post messages intended to demean and harass his coworkers. His second proposed accommodation would have forced the company to exclude sexual orientation from its workplace diversity program. Either choice would have created undue hardship for Hewlett-Packard because it would have inhibited its efforts to attract and retain a qualified, diverse workforce, which the company reasonably views as vital to its commercial success.*[78]

Practical Considerations

How should employers deal with religious advocacy or proselytizing by employees?

The court also distinguished between actions that some coworkers find irritating or unwelcome and actions that "demean or degrade," holding that although employers might have to tolerate the former when they entail religious expression, the latter constitutes undue hardship.

Sometimes employers rather than employees are the ones expressing their religious views. In one important case, the owners of a company wanted it to be a "Christian, faith-operated business."[79] The company required all employees to attend a weekly devotional service that lasted up to forty-five minutes and included prayer and Scripture reading (as well as some business matters). An employee who was an atheist objected to this requirement. The court ruled that although an employer could hold such services, it needed to reasonably accommodate employees who found participation contrary to their own religious beliefs, unless doing so would impose undue hardship on the operation of the business. Because the employer could have simply excused objecting employees, the employer violated Title VII. In contrast, the Massachusetts Supreme Court held that a mandatory week-long nondenominational seminar for managers that used references to Scripture was not discriminatory.[80]

Public employers are subject to the U.S. Constitution as well as Title VII. This further complicates the handling of religion in the workplace for government agencies. A detailed discussion of the First Amendment's protections of speech and religion is not possible here. Suffice it to say that the First Amendment protects the "free exercise" of religion from infringement by the government (the **free exercise clause**) but also prohibits governmental entities from "establishing" (i.e., sponsoring, supporting) religion (the **establishment clause**). *Thus, public employers need to be especially careful to not unduly limit the religious speech and conduct of employees, while at the same time not allowing the workplace to become infused with religious content.* The importance of striking the right balance is illustrated by a case in which a computer analyst at the California State Department of Education incorporated the phrase "Servant of the Lord Jesus Christ" into all of his work.[81] The department responded by disciplining him and issuing rules prohibiting all religious advocacy in the workplace, as well as the storage or display of religious materials anywhere except in a person's own office or cubicle. The court concluded that the agency's rules restricting religious expression went too far and were unconstitutional. In contrast, a state government agency was upheld in disciplining two employees who, as "born-again Christians," proselytized to agency clients.[82] One of the salient differences between the two cases is that the latter employees were in the position of representing their agency to external clients. Thus, the state's concerns about meeting its

---

[78]*Peterson v. Hewlett-Packard*, 358 F.3d 599 (9th Cir. 2004).

[79]*Townley Engineering & Manufacturing Co.*

[80]*Kolodziej v. Smith*, 588 N.E.2d 634 (Mass. 1992), *cert. denied*, 522 U.S. 1029 (1997).

[81]*Tucker v. California Department of Education*, 97 F.3d 1204 (9th Cir. 1996).

[82]*Knight v. Connecticut Department of Public Health*, 275 F.3d 156 (2d Cir. 2001).

responsibility under the establishment clause to remain neutral played a larger role in the case. A county violated the First Amendment rights of its sheriff's deputies by requiring their attendance for meetings at which they were addressed by representatives of the "Fellowship of the Christian Centurions."[83] The fact that the group appeared multiple times at the request of the Sheriff and delivered expressly religious messages conveyed endorsement of these views by the county.

Clippings

A science teacher who was popular with students and who had won several teaching awards was terminated by the Mount Vernon, Ohio, school district. The teacher was charged with teaching creationism, burning crosses onto the arms of at least two students, and refusing an order from the principal to remove a Bible from his desk. One colleague testified that she had to reteach evolution to his students because they did not get it in his class. The teacher claims that the "cross burning" incident was part of a science demonstration and not harmful or meant as religious symbolism. In addition to the Bible on his desk, the teacher's classroom was decorated with multiple copies of the Ten Commandments and verses from Scripture. The teacher has filed a lawsuit against the school board, alleging religious discrimination. An attorney for the board said that "We see this as a basic issue about students having a constitutional right to be free from religious indoctrination in the public schools."

Ian Urbina. "A Zealot Who Pushed Religion in Class, or a Hero Who Stood Up for His Beliefs?" *New York Times* (January 20, 2010), A11.

Religious Organization Exemption

If it is illegal to discriminate based on religion, does that mean that churches must hire persons of other faiths and attempt to reasonably accommodate their divergent practices? Title VII contains a **religious organization exemption** that absolves churches of any liability for discriminating *on the basis of religion.* Thus, religious organizations can limit employment to or have a preference for persons sharing the same faith. And they can facially discriminate in these ways without bearing the burden of establishing BFOQs based on religion. This exemption includes not only church activities but also more secular endeavors (e.g., church-sponsored schools, hospitals), at least insofar as the latter are nonprofit entities.[84] Furthermore, for constitutional reasons, discrimination on other grounds is not contested where positions with spiritual functions, such as clergy, are involved (the "ministerial exception"). Because the definition of religion is fuzzy, it should not be surprising that it is also difficult to pin down exactly what constitutes a religious organization. The mere fact that the owners of a company hold strong religious beliefs is not sufficient to convert a profit-making company into a religious organization.[85] However, a Jewish community organization was able to successfully invoke the religious organization exemption in response to a lawsuit by a Christian employee who

---

[83]*Milwaukee Deputy Sheriffs' Association v. Clarke*, 588 F.3d 523 (7th Cir. 2009).

[84]*Corporation of the Presiding Bishop of the Church of Jesus Christ of Latter-Day Saints v. Amos*, 483 U.S. 327 (1987).

[85]*Townley*, at 619.

claimed that he was fired for attending a "Jews for Jesus" concert.[86] Even though the center conducted secular activities (e.g., operating a summer camp and preschool), had mostly non-Jewish employees, served non-kosher foods, and accepted United Way funds, it was deemed to be a religious organization. The court looked to the center's connection to religious institutions and its underlying purpose of developing and sustaining a cohesive Jewish community to conclude that it was sufficiently religious in nature.

Key Terms

Americans with Disabilities Act
  (ADA), p. 309
Rehabilitation Act, p. 309
disability, p. 310
ADA Amendments Act (ADAA),
  p. 311
physical/mental impairment, p. 311
major life activities, p. 312
substantially limited, p. 312

record of disability, p. 315
regarded as being disabled, p. 315
qualified, p. 316
essential functions, p. 316
direct threat, p. 317
reasonable accommodation, p. 318
interactive process, p. 319
undue hardship, p. 329
religion, p. 329

prima facie case of failure to
  reasonably accommodate
  religion, p. 332
religious advocacy, p. 339
religious harassment, p. 339
free exercise clause, p. 340
establishment clause, p. 340
religious organization exemption,
  p. 341

Chapter Summary

The ADA Amendments Act (ADAA) prohibits discrimination against qualified individuals on the basis of disability. Persons covered by the law are entitled to both nondiscrimination and reasonable accommodation. A fundamental premise of the ADA is that being disabled does not necessarily mean being unable to work, particularly if barriers to employment are removed through reasonable accommodation. Determining who is qualified and disabled is complex. The major thrust of the ADA Amendments Act of 2008 was to broaden coverage under the law by rejecting the narrow definition of disability that courts had been employing. To be considered disabled under the ADA, an individual must have a physical or mental impairment that substantially limits the performance of a major life activity, have a record of such an impairment, or be regarded as having such an impairment. The substantial limitation requirement means that not all medical problems, even serious ones, will qualify as disabilities under the ADA. The central issue is whether, compared to most people in the general population, the individual's impairment substantially limits the conditions, manner, or duration of time it takes to perform a major life activity. Conditions that are chronic in nature are more likely to be deemed disabilities. However, impairments that are episodic or in remission can still be disabilities if they substantially limit a major life activity when active.

Furthermore, mitigating measures used by disabled persons to lessen the impact of their disabilities must not be considered when determining whether impairments are substantially limiting.

Disabled individuals must also be qualified to be protected by the law. Qualified disabled persons have the skills, education, experience, and other requirements for a job and can perform the essential functions of that job with or without reasonable accommodation. The "essential functions" of a job are the main reasons the position exists, are relatively specialized, and are not readily distributed to other employees. Not all the tasks attached to jobs are essential functions. Inability to perform marginal functions of a job does not render a disabled person unqualified for that job. An individual can be capable of carrying out essential functions, but still not be qualified if his disability is such that he poses a "direct threat" to the health and safety of himself or others.

Qualified disabled persons are entitled to reasonable accommodation provided that this does not impose undue hardship on the employer. Accommodations are provided to make it possible for disabled persons to participate in the recruitment and hiring process, enable disabled persons to perform essential functions of jobs, and allow disabled persons to enjoy the benefits and privileges of employment. The accommodations that must be provided are limited to those that are

---

[86]*LeBoon v. Lancaster Jewish Community Center Association*, 503 F.3d 217 (3d Cir. 2007), *cert. denied*, 2008 U.S. LEXIS 3671.

"reasonable." Provided that an effective accommodation is offered, employers need not implement the employee's preferred accommodation, provide items that are primarily for personal rather than work use, eliminate essential functions from the job or lower production standards, create new jobs that disabled employees can perform, excuse or refrain from disciplining conduct stemming from a disability, and provide paid leave not available to all employees. Leaves of absence and reassignment to vacant positions are among the reasonable accommodations that might be required, although courts differ in their views of how far employers must go in providing these accommodations. Accommodations that are reasonable in general might still impose undue hardship on particular employers. If a proposed reasonable accommodation causes an employer to incur "significant difficulty or expense," that accommodation is an undue hardship and the employer does not have to provide it.

Employers are required to reasonably accommodate religion unless doing so would impose undue hardship. Religion is defined broadly under Title VII to include all sincerely held religious beliefs and practices. To show that an employer has violated Title VII by failing to reasonably accommodate religion, a plaintiff must establish a prima facie case by showing the existence of a sincere religious belief or practice that conflicts with an employment requirement, that the employer was notified regarding the conflicting belief or practice, and that the employee was subjected to adverse employment action for failing to comply with the conflicting workplace requirement. The legal obligation to reasonably accommodate religion is far more limited than for disability. Employers need not incur more than minimal expense or difficulty in accommodating religion. Nevertheless, employers are required to engage in good faith efforts to accommodate employees whose religious beliefs conflict with workplace requirements and to be flexible in scheduling and the administration of policies.

Employees who engage in religious advocacy in the workplace pose a difficult problem for employers. Religious speech is an aspect of religion that requires at least an effort at accommodation. Yet, employers also have a legal obligation to protect other employees from religious harassment. This issue is particularly challenging for public employers that must abide by the Constitution's mandates to permit the "free exercise" of religion and at the same time avoid sponsoring religion. Religious organizations are exempt from Title VII to the extent that they are permitted to discriminate based on religion.

Practical Advice Summary

- Employers must consider only the ability to perform essential functions of jobs in determining whether disabled persons are qualified for employment
- Employers must identify and document the essential functions of jobs. This is best done through a job analysis, the results of which are used as the basis of a job description
- Job descriptions should
  — Distinguish essential from marginal functions.
  — Include all essential functions.
  — Specify the tasks that need to be accomplished, rather than particular means of task accomplishment
- If employment requirements tend to screen out individuals with disabilities, employers must be prepared to show that these requirements are job-related and consistent with business necessity
- Employers can deny employment opportunities to disabled persons on the grounds that they pose a threat to the health or safety of themselves and others only if the threat is significant, current, and based on objective medical evidence

- It is important for managers to have a clear understanding of any medical restrictions placed on their employees before making decisions about their suitability for employment opportunities
- If a disabled person is unable to perform the essential functions of a job, the employer must consider whether any reasonable accommodation would enable the disabled person to perform the job
- Employers must reasonably accommodate qualified disabled persons unless doing so would impose undue hardship
- Employers should consider these measures, among others, when presented with the need for reasonable accommodation of disability:
  — Making facilities accessible and usable
  — Restructuring jobs
  — Devising part-time or modified work schedules
  — Acquiring or modifying equipment
  — Modifying policies
  — Adjusting exam procedures
  — Providing readers or interpreters

— Reassigning disabled employees to vacant positions

- Reassignment to a vacant position should be considered only if it is not possible to accommodate the employee in her current position.
- Employers must recognize when requests for accommodation are being made and cannot insist that requests be made using legal terminology.
- In responding to a request for accommodation, an employer should
  — Act on requests for accommodation as expeditiously as possible.
  — Fully engage in the interactive process.
  — Work closely with the disabled employee to identify potential accommodations.
  — Select a mutually acceptable accommodation.
  — Appraise whether the accommodation provided is effective.
  — Document all aspects of the accommodation process.
- Reasonable accommodation policies are helpful to managers and should address
  — The manner in which requests for accommodation are to be initiated.
  — Any required medical documentation of the need for accommodation.
  — The process for identifying reasonable accommodations.
  — Criteria for choosing among possible accommodations.
  — Procedures for formally notifying employees of the outcome.
- Inquiries from employers to health care providers should be limited to information needed to document the functional limitations imposed by an individual's disability.
- Requests for reasonable accommodation must be considered regardless of whether other accommodations have been provided in the past. Accommodations must be maintained for as long as they are needed.
- Absent strong reasons for preferring alternatives, employers should lean toward providing the accommodations preferred by disabled employees.
- Information about reasonable accommodations and the reasons they are needed should not be shared with other employees, beyond notifying supervisors.

- Employers claiming undue hardship from a proposed accommodation of disability must
  — Be prepared to document the significant expense or difficulty.
  — Consider the availability of external funding.
  — Offer the disabled person the opportunity to pay for the portion of the cost that would create undue hardship.
- Employers are required to reasonably accommodate the sincere religious beliefs and practices of employees unless doing so would cause undue hardship.
- Employers should generally accept the sincerity of employees' stated religious beliefs and practices and focus on whether reasonable accommodation can be made.
- Religious conflicts can be minimized by making workplace policies as flexible as possible.
- Although employers do not have to incur more than minimal expense or difficulty in accommodating religion, it is still necessary to
  — Take requests for accommodation of religion seriously.
  — Engage in an interactive process.
  — Make good faith efforts to identify reasonable accommodations.
- To accommodate scheduling conflicts, employers should
  — Allow and facilitate private swaps between employees.
  — Permit employees to use available personal time.
  — Allow flexible schedules.
  — Consider changes in shifts or positions when these would not adversely affect other employees.
- Exceptions should be made to grooming and appearance policies to accommodate religious practices unless doing so creates undue hardship.
- Employers should attempt to accommodate religious advocacy by providing forums for such communication that allow other employees to choose whether they want to listen.
- Employers, and especially public employers, should not allow the workplace to become infused with religious content.
- Employers must not allow religious communication that is unwelcome to other employees to become severe or pervasive and interfere with the employees' ability to do their jobs.

Chapter Questions

1. A woman worked part-time as a clerk at a drug store. She worked mostly on weekdays from 5 PM to 9 PM, but was occasionally given other shifts. Due to glaucoma, she eventually lost all sight in her left eye. She had no difficulty performing her job, but she did experience problems getting to work. She asked to be given a "day shifts only" schedule because of the danger of driving home at night and the complete unavailability of public transportation. Her supervisor said that she would not be given the schedule she requested because that would not be fair to the store's other employees. The woman provided a doctor's note recommending that she not drive during evening hours, but the store did not change its position. Her union representative met with store officials and reported that he "got nowhere." Other attempts to arrange meetings involving the woman fell through. She received rides from family members and did not miss any work following the denial of her request. However, it became too difficult to continue to arrange rides and she quit. Did the store fail to reasonably accommodate this employee? Why or why not? (*Colwell v. Rite Aid*, 602 F.3d 495 [3d Cir. 2010])

2. A woman with severe, chronic back problems that resulted in multiple surgeries returned to her job as an inspector at a candy factory. Her physician cleared her for light work that required no bending, stooping, or lifting of more than twenty pounds. The factory had three lines on which inspectors worked. On two of them, inspectors could remain seated while performing their tasks. On the third (line 7), inspectors had to stand and repeatedly bend and twist to sort different-sized candies moving down the conveyor. Initially, on her return, the woman was assigned to only one of the less physically demanding lines. However, the company subsequently decided, due to the high incidence of repetitive stress injuries at the plant, to implement a job rotation system. Under this system, the woman would sometimes have to work on line 7. The woman requested an exemption from the job rotation system, but this was denied. The woman was unable to continue on the job. Has this employer failed to reasonably accommodate this employee? Why or why not?

(*Turner v. Hershey Chocolate USA*, 440 F.3d 604 [3d Cir. 2006])

3. A bank loan officer who was taking medication for depression had numerous drinks at a local bar, went to a cemetery, and, with a gun in his hand, threatened to commit suicide. He eventually drove off but was intercepted by the police and committed to a psychiatric facility for four days. His physician certified that he would be able to resume all of his duties in a week, but the bank balked at reinstating him. Officials at the bank expressed their shock that he was released from the hospital so quickly after threatening to kill himself. He was told that he could not be immediately reinstated because of "the impact of your action in the community and on the ability to perform your job." He was placed on a leave of absence and then terminated. Did the bank violate the ADA? Why or why not? (*Lizotte v. Dacotah Bank*, 2010 U.S. Dist. LEXIS 1223 [D.N.D.])

4. A delivery person injured his back on the job, resulting in a serious disc problem that required surgery. Following surgery, the employee's doctor imposed a lifting restriction of twenty-three pounds. This restriction precluded a return to his former position. The employee requested reassignment to another vacant job. The employer's established procedure was to post all job openings and to require that employees initiate any requests for transfer. The employee completed one transfer request for a computer/clerical position but was judged to be unqualified due to his limited computer and office skills. The company also considered him for a telephone sales position and contacted him to set up an interview. At the interview, it was determined that the employee did not have sufficient motivation for sales. Within about a month of his request for reassignment, it was concluded that there were no positions available for which he was qualified and the employee was fired. The employee sued. What should the court decide? Why? (*Burns v. Coca-Cola*, 222 F.3d 247 [6th Cir. 2000])

5. A call center representative suffered from a rare condition known as "brittle bone disease" that permanently confined him to a wheelchair. The call center has a strict policy on tardiness.

Employees are penalized for reporting to work or returning from lunch more than three minutes late. The representative was frequently late, especially returning from lunch. His tardiness was caused by a variety of factors including an insufficient number of disabled accessible parking spots in the company lot, a policy of not assigning specific cubicles to representatives, cluttered aisles that made it difficult to maneuver between cubicles, and lack of equipment in some cubicles. The representative requested that he be given a grace period of an additional fifteen minutes when returning from lunch. He would be responsible for working the same total amount of time, but he would be allowed to start a few minutes later if needed. Adjusting his work schedule in this manner would have eliminated almost all of the incidents of tardiness. His supervisors refused the grace period request and terminated the representative. Did this employer fail to reasonably accommodate this employee? (*EEOC v. Convergys Customer Service Group*, 491 F.3d 790 [8th Cir. 2007])

6. A woman with epilepsy worked as a regional medical director for an insurance company. Following a seizure, she was banned from driving for six months by her doctor. She requested that she be allowed to work from home as a reasonable accommodation. The employer refused, resulting in her termination. Except for occasional seizures, the woman's condition was controlled by medication. At least prior to the seizure that resulted in the driving ban, her seizures had been rare and brief in duration. Besides driving, she was restricted by her doctor in activities such as diving, piloting a plane, working in elevated places, and swimming alone. The position of medical director involved interaction with nurses and insurance adjusters. Her replacement testified that he spent 25–30 percent of his time in face-to-face communication with nurses and adjusters. The job description did not specify any number of hours that were required but did refer to "on-site support" as a task and "good ability to work in a team/organization" as a qualification for the job. However, the woman testified that she performed 95 percent of her job on the phone or online. For two and a half months following her seizure, she performed the job from home without any problems. Did the employer violate the ADA by refusing to allow

this employee to work from home for six months? Why or why not? (*Carlson v. Liberty Mutual Insurance*, 237 Fed. Appx. 446 [11th Cir. 2007])

7. A medical resident has Asperger's disorder. Evaluations of his work by supervising physicians were mixed, citing problems with communication skills, self-awareness, social competence, and relationship management. After the hospital informed the resident that they intended to terminate his residency, he provided them with information about his condition and suggested that he could successfully complete the program if the other nurses and physicians were informed about his condition, its symptoms, and the things that trigger it. The hospital said that it lacked the resources to comply with his request, but that it would assist him in locating a residency in a field such as pathology that requires little patient interaction. The terminated medical resident sued. Did the hospital fail to reasonably accommodate the resident? Why or why not? (*Jakubowski v. Christ Hospital*, 627 F.3d 195 [6th Cir. 2010])

8. A department store clerk is a devout Catholic. The employee decided that she needed to make a religious pilgrimage to a site in Yugoslavia where several persons claimed that the Virgin Mary appeared to them. The department store grants unpaid leave at management's discretion and prohibits the use of vacation time between October and December—the store's busiest season. The employee requested unpaid leave for the period from October 17 to October 26 to make the pilgrimage. The employee believed she had to go at that time, although the dates held no other particular religious significance. Citing general policy against taking time off during the busy season, her boss refused the leave. She went anyway and was terminated. She sued. What should the court decide? Why? (*Tiano v. Dillard Department Stores*, 139 F.3d 679 [9th Cir. 1998])

9. The younger brother of an employee committed suicide. The employee was profoundly upset by the death, considered taking his own life, and experienced mental health problems for years thereafter. The brothers had been raised in a strict religious family, but both had subsequently rejected their religious upbringing. About six years after the suicide, the employee was approached by the wife of the owner of the

company for which he worked. The wife, who was also a receptionist, said that she had a gift for speaking to the dead, that she had been communicating with the employee's brother, and that the brother wanted the employee to know that he was suffering in hell and that the employee should turn to God so that he could avoid the same fate. The employee became very upset and told the woman not to speak with him again about his brother. Undaunted, the wife continued to speak to him in the same manner each day for three and a half weeks. After the employee complained to the woman's husband, the daily communications stopped, although the wife would bring up the topic of finding religion every week or two. About six months later, the employee got into a heated argument with the wife at work and quit. He sued for religious harassment and constructive discharge. What should the court decide? Why? (*Winspear v. Community Development*, 574 F.3d 604 [8th Cir. 2009])

10. An employee was a member of the Old Path Church of God, which observes its Sabbath from sundown on Friday until sundown on Saturday. He had worked for the company for twenty-five years. During that time, a supervisor had accommodated the employee by finding volunteers to replace him when necessary. The employee transferred to a job on another shift. Initially, there was no problem because he was scheduled to work from Sunday through Thursday. But after the company went to a 24/7 operation and all employees were required to work overtime, the employee was forced to work on Friday evenings. The company permitted the man to find someone who would work additional hours for him but did not provide any assistance in locating such a coworker and apparently stipulated that a complete shift swap was not allowed. When he failed to find a coworker to take his hours and was unable to work a Friday evening, he was fired. He sued. What should the court decide? Why? (*EEOC v. Robert Bosch Corp.*, 169 Fed. Appx. 942 [6th Cir. 2006])

11. A Muslim woman who wears a khimar (religious garb that covers the head, shoulders, chest, and sometimes extends to the waist) sought referral to a factory job at a commercial printing company. The temp agency refused to refer her because the printing company had a strict policy prohibiting the wearing of any head coverings or loose-fitting clothes. The policy was enacted for safety reasons. The temp agency later offered to refer her to jobs with other employers. The woman sued the temp agency. What responsibilities, if any, does a *temp agency* have for reasonable accommodation of an employee's religion? What should the court decide? Why? (*EEOC v. Kelly Services*, 598 F.3d 1022 [8th Cir. 2010])

12. An evangelical Christian worked for a county social services agency. He placed a Bible on his desk and posted a sign in his work area saying "Happy Birthday, Jesus." The sign and Bible were clearly visible to clients and coworkers. He was told not to display religious items in this manner. He was also ordered not to talk with clients about religion. This prohibition did not extend to coworkers. The employee organized a monthly employee prayer meeting during lunchtime that was held in the department's conference room. He was informed that the conference room could not be used for that purpose, but that he could pray in the employee break room during lunch hours or go outside the building to do so. The conference room was, in fact, used only for department business, with the exception of its occasional use for birthday parties and baby showers. The employee sought a court order authorizing him to share his religious views with clients when they initiated discussions or were receptive to such discussions, to display religious objects in his cubicle, and to use the conference room for voluntary prayer group meetings. Did the agency infringe on his rights? Should the agency be required to permit his desired forms of religious expression? (*Berry v. Department of Social Services, Tehama County*, 447 F.3d 642 [9th Cir. 2006])

13. A Starbucks "barista" wore a Wiccan medallion on a chain around her neck as part of her practice of the Wiccan religion. The store manager regularly made negative comments about the pendant, saying that it might offend customers. The store manager also told the woman on several occasions to remove the pendant or tuck it inside her shirt. An assistant store manager said that wearing the pendant might lead customers to think that the employee was a "Satan worshipper." Other employees wore pieces of Christian jewelry as large as her medallion but

were not told to remove them or otherwise criticized. Despite the negative comments, the woman was never formally disciplined for wearing the Wiccan pendant. The woman was subsequently terminated for missing a scheduled day of work. She claimed that she was not aware of being scheduled on that day and that the real reason for the termination was religious discrimination due to her Wiccan faith. What should the court decide? Why? (*Hedum v. Starbucks,* 546 F. Supp. 2d 1017 [D. Or. 2008])

14. A church organist was fired, allegedly for poor performance. He had served as organist for many years. His principal duty was to play organ music during church services and for choir practices. He did not plan or select the music. He was not a member of the church's staff and did not participate in staff meetings. However, his formal job description included planning and selecting music for liturgies, participating in special services, and serving on all church committees related to liturgy. The church argues that his lawsuit should be dismissed because the liturgical significance of the position brought it within the ministerial exception to Title VII. What should the court decide? Why? (*Archdiocese of Washington v. Moersen,* 925 A. 2d 659 [Ct. of App., Md. 2007], *cert. denied,* 2008 U.S. LEXIS 1337)

15. Should employers be required to allow disabled employees to work from home as a reasonable accommodation? If so, under what circumstances? (See U.S. Equal Employment Opportunity Commission. *Work at Home/Telework as a Reasonable Accommodation.* Viewed July 17, 2007 (http://www.eeoc.gov/)

CHAPTER 11

Work-Life Conflicts and Other Diversity Issues

This chapter concludes our discussion of managing diversity by examining other employment law issues posed by diverse workforces. Workforces that are more female, older, and include disabled persons have a greater need to take leave from employment for parenting and medical problems. Work-life conflicts can also arise from responsibilities that employees have as citizens, such as serving in the military. Diverse workforces include a wide variety of national origins and languages. Language requirements such as English-only policies can clash with this basic aspect of diversity and raise legal issues. No discussion of diversity would be complete without also considering the treatment of gay, lesbian, bisexual, and transgender persons in the workplace.

Clippings

What about a single parent and soldier in the Army, who, on the eve of a deployment to Afghanistan, finds out that her child care arrangements have fallen through? That was the situation in which 21-year-old Army Specialist Alexis Hutchinson found herself. Specialist Hutchinson had been counting on her mother to care for her 10-month-old son Kamani during her yearlong deployment. But Ms. Hutchinson's mother—with her own child, an ill sister for whom she was providing care, and the responsibility of operating a day care center from her home—quickly became overwhelmed and was unable to take care of Kamani. Ms. Hutchinson chose to stay home with her child and missed her flight to Afghanistan. She was arrested and charges were brought against her that could have led to a court martial and jail time. Eventually, she received an other-than-honorable discharge from the Army. While the legal charges brought in this case were perhaps unprecedented, administrative discharges of service members with child care issues have been numerous in recent years. In 2009, more than 10,000 single parents were on active duty and deployed to other countries.

James Dao. "Single Mother Is Spared Court-Martial." *New York Times* (February 12, 2010), A16.

THE CHANGING WORKPLACE
Workforce Diversity and Work-Life Conflicts

More than anything else, the increased labor force participation of women provides the demographic backdrop to concerns about work-life conflicts. The substantial presence of women in most workplaces is thoroughly unremarkable when viewed from a contemporary perspective but, in fact, represents a major social transformation. In 1940, 28 percent of women were in the workforce, compared to slightly over 59 percent in 2009.[1] Almost three out of four women with children are in the workforce, including 63.6 percent of women with children under the age of 6.[2] The rate of growth in female participation in the labor force has slowed in recent years, but the longer-term trends have produced a workforce that is about half female, including a large number of mothers with young children. Dual-wage-earner families have become the norm. Among families of married couples, over 57 percent of husbands and wives were dual wage earners in 2005, compared to about 18 percent of married couple families in which only the husband was employed.[3] Additionally, the proportion of families headed by single parents has increased substantially and stands at nearly 25 percent. And to no one's great surprise, the DOL has documented that, on average, working women spend about twice as much time on household chores and childcare as do working men.[4]

In 2005, some 77 million workers were eligible for leave under the FMLA (their employers were large enough and the workers met the duration and hours of employment requirements).[5] Of these eligible employees, approximately 7 million took leave. The leaves were mostly for continuous blocks of time, but 1.7 million leaves were taken on an intermittent (periods of leave interspersed with periods of work) basis. An earlier study had found that the most common reason for taking FMLA leave was employees' own health problems.[6] The same study also found that over a third of leave-takers received no pay during their leaves and that financial concerns kept many employees from remaining on leave or using it at all.

Worker advocates have been particularly concerned about the absence of a paid leave requirement under the FMLA. Many workers are not entitled to paid leave of any type, including sick days. California, Washington, and New Jersey have enacted legislation providing for periods of paid family and medical leave.[7] California's Paid Family Leave (PFL) program provides up to six weeks of partial wage replacement (55 percent of usual weekly wages subject to a cap) for leave takers, funded by an employee-paid payroll tax. An analysis of the law's effects found that it appears to have caused relatively few problems for employers, while increasing employees' satisfaction with their leaves, especially among holders of low-quality jobs.[8] In 2011, Connecticut became the first state to require that large (50 or more employees) employers provide service workers with paid sick leave.[9]

It is little wonder that people experience difficulty in juggling work, caregiving, and the rest of their life activities. But this issue is larger than simply helping individuals manage work-life conflicts, worthwhile as that is. There is an intimate connection between leave for family purposes and sex discrimination. This link was highlighted by the Supreme Court in a decision authored by the late Chief Justice William Rehnquist:

> Stereotypes about women's domestic roles are reinforced by parallel stereotypes presuming a lack of domestic responsibilities for men. Because employers continued to regard the family as the woman's domain, they often denied men similar accommodations or discouraged them from taking leave. These mutually reinforcing stereotypes created a self-fulfilling cycle of discrimination that forced women to continue to assume the role of primary family caregiver, and fostered employer's stereotypical views about women's commitment to work and their value as employees. These perceptions, in turn, Congress reasoned, lead to subtle discrimination that may be difficult to detect on a case-by-case basis.[10]

However, while the law protects employees from discrimination and confers the right to take a modest amount of parental leave, it does not go so far as to require that workplaces be "family-friendly" or deliver employees—particularly women—from having to make painful choices between their families and careers. In dismissing a pattern or practice of pregnancy discrimination case brought by the EEOC against Bloomberg,

L.P., Chief U.S. District Judge Loretta A. Preska said the following:

> At bottom, the EEOC's theory of this case is about so-called "work-life balance." * * * It amounts to a judgment that Bloomberg, as a company policy, does not provide its employee-mothers with a sufficient work-life balance. There is considerable social debate and concern about this issue. Former General Electric CEO Jack Welch stated, "There's no such thing as work-life balance. There are work-life choices, and you make them, and they have consequences." * * * In a company like Bloomberg, which explicitly makes all-out dedication its expectation, making a decision that preferences family over work comes with consequences. But those consequences occur for anyone who takes significant time away from Bloomberg, not just for pregnant women and mothers. To be sure, women need to take leave to bear a child. And, perhaps unfortunately, women tend to choose to attend to family obligations over work obligations thereafter more often than men in our society. Work-related consequences follow. Likewise, men tend to choose work obligations over family obligations, and family consequences follow. Whether one thinks those consequences are intrinsically fair, whether one agrees with the roles traditionally assumed by the different genders in raising children in the United States, or whether one agrees with the monetary value society places on working versus childrearing is not at issue here. Neither is whether Bloomberg is the most "family-friendly" company. The fact remains that the law requires only equal treatment in the workplace. Employment consequences for making choices that elevate non-work activities (for whatever reason) over work activities are not illegal.

> Creating different consequences for pregnancy and motherhood is. Because Bloomberg does not create different consequences for women from the consequences for others who take leave, its conduct does not violate the law. * * * The law does not require companies to ignore or stop valuing ultimate dedication, however unhealthy that may be for family life. Whether an individual in any family wishes to make that commitment is an intensely personal decision that must account for the tradeoffs involved, and it is not the role of the courts to dictate a healthy balance for all. * * * Choices are available—and the Court acknowledges that the individual's decisions are among the most difficult that anyone must make. The women involved in the allegations here are talented, well-educated, motivated individuals working in highly paid jobs. To attain the success they enjoy, much is expected of them at work, but they have options (unlike many others).[11]

[1]U.S. Bureau of Labor Statistics. *Women in the Labor Force: A Databook.* (December 2010) Table 1 (http://www.bls.gov/cps/wlf-databook-2010.pdf).
[2]*Women in the Labor Force,* Table 7.
[3]*Women in the Labor Force,* Table 23.
[4]Edmund L. Andrews. "Survey Confirms It: Women Outjuggle Men." *New York Times* (September 15, 2004), p. A-22.
[5]73 F.R. 7876 (February 11, 2008).
[6]Jane Waldfogel. "Family and Medical Leave: Evidence from the 2000 Surveys." *Monthly Labor Review* (September 2001), 20–21.
[7]"Newly Enacted New Jersey Law Creates Paid Family Leave Insurance Plan in 2009." *Daily Labor Report* 86 (May 5, 2008), A-8.
[8]Eileen Applebaum and Ruth Milkman. *Leaves that Pay: Employer and Worker Experiences with Paid Family Leave in California.* (January 2011) (http://www.cepr.net/documents/publications/paid-family-leave-1-2022.pdf).
[9]Martha Kessler. "Connecticut Governor Signs Law Requiring Paid Sick Leave." *Daily Labor Report* 130 (July 7, 2011), A-3.
[10]*Nevada Department of Human Resources v. Hibbs,* 538 U.S. 721, 736 (2003).
[11]*EEOC v. Bloomberg, L.P.,* 2011 U.S. Dist. LEXIS 92677, at 73-79 (S.D.N.Y.).

Leave Policies Under the Family and Medical Leave Act

Leave policies are one of the major ways in which the work-life conflicts of employees can be addressed. What does the law require in terms of leave policies? The **Family and Medical Leave Act (FMLA)**[1] is the principal federal law governing the provision of

[1]29 U.S.C.S. §§ 2601–2654 (2011); 29 C.F.R. §§ 825.100–825.800 (2011).

leave to employees for parental and medical reasons. All government agencies, regardless of their size, are covered by this law, as are private sector employers with at least fifty employees. The FMLA provides a minimum standard for the leave policies of covered employers. *Parental and medical leave policies must be consistent with the provisions of the FMLA* outlined in this chapter, although employers are free to exceed the law's minimum requirements.

ELEMENTS OF A CLAIM

Interference with FMLA Rights

In a FMLA interference claim, the plaintiff must show:

1. She was eligible for FMLA benefits and protections
  - worked for this employer for at least 12 months
  - worked at least 1250 hours in the 12 months prior to taking leave or attempting to do so

2. Her employer was covered by the FMLA
  - is a private sector employer with 50 or more employees at the same work-site or spread across multiple worksites within a 75 mile radius
  - is a public agency with any number of employees

3. She experienced a qualifying event entitling her to FMLA leave
4. She provided her employer with sufficient notice of intent to take leave
5. She had not already exhausted her maximum leave entitlement for the relevant 12-month period
6. FMLA benefits to which she was entitled were delayed or denied by the employer

© Cengage Learning 2013.

Who Is Entitled to FMLA Leave?   Entitlement to FMLA leave depends on a number of factors including the size of the employer, the duration of the employee's tenure with that employer, the number of hours worked by the employee in the twelve months preceding the taking of leave, the occurrence of a "qualifying event" for which leave is needed, and provision of adequate notification to the employer of the need for leave (see "Elements of a Claim"). The employment duration and hours requirements must be met as of when leave would commence rather than at the point in time at which leave is requested. Thus, *an employee cannot be deemed ineligible for leave that would commence in the future simply because the duration or hours requirement is not currently met.* However, a schoolteacher whose annual contract of employment was not renewed after she requested parental leave was not protected by the FMLA because she had not been working for a year at the time that she first requested leave *and* at the point at which the requested leave would have commenced.[2] Tallying the number of hours worked during the past twelve months is not always a straightforward proposition. In a case involving a part-time radiological technician, the court allowed the employee's FMLA claim to proceed even though the employer's time sheets showed that she had

---

[2]*Walker v. Elmore County Board of Education,* 379 F.3d 1249 (11th Cir. 2004).

worked about sixty-five hours less than the 1,250 hours required for coverage.[3] The reason was that she had a good chance of being able to show that time spent each day prior to her shift preparing equipment for use and time spent at employer-mandated continuing education courses were work hours that should have been counted. In contrast, a mail handler who worked 1,248.8 hours in the preceding twelve months was lawfully terminated for absences that might have been covered by the FMLA.[4] Her argument that a two-hour suspension administered a month before her termination should not have been considered was rejected because she had failed to file a timely grievance challenging the suspension.

JUST THE FACTS

An employee was hired and began work on August 25, 2005. His fiancée unexpectedly went into labor on August 8, 2006. The employee notified his supervisor of the situation and requested to use several days of accrued paid leave. The request was granted. The employee returned to work on August 16, 2006. The child had been born several months premature and would remain in the neonatal intensive care unit for at least three months. The fiancée was using her own leave while their child was in the hospital. The employee informed the employer that he would need to take FMLA leave to care for the child when the child returned home in mid-November of 2006. The employee was promptly terminated. His employer argued that because the employee had not been employed for twelve months at the time of his termination he had no FMLA rights to assert. What should the court decide? Why?

See, *Reynolds v. Inter-Industry Conference on Auto Collision Repair*, 2009 U.S. Dist. LEXIS 4686 (N.D. Ill.).

What Are FMLA Qualifying Events?   An employee who is otherwise eligible for FMLA leave must still experience a qualifying event to be entitled to take leave. Qualifying events are circumstances under which eligible employees are entitled to take FMLA leave. The following are **qualifying events** under the FMLA:

- The birth of a son or daughter of the employee
- Placement of a son or daughter with the employee by adoption or foster care
- The need to care for a spouse, son, daughter, or parent with a serious health condition
- The inability of an employee to perform the functions of his job due to a serious health condition
- The need to care for a service member who suffered a serious injury or illness while on active duty ("military caregiver leave")
- Any "qualifying exigency" (e.g., short notice deployment, military events, financial and legal arrangements, counseling, post-deployment activities) arising from the fact that a family member in the military is, or soon will be, placed on active duty

The "family" portion of family and medical leave is limited to childbirth, adoption, or foster care placement. It does not include time off for other family-related activities such

---

[3]*Kosakow v. New Rochelle Radiology Associates, P.C.*, 274 F.3d 706 (2d Cir. 2001).

[4]*Pirant v. U.S. Postal Service*, 542 F.3d 202 (7th Cir. 2008), *cert. denied*, 2009 U.S. LEXIS 6956.

as attending parent-teacher conferences or obtaining counseling for marital problems. Both males and females are entitled to parental leave. Entitlement to parental leave under the FMLA generally expires twelve months from the date of the birth, adoption, or foster care placement. If an expectant mother's medical condition warrants that leave begin before the birth of a child, such leave is available under the qualifying event of a serious health condition.

Clippings

Colby Lewis, a pitcher for the Texas Rangers, has the distinction of being the first professional baseball player to take parental leave. He missed a scheduled start but was present for the birth of his second child, Elizabeth Grace. Under a new policy implemented in the 2011 season, major league baseball players are entitled to twenty-four to seventy-two hours of paternal leave. Lewis's decision to take leave was praised by many commentators but drew criticism from other quarters. Richie Whitt, a writer for the *Dallas Observer*, blasted the pitcher's decision to forgo a start and said in a blog that "I don't care if Lewis is a good dad. If I wanted to root for a team of great role models, I'd renew my season tickets to watch the deacons at my Sunday church. I want—always have, always will—the Rangers to win."

James Burger. "Home Run Call? Local Major Leaguer Chooses Family Over Game." *The Bakersfield Californian* (April 22, 2011) (http://www.bakersfield.com/).

The definition of *serious health condition* is complex. This term is far more inclusive than *disability,* but it still does not encompass all medical problems of an employee or a family member. Basically, **serious health conditions** are medical conditions that involve inpatient care in a hospital (or similar medical facility) or continuing treatment by a health care provider. A *serious health condition involving inpatient care* includes not only the actual period of hospitalization but also any **period of incapacity** (inability to work, attend school, or engage in other regular daily activities) and time needed for subsequent treatment of the condition. *Serious health conditions involving continuing treatment by a health care provider* include the following:

- Conditions that result in periods of incapacity of more than three consecutive calendar days and either two or more treatments by health care providers or one treatment followed by a regimen of continuing care supervised by a health care provider (the first of these treatments must generally occur within seven days of the onset of incapacity and at least one other treatment must generally occur within thirty days of becoming incapacitated)
- Any periods of incapacity relating to pregnancy or prenatal care
- Any periods of incapacity, including subsequent treatment, due to chronic, serious health conditions (e.g., asthma, diabetes) for which at least two visits to a health care provider are made per year
- Long-term periods of incapacity due to conditions for which treatment may not be effective (e.g., stroke, terminal diseases)
- Any absences to receive multiple treatments from health care providers for conditions that would likely result in periods of incapacity of more than three consecutive calendar days if left untreated

Not surprisingly, the existence of a serious health condition is sometimes disputed and must be decided by a court. Department of Labor (DOL) regulations state that:

Ordinarily, unless complications arise, the common cold, the flu, earaches, upset stomach, minor ulcers, headaches other than migraine, routine dental or orthodontia problems, periodontal disease, etc. are examples of conditions that do not meet the definition of a serious health condition and do not qualify for FMLA leave.[5]

Although these are useful examples, ultimately the criteria mentioned earlier determine the existence of a serious health condition. In a case involving a woman who was absent with the flu, the court concluded that she nonetheless had a serious health condition because she was incapacitated for more than three days and had several treatments from a health care provider.[6] Importantly, the court emphasized that "treatments" include visits to doctors for purposes of diagnosis and evaluation.

The right to take leave for the serious health conditions of family members is limited to immediate family members. Thus, employers are not required to grant leave so that employees can provide care to grandparents, aunts or uncles, or even in-laws. Leave to care for sons or daughters generally applies to children under 18 years of age unless the children are disabled and incapable of self-care. However, a "parent" eligible to take leave to care for a child (and for the birth of a child as well) need not have a biological or legal relationship to that child.[7] Instead, multiple individuals, including same-sex partners, who act as parents can qualify for such leave. In the case of military caregivers, leave is available to care for children of any age, as well as "next of kin." The element of "caring for" is also important here. A person taking leave based on the serious health condition of a family member must actually be involved in the ongoing treatment of the condition by providing physical or psychological care. An airline employee who took leave due to the medical complications of his wife's pregnancy was not protected by the FMLA when he was terminated for unexcused absences.[8] The employee's vehicle broke down shortly after the leave commenced and he flew to another city where he owned a second car. He then drove the car back cross-country. The car trip lasted four days. Although the employee's sister-in-law stayed with his wife and the employee remained in regular contact with his wife via cell phone, the court concluded that this was not the type of care required by the FMLA. Finally, the FMLA does not provide leave for periods of bereavement or funeral attendance.

Employers may, and generally should, require that requests for leave based on serious health conditions be supported by certifications from health care providers. Employees must be given at least fifteen days to obtain this medical documentation. The process of documenting a serious health condition should not be made onerous, and the information provided by an employee's own doctor should generally be sufficient. *When the information provided is deemed inadequate, employers are required to notify the employee in writing, indicate what information is missing, and afford the employee at least seven calendar days to provide the information.* Employers are also permitted, at their own expense, to require employees to obtain second medical certifications from other doctors. If the first and second opinions conflict, employers have the option of requiring a third assessment by a different health care provider approved by both parties. The third opinion is final and binding. Employers may contact employees while they are on leave to receive information on their status and verify their intent to return to work following leave. An employee on

---

[5]29 C.F.R. § 825.113 (d) (2011).

[6]*Miller v. AT&T Corp.,* 250 F.3d 820 (4th Cir. 2001).

[7]U.S. Department of Labor, Wage and Hour Division. *Administrator's Interpretation No. 2010-3.* Issued by Deputy Administrator Nancy J. Leppink (June 22, 2010).

[8]*Tellis v. Alaska Airlines,* 414 F.3d 1045 (9th Cir. 2005).

FMLA leave for an anxiety condition was disciplined by his employer when the employee violated a policy requiring employees with bad sick leave records to notify their employer if they were leaving the home. The court stated that while employers' sick leave policies cannot conflict with the FMLA, "Nothing in the FMLA prevents employers from ensuring that employees who are on leave from work do not abuse their leave, particularly those who enter leave while on the employer's Sick Abuse List."[9]

Employers are also permitted to require medical certification of fitness upon an employee's return to work, provided that this is their general practice. However, an employer ran afoul of the law when it subjected an employee returning from FMLA leave to repeated requests for proof of his fitness to work, failed to inform the employee as to precisely what information was needed, and arbitrarily refused to accept the documentation he provided.[10]

What Must Employees Do to Obtain Leave?   Employees are responsible for notifying their employers that a qualifying event has occurred for which leave is needed. This notification can be verbal and need not specifically refer to the FMLA, but it must provide enough information to alert the employer that the FMLA might apply. Calling in sick, by itself, is not sufficient notification. *If the need for leave is foreseeable, such as a birth or planned medical treatment where at least the approximate leave dates are known, employees can be required to provide thirty days' advance notice.* Failure to provide adequate notice when the need for leave is foreseeable can result in delay of the leave until the thirty-day notice requirement is satisfied. *If the need for leave is not foreseeable, such as when a serious health problem suddenly emerges, employees are responsible for providing notice "as soon as practicable."* The DOL expects employees to comply with their employers' "usual and customary notice and procedural requirements for requesting leave, absent unusual circumstances."[11] But in the case of serious medical emergencies, notification might be made during, or possibly after, periods of absence. Likewise, employers' requirements for written notification of the need for leave cannot be enforced in emergency medical situations. When leave is needed for planned medical treatment(s), employees are expected to first consult with their employers regarding the timing of the treatment and attempt to schedule leave to lessen its disruptiveness.

JUST THE FACTS

A sales representative was at a mandatory training seminar in Indianapolis when he learned that his elderly mother was experiencing a medical emergency. He immediately left and returned to Illinois to be with his mother. The next day, he e-mailed his supervisor to explain that he needed "the next couple days off" to make arrangements for his mother's care. He said in his e-mail that he had vacation time available or "could apply for the family care act, which I do not want to do at this time." His supervisor tried unsuccessfully for more than a week to reach him by telephone to clarify his request for leave. The sales rep did not return these calls or otherwise contact his employer. He returned to work nine days later and was fired for violating his employer's leave policy. Did this termination violate the FMLA? Why or why not?

See, *Righi v. SMC Corp. of America,* 632 F.3d 404 (7th Cir. 2011).

---

[9]*Callison v. City of Philadelphia,* 2005 U.S. App. LEXIS 6770, 9-10 (3d Cir.), *cert. denied,* 126 S. Ct. 389 (2005).
[10]*Stevens v. Coach U.S.A.,* 2005 U.S. Dist. LEXIS 19889 (D. Conn.).
[11]29 C.F.R. § 825.303 (2011).

The adequacy of employees' notification of their need for FMLA leave is an oft-contested issue. In one relevant case, an employee without a telephone had her mother deliver a note to her employer. The note said that the woman "was having a lot of pain in her side" and would not be able to come to work. The court concluded that the woman had not provided enough information for the employer to be aware that she was requesting FMLA leave for a serious health condition.[12] Likewise, an employee informing her employer that her doctor had advised that she perform only "light duty" work was deemed to not have provided sufficient notice of need for FMLA leave.[13] In contrast, an employee's report that he missed work because he "had a headache" was deemed sufficient notice of need for FMLA leave when the employer had prior knowledge that he suffered from migraines.[14] Employees who provide prior (rather than after the fact) notice of the need for leave, who indicate at least an approximate date of return, and who maintain contact with their employers during leave appear to fare better legally than those who do not do these things.[15]

In *Scobey v. Nucor Steel-Arkansas*, the court must decide whether an employer was provided with adequate notification of the existence of an employee's serious health condition.

Scobey v. Nucor Steel-Arkansas
580 F.3d 781 (8th Cir. 2009)

OPINION BY CIRCUIT JUDGE SHEPERD:

Talmadge Scobey appeals the district court's dismissal on summary judgment of his lawsuit alleging violations of the Family and Medical Leave Act ("FMLA"). We affirm.

In 1998, Scobey began working at Nucor Steel in Hickman, Arkansas. From 1999 to 2005, he worked as a "ladle man" at the steel mill, a dangerous and demanding position that involved the handling of thousands of pounds of molten steel. * * * This suit arises from Nucor's demotion of Scobey to a position in the company's shipping department for having incurred four unexcused absences from April 10–13, 2005, due to drunkenness. Scobey also had two prior unexcused absences in February 2005. Under Nucor's attendance policy, on the "fourth occasion" of an employee's unexcused absence that employee may be terminated from the company.

On Saturday, April 9, 2005, Scobey attempted to contact his direct supervisor, Kirby Teeter, and left him a message asking him to return Scobey's call,

apparently without explaining the reason for the call. Although Teeter attempted to return the call on April 10, he did not speak with Scobey until April 11. Later on April 9, Scobey called Randy Blakemore, another supervisor and a friend of Scobey's, and disclosed that his ex-wife's father had passed away and asked how to arrange time off from work in order to attend the funeral. Blakemore told him that he should call into work and arrange a swap with another employee. * * * On Sunday, April 10, Scobey did not come to work and called Seratt while intoxicated. Seratt stated that: [Scobey] said he was through and done with us, he was very emotional and I was very concerned over his mental state at the time. I asked him not to do anything stupid, call in for Monday and come and talk to Kirby [Teeter], … or myself over what he wanted to do or what his options were.

Seratt then called Blakemore to express his concerns about Scobey's welfare. Later that night, Scobey called and told Blakemore that he was "done, through" and then hung up the phone. Worried about Scobey's

[12]*Satterfield v. Wal-Mart*, 135 F.3d 973 (5th Cir. 1998), *cert. denied*, 525 U.S. 826 (1998).

[13]*Scott v. UPMC*, 2011 U.S. App. LEXIS 13479 (3d Cir.).

[14]*Ware v. Stahl Specialty Co.*, 1998 U.S. Dist. LEXIS 5506 (W.D. Mo.).

[15]*Brannon v. OshKosh B'Gosh*, 897 F. Supp. 1028 (M.D. Tenn. 1995); *Collins v. NTN-Bower Corp.*, 272 F.3d 1006 (7th Cir. 2001).

state of mind, Blakemore called Scobey back and then met with him in person. During their conversation Scobey complained to Blakemore about the pressure Nucor put on its employees.

On Monday, April 11, Teeter spoke with Scobey concerning his call on April 9. Scobey told Teeter that he had suffered a nervous breakdown and then hung up the phone without any further explanation. Teeter stated in an affidavit that Scobey's speech was slurred and that he had the impression that Scobey was intoxicated. Due to previous incidents of dishonesty, Teeter did not believe Scobey's claim of a nervous breakdown and thought he was making excuses to avoid work because he was intoxicated. Then, Scobey called Steve Segars, a shift manager at Nucor, and told him that, due to the death of his former father-in-law and some personal problems, he would not be back at work for a while. * * * On April 12, Scobey did not show up at work and did not contact anyone at Nucor. On April 13, Scobey missed work for the fourth consecutive day. He called and left a message with Kellie Crain, Nucor's Human Resources Manager and the person in charge of designating FMLA leave, saying that he would call her the next day. On April 14, Scobey called Blakemore and told him that he could not recall the previous four days and that he wanted some help. Blakemore told Scobey to contact HR Manager Crain. However, Scobey and Crain were unable to reach each other until April 19. * * * When Scobey and Crain spoke on April 19, Scobey told Crain that he had an alcohol problem and that he was depressed. Crain set up an appointment with the Employee Assistance Program ("EAP") for the next day.

On April 20, Scobey was assessed at Nucor's EAP, which referred him to Lakeside Behavioral Health System for inpatient treatment of alcoholism and depression. On April 26, Lakeside discharged Scobey and transferred him to outpatient care following diagnoses for alcohol dependence, alcohol withdrawal, depression, post-traumatic stress disorder, hypertension, and job/family impairment. * * * Nucor did not designate Scobey's absences for treatment as FMLA leave, but designated it as paid leave from the company.

On May 20, Scobey met with Nucor's plant manager, Sam Commella, to determine the appropriate discipline. During the meeting, Commella reminded Scobey that Nucor's absenteeism policy permitted termination after four consecutive, unexcused absences. Although he admitted to having a "taste" of beer a few days earlier, Scobey asked for a second chance. Commella agreed that Scobey had made efforts to improve his behavior, and that he could continue his employment with Nucor. However, Commella suspended Scobey for three days and demoted him to an entry-level position in Nucor's shipping department. This new position resulted in a 40–50 percent reduction in Scobey's pre-demotion pay and required that he work the night shift. Scobey now states that he interpreted his demotion as an attempt by Nucor to force him to quit. Nonetheless, Scobey did not object at the time to his demotion and, during the first two weeks of his new position, he received a pay raise. Soon thereafter and without notifying Nucor of his intent to leave, Scobey stopped coming to work. * * *

"Under the [FMLA], an eligible employee is entitled to up to twelve weeks of unpaid leave during a twelve-month period '[b]ecause of a serious health condition that makes the employee unable to perform the functions of the position of such employee.'" * * *

"In order to state a claim for interference under the FMLA, [Scobey] must have given notice of [his] need for FMLA leave." Although the FMLA statute does not define the type and timing of the notice required when the need for leave is unforeseeable, the Department of Labor's ("DOL's") regulations provide some considerable guidance, and they are generous to employees. Notice must be given "as soon as practicable," but "the employee need not explicitly assert rights under the FMLA or even mention the FMLA" to require the employer to determine whether leave would be covered by the FMLA.

Although recent amendments to the DOL's regulations have somewhat curtailed this generosity, the regulation in place during the events giving rise to this lawsuit stated that, after notice had been given

> [t]he employer will be expected to obtain any additional required information through informal means. The employee or spokesperson will be expected to provide more information when it can readily be accomplished as a practical matter, taking into consideration the exigencies of the situation.

However, even before the recent amendments, we have held that an employee must do more than merely call in sick to trigger an employer's duties under the FMLA. "Although the employee need not name the statute, he must provide information to suggest that his health condition could be serious." "Employees thus have an affirmative duty to indicate both the need and the reason for the leave, and must let employers know when they anticipate returning to their position." "The employer must be made aware that the absence is due to a serious illness so the employer can distinguish it from ordinary 'sick-days,' or even malingering, as a type of unusual and privileged absence." "To hold otherwise would create an unreasonable burden for employers, requiring them to investigate virtually every absence to ensure that it does not qualify for FMLA leave."

* * * Scobey contends that he provided Nucor with sufficient and timely notice that he had a serious health condition requiring FMLA leave during the four unexcused absences from April 10–13. Having received proper notice, he argues, Nucor failed to follow the FMLA's procedures designed to protect employers by not requesting a medical certification form from a health care provider corroborating that Scobey was unable to work. * * * Scobey's principal case in support of this argument is *Thorson v. Gemini, Inc.* In *Thorson*, an employee missed more than three days of work and, during her absence, provided two notes from her physician stating that she was unable to work. Without requesting a medical certification form, the employer summarily terminated her employment for violating its attendance policy. The employer did not request a medical evaluation until the employee filed suit several months later. In that situation, this court held that the employee's submission of two doctor's notes advising that she should not work put the employer on notice that she might be eligible for FMLA-protected leave. This notice triggered the employer's responsibility to count the employee's absence as FMLA leave or inquire further into the matter by requesting a medical certification form. Having failed to make further inquiries, the employer could not use later medical evaluations to create a genuine issue of material fact as to the validity of the notes from the employee's physician excusing her from work.

Whether *Thorson* applies, however, depends first and foremost on whether Scobey put Nucor on notice that he might be entitled to leave under the FLMA. Only if he provided adequate notice do we need to examine whether Nucor defaulted on any obligation to inquire further. Having examined the record, we conclude that there is no genuine issue of material fact that Scobey did not adequately put Nucor on notice. * * *

[I]n *Spangler v. Federal Home Loan Bank of Des Moines*, the employer had known for many years that the employee's depression had periodically necessitated time off from work. Within this context, the employee's statement that she would be absent from work because of her "depression again" put the employer on notice that she might be entitled to FMLA leave. In other circumstances we have found

notice to be insufficient. In Woods, we held that notice must contain an explanation of the condition rendering the employee unable to work in order to adequately apprise the employer that the condition may be protected by the FMLA. Similarly, in Rask, we held that an employee who informed her employer that she had been diagnosed with depression had not given adequate notice because "[d]epression … is a condition with many variations" and the employer would need additional details before being on notice that her condition rendered her unable to work. Rask distinguished Spangler on the ground that the employer had no previous knowledge of the employee's depression and lacked any indication that it was so serious as to render her unable to work.

* * * Prior to his four absences from April 10 to April 13, 2005, Scobey had incurred two unexcused absences in February of the same year. Scobey initially requested a day off to attend a funeral, which is not protected by the FMLA. He then called in while intoxicated and stated that he wanted to terminate his employment at Nucor. This was not notice that he needed time off from work. This was notice that he intended to terminate his employment at Nucor. He was intoxicated throughout the four days of his absence and cannot remember any details of this period. While absences for treatment of alcoholism are protected by the FMLA, absences caused by the use of alcohol are not. Furthermore, Scobey had several conversations, both over the telephone and in person, with Nucor's representatives during this period. During these conversations, Scobey made no mention of anything that could even plausibly have constituted notice of a need for FMLA leave until April 11, when he remarked to his supervisor Kirby Teeter that he believed he was having a "nervous breakdown" and was "f***ed up." Although he acknowledges that intoxication is not a serious health condition protected by the FMLA, Scobey argues that such comments should have demonstrated to Nucor that his inebriated state was a manifestation of his underlying depression. However, these comments—especially in the context of Scobey's previous unexcused absences, drunken behavior, and shifting explanations of why he could not come to work—were inadequate to apprise Nucor of any possible obligations under the FMLA. Moreover, even if we assume … that Scobey's remark on April 14 to Blakemore that he "wanted to get some help" constituted sufficient notice that Scobey might need some time off in the future for treatment for alcoholism or depression, that remark did not alter the fact that Scobey's immediately preceding absences

were not, and did not appear to Nucor to be, protected by the FMLA.

* * * Having failed to provide notice, Scobey's claim that Nucor interfered with his FMLA rights by demoting him for his four unexcused absences from April 10 to April 13 must fail. For this reason, it is unnecessary to reach Scobey's other arguments concerning whether he has successfully demonstrated that he had a serious health condition protected by the FMLA. We can only reach a claim that an employer interfered with an employee's right under the FMLA to take leave for a serious health condition if that employee first demonstrates that he or she notified the employer of the possible need for leave. Having failed to provide adequate and timely notice, any argument about whether Scobey actually had a serious health condition during the relevant time period is moot.

DISSENTING OPINION BY CIRCUIT JUDGE BYE:

The majority is correct in the context of Scobey not being entitled to FMLA leave on the basis of alcohol use, as opposed to alcohol abuse treatment. However, I believe there is a genuine issue of material fact as to whether Scobey put Nucor on notice as to his being in need of FMLA leave on the basis of severe depression.* * *

Scobey gave Nucor sufficient notice as to his being in need of FMLA leave on the basis of severe depression because he twice stated he was having a "nervous breakdown." In addition, his other statements ..., while they could have just as easily related to his alcohol use and intoxication, led Nucor employees to express concern over his mental state and even possible suicide. * * * Blakemore was so concerned over Scobey's mental health, including possible suicidal thoughts, that he went to Scobey's house to check on him. And, when Scobey finally spoke with HR Manager Crain, Scobey told her he had both alcohol and mental problems. These statements indicated more than generic depression and gave Nucor notice that Scobey's absences may be the result of a serious health condition entitled to FMLA protection.

Scobey's notice was also timely. Nucor argues Scobey did not give notice he needed treatment until April 14, which it claims was beyond the one or two days notice contemplated by the statute. I disagree. Rather, the statements indicating a possible need for leave for mental health issues began much earlier. Scobey first expressed his belief he was having a "nervous breakdown" on April 11, only one day after his first absence. His other comments which led Nucor employees to express concern over his mental state began on the day of his first absence, April 10. Therefore, Scobey commenced giving notice on April 10, and this notice became sufficient, at the latest, on April 11, when he stated he was having a "nervous breakdown." While it is probable Nucor simply believed these statements to be excuses or exaggerations because of his obvious intoxication, the statute was satisfied because Scobey gave enough information to indicate a possibility he was incapacitated from work because of mental problems. Once Scobey raised this possibility, it was then incument upon Nucor to require substantiation to differentiate between the possible causes. I therefore respectfully dissent.

CASE QUESTIONS

1. What were the legal issues in this case? What did the court decide?
2. Why does the court conclude that adequate notice was not given? Why does the dissenting judge say otherwise? Which side has the better argument? Why?
3. The court decides this case without reaching the question of whether the plaintiff had a "serious health condition." Does it appear that he did? Why or why not?
4. Look up the current regulations regarding "employee notice requirements for unforeseeable FMLA leave" (29 C.F.R. § 825.303). What do the regulations now say?
5. What, if anything, should this employer have done differently?

What Does the FMLA Require Employers to Provide?   The FMLA requires that employers provide the following to eligible employees who experience qualifying events:

1. Up to a total of twelve workweeks of leave over a twelve-month period (however, when the qualifying event is the serious injury or illness of a service member incurred during active duty, the maximum period of leave is extended to twenty-six weeks)

2. Maintenance of health insurance under the same conditions as if the employee had not taken leave

3. Restoration to the same position held before leave commenced or to an equivalent position with the same pay, benefits, and other terms and conditions of employment

These three core requirements reinforce one another. The right to take leave would be rendered meaningless if employees did not retain their health insurance. After all, entitlement to leave is predicated on events (serious illnesses, childbirth) that are necessarily accompanied by medical services and bills. Likewise, the promise of a right to take leave would be illusory if employees had to take leave without a reasonable guarantee that their jobs would still be there upon returning from leave. The FMLA's provisions are further buttressed by requirements that *employers must refrain from discriminating against employees for taking FMLA leave or otherwise interfering with, restraining, or denying the exercise of FMLA rights.*

Bachelder v. America West Airlines considers whether an employee is entitled to FMLA leave and whether her employer violated the act's prohibition against interference with the exercise of FMLA rights.

Bachelder v. America West Airlines
259 F.3d 1112 (9th Cir. 2001)

OPINION BY CIRCUIT JUDGE BERZON:

Penny Bachelder claims that her employer, America West Airlines, violated the Family and Medical Leave Act of 1993 ("FMLA" or "the Act") when it terminated her in 1996 for poor attendance. The district court granted partial summary judgment to America West, holding that Bachelder was not entitled to the Act's protection for her 1996 absences. * * * This appeal requires us to interpret both the Act and the regulations issued pursuant to it by the Department of Labor. * * *

[T]he regulations provide employers with a menu of choices for how to determine the "twelve-month period" during which an employee is entitled to twelve weeks of FMLA-protected leave:

1. The calendar year;
2. Any fixed 12-month "leave year," such as a fiscal year, a year required by State law, or a year starting on an employee's "anniversary" date;
3. The 12-month period measured forward from the date an employee's first FMLA leave begins; or,
4. A "rolling" 12-month period measured backward from the date an employee uses any FMLA leave.

This "leave year" regulation is at the heart of Bachelder's appeal.

Bachelder began working for America West as a customer service representative in 1988. From 1993 until her termination in 1996, she was a passenger service supervisor.... From 1994 to 1996, Bachelder was often absent from work for various health- and family-related reasons. In 1994, she took five weeks of medical leave to recover from a broken toe, and in mid-1995, she took maternity leave for approximately three months. It is undisputed that these two leaves were covered by, and protected by, the FMLA. In addition to these extended absences, Bachelder also called in sick several times in 1994 and 1995.

On January 14, 1996, one of America West's managers had a "corrective action discussion" with Bachelder regarding her attendance record. Among the absences that concerned the company were several occasions on which Bachelder had called in sick and the 1994 and 1995 FMLA leaves. Bachelder was advised to improve her attendance at work and required to attend pre-scheduled meetings at which her progress would be evaluated.

In February 1996, Bachelder was absent from work again for a total of three weeks. During that time, she submitted two doctor's notes to America West indicating her diagnosis and when she could return to work. Bachelder's attendance was flawless in March 1996, but in early April, she called in sick for one day to care for her baby, who was ill. Right after that, on April 9, Bachelder was fired. * * *

Bachelder filed this action, alleging that America West impermissibly considered her use of leave protected by the FMLA in its decision to terminate her. In response, America West maintained that it had not relied on FMLA-protected leave in firing Bachelder, because none of her February 1996 absences were protected by the Act, and because her 1994 and 1995 FMLA leaves did not factor into its decision. None of Bachelder's February 1996 absences were covered by the Act, argued America West, because the company used the retroactive "rolling" year method—the fourth of the four methods permitted by the leave year regulation—to calculate its employees' eligibility for FMLA leave. If that method was used, Bachelder had exhausted her full annual allotment of FMLA leave as of June 1995, and was entitled, according to the company, to no more such leave until twelve months had elapsed from the commencement of her 1995 maternity leave. * * *

Bachelder countered that according to the regulations implementing the FMLA, she was entitled to have her leave eligibility calculated by the method most favorable to her. Under a calendar year method of calculating leave eligibility, she contended, her February 1996 absences were protected by the FMLA, and America West had violated the Act by relying on those absences in deciding to fire her. * * *

Congress made it unlawful for an employer to "interfere with, restrain, or deny the exercise of or the attempt to exercise, any right provided" by the Act. The regulations explain that this prohibition encompasses an employer's consideration of an employee's use of FMLA-covered leave in making adverse employment decisions:

> Employers cannot use the taking of FMLA leave as a negative factor in employment actions, such as hiring, promotions or disciplinary actions; nor can FMLA leave be counted under "no fault" attendance policies.

* * * [E]mployer actions that deter employees' participation in protected activities constitute "interference" or "restraint" with the employees' exercise of their rights…. [Attaching negative consequences to the exercise of protected rights surely "tends to chill" an employee's willingness to exercise those rights: Employees are, understandably, less likely to exercise their FMLA leave rights if they can expect to be fired

or otherwise disciplined for doing so. The Labor Department's conclusion that employer use of "the taking of FMLA leave as a negative factor in employment actions," violates the Act is therefore a reasonable one. * * *

In the case before us, there is direct, undisputed evidence of the employer's motives: America West told Bachelder when it fired her that it based its decision on her sixteen absences since the January 1996 corrective action discussion. If those absences were, in fact, covered by the Act, America West's consideration of those absences as a "negative factor" in the firing decision violated the Act.

The FMLA "leave year" regulation, while allowing employers flexibility in deciding how to comply with the Act, also includes various safeguards for employees. First, the employer must apply its chosen calculating method consistently to all employees. Second, if the employer has failed to select a calculating method, the regulations state that the method "that provides the most beneficial outcome for the employee will be used." By preventing employers from calculating FMLA leave eligibility in their own favor on an ad hoc, employee-by-employee basis, the "leave year" regulation encourages the employer to choose its calculating method prospectively. By doing so, the regulation not only prevents unfairness to employees through retroactive manipulation of the "leave year," but also encourages a system under which both employees and employers can plan for future leaves in an orderly fashion.

The regulations allow employers to choose among four methods for calculating their employees' eligibility for FMLA leave, but they do not specifically state how an employer indicates its choice. America West contends, correctly, that the FMLA's implementing regulations do not expressly embody a requirement that employers inform their employees of their chosen method for calculating leave eligibility. The regulations nonetheless plainly contemplate that the employer's selection of one of the four calculation methods will be an open one, not a secret kept from the employees, the affected individuals. * * *

The question remains whether America West adequately notified its employees that it had chosen the retroactive rolling "leave year" calculation method. America West contends, and the district court agreed, that, because its employee hand book states that "employees are entitled to up to twelve calendar weeks of unpaid [FMLA] leave within any twelve month period," it provided sufficient notice to its employees that it uses the "rolling method" for calculating leave eligibility. We disagree. * * * [T]he very fact that the regulation permits employers to use any of four calculating methods is fatal to America West's argument: Because the statute can reasonably be read to allow the four different methods spelled out, merely parroting the statutory language cannot possibly inform employees of the method the employer has chosen. By paraphrasing the statutory language, in other words, America West has done no more than announce its intention to comply with the Act.

Because choosing a calculating method carries with it an obligation to inform employees of that choice and America West has failed to fulfill this obligation, it has "failed to select" a calculating method. Thus, "the option that provides the most beneficial outcome for the employee" must be used to determine whether Bachelder's 1996 absences were covered by the FMLA. The calendar year method provides the most favorable outcome to Bachelder. Under this approach, it is immaterial that Bachelder had utilized her full allotment of FMLA-protected leave between April and June 1995.... Because she began 1996 with a fresh bank of FMLA-protected leave, Bachelder's February 1996 absences were covered by the Act. * * *

[I]t is the employer's responsibility, not the employee's, to determine whether a leave request is likely to be covered by the Act. Employees must notify their employers in advance when they plan to take foreseeable leave for reasons covered by the Act, and as soon as practicable when absences are not foreseeable. Employees need only notify their employers that they will be absent under circumstances which indicate that the FMLA might apply. * * * [T]he employer is responsible, having been notified of the reason for an employee's absence, for being aware that the absence may qualify for FMLA protection.

Bachelder provided two doctor's [*sic*] notes to America West regarding her absences in February 1996. The company was therefore placed on notice that the leave might be covered by the FMLA, and could have inquired further to determine whether the absences were likely to qualify for FMLA protection.

Because we hold that Bachelder's February 1996 absences were protected by the FMLA, and because America West used these absences as a negative factor in its decision to fire her, we reverse the district court's grant of summary judgment for America West.

CASE QUESTIONS

1. What were the legal issues in this case? What did the court decide? Why?
2. What errors did the airline make in this case? What does this case tell us about things that employers must do to comply with the FMLA?
3. Why are "no-fault" attendance policies in conflict with the FMLA?
4. The court selected the calendar year as the method most favorable to Bachelder. Would any of the other three methods have entitled Bachelder to leave for her 1996 absences? Explain.

The FMLA creates an entitlement to leave, regardless of if or when an employer would prefer to grant leave. *If an eligible employee experiences a qualifying event and notifies her employer that she needs to take leave, the employer must grant the leave. The amount of leave that must be provided is the amount needed by the employee, up to a total of twelve workweeks over a twelve-month period.* As the *Bachelder* case illustrates, employers have four basic options for defining the twelve-month period: (1) the calendar year, (2) any other fixed twelve-month period, (3) a twelve-month period measured forward from the first day that any FMLA leave is taken by the employee, and (4) a rolling twelve-month period measured backward from the most recent day in which leave was used. The latter two methods are more complex but prevent employees from stacking periods of leave on top of one another (e.g., twelve weeks at the end of a calendar year followed by twelve weeks at the beginning of the next year). *Employers must adopt one of these methods, use it consistently, and notify employees regarding their choice of method.*

"Leave" means that the employee is relieved of all work duties and the obligation to come to work. Although employers can require that employees on FMLA leaves comply with reasonable, nondiscriminatory policies applied to ensure that leaves are not being abused, *employers are not free to assign work duties to employees on FMLA leave.* An employee who took FMLA leave to have a child received regular phone calls regarding various accounting and payroll problems at work, beginning when she was still in the hospital. In one of these calls, the employee was "chewed out" for deficient training procedures in the accounting department. On another occasion, the employee was asked to come to work to help resolve some problems and she went in for three to four hours. The employee was then laid off on her return to work. The court concluded that "By essentially requiring Plaintiff to work while on leave, and by terminating her for failing to do so, Defendant has 'interfered' with Plaintiffs attempts to take leave, and 'discriminated' against her for taking it."[16] Likewise, when a bookkeeper who had been taking periods of leave to care for her ailing parents was terminated—allegedly for poor performance—the court observed that the woman's FMLA leave was "illusory."[17] The fact that her employer continued to expect that she fulfill all of her duties as if she were present full-time bolstered the bookkeeper's argument that her termination was in retaliation for taking FMLA leave.

Whether leave must be taken on a **continuous** basis (i.e., all in one block with no work occurring between the beginning and end of leave) or whether it can **be intermittent** (i.e., periods of leave mixed with periods of work) depends on which qualifying event necessitated the leave. Leaves for childbirth, adoption, or foster care placement must be continuous unless the employer allows otherwise. Leaves for serious health conditions of employees or their family members can be either continuous or intermittent depending on the employee's needs. For example, intermittent leave might be needed to receive ongoing treatments or to deal with chronic conditions that occasionally flare up. One particular type of intermittent leave is a **reduced leave schedule**. This means that the employee's normal daily or weekly hours of work are reduced. Periods of intermittent leave can be as short as one hour, and *employees cannot be required to take longer periods of leave than they need simply for the administrative convenience of employers.*

Practical Considerations How should situations where employees need to take frequent intermittent leave be handled?

A critical issue for employees is whether the time off from work comes with pay. Under the FMLA, *employees may choose—or their employers may require them—to substitute available paid leave for unpaid FMLA leave.* Thus, although the FMLA does not entitle employees to paid leave, many employees are able to use vacation, personal days, sick days, or other paid leave to cover some or all of their FMLA leaves. Any paid leave that is substituted must fit the qualifying event that necessitated FMLA leave and any other neutral requirements of the employer's normal leave policies. Whether, for example, an employee can use sick leave to stay home and care for a family member with a serious health condition depends on whether the employer customarily permits sick leave to be used for that purpose or only for an employee's illness.

The FMLA specifically requires that health benefits be maintained under the same conditions that would pertain if the employee did not take leave. Thus, *assuming that the employer offers a group health plan, that coverage must remain in place, including any coverage of family members, with the employer paying what it usually pays for the coverage and the employee on leave paying whatever employee share is normally paid.* The FMLA permits employers to recover health insurance premiums paid if the leave-taker does not return to work for reasons other than inability to work due to a serious medical condition or other circumstances beyond the employee's control. Seniority and benefits related to time of service, including paid time off, need not continue to accrue while an employee is on unpaid FMLA leave. However, an employee cannot lose seniority or other benefits that were accrued prior to taking leave. Also, although benefits such

---

[16]*Sherman v. AI/FOCS, Inc.,* 113 F. Supp. 2d 65, 70-1 (D. Mass. 2000).

[17]*Lewis v. School District #70,* 523 F.3d 730, 743 (7th Cir. 2008).

as life insurance need not be maintained during periods of leave, the requirement that employees be restored following leave usually means, as a practical matter, that these other benefits must be kept in place.

On return from FMLA leave, an employee must be restored or reinstated to the same position held when leave was taken or to a position that is equivalent in pay, benefits, terms, and conditions of employment. To be equivalent, a position should be generally located in the same work site as the previous position; entail the same work schedule; offer equivalent opportunity for bonuses, profit sharing, and other payments; and be similar in duties and authority. A store manager who, on returning from FMLA leave, was offered positions in the procurement office or as a sacker/stocker at $7/hr and with increased health insurance premiums and no life insurance coverage was clearly not restored to an equivalent position.[18] In contrast, a laundry worker who was restored to a different position that involved somewhat more standing, lifting, and exposure to foul odors was unable to show that she had not been placed in a position equivalent to her prior position. This was true even though the employee was told that although her pay would remain the same for about a month, it "might go down" thereafter.[19] Likewise, an account manager was deemed restored even though her sales territory and the hospitals she dealt with were altered following her return from parental leave.[20] The court focused on the employee retaining the same job title, job responsibilities, and benefits. It dismissed her perception that the new accounts were less desirable and that her status and prospects for promotion had been diminished, labeling any such differences between the positions as "the sorts of de minimis, intangible, and unmeasurable aspects of a job that the regulations specifically exclude."[21] Employers are permitted to temporarily transfer employees on intermittent leave or reduced leave schedules to positions equivalent in pay and benefits to their existing jobs, but for which the intermittent leave would be less disruptive.

Taking leave does not immunize an employee from a layoff or termination that would have occurred anyway. "An employee has no greater right to reinstatement ... than if the employee had been continuously employed during the FMLA leave period."[22] If, for example, an employer can show that the leave-taker's position was eliminated due to restructuring or that the project for which the employee was hired is now completed, restoration would not be required. But notice that the fact of leave-taking raises legal questions that would not otherwise arise in terminating the employment of at-will employees. Thus, *decisions adversely affecting employees on FMLA leave or recently returned from leave should be very closely scrutinized.* A common issue in FMLA cases, including *Bachelder,* is employees being disciplined or terminated based on absences due to FMLA leave. Whether framed as "interference" or "discrimination," *employers cannot base adverse employment decisions on the taking of FMLA leave.* After the court determined that Bachelder was entitled to FMLA leave for her absences in 1996, her termination for excessive absences that included those in 1996 violated the FMLA. *"No-fault" attendance policies, which count absences without regard to the reasons for them, are inherently in conflict with the FMLA and must be eliminated or allow for exceptions.*

What if a high-level manager is having a baby? Is she still entitled to FMLA leave and restoration following leave? There is a narrow exception to the restoration requirement when "key employees" take leave. **Key employees** are salaried employees who are among the top 10 percent of a company's employees (i.e., those within a seventy-five-mile radius of the employee's workplace) in pay. *Employers cannot refuse leave to key employees but can*

---

[18]*Hanna v. Pay-and-Save, Inc.,* 2001 U.S. Dist. LEXIS 20095 (N.D. Tex.).

[19]*Vasquez v. Northern Illinois Hospital Services,* 2002 U.S. Dist. LEXIS 5257 (N.D. Ill.).

[20]*Breeden v. Novartis Pharmaceuticals Corp.,* 2011 U.S. App. LEXIS 13906 (D.C. Cir.).

[21]*Breeden,* at 24.

[22]29 C.F.R. § 825.216(a) (2011).

Practical Considerations An employee who is expecting a child is eligible and makes a timely request for parental leave. Draft a letter responding to her request for leave and notifying her that it will be considered FMLA leave. What should be included in this letter?

decline to restore them if restoration would "cause substantial and grievous economic injury" to the employer's operation. It is important that employers clearly inform employees regarding both their status as key employees and the employer's intent to not reinstate them. An employer violated the FMLA by terminating a nursing home administrator who had taken medical leave to deal with some serious health problems.[23] Although the employer designated her as a key employee and informed her regarding the possibility of non-restoration, it did not clearly convey that she would not be reinstated, it failed to explain the grounds for its determination that restoration would cause substantial harm to the firm, and it did not give her sufficient time to return from leave rather than lose her job. One of the main reasons for denying restoration is that it was necessary to find a permanent replacement for the key employee on leave. An employee denied restoration on the grounds of being a key employee was allowed to go to trial because there was evidence that his replacement as county tax assessor was hired on an interim basis and could have been returned to his prior position without cost to the county.[24] *Key employees must be informed of their status when they seek leave, and if the employer decides that their restoration would cause substantial and grievous economic injury, they should be given a reasonable amount of time to return from leave.*

How Should Employers Respond to Requests for FMLA Leave?   *Employers presented with requests for time off related to childbirth or medical problems must carefully consider whether the leave is required under the FMLA and respond promptly.* "The FMLA envisions a cooperative dialogue between employers and employees through which a balance between their competing needs can be struck…. [M]ost litigation arising under the FMLA results from a breakdown of that hoped-for cooperative dialogue."[25] However, this "dialogue" must proceed from the basic premise that employees have an entitlement to leave under the FMLA. Generally, employers do not have the right to deny or delay FMLA leave. Thus, a court held that an employer's effort to get an employee to delay a continuous period of leave until a less busy time could constitute interference with FMLA rights even though the employer subsequently relented.[26]

The DOL regulations call for employers to *provide written notice to employees requesting leave that the leave is being designated as FMLA leave, generally within five business days after notification of the need for leave.* The Supreme Court has determined that the DOL cannot punish employers who fail to provide the timely notification by not allowing them to count the days of leave against an employee's maximum entitlement under the FMLA,[27] but the basic principle remains: *Employers are responsible for promptly designating leave as FMLA leave and for informing employees of their rights under the FMLA.* In a relevant case, an employee who needed time off due to a serious health condition was not told his leave would be designated FMLA leave or that such leave is limited to a maximum of twelve workweeks. The employee was eventually fired based on his absences. The court concluded that the employee could go to trial on his claim that the employer interfered with his FMLA rights by failing to properly advise him. This failure impaired the employee's exercise of his rights because he was apparently not aware that FMLA leave is limited to a maximum duration of twelve workweeks over a twelve month period.[28]

What should this notification to employees look like? The DOL's Wage and Hour Division has a form that can be used for this purpose. Whether the government's form

---

[23]*Neel v. Mid-Atlantic of Fairfield*, 2011 U.S. Dist. LEXIS 42807 (D. Md.).

[24]*Kephart v. Cherokee County*, 2000 U.S. App. LEXIS 18924 (4th Cir.).

[25]*Shtab v. Greate Bay Hotel and Casino*, 173 F. Supp. 2d 255, 257 (D.N.J. 2001).

[26]*Shtab*, at 268.

[27]*Ragsdale v. Wolverine Worldwide, Inc.*, 122 S. Ct. 1155 (2002).

[28]*Conoshenti v. Public Service Electric & Gas Company*, 364 F.3d 135 (3d Cir. 2004).

or an employer's own document is used, *employer notices designating leave as FMLA leave should contain the following:*

- A specific statement that the leave is designated FMLA leave and will be counted against the employee's leave entitlement
- Any requirements for producing medical certification of a serious health condition and the consequences of failing to do so
- A statement of the employee's right to substitute paid leave for FMLA leave, a statement of whether the employer will require that to be done, and any conditions related to the substitution
- Any requirements for payment of the employee's share of health insurance premiums, arrangements for making those payments, and the right of the employer to recover premium payments if the employee chooses not to return from leave
- Any requirements for the employee to present fitness-for-duty certification prior to being restored
- A statement of the employee's right of restoration to the same job or an equivalent position
- Designation of key employee status if the employee meets the criteria and explanation of the circumstances under which restoration might be denied

Leave Policies Under the Pregnancy Discrimination Act

Because of the relatively high employer-size threshold for coverage under the FMLA, many employees do not receive its protection. In light of the limited coverage of the FMLA, the **Pregnancy Discrimination Act (PDA)** continues to have a significant influence on leave policies. The PDA confirms that discrimination based on pregnancy, childbirth, or related medical conditions is sex discrimination and violates Title VII.[29] The PDA does *not* require that employers provide leave for childbirth or medical problems associated with pregnancy. However, employers must treat persons with pregnancy-related conditions in the same manner as persons with other medical conditions who are similar in their ability or inability to work. *If sick leave, disability leave, or other forms of paid or unpaid time off are available to a company's employees, the same forms of leave on the same terms must be available to its pregnant employees.* This is also true regarding reassignment to light-duty positions or other alternative working arrangements if these are made available to employees with other temporarily disabling conditions. However, a trucking company did not violate the PDA by having a policy that made light-duty assignments available only to employees who had been injured on the job. The court viewed such a policy—presumably motivated by a desire to minimize workers' compensation payments—as "pregnancy blind" because it was the existence of a work-related condition, and not pregnancy, that determined eligibility for light-duty work.[30]

Pregnant employees are entitled to continue working for as long as they can perform their jobs (except in those rare cases where not being pregnant is a BFOQ). *Employers are prohibited from requiring pregnant employees who can perform their jobs to take leave or from establishing arbitrary timelines for when parental leave must commence or end.* Pregnancy-related conditions cannot be singled out for special procedures for determining ability to work. However, *any medical certification that is generally required before granting leave or for documenting fitness for duty on return from leave can also be required of employees who take leave for pregnancy-related conditions.* There is no specific restoration requirement under the PDA. Instead, parity is again the rule. *Jobs must*

---

[29]42 U.S.C.S. § 2000e(k) (2011).

[30]*Reeves v. Swift Transportation*, 446 F.3d 637, 641-42 (6th Cir. 2006).

be held open for employees on pregnancy-related leave at least as long as they are for employees who take sick or disability leave for other medical conditions.[31]

Leave to Perform Civic Duties

As citizens, employees are sometimes called on to perform duties that require their absence from work. One example of this is serving on a jury. The federal **Jury System Improvements Act**[32] protects persons who serve on federal juries from discharge, intimidation, or coercion by their employers. Most states also have laws protecting from discharge employees who serve on juries. Some states require that employees be paid while on jury duty, but that is not always the case. Voting is another civic duty addressed by state laws.[33] Most states require that employees be given a specified number of hours (generally two or three) off to vote when there is not sufficient nonwork time to do so. Most often the laws specify that this is paid time off but allow employers to determine the particular hours to be used for voting. Thus, although the details vary between states, *employers must generally provide employees with time off to serve on juries and to vote.*

Leave for Military Service

Extensive legal requirements surround military service, which are detailed in the **Uniformed Services Employment and Reemployment Rights Act (USERRA).**[34] Employers of any size are prohibited from discriminating against people who are members of, apply to become members of, or have obligations to serve in a uniformed military service. Often, complying with this law means allowing an employee in the National Guard to attend scheduled annual drill training and treating the employee as if he had not been absent. However, in a time of ongoing military operations, National Guard members and reservists are increasingly being called into active duty and required to perform lengthy military service—sometimes on multiple tours.[35] Employers must be aware that such employees retain many important rights under the USERRA.

ELEMENTS OF A CLAIM

USERRA—Failure to Reinstate

In a case alleging failure to reinstate following military leave, the plaintiff must show:

1. The employer was informed that the employee needed leave to fulfill military duties.
2. The employee received an honorable discharge from active military service.
3. The employee made a timely (usually within 90 days) request to be reinstated.
4. The employer delayed reinstatement, denied reinstatement, or failed to fully reinstate by restoring the employee to the terms and conditions of employment that would have prevailed had the employee not left to engage in military service.

---

[31]U.S. Equal Employment Opportunity Commission. "Facts About Pregnancy Discrimination." (January 1994).

[32]28 U.S.C.S. § 1875(a) (2011).

[33]"Most Workers are Guaranteed Time to Vote, But Specifics Vary Widely under State Laws." *Daily Labor Report* 208 (October 28, 2008), C-1.

[34]38 U.S.C.S. §§ 4301-4334 (2011); 20 C.F.R. §§ 1002.1-1002.314 (2011).

[35]Thom Shanker. "Army Is Worried by Rising Stress of Return Tours." *New York Times* (April 6, 2008), A1.

As a general rule, *employees are entitled to reemployment following up to five years of cumulative absence* (not counting periods of required training) for military service. An employee taking leave for military service must notify his employer to that effect but is not required to await permission or to decide at that time whether reinstatement will be sought following the period of military service. *Provided that an honorable discharge is received and a timely request made for reemployment, an employee returning from military service must be reemployed.* Service members have to report more or less immediately following service periods of less than 31 days and within 90 days of discharge when the service period exceeds 180 days. Service members injured or disabled during service are given up to two years to return to their jobs. The main exceptions to this reinstatement requirement are where (1) the employer's circumstances have changed, rendering reemployment "impossible or unreasonable" (e.g., a business closure); (2) the necessary training or other accommodations needed to successfully reemploy the individual would impose "undue hardship"; or (3) the prior employment was for a brief, nonrecurrent period and carried no expectation of continued employment (e.g., temporary employment to complete a specific project).[36]

JUST THE FACTS

Michael Serricchio went to work for Prudential Securities in 2000 as a financial advisor. He was also a member of the United States Air Force reserve. Mr. Serricchio was called to active duty following September 11, 2001. At the time of his activation, he was managing 237 client accounts and earning about $76,000 per year. Mr. Serricchio was honorably discharged in October 2003. In the interim, the business had been sold to Wachovia and many of his clients had been transferred to a national call center that was being used to service low volume, less affluent clients. On December 1, 2003, Mr. Serricchio requested reinstatement. He was offered reinstatement as a financial advisor with a small number of his remaining clients, a $2,000 per month advance against his commissions, and the opportunity to cold-call for new clients. Mr. Serricchio left the office that day and never returned. He was terminated for job abandonment. Did this employer violate the USERRA by failing to properly reinstate this employee?

See, *Serricchio v. Wachovia*, 556 F.Supp. 2d 99 (D. Conn. 2008).

Delaying reinstatement of an employee from military leave can also violate the USERRA, as *Petty v. Metropolitan Gov't of Nashville & Davidson County* shows.

Petty v. Metropolitan Gov't of Nashville & Davidson County
2008 U.S. App. LEXIS 17549 (6th Cir.)

OPINION BY CIRCUIT JUDGE BATCHELDER:

* * * The central dispute in this case is whether Metro violated USERRA in its treatment of Petty, a former police officer who left the department for active duty with the United States Army and who sought reemployment with the department after completion of his military service. * * *

Plaintiff joined the Army National guard in 1986 and opted into the Army Reserve with the Army National Guard ... in 1989. * * * Metro promoted

---

[36]38 U.S.C.S. § 4312(d)(1) (2011).

the Plaintiff to the rank of sergeant in January 2000…. All Metro police officers must get approval for off-duty work, and the Plaintiff sought and received Metro's approval to work as a security guard at … [two] restaurants prior to his deployment. Plaintiff remained in the Army Reserve through 2003. In October of 2003, the Army called Plaintiff at work to tell him that he "was being transferred to another unit to take command as they were being mobilized" for service in Operation Iraqi Freedom. Plaintiff told his lieutenant at Metro, Kim Dillingham, of his upcoming military leave the same day that the Army informed him. The week after the Army contacted him, the Plaintiff took his first trip to Chattanooga to begin preparations for deployment, and he stopped working at Metro altogether on November 30, 2003. * * *

The Army assigned the Plaintiff to run the "mayor's cell" at Camp Navistar. Plaintiffs unit ran the camp on a day-to-day basis—moving supplies; setting out bottled water for soldiers; handling any problems with housing, etc. The job also required Plaintiff to empty and store contraband from "amnesty boxes." In June or July, 2004, Command Sergeant Thomas Seuberling conducted a health and welfare inspection of Plaintiffs quarters. During the initial inspection, CSM Seuberling found a five-gallon jerry can (which looks like a gas can) that Plaintiff was using to manufacture homemade wine. * * * Based upon CSM Seuberling's health and welfare inspection, and the resulting investigation, Plaintiff was charged with a violation of the Military Code of Justice. * * *

In late 2004, Plaintiff appeared in front of a military judge, where he was arraigned. In lieu of going forward with court martial proceedings, Plaintiff submitted a request to resign his commission "for the good of the service." When Plaintiff submitted his request to resign "for the good of the service," the Army relieved him of his command, meaning that he was relieved of his supervisory responsibilities. Plaintiff was notified on January 15, 2005 that his resignation "for the good of the service" had been approved. The Army formally dismissed all charges against him in January 2005. * * * Plaintiffs discharge was characterized as "under honorable conditions (general)." The Army returned Plaintiff to Fort Stewart, Georgia on or about February 1, 2005.

Plaintiff visited Metro to request reinstatement on February 28, 2005. The Police Department has a return-to-work process for officers who have been away from the Police Department for an extended period of time. This return-to-work process applies to all officers who have been away from the Police Department for an extended period of time, regardless of the reason for their separation. [The] … process includes a personal history update questionnaire, a medical examination, a computer voice stress analysis, a drug screening, and a debriefing with a Police Department psychologist. In addition, the Police Department requests that returning officers execute a medical records authorization, and for individuals returning from military duty, an authorization to obtain military records. * * *

One of the questions on the personal history questionnaire Plaintiff filled out during the return-to-work process asked: "During your absence were you arrested, charged, detained, or a suspect in any criminal action or military disciplinary action for any reason or do you have any action pending? If yes, explain in detail (use back if necessary)." Plaintiff answered "Yes." He also attached a narrative explanation of his response in which he admitted facing military charges in Kuwait. The narrative description did not disclose: (1) that Plaintiff was accused of giving alcohol to an enlisted soldier; and (2) that Plaintiff was accused of manufacturing alcohol. * * *

On March 21, 2005, Defendant returned the Plaintiff to work. Defendant did not, however, return the Plaintiff to his original position of patrol sergeant, or a substantially similar position. Plaintiff contends that he was assigned to an office job in which he primarily answered telephone calls from the public. * * * The Metropolitan Police * * * initiated an investigation focused on whether Plaintiff was honest and truthful when he completed return-to-work paperwork after returning from military service. * * * [It was] discovered that the DD-214 [a form issued by the Defense Department upon discharge] Plaintiff submitted to the Metropolitan Government appeared to have been "altered." * * * The form submitted by the Plaintiff to Metro omitted a few boxes at the bottom, including Box 28, which listed Plaintiffs "Narrative Reason for Separation" as "in lieu of trial by court martial." The form also omitted Blocks 29 and 30.

During his deposition testimony and in response to Defendant's requests for admission, Plaintiff admitted that he did not provide a complete copy of his DD-214 to Metro. * * * Plaintiff testified that when he copied his DD-214, the copy was enlarged, which cut off Boxes 28, 29 and 30. He testified that he did not intentionally enlarge the form. * * * Since approximately

October 10, 2005, Defendant has assigned Plaintiff to the Central Station "bubble," where he has continued answering telephone calls from the public. Traditionally, Metro staffs the bubble with officers facing discipline or who are otherwise "disempowered." On December 21, 2005, Plaintiff requested Metro's permission to return to his off-duty security jobs.... Metro denied Plaintiffs request for off-duty employment.

Petty's complaint alleged that Metro violated his rights under USERRA in that: (1) Metro delayed rehiring him for the purpose of subjecting him to the department's return-to-work process; (2) Metro did not properly rehire him because he was not placed in the position to which he was entitled; and (3) Metro impermissibly denied him the ability to work off-duty security jobs. * * *

For the purposes of this case, USERRA performs four key functions. First, it guarantees returning veterans a right of reemployment after military service. Second, it prescribes the position to which such veterans are entitled upon their return. Third, it prevents employers from discriminating against returning veterans on account of their military service. Fourth, it prevents employers from firing without cause any returning veterans within one year of reemployment. * * * [One section of the USERRA] protects service members at the instant of seeking reemployment, entitling the service member to reemployment in either the position she would have been in had she not left for military service "or a position of like seniority, status and pay, the duties of which the person is qualified to perform." [Another section] ... applies after reemployment has occurred and "prohibits discrimination with respect to any benefit of employment against persons who serve in the armed services after they return from a deployment and are reemployed." * * *

A. PETTY'S FIRST TWO CLAIMS—DELAY IN REHIRING AND FAILURE TO HIRE AT PROPER POSITION:

Congress has clearly prescribed the prerequisites Petty was required to satisfy to qualify for USERRA's reemployment protection. First, he was required to notify his employer in advance of his departure that he would be leaving for military service. Second, the cumulative length of such military service must be less than 5 years. Third, upon his return, he was required to request reemployment from Metro within the time frame ... and with the documentation specified by

[the USERRA]. Fourth, his separation from service must have been under "honorable conditions." Metro contends only that Petty failed to ... provide documentation establishing that he has satisfied these four prerequisites.

In [the regulations for implementing the USERRA], the Department of Labor lists documents that satisfy the documentation requirements.... Among those listed is a form DD-214, which Metro concedes Petty provided. But Metro argues that Petty's DD-214 is not sufficient, because the copy of the form that Petty sent Metro did not include three fields at the bottom of the form—most notably one including the statement "Narrative Reason for Separation: In lieu of trial by court-martial." Furthermore, Metro argues, the DD-214 was "void" because the failure to include all fields constituted an alteration voiding the form. Petty counters that his DD-214 included all the information necessary under the ... [USERRA].

We conclude that it would be inconsistent with the goals of USERRA to prevent Petty from exercising his right to reemployment because he failed to provide forthrightly information that is statutorily unnecessary to his establishing the right in the first place. First, ... the types of documentation necessary to establish eligibility for reemployment may vary from case to case. The focus of USERRA is on securing rights to returning veterans, not on ensuring that any particular documentation is produced. Second, in compliance with Metro's return-to-work process, Petty signed an authorization granting Metro unfettered access to all of his medical and military records, including a complete DD-214. Accordingly, we find that Petty satisfied USERRA's documentation requirement, and, inasmuch as Metro does not dispute his having satisfied the other statutory prerequisites, it is apparent that he established his right to reemployment....

Metro, therefore, was not permitted to delay or otherwise limit Petty's reemployment rights in any way; in particular, Metro was not permitted to limit or delay Petty's reemployment by requiring him to comply with its return-to-work process. [The] USERRA "supersedes any ... contract, agreement, policy, plan, practice, or other matter that reduces, limits, or eliminates in any manner any right or benefit provided by this chapter, including the establishment of additional prerequisites to the exercise of any such right or the receipt of any such benefit." By applying its return-to-work process to Petty, Metro not only delayed his reemployment, but as we shall explain, it also limited and withheld benefits to which Petty was entitled under USERRA.

It is of no consequence here that Metro believes it is obligated to "ensure that each and every individual entrusted with the responsibility of being a Metropolitan Police Officer is still physically, emotionally, and temperamentally qualified to be a police officer after having been absent from the Department." In USERRA, Congress clearly expressed its view that a returning veteran's reemployment rights take precedence over such concerns. Metro does not question Petty's physical qualifications; instead, it questions only whether his conduct during his military service would disqualify him from returning to service in the police department. But Petty's separation from military service is classified as "under honorable conditions," which Congress has made clear suffices to qualify him for USERRA benefits. To the extent that his military service may have in fact left Petty unfit to carry out his duties as a police officer but is not reflected in the classification of his separation from service, USERRA would allow, after his reemployment, a "for cause" termination of that employment. * * * The district court determined that Metro's return-to-work procedures could be applied to Petty, finding that because they are applicable to all individuals regardless of military service, these procedures did not constitute "additional prerequisites." In this, the district court erred. * * * It is important to note that Petty was not required to make any showing of discrimination in order to sustain either of his reemployment claims. * * *

... [W]e must now determine whether Metro violated [the USERRA] in failing to rehire Petty at the appropriate level of employment. * * * Metro does not dispute that Petty was not placed in any of the positions apparently mandated by [the USERRA] (e.g., his former position as patrol sergeant). Rather, Metro argues only that it did not violate [the USERRA] because, having perhaps been dishonest in the return-to-work process, Petty may not be qualified to hold these positions. This argument is without merit. At the point at which Petty was entitled to reemployment ..., Metro had no basis on which to question his qualifications. Petty had satisfied the only prerequisites to ... [reemployment] and Metro's attempt to impose additional prerequisites through its return-to-work process was ... wholly impermissible. The process, then, including Petty's alleged "dishonesty" therein, cannot serve as a basis for delaying or otherwise limiting Petty's right to reemployment.

Furthermore, Metro cannot avoid this conclusion by arguing that its second investigation into Petty's conduct during the return-to-work process had not been completed at the time of Petty's filing of this action, and Metro therefore had not been able to determine whether Petty was qualified for reemployment in his original position with the police department. [The USERRA] includes a promptness requirement that Metro clearly violated notwithstanding any concerns that it may have harbored regarding Petty's truthfulness. "Prompt reemployment" ... [according to the DOL] means reemployment as soon as practicable under the circumstances of each case. *Absent unusual circumstances, reemployment must occur within two weeks of the employee's application for reemployment.* For example, prompt reinstatement after a weekend National Guard duty generally means the next regularly scheduled working day. On the other hand, prompt reinstatement following several years of active duty may require more time, because the employer may have to reassign or give notice to another employee who occupied the returning employee's position.

Because of its return-to-work process, Metro took three weeks to "rehire" Petty, and even then it did not place Petty in the correct position.... Metro cannot justify these delays; neither a return-to-work process that has been superseded by statute nor any investigations resulting from that process constitute the "unusual circumstances" that the Department of Labor has specified may justify a less timely reinstatement. [I]n any event, the burden of proving that a returning veteran is not qualified ... falls on the employer, not on the employee. Metro cannot defeat the "prompt reemployment" guarantee ... by engaging in never-ending investigations into Petty's qualifications. * * * Metro has never *proved* Petty's disqualification for reemployment. Indeed, even today, approximately three years after Petty originally sought reemployment, Metro simply argues that, pending the outcome of its second investigation, it believes that Petty *may* be unqualified. * * *

B. PETTY'S THIRD CLAIM—DENIAL OF HIS REQUEST FOR OFF-DUTY WORK:

* * * The ability to obtain additional income by working as an off-duty security officer was certainly a "benefit" of serving as a Metro police officer, so any discrimination with respect to this benefit on account of Petty's military service would violate [the USERRA]. An individual bringing a [discrimination] claim has

the initial burden of proving a prima facie case of discrimination by showing, by a preponderance of the evidence, that his protected status was a substantial or motivating factor in the adverse employment action(s). The burden then shifts to the employer to prove the affirmative defense that the employment action(s) would have been taken in the absence of the employee's protected status. For Petty's military service to have been "[a] motivating factor does not mean that it had to be the sole cause of the employment action. Instead, it is one of the factors that a truthful employer would list if asked for the reasons for its decision." * * *

Metro argues that Petty was denied permission to engage in off-duty employment because he was being investigated at the time of his request and Metro has a policy against approving off-duty requests for officers under investigation. The district court concluded that this policy was the motivating factor behind Metro's denial, that the policy was a legitimate reason and not a pretext for that decision, and that Metro's action was not discriminatory and did not violate USERRA. We conclude that the district court erred in its analysis. In accepting Metro's justification regarding its policy, the district court failed to consider Metro's motivations for launching the investigation that triggered the policy's application to Petty in the first place. * * * Petty came within the ambit of the "legitimate" policy only because he was under investigation. If that investigation was motivated by an improper purpose, then it follows that the denial of benefits on the basis of the investigation's existence was also motivated, at least in part, by an improper purpose. * * *

Metro has undertaken two separate investigations of Petty. The first was launched on April 14, 2005, to investigate concerns about Petty's honesty in disclosing the details of his military arrest and discharge. These concerns were determined to be "unfounded" in May of 2005, and the investigation was formally closed on July 22, 2005. The second investigation was launched on October 21, 2005, and was aimed at determining whether Petty's submission of a form DD-214 with three fields missing violated department rules against the withholding of information. * * * Metro contends

that the second investigation * * * although indirectly involving his military service, is solely motivated by concerns for Petty's honesty and truthfulness.

* * * The record contains a chain of email correspondence that took place after the first investigation was concluded but prior to the second investigation. * * * This email establishes: (1) that after the first investigation was complete, there was still concern regarding Petty's *conduct in service*, not his honesty, amongst those who initiated the second investigation, and (2) that the informal investigation that led to the second, formal investigation was quite possibly motivated by those concerns about Petty's military service. Indeed, [the lead investigator] … testified that she continued to investigate Petty—even after signing off on the first investigation's conclusion that the concerns about his honesty were "unfounded"—because she was "uncomfortable with the fact that [Metro] [was] not able to get as much information as [she] wanted with regard to the actual circumstances" of Petty's offense and discharge. * * *

For the foregoing reasons, we **REVERSE** * * * and **REMAND** this matter to the district court with instructions to enter summary judgment in favor of Petty on the reemployment claims and to determine the resultant damages, and with regard to the discrimination claim, to conduct further proceedings not inconsistent with this opinion.

CASE QUESTIONS

1. What were the legal issues in this case? What did the court decide?
2. How were the reemployment provisions of the USERRA violated in this case?
3. Was the plaintiff still qualified to be a police officer? Wasn't the department justified in being concerned about possible misconduct that occurred while the officer was in Iraq? Explain.
4. Why does the court conclude that Petty has a claim for discrimination under USERRA? How does a discrimination claim under USERRA differ from a re-employment claim?
5. What should the police department have done differently?

Under the **escalator principle,** *employers must attempt to place individuals returning from military service into the positions, including promotions, they likely would have attained absent the service.* Employers must make reasonable efforts, such as by providing training, to permit returning service members to perform their jobs. If individuals are not qualified to perform the jobs that they would otherwise have attained, reinstatement to the position held prior to military service or an equivalent position must occur. Reemployment under the USERRA also means that an employee returns with the seniority he would have had if he were continuously employed and any other benefits related to length of service (e.g., pay raises). Benefits unrelated to seniority must be maintained on the same basis as for other employees receiving comparable, nonmilitary leaves of absence.[37] Fred Meyer Stores settled a lawsuit alleging that it had violated the USERRA by failing to award longevity-based step increases to employees who were away on military leave.[38] Consequently, the leave takers were underpaid on their return to work and the proper amounts were also not paid into the pension plan on their behalf.

Employers are not required to pay employees while they are gone performing military service, although some do so. *Health insurance must be maintained for short stints of service (less than thirty-one days) and for longer periods (up to twenty-four months) if the employee pays the full cost of group coverage.*[39] Pension benefits generally continue to accrue while employees are in the military service, although employee contributions might still be required.

The substantial nature of service members' reemployment rights is underscored by the fact that after they are reemployed, service members can be subsequently terminated only "for cause" for the next six months to a year (depending on length of service). USERRA defines "for cause" termination as being based on the employee's conduct or on the application of other legitimate, nondiscriminatory reasons.[40] The employer bears the burden of proving that the termination was for cause and that the employee had express or implicit notice that the conduct in question was cause for termination. Thus, employees are protected against "sham" reemployment that attempts to circumvent the strong reinstatement rights provided under the USERRA.

Language Requirements and National Origin Discrimination

One of the more obvious manifestations of diversity is a workforce in which a variety of languages and accents are heard. Language is closely tied to national origin. Legal issues can arise when employers make employment decisions based on English fluency or the presence of an accent and when employers adopt English-only rules to curtail the use of other languages in the workplace.

English Fluency and Accents

As if calculus was not hard enough by itself, you're crammed into a lecture hall, staring at a jumble of strange symbols and straining to comprehend the heavily accented words of your foreign-born instructor. That experiences like this might be viewed as valuable lessons in diversity—preparation for a world in which not everyone we work or do business with speaks in a familiar manner—is understandably lost on frustrated students. But is it national origin discrimination for universities or other employers to insist that employees be fluent in English and not speak with heavy accents?

---

[37]38 U.S.C.S. § 4316(a) (2011)

[38]Michael Rose. "Fred Meyer to Pay Back Wages to Veterans Who Did Not Receive Raises While Serving." *Daily Labor Report* 57 (March 24, 2011), A-5.

[39]38 U.S.C.S. § 4317(a) (2011).

[40]20 C.F.R. § 1002.248 (2011).

The EEOC "defines national origin discrimination broadly as including, but not limited to, the denial of equal employment opportunity because of an individual's, or his or her ancestor's, place of origin; or because an individual has the physical, cultural or *linguistic characteristics* [emphasis added] of a national origin group."[41] Most courts do not go quite as far in equating linguistic and national origin discrimination, but courts recognize the close nexus between language and national origin and the ease with which subjective assessments of language can merge into national origin discrimination. In one important case, a Filipino emigrated to Hawaii and scored highest in the state on a civil service exam for motor vehicle bureau clerks. The exam included, among other things, word usage, grammar, and spelling. However, when the man was interviewed for the position, the two interviewers concluded that he had a "heavy accent" that would be difficult for customers to understand, particularly over the phone. The Filipino man was not hired. The court found for the employer because of the following:

> *The record conclusively shows that Fragante [the plaintiff] was not selected because of the deleterious effect his Filipino accent had upon his ability to communicate orally, not merely because he had such an accent. This is a crucial distinction. Employers may lawfully base an employment decision upon an individual's accent when—but only when—it interferes materially with job performance.*[42]

Thus, *an employee or job applicant's accent can be lawfully considered in making employment decisions when communication is a significant part of the job in question and the individual's accent substantially interferes with the ability to communicate.* The critical issue is comprehension and not that the person sounds different or "foreign" or that understanding the person requires extra effort on the part of listeners. *Fluency in English should be considered only to the extent that it is job related*, since this selection criterion is otherwise a strong candidate for adverse impact claims. The linguistic demands of different jobs can vary widely even with the same organization, making it important to distinguish between positions when establishing fluency requirements.[43]

Universities have been upheld by the courts in cases where they reasonably took into account the communication skills of faculty. For example, the termination of a professor from Trinidad was upheld despite the fact that the university's evaluation of his teaching was based on student evaluations that included negative comments about the professor's accent (among other complaints). The court wrote the following:

> *[R]equiring that a professor speak the native tongue in order to convey his ideas is not any form of discrimination.... This sentence [one student evaluation said "hire a professor who speaks English"] merely expresses the frustration of a student stymied by a professor not conversant in the language of his students.*[44]

However, where complaints about an accent were combined with derogatory comments about foreign faculty, inconsistent evaluations of the faculty member, and a highly subjective evaluation system, they supported a finding of national origin discrimination.[45] A bank discriminated when it refused to promote an employee because

---

[41]29 C.F.R. § 1606.1 (2011).

[42]*Fragante v. City and County of Honolulu*, 888 F.2d 591, 596 (9 Cir. 1989), *cert. denied*, 494 U.S. 1081 (1990).

[43]Michael Bologna. "EEOC Commissioner Calls for Examination of Employers' English-Only Work Policies." *Daily Labor Report* 215 (November 8, 2010), C-1.

[44]*Jiminez v. Mary Washington College*, 57 F.3d 369, 380 (4th Cir. 1995), *cert. denied*, 516 U.S. 944 (1995).

[45]*Saleh v. Upadhyay*, 2001 U.S. App. LEXIS 11322 (4th Cir.).

of his Cambodian accent. The employee had completed management training, had taken English classes to improve his language skills, and had good performance appraisals, but he was told that he could not be promoted because of his foreign accent.[46]

English-Only Rules

Employers with bilingual or multilingual employees sometimes institute **English-only rules** that prohibit or restrict the speaking of languages other than English in the workplace. These policies vary in breadth, from total bans to time and place restrictions on when other languages can be spoken in the workplace. The impetus for establishing these policies is often the complaints of monolingual English-speaking employees who believe that they are being denigrated. Safety concerns, customer preferences, and problems in supervision are also cited as motives. Data from the 2000 census showed that 18 percent of the U.S. population (47 million people at the time) spoke a language other than English at home and this number has likely increased since then.[47] Given the demographics of the U.S. workforce, English-only policies most often have the effect of limiting Latino employees from speaking Spanish on the job.

Practical Considerations Would you advise employers with multilingual workforces to adopt English-only rules? If so, under what circumstances?

Clippings

A company that operates skilled nursing facilities in several states agreed to pay up to $450,000 to settle a national origin discrimination claim brought by the EEOC on behalf of Latino employees. The suit centered on the company's strict English-only rule, under which employees were allegedly prohibited from using Spanish to converse with Spanish-speaking nursing home residents and disciplined for speaking Spanish in the parking lot during breaks. EEOC Acting Chair Stuart J. Ishimaru commented that "As our workforce becomes increasingly diverse, employers must be vigilant in ensuring that if English-only rules are necessary, they are not discriminatory." The EEOC handled 204 cases involving English-only rules in fiscal year 2008.

Tom Gilroy. "Skilled Nursing Firm to Pay $450,000 to Settle National Origin Bias Claims." *Daily Labor Report* 71 (April 16, 2009), A-10.

The EEOC's guidelines hold that broad English-only rules applied at all times are presumptively discriminatory. More narrowly tailored policies applied only at certain times are legal, provided that employers can demonstrate their business necessity. The EEOC also maintains that unless employers notify employees of the existence of an English-only rule, any disciplinary actions taken against noncomplying employees will be viewed as evidence of discrimination.[48] Courts have not always concurred with the EEOC's position. Some courts have held in adverse impact claims that English-only rules do not adversely affect the employment opportunities of bilingual employees because they are

---

[46]*Xieng v. Peoples National Bank,* 844 P.2d 389, 392 (Wash. 1993).

[47]Bologna.

[48]29 C.F.R. § 1606.7 (2011).

able to comply with the policies. Consequently, there is no need for the employers to even show the business necessity for their English-only rules.[49] Courts have also found for employers when the English-only rules were not overly broad and rigidly enforced. In one such case, retail store employees were required to speak English when on the sales floor and in the presence of customers—and expressly permitted to speak other languages in the workplace at all other times. The court agreed with the employer that the policy served the business necessity of promoting customer service by rendering salespeople more polite and approachable.[50] But none of this amounts to blanket authorization for English-only rules. Monolingual employees who speak languages other than English are clearly unable to comply and are disadvantaged if the policies are enforced against them. Combined with other forms of hostility to "foreigners," rigidly enforced English-only policies contribute to hostile environments and national origin harassment. Public employees may be able to assert First Amendment speech rights if their government employers limit them to speaking English on the job.[51] *If used at all, English-only rules should be no broader than absolutely necessary to accomplish legitimate business purposes. Enforcement of the rules should not be rigid, and employees must be clearly notified that the rules are in effect.*

JUST THE FACTS

A taxi company instituted an English-only policy for its dispatch office. All of the employees spoke English, although some spoke Spanish as well. The memo announcing the policy stated that "there is to be no Spanish spoken in the main office" unless a customer did not speak English. The policy applied to business conducted in the main office but not to conversations outside the main office during breaks. Violations of the policy subjected employees to termination. The employer claimed that the policy was needed to help cut down on miscommunication between drivers and dispatchers. Is this English-only policy discriminatory?

See, *Gonzalo v. All Island Transportation*, 2007 U.S. Dist. LEXIS 13069 (E.D.N.Y.).

Discrimination Based on Sexual Orientation

Sexual orientation has become quite prominent among forms of diversity. Whether a person identifies himself or herself as gay, lesbian, bisexual, or heterosexual often has real consequences for that individual—both in the larger society and in the workplace. While its precise extent is difficult to gauge, there is considerable evidence that gays and lesbians face discrimination in the workplace.[52] What, if any, laws protect employees from discrimination based on their sexual orientation?

---

[49]*Garcia v. Spun Steak*, 998 F.2d 1480, 1488 (9th Cir. 1993), *cert. denied*, 512 U.S. 1228 (1994).

[50]*Equal Employment Opportunity Commission v. Sephora USA*, 2005 U.S. Dist. LEXIS 20014 (S.D.N.Y.).

[51]*Ruiz et al. v. Hull, Governor of Arizona*, 957 P.2d 984 (Ariz. 1998), *cert. denied*, 525 U.S. 1093 (1999).

[52]M.V. Lee Badgett, Holning Lau, Brad Sears, and Deborah Ho. *Bias in the Workplace: Consistent Evidence of Sexual Orientation and Gender Identity Discrimination*. The Williams Institute, UCLA School of Law (June 2007) (http://www.law.ucla.edu/williamsinstitute/publications/Bias in the Workplace.pdf).

Protection Under Federal Law

Title VII of the Civil Rights Act of 1964 refers to "sex" as a protected class, but courts have consistently held that protection against discrimination based on sexual orientation cannot be read into the Act.[53] Attempts to amend Title VII to include sexual orientation (and, more recently, gender identity) as a protected class have become regular events, but thus far none of these bills have become law. The U.S. Constitution offers somewhat more protection against sexual orientation discrimination, albeit only to public employees. When government agencies make adverse employment decisions based on a person's sexual orientation, those decisions or policies can be challenged as unconstitutional (as denials of equal protection of the law or perhaps violations of associational rights) if they are not "rationally related to a legitimate government purpose or interest." As one court has described the **rational relationship standard** of constitutional scrutiny:

> [T]he state [government] action must still bear a rational relationship to the legitimate state objectives and interest. Under the rational relationship standard, a court presumes that the classification is constitutional and the Plaintiff bears the burden of demonstrating that the classification at issue bears no legitimate purpose. Although most state actions survive legal analysis because of at least some tenuous rational relationship between the class distinction and the state interest, the rational relationship test is not entirely toothless. The Supreme Court has used the Equal Protection Clause to protect individuals ... from "invidious discrimination" and "irrational prejudice."[54]

Though not inherently "toothless," constitutional challenges to sexual orientation discrimination by government agencies generally have not fared well. Many of these cases have involved government agencies with security or law enforcement missions. For example, the FBI s refusal to hire a lesbian was upheld as constitutional[55] (based on concerns that homosexuals would be more subject to blackmail to prevent themselves or their partners from being "outed"). Courts also upheld the Georgia Attorney General's decision to rescind an offer of employment on learning that a woman had engaged in a commitment ceremony with her female partner[56] (based on the state's claims that citizens would be confused about what the law is regarding same-sex marriage and that the Office's public image would be harmed).

Clippings

In a historic action, the U.S. Senate voted on December 18, 2010, to repeal the law that had established the military's "don't ask, don't tell" policy. An estimated 14,000 service members were forced to leave the military under this policy. While this action cleared the way for gays and lesbians to serve openly in the military, the change would not go into effect until sixty days after completion of a review and certification by the Secretary of Defense that policies are in place to ensure that

---

[53]*DeSantis v. Pacific Telephone & Telegraph*, 608 F.2d 327 (9th Cir. 1979), *overruled* in part by *Nichols v. Azteca Restaurant Enterprises*, 256 F.3d 864, 875 (9th Cir. 2001).

[54]*Baumgardner v. County of Cook*, 108 F. Supp. 2d 1041, 1054 (E.D. Ill. 2000).

[55]*Padula v. Webster*, 822 F.2d 97 (D.C. Cir. 1987).

[56]*Shahar v. Bowers*, 114 F.3d 1097 (11th Cir. 1997), *cert. denied*, 522 U.S. 1049 (1998).

> troop readiness and effectiveness, unit cohesion, recruiting, and retention will not
> be compromised by the change.
>
> Carl Hulse. "Senate Ends Military Ban on Gays Serving Openly." *New York Times*
> (December 19, 2010), A1.

Gays in the Military: "Don't Ask, Don't Tell"   More than any other governmental
institution, the military has experienced ongoing controversy and legal challenges regarding its treatment of gays and lesbians. The stated concern of the military was that people
who engage in homosexual behavior and are known to be gay or lesbian might undermine the group cohesion and morale that is vital to military service. A compromise policy—dubbed **"don't ask, don't tell"**—was crafted in 1993. The gist of the policy was that
gay and lesbian service members were expected to be discreet and not talk about or
openly engage in homosexual behavior. In return, the military was to refrain from engaging in fishing expeditions to ferret out gays and lesbians in the ranks. Despite the fact
that the policy was intended to be more permissive, discharges of gays and lesbians
surged following adoption of the "don't ask, don't tell" policy.[57] In November 2010, a
draft report by the Pentagon was released concluding that repeal of the policy might
cause some temporary problems, but would not result in overall harm to the military.[58]
In December 2010, the Senate voted to repeal "don't ask, don't tell" and President
Obama quickly signed the legislation. However, this legislation put in place a
very deliberate process for implementing the change. Discharges of gays and lesbians
from the military continued to take place and lawsuits challenging the policy continued
to be filed.[59] The required certification by the Secretary of Defense that the military is
ready for the change was eventually issued and the "don't ask, don't tell" policy ended
September 20, 2011.

Legislative repeal of "don't ask, don't tell" does not necessarily end litigation over this
issue. For one thing, the repeal does nothing to compensate or reinstate the many thousands of service members who were discharged under the policy. The military has indicated that it does not intend to reinstate these service members or confer any preference
on them with respect to reenlistment. Additionally, it is not beyond the realm of possibility that a shift in political winds could resurrect the policy. If so, its constitutionality
would have to be decided. Earlier decisions upholding the policy under a rational basis
standard[60] would seem to be on shakier ground following the military's own assessments
that the policy is not essential to military readiness. The Supreme Court's decision, on
broad privacy grounds, to strike down as unconstitutional a state law criminalizing consensual sodomy[61] influenced subsequent appeals court decisions in challenges to the
"don't ask, don't tell" policy[62] and would likely be at the center of any future cases.

---

[57]John Files. "Rules on Gays Exact a Cost in Recruiting, a Study Finds." *New York Times* (February 24, 2005),
A-16.

[58]Elisabeth Bumiller. "Little Harm Found if Gay Ban Is Lifted." *New York Times* (November 12, 2010), A16.

[59]John Schwartz. "'Don't Ask, Don't Tell' Remains in Effect Months after Passage of Law to End It." *New York
Times* (February 23, 2011), A13.

[60]For example, *Able v. United States*, 155 F.3d 628 (2d Cir. 1998).

[61]*Lawrence v. Texas*, 539 U.S. 558 (2003).

[62]*Witt v. Department of the Air Force*, 527 F.3d 806 (9th Cir. 2008); Cook v. Gates, 528 F.3d 42 (1st Cir.
2008).

Protection Under State and Local Laws

For most employees, the availability of legal protection from discrimination based on sexual orientation depends on the geographic location of their workplace. Employees in about twenty-one states, in addition to the District of Columbia, enjoy protection under state law.[63] In some other states, only public sector employees are covered. State laws typically proscribe discrimination against any sexual orientation (including heterosexuals) and usually include perceived sexual orientation (regardless of whether the person so identifies). A sizable number of cities address sexual orientation discrimination under municipal laws. *Employers must be aware of and abide by any state and local laws prohibiting discrimination based on sexual orientation.*

Discrimination Based on Gender Identity

Whatever their sexual orientation, some people ("transsexuals") believe that the gender assigned them at birth does not comport with their gender identity and they seek to live as members of the opposite sex (sometimes undergoing hormonal treatments and surgical procedures in the process). *Transgender* is an umbrella term that includes not only transsexuals but also people who cross-dress while retaining their established gender identities and androgynous persons with ambiguous, shifting, or unconventional gender identities. About fourteen states and the District of Columbia have laws prohibiting discrimination based on gender identity or transgender status.[64]

> ### *Clippings*
>
> El' Jai Devoureau was born biologically female but has lived virtually all of his life as a male. He began taking male hormones in 2006 and subsequently had sex change surgery. He has a new birth certificate that identifies him as male. His driver's license identifies him as male and the Social Security Administration changed its records to indicate that he is male. In 2010, Mr. Devoureau was hired as a urine monitor at a drug treatment center. His job was to observe male clients as they produced urine samples for drug testing to ensure that they were not cheating. On his second day on the job, Mr. Devoureau was approached by a manager who said that she had heard that he was transgender. Mr. Devoureau replied that he is male and refused to answer questions about whether he had undergone any surgery. He was immediately terminated. The treatment center claims that being male is a BFOQ for the job and that as a transgender person born female, Mr. Devoureau does not meet that requirement. New Jersey, where this case arose, has a state law prohibiting discrimination based on transgender status.
>
> Richard Pérez-Peña. "In New Jersey, a Job Discrimination Lawsuit's Unusual Question: Who Is a Man?" *New York Times* (April 11, 2011), A18.

Discrimination claims brought by transgender persons under federal law have often been rejected by the courts on the grounds that any such discrimination is not

---

[63]U.S. Government Accountability Office (GAO). *Sexual Orientation and Gender Identity Employment Discrimination: Overview of State Statutes and Complaint Data.* GAO-10-135R (October 1, 2009).

[64]William H. Carlile. "Nevada Governor Signs Bill Banning Discrimination on Basis of Gender Identity." *Daily Labor Report* 100 (May 24, 2011), A-11.

"because of sex." However, in a case involving a firefighter who was subjected to adverse employment actions after he informed his employer regarding his gender identity disorder and began assuming a more feminine appearance in the workplace, the court found that there was sex discrimination in violation of Title VII:

> *Sex stereotyping based on a person's gender non-conforming behavior is impermissible discrimination, irrespective of the cause of that behavior; a label, such as "transsexual" is not fatal to a sex discrimination claim where the victim has suffered discrimination because of his or her gender non-conformity.*[65]

The court distinguished this case from the earlier decisions because, in the interim, the Supreme Court had firmly endorsed the theory of sex-stereotyping in Title VII cases. Another case involving a transsexual police officer removed from a promotional position for being "not masculine enough" was also decided in favor of the plaintiff, and the Supreme Court opted not to review the decision.[66] Perhaps the most sweeping ruling in this area is a decision in favor of a woman whose job offer from the Library of Congress was rescinded after she informed her employer that she would be transitioning from male to female.[67] The court ruled for the plaintiff under the sex-stereotyping theory but also found that discrimination against transgender persons falls directly under the protected class of sex in the same manner that discrimination against an employee who decides to convert to another religion is based on religion. Overall, the law surrounding discrimination against transgender persons is still quite uncertain, but it appears to be shifting in the direction of greater legal protection.

Key Terms

Family and Medical Leave Act (FMLA), p. 351
qualifying event, p. 353
serious health condition, p. 354
period of incapacity, p. 354
continuous leave, p. 364
intermittent leave, p. 364

reduced leave schedule, p. 364
restoration, p. 365
key employee, p. 365
Pregnancy Discrimination Act (PDA), p. 367
Jury System Improvements Act, p. 368

Uniformed Services Employment and Reemployment Rights Act (USERRA), p. 368
escalator principle, p. 373
English-only rules, p. 376
rational relationship standard, p. 378
"don't ask, don't tell" policy, p. 379

Chapter Summary

The Family and Medical Leave Act (FMLA) is the principal federal law affecting the provision of leave for parental and medical reasons. The FMLA entitles employees to up to a total of twelve weeks of leave over a twelve-month period (twenty-six weeks for military caregivers), maintenance of health insurance benefits during leave, and restoration from leave to the same position held prior to leave or an equivalent position. The FMLA prohibits both interference with the exercise of these substantive rights and discrimination (retaliation) against employees for taking leave or filing

charges. Employees are entitled to leave if they work at a site where the employer has at least fifty employees within a seventy-five-mile radius, have worked at least twelve months for that employer, have worked at least 1,250 hours within the past twelve months, and have experienced a "qualifying event." Qualifying events for FMLA leave include the birth, foster care placement, or adoption of a child; the serious health condition of the employee; the serious health condition of a spouse, child, or parent; the serious injury or illness of a family member incurred during active military duty; and

---

[65]Smith v. City of Salem, Ohio, 378 F.3d 566, 575 (6th Cir. 2004).

[66]*Barnes v. City of Cincinnati*, 401 F.3d 729 (6th Cir. 2005), *cert. denied*, 2005 U.S. LEXIS 8238.

[67]*Schroer v. Billington*, 577 F. Supp. 2d 293 (D.D.C. 2008).

"qualifying exigencies" related to the active military duty of a family member. Serious health conditions involve either inpatient care in a medical facility or continuing treatment by a healthcare provider that meets certain other criteria.

Leave policies also must meet the requirements of the Pregnancy Discrimination Act (PDA). The PDA prohibits discrimination based on pregnancy, childbirth, and related medical conditions. Although the PDA does not require that employers offer parental leave, it does mandate that pregnant women be treated the same under employer leave programs as others employees who are similar in their ability or inability to work.

Employees sometimes need time off to attend to civic duties, and there is some legal protection for employees who perform these services. The rights of persons who serve in the military are protected by the Uniformed Services Employment and Reemployment Act (USERRA). The USERRA protects employees from discrimination based on military service and provides for extensive reinstatement rights on return from military service.

Language is an important aspect of diversity. Employer requirements related to language can result in national origin discrimination and violations of Title VII. Accents can lawfully be considered in making employment decisions to the extent that communication is an important aspect of the job in question and the accent interferes with comprehension of the person's words. English-only rules, particularly when broadly applied, are potentially discriminatory, either for their adverse impact or as evidence of harassment or other disparate treatment.

Neither Title VII nor any other federal statute prohibits discrimination based on sexual orientation. Public employees have some protection under the equal protection provisions of the Constitution, but usually only to the extent that the public employer's discrimination based on sexual orientation or behavior bears no rational relationship to a legitimate government purpose. The treatment of gays and lesbians by the military has been the focus of controversy and legal challenges. The military's "don't ask, don't tell" policy has been repealed, but legal questions about the constitutionality of the policy will likely remain. Any protection for private sector employees from discrimination based on sexual orientation comes under state and city laws. Legal protection against discrimination based on gender identity appears to be expanding, under both state laws and Title VII. The latter cases typically depend on the theory of sex-stereotyping to argue that discrimination against transgender persons is due to their nonconformance with established gender roles.

Practical Advice Summary

- For employees who experience qualifying events, request leave, and meet the other eligibility requirements for FMLA leave, employers must
  - Provide up to twelve workweeks of leave over a twelve-month period.
  - Maintain the health insurance of employees on FMLA leave under the same terms that would have prevailed had leave not been taken.
  - Restore employees from FMLA leave by reinstating them to their same jobs or to positions that are equivalent in pay, benefits, and working conditions.
- Employees must be allowed to use any applicable paid leave provided by their employers to substitute for unpaid FMLA leave.
- Employees must be allowed to take leaves on an intermittent basis or as reduced leave schedules when needed to care for serious health conditions.
- In responding to requests for leave, employers must

  - Not attempt to discourage eligible employees from taking leave or attempt to delay the taking of leave.
  - Assess eligibility for leave as of the point in time when leave would commence rather than when leave is initially requested.
  - Promptly respond to employees.
  - Notify employees in writing whether any leave will be designated as FMLA leave.
- If medical certification is required to document the existence of a serious health condition
  - Employees' own doctors should be the primary sources for this information.
  - Employees must be given at least fifteen days to provide such information.
  - Employers must inform employees if their medical documentation is insufficient and provide at least seven additional calendar days to correct the deficiencies.

— Certification by another health care provider can be required at employers' expense if employees provide inadequate information.

- Employers can require that employees
  — Provide at least thirty days' advance notice when the need for leave is foreseeable.
  — Cooperate in minimizing disruptiveness when scheduling medical treatments.
- If certification of fitness for duty is required of other employees returning from medical leaves, an employer should require the same for employees taking FMLA leave.
- Key employees must
  — Be informed of their status.
  — Be told if the employer does not intend to restore them.
  — Be given adequate opportunity to decline or return from leave.
  — Be restored unless restoration would cause substantial and grievous economic injury to the employer.
- Adverse employment decisions should be scrutinized very closely if they involve employees on or recently returned from FMLA leave.
- Employers cannot base adverse employment decisions on the taking of FMLA leave. "No-fault" attendance policies must be discontinued or include exceptions for FMLA leave.
- Employer leave policies
  — Must be included in any employee handbooks that are provided.
  — Must be consistent with the requirements of the FMLA (although they can exceed these).
  — Should spell out the employer's choices about how to administer FMLA leave, including how the relevant twelve-month period is defined.
- If an employer provides sick leave, disability leave, and other forms of leave to people with medical conditions, the same forms of leave on the same terms must be available to pregnant employees.
- Employers must generally allow pregnant employees to work for as long as they can perform their jobs and cannot specify when parental leaves will commence or terminate.
- Employers generally must allow employees time off to vote and serve on juries.
- Employees who have served in the military for up to five years, have been honorably discharged, and have made a timely request for reemployment
  — Must be reinstated by their employers.
  — Must be reinstated into positions they would have attained had they been continuously employed, unless they are unable to perform those jobs.
  — Must be provided with training needed to be able to perform their jobs.
  — Must be reemployed with accrued seniority and benefits.
  — Cannot be terminated for up to a year unless "for cause."
- Employers should consider an applicant or employee's accent only to the extent that
  — Communication is a significant part of the job in question.
  — The individual's accent interferes with the ability to communicate and be understood.
- If employers use English-only rules at all
  — Employees should be clearly informed that these policies are in effect.
  — The rules should be no broader than necessary to accomplish business purposes.
  — Enforcement should not be rigid.
- Employers need to be aware of and abide by any state or local laws that prohibit discrimination based on sexual orientation and gender identity.

Chapter Questions

1. A car salesperson was fired after he missed thirteen days of work to receive treatment for a ruptured disc in his back. The salesperson had worked at this large dealership for five years and then left to work elsewhere. Five years later he returned to the original dealership. After seven and a half months on the job, during which he worked full-time (averaging forty-eight hours per week), the employee suffered the back problem that led to his termination for missed work. He sued. Was the salesperson eligible for FMLA leave? (*Rucker v. Lee Holding Co.,* 471 F.3d 6 [1st Cir. 2006])

2. A company's attendance policy provides that seven chargeable absences within a twelve-month period subject an employee to termination. Categories of absence considered "chargeable" include late arrivals; early departures; unexplained absences; and absences related to illness, injury, or nonqualifying personal reasons. An

employee was absent due to sickness. Because this was her sixth chargeable absence in twelve months, she received a final warning for habitual absenteeism. On October 15, she reported to work, told her supervisor that she was "sick," and left early. The supervisor did not inquire about her sickness or request medical documentation. Nevertheless, the employee submitted a form to the employer indicating that she was seen at the Comprehensive Health Center that day and should be off work from October 15 until October 19. The three days she then took off work resulted in another chargeable absence. She was subsequently terminated for excessive absenteeism. The employee, who was later diagnosed with a head tumor, sued. Did the employer violate the FMLA in enforcing its attendance policy? (*Phillips v. Quebecor World RAI Inc.,* 450 F.3d 308 [7th Cir. 2006])

3. An autoworker who had been on FMLA leave for a serious health condition was given clearance by her doctor and reported to work on June 27, 2000. She had previously worked on the engine line in a position that accommodated physical restrictions that she had from a back injury. The employee was told that no such positions were currently available. A "placement review" was conducted, but a position was not found until July 26. She returned to the engine line on July 31. However, this was a part-time position, and she did not resume full-time work on the engine line until September 18. The employer contended that this delay was due to the combination of her unexpected return, a changeover in models that affected the production process, and the difficulty of finding a position that accommodated her physical restrictions. The employee sued. What should the court decide? Why? (*Hoge v. Honda of America Mfg.,* 384 F.3d 238 [6th Cir. 2004])

4. A company's employees were offered "stay bonuses" as an inducement to remain with the firm during an acquisition by another company. The bonus was offered in 2000 and predicated on employees remaining "employed and actively working for the company as of September 30, 2001." On May 7, 2001, an employee of the company was granted twelve weeks of FMLA leave for the adoption of a child. The employee returned from leave in early August 2001 and remained with the company. However, her stay

bonus was prorated to reflect the twelve weeks that she had been on FMLA leave, resulting in a reduction of some $8,000. The employee sued. What should the court decide? Why? (*Dierlam v. Wesley Jessen Corp.,* 222 F. Supp. 2d 1052 [N.D. Ill. 2002])

5. After becoming pregnant, an employee took occasional FMLA leave to attend medical appointments. The employee subsequently received a doctor's slip diagnosing her with pregnancy and gestational edema and identifying her as totally disabled from that date until "6 wks post partum." The employee gave the employer the doctor's slip and a disability form indicating her "Estimated" return to work date as "6 wk post partum" and her "Expected" delivery date. FMLA leave was granted. The woman delivered her baby and was cleared to return to work seven weeks after the birth of her child. When the employee returned to work, she had taken FMLA leave for a total of fifty-seven workdays during the relevant twelve-month period. She was informed by her employer that she had been expected back at work six weeks after giving birth —and not seven. As such, the employer applied attendance points for each day the employee failed to report to work or notify management of her absence. These absences led the employer, in accordance with its attendance policy, to terminate the employee. She sued. What should the court decide? Why? (*Morr v. Kamco Industries,* 548 F. Supp. 2d 472 [N.D. Ohio 2008])

6. A couple is having a child. They both work for the same employer. Several months before the anticipated birth date, both inform the employer of their need for leave. The employer says that they are limited to a total of twelve weeks of leave between them for the birth. Is the employer correct? Explain. (29 C.F.R. § 825.202 [2011])

7. While on vacation in Honduras, an employee's daughter fell and suffered a serious head injury. The daughter was airlifted to Miami for emergency surgery. The employee contacted his employer and was told to take all of the time he needed. He was forwarded and completed an FMLA leave request form. About three weeks later, while the daughter was still recovering, the employee's wife stayed in Miami with the daughter while the employee returned to the family home in Texas. The return was prompted,

in part, by complaints to the neighborhood association about the untended yard. However, the employee also made modifications to the house, including adding padding to sharp edges, to make the house safer for his daughter's return. The employee remained in daily phone contact with his wife and daughter until they arrived home about two weeks later. The employee returned to work about a week later, which was also the return date indicated on his FMLA leave request. Two days after his return to work, the employee was terminated. Did this employer violate the FMLA? Why or why not? (*Baham v. McLane Foodservice*, 2011 U.S. App. LEXIS 13620 [5th Cir.])

8. An employee's job included receiving merchandise, finding lost delivery items, tracking outgoing packages, filing claims for UPS and Federal Express, devising shipping solutions, developing packaging materials, and formulating process improvements for assembly lines. The employee saw his job responsibilities grow substantially over time. He was given the title of Process Analyst to match his new responsibilities. The employee took FMLA leave to receive treatment for gastroesophageal reflux. He had previously taken leave at least a dozen times without incident. But this time when he returned from leave, he was told to work on the keypad line. This was a production line position, and it required the employee to lift heavy boxes and manually press buttons on phone keypads to ensure the phones functioned properly. He worked in the keypad position for eight days before taking leave for esophageal surgery. When he returned to work again, he had exhausted his annual entitlement to FMLA leave. He was informed that his former Process Analyst position had been permanently phased out because of business needs, but his pay and benefits would not be affected. A manager explained that "in our service business it's hard to hold positions open when we've got to take care of customers every day. So we found a way of working through [his leaves]." The employee sued. Was he restored from leave? Discriminated against for taking leave? (*Breneisen v. Motorola*, 512 F.3d 972 [7th Cir. 2008])

9. A delivery truck driver was in the Army National Guard. He was required to report for drills one weekend per month and for at least two weeks in the summer. His requests for time off were routinely met with resistance by managers. He was told that he should get out of the National Guard and that it was placing a burden on others to cover his shifts. At his supervisor's insistence, the driver had his weekend obligations changed to Wednesdays, his usual day off. However, after 9/11, the National Guard no longer allowed this and he had to report on weekends. When the driver informed his employer that he would be taking time off to fulfill his two-week summer Guard duty, he was told again to "get out" of the Guard. He was given the time off only after the intervention of the HR department. While the driver was away on military duty, an incident was reported in which the driver had hugged an employee of a nursing home that was on his delivery route and left a bruise on her arm. Although the employee said that he was "just fooling around," the nursing home insisted that he not be allowed to deliver to them. The driver was informed on his return from summer drills that he had been terminated based on this incident. The driver sued. What should the court decide? Why? (*Mills v. Earthgrains Baking Companies*, 2004 U.S. Dist. LEXIS 14582)

10. A city police department had a policy allowing police officers who missed shifts due to weekend National Guard activities to work on scheduled days off. This policy made it possible for the officers to perform their National Guard duties and still receive their full week's pay. After about nine years, the policy was rescinded. The police chief cited the potential for scheduling conflicts as the reason for eliminating the policy. A police officer who served in the National Guard sued. Did the city violate the USERRA by changing its policy? Why or why not? (*Crews v. Mt. Vernon*, 567 F.3d 860 [7th Cir. 2009])

11. A supervisor served in the Army Reserve. He reentered active status in February 2007, making it likely that he would soon be deployed. In July 2007, following receipt of an unusually low performance rating, he was placed on a Performance Improvement Program (PIP). Placement on a PIP renders an employee ineligible for promotion and potentially subjects him to discipline or termination. He completed his assigned PIP goals but was informed in November 2007 that his PIP would be extended until after he returned from

military service. The supervisor began a lengthy military deployment in that same month. The stated reasons for the extension were a disrespectful e-mail that he had allegedly sent, but also to allow for verification of his behavior and work habits following his military leave. The supervisor sued. Did the employer violate the USERRA by extending the PIP? Why or why not? (*Vega-Colon v. Wyeth Pharmaceuticals*, 625 F.3d 22 [1st Cir. 2010])

12. Does the Family & Medical Leave Act go far enough? Too far? What, if any, changes would you make to the FMLA?

13. Look again at Chief District Judge Preska's comments in the Bloomberg, L.P. pregnancy discrimination case (see "The Changing Workplace"). What is your reaction to her comments? (See Elissa Gootman, "In Bloomberg L.P. Ruling, Seeing Scorn for Working Mothers, or a Shot of Reality." *New York Times* [August 19, 2011], A18).

14. Should Title VII be amended to prohibit discrimination on the basis of sexual orientation? Gender identity? Why or why not?

PART 4

Pay, Benefits, Terms and Conditions of Employment

CHAPTER 12

Wages, Hours, and Pay Equity

"A fair day's work for a fair day's pay." But what is "fair"? The law does not resolve the question of what is fair pay or impose a general requirement that employees be paid fairly. Instead, employers are prohibited from paying below certain legislatively determined minimum levels of pay and from discriminating in pay. The law has even less to say about what is a fair amount of work time and effort. Rather than regulate hours directly, federal law affects work hours primarily by requiring premium pay for overtime work and by restricting the work hours of minors. This chapter focuses on the Fair Labor Standards Act (FLSA), the principal federal statute regulating wages and hours. It also discusses the Equal Pay Act and other laws bearing on wages, hours, and pay equity.

Wage and Hour Standards: Fair Labor Standards Act

The **Fair Labor Standards Act (FLSA)**[1] establishes a federal minimum wage and requires premium pay for overtime work. It also sets out certain work-hour limitations for minors. The FLSA's main requirements are straightforward. The law's complexity derives from problems in applying its general provisions to the enormous variety that exists among workplaces and compensation practices of employers. Analysis of wage and hour issues is also complicated by the existence of many exceptions ("exemptions") to the FLSA's general requirements.

> *Clippings*
>
> Violations of wage and hour laws are disturbingly common. A study of low-wage workers in Chicago, Los Angeles, and New York found that 68 percent of the more than 4,000 employees interviewed had experienced at least one violation of wage and hour laws in the previous week. The violations amounted on average to a 15 percent reduction in pay for these already low-paid workers. Denial of proper overtime pay was especially common; while 26 percent of the workers interviewed had not been paid at least the minimum wage in the previous week, fully 76 percent of interviewees who had performed overtime work in the previous

---

[1] 29 U.S.C.S. §§ 201–219 (2011); 29 C.F.R. §§ 516–794 (2011).

> week had not received the correct amount of overtime pay for their efforts. Working off the clock, non-receipt of pay stubs, and misappropriation of tips were also widely reported.
>
> Steven Greenhouse. "Low-Wage Workers Are Often Cheated, Study Says." *New York Times* (September 2, 2009), A11.

Minimum Wage

Under the FLSA, *employers must pay employees at a rate no less than the minimum wage for each hour worked during a workweek*. The federal **minimum wage** was increased to $7.25/hr in July 2009 and will remain at that level until such time as Congress decides to change it. The fact that the minimum wage is stated as an hourly rate does not mean that other rates (e.g., weekly pay, piece rates) are prohibited; it only means that when the amount paid for each workweek is converted to an hourly rate, that rate must be equal to or greater than the minimum wage. Nor does the FLSA specify any particular pay period. Payment of the minimum wage and overtime must be prompt, but that generally means in the paycheck covering the relevant workweek (unless state law contains more stringent requirements). To determine whether the minimum wage has been paid, total straight-time (i.e., not overtime) pay for a workweek is divided by total hours worked during that workweek. For example, if an employee worked 35 hours the previous workweek and received $200 in pay for the week, the employee did not receive the full payment due under the FLSA because $200/35 = $5.71/hr. The employer would have had to pay at least $253.75 (35 * $7.25) to be in compliance with the FLSA.

One exception to the general requirement of hourly pay at least equal to the minimum wage is the **opportunity wage**. Employers are permitted to pay employees under 20 years of age at the rate of $4.25/hr for their first ninety calendar days on the job. A condition of the opportunity wage is that it cannot be used to displace or reduce the hours of existing employees.

Another significant exception is for **tipped employees**. These are employees who customarily and regularly receive at least $30 per month in tips. *Under the FLSA, employers can meet their minimum wage obligations to tipped employees by paying them at least $2.13/hr, provided that this amount plus tips equals at least the minimum wage. However, to take advantage of the tip credit, employers must inform employees about it beforehand and allow employees to retain all tips, either individually or pooled among employees.* New DOL regulations elaborate on employers' responsibility to clearly inform employees about such matters as the size of the tip credit being claimed.[2] If tips do not bring employees up to the minimum wage, employers must make up the difference. "Pools" must include only those employees who customarily participate in the sharing of tips and not people unrelated to the services provided. An employer cannot participate in a tip pool, even when the employer performs work that is normally tipped. Thus, a bar owner who also tended bar violated the FLSA by taking the employer tip credit and sharing in pooled employee tips.[3] There appears to be considerable leeway in structuring tip pools. A pooling arrangement in which table servers were required to contribute 3 percent of their gross sales was upheld despite the servers' claim that low tipping rates and the sale of merchandise for which tips were not obtained (e.g., T-shirts) effectively

---

[2] 29 C.F.R. § 531.59 (b) (2011).

[3] *Gionfriddo v. Jason Zink LLC*, 769 F. Supp. 2d 880 (D. Md. 2011).

required them to surrender over a third of their tips.[4] Because pooling of tips is permitted and none of the servers earned less than the minimum wage, it was legal. Employers are also permitted to deduct from tips the transaction fees charged by credit card issuers when tips are paid using credit cards.[5] However, compulsory service charges (e.g., 18 percent added to the bill) are not considered tips and cannot be used for purposes of the tip credit.

JUST THE FACTS

Servers and bartenders at Applebee's are paid $2.13/hr, while the chain avails itself of the tip credit. The servers and bartenders spend a considerable amount of their time performing preparation and cleanup activities that do not generate tips. These employees contend that they should be paid $7.25/hr for the time they spend performing these ancillary duties, rather than $2.13/hr plus tips. What does the FLSA require regarding the payment of employees with "dual jobs" that incorporate substantial amounts of both tipped and non-tipped activities?

See, *Fast v. Applebee's*, 638 F.3d 872 (8th Cir. 2011).

The minimum wage requirement applies to gross pay. Employers are required to withhold income taxes from employees' gross pay as well as the employees' share of Social Security. With employees' consent, deductions can be made for items such as employee contributions to insurance plans, union dues, and savings plans. Additional sums (generally limited to 25 percent of disposable earnings) may be deducted because a court or government agency has ordered an employee's pay to be "garnished" to recover money owed for obligations such as child support, alimony, and student loans. Although deductions for these and other purposes do not affect compliance with the FLSA, *employers are not free to charge employees for items that primarily benefit the employer (e.g., uniforms or the laundering of uniforms, fees to cover breakage) when the effect of those deductions would be to push an employee's hourly wage rate below the minimum wage.* Furthermore, a restaurant that uses the tip credit cannot lawfully deduct any uniform and cleaning expenses from the pay of tipped employees. The reason is that all tips beyond the tip credit that brings the employee up to the minimum wage are employees' property rather than wages. Thus, the effect of any deduction for uniforms would be to take wages below the minimum wage.[6]

Overtime Pay

Under the FLSA, *employers must pay at least one and one-half times an employee's regular rate of pay for each hour worked in excess of forty in a workweek.* Other than for minors, the FLSA does not limit the number of hours employees can be required to work. Instead, the act gives employers a financial incentive to limit **overtime** because those hours of work must be compensated at a premium. That premium is expressed in terms of an employee's **regular rate of pay**. If an employee is paid an hourly wage, the

---

[4]*Kilgore v. Outback Steakhouse of Florida*, 160 F.3d 294 (6th Cir. 1998).

[5]*Gillis v. Twenty Three East Adams Street Corp.*, 2006 U.S. Dist. LEXIS 12994 (N.D. Ill.).

[6]Michael R. Triplett. "Tipped Workers Cannot Agree to Deductions for Uniform Cleaning, DOL Says in Letter." *Daily Labor Report* 131 (July 10, 2006), AA-1.

**Practical
Considerations**
Employers generally
seek to minimize costs
related to overtime
work. What are some
options for
accomplishing this
goal in a lawful
manner?

hourly wage is the regular rate (barring receipt of certain other payments). An employee who earns $8/hr and works forty-four hours in a workweek would be entitled to $8/hr for the first forty hours of work ($8 * 40 = $320) plus $12/hr ($8 * 1.5) for the four overtime hours ($12 * 4 = $48), for a total of $368 for the week. If an employee is paid a weekly sum based on a specified number of hours, such as forty, the regular rate would be the weekly pay divided by 40. However, if the employee is paid a weekly salary for a fluctuating number of hours, the regular rate would be the weekly salary divided by the number of hours actually worked each week. Under this scenario, the regular rate varies from week to week and decreases as the number of overtime hours increases. Computing the regular rate in this manner is nonetheless legal (although a potential labor relations nightmare) provided that the employer previously informed the employee that overtime pay would be calculated in this manner.[7]

The basic unit of time for determining compliance with both the FLSA's minimum wage and overtime requirements is the **workweek**. The workweek is any fixed and recurring period of seven consecutive days (168 hours). The workweek does not necessarily correspond to the calendar week or begin at the start of a workday. Work does not necessarily occur on every day of the workweek. With just a few exceptions, FLSA overtime is earned on a weekly basis. It does not matter how many hours an employee works on a particular day; the relevant issue is the number of hours worked in the workweek. (However, daily overtime might be required under a collective bargaining agreement or state law.) Just as there is no daily overtime under the FLSA, *hours of work generally cannot be averaged across workweeks (e.g., a long workweek followed by a short one) to avoid overtime liability*. However, employers can rearrange hours *within* workweeks (e.g., a long day followed by a shorter day or day off in the same workweek) to avoid incurring overtime liability.

Clippings

Husky Energy Corp. has paid nearly $1 million in back overtime pay to 173 employees at its Lima, Ohio, refinery. When the refinery changed from eight- to twelve-hour shifts, it resulted in employees having alternating workweeks of sixty and twenty-four hours. Rather than pay at the rate of time and a half for the twenty overtime hours worked during employees' sixty-hour weeks, the firm violated the FLSA by establishing a single, adjusted rate for all hours of work. Additionally, the refinery failed to include a shift differential in the regular rate of pay on which overtime pay was based.

Gayle Cinquegrani. "Husky Energy Pays $969,182 in Overtime to 173 Petroleum Refinery Workers in Ohio." *Daily Labor Report* 42 (March 5, 2010), A-2.

Compensatory Time What if an employee who has been working long hours would prefer more time off to overtime pay? The legality of **comp time**—that is, paying for overtime work with compensatory time off rather than overtime pay—depends on whether the employer is in the private or public sector. *Private employers cannot pay for overtime required under the FLSA with compensatory time off in the future, whereas government agencies can.* The explanation for this difference is essentially that public employers were not originally covered by the FLSA, and Congress seized upon comp

---

[7]*Samson v. Apollo Resources*, 242 F.3d 629 (5th Cir. 2001), *cert. denied*, 122 S. Ct. 63 (2001).

time as a means of softening the fiscal impact when public employers became subject to the law.

The ability of public employers to provide comp time in lieu of cash payment for overtime work is subject to certain restrictions. First, it must be in accordance with an agreement to that effect, either with individual employees or with their collective bargaining representative when the public employees are unionized. For most public employees, the maximum amount of comp time that can be banked is capped at 240 hours. Any additional overtime must be paid for in cash. Public employees have the right to use their accrued comp time "within a reasonable period after making the request," but not if taking the compensatory time off would "unduly disrupt the operations of the public agency."[8] However, the need to pay overtime to other employees to provide requested time off does not by itself show that operations of a public agency are being unduly disrupted.[9] The right to use comp time within a reasonable period does not require that the public employer provide time off on the specific day(s) requested, as long as it is provided within a reasonable amount of time.[10] Furthermore, the Supreme Court has ruled that public employers can require that their employees use up accrued comp time against their will.[11] Public employers are also allowed to cash out employees' accrued comp time if they so choose, and employees terminating their employment are entitled to be paid for their unused comp time.

Determining Compliance with Wage and Hour Standards

Determining whether the minimum wage and overtime pay requirements of the FLSA have been met requires accurate information on compensation received, compensable work hours, and the exempt or nonexempt status of employees.

Compensation Received

Compensation takes many forms. Employees receive not only hourly wages or salaries but also tips, commissions, piecework earnings, bonuses, and merit pay; lodging and meals; pay for holidays, vacations, and sick days; premium pay for working on weekends or night shifts; and profit sharing and benefits—among other forms of payment for work. Although wages must generally be paid in cash (i.e., a paycheck), the "reasonable cost" of goods customarily provided by employers for their employees' benefit, such as lodging and meals, can be credited against minimum wage and overtime pay obligations.

Depending on what types of compensation are considered, some of which may be occasional (e.g., certain bonuses) or may not be attached to work performed (e.g., paid sick days), an employee's regular rate of pay might vary substantially. When calculating the regular rate of pay on which overtime pay is based, most forms of compensation must be included. The primary *exclusions* are the following:

- Most paid absences (e.g., vacation, holiday, illness)
- Discretionary bonuses (e.g., not based on merit or attendance) and prizes
- Reimbursements for expenses (e.g., travel, materials)

---

[8]29 U.S.C.S. § 207(o)(5)(B) (2011).

[9]*Beck v. City of Cleveland*, 390 F. 3d 912 (6th Cir. 2004), *cert. denied*, 125 S. Ct. 2930 (2005).

[10]*Mortensen v. County of Sacramento*, 368 F.3d 1082 (9th Cir. 2004).

[11]*Christensen v. Harris County*, 529 U.S. 576 (2000).

Practical Considerations To properly comply with the FLSA's overtime pay requirements, how should employers deal with performance-based bonuses earned on an annual basis?

- Employer payments for pensions and other employee benefits
- Profit-sharing plans
- Many forms of premium pay (e.g., extra pay for working on holidays)
- Daily or other non-FLSA required overtime pay

The city of Albuquerque violated the FLSA by failing to include compensation for unused sick leave ("buy-backs") in the regular rate of pay. Even though paid sick days can be excluded, the buy-backs are more like performance-based bonuses (for good attendance) that must be included when calculating overtime pay.[12]

Not surprisingly, the FLSA contains substantial record-keeping requirements regarding payments to workers and their hours of work. Because FLSA claims can go back as far as three years (for willful violations), *records of wages paid and hours worked must be kept for at least three years.* Shoddy or nonexistent records do not redound to an employer's benefit in court. Inadequate record keeping is a violation in itself, and in the absence of employer documentation, courts will accept employees reasonable estimates of what they are owed.[13] The Department of Labor recently made it easier for employees to systematically track and record their own work hours by offering a free electronic timesheet application for smartphones.[14]

Compensable Time

Besides compensation received, the number of hours worked in a workweek must also be known to determine compliance with the FLSA's requirements. This can be more complicated than simply consulting timesheets. Questions about **compensable time** arise because the workday is often punctuated with breaks, periods of waiting or downtime, and other activities different from the principal work duties of an employee. Conversely, work duties sometimes intrude on time off. Further, it is not always obvious when work begins or ends. Table 12.1 provides examples of activities that are generally treated as compensable time and those that are not compensable.

TABLE 12.1 EXAMPLES OF COMPENSABLE AND NONCOMPENSABLE TIME

GENERALLY COMPENSABLE	GENERALLY NONCOMPENSABLE
Fire drills; and rest periods of twenty minutes or less	Preemployment tests
Employer-required training	Voluntary training that is not related to regular duties, that is outside work hours, and that is during time when work is not performed
Traveling between work sites	Traveling from home to work site
Waiting while on duty	Waiting to start work and waiting after being relieved from duty for a definite and useful time
Restrictive on-call arrangements	Most on-call duty performed outside the workplace
Meal periods when not substantially relieved from duties	Meal periods free of duties (and usually at least thirty minutes)

© Cengage Learning 2013.

---

[12]*Chavez v. Albuquerque*, 630 F.3d 1300 (10th Cir. 2011).

[13]*Marshall v. Partida*, 613 F.2d 1360, 1363 (5th Cir. 1980).

[14]U.S. Department of Labor, Wage & Hour Division. "Wage and Hour Highlights." (May 9, 2011) Viewed August 26, 2011 (http://www.dol.gov/whd/).

There are a few basic principles for determining whether activities are compensable. A starting point is that employers are required to compensate all work that they "suffer or permit." Employers' claims that employees have contributed work without employers' knowledge and against their will are rightly viewed with skepticism. This does not mean that employers are expected to be aware of everything that employees do or that employees can simply perform work anywhere or at any time and present their employers with the bill. *If employers do not want their employees to work extra hours, thereby incurring overtime liability, they must communicate and enforce policies prohibiting employees from working outside of assigned work hours without prior authorization. For these policies to be genuine, supervisors cannot ignore workers starting work early, staying late, or coming in on scheduled days off. Nor should employees be assigned work and given deadlines that effectively require them to work late or take work home. Similarly, employees should not be pressured or allowed to underreport hours worked.* The amount of time actually spent performing work duties—not norms or expectations (e.g., "it usually takes an hour to clean up after the restaurant closes")—determines compensable time. Taking "too long" to carry out some task might need to be addressed as a performance issue, but it is not an excuse for withholding pay from the employee in violation of the FLSA.

Clippings

In recent years, Wal-Mart has experienced an avalanche of suits alleging violations of wage and hour laws. In December 2008, the retailer agreed to pay at least $352 million to settle sixty-three cases that were pending in forty-two states. The cases involved hundreds of thousands of current and former employees. The suits alleged that Wal-Mart managers used a variety of illegal means to keep labor costs low, including forcing employees to work off-the-clock, erasing hours from time cards, and denying breaks and meal periods to employees. This settlement followed other multimillion-dollar settlements of cases brought in California, Pennsylvania, and Minnesota.

Steven Greenhouse and Stephanie Rosenbloom. "Wal-Mart to Settle Suits over Pay for $352 Million." *New York Times* (December 24, 2008), B1.

In *Chao v. Gotham Registry*, the court must decide whether a staffing agency is responsible for overtime work performed by the nurses it provides to hospitals. In so doing, the court makes a strong statement of the principle that work that is "suffered or permitted" is compensable time.

Chao v. Gotham Registry
514 F.3d 280 (2d Cir. 2008)

OPINION BY CIRCUIT JUDGE CARDAMONE:

A typical Gotham placement begins when one of its client hospitals requests a nurse to fill a temporary vacancy or to support hospital personnel during a peak period. Gotham then offers the assignment to a nurse on its register, and the nurse who accepts the position reports directly to the hospital. The nurse is required to sign in and out on daily time sheets, which are compiled and reviewed by the hospital and forwarded to Gotham each week. Gotham is not permitted to go on hospital premises to verify the nurse's hours or otherwise supervise his or her performance. The hospital pays Gotham an hourly fee multiplied by the number of hours worked by the nurse and Gotham pays most of this money to the nurse. * * *

Gotham's clients do not pay Gotham a premium for overtime hours in all cases.... After seeking advice of counsel, the staffing agency adopted a policy designed to check unauthorized overtime or, failing that, insulate itself from claims for time and one-half compensation for unauthorized hours. Gotham's overtime policy is printed on the time sheets completed by its nurses and reads: "You must notify GOTHAM in advance and receive authorization from GOTHAM for any shift or partial shift that will bring your total hours to more than 40 hours in any given week. If you fail to do so you will not be paid overtime rates for those hours."

In the course of their assignments at client hospitals, Gotham nurses are sometimes asked to work overtime by hospital staff. Nurses who agree to work an unscheduled shift will on occasion contact Gotham first to request approval in compliance with Gotham's rule. If Gotham authorizes an assignment, the nurse is guaranteed premium wages for any resulting overtime. But three out of four approval requests are denied. At other times, nurses accept unscheduled shifts without obtaining the staffing agency's approval. When these nurses report their overtime for the preceding week, Gotham attempts to negotiate with the hospital to procure an enhanced fee for the overtime hours already worked. If Gotham succeeds—as it does ten percent of the time—it pays the nurse time and one-half wages for the unauthorized overtime hours. Otherwise, the nurse receives straight-time wages for the extra hours worked. * * *

Gotham is liable for the nurses' compensation for the overtime hours only if it employed the nurses during this time, that is, if it suffered or permitted the nurses to work. It is clear an employer's actual or imputed knowledge that an employee is working is a necessary condition to finding the employer suffers or permits that work.

Information that Gotham's nurses regularly worked overtime was communicated to Gotham each week on the nurses' time sheets. Gotham's insistence that it acquired its knowledge only after the fact misses the point. We have never suggested that an employer's knowledge need arise *concurrently* with the performance of overtime, for good reason. The Act's over-

time provisions apply to work performed off premises, outside of the employer's view and sometimes at odd hours, where an employer's concurrent knowledge of an employee's labor is not the norm. It would appear impractical, for example, to require a K-9 officer to report to his supervisor before and after grooming his dog. Moreover, a requirement of concurrent knowledge would allow employers to escape their obligations under the Act by purposefully eschewing knowledge as to when such work was performed.

We regard Gotham's knowledge as sufficient to afford it the opportunity to comply with the Act. An employer who has knowledge that an employee is working, and who does not desire the work be done, has a duty to make every effort to prevent its performance. This duty arises even where the employer has not requested the overtime be performed or does not desire the employee to work, or where the employee fails to report his overtime hours.

Gotham endeavored to reduce unwanted overtime by promulgating a rule requiring its employees to obtain prior approval for any work that would result in overtime and informing them that, absent such approval, they would be paid straight-time wages for the ensuing overtime. We do not agree with the Secretary's interpretation of Gotham's rule as one that disclaims liability for unauthorized overtime without barring its performance outright. A straightforward reading indicates the rule serves as both a prohibition and a warning as to the consequence of its violation.

Whether Gotham's pre-approval rule satisfied its legal obligation to prevent unwanted overtime involves a question of first impression in this Circuit, complicated by Gotham's limited control over the nurses. Our starting point is the Department of Labor (Department) regulation addressing such rules.

In all such cases it is the duty of the management to exercise its control and see that the work is not performed if it does not want it to be performed.... The mere promulgation of a rule against such work is not enough. *Management has the power to enforce the rule and must make every effort to do so.*

In *Reich v. Dep't of Conservation,* the Eleventh Circuit ... held liable an employer that, like Gotham, had limited concurrent control over its employees' work schedules. The case involved a state agency charged with enforcing game and fish laws, which employed enforcement officers posted throughout the state. The officers, whose job it was to answer citizen complaints around the clock, worked from home under minimal supervision. The state agency promulgated a rule forbidding officers to work more than 40 hours per week, but had actual and constructive knowledge that some officers continued to work overtime without reporting the extra hours. The Eleventh Circuit concluded the agency could not avoid overtime compensation simply by adopting a policy against overtime and issuing periodic warnings.

Gotham's efforts to distinguish *Reich v. Dep't of Conservation* do not convince us. The staffing agency points out that the majority of employees involved in the Eleventh Circuit's case were unable to perform their duties within a 40 hour workweek, while Gotham nurses can fulfill their obligations—at least to Gotham—without incurring overtime. Given this difference, Gotham urges us instead to follow *Lindow v. United States,* where the Ninth Circuit held an employer may insulate itself from overtime claims by notifying its employees that overtime is not expected, so long as the employees can complete their duties within regular hours and are under no pressure to perform overtime. In *Lindow,* employees of the Army Corps of Engineers were in the habit of arriving fifteen minutes early to exchange information with their colleagues working the earlier shift, review the log book, drink coffee, and socialize. A portion of this time was classified by the court as working time. The Corps issued a letter informing its employees that they were not required to arrive early, but some employees continued to do so. The Ninth Circuit held that the letter relieved the Corps of liability for overtime compensation because the Corps did not require or pressure the employees to work overtime and the work could have been performed during regular hours.

In the instant case, the district court found the unauthorized shifts were controlled and required by the hospitals *and* by the employees. It is not obvious to us that the nurses do not on occasion work overtime because they feel unable to satisfactorily perform their duties to hospital supervisors or patients within their scheduled hours. It is plain that *Lindow's* rationale does not extend to employees whose jobs require them on occasion to work beyond regular hours, whether the requirement is enforced by the employer or inherent in the nature of the work.

Even setting aside this concern and assuming that the nurses elect to work overtime without any compulsion to do so, we decline to follow *Lindow.* First, the Supreme Court has rejected the argument that an employer may avoid its obligations under the Act upon proof that its employees voluntarily engage in inadequately compensated work. More generally, … "[t]he reason an employee continues to work beyond his shift is immaterial; if the employer knows or has reason to believe that the employee continues to work, the additional hours must be counted." In other words, once it is established that an employer has knowledge of a worker's overtime activities and that those activities constitute work under the Act, liability does not turn on whether the employee agreed to work overtime voluntarily or under duress. * * * In addition, the scenario presented to us differs from *Lindow* inasmuch as the nurses who were asked to work overtime provided services in addition to those performed during their regular hours and so by definition were unable to complete their work within those regular hours. * * *

In an ordinary employer-employee relationship, management is believed to have ready access to a panoply of practical measures to induce compliance with its formal rule against overtime. In such cases, a presumption arises that an employer who is armed with knowledge has the power to prevent work it does not wish performed. Where this presumption holds, an employer who knows of an employee's work may be held to suffer or permit that work. * * * Gotham seeks to rebut this presumption on the basis that its power to control the nurses is severely constrained by the nature of its business and the labor market in which it deals. Gotham portrays its role as nothing more than an employment agency matching the requirements of hospitals with the qualifications of nurses and maintains that it has no ability to control nurses who violate its rule.

We recognize that Gotham does not have at its disposal all the instruments of control available to ordinary employers. That said, the law does not require Gotham to follow any particular course to forestall unwanted work, but instead to adopt all possible measures to achieve the desired result. Gotham has not persuaded us that it made every effort to prevent the nurses' unauthorized overtime: for example, it did not explain why it could not keep a daily, unverified tally of its nurses' hours and reassign shifts later in the week that would result in overtime; or refuse to assign any shifts to nurses who habitually disregard Gotham's overtime rule. Notably, Gotham admitted at trial that a nurse who disregards its pre-approval rule faces no adverse consequences beyond straight-time wages for the ensuing overtime, while one who disregards Gotham's other policies is subject to contractual penalties. If Gotham were serious about preventing unauthorized overtime, it could discipline nurses who violate the rule. It could also entirely disavow overtime hours, announcing a policy that it does not, under any circumstances, employ a nurse for more than 40 hours in a week. Any hours over the limit would not be billed to the hospital and would not result in any compensation for the nurse (as opposed to the current policy of regular pay). Alternatively, Gotham could simply contract in advance with the hospitals to charge a higher fee when nurses are working overtime, thus shifting the decision to those best placed to judge when overtime is cost-effective and avoiding the need for an anti-overtime policy to begin with.

We confess we are skeptical whether an employer with full knowledge respecting the activities of its employees ever lacks power, at the end of the day, to require those it retains to comply with company rules that implicate federal law. Gotham in any event has not overcome the presumption here that it possessed

such power. It follows that Gotham suffered or permitted the nurses' overtime and, by failing to compensate them in accordance with … [the FLSA]. * * *

CASE QUESTIONS

1. What was the legal issue in this case? What did the court decide?
2. Why did it ultimately not matter that the staffing agency had a policy requiring prior approval of overtime work? That the agency was not in the workplace and had no prior notification of the disputed overtime work?
3. What should the staffing agency have done instead? Would the court's suggestions be workable? Legal?
4. Do you agree with the decision in this case? Should the hospitals that requested the overtime work share in liability for any violations of the FLSA? Explain.

Many questions about compensable time hinge on whether the time in question was or was not spent "predominantly for the benefit of the employee." In cases involving periods of waiting during work hours, courts focus on whether waiting periods were sufficiently long and the surrounding circumstances (e.g., was the employee out somewhere without a vehicle or next door to a mall?) conducive to employees using the time for their own benefit. Employees of an insulation contractor successfully argued that their employer failed to pay them for time spent waiting for assignments and loading the trucks they used to travel to work assignments.[15] The time was compensable because there was evidence that the owner expected them to show up before the official starting time, they needed to be there to get work assignments and meet up with other members of the work crews, and at least part of the time was spent loading trucks with equipment. That they also drank coffee and socialized with one another during this time did not negate the fact that it was spent primarily for the employer's benefit. Situations in which employees are required to remain on-call often raise the same issue. In one such case, nurses required to be on-call while at home were not entitled to compensation for that time because they remained largely free to pursue their own interests.[16] Calls were relatively infrequent. The nurses did not have to remain in their homes provided that they could be contacted and report to the hospital within twenty minutes. The primary restriction on their activities was that they could not use alcohol.

Another principle used by courts is that activities must be sufficiently related to employees' primary job duties to be deemed compensable. Time spent performing activities that are clearly preliminary (i.e., prior to) or postliminary (i.e., following) to the employee's main activities is not compensable unless made so by "contract, custom, or practice."[17] Thus, time spent commuting to and from work is usually not compensable.

Practical Considerations How should employers who need employees to be on-call structure these arrangements to conform with the law while minimizing overtime liability?

[15]*Chao v. Akron Insulation & Supply Inc.*, 184 Fed. Appx. 508 (6th Cir. 2006).
[16]*Reimer v. Champion Healthcare*, 258 F.3d 720 (8th Cir. 2001).
[17]Portal-to-Portal Act, 29 U.S.C.S. § 254(a) (2011).

THE CHANGING WORKPLACE

The Blurring of Work and Nonwork Time

Employer demands on employees outside the workplace raise questions about compensable time that are likely to become more common as communications technology advances and further blurs the boundaries between home and work, and work and nonwork time.[1] For example, it might be "strongly suggested" or required that employees read and respond to e-mail on the weekends. Or employees might be expected while "off the clock" to make arrangements for future travel, look up information, or respond to customer requests—all of which can be easily accomplished from home. As one attorney has put it, "with universal wireless connectivity coming on strong ... it won't be long before nonmanagerial rank-and-file workers are given electronic access to the workplace. And once that happens, lawsuits will follow."[2] And because these devices inherently maintain electronic records of their use, it could prove more difficult for employers to contest the performance of work on their behalf.

A retail specialist for Black & Decker who worked out of his home and commuted to Home Depot stores where the company's products were sold contended that he was pressured to not report the significant amount of time that he spent dealing with company e-mails, voice mails, and sales reports.[3] The plaintiff further argued that since these at-home tasks, which he typically performed right before and after completing his visits to stores, were integral and indispensable to his principal work activity of visiting stores, the time that he spent commuting to the first store visited and back home from the last store visited during the day should also be compensable. The court rejected the latter argument on the grounds that the timing of his at-home work was at his own discretion and that the general rule of commuting time not being compensable still applied. However, the court permitted his claim for uncompensated overtime based on his unreported at-home work to go forward. The employer is ultimately responsible for keeping accurate records and there was sufficient evidence

presented that the employee had performed overtime work of which his supervisors were aware to justify allowing the case to proceed. Likewise, an employee who installed and repaired vehicle recovery systems at clients' locations had to transmit data about his daily activities via a modem provided by his employer. The process could be done only at certain times and the transmissions were not always successful, necessitating additional attempts. The court concluded that this work was integral to the employee's principal activities and that it was not clearly "de minimis."[4]

In contrast, the mere fact that airport police who were issued pagers were required to carry the pagers while off duty and subject to discipline for failing to do so did not render that time compensable.[5] The officers were unable to show that this on-call arrangement was so restrictive that their time was being spent primarily for the benefit of their employer. In perhaps a glimpse of things to come, ABC confiscated company-issued BlackBerry devices from some news employees who refused to sign agreements waiving overtime pay for work performed on the devices outside of scheduled work hours.[6] The situation was resolved through an agreement between the company and the employees' union that some work performed outside work hours using the BlackBerry devices (such as tracking breaking news stories or booking shows) would be compensable, but that routine checking of e-mail would not require overtime pay.

---

[1]Michael Sanserino. "Lawsuits Question After-Hours Demands of Email and Cellphones." *The Wall Street Journal* (August 10, 2009), B1.
[2]David Shadovitz. "Nonexempts Going Wireless?" *Human Resource Executive Online* (May 6, 2008) Viewed May 14, 2008 (http://www.hreonline.com).
[3]*Kuebel v. Black & Decker*, 643 F.3d 352 (2d Cir. 2011).
[4]*Rutti v. Lojack Corp.*, 596 F.3d 1046 (9th Cir. 2010).
[5]*Adair v. Charter County of Wayne*, 452 F.3d 482 (6th Cir. 2006).
[6]"ABC News and Writers Guild Members Agree That Some Blackberry Work Should Be Paid." *Daily Labor Report* 126 (July 1, 2008), A-8.

What about time spent putting on ("donning") and taking off ("doffing") protective clothing and safety equipment? Such time is compensable when these activities are "integral and indispensible" parts of employees' principal work activities—that is, they are required by the nature of the job and not merely matters of personal preference. The Supreme Court determined that the time employees of a meatpacking plant spent walking from the locker rooms in which they donned necessary garb and safety equipment to their workstations—and back at the end of the shift—was compensable.[18] Since the equipment was required to do the job, putting the equipment on was itself a principal activity and the walking time was like any other brief periods of time spent moving about during the workday. However, time spent waiting in line to be issued safety equipment was a step further removed from principal work activities and was not compensable.

Clippings

Polo Ralph Lauren Corporation settled a class action lawsuit brought on behalf of former employees of its stores in California. The suit was based on the stores' practice of making employees wait for up to thirty minutes following the end of their shifts to perform "loss prevention searches" during which employees' bags and other belongings were searched. The employees were not free to leave and were also not paid for their time.

Janet Cecelia Walthall. "Polo, Workers Agree to Settle for $4 Million Claims Based on Bag Searches, Court Says." *Daily Labor Report* 99 (May 25, 2010), A-1.

JUST THE FACTS

Construction workers were hired to complete a building project at the Miami International Airport. To get to the work site, the workers had to pass through a security checkpoint and then ride authorized buses or vans supplied by the construction company. Workers signed in when they reached the work site and received their instructions for the day at that point. Workers were required to carry their personal safety equipment with them through security and on the vans, but otherwise performed no other tasks. A group of workers sued under the FLSA. Was the time spent going through security compensable? The time spent waiting for and riding the company-provided transportation to and from the work site?

See, *Bonilla v. Baker Concrete Construction*, 487 F.3d 1340 (11th Cir. 2007).

Exemptions from FLSA Requirements

Thus far, the FLSA's requirements have been stated as though they apply to all employees. They do not. Employers are exempted (excused) from having to follow some or all of the FLSA's rules for certain types of employees. Some of these exemptions are full

---

[18]*IBP v. Alvarez/Tum v. Barber Foods*, 126 S. Ct. 514 (2005).

FIGURE 12.1 Examples of FLSA Exemptions*

Full Minimum Wage Exemptions	Outside salespersons
	Employees of amusement or recreational establishments having seasonal peaks
	Employees engaged in the fishing industry
	Agricultural employees who work on certain types of farms
Partial Minimum Wage Exemptions	Certain workers with disabilities (subminimum wage allowed with DOL certification)
	Students employed at colleges and universities (payment at 85 percent of the minimum wage is allowed with DOL certification)
Full Overtime Exemptions	Executive, administrative, or professional employees
	Outside salespersons
	Most transportation employees (e.g., motor carriers, railroads, and airlines)
	Taxicab drivers
	Agricultural employees
	Employees of motion picture theatres
Partial Overtime Exemptions	Commission-paid employees of retail and service establishments (commissions take the place of overtime pay if the regular rate of pay is greater than one and a half times the minimum wage and commissions make up at least half of the employee's total compensation)
	Hospital and nursing home employees (14-day period, rather than the workweek, can be used to calculate overtime if the employee is paid overtime for biweekly hours in excess of 80 and for daily hours in excess of 8)

*29 U.S.C. §§ 207(i), (j), 213–214 (2011).

© Cengage Learning 2013.

exemptions (i.e., the rule can be completely disregarded for exempt employees), and other exemptions are partial (i.e., something other than the general rule applies to exempt employees). The terms **exempt** and **nonexempt employees** are used to contrast employees for whom employers do not have to follow FLSA requirements (exempt) with employees entitled to the act's protections (nonexempt). Figure 12.1 lists some examples of FLSA exemptions.

White-Collar Exemptions   The most significant exemptions are for executive, administrative, and professional employees. These occupations are found in all types of businesses and comprise an estimated 20 to 27 percent of the full-time U.S. work-force.[19] Employees holding these jobs often work long hours and earn relatively high rates of pay. That the so-called **white-collar exemptions** (which also include "outside" salespersons) free employers from the obligation to pay overtime to these employees is no small matter. But who is an exempt executive, administrative, or professional employee?

Given the stakes, it is not surprising that employers tend to take a broad view of which employees fit under the umbrella of the white-collar exemptions, whereas

---

[19]United States General Accounting Office. *Fair Labor Standards Act: White-Collar Exemptions in the Modern Work Place.* GAO/HEHS-99-164 (September 1999), 8.

employees are likely to claim that they are nonexempt and entitled to overtime pay. In the face of legal challenges, employers bear the burden of proving that employees denied the act's protections are, in fact, exempt. A common misconception is that whether an employee is exempt turns solely on whether that employee is paid a salary. This is not true—or at best, it is incomplete. To determine whether an individual is or is not an exempt **executive**, **administrative**, or **professional employee**, the nature of that individual's duties and responsibilities must be closely examined (duties test), as well as the manner in which the person is paid (salary basis test). Not everyone paid a salary is an exempt employee. Criteria for determining whether employees fit within the white-collar exemptions are listed in Figure 12.2.

Duties Test As Figure 12.2 shows, exempt status rests in part on applying a **duties test** to determine whether employees' duties are genuinely executive, administrative, or professional in nature. Job titles, by themselves, mean nothing. Calling a secretary an "Administrative Assistant I" does not transform that person into an exempt employee. The burden on employers to establish exempt status provides yet another reason to maintain accurate and up-to-date job descriptions. *An employee's job description should clearly support the determination that he or she is an exempt employee.* The same occupation can be exempt or nonexempt depending on the particular circumstances. For example, reporters, producers, and directors for a TV news program were determined to be nonexempt employees.[20] The court's rationale was lengthy, but it basically came down to the fact that they did not manage other employees (hence, they were not executives), their work was directly related to producing the station's product (hence, they were not administrators), and the news program they worked on was more formulaic than creative or original (hence, they were not creative professionals). Yet, in another case involving TV news writers and producers at a different station, the court found that their duties were sufficiently original and creative to warrant exemption as professionals.[21]

FIGURE 12.2 Tests for Executive, Administrative, and Professional Employee Status*

Executive Employees	• Have as their primary duty the management of an enterprise, department, or other customarily recognized sub-unit of a company. • Customarily and regularly direct the work of two or more full-time employees or their equivalent. • Have the authority to hire or fire other employees or have particular weight given to suggestions and recommendations concerning hiring, firing, advancement, promotion, or any other change in the status of other employees. • Paid a salary of at least $455/wk. • "Highly compensated" employees paid at least $100,000 annually (which must include at least $455/wk paid on a salary basis) are exempt if they have an identifiable executive function, even if they do not meet all the duties test criteria.

[20]*Dalheim v. KDFW-TV*, 918 F.2d 1220 (5th Cir. 1990).

[21]*Freeman v. National Broadcasting Co.*, 80 F.3d 78 (2d Cir. 1996).

FIGURE 12.2 continued

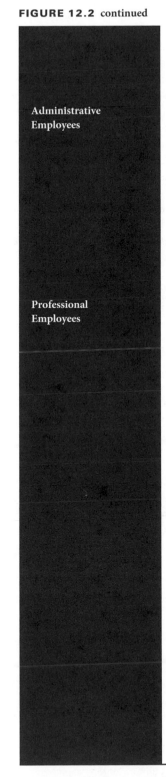

Administrative Employees	• Employees who have at least a 20 percent ownership interest in the enterprises that employ them and who are actively engaged in management of those enterprises are exempt without regard to the above criteria.
	• Primary duty is performing office or nonmanual work directly related to the management or general business operations of an employer or the employer's customers.
	• Primary duty includes the exercise of discretion and independent judgment with respect to matters of significance.
	• Paid a salary of at least $455/wk.
	• "Highly compensated" employees paid at least $100,000 annually (which must include at least $455/wk paid on a salary basis) are exempt if they have an identifiable administrative function, even if they do not meet all of the duties test criteria.
Professional Employees	• Primary duty is work that requires advanced knowledge, is predominantly intellectual in character, and entails the consistent exercise of discretion and judgment. The advanced knowledge must be in a field of science or learning and be customarily acquired by a prolonged course of specialized intellectual instruction ("learned professionals") or have as their primary duty work that requires invention, imagination, originality, or talent in a recognized field of artistic or creative endeavor ("creative professionals").
	• Paid a salary of at least $455/wk (or for skilled computer employees only, an hourly rate of at least $27.63).
	• Teachers are exempt without regard to other criteria if their primary duty is teaching, tutoring, instructing, or lecturing in the activity of imparting knowledge and if they are employed in this activity by an educational establishment.
	• Computer employees are exempt if they are employed as systems analysts, programmers, software engineers, or other similarly skilled occupations. Their primary duties must include the likes of applying systems analysis techniques, consulting with users, and designing or developing computer systems and programs.
	• Employees holding valid licenses or certificates to practice law or medicine and who are actively engaged in such practice are exempt without regard to other criteria.
	• "Highly compensated" employees paid at least $100,000 annually (which must include at least $455/wk paid on a salary basis) are exempt if they have an identifiable professional function, even if they do not meet all the duties test criteria.

*29 C.F.R. §§ 541.119, 541.214, 541.303, 541.314, 541.315 (2011).

Jobs frequently entail a mixture of exempt and nonexempt activities. Courts have to determine whether the **primary duties** of an employee are exempt in nature. While exempt work normally consumes more than half of an exempt employee's work time, the primary duties of an employee are not necessarily those performed most regularly. In addition to the share of work time allocated to the activity, other factors to consider include the relative importance of the exempt duties as compared with other types of duties; the employee's relative freedom from direct supervision; and the relationship between the employee's salary and the wages paid to other employees for the kind of nonexempt work performed by the employee.[22] The manager of a Family Dollar Store was found to be an exempt executive even though she alleged that she spent as much as 99 percent of her time performing such nonexempt duties as unloading merchandise, stocking shelves, running a cash register, and cleaning the store.[23] The court emphasized that at all times she was the person responsible for the store and its employees. She carried out this basic oversight duty concurrent with her nonexempt activities and with relative freedom from supervision.

Correctly identifying "administrative" employees poses particular problems. Merely performing office work or brushing shoulders with managers is not enough to confer exempt status. The fundamental criterion is whether the individual performs primarily office or nonmanual duties that relate to the general operations and policies of the company, as opposed to producing the goods or services that it sells. In a case involving a woman who was the "office manager" and "bookkeeper" for a consulting firm, the court decided that her job included enough exempt activities to make her a bona fide administrative employee.[24] The woman spent much of her time keeping the books, an activity that DOL regulations indicate is not sufficient to demonstrate exempt administrative work. However, she was also involved in policy decisions and supervised accounts receivable and payable, purchase orders, and payroll records.

Another important criterion for identifying administrative employees is the "exercise of discretion and independent judgment with respect to matters of significance."[25] This is often a telling factor in distinguishing bona fide administrative employees from glorified secretaries and clerical workers. To exercise discretion and independent judgment, an employee, free from immediate supervision or direction, must have the authority to consider possible courses of action and make independent choices regarding significant matters. The employee must do more than merely use skill "in applying well-established techniques, procedures, or specific standards described in manuals or other sources."[26] In the case of the office manager mentioned earlier, the court found evidence of independent judgment in the fact that the woman participated in senior staff meetings and made recommendations in the areas of insurance policies, hiring, firing, and banking. In contrast, an interviewer who merely screens candidates for hiring according to preestablished criteria is not exercising discretion and independent judgment.

Clippings

Levi Strauss & Co. has agreed to pay more than $1 million in back overtime pay to 596 employees. The Wage and Hour Division of the Department of Labor had

---

[22]29 C.F.R. § 541.700 (2011).

[23]*Grace v. Family Dollar Stores*, 637 F.3d 508 (4th Cir. 2011).

[24]*Gagnon v. Resource Technology, Inc.*, 19 Fed. Appx. 745 (10th Cir. 2001).

[25]29 C.F.R. § 541.202(a) (2011).

[26]29 C.F.R. § 541.202(e) (2011).

found that the firm misclassified assistant store managers as exempt, along with a variety of office employees who worked out of the company's headquarters.

Gayle Cinquegrani. "Levi Strauss to Pay $1 Million in Overtime to 596 Store and Headquarters Employees." *Daily Labor Report* 61 (March 30, 2011), A-2.

In *Whalen v. J.P. Morgan Chase*, the court considers an employer's attempt to invoke the administrative employee exemption to defend an employee's FLSA claim for unpaid overtime work. The court's decision rests squarely on its application of the duties test criteria.

Whalen v. J.P. Morgan Chase
587 F.3d 529 (2d Cir. 2009), *cert. denied*, 130 S. Ct. 2416 (2010)

OPINION BY CIRCUIT JUDGE LYNCH:

This appeal requires us to decide whether underwriters tasked with approving loans, in accordance with detailed guidelines provided by their employer, are administrative employees exempt from the overtime requirements of the Fair Labor Standards Act. Andrew Whalen was employed by J.P. Morgan Chase ("Chase") for four years as an underwriter. As an underwriter, Whalen evaluated whether to issue loans to individual loan applicants by referring to a detailed set of guidelines, known as the Credit Guide, provided to him by Chase. The Credit Guide specified how underwriters should determine loan applicant characteristics such as qualifying income and credit history, and instructed underwriters to compare such data with criteria, also set out in the Credit Guide, prescribing what qualified a loan applicant for a particular loan product. Chase also provided supplemental guidelines and product guidelines with information specific to individual loan products. An underwriter was expected to evaluate each loan application under the Credit Guide and approve the loan if it met the Guide's standards. If a loan did not meet the Guide's standards, certain underwriters had some ability to make exceptions or variances to implement appropriate compensating factors. Whalen and Chase provide different accounts of how often underwriters made such exceptions.

Under the Fair Labor Standards Act (FLSA), employers must pay employees overtime compensation for time worked in excess of forty hours per week. Whalen claims that he frequently worked over forty hours per week. A number of categories of employees are exempted from the overtime pay requirement. * * * One categorical exemption is for employees who work in a "bona fide executive, administrative, or professional capacity."

At the time of Whalen's employment by Chase, Chase treated underwriters as exempt from the FLSA's overtime requirements. Whalen sought a declaratory judgment that Chase violated the FLSA by treating him as exempt and failing to pay him overtime compensation. * * * The district court denied Whalen's motions and granted Chase's motion, dismissing Whalen's complaint. This appeal followed. * * *

Exemptions from the FLSA's requirements "are to be narrowly construed against the employers seeking to assert them and their application limited to those establishments plainly and unmistakably within their terms and spirit." * * * Federal regulations specify ... that a worker is employed in a bona fide administrative capacity if she performs work "directly related to management policies or general business operations" and "customarily and regularly exercises discretion and independent judgment." Regulations further explain that work directly related to management policies or general business operations consists of "those types of activities relating to the administrative operations of a business as distinguished from 'production' or, in a retail or service establishment, 'sales' work." Employment may thus be classified as belonging in the administrative category, which falls squarely within the administrative exception, or as production/sales work, which does not. * * *

The line between administrative and production jobs is not a clear one, particularly given that the item being produced ... is often an intangible service rather than a material good. Notably, the border between administrative and production work does not track the level of responsibility, importance, or skill needed to perform a particular job. The monetary value of the loans approved by Whalen as an underwriter, for example, is irrelevant to this classification: a bank teller might deal with hundreds of thousands of dollars each month whereas a staffer in human resources never touches a dime of the bank's money, yet the bank teller is in production and the human resources staffer performs an administrative position. Similarly, it is irrelevant that Whalen's salary was relatively low or that he worked in a cubicle. What determines whether an underwriter performed production or administrative functions is the nature of her duties, not the physical conditions of her employment.

* * * In 2004, the Department of Labor promulgated new regulations discussing, among other things, employees in the financial services industry. Although these regulations were instituted after Whalen's employment with Chase ended, the Department of Labor noted that the new regulations were "[c]onsistent with existing case law." The regulation states:

> Employees in the financial services industry generally meet the duties requirements for the administrative exemption if their duties include work such as collecting and analyzing information regarding the customer's income, assets, investments or debts; determining which financial products best meet the customer's needs and financial circumstances; advising the customer regarding the advantages and disadvantages of different financial products; and marketing, servicing or promoting the employer's financial products. However, an employee whose primary duty is selling financial products does not qualify for the administrative exemption.

As an under writer, Whalen's primary duty was to sell loan products under the detailed directions of the Credit Guide. There is no indication that underwriters were expected to advise customers as to what loan products best met their needs and abilities. Underwriters were given a loan application and followed procedures specified in the Credit Guide in order to produce a yes or no decision. Their work is not related either to setting "management policies" nor to "general business operations" such as human relations or advertising, but rather concerns the "production" of loans—the fundamental service provided by the bank.

Chase itself provided several indications that they understood underwriters to be engaged in production work. Chase employees referred to the work performed by underwriters as "production work." Within Chase, departments were at least informally categorized as "operations" or "production," with underwriters encompassed by the production label. Underwriters were evaluated not by whether loans they approved were paid back, but by measuring each underwriter's productivity in terms of "average of total actions per day" and by assessing whether the underwriters' decisions met the Chase credit guide standards. Underwriters were occasionally paid incentives to increase production, based on factors such as the number of decisions underwriters made. * * * Paying production incentives to underwriters shows that Chase believed that the work of underwriters could be quantified in a way that the work of administrative employees generally cannot.

We conclude that the job of underwriter as it was performed at Chase falls under the category of production rather than of administrative work. Underwriters at Chase performed work that was primarily functional rather than conceptual. They were not at the heart of the company's business operations. They had no involvement in determining the future strategy or direction of the business, nor did they perform any other function that in any way related to the business's overall efficiency or mode of operation. It is undisputed that the underwriters played no role in the establishment of Chase's credit policy. Rather, they were trained only to apply the credit policy as they found it, as it was articulated to them through the detailed Credit Guide.

Furthermore, we have drawn an important distinction between employees directly producing the good or service that is the primary output of a business and employees and performing general administrative work applicable to the running of any business. * * * [A]dministrative functions such as management of employees through a human resources department or supervising a business's internal financial activities through the accounting department are functions that must be performed no matter what the business produces. For this reason, the fact that Whalen assessed creditworthiness is not enough to determine whether his job was administrative. The context of a job function matters: a clothing store accountant deciding whether to issue a credit card to a consumer performs a support function auxiliary to the department store's primary function of selling clothes. An underwriter for Chase, by contrast, is directly engaged in creating the "goods"—loans and other financial services—produced and sold by Chase.

This conclusion is also supported by persuasive decisions of our sister circuits. In *Bratt v. County of Los Angeles*, the Ninth Circuit held that the "essence" of an administrative job is that an administrative employee participates in "the running of a business, and not merely … the day-to-day carrying out of its affairs." * * * More recently, the Ninth Circuit expanded, "The administration/production distinction thus distinguishes between work related to the goods and services which constitute the business' marketplace offerings and work which contributes to 'running the business itself.'" The Third Circuit has also noted that production encompasses more than the manufacture of tangible goods. * * * The Third Circuit held that telephone salespersons were production employees because the goal of the salespersons was "to *produce* wholesale sales." [In contrast], the First Circuit held that marketing representatives charged with cultivating and supervising an independent sales force were exempt administrative employees, as their primary duties of educating and organizing salespeople were "aimed at promoting … customer sales *generally*," not "routine selling efforts focused simply on particular sales transactions."

Other out-of-circuit cases similarly support the logic that context matters. An employee whose job is to evaluate credit who works in the credit industry is more likely to perform a production job. Employees who evaluate and extend credit on behalf of a company that is not in the credit industry—extending credit in order to allow customers to purchase a tangible good that the employer manufactured, for example—are generally considered administrative employees. But in the context of such businesses, such employees provide adjunct, general services to the overall running of the business, while at Chase, underwriters such as Whalen are the workers who produce the services—loans—that are "sold" by the business to produce its income.

* * * Accordingly, we hold that Whalen did not perform work directly related to management policies or general business operations. Because an administrative employee must *both* perform work directly related to management policies or general business operations *and* customarily and regularly exercise discretion and independent judgment, we thus hold that Whalen was not employed in a bona fide administrative capacity. We need not address whether Whalen customarily and regularly exercised discretion and independent judgment.

The judgment of the district court in favor of the appellee is REVERSED.

CASE QUESTIONS

1. What is the legal issue in this case? What did the court decide?
2. What are the criteria for determining whether an employee is exempt as an administrative employee? How does the court apply these criteria to the facts of this case to reach its decision?
3. Although the court did not need to decide this issue, does it appear that this employee regularly exercised discretion and independent judgment?
4. Are production and administration really a dichotomy? Isn't it possible for a job to be neither of these?

JUST THE FACTS

An employee was hired as a "product design specialist II." The job pays an annual salary of $62,000. The job description calls for at least twelve years of experience, but it does not specify any educational requirements. The employee came to the job with twenty years of experience as a draftsperson, detailer, and designer. He also had three years of experience with hydraulic power units (HPUs). However, he did not have a college degree. He was given principal responsibility for drafting plans for HPUs. The company classified the position as exempt and the employee did not contest this designation or demand overtime pay during the three years that he worked for the company. However, after he was terminated in a downsizing, the employee sued, claiming that he should have been paid for his overtime work. The company claimed that he was exempt. What should the court decide?

See, *Young v. Cooper Cameron*, 586 F.3d 201 (2d Cir. 2009)

Salary Basis Test   To be exempt, executive, administrative, and professional employees must also be paid salaries. Employees must be paid at least $455/week to qualify for any of the white-collar exemptions. Pay of more than $100,000/year creates a presumption of exempt status. But the most interesting legal questions surround not the amount of pay, but whether the method of payment is truly a salary.

A salary can be contrasted with an hourly wage, in which pay is closely calibrated to time put in, or with a piece-rate system, in which pay is directly geared to the volume of output. A **salary** is a pre-specified sum that an employee is paid for discharging the responsibilities associated with a position. The amount of time needed to do so and the quality or quantity of work output will likely vary from week to week and are not the bases for payment. Employers certainly benefit when salaried, exempt employees put in long hours for no extra pay. But what about when salaried employees work fewer hours than expected? Certain employer policies can pose questions about whether employees are truly paid on a salary basis and, hence, whether those employees are exempt from the FLSA's overtime pay requirements.

Suppose, for example, that an exempt employee takes the afternoon off to attend to personal business and her employer deducts these hours from her pay. Or suppose that the computer system crashes and the employer sends everyone besides the IT people home, while subsequently reducing the pay of exempt employees. If employees have their pay reduced for time not worked on such occasions, are they really being paid on a **salary basis**? Employers cannot have it both ways—enjoying the benefit of employees' lengthy hours without overtime obligations, but penalizing employees for working fewer hours than expected. And if employees are not paid on a salary basis, they are not exempt from the FLSA's requirements, regardless of how obviously executive, administrative, or professional their duties. This approach to determining whether employees are paid on a salary basis is known as the DOL's **pay docking rule**.

Clippings

A federal judge ruled in favor of some 400 store managers of the Gristedes grocery chain on their FLSA and state law claims for overtime pay. The company had failed to properly record and compensate overtime work by store managers. The store managers were not exempt executive employees because, in the words of the judge, Gristedes had "clearly sought to treat workers as 'hourly' for some purposes (i.e., docking them for hours not worked during the workweek), but 'salaried' for other purposes (i.e., not paying them overtime for hours worked in excess of the workweek)." The evidence in the case, including the payroll director's testimony that store managers were paid only for time worked, led to the conclusion that

> "no reasonable juror could find that Gristedes intended to compensate the class members on a salary basis."
>
> John Herzfeld. "New York City Grocery Chain Employees Win Summary Judgment in Overtime Case." *Daily Labor Report* 172 (September 5, 2008), A-5.

Under the pay docking rule, exempt employees must receive predetermined amounts of pay not subject to reduction due to variations in the quantity or quality of work performed. Employers cannot reduce pay for partial-day absences for personal reasons; time missed due to jury duty, court appearances as a witness, and temporary military leave; and for absences occasioned by the employer or the operating requirements of the business when the employee is otherwise ready and able to work. However, exempt status is not jeopardized by deductions for absences of a day or more for personal reasons, for absences due to sickness or accidents (provided that the employer has a policy for compensating employees when days are lost to sickness or accidents), for unpaid disciplinary suspensions of one or more full days "imposed in good faith for infractions of workplace conduct rules," for hours not worked in the first and last week of employment, and for periods of unpaid leave under the FMLA.[27]

To be absolutely clear, the pay docking rule does not make it illegal for an employer to do any of these things. Rather, the consequence of making prohibited deductions from the pay of exempt employees is that those employees may no longer be considered exempt because they are not paid a genuine salary. If the employer is found to have an actual practice of making improper deductions, exempt status will be lost for all employees who have the same job classification as the employee bringing the complaint and who work for the same manager(s) responsible for the deductions. However, an employer can still avoid this outcome by having a clearly communicated policy prohibiting improper deductions and providing a complaint mechanism, reimbursing employees for any improper deductions, and making a "good faith commitment" to comply in the future.[28]

A group of otherwise exempt white-collar employees was found to be not exempt because their employer made deductions from their base salary.[29] The deductions were made to recover monthly bonus payments based on year-to-date performance in situations where the employees' subsequent performance fell below minimum expectations. In contrast, the exempt status of a group of employees was not lost even though the employer used a single payroll system that required all of its employees, exempt and nonexempt, to report their hours and did not pay salaried employees their full salaries unless they reported at least forty hours of work. Additionally, the employer elected to pay exempt employees at their straight time rate for hours worked in excess of forty in a workweek. The court was satisfied that the employer had a policy against pay docking and that improper payments due to incorrect reporting of hours or other errors were relatively few in number, inadvertent, and corrected by the employer. The tracking of hours—although arguably inconsistent with exempt status—did not by itself violate DOL regulations. Nor did the voluntary provision of overtime pay at a straight-time rate; the regulations only proscribe reductions in pay.[30]

---

[27]29 C.F.R. § 541.602 (2011).

[28]29 C.F.R. § 541.603 (2011).

[29]*Baden-Winterwood v. Life Time Fitness*, 566 F.3d 618 (6th Cir. 2009).

[30]*Acs v. Detroit Edison Co.*, 444 F.3d 763 (6th Cir. 2006).

While it should be relatively easy for employers to avoid running afoul of the pay docking rule, payment on a salary basis is still a requirement for exempt status. Thus, *employers should be careful not to dock the pay of exempt executive, administrative, or professional employees for lack of available work to perform, partial-day absences for personal reasons, and time spent on jury duty. Employers should establish and communicate clear policies prohibiting improper deductions from the pay of exempt employees and providing a mechanism for handling complaints about any such deductions. Employees who are nonetheless subjected to improper deductions should be promptly reimbursed.*

Other Wage Laws

Most states have their own wage and hour laws. The FLSA permits states to establish minimum wages higher than the federal minimum wage. Eighteen states (e.g., California, Alaska, Vermont, Massachusetts) had state minimum wages higher than the federal minimum wage in 2011. Four had minimum wages lower than the federal minimum, but these applied only to small firms not covered by the FLSA (generally, companies with revenues less than $500,000 per year).[31] Minimum wage laws in several states (e.g., Ohio, Colorado) have the interesting feature that, unlike the federal minimum wage, the state minimum wage is adjusted annually with changes in the cost of living. Thus, state wage and hour laws define minimum pay levels for a large part of the U.S. workforce. State wage laws are also important because they serve as a basis for suits to recover unpaid wages and establish requirements for when wages, including final paychecks, must be paid.

Employers incur additional legal obligations to their employees (e.g., affirmative action) when they contract to provide goods or services to the government. Several federal laws require payment of a **prevailing wage** for government contract work. These laws include the **Davis-Bacon Act** (construction contracts) and the **McNamara-O'Hara Service Contract Act** (contracts for many different types of services). The prevailing wage is the average wage paid to a class of employees in the relevant geographic area. This amount is determined by the DOL.

The inadequacy of the minimum wage has sparked campaigns for **living wage** laws. These laws mandate levels of hourly pay in excess of federal and state minimums. Nearly 150 communities have passed living wage laws, including the cities of Baltimore, Chicago, Los Angeles, New York, Milwaukee, Minneapolis, and Cincinnati. In 2007, Maryland became the first state to enact a statewide living wage law.[32] This law requires that employers with state contracts pay employees at least $11.30/hr in the Baltimore-Washington area and at least $8.50/hr in the rural counties of Maryland. However, the reach of these laws is limited. They typically apply only to companies doing business with and/or receiving some form of financial assistance (e.g., tax abatements, grants) from municipalities—and sometimes to municipal employees. Further, some of the laws require payment of a living wage only for particular types of contracts (e.g., janitorial services). So far, living wage laws have weathered the inevitable legal challenges from employers. Berkeley, California's living wage ordinance has been upheld against a constitutional challenge.[33] Santa Fe's living wage law, which—unlike most such statutes—applies to all private businesses in the city with at least twenty-five employees, has also been upheld.[34]

---

[31]U.S. Department of Labor. "Minimum Wage Laws in the States—January 1, 2011." Viewed August 27, 2011 (http://www.dol.gov/whd/minwage/america.htm).

[32]Steven Greenhouse. "Maryland Is First State to Require Living Wage." *New York Times* (May 9, 2007), A-18.

[33]*RUI One Corp. v. City of Berkeley*, 371 F.3d 1137 (9th Cir. 2004), *cert. denied*, 2005 U.S. LEXIS 290.

[34]*New Mexicans for Free Enterprise v. City of Santa Fe*, 138 N.M. 785 (App. Ct. 2005).

Thus, employers must be aware that, depending on geographic location and dealings with government entities, they might be required to pay a state minimum wage, prevailing wage, or municipal living wage that exceeds the federal minimum wage.

What about Farmworkers?

The people who put food on our tables, many of them migrant laborers who follow the crops that need harvesting, have historically endured some of the lowest wages and most substandard living and working conditions of all employees. Despite their often wretched working conditions and the fact that many farmworkers are employed by large agribusinesses, the image of bucolic family farms has dominated policy making and left agricultural workers with minimal legal protection. The FLSA does little for farmworkers. Agricultural employees, even if they work for covered firms, are completely exempted from the act's overtime provisions, largely exempted from the minimum wage, and in some cases even excluded from the FLSA's child labor provisions.

The **Migrant and Seasonal Agricultural Worker Protection Act (MSPA)**[35] covers most seasonal agricultural employees. Its provisions are basic but nonetheless important to farmworkers. The MSPA requires registering farm labor contractors with the DOL, making full written disclosure of the terms and conditions of employment in the employee's language at the time of recruitment, paying all wages owed to employees, maintaining and retaining wage and hour records, refraining from the practice of forcing employees to purchase services from their employers (the "company store"), giving assurance that any housing provided is safe and sanitary, and providing for the safe transportation of employees. Notably, the MSPA does not establish a minimum pay level, much less an entitlement to overtime pay.

Nor is agriculture the only industry where nonpayment of wages and subhuman working conditions are problems. The garment industry, both internationally and domestically, has long been known for its **sweatshops**. The term *sweatshop* is not a legal term but generally refers to firms that pay very low wages for long hours of work, provide unsafe conditions, and staunchly oppose unionization. Consumers, including college students purchasing pricey hats and sweatshirts with university logos, are increasingly questioning the terms and conditions under which those items are produced. Although the FLSA ostensibly applies to many garment workers in the United States, fly-by-night operations and intimidation of immigrant workers undermine the enforcement of basic standards. For many workers at or near the bottom of the labor market, even the minimum standards of the FLSA and other wage laws remain elusive.

Limitations on Work Hours

The FLSA provides employers with an economic incentive to minimize overtime work (i.e., the premium that must be paid for each overtime hour worked by a nonexempt employee), but it does not directly limit the number of hours that most employees can be required to work. Nor does the act require that employers provide rest periods, breaks, or time for meals. There are compelling safety, productivity, and labor relations reasons for doing so anyhow, but with the exception of regulations pertaining to particular groups such as airline pilots and truck drivers, federal law is largely silent on this matter. Some states, however, mandate breaks or meal periods. An interesting recent development is that, as part of health insurance reform, the FLSA was amended to require employers with fifty or more employees (and smaller employers, if they would

---

[35]29 U.S.C.S. § 1801 *et seq.* (2011).

not incur undue hardship) to provide reasonable amounts of break time (unpaid) and private places for nursing mothers to express breast milk.[36]

Although the FLSA does not generally limit hours worked, it does prohibit **oppressive child labor**. This requirement affects hours of work for minors. The federal minimum age for employment is 16. However, to perform certain hazardous occupations (e.g., mining, logging, roofing, using power-driven meat slicers), employees must be at least 18 years of age. *Minors (14–15 years of age) can be employed in certain service or retail occupations, subject to restrictions on their hours of work. When school is in session, minors must be employed outside of school hours between 7 A.M. and 7 P.M., not more than three hours per day, and not more than eighteen hours per week. When school is not in session, minors can work up to eight hours in a day and forty hours in a week. In the summer, the workday of minors can be extended to 9 P.M.*

To comply with the FLSA's child labor requirements, employers must ascertain the ages of their youthful employees. Doing so, even in a preemployment context, does not violate the ADEA because the protected class is employees 40 years of age and older. "Working papers" are not mandated by the FLSA, although some states require them. *Managers putting together work schedules should take into account the lesser flexibility they have in assigning minors* (e.g., minors cannot be asked to "hang around for another hour because it's busy" if doing so would violate the FLSA). Undoubtedly, in many cases, the FLSA's hours limitations for minors are winked at by employers and employees alike, but there is evidence that excessive work hours can harm teens (e.g., lower grades, greater alcohol use).[37] No matter how complicit minors are in violating the law, it is employers who are legally responsible for compliance.

Discrimination in Pay: Equal Pay Act

Pay disparities based on any protected class characteristics are discriminatory, but pay discrimination based on sex is a particular concern. A substantial gap still exists between the earnings of full-time male workers and full-time female workers. In terms of median weekly pay, full-time female workers earned about 81 percent of what their male counterparts earned in 2010.[38] Many factors undoubtedly account for the persistent male-female earnings gap. To what extent is discrimination in pay one of these?

Identifying discrimination in pay is particularly challenging. Pay determinations are often highly individualized. Pay is influenced by a multitude of factors, including the going rate in the labor market, an organization's pay policies and pay structure, the conditions under which the job is performed (e.g., shift, location), the demands of the job, and a host of individual characteristics (e.g., seniority, education, merit). More than most other employment decisions, pay determinations are subject to negotiation and are affected by prior decisions that might reach back far in time (e.g., starting pay, adjustments in pay structures intended to deal with particular problems and carried forward in time). Sorting through these complexities requires an approach somewhat different from that used in other discrimination cases. A methodology for proving pay discrimination has been developed for **Equal Pay Act (EPA)**[39] cases. The Equal Pay Act is targeted specifically at pay discrimination based on sex. *Employers are prohibited from*

---

[36]29 U.S.C.S. § 207 (r) (2011).

[37]Steven Greenhouse. "Problems Seen for Teenagers Who Hold Jobs." *New York Times* (January 29, 2001), A-1.

[38]"BLS Says Wage Gap Narrowed in 2010 as Women Earned 81.2 Percent of Men's Pay." *Daily Labor Report* 137 (July 18, 2011), A-10.

[39]29 U.S.C.S. § 206(d) (2011).

paying a person of one sex at a lower rate of pay than a person of another sex for perform-ing substantially equal work in the same establishment—unless the differential in pay is accounted for by a legitimate "factor other than sex."

ELEMENTS OF A CLAIM

Pay Discrimination

To establish a **prima facie case of pay discrimination** under the Equal Pay Act, the plaintiff must show the following:

- There is one or more persons of the opposite sex working in the same estab-lishment (i.e., the comparator)
- The comparator receives a higher rate of pay
- The comparator performs work substantially equal to that performed by the plaintiff.

   If a prima facie case is established, the employer must show that the challenged differential in pay is explained by one or more of the following:

- A seniority system
- A merit pay system
- A system that bases pay on the quality or quantity of production
- Some other factor other than sex

Proving Pay Discrimination under the Equal Pay Act

Proving pay discrimination first involves identifying one or more **comparators**, which are people of the opposite sex who are in the same workplace and receive a higher rate of pay for performing the same type of work as the plaintiff. Importantly, comparators are usually limited to people employed in the same establishment. Pay comparisons across companies—or even among personnel in different divisions, offices, or plants of the same company—usually will not suffice. A female head grocery buyer for a food dis-tribution center was unable to establish a prima facie case of pay discrimination based on the higher pay of males who were the head grocery buyers for other distribution centers operated by the same company.[40] Likewise, a director of rehabilitation who worked for a company in its Corpus Christi network was unable to base an Equal Pay Act claim on the higher pay of his counterpart holding the same job in the company's San Antonio network. However, this plaintiff was able to challenge his lower rate of pay relative to the female who immediately succeeded him as Director of Rehabilitation.[41]

Equal Work

Equal Pay Act cases often hinge on whether the plaintiff can show that she and the com-parator perform substantially equal work. The two jobs do not have to be identical or carry the same job title; however, duties and tasks performed on the two jobs must over-lap substantially. Given a core of common tasks, the analysis then focuses on the tasks that differentiate the jobs. At this point, the Equal Pay Act incorporates the logic of job

---

[40]*Renstrom v. Nash Finch Co.*, 2011 U.S. Dist. LEXIS 41858 (D. Minn.).

[41]*Perales v. American Retirement Corp.*, 2005 U.S. Dist. LEXIS 22630 (W.D. Tex.).

evaluation. **Job evaluation** is a systematic process for rating jobs in terms of certain **compensable factors**. The requirements of jobs, rather than the performance of individuals, are the basis for job evaluations. Jobs that are rated higher are more demanding and valuable to employers and tend to be paid more.

The Equal Pay Act cites four compensable factors to be used in determining whether jobs are substantially equal: skill, effort, responsibility, and working conditions. **Skill** refers to what one needs to know and be able to do to perform a job. **Effort** is the amount of physical and mental exertion required by a job. **Responsibility** refers to things such as accountability for outcomes, supervisory duties, and involvement in important decisions. **Working conditions** has a more restricted interpretation under the Equal Pay Act than it does in other areas of employment law. It refers to "hazards" (how dangerous the job is in terms of physical hazards) and "surroundings" (e.g., elements such as fumes, outside work in cold weather). For jobs to be substantially equal, there must be significant commonality in duties; the jobs must require substantially equal levels of skill, effort, and responsibility; and they must be at least similar in terms of working conditions.

What if one or more potential comparators are earning a higher rate of pay and others are not? Courts have generally recognized prima facie cases of pay discrimination where some comparators of the opposite sex, but not all, earned a higher rate of pay than the plaintiff. In one such case, the court explained:

> *Taken literally … the "some males made the same or less" rule would force a court to hold that a female employee could not make out a* prima facie *case of wage discrimination where she was one of ten females paid half as much as nine males for "equal work," so long as a tenth male was paid the same or less than the female workers. In such circumstances … it seems as least highly likely that the employer is "discriminating between employees on the basis of sex," but the employer would nevertheless be insulated from suit.*[42]

JUST THE FACTS

Tammy Drum worked as a human resource manager, earning $41,548. She was promoted to a different position paying $45,600. Her replacement, a male, was hired from outside the company at $62,500. The company explained that the higher pay was because the male was the most qualified candidate available for the job and he had demanded a higher salary. Drum sued for pay discrimination under the Equal Pay Act. What should the court decide? Why?

See, *Drum v. Leeson Electric*, 565 F.3d 1071 (8th Cir. 2009).

Factors Other Than Sex

As in other discrimination cases, establishing a prima facie case creates an inference that pay discrimination has occurred, but does not resolve the matter. The employer in Equal Pay Act cases has the opportunity to justify the differential in pay as being due to a seniority system, a merit pay system, a system that bases pay on the quality or quantity of production (e.g., piece-rate system), or any other **factor other than sex**. Factors other than sex that might justify pay differentials for equal work include differences in

---

[42]*Hennick v. Schwans Sales Enterprises*, 168 F. Supp 2d 938, 950 (N.D. Iowa 2001).

educational attainment, experience levels, or training; shift premiums; and different rates for full- and part-time workers—to cite just a few. Although there are many possible factors other than sex, some justifications raise more questions than others. For example, to the extent that women receive lower pay in the labor market, using prior salary level as a basis for offers tends to perpetuate this problem. Does this violate the Equal Pay Act? Some courts maintain that *any* factor other than sex will suffice to defend a pay discrimination claim, even factors that lack any apparent business rationale. Under this view, basing pay on prior salary level is lawful despite its potential discriminatory effect.[43] More often, courts have held that employers bear the burden under the Equal Pay Act of proving that a factor other than sex serves a legitimate business purpose. Courts that take this view require employers to show business reasons for considering prior salary (e.g., particular skills, the desire to woo the employee away from another job).[44] An employer's market factors and salary history arguments were unpersuasive when the higher paid male had been unemployed for six months prior to being hired and admitted during his interview that he was "desperately" trying to find a job.[45] The claim that his prior salary level justified higher starting pay was undercut by the fact that he was given some $12,000 more, while the female plaintiff was given only $2,000 more than her previous salary. Women may also be disadvantaged by reliance on negotiation demands to determine pay offers because there is some evidence that women are reluctant to initiate salary negotiations and to drive a hard bargain.[46] The claim that a particular employee was paid more because he demanded a higher rate of pay in negotiations with the employer could easily serve as a pretext for discriminatory pay decisions. Because employers do not have to accede to pay demands simply because they are made, *employers justifying differential pay on the basis of individual salary negotiations should be able to point to abilities or experience that justify acceptance of a demand for higher pay.* Differences in the revenues or profits accounted for by positions have also been advanced as a factor other than sex (or as a basis for finding unequal work).[47] *Employers making this claim should ensure that the more lucrative positions are open to both male and female employees and that the differential profitability is not itself a product of discrimination.*

In *Vehar v. Cole National Group*, the court considers whether the markedly lower pay received by a female programmer was discriminatory.

Vehar v. Cole National Group
251 Fed. Appx. 993 (6th Cir. 2007)

OPINION BY CIRCUIT JUDGE GRIFFIN:

Plaintiff Wendy Vehar appeals the district court's grant of summary judgment for defendants regarding Vehar's sex discrimination claims under the federal Equal Pay Act.... [W]e reverse the decision of the district court and remand for further proceedings.

* * * Vehar originally began working for Cole as a Data Analyst in the Systems Management Department at a salary of $46,000. Her qualifications for the position included a bachelor's degree in mathematics from the University of Toledo, with a minor in computer science. In addition, she possessed six years, eight

[43] *Wernsing v. Department of Human Services, State of Illinois*, 427 F.3d 466 (7th Cir. 2005).
[44] *Price v. Lockheed Space Operations*, 856 F.2d 1503 (11th Cir. 1988).
[45] *Mickelson v. New York Life Insurance Co.*, 460 F.3d 1304, 1313-14 (10th Cir. 2006).
[46] Linda Babcock and Sara Laschever. *Women Don't Ask* (Princeton University Press, 2003).
[47] *Hodgson v. Robert Hall Clothes*, 473 F.2d 589 (3d Cir. 1973), *cert. denied*, 414 U.S. 866 (1973).

months' experience as a computer programmer.... Through her work …, Vehar acquired extensive experience with database management systems…, operating systems…, and computer programming languages…. * * *

During her first year in Cole's Systems Management Department, Vehar was called upon to develop the guide for the Pearle Business System ("PRO"), the application code for Cole's in-house language "PROGRESS." Vehar's guide became known as the "PRO bible" within the company. Due to the fact that the PRO system was relatively new to Cole, Vehar provided informal instruction to other employees, including her supervisor Lyle Turner, concerning the use of the system. Turner stated that Vehar had "truly made a difference with [her] efforts and perseverance … and taken the lead to bring us all to common understanding of PRO processing/flow." * * * After her first year, Vehar was given a one-percent raise, bringing her salary to $46,400.

In June of 2002, Vehar was offered a lateral transfer to the Retail Systems Group. Vehar asserts that, although her employment offer letter stated that she was to be hired as a "Programmer Analyst," she was actually appointed to the lower position of "Programmer II" without her consent. Moreover, she remained in pay grade 28, at a salary of $46,400, in this new position. This salary was below the midpoint for the $38,100 to $57,000 salary range applicable to pay grade 28. The Retail Systems Group was responsible for maintaining all computer technology in approximately 1,900 Pearle Vision, Sears Optical, Target Optical, and BJ's Optical stores. This technology included operating systems, point-of-sale applications, and order entry applications. Vehar was assigned primary PRO support duties within four weeks of her start in the Retail Systems Group.

In this group, Vehar worked with fellow programmers Erich Leipold and Dave Crosley. Cole hired Leipold as a Programmer Analyst in May of 2000. This position had a salary grade of 29. At the time of his hire, Leipold was paid $60,000. By September of the next year, Leipold had been promoted to Senior Programmer Analyst, increasing his salary to $67,307.63. At the time of his initial hire, Leipold had nine years of industry experience, but no college degree. By his own admission, Leipold demonstrated weak or nonexistent project management and communication skills during his tenure at Cole. Snyder consistently evaluated him as "M" for "meets expectations" commensurate with

his position. In July 2004, just before his eventual departure from Cole, Leipold was promoted to Senior System Analyst, earning $78,622.

Crosley was hired as a Systems Analyst, a position superior to that of Programmer II, about six months prior to Vehar's start date. * * * As a Systems Analyst, Crosley's salary grade was 31 and he earned $68,500 annually. He held a technical degree and eight years of experience prior to his time at Cole. After serving three years as an independent consultant to Cole, from 1997 to 2000, Crosley was hired as a full time employee. In his position as a Systems Analyst, Crosley acted in a supervisory capacity to Leipold and Vehar. Snyder rated Crosley as "M" or "meets expectations" commensurate with his position. Crosley's supervisory role continued until about February of 2003, when he was functionally demoted and replaced as supervisor. He continued on as a Senior Programmer Analyst, working alongside Leipold and Vehar and earning $73,733.40. At this time, Vehar was earning $46,460.

From June 2002 onward, Vehar and Leipold worked together and reported to the same manager. Snyder described their major work responsibilities as including the writing of code and retail store support. Cole regarded this latter duty as the "most important role" of the Retail Systems Group. After Crosley's demotion in February 2003, all three programmers reported to the same supervisor and were tasked with writing code and providing support to retail stores. * * * Between November 2002 and November 2004, Vehar authored more than 36 percent of Pearle Retail Systems development changes, while Crosley authored 34 percent and Leipold 26 percent. In addition to store support, the Retail Systems Group was assigned various projects, which were categorized as either "low priority" or "high priority." Vehar states that while Leipold and Crosley were assigned to some low priority projects, she was assigned to only high priority projects. * * * For the Perpetual Inventory Project and RGIS Inventory Project, Vehar assumed a leadership role and assigned, supervised, and corrected Crosley's project work. Vehar was eventually promoted to Programmer Analyst in March of 2003, moving her into pay grade 29, and earning a salary of $48,783. This figure is near the bottom of the $42,700 to $64,000 salary range for a pay grade of 29.

In October of 2003, Vehar complained to Snyder that she received less pay than her male coworkers and that she sought a raise. Snyder responded that

Vehar needed "to be patient these things take time." Snyder did not indicate at the time that Leipold's and Crosley's pay was a product of greater experience and/or skills. Snyder eventually discussed Vehar's complaints with his supervisor, John Broerman, and learned that Vehar had already discussed the matter with Broerman. Broerman looked into Vehar's complaint and later reported back to Snyder that Vehar's pay would not be increased because of her promotion to Programmer Analyst three months earlier. Vehar continued to work in the Retail Systems Group and received an "E" or "exceeds expectations" performance review. This resulted in a six percent merit increase in pay, bringing Vehar's salary to $51,709.

* * * On November 8, 2004, Vehar reiterated her concern over the apparent pay discrepancy between her and her male coworkers in a letter to Snyder, Broerman, and Human Resources Director Steven Hurd. * * * [After being overlooked for another position with the company] Vehar then applied for work outside of Cole and found a job at National City Bank as a "Project Lead II" at a salary of $73,000, thirty percent higher than her highest salary at Cole. * * *

To establish a prima facie case of wage discrimination under the EPA, the plaintiff must demonstrate that an employer pays "different wages to employees of opposite sexes 'for equal work on jobs the performance of which requires equal skill, effort, and responsibility, and which are performed under similar working conditions.'" The job functions of two individuals need not be identical to be considered "equal work" under the EPA. Instead, there only needs to be a "substantial equality of skill, effort, responsibility, and working conditions." The question of whether the work of two employees is substantially equal "is determined on a case-by-case basis and 'resolved by an overall comparison of the work, not its individual segments.'" The focus ... is on actual job requirements and duties, rather than job classifications or titles.

The district court was correct in finding that Vehar successfully established a prima facie case of sex discrimination ... [in pay]. The record supports the conclusion that Vehar, Crosley, and Leipold performed substantially equal work. All three worked as programmers in Cole's Retail Systems Group and reported to the same manager. They were assigned to the PRO/Pearle Support subgroup and provided additional support to the RIS Support subgroup, which they did with

no distinction between duties or responsibilities. The programmers were responsible additionally for writing code and authoring development changes to the system. Vehar, Crosley, and Leipold were also responsible for completing a variety of projects, on which they sometimes collaborated. The programmers were called upon to perform both programming and leadership duties in these projects. For one such assignment, a Perpetual Inventory Project and RGIS Inventory Project, Vehar assumed a leadership role, supervising and assigning work to Crosley. Vehar has offered sufficient evidence that she performed work substantially equal to that of Crosley and Leipold.

It is also plain that Vehar received less pay for this comparable work. When Vehar first came to the Retail Support Group, she was classified as a Programmer II, despite Cole's earlier representation that she would begin as a Programmer Analyst. She was paid $46,400 in this role. Leipold was allowed to begin his employment as a Programmer Analyst at a salary of $60,000, a twenty-percent increase over the pay Vehar received in the same position. By September of 2001, Leipold was promoted to Senior Programming Analyst, earning $67,307.63. Crosley, while a Systems Analyst, earned $68,500. After the restructuring of the Retail Support Group and his functional demotion to Senior Programming Analyst, Crosley earned $73,733.40. This indicates that not only were the employees performing substantially equal work under disparate job titles, leading to an imbalance in pay, but that even within equivalent job titles, Vehar received less pay than her male counterparts. * * *

Once a plaintiff establishes a prima facie case of wage discrimination, the burden shifts to the defendant to prove that the difference in wages is justified by one of the affirmative defenses enumerated in ... [the EPA]. These defenses are: (1) a seniority system; (2) a merit system; (3) a system that measures earnings by quantity or quality of production; or (4) any factor other than sex. Here, defendants assert the fourth factor as the basis for Vehar's lower salary. This "catchall" provision "does not include literally any other factor, but a factor that, at a minimum, was adopted for a legitimate business reason." The defendant bears the heavy burden of proving that a factor other than sex is the basis for a wage differential; in other words, it must be shown that the factor of sex provides absolutely no part of the basis for the pay disparity. The district court ultimately held that defendants satisfied the fourth factor…. In reaching this conclusion, the district court mainly relied on Crosley's and Leipold's additional work experience. Although experience and skills may justify a pay differential in some instances, here the differences are not significant enough to support summary judgment. On this record, we hold that a reasonable jury could determine that sex played a role in determining Vehar's wage.

Cole's description of the requirements for the programmers' respective positions set forth the following educational and work experience prerequisites: Programmer Analyst (Salary Grade 29): Position requirements include a Bachelor's degree or equivalent experience typically achieved with 5+ years work experience…. * * * Senior Programmer Analyst (Salary Grade 31): Position requirements include a Bachelor's degree or equivalent experience typically achieved with 7+ years work experience…. * * * Systems Analyst (Salary Grade 31): Position requirements include a Bachelor's degree or equivalent experience typically achieved with 10+ years work experience….

These position listings indicate that education is a desired trait in employees, an attribute that can serve as a substitute for relevant work experience. Here, Vehar is the only programmer of the three to hold a degree from a four-year institution at the time of her hire. It appears, however, that her degree was apparently not factored into either pay or promotion considerations. When Vehar first questioned Snyder about her disparate pay, he did not state that Leipold's or Crosley's larger salaries were in any way based on their greater experience. Further, at the time Leipold was hired, he possessed nine years of experience, which qualified him for the position of Programmer Analyst. At the time of Vehar's transfer to Snyder's group, she possessed approximately eight years of experience and a four-year degree, yet she was only hired on as a Programmer II, a position below her education level and experience. By the time of her promotion to Programmer Analyst in March of 2003, she had nearly nine years of experience, the same amount of experience Leipold possessed at the time of his hire. Despite her roughly equal experience and superior education, Vehar earned almost twenty percent less than Leipold in the same position.

Crosley possessed more experience than Vehar, but again, he did not have a comparable educational background. Moreover, the record indicates that Crosley's experience did not translate to increased performance or productivity. When Vehar first joined the Retail Systems group, Crosley, as a Systems Analyst, acted in a supervisory role over Vehar and Leipold. After his demotion to Senior Programming Analyst and the elimination of these supervisory duties, Crosley would earn even more. Crosley operated in the same work space as Vehar and Leipold and performed substantially equal tasks. Vehar actually supervised him on some project work, with Crosley performing some of the less complicated programming changes. While Crosley was under her supervision, he occasionally submitted his work late. Based on his observations of Crosley's work product, Leipold regarded Crosley as "weak" in terms of knowledge of programming standards.

Defendants repeatedly emphasize the "more advanced skills" of both Crosley and Leipold as justifying the difference in pay among the three programmers. It is true that Crosley, Leipold, and Vehar all possessed diverse and varied aptitudes. For example, unlike Vehar, her supervisor Snyder is not proficient in Linux, Unix, C++, or Java. We recognize the difficulty in making qualitative distinctions in such a narrow and technical field of expertise, particularly at the summary judgment stage. Indeed, the invitation to determine whether C++ is more useful than Java for a particular programming task is one we must decline. Analysis of such technical specifics is better suited to trial….

Similarly unavailing is defendants' argument that Vehar's experience prior to her employment at Cole was outmoded or otherwise obsolete. The record suggests the opposite conclusion, as Vehar consistently garnered "E" (exceeds expectations) performance ratings during her time in the Retail Systems group. As Leipold described: "All programming languages have pretty much the same foundation…. If you understand one in terms of the linear programming language, you can probably understand three, four, five or six…. It doesn't take too long to transition [into a new language]." He further stated that based on his own experience, proficiency in unknown languages can be acquired on the job. This view is supported by Vehar's quick comprehension of the "PRO" application code for Cole's mainframe language, "PROGRESS."

Although it is clear that Leipold and Crosley possessed more experience than Vehar, defendants have not met their burden of establishing that this distinction was the reason for the pay disparity. For example, defendants have not demonstrated that Cole valued work experience more than other attributes, such as education, in determining salary. Indeed, the job descriptions of Programmer Analyst, Senior Programmer Analyst, and Systems Analyst suggest that education could serve as a substitute for five, seven, or even ten years of experience. To grant summary judgment on the basis of an identified distinction, without requiring proof of a qualitative difference, essentially nullifies the burden of proof on this issue. * * *

CASE QUESTIONS

1. What were the legal issues in this case? What did the court decide?
2. What was the basis for the court's conclusion that the plaintiff and her two male comparators engaged in equal work?
3. What factor other than sex is cited by the employer? Why is it not sufficient to avoid a trial?
4. What should the employer have done differently?

In short, *employers should be prepared to account for pay decisions, particularly when males and females performing similar jobs in the same workplace are paid differently.* Defending pay decisions is much easier if employers *establish and consistently apply specific job-related criteria for making those decisions.* Employers should *avoid basing pay decisions on the pay level in a prior position or on demands made in negotiations unless these actually reflect the abilities of the individuals in question.* Finally, *if pay discrimination exists, it must be remedied by raising the pay of the lower-paid individual(s).*

Pay Secrecy Policies

Shhh! **Pay secrecy policies** discourage employees from sharing information about their pay and sometimes go as far as to require the termination of employees who violate the policies. A 2010 study found that 19 percent of surveyed employees worked in organizations with formal pay secrecy policies.[48] Informal practices of discouraging discussion of pay among coworkers appear to be common, with the same study finding that 61 percent of private sector respondents were subject to such pressures. Whatever the advantages of these policies, they clearly pose obstacles to employees seeking to determine whether they are victims of pay discrimination. They also interfere with employees' rights under the National Labor Relations Act (NLRA) to join together and communicate about workplace concerns.

In one case, a dietary aide at a nursing home was told several times by supervisors that employees were not to discuss their paychecks with anyone. Several coworkers came to her with problems they were having with shortages in their paychecks. She agreed to convey their concerns to the supervisor. Shortly thereafter, she was fired. The National Labor Relations Board (NLRB) decided, and an appeals court affirmed, that the aide's rights had been violated. The court held that "A rule prohibiting employees from communicating with one another regarding wages, a key objective of organizational activity, undoubtedly tends to interfere with the employees' right to engage in protected concerted activity."[49] The home was ordered to reinstate her with back pay. We will discuss the NLRA further in Chapter 14. The point for now is that pay secrecy policies are likely to violate employees' rights regardless of whether the policy is written or only spoken, whether or not the policy is strictly enforced, and whether the workplace is unionized or not unionized. Thus, *employers should refrain from establishing and enforcing pay secrecy policies.*

---

[48]National Women's Law Center. "Combating Punitive Pay Secrecy Policies." (April 12, 2011) Viewed April 13, 2011 (http://www.nwlc.org/).

[49]*NLRB v. Main Street Terrace Care Center,* 218 F.3d 531 (6th Cir. 2000).

Key Terms

Fair Labor Standards Act (FLSA),
    p. 389
minimum wage, p. 390
opportunity wage, p. 390
tipped employee, p. 390
overtime, p. 391
regular rate of pay, p. 391
workweek, p. 392
comp time, p. 392
compensable time, p. 394
exempt employee, p. 401
nonexempt employee, p. 401
white-collar exemption, p. 401
executive employee, p. 402
administrative employee, p. 402

professional employee, p. 402
duties test, p. 402
primary duties, p. 404
salary, p. 408
salary basis test, p. 408
pay docking rule, p. 408
prevailing wage, p. 410
Davis-Bacon Act, p. 410
McNamara-O'Hara Service
    Contract Act, p. 410
living wage, p. 410
Migrant and Seasonal Agricultural
    Worker Protection Act (MSPA),
    p. 411
sweatshop, p. 411

oppressive child labor, p. 412
Equal Pay Act (EPA), p. 412
prima facie case of pay
    discrimination, p. 413
comparator, p. 413
job evaluation, p. 414
compensable factor, p. 414
skill, p. 414
effort, p. 414
responsibility, p. 414
working conditions, p. 414
factor other than
    sex, p. 414
pay secrecy policies, p. 419

Chapter Summary

The principal federal law regulating wages and hours is the FLSA. The FLSA requires that most employees be paid at least the minimum wage for each hour of work in a workweek. Employers are also required to pay most employees at least one and one-half times their regular rate of pay for hours worked in excess of forty in a workweek. The FLSA also prohibits oppressive child labor, limiting hours of work for minors under 16 and restricting certain dangerous jobs to people 18 and over. Under the Davis-Bacon Act and the McNamara-O'Hara Service Contract Act, federal government contractors are sometimes required to pay the "prevailing wage" in a locality to employees performing contract work. States have their own wage and hour laws, and a number of states have established minimum wages in excess of the federal minimum wage. Numerous cities have enacted laws requiring that companies doing business with and/or receiving financial support from the city pay their employees a "living wage" well in excess of the minimum wage.

Enforcement of the wage and hour standards of the FLSA or other statutes requires knowledge of compensation received and hours worked and whether the particular employees are covered by or exempt from the standards. Disputes frequently arise over the number of hours worked (compensable time) because it is not always clear when work begins and ends, not all work hours are spent performing principal duties, and work duties sometimes intrude on nonwork time. In general, any work that an employer "suffers or permits" is compensable time. Employers are not required to pay for

activities that are clearly preliminary or postliminary to employees' principal duties, but drawing the line between these and setup or cleanup activities integral to the principal duties of a job is difficult. Cases involving breaks in work activity or work demands imposed during nonwork time typically turn on whether the time is spent principally for the employer's or the employee's benefit.

The FLSA contains many exemptions that permit employers not to comply with the act's requirements when compensating certain types of employees. Groups of employees not covered by particular provisions of the FLSA are labeled "exempt," whereas employees covered by those provisions are termed "nonexempt." The "white-collar exemptions" to the FLSA excuse employers from the obligation of paying overtime to executive, administrative, and professional employees. Whether employees fit these categories depends on the nature of their duties and responsibilities (the duties test), their salary level, and whether they are genuinely paid on a salary basis (the salary basis test). A salary is not calibrated to the number of hours worked or the quantity or quality of production. Instead, salaried employees are expected to accomplish their tasks and to put in the amount of time and effort needed to do so, in return for a predetermined sum. The DOL's pay docking rule is used to determine whether employees are being paid on a salary basis.

The Equal Pay Act promotes fair pay by prohibiting pay discrimination based on sex. Employers are prohibited from paying an employee of one sex at a lower rate of pay than an employee of the opposite sex when those employees perform substantially equal work in the same establishment. To establish a prima facie case of pay discrimination under the Equal Pay Act, an employee must identify one or more comparators of the opposite sex who work in the same establishment and earn a higher rate of pay for performing substantially equal work. To be substantially equal, jobs must have a significant number of overlapping duties; require substantially equal skill, effort, and responsibility; and be carried out under similar working conditions. If a prima facie case is established, an employer can defend the pay discrimination claim by showing that the pay differential was due to a seniority system, a merit pay system, a system of compensation based on the quantity or quality of production, or any factor other than sex.

Practical Advice Summary

- Employers must pay nonexempt employees an hourly rate at least equal to the minimum wage for each hour worked in a workweek.
- Deductions must not be made from the pay of employees for items that primarily benefit employers (e.g., uniforms) when the effect of those deductions is an hourly wage rate lower than the minimum wage.
- Employers can pay "tipped employees" $2.13/hr, provided that
  — Employees are so informed.
  — They (individually or collectively) retain all their tips.
  — Their pay plus tips equals at least the minimum wage.
  — State law does not provide for higher payment.
- Employers will be required to pay employees at a rate higher than the federal minimum wage if
  — They perform contract work for the federal or state governments that requires payment of the prevailing wage for that class of employees in the locality.
  — They perform contract work for or receive financial assistance from cities that require payment of a specified living wage.
  — The work is performed in a state with a higher minimum wage.
- Employers must pay nonexempt employees at least one and one-half times their regular rate of pay for hours worked in excess of forty in a workweek.
- In meeting their overtime pay obligations, employers generally cannot
  — Average work hours over periods of time longer than workweeks for purposes of determining overtime eligibility.
  — Provide compensatory time off (comp time) in lieu of overtime pay.
- However, public employers can use comp time if
  — It has been agreed to by employees or their representatives.

- Comp time accrual is capped (a maximum of 240 hours for most employees).
- Employees are permitted to use their comp time within a reasonable period after asking to do so unless fulfilling the request would disrupt agency operations.
- Employees are paid for any unused comp time when they leave employment.
- Wage and hour records must be maintained and kept for at least three years.
- To limit unwanted hours of work and overtime liability, employers should
  — Communicate and enforce policies prohibiting employees from working outside of assigned work hours without prior authorization.
  — Not ignore employees starting work early, staying late, or coming in on scheduled days off.
  — Not assign work or set deadlines that require work outside of work hours.
  — Not pressure or allow employees to underreport work hours.
- To limit overtime liability, on-call employees should
  — Be provided with cell phones, beepers, or pagers.
  — Not be called in repeatedly.
  — Be given a reasonable amount of time to respond to calls.
  — Be allowed to handle calls from home as much as possible.
  — Not be disciplined for isolated failures to respond.
- Job descriptions should be accurate, be up-to-date, and clearly support determinations of exempt status.
- To maintain the exempt status of executive, administrative, and professional employees, employers should not make deductions from salaries for
  — Partial-day absences for personal reasons.
  — Absences due to jury duty, appearances in court as a witness, and temporary military leave.
  — Lack of available work to perform when the employee is ready and able to work.

- Employers should establish and communicate clear policies prohibiting improper deductions from the pay of exempt employees and providing a mechanism for handling complaints about any such deductions. Employees who are nonetheless subjected to improper deductions should be promptly reimbursed.
- Employers must verify that young employees are old enough to employ. Employers must not use employees under 18 years of age for certain dangerous jobs. People 16 and over can be employed at all other jobs. Those who are 14 and 15 years old can be used for certain retail and service jobs.
- While school is in session, employers must not permit minors (under 16) to work
  — During school hours.
  — More than three hours a day.
  — More than eighteen hours a week.
  — Outside the hours of 7 A.M. to 7 P.M.
- When school is not in session, employers must not permit minors to work more than eight hours per day and forty hours per week.

- Employers must not pay people of one sex at lower rates of pay than people of the opposite sex for performing substantially equal work in the same establishment unless the different pay is due to
  — A seniority system.
  — A merit pay system.
  — A system for compensating according to the quantity or quality of production.
  — Any additional factor other than sex.
- Employers should
  — Be prepared to explain pay disparities between men and women performing similar jobs in the same workplace.
  — Establish and consistently apply clear criteria for making pay decisions.
- Employers must correct any pay discrimination by raising the pay of the lower-paid individual(s).
- Employers should refrain from establishing and enforcing pay secrecy policies.

Chapter Questions

1. A restaurant in Oregon paid its food servers the full state minimum wage ($7.95/hr at the time). Servers were required to contribute their tips to a tip pool. All employees of the restaurant other than managers shared in the tip pool based on their number of hours of work. The servers objected to sharing their tips with dishwashers and cooks. A server sued. What should the court decide? Why? (*Cumbie v. Woody Woo Inc.*, 596 F.3d 577 [9th Cir. 2010])

2. Employees of a county public works department used county-owned vehicles to travel to job sites where they inspected the work of subcontractors. The vehicles contained the tools and equipment the employees used on the job and served as their offices at the job sites. The employees were not allowed to drive the vehicles to their homes at the end of the day. Instead, they were required to bring them back to secure county-owned parking areas, where they also retrieved their own private vehicles. The employees were not paid for the time spent traveling from the remote parking areas to their first job site of the day. Nor were they compensated for the time spent bringing the vehicles back to the parking areas from their last job site of the day. Is this travel time compensable under the FLSA? (*Burton v. Hillsborough*

County, Florida, 181 Fed. Appx. 829 [11th Cir. 2006], *cert. denied*, 2006 U.S. LEXIS 8396)

3. In addition to their normal hours of work, electronic technicians at a power plant were required to remain on-call from 4:30 P.M. to 7:30 A.M. on Monday through Friday and for twenty-four hours on the weekend. While on call, the technicians typically responded to three to five alarms per evening. Each alarm took, on average, about forty-five minutes of work. Technicians were expected to respond to alarms within fifteen minutes. Failure to respond was grounds for discipline. The technicians were given pagers, but these did not work properly, forcing the technicians to remain at or near home. The technicians were paid for the time they spent responding to problems, but not for the remainder of the on-call time. The technicians sued for unpaid overtime. What should the court decide? Why? (*Pabst v. Oklahoma Gas & Electric*, 228 F.3d 1128 [10th Cir. 2000])

4. Fire alarm inspectors for the city of New York visited the home office once per week. On the other days of the week, they commuted directly to the sites where they conducted their first inspections of the day. The inspectors, most of whom commuted by bus or train, were required

to carry bulky briefcases weighing fifteen to twenty pounds and containing the inspection files needed for the week. Inspectors reported that the bulky briefcases added time to their commutes, sometimes caused them to miss trains, and required them to return directly home after work rather than attend social events. They argued that the carrying of the files rendered their commutes compensable time. What should the court decide? Why? (*Singh v. New York City,* 524 F.3d 361 [2d Cir. 2008])

5. An employee worked as a "field service engineer" for a company that sells robotic test and inspection equipment. He was paid a salary. He was the company's main contact with one of its largest clients, Max Media. His primary duty was to install, troubleshoot, and maintain the company's equipment used by Max Media. He also acted as a conduit for information between his employer and Max Media. Over the past year, he worked with crews to install ten machines, accounting for about 40 percent of his work time. He spent the remainder of his work time maintaining machines, responding to customer calls, learning about new systems, and completing paperwork. He was expected to keep his supervisor apprised of all his activities. Replacement parts for machines were stored at the home office and could be obtained only by going through his supervisor. The employee sued for unpaid overtime. The employer said that he was an exempt administrative employee. What should the court decide? Why? (*Bothell v. Phase Metrics,* 299 F.3d 1120 [9th Cir. 2002])

6. A city children's services department required that its case workers have a bachelor's degree in social work or a related field, along with at least three years of related work experience. Candidates without bachelor's degrees would also be hired, but only if they had at least seven years of experience. Truancy prevention case managers are responsible for assessing the needs of children and families, visiting schools and homes, recommending treatment, arranging resources for families, and testifying in court. They are subject to supervision. A man with a bachelor's degree in psychology and three years of social work experience was hired. At the time, he was told that he would be paid an annual salary of $35,000, work from 9 A.M. to 5 P.M., and be responsible for twenty-five clients. He ended up working sixty

hours per week and taking care of forty clients. He received no overtime pay. The man sued. What should the court decide? Why? (*Chatfield v. Children's Services,* 555 F.Supp. 2d 532 [E.D. Pa. 2008])

7. Store managers at a gasoline station/convenience store chain earn a base salary of $522/wk and are eligible for a bonus that can bring their pay to a maximum of $2,500/month. Managers work at least fifty hours per week and are on call 24/7. They spend about 60 percent of their time performing nonmanagerial tasks such as stocking shelves, operating registers, and cleaning bathrooms. Store managers also perform managerial tasks, including supervising employees, hiring, training, scheduling, and disciplining employees. Store managers recommend pay increases and terminations to district managers, but they do not decide these matters unilaterally. District managers typically visit stores once or twice a week and communicate frequently with store managers via phone and e-mail. Are the store managers exempt executives? (*Thomas v. Speedway SuperAmerica,* 506 F.3d 496 [6th Cir. 2007])

8. Pharmacists at Wal-Mart were paid a salary based on an expected number of hours of work. During slow times of the year, pharmacists' hours and salaries were reduced in response to lower sales. The pharmacists claim that this practice makes them not exempt. They sue for unpaid overtime work. What should the court decide? Why? (*In Re: Wal-Mart Stores, Fair Labor Standards Act Litigation,* 395 F.3d 1177 [10th Cir. 2005])

9. If during a snowstorm a company remains open for business, can the employer deduct from the pay of salaried employees who do not come to work without jeopardizing their exempt status? If the employer closes its offices due to the storm, can salaried employees be required to use paid time off (e.g., vacation) to cover the day? (Michael R. Triplett. "DOL Gives Advice on Salary Deductions for Weather-Related Absences, Closures." *Daily Labor Report* 218 [November 14, 2005], A-8)

10. A woman worked for a manufacturing company as a "tool crib attendant." She started in the position at $6.31/hr and after two years earned $7.52/hr. A man who worked at the plant as a security guard (at $7.42/hr) was hired to be the tool crib attendant on the third shift. He was

offered the job at the rate of $7.75/hr. The HR manager attributed the pay level to the man's "computer skills and his potential." The man had a bachelor's degree in anthropology and master's degrees in education and urban planning. The woman had a high school diploma. The tool crib attendant job did involve some work with computers, and it was acknowledged that the man's computer skills were superior to those of the woman. However, there was also evidence that another female who had taken computer classes and who had clearly indicated her interest in the job was not even considered for the position. Has the employer violated the Equal Pay Act? Why or why not? (*Warren v. Solo Cup Co.*, 516 F.3d 627 [7th Cir. 2008])

11. The coach of a women's college basketball team demands to receive the same salary as the (male) coach of the men's basketball team. Are these jobs "equal work"? If they are, what "factors other than sex" might justify paying one coach more than the other? (*Stanley v. University of Southern California,* 178 F.3d 1069 [9th Cir. 1999]; Equal Employment Opportunity Commission. "Enforcement Guidance on Sex Discrimination in the Compensation of Sports Coaches in Educational Institutions." No. 915.002 [October 29, 1997])

12. Should private sector employers be allowed to use comp time to meet their overtime pay obligations? What are the potential benefits? Problems? (David J. Walsh. "The FLSA Comp Time Controversy: Fostering Flexibility or Diminishing Worker Rights?" *Berkeley Journal of Employment and Labor Law* 20, 1 [1999])

13. Does the Equal Pay Act go far enough in prohibiting pay discrimination? Should the proposed amendments to the EPA found in the Fair Pay Act (2011 S. 788; H.R. 1493) be enacted?

14. There are many cases of serious wage and hour violations by employers, particularly in the retail sector. These cases feature employers failing to provide breaks; pressuring workers to underreport hours of work; requiring that work be performed both before and after shifts; and, crudest of all, "shaving time." The latter refers to the practice of simply deleting work hours from computerized payroll records. Is this any different from stealing? Is there any justification for such acts? (Steven Greenhouse. "Time Records Often Altered, Job Experts Say." *New York Times* [April 4, 2004], A-1; Steven Greenhouse. "Forced to Work Off the Clock, Some Fight Back." *New York Times* [November 19, 2004], A-1)

CHAPTER **13**

Benefits

Benefits are an important part of compensation. The availability of benefits, such as pensions and health insurance, matters a great deal to employees. For employers, benefit plans are a significant part of labor costs and require considerable expertise to administer. Many laws, both employment and tax laws, affect benefit plans. This chapter focuses on the Employee Retirement Income Security Act (ERISA), the principal federal law regulating benefit plans. Laws specifically regulating group health insurance plans will also be discussed, as will the application of general antidiscrimination statutes to benefit plans.

The law surrounding benefits is very much in flux. Significant public policy questions are being debated about how best to provide and pay for the health care and retirement income needs of an aging population. Employer-provided benefits will no doubt remain central to how most people in the United States meet these basic needs, but employers are clearly seeking to minimize benefit costs and to shift some of the risk and cost associated with them to employees and the public.

What Benefits Must Employers Provide?

Employers are required to make contributions on behalf of employees into several social insurance programs. These include Social Security, unemployment insurance, and workers' compensation (for replacement income and medical expenses arising from workplace injuries). Leave provided under the Family and Medical Leave Act can also be thought of as a type of legally mandated benefit, although the FMLA does not require that any more paid time off be provided than is already available under an employer's own leave policy. Recent changes in federal law governing health insurance plans do not go so far as to require that employers offer group health plans, but they do define certain essential health services that plans must cover and subject large employers to monetary penalties if they fail to offer such coverage to their employees.[1] Some states and cities have attempted to mandate employer contributions toward the health insurance of their employees or provision of paid time off.[2] But these are exceptions to the

---

[1]Victoria A. Judson and Anne E. Moran. "Health Reform: What Employers Need to Consider." *Employee Relations Law Journal* 36, 2 (2010), 59–83.

[2]Pam Belluck. "Massachusetts Sets Health Plan for Nearly All." *New York Times* (April 5, 2006), A1; Lee Romney. "San Francisco Labor Hails Passage of Sick Leave Measure." *Los Angeles Times* (November 9, 2006).

general rule that employers are *not* legally required to provide health insurance, pensions, paid sick days, severance pay, or any other benefits. Thus, although the laws discussed in this chapter come into play after an employer decides to have benefit plans, employers generally get to decide which, if any, benefits they will offer to their employees and how generous those plans will be.

What Does ERISA Require?

Despite its name, the **Employee Retirement Income Security Act (ERISA)**[3] governs benefit plans broadly and is not concerned only with pensions. ERISA covers most employer- and labor union–sponsored benefit plans, but not government employer plans. The social insurance programs mentioned earlier are also not covered by ERISA. Under ERISA, benefit plans are classified as either pension plans or welfare plans. **Pension plans** are designed to provide retirement income to employees or to otherwise defer income until after employment ends (e.g., defined benefit pensions, 401[k]s, ESOPs, profit sharing). **Welfare plans** are essentially any other benefit plans covered by ERISA that are not pension plans (e.g., health insurance, childcare subsidies, prepaid legal services). There are a number of exclusions from this broad category. Without attempting to list them all, the exclusions center on premium pay (e.g., for shift, overtime, or holiday work), payment for nonwork time that comes out of general assets rather than a separate trust fund (e.g., sick pay, vacation pay), scholarship or tuition reimbursement plans, and occasional gifts (e.g., holiday gifts). Benefits that are excluded need not meet ERISA requirements.

Throughout this book, we have pointed to the important role that state laws play in our system of employment law. States often address issues not covered by federal laws or provide for greater protection of employees. In general, states are free to fill in where federal law is silent and to mandate greater protection of employees. However, such is not the case when it comes to benefit plans covered by ERISA. ERISA is unusual among employment laws in its sweeping **preemption** language. ERISA preempts (supersedes) state laws even remotely relating to the regulation of benefit plans. This technical legal issue has real consequences. For example, since ERISA does not require employers to offer health benefits, efforts by states to achieve universal coverage by mandating that employers provide health insurance for their employees have sometimes been preempted.[4] And because the remedies and requirements of ERISA, particularly those that apply to welfare plans, are quite limited, achieving uniformity across states in the legal rules for benefit plans has often come at the price of less employee protection.

ERISA is a complex law that contains four main parts (titles). It combines provisions relating to employee rights with rules relating to the treatment of benefit plans under the tax code. Although the United States relies very heavily on employer-provided benefits (as opposed to government-provided benefits such as national health insurance), employee benefit plans are heavily subsidized through tax deductions. "Qualified" plans receive favorable tax treatment, which provides employers with a strong incentive to conform to ERISA's requirements.

The following overview of ERISA's requirements focuses on the employee rights provisions of Title I. Under ERISA, *employers are required to inform employees about their benefits, deliver promised benefits, provide claims and appeals procedures, manage plans wisely and in employees' interests, and refrain from interfering with or retaliating against beneficiaries.*

---

[3]29 U.S.C.S. §§ 1001–1461 (2011).

[4]*Retail Industry Leaders Association v. Fielder*, 475 F.3d 180 (4th Cir. 2007); *Golden Gate Restaurant Association v. San Francisco*, 2008 U.S. App. LEXIS 20574 (9th Cir.), *cert. denied*, 2010 U.S. LEXIS 5478.

Inform Employees about Their Benefits

A basic premise of ERISA is that informing employees about their benefits helps ensure that employees actually receive the benefits to which they are entitled. Benefit plan administrators are required to periodically (and at no charge) provide employees with reports and respond to employee requests for other information about their benefits. Required reports include the Summary Plan Description (outlining the basic terms of benefit plans), Summary of Material Modifications (listing changes in plans), Summary Annual Report (giving financial data on pension plans), Individual Benefit Statement (covering individual employees' pension accruals), and Disclosure Notice (alerting employees of certain funding problems with their pension plans). DOL regulations now also require that 401(k) plans provide plan participants and beneficiaries with both plan-wide and individual fee and expense information.[5]

Summary Plan Descriptions (SPDs) are important documents. *Summary Plan Descriptions must be provided to employees within ninety days of their becoming covered under benefit plans.* Typically distributed in booklet form (or online), *SPDs must be written with a minimum of legalese and be sufficiently comprehensive and accurate to inform employees about their rights and obligations.* In general terms, SPDs must identify the plan administrator, conditions for benefit eligibility, benefits offered, and procedures for claiming benefits and appealing denials of benefits. Full disclosure of the circumstances under which participants will become ineligible for or lose benefits is particularly important. The SPD for a health insurance plan should specify any premiums, deductibles, or copayments required of employees; annual or lifetime maximums; limits on coverage for experimental procedures or drugs; limits on choice of health care providers; conditions for receiving emergency care; and requirements for preauthorization or review of the necessity of medical treatment.

Apart from reports provided to employees, *ERISA requires that employers detail their benefit plans in written plan documents.* In cases involving disputes over whether promised benefits were provided, courts strongly prefer written plan documents over statements made by company representatives incorrectly advising employees that they were entitled to certain benefits. As one court has put it, "We have made clear … that the oral representations of an ERISA plan may not be relied upon by a plan participant when the representation is contrary to the written terms of the plan and those terms are set forth clearly."[6] Thus, employees take risks when they seek and rely on statements about expected benefits. At the same time, employers who misrepresent the terms of benefit plans to employees potentially run afoul of ERISA. *Employers should be careful in advising employees regarding their benefits and refer them to SPDs and other plan documents.*

Deliver on Promised Benefits

Employers are required to provide the benefits they promise. Employees have the right under ERISA to sue their employers for denial of benefits. For example, a health plan might refuse to authorize treatment or decline to pay for care already received because it is deemed "not medically necessary" or "experimental." If a denial of benefits case ends up in court, the nature of the review depends on whether the plan gives its administrator discretionary authority to determine eligibility for benefits or to interpret the terms of the plan.[7] Because plan documents typically provide plan administrators with such authority, courts most

---

[5]Tom Stamer. "HR's Role in New ERISA Regulation." *Human Resource Executive Online* (November 10, 2010) Viewed November 22, 2010 (http://www.hreonline.com/).

[6]*Bowerman v. Wal-Mart*, 226 F.3d 574, 588 (7th Cir. 2000).

[7]*Firestone Tire & Rubber Co. v. Bruch*, 489 U.S. 101 (1989).

often confine themselves to determining whether plan administrators abused their discretion by making decisions in an arbitrary and capricious manner, rather than substituting their reading of plans for that of administrators. This is known as an **abuse of discretion** standard. The relevant question under this standard is whether the plan administrator's decision was unreasonable, not whether it was correct. Questions about the appropriate standard for review also arise because there is sometimes a conflict of interest, such that the entity administering the benefit plan has a direct financial stake in limiting access to benefits. The Supreme Court has said that courts are entitled to weigh such conflicts of interest as a factor when considering whether plan administrators have violated ERISA by denying promised benefits, but that abuse of discretion is still the relevant standard.[8] The Court has also held that even when a plan administrator is found to have abused its discretion in an initial benefits determination, subsequent interpretations are still entitled to deference.[9]

This *abuse of discretion* standard commonly used in ERISA denial-of-benefits cases is deferential to plan administrators but does not give them license to unreasonably withhold benefits. A health plan's decision not to authorize high-dosage chemotherapy (HDCT) for an employee with breast cancer was found to be arbitrary and capricious.[10] ERISA was violated because the administrator demanded evidence that HDCT is superior to more conventional treatments not to exclude it as an experimental treatment, even though the plan documents required only that a proposed treatment be recognized by the medical community and have demonstrated effectiveness to be covered. The administrator also erred by ignoring expert medical testimony favorable to the employee. In another case in which the administrator of a health plan abused its discretion, coverage for inpatient treatment in a psychiatric facility was denied despite the fact that the treating physician saw it as essential to the patient's health. The decision to deny coverage was made by another doctor who had never met the patient and who based her decision on old medical records.[11]

JUST THE FACTS

An employee with a history of coronary artery disease underwent a difficult operation for her condition. Several weeks later she was re-hospitalized, suffering from a severe staph infection in the area of the incision from her earlier surgery. She became seriously ill and is now disabled. She applied for benefits under her employer's long-term disability plan, but she was rejected on the grounds that her claim was "caused by, contributed to by, or resulting from [a] pre-existing condition." The plan defines this as a condition for which medical treatment is received in the three months just prior to becoming covered under the plan and where the disability begins in the first twelve months after coverage begins. Her disability did, in fact, occur within a year after she became covered under the plan. She had also received treatment for her coronary artery disease in the three months prior to becoming covered under the plan. The in-house review of the decision to deny benefits took one day to complete and produced a one-paragraph decision noting that "medical records from this period

---

[8]*Metropolitan Life Insurance v. Glenn*, 128 S. Ct. 2343 (2008).

[9]*Conkright v. Frommert*, 130 S. Ct. 1640 (2010).

[10]*Zervos v. Verizon*, 277 F.3d 635 (2d Cir. 2002).

[11]*Salley v. E.I. DuPont de Nemours & Co.*, 966 F.2d 1011 (5th Cir. 1992).

could further strengthen this opinion." The report acknowledged that the staph infection was not a preexisting condition but asserted that it resulted from surgery for her preexisting coronary problem. Did the plan administrator violate ERISA by denying disability benefits to this woman? Does it matter that the disability benefits would have come directly out of the profits of the insurance company that denied her claim?

See, *Fought v. UNUM Life Insurance Company of America*, 379 F.3d 997 (10th Cir. 2004), *cert. denied*, 2005 U.S. LEXIS 3888.

Administrators of benefit plans must base benefit determinations on plan documents, have reasons for their decisions, and use all the current and relevant information available to them.

Provide Claims and Appeals Procedures

Employers are required to provide "reasonable" claims and appeals procedures for their benefit plans. This means meeting certain minimum procedural standards. The standards for handling claims for health benefits are more stringent than those that apply to claims for other types of benefits. To be "reasonable," claims procedures cannot inhibit the filing or processing of claims, such as by imposing filing fees. *Decisions on initial claims generally must be made within ninety days. However, benefit determinations under health plans must be made more quickly.* Urgent care claims must be decided within seventy-two hours, whereas claims for treatment already received must be decided within thirty days. These and other time limits on benefit determinations can be extended under certain circumstances.

If a decision is made to deny a benefit claim, the specific reasons for the denial must be provided to the employee in writing. There must be a procedure for appealing adverse benefit determinations, and the procedure must allow at least sixty days (180 days under group health plans) for appeals to be filed. The results of these reviews must be communicated to employees within sixty days (more quickly for some health insurance claims). Reviews of adverse determinations under health plans must not be conducted by the original decision makers or their subordinates.

Unlike most other employment laws, employees are generally required under ERISA to use their employers' claims and **appeals procedures** before going to court to sue for denial of benefits. Thus, an employee was unable to sue his health plan for refusing to pay for a prescription drug that he needed because he had made only a single telephone inquiry about whether the drug was covered and had never used the appeals process.[12] On the other hand, an employee did not fail to exhaust the internal appeals procedure when she sent a number of letters seeking severance pay but the letters were addressed to the wrong individual in the company's human resources department.[13] The letters could easily have been forwarded to the correct individual, and the employee was never given the correct information about the claims and appeals procedure. Likewise, an insurer's failure to provide a response to an employee's appeal of the decision to end her disability benefits within the time period specified by ERISA meant that she had exhausted the appeals process and was entitled to sue for denial of benefits.[14]

---

[12]*Harrow v. Prudential Insurance*, 279 F.3d 244 (3d Cir. 2002).

[13]*Patterson v. J.P. Morgan Chase & Co.*, 2002 U.S. Dist. LEXIS 2014 (S.D.N.Y.).

[14]*Nichols v. The Prudential Insurance Company of America*, 406 F.3d 98 (2d Cir. 2005).

Manage Plans Wisely and in Employees' Interests—Fiduciary Duties

In general, anyone who exercises discretionary authority or control over the administration of a benefit plan or its funds is considered a **fiduciary**. This usually includes such people as directors, officers, plan administrators, and trustees. Outside parties that regularly render investment advice for a fee are also fiduciaries. The people or entities that control and manage benefit plans have a number of important responsibilities or **fiduciary duties**. First and foremost, *fiduciaries are responsible for managing benefit plans and funds solely in the interest of plan beneficiaries and for the purpose of providing them with benefits. Fiduciaries must manage benefit plans with skill, care, and prudence. They must ensure that plans operate in accordance with plan documents and the requirements of ERISA. With pension plans, fiduciaries are responsible for diversifying plan assets to minimize the risk of large losses, selecting proper investments, monitoring investment performance, and ensuring that plans can meet their obligations. Fiduciaries must also refrain from engaging in certain transactions that have the potential to create conflicts of interest.*

The fiduciary duties of employers extend to information provided to employees regarding their benefits. An employer violated ERISA when it knowingly misled employees, inducing them to make a disadvantageous switch in benefit plans. The employer told employees that their benefits would remain secure if they voluntarily transferred to the benefit plans of its new subsidiary even though the employer knew full well that the subsidiary was already insolvent. The Supreme Court concluded that there was a clear breach of fiduciary duty: "To participate knowingly and significantly in deceiving a plan's beneficiaries in order to save the employer money at the beneficiaries' expense is not to act 'solely in the interest of the participants and beneficiaries.'"[15] *Employers and other ERISA fiduciaries must provide accurate information about benefit plans and not withhold material facts that would likely affect the choices and interests of plan beneficiaries.*

In *Livick v. Gillette*, an employee tries to prove that his employer breached its fiduciary duty under ERISA by providing him with inaccurate information about his retirement benefits.

Livick v. Gillette
524 F.3d 24 (1st Cir. 2008)

OPINION BY CIRCUIT JUDGE LYNCH:

John Livick appeals a grant of summary judgment to his former employer, the Gillette Company ... in a dispute over the amount of his pension benefits under Gillette's employee benefit plan ("Plan"). Livick sued Gillette under ... ERISA, arguing that Gillette must pay him the amount of the erroneous benefit estimates he received before he left Gillette instead of the lesser amount he was entitled to under the Plan. We affirm the district court's grant of summary judgment for defendants.

Livick began working for Parker Pen Company in Janesville, Wisconsin in 1976. In 1993, Parker Pen was bought by Gillette Stationary [sic] Products Group ("Gillette SPG"), a division of Gillette, and the pension plans of the two companies were merged together at the end of 1995. In 1997 and again in 1998, Livick received letters from Gillette SPG explaining how the Parker Pen pension he had already accrued would be treated under Gillette's Plan. These letters enclosed an estimate of Livick's Parker Pen pension—$1047 a month—and stated in the opening paragraphs that

---

[15]*Varity Corp. v. Howe*, 516 U.S. 489, 506 (1996).

Livick would receive this pension "in addition to any benefit you accrue under the Gillette Plan for your service on and after January 1, 1996." The official Plan terms also included similar clear language under the heading "Former Participants in The Parker Pen Pension Plan."

Gillette decided to close the Janesville plant in 1999, so Livick moved to Boston to take another position within Gillette SPG. A year later, Gillette announced the sale of Gillette SPG to another company, resulting in the elimination of Livick's position. Livick attended a meeting in October 2000 in which Gillette explained what benefits would be available for the Gillette SPG workers like Livick who were losing their jobs. This is the first time someone from Gillette suggested that Livick's Gillette pension might cover the years he worked for Parker Pen. Following up on that meeting, Livick met individually with Wayne Brundige, a human resources representative, the next week. Brundige calculated an estimate of Livick's Gillette pension based on a hire date of 1976 instead of the appropriate Gillette hire date of 1996. That estimate put Livick's Gillette pension at $2832 a month.

While still employed at Gillette SPG, Livick went online to check Brundige's estimate against Gillette's pension estimator ("Estimator"). Before the online Estimator can be accessed, the user must pass through a "Disclaimer" page that emphasizes repeatedly that the site only provides estimates. That page also notes that the Estimator does not take into account "some very specific features of the Gillette Retirement Plan." In capital, bold letters at the bottom of this disclaimer page, the Estimator website states "IN THE EVENT THERE IS ANY DISCREPANCY BETWEEN THE INFORMATION PROVIDED BY THE ESTIMATOR AND THE BENEFITS TO WHICH YOU ARE ENTITLED, THE TERMS OF THE GILLETTE PLANS WILL APPLY." In a more detailed "Definitions and Additional Information" section of the website, a subsection entitled "Parker Frozen Benefit" explains that former Parker Pen employees would receive their earned pension under the Parker Pen plan "plus the benefit [they] earn under the terms of the Gillette Retirement Plan for service after [December 31, 1995]." Livick printed this portion of the website in December 2000 while researching how his pension would be calculated. The website's calculator generated a pension estimate for Livick of $2914 a month based on a hire date of 1976, which was the incorrect date under the Parker Pen frozen benefit policy.

Livick's job was formally terminated on January 12, 2001. Livick turned down another job offer, he says in reliance on the higher-than-expected pension estimates. In 2002, after Livick again visited the online Estimator and generated yet a higher estimated benefit, Livick called Gillette's Human Resource Center to ascertain which estimate—Brundige's or the Estimator's—was more correct. He was told that the online estimate was likely more correct, but that he would be sent a new estimate of his pension benefit. That new benefit statement correctly showed that Livick's Gillette pension would be based solely on the years he worked for Gillette. This dropped his Gillette pension down to $789 a month; his Parker Pen pension ($1047 a month) presumably remained unchanged.

Livick sued … claiming that Gillette was in breach of its fiduciary duty to Livick under ERISA because of these "misrepresentations. * * * We disagree…. *** Livick also argued before the district court that Gillette should be held liable … based on a theory of estoppel. * * * Livick's theory of his case is largely built on a reliance argument: that he relied to his detriment on the mistaken pension estimates he received. Thus we briefly address the estoppel theory, though we find it also unavailing.

Under ERISA, a fiduciary is defined functionally: a party is a fiduciary "to the extent" that he or she exercises discretion over the management of the plan or its funds or over its administration. A fiduciary named in an ERISA plan can undertake non-fiduciary duties, and a party not identified as a plan fiduciary can become one if, but only to the extent that, he or she undertakes discretionary tasks related to the plan's management or administration. Thus in cases alleging breach of ERISA fiduciary duty, "the threshold question is not whether the actions of some person employed to provide services under a plan adversely affected a plan beneficiary's interest," which is the heart of Livick's complaint, "but whether that person was acting as a fiduciary (that is, was performing a fiduciary function) when taking the action subject to complaint."

As Livick acknowledges, Brundige (the human resources representative) is not a named fiduciary under the Plan. Brundige was also not a functional fiduciary because providing Livick with an estimate of his future pension benefits was not a fiduciary task. Rather, the "[c]alculation of benefits" and "[p]reparation of reports concerning participants' benefits" are "ministerial functions," and "a person who performs purely ministerial functions … within a framework of policies, interpretations, rules, practices and procedures made by other persons is not a fiduciary." Livick tries to argue that this case is like those in which the employee was given misleading information while seeking advice about the security of his future benefits. On the face of the complaint, however, all Livick sought and received from Brundige was an estimate: his benefits had already accrued, he was not choosing among different options, and there was no discussion of the plan itself. This was purely a ministerial request.

Livick also asserts that Gillette breached its fiduciary duty when it hired, retained, and failed to properly train Brundige to perform such non-fiduciary tasks. This argument fails as well. * * * The regulations do require a fiduciary to exercise "prudence in the selection and retention" of persons charged with merely ministerial tasks, but only to the extent that the fiduciary "rel[ies] on information, data, statistics, or analyses" provided by these ministerial agents. Gillette did not rely on Brundige's, or anyone else's, estimates in its management and administration of the Plan.

Some courts have held named fiduciaries liable when non-fiduciary representatives provided beneficiaries with misleading information, but they have done so in situations where the fiduciaries failed to provide clear and accurate information in the first place. We do not decide whether to follow those cases; they are plainly distinguishable. Gillette provided Livick with clear, accurate, and complete information in multiple documents: in the letters mailed directly to him in 1997 and 1998, on the Estimator's website, and in the Plan itself. Indeed, Livick was quite aware of the policy as to former Parker Pen employees. Providing estimates of benefits is not a fiduciary function, nor is hiring someone to provide such estimates purely for plan members' use. With no fiduciary function involved, there can be no breach of fiduciary duty.

We turn briefly to the estoppel theory. * * * ERISA plans must be in writing and cannot be modified orally…. [A] plan beneficiary might reasonably rely on an informal statement interpreting an ambiguous plan provision; if the provision is clear, however, an informal statement in conflict with it is in effect purporting to modify the plan term, rendering any reliance on it inherently unreasonable. * * * Livick concedes that he understood the Parker Pen policy, and he is receiving the pension that accounts for his service with both Gillette and Parker and that he was guaranteed under the terms of the Plan. He cannot now argue estoppel because it was unreasonable for

him to rely on informal communications which contradicted clear plan terms.

Livick points to the company's retention of the right "to amend the Plan … in any respect and at any time." Livick asserts that the repeated mistaken estimates, because they consistently used the wrong start date, led him to believe that the Plan had indeed been changed regarding the calculation of Parker Pen employees' pensions, perhaps as part of the special severance package. * * * Livick's argument that he reasonably believed the mistaken estimates he received indicated a change in the Plan fails. By the clear terms of the Plan, any change to the method of calculation could only have come from on high: the Compensation Committee of the Board of Directors. Both Brundige and the online Estimator lacked the actual authority to modify the plan terms. They also lacked apparent authority to do so, as every estimate given to Livick was clearly labeled an estimate. Further, the online Estimator had a prominent disclaimer that the terms of the Plan trumped any estimates. There was nothing to suggest that the Plan had in fact been modified to double-count his Parker Pen years or to calculate his pension under only the Gillette plan (which also would have resulted in a higher total benefit).

Livick's situation is not an unusual one. Even assuming utter good faith on Livick's part, other courts have denied claims on facts much more compelling than his. In *Mello*, an employee of Sara Lee was entitled to the pension he had accrued under a company acquired by Sara Lee as well as subsequent pension benefits earned for his time at Sara Lee. Mello had received, however, annual statements from Sara Lee for six years erroneously double-counting his time working for the acquired company. When the error was finally caught, the estimate of Mello's monthly pension benefit dropped by $5500. Based primarily on the unambiguous plan terms, the Fifth Circuit denied Mello's … ERISA claim. In *Christensen* …, a clerical error resulted in five mistaken estimates of the plaintiff's pension benefits. Christensen relied on these estimates to decide when to retire. The Eighth Circuit rejected Christensen's claim that Qwest's plan administrators were in breach of their fiduciary duty due to their hiring of a company that used an informal process that was known to result in occasional mistaken estimates, given the multiple clear disclaimers accompanying the estimates and the need to respond quickly to a high volume of estimate requests.

The pension Livick is receiving accounts for all his years of service at Parker Pen and Gillette. It is the amount provided for under the clear terms of the Plan. Livick understood (or should have understood) these clear terms due to multiple personal letters he received from the company and from his own research on the company website. Nothing in ERISA secures to him a windfall when a ministerial employee makes a mistake in an estimate, a mistake of which the beneficiary is or should be aware because of the company's clear and accurate ERISA disclosures.

There was no breach of fiduciary duty and there was no reasonable reliance on the pension estimates. The grant of summary judgment is affirmed.

CASE QUESTIONS

1. What were the legal issues in this case? What did the court decide?
2. Who is a "fiduciary" under ERISA? Why was the human resources representative not a fiduciary?
3. Why did the plaintiff's estoppel claim also fail? Why was it not reasonable for him to rely on multiple estimates of a higher pension?
4. What are the practical implications of this decision and others like it for employees?

Refrain from Interference or Retaliation

ERISA prohibits discrimination against a benefit plan participant or beneficiary "for exercising any right to which he is entitled" under a benefit plan or "for the purpose of interfering with the attainment of any right to which such participant may become entitled" under a benefit plan.[16] An employer must not, for example, fire an employee to prevent him from becoming entitled to receive a pension. Moreover, this protection applies to both pension and welfare plans.[17] Although the statutory language appears relatively broad, courts have restricted this protection to cases in which an adverse employment decision was made for the express purpose of interfering with benefit entitlement. The mere fact that a loss of benefits accompanies a termination does not render that termination a violation of ERISA. Additionally, some courts have declined to recognize claims brought by employees who were retaliated against after making unsolicited, internal complaints about problems with the administration of benefit plans, rather than for statements made in the course of formal enforcement proceedings.[18]

JUST THE FACTS

In 2000, the Ford Motor Company "spun off" its automotive parts subsidiary Visteon. This resulted in the transfer of some salaried employees from Ford to Visteon. In 2006, Visteon transferred some of its facilities back to Ford. In 2008, Ford conducted a major reduction in force. It offered severance pay to downsized salaried employees based on years of service with Ford. The plaintiffs in this case were salaried employees who had been transferred to Visteon and then returned to Ford. On their return to Ford, they were classified as "rehired," rather than as "reinstated," and given new Ford employment service dates. Consequently, their severance pay was based only on their service since 2006. Did Ford violate ERISA by classifying the employees as "rehired" rather than reinstating them with their original Ford service dates?

See, *Maczko v. Ford Motor Co.*, 2010 U.S. Dist. LEXIS 133071 (E.D. Mich.).

---

[16]29 U.S.C.S. § 1140 (2011).

[17]*Inter-Modal Rail Employees Ass'n v. Atchison, Topeka and Santa Fe Railway Co.*, 520 U.S. 510 (1997).

[18]*Edwards v. A.H. Cornell & Sons*, 610 F.3d 217 (3d Cir. 2010), *cert. denied*, 2011 U.S. LEXIS 2092.

In one case, an employee with AIDS began filing health insurance claims and informed his employer about his condition. The employer responded by cutting the $1 million lifetime maximum under the health plan for other conditions to $5,000 for treatment of AIDS. Despite the fact that this person was the only employee known to have AIDS and the cut was made immediately after he started to file claims, the court concluded that ERISA was not violated. The reduction would affect everyone with AIDS and not just this individual. More importantly, the employer was free to change the plan at any time. Thus, there was no continuing entitlement to the higher level of coverage.[19] In contrast, when a real estate company terminated its salespeople and offered to allow them to continue as independent contractors without benefits, ERISA was violated.[20] The employer's stated purpose was to avoid paying for health insurance and a 401(k). A key distinction between this and the prior case is that the employer did not change the terms of or discontinue its benefit plans. Instead, it used the terminations to deny to the salespeople benefits that remained in place for other employees.

Employers must not discharge or otherwise discriminate against employees because they have used benefits to which they are entitled or to prevent them from using benefits to which they are entitled.

Pensions

Imagine an employee nearing retirement and looking forward to doing nothing more ambitious than walking on the beach every morning. What if he suddenly learns that the pension he was counting on will not be there for some reason? Individuals depend on the income that is deferred into pension plans to provide for their retirements. If problems with a pension plan are not discovered until retirement is at hand, it is far too late to do anything about it. ERISA was created in large part to prevent such disasters, and it contains many complex requirements specific to pension plans. However, some types of pensions are more closely regulated than others. The less regulated variety is now the most common.

Vesting and Participation

In general, employers are free to alter or discontinue benefit plans at any time. The reduction or elimination of any benefit can be detrimental to employees, but pensions present a particular problem. ERISA allows pension plans to be modified or terminated, but it requires that plan participants and beneficiaries retain the benefits accrued prior to these changes. Under ERISA, *employers with pension plans are required to provide for the vesting of pension rights.* **Vesting** means that after a specified number of years of service, employees covered under a pension plan acquire a nonforfeitable right to receive a pension. That period of time is usually either five years (for "cliff vesting," in which vesting occurs all at once at the end of the fifth year of service) or seven years (for "gradual vesting," in which the nonforfeitable portion increases in increments of 20 percent starting in the third year). Vesting pertains to an employer's contributions to a pension plan. Any employee contributions vest immediately.

Once vested, an employee is entitled to a pension from the employer (or under certain circumstances, to roll the funds into another retirement fund) even if the employee goes to work for another company. This does not mean that a 28-year-old who works seven years for a company and then quits is entitled to a pension at that time. It only means that upon reaching the plan's normal retirement age, the former employee is entitled to a pension.

---

[19]*McGann v. H&H Music Co.*, 946 F.2d 401 (5th Cir. 1991), *cert. denied*, 506 U.S. 981 (1992).

[20]*Seaman v. Arvida Realty Sales*, 985 F.2d 543 (11th Cir. 1993), *cert. denied*, 510 U.S. 916 (1993).

Because the size of a pension is closely related to length of service, the amount would probably be small in this case. Employers are required not only to vest the pension rights of employees but also to offer benefits to survivors of deceased employees.

Employers are also prohibited from making changes to pension plans that reduce pension benefits already accrued by employees. This is known as ERISA's **anti-cutback rule.** The application of this rule is at issue in the *Battoni v. IBEW Local Union No. 102 Employee Pension Plan* case that follows.

Battoni v. IBEW Local Union No. 102 Employee Pension Plan
594 F.3d 230 (3d Cir. 2010)

OPINION BY CIRCUIT JUDGE SMITH:

This appeal requires us to consider the scope of the Employee Retirement Income Security Act's ("ERISA") Anti-Cutback rule. Certain current and retired members of a union challenged an amendment to their welfare plan (the "Disputed Amendment") as an unlawful cutback of their accrued benefits under their pension plan. We must determine whether the Disputed Amendment, which conditions receipt of healthcare benefits under a welfare plan on non-receipt of an accrued benefit under a pension plan, violates the Anti-Cutback rule…. [W]e conclude that the Disputed Amendment violated the Anti-Cutback rule by constructively amending the pension plan in a manner that decreased an accrued benefit under that plan. Accordingly, we will affirm the District Court's judgment in favor of the Battoni Plaintiffs.

In November 1999, the Local 675 and the Local 102 chapters of the International Brotherhood of Electrical Workers ("IBEW") merged. * * * After the merger, the two pension plans were combined into one—the Local 102 Pension Plan. * * * [T]he Local 102 Welfare Plan was amended to include a new condition on the receipt of healthcare benefits. This amendment, the Disputed Amendment, conditioned a retiree's receipt of healthcare benefits on the retiree's not choosing the lump sum pension benefit offered under the Local 102 Pension Plan. The Disputed Amendment stated, in relevant part, that:

Retired employees who elect a lump sum pension benefit in lieu of periodic monthly benefits from [the] IBEW Local 102 Pension Plan and/or from another Local Union IBEW Pension Plan shall not be eligible for continued [healthcare] coverage.

Before the addition of the Disputed Amendment, a former Local 675 member could elect to receive the lump sum pension benefit provided under the Local 102 Pension Plan and still receive healthcare benefits under the Local 102 Welfare Plan. A group of current and retired members of the Local 102 chapter who were formerly members of the Local 675 chapter, the Battoni Plaintiffs, challenged the Disputed Amendment, alleging, among other things, that it violated the Anti-Cutback rule. * * *

To state a claim for violation of ERISA's Anti-Cutback rule one must show (1) that a plan was amended and (2) that the amendment decreased an accrued benefit. The Union concedes that the lump sum pension benefit offered under the Local 102 Pension Plan was an "accrued benefit." It argues that the Disputed Amendment lawfully amended a welfare benefit plan—such benefits are exempt from coverage under the Anti-Cutback rule—without disturbing the Battoni Plaintiffs' rights to the lump sum pension benefit offered under the Local 102 Pension Plan. This argument cannot succeed in this case.

The first question that must be resolved is whether the Disputed Amendment, by conditioning the receipt of welfare benefits on a retiree not exercising her right to receive a lump sum pension benefit under the Local 102 Pension Plan, constituted an amendment to the Local 102 Pension Plan. Because the Disputed Amendment constructively amended the right to receive a lump sum pension benefit under the Local 102 Pension Plan, we conclude that the first requirement of an Anti-Cutback claim was satisfied.

* * * "ERISA recognizes two types of employee benefit plans: pension plans and welfare plans." Welfare plans provide "medical, surgical, or hospital care or benefits, or benefits in the event of sickness, accident, disability, death or unemployment[.]" Pension plans provide retirement income to employees or result in a deferral of income by employees for periods extending to the termination of covered employment or beyond.

According to the Union, the Disputed Amendment amended the welfare plan and thus was exempted from the Anti-Cutback rule. The Anti-Cutback rule, however, cannot be employed in such an overly simplistic, robotic fashion.

* * * The Disputed Amendment constructively amended the pension plan by adding a condition to the receipt of a benefit accrued under that plan. If a retiree elects to receive the lump sum pension benefit under the Local 102 Pension Plan she loses healthcare benefits under the Local 102 Welfare Plan. Thus, the Disputed Amendment necessarily, "by its express terms or as a result of surrounding circumstances," amended the Local 102 Pension Plan. * * * Thus, even though the Disputed Amendment was added to the Local 102 Welfare Plan and certainly dealt with healthcare benefits, it also "function[ed]" to condition receipt of the lump sum pension benefit under the Local 102 Pension Plan on non-receipt of healthcare benefits under the Local 102 Welfare Plan.

Having determined that the Disputed Amendment amended the Local 102 Pension Plan, the next inquiry is whether the amendment decreased an accrued benefit. The Union argues that the Disputed Amendment merely restricts access to healthcare benefits and does not decrease any accrued benefit. But because the Disputed Amendment imposed a condition on the receipt of the lump sum benefit under the Local 102 Pension Plan, it decreased an accrued benefit. * * *

In *Central Laborers' Pension Fund*, the Supreme Court considered "whether the [Anti-Cutback] rule prohibits an amendment expanding the categories of postretirement employment that triggers suspension of payment of early retirement benefits already accrued." It held that such an amendment was prohibited in part because the imposition of a new condition on an accrued benefit decreased the value of that accrued benefit. Thomas Heinz, a retiree who participated in a pension plan administered by the Central Laborers' Pension Fund, worked in the construction industry before retiring. Heinz's pension plan contained a "disqualifying employment" provision that stated that monthly retirement payments would be suspended if he accepted work as a "union or non-union construction worker." The provision did not cover work as a "construction supervisor." After retiring, Heinz began working as a construction supervisor while receiving pension payments. Approximately two years later, the pension plan's "disqualifying employment" provision was amended to include any job in the construction industry. Heinz was warned that he would lose his

monthly pension payment if he continued to work as a construction supervisor. Despite the warning, Heinz continued to work as a construction supervisor and his monthly pension payments were suspended because of his ongoing violation of the amended "disqualifying employment" provision. Heinz sued the pension fund to recover the suspended benefits, alleging that the amended "disqualifying employment" provision violated the Anti-Cutback rule.

In its defense, the Central Laborers' Pension Fund argued that it did not decrease an accrued benefit because Heinz's monthly pension payments were merely suspended, not outright eliminated. The Supreme Court explained that the pension fund's distinction between suspension and elimination "misse[d] the point" of the Anti-Cutback rule. The imposition of the condition itself was what devalued the accrued benefit:

> The real question is whether a new condition may be imposed after a benefit has accrued; may the right to receive certain money on a certain date be limited by a new condition narrowing that right? In a given case, the new condition may or may not be invoked to justify an actual suspension of benefits, but at the moment the new condition is imposed, the accrued benefit becomes less valuable, irrespective of any actual suspension.

The same reasoning applies here. The Local 102 Pension Plan, like Heinz's pension plan, imposed a new condition on the receipt of an accrued benefit. The Battoni Plaintiffs' lump sum pension benefits accrued before the Disputed Amendment was added to the Local 102 Welfare Plan. Yet the Disputed Amendment conditioned the receipt of those accrued benefits on forfeiting healthcare benefits. This "new condition," in and of itself, decreased the value of the lump sum pension benefit. * * *

Thus, we will affirm the District Court's judgment that the Disputed Amendment violated ERISA's Anti-Cutback rule.

CASE QUESTIONS

1. What were the legal issues in this case? What did the court decide?
2. Since the anti-cutback provisions of ERISA apply only to pensions and not welfare plans, why did changing the conditions under which retiree health care benefits were available run afoul of the anti-cutback rule?
3. In what sense were the accrued pension benefits of these employees reduced?
4. What should the benefit plan have done instead?

In addition to mandatory vesting, ERISA has **participation** requirements for pension plans aimed at broadening coverage. As a general rule, *pension plans cannot exclude employees who are at least 21 and have at least one (if gradual vesting) or two (if cliff vesting) years of service.* Limitations other than those based on age or years of service (e.g., division, occupation) can still be imposed. However, qualified pension plans enjoying tax-exempt status are subject to the additional participation requirement that the lesser of fifty employees or 40 percent of the workforce must be covered.

Types of Pension Plans

Under ERISA, pension plans are categorized as either defined benefit or defined contribution plans. Legal requirements vary depending on the type of plan, with defined benefit plans being subjected to greater scrutiny.

As the name suggests, **defined benefit plans** promise a specific pension benefit upon retirement. The size of an individual's pension is typically determined by a formula based on years of service and earnings. In establishing a defined benefit plan, an employer undertakes a long-term obligation to provide a specified level of retirement income to its employees. A pension fund is maintained separate from the employer's other assets, and benefits are paid from the fund. However, no separate accounts or funds are set aside for individual employees. The employer bears the burden of providing funding sufficient to meet the plan's obligations to its retired employees. If the investments made by the pension fund do well, the employer has to contribute less. If the investments do poorly, the employer has to make up the difference. In either case, the pensions received by employees remain the same.

Obviously, adequate financing is the key to the operation of a defined benefit plan. ERISA's funding requirements for defined benefit pension plans are well beyond the scope of this book. Suffice it to say that there are many such rules, including minimum funding standards and financial penalties for underfunding. Defined benefit pension plans can be terminated or frozen, but funding has to be maintained to pay the benefits that have already been accrued by vested employees and retirees. In cases where the employer is unable to meet its obligations to retirees, the **Pension Benefit Guaranty Corporation (PBGC)** intervenes. Employers with defined benefit pension plans pay termination insurance and these funds are used by the PBGC to provide at least partial retirement benefits to retirees and vested employees. Failures of pension funds at large employers have placed a major strain on the finances of the PBGC and prompted Congress to enact more stringent rules for employer funding of defined benefit plans. One of the key objectives of the **Pension Protection Act of 2006**[21] was to place defined benefit plans on firmer financial footing. The Pension Protection Act aimed to do this by, among other things, requiring that more realistic interest rate assumptions be used, increasing termination insurance premiums for companies with underfunded plans, further restricting the ability of underfunded plans to increase benefits, and (most directly) requiring full funding of (most) plans within seven years. But shoring up the pension system requires striking a delicate balance between pressuring employers to adequately fund their obligations while not accelerating the trend toward termination of defined benefit plans. The grim economic reality of the stock market and massive losses suffered by pension plans in 2008 led Congress to subsequently relax its funding requirements.[22]

---

[21]P.L. 109-280; 120 Stat. 780 (2006).

[22]Mary Williams Walsh. "Pensions Get a Reprieve in Congress." *New York Times* (December 12, 2008), B1.

Clippings

ERISA does not cover the pension plans of public employers. There is growing concern about the ability of states and municipalities to meet their pension obligations to public employees. The city of Prichard, Alabama, ignored years of warnings about underfunding of its pension fund. In 2009, the fund ran out of money. Despite a state law requiring cities to pay promised pension benefits in full, the city stopped sending pension checks out to its 150 retirees. The city, which has twice filed for bankruptcy, maintains that it cannot afford to pay the pension benefits. There are many unanswered legal questions about whether, or under what circumstances, governments can eliminate already-earned pension benefits. Michael Aquirre, a former city attorney for San Diego, offered the pessimistic assessment that "Prichard is the future…. We're all on the same conveyor belt. Prichard is just a little further down the road."

Michael Cooper and Mary Williams Walsh. "Alabama Town Shows the Cost of Neglecting a Pension Fund." *New York Times* (December 23, 2010), A1.

The many types of **defined contribution plans** include 401(k)s, profit-sharing plans, stock bonus plans, and employee stock ownership plans (ESOPs). In all these plans, contributions are made into individual employee accounts. The pension benefit that employees receive is not specified beforehand but depends instead on the amounts in these individual employee accounts at the time of retirement. In turn, those amounts are linked to choices about how much income to defer, whether employee contributions are matched by their employers, what investments are selected, and what the gains or losses are from those investments. Thus, with defined contribution plans, employers establish plans and define what their own contributions, if any, will be (e.g., match employee contributions up to specified amounts, provide certain amounts of company stock). They make no promises regarding the eventual payout to employees.

THE CHANGING WORKPLACE

Defined Contribution Plans and Shifting Risk to Employees

Many contemporary workplace developments can be viewed as shifting risk and uncertainty from employers to employees. For example, less stable and more contingent forms of work place the burden of fluctuations in the need for labor squarely on workers and relieve employers from commitments to use corps of relatively permanent employees. Likewise, when employers move toward "variable compensation" linked to the performance of employees (e.g., merit pay) or organizations (e.g., profit sharing), risk is shifted from employers to employees. In the area of benefits, health plans increasingly take the form of "consumer-directed" plans that combine high deductibles with

health savings accounts (to which employers might, or might not, contribute) out of which employees are expected to pay for most of their own medical expenses. However, this shifting of risk to employees is most clearly seen in the movement away from defined benefit pensions to defined contribution plans.

About 59 percent of Americans have access to a pension plan through their employment, but only about 45 percent actually participate in such a plan.[1] For those employees fortunate enough to participate in pension plans, defined contribution plans have become the preeminent type over the past few decades. In 1983, approximately 62 percent of employees with pensions were covered by defined benefit plans only, 12 percent by defined contribution plans only, and 26 percent by both. By 2004, the situation had almost reversed itself. Only 20 percent of employees with pensions had defined benefit plans only, 63 percent had defined contribution plans only, and 17 percent had both.[2] Among firms with fewer than 1,000 employees, there was a 70 percent decline in the number offering defined benefit plans between 1990 and 2004. The shift from defined benefit to defined contribution plans has been especially marked in the private sector. The 112,000 single employer defined benefit pension plans that existed among private sector firms in 1985 had dwindled to 27,650 by 2009.[3]

Shifting from defined benefit pension plans to defined contribution plans like 401(k)s means that employees bear much more, if not the entirety, of the pension funding burden. Employees, rather than expert fund managers, are responsible for setting aside sufficient funds for retirement and making wise investment choices. If those investments turn out poorly, that is not the problem of their employers. While many arguments can be made for the superiority of defined benefit over defined contribution pension plans, that train has already left the station. The question is what legal responsibility employers have regarding these inherently risky arrangements that are now at the center of how the retirement income needs of employees are provided for.

---

[1]Brian Perlman, Kelly Kenneally, and Ilana Boivie. *Pensions and Retirement Security 2011: A Roadmap for Policy Makers* (March 2011). National Institute on Retirement Security (http://www.nirsonline.org/).
[2]Alicia H. Munnell and Pamela Perun. "An Update on Private Pensions." *Issues in Brief* (Center for Retirement Research at Boston College, August 2006), 5.
[3]Ilana Boivie. *Issue Brief: Who Killed the Private Sector DB Plan?* (March 2011). National Institute on Retirement Security (http://www.nirsonline.org/).

Policy makers have begun to respond to the reality of a pension system in which defined contribution plans now dominate. The Sarbanes-Oxley Act[23] requires (among many other corporate governance measures) that *employees receive a thirty-day notice of blackout periods (i.e., lockdowns) that would affect their ability to direct investments in or receive distributions from their 401(k)s.* The law provides that corporate insiders will also be subject to any blackout periods, meaning that they will be unable to sell shares or exercise stock options when employees with 401(k)s are so restricted. The Pension Protection Act of 2006 also has many provisions affecting defined contribution plans (but not ESOPs). One of the most significant is that employees must be allowed at any time to divest themselves of their employers' publicly traded stock when that stock was purchased with employees' own contributions.[24] Employer stock purchased through employer contributions can be divested after employees have reached three years of service. Employers are required to provide at least quarterly windows for divesting company stock and to offer at least three investment alternatives (each with different risk and return characteristics) to company stock. The basic purpose of these requirements is to promote greater diversification of the investments found in employees' defined contribution accounts. This is important because many employees fail to adequately diversify the investments in their retirement plans, particularly by over-investing in their own employers' stock.[25]

Another significant feature of the Pension Protection Act of 2006 is its authorization of "qualified automatic contribution arrangements."[26] Subject to many stipulations,

---

[23]P.L. 107-204, 116 Stat. 745 § 306 (2002).

[24]P.L. 109-280 § 901 (2006).

[25]Richard A. Oppel. "The Danger in One-Basket Nest Egg Prompts a Call to Limit Stock." *New York Times* (December 19, 2001), C1.

[26]P.L. 109-280 § 902 (2006).

Practical Considerations Would you recommend that an employer with a 401(k) plan automatically enroll all of its employees in that plan? If so, how should this be done?

employers are permitted to automatically establish 401(k)s for employees, withhold between 3 and 10 percent of employees' earnings, and place those funds in certain investments on employees' behalf. Employers utilizing these arrangements are required to make certain matching contributions on behalf of their employees who are "not highly compensated." Employees can still opt out and choose to have less or none of their earnings put into 401(k)s, but they have to take the affirmative step of notifying their employer to this effect. Under these arrangements, the default option is participation. Finally, employers are now freer to arrange for "qualified fiduciary advisers" to provide individualized investment advice to employees without fear of breaching their fiduciary duties, subject again to numerous qualifications.[27]

Recent changes in the law notwithstanding, defined contribution plans are not governed by the extensive funding and administrative requirements that apply to defined benefit plans. However, employers and other decision makers still have a basic fiduciary duty toward participants in defined contribution plans. In a case involving a 401(k) plan participant who sued his employer for breaching its fiduciary duty under ERISA by failing to follow his investment instructions (costing him approximately $150,000), the Supreme Court agreed that he could sue under a section of the law that authorizes recovery for fiduciary breaches that diminish the value of plan assets.[28] The relevance of this decision for our purposes is that the Court clearly recognized that most pensions now take the form of defined contribution plans. The fact that plan assets were contained in individual accounts rather than a single pension fund did not preclude enforcement of the law. Cases alleging fiduciary breaches by companies administering defined contribution plans are clearly a "growth" area in employment law. In one such case, the court found that defendants responsible for managing an employee stock ownership plan (ESOP) breached their fiduciary duty to plan participants by purchasing stock on behalf of the ESOP without investigating properly and by overpaying for the stock. Reliance on an outside expert to establish a fair market value for the stock was not sufficient evidence of prudence in this case because the expert was not supplied with complete and accurate information. Beyond the problem of the faulty stock valuation, the court summed up the case as follows:

> [T]he facts demonstrate that the Hall Chemical ESOP was established in an environment where the trustees were unaware of what was going on, the trustees were not consulted on major decisions ..., there was not negotiation as to the price of the ... stock, there was more concern for the return on investment for the Master Trust, and the inconvenience of dealing with uneven numbers could justify charging the Hall Chemical ESOP an additional $44,900.00 for the stock it purchased. Such facts demonstrate not only the uniquely careless and haphazard manner in which the Hall Chemical ESOP was created, but also clear violations of defendant's fiduciary duties.[29]

Lawsuits (known as "stock-drop" cases) are proliferating in the courts alleging breach of fiduciary duty by employers who continue to offer company stock as an investment option for employee retirement accounts and fail to inform employees of known problems with that stock, resulting in large losses. Numerous companies have settled such claims. Other cases are slowly wending their way through the court system, with varying outcomes. Cases have been decided or are ongoing against

---

[27]P.L. 109-280 § 601 (2006).

[28]*LaRue v. DeWolff, Boberg & Associates*, 128 S. Ct. 1020 (2008).

[29]*Chao v. Hall Holding Company*, 285 F.3d 415, 433-34 (6th Cir. 2002), *cert. denied*, 2003 U.S. LEXIS 887.

companies whose officials remained heavily invested in company stock even though its value had fallen by nearly 80 percent because of regulatory changes that undermined the company's business model;[30] offered a few, overly expensive, investment options and had conflicts of interest;[31] continued to offer company stock as an investment option while they were busy backdating stock options and making fraudulent transactions that artificially inflated the stock's value—until it plummeted;[32] offered company stock as an investment while engaging in accounting gimmickry and serious mismanagement;[33] permitted investments in company stock to continue while failing to divulge known information about manufacturing defects in one of the company's main products;[34] and disseminated misleading Securities and Exchange Commission filings to participants in an ESOP.[35] Defendants have generally not been successful in arguing that insider trading laws would prohibit the disclosure of relevant, nonpublic information to plan participants.[36]

Clippings

Caterpillar Inc. agreed to a $16.5 million settlement of a class-action lawsuit brought on behalf of participants in its 401(k) plans. The suit had alleged that Caterpillar breached its fiduciary duties under ERISA by including more costly retail mutual funds in the plan rather than demanding investment management through low-cost institutional structures, maintaining excessive cash in the company stock fund, and paying excessive fees to a financial subsidiary of Caterpillar.

Michael Balogna. "Caterpillar Agrees to Pay $16.5 Million Under Settlement of Alleged ERISA Violations." *Daily Labor Report* 214 (November 9, 2009), A-9.

A class-action lawsuit alleging violation of Comcast's fiduciary duty in administering its 401(k) plan was settled. The plaintiffs charged that the price of Comcast stock had been artificially inflated, making it an imprudent investment option for the plan. Besides the monetary settlement, the company agreed to provide certain investment advisory services for a three-year period, send annual diversification notices to plan participants whose accounts balances include more than 10 percent Comcast stock, and remove any limits on the ability of plan participants to divest themselves of company stock for the next three years.

Jo-el J. Meyer. "District Court OKs $5 Million Settlement, Ends Comcast 'Stock-Drop' Class Action." *Daily Labor Report* 17 (January 26, 2011), A-13.

---

[30]*Peabody v. Davis*, 636 F.3d 368 (7th Cir. 2011).

[31]*Braden v. Wal-Mart Stores*, 588 F.3d 585 (8th Cir. 2009).

[32]*Lanfear v. Home Depot*, 536 F.3d 1217 (11th Cir. 2008)..

[33]*In re Goodyear Tire & Rubber Co, ERISA Litigation*, 438 F. Supp. 2d 783 (N.D. Ohio 2006).

[34]*In re Guidant Corp. ERISA Litigation*, 2008 U.S. Dist. LEXIS 47535 (S.D. Ind.).

[35]*In re General Motors ERISA Litigation*, 2007 U.S. Dist. LEXIS 63209 (E.D. Mich.).

[36]*Rankin v. Rots*, 278 F. Supp. 2d 853 (E.D. Mich. 2003).

There are also many cases alleging breach of fiduciary duty in the administration of defined contribution plans that have gone against employees. For example, a group of employees sued under ERISA when their employer offered 401(k) plan participants an investment option (described by the employer as a "conservative" investment intended to return principal and interest) that was based on junk bonds and the investment subsequently lost money. After several rounds of litigation, the court concluded that the employer had not breached its fiduciary duties to offer prudent investments, diversify (the bad investment comprised 20 percent of the fund), or disclose material information to participants.[37] The court stressed that it is the fiduciary's conduct in arriving at an investment decision (e.g., conducting appropriate research before purchasing investments), and not the financial outcome, that establishes prudence. Likewise, 401(k) participants were unsuccessful in a suit based on the heavy investment of nonvested funds in company stock. The price of that stock had plummeted following the release of negative information to the public. The employees' claim that the employer knew the stock was overvalued yet did not disclose this to plan participants and continued to allow it to be purchased as a plan investment foundered largely on the issue that the company itself, as opposed to the plan committee, had little fiduciary responsibility under the plan.[38] The court allowed a separate securities fraud claim to continue, but it stressed that a distinction exists between ordinary business decisions that have an effect on benefits and actions specifically directed toward a plan. It is only the latter that implicate fiduciary duties under ERISA.

A major obstacle for plaintiffs in stock-drop cases is the **presumption of prudence** adopted by many courts. Under this presumption, companies that offer their own stock as an investment option when the documents of the defined contribution plan call for that will generally be deemed to have acted prudently, even if there are problems with the stock.[39] Thus, even though American Express stock lost nearly 78 percent of its value in 2008, the company laid off 10 percent of its workforce, and an infusion of $3 billion in federal TARP (Troubled Asset Relief Program) funds was needed, the company did not breach its fiduciary duty by continuing to offer company stock as an investment option.[40] Courts have also found for employers when company officials—prior to a merger that greatly reduced the value of its stock—sold off most of their shares without disclosing that fact to plan participants;[41] when the employer was engaged in sham transactions that artificially inflated its stock value, but plan documents specifically called for company stock to be available as an investment option and for employer matches to be made in this form;[42] and when an employer failed to disclose information about fees and costs to plan participants and paid excessive fees to the financial services company that managed investments.[43]

In *DeFelice v. U.S. Airways*, large financial losses suffered by employees who invested in the airline's stock are not enough to show a breach of fiduciary duty.

---

[37]*In Re: Unisys Savings Plan Litigation*, 173 F.3d 145 (3d Cir. 1999), *cert. denied*, 528 U.S. 950 (1999).

[38]*Hull v. Policy Management Systems*, 2001 U.S. District LEXIS 22343 (D. SC).

[39]*Moench v. Robertson*, 62 F.3d 533 (3d Cir. 1995); *Quan v. Computer Sciences Corp.*, 623 F.3d 870 (9th Cir. 2010).

[40]*In re American Express Co. ERISA Litigation*, 762 F. Supp. 2d 614 (S.D.N.Y. 2010).

[41]*Nelson v. Hodowal*, 512 F.3d 347 (7th Cir. 2008).

[42]*Kirschbaum v. Reliant Energy*, 526 F.3d 243 (5th Cir. 2008).

[43]*Hecker v. Deere & Co.*, 556 F.3d 575 (7th Cir. 2009), *cert. denied*, 2010 U.S. LEXIS 675; *Renfro v. Unisys Corp.*, 2011 U.S. App. LEXIS 17208 (3d Cir.).

DiFelice v. U.S. Airways
497 F.3d 410 (4th Cir. 2007)

OPINION BY CIRCUIT JUDGE MOTZ:

In August 2002, following a period of severe financial stress exacerbated by the September 11th attacks, U.S. Airways, Inc (Group), filed for relief under Chapter 11 of the Bankruptcy Code. As a consequence, all Group stock was cancelled without distribution to stockholders. Vincent DiFelice then brought this action seeking recovery under ... ERISA on behalf of U.S. Airways employees (the Employees) who held Group stock from October 1, 2001 to June 27, 2002 through a U.S. Airways 401(k) plan. The district court ... after a bench trial, granted judgment to U.S. Airways. * * *

Throughout the class period, U.S. Airways maintained a defined contribution § 401(k) plan for qualified employees.... U.S. Airways, the named administrator of the Plan for tax and ERISA purposes, delegated its duties to the Pension Investment Committee (PIC), a group of high-ranking company officers, including the Chief Financial Officer, who reported, through the Human Resources Committee of the Board of Directors, to the full Board. The PIC, which had both the responsibility and the authority to make decisions regarding investment options under the Plan, met regularly to review the performance of the Plan's investment options and to confer with outside financial advisors and investment consultants. * * *

The Plan "permitted participants to contribute up to 15% of their salaries ... on a pretax basis"; U.S. Airways matched certain employee contributions up to a specified level. Each employee who chose to invest through the Plan had his own individual account; the balance in a participant's account consisted of his contributions and any matched funds, "plus any earnings and less any losses or allocated expenses." The Plan granted U.S. Airways the authority to "'determine the number and type of Investment Funds and select the investments for such Investment Funds.'"" [I]n its discretion,'" U.S. Airways could "'terminate any ... Investment Fund.'" The Plan stated that the menu of Investment Funds could, but need not, include a Fund consisting of Group stock. If the Plan did include such a Fund, it required that U.S. Airways "'continually monitor the suitability ... of acquiring and holding Company Stock.'"

During the class period, the Plan offered twelve diversified Investment Funds, including a money market fund, a fixed income fund, various mutual funds, and several diversified portfolio funds. The Plan also offered a Company Stock Fund ("Company Fund")....Within this thirteen-Fund menu, participants had an almost unlimited ability to allocate their investments. * * * U.S. Airways, however, did provide participants with a Summary Plan Document (SPD), as well as other brochures and pamphlets, which provided general information about the Plan ... and specific warnings about the Company Fund. The materials identified the Company Fund as the riskiest, most volatile offering, and stated that investment in this Fund was appropriate for "'[s]omeone who does not rely on this fund for his/her entire portfolio.'" * * * In the same vein, the Plan literature emphasized the importance of spreading investment dollars among three basic asset types—stocks, bonds, and short-term investments— and among three basic strategies—growth, income, and preservation of principal—in order to minimize the risk of significant losses in one particular investment or investment type. The SPD informed participants that U.S. Airways did not "'guarantee the performance of the [Company] Fund,'" or any other Fund, and that participants alone were responsible for any losses which resulted from their Plan selections. The SPD also stated, in bold print, that Plan participants should consider seeking professional advice when deciding how to allocate their contributions.

Throughout the class period, U.S. Airways remained an embattled company "facing serious hurdles, with its long-term success, and indeed viability, in doubt." * * * On September 10, 2001, the Group stock price closed at $11.62 per share. In the days after the September 11th attacks, Group stock never closed lower than $4.10 per share, its closing price on September 27, 2001. * * * [From] October 1, 2001 to June 27, 2002, U.S. Airways implemented cost-cutting measures. * * * At the end of the 2001 calendar year, the Group stock price had rebounded to $6.34 per share. * * * By April 2002, U.S. Airways recognized that cost-cutting would not generate sufficient liquidity for its survival and the company announced that it would seek government assistance from the Air Transportation Stabilization Board (ATSB) as well as concessions from key stakeholders. Despite this news, in mid-April, the Group stock price was largely unchanged from four months earlier, trading at $6.25 per share on April 15th.

Over this same seven-month period—from September 2001 to April 2002—as U.S. Airways's [sic] financial situation, and liquidity, generated both cautious optimism and cause for concern, the PIC not only met internally, but also sought outside advice from U.S. Airways's Associate General Counsel, and later from outside legal counsel, about whether it should retain the Company Fund as an option under the Plan. All parties … believed it unnecessary, at that time, to cease offering the Company Fund. The Human Resources Committee of the Board of Directors and, later, the full Board considered and approved the PIC's decision to retain the Fund.

In May 2002, … the PIC recommended the appointment of an independent fiduciary to assume U.S. Airways's [sic] duties vis-a-vis the Company Fund. In a special meeting on May 9, 2002, the Board of Directors voted to retain an independent fiduciary for the Company Fund and authorized prompt steps to retain one. * * * By June 27, 2002, after an initial false start, U.S. Airways had retained Fiduciary Counselors … to serve as an independent fiduciary for the Company Fund. * * * At this point, the stock price was $3.72 per share. Once appointed, Fiduciary Counselors moved immediately to increase the cash component of the Company Fund from 10% to 20%, which required selling some Group stock. Shortly thereafter, on July 3, 2002, Fiduciary Counselors halted the purchase of additional shares of Group stock for the Company Fund, although it continued to allow participants to move freely in and out of the Company Fund. * * * [T]he company voluntarily filed for bankruptcy on August 11, 2002. On that date, Fiduciary Counselors directed that the Company Fund be closed. * * * On December 20, 2002, Fiduciary Counselors advised participants that existing Group stock would be cancelled and stockholders would receive no distribution under the Plan. * * *

Under ERISA, plan fiduciaries "are assigned a number of detailed duties and responsibilities, which include the proper management, administration and investment of plan assets, the maintenance of proper records, the disclosure of specific information, and the avoidance of conflicts of interest." * * * ERISA requires that a fiduciary shall act "with the care, skill, prudence, and diligence under the circumstances then prevailing that a prudent man acting in a like capacity and familiar with such matters would use in the conduct of an enterprise of a like character and with like aims." It also requires that a fiduciary "shall discharge his duties … solely in the interest of the participants and beneficiaries." Thus, in common parlance, ERISA fiduciaries owe participants duties of prudence and loyalty. To enforce these duties, "the court focuses not only on the merits of [a] transaction, but also on the thoroughness of the investigation into the merits of [that] transaction." * * * The district court concluded that U.S. Airways fulfilled its duties as a fiduciary, by acting both prudently and with loyalty toward the Plan participants. The Employees, however, challenge the district court's judgment on a variety of grounds. All are meritless…. But in light of the importance of this case and the lack of precedent in the field, we address the Employees' primary challenges to the district court's findings and then to its methodology. * * *

[T]he Employees contend that the district court erred in finding that U.S. Airways met its fiduciary duty to hold only prudent investments over the class period. The Employees principally argue that U.S. Airways insufficiently monitored the performance and prospects of the Company Fund…. The Employees' claim appears to be that had U.S. Airways acted prudently, it would have removed the Company Fund as an option for investment at some point during the class period. When deciding whether a plan fiduciary has acted prudently, a "[c]ourt must inquire whether the individual trustees, at the time they engaged in the challenged transactions, employed the appropriate methods to investigate the merits of the investment and to structure the investment." * * *A similar inquiry must take place when plaintiffs allege, as the Employees do here, that a fiduciary's failure to engage in a transaction, such as removal or closure of a company fund, breaches a duty. * * *

The district court found … that … [i]n addition to the Company Fund, U.S. Airways offered twelve diversified, and less risky, alternatives for investment and allowed participants to transfer their investment funds freely between these diversified options, always allowing participants to remove funds from the Company Fund without restriction. The Plan placed no conditions on investment of "matched" funds, except to disallow their investment in company stock (differentiating U.S. Airways's [sic] plan from those involved in the Lucent and Enron suits, which compelled investment in company stock). Furthermore, Plan literature repeatedly noted the risks associated with a non-diversified retirement portfolio in general, and the Company Fund in particular; U.S. Airways explicitly informed participants ... that the Company Fund carried the highest risk of the available options.

In addition, the district court found that U.S. Airways, through the PIC, monitored the performance of the Company Fund, and evaluated its continued suitability. During the class period, in addition to meeting informally, the PIC met formally four times, and at each of these meetings considered whether to continue to offer the Company Fund. Moreover, on at least two occasions, the PIC sought outside legal opinions with regard to ERISA's fiduciary duty requirements and those outside advisors indicated that it was consistent with the "prudent man" duty to maintain the Company Fund.... U.S. Airways [eventually] appointed an independent fiduciary to ensure that a non-company fiduciary would determine the future of the Company Fund in the Plan. Additionally, U.S. Airways's [sic] PIC continued reasonably to believe, throughout the class period, that U.S. Airways had a "credible and viable voluntary restructuring plan with a reasonable chance of success," and that it "would be able to avoid bankruptcy."

* * * Based on these facts, the court correctly concluded that U.S. Airways met its fiduciary duty to engage in a reasoned, "prudent" decision-making process, using "appropriate methods to investigate the merits" of retaining the Company Fund as an investment option. We stress that U.S. Airways twice engaged independent advisors—once during the class period, and once marking its end. Although plainly independent advice is not a "whitewash," it does provide "evidence of a thorough investigation."

* * * Under ERISA, it is not fatal that a plan fiduciary has "financial interests adverse to beneficiaries." There is no per se breach of loyalty if an "officer, employee, agent, or other representative" of the plan sponsor also serves as a plan fiduciary, even if that fiduciary purchases company securities on behalf of that plan. Thus, the fact that corporate officers comprised the PIC does not, in and of itself, create an illegal conflict of interest.

Beyond the bare allegation of a conflict based on the corporate position of the plan fiduciary, the Employees have provided no evidence that U.S. Airways continued to offer the Company Fund based on anything other than the best interests of the Plan participants—those who had already invested in the Company Fund as well as those who might elect to do so in the future. The district court found no evidence of other indicators of a breach of a duty of loyalty, e.g., that high-ranking company officials sold company stock while using the Company Fund to purchase more shares, or that the Company Fund was being used for the purpose of propping up the stock price in the market. Indeed, the court found that, throughout the class period, the PIC had a "well-founded" belief that the company would avoid bankruptcy. If the PIC had been correct, holding Group stock could have been a very profitable venture and one that would have been in the best interest of participants. Furthermore, if U.S. Airways had closed the Company Fund prematurely, and Group stock had rebounded further, the PIC would have succeeded only in locking in participant losses and precluding Plan participants from benefitting from the increase in stock price. * * *

The Employees ... assert that the district court's holding "is fatally flawed by its misunderstanding of modern portfolio theory." The district court properly noted that "the portfolio management theory ... teaches that an investment in a risky security as part of a diversified portfolio is, in fact, an appropriate means to increase return while minimizing risk." * * * However, the court may have overstated the appropriate relevance of modern portfolio theory to this case. Standing alone, it cannot provide a defense to the claimed breach of the "prudent man" duties here. "Under ERISA, the prudence of investments or classes of investments offered by a plan must be judged individually." That is, a fiduciary must initially determine, and continue to monitor, the prudence of each investment option available to plan participants. * * * This is so because a fiduciary cannot free himself from his duty to act as a prudent man simply by arguing that other funds, which individuals may or may not elect to combine with a company stock fund, could theoretically, in combination, create a prudent portfolio. To adopt the alternative view would mean that any single-stock fund, in which that stock existed in a state short of certain cancellation without compensation, would be prudent if offered alongside other, diversified Funds. * * * Although the district court may have relied too heavily on modern portfolio theory, this reliance in no way affected the validity of its ultimate holding. For the reasons stated earlier, even considered individually the Company Fund was a viable and prudent option for investment over the class period.

At the heart of the Employees' case seems to be the view that, given their losses and U.S. Airways's [sic] undisputed knowledge of its uncertain financial condition over the class period, U.S. Airways must have violated ERISA's "prudent man" duty when it continued to offer the Company Fund as a Plan option. Although we are not unsympathetic to the Employees' losses, such a contention is not tenable.

First and foremost, whether a fiduciary's actions are prudent cannot be measured in hindsight, whether this hindsight would accrue to the fiduciary's detriment or benefit. Put another way, an investment's diminution in value is neither necessary, nor sufficient, to demonstrate a violation of a fiduciary's ERISA duties. Furthermore, although placing retirement funds in any single-stock fund carries significant risk, and so would seem generally imprudent for ERISA purposes, Congress has explicitly provided that qualifying concentrated investment in employer stock does not violate the "prudent man" standard per se. We agree with the Employees that the risks of concentration are especially great when the employer stock at issue is volatile or the company's prospects in peril. * * * Congress, however, has chosen to follow a "strong policy and preference in favor of investment in employer stock." * * *

As more employers shift toward participant-driven, defined-contribution plans ... , Congress may reconsider the necessity of more safeguards for participants. For example, ERISA already limits the amount of employer stock that can be held in any defined-benefit pension plan to 10% of total plan assets. In light of the losses that have accrued to the Employees here, and others similarly situated, Congress may well decide that a similar limitation is appropriate for participant-driven, non-ESOP, defined-contribution plans. However, this policy decision is one for Congress and not for the courts. Accordingly, the Employees cannot succeed in this lawsuit simply by demonstrating that U.S. Airways offered the Company Fund during a time of grave uncertainty for the company, no matter how significant the Employees' ultimate financial losses. * * *

CASE QUESTIONS

1. What was the legal issue in this case? What did the court decide?
2. On what grounds did the employees challenge the airline's handling of its own stock as an investment option? Why did the court find these claims to be "meritless"?
3. In practical terms, what does this case say about what companies should do or not do when administering defined contribution plans?
4. Should Congress follow the court's suggestion and institute diversification requirements for defined contribution plans that specifically limit the percentage of company stock that can be held by employees? Why or why not?

The law in this area is still developing, but employers should do a few basic things regarding 401(k)s and other defined contribution plans. First, *employers must invest the funds deducted from employees' pay no later than fifteen business days after the end of the month in which deductions are made. Second, employers should carefully research investments, offer a range of investment types and investment companies from which to choose, and warn employees regarding the dangers of inadequate diversification. Obtaining independent financial advice is often prudent. Third, employers must provide regular opportunities for employees to divest themselves of company stock and place those funds in other investments. Fourth, employers should make impartial investment information available to employees. Fifth, employers should consider placing reasonable limits on the extent to which employee accounts are comprised of company stock and should remove company stock as an investment option when it is no longer a prudent investment. Finally, employers must not violate their fiduciary duty to manage plans in the best interests of employees by imposing lockdowns for illegitimate purposes.*

Cash Balance Plans Defined benefit pension plans that also include some features of defined contribution plans are known as **cash-balance plans**. These plans first appeared in 1985. About one-fourth of large employers with defined benefit plans had converted to cash balance plans by 2003.[44] As with other defined benefit plans, employers sponsoring cash balance plans are responsible for providing a promised level of benefits, employees are entitled to receive their benefits in the form of lifetime annuities if they choose (as opposed to lump-sum distributions), and the plans are insured through the PBGC. Unlike other defined benefit plans, the pension benefit is defined by the accumulation of annual employer contributions based on a percentage of an employee's salary plus a specified interest rate. A hypothetical account is created for each employee to track the accrual of pension benefits over the course of employment. The accounts do not actually exist, and employees do not have the ability to make investment decisions for their pension funds, but the pension benefit to which employees are entitled upon leaving employment is the amount accrued in these hypothetical accounts (i.e., the cash balance). Thus, there is greater portability of benefits under cash-balance plans than under traditional defined benefit plans.

Cash balance plans have been subjected to numerous legal challenges stemming from adverse effects on older workers associated with the process of converting from traditional defined benefit plans, but it now appears that they will generally be found lawful.[45] In a case involving IBM's conversion of its defined benefit plan to a cash balance plan, the court held that IBM did not reduce the rate of employees' benefit accrual. While acknowledging that older workers would generally fare worse under a cash balance plan, "the court said that removing a feature that gave extra benefits to the old differs from discriminating against them."[46] The Pension Protection Act of 2006 also contains language supporting the use of these plans.[47] *Employers should nonetheless proceed cautiously in converting to cash balance plans, fully inform employees about the nature of this change, and attempt to minimize the detrimental effects on older workers.*

Health Insurance

Health insurance is far and away the most important type of welfare plan covered by ERISA. Legal issues surrounding this costly but very necessary benefit include removing barriers (such as preexisting condition exclusions) to obtaining coverage,; preventing loss of coverage; and contesting discrimination—particularly against disabled persons and pregnant women. Fundamental changes have been made to the law governing health insurance plans in recent years.

Health Insurance Reform

In 2010, the **Patient Protection and Affordable Care Act (PPACA)** was signed into law.[48] This law is intended to ensure that most Americans will have adequate health insurance coverage. At the same time, the law includes a number of measures aimed at reining in the cost of health care. Some of the main provisions of the PPACA are outlined in Figure 13-1.

The PPACA is a complex statute. Its complexity stems from a number of sources. First, a policy and political judgment was made to build on the numerous existing sources of health insurance coverage rather than to create a single-payer system modeled after the Medicare program that serves as the primary health insurance for most older persons. Second, the many changes called for by the PPACA could not be implemented

---

[44]Elizabeth White Grover. "Shift to 'Hybrid' Pension Plans Slows; Employers Considering HSAs, EPF Says." *Daily Labor Report* 164 (August 25, 2005), A-10.

[45]*Engers v. AT&T*, 2011 U.S. App. LEXIS 12675 (3d Cir.).

[46]*Cooper v. IBM Personal Pension Plan*, 457 F.3d 636, 642 (7th Cir. 2006), *cert. denied*, 127 S. Ct. 1143 (2007).

[47]P.L. 109-280 § 701 (2006).

[48]P.L. No. 111-148 (2010), as amended by the Health Care and Education Reconciliation Act, P.L. No. 111-152 (2010).

FIGURE 13.1 Major Provisions of the Patient Protection and Affordable Care Act, as Amended, by Date of Implementation

---

June 21, 2010

Beginning on this date and until January 1, 2014 (the date by which insurance exchanges are required to be operational), individuals who have pre-existing conditions and who have not had group health coverage for at least six months will be able to obtain coverage through a "**temporary insurance program for high-risk individuals.**"

Beginning on this date and until January 1, 2014, a "**temporary reinsurance program for early retirees**" will be established to provide reimbursement to employer health plans for a portion of the costs of providing health insurance coverage to early retirees.

September 23, 2010

Health plans are prohibited from enforcing **pre-existing condition exclusionary periods** against enrollees *under the age of 19.*

Health plans that offer family coverage are required to cover **dependent children** until they reach the age of 26.

Health plans must distribute simple, plain language plan summaries. **Notice of material modifications to plans** must be distributed 60 days in advance of the effective date of the change.

Health plans are required to cover immunizations and other **preventive care services**. They are prohibited from imposing any cost-sharing requirements for that care.*

Prior authorization cannot be required as a condition of reimbursement for **emergency services**. Such services must generally be treated as in-network care.

Health plans are required to establish appeals procedures that include an **external review process** for disputed claims.*

Health plans are prohibited from discriminating in favor of highly compensated employees.*

Health plans are prohibited from including **lifetime limits** on the dollar value of essential health benefits.

Health plans are prohibited from **rescinding coverage** of otherwise eligible individuals, except in cases of fraud or misrepresentation.

Group health plans must offer a package of **essential health benefits** (e.g., maternity and newborn care, mental health and substance abuse services, prescription drugs).

Employers with at least 200 full-time employees who offer health insurance coverage are required to **enroll all new, full-time employees automatically**. An employee who objects would have to opt out of coverage.*

Any health care provider willing to accept the terms and conditions of participation established by the health plan or insurer must be allowed to participate in the network of providers (i.e., "**any willing provider requirement**").

March 1, 2013

Employers are required to **notify** employees that they can obtain coverage through an **exchange**.

January 1, 2014

Group health plans are prohibited from establishing **excessive employee cost-sharing and deductibles**.

Health plans are no longer able to include **lifetime and annual limits** on the dollar value of essential health benefits.

All **pre-existing condition exclusions** in health plans are prohibited.

Health plans (but not self-insured employer plans) are prohibited from charging different **premiums** to individuals except based on age, geographic area, family coverage, and tobacco use. However, employers with **wellness programs** are permitted to provide **incentives** up to thirty percent of the cost of coverage based on employees meeting health standards.

Health plans are prohibited from applying **waiting periods** of more than 90 days.

Insurance companies must **renew** group health plans if requested to do so by employers (although they are free to increase the price).

Each state is required to establish an **exchange** through which coverage under qualified health plans can be purchased. Individuals and small (less than 100 employees) employers will have access to these exchanges. Qualified health plans must provide an essential health benefits package in order to be offered on an exchange. Households with incomes between 100 and 400 percent of the poverty

FIGURE 13.1 Continued

line will be eligible for a tax credit on coverage that they purchase through an exchange. Small (less than 25 employees) employers will be eligible for a tax credit for 50 percent of the contributions made toward the premiums for health plans purchased through an exchange.

Once exchanges are established, individuals who fail to obtain minimum essential coverage for themselves or family members will be subject to a **monetary penalty**.

Once exchanges are established, large employers that do not offer minimum essential coverage under an employer-sponsored health plan to all of their full-time employees and dependents will be subject to a penalty if one or more of their full-time employees opt to purchase coverage through an exchange and receive government assistance in doing so. The penalty amount will start at approximately $167 per full-time employee in 2014 and be indexed to health care inflation.

After 2014

As of 2018, plans that cost more than $10,200 (individual coverage) or $27,500 (family coverage) will be subject to a 40 percent **excise tax** on the amount by which the cost of the plan exceeds these amounts (i.e., a tax on "Cadillac" plans).

*Indicates provisions that do not apply to "grandfathered" plans. Applicable provisions must be adopted by the beginning of the plan year that commences on or after the specified dates.

© Cengage Learning 2013.

Practical Considerations

Suppose that you are an employer with 110 employees and a group health plan. How will the new health insurance law affect you? Is it worth your while to avoid making changes that affect the grandfathered status of your plan?

immediately and all at once. Instead, implementation of the law's provisions was spread out over several years and includes a number of temporary patches. While many new requirements are being phased in, the full effect of the law will not be felt until at least 2014. Even then, there will still be different requirements depending on whether a particular health plan is "grandfathered." Plans are considered **grandfathered** if they existed prior to enactment of the PPACA and no significant changes resulting in reduced benefits or increased cost to plan beneficiaries were made to the plans.[49] Grandfathered plans are exempted from some requirements, although it is expected that over time, most plans will be altered in ways that will bring them under the full set of PPACA requirements. *Employers contemplating changes to their health plans need to consider whether those changes will remove their plans from "grandfathered" status.* A final source of complexity is the fact that the law contains different provisions for different types of health plans and different sizes of employers. In many respects, the implications of the PPACA are more far-reaching for the individual health insurance market than for employer-sponsored group plans.

Health insurance reform has proven to be controversial and politically incendiary. Numerous lawsuits have been filed challenging the PPACA.[50] The suits center on the issue of whether the government exceeded its authority under the commerce clause of the U.S. Constitution by requiring that individuals purchase health insurance or pay a penalty. This mandate is seen as integral to the PPACA because uninsured individuals increase health care costs for everyone when they put off seeking treatment until their conditions are severe and then obtain medical services from relatively costly sources (e.g., hospital emergency rooms) legally required to treat them. To date, legal challenges to the PPACA have resulted in conflicting decisions, including at the appellate court level.[51] The Supreme Court is expected to weigh in on this matter and may have already done so by the time that

[49]Sara Hansard. "Regulations for Grandfathered Plans Forbid Big Increases in Copayments." *Daily Labor Report* 113 (June 15, 2010), A-14.

[50]Kevin Sack. "Battle Over Health Care Law Shifts to Federal Appellate Courts." *New York Times* (May 9, 2011), A14.

[51]*Thomas More Law Center v. Obama*, 2011 U.S. App. LEXIS 13265 (6th Cir.) (finding that the law is constitutional); *Florida v. United States HHS*, 2011 U.S. App. LEXIS 16806 (11th Cir.) (finding that the individual mandate exceeded government authority under the commerce clause, but not invalidating the entire statute); *Virginia ex rel. Cuccinelli v. Sebelius*, 2011 U.S. App. LEXIS 18632 (4th Cir.) (finding that the state lacks standing to bring a suit challenging the law).

you read this book. Apart from whatever action the Supreme Court takes, Congress might also amend or repeal the law. But whatever twists and turns the story of health insurance reform takes in the future, the reality of ever-increasing health care costs and our failure to provide adequate health care for all will not magically disappear.

Maintaining Coverage: COBRA and HIPAA

In any given year, large numbers of Americans go without health insurance. If the PPACA remains in place and works as envisioned, the problem of the uninsured should be greatly diminished (but not, even under the most optimistic projections, eliminated). A much earlier effort to deal with problem of the uninsured focused on circumstances that caused individuals to lose their coverage and provided them with a means of staying insured until they became covered under other group health plans. The **Consolidated Omnibus Budget Reconciliation Act (COBRA)**[52] requires that employers who have group health insurance plans and at least twenty employees offer continuation coverage to employees (and other beneficiaries if there is family coverage) who experience **qualifying events** that would otherwise cause the loss of their health insurance. COBRA qualifying events and the periods of time for which coverage (if chosen by an employee or beneficiary) must be maintained are as follows:

Continue coverage for up to eighteen months

- Voluntary or involuntary termination of employment for reasons other than "gross misconduct"
- Reduced hours of employment

Continue coverage for up to thirty-six months

- Divorce or legal separation
- Death of an employee
- Loss of dependent child status under the terms of the health plan
- Covered employee becoming entitled to Medicare

Practical Considerations What specific steps should employers take to administer continuation of health insurance under COBRA?

If one of these qualifying events occurs, an employer must offer continuation coverage to the employee and other family members who have been covered under the employee's health insurance. Employees cannot simply be "dropped" from health plans without following COBRA's procedures. The continuation coverage must be the same coverage enjoyed by employees who have not experienced a qualifying event. There is a heavy emphasis under COBRA on providing proper notification. *Information about COBRA rights must be provided to covered employees and their spouses and be included in health plan SPDs at the time health plan coverage begins.* Employers must notify plan administrators of the occurrence of qualifying events within thirty days. Because employers would not necessarily know of divorces, separations, or loss of dependent child status, employees or other beneficiaries are responsible for bringing these events to the attention of plan administrators within sixty days. *After they are alerted that a qualifying event has occurred, plan administrators have fourteen days to offer continuation coverage. Notice of the availability of continuation coverage should go to all adult beneficiaries, and not just to covered employees. Beneficiaries must be given at least sixty days from when their health coverage ends or from when they are notified of their COBRA rights, whichever is later, to elect continuation coverage and an additional forty-five days to make the first payment.*

Continuation coverage under COBRA is not free. Beneficiaries can be charged up to 102 percent of the cost to the employer of providing coverage under the group health

---

[52]29 U.S.C.S. §§ 1161-1167 (2011).

plan. Although this is a major expense for most employees, it may still be preferable to the option of being uninsured or trying to purchase an individual policy from an insurance company, especially if the employee or family members have known health problems. *If an employee elects continuation coverage, the coverage must continue for up to eighteen or thirty-six months unless the employee fails to make the payments, the employer discontinues offering group health insurance to its employees, or the employee becomes covered under another group health plan (e.g., gets another job).*

JUST THE FACTS

An employee was terminated in the aftermath of a change of ownership at a company. The employee's wife had breast cancer at the time, and he wanted to maintain health insurance coverage for the two of them. He asked at the office whether he would be able to continue coverage after his termination. On his last day of work, he was informed verbally that his health insurance would be continued. However, when his wife sought medical treatment about nine months later, she was told that she had no insurance coverage. Did this employer violate COBRA?

See, *McDowell v. Krawchison*, 125 F.3d 954 (6th Cir. 1997).

Another obstacle to obtaining health benefits or maintaining coverage when changing jobs is the preexisting condition exclusions commonly incorporated into health plans. A **preexisting condition exclusion** denies coverage for a specified period of time for the treatment of conditions that existed before an individual enrolled in a health plan. The PPACA provides for the elimination of all preexisting condition exclusions from health plans by 2014. Until such time as that occurs, the **Health Insurance Portability and Accountability Act (HIPAA)**[53] remains important in this regard. HIPAA greatly restricts but does not eliminate the use of preexisting condition exclusions by health plans. First, it restricts preexisting conditions to those "for which medical advice, diagnosis, care, or treatment was recommended or received within the 6-month period ending on the enrollment date."[54] Pregnancy cannot be deemed a preexisting condition. Second, *exclusionary periods can last no longer than twelve months* (eighteen months for late enrollees). Third, *exclusionary periods must be reduced by any periods of prior coverage under a group health plan (including COBRA coverage) provided that no more than sixty-three days elapsed between the prior coverage and enrollment in the new plan.* Prior coverage under a group health plan is documented in a **certificate of creditable coverage**. *Certificates of creditable coverage must be provided automatically and free of charge to employees when they lose coverage or exhaust their COBRA continuation coverage.*

Retiree Health Benefits

The need for medical care generally increases during a person's retirement years. Medicare is designed to be the primary health insurance for retired persons, but it provides only partial coverage of medical costs and is not available to younger retirees. In the face of rapidly rising health costs, many employers have cut back on or completely

---

[53]P.L. No. 104-191, § 101, 110 Stat. 1936 (1996).

[54]42 U.S.C.S. § prec 300gg(a)(1) (2011).

eliminated health insurance coverage for their retirees. This has raised the question of whether employers are ever legally bound to continue providing health insurance coverage to retirees. The principal issue in these cases is whether the employer intended to confer an irrevocable right to receive health benefits on retirees. Unionized employees have had some success in arguing that retiree health benefits obtained through collective bargaining are not revocable, particularly in the absence of any clear contract language authorizing the employer to modify or terminate the benefits.[55] An employer violated its fiduciary duty under ERISA by failing to make clear to its employees that its promises of free or low-cost medical benefits throughout their retirements or lives were subject to change.[56] But overall, retirees have had a difficult time convincing courts that their former employers should be bound to providing this welfare benefit that, unlike pensions, does not vest.[57]

Discrimination and Benefits

Some benefits, including life insurance, disability insurance, and health insurance, are more expensive to provide for older workers. The **Older Workers Benefit Protection Act**,[58] which amended the ADEA, takes account of this fact. *Employers are permitted to provide less extensive coverage for older workers so long as the amount spent to provide benefits to older workers is at least equal to the amount spent providing those benefits to other workers.* This cost-equalization principle applies only to welfare plans whose cost is age-related, and not to pension plans. Certain offsets or deductions from benefits received by older workers in exchange for other benefits (e.g., less severance pay in exchange for retiree health insurance) are also permitted. Employers that provide retiree health insurance can lawfully reduce (or eliminate) health benefits for retirees when they turn 65 and become eligible for Medicare coverage.[59] Regarding pensions, plans can establish minimum ages for receipt of pension benefits (e.g., employees must be at least 52 regardless of how many years of service they have) and "normal" retirement ages (e.g., 65). However, as a general rule, *older workers must be allowed to participate in and continue accruing benefits under pension plans regardless of how old they are when first employed or whether their age now exceeds the normal retirement age under the plans.*

Clippings

The EEOC settled a lawsuit alleging that the Minnesota Department of Human Services violated the ADEA by offering an early retirement incentive that treated employees who retired before age 55 better than employees who retired at a later age. Under the plan, contributions were made toward the health and dental premiums of younger retirees until they turned 65 and were eligible for Medicare, while no premium subsidies were available for older retirees. A federal district court had already found the Minnesota Department of Correction's use of the

---

[55]*International Union, UAW v. Yard-Man*, 716 F.2d 1476 (6th Cir. 1983), *cert. denied*, 465 U.S. 1007 (1984); *Quesenberry v. Volvo Trucks N. America*, 2011 U.S. App. LEXIS 14161 (4th Cir.).

[56]*Adair v. Unisys Corp.*, 579 F.3d 220 (3d Cir. 2009), *cert. denied*, 130 S. Ct. 1546 (2010).

[57]*Vallone v. CNA Financial*, 375 F.3d 623 (7th Cir. 2004), *cert. denied*, 125 S. Ct. 670 (2004).

[58]P.L. 101-433, 104 Stat. 978 (1990).

[59]Robert Pear. "Many Retirees May Lose Benefit from Employers." *New York Times* (December 27, 2007), A1.

same early retirement incentive to be "facially discriminatory" against employees over 55.

Kevin P. McGowan. "EEOC, Minnesota Agency Settle for $467,000 Lawsuit Alleging Age Bias in Retiree Benefits." *Daily Labor Report* 70 (April 12, 2011), A-3.

Disabled persons have a particularly great need for health insurance. At the same time, this might provide some employers concerned about the rising cost of health insurance with an incentive to discriminate against them. Clearly, *employers cannot refuse to hire or terminate disabled persons based on the assumption, or even fact, that they are more expensive to insure.* Basing employment decisions on disability is disparate treatment and violates the Americans with Disabilities Act. *Employers are also prohibited from discriminating against an employee because that employee is associated with a disabled family member who might be a heavy user of health benefits. An employer also violates the ADA by refusing to provide health coverage to employees with disabilities if health coverage is provided to nondisabled employees.* Thus, the ADA was violated when an employer changed group health plans and the new insurer refused to cover an employee who previously had cancer and was currently afflicted with AIDS.[60] Under HIPAA, *group health plans are prohibited from limiting eligibility based on the health status, medical condition, claims experience, medical history, genetic information, or disability of an employee or dependent.*

Group health plans and the issuers of health insurance coverage under group plans also must comply with the Genetic Information Nondiscrimination Act (GINA). This law requires that premiums and contribution amounts for groups must not be adjusted on the basis of genetic information. Additionally, group health plans and insurers offering them cannot request or require employees or their family members to undergo genetic testing and are prohibited from collecting in any way genetic information about employees prior to their enrollment in or coverage under a group health plan.[61]

Can group health plans provide less coverage or impose higher copayments for mental health services or substance abuse treatment than for other medical services? Insurers had traditionally done so, but the **Mental Health Parity and Addiction Equity Act** requires that employers with fifty or more employees that choose to cover mental health and substance abuse treatment at all must do so at the same level and under the same terms as medical and surgical treatments.[62] Since the PPACA includes mental health and substance abuse care among the essential health services that must be covered, the option of not covering these services at all appears to no longer be available.

The Pregnancy Discrimination Act (PDA) is another antidiscrimination statute with implications for the design of health plans. The basic principle of the PDA is that pregnant employees are entitled to the same treatment as nonpregnant employees with similar ability to work. *Health plans must cover expenses for pregnancy-related medical care on the same basis as for other medical conditions.* An exception is that health plans can refuse to pay the cost of abortions where the life of the mother is not endangered. Not

---

[60]*Anderson v. Gus Mayer Boston Store*, 924 F. Supp. 763 (E.D. Tex. 1996).

[61]110 P.L. 233; 122 Stat. 881, Title I, Sec. 101 (2008).

[62]The Paul Wellstone and Pete Domenici Mental Health Parity and Addiction Equity Act, 110 P.L. 343, § 512, 122 Stat. 3765 (2008).

only must pregnancy-related medical costs be covered, but *health plans are prohibited from imposing additional deductibles or copayments for pregnancy-related treatments.* Additionally, *coverage of pregnancy-related treatment cannot be limited to married employees, and the same level of coverage must be provided for the spouses of male employees as is provided for the spouses of female employees.*

JUST THE FACTS

Prior to when the Pregnancy Discrimination Act went into effect in 1979, Pacific Telephone & Telegraph (now part of AT&T) allowed employees taking maternity leave a maximum of thirty days of service credit. No similar limitation was placed on other forms of temporary disability leave. A group of women who had taken maternity leave during the 1970s and whose pensions were lower at the time of their retirements than they would have been if service credit had been received for the entire period of maternity leave sued. Should the employer be liable for the adverse effect on these employees' pensions of a policy that was contrary to the PDA but that occurred prior to passage of the law?

See, *Hulteen v. AT&T Corp.,* 129 S. Ct. 1962 (2009).

Domestic Partner Benefits

Many people become entitled to benefits through their associations with others. For example, health insurance plans typically allow employees to opt for family coverage to insure their spouses and dependents. To the extent that eligibility to share benefits is based on a marital relationship, a person who is not married but is living with another person is disadvantaged. This is particularly true of gays and lesbians, who in most parts of the United States do not have the option of becoming legally married to their partners.

Because federal law does not currently prohibit discrimination based on sexual orientation, it also does not require that benefits be made available to domestic partners. The Montana Supreme Court decided on constitutional grounds (equal protection of the law) that public universities in that state must provide gay and lesbian employees with health insurance coverage for their domestic partners.[63] However, the Michigan Supreme Court determined that a marriage amendment to the state's constitution prohibited public agencies from offering health insurance to the same-sex partners of their employees.[64] The amendment's wording ("the union of one man and one woman in marriage shall be the only agreement recognized as a marriage or similar union for any purpose") was construed by the court as meaning that domestic partnerships are "similar unions" that cannot be "recognized … for any purpose" including provision of health benefits.

For the most part, employers decide whether to offer **domestic partner benefits**. A number of state and city governments provide domestic partner benefits voluntarily, as do numerous private employers. The Bureau of Labor Statistics estimated that about 36 percent of full-time, private sector employees had access to health insurance for same-sex

---

[63]*Snetsinger v. Montana University System,* 104 P.3d 445 (Mont. 2005).

[64]*National Pride at Work v. Governor of Michigan,* 748 N.W.2d 524 (Mich. 2008).

domestic partners (and 31 percent had access to coverage for opposite sex domestic partners).[65] Although domestic partner benefits are often made available to both same-sex and different-sex partners, a court has ruled that a program limited to same-sex domestic partners does not constitute sex discrimination.[66]

Key Terms

Employee Retirement Income
  Security Act (ERISA), p. 426
Pension plans, p. 426
welfare plans, p. 426
preemption, p. 426
Summary Plan Descriptions
  (SPDs), p. 427
abuse of discretion, p. 428
appeals procedures, p. 429
fiduciary, p. 430
fiduciary duties, p. 430
vesting, p. 434
participation, p. 437
defined benefit plans, p. 437

Pension Benefit Guaranty
  Corporation (PBGC), p. 437
Pension Protection Act of
  2006, p. 437
defined contribution plans, p. 438
presumption of prudence, p. 442
cash balance plans, p. 446
Patient Protection and Affordable
  Care Act (PPACA), p. 447
grandfathered, p. 449
Consolidated Omnibus Budget
  Reconciliation Act
  (COBRA), p. 450
qualifying events, p. 450

preexisting condition
  exclusion, p. 451
Health Insurance Portability and
  Accountability Act
  (HIPAA), p. 451
certificate of creditable
  coverage, p. 451
Older Workers Benefit Protection
  Act, p. 452
Mental Health Parity and
  Addiction Equity
  Act, p. 453
domestic partner
  benefits, p. 454

Chapter Summary

The Employee Retirement Income Security Act (ERISA) is the principal federal law regulating the benefit plans of private sector employers. ERISA covers plans that defer income for retirement (pension plans), as well as a host of other benefits such as health insurance and severance pay (welfare plans). Under ERISA, employers must provide reports and other information to employees about their benefits, ensure that promised benefits are actually provided, establish reasonable claims and appeals procedures, manage plans wisely and solely in the interest of beneficiaries, and refrain from interfering with or retaliating against plan participants. Many ERISA cases involve claims in which promised benefits were denied or a breach of fiduciary duty occurred. Fiduciaries are those parties who exercise discretionary authority or control over the management or administration of a benefit plan or its assets. They have many responsibilities under ERISA, including managing plans in compliance with ERISA and plan documents, exercising skill and prudence, being loyal to the interests of plan participants and beneficiaries, diversifying investments, avoiding conflicts of interest, and not misrepresenting

or knowingly withholding material information about benefit plans.

ERISA regulates pension plans more closely than welfare plans. Unlike other benefits, employee pension rights vest after a specified period of service, resulting in a nonforfeitable right to a pension. ERISA's participation rules encourage pension plans to have broad coverage. The law distinguishes between defined benefit and defined contribution pension plans. Defined benefit plans specify a particular benefit that vested employees will receive upon retirement. Defined contribution plans do not promise any particular level of payment upon retirement. Instead, the size of the pension is determined by the sum of money that has accrued in an employee's account as the result of contributions and the manner in which they were invested. Employers with defined benefit plans must comply with many rules intended to ensure that their plans are adequately funded. The Pension Benefit Guaranty Corporation exists to deal with problems created by the termination of defined benefit pension plans and to ensure that vested employees do not lose their pensions in plan terminations.

---

[65]Alicia Biggs. "Over One-Third of Workers Have Access to Same-Sex Domestic Partner Benefits." *Daily Labor Report* 143 (July 26, 2011), D-1.

[66]*Foray v. Bell Atlantic*, 56 F. Supp. 2d 327 (S.D.N.Y. 1999).

With defined contribution plans, the risk of producing adequate retirement income is placed squarely with employees. As employers have shifted away from defined benefit plans to defined contribution plans, particularly 401(k)s, concerns have arisen regarding lack of diversification in investments, lack of good information about investments, delays in or misappropriation of investments, and misuse of administrative mechanisms such as lockdown periods. Many suits have been brought against the fiduciaries of defined contribution plans alleging that company stock was imprudently offered as an investment or plan participants were subjected to excessive fees. Outcomes have varied, depending in part on whether the courts applied a presumption of prudence to plan administrators who followed plan documents in offering company stock as an investment option.

Health insurance is the most important type of welfare plan covered by ERISA. Lack of health insurance, inadequate coverage, and the high cost of coverage have long been concerns of policy makers. The Patient Protection and Affordable Care Act (PPACA) is a complex statute intended to address these problems. Its many provisions are being implemented over a number of years. Whether the law will be fully implemented depends on future political developments and the outcomes of legal challenges. A far more modest but long-standing approach to dealing with the problem of uninsured persons is the law known as COBRA. This law requires that employers provide the option of continuation coverage when qualifying events occur that would otherwise cause coverage to be lost (for the employee or other beneficiaries). These qualifying events include termination for reasons other than gross misconduct, reduction in hours, legal separation or divorce, death of a covered employee, entitlement of a covered employee to Medicare, and loss of dependent child status by a beneficiary. The Health Insurance Portability and Accountability Act (HIPAA) greatly restricts but does not eliminate the use of preexisting condition exclusions. HIPAA also makes it illegal for health plans to base eligibility on any aspect of health status.

Discrimination in benefits, like other employment opportunities, can be challenged. The ADEA addresses issues related to the greater cost of providing some benefits for older workers and allows adjustments to be made in benefits provided employers pay no less toward the benefits of older workers than is expended for younger workers. Employers are prohibited by the ADA from excluding disabled persons from employment opportunities based on concerns about their use of medical services. Under the PDA, pregnancy must be treated like other medical conditions under health plans. GINA prohibits the adjustment of health insurance premiums on the basis of genetic information and the collection of employees' genetic information prior to their enrollment in or coverage under a group health plan. The Mental Health Parity and Addiction Equity Act requires larger employers with health plans that cover mental health treatments to cover those services on the same terms as other medical treatments. Finally, it is generally up to employers whether to extend benefit coverage to the domestic partners of gay or other unmarried employees.

Practical Advice Summary

- Benefit plans must be detailed in writing in plan documents.
- Summary Plan Descriptions (SPDs) must be
  — Written in plain language.
  — Sufficiently comprehensive and accurate to inform employees about their rights and responsibilities under benefit plans.
  — Provided to employees within ninety days of their becoming covered under benefit plans.
- Employers should be careful in advising employees about their benefits and refer them back to SPDs and other plan documents.
- Benefit plan administrators must
  — Base benefit determination decisions on plan documents.
  — Have reasons for their decisions.
  — Use all the current and appropriate information available to them.
- Employers must establish "reasonable" claims and appeals procedures for their benefit plans. This requirement includes
  — Generally making decisions on benefit claims within ninety days (more quickly for claims under health plans).
  — Providing written notice when benefits are denied, including the specific reason(s) for the denial.
  — Allowing at least 60 days (180 days for group health plans) to appeal adverse decisions regarding benefit claims.

- Parties acting as fiduciaries are responsible for managing benefit plans and funds solely in the interest of plan participants and beneficiaries and for the purpose of providing them with benefits.
- The duties of fiduciaries include
  — Managing plans with skill, care, and prudence.
  — Ensuring that plans comply with plan documents and ERISA.
  — Diversifying the assets of pension plans to minimize the risk of large losses.
  — Selecting proper investments for pension plans and monitoring their performance.
  — Refraining from transactions that would create conflicts of interest.
  — Providing accurate information about benefit plans and not withholding material facts that would likely affect the choices and interests of beneficiaries.
- Employers must not discharge or otherwise discriminate against employees because they have used benefits to which they are entitled or interfere with their use of benefits to which they are entitled.
- Employers with pension plans must allow
  — Vesting of pension benefits, usually after no more than five or seven years of service.
  — Employees who are at least 21 years of age and have served for at least one (if gradual vesting) or two (if cliff vesting) years to participate in pension plans, although other limitations can be imposed.
- Employers with defined contribution plans
  — Must ensure that funds deducted from pay are invested no later than fifteen days after the end of the month.
  — Should offer a range of investment types and investment companies from which employees can choose.
  — Should make impartial investment information available to employees.
  — Must provide regular opportunities for employees to divest themselves of company stock and place those funds in other investments.
  — Should consider placing limits on investment in company stock and remove company stock as an investment when it is no longer a prudent investment option.
  — Should not impose lockdowns for illegitimate purposes.
  — Must provide a thirty-day notice of blackout periods (i.e., lockdowns).

- Employers converting to cash-balance pension plans should
  — Proceed with caution.
  — Fully inform employees about the nature of this change.
  — Strive to minimize the detrimental effects on older workers.
- With just a few exceptions, employers must not establish mandatory retirement ages.
- Older workers cannot be denied benefits, but employers can provide less extensive benefits to older workers when
  — The cost of providing those benefits is greater for older workers.
  — The total amount spent on benefits for older workers is at least equal to the amount spent for other employees.
- Employers contemplating changes to their health plans need to consider whether those changes will remove their plans from "grandfathered" status.
- Group health plans that are not grandfathered must (currently or by 2014):
  — Cover dependents until they are 26 years of age.
  — Provide preventive services without cost-sharing.
  — Offer a package of essential health benefits.
  — Not have annual or lifetime limits on the dollar value of essential health benefits.
  — Not impose excessive deductibles or cost-sharing on participants.
  — Establish an external review process for disputed claims.
  — Not require prior authorization of emergency services.
  — Not charge different premiums based on health status or any basis other than age, geographic area, family coverage, and tobacco use (does not apply to self-insured plans).
  — Not impose waiting periods of more than ninety days.
- Employers with group health plans and at least twenty employees must offer continuation coverage to employees and other beneficiaries who would otherwise lose their health insurance due to one or more qualifying events.
  — An employee can be charged up to 102 percent of the cost of covering the employee under the group health plan for continuation coverage.
  — Information about COBRA continuation coverage must be provided to covered employees and their spouses at the time health plan coverage begins.

— Notice of the availability of continuation coverage following occurrence of a qualifying event must go to covered employees and their spouses.

— Beneficiaries must be given at least sixty days from when their health coverage ends or notice is received, whichever is later, to elect continuation coverage.

- Employers should
  — Carefully document when COBRA notifications are sent.
  — Request that all employees respond regardless of whether they are accepting or declining.
  — Maintain up-to-date contact information.
  — Arrange for how payment will be made.
  — Track coverage periods.

- When continuation coverage is chosen, that coverage must continue for up to eighteen or thirty-six months (depending on the qualifying event) unless
  — The employer discontinues offering group health insurance.
  — The employee fails to pay.
  — The employee obtains coverage under another group health plan.

- Preexisting condition exclusionary periods
  — Can be applied only to conditions for which diagnosis, care, or treatment was recommended or received within the six months prior to plan enrollment (and never to pregnancy).
  — Can last no more than twelve months (eighteen months for late enrollment).
  — Must be reduced by any periods of prior coverage under a group health plan that ended no more than sixty-three days before enrollment in the new health plan.
  — Must be eliminated from health plans starting in 2014.

- Certificates of creditable coverage must be provided automatically and free of charge to employees when they lose health insurance coverage or exhaust their COBRA continuation coverage.

- Employers cannot refuse to hire or terminate disabled persons or employees with disabled family members based on concerns about the cost of providing them with health insurance.

- Group health plans must not limit eligibility based on health status, medical condition, claims experience, medical history, genetic information, or the disability of an employee or dependent.

- Health plans must
  — Cover costs of pregnancy-related medical treatment (except abortion).
  — Not impose additional deductibles or co-payments for such treatments that are not required for other medical treatments.
  — Provide the same level of coverage for pregnancy-related medical treatment to both married and unmarried employees and for the spouses of both male and female employees.

- The health plans of employers with more 50 or more employees must cover treatment for mental health and substance abuse problems on the same terms as coverage for other medical treatments.

Chapter Questions

1. Following a merger in 1998, a Lucent Technologies employee received several written communications from the company stating that the date of first service that would be used in computing his pension benefit was 1980. This was the year in which the employee had begun to work for a company that was subsequently acquired by Lucent. Based on the information received, the employee determined that he would be able to retire with a full pension in 2005 and that his wife could afford to go ahead and retire from her job at the end of 2003. Shortly after the wife's retirement, and in the face of an impending lay-off, the employee requested a pension benefit calculation from the company. They first sent an estimate of $1,469.25, based on the 1980 start date. Two weeks later, the company sent a revised pension worksheet that indicated less than 15 years of total service and a monthly pension benefit of $880.54. In fact, plan documents provided that the merger date of 1998 would be used to determine length of service for pension purposes. Did the employer violate ERISA through misrepresentations that were relied on in making the decision for the wife to retire? (*Shook v. Avaya*, 625 F.3d 69 [3d Cir. 2010])

2. A 44-year-old project manager and plumber was diagnosed with multiple sclerosis. She applied for and received benefits under her employer's disability plan. While she was receiving benefits, she was encouraged also to apply for Social Security

disability. Receipt of the latter would reduce but not end payments under the employer's plan. She applied for the Social Security disability benefits, was determined to be disabled by the Social Security Administration, and began to receive Social Security disability. At about the same time, the administrator of the employer's disability plan undertook an examination of her case. Several physicians were hired to conduct peer reviews of her medical files. One of the reviewing physicians concluded from examining her file that the woman "was not credible" and that she could, in fact, work. Her benefits under the employer's disability plan were discontinued. No examinations of the woman were conducted, and the ruling that she was eligible for Social Security disability was not considered. Was ERISA violated by the termination of this woman's disability benefits? (*Bennett v. Kemper National Services*, 514 F.3d 547 [6th Cir. 2008])

3. A flight attendant got into an altercation with another employee while performing between-flight duties on a plane. The flight attendant threw an apple at the other employee, who then threw it back. The flight attendant used a racial epithet to refer to the other employee, who was African American. The two ended up tussling on the floor of the aircraft, with choke holds being applied. The fight was eventually broken up by two first-class passengers boarding the plane. Both employees were fired. The airline failed to notify the flight attendant of her right to continuation of health coverage, and she sued. What should the court decide? Why? (*Nakisa v. Continental Airlines*, 2001 U.S. Dist. LEXIS 8952)

4. A company terminated an employee and sent him notification of his COBRA rights via certified mail with return receipt requested. The former employee was out of the house on two occasions when the postal service attempted to deliver the letter. It left a note that he could pick it up at the post office. However, when he went to the post office, the letter could not be found. The letter was later found and sent back to the employer marked "undelivered." The employer made no further attempt to contact the former employee. The employee incurred medical expenses for which he wanted continuation coverage. The employer denied continuation coverage because he did not elect it within the required sixty days. The former employee sued. What

should the court decide? Why? (*Degruise v. Sprint Corp.*, 279 F.3d 333 [5th Cir. 2002])

5. An employee got hurt on the job, was unable to work for a period of time, and received workers' compensation benefits. His employer did not deduct the employee's share of health insurance premiums from his worker's compensation payment or otherwise notify the employee as to how he should continue to make contributions toward his health insurance. The health insurance was maintained by the employer for six months. Thereafter, the employee was informed that his health insurance coverage had been terminated. The employer claimed that the reason for the termination was nonpayment of the employee's premiums and, thus, no COBRA notification was required. Did this employee experience a qualifying event? Were his COBRA rights violated? (*Aquilino v. Solid Waste Services*, 2008 U.S. Dist. LEXIS 47168 [E.D. Pa.])

6. DuPont amended its pension plan to create a Temporary Pension System (TPS) that would provide an enhanced retirement benefit to employees who chose early retirement. In a written communication detailing the plan, employees were told that "If taken as a lump sum, all or part of the lump sum can be rolled into the DuPont Savings and Investment Plan (SIP) or any other qualified IRA, within 60 days." The advantage of "rolling over" a lump sum payment of this sort is that the employee avoids a large tax payment. However, the communication failed to mention that under IRS rules, not all employees would be entitled to roll over the TPS payment. Two weeks before the retirement date of an employee who had opted to accept the offer, largely because of the extra benefit that would be free from tax liability, company personnel processing his paperwork discovered that the employee would not be entitled to roll over the funds. The employee was not informed of this, and after retiring, he was assessed approximately $50,000 in taxes on the lump sum that he received. He sued. What should the court decide? (*Griggs v. DuPont*, 237 F.3d 371 [4th Cir. 2001])

7. Under a Force Management Plan (FMP) adopted by Lucent in July 2001, employees who were downsized would receive severance pay and other benefits. Employees were told that the facility that they worked at would be closing and that they "should consider themselves FMP'd at some

future date." A couple of months later and prior to closure of the facility, several employees were told that they were under investigation for failing to work forty hours per week at the facility. The employees subsequently received letters indicating that they were being terminated "for cause" and would not be entitled to FMP benefits. The fact that these employees performed some of their work hours off-site had been known by the company for some time. The company had not warned or taken any previous action against the employees for this alleged violation of company policy. The terminated employees sued. What should the court decide? Why? (*Leszczuk v. Lucent Technologies*, 2005 U.S. Dist. LEXIS 11552)

8. A public employee pension plan for the state of Kentucky adds unearned years of service to years of actual service in determining pension benefits for employees in certain high-risk occupations (e.g., firefighters) who become disabled before they reach the minimum retirement age under the plan. The plan does not do so for employees who become disabled after having already reached the plan's minimum retirement age (instead, basing benefits only on actual years worked). The purpose is to provide benefits to disabled employees that are on par with normal retirement benefits. The effect of the provision is that some older disabled workers receive pension benefits that are less than those that younger disabled workers can receive. Does this violate the ADEA? (*Kentucky Retirement System v. EEOC*, 128 S. Ct. 2361 [2008])

9. An employee's wife had a liver disease and eventually received a transplant. The employer is a relatively small company that has a self-insured health plan. The wife's numerous treatments caused the company to incur substantial costs. Managers attempted to convince the couple to accept some alternative arrangement for insuring the wife, but because no viable alternative existed, she remained under the plan. The employee was told at one point that the company's options were to fire him or make him an independent contractor without benefits, but nothing was done at the time. About a year later, the employee was fired and he sued. What should the court decide? Why? (*Jackson v. Service Engineering*, 96 F. Supp. 2d 873 [S.D. Ind. 2000])

10. Is the broad preemption language of ERISA necessary? Does preemption unduly constrain the ability of employees to hold employers accountable for the manner in which benefit plans are administered?

11. Now that you have learned a little bit about what the new health insurance law (the PPACA) entails, are you in favor of or opposed to this law? Why?

CHAPTER 14

Unions and Collective Bargaining

Most of the law discussed in this book concerns rights conferred on individual employees, such as the right not to be discriminated against and the right to be paid at least the minimum wage. The labor laws discussed in this chapter take a fundamentally different approach to protecting workers. Their focus is on protecting employees who join together in groups and seek to engage in collective bargaining with their employers. Rather than legislators, courts, or administrative agencies deciding what is acceptable treatment of employees, collective bargaining allows for employers and employees to decide many of the rules that will govern their workplaces—and to do so on relatively equal terms. This chapter focuses on the principal federal labor law that governs collective bargaining by private sector employees, the National Labor Relations Act.

Not all employees have union representation. In fact, the vast majority of private sector employees are not currently unionized. This does not negate the importance of understanding the NLRA and other labor laws. For one thing, employees who are currently not represented by unions might opt for unionization at some point in the future. Nonunion employers often have dealings with contractors and suppliers whose employees are unionized. Mergers or acquisitions might bring unionized employees into the fold. Even if an employer does not have any dealings with unionized employees, nonunion employees still have certain rights under the NLRA that must be respected. The *NLRA and other labor laws also affect nonunion workplaces and cannot safely be ignored by those employers.*

The Idea of Collective Bargaining

When people want to get things done, they organize. Joining together with other like-minded people often makes it possible to accomplish objectives that elude individuals acting alone. This is particularly true when employees seek to influence their powerful and well-organized employers. The institution of **collective bargaining** recognizes the value of employees banding together to deal with their employers and the fact that the desires of employees and employers sometimes clash. Both employers and employees care a great deal about and are apt to disagree on wages, hours, and many other terms and conditions of employment. Collective bargaining provides employees with representation, greater power in dealing with their employers, and a means of resolving issues in ways that meet the requirements of both parties.

Labor unions play a critical role in collective bargaining. Unions are organizations of employees that represent employees in their dealings with employers. Employees have the opportunity to choose, by majority rule, whether they want to have union representation. Unions negotiate with employers to obtain **labor agreements**—contracts specifying the wages and many other terms and conditions of employment for the employees they represent. However, the collective bargaining process does not end with the signing of labor agreements. Unions have an ongoing role in representing employees, including filing grievances when disputes arise about whether employees' contractual rights have been violated.

There is much to recommend about collective bargaining. Providing employees with a means of influencing important workplace issues that directly affect their well-being is entirely consistent with our democratic values. Rather than having to accept their employers' dictates or quit, collective bargaining gives employees the opportunity to exert a strong voice in the workplace. Another laudable feature of collective bargaining is that the parties most directly affected by decisions about terms and conditions of employers—the employees and the employers—get to decide the rules by which they will live. As a consequence, the rules contained in labor agreements can be responsive to the particular needs of individual industries, firms, or workplaces—as opposed to government-mandated one-size-fits-all standards.

Despite these and other benefits, collective bargaining is wildly unpopular with U.S. employers. The reasons for this are simple enough: money and power. Unions do a reasonably good job of increasing the share of corporate revenues claimed by employees and make it more difficult for employers to implement policies not favored by employees. Certainly, employer views vary concerning collective bargaining, but the typical response is hostility. Thus, even though collective bargaining is a vital piece of U.S. public policy governing the workplace, the process of attempting to form unions and bargain with employers is often contentious and produces many legal claims.

The **National Labor Relations Act (NLRA)**[1] is the principal federal law concerning self-organization and collective bargaining by private sector employees. The **National Labor Relations Board (NLRB)** is the agency that administers the NLRA, including holding elections to determine whether employees desire union representation and determining whether unfair labor practices (ULPs) have been committed. The **Railway Labor Act (RLA)**[2] is a federal labor law that governs collective bargaining in the highly unionized railroad and airline industries. The RLA is administered by the **National Mediation Board (NMB)**. State laws or executive orders provide for collective bargaining by (some or all) state and local government employees in more than forty states. Collective bargaining by federal government employees is governed by the **Civil Service Reform Act (CSRA)**[3] and overseen by the **Federal Labor Relations Authority (FLRA)**. The details of these labor laws vary, but they have procedures in common for determining desire for union representation as well as provisions to protect employees' right to engage in collective bargaining.

---

[1] 29 U.S.C.S. §§ 151 *et seq.* (2011).

[2] 45 U.S.C.S. §§ 151 *et seq.* (2011).

[3] 5 U.S.C.S. §§ 7101 *et seq.* (2011).

The National Labor Relations Act (NLRA)

In contrast to most of the other laws discussed in this book that apply to all employees regardless of organizational position, the National Labor Relations Act's protections do not apply to supervisors and managers. Determining who is a **supervisor** is sometimes problematic. Under the NLRA, supervisors are individuals who have the authority, in the interest of the employer, to make personnel decisions (e.g., hire, discharge, discipline, and promote), to responsibly direct other employees, to settle their grievances, or to effectively recommend such actions. For supervisory status to be conferred, these activities must also entail the use of independent judgment. This definition of supervisor is intended to distinguish positions that are genuinely part of management from lower-level employees with some of the trappings of managerial authority (e.g., "team leaders") and from professionals in general (who are covered by the NLRA when they are not supervisors or managers).

The supervisory status of nurses has been a hotly contested issue. In one such case, the nurses did not hold the title of supervisor, but they were often the most senior employees on duty, ensured adequate staffing, made daily work assignments for aides, and monitored the work of the less skilled aides. The Supreme Court held that the nurse's actions undertaken in the course of providing care to patients constituted supervisory actions taken "in the interest of the employer."[4] In another nurse case, the Supreme Court acknowledged that employers bear the burden of proving that particular employees are supervisors, but it rejected the NLRB's position that the use of "independent judgment" requisite for supervisory status is not evidenced by the exercise of "ordinary professional or technical judgment in directing less-skilled employees to deliver services in accordance with employer-specified standards."[5] Following these Supreme Court cases, the NLRB issued decisions in a set of cases dealing with supervisory status that can be viewed as substantially broadening the definition of supervisor under the NLRA. In one of these cases, the NLRB found that full-time "charge nurses" (RNs who were given the additional tasks of overseeing patient care units and assigning other staff to particular patients and work areas) were supervisors.[6] While their jobs resembled those of their RN colleagues in most respects and they were paid only slightly more for their additional responsibilities, the charge nurses were deemed supervisors based on their use of discretion and independent judgment in carrying out the single supervisory function of assigning other employees to patients and work areas.

Managerial employees, who "formulate and effectuate management policies by expressing and making operative the decisions of their employer," are also excluded from coverage.[7] It was no doubt news to many professors at Yeshiva University, a private college, when the Supreme Court ruled that they were managers. The Court reasoned that the faculty's role in making decisions about such basic matters as determining curriculum, hiring faculty, and granting tenure was managerial authority exercised in the employer's interest.[8] Although the *Yeshiva* decision closed the door to the unionization of most full-time faculty at private universities, state public employee collective bargaining statutes have generally been interpreted as covering faculty

---

[4]NLRB v. *Health Care & Retirement Corp.*, 114 S. Ct. 1778 (1994).

[5]NLRB v. *Kentucky River Community Care*, 121 S. Ct. 1861, 1867 (2001).

[6]*Oakwood Healthcare*, 348 NLRB No. 37 (2006).

[7]*NLRB v. Bell Aerospace Co.*, 416 U.S. 267, 288 (1974).

[8]*NLRB v. Yeshiva University*, 444 U.S. 672 (1980).

members. Thus, if you are a student at a public university, the faculty members at your school might be unionized.

There is one significant exception to the general rule that supervisors and managers fall outside of the NLRA's protections. In a case involving a manufacturing supervisor who claimed that he was terminated in retaliation for his refusal to help the company "build a case" that it could use to fire two employees who were attempting to organize a union, the court made it clear that a supervisor or manager who is disciplined for refusing to commit unfair labor practices is protected by the NLRA.[9]

Employee Rights under the NLRA

The NLRA does not directly affect employment outcomes for workers; instead, it provides employees with a means of acting in their own interest to improve their terms and conditions of employment. The fundamental rights conferred by the NLRA (often termed *Section 7 rights*) include the right to do the following:

- Engage in self-organization
- Form, join, or assist labor organizations
- Bargain collectively with their employer through representatives of the employees' own choosing
- Go on strike
- Engage in other concerted activities for the purpose of collective bargaining or other mutual aid or protection
- Refrain from such activities

Concerted Activity   The self-organization and concerted activity protected by the NLRA is broadly construed. Concerted or group activity is not confined to formal collective bargaining conducted by unions. Instead, any efforts by employees to join together for "mutual aid or protection" can qualify as protected **concerted activity**—even if those employees are not represented by a union.

What makes employee actions "concerted"? In general, conduct must be "engaged in with or on the authority of other employees, and not solely by and on behalf of the employee himself" to be concerted.[10] An employee who voices a personal gripe is not engaging in concerted activity. In one relevant case, a nonunion employee who distributed flyers criticizing the layoffs of coworkers and asking that red ribbons be worn in support of those laid off was found to have engaged in protected concerted activity for mutual aid or support.[11] Likewise, a financial consultant's complaints about his employer's compensation practices and his meeting with other financial consultants to discuss their concerns was protected concerted activity.[12] Evidence of group activity—such as an individual employee attempting to rally coworkers, discussions among employees, a group of employees approaching management together, or the delegation of an employee to speak with management—is generally necessary to demonstrate that activity is concerted. However, for unionized employees, a complaint or grievance that relates to enforcement of rights under a labor agreement is concerted activity even if the complaint is raised only by an individual.

---

[9]*Lewis v. Whirlpool Corp.*, 630 F.3d 484 (6th Cir. 2011).

[10]*Meyers Industries (II)*, 281 NLRB 882, 885 (1986), *affirmed sub nom.*, *Prill v. NLRB*, 835 F.2d 1481 (D.C. Cir. 1987).

[11]*United Services Automobile Association v.* NLRB, 387 F.3d 908 (D.C. Cir. 2004).

[12]*Citizens Investment Services Corp.*, 430 F.3d 1195 (D.C. Cir. 2005).

The reason is that this activity is part of the collective bargaining process and clearly affects the rights of all employees covered by the contract.[13]

The NLRA is also violated when an employer terminates an employee to *prevent* that employee from exercising her right to engage in concerted activity (the "preemptive strike" theory).[14] Thus, when a nurse discussed her concerns about possible pay discrimination with a coworker, was subsequently called into a meeting with managers, was asked whether she had said anything about this to other workers (she said that she had not done so), and was summarily terminated, her termination violated the NLRA. Even if her original conversation was not concerted activity, the Board concluded that the employer's attempt to "erect 'a dam at the source of supply' of potential, protected activity" constituted illegal interference.[15]

To receive protection, an employee's actions must be "concerted" and be for the purpose of "mutual aid or support." These two requirements tend to coincide but are nonetheless distinct. In a controversial decision, the Board decided that an employee who was fired after she attempted to persuade a coworker to testify before a state agency in her harassment case was not protected by the NLRA.[16] This was so even though the Board determined that she did engage in concerted activity (seeking support from a coworker) and that her concerted activity was the basis for the termination. However, because she was viewed as acting solely to further *her own legal claim*, the concerted activity was not protected.

Even when it is for mutual aid or support, concerted activity by employees is not always protected. For one thing, the activity must be related to employees' concerns regarding their wages, hours, terms, and conditions of employment. Second, the manner in which the activity is carried out must not be extreme or abusive. Conduct that is flagrant, egregious, or abusive and speech that is malicious, defamatory, or highly profane are not protected. The occasional use of profanity in emotionally charged situations or the ruffling of managerial feathers is not sufficient to cause a loss of protection. Two union-represented electricians were fired for violating a zero-tolerance policy toward workplace violence after they told a supervisor who had disciplined a group of their coworkers for taking overly long breaks that "it's going to get ugly" and he "better bring boxing gloves." The court found that the statements, although intemperate, were not actual threats of violence and were protected.[17] In contrast, a nurse who made statements on a television program alleging that the hospital was "jeopardizing the health of mothers and babies" by cutting staff was not protected by the NLRA. Although her conduct (which occurred in the midst of efforts to organize a union) was concerted activity, it was not protected "because her false and disparaging public statements alienated her from her most important coworkers and made her continued employment untenable."[18]

In *MasTec Advanced Technologies*, the NLRB must decide whether comments made by employees appearing on a TV news program were protected concerted activity.

---

[13]*NLRB v. City Disposal Systems*, 465 U.S. 822 (1984).

[14]*Paraexel International*, 356 NLRB No. 82 (2011).

[15]*Paraexel*, at 4.

[16]*Holling Press*, 343 NLRB No. 45 (2004).

[17]*Kiewit Power Constructors v. NLRB*, 2011 U.S. App. LEXIS 15920 (D.C. Cir. 2011).

[18]*St. Luke's Episcopal-Presbyterian Hospitals v. NLRB*, 268 F.3d 575, 582 (8th Cir. 2001).

MasTec Advanced Technologies
357 NLRB No. 17 (2011)

BY CHAIRMAN LIEBMAN AND MEMBERS BECKER AND HAYES:

This case presents the question of whether 26 former service technicians employed by Respondent Advanced Technologies, a division of MasTec, Inc. (MasTec), lost the protection of the Act by appearing on a television news broadcast in which statements were made about their employer and Respondent DirecTV, Inc., for which MasTec provides installation services. The technicians' participation in the newscast grew out of their opposition to a new compensation formula that MasTec implemented in response to DirecTV's dissatisfaction with MasTec's performance.

Applying the principles set forth by the Supreme Court in *Jefferson Standard*, regarding the extent to which employees' disparaging statements to third parties about their employer's product or service enjoy the Act's protection, the judge concluded that the technicians' statements were unprotected and thus that neither MasTec, by terminating its employees, nor DirecTV, by causing their termination, violated [the NLRA]. In his exceptions, the General Counsel challenges the judge's finding that the employees' statements were unprotected. As explained below, we find merit in the General Counsel's position.

MasTec operates as a home service provider (HSP), installing and maintaining satellite television equipment under contract with satellite television providers. In the Orlando, Florida area MasTec's only client is DirecTV. * * * The Respondents consider connecting the satellite receiver to an active telephone land line to be part of a standard installation. Such connections allow customers (1) to order pay-per-view by using the remote control; (2) to have caller ID information displayed on their television screen; and (3) to receive downloads of DirecTV software upgrades. In addition, phone line connections provide a record of what customers are viewing, thereby assisting DirecTV in making programming decisions. Although these features may be attractive to many consumers, and have potential benefits for DirecTV's business, telephone line connections are not essential for the system to function. The record establishes that a satellite receiver will properly transmit the signal to a television set without a telephone connection. Many customers resist having the telephone connection made, even

though there is no extra charge for a standard connection. Receivers that are connected to phone lines are referred to as "responders" because they respond to a verification signal; unconnected receivers are called "non-responders."

Because of the business importance of telephone connections, the Respondents have emphasized to technicians the need to make as many connections as possible. Despite the Respondents' efforts, however, it is undisputed that connections were often not made. In early 2006, therefore, DirecTV informed MasTec that if it did not improve its responder installation rates, it would be penalized. * * * By memo of January 17, MasTec, in turn, informed technicians that their piece work pay structure would be modified to reflect the increased emphasis on improving responder installation rates. Beginning February 1, technicians would be paid $2 less for basic and additional outlet installations, but would earn $3.35 for each receiver they connected to a phone line. In addition, technicians would incur a back-charge of $5 for every new non-responding receiver installed during a 30-day period if they failed to connect at least 50 percent to phone lines. Technicians failing to meet the 50 percent threshold for 60 consecutive days would be subject to termination.

Technicians voiced strong opposition to the new pay formula at several team meetings, arguing that reaching the 50-percent responder rate threshold would be problematic. They pointed out that making the phone connection was not always possible, because of customer resistance or other circumstances beyond their control. * * * MasTec supervisors suggested ways around these problems, including making the connection without telling customers they were doing so or telling customers, falsely, that the receiver would not work without it. At one meeting, after hearing a group of technicians repeating the arguments about why the new target percentage rate was unattainable, Regional Operations Manager Chris Brown told them to tell customers anything, "whatever you have to tell them" and "whatever it takes" to make the connection, even jokingly suggesting that technicians tell customers that the receiver would "blow up" if it was not connected.

In addition, MasTec showed the technicians a DirecTV-produced video addressing the importance of making the receiver-phone line connection. In the video, DirecTV's vice president for field operations, Stephen Crawford, said MasTec was not to blame for the increased emphasis on improving responder rates and that the pressure was coming instead from DirecTV. He and another DirecTV vice president, Scott Brown, suggested that technicians might have greater success in connecting receivers to phone lines if they did not tell customers they were doing so or simply told them—again, falsely—that the connection was "mandatory" and necessary "for the equipment to function correctly." * * *

Technicians received their first paychecks under the new compensation system in late March. Many had been back charged for failing to reach the target responder installation rate. A number of technicians assembled at the Orlando facility parking lot on the mornings of March 27 and 28 and expressed their dissatisfaction to Brown and Facility Supervisor Herbert Villa, reiterating many of the same complaints they had raised with them in previous meetings. Despite their protestations, they were unable to persuade MasTec to rescind the new policy. Frustrated by their failed efforts, a group of technicians decided that management might reconsider its adherence to the pay system if they took their complaints public. Technician Frank Martinez contacted a local television reporter, Nancy Alvarez from WKMG-TV Channel 6, and set up a meeting. On the morning of March 30, Martinez and 27 fellow technicians, dressed in their work uniforms, drove from the MasTec facility to Channel 6 in their company vans. Alvarez met the technicians in the station's parking lot and invited them into Channel 6's studio where she interviewed them on film as a group. * * *

On Friday, April 28, Channel 6 aired a "teaser" promoting the story. It began with a reporter asking, "Why did over 30 employees of a major company show up at [Channel] 6?" A video of this exchange followed:

Interviewer: "So you've basically been told to lie to customers?"

Technician: "Yeah." * * *

The full news story first aired ... on Monday, May 1. The story begins with the following exchange among the anchors and reporter:

News Anchor 1: Only on 6 ... a problem solver investigation with a bit of a twist ... this time they came to us.

News Anchor 2: Yeah ... technicians who have installed hundreds of DirecTV satellite systems across

Central Florida ... they're talking about a company policy that charges you for something you may not ever use. And as problem solver Nancy Alvarez found, if you don't pay for it, the workers do.

Reporter Alvarez: They arrived at our Local 6 studios in droves. DirecTV trucks packed the parking lot and inside the technicians spoke their minds. (accompanying video showed more than 16 DirecTV vans in the parking lot followed by a shot panning a group of technicians wearing shirts bearing the DirecTV logo). The scene shifts to a room where more than 20 technicians were seated, facing Alvarez.

Technician Lee Selby: We're just asking to be treated fairly.

Alvarez: These men have installed hundreds of DirecTV systems in homes across Central Florida but now they admit they've lied to customers along the way.

Technician Hugh Fowler: If we don't lie to the customers, we get back charged for it. And you can't make money.

Alvarez: We'll explain the lies later but first the truth. Phone lines are not necessary for a DirecTV system ... * * * But every phone line connected to a receiver means more money for DirecTV and MasTec, the contractor these men work for. So the techs say their supervisors have been putting pressure on them. Deducting five bucks from their paychecks for every DirecTV receiver that's not connected to a phone line. * * *

Alvarez (questioning a room full of technicians): How many of you here by a show of hands have had $200 taken out of your paycheck? (Accompanying video shows virtually every technician in the room raising his hand.)

Martinez: More.

Alvarez: Want to avoid a deduction on your paycheck? Well, according to this group, supervisors have ordered them to do or say whatever it takes.

Martinez: Tell the customer whatever you have to tell them. Tell them if these phone lines are not connected the receiver will blow up.

Alvarez: You've been told to tell customers that ...

Martinez: We've been told to say that. Whatever it takes to get the phone line into that receiver. * * *

This report reaired, in slightly different versions, over a 2-day period. Chris Brown sent the recorded broadcasts to his superiors, who, in turn, forwarded them to DirecTV. After discussing their mutual concerns, DirecTV's Crawford told MasTec's Retherford that he did not want any of the technicians who appeared on the broadcast to represent his company in customers' homes. Thereafter, Retherford directed Chris Brown to identify the technicians who appeared in the newscast. After receiving the list of names, on May 2, Retherford instructed Brown to tell Villa to notify each of the identified technicians that he was being terminated "at will." Following Retherford's directions, Villa informed the technicians of their terminations at the end of the work day on May 3. * * *

Section 7 of the Act provides, in part, that "[e]mployees shall have the right … to engage in … concerted activities for the purpose of … mutual aid or protection." However, that right is not without limitation. In *Jefferson Standard*, the Court upheld the employer's discharge of employees who publicly criticized both the quality of the employer's product and its business practices without the employees relating their complaints to any labor controversy. The Court found that the employees' conduct amounted to disloyal disparagement of their employer and was outside the Act's protection. In cases decided since *Jefferson Standard*, "the Board has held that employee communications to third parties in an effort to obtain their support are protected where the communication indicated it is related to an ongoing dispute between the employees and the employers and the communication is not so disloyal, reckless or maliciously untrue as to lose the Act's protection."

The first prong of this test is not at issue here. The Respondents do not contest the judge's finding, with which we agree, that the employee communications here were clearly related to their pay dispute. As to the second prong of the test, we find that the judge clearly erred in finding that the employee communications and/or participation in the Channel 6 newscast were either maliciously untrue or so disloyal and reckless as to warrant removal of the Act's protection. Statements are maliciously untrue and unprotected, "if they are made with knowledge of their falsity or with reckless disregard for their truth or falsity. The mere fact that statements are false, misleading or inaccurate is insufficient to demonstrate that they are maliciously untrue.

None of the statements made by the technicians were maliciously untrue under these well-established legal principles. Indeed, for the most part, the statements were accurate representations of what the Respondents had instructed the technicians to tell customers. Contrary to the judge, the technicians were essentially told to lie, as certain technicians stated during the telecast. The record clearly establishes that although the Respondents may have avoided expressly using the word "lie" when suggesting ways to overcome obstacles to making receiver phone line connections, both Respondents affirmatively encouraged the technicians to do just that. * * * Indeed, Brown instructed technicians to tell customers "whatever you have to tell them" and "whatever it takes" to make the connection. The technicians would readily understand these instructions to include "lie if you have to." * * * Thus, whether the Respondents' officials expressly told the technicians to lie is immaterial. They expressly encouraged technicians to make statements known by the Respondents' managers to be false and intended to deceive customers into believing, erroneously, that their satellite receivers would not work if they were not connected to a land line telephone. Similarly, the technicians did not make maliciously false statements by failing to specify that they would be back charged only if they failed to connect 50 percent of the receivers they installed. The statements the technicians did make fairly reflected their personal experiences under the new pay scheme. * * * [T]he failure to fully explain the 50 percent connection rule was at most an inaccuracy. There is no basis in the record to find that the technicians knowingly and maliciously withheld that information in order to mislead the viewing public. * * *

We also find that none of the technicians' statements constituted unprotected disloyalty or reckless disparagement of the Respondents' services. Statements have been found unprotected where they constitute "a sharp, public, disparaging attack upon the quality of the company's product and its business policies, in a manner reasonably calculated to harm the company's reputation and reduce its income." The Board has stated that it will not find a public statement unprotected unless it is "flagrantly disloyal, wholly incommensurate with any grievances which they might have." Further, "[i]n determining whether an employee's communication to a third party constitutes disparagement of the employer or its product, great care must be taken to distinguish between disparagement and the airing of what may be highly sensitive issues."

In this case, the technicians participated in the Channel 6 newscast only after repeated unsuccessful attempts to resolve their pay dispute in direct communications with the Respondents. The newscast shed unwelcome light on certain deceptive business practices, but it was nevertheless directly related to the technicians' grievance about what they considered to be an unfair pay policy that they believed forced them to mislead customers. While the technicians may have been aware that some consumers might cancel the Respondents' services after listening to the newscast, there is no evidence that they intended to inflict such harm on the Respondents, or that they acted recklessly without regard for the financial consequences to the Respondents' businesses. We therefore find that the technicians did not engage in unprotected disloyal or reckless conduct, as previously defined by Board and court precedent.

Based on the foregoing, we find that the technicians' participation in the Channel 6 newscast was protected concerted activity directly and expressly related to and in furtherance of an ongoing labor dispute. Accordingly, we reverse the judge and find that by causing the discharge of the technicians for their participation in the newscast, and by discharging them, Respondents DirectTV and MasTec, respectively, violated [the NLRA].

CASE QUESTIONS

1. What was the legal issue in this case? What did the court decide?
2. What was the concerted activity in which the technicians engaged? What made that activity "concerted"?
3. Why was this activity "protected"?
4. What if the companies had shown that they suffered substantial losses in sales and revenues stemming from the news program? Would that have made a difference in the outcome of this case? Why or why not?
5. Do you agree with this decision? Why or why not?

Company policies can run afoul of the NLRA due to the constraints that they place on concerted activity. "Pay secrecy" policies that restrict employees from talking with one another about the central issue of wages are invalid for this reason (see Chapter 12). Policies limiting "solicitation" and access to the workplace are also problematic. A casino restaurant's rules that employees could not report to the "property" more than thirty minutes prior to the start of shifts or remain longer than thirty minutes after shifts and that employees were prohibited from returning to the "premises" during unscheduled hours other than as paying guests were struck down by the NLRB.[19] Similarly, a policy prohibiting "negative conversations" about coworkers or managers violated the NLRA due to the likelihood that employees would view the rule as prohibiting complaints about management decisions.[20] But another employer's more general rules prohibiting "abusive and profane language," "harassment," and "verbal, physical, and mental abuse" were deemed lawful. Although these rules could conceivably be invoked to punish employees criticizing management or seeking to persuade their coworkers to unionize, the NLRB determined that the rules did not explicitly restrict protected activity. Thus, for the rules to be invalidated, there must be evidence that employees would reasonably construe the language to prohibit protected activity, the rules were created in response to protected activity, or the rules had been applied to restrict such activity. None of these were shown.[21] However, an appeals court overturned part of an NLRB decision that had upheld a rule prohibiting security guards from at any time fraternizing, dating, or "becoming overly friendly" with coworkers or employees of client companies.[22] The court concluded that employees could reasonably view this language as prohibiting them from banding together to address their workplace concerns and not simply as a limitation on romantic or "personal entanglements."

[19]*Ark Las Vegas Restaurant Corp.*, 343 NLRB No. 126 (2004).
[20]*KSL Claremont Resort*, 344 NLRB No. 105 (2005).
[21]*Lutheran Heritage Village-Livonia*, 343 NLRB No. 75 (2004).
[22]*Guardsmark* v. NLRB, 475 F.3d 369 (D.C. Cir. 2007).

Even if a policy unlawfully restricts protected activity, an employee terminated under that policy—but for reasons completely unrelated to engaging in protected activity—would not be protected by the NLRA. Thus, even though an employer's overly broad rule prohibiting access to company property by off-duty employees was unlawful, disciplining an employee for sleeping in and living out his car parked in the employer's parking lot did not violate the NLRA.[23] But the general rule is that a termination (or other discipline) imposed under the terms of an overly broad policy for conduct that would be protected, or that is closely related to protected activity, violates the NLRA.[24] However, employers still have the opportunity in such cases to assert an affirmative defense by showing that the disruptiveness of the act, and not merely its violation of the policy, was the reason for imposing the discipline.[25] *Clearly, employers should consider the possibility that broad policies regulating employee conduct will interfere with the exercise of employees' NLRA rights and not adopt or enforce such policies (at least not when the conduct is arguably protected).*

Clippings

In the first NLRB case of its kind, the ambulance company American Medical Response terminated an employee after learning that she had criticized her supervisor on Facebook from her home computer. Coworkers had responded to the posting and added their own comments. The NLRB alleged that by disciplining the employee for her airing of workplace issues on the social networking site, the company violated the National Labor Relations Act. The company settled with the NLRB, agreeing to revise its overly broad policy prohibiting such communications and to not discipline employees for engaging in conversations of this sort.

"Company Settles Case in Firing Tied to Facebook." *New York Times* (February 8, 2011), B7.

Today, employee complaints about their terms and conditions of employment are as likely to be aired electronically through social media sites as in-person around the water cooler. The case against the ambulance company (see "Clippings") was just the first of a line of similar cases being brought to the NLRB. Certainly, there are aspects of such communications that distinguish them from face-to-face conversations and other media through which concerted activity has traditionally occurred, including the relative permanence of Facebook postings, their potential distribution to much larger audiences that include non-employees, and their ability to incorporate photographs and other visual media. But fundamentally, the issue is still whether the employees initiating such communications and any coworkers responding to them are engaged in protected concerted activity. The NLRB does not always find merit in these cases.[26] Perhaps more so than in cases not involving social media, the NLRB appears to be focusing on the reactions of coworkers as a means of distinguishing individual gripes

---

[23]*Continental Group*, 357 NLRB No. 39 (2011).

[24]*Double Eagle Hotel & Casino*, 341 NLRB 112 (2004), *enforced*, 414 F.3d 1249 (10th Cir. 2005).

[25]*Continental Group*, at 4.

[26]Lawrence E. Dubé. "NLRB Advice Division Finds No Protection for Some Complaints Posted on Facebook." *Daily Labor Report* 144 (July 27, 2011), AA-1.

from concerted activity. A Wal-Mart employee who was suspended after posting the comment "Wuck Falmart! I swear if this tyranny doesn't end in this store they are about to get a wakeup call because lots are about to quit!" on his Facebook page was not protected.[27] Even though at least one other employee responded to his posting and said "hang in there," it was concluded that the comment was not intended to induce collective action by coworkers. In contrast, an administrative law judge (ALJ) found that a nonprofit social service agency violated the NLRA when it terminated five employees for responding on Facebook to a coworker's criticism of their job performance.[28] The terminated employees were "taking a first step toward group action to defend themselves against the accusations they could reasonably believe [the coworker] was going to make to management."[29] The concerted activity was protected because it was not engaged in during work time and did not constitute harassment of the coworker.

Employers in both unionized and nonunion workplaces must respect the right of employees to join together in contesting or expressing concerns regarding their terms and conditions of employment, whether this occurs in-person or electronically. Policies that limit this right should not be maintained or enforced.

JUST THE FACTS

A beverage distributor announced that it was consolidating its operations and closing one of its unionized facilities. The union subsequently entered negotiations with the employer over the effects of the closure on employees. Six drivers heard that there would be a negotiation session held later that morning. They decided to leave work to try to get information about how the consolidation would affect their future employment. The drivers first met at a coffee shop to formulate their questions and then proceeded to the union hall where the negotiating session was being held. When they showed up at the union hall, a union officer advised them to return to work. The drivers persisted and it was agreed that they would be allowed to introduce themselves to the management representatives. After doing so, the drivers returned to work. All told, they had been gone from work for about three hours. They were subsequently terminated for leaving work without authorization. Did this employer violate the NLRA by terminating these employees for engaging in protected concerted activity?

See *Northeast Beverage Corp. v. NLRB*, 554 F.3d 133 (D.C. Cir. 2009).

Unfair Labor Practices (ULPs)

To protect employees' rights to self-organization and give collective bargaining a chance to work, the NLRA prohibits certain actions by employers and unions. These **unfair labor practices (ULPs)** are listed here.

Employers must refrain from the following activities:

1. Interfering with, restraining, or coercing employees in the exercise of their rights under the NLRA

---

[27]Dubé.

[28]*Hispanics United of Buffalo,* Case No. 3-CA-27872 (September 2, 2011)

[29]*Hispanics United of Buffalo,* 8–9.

2. Dominating or interfering with the formation or administration of a labor organization
3. Discriminating against employees for the purpose of encouraging or discouraging membership in any labor organization
4. Retaliating against employees for filing charges or giving testimony under the act
5. Refusing to engage in collective bargaining

Labor organizations must refrain from the following activities:

1. Restraining or coercing employees in the exercise of their rights under the act
2. Causing an employer to discriminate against an employee for the purpose of encouraging or discouraging membership in a labor organization
3. Refusing to engage in collective bargaining
4. Broadening labor disputes to include neutral employers ("secondary boycott")
5. Charging excessive or discriminatory initiation fees or dues
6. Causing an employer to pay for work not performed ("featherbedding")
7. Picketing for more than thirty days for the purpose of obtaining union recognition

Because our primary concern is with the legal obligations of employers, we will focus on employer ULPs. The first category of employer ULP—interfering with, restraining, or coercing employees in the exercise of their NLRA rights—encapsulates employers' legal obligations under the NLRA. The remaining employer ULPs are elaborations on this general requirement. The cases discussed earlier involving employees being terminated or otherwise disadvantaged for engaging in protected concerted activity exemplify employer interference with and restraint of NLRA rights.

The prohibition against employer domination of a labor organization or interference in its administration (including providing financial support) requires more explanation. The underlying notion is that to be bona fide employee representatives, labor organizations must be independent of employers. This requirement of independence holds not just for labor unions but also for labor organizations of any kind. The definition of labor organization under the NLRA is broad. A **labor organization** is "any organization … or employee representation committee or plan, in which employees participate and which exists for the purpose, in whole or in part, of dealing with employers concerning grievances, labor disputes, wages, rates of pay, hours of employment, or conditions of work."[30] Clearly, employers are prohibited from creating or controlling "company unions" that do not genuinely represent employees' interests. But the NLRA also has implications for employee involvement groups and work teams.

The idea of the employee involvement or participation programs that have proliferated in the past few decades is to improve productivity, quality, and organizational effectiveness by including employees in decisions previously reserved for management and eliciting their active involvement in solving organizational problems. Employee involvement takes many forms but typically involves groups of employees interacting in some fashion with managers to discuss production, safety, and other issues. The NLRA comes into the picture because employee involvement groups can be deemed "labor organizations" dealing with employers regarding employment matters. And if the groups are labor organizations, they will almost certainly be considered "dominated" because they are initiated by employers. Thus, their existence can violate the NLRA.

In one important case, a nonunion employer responded to employee dissatisfaction by creating a number of "action teams." The teams included employee representatives and managers. Separate teams were created to deal with issues of absenteeism, a

---

[30]29 U.S.C.S. § 152(5)(2011).

no-smoking policy, communication, pay progressions, and an attendance bonus program. The teams were eventually disbanded after a union organizing campaign began, but the NLRB ruled and an appeals court affirmed that the teams violated the NLRA.[31] The teams constituted labor organizations because employees participated and they dealt with management regarding the types of issues typically taken up in collective bargaining. The decision stressed that "dealing with" is not limited to formal negotiations. When, as in this case, there is an exchange of views between employees and management and an attempt to influence decision outcomes, there is "dealing." Some board members also attributed particular significance to the fact that employees on the action teams were expected to represent the views of other employees. The action teams were also employer-dominated. The employer initiated the teams, established their purpose, limited the number of teams employees could serve on, provided materials, and paid employees for their time.

A unionized employer also violated the NLRA by setting up company-dominated employee involvement teams that dealt with such issues as safety and benefits.[32] Furthermore, the Board concluded that the employer was bypassing the employee's representative and not meeting its legal obligation to bargain only with the union on these issues. However, the law was not violated when a unionized employer sought employee volunteers to serve on a committee to make recommendations regarding the process for selecting "crew leaders." The recommendation was used by the employer to formulate its own proposal in bargaining over the issue with the union.[33] Nor was the NLRA violated when a nonunion company created seven employee committees that functioned as "self-managing" work teams. The Board concluded that because the decision-making authority on a range of issues was delegated to the teams and the plant manager rarely overruled committee recommendations "it cannot be doubted that each committee exercises as a group authority that in the traditional plant setting would be considered to be supervisory.... . [T]he seven committees are not labor organizations because their purpose is to perform essentially managerial functions, and thus they do not 'deal with' the [employer]."[34]

Practical Considerations How should employers with employee involvement programs structure those programs so as to not run afoul of the NLRA?

Employers also commit a ULP by discriminating against employees for the purpose of either encouraging or discouraging membership in a labor organization. Thus, employers cannot refuse to hire, fire, demote, or otherwise limit the employment opportunities of employees because they are known or suspected to be union activists or supporters. In one NLRA discrimination case, a mechanic applied for work on a highway construction project. Despite having been referred from the union hiring hall (the typical procedure for filling such jobs) and being well qualified, the company declined to hire the mechanic. In a letter to the union, the company cited "past performance and personality conflicts" (the mechanic had worked on other projects with this construction company) as its reason for not hiring him. The mechanic questioned the company owner about the alleged personality conflict, and the owner said that "maybe you was too union for us." The NLRB found for the mechanic on his discrimination charge, and on appeal, a court agreed.[35] In another case, a hospital contracted out the work of its respiratory care unit two weeks before an election that would determine if employees desired union representation. In ruling for the employees, the court observed that "we would need to ignore a

[31]*Electromation, Inc.*, 309 NLRB 990 (1992), *enforced, Electromation, Inc.* v. NLRB, 35 F.3d 1148 (7th Cir. 1994).

[32]*E.I. DuPont & Co.*, 311 NLRB 893 (1993).

[33]*Georgia Power Company*, 342 NLRB No. 18 (2004).

[34]*Crown Cork & Seal Company*, 334 NLRB 699, 701 (2001).

[35]*Mashuda Corp.* v. *NLRB*, 135 Fed. Appx. 574 (4th Cir. 2005).

powerful string of coincidences to conclude that [the hospital] would have implemented subcontracting, *when and as it did,* in the absence of union activity."[36] Employees had openly campaigned for union representation, and the respiratory care therapists were strongly pro-union. The hospital's discussions about outsourcing closely coincided in time with an intensification of employees' efforts to unionize. The hospital accepted a proposal for outsourcing on the same day that it was received. The management problems that the hospital claimed to be addressing by outsourcing had existed for many years, and there was no evidence that the move would resolve those problems.

As in other disparate treatment discrimination cases, proving the motive for a challenged employment decision is crucial. However, a somewhat different approach is used in NLRA cases.[37]

ELEMENTS OF A CLAIM

Discrimination Under the NLRA

To establish a prima facie case of discrimination, the General Counsel of the NLRB must show the following:

1. The employee engaged in protected activity.
2. The employer was aware of the protected activity.
3. The employer demonstrated hostility toward the protected activity.
4. There was a causal connection between this hostility and the decision to deny an employment opportunity.

If a prima facie case is established, the NLRA is violated unless the employer can show that the same decision would have been made regardless of whether the employee engaged in protected activity.

© Cengage Learning 2013.

Union Organizing and Representation Elections

Legal claims under the NLRA, particularly charges of interference with self-organization and discrimination against union supporters, are especially common during periods when employees are attempting to form unions. The NLRA places many constraints on employer behavior under these circumstances. The act also spells out a set of procedures for holding representation elections to determine whether employees desire union representation.

Union Organizing Campaigns

Why are there unions in some workplaces but not others? Unions are formed over a period of time—sometimes months, sometimes years—in which employees dissatisfied with their terms and conditions of employment become convinced that unionization is the best way to improve their lot. As an organizing campaign develops momentum, there is typically much discussion and persuasion among workers, distribution of literature, wearing of buttons and other symbols of support for unionization, rallies, and requests to sign petitions or "authorization cards" (indicating desire for representation). Nonemployee organizers from established unions often play an important leadership

---

[36]*Healthcare Employees Union Local 399 v. NLRB,* 463 F.3d 909 (9th Cir. 2006).

[37]*NLRB v. Transportation Management Corp.,* 103 S. Ct. 2469 (1983).

role, but for the most part, employees organize themselves. At some point, if sufficient support is enlisted, the NLRB might be petitioned to hold an election to determine whether a union will be certified as the legal representative of the employees.

Clippings

Dissatisfied with what they said was minimum wage pay, poor working conditions, and inability to take sick leave without finding their own replacements, about 200 workers at ten Jimmy John's sandwich shops in the Minneapolis area formed the first chapter of the Jimmy John's Workers Union. The union affiliated with the Industrial Workers of the World (IWW) and sought recognition as the bargaining representative for employees at these stores. An NLRB election, the first in the nation involving this restaurant chain, was held in October 2010. The outcome was a vote of 87–85 against union representation, with two challenged ballots. However, the union alleged that the shop owners had engaged in numerous unfair labor practices, including threatening and terminating union supporters. The parties subsequently entered into a settlement, providing for a new election to be held on an expedited basis if one is sought. Additionally, the employer, without admitting to wrongdoing, agreed to refrain from engaging in certain anti-union activities and to hold mandatory meetings at which a notice from the NLRB regarding the case would be read to employees.

Susan R. Hobbs. "NLRB Settlement Nullifies Results of Jimmy John's Representation Election." *Daily Labor Report* 6 (January 10, 2011), A-1.

In the following excerpts from two cases involving the same employer and union, but different workplaces, the court must sort through the employer's actions to determine which, if any, violated the NLRA.

United Food and Commercial Workers Union, Local 204 v. NLRB (I)
447 F.3d 821 (D.C. Cir. 2006)

PER CURIAM:

In 1992, the Smithfield Packing Company opened a large pork processing plant in Tar Heel, North Carolina. Shortly after the plant opened, the United Food and Commercial Workers Union took steps to organize the plant's employees. Those efforts culminated in two elections, one in 1994 and the other in 1997, both of which the Union lost. From the outset, Smithfield was exceptionally hostile to union organizing activities at the Tar Heel plant. According to National Labor Relations Board findings unchallenged here, the company threatened to fire employees who voted for the Union, to freeze wages and shut the plant if the

employees unionized, and to discipline employees who engaged in union activity. It also interrogated employees about their union support, confiscated union materials, and videotaped and otherwise spied on its employees' union activities. * * *

We first address Smithfield's argument that the Board lacked substantial evidence to find that the company ... establish[ed] an overly broad no-solicitation/no-distribution policy. The Board's conclusion rests on testimony that Smithfield posted a sign outside the Tar Heel facility's parking lot describing an unlawfully broad policy [stating that no solicitation could occur on company time or property]. * * * Smithfield ... argues that no reasonable employee would have believed the concededly unlawful policy on the sign trumped the lawful policy the company published in its employee handbook. But the Board reasonably found that, in the atmosphere of intimidation and coercion under which Smithfield employees operated, employees might well have believed that the parking-lot sign stated Smithfield's real nosolicitation/ no-distribution policy.

Second, Smithfield challenges the Board's determination that it unlawfully coerced Fred McDonald, a known union supporter, when McDonald's supervisor approached him and said, "Why do you all guys want a Union, the Union can't do anything for you but cause trouble between the workers and the Company." … [T]he Board concluded that "the employer's conduct put the employee in a defensive posture because the employer, which controlled his livelihood, did not approve of his union activity." * * * [A]n employer's statement that union support would "cause trouble" can put an employee in a "defensive posture" and be unduly coercive under the right circumstances … [such as] the intense and widespread coercion prevalent at the Tar Heel facility….

Third, Smithfield argues that the Board lacked substantial evidence to conclude that it harassed and coerced Chris Council, a known union supporter. Although Council's supervisor, James Hargrove, ordered him to stamp hogs with a "Vote No" stamp, Smithfield insists that "the assignment did not unlawfully coerce Council to participate in Smithfield's anti-union effort" because Hargrove never "tricked" Council. But we think the Board could have reasonably concluded that Council's supervisor ordered him to engage in campaign activities in which Council never meant to participate; this amounts to coercion, plain and simple, whether or not Council was ever "tricked."

Fourth, Smithfield claims that the Board lacked substantial evidence to find the company violated [the] NLRA by discharging Rayshawn Ward, Lawanna Johnson, Margo McMillan, and Ada Perry. Reviewing the record, we find substantial evidence to support each decision. When Rayshawn Ward acted as a union observer at the 1997 union election, a fight broke out after the ballots were counted. Although Ward claimed he never hit anyone, law-enforcement officials arrested him. Ward testified that three days after the fight, a Smithfield manager named Larry

Johnson told him "I'm just tired of this Union shit and I'm ready to get my company back where it belong [sic]." Ward was fired two days later, ostensibly for his involvement in the fight. Because Johnson's statement exhibits powerful anti-union animus, even standing alone it provides substantial evidence for the Board's conclusion that Ward would not have been fired but for his union support. * * *

Similarly, the Board refused to credit Larry Johnson's testimony that he fired Lawanna Johnson for an attendance violation. Instead, it credited testimony that Larry threatened Lawanna with termination if she encouraged people to vote for the Union—and that Larry then fired Lawanna just three days later. Without more, the Board could reasonably have concluded that this supported a finding of anti-union animus. Although Lawanna had signed a last-chance agreement making her employment contingent on perfect attendance, the Board found that Smithfield had sometimes been lenient with other employees on "final warnings" for repeated attendance violations. Substantial evidence therefore supports the Board's conclusion that Smithfield fired Lawanna for her union support, not for her attendance violation.

* * * [S]ubstantial evidence [also] supports the Board's conclusion that McMillan and Perry were fired for their union support. Shortly after Smithfield unlawfully interrogated McMillan about her position on unionization, McMillan was fired for her "continued negative approach." But according to McMillan's supervisor, Smithfield failed to follow its progressive discipline policy, instead firing her before she had accrued enough warnings. From this, the Board was entitled to infer … that her union support, and not her "negative approach," was the real reason for her discharge.

As for Perry's termination, Smithfield never contests that it threatened Perry for her pro-union beliefs, arguing instead that it would have fired Perry regardless of her union support because she threatened a co-worker. Known around the plant as "Granny," Perry was sixty-one years old at the time of the alleged threat, and the person she supposedly threatened was a man in his early twenties. Even her supervisor, who witnessed the purported threat, testified that he didn't take it seriously. The Board had ample reason to refuse to credit this flimsy justification and instead find that Perry's termination violated NLRA section 8(a)(3). * * *

United Food and Commercial Workers Union, Local 204 v. NLRB (II)
506 F.3d 1078 (D.C. Cir. 2007)

OPINION BY CIRCUIT JUDGE TATEL:

Following a union's unsuccessful effort to organize a plant, the National Labor Relations Board found that over the course of the union's campaign the employer committed several unfair labor practices in violation of the National Labor Relations Act. Although the employer contests none of the Board's conclusions, the union challenges the Board's decision to dismiss two of its claims: (1) that statements by high-level company management constituted unlawful threats of plant closure; and (2) that the company's decision to train a security camera on union organizers created an illegal impression of surveillance.... [W]e deny the union's petition for review on both claims. * * *

The Supreme Court [has stated]:

> [A]n employer is free to communicate to his employees any of his general views about unionism or any of his specific views about a particular union, so long as the communications do not contain a "threat of reprisal or force or promise of benefit." He may even make a prediction as to the precise effects he believes unionization will have on his company. In such a case, however, the prediction must be carefully phrased on the basis of objective fact to convey an employer's belief as to demonstrably probable consequences beyond his control or to convey a management decision already arrived at to close the plant in case of unionization. If there is any implication that an employer may or may not take action solely on his own initiative for reasons unrelated to economic necessities and known only to him, the statement is no longer a reasonable prediction based on available facts but a threat of retaliation based on misrepresentation and coercion, and as such without the protection of the First Amendment.

* * * [I]n a case like this, which deals only with predictions of adverse economic consequences, ... a two-part inquiry [is used] to distinguish "permissible predictions" from "forbidden threats." First, did the employer predict "adverse economic consequences" as a result of unionization? If not, the inquiry ends. But if the employer made such predictions, then we proceed to the second question: did those predictions rest on objective facts outside the employer's control?

Guided by these questions, we turn to the union's claim that communications by high-level Smithfield managers during the unionization campaign constituted unlawful threats of plant closure. In a series of speeches and letters designed to combat the UFCW's unionization campaign, Plant Manager Phil Price and Smithfield President and Chief Operating Officer Lewis Little repeatedly told employees that three other companies had previously operated the Wilson plant, that the UFCW had unionized the plant under each of those companies, and that each company ultimately shut down the plant. Both managers, however, carefully avoided linking the previous closures directly to the union. For example, in one speech Price mentioned the three previous plant closures but made clear he had no idea whether the UFCW had caused them:

> In none of these three cases did a union contract provide long-term job security for employees. Maybe it was just the opposite. Maybe the union forced inflexible rules on these companies so that they could not compete in today's environment. Maybe this union made it so these companies couldn't satisfy their customers' demands. It really doesn't matter. Whether this union caused these other three plants to close is not for me to say. I don't know what happened. I do know that Smithfield wants this plant to be a success... .

Later in the unionization campaign, Price sent a letter to all Smithfield employees that again emphasized the Wilson plant's repeated failures under previous management. Offering no prediction about the company's intentions, he stated, "I can't predict the future, especially if the union were to get in," and he again disclaimed any direct link between the union and the previous plant closures. Price wrote:

> Did the UFCW cause these three companies to close the plant here on Wilco Boulevard? I don't know the

answer to that. Maybe they did, maybe not. But I can spot a bad trend.... The UFCW is obviously a jinx for this plant. They have struck out for Wilson employees three times. It's time for another approach.

* * * Although this appeal concerns statements by Price and Little, the two were not the only company representatives encouraging Smithfield employees to reject the union. During the unionization campaign, lower-level Smithfield supervisors held smaller meetings with various plant workers. Less circumspect than Price and Little, they expressly warned that the company could close the Wilson plant if employees chose to unionize. * * * Rounding out Smithfield's anti-union effort, another high-level executive, Human Resources Director Sherman Gilliard, appeared in a video shown to employees prior to the election. In contrast to Price and Little, Gilliard linked one of the previous plant closures directly to the union, opining, "If anything, [the UFCW] pretty much ran the company out of business." * * *

Reviewing all the evidence "in context," the Board, over one member's dissent, found no threat or coercion in Price's and Little's statements and concluded that they merely contained "relevant, factual information about the union's history at the facility." The Board emphasized that the two managers "never mentioned closure" and "expressly disclaimed any certainty about the connection between the previous closures at the Wilson facility and the union." Turning to the lower-level supervisors, the Board ... conclu[ded] that their statements violated [the] NLRA because these more explicit threats "offer a clear contrast with the speech by Plant Manager Price."

The union ... argues that ... an employer can violate the Act by merely suggesting that it may close a plant as a result of unionization; it need not definitively assert that it will do so. Placing the statements recounted above in the context of the company's overall antiunion campaign, the union contends that the unmistakable effect of Price's and Little's remarks was to threaten workers with the specter of a plant shutdown. That being the case, the union argues, the managers violated the Act by failing to provide any objective justification for the previous plant closures. Instead, "Smithfield's top managers expressly blamed the past closures at Wilson on the union," leaving employees to believe that if they chose UFCW

representation, they would suffer the same fate as the plant's previous occupants.

* * * [W]e conclude that substantial evidence supports the Board's finding that neither Price nor Little threatened to close the Wilson plant in the event of unionization. As the Board found, neither executive predicted that the company would take any particular course of action, nor did either ever suggest closing the plant. To the extent that Little made any prediction at all, he told employees that he intended to invest in the Wilson facility and was "committed" to its success. The record also reveals that when asked whether Price ever said that "the plant would close if the union got in," one employee responded, "No, he just asked what would—what do we think would happen." * * * We are also satisfied that the Board took the Gilliard video and the lower-level supervisors' statements into account when examining the overall context in which Price and Little made their remarks.

In upholding the Board's decision, we acknowledge that the record could be read differently. * * * Nevertheless, ... it is the Board's duty, not ours, to "focus on the question: 'What did the speaker intend and the listener understand?'" Here, the Board determined that threats were neither intended nor understood. Had the Board reached the opposite conclusion, we likely would have deferred to that determination as well. * * * The union argues that the Board departed from its own precedent.... There, the employer had displayed a poster depicting a row of tombstones bearing names of plants that had previously closed after unionization. The last tombstone bore the employing plant's own name with a question mark beneath it. Although the Board concluded that the employer's actions violated the Act, the case is ... distinguishable ... because there the Board found that "no member of the [employer's] management ever sought to clarify the message, or to assure employees that it was not predicting that the same fate awaited [them] as had befallen other plants," while here the Board found exactly the opposite. * * *

While Smithfield executives delivered antiunion messages inside the plant, union representatives gathered outside the facility's front gate to encourage entering employees to join the UFCW. When union organizers began their campaign, Smithfield painted a red line on the plant's driveway to distinguish public property from company property. From late March 1999 until the election on July 8, union representatives congregated at the driveway and distributed handbills to employees as they went to work. Early in the organizing effort, Smithfield's security guard, Joe Pittman, saw union representatives cross the red line onto company property "seven to ten times" over the course of one day. Approaching the organizers, Pittman asked them to stay behind the line and then escorted them back to public property. When the union representatives immediately followed him back onto company property, Pittman warned he would call the police unless they stayed on their side of the line. When they ignored him, Pittman carried out his threat. The police arrived and informed the organizers that they had to remain on public property or risk arrest. * * *

[F]ollowing this trespassing incident, he reoriented a security camera—which normally monitored the plant's parking lot and front gate—to focus farther down the driveway on the union organizers "in case [the company] needed some type of documentation that they were in fact on [company] property." The images from the camera appeared on television monitors inside a guard shack near the plant entrance, which was manned by one or two guards. Employees on their way to work could see the screens as they walked through the guard shack, but neither they nor the guards could make out facial features or identify individuals from the images. The camera usually recorded onto a videotape, and the guards typically rewound the tape at the end of each shift to record over the images the following day. * * * Smithfield left the camera trained on the union organizers until the July 8 election, more than three months after the initial trespassing incident. After the unionization campaign ended, the company returned the camera to focus on its original target.

… [E]mployers may not photograph or videotape employees engaged in concerted collective activities without legitimate justification. Preventing trespass may qualify as a legitimate justification for videotaping…. [T]o assess the legality of an employer's surveillance activity, the Board asks "whether there was proper justification and whether it reasonably tends to coerce employees. "The Board rul[ed] that Smithfield's reasonable concern over continued union trespassing justified the company's decision to reposition the camera. The dissenting Board member found a single trespassing incident insufficient to justify continuous video monitoring over the course of a three-month unionization campaign. The majority dismissed that objection because the union "never offered assurances that it would not trespass again." * * * The union argues that the Board should have discredited Smithfield's trespassing rationale because the company taped over the recorded images each day and sometimes even failed to insert videotapes into the camera's recording device. According to the union, these facts belie Smithfield's purported concern over trespass and reveal that its true purpose in repositioning the camera was to chill employees' exercise of their rights under NLRA section 7. * * *

Considering the record as a whole, we conclude that substantial evidence supports the Board's finding that Smithfield acted to protect its property rather than to intimidate its employees. To begin with, union organizers trespassed onto company property and "openly mocked" Pittman when he tried to escort them back across the red line. Second, after the trespassing incident, union organizers continued distributing handbills at the very boundary line separating company property from public land. Finally, giving added support to the Board's finding that the company sought merely to protect its property, not to coerce or intimidate its employees, Smithfield reoriented its camera only after the union trespassed, and … "[d]etails such as facial identification could not have been determined by looking at the camera monitors." * * *

For the reasons given above, we deny the union's petition for review.

CASE QUESTIONS

1. What were the legal issues in these two cases? What did the court decide?
2. Why were the employer's actions discussed in the first case deemed unfair labor practices?
3. Why did the employer's statements about prior plant closings not violate the NLRA? Couldn't they reasonably be viewed as implied threats? Are you persuaded that the employer had a legitimate business reason for its videotaping? What effect does videotaping likely have on employees?
4. How should employers respond to union organizing?

Clippings

In December 2008, workers at the world's largest hog-slaughtering plant, located in Tar Heel, North Carolina, voted for union representation. The vote came after a fifteen-year-long struggle that included two election losses in 1994 and 1997, the issuance of numerous unfair labor practice charges by the NLRB, a mass deportation of immigrant workers, and years of litigation. The vote was 2,041 for unionization and 1,879 against unionization. One union supporter said afterward "I favored the union because of respect…. We deserve more respect than we're getting. When we were hurt or sick, we weren't getting treated like we should." Another said, "People wanted fair treatment. We fought so long to get this, and it finally happened." A first contract was successfully negotiated and went into effect in July 2009. The contract provided for wage increases of $1.50/hr over four years, continued health insurance coverage, more paid time off, and guaranteed minimum hours.

Steven Greenhouse. "Workers at Pork Plant in North Carolina Vote to Unionize After a 15-Year Fight." *New York Times* (December 13, 2008), A9; Andrew M. Ballard. "First Contract OK'd by UFCW Members at Raleigh, North Carolina Smithfield Facility." *Daily Labor Report* 125 (July 2, 2009), A-10.

Employer Responses to Union Organizing

Employers faced with organizing campaigns might be tempted to ask employees what their attitudes are toward having a union or whether they intend to vote for a union. Making these types of inquiries is not a per se (automatic) violation of the NLRA,[38] but it tends to be intimidating and coercive even if not accompanied by explicit threats. Employees are apt to suspect that their employer wants this information to single out union supporters for disadvantageous treatment. Under certain limited circumstances, systematic polling of employees regarding their union views is allowed, but by and large, *employers should refrain from either interrogating individuals or polling employees to find out who supports unionization, why employees want a union, and how employees intend to vote in representation elections.* Videotaping or photographing employees engaged in lawful organizing activity is also likely to be intimidating. Absent legitimate justification, such as the claim in the excerpted case that doing so was necessary to prevent trespassing on company property, these actions violate the NLRA.[39]

Although some employers agree to remain neutral during organizing campaigns, the NLRA does not require that employers remain on the sidelines. Employers are generally free to make their views about the merits of unionization known to employees. Except for the twenty-four-hour period immediately preceding a NLRB representation election, employers are free to require employees to attend meetings ("captive audience meetings") where the employer's views about unionization are presented.[40]

---

[38]*Hotel & Restaurant Employees, Local* 11 v. *NLRB,* 760 F.2d 1006 (9th Cir. 1985).

[39]*The Timken Co.* v. *NLRB,* 29 Fed. Appx. 266 (6th Cir. 2002).

[40]*Peerless Plywood Co.,* 107 N.L.R.B. 427 (1953). However, under an Oregon State law (the Worker Freedom Act—S.B. 15), it is illegal to discipline employees for declining to attend or participate in employer-sponsored meetings if the primary purpose of the meeting is to communicate the employer's opinions about religious or political (including unionization) matters. Susan J. McGolrick. "Business Groups Bring Legal Challenge to Oregon Statute on Mandatory Meetings." *Daily Labor Report* 245 (December 24, 2009), AA-1.

For that matter, employers (and unions) are generally free to engage in another staple of electoral politics—lying. The NLRB does not police the truthfulness of statements made in the course of organizing campaigns unless the Board's processes are misrepresented, forged documents are presented, or inflammatory appeals based on racism are made.

However, *employers (and unions) are prohibited from making statements that contain threats of reprisal or force or promises of benefit.* Typical threats include claims that unionization will inevitably result in plant closure, loss of employment, diminished wages or benefits, and strikes. More subtle but potentially unlawful are employer claims that unionization will be futile. In one such case, employees were told that bargaining would "start at zero" (implying that the outcome would be inferior to current terms); the union would likely seek to gain control of the 401(k) plan, resulting in loss of the plan; and work could be quickly shifted to another facility if a strike occurred. The Board concluded and a court agreed that these statements constituted unlawful threats.[41] *Employers must refrain from threatening employees as a means of influencing their decisions regarding unionization.*

JUST THE FACTS

During a union organizing campaign, two employees eating lunch in the dining room asked other employees whether they would like to sign cards indicating their support for the union. The vice president for HR was also eating lunch and observed the encounter. She approached the employees and said, "I would like to make sure that you have all of the facts before you sign that card." She went on to explain that the cards were "legal and binding" and that they would have to pay union dues if the union won an election. She also stated that there was no guarantee that the union would be able to obtain improvements in health benefits. The entire conversation lasted about eight minutes. In a second incident in the dining room, an employee was signing a union authorization card and a different HR manager came up and said that the employee "shouldn't be signing things that she wasn't sure about because what she was signing was something like a contract" and that the organizer was "probably promising something that [the union] wasn't going to be able to give her." Did these intrusions into the union organizing process violate the NLRA?

See, *Local Joint Executive Board of Las Vegas* v. NLRB, 515 F.3d 942 (9th Cir. 2008).

Deciding what statements constitute threats is not always straightforward. Although employees cannot be threatened, employers can make "predictions" about the likely consequences that unionization will have for the business—consequences that are objectively probable due to economic reality that is beyond the employer's control.[42] An employer violated the NLRA by making each of the following statements: that a client company could terminate its contract with the employer if the union won the election, that employees might lose their jobs, and that the employer would close down the business

---

[41]*Federated Logistics and Operations*, 400 F.3d 920 (D.C. Cir. 2005).

[42]*NLRB v. Gissel Packing Co.*, 395 U.S. 575, 618 (1969).

if employees unionized.[43] Although the first two comments were relatively conditional, the Board viewed them as more akin to threats than predictions because they lacked any objective basis and they were explicitly linked to the unionization decision. Threats that violate the NLRA still might not warrant the holding of a new election. In one case, an employee was told by a production manager shortly before a representation election that if the employees voted to unionize, the employer would move the facility at the end of the year when the lease expired. The union lost the election by a slim margin and asked the NLRB to order a rerun election due to the illegal threat. The Board decided that in such cases, the objecting union bears the burden of proving that the threat made to one or a few employees had spread throughout the larger workforce. Dissemination of the coercive threat would not be presumed.[44]

Providing, rather than merely promising, benefits is also problematic. After *an organizing campaign is underway, and especially if an election has been ordered, employers risk violating the NLRA if they raise wages or make other previously unscheduled changes in employment benefits.* Although this might seem like a reasonable way to respond to dissatisfied employees, it is usually done as a last-ditch effort to sway employees prior to an impending election. Overnite Trucking, faced with organizing campaigns at a number of its service centers, violated the law with a pay raise because the raise was virtually simultaneous with several elections, it was the second pay raise in several months and a departure from the company's usual practice, and it occurred in the context of other ULPs committed by the company. In contrast, a pay increase the following year was not a ULP because it occurred at the usual time for pay increases and few elections were pending.[45]

Termination of pro-union employees for their organizing activity is an all-too-common occurrence. *Employers must not discharge or otherwise discriminate against employees because of their efforts to organize a union.* This does not mean that employees can never be terminated in the midst of organizing campaigns. But terminations under these circumstances are suspect, particularly if the employer offers conflicting reasons, the discipline is unusually harsh, or the termination is for behavior that has been condoned in the past. These terminations are a clear affront to the rule of law and any sense of fair play. Claims that employees are no longer interested in unionization carry little weight when employers regularly resort to terminations and the threat of terminations to defeat employees' desire for unions.[46]

The high degree of control over employee conduct exercised by many employers must give way somewhat to the right of employees to organize. *In general, employers must allow employees to engage in discussions about unionization in the workplace during nonwork time.* However, restricting organizing to nonwork time presupposes that the employer has a fairly enforced, nondiscriminatory policy prohibiting other similar forms of "solicitation" during work time. In some workplaces (e.g., hospitals, retail stores), organizing can be restricted to nonwork areas. *In general, employees must be allowed to wear union buttons or display other insignias and to engage in activities such as lunchtime rallies.*

---

[43]*Tellepsen Pipeline Services Co.,* 335 NLRB 88 (2001).

[44]*Crown Bolt, Inc.,* 343 NLRB No. 86 (2004).

[45]*Overnite Transportation Co. v. NLRB,* 280 F.3d 417 (4th Cir. 2002).

[46]Kate Bronfenbrenner. *No Holds Barred: The Intensification of Employer Opposition to Organizing.* EPI Briefing Paper #235. Economic Policy Institute: Washington, DC (May 20, 2009); John Schmitt and Ben Zipperer. *Dropping the Ax: Illegal(illegal) Firings during Union Election Campaigns, 1951–2007.* Center for Economic and Policy Research: Washington, DC (March 2009).

JUST THE FACTS

A union organizing campaign was underway at a company that makes parts used by auto manufacturers. A high company official held monthly meetings with workers. Statements made during these meetings included "If we got [a] Union into the plant [auto makers] wouldn't probably do business with us and we wouldn't have jobs"; "If Honda or Toyota or any other customer became concerned about reliability of DTR's production flow, ... those customers would look for other sources"; "We had a sole supplier deal going with some of our customers where we were the only company that made particular parts for them. If the UAW was to get into DTR we would lose that sole supplier status because the companies would no longer feel confident with us being their only supplier because the UAW would make us more unreliable"; "Competition from other companies would result in layoffs"; and "DTR had never laid anyone off in the time that they'd been a company, but if the UAW came there that that policy would have to change." Did this employer violate the NLRA by unlawfully threatening its employees?

See *DTR Industries v. NLRB*, 297 Fed. Appx. 487 (6th Cir. 2008).

What about discussions of unionization that occur in the workplace and use employer-provided e-mail systems? Since e-mail is a primary mode of workplace communication for many employees, employers' ability to restrict solicitation via e-mail is of great practical significance. In a controversial 2007 decision, the NLRB had determined that employees "have no statutory right to use [their employer's] e-mail system for Section 7 purposes."[47] The case involved a union president who was disciplined for sending several e-mail messages requesting employees' participation in activities supportive of the union. The employer's policy prohibited use of the e-mail system to "solicit or proselytize for commercial ventures, religious causes, outside organizations, or other non-job-related solicitations." The e-mail system was widely used by employees to convey personal messages to one another, although the Board found that there was no evidence that the system had been used to solicit support for any outside causes or organizations except for the United Way. The decision emphasized the property rights of employers and departed from previous NLRB decisions by holding that only those restrictions that specifically disadvantage activity protected under the NLRA would violate the law. Thus, under the NLRB's 2007 ruling, policies permitting solicitations of a personal nature, but prohibiting invitations to join organizations or buy products, would have been lawful because union organizing was treated the same as communications about joining other organizations. However, this decision was appealed and overturned.[48] While the appeals court did not go so far as to say that a truly neutral e-mail use policy that had the effect of prohibiting union-related communications would be unlawful, it rejected the NLRB's view that the company had not discriminated against the union president for engaging in protected activity. The court said that the employer had enforced its no-solicitation policy only when union-related communications were involved and had not attempted to draw the distinction between personal and organizational solicitations that the NLRB relied on in its ruling. Thus, while the law is still a bit

Practical Considerations What kind of distribution/solicitation policy would you recommend that an employer adopt regarding e-mail use?

---

[47] *Guard Publishing*, 351 NLRB No. 70 (2007).

[48] *Guard Publishing Co. v. NLRB*, 571 F.3d 53 (D.C. Cir. 2009); *remanded*, 2011 NLRB LEXIS 380.

murky on this question, *employers should generally avoid maintaining sweeping policies prohibiting e-mail solicitations*, since such policies are likely to be selectively and discriminatorily enforced.

Nonemployee organizers (e.g., union employees, community activists) who assist employees in forming unions are often critical to employees acting on their rights under the NLRA. However, providing outsiders with access to employees can clash with the property rights of employers. In one important case, nonemployee organizers sought to communicate with the employees of a retail store. The store was located in a shopping center with a parking lot. The store was part-owner of the privately owned lot. When organizers attempted to place handbills on the windshields of employee cars, the store had the organizers removed from the parking lot. The Supreme Court held that as long as the location of a workplace and the living quarters of employees do not place them beyond the reach of reasonable communication means, nonemployee organizers need not be provided with access to employees on the private property of employers.[49] Because the union in this case had some ability to contact employees at their homes and to communicate with employees in a public area located between the parking lot and a highway, the employer did not violate the NLRA by barring the nonemployee organizers. The examples cited by the Court of cases in which private property rights would have to yield to organizing efforts (remote logging and mining camps) suggest that accommodation of nonemployee organizers is rarely required. Thus, *provided that nonemployee organizers have some viable means of communicating with employees, employers with nondiscriminatory no-solicitation policies can deny nonemployee organizers access to workplaces and private property surrounding them.*

The employee/nonemployee dichotomy ignores another significant category of potential union organizers—employees of the same company who work at other facilities. Such "off-site employees" have a direct stake in the success of union organizing at other facilities: "'[W]hen offsite employees seek to organize similarly situated employees at another employer facility, the employees seek strength in numbers to increase the power of their union and ultimately to improve their own working conditions.'"[50] The NLRB and courts have generally held that off-site employees must be allowed access to nonwork areas surrounding the workplace even if these are otherwise treated as private property by the employer.

Questions remain about exactly what areas are private, particularly in workplaces that are open to the public. In a case involving nonemployee organizers distributing literature and picketing in a privately owned parking lot and walkway outside a grocery store, the court concluded that the grocery store owner violated the NLRA by having the organizers removed.[51] The key difference from the Supreme Court case cited earlier was that under California State law, the peaceful exercise of free speech is favored over property rights in areas open to the public, such as shopping centers and malls. State property laws, not the NLRA, determine whether employers have property rights to assert in denying access to nonemployee organizers. Unions also sometimes resort to colorful means of drawing attention to organizing campaigns and other labor disputes. With increasing frequency, these include the display of large (often ten feet tall or more) inflatable rats. Questions arise whether employers or local government officials must tolerate such displays. When it is government officials that object, constitutional questions are

---

[49]*Lechmere Inc. v. NLRB*, 112 S. Ct. 841 (1992).

[50]*ITT Industries* v. *NLRB*, 413 F.3d 64, 70-1 (D.C. Cir. 2005).

[51]*NLRB v. Calkins*, 187 F.3d 1080 (9th Cir. 1999), *cert. denied*, 529 U.S. 1098 (2000).

raised. The New Jersey Supreme Court struck down as unconstitutional the use of a local sign ordinance to prohibit the display of an inflatable rat on a public sidewalk outside of a construction site because the ordinance distinguished between types of signs based on their content.[52] The NLRB has taken the position that the display of banners and inflatable rats is expressive activity protected by the First Amendment and, thus, the NLRA should generally be interpreted to allow such speech and avoid possible infringement on employees' free speech rights.[53]

Representation Election Procedures

The NLRA (in common with other labor laws) sets out procedures for determining employee choice through **representation elections**. But the next question is, Which employees will be represented? Employees of a company hold many different job titles and are often spread across numerous workplaces, departments, and divisions. The NLRB is responsible for ensuring that the group of employees for which representation is being sought constitutes an **appropriate bargaining unit**. This determination is very important. As every gerrymandering politician knows, the outcome of an election is often a direct function of how the electorate is defined. Furthermore, if union representation is chosen, the success of collective bargaining is affected by whether the employees in the bargaining unit have sufficient common interests.

For the most part, the NLRB determines the appropriateness of proposed bargaining units on a case-by-case basis. The primary criterion used by the Board is whether the employees "share a community of interest." Among the indicators used to determine community of interest are similarity in skill levels; interrelationship of tasks; and common pay systems, supervision, and personnel policies. Certain provisions of the NLRA also limit the makeup of bargaining units. For example, professional employees cannot be included in bargaining units with nonprofessionals unless a majority of the professional employees choose to be included in such units. Plant guards and other security personnel cannot be included in bargaining units with other employees under any circumstances. In a case involving employees of a cable company, the NLRB departed from customary practice and determined that an appropriate bargaining unit would encompass employees at all four of the company's facilities in a geographic area rather than just employees at a single work site.[54] Even though the distance between work sites was considerable, the Board emphasized the centralized nature of the employer's daily operations and labor relations policies in deciding that the larger grouping would be appropriate. This was an unfortunate outcome for the employees because they had attempted to organize only one of the facilities.

The typical (but not the only) path to union representation under the NLRA proceeds from an organizing campaign to employees (or a union on their behalf) petitioning the NLRB to hold a representation election. One of the main requirements for the Board to order an election is a showing that at least 30 percent of the employees in an appropriate bargaining unit desire union representation. This showing is typically made by employees signing **authorization cards**. To be valid, these cards must be current and indicate a desire for representation by a particular union (as opposed to merely the holding of an election). Under the NLRB's formal certification process, the authorization cards are not the representation election, but rather evidence that an election is warranted. The Board will not hold repeated elections for the same group of workers. If there was a prior election within the past twelve months, an election will not be ordered (this is known as the

---

[52]*State v. DeAngelo*, 197 N.J. 478 (2009).

[53]*Sheet Metal Workers, Local 15*, 356 NLRB No. 162, at 3-4 (2011).

[54]*Prince Telecom*, 347 NLRB No. 73 (2006).

election bar). Also, if the employees are already represented by a union and covered by a collective bargaining agreement, an election to change representatives will be ordered only during a brief window period prior to contract expiration or after contract expiration (the *contract bar*).

If an election is ordered, the employer is required to provide to the NLRB within seven days a list of names and addresses of all employees in the bargaining unit to give the union a chance to contact all employees who might be interested in unionization. During this time between when an election is ordered and when the election is held, employer and union conduct is subject to particularly close scrutiny. Misconduct by an employer or union that upsets the "laboratory conditions" for free choice by employees can cause the NLRB to order a rerun election even without a finding that the misconduct amounts to a ULP.[55] In rare cases, an employer's misconduct prior to an election is so severe that the Board will certify a union that had shown majority support through authorization cards and require the employer to bargain even though the union lost the election.[56] Representation elections are secret ballot elections held under the supervision of the NLRB and generally in the workplace during work time. Election observers can be chosen, but these must not be managers or supervisors. If the majority of employees who actually cast votes choose union representation, the NLRB will certify the union as the "exclusive representative" of all employees in the bargaining unit.

Although the usual purpose of elections is to determine whether currently unrepresented employees desire representation, the NLRA also provides for **decertification elections**, in which employees decide whether they want to continue to have union representation. *Employers can neither petition for decertification elections to be held nor interfere by encouraging employees to decertify their unions.*

Voluntary recognition of a union by an employer is also permitted under the NLRA as an alternative to certification following the holding of a representation election, provided there is evidence of uncoerced, majority support for the union. Frustrated by delays and by what they see as employer manipulation of the representation election process, unions are increasingly seeking to obtain recognition through a **card-check procedure**. In general, this entails obtaining the employer's agreement to recognize the union if a majority of employees sign authorization cards. A neutral third party is designated to verify the results. Under this procedure, authorization cards serve as the decisive indicators of employee preference and not merely as means to obtain elections. Unions going this route also typically attempt to negotiate **neutrality agreements**, whereby employers pledge to remain neutral and not oppose unionization. One of the central provisions of the proposed **Employee Free Choice Act** (EFCA) is a requirement that employers recognize unions chosen through a card-check procedure.[57] While EFCA would make card-check the primary means through which employee desire for representation was determined, the prospects for passage of this law now seem remote. However, the NLRB has proposed new regulations aimed at expediting the holding of elections and eliminating opportunities for delay.[58] The Board has also put in place regulations requiring for the first time the posting in most private sector workplaces of fairly detailed information about employees' rights under the NLRA.[59]

Since under existing law the use of card-check results in voluntary recognition, questions arise as to when and how such recognition can be withdrawn. The Board's answer

Practical Considerations How should an employer respond to a request for voluntary recognition by a union? Are there any advantages to an employer of using the card-check procedure and remaining neutral?

---

[55]*General Shoe Corp.*, 77 NLRB 124 (1948).

[56]*Gissel Packing.*

[57]110 H.R. 800; 110 S. 1040 (2007).

[58]76 Fed. Reg. 36812 (June 22, 2011).

[59]76 Fed. Reg. 54006 (August 30, 2011).

for many years was that while voluntary recognition might not be owed the same degree of deference as representation election results (remember, under the election bar, petitions for another election will generally not be accepted for twelve months), the parties should be afforded a "reasonable period" of time following recognition to form a relationship and give collective bargaining a chance to work. Thus, during this reasonable period, the NLRB would not process any election petitions, including petitions to decertify (the *recognition bar*). In 2007, the Board changed its mind and instituted a set of procedures that opened the representative status of voluntarily recognized unions to immediate challenge.[60] In practice, this change had the effect of discouraging, or at least delaying, meaningful collective bargaining, since employers would be inclined to wait and see whether their employees would continue to be represented and by whom. Then, in 2011, the NLRB—as it is notorious for doing—once again reversed course and went back to its earlier practice of barring elections for a reasonable period of time.[61] The Board also indicated that it would henceforth define "reasonable period" as between six months and a year, with the precise length of time depending on the status of negotiations.

The union's status as **exclusive representative** is important. In practice, it means that *unionized employers must generally refrain from dealing with individual employees regarding their wages, hours, terms, and conditions of employment.* Even if an individual employee is willing to accept terms other than those provided for under the labor agreement, deals of this sort are not permitted. It also means that the union represents all employees in the bargaining unit regardless of whether those employees voted for the union or want it now.

Representation by a union is distinct from membership. Many employees choose to become union members. However, because a union is legally required to represent all the employees in a bargaining unit and some employees might be tempted to enjoy the benefits of representation without paying for it, unions commonly negotiate with employers to include **union security** provisions in their labor agreements. There are different types of union security provisions (e.g., union shop, agency shop), but in general, these clauses require all employees in a bargaining unit to pay union initiation fees and dues (or equivalent amounts) within a specified period of time (not less than thirty days after hire) under penalty of discharge by the employer. Employees who do not want to be union members and who object to paying full dues can inform their unions of that fact and pay a lesser amount that covers the cost of representation, but not other union activities deemed by the courts to be outside the realm of representation (e.g., political action).[62] Costs related to organizing new members can legitimately be passed along as part of representation,[63] but the union will likely have to prove that getting more employees under contract increases its ability to negotiate favorable terms for all of its members.[64] The Supreme Court has also approved assessing nonmembers for litigation costs incurred by a national union, insofar as those costs were related to the union's collective bargaining activities and part of a reciprocal relationship between the national union and its locals.[65]

---

[60]*Dana Corp.*, 351 NLRB No. 28 (2007).

[61]*Lammons Gasket Company*, 357 NLRB No. 72 (2011).

[62]*Communication Workers of America v. Beck*, 108 S. Ct. 2641 (1988).

[63]*United Food and Commercial Workers, Local 1036 v. NLRB*, 307 F.3d 760 (9th Cir. 2002), *cert. denied*, 537 U.S. 1024 (2002).

[64]*Pirlott v. NLRB*, 522 F.3d 423 (D.C. Cir. 2008).

[65]*Locke v. Karass*, 555 U.S. 207 (2009).

THE CHANGING WORKPLACE

Collective Bargaining and Public Employment

Union membership is not equally distributed throughout the workforce. Public sector (i.e., government) employees are far more likely to have union representation than private sector employees. In 2010, 36.2 percent of public sector workers were union members, compared to 6.9 percent of private sector workers.[1] Even though the public sector is far smaller than the private sector (accounting for roughly 17 percent of total U.S. employment), the number of unionized public employees (7.6 million) exceeded the number of unionized private sector employees (7.1 million) for the first time in 2010.

This concentration of union membership in the public sector is a relatively recent phenomenon. While the National Labor Relations Act was enacted in 1935, state laws governing collective bargaining by public employees are of much more recent vintage. Many of these laws were passed in the late 1960s and 1970s, both in response to growing labor activism among public employees and, in turn, facilitating a period of rapid expansion. This explosive growth in public sector unionism has cooled in recent decades, but the earlier gains by public employees have generally been maintained, while unionization in the private sector has continued to decline.[2] Questions were initially raised about the appropriateness of bargaining in the public sector and whether it represented an unwarranted incursion on the sovereignty of government,[3] but these concerns appeared to subside with years of experience in public sector bargaining. Still, a number of states (about 10) have never allowed collective bargaining by public sector employees, others permit it only for certain groups, and almost all place greater restrictions on it, particularly regarding the right to strike.[4]

Despite fears that public sector unions would have excessive power due to their lobbying ability, the capacity of governments to impose taxes to fund agreements, the fact that public agencies must stay open and cannot relocate, and perhaps a lesser incentive for public officials to resist employee demands, the evidence suggests that, on the whole, public employees are paid less than comparable private sector employees.[5] This is particularly true for more highly educated workers.[6] Furthermore, while government employees generally enjoy benefits that are superior to the private sector and benefits comprise a larger portion of their total compensation (which is true among unionized workers generally), total compensation costs—including benefits—also appear to be somewhat lower for public employees.[7] To be sure, government services are relatively labor-intensive and personnel costs are a major part of municipal and state budgets. There are also serious concerns regarding the ability of states and cities to fund the commitments made to their public employees' health care and pensions.[8] But the experience with public sector collective bargaining to date does not support the conclusion that it is the cause of the fiscal problems of state and city governments or that stripping away the collective bargaining rights of public employees is required as a solution to those problems.

Nevertheless, massive budget deficits, political realignments, an aggressive campaign by opponents of unions, and more than a little political opportunism have combined to throw the future of collective bargaining by public employees into serious doubt. Legislators and governors in a number of states have proposed or enacted laws that eliminate collective bargaining rights entirely for some public employees, restrict the issues subject to negotiation for others, limit the potential outcomes of bargaining, take away certain alternatives for resolving negotiation disputes, and leave decision making power firmly in the hands of government officials. Wisconsin and Ohio have gone the farthest down this road to date, but similar measures are under consideration in other states and the fate of the Wisconsin and Ohio efforts is being closely watched.[9]

---

[1]U.S. Bureau of Labor Statistics. "Union Members—2010." *News Release* (January 21, 2011) (http://www.bls.gov/).

[2]Kate Bronfenbrenner and Tom Juravich. *Union Organizing in the Public Sector: An Analysis of State and Local Elections.* ILR Bulletin 70. Ithaca, NY: ILR Press (1995).

[3]Harry Wellington and Ralph Winter. "The Limits of Collective Bargaining in Public Employment." *Yale Law Journal* 78, 7 (1969), 1107–1127.

[4]John Lund and Cheryl Maranto. "Public Sector Labor Law: An Update." In Belman, Gunderson, and Hyatt, eds. *Public Sector Employment in a Time of Transition.* Madison, WI: Industrial Relations Research Association (1996), 29–30.
[5]David Lewin et al. "Getting It Right: Empirical Evidence and Policy Implications from Research on Public-Sector Unionism and Collective Bargaining." Employment Policy Research Network, Labor and Employment Relations Association (March 16, 2011), 2.
[6]Michael Luo and Michael Cooper. "A State Worker's Worth." *New York Times* (February 26, 2011), A11.

[7]Jeffrey Keefe. *Debunking the Myth of the Overcompensated Public Employee.* EPI Briefing Paper #276. Economic Policy Institute (September 15, 2010), 6.
[8]David Leonhardt. "Union Pay Isn't Busting State Budgets." *New York Times* (March 2, 2011), B1; Steven Greenhouse. "Pensions on the Move: States Want Workers to Pick Up a Burden." *New York Times* (March 1, 2011), B1.
[9]Michael Cooper and Katharine Q. Seelye. "Wisconsin Leads Way as Workers Fight State Cuts." *New York Times* (February 19, 2011), A1; Steven Greenhouse. "Ohio's Anti-Union Law Is Tougher than Wisconsin's." *New York Times* (April 1, 2011), A16.

Union security provisions are legal under the NLRA because the section of the law that prohibits discrimination by an employer for the purpose of encouraging or discouraging membership in a labor organization makes an exception for the discharge of employees who do not meet their obligations to financially support their unions. However, the NLRA also permits states to pass laws making it illegal to incorporate union security provisions into labor agreements. These laws, known as **right-to-work laws,** exist in more than twenty states.

Bargaining

Employees unionize in large part to obtain the legal right to engage in collective bargaining with their employers and to negotiate contracts containing improved wages, hours, terms and conditions of employment. It is a ULP for an employer (or a union) to refuse to engage in collective bargaining. But what does an employer have to do to meet its obligation to bargain? And if agreement proves elusive, what rights do the parties have to use strikes and other economic weapons?

Duty to Bargain in Good Faith

The law does not and cannot ensure that collective bargaining will result in agreement; however, **good faith bargaining** is required. The NLRA does not go very far in defining what this means; it refers to the obligation to *"confer in good faith with respect to wages, hours, and other terms and conditions of employment," the "mutual obligation of the employer and the representative of the employees to meet at reasonable times," and the "execution of a written contract incorporating any agreement reached."*[66] Because parties to a collective bargaining relationship are free to engage in "hard" bargaining and need not reach agreement or even make concessions to the other party, identifying when there is a lack of good faith is difficult. However, *actions such as imposing conditions on the holding of negotiations, attempting to dictate which union representatives can be present at negotiations, inhibiting or delaying negotiations, withdrawing accepted offers, or simply going through the motions of negotiating without making a genuine effort to reach agreement are indicators of lack of good faith and should be avoided.*

Good faith bargaining entails sharing information. As a general matter, *employers are required to supply unions with information, if requested, that is "relevant and*

---

[66]29 U.S.C.S. § 158(d) (2011).

necessary" to representing effectively. This information is usually limited to wage and other employment data directly related to bargaining issues, rather than financial data. However, if an employer asserts that a union demand cannot be met due to financial constraints, the employer will have to provide financial information, if it is requested, to substantiate that claim.[67] *Bypassing union representatives and appealing directly to employees constitutes refusal to bargain with the legal representative of employees. Employers also fail to show good faith when they make material changes in employees' terms and conditions of employment without informing and negotiating with unions over these changes.*

JUST THE FACTS

During bargaining over a new contract, the company presented demands for smaller wage increases, discontinuation of its 401(k) contributions, and elimination of company-provided meals. When the union representative asked whether the company could afford the union's proposals, the general manager responded that "things are tough" and that "No, I can't. I'd go broke." The union requested to see financial records, but the general manager refused and stated in a letter that "at no time have I ever told you that we cannot afford your proposals." During another bargaining session, the general manager responded to a union question about whether business was really as bad as she was suggesting by stating "Have you seen sales lately?" A union request for corroborating financial information was again rejected. About two months later, the employer temporarily laid off most of the employees in the bargaining unit, citing poor financial results as the reason. Has this employer failed to bargain in good faith?

See *International Chemical Workers Union Council v. NLRB*, 467 F.3d 742 (9th Cir. 2006).

NLRB v. Whitesell Corp. illustrates the difficulty of deciding whether an employer has done enough to meet its legal obligation to bargain in good faith.

NLRB v. Whitesell Corp.
638 F.3d 883 (8th Cir. 2011)

OPINION BY CIRCUIT JUDGE SHEPHERD:

The National Labor Relations Board ("NLRB" or "the Board") petitions for enforcement of its order finding that Whitesell Corporation ("Whitesell") violated various provisions of the National Labor Relations Act ("NLRA") while negotiating a new collective-bargaining agreement ("CBA") with the Glass, Molders, Pottery, Plastics, and Allied Workers International Union, AFL-CIO ("Union"). * * * Whitesell challenges, for lack of substantial evidence, the NLRB's determinations that Whitesell failed to (1) bargain in good faith to impasse; (2) give the required timely notice to the Federal Mediation and Conciliation Service ("FMCS"); and (3) bargain in good faith by failing to provide information requested by the Union while negotiating the new CBA.

---

[67] *NLRB v. Truit Manufacturing*, 351 U.S. 149 (1956).

In January 2005, Whitesell purchased Fansteel Washington Manufacturing, Inc., a wire manufacturer in Washington, Iowa. Pursuant to the purchase, Whitesell recognized the Union that had represented the plant's production and maintenance employees for more than 40 years and adopted the existing CBA, which was set to expire on June 12, 2006. The employees at Whitesell's other facilities do not have union representation. * * *

On March 2, 2006, Whitesell's human resources manager, Cris Libera, sent the Union a letter, declaring Whitesell's "intent to terminate" the CBA upon its expiration on June 12, 2006. Attached to this letter was a copy of the F-7 form that a party seeking to modify or terminate a CBA must file with the FMCS within 30 days of notifying the other party of the dispute. However, the FMCS never contacted the parties, a fact that both sides noted was odd during the subsequent negotiations. When Union negotiator Dale Jeter contacted the FMCS to request a mediator on July 10, almost a month after Whitesell declared impasse and ended the negotiations over the new CBA, the FMCS replied that it had no knowledge of the dispute. Although Whitesell claims it mailed the F-7 form on March 2, the same day it sent the letter to the Union, the FMCS did not receive an F-7 form from Whitesell until August 11.

On May 1, 2006, Whitesell negotiator Robert Janowitz provided Jeter with the company's initial proposal for a new CBA. Janowitz also informed Jeter that Whitesell would not negotiate beyond the existing CBA's expiration on June 12, 2006. Whitesell's stated intention was "to negotiate a new agreement from start to finish" and "to equalize labor costs with that of other [non-union] locations and facilities." Accordingly, Whitesell proposed a number of significant changes, including: elimination of the dues check-off provision; elimination of the provision prohibiting the company from discriminating against union members when making employment decisions; replacement of the "just cause" provision with a requirement that the Union demonstrate that Whitesell acted arbitrarily; elimination of Union representation at disciplinary meetings other than those regarding termination or suspension; imposition of Whitesell's unilateral right to change any policy or procedure affecting overtime pay, holidays, vacations, and sick pay, in accordance with the company's practice at its other facilities; extension of the probationary period for new employees to 90 days; and consideration of factors in addition to seniority for layoffs and recalls.

Beginning on May 26, the parties held eight bargaining sessions. The first and last sessions did not involve substantive bargaining. The Union presented its initial proposals to Whitesell on May 26, which included a yearly wage increase of $1 per hour, two additional holidays, and increases in the company's defined pension contributions, sickness, and accident benefits. * * * At the second meeting on June 6, Whitesell provided Jeter with the specifics of the company-wide policies that it proposed to implement. These included the replacement of the Union-defined contribution pension plan with the company's 401(k) plan, a four- or five-fold increase in the insurance premiums for employees with less than ten years of service, an increase in the number of years of service required for certain vacation benefits, and a decrease in the number of paid holidays from ten to eight days. * * * Whitesell's proposal also eliminated overtime pay for weekend work.

At the third meeting on June 7, Whitesell proposed for the first time replacing annual wage increases with a merit-based system based on annual performance reviews. At the fourth meeting on June 8, Whitesell provided Jeter with cost estimates for employees participating in its various benefit programs and asked the Union to propose a final offer. At the fifth meeting on June 9, Whitesell offered a modified wage proposal, whereby it would increase wages by $0.25 per hour for the first year of the CBA and increase the shift differentials for those working second and third shifts. Whitesell also conceded that the Union could represent employees during performance evaluations. Although the parties agreed on several of Whitesell's proposals, the Union requested that the existing CBA be extended until July 16 to provide the Union with time to understand some of Whitesell's more substantial changes. In particular, Jeter requested information regarding the impact of the company's proposed vacation plan. The company refused to delay the expiration date of the existing CBA. At the sixth meeting on June 10, the Union lowered some of its wage demands and indicated that it would be willing to accept a modified merit-pay system. However, the Union reiterated its objection to some of Whitesell's proposals. With regard to the company's proposal to replace the "just cause" standard for employee discipline with a prohibition on "arbitrary action" by the company, Jeter told Whitesell's negotiator that the Union would never accept such a standard and that this was the Union's "final position."

The last substantive bargaining between the parties took place at the seventh meeting on June 11. At this meeting, the parties agreed on a number of important issues. In exchange for Whitesell's acceptance of the Union's dues-checkoff proposal, the Union accepted Whitesell's proposals on holiday, vacation, and funeral leave. Whitesell also made a counterproposal on seniority. On June 12, the expiration date of the existing CBA, Whitesell presented its final offer after the Union agreed to adopt the company's proposed health insurance plan. Jeter was dissatisfied with the offer and refused to present it to Union membership for a vote. Later that evening, Jeter requested further negotiations. Whitesell refused, declaring that the negotiations were at an impasse. At this time, the parties had reached tentative agreements on approximately 30 issues.

Whitesell then implemented selected portions of its final offer. However, despite Whitesell's inclusion of the Union's dues-checkoff provision in its final offer, Whitesell stopped collecting Union dues after June 12. Whitesell also canceled a voluntary accident program and refunded the money to employees who had contributed, even though cancelling the program had not been one of the terms presented in the company's final offer. In addition, Whitesell prohibited Union members from using their break and unpaid time to post notices about Union meetings on the company's bulletin boards. * * *

[T]he NLRB found that Whitesell had violated the NLRA by prohibiting Union members from posting notices about Union meetings on company bulletin boards during their break and unpaid time; … terminating the existing CBA and implementing portions of its final offer without providing notice to the FMCS; … failing to provide relevant information requested by the Union; … and unilaterally implementing certain provisions of its final offer without first bargaining to a valid impasse. Based upon these findings, the NLRB ordered Whitesell to cease and desist from its termination of the previous CBA and to restore the previous CBA until the parties sign a new agreement or, in good faith, reach a valid impasse. * * * The NLRB now petitions this court for enforcement of its order. * * *

First, we address the issue of whether substantial evidence supports the NLRB's findings that Whitesell failed to negotiate to a valid impasse. * * * [T]he Supreme Court [has] held that an employer violates … the NLRA when the employer makes a unilateral change in a term or condition of employment without first bargaining to an impasse on that term. An impasse occurs when "good faith negotiations have exhausted the prospects of concluding an agreement, leading both parties to believe that they are at the end of their rope." "Whether the parties have reached this point is a case-specific inquiry; there is no fixed definition of an impasse or deadlock which can be applied mechanically to all factual situations." "Among the factors that the [NLRB] considers in evaluating the existence of an impasse are the bargaining history, the good faith of the parties in negotiation, the length of the negotiations, the importance of the issue or issues as to which there is disagreement, [and] the contemporaneous understanding of the parties as to the state of negotiations."

The NLRB's finding that Whitesell did not negotiate to a valid impasse is supported by substantial evidence. * * * Whitesell's negotiator, Janowitz, informed the Union of Whitesell's intention not to negotiate beyond the expiration of the existing CBA when he sent the company's initial proposals to the Union, and he reiterated this intention at the first bargaining session. * * * While there were eight bargaining sessions, the parties spent much of the time caucusing with their respective sides, and two of these sessions did not involve any substantive bargaining. Whitesell first presented its proposal to replace the Union's system of annual wage increases with a merit-based system at the third meeting. [In another case, the NLRB found] that a party failed to bargain in good faith when that party sought extensive changes to an existing agreement, but imposed "an artificial, relatively short, deadline for concluding a new agreement and then declared impasse when that deadline could not be met." Moreover, despite Whitesell's claims of impasse, the parties came to agreement on 30 issues and were continuing to come to agreement on important issues up until the final meeting on June 12. * * * Whitesell claims that the parties were deadlocked on a number of important issues on the final day, in particular the standard for disciplinary action, retirement plan, wage increases, the company's insurance plan, vacation, seniority, overtime, and the leave of absence and sick leave provisions. However, the disagreements over the standard for disciplinary action and overtime are the only issues over which the parties were clearly deadlocked. Concerning the retirement plan, Jeter testified that he did not understand the parties to be "at the end of their rope" because they had not yet fully discussed the differences between the Union's existing defined contribution pension and Whitesell's 401(k), or how the company's plan would affect the benefits accrued under the existing plan. Nothing in the record contradicts Jeter's belief that the parties were not at an impasse over the retirement plan. Whitesell's claim that the parties were deadlocked over wage increases is belied by the fact … that the Union reduced its proposed wage increases for the second and third year of the CBA and agreed to accept a modified version of the company's proposed merit-pay system two days before Whitesell declared impasse. Similarly, although the parties had not reached an agreement on the time frame within which to introduce the increases in employee insurance premiums, at their final meeting the parties came to the more fundamental agreement that the Union would accept Whitesell's group health insurance proposal. Moreover, Whitesell compromised on its proposal to use performance evaluations in addition to seniority to determine layoffs and recall, a fact that undermines Whitesell's contention that the parties were deadlocked concerning seniority. Finally, Whitesell concedes that the provision concerning leaves of absence and sick leave was relatively unimportant to the parties, thereby diminishing the relevance of any disagreement over this provision to the question of whether the entire bargaining process had broken down. * * *

Further, the cases cited by Whitesell do not support its claims of impasse. In *TruServ*, the court reversed the NLRB's finding that the parties had not bargained to a valid impasse. However, unlike the company in *TruServ*, Whitesell has made no demonstration of economic exigencies that justified the haste with which it wanted to conclude the bargaining process. Moreover, the parties in *TruServ* had an extensive bargaining history with one another, whereas the parties here were negotiating for the first time. Similarly, in *AMF Bowling Co.*, the court held that the parties had reached a genuine impasse where the union had twice voted on and rejected the company's final offer without making any counteroffers that would indicate a willingness to compromise. There is no such indication of obstinacy on the part of the Union here.

Whitesell's claim that the parties were at a good-faith impasse is further undermined by the NLRB's finding that Whitesell failed to provide information about the vacation plan … . Although the Union ultimately accepted Whitesell's vacation proposal, the parties continued to disagree over whether, and to what extent, the company's plan would deprive employees of the vacation benefits they had earned under the

expiring CBA. This disagreement was prolonged by Whitesell's failure to provide the information requested by the Union. * * * Whitesell also cancelled the voluntary supplemental accident fund without bargaining for the issue or including such a provision in its final offer. * * * "It is settled law that where an employer bargains in good faith to impasse, … it may implement unilateral changes in working conditions so long as the changes are reasonably comprehended within its pre-impasse proposals to the union."

Whitesell also contests the NLRB's finding that it failed to provide notice to the FMCS as required by … the NLRA. * * * [T]he NLRB found that the failure to provide the requisite … notice constituted a separate violation of the duty to bargain … and that the remedy for this violation was to extend the dues-checkoff provision until 30 days after the FMCS received the proper notice from Whitesell. * * * [T]he obligation is on "the party desiring such termination or modification" to "notif[y] the [FMCS] within thirty days after such notice of the existence of a dispute." Whitesell bears the burden of showing that the FMCS received the notice that a dispute had arisen between Whitesell and the Union. Merely stating that the notice was mailed does not show that notice was received by the FMCS. Further, because Whitesell was the party seeking to modify the CBA, the obligation rested with Whitesell to perfect the notice. Thus, the Union's communication with the FMCS on July 10 to request a mediator does not meet the clear mandate … that Whitesell serve as the notifying party. * * * [D]ues-checkoff provisions are not terms or conditions of employment that will continue to be in effect until the parties reach a new agreement or bargain to a genuine impasse. Therefore, Whitesell is only required to reimburse uncollected dues for the period ending 30 days after it gives the notice it is statutorily obligated to provide. If the dues-checkoff provision was a term or condition of employment, Whitesell would be expected to comply with the provision until it reached a bargain or impasse, rather than for the finite period ending 30 days following proper notice. Whitesell, of course, could have avoided this obligation altogether had it insured that the proper notice was timely given to the FMCS.

Finally, we address the claim that Whitesell failed to bargain in good faith by not providing information regarding changes in Whitesell's proposed vacation plan as requested by the Union …. "There can be no question of the general obligation of an employer to provide information that is needed by the bargaining representative for the proper performance of its duties." "Similarly, the duty to bargain unquestionably extends beyond the period of contract negotiations and applies to labor-management relations during the term of an agreement." * * * We agree with the NLRB's findings that Whitesell violated [the NLRA] by not providing the requested information concerning how its vacation proposal would impact the employees. Prior to the negotiations, Whitesell provided the Union with a seniority list and indicated the Union would be able to determine, using the list, how the vacation proposal would impact the employees. When the Union stated it calculated that one-third of the employees would be adversely impacted by the vacation proposal, Whitesell responded that the Union's calculation was close but not accurate. This response resulted in the Union's request for a complete list of employees along with an explanation of how the vacation proposal would affect each employee.

Whitesell argues we should not enforce this part of the NLRB's findings because Whitesell provided the Union with a seniority list and the Union "was as fully capable as [Whitesell] of determining who

would be affected immediately and in the future by [Whitesell]'s vacation proposal." This argument is belied by Whitesell's response that the Union's calculation was close but not accurate. The Union was entitled to the information upon which Whitesell was basing its individual vacation calculation.* * * .

Accordingly, we enforce the NLRB's order as supported by substantial evidence.

CASE QUESTIONS

1. What were the legal issues in this case? What did the court decide?
2. Why was it concluded that a valid impasse did not exist at the time that the employer ceased to negotiate? Since the employer wanted to eliminate the just cause provision in the contract and the union said that it would never agree to that, why wasn't that fact alone enough to show the existence of an impasse?
3. So, what happens now? What if the parties still cannot come to agreement?
4. What specific things should this employer have done differently to avoid the outcome in this case?

Does the duty to bargain extend to every issue that might be raised by one of the parties? For example, a union might be concerned about the firm's business strategy, the excessive pay of top management, the prices charged for a company's products, or any of a host of other issues. The duty to bargain pertains to "wages, hours, terms and conditions of employment." This phrase is given a broad reading under the NLRA, but it does have boundaries. The NLRB distinguishes between "mandatory" and "permissive" (or voluntary) topics of bargaining.[68] Mandatory topics are issues that, if raised by either party, must be negotiated over. Furthermore, disagreement over a **mandatory topic** is a sufficient reason for failing to reach agreement in negotiations. In contrast, if a **permissive topic** is raised, the other party can decline to discuss it. And if a permissive topic is discussed but not agreed on, it cannot be the basis for failing to come to terms. The many mandatory topics of bargaining include wages, bonuses, benefits, work schedules, safety, layoff and recall procedures, and grievance procedures, to cite only a few. Permissive topics are all nonmandatory topics that are not illegal to incorporate into a labor agreement. The firm's business strategy, CEO pay, and pricing policy are examples of permissive topics that an employer is not required to discuss.

What Happens When Parties Cannot Reach Agreement?

Proposals in collective bargaining come from both unions and employers. When employers are facing severe financial or operational problems, they are usually anxious to reach agreement on terms that will enable them to lower their labor costs or operate more

---

[68]*NLRB v. Wooster Division of Borg-Warner Corp.*, 356 U.S. 342 (1958).

efficiently. Although employers are generally prohibited from making unilateral changes in the terms and conditions of employment for their unionized employees, an employer can unilaterally implement its last, best offer made during negotiations if an impasse is reached (and any existing contract has expired). An **impasse** is reached when negotiations over one or more mandatory topics have become deadlocked and both parties are warranted in assuming that further negotiation would be futile. An impasse is not necessarily a permanent state of affairs and can be broken by one or both parties later relenting and making further concessions to the other.

Distinguishing a genuine impasse justifying unilateral implementation of terms from an illegal refusal to bargain in good faith is difficult. In one case, the employer and union negotiated over a new contract, made progress in compromising on their differences, but remained far apart on several important issues as the contract expiration date approached. In the last negotiating session, the employer announced that it was making its "last, best, and final offer" and that it intended to implement those terms shortly thereafter if they were not accepted. An appeals court overruled the NLRB and found that the employer had not violated the act. Despite the relatively small number of negotiation sessions (eight) prior to the declaration of impasse and the abruptness of the final offer, the court concluded that the company had reached the point where it was no longer willing to compromise, that it had engaged in good faith bargaining by altering its positions in the direction of union demands previously, that it was experiencing economic duress that necessitated a firm bargaining stance, and that the union's expressed desire to continue negotiations was not accompanied by a concrete indication that it was willing to change its demands.[69] In contrast, the court in *NLRB v. Whitesell Corp.* found that a valid impasse had not been reached because, despite the same number of negotiating sessions, the employer delayed making substantive proposals, announced at the outset that negotiations would cease with the expiration of the contract, failed to provide relevant information, ceased negotiating despite progress continuing to be made, and failed to show that it was forced to act due to economic duress.

Third-Party Intervention For the most part, unions and employers are on their own when it comes to bargaining. The assistance of outside parties can be helpful in negotiations but usually is not legally required. **Mediators** are neutral third parties who, by entering negotiations and exerting control over the bargaining process, help unions and employers reach their own negotiated settlements. Mediators can only facilitate negotiations; they have no authority to impose agreement or any particular terms on the negotiating parties. The NLRA requires that the Federal Mediation and Conciliation Service (FMCS) be notified within thirty days after bargaining is requested if an agreement has not been reached in the negotiations. The agency, at its own initiative or at the request of the parties, is charged with promptly communicating with the parties and using mediation to produce agreements and avoid strikes. However, if the negotiating parties do not want to settle, there is little that a mediator can do.

Mediators have a stronger hand under the Railway Labor Act (RLA). Only when the National Mediation Board (NMB) concludes that further negotiations would be fruitless are the parties released from mediation and allowed to pursue a strike or other "self-help" approaches. Airline industry negotiations overseen by the NMB sometimes take several years to conclude. Fact-finding procedures that delay strikes are used in rare circumstances under the NLRA (in "national emergency" disputes) and somewhat more frequently under the RLA (appointment of "presidential emergency boards"). Only rarely does the law require that negotiating parties turn over unresolved issues

---

[69]*TruServ Corp. v. NLRB*, 254 F.3d 1105 (D.C. Cir. 2001), *cert. denied*, 122 S. Ct. 1070 (2002).

for resolution by an arbitrator (e.g., state collective bargaining laws requiring arbitration for contract disputes involving police officers and firefighters in lieu of the right to strike).

Strikes and Other Economic Weapons Perhaps the most highly publicized and dramatic manifestation of labor relations is the **strike**. However, despite the hold that strikes have on the public's imagination, the vast majority of negotiations conclude successfully without strikes. In a strike, employees withhold their labor, refusing to resume work until their employer agrees to more favorable terms and conditions of employment or refrains from engaging in ULPs. Strikers are not quitting their jobs. Rather, they are attempting to place pressure on their employers to act differently. Strikes and the threat of strikes play a vital role in negotiations. Because employees can credibly threaten to impose unwanted costs on employers through the disruption of production, employers have a strong incentive to bargain seriously, compromise, and attempt to reach agreement. Strikes also impose costs and pose potential dangers for employees and their unions; there is no guarantee that strikes will succeed. Thus, the strike option gives both management and labor good reason to bargain seriously.

Strikes and associated activities, such as picketing, are concerted activity. As such, strikers are generally protected by the NLRA and *private employers must not terminate employees for engaging in lawful strikes.* Although the right to strike is protected under the NLRA (and the RLA), federal government employees do not have the right to strike. Many state and local government employees are also prohibited from striking.

Clippings

A decision by the NLRB's Acting General Counsel Lafe Solomon to pursue unfair labor practice charges against Boeing has proven to be enormously controversial. Solomon alleges that Boeing decided to establish a second assembly line at a newly constructed facility in South Carolina and to transfer some of the work on the new "Dreamliner" there from Washington State because union employees had engaged in five strikes since 1977. In numerous public statements and internal communications, company officials had attributed the move to the prior strikes. In Solomon's view, Boeing interfered with the exercise of its employees' Section 7 rights by punishing them for their legal strikes and discriminated against its unionized Washington State employees by shifting employment opportunities to the South Carolina plant (which is nonunion, following a vote to decertify that shortly preceded the decision to transfer work). The remedy being sought includes an order to bring the second assembly line back to Washington State. An administrative law judge rejected Boeing's efforts to get the case thrown out and is now considering the merits of the charges. In the meantime, Congress has entered the fray. The House of Representatives passed the "Protecting Jobs from Government Interference Act" that prohibits the NLRB from ordering the transfer or relocation of employment or operations under any circumstances. Whether the bill will become law is unclear at this point, but it represents a major incursion into the independence of the NLRB.

Steven Greenhouse. "Union Issue May Upend Boeing Plan." *New York Times* (April 21, 2011), B1; Steven Greenhouse. "In Boeing Case, House Passes Bill Restricting Labor Board." *New York Times* (September 16, 2011), B3.

Strikers engaging in lawful strikes cannot be terminated, but they can be "replaced." The rights of strikers hinge on whether the strike is an economic strike or a ULP strike. **Economic strikes** are undertaken to pressure employers to meet employee negotiation demands. The issues in dispute need not be money issues. **Unfair labor practice strikes** are undertaken in response to employer ULPs (e.g., refusal to bargain in good faith) for the purpose of pressuring employers to comply with the law. In any strike, employers have a number of options. They can, for example, cease operating during the course of a strike or operate using management personnel only. If employers choose to operate by using replacements for the striking employees, the distinction between economic and ULP strikes becomes relevant. In economic strikes, employers can hire either temporary (for the duration of the strike) or permanent replacements.[70] *Strikers who are permanently replaced remain employees and have the right, when the strike is over, to be placed on a recall list, notified of available job vacancies, and rehired if a job substantially equivalent to their previous position becomes available and they do not have substantial employment elsewhere.* Strikers in a ULP strike can be temporarily, but not permanently, replaced.[71] *Employers must reinstate ULP strikers upon their making unconditional requests to return to their jobs.*

Whether a strike is a ULP strike is not certain until after the NLRB, and often the courts, have ruled. This fact creates risk for both employers and unions. If the NLRB decides that a strike was in response to a ULP, replaced strikers are entitled to immediate reinstatement and substantial back pay. At the same time, if employers confer "permanent" status on replacements in strikes that turn out to be ULP strikes, the replacement workers who must be discharged have grounds to sue for breach of contract.[72] However, the fact that workers hired as "permanent" replacements are required to sign application forms indicating that they are employed at will does not prove that they are not permanent replacements.[73] No guarantee of greater job security is required for permanent replacement status.

Practical Considerations How should employers respond to strikes?

Strikers sometimes lose legal protection due to behavior engaged in during a strike. Picketing is common behavior during strikes (although it also occurs apart from strikes). Picketers establish a presence near their workplace and through words or signs make it known that they have a dispute with their employer. Emotions run high and harsh words can be expected on picket lines. However, picketing that restrains or coerces other employees who have the right to refrain from concerted activity is not protected and, under some circumstances, violates state criminal laws. Thus, mass picketing that does not allow picket lines to be crossed, actual violence or clear threats of violence against nonstrikers, destruction of employer property, and similar conduct is not protected. Picketing generally must be limited to the primary employer. Other secondary neutral employers cannot lawfully be picketed. For example, a union cannot picket a supplier that provides the major components for a manufacturer's product as a means of placing pressure on the manufacturer. This would be a type of "secondary boycott" that the NLRA makes a union ULP. However, if a secondary employer is not truly neutral because it is performing work on behalf of a struck employer, then it is a business ally that can lawfully be picketed.[74] Also, unions can picket at retailers to urge consumer boycotts of products produced by their primary employer if it is clear that they are not

[70]*NLRB v. Mackay Radio & Telegraph Co.*, 304 U.S. 333 (1938).

[71]*Mastro Plastics Corp. v. NLRB*, 350 U.S. 270 (1956).

[72]*Belknap v. Hale*, 463 U.S. 491 (1983).

[73]*United Steelworkers v. NLRB*, 2008 U.S. App. LEXIS 19562 (7th Cir.).

[74]NLRB v. *Business Machine & Office Appliance Mechanics Conference Board, IUE, Local 459*, 228 F.2d 553 (2d Cir. 1955), *cert. denied*, 351 U.S. 962 (1956).

urging a boycott against the retailer generally and the product in question does not account for a substantial portion of the neutral retailer's business.[75]

Under certain circumstances, employers can legally engage in a **lockout** of employees. Following the expiration of any labor agreement, an employer might choose to withhold from employees the opportunity to work despite their willingness to remain on the job and continue negotiating. The employer might do so because it fears that a strike will take place later at a disadvantageous time (e.g., while the employer has a large inventory of perishable goods), or it might do so to put more pressure to settle on a union that is reluctant to strike. Courts have allowed employers to use temporary replacements for locked-out employees.[76] Lockouts have become commonplace in professional sports. However, a lockout is illegal if the purpose of the lockout is to defeat employees' right to have a union. In one relevant case, an employer continued to operate in the face of a strike. A number of employees crossed the picket line. The union decided to end the strike and make an unconditional offer to return to work. The employer responded by locking out all of the strikers until a contract was obtained, but allowing the employees who previously crossed the picket line to continue working. This "partial lockout" that punished employees for exercising their right to strike and that did not have a substantial business justification violated the NLRA.[77]

Labor Agreements

Negotiations that conclude successfully, either without or after a strike, result in written, signed labor agreements. Most unions require that agreements be approved, or ratified, by their members before they become final, but ratification procedures are internal to unions and not a legal requirement. Labor agreements are very important documents. They are the basic source of rules governing the wages, hours, terms, and conditions of employment for unionized employees. The provisions they contain typically go well beyond minimum legal requirements. Labor agreements contain enforceable contractual protections for employees. *Employers must abide by the terms of labor agreements when making human resource decisions regarding employees represented by unions. Thus, managers must be thoroughly familiar with any labor agreements that cover their employees.*

Enforcing Labor Agreements: Grievance Procedures and Arbitration

What happens when an employee believes that her employer has violated a labor agreement? For example, an employee might be passed over for a promotion and believe that the contract's language regarding criteria for making promotional decisions was not followed. Disputes of this sort are inevitable. Rather than require lawsuits for breach of contract every time an employee's rights have been violated, labor agreements almost universally provide for grievance procedures, ending with arbitration if necessary. Employees who believe that their contractual rights have been violated can file **grievances** (or unions will do so on their behalf). The grievances will be considered by successively higher levels of management and union personnel. The representative role of the union must be respected in the contract administration process, as during the negotiations. *Thus, although individual employees can choose to file and pursue their own grievances, unions must be notified and given the opportunity to have a*

---

[75]NLRB v. *Fruit & Vegetable Packers & Warehousemen, Local 760*, 377 U.S. 58 (1964).

[76]*American Ship Building Co. v. NLRB*, 380 U.S. 300 (1965).

[77]*Local 15, International Brotherhood of Electrical Workers v. NLRB*, 429 F.3d 631 (7th Cir. 2005).

representative present at any meeting about the grievance. Most importantly, individual employees and employers cannot agree to resolve grievances in ways that would alter or conflict with the labor agreement. The availability of a grievance procedure also means that employees cannot take contract enforcement into their own hands, such as by refusing to follow orders that they believe are contrary to the labor agreement. Instead, they are required to follow the orders and file a grievance (situations threatening employee safety are an exception). If the grievance is upheld, the employee will receive a remedy for the violation.

Grievances that cannot be resolved by conferences between representatives of labor and management are sometimes submitted to arbitration. Ultimately, the union decides whether to take a case to arbitration. Recall that in arbitration, a neutral third party acts like a judge in rendering a decision that is generally final and binding on the parties. In **grievance arbitration**, the arbitrator decides disputes regarding the interpretation and enforcement of an existing labor agreement.

The courts have made it clear that arbitration is the preferred means of resolving disputes about rights under labor agreements and that arbitrator's decisions generally are final.[78] Arbitrators have a great deal of leeway in interpreting labor agreements, but their decisions still must be grounded in or "draw their essence from" the language of those agreements. One of the circumstances under which courts will overturn an arbitrator's decision is when the arbitrator clearly disregards the contract. In a case involving a dispute over commissions paid to delivery drivers, a court overturned ("vacated") an arbitrator's decision because the arbitrator had ignored the clear and unambiguous language of the contract. The court noted the limited and highly deferential nature of its review:

> *[O]ur concern is limited to whether the arbitrator went beyond, or outside the bounds of interpreting the contract before him.... The question is not whether the arbitrator misinterpreted the agreement, but only whether the arbitrator's inquiry disregarded the very language of the agreement itself.*[79]

The court concluded that the arbitrator had, in fact, ignored clear contract language in favor of his own view of what would be fair, based on what he took to be the past practice of the parties regarding the payment of commissions. Likewise, a court vacated an arbitrator's decision that a hospital had violated its labor agreement by instituting a policy prohibiting employees from smoking when on hospital property.[80] The contract was silent on the issue of smoking but reserved the right of the hospital to establish and revise reasonable employment policies.

Labor agreements between unions and employers are more than words written on paper. Grievance procedures and arbitration are critical in defining the rights of the parties under a labor agreement. Thus, *employers should handle grievances and arbitration cases very carefully, including gathering the facts and carefully considering which cases should be settled or allowed to go to arbitration.* An adverse arbitration decision can amount to the same thing as negotiating unfavorable terms. The labor agreement sometimes extends to ongoing practices of the parties, even when these are not explicitly (or not at all) mentioned in the labor agreement. Arbitrators may find a **binding past practice** to exist when a practice is clear, it has been consistently engaged in over a substantial period of time, and the practice existed with the knowledge and at least

---

[78]*United Steelworkers v. Enterprise Wheel & Car Co.*, 363 U.S. 593 (1960).

[79]*Anheuser-Busch, Inc. v. Teamsters Local 744*, 280 F.3d 1133 (7th Cir. 2002), *cert. denied*, 537 U.S. 885 (2002).

[80]*Armstrong County Memorial Hospital v. United Steelworkers, Local 158-06*, 419 Fed. Appx. 217 (3d Cir. 2011).

tacit consent of both the union and the employer. For example, if an employer has regularly provided coffee or food for employees despite the absence of any contractual requirement to do so, an arbitrator might overrule the unilateral discontinuation of this practice. A binding past practice is more likely to be found when some type of employee privilege or benefit is concerned than when work schedules or other managerial decisions are involved.

A change in circumstances (e.g., installation of new equipment) or in contract language is likely to invalidate a prior practice. Past practice cannot be cited to create rights that conflict with clear and unambiguous contract language, but it can be important in supplementing labor agreements when they are silent on a given matter or where there is more than one reasonable interpretation of the contract language. After all, it is reasonable to assume that the issue presented in a grievance has been dealt with before and the manner in which it was dealt with conveys important information about how the parties understand their agreement. In light of the importance of past practice in arbitration, *unionized employers should not establish informal practices of conferring benefits or privileges not specified in the labor agreement unless they are willing to sustain those practices (or bargain over changes in them). Both employers and unions have a responsibility to actively "police" the contract and ensure that it is being enforced in a manner consistent with the understandings at the time the agreement was reached.*

Key Terms

collective bargaining, p. 461
labor unions, p. 462
labor agreements, p. 462
National Labor Relations Act (NLRA), p. 462
National Labor Relations Board (NLRB), p. 462
Railway Labor Act (RLA), p. 462
National Mediation Board (NMB), p. 462
Civil Service Reform Act (CSRA), p. 462
Federal Labor Relations Authority (FLRA), p. 462

supervisor, p. 463
concerted activity, p. 464
unfair labor practices (ULPs), p. 471
labor organization, p. 472
representation elections, p. 485
appropriate bargaining unit, p. 485
authorization cards, p. 485
decertification elections, p. 486
card-check procedure, p. 486
neutrality agreements, p. 486
Employee Free Choice Act, p. 486
exclusive representative, p. 487
union security, p. 487

right-to-work laws, p. 489
good faith bargaining, p. 489
mandatory topic, p. 494
permissive topic, p. 494
impasse, p. 495
mediators, p. 495
strike, p. 496
economic strikes, p. 497
unfair labor practice strikes, p. 497
lockout, p. 498
grievances, p. 498
grievance arbitration, p. 499
binding past practice, p. 499

Chapter Summary

Labor laws protect the rights of employees to join together and engage in collective bargaining with their employers. In collective bargaining, employees are represented by labor unions in negotiating with employers over wages, hours, and a host of other terms and conditions of employment. The rules of the workplace are negotiated and incorporated into enforceable labor agreements rather than left to management or legal mandates imposed by government. The National Labor Relations Act (NLRA) is the

principal federal labor law covering private sector workplaces. The NLRA is administered by the National Labor Relations Board (NLRB).

The NLRA confers on employees the basic rights to self-organization; to form, join, or assist labor organizations; to bargain collectively with employers through representatives of employees' own choosing; to go on strike; to engage in concerted activities for the purpose of collective bargaining or other mutual aid or protection; and to refrain from such activities. Concerted or group activity by employees aimed at influencing employers regarding wages, hours, terms, and conditions of employment goes beyond union formation and formal collective bargaining. Employees who are not currently unionized and not seeking to form unions can still engage in protected concerted activity. To be protected, the activity must be engaged in with other employees or with their backing rather than only by or on behalf of an individual. For unionized employees, conduct related to enforcing rights under a labor agreement can be concerted activity even if engaged in solely by an individual. Protection for concerted activity can be lost if the conduct or speech is extreme or abusive.

The NLRA prohibits certain activities by employers and unions and labels these unfair labor practices (ULPs). Employer ULPs include interfering with, restraining, or coercing employees in the exercise of their NLRA rights; dominating or interfering with the administration of a labor organization; discriminating against employees for the purpose of encouraging or discouraging membership in a labor organization; retaliating against employees for filing charges or giving testimony under the act; and refusing to engage in collective bargaining. The ULP of dominating a labor organization aims at ensuring the independence of labor organizations by prohibiting company unions established or controlled by employers. The NLRA's broad definition of labor organization includes any organization or committee in which employees participate and that deals with employers regarding employment issues. If care is not taken to limit the issues dealt with or the manner in which employees on employee involvement teams interact with management, these teams can constitute dominated labor organizations and violate the NLRA. The ULP of discriminating against employees for the purpose of encouraging or discouraging membership in labor organizations requires the NLRB to establish a prima facie case that an employee's protected conduct was the motivation for a discharge or other adverse employment decision. If the NLRB can show this, the employer has violated the NLRA unless it can show that the same decision would have been made absent the discriminatory motive. Although employers are prohibited from discriminating to either encourage or discourage union membership, it is legal under the NLRA but not state right-to-work laws to negotiate union security provisions in labor agreements. These clauses obligate employees to pay for the services they receive from

unions and require the discharge of employees who fail to meet this obligation.

The NLRB attempts to closely police employer and union conduct during organizing campaigns for ULPs and other conduct that would disturb "laboratory conditions" for the free exercise of employee choice regarding unionization. The NLRA provides for representation elections to determine whether employees desire union representation. These secret ballot elections are overseen by the NLRB. If the majority of employees who vote choose union representation, the union will be certified as the exclusive representative of all employees in the bargaining unit. The NLRB determines whether a proposed bargaining unit is an appropriate bargaining unit by considering whether the employees share a community of interest. Increasingly, unions are organizing new members through the alternative means of receiving voluntary recognition from employers following card-checks.

Employers have a legal obligation to bargain in good faith with the union(s) representing their employees. Good faith bargaining requires a sincere effort to settle but does not necessitate that employers and unions actually reach agreement or make concessions from their stated positions. The duty to bargain pertains to mandatory but not permissive or illegal topics of bargaining. Third parties such as mediators are available to assist in negotiations, but under the NLRA, the negotiating parties determine whether they want to avail themselves of this assistance. The government plays a limited role in private sector labor negotiations and in most cases does not intervene to stop or delay strikes. Private sector employees have the right to strike and cannot be terminated for going on strike. In contrast, public sector collective bargaining laws usually require the intervention of third parties if agreement cannot be reached, and many public employees are prohibited from going on strike.

Although under the NLRA private sector employees cannot be fired for going on strike, they can be replaced. In economic strikes, where the aim is to place pressure on an employer to offer more satisfactory terms and conditions of employment, employees can be permanently or temporarily replaced. With permanent replacement, strikers need not be restored to their jobs at the end of a strike, but they retain the right to be recalled to their former positions or substantially equivalent ones. In ULP strikes, which are precipitated by employer ULPs and aim to place pressure on an employer to stop breaking the law, employees can be temporarily but not permanently replaced. Employees who make an unconditional offer to return to work from a ULP strike must be reinstated even if that means terminating a replacement worker.

Labor agreements are contracts that govern the wages, hours, terms, and conditions of employment for unionized employees. Labor agreements are enforced through contractual grievance and arbitration procedures. If grievances alleging violations of employee rights under labor agreements cannot be resolved in discussions between unions and employers, the disputes may be submitted to arbitration. The decisions that arbitrators make regarding the meaning and enforcement of labor agreements are usually final and binding. Arbitrators have considerable leeway in interpreting and enforcing labor agreements, but their decisions must be based on the language of those contracts. Arbitrators often look to evidence of how the parties have dealt with the same issues in the past. A binding past practice can be found where a clear practice has been consistently engaged in over a period of time with the knowledge and consent of both parties. Past practice does not negate unambiguous contract language, but it plays an important role in determining the intent of the parties when a contract is either ambiguous or silent on a matter in dispute.

The future of the institution of collective bargaining in the United States is in serious question. The private sector has seen decades of dwindling union density and escalating employer opposition to union organizing. As a result, the labor movement has become concentrated in the public sector. More recently, collective bargaining in the public sector has come under attack, with public employees and their unions portrayed as the cause of the fiscal problems of states and cities. Whatever the outcome of these efforts to curtail or eliminate collective bargaining in both the private and public sectors, the need for a powerful voice to advocate for the interests of workers will not go away.

Practical Advice Summary

- Employers must respect the right of employees to join together in contesting or expressing concerns regarding their terms and conditions of employment. Employment policies that interfere with these rights must not be maintained or enforced.
- Employers must refrain from interfering with, restraining, or coercing employees in the exercise of their NLRA rights. This includes
  — Refraining from interrogating individual employees or systematically polling employees regarding why they want a union and how they intend to vote in a representation election.
  —Not responding to organizing efforts by raising wages or making other unscheduled changes in employment benefits.
  —Not threatening employees or promising them benefits as a means of influencing their decisions regarding unionization.
  —Allowing employees to engage in discussions about unionization in the workplace during nonwork time.
  —Allowing employees to wear union buttons, display other insignias, and engage in other activities such as lunchtime rallies.
- Employers can bar nonemployee organizers from the workplace and surrounding private property provided that

  —The organizers have some viable means of communicating with employees.
  —The employer has a nonsolicitation policy.
  —The policy is applied in a nondiscriminatory manner to all outside parties.
- Employers generally must allow off-site employee organizers access to nonwork areas outside the workplace even if these are otherwise treated as private property.
- Employers must refrain from dominating or interfering with the formation or administration of a labor organization. This includes
  —Not creating or controlling "company unions."
  —Not instituting employee involvement in response to union-organizing campaigns.
  —Not using employee involvement teams to discuss or decide issues that are properly part of collective bargaining when employees are represented by a union.
- Any employee involvement teams that are used should be structured so that at least one of the following conditions is met:
  —Employees do not serve in a representative capacity.
  —Substantial decision-making authority is delegated to them.
  —Communication is not bilateral.
  —Their focus is on productivity rather than employment issues.

- Employers must refrain from discriminating against employees for the purpose of encouraging or discouraging membership in any labor organization.
- Employers cannot refuse to hire, fire, demote, or otherwise limit the employment opportunities of employees because they are known or suspected to be union supporters or activists.
- Employers must refrain from retaliating against employees who file charges or give testimony in proceedings related to enforcement of the NLRA.
- Employers must not encourage or assist employees in decertifying their unions.
- Employers must not refuse to engage in collective bargaining with employees' labor representatives.
- When employees are represented by a union, employers must refrain from negotiating or otherwise dealing with individual employees regarding their wages, hours, terms, and conditions of employment.
- Employers must be willing to bargain in good faith with their employees' representative, including
  —Meeting at reasonable times.
  —Putting any agreements into writing.
  —Refraining from imposing conditions on the holding of negotiations.
  —Not attempting to dictate which union representatives can be present at negotiations.
  —Not inhibiting or delaying negotiations.
  —Not withdrawing accepted offers.
  —Not going through the motions of bargaining without a genuine effort to reach agreement.
  —Providing unions with information, if requested, that is relevant and necessary to effective bargaining and representation.
  —Not making material changes in employees' terms and conditions of employment without first notifying and negotiating with the employees' union.
- Employers can unilaterally implement their final offers on issues only after bargaining in good faith and reaching an impasse.

- Private sector employers must not terminate employees for engaging in lawful strikes provided that they do not engage in serious misbehavior during the strikes.
- If strikers in an economic strike are permanently replaced, those employees must be
  —Placed on a recall list.
  —Notified of available job vacancies.
  —Rehired if a job substantially equivalent to their previous position becomes available and they do not have substantial employment elsewhere.
- Employers must reinstate strikers in a ULP strike who make an unconditional request to return to their jobs.
- Employers must abide by the terms of labor agreements when making human resource decisions regarding unionized employees.
- Managers must be thoroughly familiar with any labor agreements covering their employees.
- If individual employees want to present their own grievances
  —Their union must be notified.
  —The union must be given the opportunity to be present at any meeting about the grievances.
  —Resolution of the grievance must not alter or conflict with the labor agreement.
- Employers should handle grievance and arbitration cases very carefully, including carefully researching them and considering which cases should be settled rather than allowed to go to arbitration.
- Unionized employers should not establish informal practices of conferring benefits or privileges not specified in labor agreements unless they are willing to sustain those practices or bargain over changes in them.
- Employers should be vigilant in monitoring whether labor agreements are being enforced in a manner consistent with what was intended when they were negotiated.

Chapter Questions

1. An RN with the title of "weekend supervisor" spent most of her work time providing patient care and interacting with patients' families. She attended management meetings and was paid more than other nurses. She was the highest-ranking employee at the facility on weekends, but the employer provided the weekend staff with the telephone numbers of various managers to contact in case of an emergency. The RN would check to see whether employees did their tasks correctly and could correct employees if they did something wrong. If there was a gross infraction of residential care, the RN—as well as other nursing employees not alleged to be supervisors—could write up the employee on a disciplinary form. If she did so, the completed disciplinary form would be reviewed by administrators, who determined whether the infraction warranted

disciplinary action. On two occasions, the RN made an oral report that an employee was unfit for work. In both instances, she was instructed by administrators to send the employee home. In addition, on two occasions, employees came to her and expressed their need to leave work early because of severe health problems experienced by their young children. The RN—without first checking with her superiors—told both employees to leave work early. Finally, on one occasion, the RN prepared a performance evaluation of another employee. In this particular circumstance, the director of nursing asked her to fill out the evaluation because she was not familiar with the employee. The RN was discharged after circulating a petition protesting an action of the employer. Was this RN a supervisor, or was she protected by the NLRA? (*Jochims v. NLRB*, 480 F.3d 1161 [D.C. Cir. 2007])

2. The president of a nonunion company called a meeting of employees to express his dissatisfaction regarding worker productivity and scrap rates. He also announced that breaks would be more restricted. An employee questioned him about the new break policy, asking whether it was punishment for low productivity and whether it would also be imposed on workers in the office area. The employee blamed management for the productivity problems that the company was experiencing. The employee responded in the affirmative when the president asked if he should fire the managers. The president became annoyed by the employee's complaints about company management and said that the HR representative should "come up with a package" so that the employee could leave. On the same day, she was suspended for an indefinite period that turned out to be three weeks. When she returned to work, she was placed on indefinite probation. She remained in that status for almost a year. Did the employer violate the NLRA by disciplining the employee in this manner? (*NLRB v. Caval Tool Division*, 262 F.3d 184 [2d Cir. 2001])

3. A company included the following in its employee ("partner") handbook: "We honor confidentiality. We recognize and protect the confidentiality of any information concerning the company, its business plans, its partners [employees], new business efforts, customers, accounting and financial matters." A union

attempting to organize the company's workers challenges the policy. Does the policy violate the NLRA? (*Cintas Corporation v. NLRB*, 482 F.3d 463 [D.C. 2007])

4. Employees of a nonunion sanitation company that cleaned meatpacking plants overnight grew upset over their treatment by the company's safety personnel. One of their supervisors was sympathetic to their complaints. When that supervisor refused to follow a safety manager's order to discipline an employee, he was fired. This led to a walkout by employees that closed the plant for a day. The dispute was resolved for a brief period when the company agreed to make improvements and to reinstate the fired supervisor. But shortly thereafter, the company determined that it was going to fire a number of supervisors—including the one who had just been reinstated—for their failure to support the company. When word about this got out, a number of employees left their work area and congregated outside the plant. Some of the employees who walked out to protest the firing of the supervisors were also terminated. Did the employer violate the NLRA? (*Smithfield Packing v. NLRB*, 510 F.3d 507 [4th Cir. 2007])

5. A unionized employee filed more than a dozen grievances over a three-year period. His supervisors asked him why he was filing so many grievances and called him a "troublemaker." The employee got into an argument with a coworker and was told that if there was another instance, he would be fired. A few months later the employee made a derisive comment about another coworker who was not present. When the coworker later heard secondhand what had been said about him, he complained to management. The employee was suspended and then terminated for "comments directed toward another employee that were totally inappropriate, intimidating, antagonistic and offensive and could be construed as sexual harassment towards a fellow employee." Vulgar comments were common in this workplace. No written rule prohibited profanity, and no employee had ever been discharged on this basis. The employee's case was brought to the NLRB. What should the Board decide? Why? (*United Parcel Service v. NLRB*, 2005 U.S. App. LEXIS 8982 [6th Cir.])

6. Shortly before a representation election, an employer convened a series of meetings with its

security officers. At these "focus meetings," high-level managers discussed the union campaign and asked the officers about their work-related concerns. The officers were told that the purpose of the meetings was "so they could understand problems that we encountered and our working conditions," "to answer the concerns and problems officers expressed," and "to give senior management a chance to talk with officers about their desire to form a union." Shift meetings were regularly held in this workplace, but the focus meetings with top management were unprecedented. At one focus meeting, the CEO addressed the officers' concerns about overtime. Full-time officers' overtime opportunities had been greatly reduced when the employer decided to hire part-time officers to work the extra hours. The full-time officers had complained repeatedly about this change in policy, with no response from management. The CEO told the employees at the focus meeting that "it was a failed strategy to bring in a large number of part-time officers and it was being addressed and looked at." At a later focus meeting, the executive vice president repeated this comment. When the election was held, the union lost by a small margin. Do the employer's actions warrant the holding of another election? (*Mandalay Corp. d/b/a Mandalay Bay Resort & Casino*, 355 NLRB No. 92 [2010])

7. A written hospital policy prohibited solicitation and distribution in all patient care areas, including hallways adjacent to patients' rooms and other areas frequented by patients. The policy specifically permitted these activities in nonwork areas and during nonwork time. However, during an organizing campaign, nurses were instructed that organizing would not be allowed in the employee break rooms because of their proximity to patient care areas. Union literature was removed from break rooms, while the hospital's anti-union literature was allowed to remain. Disciplinary action was taken against a nurse who approached another nurse seated at the nurses' station in the intensive care unit to see if she wanted to sign a union authorization card. Again, the hospital cited proximity to patients and the potential to upset patients as grounds for this action. Charitable donations, collections for birthday gifts, and sales of various products (e.g., Girl Scout cookies, Avon products) were commonly allowed at nurses' stations. Has the employer violated the NLRA by enforcing its solicitation and distribution policy in this manner? (*St. Margaret Mercy Healthcare Centers v. NLRB*, 519 F.3d 373 [7th Cir. 2008])

8. An employer became aware that a union organizing campaign was underway in one of its plants. A union supporter was called in to a meeting with plant managers. At the end of the meeting, when the employee asked what he was supposed to do if others wanted to talk with him about unionizing, he was told "[Y]ou're to just work and not talk about the Union." After union supporters posted material on company bulletin boards, the flyers were repeatedly taken down. The company then issued a policy requiring all employees to obtain approval before placing any material on the boards. Subsequently, the company's practice was to refuse to post material of any kind from employees. A few months later, several off-duty employees attempted to distribute prounion flyers in the company parking lot but were stopped by company officials. They were warned that they were in violation of company policy. Around the same time, employees passed out union buttons in the plant and left some of them near a time clock for other employees to pick up. When company officials learned of this activity, they quickly called a meeting and warned one union advocate that "I don't want to catch you passing [buttons] out, Okay, I don't want to see them laying around…. You can pass them out when you're outside, on your own time, but when you're here working, you, you, need to be working." The officials said that this action was taken to keep the plant free of clutter and trash. Has this employer engaged in unfair labor practices in its response to the union organizing activity? (*Loparex LLC v. NLRB*, 591 F.3d 540 [7th Cir. 2009])

9. A call-in center operated 24/7. After the employees unionized, six employees from different work groups and all three shifts volunteered to serve on the committee that would be bargaining for a first contract. The union requested that the employer provide unpaid leave for the bargainers and that the union would compensate them for lost wages. The employer refused, insisting that they would have to use any paid time off available to them and do so in full-day increments regardless of the length of negotiation

sessions. The company later modified its position to allow paid time off to be used in four-hour increments. Since four of the six bargaining committee members worked days, the union requested that some evening bargaining sessions be scheduled. The company initially agreed, but when the company changed its lead negotiator, he insisted that negotiation sessions be held only during the day's "normal business hours." Three of the six committee members were not able to regularly attend negotiating sessions. Another had to use more than 100 hours of personal time to attend. After eighteen sessions, there was still no agreement on a first contract. The union filed an unfair labor practice charge. Did the employer fail to bargain in good faith? (*Ceridian Corp. v. NLRB*, 435 F.3d 352 [D.C. Cir. 2006])

10. A labor agreement stated that the employer would not subcontract work "for the purpose of evading its obligations under the Agreement," but retained the right to do so provided that it did "not result in the termination or layoff, or the failure to recall from layoff, any permanent employee qualified to do the work." On several occasions, the union sent letters requesting information about the employer's use of subcontracting. The union cited its belief that subcontracting by the employer had recently increased and that the failure to hire a replacement for a retired employee might be linked to subcontracting. However, the union had not filed a grievance alleging that the subcontracting provisions of the contract had been violated. The employer repeatedly questioned the relevance of the requested information and never provided it to the union. Did the employer violate the NLRA by failing to provide the requested information? (*Disneyland Park*, 350 N.L.R.B. No. 88 [2007])

11. An employee was terminated for making angry accusations about a manager. His union intervened, and the employer agreed to reinstate the employee subject to his signing a "last-chance"

agreement. The agreement, which he signed, specified that the employee would be fired for any similar conduct in the future and that the union "waive[d] its right to grieve such future incident." A couple of years later, in front of customers, the employee got into a loud argument with a manager, who he accused of being racist. The employee was terminated. The union again intervened. When the case went to arbitration, the arbitrator determined that the employee's behavior might be indicative of underlying psychological problems. Rather than uphold the termination, the arbitrator ordered that the employee undergo psychological treatment and evaluation at the union's expense. If after nine months of treatment the employee was certified as being fit to work, he would be reinstated (without back pay). The employer went to court to have the arbitrator's decision overturned. What should the court decide? Why? (*Hay Adams Hotel v. Hotel & Restaurant Employees, Local* 25, 2007 U.S. Dist. LEXIS 34129 [D.D.C.])

12. Is it fair that employers can permanently replace economic strikers? Should the law be changed to prohibit permanent replacement of strikers? Why or why not?

13. What if, instead of majority rule determining whether employees can have union representation, the NLRA provided recognition and bargaining rights to "minority unions" representing just their members rather than functioning as the exclusive bargaining representatives for entire bargaining units? Could this work? Is it a good idea? Why or why not? (Susan J. McGolrick. "Forty-Six Labor Law Professors Urge NLRB to Issue Rule on Members-Only Bargaining." *Daily Labor Report* 113 [June 15, 2010], A-1)

14. Is collective bargaining by public employees a cause of the fiscal problems of states and cities? Why do you say that? Should the collective bargaining rights of public employees be eliminated? Expanded? Why do you say that?

CHAPTER 15

Occupational Safety and Health

Providing safe workplaces is one of the most important responsibilities employers have to their employees. This chapter focuses on the Occupational Safety and Health Act, including its requirements for employers and the manner in which the law is enforced. In the event that workers are hurt on the job, state workers' compensation laws come into play and provide remedies to injured employees. Although workers' compensation statutes are among our oldest employment laws, they continue to generate legal questions about when employees are entitled—or limited to—workers' compensation benefits.

The Occupational Safety and Health Act

The **Occupational Safety and Health Act (OSH Act)**[1] is the principal federal law requiring private sector employers to keep their workplaces free from hazards that threaten the safety and health of employees. Three new agencies were created when the OSH Act was enacted: the **Occupational Safety and Health Administration (OSHA)**, the **Occupational Safety and Health Review Commission (OSHRC)**, and the **National Institute of Occupational Safety and Health (NIOSH)**. OSHA has overall responsibility for administering and enforcing the OSH Act. OSHA establishes safety standards, conducts inspections of workplaces, and provides information to employers and employees about workplace safety and health issues. The OSHRC is independent from OSHA and hears appeals of its enforcement actions. NIOSH provides scientific and technical support to OSHA, helping it to identify hazards and develop appropriate standards. When requested, NIOSH visits workplaces and conducts health hazard evaluations. Following the explosion of BP's Deepwater Horizon drilling rig in April 2010, NIOSH was brought in to monitor the chemical exposures of workers cleaning up the oil spilled in the Gulf of Mexico. NIOSH determined that exposure to volatile organic compounds such as benzene was well within established limits, although carbon monoxide exposures, due in part to idling boat engines, were excessive.[2]

The OSH Act protects most private sector employees but not government employees (at least not directly). The act allows states that prefer to issue and enforce their own safety and health standards to do so, as long as the state programs are certified by OSHA as being at least as effective as the federal program. Another condition for OSHA certification of state plans is that state and local government employees also be

---

[1]29 U.S.C.S. §§ 651-678 (2011).

[2]Greg Hellman. "Review of Gulf Worker Hazards Shows Limited Chemical Exposures, NIOSH Says." *Daily Labor Report* 136 (July 16, 2010), A-4.

covered. About half the states are state plan states.[3] When the OSH Act runs up against other federal laws affecting the safety and health of private sector employees (e.g., laws regulating transportation, nuclear plants), OSHA is generally prohibited from exercising its jurisdiction.

The OSH Act is aimed at eliminating, or at least lessening, safety and health hazards in the workplace. Unsafe conditions violate the law even if they have not (yet) resulted in injury, illness, or death. The latter might prompt enforcement activities or affect penalties, but unsafe conditions by themselves violate the OSH Act.

How Safe Is "Safe Enough"?

Most agree that workplaces should be safe, but some risk is involved in any activity. (As I sit here typing these words, a projectile might come crashing through the window, my back might go out when I twist to reach for some papers, the air might be full of asbestos, and so on.) How far should employers have to go in protecting employees from hazards to their safety and health? The minimum levels of safety that employers are required to provide are defined in two ways: through standards created by OSHA to address specific hazards and through the OSH Act's general duty clause.

Safety Standards   At its own initiative or at the request of other parties (e.g., NIOSH), OSHA has the authority to create (or "promulgate") **safety standards**. Separate standards are issued for general industry, maritime, construction, and agriculture. General industry standards apply to all industries unless more specific maritime, construction, or agricultural standards deal with the same issues. Figure 15.1 lists a few examples of OSHA general industry standards. *Employers must become aware of and comply with all standards that apply to their operations.* Employers arguing that they should be excused for not meeting standards because compliance would be "infeasible" must show that compliance with the standard would be impossible (or render performance of the work impossible) and that they took other steps to protect workers (or no such steps were available). An employer was unable to convince a court of the infeasibility of compliance with a standard calling for at least ten feet of clearance between the operation of mechanized equipment and energized, noninsulated power lines.[4] The fact that deenergizing the power lines while the ground-clearing operation was underway would have temporarily cut off electrical power to a number of parties and was not favored by the local utility did not render it an impossibility.

Figure 15.2 further illustrates the nature of OSHA standards by outlining the contents of OSHA's occupational noise exposure standard. Exposure to excessive noise on the job

FIGURE 15.1 Examples of OSHA General Industry Standards

Substances	lead, benzene, asbestos, formaldehyde, blood-borne pathogens
Equipment	woodworking machinery, mechanical power presses, cranes
Work processes	grain handling, arc welding and cutting, pulp and paper mills
Environmental conditions	noise, ventilation, sanitation
Safety practices	control of hazardous energy (lockout/tagout), hazard communication, respirators, eye and face protection, medical services, first aid

© Cengage Learning 2013.

---

[3]Twenty-two states currently have plans covering both private and public sector employees. Four states and the Virgin Islands have state plans covering public sector employees only (http://www.osha.gov/).

[4]*Crooker & Sons v. OSHRC*, 537 F.3d 79 (1st Cir. 2008).

FIGURE 15.2 Summary of the OSHA Occupational Noise Exposure Standard*

Establishes a permissible exposure limit (PEL) of 90 decibels (based on an 8-hour day).

When employees are subjected to sound in excess of the PEL, employers are to use appropriate, feasible engineering (e.g., adjustments to equipment to reduce vibration, sound barriers, mufflers) or administrative (e.g., limitation on work hours, job rotation, quiet break areas) controls to lessen the exposure. Personal protective equipment (e.g., ear plugs) must be used if these measures do not reduce the exposure below the PEL.

Establishes an action level of 85 decibels (based on an 8-hour day).

A hearing conservation program must be established for all employees exposed to noise above the action level. This includes monitoring workplace noise levels; making audiometric (hearing) testing available at no cost to employees; taking, within six months of an employee's first exposure at or above the action level, a baseline audiogram against which subsequent tests can be compared; taking follow-up audiograms on at least an annual basis; and evaluating audiograms for evidence of hearing loss.

Hearing protectors must be made available at no cost to employees exposed to noise at or above the action level. Employers must ensure that protectors are worn, give employees a choice among a variety of suitable protectors, provide training in their proper use, and ensure that they fit properly.

A training program must be instituted and repeated annually for all employees exposed to noise at or above the action level.

Records of exposure monitoring must be retained for two years and be made available on request to employees and their representatives. Records of individual audiometric tests must be retained for the duration of an employee's employment.

*29 C.F.R. 1910.95 (2008).

© Cengage Learning 2013.

is a serious hazard that threatens the hearing of workers in a variety of occupations, from factory workers to rock musicians.

In deciding what standards are applicable, specific standards take precedence over more general ones. Employees do not actually have to be exposed to the conditions that violated a standard (nor suffer any harm); it is enough that the nature of their work and the facility make it reasonable to expect that they might encounter the danger. Knowledge of a hazard that violates an OSHA standard can be either actual or constructive. Employers are not expected to be omniscient, but they cannot evade their responsibilities by ignoring obvious problems. Thus, if a hazard is in plain view, is known to supervisors, or is the object of employee complaints, the employer will be deemed to have known of its existence. Because employers are expected to be aware of applicable standards, professing ignorance that particular conditions violate OSHA standards is of no avail.

ELEMENTS OF A CLAIM

Violation of an Osha Safety Standard

To establish violation of a standard, OSHA must show all the following:

1. An applicable standard exists.
2. The standard was not complied with.
3. One or more employees were exposed or had access to the hazard.
4. The employer knew or should have known of the hazard.

© Cengage Learning 2013.

In *R. Williams Construction Co. v. OSHRC*, the court considers whether citations for violations of specific OSHA standards by a construction contractor should be upheld. Although safety regulations might seem bureaucratic or nitpicky, the potential consequences of failing to adhere to them—in this case, the death of a worker in a trench collapse—are sobering.

R. Williams Construction Co. v. OSHRC
464 F.3d 1060 (9th Cir. 2006)

OPINION BY CIRCUIT JUDGE FLETCHER:

Petitioner R. Williams Construction Co. ("Williams" or "the Company") petitions for review of a final order of the Federal Occupational Safety and Health Review Commission (the "Commission"), affirming violations of the Occupational Safety and Health Act ("OSHA") in the wake of a trench collapse and death of an employee at a construction site in Santa Ynez, California. We deny the petition for review.

On September 19, 2002, a trench collapse at a sewer-construction project at the Chumash Casino Project in Santa Ynez, California, killed Jose Aguiniga, a Williams employee, and seriously injured [Adam Palomar,] another Williams employee. On the day of the collapse, the trench was ten to twelve feet deep and between three and four feet wide at the bottom. The trench was about thirteen feet wide at the top and more than forty feet long. The sides of the trench rose vertically from the bottom for approximately five feet, after which they sloped backwards at about a forty-five degree angle. An earthen slope at the west end of the trench provided the workers' only access to and egress from the bottom. Ground water seeped into the soil continuously.

Williams used a number of submersible pumps to remove the ground water that seeped into the trench. Although the pumps could be pulled up and cleaned from the top of the trench, it was the practice to do so from inside the trench. Palomar and Aguiniga ... were generally responsible for cleaning the pumps and did so as needed throughout any given workday without receiving specific instructions. On the day before the accident, a hydraulic jack shoring system, which supported the trench wall, had been removed. On the day of the accident, Palomar and Aguiniga entered the unshored trench to clean the pumps, remaining there for about fifteen minutes. As the two were exiting the trench, the north wall collapsed, burying Aguiniga

completely and Palomar almost completely. Aguiniga died, and Palomar was severely injured.

OSHA conducted an investigation and cited the Company for safety violations. The first citation charged the Company with failing to instruct its employees in the recognition and avoidance of unsafe conditions and in the regulations applicable to their work environment, as required by [regulation]. The second citation charged the Company with failing to ensure that no worker would have to travel more than 25 feet to reach a safe point of egress, as required by [regulation]. The third citation charged the Company with failing to ensure that a "competent person"—i.e., one with specific training in soil analysis and protective systems and capable of identifying dangerous conditions—performed daily inspections of excavations for evidence of hazardous conditions, as required by [regulation]. The fourth violation charged the Company with failing to ensure that the walls of the excavation be either sloped or supported, as required by [regulation]. The Secretary of Labor (the "Secretary") designated the first three violations "serious" in nature and proposed penalties of $7,000 for each violation. The Secretary designated the fourth violation "willful" in nature and proposed a $70,000 penalty, for a total penalty of $91,000.

The ALJ [OSHRC administrative law judge] conducted a two-day hearing, during which several Williams employees provided testimony. Sergio Lopez and Rick Dzamba stated that they did not know that Adam Palomar and Jose Aguiniga were in the unshored trench when the wall collapsed. However, both Lopez and Dzamba had provided contrary statements to the general contractor immediately after the accident, which suggested they knew that the two men were working in the unshored trench. Based on these contradictions and their demeanor during the hearing, the ALJ determined that Lopez and Dzamba were not credible.

Joseph Goforth, an employee who started working for Williams four days before the trench collapse, testified that he occasionally worked in the trench and received no training when he started work. He was not told of any rules or shown a safety manual. No one discussed safety the day of the trench collapse.

Palomar testified that he worked for Williams for approximately nine months prior to the accident and had never received any training in trench safety. He testified that there was no safety meeting at the beginning of the workday on September 19, 2002. He was never told not to enter the trench and did not know who his supervisor was. He received all of his work instructions from Sergio Lopez, who acted as translator because Palomar speaks only Spanish.

* * * John (J.P.) Williams testified that he was the supervisor at the Santa Ynez worksite and was responsible for employee safety at the site. He admitted that he never looked at the company safety manual, which was located behind the seat of his truck; he also had not been trained as an OSHA "competent person" or received any other safety training other than on the job. He was unfamiliar with OSHA sloping and trenching requirements and did not conduct any physical tests on the soil in the trench. J.P. Williams stated that the crew talked about safety "all the time." However, he could not say when and where any specific rules—for instance, rules against entering the trench when it was unshored—were discussed. Williams stated that he and Dzamba were in charge of checking the trench the day of the accident but could not remember what, if any, warnings were provided to employees that day.

* * * Based on the testimony at the hearing, the ALJ affirmed the citations. However, the ALJ downgraded the one "willful" violation to "serious," reducing the penalty for that particular violation from $70,000 to $7,000. The ALJ reduced the penalties for each of the remaining violations from $7,000 to $5,000, based on the fact that Williams is a small employer with no history of prior injuries or OSHA violations. This resulted in a total penalty of $22,000.

Williams violated [an OSHA regulation] for failing to instruct each employee in the recognition and avoidance of unsafe conditions and for failing to eliminate other hazards: Williams provided no training in trenching hazards to at least the two employees working in the trench; moreover, no Williams supervisor was familiar with OSHA regulations. Williams argues that although Palomar testified that he did not receive instructions regarding trench safety when he was first employed by Williams, there was no evidence "that

Mr. Palomar had not received instructions on trench safety on some [other] occasion during his employment with Petitioner (nine months)." Williams seems to take the position that unless the Secretary can prove the absence of a conversation on trenching hazards, substantial evidence is lacking. But the Secretary is not required to prove a negative; moreover, evidence of broad neglect of safety is sufficient to support the ALJ decision.

Williams also violated [another OSHA regulation] by providing only one safe means of egress at the east end of the 45-foot trench. Although it appears that at least one of the pumps was located more than 25 feet away from the ramp, the exact location of the pumps, or the precise location of Palomar and Aguiniga vis-a-vis the ramp at the moment of the trench collapse, is immaterial. An employee working less than 25 feet from an exit may find it necessary to venture further from the egress point to satisfactorily complete a job. It is reasonably predictable that such an employee, already within a "zone of danger," will become exposed to the danger itself. Thus, we hold that this regulation applies regardless of whether the employees were exposed to the actual danger at the time of the collapse. A violation is established so long as employees have *access* to a dangerous area more than 25 feet from a means of egress.

In addition, Williams violated [another OSHA regulation] for failing to designate a "competent person" with sufficient training and knowledge to identify and correct existing and predictable hazards. No supervisor at the Company was familiar with the basic standards applicable to the worksite or otherwise "capable … of identifying and correcting existing and predictable hazards in their surroundings." We disagree that the Company discharged its OSHA duties merely by relying on the general work experience of Dzamba and J. P. Williams or "common sense."

The Company also violated [OSHA] for failing to protect employees from cave-ins: Williams had reason to know that its employees would enter the trench on the day of the cave-in and had actual knowledge that two of its employees entered the trench prior to the cave-in. It is unavailing for Williams to argue that *employees* must take greater care to avoid placing themselves in harm's way or that management can "expect an employee … not [to] intentionally place himself in danger." Such a claim misconstrues the purpose of the OSHA safety standards.

Williams failed to instruct its employees in proper safety measures and made no effort to ensure that employees not enter the trench on the day of the collapse. The ALJ findings, and the reasonable inferences drawn from them, easily satisfy the substantial-evidence standard. Consequently, the ALJ's decision affirming the citations is affirmed.

CASE QUESTIONS

1. What was the legal issue in this case? What did the court decide?
2. What exactly did the employer do or fail to do that violated the OSH Act?
3. Why was it "unavailing for Williams to argue that *employees* must take greater care to avoid placing themselves in harm's way"? What role, if any, should employees' actions have in determining liability under the OSH Act?
4. Ultimately, these violations that caused, or at least contributed to, the death of an employee and serious injuries to another resulted in a $22,000 fine for the employer. Is that a just outcome? Are the penalties for violations of OSHA standards sufficient?

The engineer of a commuter train that crashed into a freight train, killing and injuring numerous people, including himself, was apparently sending and receiving text messages just seconds before the crash occurred.[5] Employees *sometimes* engage in careless and unsafe behaviors that lead to accidents. Under the OSH Act, an employer can argue that a safety violation was due to unpreventable employee misconduct. However, to prevail in this argument, the employer must be able to show that it established rules designed to address the hazard, the rules were communicated to employees, efforts were made to discover violations, and people violating the rule were disciplined. This defense is also more likely to fly where isolated instances of misconduct by an individual are involved, rather than more widespread or continuous violations. In a case involving the drowning of an employee at a construction site, the employer was unsuccessful in claiming the defense of unpreventable employee misconduct. The employer's safety policies did not address the hazard at hand, the supervisor did not require foremen to report hazards if the foremen thought that they could take care of the problems by themselves, and the employer's rules on the use of personal protective equipment were discretionary rather than mandatory.[6] Likewise, an employer was unsuccessful in proving that the failure of an employee who was thrown from his tractor and killed while not wearing a seatbelt was unpreventable employee misconduct.[7] While this defense might have been sustained under other circumstances, in this case the seat belt was not operational, the supervisor did not conduct required daily checks, the seat belt went uninspected for six months even though reports were filed claiming that inspections had been performed, and the foreman did not check up on whether the supervisor was performing the required inspections.

Congress allowed OSHA to adopt national consensus standards on an expedited basis for the first two years of its existence so that it could "ramp up" quickly. These were drawn from voluntary standards that had been created by a number of nongovernmental organizations (e.g., for use by insurers), and many are still in effect. OSHA also has the authority to bypass normal procedures and adopt temporary emergency standards when there is "grave danger" from exposure to toxic or other harmful substances or from some new hazard. The process of adopting or revising permanent standards is laborious. In general terms, OSHA must develop substantial documentation to support proposed

---

[5]Randal C. Archibold. "Investigators Say Train Engineer Sent Text Messages Seconds Before Crash." *New York Times* (October 2, 2008), A-16.

[6]*Davis-Shook Joint Venture XXV v. Secretary of Labor*, 319 F.3d 805, 812-13 (6th Cir. 2003).

[7]*Secretary of Labor v. Buford's Tree Inc.*, OSHRC Case No. 07-1899 (2010).

rules, make several announcements of its intention to promulgate a new standard, seek public comments in writing, and hold hearings. New standards are initially published in the *Federal Register* and subsequently included with other OSHA standards in the *Code of Federal Regulations* (CFR). The adoption of a new standard typically precipitates a race to the courthouse in which one or more parties associated with industry or labor challenges the standard's legality. Courts sometimes stay (put off) the implementation of a standard until legal challenges are concluded. Sometimes Congress gets into the act. In short, the process of adopting new safety standards is lengthy, arduous, litigious, and politicized. OSHA officials do not create new standards on a whim. In fact, the number of new permanent standards that OSHA has managed to implement since its inception is quite small. Standards are nonexistent or outdated for many significant hazards.

Beyond the procedural and political hurdles, courts have placed certain constraints on OSHA's standard setting. The OSH Act says the following about standards:

> *The term "occupational safety and health standard" means a standard which requires conditions, or the adoption or use of one or more practices, means, methods, operations or processes, reasonably necessary or appropriate to provide safe or healthful employment and places of employment.*[8]

> *[I]n promulgating standards dealing with toxic materials or harmful agents ... [OSHA] shall set the standard which most adequately assures, to the extent feasible, on the basis of the best available evidence, that no employee will suffer material impairment of health or functional capacity even if such employee has regular exposure to the hazard ... for the period of his working life.*[9]

When OSHA reduced the **permissible exposure limit (PEL)** (the maximum allowable level of exposure to a hazard) for benzene, the Supreme Court was called on to determine whether OSHA had exceeded its authority. The Court interpreted the statutory language just quoted here (particularly "reasonably necessary or appropriate") to mean that OSHA bears the burden of demonstrating that any new or revised standard addresses a **significant risk** to the health of employees[10]. The agency is justified in establishing a new standard only if this significant risk can be shown. The revised standard for benzene was struck down because the agency had not done sufficient risk assessment to establish that workers were endangered by keeping the PEL at the existing higher level. (OSHA succeeded in lowering the PEL for benzene several years later.) An attempt by OSHA to package a large number of standards covering related hazards into a single generic ("air contaminants") standard, without showing that each of the individual hazards posed significant risk, was also rejected[11] However, courts have permitted OSHA to require the medical monitoring of employees as a means of ensuring that they are not being harmed, even where there is no current evidence of significant risk.[12]

The development of a new OSHA standard limiting worker exposure to hexavalent chromium—a toxic substance known to cause lung cancer and other health problems— illustrates the protracted and contentious nature of the standard-setting process. A PEL was initially set in 1971 following enactment of the OSH Act, based on industry standards dating back to the 1940s. It became increasingly clear that these limits were not

---

[8]29 U.S.C.S. § 652(8) (2011).

[9]29 U.S.C.S. § 655(b)(5) (2011).

[10]*Industrial Union Department v. American Petroleum Institute*, 448 U.S. 607 (1980).

[11]*AFL-CIO v. OSHA*, 965 F.2d 962 (11th Cir. 1992).

[12]*National Cottonseed Products Ass'n v. Brock*, 825 F.2d 482 (D.C. Cir. 1987), *cert. denied*, 485 U.S. 1020 (1988).

sufficiently protective of workers' health. In 1998, a court denied a petition from a labor union seeking to force OSHA to adopt a more protective standard. However, when OSHA continued to drag its feet, a court found in 2002 that the agency had unreasonably delayed its rulemaking and ordered it to expeditiously proceed with establishing a new PEL.[13] Under a revised standard proposed by OSHA in 2004, the PEL for hexavalent chromium was to be reduced from the decades-old limit of 52 micrograms per cubic meter to a limit of 1 microgram per cubic meter. However, following the required comment period and further delay, OSHA issued a final rule in 2006 that set the PEL at 5 micrograms per cubic meter.[14] A public interest group then sued OSHA on the grounds that it had adopted an insufficiently protective standard without good reason. An appeals court upheld the final PEL, even though OSHA conceded that workers would still be exposed to a significant risk.[15] The court accepted OSHA's conclusion that it was not technologically feasible to achieve the 1 microgram exposure limit in some industries (e.g., welding, electroplating, aerospace painting) and that it was preferable to have a single PEL rather than identify different feasible exposure limits for specific operations and industries. However, the court remanded for further consideration whether the standard's requirement for notification to workers of high levels of exposure was sufficient. To put all of this in perspective, it required decades of scientific studies and litigation to produce a somewhat more protective standard (but one that still allows workers to be exposed to hexavalent chromium at levels that pose a significant risk to their health) for just one of the many thousands of toxic and carcinogenic substances used in workplaces.

OSHA must conduct extensive risk assessments to justify proposed standards. Is it also required to conduct cost-benefit analyses? In a **cost-benefit analysis**, the costs to employers of complying with a standard are compared to the economic value of the expected improvement in worker health (e.g., fewer cases of cancer, fewer deaths). Standards are adopted only if the projected costs do not exceed the projected benefits. In a case involving the standard for cotton dust, which causes brown lung disease, the Supreme Court rejected the industry's arguments that OSHA is required to conduct a formal cost-benefit analysis before promulgating standards.[16] Because OSHA is authorized to set standards that eliminate health hazards "to the extent feasible," the focus must be on whether improved safety is achievable, not whether it is economically optimal. Feasibility includes economic considerations, and, in fact, Congress requires OSHA to consider and estimate the cost implications of its proposed regulations (e.g., their potential impact on small businesses). But OSHA is not required to perform a cost-benefit analysis, nor is the agency limited to adopting only those standards whose monetary benefits are demonstrably greater than their costs. A more recent Supreme Court decision concluding that the Environmental Protection Agency (EPA) is not required to perform cost-benefit analysis in adopting environmental regulations suggests that the same continues to be true for OSHA.[17]

General Duty Clause   It is impossible for OSHA to develop standards addressing all hazards to which employees might be exposed. The OSH Act's **general duty clause**

---

[13]*Public Citizen Health Research Group v. Chao*, 314 F.3d 143 (3d Cir. 2002).

[14]71 Fed. Reg. 10,100 (February 28, 2006).

[15]*Public Citizen Health Research Group v. OSHA*, 557 F.3d 165 (3d Cir. 2009).

[16]*American Textile Manufacturers Institute v. Donovan*, 452 U.S. 490, 509 (1981).

[17]*Whitman v. American Trucking Ass'ns*, 531 U.S. 457 (2001).

places basic responsibility for workplace safety with employers and can be invoked for enforcement purposes in the absence of specific standards:

> *Each employer … shall furnish to each of his employees employment and a place of employment which are free from recognized hazards that are causing or are likely to cause death or serious physical harm to his employees.*[18]

Hazards are "recognized" when there is reason to believe that they are known to the employer or to the industry in which the employer operates. Recognition refers in this context to awareness that a condition is hazardous to employees, in contrast to the "knowledge" element in standards violation cases, where it is simply awareness of the condition that is the issue. Even though the general duty clause provides OSHA with an important weapon for contesting unsafe conditions—one that does not rely on the glacial standard-setting process—it can be difficult for the agency to prove that hazards that have not been the subjects of safety standards are nonetheless recognized and that there are feasible means of abating those hazards.

ELEMENTS OF A CLAIM

Violation of the General Duty Clause

To prove a violation of the general duty clause, OSHA must show all the following:

1. A workplace hazard was allowed to exist.
2. The hazard was or should have been recognized by the employer.
3. The hazard caused or was likely to cause death or serious physical injury.
4. Feasible means exist to abate the hazard and were not used.

© Cengage Learning 2013.

JUST THE FACTS

Outside of a Wal-Mart store in Valley Stream, New York, some 2,000 eager shoppers had been gathering for hours in the cold and dark as they awaited the store's 5 AM opening for its post–Thanksgiving Day sale (a.k.a. "Blitz Day"). The crowd became increasingly unruly and Wal-Mart even called the police. But the police left without taking action and shortly before the scheduled opening time, the crowd burst through the door and into the store. A temporary worker who had been sent to the vestibule of the store to ready it for opening was trampled by the surging crowd and eventually died of asphyxiation. Although this was the first fatality, similar incidents have occurred on previous "Blitz Days," including doors knocked off hinges and shattered glass. Employees are instructed to go to the front of the store to deal with the crowd, "be safe," and help any customers who are knocked over in the melee. OSHA investigated and cited the retailer for violating the general duty clause by exposing its workers to the hazards of asphyxiation or being struck by the rushing crowd. The citation, which includes a proposed $7,000 penalty, is being appealed by Wal-Mart. On appeal, what should the OSHRC decide?

See *Secretary of Labor v. Wal-Mart Stores*, OSHRC, No. 09-1013 (March 25, 2011), *directed for review* (April 6, 2011).

---

[18]29 U.S.C.S. § 654(a)(1) (2011).

THE CHANGING WORKPLACE

Ergonomic Hazards

Ergonomics deals with the fit between the physical demands of jobs and the physical abilities of people. Work tasks, equipment, and surroundings can pose hazards to employees when they entail such things as frequent use of force, lifting of heavy loads, repetitive motions, awkward postures, excessive standing in one place, vibration, and exposure to cold temperatures These ergonomic risk factors can result in a variety of **musculoskeletal disorders (MSDs)** (also referred to as repetitive stress injuries or cumulative trauma disorders). Particular types of MSDs include carpal tunnel syndrome, rotator cuff syndrome, low back pain, sciatica, and tendonitis. These conditions range in severity but can be painful and debilitating. The number of reported MSDs suffered by workers increased enormously between the mid-1980s and 1996. The number of reported cases has dropped off considerably since then but MSDs still constitute the lion's share of recorded occupational illnesses (in contrast to injuries) and account for a significant proportion of workers' compensation claims. In 2009, MSDs accounted for 29.4 percent of all injuries and illnesses resulting in lost work time.[1] Injuries stemming from repetitive motion are associated with a high number of days away from work (the median is 21 days). Laborers, freight workers, nurses' aides, and truck drivers are among the occupations that see the largest numbers of MSDs. Not all MSDs are caused by work activities, but substantial evidence exists that many MSDs are work-related and that ergonomic interventions in workplaces can reduce the incidence of MSDs.[2]

OSHA's efforts to develop an ergonomics standard are another classic illustration of the highly contentious and politicized standard-setting process. The agency started out in the mid-1980s by offering ergonomics training to employers. It issued voluntary guidelines for the meatpacking industry in 1990. In 1992, OSHA announced that it intended to develop an ergonomics standard (it issued an "advance notice of proposed rule making"). A draft standard was released in 1995, and as former OSHA head Charles Jeffress put it, "all hell broke loose."[3] OSHA made revisions and held numerous public hearings, but industry prevailed on its allies in Congress to attach riders to OSHA's budget appro-

priations, prohibiting it from adopting an ergonomics standard. OSHA eventually issued an ergonomics standard in November 2000, requiring the establishment of ergonomics programs covering employees in manufacturing and manual handling jobs and other jobs when an MSD was reported by a job occupant. Congress responded in early 2001 by invoking the never-before-used Congressional Review Act of 1996 to repeal the ergonomics standard.[4] The end result is that there is currently no specific OSHA standard addressing this major workplace safety and health hazard. However, OSHA has issued voluntary guidelines for preventing MSDs in nursing homes, retail grocery stores, poultry processors, and shipyards.[5] OSHA has also proposed that employers explicitly record whether injuries are ergonomic in nature on their required injury and illness logs.[6]

In the absence of an ergonomic standard, OSHA must rely on the general duty clause to address ergonomic hazards. However, despite the prevalence of MSDs, OSHA has issued only a handful of citations for ergonomic violations in recent years.[7] In one ergonomics case, OSHA argued that the lifting and moving of patients was a workplace hazard that resulted in high rates of lower-back injuries among the employees of a nursing home chain.[8] The Occupational Safety and Health Review Commission (OSHRC) agreed that this was a "recognized" hazard. Even though the chain's work practices were similar to those found throughout the industry, it had unusually high injury rates relative to the already high rates in the industry, a large body of scientific evidence existed pointing to the lifting of patients as a hazard, management was aware of and clearly concerned about the large number of workers' compensation claims that stemmed from such injuries, and the chain had adopted measures intended to lessen the problem. The OSHRC also ruled that the ergonomic injuries suffered by these employees, injuries that were often long-lived and debilitating, constituted the type of "serious physical harm" needed to invoke the general duty clause. However, the case was remanded to determine whether feasible means of abating the hazard existed. While the case was on remand, the parties settled. The nursing home chain agreed to provide more training to employees and to purchase more mechanical lifting devices, but it did not admit to a violation of the OSH Act.[9] To date, OSHA has yet to successfully litigate an ergonomics case before the OSHRC.

[1]U.S. Bureau of Labor Statistics. "2009 Nonfatal Occupational Injuries and Illnesses: Private Industry, State Government, and Local Government." Charts 20 and 21 (November 9, 2010) (http://www.bls. gov/).
[2]National Research Council. *Work-Related Musculoskeletal Disorders: A Review of the Evidence.* (National Academy PressWashington, DC, 1998).

[3]Charles N.Jeffress. "Ergonomics in the Workplace." Speech at Fitchburg, Massachusetts (September 29, 1999). Archived speech viewed October 8, 2008 (http://www.osha.gov).
[4]StevenGreenhouse. "Senate Votes to Repeal Rules Clinton Set on Work Injuries." *New York Times*, March 7, 2001, A-1.
[5]U.S. Occupational Safety and Health Commission. "Ergonomics." Viewed October 8, 2008 (http://www.osha.gov/SLTC/ergonomics/Index.html).
[6]75 Fed. Reg. 4728 (January 29, 2010).
[7]GregHellman. "OSH Act General Duty Clause Used Sparingly to Cite Employers for Ergonomic Violations." *Daily Labor Report* 241 (December 16, 2010), A-5.
[8]*Secretary of Labor v. Beverly Enterprises*, 2000 OSHRC No. 38.
[9]*Beverly Enterprises*, at 3.

How Is the OSH Act Enforced?

Unlike most other employment laws, the OSH Act is enforced not only by responding to employee complaints of violations but also by OSHA going out to workplaces and conducting **inspections** to determine whether employers are complying with the law. At the same time, enforcement is not effective without the active involvement of employees or their unions bringing hazards to OSHA's attention, participating in the inspection process, and occasionally taking enforcement into their own hands.

Clippings

Michele DuFault was an undergraduate at Yale, majoring in astronomy and physics. A few weeks before she was set to graduate, Ms. DuFault was working late at night trying to finish up her senior thesis in a machine shop that was part of the chemistry lab. Her hair became caught in a lathe and she was killed. There were no witnesses to the accident and Ms. DuFault was known as someone who followed safety precautions. But lathes are powerful machines that have numerous moving parts in which hair can become caught and draw users into them. OSHA has jurisdiction because the machine shop was also used by Yale employees and it is conducting an investigation.

Lisa W. Foderaro. "Yale Student Killed as Hair Gets Caught in Lathe." *New York Times* (April 14, 2011), A18.

OSHA has proposed a fine of $75,000 against SeaWorld of Florida. This enforcement action stems from a horrifying incident in which a trainer working with a killer whale during a show was pulled underwater, thrashed about, and killed. The cause of death was drowning and traumatic injuries. SeaWorld has a history of incidents involving attacks by its killer whales. In fact, the same whale had killed a trainer in 1991. Cindy Coe, OSHA regional administrator, said that "SeaWorld recognized the inherent risk of allowing trainers to interact with potentially dangerous animals. Nonetheless, it required its employees to work within pool walls, on ledges, and on shelves where they were subject to dangerous behavior by the animals." SeaWorld announced that it planned to contest the citation.

Stephen Lee. "Proposed Fine of $75,000 Levied Against SeaWorld in Whale Trainer Death." *Daily Labor Report* 162 (August 23, 2010), A-8.

> Quality Stamping Products, a metal-stamping firm in Cleveland, has been cited by OSHA for twenty-seven violations. The proposed penalties amount to $426,100. The company has also been placed in OSHA's Severe Violator Enforcement Program, subjecting it to targeted follow-up inspections. The alleged violations include failure to report amputation injuries, properly train press operators, use needed guards on machines, conduct required inspections of machinery, institute proper lockout/tagout procedures to prevent inadvertent activation of machines, and provide hazard communication training. Additional citations were for excessive noise, improperly storing compressed gas cylinders, and exposing employees to electrical hazards.
>
> Bebe Raupe. "Metal-Stamping Firm Cited by OSHA as Severe Violator after Amputations." *Daily Labor Report* 128 (July 5, 2011), A-13.

Practical Considerations How should employers respond to OSHA inspections?

Inspections and Citations   OSHA has limited resources. In fiscal year 2010, OSHA conducted 40,993 inspections and found 96,742 violations.[19] If this sounds like a sizable number of inspections, consider that U.S. workplaces number in the millions. OSHA has to carefully prioritize when selecting sites to inspect. In order of priority, OSHA inspects workplaces where it has reason to believe there is imminent danger of death or serious physical harm to employees, where it is investigating a catastrophe or fatal accident, where it has received employee complaints of alleged violations, where the workplace was selected as part of a planned effort to conduct inspections in dangerous industries ("programmed inspections"), and where the agency wants to determine whether prior violations have been corrected (follow-up inspections).

Most OSHA inspections are unannounced. When OSHA inspectors (compliance officers) arrive at workplaces, they first locate and present their credentials to the owners or other people in charge. The OSH Act empowers OSHA inspectors to enter workplaces without delay and at reasonable times to examine records, inspect conditions, and question individuals. However, the Supreme Court has determined that the Fourth Amendment rights of employers to be free from unreasonable search and seizure permit them to refuse entry to OSHA inspectors without a search warrant.[20] This right of refusal does not apply if a clear emergency exists, the hazard in question is in plain view, or an authorized party consents to entry (even though a co-owner disagrees). Refusing entry is at best a delay tactic. OSHA can generally obtain a warrant from a court by establishing probable cause of a violation (e.g., the fatalities that occurred, credible employee complaints) or by showing that selection for a programmed inspection was based on reasonable administrative criteria (e.g., located in a dangerous industry). However, although OSHA inspections generally are not limited to examination of the particular hazards that were the objects of complaints, the scope of searches authorized by warrants might be.[21]

An inspection typically begins with an opening conference where the circumstances of the inspection are explained by the OSHA compliance officer. *An employer representative is entitled to accompany the compliance officer during a workplace inspection, but employers are prohibited from intimidating or interfering with compliance officers as they*

---

[19]U.S. Occupational Safety and Health Commission. "OSHA Enforcement: Committed to Safe and Healthy Workplaces." Viewed October 3, 2011 (http://www.osha.gov/dep/2010_enforcement_summary.html).

[20]*Marshall v. Barlow's, Inc.*, 436 U.S. 307 (1978).

[21]*In re: Inspection of Workplace (Carondelet Coke Corp.)*, 741 F.2d 172 (8th Cir. 1984).

perform their jobs. While touring workplaces, compliance officers might write down observations, take photographs, take instrument readings, and ask questions of employees. Apparent violations are pointed out. Although some violations can be corrected on the spot, this does not necessarily preclude issuance of citations for those violations. At a closing conference, the compliance officer goes over the observed violations and the OSHA appeal process.

Citations or fines are not levied by inspectors. Instead, the directors of OSHA area offices issue citations and penalties after reviewing inspection reports. **Citations** for safety violations indicate the nature of the violations, the OSHA standard(s) violated, the monetary penalties associated with the violations, and the amount of time that the employer has to correct the problems (the **abatement** period). Fines vary according to how severe the violations are and whether they are deemed willful (intentional). Although the OSH Act provides for limited criminal penalties (a maximum of $20,000 in fines and one year in jail, regardless of the number of violations), in cases where employers willfully violate standards and these violations result in employee deaths, criminal penalties are only rarely sought.[22] Stronger enforcement may require OSHA to team up with other federal agencies, particularly the EPA, that have the capability to impose more severe criminal sanctions against employers.[23] Employers that subject their employees to serious workplace hazards are often equally poor stewards of the environment.[24]

Copies of citations received must be posted in the workplace near where the violations occurred and for three working days or until the violations are corrected, whichever is longer. Employers have the right to challenge the existence of violations, penalties, and/or the length of abatement periods. *Employers have fifteen days following the receipt of a citation to contest the citation (i.e., file a written Notice of Contest with the OSHA area director who transmits the case to the OSHRC). Although all violations should be corrected promptly, employers are not legally required to correct alleged violations until their appeals have been heard and the OSHRC has issued a final order.* Besides appealing to the OSHRC (and sometimes, subsequently, the courts), employers can petition OSHA to modify abatement schedules or meet with OSHA area directors to discuss settlements. The ability to put off fixing dangerous conditions until the OSHRC appeals process is completed provides employers with considerable leverage when negotiating with OSHA over citations.

Employee Role in Enforcement   Because OSHA visits only a minuscule number of workplaces at its own initiative, employee reports of potential hazards are critical to enforcement. Not surprisingly, some employers take a dim view of such complaints. OSHA does not reveal the identities of employees who make safety complaints, but it does inform employers when inspections are prompted by complaints and provides copies of written complaints (with names deleted). In one case, a machine operator complained to coworkers and her boss about a chemical spray emitted by her machine.[25] She then filed a formal complaint with OSHA, prompting an inspection. The employer pressed the OSHA compliance officer for the identity of the complainant and expressed annoyance when it was not divulged. Three days later the complainant was fired.

---

[22]David Barstow. "U.S. Rarely Seeks Charges for Deaths in Workplace." *New York Times* (November 22, 2003), A-1.

[23]David Barstow and Lowell Bergman. "With Little Fanfare, a New Effort to Prosecute Employers that Flout Safety Laws." *New York Times* (May 2, 2005), A-17.

[24]"New Jersey Pipe Company Fined $8 Million for Environmental, Worker Safety Violations." *Daily Labor Report* 80 (April 29, 2009), A-4.

[25]*Reich v. Hoy Shoe Co.*, 32 F.3d 361 (8th Cir. 1994).

The company said that the termination was for tardiness, but it had ignored violations by other employees. The court concluded that the employee was retaliated against in violation of OSHA. It was not necessary to show that the employer had certain knowledge of the identity of the complainant to establish a causal connection between engaging in protected activity and suffering adverse employment consequences. *Employers are prohibited from retaliating against employees for making complaints about safety problems, contacting OSHA, filing complaints with OSHA, speaking with inspectors, or otherwise participating in the enforcement process.*

Employees' lives, health, and well-being are at stake in dangerous workplaces. Under the best of circumstances, there is delay between when OSHA is informed of potential hazards and when any inspections occur. Employees who refuse to work under dangerous conditions have some legal protection from termination or other punishment for their refusal to work. For one thing, walking off the job due to serious safety problems can constitute protected concerted activity under the National Labor Relations Act (NLRA). Also, a section of the NLRA specifically permits employees to stop work because of "abnormally dangerous" conditions without being in violation of contractual no-strike clauses.[26] The nonretaliation provisions of the OSH Act have been interpreted as protecting refusals to engage in very dangerous work, and the Supreme Court has concurred with this interpretation.[27] However, such refusals are protected only where the hazard poses a threat of serious injury or death, the threat is too immediate to rely on the normal enforcement process, and the employer has been informed but has not corrected the hazard. *Employers should take employee safety complaints seriously and must not punish employees for refusing to work under conditions that pose a serious and imminent threat to their health.*

An employee representative must be allowed to participate in the opening conference and to accompany the compliance officer during an inspection. The employee representative must not be chosen by the employer. As a practical matter, this right is most often exercised when employees have union representation.[28] Employees can request informal review in cases where OSHA declines to issue a citation, but only the amount of time that the employer is given to fix problems can be formally contested by employees. Employees are responsible under OSHA for following health and safety rules, although employees who fail to do so are not subject to any type of enforcement action. The reason is that employers already have available the means of obtaining employee compliance (e.g., discipline, training, supervision).

Recording and Reporting Requirements

Keeping records of occupational injuries and illnesses is important to discern patterns that might point to systemic problems and is a requirement of the OSH Act. Exempted from these recording requirements are most employers with ten or fewer employees and employers in a variety of service and retail industries. *Employers not exempted from record keeping are required to establish and communicate to their employees specific procedures for reporting workplace injuries and illnesses. Employers are required to record (within six days of their occurrence) all work-related injuries or illnesses that result in death, days away from work, restricted work, transfer to another job, loss of consciousness, or medical treatment beyond first aid—and any other "significant" injuries or illnesses diagnosed by licensed health-care professionals.* Injuries or illnesses are work-related

---

[26]29 U.S.C.S. § 143 (2011).

[27]*Whirlpool Corp. v. Marshall*, 445 U.S. 1 (1980).

[28]David Weil. "Enforcing OSHA: The Role of Labor Unions." *Industrial Relations* 30, No. 1 (1991), 28–29.

when "an event or exposure in the work environment either caused or contributed to the resulting condition or significantly aggravated a preexisting injury or illness."[29]

Because safety and health conditions can vary considerably between individual workplaces, *records must be kept for each separate establishment and not just an entire company.* Employers can use OSHA's Form 300 (Log of Work-Related Injuries and Illnesses) and Form 301 (Injury and Illness Incident Report) or maintain the same information in other comparable formats. *An annual summary of injuries and illnesses must be maintained and posted for employee inspection during the month of February (for the previous year).* (OSHA's Form 300A—Summary of Work-Related Injuries and Illnesses—can be used for this purpose.) *These records must be retained for five years and made available for OSHA inspectors.*

Records must also be maintained for documenting safety training provided and certifying that certain potentially dangerous equipment (e.g., cranes) has been examined and is in safe working order. If employees are given periodic medical tests to screen for adverse health effects or workplace conditions are monitored (e.g., air quality tests), those records must also be kept. Because occupational diseases often take a long time to develop, medical and exposure records must be retained for many years.

Although logs of injuries and illnesses are not usually sent to OSHA, *employers are required to report to OSHA (within eight hours) any fatal accident or any accident that results in the hospitalization of three or more employees. Employers are also required, if selected, to participate in the Bureau of Labor Statistics (BLS) annual survey of occupational injuries and illnesses.* This survey is a basic source of data for occupational safety and health statistics. Even firms that are otherwise exempt from the OSHA recording requirements have to participate in the BLS survey.

Violations of OSHA's recordkeeping requirements are apparently common. In one recent study, OSHA found record keeping violations in 47 percent of the inspections conducted.[30] Although difficult to detect, these violations can be costly to employers. A court upheld a penalty of $224,050 imposed against an employer for numerous willful violations in failing to record serious injuries.[31] The employer failed to record some 357 injuries (86 percent of the total) that occurred in one of its facilities during a year. The injuries included finger amputations, broken bones, eye injuries, and severe burns. In light of the seriousness of the injuries, the number of injuries not recorded, and evidence that the employer was aware of OSHA's record-keeping requirements, the company's claim that its behavior was not willful was unpersuasive. Another court ruled that penalties for willful violations of record-keeping requirements must be assessed on a per violation basis.[32] Thus, the OSHRC erred when it grouped together scores of record-keeping infractions and levied a single fine of $70,000 rather than fines of at least $5,000 for each violation.

Clippings

An independent team of investigators appointed by the governor of West Virginia to investigate the cause of a mine explosion that resulted in the deaths of twenty-nine miners in April 2010 concluded that "Ultimately, the responsibility for the

[29] 29 C.F.R. § 1904.5(a) (2011).

[30] Stephen Lee. "OSHA Says Recordkeeping Program Revealed 47 Percent Violation Rate." *Daily Labor Report* 176 (September 13, 2010), A-2.

[31] *Kaspar Wire Works, Inc. v. Secretary of Labor,* 268 F.3d 1123 (D.C. Cir. 2001).

[32] *Chao v. OSHRC,* 480 F.3d 320 (5th Cir. 2007).

explosion at the Upper Big Branch Mine lies with the management of Massey Energy.... The company broke faith with its workers by frequently and knowingly violating the law and blatantly disregarding known safety practices while creating a public perception that its operations exceeded industry safety standards." The primary cause of the explosion was a severe build-up of coal dust that resulted from the company's failure to take proper steps to control dust levels and ventilate the mine. The report flatly rejected Massey's claim that an unforeseeable inundation of methane gas was the cause of the accident. The panel said that practices at the mine prior to the explosion were focused on increasing production at any cost and amounted to a "normalization of deviance." The panel also criticized the federal Mine Safety and Health Administration for failing to use its full enforcement powers against the mine's operators.

Derrick Cain. "Massey Mine Blast Called 'Man-Made'; Report Says Explosion Was Preventable." *Daily Labor Report* 97 (May 19, 2011), AA-1.

Mine Safety and Health Act

Mining has historically been a dangerous line of work. Deaths of employees in recent mine accidents remind us that it remains perilous.[33] The **Mine Safety and Health Act (MSH Act)**[34] was enacted in recognition of the particular hazards involved with mining. This law is enforced not by OSHA but by the Mine Safety and Health Administration (MSHA). The MSH Act calls for close regulation of mines, including inspecting all underground mines four times per year. However, MSHA has been criticized for failing to perform the required inspections and being lenient in assessing and collecting penalties against mine owners.[35] Congress amended the law in 2006, mandating more rapid (within fifteen minutes of discovery) reporting of accidents, provision of communication and tracking devices, increased oxygen supplies along escape routes, and enhanced penalties for violations (up to a maximum of $220,000).[36]

Preventing Occupational Injuries and Illnesses

Clippings

A presidential commission studying the explosion of the Deepwater Horizon oil rig in the Gulf of Mexico found it to be avoidable and the product of missteps by both the companies involved and federal regulators. Eleven employees died in the blast and an enormous amount of oil was released into the gulf. BP, Transocean,

---

[33]Ian Urbina and Michael Cooper. "Deaths at Mine Raising Issues about Safety." *New York Times* (April 7, 2010), A1.

[34]30 U.S.C.S. §§ 801 *et seq.* (2011).

[35]Steven Greenhouse. "Report Cites Mine-Safety Agency Failures." *New York Times* (November 18, 2007), A14.

[36]Ian Urbina. "Stiff Overhaul of Mine Safety Rules Passes Congress." *New York Times* (June 8, 2006), A18.

> Halliburton, and a number of smaller subcontractors all played roles in the mishap. The commission cautioned that "the root causes [of the explosion] are systemic and, absent significant reform in both industry practices and government policies, might well recur."
>
> John M. Broder. "Panel Points to Errors in Gulf Spill." *New York Times* (January 6, 2011), A14.

Some OSHA standards are specific about the particular actions that employers must take, but many other standards leave it to employers to devise a set of **controls** that will effectively make their particular operations safer. For example, the occupational noise exposure standard outlined earlier specifies maximum noise exposure levels and the elements of a hearing conservation program intended to identify and respond to hearing loss, but in terms of abating the noise hazard itself, it says only that "feasible administrative or engineering controls shall be utilized" when exposure is above the maximum allowed. The standard further states that "if such controls fail to reduce sound levels within the [specified] levels, personal protective equipment shall be provided and used to reduce sound levels."[37] This and other OSHA standards reflect the safety principle of a **hierarchy of controls**.[38] The hierarchy runs from measures that might eliminate a hazard entirely (e.g., using new equipment, substituting another component for a toxic substance), to engineering controls that do not eliminate hazards but automatically provide protection from them (e.g., machine guards, venting), to administrative measures that limit the extent of exposure (e.g., job rotation, additional staffing), to training and warnings that teach employees about how to protect themselves from hazards, to personal protective equipment that is worn by employees and provides the last line of defense between the hazard and the worker. Eliminating or engineering out hazards tends to be more expensive, but is also far more effective. *Employers should focus on eliminating hazards or reducing them to the maximum extent possible through use of engineering and administrative controls.* Training and personal protective equipment are clearly necessary and important, but they do not do anything to make unsafe conditions safer, and they are vulnerable to the vicissitudes of employee behavior.

Flexibility and options are desirable in many realms, but not with respect to safety rules. *Safety rules should be clear, specific, consistent with one another, and strictly enforced.* An employer had a rule prohibiting the use of gloves near moving machinery (because gloves tend to get caught in machinery and pull their wearer's hands in with them) but gave employees the option of using gloves near a particular type of moving machinery that presented the threat of cuts and abrasions to the hand. The employer was found to have violated two OSHA standards regarding hand protection and machine guarding. The court observed:

> *Rather than adopting a hand protection policy that took into account two simultaneous hazards, Riverdale adopted one policy forbidding use of gloves around moving machinery, but then allowed employees to wear gloves when using the Peck machine in order to avoid cuts. These contradictory policies forced employees to choose which hazard to protect against, thereby exposing them to one hazard or the other, unabated.*[39]

---

[37]29 C.F.R. § 1910.95(b)(1) (2011).

[38]Gerald Wagner. "The Hierarchy of Controls: An Alternative to Behavior-Based Safety." *Occupational Hazards* (May 1999), 95–97.

[39]*Riverdale Mills v. OSHRC,* 29 Fed. Appx. 11 (1st Cir. 2002).

FIGURE 15.3 Elements of Workplace Safety Programs

Demonstrate Management Commitment	Develop a safety and health policy statement
	Communicate with employees about safety and health issues
	Establish objectives for safety and health performance; measure performance
	Assign responsibility for health and safety activities and outcomes
	Provide sufficient time, authority, and resources to safety and health staff
	Reward good safety and health performance
	Enforce safety rules
	Show direct involvement of upper-level managers in safety issues
Obtain Employee Commitment	Utilize safety and health committees (structured to also comply with the NLRA)
	Work closely with union representatives on safety issues
	Involve employees in identifying and solving safety problems
	Encourage expression of safety concerns
Perform Worksite Hazard Analyses	Consult with outside experts
	Review OSHA-required records for patterns
	Carefully investigate accidents and near misses, looking for root causes
	Conduct self-inspections, job hazard analyses
	Consider health and safety ramifications of changes in equipment, work processes, and staffing
Prevent or Control Hazards	Give priority to eliminating or abating hazards
	Use engineering, work process, and administrative controls; training; personal protective equipment; medical and exposure monitoring
	Properly maintain facilities and equipment
	Engage in emergency planning and preparation
	Ensure that medical surveillance and treatment are readily available

© Cengage Learning 2013.

Practical Considerations Think about a restaurant, store, office, or factory where you have worked. What safety and health hazards existed in that workplace? What measures were used to address those hazards? Was safety given sufficient attention?

The absence of recordable injuries and illnesses does not mean that a workplace is safe. For example, near misses may occur that, but for luck, would have resulted in serious injury. *Employers should engage in proactive efforts to identify and abate unsafe conditions in their workplaces. One of the best ways to do this is to establish an effective workplace safety program.* OSHA guidelines[40] and contemporary safety practice strongly encourage the implementation of effective **workplace safety programs**. These programs help instill a safety culture in an organization, making safety a central concern that is closely monitored, discussed, rewarded, and continuously improved. It turns out that effectively managing safety requires much the same approach as ensuring efficiency, quality, and other important objectives. Figure 15.3 outlines the basic elements of a safety program.

One of the ways in which OSHA encourages the implementation of safety programs is through its Voluntary Protection Program (VPP). This program recognizes excellence in employer safety and health practices. Firms that are certified under the VPP as having effective safety and health programs are subject to less frequent inspections. OSHA also provides free consultations, particularly to small businesses; those firms will not be cited

---

[40]U.S. Occupational Safety and Health Administration. *Safety and Health Program Management Guidelines* (1989).

for any violations observed, provided that they agree to abate the hazards. However, OSHA was thwarted when it attempted to give employers with high injury rates the choice of implementing comprehensive safety and health programs or facing wall-to-wall inspections.[41] This strategy, termed the Cooperative Compliance Program, was deemed by the court to be a revision of safety standards that had to be approved through the formal standard-setting process. It was viewed as a change in standards because safety and health programs go beyond the minimum safety levels required by the OSH Act in addressing and abating all identified hazards. The idea of promoting safety and health programs in which employers proactively seek to prevent workplace injuries and illnesses is still alive, however. OSHA has announced its intention to adopt a planned prevention program rule under which employers would be required to implement their own safety and health programs. The programs would be separate from OSHA's enforcement of safety standards and the general duty clause, although employers could presumably be cited for the absence or insufficiency of their safety and health programs.[42] Whether the planned prevention program rule will be finalized and whether it will fare better than did the Cooperative Compliance Program in the face of inevitable legal challenges remain to be seen.

Workers' Compensation

The purpose of the OSH Act is to prevent injuries and illnesses by making workplaces safer, **workers' compensation** statutes deal with the consequences of those workplace injuries and illnesses that nonetheless occur. Workers' compensation is generally provided for under state laws.

Workers' compensation statutes require coverage of almost all employees, whether full-time or part-time, private or public sector. The major exclusion from coverage is for independent contractors (some states also limit coverage of farm workers and domestics). However, companies that use the employees of contractors to perform work that would normally be performed by their own employees can be deemed "statutory employers." If a contractor does not provide workers' compensation for its employees, the statutory employer can be required to provide such coverage. Thus, *firms using employees from contract companies should ensure that those contractors are providing workers' compensation for their employees.* Furthermore, *even if an employer does not pay workers' compensation premiums for its contract employees (or temps), it is still obligated under OSHA to provide a safe workplace for those workers.* These workers are at greater risk because they are often less familiar with the workplace layout and equipment and they are frequently enlisted to perform dirty and dangerous tasks.[43]

In almost all states, workers' compensation coverage is mandatory. By law, *employers must arrange workers' compensation coverage for their employees.* They do so by contributing to state workers' compensation funds, purchasing coverage from private insurers, or (for larger employers) self-insuring. The available funding options vary by state. The amounts that must be contributed depend largely on the industry in which the employer operates and, to a lesser extent, on experience rating. Under **experience rating**, employers that have worse records of injuries and claims pay more, providing a financial incentive to invest in safety. However, rates only partially reflect claims experience and—with

---

[41]*Chamber of Commerce v. Department of Labor*, 174 F.3d 206 (D.C. Cir. 1999).

[42]Stephen Lee. "Michaels Urges Early Implementation; Howard Says NIOSH Will Push Safety Studies." *Daily Labor Report* 114 (June 14, 2011), C-1.

[43]Greg LaBar. "Contingent Worker Safety: A Full-Time Job in a Part-Time World." *Occupational Hazards* (October 1997), 92–99.

the exception of self-insurance, where the employer bears all the costs of claims—incentives to invest in safety are probably less than optimal.

What do employees who are hurt on the job get through workers' compensation? Benefit levels are fixed by law. The benefits include replacement income (if an employee is unable to work), payment of all medical costs associated with the injury or illness, and rehabilitation services. Workers' compensation statutes provide only partial income replacement, on the theory that this will give employees greater incentive to return to work. Typical payment levels are replacement of two-thirds of normal pay, up to an amount that is not more than the statewide average weekly wage. Interestingly, employees who work more than one job (i.e., "moonlight") may be entitled to replacement pay based on their combined income from those multiple jobs, rather than only on the income derived from the job being worked at the time of the injury.[44] Payments depend on whether the individual is judged to be temporarily or permanently disabled and whether the disability is full or partial. Survivors can receive payments for employee deaths. Coverage of medical costs under workers' compensation is separate from any health insurance benefits that an employee receives through an employer.

Exclusive Remedy

Workers' compensation is provided, for the most part, on a no-fault basis. Employees receive benefits without having to demonstrate in court that their employers were negligent in allowing them to get hurt. Employees need not fend off employer claims that they contributed to the harm they suffered by being careless, that a coworker caused the injury rather than the employer, or that they knowingly "assumed risk" by accepting their jobs. These traditional common law defenses to negligence claims—**contributory negligence**, the **fellow servant rule**, and **assumption of risk**, respectively—do not apply under workers' compensation. However, the right to receive workers' compensation without proving employer negligence comes at a price. Workers' compensation is the **exclusive remedy** for injuries and illnesses that arise out of and in the course of employment. Employees who are hurt on the job generally cannot sue their employers. Instead, they are limited to filing workers' compensation claims and accepting the meaningful, but comparatively limited, remedies.

An important exception to the general rule that workers' compensation is the exclusive remedy for workplace injuries is that the rule does not hold when an injury is intentional rather than accidental. For example, when an employee's fingers were crushed and partially amputated after his work glove became caught by the unguarded nip point of a machine with rollers, the injury was found to be intentional and the employee was not limited to the remedy of workers' compensation benefits.[45] Key facts in the case included that there had been a number of "near misses" reported to management in the past and company officials had removed the safety guard from the machine for "speed and convenience," putting it back in place only for OSHA inspections. The court emphasized that a "subjective desire to injure" was not required to show that the injury was intentional; instead, it was enough that the employer had "substantial certainty" that injury would occur and that the employer's actions were clearly contrary to industry norms and practices.[46] Similarly, a mill worker who suffered severe injuries to his arm and hand was not limited to workers' compensation because the machine he was working on had been

---

[44]*State ex rel. FedEx Ground Package Systems v. Industrial Commission,* 126 Ohio St. 3d 37 (2010).

[45]*Laidlow v. Hariton Machinery,* 790 A.2d 884 (N.J. 2002).

[46]*Laidlow* at 897-88.

modified in a way that made it more dangerous, the mill's cutters were unguarded, the employee was not trained to avoid using gloves near the machine, the employee was known to be prone to stumbling due to a prior injury, and the company had been cited previously for operating a mill with an unguarded cutter.[47] It did not matter that the company had operated this way for years without any injuries.

In general, though, courts are sparing in recognizing this exception to the exclusivity of workers' compensation. The fact that an employee is hurt by exposure to a known hazard that violates the OSH Act does not, by itself, render the injury intentional.[48] In one relevant case, a 17-year-old was killed when he went through a pallet shredder. The North Carolina Occupational Safety and Health Administration conducted a post-accident investigation and cited the company for eleven violations, including operating a machine whose safety guards had been removed, assigning work on heavy machinery to an underage employee, and failing to train and properly supervise that employee. Despite these facts, the court rejected the family's wrongful death suit because workers' compensation was the exclusive remedy for the employee's death. North Carolina courts recognize exceptions to the exclusivity of workers' compensation "only in the most egregious cases of employer misconduct … where there is uncontroverted evidence of the employer's intentional misconduct and where such misconduct is substantially certain to lead to the employee's serious injury or death."[49] In the view of the court, this case fell considerably short of that threshold. Likewise, in a case involving the death of an employee in a collapsed trench, the Kentucky Supreme Court stated:

> [S]ince the trench was over five feet deep Environmental failed to comply with Kentucky OSHA regulations regarding safety precautions for trench work by not sufficiently sloping the trench, shoring the trench walls, or installing a trench box. Environmental failed to provide the proper means of escape from the trench and failed to report [the employee's] death to Kentucky OSHA officials within the required eight hours. Environmental also failed to have a competent person perform daily inspections of the site. Environmental knew that injury or death could result from a failure to take the proper precautions. Nevertheless, Environmental's violation of OSHA regulations and acknowledgement of the possible consequences does not amount to a deliberate intention to produce [the employee's] death.[50]

Another exception to the exclusivity of workers' compensation as a remedy is that third parties (e.g., equipment manufacturers, suppliers of components) can sometimes be sued for workplace injuries and illnesses, even when employers cannot be. Employees who suffered severe lung disease after being exposed on the job to airborne butter flavoring (diacetyl) were limited to workers' compensation claims against their employer, but are pursuing lawsuits against companies that make the flavoring.[51] The plethora of suits brought by plaintiffs, including employees, against asbestos manufacturers for their failure to warn users of the dangers associated with their product is the leading example of this exception to the exclusivity of workers' compensation.

---

[47]*Hina v. Anchor Glass Container Corp.*, 2009 U.S. Dist. LEXIS 59391 (S.D. Ohio).

[48]*Loveria v. Portadam*, 2010 U.S. Dist. LEXIS 51250 (N.D.N.Y.).

[49]*Valenzuela v. Pallet Express*, 700 S.E.2d 76, 79 (2010).

[50]*Moore v. Environmental Construction Corp.*, 147 S.W. 3d 13 (Ky. 2004).

[51]Christopher Brown. "Jury Awards Popcorn Worker $15 Million for Lung Disease Related to Work at Plant." *Daily Labor Report* 70 (April 13, 2005), A-7.

JUST THE FACTS

An employee worked as a stock clerk at a grocery store. His duties sometimes required use of a motorized pallet jack. The employee received no formal training on how to operate a pallet jack. On several occasions, the store manager asked the employee if he had ever used a pallet jack and each time he said that he had not. Eventually, the employee figured out how to operate the pallet jacks on his own. The employee used the store's two pallet jacks for roughly four months before getting injured. During this time, he had problems with one of the jacks and repeatedly complained to the store manager that the machine would sometimes accelerate on its own and take off at top speed. The head night supervisor at the store noticed that both of the store's pallet jacks were malfunctioning, although the supervisor did not have problems with sudden acceleration and he never complained to his superiors. There was also an earlier incident in which a pallet jack pinned an employee against the wall and hurt her hand. One day, the employee was operating a pallet jack that suddenly accelerated toward him. He tried to stop it, but the braking mechanism failed and the jack, which weighed over 2,000 pounds, rolled over on his right foot, fracturing it in numerous places. Can this employee sue his employer for negligence or is workers' compensation his exclusive remedy?

See, *Skaggs v. Kroger*, 2011 U.S. Dist. LEXIS 43587 (S.D.W. Va.).

Arising Out of and in the Course of Employment

Workers' compensation is intended to deal with work-related injuries and illnesses—specifically, those that "arise out of and in the course of employment." The requirement that the injury or illness occur **in the course of employment** refers to the time, place, and setting in which it occurs. **Arising out of employment** refers to the underlying causation of the injury or illness. These phrases are deceptively simple. They have been the object of much litigation. For example, is a telecommuting employee who is assaulted by a neighbor in her home during the course of her workday entitled to workers' compensation? *Wait v. Travelers Indemnity Co.* considers this question.

Wait v. Travelers Indemnity Co.
240 S.W.3d 220 (Tenn. 2007)

OPINION BY JUDGE BARKER:

This workers' compensation action presents an issue of first impression in Tennessee. The plaintiff sought workers' compensation benefits after a third party assaulted her while she was preparing lunch in her home where she had an employer-approved office. The chancery court ... h[eld] that the plaintiff's injuries did not arise out of or occur in the course of the plaintiff's employment. On appeal, the plaintiff argues that: 1) the injuries arose out of her employment

because her work arrangement placed her in a position that facilitated the assault, and 2) the injuries occurred in the course of her employment because she was engaged in a permissible incidental activity. We * * * affirm the chancery court's holding that the plaintiff's injuries did not arise out of her employment.

... Kristina Wait, worked as Senior Director of Health Initiative and Strategic Planning for the American Cancer Society ("ACS"). Because of the lack of office space at its Nashville, Tennessee facilities, the

ACS allowed the plaintiff to work from her East Nashville home. The plaintiff converted a spare bedroom of her home into an office, and the ACS furnished the necessary office equipment, including a printer, a facsimile machine, a dedicated business telephone line, and a budget to purchase office supplies. In all respects, the plaintiff's home office functioned as her work place. Not only did the plaintiff perform her daily work for the ACS at her home office, the plaintiff's supervisor and co-workers attended meetings at the office in her house. There is no evidence in the record with respect to any designated hours or conditions of the plaintiff's employment, nature of her work space, or other work rules. Significantly, the plaintiff's work for the ACS did not require her to open her house to the public. In fact, during working hours the plaintiff locked the outside doors of her home and activated an alarm system for her protection. Unfortunately, however, on September 3, 2004, the plaintiff opened her door to a neighbor, Nathaniel Sawyers ("Sawyers"), who brutally assaulted and severely injured the plaintiff.

The plaintiff met Sawyers in May or early June of 2004 at a neighborhood cookout she attended with her husband. Thereafter, Sawyers, who lived approximately one block from the plaintiff's home, came to the plaintiff's home for a short social visit on a *weekend* day in late June. The plaintiff and her husband spoke with Sawyers for approximately five minutes, and then Sawyers left. In August, Sawyers came to the plaintiff's home on a weekday for a social visit; however, the plaintiff was preparing to leave her home office for a job-related television interview. The plaintiff told Sawyers that she was going to a business meeting. When Sawyers replied that he was on his way to a job interview in Nashville, the plaintiff allowed Sawyers to ride with her to his job interview.

On September 3, 2004, the plaintiff was working alone at her home office. Around noon, the plaintiff was in her kitchen preparing her lunch when Sawyers knocked on her door. The plaintiff answered and invited Sawyers into the house, and he stayed for a short time and then left. However, a moment later, Sawyers returned, telling the plaintiff that he had left his keys in her kitchen. When the plaintiff turned away from the door, Sawyers followed her inside and brutally assaulted the plaintiff without provocation or explanation, beating the plaintiff until she lost consciousness. As a result of this assault, the plaintiff suffered severe injuries, including head trauma, a severed ear, several broken bones, stab wounds, strangulation injuries, and permanent nerve damage to the left side of her body. * * *

This case requires us to apply the [Workers' Compensation] Act to a new and growing trend in the labor and employment market: telecommuting. An employee telecommutes when he or she takes advantage of electronic mail, internet, facsimile machines and other technological advancements to work from home or a place other than the traditional work site. In 2006, approximately thirty-four million American workers telecommuted to some degree. * * * [T]his innovative working arrangement has resulted in an issue of first impression: whether the injuries a telecommuter sustains as a result of an assault at her home arise out of and occur in the course of her employment.

It is well settled in Tennessee, and in many other jurisdictions, that for an injury to be compensable under the Act, it must both "arise out of" and "occur" in the course of employment." Although both of these statutory requirements seek to ensure a connection between the employment and the injuries for which benefits are being sought, they are not synonymous. * * * In this case, we will consider the second requirement first. An injury occurs in the course of employment "when it takes place within the period of the employment, at a place where the employee reasonably may be, and while the employee is fulfilling work duties or engaged in doing something incidental thereto."

Generally, injuries sustained during personal breaks are compensable.... [W]e affirmed an award of workers' compensation benefits for an employee who slipped and fell in his employer's parking lot while he was putting his lunch box into his vehicle after finishing his meal. We noted that "[t]he remedial policies of the Worker's Compensation Act would be undermined if too severe a line were drawn controlling the compensability of injuries that occur during the normal course of the work day after employees have arrived for work, have started working, and before they have left for the day." ... [T]he defendant here argues that the plaintiffs injuries are not compensable because the plaintiff was not "fulfilling a work duty" in admitting Sawyers into her kitchen. * * *

[A]fter careful review, we conclude that the injuries the plaintiff sustained while on her lunch break ... occurred during the course of the plaintiff's employment. The plaintiff was assaulted at a place where her employer could reasonably expect her to be. The ACS permitted the plaintiff to work from home for approximately four years. The plaintiff's supervisor and co-workers regularly came to her home office for meetings. The record does not suggest that the ACS restricted the plaintiff's activities during working hours or prohibited her from taking personal breaks. The facts do not show that the plaintiff was engaging in any prohibited conduct or was violating any company policy by preparing lunch in her kitchen. It is reasonable to conclude that the ACS would have anticipated that the plaintiff would take a lunch break at her home just as employees do at traditional work sites. Importantly, Sawyer's initial visit was very brief and spontaneous. Unless instructed otherwise by the employer, an employee working from a home office who answers a knock at her door and briefly admits an acquaintance into her home does not necessarily depart so far from her work duties so as to remove her from the course of her employment. This is not to say, however, that situations may never arise where more prolonged or planned social visits might well remove the employee from the course of the employment…. [T]he defendant maintains that the plaintiff's decision to admit Sawyers into her home was not a work duty …, [but] this argument misses the mark … because the Act does not explicitly state that the employee's actions must benefit the employer; it only requires that the injuries occur in "the course of the employment." * * * The question is not whether the plaintiff's injuries occurred while she was performing a duty owed to the ACS, but rather whether the time, place, and circumstances demonstrate that the injuries occurred while the plaintiff was engaged in an activity incidental to her employment. Accordingly, we hold that the plaintiff suffered her injuries during the course of her employment and disagree with the chancery court's conclusion on this important point.

Even though the plaintiff's injuries occurred "in the course of her employment," we nevertheless hold that they did not "arise out of" her job duties with the ACS. The phrase "arising out of" requires that a causal connection exist between the employment conditions and the resulting injury. With respect to whether an assault arises out of employment, we have previously delineated assaults into three general classifications: (1) assaults with an "inherent connection" to employment such as disputes over performance, pay or termination; (2) assaults stemming from "inherently private" disputes imported into the employment setting from the claimant's domestic or private life and not exacerbated by the employment; and (3) assaults resulting

from a "neutral force" such as random assaults on employees by individuals outside the employment relationship.

When an assault has an "inherent connection" to the employment it is compensable. On the other hand, assaults originating from "inherently private" disputes and imported into the work place are not compensable. However, whether "neutral assaults" are compensable turns on the "facts and circumstances of the employment." * * * A "neutral force" assault is one that is "neither personal to the claimant nor distinctly associated with the employment." * * * Generally, for an injury to "arise out of" employment, it must emanate from a peculiar danger or risk inherent to the nature of the employment. Thus, "an injury purely coincidental, or contemporaneous, or collateral, with the employment … will not cause the injury … to be considered as arising out of the employment." However, in limited circumstances, where the employment involves "indiscriminate exposure to the general public," the "street risk" doctrine may supply the required causal connection between the employment and the injury.

… [T]he "street risk" doctrine provides that "if the employment exposes the employee to the hazards of the street that it is a risk or danger incident to and inherent in the employment and provides the necessary causal connection between the employment and the injury." In … [one such] case, unknown assailants assaulted the claimant as he entered the cab of his employer's tractor trailer after purchasing lunch at a fast food restaurant. The assailants did not steal the claimant's money or anything from the vehicle, and their motives were never discovered. In holding that the "street risk" doctrine supplied the causal connection, we emphasized that the claimant wore a uniform identifying him with his employer, the nature of the claimant's employment exposed him to the general public, and the claimant was charged with safeguarding his employer's property while on duty, even on his lunch break.

In more recent cases, this Court has applied the "street risk" doctrine in situations that do not actually involve streets and highways. For example, … we applied the "street risk" doctrine to supply the causal connection where an employee was raped by a customer on her employer's premises while she was performing her work duties as a convenience store clerk. In that case, we rejected the employer's argument that "an employee so injured must show an employment-related motive on the part of the assailant and that a rape, standing alone, suggests a personal motive." Rather, we held that an assailant's motive is but one factor to consider in deciding whether an assault arises out of the employment. * * * [We] stated that the street risk doctrine applies where an employee's "indiscriminate exposure to the general public is one of the conditions under which her work [is] required to be performed, and the actions of those persons on the premises are reasonably considered hazards of the employment." * * * Likewise, this Court [has] held that the "street risk" doctrine satisfied the causal connection requirement where the employee was assaulted by unknown assailants as he removed paperwork from his employer's van while it was parked at his residence. We carefully limited application of the street risk doctrine to "workers whose employment exposes them to the hazards of the street, or who are assaulted under circumstances that fairly suggest they were singled out for attack because of their association with their employer...."

Unlike our previous cases in which the facts supported application of the "street risk" doctrine to provide the necessary causal connection, the facts here do not establish that the plaintiff's employment exposed her to a street hazard or that she was singled out for her association with her employer. There is nothing to indicate that she was targeted because of her association with her employer or that she was charged with safeguarding her employer's property. Additionally, the plaintiff was not advancing the interests of the ACS when she allowed Sawyers into her kitchen, and her employment with the ACS did not impose any duty upon the plaintiff to admit Sawyers to her home.

The plaintiff argues that had it not been for her employment arrangement, she would not have been at home to suffer these attacks. However, we have never held that any and every assault which occurs at the work site arises out of employment. Additionally, although Sawyers knew from a previous visit that the plaintiff was home during the day, there is nothing in the record which indicates that there was a causal connection between the plaintiff's employment and the assault. Unlike our prior decisions, the facts do not show that Sawyers attacked the plaintiff because she was identifiable as an ACS employee, or because she was performing a job duty, or because she was safeguarding the ACS's property. The "street risk" doctrine is not a limitless means of allowing recovery for every situation. As such, this case presents us with an opportunity to outline the boundaries of the doctrine. When an employee suffers a "neutral assault" within the confines of her employer's premises—whether the premises be a home office or a corporate office—the "street risk" doctrine will not provide the required causal connection between the injury and the employment unless the proof fairly suggests either that the attacker singled out the employee because of his or her association with the employer or that the employment indiscriminately exposed the employee to dangers from the public. The facts of this case clearly illustrate that the "street risk" doctrine does not apply. There is nothing in the record to fairly suggest or provide any weight to the assertion that the plaintiff's injuries were causally connected with the nature of her employment. Therefore, the chancery court's holding that the plaintiff's injuries did not arise out of her employment is affirmed.

CASE QUESTIONS

1. What was the legal issue in this case? What did the court decide?
2. How could her injury have occurred "in the course of employment" if she was hurt while taking a lunch break and not performing any job duties?
3. Why was her injury deemed not to "arise out of employment"? Would she have been hurt if she had not been a telecommuter?
4. How, if at all, should the law provide for the safety and health of telecommuters? Should the lesser degree of control that employers have over the workplaces of telecommuters be taken into account?

Many circumstances raise questions about whether injuries or illnesses arose out of and in the course of employment. For example, are employees who are injured or killed while commuting to work entitled to workers' compensation? Such injuries are typically not compensable, but if employees are commuting in company-provided transportation, performing duties en route to work (e.g., picking up materials at a supplier), or being exposed to special hazards stemming from the location of the workplace (e.g., a dangerous left turn across traffic without a light), their injuries would likely be compensable. Similarly, injuries that occur while entering or leaving the workplace or in company-owned parking lots are usually compensable. However, when a teenage employee who became ill at work was mugged while walking home at 3 AM, the court concluded that his injuries were not compensable because he was not exposed to any special hazard to which the general public was not equally subject in walking home at that time of day.[52]

Travel by employees, outside of commuting to and from work, also raises questions about coverage. In a case with an extraordinary set of facts, an accountant accepted a two-year assignment in the Philippines and moved to Manila. Four days after his arrival in the country and on an off day from work, the employee was abducted after leaving a restaurant and heading back to his hotel. The employee was held by his captors for three weeks, chained to the floor, threatened, and tortured. Despite telling the employee's wife that the company would pay the ransom demand, the employer stalled in doing so out of concern that this would create an incentive to kidnap other employees. Angry that the promised ransom had not been paid, the kidnappers cut off part of the employee's ear and sent a videotape of the event to the employer. The ransom was paid the next day, and the employee was released. In response to the numerous legal claims brought by the employee and his wife, the company asserted that workers' compensation was the exclusive remedy for the employee's injuries. The court recognized that a "traveling employee" exception, extending workers' compensation coverage to certain employees who are injured in the course of job-related travel, exists under Washington D.C.'s (the relevant jurisdiction) workers' compensation statute. However, the court refused to apply the traveling employee exception to all injuries that might occur anytime an employee relocates outside the state or country for work. Although the accountant was in the Philippines because of this work assignment, his injuries did not arise out of or in the course of his employment. He remained free to pursue tort claims against his employer.[53]

JUST THE FACTS

A carpenter arrived at a condominium complex that was under construction. He parked his truck about a block from the building that he would be working on that day and headed toward a porta-potty that was positioned on the street outside of the building. En route to the porta-potty, he tripped over some partly buried fencing and fell on top of discarded banding straps, cutting his face and injuring his leg and back. The accident occurred about fifteen minutes prior to the scheduled start of his shift. His employer did not own either the street area on which the porta-potty sat or the porta-potty itself. Materials were stored in the street and carpenters sometimes did their work out in the street. Is this employee entitled to workers' compensation for his injuries?

See, *Mularczyk v. Daimco Contracting*, 2010 Mich. App. LEXIS 165, *leave to appeal denied*, 486 Mich. 931 (2010).

---

[52]*Slagle v. White Castle System, Inc.*, 607 N.E.2d 45 (Ohio App. 1992).

[53]*Khan v. Parsons Global Services, Ltd.*, 428 F.3d 1079 (D.C. Cir. 2005), *remanded on other grounds*, 521 F.3d 421 (2008) (finding an arbitration agreement was not enforceable).

What about when employee or coworker misconduct results in injury? In *State ex rel. Gross v. Industrial Commission of Ohio,* the court considers a case in which the injured employee failed to heed workplace safety rules and repeated verbal warnings. While sympathy for such an employee is likely to be in short supply, denying benefits clashes with the bedrock principle that workers' compensation is available on a "no-fault" basis. In the course of deciding this case, the Ohio Supreme Court rescinds its own prior decision and elicits a vigorous dissent.

State Ex Rel. Gross v. Industrial Commission of Ohio
115 Ohio St. 3d 249 (2007)

OPINION BY JUSTICE LUNDBERG STRATTON:

This matter is before us on a motion for reconsideration ... * * * For the reasons that follow, we grant Gross's motion, vacate our [prior] decision ("Gross I"), and affirm the judgment of the court of appeals, which order[ed] the Industrial Commission to reinstate Gross's temporary total disability ("TTD") benefits.

In [Gross I] ... we upheld the commission's termination of TTD compensation to Gross for injuries he sustained in the course of and arising out of his employment with KFC. Gross had injured himself and two others on November 26, 2003, when he placed water in a pressurized deep fryer, heated the fryer, and opened the lid. KFC conducted an investigation into the accident and determined that Gross had violated a workplace safety rule and repeated verbal warnings. KFC terminated his employment on February 13, 2004. As a result, the Industrial Commission terminated Gross's TTD benefits on the basis that he had voluntarily abandoned his employment.

In *Gross I,* the majority determined that KFC terminated Gross for disobeying written safety rules and ignoring repeated warnings. Therefore, the court held, the conduct for which he was fired constituted a voluntary abandonment of employment that precluded continuation of his TTD compensation. Gross contends that our opinion ... wrongfully injected fault into the workers' compensation system and expanded the voluntary-abandonment doctrine.

Workers' compensation law provides that an employee who is injured in the course of employment is entitled to receive "compensation for loss sustained on account of the injury." An employee who is temporarily and totally disabled as a result of a workplace injury may be entitled to compensation for lost earnings during the period of disability while the injury heals. Generally, TTD benefits terminate when the employee returns to work, is capable of returning to work, or has reached maximum medical improvement.

In ... [an appellate decision in an earlier case] [the court] was asked to determine whether a claimant was entitled to the continuation of his TTD benefits after he permanently retired from the work force. The appellate court applied a two-part analysis to determine whether an injury qualified for TTD compensation. The ... court first focused upon the disabling aspects of the injury that prevented the claimant from returning to his former position of employment. The court next inquired whether there was any reason other than the injury that was preventing the claimant from returning to work. * * * [The court] concluded that a claimant's voluntary retirement with no intention of returning to the work force would be reason to terminate TTD benefits because his disability would no longer be the cause of his loss of earnings. The court held that "where the employee has taken action that would preclude his returning to his former position of employment, even if he were able to do so, he is not entitled to continued temporary total disability benefits since it is his own action, rather than the industrial injury, which prevents his returning to such former position of employment."

In ... [a case involving an employee] who was in prison ... [the employee] filed a motion for TTD compensation related to an industrial injury he sustained three years earlier. The commission denied his request on the ground that his incarceration amounted to an abandonment of his former position of employment. [The employee] argued that ... his incarceration was not a permanent abandonment of the work force and it could not be regarded as voluntary. The temporary nature of his abandonment of his former employment was irrelevant, the court held. Furthermore, a person who violates the law is presumed to tacitly accept the consequences of his voluntary acts so there is a voluntary nature to incarceration. The claimant was no longer in a position to return to work while incarcerated. His loss of earnings was no longer "on account of the injury".... Therefore, the court held that he had voluntarily removed himself from the work force and was not eligible for TTD benefits.

... [W]e have continued to apply the voluntary-abandonment doctrine to situations in which the claimant has left his former position of employment *following* his injury. In [one such case], we clarified that the abandonment of employment must be voluntary, not involuntary, to act as a bar to TTD compensation. In [this case], the claimant had retired while on disability. There was some evidence, however, that his retirement was causally related to his industrial injury. Therefore, we upheld the commission's determination that the claimant's retirement was not voluntary and he continued to be eligible for TTD benefits. In [another case], we were asked to determine whether an employee's termination for violating work rules could be construed as a voluntary abandonment of employment that would bar TTD compensation. In that case, the employer was notified that the claimant was medically released to return to work following a period of TTD. When the claimant did not report to work for three consecutive days, he was automatically terminated for violation of the absentee policy in the company's employee handbook.

The claimant subsequently moved for additional TTD benefits, arguing that being fired was an involuntary departure from employment. "Although not generally consented to, discharge, like incarceration, is often a consequence of behavior that the claimant willingly undertook, and may thus take on a voluntary character."" [W]e find it difficult to characterize as 'involuntary' a termination generated by the claimant's violation of a written work rule or policy that (1) clearly defined the prohibited conduct, (2) had been previously identified by the employer as a dischargeable offense, and (3) was known or should have been known to the employee." We explained that a departure under such circumstances must be considered voluntary because "an employee must be presumed to intend the consequences of his or her voluntary acts."

* * * To be eligible for TTD compensation, "the claimant must show not only that he or she lacks the medical capability of returning to the former position

of employment but that a cause-and-effect relationship exists between the industrial injury and an actual loss of earnings. In other words, it must appear that, but for the industrial injury, the claimant would be gainfully employed." "[T]he voluntary abandonment rule is potentially implicated whenever TTD compensation is requested by a claimant who is no longer employed in the position that he or she held when the injury occurred." * * *

The parties have perceived our language in *Gross I* as an expansion of the voluntary-abandonment doctrine and a potential encroachment upon the no-fault nature of our workers' compensation laws. Because of the confusion and misunderstanding that *Gross I* has generated, it is necessary for us to address the issues raised in Gross's motion for reconsideration.

First, *Gross I* was not intended to expand the voluntary-abandonment doctrine. Until the present case, the voluntary-abandonment doctrine has been applied only in postinjury circumstances in which the claimant, by his or her own volition, severed the causal connection between the injury and loss of earnings that justified his or her TTD benefits. The doctrine has never been applied to preinjury conduct or conduct contemporaneous with the injury. *Gross I* did not intend to create such an exception.

The General Assembly, in its expression of public policy, has enacted certain exceptions to a claimant's eligibility for benefits. For instance, [the Ohio workers' compensation statute] expressly prohibits a claimant from receiving benefits while incarcerated. In addition, the statute creates a rebuttable presumption that a claimant's being intoxicated or under the influence of drugs is the proximate cause of an injury, which forfeits the employee's eligibility for benefits. However, the statute contains no exception for willful or deliberate violation of workplace rules. It is the role of the legislature, not the judiciary, to carve out exceptions to a claimant's eligibility for TTD compensation. Second, it was not our intention in *Gross I* to inject fault into the analysis of voluntary abandonment or to otherwise undermine the no-fault nature of our workers' compensation system. To the extent that our opinion in *Gross I* has been interpreted as injecting fault into the system, we expressly reject that interpretation.

The no-fault nature of our workers' compensation scheme is a statutory mandate. * * * Except as expressly set out in the statute, workers' compensation benefits may not be denied on the basis of fault to a claimant who was injured in the course and scope of employment. There is no question that Gross sustained a disabling injury. The issue is whether his injury or his termination (because of the violation of a rule) is the cause of his loss of earnings. The distinctions between voluntary and involuntary departure are complicated and fact-intensive. An underlying principle, however, is that if an employee's departure from the workplace "is causally related to his injury," it is not voluntary and should not preclude the employee's eligibility for TTD compensation. The … Court of Appeals followed that principle. The court concluded from KFC's termination letter that "relator's termination was causally related to his injury. The letter states expressly that the employer's actions arose from 'the accident' that caused relator's injury."

We agree. Although KFC appears justified in firing Gross for violating workplace rules, the termination letter established that his discharge was related to his industrial injury. Gross had violated the same rules on prior occasions without repercussion. However, according to the termination letter, it was Gross's latest violation resulting in injury that triggered KFC's investigation and subsequent termination. Therefore, upon reconsideration, we hold that Gross's termination was involuntary. * * *

DISSENT BY JUSTICE O'CONNOR:

* * * In an effort to present a more palatable decision without expressly overruling our precedent (including our evidently short-lived decision in this case), the majority goes to great lengths. It obfuscates the facts of this case and our holding in *Gross I*. It ignores the abuse-of-discretion standard. In so doing, the majority steps well beyond the bench to proclaim a new exception in the law that it suggests is not the result of judicial activism but, rather, of deference to the legislature. I disagree with that characterization, and with the majority's analysis and holding in this case. I believe that the majority's decision is fraught with peril for Ohioans in service-oriented and industrial workplaces and that it is unfair to employers who rightfully attempt to enforce safety rules for the well-being of their employees and consumers. I strongly dissent.

* * * "During his orientation, [Gross] was given an employee handbook. One of the safety rules in the handbook stated:" " [The employer] wants to have a safe place for you to work—and safety is an important part of your job. To help prevent accidents—follow these safety tips:'" * * * "'Follow all warnings and instructions about the safe operation of all equipment. *Never boil* water in a cooker to clean it.'" The commission also found that the handbook set forth "critical

violations," i.e., offenses for which employees could be terminated "right away." One such critical violation was an employee's violation of health or safety guidelines that "cause or could cause illness or injury of anyone." There is no dispute that Gross received the handbook.

In addition, there was "a warning label affixed to the top of the 690 Henny-Penny gas pressure cooker at Gross's workplace [that] reminded employees that they should 'not close the lid with water or cleaning agents in the cook pot'" but that "[d]espite this warning and the one in the employee handbook, [a supervisor] observed Gross on one occasion putting water into the cooker to clean it. [The supervisor] confronted Gross, explaining the proper cleaning procedure and stressing that adding water to the cooker could cause serious injuries." On the day of the injury, a co-worker "saw Gross again putting water into the cooker. [The co-worker] immediately told him to stop and clean it out the proper way. Moments later, a second coworker warned Gross not to open the cooker's lid, as the now boiling water was under extreme pressure. Gross ignored both men and opened the lid, severely burning himself and [them]."

In other words, Gross ignored the same important safety warning he had received at least five times in two months of employment: (1) the warning in the employee handbook, (2) the warning of the manufacturer, (3) the warning of his supervisor, and (4 and 5) the two warnings of the co-workers injured by Gross's misconduct. In light of the gravity of Gross's misconduct, our original opinion noted that an immediate termination "may not have been unwarranted." * * * Contrary to the assertions of the court of appeals and the majority here, the employer's termination letter to Gross did not "establish[] that his discharge was related to his industrial injury." Rather, in the letter terminating his employment, the employer stated that it "cannot and will not tolerate employees who pose a danger to themselves and other based upon their refusal or failure to follow instructions and recognized safety procedures." * * * The letter concluded, "Pursuant to those sections of the Handbook [requiring employees to follow safety rules], and our investigation, your employment * * * is hereby terminated." * * * Thus, the employer's focus was properly on Gross's intentional (not negligent) conduct in repeatedly violating the safety rules for the workplace, *not* on his injury.

* * * The majority's decision creates an entirely new exception in our workers' compensation law, so that an

employee who was discharged for repeatedly violating safety rules can maintain compensation for temporary total disability ("TTD") if he is injured in the process of effectuating his misconduct. That exception is without any support in the law or in public policy. * * * Workers' compensation coverage is rightfully extended to employees who act unwisely, negligently, or stupidly. We have adhered to that rule for nearly one hundred years, based on the principle that workers' compensation is a "mutual compromise between the interests of the employer and the employee," in which fault plays no part. But the bargain that gives rise to workers' compensation has never extended succor to every employee or the absolute entitlement to TTD that the majority now offers to workers who happen to be injured in the workplace.

* * * [T]he new majority insists that we should ... create an entirely new exception that inures to the benefit of Gross merely because he was injured while playing Russian roulette with safety rules, a conscious decision that had a substantial likelihood of injuring him and his co-workers. I cannot countenance such a result. * * * It is absurd to create an exception to our law so that an employee who acts in clear violation of his employer's rules remains eligible for TTD while, at the same time, we adhere to our precedent for other employees so that they are denied TTD benefits if the rules they violate or the misconduct they commit is not sufficiently

inextricable from their injuries—even if there is no dispute that the misconduct is connected to a workplace injury. Let us make no mistake as to the effect of the majority's holding: its practical effect will be to afford TTD to the most dangerous and egregious workplace violators who happen to have caused injury to themselves and others, while permitting the denial of TTD to the more mundane violators. * * *

This is not an instance of horseplay in the workplace gone awry. The denial of TTD to Gross was based on the commission's finding that he had voluntary [sic] abandoned his employment by intentional disregard of his employer's rule, not because he was at fault for the injuries that ensued or because he was injured as a result of the misconduct. I am not prepared to say that that conclusion was so arbitrary or capricious that it constituted an abuse of discretion and cannot stand.

CASE QUESTIONS

1. What was the legal issue in this case? What did the court decide?
2. What is the voluntary abandonment doctrine? Should it have been applied to this case?
3. What are practical consequences of this decision? What would the consequences have been if the original decision by the court had been upheld?
4. Was the case correctly decided? Why or why not?

In a coworker misconduct case, an employee who suffered a back injury when she went to sit down in her chair, the height of which had been lowered by a coworker as a prank, was entitled to workers' compensation.[54] In general, nonparticipating employees who are injured by the horseplay or pranks of other employees are entitled to workers' compensation.[55] Even employees who actively participate in such activity can be covered if the employer condoned the conduct. A chicken plant employee who was seriously slashed by a coworker after both had been using their five-inch knives to try to cut the apron strings of the other was still entitled to workers' compensation for the injury. Playing with deboning knives was customary in this workplace, and the employer had never done anything to stop it.[56] Misbehavior that results in injury but does not constitute a substantial departure from required tasks is likely to be compensable. In an extreme example of this point, a truck driver who was hurt when the truck he was driving was struck by a train was entitled to compensation even though there was evidence that he had also been engaged in sexual activity with a coworker at the time of the mishap.[57]

[54]*Oliva v. Heath*, 35 Cal. App. 4th 926 (1995).

[55]*Coleman v. Armour Swift-Eckrich*, 130 P.3d 111 (Kan. 2006).

[56]*Bare v. Wayne Poultry Co.*, 318 S.E.2d 534 (N.C. App. 1984), *review denied*, 325 S.E.2d 484 (N.C. 1985).

[57]*Darco Transportation v. Dulen*, 922 P.2d 591 (Okla. 1996).

However, employees who are injured while under the influence of drugs or alcohol on the job are generally viewed as having abandoned their jobs and are not entitled to workers' compensation.[58] Consequently, *employers often conduct drug and alcohol tests following accidents, and they may be required to do so by insurers.*

JUST THE FACTS

Three emergency medical services employees were returning to their office in an ambulance after having had lunch. An EMT in the rear of the vehicle turned on the power to a manual cardiac defibrillator, adjusted its energy to a high setting, and picked up the defibrillator paddles. He jokingly told a female employee riding in the passenger seat of the ambulance that "I'm going to get you." She screamed and told him to get the paddles away from her. The EMT appeared to be complying, but then turned back toward her and struck her with the paddles while simultaneously activating them. The female employee lost consciousness, had cardiac arrest, and eventually died from electrocution by the charged defibrillator. The deceased employee's estate sued for negligent hiring and retention of the EMT. Is workers' compensation the exclusive remedy for the employee's death, or can the employer be sued in tort?

See, *Hilton v. Martin,* 275 Va. 176 (2008).

Heart attacks and back injuries present other problems. These conditions clearly have many causes and might be preexisting conditions that become aggravated by the demands of employment. Most courts follow the usual exertion rule, under which such injuries are compensable if the normal demands of employees' jobs are such that they might reasonably result in injury. Courts that follow the unusual exertion rule insist that only those injuries resulting from some unusual set of demands over and above what the injured employees' jobs typically entailed are compensable. Preexisting conditions that are aggravated by occupational factors are often compensable. The general principle is that employers take their employees "as they find them"—healthy or not so healthy.

Does workers' compensation cover psychological conditions also? Considerable variability exists regarding this issue. Psychological conditions that follow from physical injuries (e.g., depression following an amputation) and psychological stresses that cause physical harm (e.g., upset or stress precipitating a stroke) are likely to be compensated. In many states, psychological conditions resulting from single traumatic events at work (e.g., witnessing a coworker's death) are compensated. However, psychological conditions that develop over time and are related to ongoing stresses in the work environment are generally not compensated. In one interesting case,[59] a bank teller sought workers' compensation for her post-traumatic stress disorder caused by witnessing two bank holdups (one in which she was the teller robbed). Not only was she ineligible for benefits under Ohio law, but the Ohio Supreme Court ruled that this disadvantaging of employees with psychological injuries was constitutional because it had a rational basis (the presumed greater difficulty of diagnosing and effectively treating psychological conditions,

---

[58]*Coleman v. State ex rel. Wyoming Workers' Compensation Division*, 915 P.2d 595 (Wyo. 1996).

[59]*McCrone v. Bank One*, 107 Ohio St. 3d 272 (2005).

conservation of resources). Dissenting justices pointed to the majority's outmoded assumptions about differences between physical and mental health, but also to the fundamental irrationality of a law under which she "would be fully covered … if only the bank robber had been considerate enough of [her] compensation position to have shoved her during the robbery so that she could stub her toe and acquire the physical element that is deemed so essential to her right of recovery."[60]

Clippings

There is growing concern that the numerous blows to the head incurred by professional football players create a much higher than average risk that these players will develop dementia—and at relatively early ages. The family of Ralph Wenzel, a 67-year-old former lineman who began exhibiting signs of dementia while in his mid-50s and now requires the care of an assisted living facility, is pursuing a workers' compensation claim in California. If the Wenzels are successful in arguing that his dementia is work-related, the ramifications for the NFL could be significant. California is an especially hospitable venue for workers' compensation claims by former athletes. Players who played for teams in other states, but participated in at least one game in California during their careers, can receive benefits. And the statute of limitations for filing claims in California does not begin until an injured worker is informed by his employer of his right to workers' compensation—which NFL teams almost never do.

Alan Schwarz. "Worker Safety Case on Dementia Tests N.F.L." *New York Times* (April 6, 2010), A1.

Practical Considerations What should an employer do when an injury occurs in the workplace? How should accidents be investigated?

Responding to Workplace Injuries

Employers should require that employees report all injuries that occur in the workplace as soon as possible. This allows for any needed first aid or other treatment to be provided. *Employers should err on the side of caution in referring injured employees for medical treatment.* Prompt reporting also puts an employer on notice that a workers' compensation claim might be forthcoming and allows for effective investigation. However, most workers' compensation statutes allow employees substantial time to file claims, and the seriousness of some conditions might not become apparent until a later date. *Reports of injuries should be investigated immediately and thoroughly. Hazards that caused the injuries should be identified and abated.* If a claim is filed, a decision must be made about whether to contest the claim. *Workers' compensation claims should not be routinely contested. Reasonable grounds for contesting claims are when the severity of an injury or whether it arose out of and in the course of employment is in question.*

Employees must not be retaliated against for filing workers' compensation claims. Filing a workers' compensation claim is an injured employee's sole remedy under the law. An employer violated a New Jersey workers' compensation statute when it fired an employee for failing to attend several medical appointments scheduled during nonwork time to treat a work-related shoulder injury. The employee had returned to full-time work and missed the appointments because dissatisfaction with his treating physician led him to consult another doctor. Under the employer's policy, missed medical appointments were counted as absences from work, but only for employees with work-related

---

[60]*McCrone* at 282.

conditions. The court decided that the policy discriminated against workers' compensation claimants by treating them less advantageously than people with nonwork-related conditions. However, the court also opined that a neutral policy counting all absences, regardless of whether the absent employees are receiving workers' compensation, would be legal.[61] Importantly, protection against retaliation does not mean that an employee who is receiving workers' compensation and unable to work cannot be terminated if he or she has exhausted the leave time available under the employer's policy. As long as the motive for termination is not retaliation for filing a claim, the receipt of workers' compensation benefits does not entitle an employee to retain his or her job.[62]

Employers should stay in close contact with injured employees and their medical care providers. Information about job tasks and requirements should be conveyed to medical care providers so they can make accurate assessments about readiness to return to full-time or light-duty work. Light-duty assignments should be available and considered for injured employees who are not yet capable of fulfilling all the duties of their former positions. However, there are some important caveats. The injuries employees suffer on the job might also constitute "serious health conditions" entitling them to FMLA leave. Or they might be disabilities under the ADA, in which case the employees would be entitled to leave or other reasonable accommodations allowing them to perform their regular jobs.[63] Thus, although employers usually require acceptance of light-duty assignments and press for employees to return to work as soon as possible as part of their efforts to control workers' compensation costs, *employers need to be mindful that employees with work-related injuries might also be entitled to take leave or receive accommodations that will allow them to perform the essential functions of their regular jobs.*

Key Terms

Occupational Safety and Health Act (OSH Act), p. 507
Occupational Safety and Health Administration (OSHA), p. 507
Occupational Safety and Health Review Commission (OSHRC), p. 507
National Institute of Occupational Safety and Health (NIOSH), p. 507
safety standards, p. 508
permissible exposure limit (PEL), p. 513

significant risk, p. 513
cost-benefit analysis, p. 514
general duty clause, p. 514
ergonomics, p. 516
musculoskeletal disorders (MSDs), p. 516
inspections, p. 517
citations, p. 519
abatement, p. 519
Mine Safety and Health Act, p. 522
controls, p. 523

hierarchy of controls, p. 523
workplace safety programs, p. 524
workers' compensation, p. 525
experience rating, p. 525
contributory negligence, p. 526
fellow servant rule, p. 526
assumption of risk, p. 526
exclusive remedy, p. 526
in the course of employment, p. 528
arising out of employment, p. 528

Chapter Summary

The Occupational Safety and Health Act is the principal federal law governing safety in private sector workplaces. The OSH Act is administered by OSHA. OSHA establishes standards, provides information about how to meet those standards, and enforces them by conducting inspections. The National Institute of Occupa-

tional Safety and Health (NIOSH) provides scientific and technical advice to OSHA. The Occupational Safety and Health Review Commission (OSHRC) hears appeals of OSHA enforcement decisions.

An elaborate process exists for establishing standards. OSHA bears the burden of showing that a

---

[61]*Carter v. AFG Industries,* 782 A.2d 967 (N.J. Super. 2001), *cert. denied,* 793 A.2d 718 (2002).

[62]*Dotson v. BRP US Inc.,* 520 F.3d 703 (7th Cir. 2008).

[63]U.S. Equal Employment Opportunity Commission. *Enforcement Guidance: Workers' Compensation and the ADA.* No. 915.002 (1996).

dangerous substance or other hazard poses a significant risk to the health of employees. However, proposed standards are not required to pass a strict cost-benefit analysis. To prove a violation of an existing standard, OSHA must show that a relevant standard exists, it was violated, the employer knew or should have known of the violation, and employees were working in or had access to the area of the workplace in which the violation occurred. The general duty clause covers hazards for which no specific standard exists. To prove a violation of the general duty clause, OSHA must show that a hazard existed, the hazard was recognized by the employer or the industry, the hazard caused or was likely to cause serious physical injury or death, and feasible means existed to abate the hazard.

Situations where there is imminent risk of serious physical harm or death have the highest priority for inspection, followed by inspections in the aftermath of serious accidents, inspections in response to employee complaints, programmed inspections in high-risk industries, and follow-up inspections. Violations observed by compliance officers during inspections are reported to the OSHA area director, who decides whether to issue citations. Challenges to citations must be made to the OSHRC within fifteen days of receiving citations and can contest whether the violations existed, the penalties, or the period of time given to correct hazards. Employees and their unions play an important role in the enforcement process. Employees are protected for refusing to perform work that poses an imminent threat of death or serious physical harm when the employer was informed of the hazard but failed to fix it.

State workers' compensation laws provide remedies to employees who suffer injuries, illnesses, or death from their employment. Workers' compensation provides employees with partial replacement income, medical care, and rehabilitation. Workers' compensation is provided on a no-fault basis and is the exclusive remedy available to employees hurt on the job. Exceptions to exclusivity occur when injuries are intentional rather than accidental and when third parties are involved. Workers' compensation covers all injuries, illnesses, and deaths that "arise out of and in the course of employment."

Practical Advice Summary

- Employers must become aware of and comply with all OSHA standards that apply to their operations.
- Employers must provide employees with employment and places of employment that are free from recognized hazards that are causing or are likely to cause death or serious physical harm.
- When faced with an inspection by OSHA, employers
  - Must allow inspectors to enter the workplace and conduct inspections, although employers may require that the agency first obtain a search warrant.
  - Can and should designate a representative to accompany OSHA compliance officers.
  - Must allow an employee representative not chosen by them to participate in the inspection process.
  - Must not attempt to intimidate or interfere with inspectors as they conduct inspections.
- When cited for a safety violation, employers must
  - Correct the violation within the required abatement period unless the citation is being contested.
  - Post a copy of the citation in the workplace near the site of the violation for three working days or until the violation is corrected, whichever is longer.

- Employers must not retaliate against employees for
  - Making complaints about safety problems.
  - Contacting OSHA.
  - Speaking with inspectors or otherwise participating in the enforcement process.
  - Refusing to work under conditions that pose a serious and imminent threat to their health and about which employers have been informed.
- Employers not exempted from record-keeping requirements must
  - Establish and communicate procedures for their employees to report workplace injuries and illnesses to them.
  - Record within six days of their occurrence all work-related injuries or illnesses that meet the established criteria of seriousness.
  - Record injuries and illnesses separately for each establishment operated.
  - Complete an annual summary of work-related injuries and illnesses to be posted in the workplace during the month of February.
  - Retain records of work-related injuries and illnesses for five years and make them available to OSHA on request.

- All employers must report to OSHA within eight hours
  - All fatal accidents.
  - All accidents that result in the hospitalization of three or more employees.
- All employers must, if selected, participate in the BLS's annual survey of occupational injuries and illnesses.
- Safety rules should be
  - Clear and specific.
  - Consistent with one another.
  - Strictly enforced.
- Employers should engage in proactive efforts to identify and abate unsafe conditions in their workplaces, especially by implementing effective workplace safety programs.
- Employers must provide workers' compensation coverage for their employees.
- Firms using workers from contract companies should ensure that the contract companies are providing workers' compensation for their employees.
- Employers should require that employees report all injuries that occur in the workplace as soon as possible after they occur.

- When employees are hurt on the job, employers should
  - Err on the side of caution in referring injured employees for medical treatment.
  - Investigate reports of injuries immediately and thoroughly.
  - Identify and abate any hazards that caused the injuries.
  - Not routinely contest workers' compensation claims, but contest those in which the severity of injuries or whether they arose out of and in the course of employment is questionable.
  - Convey information about job tasks and requirements to medical care providers treating work-related injuries.
  - Make light-duty assignments available to employees who are not yet capable of fulfilling all the duties of their regular positions, provided that this does not conflict with entitlement to leave or other reasonable accommodations.
- Employees must not be retaliated against for filing workers' compensation claims.

Chapter Questions

1. Employees were making repairs on a company's huge forging press using a gear-pulling device. The device had four large steel studs weighing nearly forty pounds each. A stud broke off during the repair operation, flew 121 feet, and struck an employee in the head. There had been two prior incidents in which studs had broken off and nearly injured workers, including supervisors, in the vicinity. The lead repairperson for the day shift had repeatedly requested enhanced safety precautions during repair operations, but the company rejected these measures because they would have been too expensive or time-consuming. However, on another occasion, the company did take the lead repairperson's suggestion that it post warning signs and cordon off the area. OSHA cited the company under the general duty clause. The company appealed the citation. What should the court decide? Why? (*Caterpillar v. OSHRC*, 122 F.3d 437 [7th Cir. 1997])

2. On a day off from work, an employee visited the store at which she was employed for the purpose of signing a sympathy card for a coworker. While talking with coworkers at the back of the store, a shelf gave way and began to fall over. The employee grabbed the shelf to stop it from falling. In the process of helping to hold up the shelf, the employee severely injured her back. It was determined later that the shelf fell over because it had been improperly braced when it was put up by the employer. The employee sued for negligence, while the employer maintained that workers' compensation was her exclusive remedy. What should the court decide? Why? (*Wright v. Beverly Fabrics,* 95 Cal. App. 4th 346 [2002], *review denied,* 2002 Cal. LEXIS 3206)

3. On a snowy day, an employer offered to give several employees who were unable or reluctant to travel due to the inclement conditions rides to and from work. Employees were not required to accept the ride to work. One of the employees who decided to take the employer up on his offer was injured when she fell on the ice as she crossed a street from her home to where her employer's car was waiting to pick her up. Is the

employee entitled to workers' compensation for her injury? (*Love v. Bipo,* 146 P.3d 873 [Okla. 2006])

4. An employee often worked with a team that performed a procedure known as "die-flipping." The dies weighed between 5,000 and 25,000 pounds. Die-flipping requires employees to connect the die to a steel I-beam with a cable, permitting them to hoist the I-beam and die with a vehicle. The employee had participated in many die-flipping operations, and based on these experiences, he came to the belief that the process was unnecessarily dangerous, that the company emphasized "get[ting] it done as quick[ly] as possible" at the expense of precaution, and that there was no formal procedure for safely performing the task. He expressed these concerns to his immediate supervisors and suggested the purchase of specialized die-flipping equipment and establishment of a protocol for the procedure. Acknowledging the danger, the supervisors conveyed these requests to members of the plant's upper management, but no action was taken. During a subsequent "die-flipping," the die became stuck. Observing the process from a safe distance, the employee motioned to the vehicle operator to stop and ran across the front of the vehicle "to the other side to see if it was hung up on something." Suddenly, "[s]omething snapped" or "broke loose," causing the I-beam to fly off the forklift and to bounce off the cement and smash the employee's leg. After the accident, the plant's human resources manager told the employee that the accident never would have happened had upper management approved the purchase of new equipment. Was this an "intentional injury," or was workers' compensation the employee's exclusive remedy? (*House v. Johnson Controls,* 248 Fed. Appx. 645 [6th Cir. 2007])

5. An employee of a bear park in Montana smoked marijuana on his way to work. Later in the day, the employee went to feed the bears. The employee was subsequently mauled by a large grizzly bear and suffered severe injuries. There was evidence that employees sometimes smoked marijuana at the park and that the park owner had done so as well. Is the employee entitled to workers' compensation for his injuries? (*Hopkins v. Kilpatrick,* 359 Mont. 381 [2011])

6. A secretary who worked for Sea World was asked if she would like to be a model in publicity pictures. The pictures would show her in a bikini, riding Shamu the killer whale. The secretary was warned in general terms that there was danger involved, but she was not told that Shamu had been conditioned to allow only people in wetsuits to ride her, that the whale had previously attacked people wearing regular swimsuits who were attempting to ride her, and that Shamu had been behaving erratically in recent months. During one of the rides on Shamu for the photo shoot, a trainer noticed that the whale was showing signs of agitation. On the next ride, the woman was thrown off and bitten on the legs and hips. Her wounds required more than 100 stitches and left permanent scars. She sued Sea World. What should the court decide? Why? (*Eckis v. Sea World Corp.,* 134 Cal. Rptr. 183 [Cal. App. 1976])

7. An employee worked as a manager at an automotive service and repair shop. Typically, he spent at least 30 percent of each workday talking on the telephone with customers, other managers, and vendors. At the time of his injury, there was a thunderstorm outside. The manager was talking on a corded telephone to another manager and leaning against a metal table. The telephone was struck by lightning. The manager filed a workers' compensation claim based on serious medical problems suffered due to the lightning strike. The employer contested the claim. What should the court decide? Why? (*Ex parte Richard Byrom,* 895 So. 2d 942 [Ala. 2004])

8. A woman worked at a hotel as an assistant manager. She was required to live on the premises. She and her husband were considered to be on call at all times in order to be available to address any problems that arose. While she was off duty and changing clothes in the bathroom of the hotel, a fire broke out. The woman died in the fire. Is her estate entitled to workers' compensation for her death? (*Jivan v. Economy Inn & Suites,* 370 Ark. 414 [2007])

9. Homicides perpetrated against employees of retail establishments that operate late at night are a serious safety and health problem. What would you recommend that such establishments do to better protect their employees? (Occupational Safety and Health Administration.

Recommendations for Workplace Violence Prevention Programs in Late Night Retail Establishments. OSHA 3153-12 R [2009])

10. The "historic bargain" that resulted in workers' compensation laws occurred at a time (the early 1900s) when almost no other employment laws existed and courts routinely ruled against workers with disabling injuries caused by their employers' negligence. Is workers' compensation a fair bargain now, or does it too often shield employers from the consequences of their negligence? Why do you say that?

11. Should OSHA have to prove that its proposed standards pass a cost-benefit analysis? Why or why not?

12. Does OSHA do enough to protect the safety of workers? Does it overregulate? Should the trend toward relying on voluntary compliance by employers be continued? What is the basis for your opinion? (Stephen Labaton. "OSHA Leaves Worker Safety Largely in Hands of Industry." *New York Times* [April 25, 2007], A-1)

13. Are the penalties assessed by OSHA sufficient to deter violations? What penalties should be available when safety violations lead to deaths of workers? (David M. Uhlmann. "The Working Wounded." [Op Ed] *New York Times* [May 27, 2008], A-23)

PART 5

Managing Performance

CHAPTER **16**

Performance Appraisals, Training, and Development

Employers care about performance. "Performance management" incorporates all the aspects of an organization that affect employee performance, including rewards, supervision, discipline, performance appraisal, training, and development. This chapter focuses on legal issues surrounding performance appraisals and training and development programs. These important human resource activities raise interesting questions for the application of laws that we have already discussed. Performance appraisals and training and development programs are likely to be the objects of even more legal controversies in the future as organizations tie employment decisions more closely to assessments of performance and employees strive to remain marketable in the face of changing skill requirements and less stable employment relationships.

Performance Appraisals

Performance appraisals are a fact of life for most employees. At their best, performance appraisals provide welcome recognition of accomplishments and needed feedback on how to improve performance. At their worst, they are pointless exercises or shams perpetrated to justify questionable employment decisions. Performance appraisals hold considerable legal significance. Discrimination is the central legal concern with respect to performance appraisals.

In general, employers do not have a legal duty to conduct performance appraisals or to do so with any particular level of proficiency. However, the failure to evaluate some employees while evaluating others might result in discrimination claims. For example, a female manager sued her employer for age and sex discrimination based on its failure to evaluate her performance, a failure that she contended led to her not being promoted. Despite repeated requests and contrary to the firm's (a management consulting firm no less) stated policy, the woman did not receive any annual written performance appraisals for twelve years. When she finally received an appraisal, it was negative and lacked the type of development plan typically included in the appraisals of male employees. The plaintiff was able to show that several younger male employees received nine evaluations during the period that she received only one. The company's bid to have her case thrown out failed, and a trial was ordered.[1]

Courts generally have not recognized negative performance appraisal ratings in and of themselves as adverse employment actions on which discrimination charges can be

---

[1] *Esterquest v. Booz-Allen & Hamilton, Inc.*, 2002 U.S. Dist. LEXIS 2545 (S.D.N.Y.).

based. Thus, an employee who believes that discriminatory bias underlies a poor performance appraisal will not be able to legally challenge that appraisal. However, if the biased appraisal is used as grounds for a decision to deny an employment opportunity (e.g., not give the employee a raise, fire or demote the employee), then evidence that a discriminatory motive tainted the performance appraisal can be used to argue that the decision was discriminatory. Thus, in a disparate treatment case involving an African American employee who was selected for downsizing by Kodak on the basis of low ratings received in a "Performance Appraisal Ranking Process," the court stated:

> [The plaintiff] does not argue that Kodak has articulated a false reason for her layoff (for example, excessive tardiness) in order to disguise the actual, unrelated reason (her race).... [R]ather, she challenges the racial neutrality of the proffered reason itself. The latter ... is also ... a form of disparate treatment: if an employer evaluates employees of one race less favorably than employees of another race who have performed equivalently, and if race ... is the basis for the difference in evaluations, then the dis-favored employees have been subjected to "discrimination ... because of ... race."[2]

Furthermore, the Supreme Court's decision[3] to give a broader reading to the category of acts that can be challenged as retaliatory than is true of discrimination cases generally suggests that unwarranted negative performance appraisals could, by themselves, constitute materially adverse employment actions. If so, performance appraisals could occasion retaliation claims if they are used to punish employees for exercising their rights.

Courts are not interested in substituting their judgment for that of employers. When performance appraisals become objects of legal scrutiny, it is to determine whether they contain evidence of discriminatory or other illegal motives—and not to assess whether employers had reasonable expectations or were good judges of performance. Thus, in an employee's unsuccessful claim that excessively negative performance appraisals and inadequate feedback contributed to a racially hostile environment, the court observed:

> [W]e do not sit to appraise ... [the] appraisal. Rather, "our sole concern is whether the reason for which the defendant discharged the plaintiff was discriminatory."... There is evidence in the record that suggests Price was a tough, demanding supervisor.... Price's criticism of her may have been blunt and even at times unfair. But the types of difficulties that Hawkins encountered with Price arise routinely in employment relationships.... Her suit amounts mostly to an effort to seek judicial review of the quantity and quality of workplace criticism. The District Court properly dismissed the action, for employment discrimination law "is not a vehicle for substituting the judgment of a court for that of the employer."[4]

Clippings

Carrie Nelson, an employee at the Mountaire Farms chicken processing facility in Lumber Bridge, North Carolina, was given an unjustifiably negative performance evaluation after she complained about her supervisor's use of racially offensive language. Then, when she complained about the unfair appraisal, she was

---

[2] *Thomas v. Eastman Kodak*, 183 F.3d 38, 58 (1st Cir. 1999), *cert. denied*, 528 U.S. 1161 (2000).

[3] *Burlington Northern and Santa Fe Railway v. White*, 126 S. Ct. 2405 (2006).

[4] *Hawkins v. Pepsico, Inc.*, 203 F.3d 274, 280, 282 (4th Cir. 2000), *cert. denied*, 531 U.S. 875 (2000).

> terminated. The EEOC filed a lawsuit on Ms. Nelson's behalf and the company settled the case.
>
> U.S. Equal Employment Opportunity Commission. "Mountaire Farms to Pay $40,000 to Settle EEOC Retaliation Suit." Press Release (August 2, 2010) (http://www.eeoc.gov/).

Although there are limits to the legal challenges that can be mounted against performance appraisals, there are strong legal reasons that *employers should conduct performance appraisals regularly and maintain credible written documentation of performance.* Performance appraisals affect many employment decisions, including promotions, training and development, merit pay and bonuses, demotions, layoffs, and terminations. A sound performance appraisal process makes it much less likely that discrimination will occur in making decisions about these employment opportunities. And when legal challenges do arise, credible performance appraisals provide important documentation of the lawful motives behind employment decisions. *It behooves employers to have performance appraisals that are consistent with and support their decisions about employment opportunities.* To determine whether a performance appraisal process is legally sound and credible, it is necessary to consider performance criteria and standards, the performance appraisal process, and the manner in which feedback on performance is provided.

Performance Criteria and Standards

Practical Considerations How should employers deal with situations in which performance problems might be related to employees' disabilities?

Common **performance criteria** include work quality and quantity, attendance and punctuality, judgment, ability to work with others in a team, and leadership. In general, employers are free to establish the criteria and **standards of performance** (e.g., the level of work quality regarded as "poor" or "excellent") that they see fit in evaluating employee performance. However, performance criteria and standards must take into account the needs of disabled employees, be consistently applied, be as objective as possible, and be job-related and consistent with business necessity.

The ADA and Rehabilitation Act hold several implications for performance appraisals. As a starting point, *employers can and should hold disabled employees to the same standards of performance as nondisabled employees who do the same jobs.* Lowering or eliminating a performance standard because it cannot be met by a disabled employee is not a "reasonable" accommodation that an employer would be required to make. However, if an employee with a disability needs a reasonable accommodation to perform the essential functions of his or her job with an acceptable degree of proficiency, that accommodation must be provided unless it would impose undue hardship.[5] *Receipt of an accommodation should not be held in any way against a disabled employee, such as by lowering performance ratings because the individual is "getting help." If, due to a disability, a disabled employee is unable to perform a marginal function of a job with an acceptable degree of proficiency, that function should be removed from the job and the failure to perform it should not be reflected in performance ratings. More generally, employers should consider whether performance deficits are related to disabilities.* This is particularly true for employees with known disabilities, but sensitive inquiries can also be

---

[5]U.S. Equal Employment Opportunity Commission.*The Americans with Disabilities Act: Applying Performance and Conduct Standards to Employees with Disabilities.* (2008) (http://www .eeoc.gov/facts/performance-conduct.html).

made to determine whether a previously undisclosed (or newly developed) disability might be playing a role in observed performance problems.

Clippings

An employee worked for twelve years as a forklift operator at a Wal-Mart distribution center. He developed cancer and had surgery. He was able to return to work, but the surgery left him with extreme weakness in his right shoulder and arm. He continued to perform his forklift operator duties successfully and without incident until November 24, 2008. On that day, the employee was told that he would have to fill in for another employee in the shipping department who was taking a twenty-minute break. Because the cancer surgery rendered him unable to do any manual lifting, he was unable to perform the shipping department job and asked to remain with his forklift. This request was refused by Wal-Mart, which claimed that he was unable to perform the essential functions of his job. The employee was placed on unpaid leave—on the same day that he received a performance evaluation labeling his work as "outstanding." The employee was terminated shortly thereafter and the EEOC filed a lawsuit on his behalf.

U.S. Equal Employment Opportunity Commission. "EEOC Sues Walmart for Firing Veteran Employee over Cancer-Related Disability." Press Release (October 7, 2010) (http://www.eeoc.gov/).

In one relevant case, a woman who suffered serious neurological damage following a car accident saw her condition improve, but she still had difficulties with memory, concentration, balance, and mobility. The woman was hired on a probationary basis as a library teacher. Largely on the basis of an unannounced visit to her class by an administrator, during which she remained seated while teaching and was deemed to have not taken sufficient steps to control the class, the school decided not to grant her tenure. She sued under the Rehabilitation Act, claiming that the school district should have provided her with a teacher's aide as a reasonable accommodation. The court remanded the case to gather further facts on the reasonableness of her proposed accommodation. Significantly, and in response to the employer's claim that she was denied tenure on the basis of her poor performance rather than her disability, the court stated:

Failure to consider the possibility of reasonable accommodation for such disabilities, if it leads to discharge for performance inadequacies resulting from the disabilities, amounts to a discharge solely because of the disabilities.[6]

JUST THE FACTS

An employee was diagnosed with bipolar disorder. Following a period of leave after an "emotional breakdown" at work, she informed her supervisor and coworkers of her condition and asked for their understanding as she was seeing a therapist and dealing with medication issues. However, her symptoms grew more severe. She became

---

[6]*Borkowski v. Valley Central School District*, 63 F.3d 131, 143 (2d Cir. 1995).

increasingly irritable, easily distracted, and unable to concentrate or set priorities. During this time, her current and former supervisors met to discuss her "attitude" and her "poor job performance" as they perceived it. The supervisors decided to place her on a performance improvement plan. She was ordered to come to a meeting about the plan, but she was not told the purpose. At the meeting, she became very upset, and after conveying some choice profanities, she stormed out. The next day when she came to work, she began to have suicidal thoughts. The employer sent her to the hospital and provisionally approved her request for FMLA leave. However, just as her leave was set to begin, the employer also commenced an investigation. After hearing from some coworkers who expressed concerns about the woman returning to the workplace, she was terminated. The reason given for her termination was her outburst at the meeting. Did this employer violate the ADA by terminating a disabled employee under these circumstances?

See, *Gambini v. Total Renal Care*, 486 F.3d 1087 (9th Cir. 2007).

Performance criteria and standards must be applied in a consistent manner. Using double standards to evaluate members of different protected class groups is clearly disparate treatment. An employee's complaint that he was retaliated against when his employer changed evaluation criteria and gave the employee a low rating that led to the loss of his position was dismissed in large part because the plaintiff "was evaluated using the same standards as the other loss prevention field agents."[7] In contrast, an accountant was allowed to go to trial on an age discrimination claim based on evidence that the employer set him up for failure by establishing performance objectives that could not be met. E-mails between company managers said that the performance plan given to the accountant "will then enable us to take appropriate action *when* he fails to meet the documented objectives" and "looking at this data (*good job Janice*) can I now put [the accountant] on a verbal warning?" The court took note of the facts that the accountant was given only thirty days to familiarize himself with and complete an assignment using software not used by anyone else in the company, no training or assistance was provided, and the software was dropped shortly after the accountant was terminated and replaced by a younger employee.[8]

To lessen the chance of disparate treatment, *performance criteria should also be as objective as possible.* Performance appraisal inherently involves an element of subjectivity (the judging of Olympic figure skating illustrates this on a grand scale). Subjective performance criteria (e.g., potential for advancement) are not illegal, but they stand up less well in the face of other facts suggesting a discriminatory motive. Thus, in the case of a Latino police officer who was repeatedly (seven times) denied promotions on the basis of performance appraisals that rated his interpersonal skills as poor, the court concluded:

> *Considering the facts of this case and the potential for manipulation inherent in the use of subjective evaluations, the district court properly concluded that Officer Jauregui was a victim of disparate treatment.*[9]

---

[7]*Gresham v. Food Lion*, 31 Fed. Appx. 131 (4th Cir. 2002).

[8]*Andrews v. GlaxoSmithKline*, 2005 U.S. Dist. LEXIS 1021, at 20–22 (E.D. Pa).

[9]*Jauregui v. City of Glendale*, 852 F.2d 1128, 1136 (9th Cir. 1988).

Likewise, a court denied summary judgment to an employer and criticized the performance appraisal process used to select employees for downsizing in the following terms:

This process … consisted of a single-paragraph string of conclusory subjective judgments wholly without grounding in concrete factual reference. Indeed, … the level of reference is in some instances so vague that it is impossible to determine in a meaningful way what the criticism even means.[10]

Consistent with the desirability of specific and objective performance criteria, *"global" or overall performance ratings should be avoided unless they are based on ratings for more specific criteria that are then combined in a reasonable manner to produce the overall scores.* Job performance is too multifaceted a construct to capture in a single score without first considering specific dimensions of performance. It is also *important to have criteria that are established and known to employees beforehand.* A court noted with approval that "the subjectivity inherent in such a review is tempered by a requirement that employee goals and objectives be mapped out well in advance, in order to allow the employee the opportunity to meet articulated job expectations."[11] Subjectivity can be minimized by maintaining documentation of performance that is independent of and goes beyond supervisors' ratings on performance appraisals. Sales records, attendance records, and customer input are just a few examples of such additional documentation.

Clippings

At a conference on equal employment opportunity law sponsored by the American Bar Association (ABA), participants discussed the "unconscious biases" that affect the performance evaluations of female attorneys at large private law firms. Performance appraisals play a significant role in partnership decisions and may be one reason why the percentage of partners who are women (17 percent in 2009) remains low and has hardly budged since 1999. Surveys show that the majority of female attorneys believe that they are held to a higher standard of performance than their male peers. An empirical study of a large law firm's performance appraisals showed that both numerical ratings and qualitative comments were significantly worse for female attorneys. Interestingly, this result held regardless of the sex of the evaluator. Assumptions about the detrimental effects of child care responsibilities appear to play a role in the lower ratings for female attorneys, as do double standards for judging aggression and outspokenness on the part of male and female attorneys.

Kevin P. McGowan. "Female Lawyers Face Persistent Barriers in Advancement at Law Firms, ABA Told." *Daily Labor Report* 61 (April 2, 2009), C-2.

As "neutral" employment practices that affect employment opportunities, performance appraisals can also be challenged for their adverse impact. For example, a woman claimed that Hewlett-Packard's promotion process based on performance appraisals led to the exclusion of women from management positions. The court found that the disparity between the high ratings she received on more objective criteria (meeting sales quotas) and low ratings on more subjective criteria, combined with the fact that

---

[10]*Platero v. Baumer*, 98 Fed. Appx. 819, 821 (10th Cir. 2004).

[11]*Donaldson v. Microsoft*, 2001 U.S. Dist. LEXIS 23396 (W.D. Wa.), at 20.

no female sales representatives had ever been promoted to management, was sufficient to warrant a trial on her adverse impact claim.[12] Although an early case suggested that employers had to validate performance appraisal devices in the same manner as formal employment tests,[13] it has since become clear that the courts view performance appraisals as more akin to employment interviews—relatively discretionary devices for which evidence of a "manifest relationship to the employment in question" is required, but not formal validation studies.[14] Thus, although most cases involving performance appraisals allege disparate treatment rather than adverse impact, there are legal grounds for holding that *performance appraisal criteria should be job-related and consistent with business necessity.*

Performance Appraisal Process

Aspects of the performance appraisal process that raise legal concerns are lack of consistency in evaluations, the parties conducting appraisals, and the contents of appraisals.

Lack of Consistency in Evaluations Performance ratings that suddenly diverge from established track records of performance are apt to attract judicial notice. This is particularly true when the alleged precipitous decline in performance occurs following the filing of a charge (suggesting retaliation) or shortly before a layoff or termination (suggesting the possibility that a "paper trail" is being created to cover up an anticipated discriminatory action). For example, a 57-year-old machinist was fired five days after receiving a performance appraisal describing his work as unsatisfactory over the past five months and recommending termination. He had received consistently favorable performance reviews for years, including one from the same supervisor earlier in the year that stated, "Your work … has been exceptional. You have made a positive contribution in work and in adapting to change." In the period intervening between the two evaluations, the company had decided to downsize. Following attendance at a meeting with upper management about the impending terminations, the supervisor had said, "These damn people—they want younger people here." The court found these circumstances more than sufficient to show that the employer's claims regarding poor performance were a pretext for intentional age discrimination.[15] Likewise, an African American woman who had been a server for more than ten years was offered the choice of being terminated or becoming a busser following an incident in which a "mystery shopper" from corporate headquarters allegedly experienced inadequate service. The woman had a record of solid performance appraisals at another restaurant in the chain and had recently transferred to a facility where she was the only full-time African American employee. Despite the employer's claims that she was unable to keep up with the faster pace at her new assignment, she had received a very positive evaluation and a pay raise shortly after her arrival. Within a few weeks of that appraisal, she was effectively terminated ("constructively discharged") for poor performance. The court found that the plaintiff had stated facts sufficient to warrant a trial on her disparate treatment claim.[16] An employer suffered the same fate when its highly subjective performance appraisal, conducted on the eve of a downsizing, was used to terminate a Navajo woman. The court pointed to numerous glaring inconsistencies between the pre-downsizing appraisal and a contemporaneous appraisal by the employee's supervisor (e.g., criticism for not

---

[12]*Victory v. Hewlett-Packard Co.*, 34 F. Supp. 2d 809 (E.D.N.Y. 1999).

[13]*Brito v. Zia Co.*, 478 F.2d 1200 (10th Cir. 1973).

[14]*Watson v. Fort Worth Bank & Trust*, 487 U.S. 977 (1988).

[15]*Woodman v. Haemonetics Corp.*, 51 F.3d 1087 (1st Cir. 1995).

[16]*Logan v. Denny's Inc.*, 259 F.3d 558, 577 (6th Cir. 2001).

being a "team player" compared to high ratings on "teamwork," including "builds positive collaborative relationships"). Although the inconsistency did not necessarily mean that the appraisal used in the downsizing was biased, it was sufficient to raise doubts about the termination that could only be resolved through a trial.[17] *Performance appraisals must not be manipulated and made more negative than actual performance warrants as a means of retaliating against employees who file charges or of justifying discriminatory actions.*

Sometimes a recent change in performance ratings works to an employee's disadvantage. An employee whose performance improved markedly in the month prior to his termination was unable to show that his employer's claims of poor performance were pretext because his record for the majority of his tenure had been poor.[18] In *Senske v. Sybase, Inc.*, the court considers the case of an employee whose company-leading performance in the year prior to his termination might have been a fluke and stood in stark contrast to his overall record.

Senske v. Sybase, Inc.
588 F.3d 501 (7th Cir. 2009)

OPINION BY CIRCUIT JUDGE EVANS:

In 2005 Robert Senske was fired from his position as a high-ranking sales manager with Sybase, Incorporated, a software and systems-management company with an office in Chicago. Sybase says it fired Senske because a client complained about his performance and because he was dilatory in completing required paperwork, was persistently tardy for meetings, and was not a team player. Senske says he was fired because his manager considered him too old. Senske sued Sybase under the Age Discrimination in Employment Act (ADEA), alleging that Sybase concocted fictional reasons to fire him in an attempt to disguise age discrimination. The district court ... granted summary judgment to Sybase. Senske appeals. * * *

In the summer of 2002, when Senske was 55 years old, Sybase hired him to fill the role of Strategic Account Manager, or "SAM 2." * * * Senske's employment did not get off to a stellar start. In his first annual performance review his then-supervisor, Terry Stempel, rated his overall performance for 2003 as "marginal." Stempel characterized Senske's sales performance as "unacceptable," his pipeline of potential revenue as "insufficient," and his follow-through on paperwork as lacking in "discipline." Although his review noted that "the employee needs to be placed

immediately on a Performance Improvement Plan," Stempel opted not to discipline Senske.

In October 2004 Allan Roeder replaced Stempel as Senske's supervisor. Their first meeting didn't go well. Depending on whose story is believed, Senske was late by at least 30 minutes, and perhaps by up to 90 minutes, in picking Roeder up at the airport. Senske's tardiness on that day was not an isolated event. According to Roeder's supervisor, Barb Stinnett, Senske persistently was late to or absent from weekly conference calls with the management team.

Although in 2003 Senske met only 54 percent of his annual revenue goal, in the fourth quarter of 2004 he participated in two deals that led him to achieve 186 percent of his $2.5 million sales quota. The first involved HSBC, which had acquired Household Finance, one of the accounts Senske inherited when he joined Sybase in 2002. Senske was authorized to offer HSBC up to a 5 percent discount off of the list price for Sybase's products. When HSBC asked for more, Senske followed company policy and brought Roeder and Presales Manager Mehul Rajparia onto the deal. Problems arose during the closing process, but despite Roeder's request that he participate in the contract negotiations, Senske left it up to Roeder and Rajparia to hammer out the details. When the $940,000 deal closed in December 2004, Senske received 90 percent of the commission credit.

---

[17]*Platero*, at 821.

[18]*Olsen v. Marshall & Ilsley Corp.*, 267 F.3d 597 (7th Cir. 2001).

By far the larger of the two deals involved JPMorgan Chase, which in 2004 merged with one of Senske's clients, Bank One. Prior to the merger, Senske had proposed a $912,500 deal to Bank One. When the JPMorgan acquisition was announced in the early summer of 2004, Senske's deal with Bank One was put on hold. Following the merger, Senske got a call from Eric Johnson, the head of FSI, which is Sybase's New York–based financial services group. Johnson told Senske that FSI would handle the deal going forward but would split the resulting commission with him 50-50. FSI took a new strategy on the deal and did not ask Senske to participate in the deal's negotiation or closing. Senske continued to be involved to the extent that he communicated with his Bank One contacts and discussed with colleagues how Sybase could generate new revenue from the merger. The deal structured by FSI closed in December 2004 at $5.2 million, more than five times the size of the deal Senske originally pitched to Bank One. Nonetheless, pursuant to his agreement with Johnson, Senske was credited with $2.6 million in revenue from the deal. Without that credit, Senske would not have met his 2004 revenue quota; with it, he exceeded his quota by 86 percent and became Sybase's top North American earner for the year. Because he exceeded his 2004 sales quota, Senske was invited to join the President's Club, a reward program for high-achieving Sybase employees.

In January 2005 Roeder completed Senske's performance review for 2004. Roeder gave Senske the highest possible rating for revenue accomplishment but noted that he would not have met his quota without the JPMorgan deal. Roeder gave Senske lower scores in the categories of paperwork completion and pipeline readiness. Roeder noted that Senske "is consistently late in updating or accurately completing weekly reports," and commented that his pipeline "does not meet current or future corporate guidelines for pipeline performance." Despite these criticisms, Roeder scored Senske's overall performance in the "good" category, meaning he was "meeting all, and possibly exceeding some, performance requirements."

That same month Sybase introduced the managers to a new planning tool called "blue sheets," but Stinnett and Roeder perceived Senske as resisting the new method. In the ensuing months Senske maintained his resistance, never turning in a blue sheet (or, at most, submitting one). He also continued to be late to or absent from weekly calls. In late 2004 and the first several months of 2005, Roeder counseled Senske about problems that arose on two of Senske's accounts: Citadel and HSBC. Roeder perceived Senske as having difficulty communicating with or meeting the needs of the decisionmaker at Citadel, Matt Swan. Roeder thought that Citadel's technical problems remained unresolved for too long, but despite Roeder's prompting, Senske had not come up with an action list to address that concern. As for the HSBC account, Roeder fielded complaints from Eric Johnson, who said that Senske was not sharing his HSBC contacts or leveraging his networks with FSI, which was handling the post-merger JPMorgan account. Roeder discussed these complaints with Senske and told him it was "mandatory" that he be "a participant in a team."

In March 2005 Roeder prepared a Performance Improvement Plan (PIP) for Senske which Stinnett and Stinnett's boss, Steve Capelli, approved. The PIP informed Senske that he needed to improve his account and closing strategy and demonstrate his ability to "close competitive opportunities." Roeder noted that Senske had relied on him to close deals with HSBC and Citadel instead of taking ownership of the deals himself. He also relayed some of Swann's complaints, noting that Senske did not understand Swann's negotiating preferences and other management needs. Roeder further noted that Senske was unresponsive to his requests for timely and complete account updates and reports. Roeder informed Senske that he must improve his closing skills, respond to management requests in a timely manner, provide weekly blue sheets, and tighten up his "account plans and strategy to the point where your accuracy approaches 100%." The PIP emphasized that Senske would be fired unless he made the required improvements within 60 days.

Three key events unfolded during Senske's 60-day PIP period. First, in late May Senske arrived 45 minutes late for a meeting with Citadel and then failed to take notes during the meeting. Roeder chastised him by e-mail, saying, "It's a lack of professionalism to always be late. It sends the wrong signal." Next, in early June Swann met with Roeder and expressed his frustration with what he considered Senske's poor commitment to the Citadel account. Swann later e-mailed Roeder saying, "I have very limited confidence that Bob Senske and [another employee] are capable of providing the level of support required by Citadel." He noted Citadel's need for Sybase to "deliver consistent follow up from an account management perspective," and emphasized his desire for "quality, proactive support management." Roeder forwarded the e-mail to Stinnett, saying, "Citadel is defcon 4. I believe this is our last chance [t]o salvage this." Finally, the day after Swann e-mailed Roeder, Johnson e-mailed Stinnett to complain that Senske had "run loose" on the HSBC account and was refusing to work with other members of the team. Johnson told Stinnett, "This cannot continue. Besides being counterproductive, it is just wrong."

Five days later Roeder wrote a memo to human resources recommending Senske's termination. * * * [A] human resources executive, Nita White-Ivy * * * approved the termination. Senske was 58 years old on the day he was fired. * * *

The central premise of Senske's pretext argument is that no juror could believe that Sybase's top earner for North America in 2004 would be fired for performance deficiencies in 2005. Senske points to the undisputed fact that he exceeded his revenue quota for 2004 and argues that his success in that area overshadows the shortcomings Sybase cites to justify his termination. Senske notes that revenue generation is the most heavily weighted performance criteria in the written review for a SAM 2 and points out that Roeder gave Senske the highest possible score for that criteria in his review for 2004. Senske also relies heavily on the fact that he was invited to join the President's Club just days before Roeder recommended firing him. In essence, Senske argues that given his outstanding revenue numbers for 2004, the reasons Sybase articulates—his failures to act as a team player, complete required paperwork, or correct his persistent tardiness, along with the client complaint—are simply insufficient to warrant his termination, and accordingly a jury could find them pretextual.

Despite his efforts to cast himself as a revenue-generating wunderkind, Senske has not rebutted the voluminous evidence showing that his 2004 revenue performance was anomalous. It is undisputed that Senske made only 54 percent of his revenue quota for 2003 and that Roeder's predecessor considered his sales performance "unacceptable." In fact, Senske did not meet his revenue quota in any of the eight quarters preceding the fourth quarter of 2004. And up until that quarter, Senske was making only 29 percent of his annual quota for 2004.

What's more, Senske's success in the fourth quarter of 2004 hinged entirely on the deals with JPMorgan and HSBC, and Senske has not rebutted the evidence

demonstrating that Roeder and his superiors believed that the credit he received for those deals overstated his actual contribution. As for HSBC, Sybase showed that Senske worked on the deal for almost two years without producing any revenue, and when the $940,000 deal finally closed late in 2004, he abdicated to Roeder the task of negotiating the final details. But even if Senske fully earned the HSBC credit, he needed the 50 percent credit on the JPMorgan deal to exceed his 2004 quota.

Sybase has convincingly shown that Senske's credit for the JPMorgan deal stems from what is known in the sales industry as a "bluebird," a deal that flies in the metaphorical window with little or no work on the part of the salesperson. Senske does not dispute that the deal he pitched to Bank One was less than one-fifth the size of the deal that eventually closed, nor does he dispute that the New York office took the lead—indeed, took an entirely new strategy—in negotiating and closing the post-merger deal with JPMorgan. He also acknowledges that the decision to credit him 50 percent of the commission was made before the merger and before any of the work on the new deal began. * * *

Senske also makes much of the fact that his 2004 revenue numbers garnered him an invitation to the President's Club. The evidence shows that Sybase extends membership in the President's Club to sales managers who meet their annual quota. The parties dispute whether there are discretionary factors above and beyond the hard numbers, but the dispute is immaterial, because Senske has pointed to no evidence to show that his invitation was based on anything other than his bluebird-driven 2004 revenue achievement. Senske points to White-Ivy's e-mail saying that it was "weird" that Roeder was recommending the termination of a member of the President's Club and argues that her statement shows that his membership should have insulated him. But White-Ivy approved the termination after Capelli explained that his revenue numbers stemmed from a bluebird and Stinnett showed that in other revenue quarters Senske consistently underperformed. These responses show that supervisors other than Roeder—who is the only decisionmaker Senske accuses of discriminatory animus—agreed that Senske's 2004 revenue numbers did not accurately reflect his contributions. Accordingly, a reasonable jury would not conclude that Senske's revenue performance so outweighed the cited performance deficiencies as to raise an inference of pretext.

Not only has Senske failed to demonstrate that Sybase's explanations are insufficient to justify his dismissal in light of his revenue performance, but he has pointed to no evidence casting doubt on their sincerity. Perhaps the most solid explanation is the complaint from Swann about Senske's management of the Citadel account. As we have noted, mere days before the termination decision, Roeder received what he characterized as a "defcon 4" e-mail from Swann. In that e-mail Swann twice named Senske and another employee as the source of his dissatisfaction with Sybase and emphasized that Sybase's account management was not meeting his minimum expectations. * * *

Nor has Senske cast doubt on the sincerity of Sybase's determination that Senske failed to act as a team player on the HSBC account. In his termination recommendation, Roeder explained that Eric Johnson, the New York executive who helped coordinate the JPMorgan deal, complained repeatedly that Senske failed to return phone calls and was not perceived as a team player. Senske argues that this complaint is insincere because, he says, he followed company policy on the HSBC account by dealing directly with a global account manager rather than the New York office. But even if that were the correct protocol, it does not change the fact that Roeder had to field complaints from the New York office that Senske was cutting off the team in a way that was counter-productive. And in any event, the question is not whether Roeder correctly assessed his ability to work with the team, but rather whether he did so honestly. Given that the record shows that the team-player complaint originated with Johnson and not Roeder, no reasonable jury would conclude that Roeder fabricated this justification as pretext to hide discriminatory animus.

Because the customer and internal complaints are sufficient, standing alone, to show that Senske's age was not the but-for cause of his termination, we review Sybase's remaining explanations only to ensure that nothing about them is so fishy as to create doubt where so far none has been shown. * * * Senske does not seriously attempt to dispute the facts showing that he was commonly late but instead argues that a jury could infer pretext from what he characterizes as Sybase's "shifting position" on whether tardiness was a factor in its termination decision. As evidence of the supposed shift, Senske points to Sybase's response to a questionnaire it completed … [prior] to this suit. The questionnaire asked Sybase to respond to a number of questions if "attendance was a factor" in Senske's termination. Sybase responded that the question is "not applicable." Senske points out that one of the follow-up questions Sybase would have answered if attendance were a factor was, "what constitutes an occurrence of … tardiness." Under Senske's tortured reading of the question, Sybase's "not applicable" response shows that tardiness was not among the original explanations for his termination. But Sybase has never asserted that attendance (as opposed to tardiness) was a factor in his termination, and under a straightforward reading it was not required to answer the follow-up question about tardiness unless it agreed that attendance was a factor. Especially when held against the unrebutted evidence that Senske's bosses were frustrated by his tardiness for months, there is no obvious inconsistency that permits an inference of pretext. * * *

Next, Senske argues that there is a material fact dispute over whether Roeder's dissatisfaction with Senske's paperwork motivated his termination recommendation. Again, Senske makes only a half-hearted attempt to show that he met the paperwork requirements (he didn't), but instead argues that a jury could infer pretext because, according to him, Roeder held three younger employees—Michael Clark, Heather Jones, and Jonathan Dorsey—to lower standards even though none of them were meeting their annual revenue quotas. But Senske has not shown that any of these younger colleagues were similarly situated to him. * * * [T]he evidence shows that Senske's three colleagues were SAM 2s at the time of this litigation, but Senske has not shown that Clark or Jones held that position during Senske's employment. The evidence shows that at the time of Senske's employment Clark and Jones had less experience than Senske and held lower-ranking sales positions. Sybase was entitled to hold lower-ranking employees to lower standards than those it applied to Senske. There is conflicting evidence over whether Dorsey was a SAM 2 in 2004, but even if he was, and the same standards applied to him and Senske, Senske has not shown that Dorsey—nor any of the supposedly similar employees, for that matter—never turned in required blue sheets. Nor has he shown that they were consistently tardy or the subject of client and internal complaints. In short, Senske simply has not shown that any of his comparators were similar enough to him to render suspicious any supposed distinctions in their treatment

* * * [W]e agree with the district court's conclusion that no reasonable jury could find that his age was the real reason behind Senske's termination.

The judgment of the district court is AFFIRMED.

CASE QUESTIONS

1. What was the legal issue in this case? What did the court decide?
2. Against what performance criteria was the plaintiff being judged? What was the evidence that the employer's complaints about deficient performance were not pretext?
3. What things does the employer do that lend credibility to its performance appraisal process and its eventual decision to terminate based on deficient performance?
4. Why do you think that this employee took his former employer to court? Given the numerous expressions of dissatisfaction with his performance, is there any way that he could have honestly felt that his age, rather than his performance, was the real reason for the termination?

JUST THE FACTS

Over a four-year period, a high-level manager received consistently positive performance reviews from her direct supervisor, earned bonuses, received sizable annual salary increases, and was promoted to the senior leadership team. Some criticisms were made of her interpersonal dealings with others, but these problems were not emphasized in reviews of her performance. Subsequently, during a period of several months in which there was a restructuring and change in management, other members of the top management team grew more critical of the woman. She was passed over for a promotion that she had sought, and a 37-year-old male with far less experience was chosen instead. Responsibilities were taken away from her and given to a male employee. She was told that she would no longer be part of the senior leadership team. A new 9-point rating system was introduced at a meeting of executives. This "talent review poll" resulted in the woman being given the worst possible score. A manager described her as having "broke the record" by scoring so badly in the poll. This was the only time that this rating system was ever used by the company. During this meeting, the CEO said that he "wants her out legally" and he questioned, "How do we explain this to a jury?" Following the meeting, the woman was removed from her position and replaced by a male. After no other acceptable position was found for her, she left the company. Managers' explanations for the decisions made regarding the woman centered on the lack of support for her within the management team and a perceived lack of fit with the organization. Was this sex discrimination?

See, *Metty v. Motorola*, 2006 U.S. Dist. LEXIS 73645 (N.D. Ill.).

Who Conducts Performance Appraisals? *Employers should provide training (or at least written instructions) to supervisors and others who conduct performance appraisals.* Training should include not only instruction in applying the particular appraisal device and in using appropriate language but also in recognizing and countering the many ways in which bias can distort performance appraisals.[19] *People conducting*

---

[19]Susan Bisom-Rapp. "Bulletproofing the Workplace: Symbol and Substance in Employment Discrimination Law Practice." *Florida State University Law Review* 26 (Summer 1999), 959, 998.

appraisals must be thoroughly familiar with the jobs in question and the work of the individuals being evaluated. In concluding that an employer's performance appraisal process could be viewed as a "sham" designed to cover up its retaliatory motive, the court pointed to the fact that two of the evaluators had little firsthand knowledge of the plaintiff's performance and had not troubled themselves to even review his personnel file and previous evaluations.[20]

Coworkers sometimes play a pivotal role in performance appraisals. Tenure decisions by faculty committees are the classic example of peer review of performance and the object of considerable litigation.[21] Both peer review and 360-degree appraisals (in which employees at various organizational levels, and perhaps customers, participate in evaluating an individual) have the effect of widening the circle of people conducting, or at least contributing to, performance appraisals. *If these methods are used, the group of employees given training in proper appraisal techniques and legal issues should widen correspondingly.* Employers remain legally responsible for the actions of peer reviewers. An airline terminated an employee near the end of his probationary period. The airline cited unsatisfactory peer-pilot evaluations of his performance as the basis for the termination but refused to allow the employee the opportunity to review the evaluations. There was evidence that the employee aroused the ire of his fellow pilots by having crossed a picket line. The court upheld an arbitrator's determination that the company was liable for the termination. The employer knew that the employee had been "blacklisted" by his peers and that the outpouring of negative evaluations reflected bias; yet, it nonetheless chose to terminate him based on the tainted evaluations.[22]

Contents of Appraisals   Performance appraisals are not occasions for "unloading" on employees who have, for good reasons or not, fallen into disfavor. *Appraisers do not have to shy away from criticism, but their tone should be measured and professional.* Shrill, extreme language suggests animus or hostility and makes it less likely that performance appraisals will be deferred to in legal challenges. No less than letters of reference, statements in performance appraisals that are false, damaging to the reputation of an employee, and communicated to others are grist for defamation claims if qualified privilege is lost.[23]

Language used in performance appraisals can also betray discriminatory motives. For example, an evaluator who writes "I doubt whether at this stage in your career you will be able to acquire the new skills we need" reveals stereotypical beliefs about the inability of older workers to learn new things and bias toward older workers. More subtle is the case of an employee whose performance appraisal included a recommendation that he work with an outside consultant to improve his "perception by supervisors." This comment came on the heels of the employee filing a discrimination charge with the EEOC. The court concluded that this comment, in the context of other actions, was evidence of a "pattern of antagonism" and supported the employee's retaliatory discharge claim. The fact that the statement was incorporated into a formal performance appraisal reviewed by management made it weightier and something more than a mere "stray comment."[24] *Performance appraisals also must not include criticisms for lack of performance during periods when employees are on leave to which they are legally entitled* (doing so raises questions of discrimination under the FMLA or ADA).

---

[20]*Woodson v. Scott Paper Co.,* 109 F.3d 913, at 923 (3d Cir. 1997), *cert. denied,* 522 U.S. 914 (1997).

[21]Terry L. Leap. *Tenure, Discrimination, and the Courts,* 2nd ed. (ILR Press, 1995).

[22]*Matthewson v. Aloha Airlines, Inc.,* 919 P.2d 969, 976 (Haw. 1995).

[23]*Hyland v. Raytheon Technical Services,* 277 Va. 40 (2009), *rehearing granted by* 2010 Va. LEXIS 86.

[24]*Woodson,* at 921–22.

Courts have sometimes pointed to the fact that appraisals *contain both positive and negative comments* as an indicator of lack of bias.[25] Courts also seem impressed when appraisals go beyond the checking of boxes to *explain behaviors that are the basis for ratings*[26] and, more generally, when employers are able to *cite specific instances of poor performance or wrongdoing.*[27]

Forced Distribution Method   If your professor "grades on a curve," a type of forced distribution method is being used to appraise your performance. **Forced distribution methods** require that predetermined percentages of employees be placed into particular performance categories. Forced distribution rankings are often accompanied by fairly rigid policies calling for termination or other adverse employment consequences for those employees unfortunate enough to be ranked in the lowest category. Forced distribution methods of performance appraisal have seen wide use, although their popularity might be waning.[28] Not surprisingly, these systems have faced legal challenges.[29]

Microsoft was sued over its forced distribution appraisal system. Appraisals were conducted twice per year, and each employee was assigned a score from 1.0 to 5.0. Of employees in a work group, 25 percent had to be assigned scores of 3.0 or less, 40 percent had to be assigned a score of 3.5, and 35 percent were assigned scores at or above 4.0. The scores were used in making compensation and promotion decisions. A group of employees claimed that the system discriminated against women and African Americans. The court denied the plaintiffs' motion to bring a class-action lawsuit, stating:

> *This rating system, however, is not faulty per se. In order to satisfy the Court that Microsoft's rating system worked to the detriment of Microsoft's employees, plaintiffs would have to come forward with some evidence of either disparate treatment or disparate impact arising from the implementation of that system. Plaintiffs have failed to do either.*[30]

Practical Considerations Would you recommend that an employer use a forced distribution approach to performance appraisal? What are the pros and cons?

Thus, although forced distribution performance rankings are not illegal per se, they are likely to be perceived as unfair and to serve as lightning rods for litigation, particularly when low-ranking performers are summarily terminated and are, disproportionately, members of the same protected class group(s). Microsoft has since rethought its performance appraisal process and now uses fixed percentages to assess career potential, but not actual performance.[31]

Feedback on Performance

Performance appraisals should be part of a larger process of providing information to employees about their performance, as well as the means and opportunities to correct deficiencies. *Employers should communicate performance appraisals to employees,*

---

[25]*Gresham*, at 15.

[26]*Hawkins*, at 279.

[27]*Stovall v. General Electric Co.*, 1999 U.S. Dist. LEXIS 6953 (E.D. La.).

[28]Kelley Holland. "Performance Reviews: Many Need Improvement." *New York Times* (September 10, 2006), Bu3.

[29]Reed Abelson. "Companies Turn to Grades and Employees Go to Court." *New York Times* (March 19, 2001), A1.

[30]*Donaldson*, at 39.

[31]Holland.

provide an opportunity for discussion, and allow employees to respond to and appeal them. Failure to provide adequate, honest feedback sometimes results in legal problems. In one notable case,[32] an African American female attorney returning from maternity leave was criticized for her low volume of work. Her supervisor also took exception to the number of coworkers who were coming to meet with her "behind closed doors." The supervisor opined that the attorney "was allowing herself to become a black matriarch." The attorney was offended by the remark. Concerned that she might sue, her supervisor was told by a company attorney to avoid confrontations with the employee. Subsequent performance appraisals were not provided to her but indicated satisfactory performance. Her boss viewed these as overly high ratings given for the sake of expedience. The attorney was eventually terminated in a downsizing and sued. The court concluded that the employer discriminated by giving the employee what it knew to be overly positive reviews. This deprived her of the opportunity to learn that her performance was unsatisfactory and to avail herself of improvement measures that the company offered to other employees. In contrast, the Veteran's Administration (VA) did not discriminate when it deliberately overrated an employee who had previously filed numerous charges with the EEOC. The VA did so in the hope that this would head off future charges. It didn't. The employee alleged that the overrating kept him from being eligible for a remedial program that might have facilitated his advancement. The court distinguished this case from the case mentioned previously by observing that even in the face of the disingenuous appraisals, this employee had been told on a number of occasions that his performance was unsatisfactory and had been provided with considerable remedial assistance (e.g., several training programs, seminars, mentoring).[33]

Supervisors make choices when writing performance appraisals. Sometimes a more encouraging and less critical tone will produce a better outcome than a bluntly forthright assessment. The cases discussed earlier do not stand for the proposition that there is legal jeopardy when performance appraisals are written with tact and an eye toward encouragement. However, *employers should not attempt to avoid unpleasant confrontations by failing to provide employees with feedback about their performance and opportunities to improve performance that are routinely provided to other employees.*

Performance Improvement Programs As the *Senske* case illustrated, performance appraisals sometimes lead to identification of deficiencies and placement of employees on **performance improvement programs**. Under a *performance improvement program*, an employee is given outcomes (e.g., a certain minimum level of sales, successful completion of a project, absence of customer complaints) that must be attained over some specified—usually short—period of time, with specified negative consequences (e.g., demotion, termination) ensuing if the desired performance is not forthcoming. It is a good idea to try to correct performance problems before they become too serious and require termination. But placement on such a program is often viewed as a warning to "shape up or ship out." And while being placed on a performance improvement program is not in itself an adverse employment action,[34] *Cortez v. Wal-Mart Stores* shows that there will be legal problems if the program appears to be a device used to drive out older workers.

---

[32]*Vaughn v. Edel,* 918 F.2d 517 (5th Cir. 1990).

[33]*Cullom v. Brown,* 209 F.3d 1035 (7th Cir. 2000).

[34]*Haynes v. Level 3 Communications,* 456 F.3d 1215, 1224-25 (10th Cir. 2006), *cert. denied,* 127 S. Ct. 1372 (2007).

Cortez v. Wal-Mart Stores
460 F.3d 1268 (10th Cir. 2006)

OPINION BY CIRCUIT JUDGE MURPHY:

Plaintiff Robert Cortez sued defendant Sam's Club for discrimination in violation of the Age Discrimination in Employment Act, on account of the company's failure to promote him to the position of general manager. * * * The jury found that Sam's Club had violated the ADEA and awarded damages to Cortez. * * * [W]e affirm.

Cortez worked for Sam's Club from April 28, 1986, to April 29, 2003. On the day he resigned, he was 48 years old and had been an assistant manager of several Sam's Club stores in Texas and New Mexico. The highest level that he reached in the company was the position of co-general manager of a store in Puerto Rico, where he worked from 1996 to 1998. When Cortez returned to the United States from his Puerto Rico assignment, he let it be known generally throughout the company that he wished to be promoted to general manager. * * *

From 1998 until his resignation in 2003, Cortez continued to press for promotions that never materialized. During that same time period, however, at least three other Sam's Club assistant managers were promoted to general manager positions in Texas and New Mexico. Two of those promoted were in their early 30's and the other was in his late 20's. Cortez told several executives in the company that he was concerned that he was being passed over because of his age. However, only one, Stephanie Sallinger, the personnel manager, ever followed up with him. When she did, she was under the apparently mistaken impression that a promotion for Cortez was imminent. * * *

At trial, Cortez argued that although he was qualified for the position of general manager, Sam's Club consistently denied him promotional opportunities in favor of younger employees, many of whom he had helped to train. With respect to his qualifications, Cortez argued that his long years of assistant managerial experience taught him the requisite skills to be a general manager. He also argued that he had already demonstrated his ability to be a general manager in his position as co-general manager of the store in Puerto Rico. In addition, he adduced evidence of his laudable role in opening a new store in Albuquerque in record time for the company.

Cortez also adduced evidence of what he argued was Doubleday's [director of operations] discriminatory motive for not promoting him to the general manager position. He testified that in November 1999 in a conversation with Doubleday and Charles Wright, an assistant manager, Doubleday compared him and Wright to Troy Aikman of the Dallas Cowboys. Doubleday told them that just like Troy Aikman had reached a point in his career when it was time to step aside for a better, younger quarterback, so too was it time for Cortez and Wright to step aside in favor of younger managers. Wright corroborated this story with nearly identical testimony concerning the "Aikman conversation." Doubleday testified, however, that age never factored into his decision when it came to filling the general manager positions.

Sam's Club argued that Cortez was not promoted not because of his age, but because of the active performance "coaching" in his file, in accordance with its "Coaching for Improvement" policy. According to the *Club Manual*, "Coaching for Improvement occurs when an Associate's behavior (job performance or misconduct) fails to meet the Company's expectations." The manual goes on to explain that coaching for job performance is appropriate when an associate's behavior "does not meet the reasonable expectations/standards set for all Associates in the same or similar position." Misconduct is defined as "behavior other than job performance, which falls below stated expectations, or violates Company policy, does or may interfere with safe, orderly, or efficient operations or which creates a hostile or offensive environment for Associates, Customers, and/or Vendors." The Coaching for Improvement section of the *Club Manual* also has a subheading entitled "File Retention/Active Period." That section provides that "Coaching for Improvement documentation must be maintained in the Associate's personnel file for 12 months under an 'active' status. Twelve months after the last Coaching for Improvement session, if the behavior does not reoccur, the Coaching for Improvement documentation becomes 'inactive'."

Sam's Club adduced evidence that Cortez had received a written coaching on April 2, 2001, within one year of the promotion opportunities at issue, and it argued that under company policy, employees with an active coaching in their file are not eligible for promotion. This promotion eligibility aspect of the company's coaching policy is not mentioned in the Coaching for Improvement section of the *Club Manual*. Nonetheless, Sam's Club argued that it is a well-known, unwritten policy, and Cortez admitted on cross examination that there was such a policy when he was employed at Sam's Club. Cortez argued, however, that the coaching he received on April 2, 2001, was undeserved.

The written coaching itself, which was admitted into evidence, was issued by Greg Garner, Cortez's general manager. Garner's stated reason for the coaching was as follows:

I am challenging Robert's [Cortez's] overall performance as a merchandise manager. There are certain duties Robert is responsible [sic]. Robert went on vacation and did not plan his business accordingly. Robert did not leave any notes to be carried out. Robert did not complete the alcohol [move] that was asked of him. Robert did not leave specific training plans for his new associates to do. Robert's team leader ended up on vacation at the same time he was on vacation. Robert's overall performance as a manager needs to improve. These issues and opportunities were discussed with Robert in mid-February.

Cortez testified that he challenged this coaching when he received it because it was issued while he was on vacation and he believed that Garner had mischaracterized his performance. Specifically, Cortez testified that he had not completed the alcohol move that Garner mentioned because the store had been waiting for a layout from the home office. With respect to his vacation overlapping with his team leader's, Cortez testified that Garner had approved the team leader's vacation without his knowledge after he had left for vacation. He further testified that he confronted Garner when he returned from vacation and "told him that basically he should be doing the things that are needed to be done in the club while I'm gone in my absence or move another one of the managers over to my area to make sure that the area does not deteriorate."

Cortez also adduced evidence of Sam's Club's unwritten policy of coaching employees "out the door." He testified that Garner would encourage an employee to quit, i.e., coach him out the door, "if he didn't like the associate or the associate did have a performance issue or for any other reason he wanted that associate removed from the club." He testified that he believed Garner was trying to coach him out the door in 2001 because his store was performing badly and Garner did not want to accept full responsibility. * * * Garner testified that the "coaching out the door" policy was directed at employees who consistently failed to meet expectations. Such employees, he testified, are "either going to perform or they're not going to perform, and sometimes we have to coach people out the door because they're not successful in our business." Garner also testified that the decision of whether to coach an employee out the door was not always based on a supervisor's subjective criteria, but could be based on company expectations. He testified that he issued the April 2, 2001, coaching because Cortez went on vacation without leaving any specific instructions and left the alcohol display in an unpresentable condition. * * *

We have traditionally distinguished between employment decisions based on objective criteria, which are generally immune to employer manipulation, and those based on subjective criteria, "which are particularly easy for an employer to invent in an effort to sabotage a plaintiff's prima facie case and mask discrimination." Under this dichotomy, a plaintiff who cannot meet objective hiring or promotion criteria cannot establish a prima facie case of discrimination, and the employer is entitled to judgment as a matter of law. On the other hand, a plaintiff's failure to meet subjective hiring or promotion criteria is not automatically fatal to the plaintiff's prima facie case. In order to show that he is qualified for the position sought, the plaintiff need only establish that ... he possesses "the objective qualifications necessary to perform the job at issue." The factfinder is free to consider the employer's subjective hiring or promotion criteria in the mix of plaintiff's circumstantial evidence of discrimination, but is not required to accept the employer's version of its motivation.

It is undisputed that Cortez received a written coaching on April 2, 2001, and Cortez admitted that Sam's Club has a policy with respect to promotions whereby employees are not eligible for a promotion within one year of receiving a written coaching. The question, therefore, is whether this no-coaching qualification is a truly objective criterion, such that Cortez's failure to establish it defeated his prima facie case. Sam's Club maintains that its no-coaching qualification is an objective measure that forms part of its promotion criteria. * * * We disagree.

* * * Certainly, as Sam's Club argues, the question of whether an employee has an active coaching in his file can be objectively answered. The problem, however, is that the coaching itself can be premised on almost limitless subjective bases, and in that regard it is only facially objective. Garner's testimony that a coaching is "[n]ot always" based on the subjective opinions of a supervisor, leads to the inevitable conclusion that, at least sometimes, it is. Moreover, Cortez presented evidence that his coaching was based on Garner's subjective opinion about his performance. Cortez argued at trial that the coaching was undeserved and gave specific reasons why. * * *

[A] plaintiff cannot prove that he was discriminated against simply because an employment decision was based on subjective criteria. As one court aptly put it, however, "just as use of [subjective] criteria does not establish discrimination, cloaking such criteria with an appearance of objectivity does not immunize an employment decision from a claim of discrimination." There are undoubtedly legitimate business reasons for the no-coaching aspect of Sam's Club's promotion policy. Unlike truly objective criteria, however, … the nocoaching qualification can be used as a tool for unlawful discrimination. Therefore, we conclude that Cortez's admission that he received a coaching within one year of the promotions at issue was not fatal to his prima facie case…. * * *

[W]e must now decide whether the evidence supported the jury's finding of discrimination…. * * * At trial, Cortez presented evidence that he had more than ten years of assistant managerial experience at Sam's Club and that he had earned accolades for his leadership in opening a new store in Albuquerque during the same time period that he was seeking a promotion. He was also the co-general manager of a Sam's Club store in Puerto Rico for three years where he shared responsibility with the general manager for the entire store's operations. He also testified that he lost out on promotions even as he was receiving above-average performance ratings. * * * [W]e conclude that the evidence could have convinced a rational jury that Cortez was objectively qualified to be a general manager. This evidence, combined with the relatively young age of the individuals who received the challenged promotions was sufficient to establish a prima facie case of discrimination.

There was also sufficient evidence from which the jury could have inferred that Cortez was not promoted for reasons other than the April 2, 2001, coaching. Although both Cortez and Garner testified to Sam's Club's practice of not promoting individuals with active coachings, the policy appears nowhere in the company manual's detailed description of the "Coaching For Improvement" policy. Moreover, Sam's Club points to no evidence that it ever told Cortez that he was ineligible for promotion even though he approached several company executives about what he perceived was Doubleday's unjustified refusal to promote him. Cortez testified that he believed the coaching was undeserved and was part of a long line of coachings designed to coach him out the door. Finally, both Cortez and Charles Wright testified that Doubleday specifically told them that they needed to step aside so that "younger" managers could take over. Given that Cortez established a prima facie case of discrimination, introduced enough evidence for the jury to reject Sam's Club's explanation, and produced additional evidence of age-based animus, there was sufficient evidence for the jury to find that Sam's Club discriminated against him. * * *

CASE QUESTIONS

1. What was the legal issue in this case? What did the court decide?
2. Why does the court conclude that the active "coaching" in Cortez's file did not render him unqualified for promotion and thus unable to establish a prima facie case?
3. What was the evidence that Cortez was discriminated against?
4. How should employers address performance problems? Is it legitimate to limit the employment opportunities available to employees who have been placed on performance improvement programs?

Training and Development

Training and **development** programs can make employees more productive and help them get ahead in their careers. They are a feature of better jobs in which employers are willing to invest in their human resources. The provision of training and development is largely up to employers, but there are circumstances under which training is legally required or at least highly advisable. Significant legal questions also can arise concerning who receives training and payment for that training. Training and development opportunities are expected to be at the center of more legal disputes in the future as less stable employment relationships place a premium on acquiring skills that make employees marketable and employers attempt to ensure that they receive a return on their training investments.

THE CHANGING WORKPLACE

The New Psychological Contract and the Use of Training Contracts

There has been much talk in recent years about establishing a "new psychological contract" between employers and employees. This concept refers to beliefs about the mutual obligations that employers and employees have to each other. The "old" psychological contract was an implicit bargain that employers (especially larger ones) would provide long-term employment and career advancement within organizations to employees (particularly white-collar workers) who worked hard and remained loyal. Many employers have concluded that such an arrangement is no longer tenable.[1] In its place, employers have emphasized the responsibility of employees for their own careers and made fairly nebulous promises of trust, honest communication, opportunities to learn, and positive work environments. Some variants of the new psychological contract stress the opportunity to acquire skills and have access to experiences that will enable employees to perform well in future positions, within or outside their current organizations, as substitutes for implicit promises of job security and well-defined career ladders.[2]

While employers are loath to promise job security, greater employee mobility presents problems for them. On the one hand, changes in technology and markets require continual upgrading of skills. On the other hand, employers are reluctant to train if their investments will not be recouped because employees, who have gotten the message that they must manage their own careers, pick up and leave (or worse yet, go to work for competitors). Some employers have turned to **training contracts** as an answer to this problem. *Training contracts* are agreements entered into either prior to employment or before the receipt of some special training that require employees to either stay with the employer that provided training for a specified period of time following receipt of the training or be liable for repayment of training costs.[3] Enforcement of these agreements has not yet emerged as a major legal issue, but there have been a number of such cases. The City of Los Angeles filed a breach of contract suit against fifty-three police department employees to recover the cost of the training they received at the police academy.[4] Cadets are contractually required to remain with the LAPD for at least five years following graduation from the police academy and to reimburse the city for the cost of their training if they leave sooner. For their part, the officers claim that recovery of these funds would violate wage and hour laws. In another case, a nurse who received tuition assistance enabling her to complete a nurse anesthetist program was required to repay the hospital because she left to take a job elsewhere.[5] The contract that she signed called for the loan to be forgiven if she worked at the hospital for five years following completion of her schooling. The court rejected the nurse's argument that the contract was no longer valid because the hospital had previously breached it by not providing her with a nurse anesthetist position upon completion of her studies. Since the contract did not specifically require that the hospital place the nurse in the position she desired, the court ruled for the hospital. Likewise, apprenticeship programs have successfully sued trainees for breaching their agreements to work at sponsoring companies for a specified period of time after completion of their training.[6] In contrast, a court ruled that an employer could not enforce the stated penalty against an occupational safety consultant who left after receiving training before the one-year minimum duration of employment specified in the contract. The employer had arbitrarily established the value of the "training"—which amounted to nothing more than having her view various videos that the employer had accumulated over the years and spending twelve and a half days shadowing a coworker—at $3,000. Because this sum was grossly disproportionate to the actual damages resulting from the breach of contract, the damages sought constituted an unenforceable penalty. The employer was entitled to repayment of no more than a portion of the wages paid ($9/hr) during the training period.[7] Employers also encounter problems if the enforcement of training contracts results in deductions being made from final paychecks that violate state wage payment laws, can be construed as "kickbacks" (amounts paid to an employer to retain employment), or bring employees' compensation below the minimums allowed under the Fair Labor Standards Act.[8]

Overall, it appears that most training contracts will be enforced, but that courts will also scrutinize the details of the agreements, particularly the manner and amount of reimbursement. There are a number of features that employers should consider incorporating into training contracts to make their enforcement more likely.[9] These include *being clear with employees that they are entering into a contract and providing them with sufficient time to consider or receive legal advice regarding that choice; limiting the duration of the employment obligation to a reasonable period related to the nature of the training; framing the purpose of the contract as protection of the employer's training investment; avoiding language that is needlessly coercive in tone; setting reimbursement amounts that are closely related to the employer's actual training costs; amortizing required reimbursements according to the amount of time that the employee has already worked under the agreement; and stipulating that reimbursement will occur voluntarily or by court order, but not by unauthorized deduction from the employee's final paycheck.*

Training contracts have more than a little bit in common with restrictive covenants, such as noncompetition agreements (see Chapter 19), that exist to protect employers from the fate of having their employees develop their human capital, walk out of the door, and make that human capital available to competitors. To be sure, training contracts are distinguishable from restrictive covenants to the extent that they do not prohibit employment elsewhere, but simply make changing jobs more expensive for an employee who has not yet fulfilled the service requirement. Training contracts also do not depend on whether an employee takes a job with a competing organization; a voluntary departure under any circumstances triggers the reimbursement requirement.[10] Employers have other means of promoting loyalty and recouping the benefit of their training investments—including longevity-based pay, seniority systems, and defined benefit pension plans—that are generally viewed as beneficial to employees and not as illegal restraints on their mobility.[11] But these are precisely the types of arrangements that are rapidly disappearing under the "new psychological contract." If employers increasingly turn to training contracts to fill this void that is of their own creation, courts may have to more seriously examine the relationship between training contracts and employment at will (e.g., Does a termination without just cause trigger the reimbursement requirement?), whether entering into a training contract provides employees with a right to receive the promised training and to challenge the quality of that training, whether it makes any difference if the training provided is general or firm-specific in nature, and whether other employment-related costs (e.g., recruitment and hiring) can be assessed against employees who leave employment "too soon."

[1]The Conference Board. "*Implementing the New Employment Compact.*" HR Executive Review 4 (1997).
[2]Katherine V. W. Stone. *From Widgets to Digits: Employment Regulation for the Changing Workplace.* (Cambridge, UK: Cambridge University Press, 2004), pp. 111–12.
[3]Peter Cappelli. The *New Deal at Work.* (Boston: Harvard Business School Press, 1999), pp. 198–201.
[4]*In re Acknowledgment Cases*, 2008 Cal. App. Unpub. LEXIS 5933 (4th App. Dist.); Patrick McGreevy. "LAPD Suing Former Officers." *Latimes.com* (March 22, 2006).
[5]*Sweetwater Hospital Association v. Carpenter*, 2005 Tenn. App. LEXIS 63.
[6]*Milwaukee Area Joint Apprenticeship Training Committee* v. Howell, 67 F.3d 1333 (7th Cir. 1995).
[7]*American Consulting Environmental Safety Services v. Schuck*, 888 N.E.2d 874 (Ind. App. 2008) (decision only); "Contract Term Requiring Training Costs Be Repaid Is Penalty Clause, Court Decides." *Daily Labor Report* 115 (June 16, 2008), A-2.
[8]*Heder v. City of Two Rivers, Wisconsin*, 259 F.3d 777 (7th Cir. 2002); *Gordon v. City of Oakland*, 627 F.3d 1092 (9th Cir. 2010).
[9]C. W. Von Bergen and William T. Mawer. "Recouping Training and Development Costs Using preemployment Agreements." *Employee Responsibilities and Rights Journal* 19 (2007), 135–36.
[10]*Heder*, at 780.
[11]*Heder*, at 780–81.

JUST THE FACTS

The Armed Forces Health Professional Scholarship Program provides financial assistance for medical education in exchange for an enforceable commitment to serve on active duty as a physician for a specified period of time. At the point in time relevant to this case, the contract signed by program participants stated that "If I fail to complete the period of the active duty required by this agreement because of voluntary separation for any reason (e.g., conscientious objector, pregnancy, etc.) or involuntary separation because of substandard duty performance, misconduct (e.g., homosexuality), moral or professional dereliction, or because retention is not clearly consistent with the interest of national security, I will reimburse the United States in one lump sum for the total cost of advanced education." However, the Defense Department had also issued a memo stating that while "a service member's statement of sexual orientation, sometimes referred to as a 'coming out statement' is sufficient for grounds of separation from the armed forces, such a statement is insufficient to constitute a basis for recoupment." ... [Instead,] recoupment would be appropriate "where ... it is determined that the member made the statement for the purpose of seeking separation." John Hensala attended medical school at Northwestern University under the program, graduated, was appointed as a Captain in the Air Force Reserve, and then requested (and received) two deferments from active duty (for a total of five years). After the deferments elapsed, Hensala sent a letter to the Air Force stating that "I am gay" and that "I do not believe this will affect my ability to serve in the Air Force as a child psychiatrist." The Air Force did not respond immediately to the letter. On the eve of his placement on active duty, Hensala informed his commanding officer that he was gay and that he would be living with his partner on base. The CO indicated that this was agreeable, but Hensala's statements prompted an investigation under the military's "Don't ask, Don't tell" policy. At an investigative hearing, Hensala said that he had become more comfortable with his sexual orientation over time and had made his statements because he realized he could no longer conceal his sexual orientation from coworkers and supervisors. He stated that he was not familiar with the recoupment policy or the details of "Don't ask, Don't tell." He also indicated his continued willingness to serve in the Air Force. The investigators concluded that Hensala had informed the Air Force of his sexual orientation for the purpose of avoiding active duty. Hensala was subsequently discharged from the Air Force and ordered to pay back $71,429.53 that had been expended on his medical training. Is this former service member legally required to reimburse the Air Force?

See, *Hensala v. Department of the Air Force*, 343 F.3d 951 (9th Cir. 2003).

Practical Considerations Would you advise an employer to use training contracts? Under what circumstances? What might such contracts look like?

When Is Training Legally Required?

As a general matter, employers do not have a legal duty to train their employees. One important exception is safety and health training. Circumstances also exist under which employers could be found negligent for failing to adequately train their employees. In other situations, training is not expressly required, but it is highly desirable for legal reasons.

Safety and Health Training   The OSH Act does not require that all covered employees receive safety and health training. However, well over 100 OSHA standards call for training for employees exposed to the particular hazards at which the standards are directed. Failure to provide this training violates the OSH Act. A failure to train could also violate the general duty clause if the hazard is recognized, the hazard is likely to result in death or serious physical harm, and training is a feasible means of abating the hazard. In one relevant case, a construction company was cited for violating a construction industry standard requiring employers to instruct employees in the recognition and avoidance of unsafe conditions. Specifically, the company failed to train its employees regarding the hazard of crossing multilane highways that are in use. An employee who was part of a work team digging a trench beside an interstate highway attempted to cross to the other side of the road. He was struck by a car and killed. The OSHRC upheld the citation for failure to train, and a court agreed. The court pointed to evidence that the employer had actual knowledge of this hazard and dismissed the employer's argument that the hazard was too obvious to require instruction or training:

> *The fact that he attempted to cross a road, as he and other employees had done in the past, … suggests that the dangers inherent in crossing an active roadway were not so obvious that employees would not have benefited from systematic instruction. This was not a freak accident, but one that could have been prevented with adequate guidance about when the crossing of the highway should not be attempted and when alternative means of crossing the road should be employed.*[35]

One important OSHA standard that contains substantial information and training requirements is the **hazard communication standard**.[36] This standard is based on the principle of a **right to know**—the idea that employees have a right to receive information about the dangerous chemicals that they encounter on the job so that they can take steps to protect themselves. Substances that fall within the standard can pose either health hazards (e.g., carcinogens, toxic agents, irritants) or physical hazards (e.g., flammable liquids, compressed gases, reactive materials). Chemical manufacturers, importers of chemicals, and employers all have obligations under the standard, which is briefly summarized here:

- Chemical manufacturers and importers must evaluate the hazards of chemicals that they make or sell in light of the available scientific evidence.
- Chemical manufacturers and importers must ensure that each container of hazardous chemicals is properly labeled. Employers using these substances must keep these labels on the containers.
- Chemical manufacturers and importers must provide a **material safety data sheet (MSDS)** for each hazardous chemical produced or sold. MSDSs must be provided to downstream employers with or prior to shipment of hazardous chemicals.
- Employers must have an MSDS for each hazardous chemical used in the workplace. The MSDS must be accessible to employees for their inspection.
- MSDSs must include the chemical name of the substance that appears on the label, the common name, physical and health hazards associated with the substance, the OSHA PEL and other applicable standards, procedures for safe handling and use, and first-aid procedures.
- Employers must have written hazard communication plans. These plans must show how the standard's labeling, MSDS, and training requirements will be met. All hazardous chemicals known to be in use in the workplace must be listed in the plan. These plans must also address how chemical information will be provided to contractors.

---

[35]*W.G. Fairfield Co. v. OSHRC*, 285 F. 3d 499 (6th Cir. 2002).

[36]29 C.F.R. § 1910.1200 (2011).

- Employees must be provided with training on hazardous chemicals in their work areas when they are initially assigned and whenever a new hazard is introduced.
- Elaborate procedures are set out for providing information about hazardous substances in situations where a trade secret is involved.

Knowledge of chemical hazards is vital to employees working with these substances, to people responsible for the cleanup of facilities, and to firefighters and other emergency responders.

OSHA standards refer to the type of training that must be provided, but do not spell out exactly what must be covered or how. OSHA has issued voluntary guidelines to assist employers in conducting safety training.[37] *Identifying employees who are at risk, the particular hazards to which they are exposed, and their training needs is critical. Effective training also requires paying attention to trainees' language skills, reading comprehension, and cultural backgrounds.*

Other Circumstances in Which Training Is Legally Required or Advisable

Most employers that have contracts to supply goods or services to the federal government (or that are recipients of federal grants) must comply with the Drug-Free Workplace Act (DFWA).[38] The DFWA requires contractors to certify that they are providing drug-free workplaces to their employees. This includes publishing policies prohibiting the use, sale, or possession of drugs in the workplace; backing up those policies with sanctions against violators; and creating and maintaining drug-awareness programs. These programs must *inform employees about the drug-free policy; dangers associated with drug abuse; available options for counseling, rehabilitation, and employee assistance programs; and potential penalties for drug violations.*

Just as it is possible for employers to be negligent by failing to use adequate care to screen out applicants who are likely to harm others (negligent hiring), employers can also be negligent in failing to properly train employees. Like any other negligence claim, **negligent training** occurs when there is a duty to others (in this case to provide adequate training), when that duty is breached (no training or clearly inadequate training is provided), when there is harm to one or more parties, and when breach of the duty to train is the proximate cause of harm. The key issue is whether there is a duty to train. This rests on whether the employer knew or should have known that the employee did not have the information and skills needed to perform the job without endangering others ("knowledge"), the likelihood that an improperly trained employee would cause harm to others given the nature of the job ("foreseeability"), and any public policies relevant to the provision of training in the industry or occupation. The *duty to train is clearest for jobs where supervision is limited, sound judgment must be exercised, and poor performance can readily result in serious harm to others. Employers should assess jobs for these characteristics to determine who needs training and should provide the necessary training. Careful selection, clear policies, good supervision, and effective training all play a role in averting harm. Needed training should be provided before employees are put into sensitive jobs and not just when there is time to get around to it.*

Not surprisingly, a number of cases challenging the adequacy of training have involved police officers. Supervisors cannot regularly be out on the streets with officers, sound judgment is needed to handle tense situations that can readily escalate into violence, and police carry guns and other potentially harmful weapons. In one case, a 21-year-old reserve deputy had been on the job for just a few weeks, received no training

---

[37]U.S. Occupational Safety and Health Administration. *Training Requirements in OSHA Standards and Training Guidelines* (1995).

[38]41 U.S.C.S. § 701 et seq. (2011).

from the sheriff's department, held only a high school diploma, and lacked prior experience in law enforcement. The deputy observed a pickup truck turning around at a roadblock, pursued the vehicle, stopped it, and proceeded to force a passenger from the vehicle. His "arm-bar" technique of removing the passenger resulted in severe injuries to her knees. The court concluded:

> [T]he County's provision of no training (and no supervision) to Burns, on these facts, constitutes "deliberate indifference" to the health and safety of the citizens of Bryan County .... [W]e take it as elemental that police officers need at least some training to perform their job safely and effectively. The jury was therefore justified to conclude that it was obvious to Sheriff Moore that officers without any training have a high probability of injuring citizens, routinely and unnecessarily, through use of improper techniques, improper force, and improper judgment calls.[39]

The reference to "deliberate indifference" in this quotation is important. Suits against municipalities based on their alleged failure to adequately train or supervise must show not just negligence (which does not require intent or recklessness) but deliberate indifference to the known or obvious consequences of an action.[40]

Thus, in another police case, a woman sued the city after a police officer came to her home in the early morning (after having arrested her husband earlier on drug charges), announced that he was there to strip-search her, and proceeded to conduct a body cavity and strip search. The officer was convicted on counts of second-degree rape and sexual battery, but the woman's attempt to hold the city liable for violation of her Fourth Amendment right against unreasonable search and seizure failed. She was unable to show that inadequate training led to the violation of her rights because there had been no prior instances of such conduct to alert the city that further supervision or training was needed, the officer's actions directly violated the city's written search policy, employees were trained in the policy, and the policy was customarily followed.[41]

A basic premise of this book is that a good working knowledge of employment law is indispensable for managers, supervisors, and others involved in making employment decisions. *Training in understanding and applying antidiscrimination policies, although not expressly required by the law, is highly advisable.* The advisability of providing training in employment law stems, in the first instance, from the hope that it will prevent violations of employees' rights. If violations occur nonetheless, the existence of policies, training in those policies, and enforcement can lessen the damages for which employers will be liable. Failure to train can be a factor in the imposition of punitive damages by a court. In a case involving egregious hostile environment harassment, much of it perpetrated by a manager, the court pointed squarely to the absence of an antidiscrimination policy and any training on discrimination as grounds for ordering a trial on the issue of punitive damages. The existence of an EEOC poster, which no one ever read, on a wall in the workplace was not sufficient to show good faith.[42] Similarly, in an age discrimination case, the court upheld the "liquidated damages" (an amount up to double the award that can be assessed for "willful" violations in ADEA and FLSA cases) awarded to a plaintiff. In the court's words:

> [A]s this circuit has held, leaving managers with hiring authority in ignorance of the basic features of the discrimination laws is an "extraordinary mistake" for a company

---

[39]*Brown v. Bryan County*, 219 F.3d 450, 462 (5th Cir. 2000), *cert. denied*, 532 U.S. 1007 (2001).

[40]*Board of County Commissioners v.* Brown, 520 U.S. 397, 407 (1997).

[41]*Crownover v. City of Lindsay, Oklahoma*, 2000 U.S. App. LEXIS 22390 (10th Cir.).

[42]*Anderson v. G.D.C., Inc.*, 281 F.3d 452 (4th Cir. 2002).

to make, and a jury can find that such an extraordinary mistake amounts to reckless indifference.[43]

The employer's pro forma attempt at legal compliance—putting "boilerplate" language about age discrimination being against the law on its employment applications—was to no avail. In fact, the court pointed out that using this language while making no effort to train hiring managers about how to implement it showed that the employer was aware of the law but was indifferent as to whether its managers followed it.

The Notification and Federal Employees Anti-Discrimination and Retaliation (No FEAR) Act,[44] enacted in 2002, requires agencies of the federal government to provide training to employees on their rights under federal antidiscrimination, whistleblower protection, and retaliation laws.

Selection of Trainees

Many training and development opportunities are offered on a limited basis and present questions of selection. In *Hoffman v. Caterpillar*, an employer's decision not to make training available to a disabled employee was challenged under the ADA.

Hoffman v. Caterpillar
256 F.3d 568 (7th Cir. 2001)

OPINION BY CIRCUIT JUDGE KANNE:

Shirley Hoffman, who was born without a left arm below the elbow, brought suit alleging that Caterpillar, Inc. unlawfully discriminated against her by failing to provide training on two machines in violation of the Americans with Disabilities Act (ADA). * * *

Hoffman began working for Caterpillar's Optical Services Department ("OSD") in April 1996. * * * Hoffman's primary job responsibility is indexing—entering data relating to a scanned image into the computer. Her job also includes preparing papers to be scanned, maintaining the copy machine, running the flatbed scanner (a low-speed scanner), and ordering office supplies. Due to the fact that she is missing her lower left arm, Hoffman needs several accommodations to perform her job, including a typing stand, poster putty to raise the function key on her computer, and a compound called tacky finger to improve finger grip. It is also sometimes necessary for Hoffman to have the items in her work area rearranged…. [I]t is clear that she is now able to perform the essential functions of her job. Caterpillar concedes that, with the

exception of her first three weeks on the job, Hoffman's work has been average or better and that she performs her indexing job as fast or faster than a person with two hands.

Although Hoffman already performs all of the required functions of her job, she has repeatedly expressed a desire to be trained … to operate the high-speed scanner, a production machine that scans forty to fifty pages per minute. Operation of the high-speed scanner is a key position in the OSD because the overall productivity of the department depends on the speed at which documents are scanned. OSD employees in Hoffman's position are not required to run the high-speed scanner; out of the twenty-one people in the department as of March 1999, only seven are completely trained to operate it. Caterpillar contends that Hoffman's lack of training on the high-speed scanner does not affect her compensation, benefits, work hours, job title, or ability to advance within the OSD. Hoffman disagrees with Caterpillar's claim that the denial of training does not affect her ability to advance; she argues that she will be a more attractive candidate for promotion if she is well-trained. In

---

[43]*Mathis v. Phillips Chevrolet, Inc.*, 269 F.3d 771, 778 (7th Cir. 2001).

[44]Pub. L. No. 107–174 (2002).

addition, Hoffman maintains that she should be trained, regardless of whether it affects her ability to advance, because every other employee who has expressed an interest in operating the high-speed scanner has received the necessary training to do so.

Hoffman's supervisor and the head of the OSD, Lynn Cripe, admits that he denied Hoffman training on the high-speed scanner because she only has one hand. He claims that her disability would prevent her from being able to properly run the high-speed scanner because two hands are needed to clear paper jams and to straighten documents as they exit the machine. Paper jams occur frequently on the high-speed scanner—sometimes four to five times an hour—disrupting production for anywhere from a few seconds to fifteen minutes depending on the severity of the jam. Cripe is concerned that Hoffman would be unable to run the machine, and even if she were able to operate it, that she would be unable to maintain an acceptable speed or clear the frequent paper jams without assistance. Although Cripe is not fully trained on the high-speed scanner himself, his observation of the machine leads him to believe that Hoffman, even if able to physically run the machine, would not be able to keep up with the production standards set for the department. * * * Cripe's belief that Hoffman would be unable to run the high-speed scanner was never confirmed, however, because Hoffman was never given a chance to try. * * *

Hoffman claims that Caterpillar's denial of training on the high-speed scanner constitutes both disparate treatment and a failure to accommodate under the ADA. Because Caterpillar does not challenge Hoffman's claim that she is a qualified individual with a disability within the meaning of the ADA, we turn first to Hoffman's disparate treatment claim.

At the outset, we note that it is quite clear that Caterpillar is not obligated to train Hoffman on the high-speed scanner if she is not capable of running it. The ADA certainly does not require employers to allow employees to use equipment that they are unable to operate. Nor does anything in the ADA mandate that Caterpillar must tolerate a drop in productivity in order to allow Hoffman to run the high-speed scanner. * * *

Viewing the evidence in the light most favorable to Hoffman, we find that there is an issue of fact as to whether Hoffman would be able to operate the high-speed scanner. * * * [T]he ADA discourages employment decisions "'based on stereotypes and generalizations associated with the individual's disability rather than on the individual's actual characteristics.'"

The ADA recognizes that a non-disabled person's instincts about the capabilities of a disabled person are often likely to be incorrect. Therefore, a determination that two-handed people use both of their hands to operate the high-speed scanner, or even a determination that most one-handed people would be unable to run it, should not be the end of an employer's inquiry. In this case, it seems doubtful that Cripe made an individualized determination as to whether Hoffman could operate the high-speed scanner because he never gave her a chance to try it. Caterpillar claims that the primary reason that Hoffman lacks the capability to run the high-speed scanner is that she would be unable to effectively clear the frequent paper jams that occur. There is evidence in the record, however, that Hoffman clears paper jams from the copy machine without assistance, and Caterpillar presents no evidence to suggest that clearing paper jams from the high-speed scanner is somehow different. Nor does Caterpillar counter Hoffman's claim that she could use her left arm in a manner similar to a flat hand to hold down the paper as it is being fed into the machine. Therefore, drawing all inferences in favor of Hoffman, we must assume that she is physically capable of running the high-speed scanner. * * *

Hoffman's supervisor, Cripe, admits that he refused Hoffman's requests for high-speed scanner training because of her disability. * * * Caterpillar contends that it is clear that an alleged denial of training must materially affect an individual's employment for it to be actionable. However, none of the authorities that Caterpillar cites for the proposition that a denial of training must be materially adverse deal with denials of job training under the ADA; rather, they address failure to train claims under Title VII and the ADEA. This distinction is relevant because the ADA specifically prohibits discrimination in "regard to job application procedures, the hiring, advancement, or discharge of employees, employee compensation, job training, and other terms, conditions, and privileges of employment," while the parallel provisions of Title VII and the ADEA do not specifically include the term "job training" among the prohibited actions. * * *

While we agree that Congress did not intend the ADA to reach every bigoted act or gesture, we must believe that Congress did intend to reach conduct that it specifically prohibited in the statute. Thus, with respect to employment actions specifically enumerated in the statute, a materially adverse employment action is not a separate substantive requirement. We agree with Hoffman that, because the ADA specifically prohibits discrimination in regard to "job training," and she has direct evidence of discriminatory intent, she need not show that the denial of training was materially adverse. Hoffman is not asking for special training because of her disability, on the contrary, she is merely asking for the same training that is available to all other employees who request it. * * *

We next turn to Hoffman's failure to accommodate claim. At issue is whether Caterpillar must accommodate Hoffman in order to allow her to operate the high-speed scanner if she is unable to do so without accommodation. As we noted above, Hoffman has already been accommodated in order to perform the essential functions of her job. She now requests (assuming she needs it) accommodation so that she may operate the high-speed scanner—a non-essential function of her position. While it is admirable that Hoffman wants to perform job tasks that Caterpillar does not require her to perform, "it is the employer's prerogative to choose a reasonable accommodation; an employer is not required to provide the particular accommodation that an employee requests."

Caterpillar has chosen to accommodate Hoffman's disability by letting other employees run the high-speed scanner; and, if Caterpillar is correct that Hoffman is unable to run the high-speed scanner without assistance, we will not disturb Caterpillar's chosen method of accommodation. The ADA requires "an employer to make whatever accommodations are reasonably possible in the circumstances to perform the functions essential to his position," including removing nonessential functions from the job, but nothing in the statute requires an employer to accommodate the employee so that she may perform any nonessential function that she chooses. * * *

For the foregoing reasons, the district court erred in requiring the plaintiff to show that the denial of training on the high-speed scanner was a materially adverse employment action. Therefore, we VACATE the district court's grant of summary judgment on Hoffman's disparate treatment claim with respect to the high-speed scanner and REMAND to allow the plaintiff to attempt to show that she is entitled to recover on this claim. We AFFIRM the district court's grant of summary judgment for Caterpillar with respect to Hoffman's failure to accommodate claim....

CASE QUESTIONS

1. What were the legal issues in this case? What did the court decide?
2. Why did Hoffman have a disparate treatment claim based on denial of training?
3. Why is there a discussion of whether denial of training is a "materially adverse employment action"? Why does the court say that it doesn't matter in this case?
4. Why is Hoffman not entitled to reasonable accommodation to enable her to successfully complete the training? Is the court saying that this disabled employee should be satisfied with her current status and not attempt to improve her skills or get ahead?
5. What, if anything, should the employer have done differently?

When Hoffman's case went to trial, the jury decided for Caterpillar on the grounds that Hoffman was not qualified to operate the high-speed scanner at the employer's required level of productivity. The appeals court affirmed this verdict.[45]

In *Hoffman,* the court decided that the specific reference in the ADA to "job training" (among other employment actions for which disability discrimination is prohibited) means that ADA plaintiffs need not show that a denial of training was a materially adverse employment action. Other statutes, including Title VII and the ADEA, do not refer to job training specifically but arguably encompass it in the phrase *other terms and conditions of employment.* Courts have differed on whether denial of training by itself is a valid claim under Title VII and the ADEA.[46] However, in practice, the receipt and successful completion of training is often closely linked to employment opportunities (e.g., promotions, raises). *When employers offer training, they must not discriminate in deciding whom to train.*

[45] *Hoffman v. Caterpillar,* 368 F.3d 709 (7th Cir. 2004).

[46] *Spencer v. AT&T Network Systems,* 1998 U.S. Dist. LEXIS 10718, at 14 (denial of training not an adverse employment action); *Scurto v. Commonwealth Edison Co.,* 2000 U.S. Dist. LEXIS 16171 (failure to train actionable even if not linked to loss of a promotional opportunity).

Much of the training that employees receive is informal **on-the-job training** from coworkers. An African American woman was allowed to go to trial on her discriminatory failure-to-train claim even though the company did not have a formal training program. It was enough that the typical practice was to provide on-the-job training by experienced coworkers and that she received less of such training than did similarly situated white male employees.[47]

Another meaningful form of training is **apprenticeship programs**. These programs typically combine classroom instruction with work under the guidance of experienced coworkers. They are most often used to train employees in skilled manual crafts (e.g., electricians, carpenters). Apprenticeship programs are often sponsored by labor unions, sometimes in conjunction with employer associations. Entry into apprenticeship programs is an important avenue to better-paying jobs, but the availability of apprenticeships is often limited. Although apprenticeships are often thought of as being for younger workers, apprenticeship programs are subject to the ADEA and cannot discriminate based on age. In a case involving an apprenticeship program for maritime workers that had accepted applications only from people ages 17–35, the court observed:

> *The stereotype underlying age restrictions in apprenticeships, meanwhile, is that older people are unable to learn the skills of a trade as efficiently as their younger counterparts. Such barrier to entry may also demean the contributions to the human capital of younger workers that their more mature peers can impart…. [T]he kind of age discrimination that is alleged here contravenes the reason the statute was enacted.*[48]

Following this court ruling, the apprenticeship program settled the lawsuit brought by the EEOC for a considerable sum.[49]

JUST THE FACTS

An African American woman worked as an elevator construction "helper." She aspired to become a "mechanic." To become a mechanic and earn much higher pay, she had to successfully complete an apprenticeship. The apprenticeship program was overseen by a joint labor-management committee. Completion of the program involved working for three years in the industry, receiving classroom instruction, passing an exam, and obtaining on-the-job training from master mechanics. The woman accomplished the first three of these, but the male mechanics all refused to provide her with the necessary on-the-job training. She complained to her union but was told that nothing could be done. She sued. Has she been discriminated against? If so, who is liable? The employer? The union? Both?

See, *Maalik v. International Union of Elevator Constructors, Local 2*, 437 F.3d 650 (7th Cir. 2006).

An employer that denies training to an employee and is charged with discrimination still has the opportunity to offer a lawful reason for the decision. In *Hoffman*, this avenue

---

[47]*Hamilton v. Spraying Systems*, 2004 U.S. Dist. LEXIS 19398 (N.D. Ill.).

[48]*Equal Employment Opportunity Commission v. Seafarers International Union*, 394 F.3d 197, 206 (4th Cir. 2005).

[49]U.S. Equal Employment Opportunity Commission. "Maritime Training Facility &Union to Pay $625,000 for Age Bias in Apprenticeship Program." Press Release (November 15, 2005) (http://www.eeoc.gov/).

was precluded because the supervisor openly admitted that the employee's disability was the reason for denying her training. One of the lessons that can be drawn from this case is that *training is particularly well-suited to determining a disabled employee's ability to perform a job and is greatly preferable to indulging in speculation about what disabled employees are capable of doing.* In other cases, employers have successfully defended their decisions not to provide training by showing that the individuals in question did not meet established criteria. For example, a woman who sought entry to her employer's "administrator in training" program was unable to show that the denial of training was due to her religion because she lacked one of the minimum qualifications that state law required nursing home administrators to possess (two years of prior management experience).[50] However, a court refused to throw out the age discrimination claim of a woman who was not given accountancy training even though she had made it known that she was looking for another job and company policy appeared to require that employees working in accounting positions have degrees in the field. Evidence that she had been promised training when she took the job and employer statements conveying a discriminatory motive ("it's young women I like to train") were sufficient to avoid summary judgment.[51]

Key Terms

performance appraisals, p. 547
performance criteria, p. 549
standards of performance, p. 549
forced distribution methods, p. 560
performance improvement
    programs, p. 561

training, p. 565
development, p. 565
training contracts, p. 565
hazard communication
    standard, p. 568
right to know, p. 568

material safety data sheet (MSDS),
    p. 568
negligent training, p. 569
on-the-job training, p. 574
apprenticeship programs, p. 574

Chapter Summary

Performance appraisal and training are important aspects of performance management. Both are closely linked to attaining employment opportunities, including awarding bonuses and promotions and avoiding layoffs. Performance appraisal and training are not the objects of separate laws; instead, they raise interesting questions for the application of more general laws. Discrimination is the overriding legal concern.

Employers do not have a legal duty to conduct performance appraisals. Discrimination claims, other than retaliation, will not be recognized if they are based solely on undeservedly negative evaluations. However, performance appraisals become central to disparate treatment claims when employees who suffer the loss of employment opportunities allege discrimination and their employers attribute the decisions to poor performance. In deciding whether discrimination is the real motive, the credibility of the performance appraisal necessarily becomes an issue. Marked declines in

performance ratings shortly before adverse employment decisions are made, highly subjective criteria, lack of familiarity of raters with employees' performance, and language suggesting bias are among the circumstances that will undermine performance appraisals and make it seem more likely that employment decisions were based on protected class. Performance appraisals can also be challenged for adverse impact, although formal validation studies are not required for appraisal devices.

In general, employers do not have a legal duty to provide training and development programs for their employees. However, training in safety and health matters is required under the OSH Act when employees are exposed to certain hazards and, in general, when recognized hazards likely to result in death or serious physical harm can be feasibly abated through training. OSHA's hazard communication standard requires that employees exposed to dangerous

[50]*Roh v. Lakeshore Estates, Inc.,* 241 F.3d 491 (6th Cir. 2001).
[51]*Holtz v. Rockefeller & Co., Inc.,* 258 F.3d 62 (2d Cir. 2001).

chemicals be given information and training regarding those substances. Negligent training claims can be brought when a lack of needed skills or knowledge is known to an employer or should be known, the employee's position is one that makes serious harm to others foreseeable when occupied by an improperly trained person, harm occurs, and the harm is the proximate result of a failure to train. Employers have strong legal incentives to provide training in legal compliance to people involved in making employment decisions. Failure to do so can result in greater liability when employees' rights are violated.

The allocation of training and development opportunities is likely to become a larger issue in future years. Under the "new psychological contract," employees are being told that they must assume responsibility for their own careers. Acquiring new skills, experiences, and contacts is necessary to remain marketable. Because opportunities for training and development are often limited, it is important that employers and unions not discriminate when deciding who gets these valuable opportunities. Who pays for time spent in training and how training costs can be recouped by employers have also been contested legal issues.

Practical Advice Summary

- Employers are advised to
  - Conduct performance appraisals regularly.
  - Maintain credible written documentation of employee performance.
  - Have documentation of performance that goes beyond supervisor ratings.
- In appraising the performance of disabled employees, employers should
  - Hold disabled employees to the same standards of performance as nondisabled employees who do the same jobs.
  - Evaluate performance with any needed accommodations in place.
  - Not rate performance less positively due to the need for accommodation.
  - Not require the performance of marginal functions.
  - Not allow failure to perform marginal functions to result in lower performance ratings.
  - Consider whether performance deficits are related to disabilities before taking actions against underperforming employees.
- Performance criteria and standards should be
  - Applied in a consistent manner.
  - As specific and objective as possible.
  - Established and communicated to employees before performance is appraised.
  - Job-related and consistent with business necessity.
- Global performance ratings should be avoided unless they are derived from combined ratings on more specific criteria.
- Employers should carefully consider whether the use of forced distribution methods of rating performance is worth the risk.

- Performance appraisals must not be manipulated and made more negative than actual performance warrants as a means of getting back at employees who complain about violations of their rights or as a way to justify discriminatory actions.
- Supervisors and others who conduct performance appraisals should
  - Receive training, or at least explicit written instructions.
  - Be thoroughly familiar with the jobs in question and the work of the people being evaluated.
- Performance appraisals generally should
  - Include both positive and negative comments.
  - Detail the behaviors that are the basis of ratings.
  - Cite specific instances of good or poor performance.
  - Be neutral and professional in tone.
  - Be reviewed by higher-level managers before they are given to employees.
- After performance has been appraised, employers should
  - Communicate performance appraisals to employees.
  - Provide an opportunity for discussion.
  - Allow employees to respond to and appeal them.
- Employers should not attempt to avoid unpleasant confrontations by failing to provide feedback or opportunities to improve performance when these are provided to other employees.
- Safety and health training must be provided when employees are exposed to hazards covered by OSHA standards with training requirements or to other recognized hazards that would likely result in death or serious physical harm and for which training is a feasible means of abatement.

- Employers whose employees are exposed to hazardous chemicals must
  — Maintain material safety data sheets (MSDSs) for each of these substances.
  — Have written hazard communication plans.
  — Train employees regarding the hazardous chemicals to which they are exposed.
- Employers that have contracts with the federal government must
  — Establish drug-free workplace policies.
  — Maintain drug-awareness programs.
- Employers have a duty to train, closely supervise, or otherwise act to avert harm to others when
  — They employ people they know do not have the skills or information needed to perform their jobs without endangering others.
  — The nature of those jobs makes it likely that such harm will occur.
- Employers must not discriminate in selecting employees for training.
- Employers that use training contracts should
  — Be clear with employees that they are entering into a contract and provide them with sufficient time to consider or receive legal advice regarding that choice.
  — Limit the duration of the employment obligation to a reasonable period related to the nature of the training.
  — Frame the purpose of the contract as protection of the employer's training investment and avoid language that is needlessly coercive in tone.
  — Set reimbursement amounts that are closely related to the employer's actual training costs.
  — Amortize required reimbursements according to the amount of time that the employee has already worked under the agreement.
  — Stipulate that reimbursement will occur voluntarily or by court order, but not by unauthorized deduction from the employee's final paycheck.
- Employees must be paid for required training that occurs during work hours. Training during non-work hours must also be compensated unless
  — It is voluntary.
  — No work is performed during the training.
  — The training is not directly related to the employee's current job.

Chapter Questions

1. A hospital chain hired a woman of Asian national origin as vice president for human resources. She received two annual performance appraisals that indicated she was meeting the hospital's standards in most areas. About two years after her hiring, a new president took over and the woman was terminated. The woman was not told the reason at the time, but the hospital now cites a number of failings relating to inadequate management of legal compliance issues as the basis for the termination. These concerns were not specifically addressed in her performance appraisals. The woman contends that she was discriminated against and that several other employees had received counseling and were allowed time to correct performance deficiencies. What should the court decide? Why? (*Sakaguchi v. Legacy Health System,* 1999 U.S. Dist. LEXIS 11080)

2. A female customer services manager received a favorable performance appraisal in February. In recognition of her good work, she received a bonus in April and was given an expenses-paid trip to Hawaii in May. On returning from the trip, she was discharged because she did not "fit in" and was replaced by a male. She was not charged with violating any rules or engaging in any misconduct during her employment. In addition to suing for sex discrimination, she also filed claims of negligence and fraudulent misrepresentation based on the performance appraisals that failed to inform her of any problems with her performance. Was the employer negligent in how it conducted its performance appraisals? Did it engage in fraudulent misrepresentation? (*Mann v. The J.E. Baker Co.,* 733 F. Supp. 885 [M.D. Pa. 1990])

3. A woman received a score of 3.7 (out of 5.0) on her first performance appraisal. She began to experience severe harassment from a coworker. She complained about it to her supervisor and the human resources department on numerous occasions. On a subsequent appraisal, she received a score of 3.04. The woman was laid off shortly thereafter, with the employer citing the fact that she had the lowest overall performance rating as the basis for the decision. She sued. What should the court decide? Why?

(*Winarto v. Toshiba*, 274 F.3d 1276 [9th Cir. 2001])

4. A police department terminated an African American probationary employee shortly before he completed a one-year training program for troopers. The department cited his subpar performance in report writing and radio communications. A few months before the termination, the department had the employee professionally evaluated. It was determined that he had a possible learning disability, and a remedial training program was devised to help him overcome the problem. However, by the time the remedial efforts were to begin, his probationary period was ending. Due to his performance problems, the department chose to terminate him. The employee claimed race discrimination and pointed to another (white) trainee who had been having similar problems. That employee received special assistance for six months, starting at the outset of his training (although ultimately to no avail). The department attributed the differential treatment to the fact that the other employee's problem became apparent sooner. What should the court decide? Why? (*Kidd v. Illinois State Police*, 2001 U.S. App. LEXIS 27214)

5. A 60-year-old employee had held several positions related to quality control. While interviewing for a different position in the company, he was asked about his five-year goals and his response was that he planned to be retired within five years. He did not get the job and was told afterward by his supervisor that the "word on the street" was that he did not get the job because of his retirement plans. The supervisor then asked if the employee really was intending to retire in the next few years, and the employee said that he was. Thereafter, his relationship with the supervisor "changed drastically." Within a few days of the conversation, the supervisor completed a performance appraisal on the employee, indicating that he did not meet expectations in several areas. Previous performance appraisals, including his review from the previous year, had not indicated any problems. The parties dispute whether the most recent performance appraisal contained any specific examples of performance problems. The employee testified that he had received and signed an eight-page performance appraisal. The employer presented as part of its case a nine-page performance appraisal, with the last page listing specific performance issues. The employee testified that the signature on the longer performance appraisal was not his. The performance appraisal also referenced an incident from the previous year as evidence of poor performance even though no criticisms had been made at the time. A few weeks after the appraisal, the supervisor made a site visit to observe the employee and claimed to have observed inadequate performance. The employee was terminated for poor performance several weeks later. He sued. What should the court decide? Why? (*Maughan v. Alaska Airlines*, 2008 U.S. App. LEXIS 12552 [10th Cir.])

6. Employees of a contractor that manufactures cabinets were delivering cabinets to a house under construction. Two employees were carrying a large cabinet up a stairway to the second floor when one of them fell off the landing and was killed. There were no railings or other guards on the stairway, which was still under construction. The contractor had no written safety rules specifically addressing unguarded stairs or landings. However, delivery crews were instructed that if they encountered an "unsafe condition" while making a delivery, they should leave the cabinet downstairs and call the office. The lead delivery person testified that he had occasionally left cabinets downstairs due to dangerous obstacles, but he had never reported it to the office. He also testified that unguarded stairs do not always pose a hazard, depending on how much room there is on the steps. Another delivery person testified that he had delivered cabinets upstairs despite the absence of railings or guards because he never had any problems doing so. The contractor is cited by OSHA for failing to adequately train its employees. What should the commission decide? Why? (*Superior Custom Cabinet Co.*, 18 OSHRC 1019 [1997])

7. An apprenticeship program trains people to become electricians. One of the requirements for entry into the apprenticeship program is possession of a high school diploma or GED. Applicants without a diploma or GED who applied nonetheless were rejected. In the counties where the program operated, 89.2 percent of whites and

68.3 percent of blacks held diplomas or GEDs. Blacks comprised 18.3 percent of the potential applicant pool (defined as people who work as operators or laborers in the surrounding geographic area) but only 12.2 percent of actual applicants. Of actual applicants, blacks were several times more likely than whites to be rejected due to lack of a diploma or GED. The apprenticeship program is sued for race discrimination. What should the court decide? Why? (*EEOC v. Joint Apprenticeship Committee of the Joint Industry Board of the Electrical Industry,* 186 F.3d 110 [2d Cir. 1998])

8. Employees of a state correctional facility were required to attend a seventy-five-minute training program entitled "Gays and Lesbians in the Workplace." The program was designed to show "the facility's strong commitment to create a work environment where people are treated respectfully, regardless of their differences." Several employees objected to the program after it was announced, believing that it was "indoctrination" designed to promote a lifestyle they regarded as being contrary to the Bible's teachings. These employees attended the mandatory training but silently read their Bibles or copied Scripture during the presentation. The employees did not disrupt the meeting or prompt complaints from other employees. The employees who protested the training in this manner were given written reprimands that precluded their being promoted for two years. Other employees had been inattentive during other training meetings and were not disciplined. These employees sued. What should the court decide? Why? (*Altman v. Minnesota Department of Corrections,* 251 F.3d 1199 [8th Cir. 2001])

9. An employee was hired as a "CES Intern." He signed an agreement stating that one of the conditions of continued employment was meeting or working toward completion of an educational requirement (i.e., passing a specified set of college courses). He took a number of these courses and was partially reimbursed by the employer for the cost of the courses. However, on the grounds that the courses were required by the employer and were directly job-related, the employee argued that he should be paid for the time he spent attending classes, traveling to classes, and studying (a total of 267 hours). Has this employer violated the Fair Labor Standards Act? Why or why not? (*Loodeen v. Consumers Energy Co.,* 2008 U.S. Dist. LEXIS 19978 [W.D. Mich.])

10. Do training contracts unfairly restrict the ability of employees to use their human capital in the labor market? Why or why not?

CHAPTER **17**

Privacy on the Job: Information, Monitoring, and Investigations

Employers gather, generate, and store a great deal of information about their employees. Applications, test results, performance appraisals, attendance and payroll records, Social Security numbers, telephone numbers, medical information, grievance filings, disciplinary actions, and documents generated by investigations of misconduct are among the many records that employers typically maintain. Employers also monitor employees' actions and investigate allegations of wrongdoing. The volume of information available about employees and the means of monitoring their actions have expanded greatly with the proliferation of computers. All these record-keeping and information-gathering activities raise questions of privacy. Most people are under no illusion that they are sacrificing some privacy when they go to work and are screened, supervised, evaluated, investigated, and generally watched. What are the legal limits to incursions upon privacy in the workplace?

Overview of Workplace Privacy Protections

Many laws relate to workplace privacy. Legal protections for employee privacy can be found in constitutions, common law, and statutes. However, the protection of employee privacy rights only goes so far; courts generally view the privacy rights of employees as minimal.

Constitutional Protection

The U.S. Constitution does not explicitly provide for a right to privacy (some state constitutions do, such as California's). However, constitutionally protected privacy rights have been fashioned out of the Fourth Amendment's protection against unreasonable search or seizure. In the leading Supreme Court case on the privacy rights of public employees,[1] a public employer had placed an employee suspected of wrongdoing (harassment, inappropriate discipline, and extortion of funds from the medical residents that he supervised) on administrative leave and then conducted multiple searches of his office. The Court rejected the argument that public employees enjoy no constitutional protection from workplace searches, but also held that public employers—unlike law enforcement officers—need not establish probable cause or obtain warrants before conducting workplace searches. Instead, a reasonableness standard must be used in analyzing these cases. Plaintiffs must first show that they had reasonable expectations of privacy under

---

[1]*O'Connor v. Ortega*, 480 U.S. 709 (1987).

the circumstances. If this is shown, public employers must defend the reasonableness of their actions both at their inception and in their scope. Searches are reasonable at their inception when there are reasonable grounds for believing that they will produce evidence of wrongdoing or when they are necessary for noninvestigatory, work-related purposes (e.g., retrieving files). Searches are reasonable in scope when the measures employed are not excessive in light of the purpose of the search and the seriousness of the suspected misconduct. In this particular case, the Court concluded that the employee had a reasonable expectation in the privacy of his office and its contents because he was the only occupant of the office, the office was not used to store files needed by other staff, it was locked, he had occupied the office for seventeen years, he stored personal effects in the office, and the agency did not have a policy warning against the storing of personal items in offices or otherwise alerting employees that their offices were subject to search. The case was remanded for consideration of the reasonableness of the search. It was ultimately determined that while the search was reasonable in its inception (due to the serious allegations of wrongdoing), the scope of the search (which included conducting multiple searches and placing all of the office's contents in boxes) was overly broad.[2]

Public employers need not establish probable cause or obtain warrants before conducting workplace searches. However, they must be prepared to defend the reasonableness of searches and other actions that infringe on employees' reasonable expectations of privacy.

The idea of a **reasonable expectation of privacy** is a key concept in workplace privacy law. Although tied most directly to privacy claims based on the Constitution, this concept is also relevant to invasion of privacy claims brought on other grounds. If an employee cannot be said to have had a reasonable expectation of privacy under the circumstances, he or she will not prevail in a privacy claim. One factor often considered by the courts is the existence of a policy or prior notification to employees regarding the limits of their privacy rights. To a great extent, if employers tell employees that they are subject to monitoring, searches, and other arguably invasive actions, those employees will not be deemed to have any reasonable expectations of privacy. An employee of a public university who objected to a search of his e-mails lacked a reasonable expectation of privacy.[3] The university had a computer policy that allowed for searches relevant to ongoing litigation (which was the case here), the employee was informed in advance of the need for the search, and keywords were used that focused the search on the information needed. However, although the existence of policies often extinguishes privacy claims, the absence of such a policy does not create an expectation of privacy where it would not otherwise exist. *Employers should establish privacy policies that alert employees to the limits of their privacy rights in the workplace.*

Other circumstances under which a reasonable expectation of privacy is more likely to be found include intrusions that take place in areas of the workplace (e.g., restrooms, locker rooms) that are usually regarded as private; intrusions upon an employee's person rather than property or work area; intrusions that occur outside the workplace and not in public; and intrusions that are effected through deceptive, secretive means (e.g., hidden cameras).

Practical Considerations What might a workplace privacy policy look like? What issues should it address? What should it say about those issues?

Common Law Protection

Individuals, including employees, have a common law remedy for invasion of privacy. Most states recognize the following **privacy torts**:

- Intrusion upon seclusion
- Public disclosure of private facts

---

[2]*Ortega v. O'Connor*, 146 F.3d 1149 (9th Cir. 1998).

[3]*Biby v. Board of Regents of the University of Nebraska at Lincoln*, 419 F.3d 845 (8th Cir. 2005).

- Placement in a false light
- Appropriation of a name or likeness

One fundamental way in which privacy is violated is by others snooping, prying, or otherwise engaging in unwarranted intrusions into one's private affairs. "It's none of your business!" captures the flavor of **intrusion upon seclusion** claims. To establish that privacy has been invaded in this manner, a plaintiff must show that an intentional intrusion into his or her solitude or private affairs occurred and the nature of the intrusion was such that it would be highly offensive to a reasonable person. The objects of intrusions must be truly private (e.g., not in plain sight or divulged by the plaintiff), and the intrusion must be "highly" offensive (generally resulting in anguish or suffering). Also, if the intrusion is successfully repelled, there is no invasion of privacy. Thus, when an employee refused her employer's demand to turn over her private cell phone records for an investigation, the employee had no privacy claim.[4] One example of a successful intrusion upon seclusion claim involved a department store employee whose locker— including her purse that was in the locker—was searched by store managers without her consent or awareness. The managers were apparently searching for a watch they suspected another employee of having stolen and some missing price marking guns (bar codes and scanners were not yet in use). Each employee was provided with a locker to store personal items, but some employees, including the plaintiff, provided their own locks. Although searches regularly occurred, employees were not informed of this policy. The outcome probably would have been different if the store had supplied the locks and clearly informed employees about its search policy, but the plaintiff prevailed in her intrusion upon seclusion claim.[5] Likewise, an intrusion upon seclusion occurred when a manager installed a surveillance camera system to covertly observe female employees using the restroom.[6] The employer's argument that the system was installed to investigate rumors of the use and sale of drugs in the restroom was unavailing because the observation went on for several years.

ELEMENTS OF A CLAIM

Intrusion Upon Seclusion

Plaintiffs must show the following:

1. An intentional intrusion, physical or otherwise, occurred.
2. The objects of intrusion were truly private.
3. The intrusion would be highly offensive to a reasonable person.

© Cengage Learning 2013.

Another way that privacy can be violated is by taking private and sensitive information and indiscriminately bandying it about. To establish a **public disclosure of private facts** claim, plaintiffs must show that private facts of their lives that are of no legitimate concern to the public were broadly disclosed to others in a manner that would be highly offensive to a reasonable person. The facts must be truly private (e.g., not previously known or available to others), and the disclosure must be broad (to a large enough group so that the information essentially becomes public knowledge). A public disclosure

---

[4]*Hellanbrand v. National Waste Associates*, 2008 Conn. Super. LEXIS 249 (Dist. of Hartford).

[5]*K-Mart v. Trotti*, 677 S.W.2d 632 (Tex. App. 1984), *writ denied*, 686 S.W.2d 593 (Tex. 1985).

[6]*Johnson v. Allen et al.*, 613 S.E.2d 657 (Ga. App. 2005), *cert. denied*, 2005 Ga. LEXIS 482 (2005).

of private facts claim failed because while a trucking company had faxed the names and Social Security numbers of over two hundred of its drivers to sixteen terminal managers in six states, the release of this private information did "not constitute publication to the public or to so large a number of persons that the matter must be regarded as substantially certain to become public."[7] In a public disclosure case with a different outcome, an employee who had undergone a mastectomy and reconstruction surgery had conversations about the procedures with the company nurse. Although she had been assured of confidentiality by the nurse, the woman found out from a coworker that others in the workplace had been informed of her medical condition. In finding that these facts stated a viable claim for public disclosure of private facts, the court emphasized that although the disclosure might not have been very broad in this case, it nonetheless exposed embarrassing private information to a group of people with whom the plaintiff clearly did not want to share the information.[8]

ELEMENTS OF A CLAIM

Public Disclosure of Private Facts

Plaintiffs must show that

1. A public disclosure occurred.
2. The disclosure involved facts that were truly private.
3. The disclosure would be highly offensive to a reasonable person.
4. The disclosure was intentional.
5. The matter disclosed is not of legitimate concern to the public.

© Cengage Learning 2013.

Most privacy tort claims arising in the workplace are of the two preceding varieties. However, an individual's privacy can also be violated by placing him or her in a "false light." In **placement in a false light** claims, the plaintiff must show that characteristics, conduct, or beliefs were falsely attributed to him or her; this false information was broadly publicized; the individual publicizing the false information knew or should have known that it was false; and being placed in this false light would be highly offensive to a reasonable person. False light claims are similar to defamation but require that the information be broadly disclosed. (Defamation claims only require publication to a third party.) Erroneous statements by company officials that an employee suspected of stealing goods from the company was an "admitted thief" and a highly public investigation that included placement of numerous allegedly stolen items on the employee's lawn supported the employee's false light (and defamation) claims.[9]

Employees also occasionally allege privacy violations through **appropriation of a name or likeness**. In appropriation claims, the symbolic value of one's name or likeness (e.g., prestige, recognition), which others then use for commercial gain or for other ends, is at issue. A professor's name was included on a grant application (listing him as a "coinvestigator") without his knowledge or explicit consent. When the school obtained the grant but did not continue to employ the professor because the grant was for

---

[7]*Bodah v. Lakeville Motor Express*, 663 N.W.2d 550, 558 (Minn. 2003).

[8]*Miller v. Motorola*, 560 N.E.2d 900 (Ill. App. 1990).

[9]*Wal-Mart Stores v. Lee*, 74 S.W.3d 634 (Ark. 2002).

substantially less money than had been requested, the professor sued for appropriation of his name. The court concluded that the professor had impliedly consented to being listed on the grant application by virtue of his prior involvement in the research project and the general nature of his duties (carrying out collaborative research).[10] The outcome might well have been different if the professor had been terminated before his name was used on the grant application.

A variety of other common law tort claims are often raised in conjunction with privacy claims. Perhaps the most common of these is **intentional infliction of emotional distress**.

ELEMENTS OF A CLAIM

Intentional Infliction of Emotional Distress

Plaintiffs must show:

1. Intent to harm.
2. Behavior that is so outrageous, shocking, or atrocious as to be beyond the bounds of what is tolerable in a civilized society.
3. Severe emotional harm or distress.

© Cengage Learning 2013.

Courts are emphatic that infliction of emotional distress claims are not available for garden-variety insensitivity, abrasiveness, or incivility. The challenged conduct must truly be "outrageous." For example, when a young female cashier was accused of taking some money that a customer had placed on the counter, store personnel proceeded to take her into a restroom and conduct a strip search—in full view of the complaining customer. It is scarcely relevant that the search turned up no money and that the customer later called back saying that she had miscounted her money. This extreme course of action, undertaken to placate a troublesome customer and without the slightest apparent regard for the dignity and sensibilities of the young woman, was more than sufficient to support an infliction of emotional distress claim (against both the store and the customer). Although there was no evidence that the store personnel intended to cause harm, they were reckless in their treatment of the employee. The store's claim that she had consented to the search was contested and ultimately discounted by the court in light of her young age and probable belief that she was required to submit to the search.[11] Likewise, an infliction of emotional distress claim succeeded when two managers broke into a locked restroom and snapped a revealing photograph of a male employee while he was urinating. The managers refused the employee's demands that they return the photograph. Instead, it was circulated around the office. "Peewee" and "Splinter" were among the names with which the employee was tagged after the incident. On his transfer to another office, the picture was forwarded by the managers and quickly became common knowledge in his new workplace.[12]

---

[10]*Nemani v. St. Louis University*, 33 S.W.3d 184 (Mo. 2000), *cert. denied*, 532 U.S. 981 (2001).

[11]*Bodewig v. K-Mart*, 635 P.2d 657 (Ore. App. 1981), *review denied*, 644 P.2d 1128 (Or. 1982). But see *Navarette v. Nike*, 2007 U.S. Dist. LEXIS 6323 (D. Ore.) (clarifying that under Oregon law, the requisite degree of intent that must be shown is not determined by the existence of a special relationship).

[12]*Fotiades v. Hi-Tech Auto Collision & Painting Services, Inc.*, 2001 Cal. App. Unpub. LEXIS 2559 (4th App. Dist.).

Other tort clams that arise in the context of handling employee information or investigating employee conduct include defamation, false imprisonment, and malicious prosecution. These are discussed further in later sections of this chapter.

Statutory Protection of Privacy

A number of statutes address aspects of workplace privacy. Some of these laws (e.g., Privacy Act, Electronic Communications Privacy Act) have privacy as their central focus. Other statutes—including the ADA, NLRA, and OSH Act—are not privacy laws but nonetheless have implications for employee privacy and access to records.

Handling Records and Employee Information

Employers gather and store a great deal of information about employees. Some of it (e.g., medical information, drug testing results, reports on investigations into harassment complaints) is sensitive. Major questions arise as to what information should be kept, how accurate that information must be, whether employees have access to their personnel files, and what the circumstances are under which information from employee records can be released to other parties.

JUST THE FACTS

Someone stole from a Starbucks a laptop that contained the unencrypted names, addresses, and Social Security numbers of approximately 97,000 Starbucks employees. About three weeks later, Starbucks sent a letter alerting employees to the theft and stating that Starbucks had "no indication that the private information has been misused." The letter advised the employees to monitor their financial accounts and indicated that Starbucks had arranged with a credit reporting service to offer the employees free credit watch services for the next year. One employee whose personal information had been stolen enrolled in the free credit watch service but also spent considerable time monitoring all of her accounts and paid to have the credit watch extended. Another employee claimed that he was also forced to spend a substantial amount of time monitoring his accounts, placed fraud alerts on his credit cards, and experienced "generalized anxiety and stress regarding the situation." A bank notified one of the employees about a month after the loss of the information that someone had attempted to open a new account using his Social Security number. However, the bank had closed the account and the employee did not suffer any financial loss. The employees sued Starbucks for negligence and breach of an implied contract to handle their information with reasonable care. What should the court decide? Why?

See, *Krottner v. Starbucks*, 628 F.3d 1139 (9th 2010), *supplemental opinion at* 2010 U.S. App. LEXIS 26795.

Personnel Records

Many of the records that employers maintain about their employees are incorporated into personnel files that are kept for each employee. To a large extent, the handling of personnel records is a matter of employer policy rather than law. A number of states, but by no means all, have laws pertaining to personnel records. Most of these state laws give employees the right, under specified circumstances, to review (and perhaps copy) the contents of their personnel files. However, the most comprehensive law dealing with personnel records is the federal Privacy Act.[13] The **Privacy Act** regulates the handling of personnel records by agencies of the federal government. The act defines *record* broadly to include "any item, collection, or grouping of information about an individual that is maintained by an agency."[14] Federal employees must be given access to their personnel records under reasonable procedures established by federal agencies, allowed to copy materials from their personnel files, and permitted to contest the accuracy of records in written statements that are included with any disclosures of the records to other parties. Importantly, federal agencies must obtain the consent of employees before disclosing information from their personnel records to outside parties. The Privacy Act also limits the kinds of information that federal agencies can keep regarding their employees and imposes a duty on federal agencies to maintain accurate records.

Violations of the Privacy Act can be difficult to prove because plaintiffs must show that the violations were intentional or willful and that there were actual damages, such as an adverse employment determination. However, an applicant for a job at the Postal Service was allowed to proceed to trial on a Privacy Act claim when he listed the name of his current employer on an application, he said that he did not want his current employer contacted, the Postal Service contacted the current employer anyway, and the employee was fired from his job (and, adding insult to injury, was not hired by the Postal Service).[15]

Because the Privacy Act does not apply to private sector employers, where does this leave them? In terms of access to personnel records, *if an employer operates in a state with a personnel records law, the employer generally has to allow employees access to their personnel files.* Even absent such a law, *employers generally must allow union representatives to see pertinent information in employees' personnel files.* The duty of employers under the National Labor Relations Act (NLRA) to bargain in good faith and to provide union representatives with information relevant to proper topics of negotiations pertains not only to bargaining over new contracts but also to information needed to handle grievances and otherwise represent employees. In terms of divulging information, communication of false, damaging information to third parties without a legitimate need to know might lead to defamation claims. Even information that is true could prompt a legal claim for public disclosure of private facts if the information is genuinely private in nature and effectively made public knowledge. Employee consent is a defense to both defamation and invasion of privacy claims. Thus, *although most private sector employers are not strictly required to do so, it is advisable to obtain the consent of employees prior to divulging information from their personnel records to third parties.*

Medical Information

Employers, even those that do not self-insure or administer their own health plans, amass a considerable amount of medical information on their employees. For example, preemployment medical exams (following a conditional offer of employment) or periodic exams of employees (to assess job-related conditions) might be conducted. Employees requesting leave for serious health conditions under the FMLA submit medical documentation, and employees hurt on the job file workers' compensation claims. Employees with disabilities might make their conditions known when requesting accommodations. Information about medications paid for under group health plans is available to

---

[13]5 U.S.C.S. § 552a (2011).

[14]5 U.S.C.S. § 552a (a)(4) (2011).

[15]*Sullivan v. United States Postal Service*, 944 F. Supp. 191 (W.D.N.Y. 1996).

employers. Employee assistance programs might provide reports to employers on employees experiencing personal or substance abuse problems. Medical information is sensitive information that is subject to additional legal constraints beyond those applying to personnel records in general.

Clippings

The EEOC has sued Dillard's over its policy of requiring that employees who take sick leave reveal the specific nature of their medical conditions in order to be excused for absences. A sales associate who was out sick for several days and who submitted a doctor's note justifying her absence was told that she had to reveal the specific nature of her illness. When she refused to do so, Dillard's deemed her absences to be unexcused and terminated her employment. The EEOC contends that the policy violates the ADA and that the termination was retaliatory.

U.S. Equal Employment Opportunity Commission. "Dillard's Sued for Disability Discrimination." (September 30, 2008) Viewed October 11, 2008 (http://www.eeoc.gov/press/9-30-08.html).

The Americans with Disabilities Act places limits on the type of medical information that can be obtained from employees. According to the EEOC, Dillard's insistence that employees provide specific information about the nature of their medical conditions in order to be excused for absences violated the ADA's requirement that only medical information that is job-related and consistent with business necessity can be collected from current employees. Furthermore, the ADA requires that employers *keep information regarding an employee's medical condition or history that is obtained from a medical exam or inquiry in a location apart from other personnel records and treat it as a "confidential medical record."* However, disclosure of medical information that is voluntarily offered by an employee and not obtained through a medical exam or inquiry is apparently not prohibited by the ADA. Thus, an employer did not violate the ADA when it shared an employee's HIV-positive status with coworkers after that employee voluntarily informed the company of his status.[16] The medical confidentiality provisions of the ADA apply regardless of whether an employee is disabled.[17]

JUST THE FACTS

An employee with attention deficit hyperactivity disorder (ADHD) applied for a job and was hired, conditional on his satisfactory completion of a pre-placement medical screening that included a medical history questionnaire. The employee completed the screening and asserts that he answered the questionnaire truthfully based on his understanding of the questions. Initially, he performed his job satisfactorily without needing any accommodations. However, he was subsequently transferred to a

---

[16]*EEOC v. C.R. England*, 2011 U.S. App. LEXIS 8971, 49-51 (10th Cir.).

[17]*Giaccio v. City of New York*, 2005 U.S. Dist. LEXIS 642, at 9 (S.D.N.Y.); 502 F. Supp. 2d 380 (S.D.N.Y. 2007). (ADA claim failed because the plaintiff was unable to show damages from the release of medical information.)

different position that required more multitasking, which he found to be difficult due to his ADHD. He was counseled by his supervisor for performance problems. During that meeting, the employee disclosed that he had ADHD and that he believed that his performance problems were attributable to his ADHD. He confirmed his ADHD diagnosis with a note from his doctor and requested reasonable accommodation for his disability. The employee was sent to meet with the employer's in-house medical provider. It was the same doctor who had administered his preemployment screening. Rather than discuss his requested accommodation, the doctor interrogated the employee about his earlier responses to the questionnaire and accused him of falsification. The employee said that he had thought that the questions did not pertain to mental or emotional issues such as ADHD. The doctor reported the employee's failure to mention his ADHD during the pre-placement medical exam to company managers. A decision was made to terminate the employee because he had not disclosed his ADHD when he completed the medical questionnaire. Did this employer's handling and use of medical information violate the ADA?

See, *Blanco v. Bath Iron Works*, 2011 U.S. Dist. LEXIS 72712 (D. Me.).

The OSH Act provides employees (and unions) with a right of access to medical and exposure records created in compliance with the act. A number of OSHA standards require medical monitoring of individual employees, as well as monitoring of the workplace for levels of exposure to toxic substances and harmful physical agents. Because occupational diseases can take a long time to develop and such records are critical to identifying the occupational basis of these conditions, *exposure records must be maintained for thirty years and medical records for the duration of employment plus thirty years.* Medical records of short-term employees (less than one year) need not be retained as long as they are provided to those employees upon termination of employment. *Access to medical and exposure records produced in compliance with the OSH Act, which includes the right to examine and copy records, must generally be provided within fifteen working days.* Requests need not be in writing except where trade secrets are involved. Unions and health professionals need the specific written consent of employees to have access to their personal medical records, but they can examine exposure records without obtaining consent.

Medical privacy regulations under HIPAA are also relevant. These regulations[18] primarily affect health care providers and self-insured companies. However, any employer that receives protected health information (i.e., information about medical conditions that can be linked to individuals) from insurers or health care providers has obligations under the law. Parties with access to protected health information must limit the uses and disclosure of that information, train staff on maintaining the privacy of medical information, designate a privacy officer with responsibility for compliance, and notify employees of their rights. Employees have the right to inspect and copy their medical records and propose corrections. However, the regulations do not require that consent be obtained before using or disclosing information in employees' medical records. Additionally, the HIPAA regulations apply only to medical information derived from the administration of group health plans; other sources of medical information are not affected. The HIPAA medical privacy regulations underscore the need to handle medical information in an especially careful, confidential manner.

The case mentioned earlier in this chapter regarding unauthorized public disclosure to coworkers of the private fact that an employee had a mastectomy is a good illustration of

---

[18]45 C.F.R. Parts 160, 164 (2011).

the need to treat medical information as confidential. In another case, information about a flight attendant's medical condition was given by her gynecologist to a male supervisor who had no need to know the information and who subsequently shared it with the woman's husband. The supervisor also repeatedly pressed her to discuss the details of her condition and raised the subject in front of another manager. Under these circumstances, the court found that the employee's privacy rights had been violated.[19] However, other courts have required that private information be publicized to people outside the workplace to support a public disclosure of private facts claim. For example, an employer did not violate the privacy rights of a nuclear power plant employee when it informed her coworkers that she had a hysterectomy to counter rumors that she was suffering from radiation exposure.[20] In another case, the court acknowledged that medical records fall within constitutional privacy protections, but concluded that the employer did not violate the constitutional rights of an employee by disclosing information about his HIV status to several other managers.[21] The information was inferred from a list of heavy prescription drug users that was provided by the drug chain used under the employer's prescription drug plan. Factors that the court pointed to in reaching this conclusion included that the employer had not requested names of individuals, it had obtained the report for the legitimate purpose of controlling drug costs, and the information was divulged to only a small number of employees involved with benefit administration.

Monitoring and Surveillance of Employees

"The boss is coming down the hall. We'd better look busy!" Employees are regularly observed on the job. Electronic means of monitoring and surveillance—including using video cameras, monitoring computer keystrokes, examining Internet sites visited, and tracking employees with GPS—are more comprehensive and unrelenting than old-fashioned supervision (after all, you could always slack off when the boss left) and raise new privacy concerns.

Clippings

The National Transportation Safety Board (NTSB), a federal government agency responsible for investigating accidents involving public transportation, has recommended that surveillance cameras be placed in nearly all locomotives. The recommendation follows their inquiry into a 2008 crash in Chatsworth, California, involving a commuter train (Metrolink) and a freight train. At the time of the accident, which killed twenty-five people, the Metrolink engineer was composing a text message, while the conductor on the freight train was using his cell phone. Following the accident, Metrolink installed two cameras in the cabs of every locomotive, but this action has been challenged by the train engineers' union on the grounds that it violates California privacy laws.

Matthew L. Wald. "Panel Recommends Surveillance in Locomotives." *New York Times* (January 22, 2010), A13.

---

[19]*Levias v. United Airlines*, 500 N.E.2d 370 (Ohio App. 1985).

[20]*Young v. Jackson*, 572 So. 2d 378 (Miss. 1990).

[21]*Doe v. SEPTA*, 72 F.3d 1133 (3d Cir. 1995), *cert. denied*, 519 U.S. 808 (1996).

Video Surveillance

Video cameras have become increasingly commonplace, with people "starring" on more videotape than they realize as they go about their business using ATMs, shopping, and sometimes just walking down the street. Employers use video cameras to keep tabs on both customers and employees. In general, employers can train video cameras on their employees without significant legal concerns. Thus, a Fourth Amendment challenge to a video surveillance system installed by a public agency failed because the workspace in question was open to public view and did not include private offices, the surveillance was entirely visual and did not include microphones, employees were informed that the videotaping would occur, and the cameras recorded only what was plainly visible on the surface. In short, the court held that the Fourth Amendment does not prohibit "management from observing electronically what it lawfully can see with the naked eye."[22] Likewise, the Fourth Amendment claim of an employee of a public university who was videotaped stealing money from the university box office failed.[23] Even though the video camera was hidden and she was not warned about being subject to video surveillance, the court concluded that her constitutional rights had not been violated. In reaching the conclusion that she had no reasonable expectation of privacy, the court relied heavily on the facts that her work area was open to view by both coworkers and the public and her job involved the handling of money. However, *although informing employees that they are subject to surveillance is clearly not necessary in all cases, employers are on surer legal ground if they inform employees that they are subject to monitoring and surveillance.*

In *Hernandez v. Hillsides*, a private sector employer's installation of a concealed video surveillance camera as part of a workplace investigation was challenged. The California Supreme Court's discussion of the employees' privacy claims is thorough and informative.

Hernandez v. Hillsides
47 Cal. 4th 272 (2009)

OPINION BY JUSTICE BAXTER:

Defendants ... (Hillsides), operated a private nonprofit residential facility for neglected and abused children, including the victims of sexual abuse. Plaintiffs Abigail Hernandez (Hernandez) and Maria-Jose Lopez (Lopez) were employed by Hillsides. * * *

Beginning in 2001, plaintiffs shared an office in the administrative building at Hillsides. Each woman had her own desk and computer workstation. The office had three windows on exterior walls. Blinds on the windows could be opened and closed. The office also had a door that could be closed and locked. A "doggie"

door near the bottom of the office door was missing its flap, creating a small, low opening into the office. Several people, besides plaintiffs, had keys to their office: five administrators, including [facility director] Hitchcock, and all of the program directors. * * * According to plaintiffs, they occasionally used their office to change or adjust their clothing. Hernandez replaced her work clothes with athletic wear before leaving Hillsides to exercise at the end of the day. Two or three times, Lopez raised her shirt to show Hernandez her post-pregnancy figure. Both women stated in their declarations that the blinds were

---

[22]*Vega-Rodriguez v. Puerto Rico Telephone Co.*, 110 F.3d 174, 180 (1st Cir. 1997).
[23]*Cowles v. State of Alaska*, 23 P.3d 1168 (Alaska 2001), *cert. denied*, 122 S. Ct. 1072 (2002).

drawn and the door was closed when this activity occurred. Hernandez also recalled the door being locked when she changed clothes.

On or before August 22, 2002, Hillsides circulated an "E-Mail, Voicemail and Computer Systems Policy." This document stated that it was intended to prevent employees from using Hillsides's electronic communications systems in a manner that defamed, harassed, or harmed others, or that subjected the company to "significant legal exposure." Illegal and inappropriate activity was prohibited, such as accessing sexually offensive Web sites or displaying, downloading, or distributing sexually explicit material. The policy further contemplated the use of electronic "[p]ersonal passwords." However, it warned employees that they had "no reasonable expectation of privacy in any … use of Company computers, network and system." Along the same lines, the policy advised that all data created, transmitted, downloaded, or stored on the system was Hillsides's property, and that the company could "monitor and record employee activity on its computers, network … and e-mail systems," including "e-mail messages[,] … files stored or transmitted[,] and … web sites accessed." * * *

In order to ensure compliance with Hillsides's computer policy and restrictions, Foster, the computer specialist, could retrieve and print a list of all Internet Web sites accessed from every computer on the premises. * * * In July 2002, Foster determined that numerous pornographic Web sites had been viewed in the late-night and early-morning hours from at least two different computers. One of them was located in the computer laboratory, or classroom. The other one sat on the desk Lopez used in the office she shared with Hernandez. The evidence indicated that Lopez's computer could have been accessed after hours by someone other than her, because she did not always log off before going home at night. Hitchcock explained in his deposition that employees were expected to turn off their computers when leaving work at the end of the day, that a personal password was required to log onto the computer again after it had been turned off, and that this policy was communicated orally to employees when their computers were first assigned. He admitted that he did not remind plaintiffs of this procedure before taking the surveillance steps at issue here. * * *

Foster told … Hitchcock about the inappropriate Internet use, and showed him printouts listing the pornographic Web sites that had been accessed. Given the

odd hours at which such activity had occurred, Hitchcock surmised that the perpetrator was a program director or other staff person who had unfettered access to Hillsides in the middle of the night. Hitchcock did not … suspect [the] plaintiffs. They typically were gone from the premises when the impermissible nighttime computer use occurred.

In light of these circumstances, Hitchcock decided to use video equipment Hillsides already had in its possession to record the perpetrator in the act of using the computers at night. He told other administrators about the problem and his surveillance plan. Hitchcock explained in both his deposition and declaration that he sought to protect the children from any staff person who might expose them to pornography, emphasizing the harm they had endured before entering Hillsides. * * * [B]ecause so many people used the laboratory for legitimate reasons during and after business hours, Hitchcock decided instead to conduct surveillance in the office that plaintiffs shared. He did not inform plaintiffs of this decision. He reasoned that the more people who knew and "gossiped" about the plan, the greater the chance the culprit would hear about it and never be identified or stopped.

Hence, at some point during the first week of October 2002, … video recording equipment [was installed] in plaintiffs' office and in a storage room nearby. First, in plaintiffs' office, they positioned a camera on the top shelf of a bookcase, among some plants, where it apparently was obscured from view. They also tucked a motion detector into the lap of a stuffed animal or toy sitting on a lower shelf of the same bookcase. Second, these devices connected remotely to a television that Hitchcock and Foster moved into the storage room. A videocassette recorder was built into the unit. The television had a 19-inch monitor on which images could be viewed. * * *

Hitchcock was not the only person with access to the storage room and the video surveillance equipment inside. Plaintiffs each stated in their declarations that "several supervisory employees and program directors had keys and access to that storage room." * * * Hitchcock rarely activated the camera and motion detector in plaintiffs' office, and never did so while they were there. * * * [T]he camera and motion detector were always disabled during the workday, such that "there was no picture showing" and "no recording going on" while plaintiffs were in their office. Hitchcock further stated that between installation of the equipment in early October 2002, and his decision to remove it three weeks later, no one was videotaped or caught using the computer in plaintiffs' office. He assumed that the culprit had learned about the camera and stopped engaging in unauthorized activity.

Meanwhile, about 4:30 p.m. on Friday, October 25, 2002, plaintiffs discovered the video equipment in their office. A red light on the motion detector flashed at the time. The cord attached to the camera was plugged into the wall and was hot to the touch. Shocked by the discovery, plaintiffs immediately reported it to two supervisors, Sylvia Levitan and Toni Aikins. Levitan called Hitchcock, who was at home. * * * A short time later, Hitchcock called Hernandez in her office. He apologized for installing the camera, and said the surveillance was not aimed at plaintiffs, but at an intruder who had used Lopez's computer to access inappropriate Web sites. Hernandez expressed concern that she was videotaped while changing her clothes or that "personal stuff" in her office was somehow disturbed. Hitchcock replied by assuring Hernandez that "the only time we activated that camera and the video recorder was after you left at night and [we] deactivated the two devices before you came to work in the morning…. [A]t no time did [we] ever capture [you] or [Lopez] on the tape." * * *

Based on the foregoing facts, the trial court found no triable issue as to any cause of action stated in the complaint, granted summary judgment in defendants' favor, and dismissed the action. The court agreed with defendants that there had been no intrusion on plaintiffs' reasonable expectations of privacy. * * * The Court of Appeal reversed as to the invasion-of-privacy count. Critical to the court's analysis on appeal was the placement in plaintiffs' office of a functioning hidden camera, capable of transmitting images that could be viewed or recorded by anyone who had access to the storage room and who activated the wireless remote controls. According to the appellate court, plaintiffs had a reasonable expectation to be free from this kind of intrusion in the workplace, notwithstanding evidence that they were never viewed or recorded and that they worked in a shared office to which others had access. * * * We granted review.

*** Defendants … argue … that they did nothing wrong in attempting to videotape a nighttime intruder using the computer in plaintiffs' office, because no private information about plaintiffs was obtained. Defendants insist that plaintiffs, not being the intended targets of the surveillance plan, were never viewed or recorded, and thereby suffered no serious or actionable intrusion into their private domain. Plaintiffs disagree and urge us to adopt the Court of Appeal's approach in the present case. They insist that defendants were able to view and record plaintiffs at will, without their knowledge or consent, and unjustifiably deprived them of the privacy they reasonably expected to have while working behind closed doors in their shared office.

The foregoing arguments have been framed throughout this action in terms of both the common law and the state Constitution. [Article I, section 1 of the California Constitution states: "All people are by nature free and independent and have inalienable rights. Among these are enjoying and defending life and liberty, acquiring, possessing, and protecting property, and pursuing and obtaining safety, happiness, and privacy."] These two sources of privacy protection "are not unrelated" under California law. * * *

A privacy violation based on the common law tort of intrusion has two elements. First, the defendant must intentionally intrude into a place, conversation, or matter as to which the plaintiff has a reasonable expectation of privacy. Second, the intrusion must occur in a manner highly offensive to a reasonable person. These limitations on the right to privacy are not insignificant. Nonetheless, the cause of action recognizes a measure of personal control over the individual's autonomy, dignity, and serenity. * * *

As to the first element of the common law tort, the defendant must have "penetrated some zone of physical or sensory privacy … or obtained unwanted access to data" by electronic or other covert means, in violation of the law or social norms. In either instance, the expectation of privacy must be "objectively reasonable." … [T]his court [has] linked the reasonableness of privacy expectations to such factors as (1) the identity of the intruder, (2) the extent to which other persons had access to the subject place, and could see or hear the plaintiff, and (3) the means by which the intrusion occurred. The second common law element essentially involves a "policy" determination as to whether the alleged intrusion is "highly offensive" under the particular circumstances. Relevant factors include the degree and setting of the intrusion, and the intruder's motives and objectives. Even in cases involving the use of photographic and electronic recording devices, which can raise difficult questions about covert surveillance, "California tort law provides no bright line on ['offensiveness']; each case must be taken on its facts."

The right to privacy in the California Constitution sets standards similar to the common law tort of intrusion. Under this provision, which creates at least a limited right of action against both private and government entities, the plaintiff must meet several requirements. First, he must possess a legally protected privacy interest. These interests include "conducting personal activities without observation, intrusion, or interference," as determined by "established social norms" derived from such sources as the "common law" and "statutory enactment." Second, the plaintiff's expectations of privacy must be reasonable. This element rests on an examination of "customs, practices, and physical settings surrounding particular activities," as well as the opportunity to be notified in advance and consent to the intrusion. Third, the plaintiff must show that the intrusion is so serious in "nature, scope, and actual or potential impact [as] to constitute an egregious breach of the social norms." ... [N]o constitutional violation occurs ... if the intrusion on privacy is justified by one or more competing interests. * * *

[W]e cannot conclude as a matter of law that the Court of Appeal erred in finding a prima facie case on the threshold question whether defendants' video surveillance measures intruded upon plaintiffs' reasonable expectations of privacy. Plaintiffs plausibly maintain that defendants cannot prevail on this element of the cause of action simply because they "never intended to view or record" plaintiffs, or because defendants did not "capture [plaintiffs'] images at all." Other significant factors not considered by defendants point favorably in plaintiffs' direction on this issue.

... [W]hile privacy expectations may be significantly diminished in the workplace, they are not lacking altogether. * * * [C]ourts have examined the physical layout of the area intruded upon, its relationship to the workplace as a whole, and the nature of the activities commonly performed in such places. At one end of the spectrum are settings in which work or business is conducted in an open and accessible space, within the sight and hearing not only of coworkers and supervisors, but also of customers, visitors, and the general public. At the other end of the spectrum are areas in the workplace subject to restricted access and limited view, and reserved exclusively for performing bodily functions or other

inherently personal acts. The present scenario falls between these extremes. Plaintiffs plausibly claim that Hillsides provided an enclosed office with a door that could be shut and locked, and window blinds that could be drawn, to allow the occupants to obtain some measure of refuge, to focus on their work, and to escape visual and aural interruptions from other sources, including their employer. Such a protective setting generates legitimate expectations that not all activities performed behind closed doors would be clerical and work related. As suggested by the evidence here, employees who share an office, and who have four walls that shield them from outside view (albeit, with a broken "doggie" flap on the door), may perform grooming or hygiene activities, or conduct personal conversations, during the workday. Privacy is not wholly lacking because the occupants of an office can see one another, or because colleagues, supervisors, visitors, and security and maintenance personnel have varying degrees of access.

... [A]nother relevant factor [is] the "means of intrusion." [E]mployees who retreat into a shared or solo office, and who perform work and personal activities in relative seclusion there, would not reasonably expect to be the subject of televised spying and secret filming by their employer. * * * Courts have acknowledged the intrusive effect for tort purposes of hidden cameras and video recorders in settings that otherwise seem private. It has been said that the "unblinking lens" can be more penetrating than the naked eye with respect to "duration, proximity, focus, and vantage point." Such monitoring and recording denies the actor a key feature of privacy—the right to control the dissemination of his image and actions. We have made clear that the "'mere fact that a person can be seen by someone does not automatically mean that he or she can legally be forced to be subject to being seen by everyone.'" * * *

As emphasized by defendants, the evidence shows that Hitchcock never viewed or recorded plaintiffs inside their office by means of the equipment he installed both there and in the storage room. He also did not intend or attempt to do so, and took steps to avoid capturing them on camera and videotape. While such factors bear on the offensiveness of the challenged conduct, as discussed below, we reject the defense suggestion that they preclude us from finding the requisite intrusion in the first place. In particular, Hitchcock hid the video equipment in plaintiffs' office from view in an apparent attempt to prevent anyone from discovering, avoiding, or dismantling it. He used a camera and motion detector small enough to tuck inside and around decorative items perched on different bookshelves, both high and low. Plaintiffs presumably would have been caught in the camera's sights if they had returned to work after hours, or if Hitchcock had been mistaken about them having left the office when he activated the system. Additionally, ... the means to activate the monitoring and recording functions were available around the clock, for three weeks, to anyone who had access to the storage room. * * *

[P]laintiffs cannot plausibly be found to have received warning that they would be subjected to the risk of such surveillance, or to have agreed to it in advance. We have said that notice of and consent to an impending intrusion can "inhibit reasonable expectations of privacy." Such factors also can "limit [an] intrusion upon personal dignity" by providing an opportunity for persons to regulate their conduct while being monitored. Here, however, the evidence shows that no one at Hillsides told plaintiffs that someone had used Lopez's computer to access pornographic Web sites. Nor were they told that Hitchcock planned to install surveillance equipment inside their office to catch the perpetrator on television and videotape. Moreover, nothing in Hillsides's written computer policy mentioned or even alluded to the latter scenario. As noted earlier, the version in effect at the relevant time made clear that any monitoring and recording of employee activity, and any resulting diminution in reasonable privacy expectations, were limited to "use of Company computers" in the form of "e-mail" messages, electronic "files," and "web site" data. * * * There is no evidence that employees like plaintiffs had any indication that Hillsides would take the next drastic step and use cameras and recording devices to view and videotape employees sitting at their desks and computer workstations, or moving around their offices within camera range.

In sum, the undisputed evidence seems clearly to support the first of two basic elements we have identified as necessary to establish a violation of privacy as alleged in plaintiffs' complaint. Defendants secretly installed a hidden video camera that was both operable and operating (electricity-wise), and that could be made to monitor and record activities inside plaintiffs' office, at will, by anyone who plugged in the receptors, and who had access to the remote location in which both the receptors and recording equipment were

located. The workplace policy, that by means within the computer system itself, plaintiffs would be monitored about the pattern and use of Web sites visited, to prevent abuse of Hillsides's computer system, is distinguishable from and does not necessarily create a social norm that in order to advance that same interest, a camera would be placed inside their office, and would be aimed toward a computer workstation to capture all human activity occurring there. Plaintiffs had no reasonable expectation that their employer would intrude so tangibly into their semiprivate office.

Plaintiffs must show more than an intrusion upon reasonable privacy expectations. Actionable invasions of privacy also must be "highly offensive" to a reasonable person. * * * In context, defendants took a measured approach in choosing the location to videotape the person who was misusing the computer system. Evidently, plaintiffs' office was *not* the preferred spot. Hitchcock initially tried to capture the culprit in the computer laboratory. Based on the consistently high level of human traffic he described there, the laboratory apparently was far more accessible and less secluded than plaintiffs' office. The surveillance equipment was moved to the latter location only after Hitchcock determined it was too difficult to pinpoint who was using computers inappropriately in the open, more public laboratory setting. Defendants' surveillance efforts also were largely confined to the area in which the unauthorized computer activity had occurred. Once the camera was placed in plaintiffs' office, it was aimed towards Lopez's desk and computer workstation. There is no evidence that Hitchcock intended or attempted to include Hernandez's desk in camera range. * * * Likewise, access to the storage room and knowledge of the surveillance equipment inside were limited. * * * The spot was relatively remote and secure. Timing considerations favor defendants as well.... [T]he surveillance equipment was operational during a fairly limited window of time. Hitchcock decided to remove the equipment (and plaintiffs coincidentally discovered it) a mere 21 days later, during which time no one had accessed Lopez's computer for pornographic purposes. We can infer from the undisputed evidence that Hitchcock kept abreast of his own monitoring activities, and did not expose plaintiffs to the risk of covert visual monitoring or video recording any longer than was necessary to determine that his plan would not work, and that the culprit probably had been scared away.

Defendants' actual surveillance activities also were quite limited in scope. On the one hand, the camera and motion detector in plaintiffs' office were always plugged into the electrical circuit and capable of operating the entire time they were in place. On the other hand, Hitchcock took the critical step of connecting the wireless receptors and activating the system only three times. At most, he was responsible for monitoring and recording inside of plaintiffs' office an average of only once a week for three weeks. Such measures were hardly excessive or egregious. Moreover, on each of these three occasions, Hitchcock connected the wireless devices and allowed the system to remotely monitor and record events inside plaintiffs' office only after their shifts ended, and after they normally left Hillsides's property. He never activated the system during regular business hours when plaintiffs were scheduled to work. The evidence shows they were not secretly viewed or taped while engaged in personal or clerical activities. * * *

This case does not involve surveillance measures conducted for socially repugnant or unprotected reasons. * * * The undisputed evidence is that defendants installed video surveillance equipment in plaintiffs' office … [because] an unknown staff person was engaged in unauthorized and inappropriate computer use at night. Given the apparent risks under existing law of doing nothing to avert the problem, and the limited range of available solutions, defendants' conduct was not highly offensive for purposes of establishing a tortious intrusion into private matters. * * *

For legitimate business reasons, employers commonly link their network servers to the Internet, and provide employees with computers that have direct access to the network and the Internet. As this phenomenon has grown, employers have adopted formal policies regulating the scope of appropriate computer and Internet use. Such policies contemplate reasonable monitoring efforts by employers, and authorize employee discipline for noncompliance. Despite efforts to control the problem, the potential for abuse of computer systems and Internet access in the workplace is wide-ranging. The consequences to employers may be serious. Here, Hitchcock learned that the computer in plaintiffs' office was being used to access the Internet late at night, long after their shifts ended, by someone not authorized to use that equipment or office. Data recorded and stored inside the computer system itself convinced Hitchcock and the computer specialist, Foster, that the unauthorized user was viewing sexually

explicit Web sites. * * * Such use of Hillsides's computer equipment by an employee violated written workplace policies circulated both before and after the challenged surveillance activities occurred. As those policies warned, and case law confirms, the offending conduct posed a risk that the perpetrator might expose Hillsides to legal liability from various quarters. * * *

Plaintiffs argue that even assuming defendants acted to prevent a rogue employee from accessing pornography on Hillsides's computers, and to minimize a genuine risk of liability and harm, no claim or defense of justification has been established as a matter of law. Plaintiffs insist triable issues exist as to whether defendants could have employed means less offensive than installing the camera in their office and connecting it to the monitor and recorder nearby. Examples include better enforcement of Hillsides's log-off/password-protection policy, installation of software filtering programs, closer nighttime monitoring of the camera outside the administration building, increased security patrols at night, and receipt of plaintiffs' informed consent to video surveillance.

… [D]efendants are not required to prove that there were no less intrusive means of accomplishing the legitimate objectives we have identified above in order to defeat the instant privacy claim. In the past, we have specifically declined to "impos[e] on a private organization, acting in a situation involving decreased expectations of privacy, the burden of justifying its conduct as the 'least offensive alternative' possible under the circumstances." The argument lacks merit in any event. First, the alternatives that plaintiffs propose would not necessarily have achieved at least one of defendants' aims—determining whether a program director was accessing pornographic Web sites in plaintiffs' office. Rather, it is the same suspect group of program directors on whom plaintiffs would have had defendants more heavily rely to monitor exterior cameras and perform office patrols. Obtaining plaintiffs' consent also might have risked disclosing the surveillance plan to other employees, including the program directors. With respect to stricter regulation of employee computer use (software filters and log-off enforcement), such steps might have stopped the improper use of Lopez's computer. However, they would not have helped defendants identify the employee who performed such activity and who posed a risk of liability and harm in the workplace. * * *

We appreciate plaintiffs' dismay over the discovery of video equipment—small, blinking, and hot to the touch—that their employer had hidden among their personal effects in an office that was reasonably secluded from public access and view. Nothing we say here is meant to encourage such surveillance measures, particularly in the absence of adequate notice to persons within camera range that their actions may be viewed and taped. Nevertheless, considering all the relevant circumstances, plaintiffs have not established, and cannot reasonably expect to establish, that the particular conduct of defendants that is challenged in this case was highly offensive and constituted an egregious violation of prevailing social norms. * * *

We therefore reverse the judgment of the Court of Appeal * * *

CASE QUESTIONS

1. What were the legal issues in this case? What did the California Supreme Court decide?
2. How intrusive was the employer's surveillance? Why does the Court conclude that the plaintiffs had a reasonable expectation of privacy that was violated by their employer?
3. Why does the Court nonetheless rule for the employer?
4. How convincing is the Court's argument that potentially effective, but less intrusive, means of dealing with the situation were not available to the employer?
5. Would the outcome of the case have been different if the video surveillance occurred throughout the work day? If one of the plaintiffs had been filmed while changing clothes? Why or why not?

One circumstance in which videotaping employees has been successfully challenged is when the cameras were trained on individuals engaging in protected concerted activity. Thus, an employer violated the NLRA when it videotaped and photographed employees who were distributing union literature at the entrance to the plant. The surveillance began after a minor confrontation between a human resources manager and a prounion employee, but the fact that it continued regardless of whether any managers were present cast doubt on the employer's stated motive of protecting managers against false claims of assault and battery. The court concluded that the employer cited "no legal justification for its indiscriminate videotaping of employees who handed out union literature; under these circumstances, the NLRB's finding of a violation was proper."[24] The reason is that surveillance under these circumstances tends to be coercive and interferes with the exercise of NLRA rights. When a union is already in place, employers generally have an obligation to bargain with the union over the installation of video surveillance.[25] *Employers must not conduct surveillance of employees engaged in protected concerted activities, including union organizing.*

Video surveillance that occurs off the job is more likely to run afoul of privacy law than surveillance in the workplace. Many of these cases involve employers enlisting investigators to determine whether employees claiming workers' compensation or disability benefits are really unable to work. In one such case, an employee receiving workers' compensation for treatment of a back problem mentioned that his hobby was riding a motorcycle. A private investigator hired by the company videotaped the employee engaging in various activities around his house, including riding his motorcycle. On the basis of the video, the employer contested the employee's workers' compensation claim, and the employee sued for invasion of privacy (intrusion upon seclusion). The court concluded that the videotaping was legal because it captured him moving about in public.[26] However, if the investigator had trespassed or filmed activities transpiring

[24]*The Timken Co. v. NLRB*, 29 Fed. Appx. 266, 269 (6th Cir. 2002).
[25]*Brewers and Maltsters, Local 6 v. NLRB*, 414 F.3d 36 (D.C. Cir. 2005).
[26]*York v. General Electric Co.*, 759 N.E.2d 865 (Ohio App. 2001), *appeal not allowed*, 756 N.E.2d 116 (2001).

inside the home, the outcome would have been different. *Surveillance of employees outside the workplace, if it occurs at all, must be limited to public areas.*

Clippings

The growth of social media seems to have transformed the concept of privacy for many people. Divulging information about oneself and broadcasting even mundane aspects of daily life to numerous, often unknown, others has become common place. Besides the likes of Facebook, LinkedIn, and Twitter, there are applications that announce all of one's purchases, post personal photos updated daily, evaluate entertainment events in real time, and track one's precise whereabouts throughout the day. Beyond the practical issues of increased risk of identity theft, exploitation by marketers, and theft of physical possessions by criminals who have been conveniently informed of a person's whereabouts, this apparent need to disclose information that not so long ago would have been regarded as personal and private raises questions about how far one has to go these days before infringing on privacy. As one 38-year-old consultant and heavy user of social media put it, "I simply have nothing to hide."

Brad Stone. "Too Much Information? Hah! Sharing All Online Is the Point." *New York Times* (April 23, 2010), A1.

Electronic Communications

Computers and other electronic information processing and communications devices are ubiquitous in the workplace and elsewhere. Attempts by employers to monitor and control these communications have posed profound privacy issues.

THE CHANGING WORKPLACE

The Electronic Workplace and Employee Privacy

Most employees spend a good part of their workday, and often nonwork time as well, tethered to communications and information-processing devices. These range from the venerable telephone to voicemail systems, pagers, PDAs, e-mail, the Internet, and wireless tracking systems, among many other items. This reliance on electronic communications devices opens new vistas for the monitoring and surveillance of employees. It is now relatively easy for employers to monitor every keystroke entered by an employee, the contents of an employee's computer screen at any point in time, stored e-mails, Internet sites visited, and the employee's whereabouts. An American Management Association survey of 304 U.S. employers in 2007 found that 66 percent monitored the Internet sites visited by at least some of their employees; 65 percent blocked access to Internet sites deemed inappropriate; 45 percent monitored employees' file contents, key strokes, or time spent at the keyboard; 43 percent monitored employee e-mail; 48 percent engaged in video surveillance of at least some work areas; 45 percent tracked time spent on phone calls and the numbers called; 12 percent monitored the blogosphere to find out what was being said about their companies; 10 percent of employers reported monitoring social networking sites; and 8 percent used GPS to track employees operating company vehicles.[1] All this monitoring and tracking has had consequences for employees beyond puncturing illusions of privacy. Of the responding employers, 30 percent had terminated employees for misuse of the Internet, while 28 percent had dismissed workers for misuse of e-mail. Although the use of GPS and radio frequency identification (RFID) to track employees does not appear to be widespread at this point, many commentators are particularly concerned about the privacy implications of these technologies.[2] GPS and other location-detection technology can readily be embedded in cell phones, company vehicles, uniforms, and ID badges. Indeed, it is even possible to implant RFID chips beneath the skin of employees and several states now prohibit employers from requiring employees to submit to this procedure.[3] The possibility that tracking technology can be used to keep tabs on employees when they are off the job or to map the locations of employees to identify activities such as union organizing seems quite real. The use by employers of biometric devices such as palm scanners, iris scanners, and fingerprint readers also appears to be on the rise.[4]

Nor is monitoring employees' activities online limited to use of company computer equipment during work time. Employers have taken action against bloggers based on the contents of their blogs, even when the blogging was done on home computers. A number of employers have attempted to obtain court orders forcing Internet service providers to divulge the identities of individuals making comments critical of the companies (and arguably defamatory). This is often used as a means of identifying the offending employees, who are then terminated, rather than sued.[5] In a case involving flight attendants at Northwest Airlines, a court ordered flight attendants to turn over their personal computers to a neutral third party that would check the contents of their hard drives for evidence in a court case brought by the airline.[6] Northwest had claimed that the flight attendants were using their computers to orchestrate an illegal "sickout" in violation of the Railway Labor Act.

Employers cite numerous reasons for monitoring employees through electronic means, including the need to ensure that work time is being used productively, workplace security is maintained, company equipment is not misused, and trade secrets and other confidential information are not being divulged. Legal concerns—including preventing sexual harassment through the distribution of downloaded pornography or via offensive e-mails from coworkers—are also cited as prime reasons for monitoring computer use. A New Jersey court decision adds some force to

this argument. In this sad case, an employee spent large amounts of work time accessing and downloading pictures from pornographic Web sites, including child pornography. The employee took nude pictures of his young stepdaughter and transmitted them to a Web site featuring child pornography. The employee's activities went on for several years and were well known to supervisors and coworkers alike, but no official action was taken against the employee. Following the employee's arrest on child pornography charges, the girl's mother sued the employer. The court concluded:

> [A]n employer who is on notice that one of its employees is using a workplace computer to access pornography, possibly child pornography, has a duty to investigate the employee's actions and to take prompt and effective action to stop the unauthorized activity, lest it result in harm to innocent third-parties.[7]

Ironically, the employer in this case attempted to argue that it could not conduct such an investigation because doing so would infringe upon the privacy rights of the employee. The court dismissed this argument, holding that "[W]e readily conclude that Employee had no legitimate expectation of privacy that would prevent his employer from accessing his computer to determine if he was using it to view adult or child pornography."[8]

According to the American Management Association, most (80–85 percent) employers that engage in electronic monitoring or surveillance inform employees of that fact, often through formal policies.[9] There is general consensus that such policies, while not strictly necessary, are advisable. They provide clear indications of the extent to which any expectations of privacy are reasonable. *In general, policies should place bounds on employee use of electronic communications for purposes other than completing work assignments, rather than attempt to strictly prohibit all such communications.* IBM's "Blogging Policy and Guidelines" encourages blogging but spells out a set of guidelines for bloggers to follow (e.g., identify yourself, make it clear that you are not speaking on behalf of the company, don't provide confidential or proprietary information).[10] *Policies should address not only the type of monitoring or surveillance engaged in, but also how the resulting information will be used, how long such information will be stored, and how it will be kept secure.* Ultimately, the legitimate business purposes for monitoring and surveillance have to be balanced against the greater stress this places on employees and the negative implications for working relationships based on trust.[11]

[1]Susan R. Hobbs. "Employer Monitoring of Workers' Activities on Internet on the Rise, Survey Finds." *Daily Labor Report* 41 (March 3, 2008), A-10.

[2]John Sullivan. "Use of GPS Technology Said to Be Growing, but Monitoring Leads to Privacy Concerns." *Daily Labor Report* 228 (November 29, 2004), A-5.

[3]Marisa Anne Pagnattaro. "Getting Under Your Skin—Literally: RFID in the Employment Context." *University of Illinois Journal of Law, Technology & Policy* (Fall 2008), 247–49.

[4]David B. Caruso. "Fingerprint, Palm Scanners Help Companies Track Workers; Some Grumble about Intrusion." (March 27, 2008) (http://www.startribune.com).

[5]Margo E. K. Reder and Christine Neylon O'Brien. "Corporate Cybersmear: Employers File John Doe Defamation Lawsuits Seeking the Identity of Anonymous Employee Internet Posters." *Michigan Telecommunication and Technology Law Review* 8 (2001/2002), 195.

[6]*Northwest Airlines v. International Brotherhood of Teamsters, Local 2000*, 2000 U.S. Dist. LEXIS 22638 (D. Minn.).

[7]*Doe v. XYC Corporation*, 2005 N.J. Super. LEXIS 377, 1–2 (App. Div.).

[8]*Doe*, at 25.

[9]American Management Association. "2005 *Electronic Monitoring & Surveillance Survey:* Many Companies Monitoring, Recording, Videotaping—and Firing—Employees." Viewed June 22, 2005 (http://www.amanet.org).

[10]IBM Corp. "IBM Blogging Policy and Guidelines." (May 16, 2005).

[11]Michael R. Triplett. "As Employee Monitoring Expands, Attention Turns to Information, Policies." *Daily Labor Report* 46 (March 10, 2005), C-2.

The **Electronic Communications Privacy Act (ECPA)**[27] has been used to challenge employer incursions on the privacy of electronic communications. The ECPA amended existing federal wiretapping laws. *Employers (and others) are prohibited from intentionally intercepting (through the use of electronic, mechanical, or other devices) wire, oral, or electronic communications and from disclosing such information. The intentional, unauthorized accessing and disclosure of stored electronic communications are also prohibited.* Intent is an important element of ECPA claims. In one relevant case, hospital employees alleged that one of their coworkers covertly turned on a dictation machine and thereby illegally recorded and reported to hospital officials conversations critical of the hospital administration. Whether the dictation machine had been activated intentionally or simply left on by a prior user was disputed by the parties. The ECPA claims against individual hospital officials were dismissed because the officials had no reason to believe that the recording might have been obtained illegally, but the claims against the hospital and coworker were allowed to proceed since whether the interception was intentional or inadvertent was a material issue that would have to be resolved at trial.[28]

The distinction between intercepting and accessing has proven troublesome to apply to communications such as e-mail and Internet sites. Courts have generally held that the stricter penalties associated with interception apply only when a communication is obtained at the same time it is sent. One such case involved an agent for Nationwide Insurance who allegedly sent e-mails to two competitors, inquiring about their interest in obtaining some of Nationwide's policyholders. When Nationwide became aware of the e-mails, it searched the file server on which the agent's e-mails were stored for e-mails to or from the agent that might show similar behavior. On the basis of the search, the agent's contract (he was an independent contractor) was terminated. The court concluded:

> *While Congress's definition of "intercept" does not appear to fit with its intent to extend protection to electronic communications, it is for Congress to cover the bases untouched. We adopt the reasoning of our sister circuits and therefore hold that there has been no "intercept" within the meaning of Title I of ECPA.*[29]

[27]18 U.S.C.A. §§ 2510 *et seq.* (2011).

[28]*McCann v. Iroquois Memorial Hospital*, 622 F.3d 745 (7th Cir. 2010).

[29]*Fraser v. Nationwide Mutual Insurance*, 352 F.3d 107, 114 (3d Cir. 2003).

The agent was also not able to show that the search of his stored e-mails was illegal. Because the e-mail was stored on Nationwide's system and providers of a communication service are specifically exempted from the ECPA's restrictions on unauthorized accessing of stored communications, there was no ECPA violation.

ECPA cases involving e-mails and other forms of electronic communication not amenable to interception because they are stored prior to retrieval focus instead on whether there has been unauthorized accessing or disclosure of a stored communication (i.e., on the part of the ECPA known as the Stored Communications Act). In the case of a vice president of marketing with a personal, password-protected AOL e-mail account that she sometimes used at work, the covert accessing by her employer of hundreds of her AOL e-mails both during and following her employment violated the Stored Communications Act (SCA).[30] Likewise, the electronic communications provider of a text messaging system for a police department violated the SCA by providing the department with transcripts of employee messages.[31] Even though the police department paid for the service, they were not the intended recipients of the communications and the contents of the text messages could not be lawfully divulged to them.

There are some notable exceptions to the ECPA's general requirements. Interceptions are legal if prior consent to them was granted. Providers of wire or electronic communication services are exempted from the law's requirements to the extent that such activities are necessary to render service or protect their rights and property. Additionally, business users of equipment furnished by providers are exempted to the extent that such equipment is used in the **ordinary course of business**. This term refers to uses that are routine, for legitimate business purposes, and about which employees are notified. In the context of telephone conversations, this means that *employers can use additional extensions on business phones to monitor business calls for service quality or other business purposes but cannot listen in on personal calls.* (State laws are sometimes more restrictive, including requiring notification to all parties that calls are subject to monitoring.) *Personal calls can be monitored only to the degree needed to determine that they are indeed personal.* Thus, an employer violated the ECPA by intercepting, tape recording, and listening to all of its employees' personal calls.[32] Likewise, the business user exception did not shield a police department from an ECPA violation when, without a warrant, it tapped a police officer's pager because it believed that he was in cahoots with drug dealers. (He wasn't.) This covert monitoring without any notification was not in the ordinary course of the police department's business.[33] Under the stored communications provisions of the ECPA, only the provider of the electronic communications service on which the message is stored and users of that service (with respect to messages intended for them) can authorize the accessing of stored communications.[34]

In *Stengart v. Loving Care Agency*, the New Jersey Supreme Court considers the extent of an employee's reasonable expectation of privacy with respect to e-mails between the employee and her attorney. Even though the case is not a privacy claim against her employer, the Court's treatment of privacy issues is central to the decision.

---

[30]*Van Alstyne v. Electronic Scriptorium*, 560 F.3d 199 (4th Cir. 2009) (remanded for consideration of appropriate damages for the SCA violation).

[31]*Quon v. Arch Wireless Operating Co. and City of Ontario, CA*, 529 F.3d 892 (9th Cir. 2008), *reversed on other grounds, City of Ontario, CA v. Quon*, 130 S. Ct. 2619 (2010).

[32]*Smith v. Devers Insurance Agency*, 2002 U.S. Dist. LEXIS 1125 (M.D. Ala.).

[33]*Adams v. City of Battle Creek*, 250 F.3d 980, 984 (6th Cir. 2001).

[34]18 U.S.C.S. § 2701 (c) (2011).

Stengart v. Loving Care Agency
201 N.J. 300 (2010)

OPINION BY CHIEF JUSTICE RABNER:

In the past twenty years, businesses and private citizens alike have embraced the use of computers, electronic communication devices, the Internet, and e-mail. * * * In the modern workplace … personal use of the Internet is commonplace. Yet that simple act can raise complex issues about an employer's monitoring of the workplace and an employee's reasonable expectation of privacy.

This case presents novel questions about the extent to which an employee can expect privacy and confidentiality in personal e-mails with her attorney, which she accessed on a computer belonging to her employer. Marina Stengart used her company-issued laptop to exchange e-mails with her lawyer through her personal, password-protected, web-based e-mail account. She later filed an employment discrimination lawsuit against her employer, Loving Care Agency, Inc. (Loving Care), and others. In anticipation of discovery, Loving Care hired a computer forensic expert to recover all files stored on the laptop including the e-mails, which had been automatically saved on the hard drive. Loving Care's attorneys reviewed the e-mails and used information culled from them in the course of discovery. In response, Stengart's lawyer demanded that communications between him and Stengart, which he considered privileged, be identified and returned. Opposing counsel disclosed the documents but maintained that the company had the right to review them. Stengart then sought relief in court.

The trial court ruled that, in light of the company's written policy on electronic communications, Stengart waived the attorney-client privilege by sending e-mails on a company computer. The Appellate Division reversed and found that Loving Care's counsel had violated [rules of professional conduct] by reading and using the privileged documents. We hold that, under the circumstances, Stengart could reasonably expect that e-mail communications with her lawyer through her personal account would remain private, and that sending and receiving them via a company laptop did not eliminate the attorney-client privilege that protected them. By reading e-mails that were at least arguably privileged and failing to notify Stengart promptly about them, Loving Care's counsel [acted improperly] …. * * *

Loving Care provides home-care nursing and health services. Stengart began working for Loving Care in 1994 and, over time, was promoted to Executive Director of Nursing. The company provided her with a laptop computer to conduct company business. From that laptop, Stengart could send e-mails using her company e-mail address; she could also access the Internet and visit websites through Loving Care's server. Unbeknownst to Stengart, certain browser software in place automatically made a copy of each web page she viewed, which was then saved on the computer's hard drive in a "cache" folder of temporary Internet files. Unless deleted and overwritten with new data, those temporary Internet files remained on the hard drive.

On several days in December 2007, Stengart used her laptop to access a personal, password-protected e-mail account on Yahoo's website, through which she communicated with her attorney about her situation at work. She never saved her Yahoo ID or password on the company laptop. Not long after, Stengart left her employment with Loving Care and returned the laptop. On February 7, 2008, she filed the pending complaint. In an effort to preserve electronic evidence for discovery, in or around April 2008, Loving Care hired experts to create a forensic image of the laptop's hard drive. Among the items retrieved were temporary Internet files containing the contents of seven or eight e-mails Stengart had exchanged with her lawyer via her Yahoo account. * * *

A legend appears at the bottom of the e-mails that Stengart's lawyer sent. It warns readers that

THE INFORMATION CONTAINED IN THIS EMAIL COMMUNICATION IS INTENDED ONLY FOR THE PERSONAL AND CONFIDENTIAL USE OF THE DESIGNATED RECIPIENT NAMED ABOVE. This message may be an Attorney-Client communication, and as such is privileged and confidential. If the reader of this message is not the intended recipient, you are hereby notified that you have received this communication in error, and that your review, dissemination, distribution, or copying of the message is strictly prohibited. If you have received this transmission in error, please destroy this transmission and notify us immediately by telephone and/or reply email.

At least two attorneys from the law firm representing Loving Care, … (the "Firm"), reviewed the e-mail communications between Stengart and her attorney. The Firm did not advise opposing counsel about the e-mails until months later. * * * Stengart's attorney sent a letter demanding that the Firm identify and return all "attorney-client privileged communications" in its possession. The Firm identified and disclosed the e-mails but asserted that Stengart had no reasonable expectation of privacy in files on a company-owned computer in light of the company's policy on electronic communications.

Loving Care and its counsel relied on an Administrative and Office Staff Employee Handbook that they maintain contains the company's Electronic Communication policy (Policy). * * * The proffered Policy states, in relevant part:

> *The company reserves and will exercise the right to review, audit, intercept, access, and disclose all matters on the company's media systems and services at any time, with or without notice.*
>
> *E-mail and voice mail messages, internet use and communication and computer files are considered part of the company's business and client records. Such communications are not to be considered private or personal to any individual employee.*
>
> *The principal purpose of electronic mail (e-mail) is for company business communications. Occasional personal use is permitted; however, the system should not be used to solicit for outside business ventures, charitable organizations, or for any political or religious purpose, unless authorized by the Director of Human Resources.*

The Policy also specifically prohibits "[c]ertain uses of the e-mail system" including sending inappropriate sexual, discriminatory, or harassing messages, chain letters, "[m]essages in violation of government laws," or messages relating to job searches, business activities unrelated to Loving Care, or political activities. The Policy concludes with the following warning: "Abuse of the electronic communications system may result in disciplinary action up to and including separation of employment."

* * * Loving Care argues that its employees have no expectation of privacy in their use of company computers based on the company's Policy. In its briefs before this Court, the company also asserts that by accessing e-mails on a personal account through Loving Care's computer and server, Stengart either prevented any attorney-client privilege from attaching or waived the privilege by voluntarily subjecting her e-mails to company scrutiny. * * * Stengart argues that she intended the e-mails with her lawyer to be confidential and that the Policy, even if it applied to her, failed to provide adequate warning that Loving Care would save on a hard drive, or monitor the contents of, e-mails sent from a personal account. Stengart also maintains that the communications with her lawyer were privileged. * * *

We start by examining the meaning and scope of the Policy itself. The Policy specifically reserves to Loving Care the right to review and access "all matters on the company's media systems and services at any time." In addition, e-mail messages are plainly "considered part of the company's business … records." It is not clear from that language whether the use of personal, password-protected, web-based e-mail accounts via company equipment is covered. The Policy uses general language to refer to its "media systems and services" but does not define those terms. Elsewhere, the Policy prohibits certain uses of "the e-mail system," which appears to be a reference to company e-mail accounts. The Policy does not address personal accounts at all. In other words, employees do not have express notice that messages sent or received on a personal, web-based e-mail account are subject to monitoring if company equipment is used to access the account. The Policy also does not warn employees that the contents of such e-mails are stored on a hard drive and can be forensically retrieved and read by Loving Care. The Policy goes on to declare that e-mails "are not to be considered private or personal to any individual employee." In the very next point, the Policy acknowledges that "[o]ccasional personal use [of e-mail] is permitted." As written, the Policy creates ambiguity about whether personal e-mail use is company or private property. * * *

Under the particular circumstances presented, how should a court evaluate whether Stengart had a reasonable expectation of privacy in the e-mails she exchanged with her attorney? Preliminarily, we note that the reasonable-expectation-of-privacy standard used by the parties derives from the common law and [constitutional law]…. The latter sources do not apply in this case, which involves conduct by private parties only. The common law source is the tort of "intrusion on seclusion"…. [It] provides that "[o]ne who intentionally intrudes, physically or otherwise, upon the solitude or seclusion of another or his private affairs or concerns, is subject to liability to the other for invasion of his privacy, if the intrusion would be highly offensive to a reasonable person." A high threshold must be cleared to assert a cause of action based on that tort. A plaintiff must establish that the intrusion "would be highly offensive to the ordinary reasonable man, as the result of conduct to which the reasonable man would strongly object." * * *

A number of courts have tested an employee's claim of privacy in files stored on company computers by evaluating the reasonableness of the employee's expectation. No reported decisions in New Jersey offer direct guidance for the facts of this case. * * *

Certain decisions from outside New Jersey … are more instructive. Among them, *National Economic Research Associates v. Evans* [a 2006 Massachusetts case], is most analogous to the facts here. In *Evans*, an employee used a company laptop to send and receive attorney-client communications by e-mail. In doing so, he used his personal, password-protected Yahoo account and not the company's e-mail address. The e-mails were automatically stored in a temporary Internet file on the computer's hard drive and were later retrieved by a computer forensic expert. The expert recovered various attorney-client e-mails; at the instruction of the company's lawyer, those e-mails were not reviewed pending guidance from the court. A company manual governed the laptop's use. The manual permitted personal use of e-mail, to "be kept to a minimum," but warned that computer resources were the "property of the Company" and that e-mails were "not confidential" and could be read "during routine checks." The court denied the company's application to allow disclosure of the e-mails that its expert possessed. The court reasoned,

> *Based on the warnings furnished in the Manual, Evans [(the employee)] could not reasonably expect to communicate in confidence with his private attorney if Evans e-mailed his attorney using his NERA [(company)] e-mail address through the NERA Intranet, because the Manual plainly warned Evans that e-mails on the network could be read by NERA network administrators. The Manual, however, did not expressly declare that it would monitor the content of Internet communications…. Most importantly, the Manual did not expressly declare, or even implicitly suggest, that NERA would monitor the content of e-mail communications made from an employee's personal e-mail account via the Internet whenever those communications were*
>
> *viewed on a NERA-issued computer. Nor did NERA warn its employees that the content of such Internet e-mail communications is stored on the hard disk of a NERA-issued computer and therefore capable of being read by NERA.*

As a result, the court found the employee's expectation of privacy in e-mails with his attorney to be reasonable.

In Asia Global, the Bankruptcy Court for the Southern District of New York considered whether a bankruptcy trustee could force the production of e-mails sent by company employees to their personal attorneys on the company's e-mail system. The court developed a four-part test to "measure the employee's expectation of privacy in his computer files and e-mail": (1) does the corporation maintain a policy banning personal or other objectionable use, (2) does the company monitor the use of the employee's computer or e-mail, (3) do third parties have a right of access to the computer or e-mails, and (4) did the corporation notify the employee, or was the employee aware, of the use and monitoring policies? Because the evidence was "equivocal" about the existence of a corporate policy banning personal use of e-mail and allowing monitoring, the court could not conclude that the employees' use of the company e-mail system eliminated any applicable attorney-client privilege. * * *

According to some courts, employees appear to have a lesser expectation of privacy when they communicate with an attorney using a company e-mail system as compared to a personal, web-based account like the one used here. As a result, courts might treat e-mails transmitted via an employer's e-mail account differently than they would web-based e-mails sent on the same company computer. Courts have also found that the existence of a clear company policy banning personal e-mails can also diminish the reasonableness of an employee's claim to privacy in e-mail messages with his or her attorney. We recognize that a zero-tolerance policy can be unworkable and unwelcome in today's dynamic and mobile workforce and do not seek to encourage that approach in any way. The location of the company's computer may also be a relevant consideration. In [one relevant case] … an employee working from a home office sent e-mails to her attorney on a company laptop via her personal AOL account. Those messages did not go through the company's servers but were nonetheless retrievable. Notwithstanding a company policy banning personal use, the trial court found that the e-mails were privileged. * * *

Applying the above considerations to the facts before us, we find that Stengart had a reasonable expectation of privacy in the e-mails she exchanged with her attorney on Loving Care's laptop. Stengart plainly took steps to protect the privacy of those emails and shield them from her employer. She used a personal, password-protected e-mail account instead of her company e-mail address and did not save the account's password on her computer. In other words, she had a subjective expectation of privacy in messages to and from her lawyer discussing the subject of a future lawsuit.

In light of the language of the Policy and the attorney-client nature of the communications, her expectation of privacy was also objectively reasonable. As noted earlier, the Policy does not address the use of personal, web-based e-mail accounts accessed through company equipment. It does not address personal accounts at all. Nor does it warn employees that the contents of e-mails sent via personal accounts can be forensically retrieved and read by the company. Indeed, in acknowledging that occasional personal use of e-mail is permitted, the Policy created doubt about whether those e-mails are company or private property. Moreover, the e-mails are not illegal or inappropriate material stored on Loving Care's equipment, which might harm the company in some way. They are conversations between a lawyer and client about confidential legal matters, which are historically cloaked in privacy. * * * In addition, the e-mails bear a standard hallmark of attorney-client messages. They warn the reader directly that the e-mails are personal, confidential, and may be attorney-client communications. * * *

Under all of the circumstances, we find that Stengart could reasonably expect that e-mails she exchanged with her attorney on her personal, password-protected, web-based e-mail account, accessed on a company laptop, would remain private. It follows that the attorney-client privilege protects those e-mails. * * *

Our conclusion that Stengart had an expectation of privacy in e-mails with her lawyer does not mean that employers cannot monitor or regulate the use of workplace computers. Companies can adopt lawful policies relating to computer use to protect the assets, reputation, and productivity of a business and to ensure compliance with legitimate corporate policies. And employers can enforce such policies. They may discipline employees and, when appropriate, terminate them, for violating proper workplace rules that are not inconsistent with a clear mandate of public policy. For example, an employee who spends long stretches of the workday getting personal, confidential legal advice from a private lawyer may be disciplined for violating a policy permitting only occasional personal use of the Internet. But employers have no need or basis to read the specific contents of personal, privileged, attorney-client communications in order to enforce corporate policy. Because of the important public policy concerns underlying the attorney-client privilege, even a more clearly written company manual—that is, a policy that banned all personal computer use and provided unambiguous notice that an employer could retrieve and read an employee's attorney-client communications, if accessed on a personal, password-protected e-mail account using the company's computer system—would not be enforceable. * * *

CASE QUESTIONS

1. What were the legal issues in this case? What did the New Jersey Supreme Court decide?
2. Why does the Court conclude that the plaintiff had a reasonable expectation of privacy in her e-mail communications with her lawyer? Why was the computer use policy not sufficient to extinguish any expectation of privacy?
3. This case was not brought as a privacy tort claim, but what if it had been? Was the intrusion of the sort that would be highly offensive to a reasonable person?
4. To what extent is this decision tied to the fact that an attorney-client communication was involved? Does the outcome of this case suggest that the Court would rule on behalf of a plaintiff in a privacy tort claim based on some other type of communication using company property but not the company e-mail address or intranet? Why or why not?
5. What are some practical implications of this case for employers?

Overall, employees have fared poorly in privacy claims, whether based on the ECPA or other grounds, concerning e-mail or use of employer-provided computers. Employees are well-advised to not assume that their e-mails and other electronic communications are not going to be read by their employers, particularly when the employers are the providers of the communication system. An intrusion upon seclusion claim based on an employer's review of e-mail stored in a "personal folder" (with a separate password created by the employee) failed. The employee had been accused of sexual harassment and other offenses. While he was suspended, the company decrypted his personal password and gained access to his e-mails. The court likened the arrangement to a locker for which the employer retains the combination or a master key and found that the employee had no reasonable expectation of privacy.[35] Similarly, an employee whose intemperate e-mail remarks about company personnel were read by management, resulting in his discharge, was unsuccessful in his common law privacy (and wrongful discharge) claims. Despite the fact that employees were told by the company that their e-mail communications were confidential and would not be read by management, the employee was deemed not to have had a reasonable expectation of privacy. The court pointed to the voluntary nature of his statements and the fact that they were made on a company-provided network. Further, the court held that "the company's interest in preventing inappropriate and unprofessional comments or even illegal activity over its e-mail system would outweigh [the employee's] claimed privacy interest in those communications" in any event.[36] In another case, an employee alleged that he was terminated to keep him from obtaining stock to which he was entitled, whereas his employer claimed that he was terminated for repeatedly accessing pornographic sites on his computer at work. The employer had provided another computer for him to work on at home and went to court to obtain an order directing the employee to turn over that computer with the contents of its hard drive intact. The court reasoned that the employee had no reasonable expectation of privacy in the contents of the computer because even though it was used at home, it was still the employer's property and subject to its computer use policy. The court also asserted the existence of a "community norm," in which it is now accepted practice for employers to monitor employee computer use.[37] Even cases involving communications between employees and their attorneys do not necessarily go employees' way. A court rejected a claim that communications with an attorney via a company's e-mail system were protected by attorney-client privilege when company policy prohibited personal communications and advised employees that all electronic communications were subject to monitoring. As the court put it, "the circumstances of this case were akin to consulting her lawyer in her employer's conference room, in a loud voice, with the door open, so that any reasonable person would expect that their discussion of her complaints about her employer would be overheard by him."[38]

Practical Considerations How, if at all, should employers go about monitoring the Internet activities and other computer use of employees?

Perhaps cases such as *Stengart* signal growing judicial sensitivity to the privacy issues surrounding employees' electronic communications.[39] But it is important to not overstate the matter. The ECPA case mentioned earlier in which a police department obtained transcripts of officers' text messages also led to a Fourth Amendment privacy claim against the department.[40] An appeals court ruled for the officers and made a fairly

---

[35]*McLaren v. Microsoft Corp.*, 1999 Tex. App. LEXIS 4103 (5th Dist.).

[36]*Smyth v. The Pillsbury Co.*, 914 F. Supp. 97, 101 (E.D. Pa. 1996).

[37]*TBG Insurance Services v. Zieminski*, 96 Cal. App. 4th 443 (2002), *review denied*, 2002 Cal. LEXIS 3819.

[38]*Holmes v. Petrovich Development Co.*, 191 Cal. App. 4th 1047, 1051 (Ct. App. 2011).

[39]Dionne Searcey. "Some Courts Raise Bar on Reading Employee Email." *Wall Street Journal* (November 19, 2009) (http://online.wsj.com/).

[40]*Quon.*

strong statement regarding employees' reasonable expectations of privacy in their electronic communications—even in the face of a general computer use policy that alerted officers to the possibility that their electronic communications would be monitored. However, the department also had an established practice of not reviewing messages when overages (i.e., officers exceeding the maximum number of characters allowed) occurred. Ultimately, the appeals court concluded that the officers had a reasonable expectation of privacy in the *contents* of their text messages (as opposed to the addresses to which they were sent or from which they were received) and that the search was unreasonable in its scope because less intrusive means were available for verifying the nature of the overage problem. However, the Supreme Court granted certiorari in the case and reversed the appeals court.[41] The Court's treatment of the reasonableness of employees' expectations of privacy in their electronic communications was highly equivocal:

> *The Court must proceed with care when considering the whole concept of privacy expectations in communications made on electronic equipment owned by a government employer. The judiciary risks error by elaborating too fully on the Fourth Amendment implications of emerging technology before its role in society has become clear. * * * Prudence counsels caution before the facts in the instant case are used to establish far-reaching premises that define the existence, and extent, of privacy expectations enjoyed by employees when using employer-provided communication devices. * * * At present, it is uncertain how workplace norms, and the law's treatment of them, will evolve.[42]*

The Court assumed without deciding that the officers had a reasonable expectation of privacy in the contents of their text messages, but ruled that the search of messages was not unreasonably broad and that public employers need not employ the least intrusive method available in order to be acting reasonably under the Fourth Amendment.

Investigation of Employee Conduct

The importance of conducting immediate and thorough investigations of allegations of sexual harassment was stressed in Chapter 9. Many other situations also require investigation, including potential violations of employer policies (e.g., misuse of company property, alcohol use), civil law (e.g., discrimination, retaliation), and criminal law (e.g., assaults, drug dealing, embezzlement). Means of investigating include searches, interrogations, and even polygraph exams. Decisions must also be made about what, if anything, to disclose regarding the outcomes of investigations and what to do if allegations of wrongdoing are substantiated.

Clippings

An 18-year-old woman who worked at a McDonald's in Kentucky was strip-searched and sexually assaulted at the behest of an anonymous caller who claimed to be a police officer. The "officer" told an assistant store manager that he was investigating a recent theft at the store that had been perpetrated by a female

---

[41]*City of Ontario, CA.*

[42]*City of Ontario, CA,* at 2629–2630.

employee. He then described the "suspect" and the assistant manager thought that the 18-year-old fit the description. The assistant manager then complied with the caller's directive to bring the employee to her office. In what can only be described as an utterly bizarre series of events, the assistant manager followed the caller's "detailed instructions" regarding removal of the young woman's clothing and possessions. At some point, the assistant manager's fiancé was called in to assist the investigation. Following the "officer's" commands, the fiancé conducted a body cavity search, spanked, and otherwise sexually assaulted the young woman. The "investigation" went on for three hours despite her strenuous objections and pleas for the return of her clothes so that she could leave. An appeals court upheld a jury award of more than $6 million, including $5 million in punitive damages, for an array of claims including sexual harassment, negligence, and false imprisonment. Amazingly, the court was presented with evidence that there had been more than thirty incidents of this kind at McDonald's restaurants between 1994 and 2004!

"Strip-Search, Assault at Kentucky McDonald's Supports $6,111,312 Verdict for Teen Worker." *Daily Labor Report* 225 (November 25, 2009), A-5.

Practical Considerations Who should conduct workplace investigations? What are the pros and cons of using internal versus external investigators?

Some investigations are handled by managers or company legal staff. Others involve outside counsel or private investigators. People conducting investigations should be credible and convincing if called on to be witnesses in legal proceedings. The Fair and Accurate Credit Transactions Act of 2003,[43] which amended the Fair Credit Reporting Act, clarified that employers could use outside investigators for workplace investigations of suspected employee misconduct without bringing the prior consent requirements of the FCRA into play. However, if an adverse action is taken based on information from a third-party investigator, the employer is still required to disclose to the employee the "nature and substance" of the information that was the basis for the action.[44]

Searches

Investigations sometimes entail searches of work areas, desks, files, lockers, and other venues that might yield evidence of wrongdoing. Searches, by their nature, are intrusive because they delve into the contents of things that are not in plain view. Employers are generally free to conduct workplace searches, subject to limitations imposed by the Fourth Amendment (for public employees) and privacy torts (particularly intrusion upon seclusion). *Employers should establish policies notifying employees regarding the circumstances under which searches will occur, communicate these policies, and enforce them by conducting searches only under the stated circumstances. The searches themselves should be conducted in a reasonable (e.g., not overly broad, not resulting in destruction of employee property, nondiscriminatory) manner. Evidence obtained through searches, particularly if it relates to potential criminal activity (e.g., weapons, drugs), must be handled carefully and kept in a secure location.*

Because consent is a defense to privacy claims, *obtaining consent prior to conducting searches is desirable.* However, employers must be careful in how they go about obtaining consent. The case of a Wal-Mart employee whose home was searched for stolen goods

---

[43]P.L. 108–159 (2003).

[44]P.L. 108–159 § 611(a)(2) (2003).

provides a cautionary tale.[45] The employee was apparently told that the employer would be looking for missing life jackets and fishing poles when, in fact, the employer suspected theft of tools and equipment. The employee provided initial oral consent for a search of his home based on his understanding of the limited scope of the search. At his home, the employee signed a written consent form presented by a detective (the police had been called to assist Wal-Mart employees in what turned out to be a seven-hour search in which some 400 items were seized). However, there was evidence that the employee felt coerced into signing the consent form, that he was never told that he had the right not to sign, and that he believed he would be fired if he did not sign. Wal-Mart also argued that the employee tacitly consented to the search by standing by as the marathon search proceeded, but the employee offered evidence that his objections were ignored. In the end, the court upheld a jury's finding that the employee did not give his consent to the highly intrusive search of his home.

Some searches are more problematic than others. Strip searches, even when not conducted in the absurd manner evident in the McDonald's case (see "Clippings"), are highly intrusive and likely to inflict emotional distress. Except for unusual situations, such as prisons, *strip searches should never be conducted. Contact with employees during searches of their person (e.g., searching pockets for stolen goods or drugs) should be avoided or at least minimized.* To lessen the chance of sexual harassment claims, *any search involving contact with the person searched should be conducted by someone of the same sex.* To the extent possible, *searches should be conducted away from the view of the public and coworkers.* A search conducted in full view of others might falsely communicate to others that an employee has done something bad, occasioning a defamation claim.

Deceptive means of conducting searches in which an attempt is made to conceal the fact that a search is taking place should generally be avoided. An employer hired private investigators to "go undercover" and pose as employees. Despite the fact that the focus of the investigation was supposed to be on possible theft, sabotage, and drug use in the facility, the investigators forwarded weekly reports that included considerable amounts of personal information unrelated to the probe. These reports included information about employees' families, sex lives, future employment plans, medical problems, drinking problems, paternity disputes, and complaints about the employer. The employer did nothing to limit the scope of the reports (except to instruct the investigators not to report on union organizing that was going on). In finding that the plaintiff's intrusion upon seclusion claim could go to trial, the court observed:

> [T]he act of placing private detectives posing as employees in the workplace to solicit highly personal information about defendant's employees was deceptive. A disclosure obtained through deception cannot be said to be a truly voluntary disclosure. Plaintiffs had a reasonable expectation that their conversations with "coworkers" would remain private, at least to the extent that intimate life details would not be published to their employer.[46]

Interviews and Interrogations

Investigations of potential misconduct entail interviewing witnesses and interrogating employees accused or suspected of wrongdoing. As *Dietz v. Finlay Fine Jewelry* illustrates, interrogations that are not skillfully conducted can lead to many legal problems.

---

[45]*Lee.*

[46]*Johnson v. K-Mart Corp.,* 723 N.E.2d 1192, 1196 (Ill. App. 2000), *appeal granted,* 729 N.E.2d 496 (2000).

Dietz v. Finlay Fine Jewelry
754 N.E.2d 958 (Ind. App. 2001)

OPINION BY JUDGE BROOK:

Appellant-plaintiff Melissa Dittoe Dietz ("Dietz") appeals from the … grant of summary judgment in favor of Finlay on Dietz's claims for invasion of privacy, false imprisonment, defamation, [and] intentional infliction of emotional distress…. * * * We affirm in part, reverse in part, and remand. * * *

Finlay leases a commercial space in the L.S. Ayres retail store, from which it sells fine jewelry. Finlay did not employ its own security personnel, but instead, utilized the security services provided by L.S. Ayres. In July of 1998, Finlay hired Dietz as a sales clerk…. In September of 1998, a customer wanted to purchase a Finlay diamond ring on sale for $1,439.20. The customer intended to charge the purchase to her "top" account, but Dietz did not know how to perform that task. After she mistakenly placed the purchase on the customer's "flex" account, Dietz voided the transaction and then repeatedly sought assistance to complete the sale. Both Dietz and the customer grew frustrated. Eventually, an L.S. Ayres manager assisted Dietz. Without authorization, Dietz gave the then "irate" customer an extra ten percent discount.

L.S. Ayres security manager Dennis Bake ("Bake") learned about the transaction from another employee. He confirmed the unauthorized sales price and spoke with his supervisor. Thereafter, Bake asked Dietz to accompany him to an interview room, and Dietz complied. Two other employees were present. Kathleen Camp ("Camp"), a sales manager, witnessed the interview because, if a female is interviewed, "they call one of the female managers in on it[.]" A male security employee, Curt Seufert ("Seufert"), allegedly examined video monitors during the first five or ten minutes of the meeting, a task unrelated to the Dietz interview. Dietz sat in a chair, and Bake sat in front of her.

The ensuing interview lasted fifty-seven minutes. Dietz first signed a document acknowledging that she understood she was free to leave at any time. Bake then explained his job title and responsibilities. He told Dietz that he had access to her L.S. Ayres charge account and could determine if she had been late in making her payments. Dietz was "on guard." She described Bake's demeanor as "very gruff, very intimidating." Bake also spoke of mistakes in Dietz's account book and informed Dietz that there were six pieces of jewelry missing. Dietz claims that Bake also accused her of having a drug or alcohol problem and "suggested" that she pawned the jewelry to pay bills or to support her problem. Bake allegedly stated, "It all leads back to you. What are you going to do about it?" Several times, Bake told Dietz not to interrupt him. At one point, he also demanded that Dietz stay in the room. Dietz stated she did not feel free to leave, and she believed if she had attempted to do so, Bake would have verbally intimidated her into staying.

Bake asked Dietz if she had ever given a discount to a friend or relative, or to "anybody." Dietz disclosed the incident involving the discounted ring but insisted she had done nothing wrong. Eventually, Dietz signed a promissory note for $143.92, the amount of the discount. At Bake's direction, she also drafted and signed a document admitting she had given the unauthorized discount. Finlay dismissed Dietz for violating company policy. * * *

We first consider Dietz's invasion of privacy claim, based upon her allegation that Bake disclosed her credit problems to Camp and Seufert. The general tort, invasion of privacy, includes four distinct injuries: (1) intrusion upon seclusion, (2) appropriation of likeness, (3) public disclosure of private facts, and (4) false-light publicity. The public disclosure of private facts … occurs when a person gives "'publicity'" to a matter that concerns the "'private life'" of another, a matter that would be "'highly offensive'" to a reasonable person and that is not of legitimate public concern. * * *

[U]nder the … view adopted by most courts, a communication to a single person or to a small group of persons is not actionable because the publicity element requires communication to the public at large or to so many persons that the matter is "'substantially certain to become one of public knowledge.'" In this case, Bake allegedly discussed Dietz's credit difficulties in the presence of sales manager Camp. The record does not disclose what co-employee Seufert overheard, but release of the information to even two co-workers does not satisfy the publicity requirement…. In contrast, "a few courts, including Indiana's neighbors," have adopted a looser definition of "publicity," finding a disclosure actionable if made to a "'particular public'" with a special relationship to the plaintiff. Here, Camp was present as a female witness, and Seufert was a member of the security staff, watching video monitors. There is no evidence that Dietz had a special relationship with either so that a disclosure to them, under the circumstances, would render them a "particular public." [Because the] publicity element of Dietz's claim [was lacking], the [defendants] were entitled to summary judgment for invasion of privacy. * * *

False imprisonment involves "an unlawful restraint upon one's freedom of locomotion or the deprivation of liberty of another without [her] consent." "False imprisonment may be committed by words alone, or by acts alone, or by both and by merely operating on the will of the individual, or by personal violence, or both." [The defendants] assert immunity under the Shoplifting Detention Act which provides:

> An owner or agent of a store who has probable cause to believe that a theft has occurred or is occurring on or about the store and who has probable cause to believe that a specific person has committed or is committing the theft may:
> detain the person and request the person to identify [herself]; * * * (3) determine whether the person has in [her] possession unpurchased merchandise taken from the store; * * *
> The detention must: (1) be reasonable and last only for a reasonable time; and (2) not extend beyond the arrival of a law enforcement officer or two (2) hours, whichever first occurs.

The Shoplifting Detention Act "permits the merchant's agent to effect a warrantless arrest or detention where the facts and circumstances known to the agent at the time of the arrest would warrant a person of reasonable caution to believe the arrestee has committed or is committing a theft on or about the store." * * *

At the time of the detention, Bake had discovered and verified the unauthorized transaction. Thus, he reasonably believed that Dietz had intentionally sold the diamond ring at a price less than that approved by Finlay with the intent to deprive Finlay of part of its value. That constitutes probable cause for purposes of the Shoplifting Detention Act. That alone, however, does not mean the test of reasonableness in manner and time has been met in this case. * * * In her deposition testimony, Dietz stated that Bake also questioned her about six pieces of missing jewelry. Assuming that questioning occurred, we cannot say as a matter of law that Bake had probable cause to suspect Dietz was involved in those thefts. Without probable

cause, there is no immunity under the Shoplifting Detention Act.

Nor can it be determined as a matter of law that Dietz voluntarily remained in the room during the entire interview. Although Dietz had signed a document acknowledging that she was free to leave at any time, she also stated that she did not feel free to leave during the meeting. Allegedly, at one point Bake told Dietz to stay in the room. In addition, Dietz felt that, if she had attempted to leave, Bake would have used "verbal intimidation" to keep her there. Because the designated evidence does not conclusively establish the reasonableness of the detention, we cannot determine whether the Shoplifting Detention Act renders Finlay and Ayres immune for false imprisonment. Summary judgment on that claim was improvidently granted. * * *

[D]efamation consists of the following elements: (1) a communication with defamatory imputation, (2) malice, (3) publication, and (4) damages. A communication is defamatory per se if it imputes criminal conduct. * * * Here, as stated above, Bake was justified in questioning Dietz about the unauthorized discount and, thus, Finlay and Ayres are immunized from claims of defamation based on reasonable communications related to that investigation. Indeed, statements that Dietz gave an unauthorized discount to a customer are true and, thus, not actionable. * * *

Finlay and Ayres also seek immunity under a qualified privilege of common interest, which protects "communications made in good faith on any subject matter in which the party making the communication has an interest or in reference to which he has a duty, either public or private, either legal, moral, or social, if made to a person having a corresponding interest or duty." The privilege does not apply, however, to statements made without belief or grounds for belief in their truth. As stated above, factual issues remain concerning whether Bake had grounds for belief in the truth of his alleged statements regarding jewelry thefts to support a drug or alcohol problem.

There is a second bar to application of the privilege on the designated evidence. As our supreme court recognized, a statement may lose its privileged character if there is excessive publication of the defamatory statement. "The privilege is lost if the defamation goes beyond the group interest, or if publication is made to persons who have no reason to receive the information." In this case, sales manager Camp was present during the entire interview as a female witness. Thus, Camp was required to be present. The designated evidence, however, does not indicate what Seufert heard and whether he had a corresponding duty to be present. Bake himself stated that Seufert "didn't need to be there[.]" Thus, we cannot say as a matter of law that Seufert had a reason to receive the information.

[T]here are factual disputes regarding whether Bake had grounds to believe his alleged statements concerning additional thefts to support a drug or alcohol problem. There is also a question about whether there was excessive publication of any such statements. * * * Accordingly, the trial court erred when it granted summary judgment on the defamation claim.

We next consider whether the designated material supports a claim for intentional infliction of emotional distress. The tort … is committed when a person engages in extreme and outrageous conduct that intentionally or recklessly causes severe emotional distress to another. Rigorous requirements must be met to prove the tort. The conduct at issue must exceed all bounds usually tolerated by a decent society and must cause mental distress of a very serious kind. * * *

In this case, Dietz asserts that Bake accused her of substance abuse, shoplifting, and dishonesty in a gruff and intimidating manner. Even if the interview proceeded as asserted, Dietz's intentional infliction of emotional distress claim fails as a matter of law. Bake's actions occurred in the context of a detainment for the purpose of determining the extent of Dietz's unauthorized conduct. While, at the most, Bake may have unreasonably detained and defamed Dietz, his actions in this case do not constitute outrageous behavior. Taken in context, Bake's conduct did not exceed all bounds usually tolerated by a decent society. The trial court properly entered summary judgment in favor of Finlay and Ayres on Dietz's intentional infliction of emotional distress claim. * * *

CASE QUESTIONS

1. What were the legal issues in this case? What did the court decide?
2. What was the basis of Dietz's privacy tort claim? Her infliction of emotional distress claim? Why were they rejected?
3. What was the basis of her false imprisonment claim? Her defamation claim? Why was she allowed to go to trial on them? Is she likely to prevail at trial?
4. What, if anything, should this employer have done differently?

Interrogations like the one in *Dietz* have enormous potential for generating legal claims, especially false imprisonment and infliction of emotional distress. **False imprisonment**—the intentional restraint of the physical liberty of an individual—is "false" because employers are not the police or the courts. Employers do not have the authority to effectively incarcerate other citizens. Confinement can be achieved by physical barriers, physical force, the threat of force, or other forms of duress. In a false imprisonment case with facts less subtle than those in *Dietz*, an employee was taken to a conference room with glass windows, interviewed for more than seven hours while coworkers passed by giving her "dirty looks," followed to the restroom by security personnel, not allowed to make a call to her husband in private, and not permitted to leave to pick up her daughter from school. Her false imprisonment claim was allowed to go to trial.[47]

Shopkeeper statutes and common law allow employers to take reasonable actions to protect their property against theft, but this does not translate into a general right to force employees to submit to interrogations or to remain in the workplace against their will. *Absent the need to stop the theft of employer property, employers should not attempt to detain employees suspected of wrongdoing or force them to submit to interrogations against their will. Instead, the cooperation of employees in investigations should be requested.* If the employee refuses to cooperate, employers have the option of disciplining or terminating the employee or, if a crime has been committed, involving the police. To minimize the chance of false imprisonment or infliction of emotional distress, *make it clear that the employee is free to leave the interview, do not threaten an employee with*

---

[47]*Johnson v. Federal Express Corp.,* 147 F.Supp 2d 1268, 1277 (M.D. Ala. 2001).

harm, do not lock or physically obstruct the door, avoid making accusations, allow the employee a chance to answer rather than grilling him or her with rapid-fire questions, and keep the interrogation as brief as possible. In other words, people conducting interrogations of employees should forget all the crime shows they have ever seen with detectives "tuning up" suspects to obtain confessions. Intimidation is undoubtedly part of the art of interrogation, and employers have numerous concerns when dealing with cases of serious misconduct, but poorly trained security personnel conducting heavy-handed interrogations only make bad situations worse.

JUST THE FACTS

A single mother arrived at work to find her desk in disarray and her computer moved. She was immediately approached by her supervisor, a large man who lifts weights. He told her "we need to have a meeting" and led her into a conference room where another male supervisor was waiting. The supervisor slammed the conference door behind them. The woman was seated at the head of the conference table, and the two supervisors sat on either side of her. There were two unlocked doors to the conference room. The supervisor began to scream at the woman, pounded his fists on the table, used profanity, berated the woman, and threatened to have her charged with criminal acts. The supervisor read from a personnel file that purportedly included information about work time violations. When the woman requested to see the documents so that she could provide an explanation, her request was refused and she was told that "I don't have to show you a *#@! thing!" The supervisor continued to rant, throw things, and pound his fists on the table. After this went on for a while, he told the woman that she was being terminated but that she had the option of resigning instead. The woman asked to leave the room so that she could talk to someone, but was told that she could not leave the room until she signed the document. The woman eventually signed it and was escorted out of the workplace. Was the woman falsely imprisoned during this meeting?

See, *Ripley v. Montgomery,* 2007 Ohio 7151 (10th App. Dist.).

What if an employee demands to have someone else present during an interview or interrogation? Employees do not have the right to have attorneys present in these situations. However, *employers must allow unionized employees who are called into interviews that they reasonably believe are likely to result in discipline or discharge to have a union representative present.* This is referred to as employees' *Weingarten rights,* named after the case in which the Supreme Court decided that such representation must be permitted to unionized employees because it is a form of concerted activity for mutual aid or protection.[48] This right is limited in several ways. The presence of a union representative must be requested by employees; it need not be offered. Routine conversations not likely to result in adverse employment consequences are not covered, nor are situations in which a decision to administer discipline has already been made and the purpose of the meeting is merely to convey that fact. An interview need not be postponed because a particular union representative is not available. Finally, the union representative's role is circumscribed; he or she is there as an observer and not to engage in bargaining over the prospective disciplinary action.

---

[48]*NLRB v. J. Weingarten, Inc.,* 420 U.S. 251 (1975).

What about nonunion employees? The Supreme Court's *Weingarten* decision did not consider them, and the NLRB has vacillated over the years on this question. However, the NLRB's current view is that nonunion employees do not have any right to be accompanied by coworkers when being interviewed by management for possible discipline.[49] The Board reasons that nonunion workplaces should be treated differently because coworkers, unlike union officers, do not represent the interests of the entire workforce, cannot effectively redress the imbalance of power between employees and management, do not have the same level of skill at representation, and are more likely to compromise the confidentiality of investigations. In light of the increased frequency of workplace investigations, the Board viewed it as critical that employers "be allowed to conduct ... required investigations in a thorough, sensitive, and confidential manner," a task that "can best be accomplished by permitting an employer in a nonunion setting to investigate an employee without the presence of a coworker."[50]

Polygraphs

Although the Employee Polygraph Protection Act (EPPA) prohibits most preemployment polygraph exams by private sector employers, polygraphs can be used for "ongoing investigations" of theft, embezzlement, sabotage, and related activities that result in economic loss or injury to an employer's business.[51] However, *individuals can be asked to submit to polygraphs in connection with such investigations only if they had access to the property involved in the investigation, the employer has reasonable suspicion of their involvement, and they are given written information (signed by a representative of the employer and retained for at least three years) regarding the specific incident or activity being investigated and the basis for selecting particular employees for testing.* Reasonable suspicion must be based on evidence that goes beyond the mere fact of access or proximity. *Even for investigatory purposes, submission to a polygraph exam cannot be required or made a condition of employment.* Refusal to submit to a polygraph exam, by itself, cannot be the basis for discipline or discharge. Polygraph exams conducted as part of investigations are also subject to numerous procedural requirements:[52]

- *Employees must not be asked questions designed to "degrade or needlessly intrude" on their privacy.*
- *Employees must not be asked questions concerning religious beliefs, opinions about racial matters, political beliefs, sexual behavior, and beliefs or activities regarding labor organizations.*
- *Employees have the right to review all questions beforehand.*
- *Employees must be informed whether any observational (e.g., two-way mirrors) or recording devices are being used.*
- *Employees have the right to terminate a polygraph exam at any time.*
- *Employees must not be tested who have written documentation from a physician that their physical or mental condition might cause abnormal responses.*
- *Employees have the right to a written copy of any opinion or conclusion based on the test.*

[49]*IBM Corporation*, 341 NLRB No. 148 (2004).

[50]*IBM Corporation*, at 3.

[51]29 U.S.C.S. § 2006(d) (2011).

[52]29 U.S.C.S. § 2007 (2011).

Acting on Results of Investigations

Investigations gather information. If the wrong conclusions are drawn and are communicated to others in a manner that causes qualified privilege to be lost, defamation claims are in the offing. In *Dietz*, the alleged defamation took place in the course of the interrogation as potentially false allegations of drug use and theft were communicated to other staff. In the aforementioned case of the Wal-Mart employee whose home was searched for stolen goods, the employer compounded its error (and liability) by having the allegedly stolen items placed out in the yard in full view of neighbors and, eventually, the media. This resulted in news stories about a mass seizure of stolen equipment. Wal-Mart personnel were shown to be, however indirectly, sources of information for the articles. The problem was that there was never any good evidence that the employee actually stole the seized items. What can be said with certainty is that the county prosecutor refused to bring criminal charges. Defamation (and privacy) claims were upheld, and the employee was awarded $1.65 million.[53] In another case involving Wal-Mart, several employees were fired for eating "claims candy" (candy from open or torn bags that were removed from store shelves and put aside to be discarded or returned). Managers made a number of statements about the employees and the reasons for their termination. Although statements to the effect that the employees had engaged in theft were technically true (and hence not defamatory), additional statements implying that there were other more serious violations ("there was more to it … than just claims candy") were without foundation and defamed the former employees.[54] Even absent false allegations, broad disclosure of employee wrongdoing (such as by speaking to the press) can constitute public disclosure of private facts and an invasion of privacy.

Although all this might suggest a strategy of staying mum about the results of investigations, other employees are usually aware of the incidents in question. To quell rumors and to demonstrate the enforcement of policies, employers often need to say something about the outcomes of investigations. The general advice is to *treat such information as sensitive and limit communication to those with a legitimate need to know.*

In a relevant case, the discharge of an employee for sexually harassing a coworker (the discharged employee denied having done so) led the employer to issue (in part) the following statement:

> *The recent sexual harassment incident which resulted in an employee's termination has raised supervisory and employee questions about the subject. This particular incident was determined to be a serious act of employee misconduct, but in deference to the employees involved cannot be discussed in detail. However, deliberate, repeated, and unsolicited physical contact as well as significant verbal abuse was involved in this case.*[55]

Practical Considerations Under what circumstances should employers bring suspected criminal conduct by employees to the attention of law enforcement authorities?

The statement was distributed to approximately 140 supervisors, with instructions for them to discuss it with all their employees. The alleged harasser sued for defamation. The court held that the employer had good reason to communicate with employees regarding enforcement of its harassment policy and that "coworkers have a legitimate interest in the reasons a fellow employee was discharged."[56] The court commended the employer for not describing the events in sensationalistic detail and for including additional language from EEOC guidelines. The court also approved of distribution to the

---

[53]*Lee.*

[54]*Stringer v. Wal-Mart Stores,* 151 S.W.3d 781 (Ky. 2004).

[55]*Garziano v. E.I. DuPont De Nemours & Co.,* 818 F.2d 380, 384 (5th Cir. 1987).

[56]*Garziano,* at 387.

supervisors, but remanded the case for further consideration of whether subsequent communications by supervisors to employees amounted to overly broad publication causing qualified privilege to be lost.

Employee misconduct is sometimes criminal in nature. The evidence used by employers to reach employment decisions and the process of gathering that evidence is different from what is needed to obtain criminal convictions. Employers often choose to deal with arguably criminal activities by terminating employees rather than seeking prosecution. The latter course of action might require court appearances by company personnel and invite unwanted publicity. Occasionally, it can subject employers to claims for malicious prosecution. **Malicious prosecution** occurs when criminal proceedings are initiated against an innocent party, the party initiating criminal proceedings does so without probable cause, the criminal proceedings terminate in favor of the accused party, and the accusing party was motivated by malice. In one such case,[57] a restaurant terminated a chef and then filed a criminal complaint against the chef for allegedly stealing kitchen equipment. The chef was arrested, but the District Attorney's office subsequently went to court to have the case dismissed. The restaurant was not granted summary judgment on the chef's malicious prosecution claim because it had played an active role in prosecuting the employee (simply reporting a possible crime would not be sufficient); the criminal proceeding ended in a manner not inconsistent with innocence (there need not be a trial); the employer lacked probable cause because despite complaining about the theft of multiple items, the chef had been seen leaving with only one item and it was common for chefs to use their own equipment; and malice was shown by prior threats to have the chef arrested and to use connections in the police department against him. *Employers do not have to be correct or have iron-clad evidence that employees have committed crimes to seek their prosecution, but they do have to have reasonable grounds for pursuing legal action and not appear to be out to get an innocent person.* Deciding to terminate an employee is a weighty decision in its own right, as the upcoming chapters demonstrate.

Key Terms

reasonable expectation of privacy, p. 582
privacy torts, p. 582
intrusion upon seclusion, p. 583
public disclosure of private facts, p. 583

placement in a false light, p. 584
appropriation of a name or likeness, p. 584
intentional infliction of emotional distress, p. 585
Privacy Act, p. 587

Electronic Communications Privacy Act (ECPA), p. 600
ordinary course of business, p. 601
false imprisonment, p. 612
malicious prosecution, p. 616

Chapter Summary

Public employees are protected against unreasonable search and seizure under the Fourth Amendment of the U.S. Constitution. This protection applies only in situations where employees have a reasonable expectation of privacy. By virtue of their employment, public employees have less protection against governmental intrusion than ordinary citizens. Whether there is a reasonable expectation of privacy is a case-by-case determination based on policies, practices,

and other circumstances. If a reasonable expectation of privacy is deemed to exist, the reasonableness of a search—both at its inception and in its scope—is considered. Unlike in the law enforcement context, warrants or a showing of probable cause are not required for workplace searches. To be reasonable at their inception, searches should be based on a reasonable belief that they will uncover evidence of wrongdoing or that they are necessary for noninvestigatory,

---

[57]*Lawson v. New York Billiards Corp.*, 331 F.Supp 2d 121 (E.D.N.Y. 2004).

work-related purposes. Searches are reasonable in their scope when the measures employed are commensurate with the purposes of the search and the seriousness of the alleged misconduct.

Under common law, four different types of privacy torts are recognized in most states: intrusion upon seclusion, public disclosure of private facts, placement in a false light, and appropriation of a name or likeness. Intrusion upon seclusion occurs when the solitude or private affairs of an individual are intentionally intruded upon and the nature of the intrusion is such that it would be highly offensive to a reasonable person. Public disclosure of private facts occurs when private facts about a person that are of no legitimate concern to the public are broadly disclosed to others in a manner that would be highly offensive to a reasonable person. Placement in a false light occurs when characteristics, conduct, or beliefs are falsely attributed to an individual; this false information is broadly publicized; the person publicizing the information knew or should have known that it was false; and being placed in this false light would be highly offensive to a reasonable person. In appropriation of a name or likeness, an individual's name or likeness is used by others without consent and for their own commercial or other ends.

Situations that give rise to privacy tort claims, such as searches and interrogations, also tend to lead to other common law claims. In infliction of emotional distress claims, plaintiffs must show intent to harm; behavior that is so outrageous, shocking, or atrocious as to be beyond the bounds of what is tolerable in a civilized society; and severe emotional harm or distress. False imprisonment occurs when an individual completely restrains the physical liberty of another person, resulting in harm. Malicious prosecution occurs when criminal proceedings are initiated against an innocent party, the party initiating the proceedings does so without probable cause and with malice, and the criminal proceedings terminate in favor of the accused party.

Privacy protections are also found in statutes. Under the ADA, medical information obtained through lawful exams or inquiries must be kept separate from other personnel records and treated as confidential. HIPAA imposes a set of requirements aimed at protecting the privacy of medical information obtained through the administration of group health plans. The NLRA protects privacy by prohibiting intrusions that interfere with concerted activity. It also provides unionized employees with a right to representation during disciplinary interviews. Under the OSH Act, employees have a right of access to exposure and medical records kept in compliance with the act. The Employee Polygraph Protection Act allows private employers to use polygraphs to investigate certain types of misconduct, but it also establishes many requirements for the exams. The federal Privacy Act regulates the handling of records regarding federal government employees. Under this law, federal government employees must be allowed access to their personnel records, to make copies, and to contest information they believe to be erroneous. Federal agencies have an obligation to maintain accurate records, to limit the contents of records to appropriate information, and to obtain employee consent before disclosing information from records to outside parties.

Technological changes, particularly the extensive use of electronic communications and information-processing devices, have posed new workplace privacy issues. The Electronic Communications Privacy Act prohibits the intentional interception and disclosure of wire, oral, or electronic communications. However, there are exceptions for service providers, use in the ordinary course of business, and situations where employees have consented to the interception or disclosure. The ECPA also prohibits the unauthorized accessing of stored communications, although this does not apply to the provider of a system. The many exceptions to the ECPA and the reluctance of courts to find that employees have a reasonable expectation of privacy in matters such as their e-mail or Internet use have left employees with relatively little protection in these areas.

Practical Advice Summary

- Employers should establish privacy policies that alert employees to the limits of their privacy rights in the workplace.
- Regarding personnel files, employers
  — Should generally allow employees to view their files.

  — Should obtain consent before divulging information about employees to third parties.
  — Must allow union representatives access to information needed for representational purposes.
  — Must keep medical information separate from other personnel records and handle it as confidential.

- Regarding medical and exposure records required by the OSH Act, employers must
  - Allow employees (and union representatives) to examine and copy their records (within fifteen working days of making a request to do so).
  - Retain exposure records for thirty years.
  - Retain medical records for the duration of employment plus thirty years.
- When engaging in monitoring or surveillance of employees, employers
  - Should inform employees that they are subject to monitoring or surveillance.
  - Must not engage in surveillance of employees engaged in protected concerted activities, including union organizing.
  - Should limit any surveillance of employees outside the workplace to public areas.
  - Should refrain from surveillance in areas of the workplace typically regarded as private (e.g., restrooms).
- Employers must not intercept or disclose the contents of telephone conversations; e-mails; and other wire, oral, or electronic communications without consent unless
  - The interception occurs routinely in the ordinary course of business.
  - They are for legitimate business purposes.
  - Employees receive prior notification.
- Employers must not access stored electronic communications without authorization unless they are the service providers or have been authorized to do so by a user of that service.
- Employers must not listen in on private telephone calls. Employers monitoring business calls must get off the line after it is determined that a personal call is being made or received.
- Regarding workplace searches, employers should
  - Establish policies explaining the circumstances under which searches may occur.
  - Communicate those policies.
  - Enforce search policies in a consistent, nondiscriminatory manner.
  - Make searches no more intrusive or extensive than necessary.
  - Handle carefully and keep in a secure place any evidence or contraband obtained through searches, particularly if there is potential criminal activity.
  - Never conduct strip searches.
  - Minimize any physical contact with employees during searches of their person.
  - Conduct searches out of the view of coworkers and the public.
- Public employers, in particular, must be prepared to defend the reasonableness of searches and other actions that infringe upon employees' reasonable expectations of privacy.
- Employers can take appropriate action to prevent the theft of their property, but should not otherwise detain employees suspected of wrongdoing or force them to submit to interrogations against their will.
- When conducting interrogations of employees, it is important that
  - Employees are told they are free to leave.
  - Employees are not threatened with harm.
  - The room is not locked or the path of egress physically obstructed.
  - Employees are given the opportunity to explain events rather than being grilled with rapid-fire questions or accusations.
  - Interrogations are kept as brief as possible.
- If requested, unionized employees must be allowed to have a union representative present at meetings that are reasonably likely to result in discipline or discharge.
- Employers can request that employees submit to polygraph exams in the course of investigating thefts or other events causing economic loss, but only those individuals
  - Who had access to the property involved in the investigation.
  - Who, on the basis of additional evidence, are reasonably suspected of involvement.
  - Who are given written information (signed by a representative of the employer and retained for at least three years) regarding the specific incident or activity being investigated and the basis for selecting particular employees for testing.
- When the polygraph is used for investigatory purposes
  - Submission to a polygraph exam cannot be required or made a condition of continued employment.
  - Numerous requirements must be met regarding the questions that can be asked and procedures to be followed.
- Information about employee misconduct derived from investigations should be treated as confidential and communicated only to those individuals with a legitimate need to know.

Chapter Questions

1. The FBI received a tip that an employee of an IT company was accessing child pornography from his workplace computer. When approached by the FBI, the company confirmed that the employee had regularly visited the Web sites. Company officials entered the employee's office in the evening and made copies of the contents of his computer's hard drive. All of the computers in the workplace were the property of the employer, and the employer was able to monitor all employees' Internet activity. When they were hired, employees were told that their computer use was subject to monitoring and that computers should not be used for personal business. The employee was the only user of the office, and it was kept locked. A password created by the employee was needed to use the computer. After the employee was arrested and charged with crimes, he argued that the FBI had violated his constitutional rights by searching his computer without a warrant. Did this employee have a reasonable expectation of privacy in the contents of his workplace computer? Did the *government* violate his constitutional rights by conducting an illegal search? (*United States of America v. Ziegler,* 474 F.3d 1184 [9th Cir. 2007])

2. School officials suspected that a physical education teacher was stealing money from students. Two hidden video cameras were placed in his office. The office was also used by other gym teachers and was where the teachers changed their clothes. The office was located in the boys' locker room and was accessible only by walking through the locker room. The cameras recorded and stored camera images for thirty days. It was unclear whether any school officials actually watched live images from the cameras or reviewed the tapes. When a teacher discovered the cameras, he sued. Were the privacy rights of the teachers violated? (*Helisek v. Dearborn Public Schools,* 2008 U.S. Dist. LEXIS 25514 [E.D. Mich.])

3. At the end of her shift, a 19-year-old shoe salesperson was questioned by two store security officers. She was questioned in a small room for three hours. One of the security officers sat behind her on the right side where she could not see him (she was blind in the right eye). She was asked to sign a document stating that she was voluntarily waiving her "rights," including the right to remain silent. When she asked for further explanation of the document before she signed it, she was told that it "doesn't mean anything" unless you've "done something wrong." A security officer threatened to call the police and have her jailed unless she signed a confession. She was told that the interrogation could last all night and that if she signed a confession, she could probably keep her job. Under these circumstances, she signed. She was fired two days later. What should the court decide? Why? (*Smithson v. Nordstrom, Inc.,* 664 P.2d 1119 [Ore. App. 1983])

4. A telephone company employee was on disability leave. Company policy prohibited taking vacation while collecting disability. The employee disregarded the policy and left for his planned fishing trip. Managers became suspicious and went to his house to wait for him, finding no one home. Phone records were checked to verify that the employee had not called in from home as he had claimed or made any other calls. The employer also contacted the kennel where the employee had boarded his dog, the Canadian province where he obtained a fishing license, and the post office that he had instructed to hold his mail. The employee was fired. He was reinstated without back pay by an arbitrator, but he sued for invasion of privacy. What should the court decide? Why? (*Schmidt v. Ameritech,* 768 N.E.2d 303 [Ill. App. 2002], *review denied,* 813 N.E. 2d 229 [Ill. 2004])

5. A woman was beaten by a coworker with whom she was living, resulting in several broken ribs. She filed charges against the coworker, and the coworker's conviction for domestic violence was reported in the newspaper. The woman did not report any of this information to her employer, but managers became aware of the situation due to the newspaper account. A workplace violence team investigated, seeking to determine whether the coworker was dangerous and should be removed from the workplace. On four occasions, they attempted to interview the woman, asking

questions regarding her relationship with the coworker, the domestic violence incident, and her physical and mental health. On each occasion, she became angry and left the interview, insisting that this was private information that she did not want to share. The woman was eventually terminated for her failure to cooperate with the workplace violence program. She sued. What should the court decide? Why? (*Rowe v. Guardian Automotive Products,* 2005 U.S. Dist. LEXIS 31296)

6. An employee worked the night shift at a bakery. She was having an affair and sometimes pretended to go to work when she was really visiting her lover. One evening when she was supposed to be working, her husband called the bakery and learned that she was absent. The next day he went to the bakery and met with a human resources (HR) manager. After consulting the employee's personnel file, the HR manager informed the husband that she had been absent on a number of occasions. Shortly thereafter, the husband committed suicide. He left a note saying that he hoped his wife would be happier without him being in the way. The wife sued the bakery for divulging the information. What should the court decide? Why? (*Kobeck v. Nabisco,* 305 S.E.2d 183 [Ga. App. 1983])

7. An airline pilot created a Web site on which he posted material that was critical of both his employer and his union. He created a list of coworkers who were authorized to access his site. The log-in process for the site included providing a username and creating a password. Users of the site were informed that the conditions for use included prohibitions against any members of management viewing the site and against the disclosure of the site's contents to anyone else. Two pilots were approached by a manager and asked for permission to use their names to access the site. One of the pilots had previously logged in to the site; the other pilot had not. Both gave their permission to the manager, who subsequently accessed the site on several occasions using their names. When word got back to the pilot who had created the Web site that a manager had accessed it and was threatening to sue him for defamation, the pilot sued. Did the airline violate the Electronic Communications

Privacy Act? Why or why not? (*Konop v. Hawaiian Airlines,* 302 F.3d 868 [9th Cir. 2002], *cert. denied,* 2003 U.S. LEXIS 1186)

8. In response to reports of drug use and sales by employees at one of its auto plants, Ford enlisted the services of a security firm. Investigators from the firm posed as plant employees. They mingled with employees during the work day and socialized with them after working hours. They witnessed drug-related violations, both in the plant and outside at bars and restaurants. The investigation resulted in a number of terminations and criminal prosecutions. In one incident, an employee who was being terminated was physically escorted away from his work station, despite his objections that his arm was being hurt and that he wanted to call his attorney. Did this investigation and subsequent terminations violate any legal rights of the affected employees? (*Warriner v. North American Security Solutions,* 2008 U.S. Dist. LEXIS 44316 [W.D. Ky.])

9. In the course of a meeting regarding an employee's absences from work, a doctor at a veteran's hospital divulged the HIV-positive status and marijuana use of the employee to the employee's union representatives. The employee had told the doctor not to provide this information to union officials. Were the rights of this federal employee violated under the Privacy Act? Why or why not? (*Doe v. Department of Veterans Affairs,* 519 F.3d 456 [8th Cir. 2008])

10. An employee worked for a military contractor, performing mailroom services at a naval station. One day after work when the mailroom was closed, she returned to retrieve something from the refrigerator. In the process, she discovered fourteen opened and undelivered Christmas cards in the wastebasket. She immediately reported the situation to her supervisor. When the supervisor investigated, she found a pay stub among the pieces of undelivered mail. The stub was from the paycheck of another employee who had been working at the front desk for most of that day. All the mailroom employees were subsequently asked to submit to a polygraph exam. They were told that the exam was voluntary, and they were asked to sign general release forms. These forms were not signed by any official of the company and did not specifically

mention the mail incident or provide the basis for testing each employee. All the employees signed the form. The prime suspect was polygraphed first, and the exam suggested deception in his responses. The contractor still wanted to polygraph the other employees. By this time, the employee who had discovered the undelivered mail refused to take the exam. Less than a week later, she was fired on the grounds that she had accepted package deliveries through the mail-

room's back door in violation of naval security procedures. The employee sued, challenging both the polygraph request and her termination. What should the court decide? Why? (*Polkey v. Transtecs Corp.,* 404 F.3d 1264 [11th Cir. 2005])

11. Is the current privacy protection for e-mail and Internet use sufficient?

12. What does privacy mean to you? What is reasonable for employees to expect in terms of privacy in the workplace?

PART 6

Terminating Employment

CHAPTER **18**

Terminating Individual Employees

"You're fired!" Those dreaded words carry weighty consequences for employees and employers alike. Terminations can drastically affect the ability of employees to provide for themselves and their families, harm future career prospects, and strike devastating blows at reputations and self-esteem. For employers, terminations are stressful, occasionally dangerous, and apt to prompt legal challenges. Terminations are more likely than any other human resource activity to result in legal claims.

The legal standards governing termination differ substantially depending on whether private sector and nonunion employees or public sector and unionized employees are being considered. The first, and largest, portion of this chapter deals with the legal protections available to private sector, nonunion employees. Their legal status is captured by the term *employment at will with exceptions*. The latter part of this chapter considers the more stringent *just cause/due process* standard for terminations that generally applies to unionized and public sector employees. There are also important differences between terminations of individuals for reasons specific to those individuals and the selection of numerous employees for termination in conjunction with downsizings, plant closings, mergers, and the like. This chapter considers individual terminations. Chapter 19 deals with downsizing.

Clippings

Joseph Casias is a father of two who lives in Battle Creek, Michigan. Mr. Casias uses marijuana prescribed by his doctor to relieve the pain from inoperable brain and sinus cancer. In 2008, he was named "associate of the year" at the Wal-Mart store where he worked. In 2009, he injured his knee at work. Pursuant to a company policy requiring post-accident testing, Mr. Casias was drug tested. When the drug test results came back positive due to his use of medical marijuana, Mr. Casias was fired. Although fourteen states, including Michigan, have laws permitting marijuana to be prescribed for medical purposes, only Rhode Island's Medical Marijuana Act explicitly protects employees who are medical marijuana cardholders from termination for medical marijuana use. Medical marijuana users are caught between the federal government's staunch antidrug stance, state laws that afford the right to use medical marijuana but fail to address the employment consequences of doing so, and company policies. The American Civil Liberties Union (ACLU) has filed a wrongful termination suit on behalf of Mr. Casias. His ACLU attorney says that "The cancer is not what's keeping him from earning a living—Wal-Mart is."

Jennifer Mascia. "Medical Use of Marijuana Costs Some a Paycheck." *New York Times* (August 29, 2010), 13.

Determining Whether a Termination Has Occurred: Constructive Discharge

Disputes over whether an employee quit or was fired are not uncommon. If an employee truly resigns of his own volition, the employee cannot sue for wrongful termination. However, an employer cannot get around the law by creating intolerable working conditions designed to force an employee to quit. This is known as a **constructive discharge**. If, under the circumstances, a reasonable person would have felt compelled to quit, courts will construe the resignation as a termination and a claim for wrongful termination could still be brought. Nor can employers avoid legal problems by terminating employees and then reinstating them sometime later—even if the reinstatements are with back pay.[1]

Factors that courts examine to determine whether an employee who resigned was constructively discharged include demotions; cuts in salary; reductions in job responsibilities; reassignment to menial or degrading work; reassignment to work under a younger supervisor; badgering, harassment, and humiliation calculated to encourage resignation; and offers of early retirement on terms less favorable than the employee's former status.[2] A resignation that occurs when an employee is presented with the stark option of resigning or being immediately terminated can constitute a constructive discharge. Courts consider in these cases whether the employee was given any alternative to resignation, understood the nature of the choice to resign, was allowed a reasonable amount of time in which to make a choice, and was permitted to select the effective date of the resignation.[3] A constructive discharge did not exist when a veteran teacher retired after being told by a school superintendent that he would recommend that the school district not renew her contract at the end of the school year (six months from then).[4] The court observed that despite the superintendent's stated intention, the teacher had numerous avenues to contest nonrenewal, and the likely outcome of that process was unknown. Furthermore, this was not a case where she was assigned demeaning job duties or demoted.

In "a textbook case of constructive discharge," a former chief of surgery at a VA facility was forced to quit after being subjected to a series of humiliating actions by hospital administrators.[5] After being passed over for a vice president position, "a slow degrada-

---

[1]*Phelan v. Cook County*, 463 F.3d 773 (7th Cir. 2006).

[2]*Logan v. Denny's*, 259 F.3d 558, 569 (6th Cir. 2001).

[3]*Narotzky v. Natrona County Memorial Hospital Board of Trustees*, 610 F.3d 558, 563 (10th Cir. 2010).

[4]*Cigan v. Chippewa Falls School District*, 388 F.3d 331 (7th Cir. 2004).

[5]*Stemple v. Nicholson*, 2006 U.S. Dist. LEXIS 41885, 38 (W.D. Pa.), *affirmed*, 2008 U.S. App. LEXIS 18630 (3d Cir.).

tion of his responsibilities, status, and authority began."[6] He was stripped of the authority and resources that he needed to carry out his responsibilities. The doctor was subsequently transferred to another location where it was impossible for him to perform his duties. He was given a much lower-than-usual performance appraisal, and his office was moved to another floor, farther from the operating room. In one meeting, an administrator encouraged him to retire. On a subsequent occasion, an administrator referred to meeting with him as "a waste of my time" and said to him, "I hope you have a good retirement package." The VA's ham-handed actions finally had their intended effect when the doctor quit. However, because his resignation was a constructive discharge, he was able to successfully bring age discrimination and retaliation claims against the VA. A constructive discharge was also found where an employee returned from vacation to find that her desk was empty, all of her belongings were packed in boxes, and her office was being used as storage space. Additionally, the employee had been told by her former supervisor a month earlier to "watch your back." While she was on vacation, her new supervisor had called regarding the whereabouts of some documents. Dissatisfied with her response, the supervisor told her, "This is the last straw." The employee had also received her first negative performance appraisal ever, and some of her job duties had been shifted to a newly hired employee. Under all these circumstances, the court concluded that a reasonable person would have believed that had she not resigned, she would have been terminated.[7]

JUST THE FACTS

A long-time employee received a negative performance appraisal after some other employees and a customer had complained about him. The employee was presented with the choice of retiring with a severance package or being evaluated under a thirty-day performance improvement plan. The plan would include an assessment of his performance, leadership, support for peers and managers, teamwork, and customer satisfaction. He was also told that if his supervisor received even one complaint about him during this thirty-day period, he would be terminated without severance pay. The employee was given thirty days to consider the offer. After mulling over the choice for twenty-five days, he took the severance package. Subsequently, the employee sued his former employer for wrongful termination. Was the employee constructively discharged?

See, *Saville v. IBM,* 2006 U.S. App. LEXIS 15839 (10th Cir.), *cert. denied,* 127 S. Ct. 1143 (2007).

Note, however, that constructive discharge is not a legal claim in itself. Instead, a finding that an employee who resigned was constructively discharged allows that employee to bring any legal claims for wrongful discharge that would be available had she been formally terminated. The nature of constructive discharges, and the incredible lengths to which employers sometimes go to drive employees out, also lends itself to other legal claims. One strong possibility is harassment. Another is infliction of emotional distress. In a case involving the latter, a 60-year-old high-level manager with more than thirty

---

[6]*Stemple,* at 28.
[7]*EEOC v. University of Chicago Hospitals,* 276 F.3d 326 (7th Cir. 2002).

years of experience in the industry was demoted with a reduction in benefits to a warehouse supervisor position. He had no employees to supervise and spent his time sweeping floors and cleaning the cafeteria. He was subjected to the "silent treatment" by other managers, when he was not actively being harassed (e.g., another manager posted a sign in the workplace saying "Wilson is old"). The man suffered severe psychological problems as a result of this mistreatment. Upholding a multimillion-dollar jury verdict, the court concluded:

> *We find it difficult to conceive a workplace scenario more painful and embarrassing than an executive, indeed a vice-president and the assistant to the president, being subjected before his fellow employees to the most menial janitorial services and duties of cleaning up after entry level employees; the steep downhill push to total humiliation was complete. The evidence ... will fully support the view ... that Monarch, unwilling to fire Wilson outright, **intentionally** and **systematically** set out to humiliate him in the hopes that he would quit... . [T]his conduct was, indeed, so outrageous that civilized society should not tolerate it.*[8]

Practical Considerations Should employers offer employees the choice between resigning and being terminated? Under what circumstances?

Clearly, *employers should not attempt to avoid terminations by creating intolerable conditions designed to force employees to quit.* This strategy is a loser because employees who quit under these circumstances will be deemed constructively discharged and the process of attempting to force them out might give rise to additional claims of harassment or infliction of emotional distress.

Employment at Will with Exceptions

To understand the legal limitations on termination of most private sector, nonunion employees, it is useful to distinguish between pure employment at will, employment at will with exceptions, and just cause/due process as legal standards governing terminations. Under pure **employment at will**, there is no such thing as a wrongful termination. An employee without a contract of employment for a specified term can be terminated at any time for good reason, bad reason, or no reason. Pure employment at will describes the legal regime that existed in the United States prior to 1937. In 1937, the Supreme Court upheld the constitutionality of the National Labor Relations Act. The NLRA carved out the first major exception to employment at will: Employers could no longer lawfully terminate employees for union organizing or otherwise exercising their rights under the NLRA.

The opposite end of the spectrum, in terms of the ease with which employers can terminate employment relationships, is represented by the just cause/due process standard. Under a just cause/due process standard, employers bear the burden of proving that terminations were carried out properly and were based on good reasons. The default rule is that if an employer cannot adequately defend a challenged termination, that termination is wrongful and the employee is entitled to reinstatement, back wages, or other remedies. This standard applies to roughly 20 percent of the current U.S. workforce, including most public employees, unionized employees, employees with individual employment contracts specifying the term of employment, employees in Montana (where a "good cause" standard was established by statute), and employees recently reinstated from military service.

In contrast to both pure employment at will and just cause, most private sector, nonunion employees have their employment relationships governed by a legal regime that can best be described as **employment at will with exceptions**. Under this arrangement,

---

[8]*Wilson v. Monarch Paper Co.*, 939 F.2d 1138, 1145 (5th Cir. 1991).

employment at will is still the starting point for analyzing an employee's right not to be terminated. However, since 1937, pure employment at will has been substantially modified by legislation and judicial recognition of common law wrongful termination claims. To some observers, the number of exceptions now overwhelms the rule of employment at will, but that is an overstatement. Under employment at will with exceptions, employees bear the burden of showing that their termination was for an "illegal cause" prohibited by law. But if they fail to do so, the default rule is still employment at will; the termination is legal regardless of how dubious the reasons or circumstances. Thus, even though it might seem unfair to permit the termination of an employee like Mr. Casias (see previous "Clippings") for lawful, off-the-job medical marijuana use, a court would not find the termination of this at-will employee to be wrongful unless he could point to a specific legal right to not be terminated for medical marijuana use. As you go through this chapter, see if you can identify any types of wrongful termination claims that might apply to Mr. Casias.

Impermissible Grounds for Termination

Table 18.1 lists the primary legal protections against wrongful discharge. Terminations can be challenged on constitutional, statutory, and common law grounds. Common law grounds include both contractual and tort claims. Remedies in contractual claims are intended to restore individuals to the position they would have been in had their contracts not been breached ("make the individual whole"), whereas plaintiffs suing in tort can recover both compensatory and punitive damages for the harm done to them. The tort claims listed below the line in Table 18.1 are not wrongful discharge claims per se, but rather claims that often flow from the circumstances leading up to and following terminations.

It is important to keep this "menu" in mind when analyzing the legality of a termination. Some of the protections listed in Table 18.1 (those in italics) are available only to public sector employees, unionized employees, and other employees not employed at will. What remains is considerable, although the various protections overlap and states vary in terms of whether and how particular legal protections are recognized. To simplify

TABLE 18.1 LEGAL PROTECTIONS AGAINST WRONGFUL DISCHARGE

CONSTITUTIONAL	STATUTORY	COMMON LAW	
		CONTRACT	TORT
First Amendment (e.g., speech)	*Civil service, tenure laws*	*Individual (express) employment contract*	Public policy exception
	Antidiscrimination laws (e.g., ADA, ADEA)		Intentional interference with a contractual relationship
Fifth and Fourteenth Amendments (due process, equal protection)		*Labor agreement*	
	Noninterference provisions of statutes (e.g., NLRA, FMLA)	Implied contract	
State constitutions			
	Antiretaliation provisions of statutes (e.g., OSHA, ERISA)	Covenant of good faith and fair dealing	Infliction of emotional distress
		Promissory estoppel	
	Whistleblower protection laws		Defamation
	Civic duty laws (e.g., USERRA)		
			Privacy torts
	Off-duty conduct laws (e.g., smoking)		
			False imprisonment
	Montana WDEA		

greatly, the exceptions to employment at will for most private sector, nonunion employees boil down to the following impermissible grounds for termination: terminations that would breach an implied contract or other contract-related obligation, terminations in retaliation for employee actions that support public policy, terminations that interfere with the exercise of statutory rights, and terminations that are discriminatory.

Clippings

After a brief stint as host of *The Tonight Show* during which ratings plummeted, NBC officials decided to replace Conan O'Brien and bring back the show's longtime host, Jay Leno. Mr. O'Brien had a multiyear contract with NBC to host the show. Ousting Mr. O'Brien with two and half years left on his guaranteed contract cost NBC about $45 million. Approximately $32.5 million went to Mr. O'Brien to buy out the remainder of his contract. An additional $12 million went to other employees working on the show, many of whom had sold homes in New York and moved to Los Angeles to continue working with Mr. O'Brien. The settlement negotiations dealt with a number of other sticky issues, including when Mr. O'Brien would be free to go back on the air for another network, when he would be able to give interviews regarding his experiences at NBC, and ownership of characters and comedy routines from the show.

Bill Carter. "Fingers Still Pointing, NBC and O'Brien Reach a Deal." *New York Times* (January 22, 2010), A3.

Breach of an Implied Contract

A small number of employees including professional athletes, high-level managers, and entertainers such as Conan O'Brien (see "Clippings") have "express" (i.e., explicit, mutually acknowledged) contracts of employment that are negotiated, executed in writing, signed, and specify a particular term of employment (or specific grounds under which the contract can be terminated). If an employee with an express contract is terminated prior to the expiration of the contract, the employer will be liable for damages for breach of contract unless the employer can show that there was cause to terminate. Most often, contractual disputes of this type are settled by negotiations between the parties.

But the vast majority of employees do not have express contracts of employment and are employed at will. Nevertheless, under the **implied contract** exception to employment at will, the right of employers to terminate at will can be limited by promises of job security. Even in the absence of an express contract of employment, written or oral statements by employers—and their entire course of conduct in dealing with employees—can give rise to enforceable contractual rights to something other than employment at will. The "something other" might be employment for a specified term, termination only for certain reasons (e.g., "for cause"), or use of specified procedures when making termination decisions (e.g., progressive discipline). If an implied contract exists, discharged employees can sue for wrongful termination based on breach of the implied contract.

Criteria for Determining the Existence of an Implied Contract   Most statements made by employers, whether orally or in writing, are not contractually binding. However, the following factors point to the existence of an implied contract:

- A specific promise was made.
- The promise was made frequently and consistently.

- The source of the promise was someone with sufficient authority to offer it.
- The promise was communicated to the employee.
- The promise was not highly conditional (i.e., dependent on the employer's own judgment).
- The employer's entire "course of conduct" (e.g., policies, practices, statements, industry practices, employee tenure) was consistent with the promise.
- There was an exhaustive listing of dischargeable offenses in a handbook (and the offense for which termination occurred was not included in that list).
- A change to a less protective policy was not communicated to employees.
- There was no effective disclaimer.

Vague, stray, or highly conditional promises do not evidence intent to depart from employment at will. Statements such as "you have a promising future with the company" (lack of specificity) or "you will have a job here for as long as we are pleased with you" (conditionality) are unlikely to be enforceable. The statements relied on must be sufficiently specific to constitute "offers," rather than mere general statements of policy. Thus, inclusion of a general nondiscrimination provision in an employee handbook did not create an implied contract because it "was not specific and did not make any promises regarding disciplinary procedure or termination decisions."[9] In contrast, an employee handbook that labeled its provisions as "binding" and that outlined specific disciplinary procedures was sufficiently specific and authoritative to form the basis for an implied contract.[10] Listings of dischargeable offenses can limit employment at will if they can fairly be read to restrict terminations to those based on the stated set of reasons.

Practical Considerations Should employers issue employee handbooks? If so, how should handbooks be constructed? Disseminated to employees?

To understand whether a promise was made, some courts look not only at statements spoken by managers or written in documents but also to the entire course of an employer's conduct. The course of conduct relevant to determining the existence of an implied contract includes the employer's informal policies, past practice (e.g., practice of not terminating without cause), industry customs, and treatment of the individual employee. However, although longevity, consistent raises, promotions, and positive performance appraisals can bolster an employee's claim that employment is not strictly at will, "they do not, *in and of themselves,* ... constitute a contractual guarantee of future employment security."[11]

Specific promises made to employees regarding their term of employment, permissible reasons for termination, or termination procedures must be honored. Employers that do not want to limit their prerogative to terminate at will should refrain from making such promises. Because of the central role that employee handbooks play in many implied contract cases, *handbooks, applications, and other authoritative documents should be carefully written and vetted (reviewed) by people with legal expertise before they are put into use.*

If contractual rights limiting employment at will can stem from employers' statements in handbooks and other sources, what happens if modifications are made that adversely affect those rights? Many courts permit employers to unilaterally make such changes, provided that employees are given reasonable notice.[12] However, other courts require more. The Arizona Supreme Court, for example, has held that merely providing employees with new handbooks is not legally adequate. Instead, employees must be specifically informed of any new terms, made aware of their effect on the preexisting contract, and

---

[9]*Hessenthaler v. Tri-County Sister Help, Inc.,* 616 S.E.2d 694, 699 (S.C. 2005).

[10]*Jones v. Lake Park Care Center,* 569 N.W.2d 369 (Iowa 1997).

[11]*Guz v. Bechtel National, Inc.,* 8 P.3d 1089, 1104 (Cal. 2000).

[12]*Gaglidari v. Denny's Restaurants, Inc.,* 815 P.2d 1362 (Wash. 1991).

affirmatively consent to modifications. Modifications must be supported by separate consideration—that is, some benefit to employees beyond simply being allowed to continue their employment. The court explained its reasoning as follows:

> *To those who believe our conclusion will destroy an employer's ability to update and modernize its handbook, we can only reply that the great majority of handbook terms are certainly non-contractual and can be revised, that the existence of contractual terms can be disclaimed in the handbook in effect at the time of hiring and, if not, permission to modify can always be obtained by mutual agreement and for consideration. In all other instances, the contract rule is and has always been that one should keep one's promises.*[13]

> *If changes are made that lessen employees' rights not to be terminated at will, employees should be clearly informed of those specific changes.* Employers should not try to just "slip them by." Some states require employers to obtain a clear indication of employees' assent to those changes and to provide some benefit in exchange.

In *Dillon v. Champion Jogbra*, the court must decide whether an implied contract to use specified termination procedures exists, despite the presence of a "disclaimer."

Dillon v. Champion Jogbra
819 A. 2d 703 (Vt. 2002)

OPINION BY JUSTICE MORSE:

Plaintiff Linda Dillon appeals an order of the superior court granting summary judgment to defendant Champion Jogbra, Inc. in her action for wrongful termination. Dillon contends that the trial court erroneously concluded as a matter of law that Dillon's at-will employment status had not been modified by Jogbra's employment manual and employment practices, and that the undisputed material facts failed to give rise to a claim for promissory estoppel supporting a claim for wrongful discharge. We affirm with respect to Dillon's claim for promissory estoppel, but reverse and remand on her breach of contract claim. * * *

Jogbra has an employee manual that it distributes to all employees at the time of their employment. The first page of the manual states the following in capitalized print:

> *The policies and procedures contained in this manual constitute guidelines only. They do not constitute part of an employment contract, nor are they intended to make any commitment to any employee concerning how individual employment action can, should, or will be handled.*

Champion Jogbra offers no employment contracts nor does it guarantee any minimum length of employment. Champion Jogbra reserves the right to terminate any employee at any time "at will," with or without cause. During the period from 1996 to 1997, however, Jogbra developed what it termed a "Corrective Action Procedure." This procedure established a progressive discipline system for employees and different categories of disciplinary infractions. It states that it applies to all employees and will be carried out in "a fair and consistent manner." Much of the language in the section is mandatory in tone.

Linda Dillon … was hired on as a full-time employee in August 1997 in the position of "charge-back analyst." In the summer of 1998, the position of "sales administrator" was going to become vacant. Dillon was approached by Jogbra management about applying for the position. * * * In the course of interviewing for the position, Dillon recalls that she was told that she would receive "extensive training." More specifically, she was told by the human resources manager that she would overlap with her predecessor who would train her during those days. Originally, her predecessor was scheduled to leave August 15. In the course of Dillon's interview with

---

[13]*Demasse v. ITT Corp.*, 984 P.2d 1138, 1148 (Ariz. 1999), *cert. denied*, 528 U.S. 930 (1999).

the vice president of sales, who would be her immediate supervisor, he informed her that her predecessor was actually leaving earlier and would be available for only two days of training before Dillon started the job. He reassured her, though, that the predecessor would be brought back sometime thereafter for more training. Dillon also recalls that he told her that "it will take you four to six months to feel comfortable with [the] position," and not to be concerned about it. Dillon was offered and accepted the position. She spent most of her predecessor's remaining two days with her. Her predecessor then returned in early September for an additional two days of training. Dillon stated that she felt that, after the supplemental training, she had received sufficient training for the job.

On September 29, Dillon was called into her supervisor's office. The human resources manager was also present. They informed Dillon that things were not working out and that she was going to be reassigned to a temporary position, at the same pay and benefit level, that ended in December. She was told that she should apply for other jobs within the company, but if nothing suitable became available, she would be terminated at the end of December. According to Dillon, her supervisor stated that he had concluded within ten days of her starting that "it wasn't going to work out." Prior to the meeting, Dillon was never told her job was in jeopardy, nor did Jogbra follow the procedures laid out in its employee manual when terminating her. Dillon applied for one job that became available in the ensuing months, but was not selected for it. She left Jogbra in December when her temporary position terminated. * * *

In the implied contract context, we have noted ... that ... when an employer takes steps to give employees the impression of job security and enjoys the attendant benefits that such an atmosphere confers, it should not then be able to disregard its commitments at random. * * * [W]e have noted repeatedly that the presumption that employment for an indefinite term is an "at-will" agreement ... "imposes no substantive limitation on the right of contracting parties to modify terms of their arrangement or to specify other terms that supersede the terminable-at-will [arrangement]." Additionally, an employer may modify an at-will employment agreement unilaterally. When determining whether an employer has done so, we look to both the employer's written policies and its practices. An employer not only may implicitly bind itself to terminating only for cause through its manual and practices,

but may also be bound by a commitment to use only certain procedures in doing so. * * *

When the terms of a manual are ambiguous ... or send mixed messages regarding an employee's status, the question of whether the presumptive at-will status has been modified is properly left to the jury. This may be the case even if there is a disclaimer stating employment is at-will, as the presence of such a disclaimer is not dispositive in the determination. "The mere inclusion of boilerplate language providing that the employee relationship is at will cannot negate any implied contract and procedural protections created by an employee handbook." Furthermore, an employer's practices can provide context for and help inform the determination. * * *

In this case, we cannot agree with the trial court that the terms of Jogbra's manual are unambiguous such that, as a matter of law, Dillon's status was not modified, especially considered in light of the conflicting record before the court regarding Jogbra's employment practices. Notwithstanding the disclaimer contained on the first page of the manual quoted above, the manual goes on to establish in Policy No. 720 an elaborate system governing employee discipline and discharge. It states as its purpose: "To establish Champion Jogbra policy for all employees." It states that actions will be carried out "in a fair and consistent manner." It provides that "the Corrective Action Policy requires management to use training and employee counseling to achieve the desired actions of employees." It establishes three categories of violations of company policy and corresponding actions to be generally taken in each case. It delineates progressive steps to be taken for certain types of cases, including "unsatisfactory quality of work," and time periods governing things such as how long a reprimand is considered "active." All of these terms are inconsistent with the disclaimer at the beginning of the manual, in effect sending mixed messages to employees. Furthermore, these terms appear to be inconsistent with an at-will employment relationship, its classic formulation being that an employer can fire an employee "for good cause or for no cause, or even for bad cause."

With respect to the record before the court on Jogbra's employment practices, Dillon herself was aware of at least one employee whose termination was carried out pursuant to the terms set forth in the manual. She also testified in her deposition to conversations with the human resources manager, with whom she was friendly, in which the manager had described certain procedures used for firing employees. She stated that the manager had told her that Jogbra could not "just get rid of" people, but instead had to follow procedures. The human resources manager herself testified that, although the progressive discipline system was not generally applied to salaried employees, it was "historically" used for nonsalaried employees. She could only recall two instances in which the portion of the manual providing for documentation of progressive action was not followed, one of which resulted in a legal claim against the company and the other of which involved an employee stealing from the company. In fact, the manual specifically provides that stealing "will normally result in discharge on the first offense." Thus, it is not clear how that discharge deviated from the provisions of the manual.

In conclusion, the manual itself is at the very least ambiguous regarding employees' status, and Jogbra's employment practices appear from the record to be both consistent with the manual and inconsistent with an at-will employment arrangement. Therefore, summary judgment was not proper on Dillon's breach of implied contract claim.

Dillon also argues that the trial court's grant of summary judgment on her claim of promissory estoppel was erroneous. Dillon based her claim on two separate statements: the assurance that she would receive training and the assurance that it would take her four to six months to become comfortable with the sales administrator position. We have held that, even if an employee otherwise enjoys only at-will employment status, that employee may still be able to establish a claim for wrongful termination under a theory of promissory estoppel if that employee can demonstrate that the termination was in breach of a specific promise made by the employer that the employer should

have reasonably expected to induce detrimental reliance on the part of the employee, and that the employee did in fact detrimentally rely on the promise. We agree with the trial court in this case, however, that essential elements of promissory estoppel are absent with regard to both statements.

With respect to Jogbra's promise to Dillon that she would receive training, Dillon specifically conceded that, upon her predecessor's return in September, she had received adequate training to perform the job. In other words, Jogbra had delivered on its promise. Furthermore, even assuming that Jogbra failed to provide the full extent of promised training, Dillon has failed to explain how, as a matter of law, the promise of training modified her at-will status. * * * With respect to the assurance that it would take four to six months to become comfortable with the position, the statement cannot be reasonably relied upon as a promise of employment in the sales administrator position for a set period of time. Courts have generally required a promise of a specific and definite nature before holding an employer bound by it. An estimate of how long it would take a person to adjust to a job cannot be converted into a definite promise of employment for that period of time. Thus, the vague assurance given to Dillon is not sufficient to support her claim of promissory estoppel. * * *

CASE QUESTIONS

1. What were the legal issues in this case? What did the court decide?
2. What was the implied contract in this case? How did the employer breach it?
3. Why does the disclaimer in the employee manual not have the effect desired by the employer?
4. Why does Dillon's promissory estoppel claim fail?

Effect of Disclaimers   Employment at will is a harsh arrangement. It is difficult to put a positive "spin" on the message that "We can fire you at any time for any reason not specifically prohibited by law and without even the most elementary procedural safeguards." Most employers prefer to gain the motivational and employee relations benefits that come from communicating the desire to treat employees fairly. Most employers probably also intend to treat employees fairly. But employers do not want to be bound by promises of fair treatment and liable for breaches. In short, most employers would like to have it both ways: basking in the warm glow of assurances of fair treatment and remaining entirely free to depart from any self-imposed limitations on the right to terminate at will.

Disclaimers are used to this end. **Disclaimers** are written statements incorporated into employee handbooks, employment applications, or other important documents that "disclaim" or deny that any statements in those documents create contractual rights binding on the employer. Language disclaiming the existence of a contract is typically combined with notification to employees in clear terms that their employment is at will. The statement (capitalized) on the first page of the employee manual in *Dillon* informing employees that the manual's provisions constituted guidelines only and that no commitment was being made to employees about how terminations and other decisions would be handled is a good example of a disclaimer. As another example, a bank included the following in its employee handbook:

> *[T]he contents of this handbook DO NOT CONSTITUTE THE TERMS OF A CONTRACT OF EMPLOYMENT. Nothing contained in this handbook should be construed as a guarantee of continued employment, but rather, employment with the bank is on an "at will" basis. This means that the employment relationship may be terminated at any time by either the employee or the Bank for any reason not expressly prohibited by law.[14]*

Disclaimers also frequently include language denying the contractual effect of any conflicting statements made elsewhere, reserving the right of the employer to modify policies, and placing that authority solely with designated individuals. For example:

> *[M]y employment and compensation can be terminated, with or without cause, and with or without notice, at any time, at the option of either the company or myself. I understand that no store manager or representative of Sears, Roebuck and Co., other than the president or vice-president of the Company, has any authority to enter into any agreement for employment for any specified period of time, or to make any agreement contrary to the foregoing.[15]*

But do disclaimers, inserted in the midst of statements and other facts suggesting a departure from employment at will, actually shield employers from wrongful discharge suits based on implied contract? In many cases, the answer is yes. Thus, *employers that desire to maintain employment at will should incorporate disclaimers into employee handbooks and other important documents defining the employment relationship.* As the New Jersey Supreme Court put it in a leading implied contract case:

> *[I]f the employer, for whatever reason, does not want the manual to be capable of being construed by the court as a binding contract, there are simple ways to attain that goal. All that need be done is the inclusion in a very prominent position of an appropriate statement that there is no promise of any kind by the employer contained in the manual; that regardless of what the manual says or provides, ... the employer continues to have the absolute power to fire anyone with or without good cause.[16]*

Disclaimers often defeat contractual rights flowing from handbooks and other sources if the disclaimers themselves are clear and unequivocal and if they are presented to employees in a prominent and conspicuous manner. Fine print buried in lengthy documents is not sufficient. A disclaimer placed on the first page of an employee manual, capitalized, and printed in bold is both prominent and conspicuous.[17] *Disclaimers should be communicated to employees, and employees should be asked to acknowledge receipt in writing.* Disclaimers that are included on applications for employment, so that employees know the terms of the relationship up front, appear to be especially effective.

However, disclaimers—even those carefully crafted and prominently displayed—are not foolproof. Some courts have taken the position that the interspersing of disclaimers and

---

[14]*Chambers v. Valley National Bank,* 721 F. Supp. 1128, 1131 (D. Ariz. 1988).

[15]*Reid v. Sears, Roebuck & Co.,* 790 F.2d 453, 456 (6th Cir. 1986).

[16]*Woolley v. Hoffmann-LaRoche, Inc.,* 491 A.2d 1257, 1271 (N.J. 1985), *modified,* 499.

[17]*Hessenthaler,* at 697.

statements that appear to confer rights is inherently ambiguous. Rather than simply allow a disclaimer to override everything else, the case is given to a jury to decide what the contract, as a whole, means.[18] This is precisely the approach that the court took in *Dillon*. The "mixed messages" sent by the disclaimer, the specific "Corrective Action Policy," and the employer's practices created ambiguity as to whether an implied contract existed.

If it is determined that contractual rights limiting an employer's ability to terminate at will do not exist, an implied contract wrongful discharge claim will fail. However, if contractual rights exist, it still remains to be proven that the employer violated those rights in terminating an employee. In a case involving an employee who was hired under an implied contractual agreement to terminate only for "good cause" and who was subsequently fired for sexual harassment, the California Supreme Court held:

> [T]he question critical to defendant's liability is not whether plaintiff in fact sexually harassed other employees, but whether at the time the decision to terminate his employment was made, defendants, acting in good faith and following an investigation that was appropriate under the circumstances, had reasonable grounds for believing plaintiff had done so.[19]

Thus, under this view—shared by most other courts—the role of the courts in implied contract cases is not to start with a blank slate and decide whether the employer's judgment was correct, but instead to determine whether the employer's decision was reasonable under the circumstances. In one relevant implied contract case, the court upheld a jury's verdict that the employee was not discharged for good cause, as company policy prescribed. The employee had been terminated for violating a strict policy against taking "anything, large or small." His offense was retrieving expired meat that had been disposed of in a barrel for pickup by a salvage company, cooking the meat on a grill, and (along with coworkers) eating it for lunch.[20] The jury determined that the employer violated the implied contract by terminating the employee without a "fair and honest" reason.

JUST THE FACTS

An employee worked for a utility operated by the city of Bountiful, Utah, from March 1978 to January 2004. He was given a copy of the Personnel Policies & Procedures Manual of the City of Bountiful (the "Employee Manual"). The Employee Manual contains a disclaimer stating that "[n]o contract exists between Bountiful City and its employees with respect to salary, salary ranges, movement within salary ranges, or employee benefits." The manual also states that "City policy will not tolerate verbal or physical conduct by any employee which harasses, disrupts, or interferes with another's work performance or which creates an intimidating, offensive, or hostile environment … ." Another section provides that "[o]ral or written threats, physical assault, harassment, intentional damage, and every other act or threat of violence by City employees is strictly prohibited." The employee suffered extreme abuse at the hands of his supervisor and eventually quit. If the quit was a constructive discharge, did the termination breach an implied contract? Why or why not?

See *Cabaness v. Thomas*, 232 P.3d 486 (Utah 2010).

---

[18]*McDonald v. Mobil Coal Producing, Inc.*, 820 P.2d 986 (Wyo. 1991).

[19]*Cotran v. Rollins Hudig Hall International, Inc.*, 948 P.2d 412, 423 (Cal. 1998).

[20]*Janes v. Wal-Mart Stores, Inc.*, 279 F.3d 883 (9th Cir. 2002).

Other Contract-Related Claims   Courts have long read into contracts an implied covenant of good faith and fair dealing. As a type of wrongful discharge claim, the **covenant of good faith and fair dealing** pertains to terminations that are undertaken in bad faith and that have the effect of denying employees the benefits of their contractual employment relationship. The term is potentially misleading. It does *not* amount to a general requirement that employers operate with good faith or terminate employees only for cause. Instead, in most of the states where it is recognized, the covenant applies only where there is an express or implied contract and the employer has used a termination to deprive an employee of an already-earned benefit. For example, a wrongful discharge in violation of the covenant of good faith and fair dealing was recognized where a long-term employee was fired immediately after obtaining a large order, for the purpose of depriving him of his commission.[21] Some uncertainty remains about the reach of the covenant of good faith and fair dealing and a few states, particularly Alaska, have given it a broader reading. According to the Alaska Supreme Court, the covenant of good faith and fair dealing applies to at-will employment contracts in the following manner:

> The covenant … generally requires employers to treat like employees alike and act in a manner that a reasonable person would regard as fair. The covenant has both a subjective and an objective component: the subjective component "prohibits an employer from terminating an employee for the purpose of depriving the employee of the contract's benefits," and the objective component "prohibits the employer from dealing with the employee in a manner that a reasonable person would regard as unfair."[22]

While this formulation of the covenant of good faith and fair dealing stops little short of establishing a just cause requirement for terminations, it is the exception to the rule. In most states where this type of wrongful termination claim is recognized, it adds little protection beyond that already available under the implied contract theory.

Another contract-related claim occasionally raised in discharge cases is **promissory estoppel**. We previously considered this legal claim in the context of a job applicant accepting employment and then having the offer withdrawn prior to commencing work (see Chapter 7). The key elements are reasonable and detrimental reliance on a clear promise. If, for example, an employee remains on the job due to reasonably relying on an employer's promises of job security, turns down lucrative alternative employment offers or incurs expenses relocating to a new assignment, and is then terminated, promissory estoppel might be invoked by the courts to redress the harm to the terminated employee—even in the absence of an express or implied contract. An employer who reneged on an offer to reinstate an employee if he was found innocent of criminal charges was liable for damages based on this theory.[23] In *Dillon*, the employer's statement that it would probably take four to six months for an employee to become comfortable in her new position was not a sufficiently clear promise of job security to support a promissory estoppel claim when Dillon was terminated for unsatisfactory performance shortly following acceptance of the job.

A third contract-related claim (but one for which tort damages are available) is **intentional interference with a contractual relationship**. This occurs when intentional, improper interference causes a third party to breach or not enter into a contractual relationship (the latter is sometimes referred to as "interference with prospective business advantage") with the plaintiff. In this context, "contractual" means any type of employment relationship, including at-will employment. The interference must be improper or

---

[21]*Fortune v. National Cash Register Co.*, 364 N.E.2d 1251 (Mass. 1977).

[22]*Mitchell v. Teck Cominco Alaska*, 193 P.3d 751, 760-61 (Alaska 2008).

[23]*Mers v. Dispatch Printing Co.*, 529 N.E.2d 958 (Ohio App. 1988).

without justification. Additionally, there must be a third party that is induced to breach or not enter into a contractual relationship. Cases where a former employee is blacklisted to prevent him from obtaining other employment clearly fit this requirement. The application of this claim to terminations in which agents of an employer (e.g., supervisors) use improper means to get employees fired is less clear. Is the employer a third party in such cases? The answer depends on whether the supervisor was acting within the scope of employment when the interference occurred. An intentional interference claim was allowed to proceed to trial in the case of a manager who took actions that led to the constructive discharge of an employee who opposed his romantic relationship with a married female subordinate. Evidence that the manager was acting from the purely personal motive of maintaining his affair made it plausible to argue that he was a separate party from the employer.[24]

Retaliation for an Act Supporting Public Policy

A variety of laws protect employees against terminations that, broadly speaking, are in retaliation for actions supporting public policy or that interfere with employees' rights under the law. These include common law claims for wrongful discharge under the public policy exception to employment at will, whistleblower protection statutes, antiretaliation and noninterference provisions in employment laws, and civic duty laws.

Public Policy Exception to Employment at Will   Employees are also citizens with rights and responsibilities. Sometimes, these roles conflict. Employers occasionally find it in their interest to have employees act in ways that are contrary to the public good. Under the **public policy exception to employment at will**, employers are liable in tort for wrongful discharge when they terminate employees for taking actions that public policy requires or commends. Allowing the terminations to stand would offend and undermine public policy.

ELEMENTS OF A CLAIM

Public Policy Exception to Employment at Will

Plaintiffs must show:

1. That a clear public policy existed relevant to their conduct (*clarity element*).
2. That discouraging the conduct in which they engaged would undermine this public policy (*jeopardy element*).
3. That engaging in conduct supportive of public policy resulted in termination (*causation element*).

Plaintiffs establishing these elements will prevail unless the defendant is able to show that there was an overriding justification for the termination (*absence of justification element*).

© Cengage Learning 2013.

Courts insist that claims be firmly grounded in fundamental and well-established public policies. To be protected, employees' actions must pertain to the public or society at large, and not merely personal interests or internal company matters. Primary sources

---

[24]*Kaelon v. USF Reddaway, Inc.,* 42 P.3d 344 (Or. App. 2002).

of public policy are statutes and constitutions, although regulations, court decisions, and even professional codes of ethics are sometimes recognized as grounds for public policy claims. Decisions in public policy cases often hinge on this "clarity" element. Although constitutions are the most basic source of law and public policy, courts have generally not permitted private sector employees to use constitutions as the basis for public policy claims. Thus, an employee of a private hospice who was allegedly fired for her speech was not able to ground a public policy claim in the First Amendment's protection of free speech. The court stated:

> [T]he First Amendment free speech provision expresses a guarantee only against action taken by the government. * * * [It] does not sufficiently describe the type of conduct alleged here, a private employer terminating an employee for the exercise of free speech, to enable the employer to know the fundamental public policies expressed by the First Amendment prohibited such a termination.[25]

Danny v. Laidlaw Transit Services provides an interesting example of a public policy claim by a terminated employee. The decision focuses on whether there was a sufficient public policy basis for the employee's actions, but also considers other elements of her claim.

Danny v. Laidlaw Transit Services
193 P.3d 128 (Wash. 2008)

OPINION BY JUSTICE OWENS:

* * * [The reformulated question before this court is]: Has the State of Washington established a clear mandate of public policy of protecting domestic violence survivors and their families and holding their abusers accountable? We answer the question in the affirmative.

* * * Laidlaw Transit Services, Inc., hired plaintiff Ramona Danny in February 1997. * * * In October 2002, Laidlaw promoted Danny to the position of scheduling manager.

While she was working at Laidlaw, Danny and her five children experienced ongoing domestic violence at the hands of her husband. She moved out of her house in February 2003 after suffering serious physical abuse but had to leave her children behind. In June 2003, she told Project Manager Jeff Kaeder about her domestic violence situation. In August 2003, Danny requested time off so she could move her children away from the abusive situation at their home. The project manager initially refused because Danny was working on a large project with an October deadline. * * * On August 20, 2003, Danny's husband beat her

13-year-old son so badly that he had to be hospitalized. Danny immediately moved all five children out of the home. When she returned to work, Danny again requested time off to move her children to a shelter. The project manager approved paid time off between August 25 and September 8, 2003. The record reveals that during late August and early September 2003, Danny conferred with police regarding protection from her husband and assisted in the prosecution against him for the assault of her son. During this time, Danny also used services from the King County Department of Community and Human Services to obtain transitional housing, domestic violence education, counseling and health services, and legal assistance.

On October 9, 2003, about a month after returning to work, Laidlaw demoted Danny from manager and offered her the position of scheduler, which she accepted. Laidlaw terminated Danny's employment on December 3, 2003. Laidlaw's stated reason for termination was falsification of payroll records.

Danny filed her complaint against Laidlaw ..., alleging that Laidlaw terminated her employment in violation of public policy.... Laidlaw filed a motion ... to

---

[25]*Grinzi v. San Diego Hospice*, 120 Cal. App. 4th 72, 81 (2004).

dismiss Danny's public policy claim. The District Court stayed its decision on Laidlaw's motion and instead certified the above question to this court.

ANALYSIS

Wrongful Discharge in Violation of Public Policy. Absent a contract to the contrary, Washington employees are generally terminable "at will." An at-will employee may quit or be fired for any reason. The common law tort of wrongful discharge is a narrow exception to the terminable-at-will doctrine. The tort of wrongful discharge applies when an employer terminates an employee for reasons that contravene a clearly mandated public policy. * * * To sustain the tort of wrongful discharge in violation of public policy, Danny must establish (1) "the existence of a clear public policy (the *clarity* element)"; (2) "that discouraging the conduct in which [she] engaged would jeopardize the public policy (the *jeopardy* element)"; (3) "that the public-policy-linked conduct caused the dismissal (the *causation* element)"; and (4) "[Laidlaw] must not be able to offer an overriding justification for the dismissal (the *absence of justification* element)."

* * * To determine whether a clear public policy exists, we must ask whether the policy is demonstrated in "'a constitutional, statutory, or regulatory provision or scheme.'" Although judicial decisions may establish public policy, "'courts should proceed cautiously if called upon to declare public policy absent some prior legislative or judicial expression on the subject.'" To qualify as a public policy for purposes of the wrongful discharge tort, a policy must be "truly public" and sufficiently clear.

This court has always been mindful that the wrongful discharge tort is narrow and should be "applied cautiously." Washington courts have generally recognized the public policy exception when an employer terminates an employee as a result of his or her (1) refusal to commit an illegal act, (2) performance of a public duty or obligation, (3) exercise of a legal right or privilege, or (4) in retaliation for reporting employer misconduct.

Danny argues that she performed a public duty when she acted to protect herself and her children and that she exercised a legal right to obtain protection from her abuser. * * * We find a public policy of preventing domestic violence most clearly established in the State's legislative enactments. We also find the policy pronounced by executive and judicial sources.

Legislative Expression of Public Policy. As early as 1979, the legislature recognized that domestic violence is a community problem that accounts for a "significant percentage" of violent crimes in the nation and is disruptive to "personal and community life." * * * [T]he legislature created funding for domestic violence shelters, recognizing that many domestic violence victims are unable to leave violent situations without proper resources. Also in 1979, the legislature enacted the Domestic Violence Act (DVA) requiring law enforcement to respond to domestic violence. The legislature stressed "the importance of domestic violence as a serious crime against society and [sought] to assure the victim of domestic violence the maximum protection from abuse which the law and those who enforce the law can provide." The legislature later expanded the DVA to require the mandatory arrest of domestic violence perpetrators, and has also expanded the definition of "domestic violence" to include violence between nonmarried individuals and individuals in "dating relationship[s]. * * *

In 1984, soon after enacting the DVA, the legislature enacted a separate Domestic Violence Prevention Act (DVPA) to provide domestic violence victims with the ability to obtain a civil protection order against their abusers. * * * The legislature has since amended the DVPA several times to improve the protection order process "so that victims have … easy, quick, and effective access to the court system." * * * In 1991, following enactment of the DVPA, the legislature created an address confidentiality program (ACP) to protect domestic violence victims "attempting to escape from actual or threatened domestic violence." The law provides domestic violence victims another layer of protection by allowing the secretary of state to provide victims with a substitute address in order to prevent abusers from locating their victim.

In recent years, the legislature has expanded domestic violence protection in Washington and highlighted the need for community involvement. In 2002, apparently recognizing that fear of losing employment may hinder escape from domestic violence, the legislature enacted laws allowing domestic violence victims to receive unemployment compensation through the state if they must leave employment to protect themselves or their immediate family from violence. The legislature further facilitated escape options for domestic violence victims in 2004, by allowing victims to terminate residential leases without penalty. * * * In addition to facilitating domestic violence victims in their escape, the legislature has also emphasized the importance of prosecuting domestic violence perpetrators. * * * The legislature has been equally as adamant in demanding protection for child victims of family violence such as Danny's 13-year-old son: "[C]hild abuse and neglect is a threat to the family unit and imposes major expenses on society." * * * The legislature has also created procedures for obtaining a protective order against the abuser of a child. Significantly, the legislature has declared that individuals with the physical custody of a child "have an affirmative *duty* to assist in the enforcement of the restraining order."

The legislature's consistent pronouncements over the last 30 years evince a clear public policy to prevent domestic violence—a policy the legislature has sought to further by taking clear, concrete actions to encourage domestic violence victims to end abuse, leave their abusers, protect their children, and cooperate with law enforcement and prosecution efforts to hold the abuser accountable. The legislature has created means for domestic violence victims to obtain civil and criminal protection from abuse, established shelters and funded social and legal services aimed at helping victims leave their abusers, established treatment programs for batterers, created an address confidentiality system to ensure the safety of victims, and guaranteed protection to victims exercising their duty to cooperate with law enforcement. The legislature's creation of means to prevent, escape, and end abuse is indicative of its overall policy of preventing domestic violence. This public policy is even more pronounced when a parent seeks, with the aid of law enforcement and child protective services, to protect his or her children from abuse.

Executive's Expression of Public Policy. Washington State's public policy of preventing domestic violence is also expressed in Executive Order 96-05, issued by former Washington State Governor Mike Lowry in 1996. Governor Lowry's executive order directs each state agency to create workplace environments that provide "assistance for domestic violence victims without fear of reproach" .... The executive order further directs agencies to "assure[ ] that every reasonable effort will be made to adjust work schedules and/or grant accrued or unpaid leave to allow employees who are victims of domestic violence to obtain medical treatment, counseling, legal assistance, to leave the area, or to make other arrangements to create a safer situation for themselves." Laidlaw contends that the executive order is not a proper source of public policy because it is not a "'constitutional, statutory, or regulatory provision or scheme.'" We disagree.* * * [W]e have recognized

that while statutes and case law are "primary sources of Washington public policy," public policy may come from other sources. We have previously found public policy in a federal statute, a municipal fire code, and in zoning and building codes. Other states have recognized that executive orders may form the basis of public policy. The executive order is yet another expression of our state's public policy of preventing domestic violence by assisting victims of domestic violence to leave their abusers, protect themselves and their children, and hold their abusers accountable through cooperation with police and prosecution. * * *

This state's policy of preventing domestic violence also finds expression in the Washington Constitution's crime victim amendment * * * [and in case law].

The Significance of Evidence of Public Policy. Laidlaw insists that any evidence of public policy is meaningless unless it directly addresses employers' responsibilities in preventing domestic violence. * * * [It is argued] that in order to demonstrate a clear public policy and satisfy the "clarity" element, the plaintiff must show that the *employer* contravened the public policy. This interpretation conflates the elements of wrongful discharge. The "clarity" element does not require us to evaluate the employer's conduct at all; the element simply identifies the public policy at stake. Other elements of the tort serve to evaluate the employer's conduct in relation to that public policy. * * * Because the "clarity" element does not concern itself with the employer's actions, the public policy need not specifically reference employment. * * *

The legislature's recent actions show that this state's clear and forceful public policy against domestic violence supports liability for employers who thwart their employees' efforts to protect themselves from domestic violence. The 2008 legislature unanimously passed Substitute House Bill 2602: "AN ACT Relating to increasing the safety and economic security of victims of domestic violence...." * * * [T]he new law provides for "reasonable leave" for domestic violence victims to seek legal remedies, law enforcement assistance, treatment for injuries, services from shelters and other agencies, or to relocate themselves or their families, among other things. Though the legislature had not yet considered such a bill at the time of Danny's discharge, the fundamental public policy underlying the bill had long been established at that time. * * *

Limitations of This Holding. * * * Laidlaw argues that recognizing the clearly established public policy in this case will "require employers to serve as a functional equivalent of the Department of Social and Health Services." Laidlaw also argues that "[a]n employee fearing discharge for what may be legitimate reasons need only claim to be a victim of domestic violence to be half way to a valid public policy claim when they are discharged." Laidlaw's parade of horribles is unfounded. Our holding will in no way open the floodgates of litigation. The clarity element is merely one of the elements Danny and future plaintiffs must successfully establish in order to maintain a wrongful discharge claim. Plaintiffs like Danny must also satisfy the jeopardy, causation, and absence of justification elements of the wrongful discharge tort. * * *

To satisfy the "jeopardy" element, the employee "must prove that discouraging the conduct in which [she] engaged would jeopardize the public policy." ... [I]n order to satisfy the jeopardy element, the employee must show that her conduct "*directly relates* to the public policy, or was *necessary* for the effective enforcement of the public policy." Accordingly, the employee must show that other means of promoting the policy are inadequate.

The "jeopardy" element strictly limits the scope of claims under the tort of wrongful discharge. In this case, for example, in order for Danny to show that her conduct satisfies the "jeopardy" element, she will have to show that the time that she took off work was the *only available adequate means* to prevent domestic violence against herself or her children or to hold her abuser accountable. This inquiry will turn on the nature of the danger, the particular actions that Danny took, and the details of her work schedule. For example, if she wished to get a protection order, but the court was open only during her scheduled work hours, time off may have been necessary. The amount of time off would turn on her distance from the court and other relevant factual circumstances. On the other hand, if she worked at night, her employer would likely not have been obligated to give her any time off work to seek a protection order. Time off would only be required if she could not obtain the order outside of work hours. Likewise, if she were called to testify against her abuser, time off would have been necessary if the hearing were during her work hours. If she needed to move her family to a shelter, the inquiry would turn on whether constraints such as the shelter's rules or her abuser's schedule made moving during work hours the *only adequate means* of protecting herself and her children.

We keep in mind that the critical inquiry in the four-part wrongful discharge test is not whether the employer's actions *directly* contravene public policy, but whether the employer fired the employee because the *employee* took necessary action to comply with public policy. The authors of all three opinions in this case agree that Washington State has a clearly defined public policy of protecting domestic violence survivors and their families and holding abusers accountable. The tort serves to safeguard that important public policy by allowing employees to do what they must to prevent domestic violence, without fear of losing their economic independence. ... [L]imiting the tort's application... [to] discharge[s] based on their *status* as victims of domestic violence ... would leave exposed any employee who took an absolutely necessary morning off work to get a protection order, to give a statement to police, or to move her children out of imminent harm's way. Discouraging this conduct will directly endanger our community's efforts to end domestic violence. * * *

We hold that Danny has satisfied her burden of proving the clarity element of a claim for wrongful discharge in violation of public policy. Washington State has unequivocally established, through legislative, judicial, constitutional, and executive expressions, a clear mandate of public policy of protecting domestic violence survivors and their families and holding abusers accountable. Having answered the reformulated certified question in the affirmative, we return the case to the District Court.

CASE QUESTIONS

1. What was the issue in this case? What did the Court decide?
2. How convincing is the evidence of a clear, dominant public policy? Why does it not matter that these legislative enactments do not address the responsibilities of private sector employers to their employees who are victims of domestic abuse?
3. Does it appear that the plaintiff will be able to satisfy the other elements of her public policy claim? Why or why not?
4. Should the fact that the Washington State legislature enacted a law requiring employers to provide leave to victims of domestic abuse, but did so in 2008 after the events of this case had already occurred, have any bearing on this decision? Why or why not?
5. What are the implications of this decision for employers? How should employers handle this type of situation?

The "jeopardy element" in a public policy claim points to the fact that even when an employee's actions relate to a clear public policy, the employee will not be protected unless allowing the termination would tend to undermine the public policy in question. Courts will inquire into whether alternative means exist to promote the public policy. In *Danny*, the court suggested that the plaintiff would have to show that taking the time off from work that arguably led to her termination was necessary to the furtherance of a clear public policy against domestic abuse. The availability of other avenues for enforcement is also relevant here. This is a particularly murky aspect of the public policy exception, but in general, it can be said that the tort does not apply to cases where legislators have enacted laws with comprehensive enforcement schemes and remedies for terminated employees sufficient to protect the public policy in question.[26] Thus, despite the fact that laws prohibiting discrimination are central parts of public policy, every case of discriminatory termination does *not* simultaneously become a public policy tort claim because enforcement procedures and adequate remedies already exist under antidiscrimination statutes. In a case involving a manager who said that he was fired for correcting an erroneous time card, the court agreed that wage and hour laws establish a clear requirement that employers maintain accurate records of work hours, but held that this public policy was adequately protected through numerous civil and criminal penalties against offending employers. Thus, the policy was not jeopardized by termination of the employee.[27] In contrast, an employee who was fired after he filed a wage claim under state law was able to go to trial with his public policy tort claim. The court noted that state wage and hour law addressed underpayment of wages but not termination, did not provide for jury trials, and offered relatively little in terms of potential remedies.[28]

The "causation element" is common to any type of retaliation claim and would be satisfied by evidence regarding the timing of the termination and other indicators of a motive of retaliating for the action taken in support of public policy. If an employee can establish the first three elements, an employer can still prevail by showing that the termination was also motivated by another overriding factor.

JUST THE FACTS

Prior to his termination, an employee was the financial controller for a privately held company whose principal owners were three brothers. The employee became aware that one of the owners had misappropriated $15,000 of inventory for use in another business that he owned, altered financial records to cover up his dealings, and was the cause of a $150,000 decline in company revenue. The employee reported his concerns about this financial misconduct that he believed constituted criminal embezzlement and larceny to the other two brothers. The brother that allegedly engaged in these acts began to pressure the employee to quit and eventually terminated him. Is the employee likely to prevail in a wrongful termination claim based on the public policy exception to employment at will? Why or why not?

See *Swears v. R.M. Roach & Sons*, 225 W. Va. 699 (2010).

---

[26]*Leininger v. Pioneer National Latex*, 115 Ohio St. 3d 311, 317 (2007).

[27]*White v. Sears, Roebuck & Co.*, 163 Ohio App. 3d 416 (2005), *appeal not allowed*, 108 Ohio St. 3d 1475 (2006).

[28]*Campbell v. Husky Hogs LLC*, 292 Kan. 225, 236-37 (2010).

Four varieties of the public policy exception to employment at will are recognized: termination for (1) refusing to commit an illegal act, (2) exercising a legal right, (3) performing a public duty, and (4) reporting illegal activity (i.e., whistleblowing). *Employees must not be terminated for refusing to commit illegal acts, exercising their legal rights, performing important public duties, or reporting illegal activities of employers and their agents.*

The first case in which the public policy exception to employment at will was recognized involved the termination of an at-will employee for **refusal to commit an illegal act**. Employed by the Teamsters Union, the man was called to testify at a state legislative hearing probing the union's activities.[29] When he refused his employer's instructions to give false testimony, he was summarily fired. Citing the state's criminal code and its prohibition of perjury, the court held that allowing the termination would undermine a public policy basic to law enforcement. Employees could be placed in the untenable position of either breaking the law by testifying falsely or losing their jobs. Other examples of successful public policy claims based on refusal to commit illegal acts include cases where employees were fired for refusing to pollute a waterway,[30] fill a vehicle designed for unleaded gas with leaded gas,[31] and drive a vehicle without a valid inspection sticker.[32] In contrast, a nurse's public policy claim that she was fired for refusing to backdate a Medicare form was rejected because signing a backdated form does not violate the law.[33] This was not a case of Medicare fraud. The services had, in fact, been performed, and a doctor had certified that they were necessary.

Public policy wrongful discharge claims are also recognized when employees are terminated for **exercising legal rights**. Successful claims have been raised by employees fired for such things as filing workers' compensation claims,[34] exercising their voting rights as stockholders in a manner contrary to their employer's wishes,[35] and having wages withheld (garnished) for child support.[36] However, in a troubling case, a cashier who was fired for refusing to drop assault and battery charges against her supervisor failed in her public policy claim.[37] The supervisor had assaulted her after she made known her suspicions that he was embezzling money from their employer. The employee was terminated a few weeks before the criminal trial (in which the supervisor was convicted). The court held that laws against obstruction of justice are aimed at preserving the integrity of the criminal justice system and not at preventing intimidation of individuals. Hence, the laws did not provide a sufficient public policy basis for a wrongful discharge claim.

The most nebulous and least often recognized variety of public policy claims is termination for **performing a public duty**. The duty in these cases is something that is not strictly required by law (if it was, this would place it in the category of termination for refusal to act illegally), but it is clearly an action undertaken in the public interest. The Washington State Supreme Court ruled for an armored car driver who left his armored car to intervene in a likely homicide, even though he had no legal obligation to do so,

[29]*Petermann v. International Brotherhood of Teamsters, Local 396,* 344 P.2d 25 (Cal. App. 1959).

[30]*Sabine Pilot Service v. Hauck,* 687 S.W.2d 733 (Tex. 1985).

[31]*Phipps v. Clark Oil & Refining Corp.,* 408 N.W.2d 569 (Minn. 1986).

[32]*Adams v. G.W. Cochran & Co.,* 597 A.2d 28 (D.C. App. 1991).

[33]*Callentine v. Staff Builders, Inc.,* 271 F.3d 1124 (8th Cir. 2001).

[34]*Kelsay v. Motorola,* 384 N.E.2d 353 (Ill. 1978).

[35]*Bowman v. State Bank,* 331 S.E.2d 797 (Va. 1985).

[36]*Greely v. Miami Valley Maintenance Contractors,* 551 N.E.2d 981 (Ohio 1990).

[37]*Rowan v. Tractor Supply Co.,* 559 S.E.2d 709 (Va. 2002).

and he was acting contrary to a strict company policy.[38] The court found that "protection of human life" is a fundamental public policy "evidenced by countless statutes and judicial circumstances." Because the driver was terminated for acting on behalf of this dominant public policy and the employer lacked an overriding justification for the termination (although it had a number of sound reasons for maintaining its "don't ever leave the armored car" policy), the driver had a viable public policy claim. The *Danny* case straddled the "performing a public duty" and "exercising legal rights" categories, as she claimed that she was performing a public duty when she acted to protect herself and her children and exercising a legal right by obtaining protection from her abuser. Most courts, however, have been very reluctant to protect employees who "do the right thing" absent a specific legal requirement.

The last type of public policy claim is termination for reporting illegal activity, or **whistleblowing**. Whistleblowers report activities engaged in by employers or their agents that are illegal or otherwise injurious to the public. The willingness of insiders to come forward is often critical to bringing corporate wrongdoing to light and enforcing the law. However, society's gratitude for this service is usually not matched by the reaction of employers. To put the matter succinctly, whistleblowers often get hammered by their employers. Whether reports of wrongdoing are raised internally or externally can affect the outcome of cases. Some courts have declined to protect internal reports, viewing them as more akin to internal policy disputes than to efforts to enforce public policy (at least in the absence of threats to go public if changes are not made).[39] Other courts require that internal reports occur before employees "go outside" the organization with their suspicions of wrongdoing. In either event, the subject of the report must be a matter that truly affects the public, rather than simply an alleged violation of company policy. This distinction is sometimes not so easily drawn. Courts have differed, for example, on whether hospital employees reporting problems with patient care are merely disputing internal hospital policies or reporting problems affecting public health.[40]

Whistleblower Protection Statutes

Whistleblowers also enjoy protection under a variety of statutes. Most states have whistleblower protection laws, although some of these statutes apply only to public sector employees. Some whistleblowers are protected under laws that pertain to specific safety-sensitive industries, including aviation and nuclear power. A variety of federal environmental laws incorporate whistleblower protections for employees reporting environmental violations by their employers. The Patient Protection and Affordable Care Act includes language protecting employees who blow the whistle regarding violations of the new law.[41] OSHA has been charged with enforcement of approximately twenty different federal whistleblower statutes.[42] Whistleblower protections for employees who bring to light financial wrongdoing have been the focus of recent enactments.

---

[38]*Gardner v. Loomis*, 913 P.2d 377 (Wash. 1996).

[39]*House v. Carter-Wallace*, Inc., 556 A.2d 353 (N.J. Super. 1989), cert. denied, 564 A.2d 874 (N.J. 1989).

[40]*Wright v. Shriners Hospital for Crippled Children*, 589 N.E.2d 1241 (Mass. 1992) (report about patient care not protected); *Witt v. Forest Hospital*, 450 N.E.2d 811 (Ill. App. 1983) (report about patient care protected).

[41]111 P.L. 148, Sec. 1558 (2010).

[42]U.S. Government Accountability Office. *Whistleblower Protection: Substantial Management Attention Needed to Address Long-standing Program Weaknesses.* GA0-10-722 (August 2010), 15–16.

THE CHANGING WORKPLACE

Whistleblower Protection in an Age of Financial Scandal

Improper and illegal financial dealings are hardly a new story, but their frequency and scale seem to have increased in recent years. From the insider trading and savings and loan scandals of the 1980s, to the demise of Enron in 2001, to the Madoff Ponzi scheme and the near collapse of an investment banking system overexposed to home mortgages that could not be repaid, bank customers, investors, employees, and ultimately taxpayers have been repeatedly victimized. Government regulators have lacked the ability, will, or political support to vigorously monitor and control risky financial dealings. It is clear that if anyone has the information needed to prompt timely intervention and avert full-fledged financial scandals, it is the employees of these firms. Yet, particularly in the financial sector, persons willing to blow the whistle on the misdeeds of firms have been few and far between.

The **Sarbanes-Oxley Act** (SOX Act), passed in response to a wave of corporate scandals in the 1990s that included Enron's adventure in creative accounting, was intended to encourage the reporting of financial wrongdoing by protecting employees of publicly traded companies (as well as officers, contractors, subcontractors, and agents of such companies) who disclose information, assist in investigations, file charges, testify, or otherwise assist in proceedings related to fraud against shareholders of publicly traded companies.[1] However, plaintiffs have established a track record of mostly futility in pressing Sarbanes-Oxley whistleblower claims.[2] One reason is that the law as initially written provided a very brief limitations period (ninety days). Also, courts ruled that the privately held subsidiaries of publicly traded companies were not covered by the law. Courts have construed the activities protected by the SOX Act narrowly and ruled in numerous cases that the plaintiffs did not have a reasonable belief that the defendant company was violating federal securities law or otherwise engaging in fraud against stockholders.[3] A financial officer's complaints about accounting irregularities (misreporting loan losses, permitting unqualified people to make ledger entries) did not form the basis for a successful Sarbanes-Oxley whistleblower claim because he failed to show how these complaints related to the specific securities laws referenced in the statute.[4] Likewise,

three employees who were downsized after reporting their concerns about their employer's accounting practices were found not to have reasonably believed that their employer was engaging in securities fraud.[5] The court in this case made much of the fact that one of the complainants was a CPA who should have known that the disputed financial statements were for internal use and not submitted to the SEC. Their reports about errors with a computer program used to calculate interest payments were also not grist for their whistleblower claim because the errors were not intentional, they were not concealed from stockholders, and the company made efforts to correct them. To whom a report is made also matters under the SOX Act. Two Boeing auditors who provided information to a newspaper reporter about alleged pressure on auditors to ignore deficiencies in the company's internal financial controls were not protected because the act specifies parties to whom protected reports can be made and these do not include the press.[6]

The **Dodd-Frank Wall Street Reform and Consumer Protection Act**[7] was enacted in 2010 in response to the banking crisis that led to the failure of numerous banks and investment firms, consolidation of others, and a controversial "bail-out" of large financial institutions. The legislation is wide-ranging in its efforts to strengthen oversight of the financial industry and incorporates several different whistleblower provisions. Dodd-Frank amends and addresses some of the weaknesses of the SOX Act by doubling the limitations period for bringing whistleblower claims (from 90 to 180 days), extending coverage to persons who are employed by the private subsidiaries of publicly traded companies when the financial results of the companies are reported together, providing plaintiffs with the right to a jury trial, and prohibiting the application of arbitration agreements (which are widely used in the financial industry) to suits brought under the SOX Act, as well as the waiver of SOX Act claims in settlement agreements.[8] On the theory that people who work in the financial sector are motivated by financial incentives, this section of Dodd-Frank also contains whistleblower bounty provisions similar to those found in the False Claims Act. Whistleblowers who provide original information to the Securities and Exchange Commission

(SEC) that results in the recovery of $1 million or more will be entitled to between 10 and 30 percent of the amount recovered. Whistleblowers will be permitted to remain anonymous until such time as they claim their share of the recovery. Dodd-Frank also opens new vistas of potential whistleblowing by providing protection to employees who perform work related to offering financial products and services to consumers (ostensibly, the broad job description of most persons working in the financial sector) when they provide information to the newly minted Bureau of Consumer Financial Protection or other government authorities regarding possible violations of Dodd-Frank or bureau rules.[9]

While this expansion of legal protections for financial whistleblowers seems impressive, it remains to be seen whether these laws will provide real protection to either employees or the public. Legislators' responses to scandals and crises often become subverted when the spotlight moves elsewhere and there is a return to business as usual.

---

[1] 18 U.S.C.S. § 1514A(a) (2011).
[2] Richard E. Moberly. "Unfulfilled Expectations: An Empirical Analysis of Why Sarbanes-Oxley Whistleblowers Rarely Win." 49 *William & Mary Law Review* 65 (October 2007).
[3] *Gale v. U.S. Department of Labor*, 384 Fed. Appx. 926 (11th Cir. 2010).
[4] *Welch v. Chao*, 536 F.3d 269 (4th Cir. 2008).
[5] *Allen v. Administrative Review Board*, 514 F.3d 468 (5th Cir. 2008).
[6] *Tides v. Boeing*, 644 F.3d 809 (9th Cir. 2011).
[7] 111 P.L. 203; 124 Stat. 1376 (2010).
[8] 111 P.L. 203, Sec. 922 (2010).
[9] 111 P.L. 203, Sec. 1057 (2010).

In *Sharkey v. J.P. Morgan Chase & Co.*, a bank vice president who made numerous reports regarding the suspicious financial transactions of a bank client had client accounts removed, was excluded from important meetings regarding clients, was denied a bonus, and was ultimately terminated. The court had to decide whether her reports were protected activity under the Sarbancs-Oxley Act.

Sharkey v. J.P. Morgan Chase
2011 U.S. Dist. LEXIS 92953 (S.D.N.Y.)

OPINION BY DISTRICT JUDGE SWEET:

Defendants J.P. Morgan Chase & Co. ("JPMC"), Joe Kenney ("Kenney"), Adam Green ("Green") and Leslie Lassiter ("Lassiter") (collectively, "Defendants") have moved ... to dismiss the Amended Complaint (the "AC"), filed by Plaintiff Jennifer Sharkey ("Plaintiff" or "Sharkey"). Based on the conclusions set forth below, Defendants' motion to dismiss is denied.

PRIOR PROCEEDINGS

On October 22, 2009, Sharkey filed a timely complaint with the Occupational Safety and Health Administration of the U.S. Department of Labor ("OSHA") alleging violations of the Sarbanes-Oxley Act of 2002 ("Sarbanes-Oxley" or "SOX"). On or about April 12, 2010, OSHA issued its findings and preliminary order dismissing her complaint. Sharkey filed her complaint with this court on May 10, 2010, alleging claims under SOX.

The Defendants moved to dismiss the complaint. The Opinion and Order dated January 14, 2011 of this court (the "January 14 Order") held that Sharkey engaged in a protected activity under SOX when reporting with respect to a third party, the Suspect Client, but that the illegal activity reported was not adequately alleged in the original complaint.... Sharkey was granted leave to replead her SOX claims. Sharkey filed the AC on February 14, 2011. * * *

FACTS ALLEGED

* * * Shortly after Sharkey was assigned to the Suspect Client's account, members of J.P. Morgan's compliance and risk management team contacted her to express concerns regarding the Suspect Client's alleged involvement in illegal activities, including mail fraud, bank fraud and money laundering. Around the same time in the first half of 2009, the Office of the Comptroller of the Currency, a bureau of the U.S.

Department of the Treasury conducted an audit of J.P. Morgan's Northeast Region's Private Wealth Management group and J.P. Morgan's compliance with Know Your Customer ('KYC') requirements. The AC alleges that … "OCC's investigation and audit was focused in great part on the Suspect Client, several Private Wealth Management accounts that the Suspect Client created, and J.P. Morgan's compliance—or lack thereof—with respect to KYC requirements on these accounts."

* * * The AC alleges that Plaintiff "believed that the Suspect Client was engaging in fraud, money laundering, mail fraud, bank fraud, and/or federal securities laws violations" based on … the following allegations:

- The Suspect Client, when he would provide requested documentation, would use unusual or suspicious identification documents that could not be readily verified, such as foreign passports or documents in foreign languages.
- The Suspect Client refused to provide complete information about the nature and purpose of its business, anticipated account activity, prior banking relationships, the names of its officers and directors, or information on its business locations, or tax returns.
- The Suspect Client would make frequent or large transactions with no record of past or present employment experience.
- Some of the Suspect Client's accounts, at times, acted as a trust or shell company, and the Suspect Client was reluctant to provide information on controlling parties and/or signatories on these accounts.
- The Suspect Client either refused or was reluctant to provide Plaintiff with information needed to complete the mandatory KYC report.
- Funds transfer activities in the Suspect Client's accounts were unexplained, repetitive, and/or would show unusual patterns.
- Payments or receipts with no apparent links to legitimate contracts, goods, or services would be received in the Suspect Client's accounts.
- Funds transfers would be sent or received within and between the Suspect Client's own accounts.
- Unusual transfers of funds would occur among the Suspect Client's related accounts or among accounts that involved the same or related principals.
- The Suspect Client would secure loans or margins by deposits or other readily marketable assets, such as securities.

- The Suspect Client was involved in potentially higher-risk activities, including activities that may be subject to export/import restrictions.
- Plaintiff was unable to obtain from the Suspect Client sufficient information to positively identify originators, beneficiaries and/or signatories of accounts.
- Payments to or from the Suspect Client's accounts and/or companies would have no stated or legitimate business purpose.
- The Suspect Client's transacting businesses, although not similar in their lines of business, would share the same address and/or exhibited other address inconsistencies, such as not in fact maintaining an office where one was listed.
- The Suspect Client maintained accounts and transacted deposits through multiple branches of J.P. Morgan across various geographical areas.
- The Suspect Client established multiple accounts in various corporate or individual names that lacked sufficient business purpose for the account complexities and/or appeared to be an effort to hide the beneficial ownership from J.P. Morgan.
- The Suspect Client would maintain several accounts with a zero balance, but would refuse to allow them to be closed.

Sharkey alleges that Suspect Client set up an account in the name of a law firm, which she was told was established as an escrow account to hold licensing fees associated with one of the Suspect Client's businesses. However, Suspect Client would trade securities in and from this account and would wire transfer the proceeds from the trade to personal checking accounts maintained by the Suspect Client at various J.P. Morgan commercial branches, without authorization or knowledge of the law firm. Under this same account, the Suspect Client purchased several million dollars worth of securities on margin, i.e., on a loan from J.P. Morgan.

Plaintiff alleges that she inquired with "established figures in the business area that the Suspect Client was involved" but none of them had heard of the Suspect Client or his businesses. Plaintiff learned that one of the Suspect Client's businesses dealt in merchandise from Columbia, a nation with which she states J.P. Morgan was not supposed to transact any business. Suspect Client established a limited liability corporation with respect to two properties in Westchester, New York, but never provided, despite Plaintiff's repeated requests, corporate formation documents, property deeds, purchase contracts, mortgage documentation, tax returns, or necessary proof of income. Suspect Client's son requested that J.P. Morgan, through Ms. Sharkey, provide a mortgage for his primary residence located at one those addresses, but the Suspect Client and his son refused to provide proper documentation to secure the mortgage and, on one or more occasions, provided Plaintiff with suspect and potentially false documentation regarding proof of income, resulting in Plaintiff denying the request. Suspect Client's son suggested that Plaintiff issue him a loan secured against a high-balance account maintained by his father, such as the law firm escrow account discussed above.

* * * Sharkey maintains that she communicated her complaints regarding the illegal and/or suspicious activities alleged above to Kenney, Green and Lassiter over an extended period of time by way of e-mail, telephone calls, telephone conferences, and in-person meetings.

THE COURT HAS JURISDICTION OVER THE FACTS ALLEGED IN THE AMENDED COMPLAINT

* * * "Before an employee can assert a cause of action in federal court under the Sarbanes-Oxley Act, the employee must file a complaint with [OSHA] and afford OSHA the opportunity to resolve the allegations administratively." * * * "[A] federal court can only conduct a de novo review of those [SOX whistleblower] claims that have been administratively exhausted. * * * [W]here Plaintiff's claims, including specific adverse employment actions, protected activity, and the general nature of the facts that formed Plaintiff's belief in violations of the enumerated statutes giving rise to the protected activity, were timely presented in her OSHA Complaint, and where more specific allegations naturally originating from those assertions have been alleged in the AC in direct response to this Court's decision to grant Plaintiff leave to do so, the entirety of the AC is appropriately subject to the jurisdiction of this Court.

A CLAIM UNDER THE SARBANES-OXLEY WHISTLEBLOWER PROVISION HAS BEEN STATED

The whistleblower provision of SOX provides, in relevant part:

> No company with a class of securities registered under section 12 of the Securities Exchange Act of 1934 … or that is required to file reports under section 15(d) of the Securities Exchange Act …, or any

officer, employee … or agent of such company, may discharge, demote, suspend, threaten, harass, or in any other manner discriminate against an employee in the terms and conditions of employment because of any lawful act done by the employee—(1) to provide information, cause information to be provided, or otherwise assist in any investigation regarding any conduct which the employee reasonably believes constitutes a violation of section 1341 [mail fraud], 1343 [wire fraud], 1344 [bank fraud], or 1348 [securities fraud], any rule or regulation of the Securities and Exchange Commission, or any provision of Federal law relating to fraud against shareholders, when the information or assistance is provided to or the investigation is conducted by—(C) a person with supervisory authority over the employee (or such other person working for the employer who has the authority to investigate, discover, or terminate misconduct).

To assert a whistleblower claim under SOX, Sharkey must show that: (i) she engaged in protected activity; (ii) the employer knew of the protected activity; (iii) she suffered an unfavorable personnel action; and (iv) circumstances exist to suggest that the protected activity was a contributing factor to the unfavorable action.

Defendants contend that the AC fails to allege which statute Plaintiff believed the Suspect Client violated, that it fails to allege protected activity because it does not specify the illegal conduct Plaintiff allegedly reported to Defendants, and that J.P. Morgan did not know that Plaintiff engaged in a protected activity. * * *

In order to state a whistleblower claim under SOX, "[a] plaintiff need not show an actual violation of the law, nor must a plaintiff cite a particular statute that he believed was being violated." Instead, "SOX protects employees who provide information which the employee 'reasonably believes constitutes a violation' of any SEC rule or regulation or 'Federal law relating to fraud against shareholders.'" In assessing the reasonableness of a plaintiff's belief regarding the illegality of the particular conduct at issue, courts look to the "'basis of knowledge available to a reasonable person in the circumstances with the employee's training and experience.'" * * * "The threshold is intended to include all good faith and reasonable reporting of fraud, and there should be no presumption that reporting is otherwise, absent specific evidence." * * *

Here, Plaintiff has alleged a myriad of allegations that when taken together prevent a finding, at this stage, that Sharkey's belief that Suspect Client was engaged in violations of the enumerated SOX statutes was unreasonable. * * * SOX prohibits an employer from retaliating against an employee who complains about any of the six enumerated categories of misconduct. Here, Plaintiff has surpassed that bar and adequately pled that she formed a reasonable belief that the Suspect Client was engaged in one or more violations of the SOX enumerated categories of misconduct and ... that she complained to Defendants about each of these.

* * * [A] whistleblower "need not 'cite a code section he believes was violated' in his communication to his employer, but the employee's communications must identify the specific conduct that the employee believes to be illegal." Here, "Plaintiff has properly pled that she engaged in conduct protected by when she repeatedly reported her concerns regarding the [Suspect] Client's illegal activity to the Individual Defendants and JPMC's risk and compliance team." Plaintiff's communications regarding the Suspect Client culminated in Sharkey's communication to Defendants on July 30, 2009—via her final KYC report—that J.P. Morgan exit its relationship with the Suspect Client due to the concerns Sharkey had previously reported. The prior reports ... include ... that the Suspect Client would secure loans or margins by deposits or other readily marketable assets, such as securities, which in effect would put J.P. Morgan and its shareholders at risk if any of said loans or margins defaulted; the Suspect Client was involved in potentially higher-risk activities, including activities that may be subject to export/import restrictions; under the several million dollar purported escrow account, the Suspect Client purchased several million dollars worth of securities on margin, i.e., on a loan from J.P. Morgan for which it and its shareholders would bear the risk. By alleging that she communicated these concerns to Defendants, Sharkey properly asserts that she informed J.P. Morgan and the Individual Defendants of the suspected fraudulent and illegal activity perpetrated by the Suspect Client against the Company. This was protected activity under SOX.

The Defendants further contend that Plaintiff fails to allege that Defendant J.P. Morgan "knew or should have known that Plaintiff engaged in such [protected] activity." However, the AC alleges how, when and to whom Plaintiff reported her concerns of fraudulent and illegal activity on the part of the Suspect Client. This includes Plaintiff's allegations that "[s]tarting in January 2009 ... [Plaintiff] repeatedly informed her superiors of the potential unlawful activities of the Suspect Client"; within days of Plaintiff being assigned to the Suspect Client's account, "members of J.P. Morgan's compliance and risk management team contacted Ms. Sharkey to express their concerns regarding the Suspect Client's alleged involvement in illegal activities, including allegations of mail fraud, bank fraud and money laundering" and that Plaintiff "immediately relayed this information" to Lassiter; Plaintiff shared her conclusions regarding her research into and belief that "Suspect Client was engaged in fraud, money laundering, mail fraud, bank fraud, and/or violating federal securities laws" with Kenny, Green, and Lassier [*sic*]; Plaintiff "informed J.P. Morgan's compliance department of her good faith belief that the Suspect Client was ... engaged in fraud, money laundering, bank fraud, mail fraud, and/or federal securities laws violations"; and on July 30, 2009 she submitted a Know Your Client audit on the Suspect Client's account, which Kenny, Green, and Lassiter received, that recommended that J.P. Morgan terminate its relationship with the Suspect Client. * * *

* * * Accordingly, Plaintiff adequately alleges conduct she reported to Defendants and that Defendants had knowledge of Sharkey's protected activity. * * *

CASE QUESTIONS

1. What was the legal issue in this case? What did the court decide?
2. The allegations of fraud in this case involved a client, rather than the plaintiff's employer. Why is she still able to sue her employer under the SOX Act?
3. What does a plaintiff have to show in a whistleblower complaint under the SOX Act? What is the evidence that these requirements were met in this case?
4. Assuming that there is evidence that the plaintiff was retaliated against and ultimately terminated due to her reports, why might her superiors at the bank have acted in this way?

Federal government employees are covered by the federal **Whistleblower Protection Act (WPA)**.[43] The WPA prohibits taking or failing to take a personnel action because an employee or applicant has disclosed information that is reasonably believed to show (1) a violation of a law, rule, or regulation or (2) gross mismanagement, gross waste of funds, abuse of authority, or a substantial and specific danger to public health or safety. The definition of protected reports is relatively broad under the WPA because the "internal" affairs of federal government agencies nonetheless concern the public. The act's prohibition against retaliation is also broad, extending to decisions to order psychiatric testing and "any other significant change in duties, responsibilities, or working conditions." Not all disclosures relating to these matters trigger the WPA, however. Reports made to a supervisor about the supervisor's own conduct or those made through normal channels as part of employees' job responsibilities are not covered. On the other hand, complaints made to a supervisor about other employees' misconduct are protected reports.[44] Despite the apparent breadth of the WPA, the federal appeals court hearing these cases has almost always ruled against plaintiffs.[45]

Practical Considerations How should employers respond to whistleblowing by their employees?

One other federal whistleblower law deserves mention. The **False Claims Act**[46] applies to individuals who come forth with information about a knowingly false or fraudulent claim made against the federal government. The law allows the Department of Justice to join in suits to recover the amounts lost through fraud or individuals to sue on behalf of the government. Because these cases often involve large amounts of money (e.g., defense contracts, Medicare payments to hospitals) and the act allows recovery of three times the actual damages to the government—with 15 percent to 30 percent going to the individual initiating the action—whistleblowing under the False Claims Act can be lucrative. The False Claims Act also protects employees against retaliation based on their investigating or otherwise pursuing actions intended to uncover fraud against the federal government. Employees whose normal job responsibilities include making reports to their employers about issues that are the subject of whistleblower claims must show that their actions went beyond just doing their jobs. A chief contract negotiator for a defense contractor was protected under the False Claims Act when he was suspended shortly after he told the Navy to "continue to challenge" the contractor's cost data.[47] An office manager who repeatedly warned company officials that their Medicare billing practices were unlawful and exposed them to "significant criminal and civil liability" was able to sue under the False Claims Act, even though her reports were made internally within the company and did not explicitly threaten legal action.[48] It was enough that the "employee's actions … [were] sufficient to support a reasonable conclusion that the employer could have feared being reported to the government for fraud or sued [on behalf of the government] by the employee."[49]

---

[43] 5 U.S.C.S. § 2302 (2011).

[44] *Huffman v. Office of Personnel Management,* 263 F.3d 1341 (Fed. Cir. 2001).

[45] David Cay Johnston. "Court Says Ex-I.R.S. Employee Deserves Whistle-Blower Status." *New York Times* (September 2, 2004), C4.

[46] U.S.C.S. §§ 3729–3730 (2011).

[47] *United States of America, ex rel. Williams v. Martin-Baker Aircraft,* 389 F.3d 1251 (D.C. Cir. 2004).

[48] *United States of America ex rel Sanchez v. Lymphatx,* 596 F.3d 1300 (11th Cir. 2010).

[49] *Sanchez,* at 1304.

> ## Clippings
>
> Blackwater Worldwide has received billions of dollars in federal government contracts to provide various security-related services in Iraq, Afghanistan, and elsewhere. A married couple who were formerly employees of Blackwater have accused the company of defrauding the government by filing phony receipts, double billing for services, ignoring excessive force used against Iraqi civilians, and even charging the government for the procurement of strippers and prostitutes. The couple say that they decided to speak out and take legal action because "it's the right thing to do" and because it is important for the public to know what has been going on inside of this company. The couple's lawsuit was brought under the False Claims Act.
>
> Mark Mazzetti. "2 Ex-Workers Accuse Blackwater Security Company of Defrauding the U.S. for Years." *New York Times* (February 11, 2010), A20.

Civic Duty Laws   A number of statutes protect employees against discharge for engaging in specific civic duties. One of these is jury service. Under the Jury System Improvements Act,[50] permanent employees are protected from termination because of their service on federal court juries. Most states have similar laws covering employees who serve on state court juries. Another important civic duty is military service. The extensive reinstatement rights of veterans under the Uniformed Services Employment and Reemployment Rights Act (USERRA) were discussed in Chapter 11. A significant addition to these rights is that *uniformed services members who are reinstated cannot be terminated without cause for specified periods of time.* In the case of employees who serve in the military for between 30 and 180 days prior to reinstatement, any termination must be for cause for a period of 180 days. If the military service is for more than 180 days, the period during which termination is limited is a year.[51] An employee who was downsized four months after returning from active duty had a successful USERRA claim. Although the company was losing money and had laid off large numbers of employees, his termination was not "for cause" because he was given a position with less responsibility following his deployment (another violation) and thereby disadvantaged when his performance was compared to that of other employees.[52]

Antiretaliation and Noninterference Provisions of Other Laws   Most of the statutes discussed throughout this book contain protections against retaliation. These include Title VII of the Civil Rights Act, Fair Labor Standards Act (FLSA), Occupational Safety and Health Act (OSH Act), National Labor Relations Act (NLRA), Employee Retirement Income Security Act (ERISA), and Family and Medical Leave Act (FMLA). The breadth of protection varies somewhat across these laws, but in general, employees who file charges, give testimony, and take other actions involved in the enforcement of these laws are protected from all forms of retaliation, including discharge. Under the OSH Act, protection against retaliation extends to situations where employees refuse work that presents an imminent threat of injury or death. The message is simple: *Employers must not terminate employees because they have filed charges, given testimony, participated in the enforcement of employment laws, or opposed violations of these laws.*

---

[50]28 U.S.C.S. § 1875 (2011).

[51]38 U.S.C.S. § 4316(c) (2011).

[52]*Duarte v. Agilent Technologies,* 366 F. Supp. 2d 1039 (D. Co. 2005).

Several statutes also prohibit terminations that have the effect of interfering with or restraining employees in the exercise of their statutory rights. For example, it violates the FMLA to "interfere with, restrain, or deny the exercise of" any rights provided by the act.[53] Termination of an employee for requesting leave or for excessive absenteeism based on the taking of FMLA leave violates the FMLA. Thus, a law that is ostensibly about leave nonetheless confers a right not to be terminated at will under certain circumstances. Does this mean that employees taking family and medical leave are immune from discharge? After all, a basic FMLA right is restoration from leave. Employees who take FMLA leave acquire no greater right to retain their jobs than they would have enjoyed had they not taken leave. They can still be terminated, provided that the termination would have occurred regardless of their FMLA leave. Thus, the FMLA was not violated when a nurse who was experiencing psychological problems and who continued to act in an aberrant fashion while on leave for her condition was terminated.[54] Thus, although taking FMLA leave does not shield employees from adverse employment actions that would have occurred anyway, it creates another exception to employment at will and places employers in the position of having to account for terminations of leave takers.[55] *Employers should be especially careful in terminating employees who are on FMLA leave or have recently returned from leave and must not terminate them because they have taken leave.*

Off-Duty Conduct Laws Most employees believe that their personal lives off the job are none of their employer's business and certainly not something that should affect their employment status. Alas, the legal reality is much different. About half of all states have off-duty conduct laws on the books. However, the reach of these laws is limited. Most of these statutes protect employees only for their use of tobacco and other lawful products when off the job. In states with these laws, smokers cannot be refused hire, terminated, or otherwise discriminated against (although they need not be allowed to smoke in the workplace). Elsewhere, it is legal for employers to discriminate against smokers if they so choose. One of the broadest off-duty conduct laws is New York's. This statute protects against discrimination for using lawful products and for engaging in union activity, political activity, and lawful recreational activity. However, "lawful recreational activity" does not reach romantic relationships and dating. Two employees fired for violating their employer's policy against married employees dating employees to whom they are not married were unsuccessful in pursuing claims for wrongful discharge under New York's off-duty conduct law.[56] A subsequent case in which both parties were unmarried and there was no policy regarding fraternization had the same outcome.[57]

Discriminatory Termination

Terminations based on the protected class characteristics of employees, no less than any other adverse employment decisions, are discriminatory disparate treatment. Discriminatory discharge cases present fundamentally the same issues as other discrimination cases. However, some modifications are required to apply the methodology for analyzing disparate treatment cases to discharges.

---

[53]29 U.S.C.S. § 2615(a)(1) (2011).

[54]*Throneberry v. McGehee Desha County Hospital,* 403 F.3d 972 (8th Cir. 2005).

[55]*Sanders v. City of Newport,* 657 F.3d 772 (9th Cir. 2010).

[56]*State v. Wal-Mart Stores,* 1995 N.Y. App. Div. LEXIS 17.

[57]*McCavitt v. Swiss Reinsurance America Corp.,* 237 F.3d 166 (2d Cir. 2001).

ELEMENTS OF A CLAIM

Disparate Treatment in Termination

To establish a prima facie case of discriminatory discharge, plaintiffs must show:

1. The protected class characteristic(s) relevant to the case;
2. Up to the point of the termination, the employee had been meeting the employer's legitimate performance expectations;
3. The employee was terminated (formally or constructively);
4. The employer sought a replacement or hired one with contrasting protected class characteristics; or
5. A similarly situated person with different protected class characteristics engaged in similar conduct but was not terminated.

If a prima facie case is established, the case is analyzed like other pretext cases, with the employer needing to articulate a nondiscriminatory reason for the termination and the plaintiff having the opportunity to show that the articulated rationale is pretext and that the decision was more likely motivated by discrimination.

© Cengage Learning 2013.

Inconsistency in applying disciplinary rules is frequently an issue in discriminatory discharge cases. An African American employee was terminated for violating a store's "progressive discipline policy" after being written up three times for cash discrepancies. She was the only employee suspended or terminated for violating the policy even though at least sixteen other cashiers, most of them white, had enough discrepancies to warrant suspension or termination under the policy. Even taking account of a change in management, the store could not show that it had been consistent in enforcing the policy and that the alleged violation was not a pretext for race discrimination. Thus, the employee's case was allowed to go to trial.[58] Similarly, a city street crew worker in Tennessee was able to prove race discrimination based on his termination for throwing a firecracker while on the job.[59] Apparently, the use of fireworks by employees was commonplace among the city's workers and sometimes even occurred in the presence of supervisors. When a white employee set off fireworks right outside the main garage with a supervisor viewing, the action drew no more than a mild admonition from another manager ("Okay, guys. Knock off the horseplay."). Under these circumstances, the employer's arguments that it enforced the policy out of concern about safety and that it was unaware of similar incidents involving white employees did not hold water.

Courts differ in terms of how strictly comparable the situations of employees must be to show that they are sufficiently **similarly situated** to serve as evidence of disparate treatment. In one case, a lieutenant who worked at a correctional facility was terminated after he was arrested and charged with felony assault in the off-duty stabbing of another person at a bar (the charges were later dismissed). The lieutenant, a Latino, contended that he had been treated more harshly than other non-Latino employees who had gotten into scrapes with the law. A jury, instructed by the trial court judge that the "quantity and quality of the other employees' misconduct must be of comparable seriousness to the misconduct of the plaintiff" to show that they were similarly situated, found for the

---

[58]*Curry v. Menard,* 270 F.3d 473 (7th Cir. 2001).

[59]*Madden v. Chattanooga City Wide Service Department,* 549 F.3d 666 (6th Cir. 2008).

plaintiff in his disparate treatment claim.[60] An appeals court vacated the decision on the grounds that the employees' circumstances must be "nearly identical" to conclude that they are similarly situated. There were circumstances that differentiated the employees in question, including that the plaintiff had refused to explain his actions to investigators and that his was the only case involving a formal Internal Affairs investigation.[61] Under this stringent view of the meaning of "similarly situated," adverse employment actions will be deemed to have been taken under nearly identical circumstances only when the employees being compared held the same job or responsibilities, shared the same supervisor or had their employment status determined by the same person, had comparable violation histories, and engaged in conduct "nearly identical" to that of comparators who were treated more leniently.[62] This doesn't mean that the situations of the employees being compared have to be literally identical—which would almost never be the case—but it does mean that acceptable comparators will often be hard to find.

Not all courts set the bar so high, and some differentiate between what must be shown to establish a prima facie case and what must be shown to establish pretext. Thus, in the case of an African American bank teller, the court found that she had established a prima facie case by showing that she was involved in or accused of conduct similar to that engaged in by employees of other races (violating a bank rule against conducting transactions on a teller's own account), but disciplined more harshly (she was fired and a white employee received no discipline). However, she was ultimately unsuccessful in establishing pretext because she could not show that she and the other employee were similarly situated in "all relevant respects." Her offense had involved a much larger sum of money, there were multiple questionable transactions rather than only one, and the white teller had attempted to immediately correct the mistake that she had made.[63] In a case involving an employee who was terminated after being given a low performance rating, the appeals court held that the lower court's "narrow definition of similarly situated effectively removed [the employee] from the protective reach of the anti-discrimination laws."[64] Rather than insist that the plaintiff match potential comparators in all respects, courts should determine which factors are relevant to the facts of particular cases.

Although it can be difficult for plaintiffs to prove discrimination by showing that they were disciplined more harshly than other similarly situated employees, consistent, evenhanded treatment is still the goal. *One of the best ways to avoid discriminatory terminations is to enforce policies in a consistent manner, treating like situations in a like manner, regardless of the individuals involved.*

Just Cause/Due Process

Employees regularly overestimate their rights in the workplace, particularly when it comes to terminations. Commonly, employees believe that they have the legal right not to be fired without good reason.[65] We have seen that such is not the case for the vast majority of the workforce. Nonunion, private sector employees can be terminated for

---

[60]*Perez v. Texas Department of Criminal Justice, Institutional Division,* 395 F.3d 206, 212 (5th Cir. 2004), *cert. denied,* 2005 U.S. LEXIS 7862.

[61]*Perez,* at 214.

[62]*Lee v. Kansas City Southern Railway,* 574 F.3d 253, 259-61 (5th Cir. 2009).

[63]*Rodgers v. U.S. Bank, N.A.,* 417 F.3d 845 (8th Cir. 2005).

[64]*Jackson v. FedEx Corporate Services,* 518 F.3d 388, 397 (6th Cir. 2008).

[65]Pauline T. Kim. "Bargaining with Imperfect Information: A Study of Worker Perceptions of Legal Protection in an At-Will World." *Cornell Law Review* 83 (November 1997), 133–34.

any reason that is not specifically illegal through the use of whatever decision process the employer deems appropriate. However, some segments of the workforce enjoy much greater protection against wrongful termination than is available under employment at will with exceptions. Terminations of employees who are unionized, work for government agencies, reside in Montana, have individual contracts of employment, or were recently reinstated from military service must generally meet a just cause/due process standard. Under this standard, employers bear the burden of showing that they had good reasons for their termination decisions and followed reasonable procedures.

Unionized Employees

The distinct legal status of unionized employees derives first and foremost from language in labor agreements that limits discipline and discharge to situations in which there is just cause. Labor agreements almost universally include just cause provisions, as well as grievance procedures to challenge discipline and discharge decisions (and other alleged contract violations). Grievance procedures in unionized workplaces almost always provide for the arbitration of grievances that are not otherwise resolved. Thus, determinations as to whether unionized employees have been terminated for just cause are made by arbitrators rather than courts. Arbitrators are typically given broad authority. If an arbitrator decides that a discharge was not for just cause, the arbitrator can overturn the decision entirely or modify it to provide for a lesser penalty.

Just cause is clearly a central concept in understanding the legal rights of unionized employees. But what does just cause actually mean? Arbitrators consider the following factors to determine whether employers had **just cause** for discipline or discharge:

- Was there a rule or standard prohibiting the behavior engaged in by the employee?
- Was the rule or standard clearly communicated to employees?
- Is the rule or standard a reasonable one, related to efficiency and safe operation?
- Has the rule or standard been consistently enforced?
- Was the employee afforded due process?
- Is there sufficient proof that a rule or standard was violated?
- Was progressive discipline applied?
- Was the discipline commensurate with the offense?
- Are there any mitigating factors that call for imposition of a lesser penalty?

Arbitrators are concerned that employees have prior notice that their behavior will subject them to discipline or discharge. Typically, this requires that unionized employers *establish rules, standards, and policies and communicate these to employees.* This does not apply if the behavior in question is something that any reasonable person would know is wrong. For example, an employee who sprays the office with an AK-47 cannot benefit from the absence of an explicit rule prohibiting the strafing of coworkers with high-powered weapons. However, an arbitrator overturned discipline imposed by the Federal Aviation Administration on a group of air traffic controllers for taking extended breaks (sometimes lasting four hours or more) in their cars during work time because the agency had no rules about breaks, the breaks were taken during periods when air traffic was slow, and supervisors tacitly condoned the breaks.[66]

Policies become real and enforceable not merely by being formalized and communicated in some fashion to employees, but more importantly, by being consistently enforced. *Enforcement of rules must be consistent across both time and different individuals engaging in the same conduct.* Unionized employers cannot suddenly decide to "get tough" and make an example of a particular employee when violations of the same

---

[66]*Federal Aviation Administration, Denver Air Route Traffic Control Center,* 99 L.A. 929 (Corbett, 1992).

rule have been ignored in the past or subjected to only lax enforcement. *Unionized employers must clearly communicate changes in policies before attempting to enforce new, more stringent standards.* Nor are arbitrators likely to uphold harsh discipline meted out to one employee when other employees committing the same offense at the same time are treated more leniently. The discrimination in such cases need not be along protected class lines; it is enough that one individual is treated differently than others without good reason, regardless of whether his race or sex are the same as those who benefited from leniency.

Although employers have the right to establish rules and these rules are entitled to deference, arbitrators ask whether challenged disciplinary actions are based on reasonable rules related to efficiency, safety, and other important business purposes. Discipline for off-duty conduct sometimes fails this test of reasonableness. In general, arbitrators do not uphold discharges for off-the-job activities unless the misconduct renders the employee unable to perform his job properly (e.g., the employee is shunned by coworkers) or has an adverse effect on the employer's business (e.g., harm to the employer's reputation). For example, the termination of an LPN after she pled guilty to shoplifting was reduced to a suspension. In concluding that the employer suffered little harm, the arbitrator relied on the facts that a newspaper account of the incident did not identify the individual as an employee of the hospital, the infraction was a misdemeanor, and shoplifting had little relationship to the job of LPN.[67] Similarly, an employee was reinstated (without back pay) despite having pled guilty to six off-the-job assaults within a sixteen-month period. The arbitrator noted that the employee had virtually no contact with the public (he was a relief "coal man" at a power plant), the assaults had not been widely publicized, and the employee was having problems with alcohol and drug addiction for which he subsequently received treatment.[68] In contrast, an arbitrator upheld the termination of a hotel employee who stole four car tires from a service station and served five days in jail for the offense. Even though media coverage was minimal and did not mention the hotel, the employee's job was cleaning air conditioner filters, which meant that he had unsupervised access to guests' rooms and possessions. Given the degree of trust needed to perform his job, it was reasonable for the employer to conclude that the theft rendered him unqualified to perform his job. Additionally, the employer had consistently terminated employees found guilty of off-duty theft.[69]

Grievance procedures and arbitration provide for substantial **due process** following termination. However, arbitrators typically require that elements of due process be present before termination decisions are made as well. *Unionized employers must adequately investigate alleged misconduct, notify employees of charges against them, provide employees with a chance to respond to those charges, and respect the Weingarten rights of employees* (to have union representatives present at meetings likely to result in the imposition of discipline). The aim is to ensure a careful, deliberative process and avoid any "rush to judgment."

To have just cause, the investigation must produce sufficient evidence that the accused employee is actually guilty of wrongdoing. The employer bears the burden of proving a violation. In arbitration, it is not enough that the employer reasonably believed a violation occurred or that the employer was not motivated by unlawful factors in reaching that conclusion; arbitrators will assess an employer's case to determine whether there is sufficient evidence of guilt. There is no single standard for what is "sufficient." Sometimes the standard is a "preponderance of the evidence" (overall, does the evidence

---

[67]*Fairmont General Hospital,* 91 L.A. 930 (Hunter, 1988).

[68]*Iowa Public Service Company,* 95 L.A. 319 (Murphy, 1990).

[69]*CSX Hotels,* 93 L.A. 1037 (Zobrak, 1989).

weigh in the direction of innocence or guilt?). Other times, arbitrators require "clear and convincing" evidence of guilt; and in some cases, evidence is required that establishes guilt "beyond a reasonable doubt." The more stringent standards tend to be used when the alleged offense involves criminal activity or acts of moral turpitude such that termination on these grounds would seriously impair an employee's ability to obtain future employment.

Arbitrators view discipline as corrective rather than punitive. Although some offenses are so serious that they warrant termination following a single occurrence (e.g., assaults, theft), arbitrators generally expect to see **progressive discipline**. That is, the first instance of a violation is met with a warning or with other relatively mild discipline. Subsequent offenses result in progressively more severe discipline and, if the undesirable conduct continues, discharge. The aim is to provide employees with the chance to learn what is expected of them and to alter their conduct accordingly. *Unionized employers should generally use progressive discipline. Progressive discipline entails making a genuine effort to correct undesirable behavior, not just going through the motions and creating a paper trail before terminating an employee.*

Arbitrators are also concerned that the "punishment fits the crime." An employee might be guilty of violating a rule, but if the penalty of discharge is disproportionate to the nature of the offense, a lesser penalty might be ordered. Finally, *mitigating factors are considered when imposing discipline.* Mitigating factors do not affect the finding that an employee did something wrong, but can call for a reduction in the severity of the discipline imposed. Arbitrators are empowered to reduce the penalties given to offenders when the arbitrators conclude that these penalties are excessive, but they are not free to substitute their own preference for leniency in the face of otherwise appropriate penalties. Potentially mitigating factors include the employee's past record (e.g., no prior infractions or multiple prior infractions), length of service, compelling personal or medical problems that might explain aberrant behavior, and situational factors (e.g., if the employee was in a fight, did he instigate it or engage in self-defense?).

Arbitrators do not apply these criteria in a mechanical fashion or insist that every factor clearly support an employer's position before upholding a termination. However, *unionized employers should carefully consider these just cause factors when making discharge decisions.* These criteria provide excellent guidance for making reasonable and legally defensible termination decisions. Unionized employers that fail to substantially meet these criteria can expect that their termination decisions will be challenged and most likely not upheld in arbitration.

Public Employees

A number of legal protections converge to generally remove public employees from employment at will. For one thing, public employees are far more likely than private sector employees to have union representation and to be protected by just cause language in labor agreements. Unique to public employees are statutory protections under civil service and tenure laws and constitutional protections generally requiring due process and regard for speech and associational rights.

Civil Service and Tenure Laws

Most cities, counties, and states—as well as the federal government—have **civil service laws** that are intended to ensure that merit, and not political patronage, guides employment decisions. Besides specifying job classification, testing, hiring, and promotion procedures for public employment, civil service laws usually incorporate processes for review of disciplinary decisions. Often, civil service laws provide that nonprobationary employees can be terminated only for cause. The Civil Service Reform Act covers most federal government employees. Disciplinary actions, including terminations, can be appealed to the Merit Systems Protection Board (MSPB). The federal agency imposing the discipline bears the burden of showing, by the preponderance of evidence, that the alleged misconduct actually occurred and that the penalty is reasonable in light of the severity of the offense.

Teachers and professors in public schools and universities sometimes enjoy the protection of tenure laws. In private schools, tenure systems are matters of policy and contract rather than law. **Tenure** is typically conferred following a relatively lengthy probationary period and a formal assessment of past and likely future performance. Tenure is not an absolute guarantee of a job for life. Even when tenure is provided for by law, the employment of tenured faculty can be terminated due to financial exigencies or serious misconduct. Tenure recognizes some unique facts of academic life. The freedom to raise questions, express controversial or unpopular ideas, examine chosen research topics, and pursue the truth wherever it leads are central to the purposes of academia. Absent the institution of tenure, faculty would feel less able to do these things. At a time when schools, both public and private, are chasing every dollar that can be wrung out of private sources, the potential for the free exchange of ideas to be inhibited (e.g., "Don't say anything critical of Company X; the CEO is contributing millions for a new business school") is all the more real.

Constitutional Protections

The U.S. Constitution protects public employees from wrongful termination in two ways. The Fifth and Fourteenth Amendments generally require that public employees be provided with due process before being deprived of their employment. Public employees also have substantive constitutional rights under the First Amendment—freedom of religion, speech, association—that can be invoked when a termination or other discipline is used to suppress those rights.

Property and Liberty Interests in the Job: Due Process   The U.S. Constitution requires that due process be provided before the government can deprive individuals of property rights. The Fourteenth Amendment says, in part, that states shall not "deprive any person of life, liberty, or property without due process of law." The Fifth Amendment places the same restriction on the federal government. Most, but not all (e.g., probationary and temporary employees), public employees can be said to hold a **property interest** in their jobs. The existence of a property interest is defined by state laws, employment policies, and express or implied contracts. The Supreme Court has considered the nature of the due process to which public employees with a property interest in their jobs are entitled prior to termination. Although a *pretermination* hearing "need not be elaborate" (assuming that a fuller *post-termination* hearing will be available), the public employee is still "entitled to oral or written notice of the charges against him, an explanation of the employer's evidence, and an opportunity to present his side of the story" prior to discharge.[70] This preliminary due process serves as "an initial check against mistaken decisions." The existence of a "last chance agreement," under which an employee was on notice that any future work rule violations would result in immediate termination, did not excuse a public employer from providing the requisite due process prior to termination.[71]

---

[70]*Cleveland Board of Education v. Loudermill,* 470 U.S. 532, 545–46 (1985).

[71]*Walls v. Central Contra Costa Transit Authority,* 653 F.3d 963 (9th Cir. 2011).

Public employees are also sometimes deemed to have a **liberty interest** that is jeopardized through termination. The focus of this liberty interest is on maintaining the employee's good name. The charges that are the basis for termination must be stigmatizing (e.g., theft, drug use), false, and made public without a meaningful opportunity for the employee to clear his name.[72] For example, a paramedic who was removed without adequate notice or a hearing from his position because he allegedly botched an emergency call had a liberty interest in being able to pursue his chosen career.[73] Employees who successfully assert a liberty interest of this kind are entitled to due process in the form of an opportunity to establish the falsity of the charges brought against them.

In general, public employers are responsible for affording their employees due process, both before and after termination. Prior to termination, a hearing must be held that provides public employees with notice of the charges against them, explanation of the evidence, and opportunity to present their side of the story. Following termination, a more elaborate hearing with opportunities to confront witnesses and present evidence is required if requested by terminated employees.

Substantive Constitutional Rights   Public employees, like other citizens, have rights under the **First Amendment** concerning the manner in which they are treated by the government. These rights include freedom of religion, speech, and association. Terminating or otherwise disciplining employees for exercising these rights is unconstitutional. But because the relationship between the government and individual citizens is different from that between government agencies and their employees, a more delicate balancing of constitutional rights and the government's prerogatives as an employer is required in the latter situation. The government employer's interests in efficient and effective operations provide less room for the play of constitutional rights, but do not completely override those rights.

Clippings

Until the nonrenewal of his contract in May 2010, internationally known hurricane expert Dr. Ivor van Heerden was the deputy director of the Louisiana State University (LSU) Hurricane Center. In the years before Hurricane Katrina, Dr. van Heerden regularly voiced his concerns about the potentially devastating effects of a major storm hitting New Orleans. Following the 2005 hurricane, he blasted the Army Corps of Engineers on television and in newspaper articles for engineering errors that had allowed breaches in the system designed to protect New Orleans from hurricanes. University administrators told him that his criticisms of a government agency would result in a loss of funding for the school. In his wrongful termination suit against LSU, Dr. van Heerden charges that the school "placed the bureaucratic interests of university officials above the health and safety of the millions of people who live in the path of the hurricanes that threaten the Gulf Coast every year." He has also stated that LSU was "trying to deny me my freedom of speech" and that his termination sent the message to other academics that "If you speak up on things that we are not happy about, we are going to get rid of you."

John Schwartz. "Hurricane Expert Sues over Dismissal." *New York Times* (February 11, 2010), A19.

---

[72]*Wells v. Doland*, 711 F.2d 670, 676 (5th Cir. 1983).

[73]*Braswell v. Shoreline Fire Department*, 622 F.3d 1099 (9th Cir. 2010).

Constitutional protection against termination or other disciplinary actions based on public employee speech depends, first of all, on whether the employee was speaking as a citizen on a **matter of public concern**. In a case involving a deputy district attorney who was retaliated against after writing a memo recommending dismissal of a case due to misconduct by investigators, the Supreme Court made it clear that the First Amendment protects only speech engaged in as a private citizen and not statements made pursuant to a public employee's official duties.[74] This is because the latter form of speech owes its existence to the employee's professional responsibilities, the performance of which public employers must be free to evaluate and criticize. Since writing legal memos and advising on the disposition of pending cases were aspects of the deputy district attorney's official duties, his speech in the course of carrying out these duties was not constitutionally protected. A public school teacher was not speaking as a citizen when he filed a union grievance challenging the failure of the school administration to take disciplinary action against a disruptive student.[75] Even though filing grievances was not one of the teacher's prescribed duties, his grievance was directly related to his core responsibilities as a teacher and was an avenue of expression that was available only because he was an employee.

To be constitutionally protected, public employees' speech must also be related to matters of public concern. The voicing of private grievances and disputes in the workplace does not implicate the Constitution. A doctor who openly questioned the fitness and decisions of the director of his medical center was not engaging in speech on matters of public concern. The court concluded that comments "arising from a purely private disagreement between colleagues about the manner in which a personnel matter should be handled do not constitute protected speech for purposes of the First Amendment."[76] Instead, speech is on a matter of public concern and is potentially protected when it pertains to political or social matters that concern the larger community. The employee is speaking as a citizen about matters relevant to the public rather than as an employee regarding matters of personal interest. The hurricane expert's (see "Clippings") criticisms of the Army Corps of Engineers in the wake of Hurricane Katrina were certainly related to matters of public concern. The causes of the devastation and what the government should do to prevent future disasters were political and social issues of the highest order. Whether he was acting in a work capacity or as a citizen when he made his statements is more difficult to say. Relevant considerations would include whether the comments were made on work time and through the auspices of the hurricane center, whether any effort was made to distinguish his personal views from the positions of the center, and whether the making of public statements was part of his job.

In *Decotiis v. Whittemore*, the court must decide whether a speech therapist who urged her patients' parents to contact local advocacy organizations regarding possible legal violations by a county social service agency was engaging in constitutionally protected speech.

---

[74]*Garcetti v. Ceballos*, 126 S. Ct. 1951 (2006).

[75]*Weintraub v. Board. of Education of the City School District of the City of New York*, 593 F.3d 196 (2d Cir. 2010).

[76]*Hellstrom v. United States Department of Veterans Affairs*, 178 F. Supp. 2d 164 (N.D.N.Y. 2001), *affirmed*, 46 Fed. Appx. 651 (2d Cir. 2002).

Decotiis v. Whittemore
635 F.3d 22 (1st Cir. 2011)

OPINION BY DISTRICT JUDGE SMITH:

In this case we must consider the *First Amendment* rights of a speech and language therapist working as a state contractor. * * * Plaintiff Ellen H. Decotiis brought suit against Child Development Services-Cumberland County ("CDS-Cumberland"), Lori Whittemore individually and in her official capacity as Director of CDS-Cumberland, and Debra Hannigan in her official capacity as State Director of Child Development Services ("CDS") (collectively the "Defendants").... Decotiis alleges that she was retaliated against in violation of her *First Amendment* free speech rights for expressing her opinion to parents that CDS-Cumberland was not in compliance with state regulations and urging parents to contact advocacy organizations to address this problem. She seeks a declaration that the non-renewal of her CDS-Cumberland contract was a violation of her *First Amendment* rights ... . * * *

On appeal, Decotiis argues that the district court erred in holding that her speech was not protected by the *First Amendment*.... * * * [W]e conclude that the complaint sufficiently alleges a constitutional violation, particularly in light of two holdings of this Court that came after the district court's ruling.... * * *

CDS ... provide[s] early intervention and special education services under the Individuals with Disabilities Education Act ("IDEA") for children with disabilities from birth to five years old. It is supervised by the Maine Department of Education. * * * Decotiis is a speech and language therapist licensed by the state of Maine who over the previous eighteen years, and at the time of the events giving rise to this action, had contracts with various regional CDS sites to provide speech and language therapy and evaluations for children.

In May 2008, Chapter 101 of the Maine Unified Special Education Regulation ("Unified Rule 101") was adopted. Prior to its adoption, eligible children generally received services for the full calendar year .... Unified Rule 101, however, limited these services for children aged three to five years old to the school year (September through June). As a result, services were not provided to children over the summer unless they were deemed eligible for extended school year services ("ESY services"). In response to

this new regulation, the state CDS adopted a policy offering ESY services as "the exception and not the rule." That is, ESY services were to be provided only when [it was] decided that the services were necessary to give the child a free and appropriate public education under IDEA.... Unified Rule 101 and CDS's new policy generated a stir; the CDS regional sites, service providers, and parents of children with disabilities throughout Maine were confused and concerned. This concern stemmed particularly from the absence of a clear procedure outlining the objective standards that would support eligibility determinations for ESY services.

In the spring of 2008, Decotiis was working under contracts with three regional CDS sites, including CDS-Cumberland, to provide speech and language services to children. It was around this time that Whittemore ... [and other sources] informed Decotiis about CDS-Cumberland's approach to ESY-service determinations. Specifically, Decotiis was told that it was unlikely that children would receive ESY services unless they were considered severely disabled, and that children who received a single service (for example, only speech therapy) would not qualify for ESY services. Moreover, Decotiis was told that eligibility determinations were being made without the benefit of IEP ["Individualized Education Plan"] meetings and that IEP meetings discussing children's eligibility for ESY services were only held at the insistence of parents. Decotiis also learned that Whittemore no longer trusted her clinical judgment as a result of what Whittemore perceived to be Decotiis's high rate of ESY-service recommendations, and that Whittemore would no longer accept her recommendations. In contrast to the practices of CDS-Cumberland, at the other two regional CDS sites for which Decotiis worked, Decotiis submitted quarterly reports for her caseload, including her recommendations for ESY services; she would then be notified of IEP meetings; and at these meetings, the team would review her recommendations and make decisions about ESY services.

After learning about CDS-Cumberland's approach to ESY services, * * * Decotiis contacted two advocacy groups in Maine, which advised her that CDS-Cumberland did not appear to be in compliance with state and federal law. Shortly thereafter, Decotiis "informed parents of children she was treating that she was confused and concerned about the criteria CDS-Cumberland was using for eligibility for [ESY] services and that parents should contact [advocacy organizations] for guidance concerning their rights under IDEA." She also posted a notice in her office with the names and telephone numbers of the advocacy organizations for the benefit of parents, because she believed that CDS-Cumberland had given parents the incorrect number for one of the organizations.

In a letter dated July 29, 2008, CDS-Cumberland informed Decotiis that her contract, due to expire on September 1, 2008, would not be renewed. * * *

Decotiis … argues on appeal that the district court erred in holding that she did not speak as a citizen. Though the question is a close one, we agree that the district court erred in so holding, particularly when we consider our recent decisions interpreting *Garcetti* [the Supreme Court's 2006 *Garcetti v. Ceballos* decision]. * * *

We begin with some fundamentals. Government employees undoubtedly walk a tight rope when it comes to speaking out on issues that touch upon their fields of work and expertise. It is well settled that "as a general matter the First Amendment prohibits government officials from subjecting an individual to retaliatory actions … for speaking out." This right is not absolute, however; while public employees do not forfeit all of their *First Amendment* rights by undertaking public employment, "in recognition of the government's interest in running an effective workplace, the protection that public employees enjoy against speech-based reprisals is qualified."

To determine whether an adverse employment action against a public employee violates her *First Amendment* free speech rights, this Court has articulated a three-part inquiry. First, a court must determine "'whether the employee spoke as a citizen on a matter of public concern.'" Second, the court must "balance … the interests of the [employee], as a citizen, in commenting upon matters of public concern and the interest of the State, as an employer, in promoting the efficiency of the public services it performs through its employees." Third, the employee must "show that the protected expression was a substantial or motivating factor in the adverse employment decision." If all three parts of the inquiry are resolved in favor of the plaintiff, the employer may

still escape liability if it can show that "it would have reached the same decision even absent the protected conduct."

The Court must first determine whether the speech touched upon a matter of public concern. Where speech relates to a matter of inherent public concern, such as official malfeasance or the neglect of duties, this inquiry is confined to the subject matter of the speech. Here, Decotiis informed the parents of children receiving speech and language services from CDS-Cumberland, the public agency charged with providing these services, that CDS-Cumberland may have been withholding certain services to which the children were legally entitled. She also urged the parents to contact advocacy groups for guidance on the matter. The subject matter of her speech plainly relates to a matter of inherent concern, and we therefore easily conclude that Decotiis's speech touched upon a matter of public concern. However, whether Decotiis was speaking as a citizen, and the merits of the *Pickering* balancing test, are up for debate.

* * * In *Garcetti*, the Supreme Court held that public employees do not speak as citizens when they "make statements pursuant to their official duties," and that accordingly, such speech is not protected by the *First Amendment*. In *Garcetti* itself, there was no dispute about whether the speech in question had been made pursuant to the plaintiff's employment duties, and so the Court noted that it had "no occasion to articulate a comprehensive framework for defining the scope of an employee's duties in cases where there is room for serious debate." The Court did, however, provide some guidance as to how such a determination should be made. In describing speech made pursuant to employment duties, the Court included "speech that 'owes its existence to a public employee's professional responsibilities', speech that the employer 'has commissioned or created', speech that the employee 'was paid to' make, speech that the employee's 'duties … required him to' make, speech that amounts to the employee's 'work product', and speech that is an 'official communication[].'"

* * * We recently considered the application of *Garcetti* in two cases, *Foley v. Town of Randolph* and *Mercado-Berrios,* both of which inform the analysis. In *Foley,* the chief of the town's fire department brought a *First Amendment* retaliation claim alleging that the town and town officials suspended him for publicly criticizing the fire department's lack of funding and staffing during a press conference he gave at the scene of a fatal fire. In concluding that the fire

chief's speech took on the character of an "official communication" rather than that of citizen speech, we stressed the importance of context in applying the *Garcetti* test, noting that it was not determinative that the plaintiff "was not required to speak to the media." Specifically, we found three contextual factors significant: the fire chief "spoke while in uniform and on duty; he spoke from the scene of a fire where he had been in command as the Chief of the Fire Department; and his comments were bookended by those of another official—the State Fire Marshal." The fire chief's speech was moreover "entirely related to matters concerning the Fire Department." The combination of these contextual factors gave the appearance that the comments had the fire department's imprimatur and were not citizen speech.

In *Mercado-Berrios*, we again considered the character of public employee speech. Mercado-Berrios was a transitory employee of the Puerto Rico Tourism Company, a public corporation charged with "regulating, investigating, overseeing, intervening and imposing sanctions" on persons providing tourism-related ground transportation in Puerto Rico. After she and her colleagues were told to "hold your horses" and cease issuing citations to certain luxury vehicles, Mercado-Berrios complained to three other employees, two shift supervisors and an attorney. Shortly thereafter, she applied for a permanent position but was passed over. On the heels of this rejection, she brought suit alleging retaliation. In *Mercado-Berrios* we emphasized the importance of the two-step, context-specific inquiry needed to determine whether speech is "made pursuant to the employee's official duties." First, a court must ask, "what are the employee's official responsibilities?," and second, "was the speech at issue made pursuant to those responsibilities?" After undertaking this two-part inquiry, we concluded that both sides had strong arguments and affirmed the district court's decision in Mercado-Berrios's favor because the defendant had failed to adequately brief the issue.

The instant case presents what may be a not uncommon scenario: a public employee who is hired to perform certain specific functions believes her employer is not complying with the law and suggests to constituents a method to exert pressure on the public agency to encourage compliance. The question presented by such a case is: when does the public employee take off her employee hat and put on her citizen hat? In identifying Plaintiff's official

responsibilities, "the proper inquiry is 'practical' rather than formal, focusing on 'the duties an employee actually is expected to perform,'" and not merely those formally listed in the employee's job description. It appears that the bulk of Decotiis's official duties related to evaluating and providing services to clients and participating in IFSP/IEP meetings. Neither party argues that she was expected to perform duties substantially different from these formal job duties; however, Defendants argue that the job description presumed communication with parents.

Once the employment duties have been identified, the next question is: "was the speech at issue made pursuant to those responsibilities?" Decotiis alleges retaliation for speech that occurred when she "informed parents of the children she was treating that she was confused and concerned about the criteria CDS-Cumberland was using for eligibility for [ESY] services and that parents should contact [advocacy groups] for guidance concerning their rights under the IDEA." To determine whether such speech was made pursuant to official responsibilities, the Court must take a hard look at the context of the speech. Although no one contextual factor is dispositive, we believe several non-exclusive factors, gleaned from the case law, are instructive: whether the employee was commissioned or paid to make the speech in question, the subject matter of the speech, whether the speech was made up the chain of command, whether the employee spoke at her place of employment, whether the speech gave objective observers the impression that the employee represented the employer when she spoke (lending it "official significance"), whether the employee's speech derived from special knowledge obtained during the course of her employment, and whether there is a so-called citizen analogue to the speech.

Applying these factors, … Decotiis was not literally authorized or instructed to make the speech at issue. Indeed, the facts are quite the contrary; Decotiis's speech was "not made 'pursuant to' her job duties in the most literal sense." Nothing in the complaint suggests that CDS-Cumberland authorized or commissioned Decotiis to urge parents to contact advocacy groups. Her speech may have been related to the subject matter of her job, but it was not, strictly speaking, among her enumerated duties to make such speech. That being said, it is not determinative that an employee was not required to make the speech at issue. An employee's job description is neither necessary nor sufficient to dictate the bounds of speech made pursuant to her employment duties. By the same token, it is not dispositive that Decotiis's speech "concerned the subject matter of [her] employment." Nothing in *Garcetti* or the decisions interpreting it can fairly be read to suggest that all speech tangentially or broadly relating to the work of a public employee is per se unprotected.

Beyond this, the analysis becomes more difficult.... * * * It is ... not apparent from the complaint whether the speech was made during Plaintiff's work hours, or perhaps more relevantly, during a therapy session. Although the district court presumed "that the speech at issue here occurred during therapy sessions and/or evaluations conducted by the Plaintiff on behalf of CDS-Cumberland," we find no basis for this conclusion within the four corners of the complaint. * * * Furthermore, ... we cannot conclude that her speech bore the appearance of official status or significance. The complaint states that she spoke to the parents of her clients, and it is true that speech made to an audience to which an employee only has access through her job is generally less akin to citizen speech. However, the complaint does not suggest, for example, that parents were led to believe that Decotiis was speaking on behalf of CDS-Cumberland, or that Decotiis used her position of authority and trust, as the children's therapist, to lend her advice greater credence or persuasiveness. * * * [T]he complaint does not reveal whether Decotiis's speech was confined to information she had obtained through her employment, that is, whether her speech reflected "special knowledge" attributable to her work. The complaint states that Unified Rule 101 and CDS's related policies had generated consternation among service providers and parents throughout the state. In light of this, it is reasonable to infer that such concern was the subject of public discussion and that Decotiis's knowledge was therefore publically available and not unique to her and those in her employment position. Finally, we look to whether there is a so-called citizen analogue to Decotiis's speech. Plaintiff argues that her speech was analogous to the speech of other citizens; she says that parents of children, advocacy groups, therapists, professional associations, and lawyers were all discussing the issues about which she spoke. Viewing the facts alleged in the complaint in the light most favorable to Decotiis, her speech appears to have

been sufficiently analogous to the speech of other citizens in the community troubled by the new regulation and policy.

In short, while we cannot conclusively say that Plaintiff's speech was made as a citizen, the scope of our review on a motion to dismiss does not demand as much; it is sufficient that the complaint alleges facts that plausibly set forth citizen speech. * * *

Defendants argue alternatively that even if Decotiis was speaking as a citizen on a matter of public concern, her speech was nevertheless unprotected under the *Pickering* test. The *Pickering* test attempts to "balance the value of an employee's speech—both the employee's own interests and the public's interest in the information the employee seeks to impart—against the employer's legitimate government interest in 'preventing unnecessary disruptions and inefficiencies in carrying out its public service mission.'"

In assessing the government's interest in allaying disruption and inefficiencies in the workplace, a court should include in its considerations (1) "the time, place, and manner of the employee's speech," and (2) "the employer's motivation in making the adverse employment decision." * * *

Defendants argue that CDS-Cumberland has a strong interest in restricting Decotiis's speech to prevent her from interfering with its ability to effectively communicate with the vulnerable population it serves. In their view, CDS's mission was undermined when Decotiis urged parents to contact advocacy agencies and planted seeds of doubt as to the legality of CDS-Cumberland's policies. Decotiis responds that Defendants' bald assertions of workplace disruption are insufficient to meet the *Pickering* standard.

Considering Plaintiff's interests first, the value of the employee's speech appears significant. In addition to Decotiis's interest in her own speech, the public also had a non-trivial interest in the information Decotiis sought to convey, i.e., that a state-supervised agency may have been illegally denying special education services to the children it was charged with serving. On Defendants' side, the complaint does not reveal the exact time, place, and manner of Decotiis's speech, but it does state that Decotiis spoke to her clients' parents. While questioning the legality of CDS-Cumberland's policies in the presence of its clients' parents could result in significant disruption and inefficiency, with only the facts in the complaint before us, we cannot say that such a risk of disruption and inefficiency outweighs the important interests served by Decotiis's speech. This is especially so because we must consider the motivation underlying the non-renewal. Accepting the complaint's well-pleaded facts as true, the sole motivation behind the non-renewal was retaliation, not the furtherance of governmental interests. Having concluded that the *Pickering* balancing test tips in Plaintiff's favor, we hold that the complaint alleges a plausible constitutional violation. * * *

CASE QUESTIONS

1. What were the legal issues in this case? What did the appeals court decide?

2. What factors should be considered when deciding whether a public employee spoke *as a citizen* on a matter of public concern? Why does the court decide that there was sufficient evidence that the plaintiff spoke as a citizen in this case?

3. How does the court apply the *Pickering* balancing test to this case?

4. The plaintiff in this case is actually an independent contractor rather than a public employee. Why is she nonetheless able to sue under the First Amendment? Does her status as an independent contractor have any bearing on the agency's legitimate interests in controlling her speech?

5. Do you agree with the decision? Why or why not?

Words are often uttered quickly and are apt to be misunderstood. Employers, if they hear of statements at all, usually learn about them secondhand and with no enduring record to inspect. What responsibility do public employers have to determine that any speech that they believe warrants discipline was correctly reported? The Supreme Court considered this issue when dealing with the case of a nurse who was fired after several coworkers claimed that she spoke disparagingly of her boss and department and attempted to dissuade another nurse from transferring to her department.[77] The nurse and several other witnesses who overheard the conversation maintained that she had not attempted to discourage the other nurse's transfer and that any criticisms of the boss and department were in the context of her repeatedly voiced concerns that cross-training of staff was detrimental to patient care. The Court did not reach the important question of whether statements about policies that might affect patient care are related to matters of public concern. However, the Court held that a public employer does not have to be correct in its beliefs about what an employee said; instead, it can act on what it reasonably thought was said. For their beliefs to be reasonable, *public employers should conduct some type of inquiry, gather evidence about what was said, and not ignore evidence that is plainly available.*

Protected speech is often speech that we would rather not hear. The mailing of pamphlets advocating racial hatred and white supremacist views by a police officer was treated as speech related to a matter of public concern (race relations).[78] Upon hearing of an attempt to assassinate former President Reagan, an employee in a county constable's office stated, "If they go for him again, I hope they get him."[79] The comment, prompted by a news report of the assassination attempt and uttered in the context of a broader criticism of Reagan's social policies, was deemed to be on a matter of public concern. In the aftermath of the attacks of September 11, 2001, a college professor posted an essay on a Web site in which he conveyed his lack of sympathy for the victims that worked at financial firms, labeling them "technocrats" and "little Eichmanns" (referring

---

[77]*Waters v. Churchill*, 511 U.S. 661 (1994).

[78]*Pappas v. Giuliani*, 290 F.3d 143 (2d Cir. 2002), *cert. denied*, 123 S. Ct. 2642 (2003).

[79]*Rankin v. McPherson*, 483 U.S. 378, 380 (1987).

to the Nazi war criminal, Adolph Eichmann).[80] His remarks generated enormous controversy when they came to light and were highly distasteful to many, but it is clear that he was addressing the paramount social and political issue of the day, and hence, commenting on a matter of public concern.

Public employees who speak out on matters of public concern still might not be protected from termination or other discipline if their employers' interests in efficiently and effectively delivering services outweigh employee speech rights. Speech that harms supervisory relationships, promotes lack of harmony in the workplace, has a detrimental effect on close working relationships requiring loyalty and confidence, or renders employees unable to perform their duties will not be protected. In other words, the public employee's speech rights are "balanced" against the public employer's interests and the effects of the speech.[81] In the case of the police officer who mailed racist pamphlets, the court pointed to his status as a police officer (albeit one assigned to work on the computer system), the fact that he actively disseminated his materials, and the high potential for disruption stemming from his stated views to reach the conclusion that the police department's interests trumped the employee's constitutional rights.[82] In contrast, the Supreme Court found that the statement of the employee who responded to news of an attempted assassination of President Reagan by saying "if they go for him again, I hope they get him" did not unduly interfere with the efficient functioning of the constable's office. The Court emphasized the private nature of the conversation (the comment was made to a coworker but was overheard by another employee and reported to the constable); the employee's low-level, essentially clerical position; the absence of any direct reporting or working relationship with the constable; and the limited law enforcement function of the agency.[83] Under these circumstances, the comment, however impertinent, did not unduly interfere with the functioning of the agency and was constitutionally protected. A jury determined that the college professor who criticized 9/11 victims was terminated for his constitutionally protected speech and that the university lacked any overriding justification for the action.[84] However, to date, the professor has been unsuccessful in his quest to receive damages from the university and be reinstated to his position.

Public employers must respect the constitutional rights of public employees, including their freedoms of religion, speech, and association. Termination or other disciplinary action should be imposed only when the exercise of these rights clearly interferes with an employee's ability to do her job or with accomplishment of the public agency's mission.

Montana Wrongful Discharge from Employment Act

Many employers were alarmed by the growing recognition of common law wrongful discharge claims in the 1970s and 1980s. Outcomes of cases were unpredictable, and damages could be enormous. Although these concerns were widespread and legislation was proposed in a number of states, only Montana enacted a comprehensive wrongful discharge statute. **The Montana Wrongful Discharge from Employment Act (WDEA)**[85] effectively eliminated employment at will in Montana. It replaced a patchwork of common law wrongful discharge claims with a statutory framework that more clearly spelled out the

---

[80]*Churchill v. University of Colorado at Boulder,* 2010 Colo. App. LEXIS 1745 (Div. Five), *cert. granted in part and denied in part,* 2011 Colo. LEXIS 450.

[81]*Pickering v. Board of Education of Township High School District 205, Will County,* 391 U.S. 563 (1968).

[82]*Pappas,* at 146–50.

[83]*Rankin,* at 389–91.

[84]*Churchill,* at 10.

[85]*Mont. Code Ann.* § 39-2-901 *et seq.* (2011).

rights of employees, but also limited the liability of employers for wrongful discharge and offered incentives to use alternative dispute-resolution procedures.

Under the Montana WDEA, a discharge is wrongful if any of the following is true:

1. It was in retaliation for an employee's refusal to violate public policy or for reporting a violation of public policy.
2. The discharge was not for good cause, and the employee had completed the employer's probationary period.
3. The employer violated the express provisions of its own written personnel policy.

JUST THE FACTS

Shelley Evans-Marshall was a high school English teacher. She assigned Ray Bradbury's *Fahrenheit 451* to her ninth graders. To explore the book's theme of government censorship, she distributed a list compiled by the American Library Association of the "100 Most Frequently Challenged Books." Evans-Marshall asked groups of students to select books from the list and to lead in-class debates about them. Two groups chose the book *Heather Has Two Mommies*. A parent complained about the book and the principal asked Evans-Marshall to tell the students to choose a different book. She complied, explaining to her class that "they were in a unique position to ... use this experience as source material for their debate because they [had] ... actually experienced censorship in preparing to debate censorship." At a school board meeting, twenty-five or so parents complained about the curricular choices in the schools, including *Siddhartha* (another book assigned by Evans-Marshall) and the book-censorship assignment. The next day, the principal called a meeting of the English department and told Evans-Marshall that she was "on the hot seat." Nearly 100 parents, as well as the local news media, attended the board's next meeting. For over an hour, parents expressed concerns about books in the curriculum and in the school libraries, raising particular objections to the materials in Evans-Marshall's classroom. Another incident involved student writing samples that Evans-Marshall shared with students who asked for additional guidance on assignments. Several of these writing samples dealt with sensitive themes, including a firsthand account of a rape. The principal indicated his displeasure with the materials she was using in her classroom and the themes of her in-class discussions and said that he "intended to rein it in." After several more run-ins with the principal, he wrote a performance appraisal criticizing Evans-Marshall's attitude and demeanor as well as her "use of material that is pushing the limits of community standards." A few months later, the school board voted unanimously not to renew the teacher's contract. She sued, alleging a violation of her First Amendment speech rights. What should the court decide? Why?

See, *Evans-Marshall v. Bd. of Education of Tipp City Exempted Vill. School District,* 624 F.3d 332 (6th Cir. 2010), *cert. denied,* 131 S. Ct. 3068 (2011).

The WDEA incorporates variants of the public policy exception to employment at will and implied contract into its statutory language, but goes much further in conferring a right on nonprobationary employees to not be terminated without good cause. *Good cause* is defined in the statute as "reasonable, job-related grounds for dismissal based on a failure to satisfactorily perform job duties, disruption of the employer's operation, or other legitimate business reason."[86]

In a case involving an airline employee terminated for intentionally submitting time-sheets overstating her hours of work, the court concluded that it was not enough for the employer to act in good faith and reasonably believe the offense had been committed.[87] Good cause is lacking when a termination rests on an employer's mistaken interpretation of facts as well as on grounds invalid as a matter of law under the WDEA (e.g., reporting a violation of public policy) or when the stated reason for discharge is a pretext for some other illegitimate reason. A jury found that the airline employee's recording errors were unintentional; thus, she was terminated without good cause. To have good cause for termination under the WDEA, the airline had to be honest about its reasons for the termination and have its facts straight. The first of these, by itself, was not enough.

The WDEA was passed largely at the behest of Montana's employers. What's in it for them? The main thing that the WDEA accomplishes for employers in Montana is that it limits their potential liability for wrongful discharge. In contrast to common law tort claims, in which the sky is the limit, damages under the WDEA are limited to the award of lost wages and benefits for a period not to exceed four years from the date of discharge, including interest and reduced by interim earnings. Punitive damages are available only when clear and convincing evidence exists that an employer engaged in actual fraud or malice in terminating an employee for refusing to violate or for reporting a violation of public policy. Damages for pain and suffering, emotional distress, and other compensatory and punitive damages are specifically disallowed.

Claims brought under the WDEA must be filed within one year after the date of discharge, a much shorter period of time than typically allowed for common lawsuits. The WDEA encourages employers to establish internal appeals procedures. When employers have such procedures in place, they must be used and exhausted (completed) before a suit can be filed under the WDEA. However, this does not give employers license to sit on appeals indefinitely. Appeals not concluded within ninety days are deemed to be denied, and employees are allowed to proceed to court under the WDEA. Additionally, employers are required to supply discharged employees with a written copy of their appeals procedures within seven days of termination.

Handling Terminations

Even when employed at will, employees cannot be terminated for illegal reasons. These illegal reasons have been discussed, and practical advice for avoiding unlawful terminations has been sprinkled throughout this chapter. This chapter concludes with some generally applicable advice for handling the termination process (the more extensive due process requirements for the termination of unionized employees and public employees are not reiterated here).

A wrongful termination claim cannot be brought absent a termination or constructive discharge. *Alternatives to termination—including retraining, transferring, demoting, suspending, and executing last chance agreements—should be considered.* To the extent that these are adverse employment actions, they still present legal concerns, but they are less apt to be challenged than terminations. Last chance agreements are sometimes a viable alternative to termination and are generally taken seriously by both arbitrators and courts in the event of subsequent transgressions by the employee. However, the existence of a last chance agreement does not preclude the filing of a discrimination suit by an

---

[86]*Mont. Code Ann.* § 39-2-903 (5) (2011).

[87]*Marcy v. Delta Airlines*, 166 F.3d 1279 (9th Cir. 1999).

employee if the employee is terminated for allegedly violating the agreement by committing another infraction. An employer drafted its last chance agreement to state that the employee would not have recourse to either arbitration or the courts if terminated for violating the agreement, but the court ruled that this type of prospective waiver of rights was not enforceable.[88] Employees also can be encouraged to resign, although presenting an employee with the stark choice of resigning or being fired or putting undue pressure on an employee to resign is apt to be viewed as constructive discharge. The *option of resignation is best pursued when there are growing concerns about the performance or conduct of an employee but a termination is not yet imminent. Resignations should be documented in written resignation agreements that stipulate the voluntary nature of the resignation.*

Termination decisions should receive careful higher-level review. Terminations tainted by discriminatory or retaliatory motives are particularly likely to be identified by this type of dispassionate internal review. Termination decisions should not be made on the spot by single individuals. *Employees should be placed on administrative leave if circumstances warrant their removal prior to completion of an investigation or proper review of a termination decision.*

Employers do not have to be correct about their reasons for terminating at-will employees. Nevertheless, an employer without good documentation of the reasons for a termination and the process followed will be at a distinct disadvantage in defending against wrongful discharge claims. In the face of facts suggesting a discriminatory or retaliatory motive, the absence of documentation makes the illegal motive appear more plausible. Thus, *the reasons for termination decisions and the process followed should be solidly documented.* This documentation includes performance appraisals, prior disciplinary actions, warnings, investigation results, and other pertinent items. *These materials should be in writing, produced prior to the termination decision, and support the decision to terminate.*

Employees should not be kept in the dark about the reason(s) for their termination. For one thing, a number of states have "service-letter" laws mandating that terminated employees be given written documentation of their term of service with the employer and (sometimes) the reasons for termination. In the absence of such requirements, an employee who is being terminated might view the refusal to provide a reason as an indication that the termination is, in fact, wrongful. And if it comes down to a legal challenge, vague or inconsistent explanations look highly suspicious. *Provide employees with a clear and succinct statement of the reason(s) for their termination. Employers should generally avoid making public statements about terminated employees and the reason for their termination.*

Discharges should be handled in a reasonable, dignified manner. There is no way to make termination pleasant or comfortable. Instead, the aim is to communicate the reality of termination without any ambiguity, keep the situation under control, and possibly dampen the former employee's desire for revenge through litigation or worse. Employees should be notified of termination in person. The meeting should be brief and occur in a private setting away from the view of coworkers. If possible, the meeting should not occur at the end of the week or immediately before a holiday. *Unless there are compelling security concerns, terminated employees should be allowed a reasonable amount of time to clear out their offices and take care of other business rather than be ushered out of the workplace.* The fact of termination and the reasons should be clearly communicated but not discussed or debated. Information should be provided regarding final paychecks and

---

[88]*Hamilton v. General Electric*, 556 F.3d 428 (6th Cir. 2009), *rehearing en banc denied*, 2009 U.S. App. LEXIS 12985 (6th Cir.).

benefits. *Final wages should be paid quickly within any period provided for under state law. Unless termination is for gross misconduct, terminated employees should be notified of their right to continuation of health insurance coverage under COBRA.*

Employees do not have a legal right to receive severance pay absent any contractual agreement to provide it. However, *employers should consider offering severance pay in exchange for releases of legal claims related to terminations.* In general, releases of legal claims by terminated employees are legal and enforceable. Such releases must be knowing, voluntary, and supported by consideration.[89] The consideration can come from severance pay, outplacement services, payment of health insurance premiums, early retirement incentives, or other inducements to accept the detriment of forgoing legal claims. In deciding whether a waiver of legal claims by a terminating employee is knowing and voluntary, courts usually consider first the clarity of the agreement, but often go beyond this to consider the likes of the employee's education and business experience, the extent of the employee's involvement in negotiating the terms of the agreement, the amount of time allowed for deliberation over whether to accept the deal, whether the document was actually read and considered prior to signing, whether an attorney was present or consulted, whether the consideration exceeded benefits to which the employee was already entitled, and whether there is any evidence of employer wrongdoing in executing the agreement.[90] The ADEA, as amended by the Older Workers Benefit Protection Act,[91] imposes specific and more exacting *requirements for waivers of ADEA claims to be valid: (1) Waivers must be plainly worded written agreements that specifically reference the ADEA and suggest consultation with a lawyer prior to acceptance, (2) consideration must be provided for acceptance, (3) employees must be given at least twenty-one days to consider waivers (forty-five days for group early retirement offers), and (4) waiver agreements do not become final—and can be revoked—until seven days after acceptance.* Only claims that arose prior to the date of the waiver can be waived. An employer that fails to meet these requirements will have an unenforceable waiver and is not entitled to recover the severance pay or other consideration provided to support the agreement.[92]

Key Terms

constructive discharge, p. 626

employment at will, p. 628

employment at will with exceptions, p. 628

implied contract, p. 630

disclaimer, p. 634

covenant of good faith and fair dealing, p. 637

promissory estoppel, p. 637

intentional interference with a contractual relationship, p. 637

public policy exception to employment at will, p. 638

refusal to commit an illegal act, p. 644

exercising legal rights, p. 644

performing a public duty, p. 644

whistleblowing, p. 645

Sarbanes-Oxley Act, p. 646

Dodd-Frank Wall Street Reform and Consumer Protection Act, p. 646

Whistleblower Protection Act (WPA), p. 651

False Claims Act, p. 651

similarly situated, p. 654

just cause, p. 656

due process, p. 657

progressive discipline, p. 658

civil service laws, p. 658

tenure, p. 659

property interest, p. 659

liberty interest, p. 660

First Amendment, p. 660

matter of public concern, p. 661

Montana Wrongful Discharge from Employment Act (WDEA), p. 667

---

[89]U.S. Equal Employment Opportunity Commission. *Understanding Waivers of Discrimination Claims in Employee Severance Agreements.* Viewed July 16, 2009 (http://www.eeoc.gov/).

[90]*Hampton v. Ford Motor Co.*, 561 F.3d 709, 716-17 (7th Cir. 2009).

[91]Pub. L. No. 101–433, § 1, 104 Stat. 978 (1990).

[92]*Oubre v. Entergy Operations, Inc.*, 522 U.S. 422 (1998).

Chapter Summary

The legal framework governing the termination of most private sector, nonunion employees can best be described as employment at will with exceptions. Terminations are legal no matter how dubious the reasons or circumstances unless plaintiffs can prove that their terminations occurred for reasons or under circumstances that are specifically illegal. The exceptions to employment at will fall into the broad categories of terminations breaching implied contracts or other contract-related rights, terminations in retaliation for acts supporting public policy, terminations that interfere with the exercise of statutory rights, and terminations based on the protected class characteristics of employees.

Quits or resignations that occur when an employer creates intolerable working conditions with the intent of forcing an employee out are constructive discharges. If a reasonable person would have felt compelled to quit under the circumstances, the quit is treated as a termination. Constructive discharge is not a legal claim, but rather a finding that permits an employee who resigned to pursue any claims for wrongful discharge that would have been available had the employee been formally terminated. The behavior involved in creating intolerable working conditions also lends itself to harassment and infliction of emotional distress claims.

The right of employers to terminate at will can be limited by employer policies, handbook provisions, managers' statements, and the entire course of conduct between employers and their employees. The breach of an implied contract not to terminate at will is a type of wrongful discharge claim. Specific promises to terminate only for good reasons or to use specified disciplinary procedures that are communicated to employees and not effectively disclaimed can be enforceable. Apart from any express or implied contract, employees who reasonably rely on clear promises of job security and suffer a specific detriment for doing so can sue under the theory of promissory estoppel. Employees also can sometimes sue (in tort) for intentional interference with a contractual relationship when intentional, improper interference causes termination of employment or inability to establish a new employment relationship.

Under the public policy exception to employment at will, employers are liable in tort for terminating employees in retaliation for their taking actions that public policy requires or commends. The public policy exception has been recognized for terminations based on an employee's refusing to engage in illegal activity, exercising a legal right, performing a public duty, and reporting illegal activity. Public policy claims must be firmly grounded in fundamental and well-established public policies as spelled out in statutes, constitutions, and other sources, and not merely in individual judgments about what is right or in the public interest. Reporting illegal activity—whistleblowing—is also protected under a variety of state and federal statutes. The federal Whistleblower Protection Act (WPA) protects federal government employees who make reports about violations of laws, rules, and regulations; gross mismanagement; gross waste of funds; abuse of authority; and substantial and specific dangers to public health and safety. Under the False Claims Act, parties with knowledge of intentional fraud against the federal government can bring suits to recover government funds and share substantially in the recovered funds. The Sarbanes-Oxley Act includes provisions protecting employees who blow the whistle on possible violations of securities laws or other fraud against shareholders of publicly traded companies. The Dodd-Frank Wall Street Reform and Consumer Protection Act strengthens Sarbanes-Oxley's whistleblower protections and extends protection to a broad swath of employees whose jobs involve the provision of financial services to customers.

Employees reinstated following military service are protected by the Uniformed Services Employment and Reemployment Rights Act (USERRA). Such employees can be terminated only for cause for up to a year following reinstatement. Most federal employment laws protect employees who file charges or give testimony against termination or other retaliation for participating in the enforcement process. Additionally, the NLRA, ERISA, and the FMLA prohibit employers from using terminations to interfere with the exercise of employees' statutory rights.

To establish a prima facie case of disparate treatment in a discharge situation, plaintiffs must show the protected class characteristic(s) relevant to the case; that up to the time of discharge, they were performing acceptably; that they were discharged; that their employer sought or hired a replacement; or that a similarly situated person outside the protected class engaged in similar conduct but was not terminated. Many discriminatory discharge cases center on the question of whether other similarly situated employees with contrasting protected class characteristics were treated less harshly.

The legal framework governing the termination of most employees who are unionized, work for government agencies, reside in Montana, or have express contracts of employment for specified durations can be described as a just cause/due process standard. For unionized employees, labor agreements typically specify that discipline or discharge must be for just cause only. If a discharge is challenged, an arbitrator decides whether there was just cause, taking into account the following factors: (1) Was there a rule prohibiting the behavior? (2) Was the rule communicated to employees? (3) Is the rule reasonable? (4) Was the rule consistently enforced? (5) Was the employee afforded due process? (6) Is there sufficient proof that the rule was violated? (7) Was progressive discipline applied? (8) Was the discipline commensurate with the severity of the offense? (9) Are there mitigating factors that call for imposition of a lesser penalty? Employers bear the burden of proving that discipline or discharge was for just cause.

Public employees are generally removed from employment at will by virtue of the combination of their high rate of unionization, civil service and tenure laws, and constitutional protections. Public employees deemed to have a property interest in their jobs are entitled to due process under the Fifth and Fourteenth Amendments before their employment can be terminated. Due process includes both pre-termination and post-termination hearings. Public employees deemed to have a liberty interest in their employment are entitled to an opportunity to clear their names. Like other citizens, public employees also have religious, speech, and associational rights under the First Amendment. Public employers cannot use terminations or other discipline to suppress these rights. However, First Amendment freedoms must be balanced against the government's interests in the efficient operation of public agencies. Public employees' speech is constitutionally protected to the extent that it is engaged in as a private citizen, relates to matters of public concern, and is not unduly disruptive. Factors to be weighed include the effects of speech on supervisory relationships, workplace harmony, close working relationships requiring loyalty and confidentiality, and employees' ability to perform their duties. Public employers can act on what they reasonably believe employees have said, even if those beliefs ultimately turn out to be incorrect.

Termination is the human resource decision most likely to result in legal action. The law gives employers, especially nonunion employers in the private sector, considerable latitude in making this decision. But employers still must carefully consider the grounds for any termination, and the termination process itself should be as humane and dignified as possible.

Practical Advice Summary

- Employers should not attempt to avoid terminations by creating intolerable conditions designed to force employees to quit.
- When communicating with employees via handbooks and other means, employers should
  - Refrain from making specific promises to employees regarding duration of employment, grounds for discharge, or termination procedures unless they are willing to honor those promises.
  - Ensure that employee handbooks, employment applications, and other documents are carefully written and reviewed by someone with legal expertise before they are put into use.
  - Clearly inform employees regarding changes in policies that have the effect of lessening protection against termination.
  - Incorporate disclaimers and employment-at-will statements if that is the type of employment relationship desired.
- If disclaimers are used, they must be
  - Clear and specific in their language.
  - Presented in a prominent and conspicuous manner.
  - Communicated to employees, with receipt of the information acknowledged in writing.
- Employees must not be terminated for
  - Refusing to commit illegal acts.
  - Exercising their legal rights.
  - Performing important public duties.
  - Reporting illegal activities of employers and their agents.
- Employers should
  - Provide credible internal procedures for reporting wrongdoing by the company or its agents.
  - Investigate reports of wrongdoing and not punish whistleblowers for making them.
- Employers must not terminate reinstated military service members without cause for a period of time (180 days or a year, depending on length of service) following reinstatement.
- Employers should be cautious about terminating employees who are on or have recently returned

from FMLA leave and must not terminate them because they have taken leave.

- Employers should enforce disciplinary policies in a consistent manner, treating like situations in a like manner, regardless of the individuals involved.
- Employers must not terminate employees because they have filed charges, given testimony, or otherwise participated in the enforcement of employment laws.
- If resignation is offered as an alternative to termination
  - The employee should not be presented with the stark choice of quitting or being immediately terminated.
  - Acceptance of the offer should be documented in a written resignation agreement that stipulates the voluntary nature of the quit.
- Before arriving at the decision to terminate, employers should
  - Consider alternatives, including retraining, transferring, demoting, suspending, and signing last-chance agreements.
  - Subject the decision to careful higher-level review.
  - Place employees on administrative leave if immediate removal is warranted, but time is needed to properly conduct an investigation.
  - Have documentation of the process and the reasons for termination that is written, produced prior to termination, and consistent with the decision to terminate.
- After a decision to discharge has been made

- The discharge should be handled in a reasonable, dignified manner.
- A brief termination meeting should be held in a private setting.
- A clear, succinct statement of the reason(s) for the termination should be given to the employees (in some states, a service letter is required).
- Absent compelling security concerns, terminated employees should be allowed a reasonable amount of time to clear out their offices.
- Final wages should be paid quickly within any period of time specified under state law.
- Unless termination is for gross misconduct, terminated employees should be notified of their right to continuation of health insurance coverage under COBRA.
- Consideration should be given to offering severance pay in exchange for releases of legal claims.
- Waivers of legal claims in exchange for severance pay or other benefits must be written and executed in a manner that renders them knowing and voluntary agreements
- Waivers of ADEA rights must meet the additional requirements that they
  - Are plainly worded written documents that specifically refer to the ADEA and that suggest consultation with a lawyer prior to acceptance.
  - Are supported by consideration.
  - Allow employees at least twenty-one days to consider acceptance.
  - Not take effect until at least seven days after acceptance.

Chapter Questions

1. A manager at an airline raised concerns about the airline's pay practices. She also complained that the performance appraisal process discriminated against female employees. After a number of run-ins with her supervisor, the supervisor determined that the woman "could not be trusted in a leadership position." At a subsequent meeting between the employee, the supervisor, and an HR representative, the employee was told that she had the option of resigning or accepting a non-management, part-time customer service position in a different state. The woman said that she could not leave Colorado because of her three children. She eventually submitted a letter of resignation. Can the woman still sue for wrongful termination? Why or why not? (*Barone v. United Airlines*, 355 Fed. Appx. 169 [10th Cir. 2009])

2. Who let the Ice Dogs out? Actually, the question is whether the ownership of the Bozeman Ice Dogs, a Junior A hockey team, violated its written contract of employment with the team's coach and general manager when it terminated him for poor performance based on the team's losing record (eighteen wins, thirty-five losses, and seven ties in his last full season). At the time of the termination, the coach had a five-year contract specifying that he would be entitled to his salary and bonus for a full calendar year if he was terminated for other than cause. The contract did not specify any particular win/loss record or other team performance standard for the coach. The team argued that it was not required to provide the specified payment because the termination was "for cause." What

should the court decide? Why? (*Cole v. Valley Ice Garden,* 113 P.3d 275 [Mont. 2005])

3. A store employee observed a woman being physically assaulted across the street from the store. The employee grabbed a baseball bat that was kept under the checkout counter, ran outside, and succeeded in scaring off the attacker. The employee was terminated for violating store policy by leaving the workplace to assist the woman. The termination letter referred to the employee leaving his workstation while still on company time, involving himself in a situation that was "none of our business," and exposing the store to potential liability. The employee sued. What should the court decide? (*Little v. Eastgate Discount Beer & Tobacco,* 2007 Tenn. App. LEXIS 242)

4. A security guard at a private university was on duty during a university-sponsored street festival. He observed what he thought was an altercation. A white female student was being held in the air by an African American male student (who was also a football player). The female was kicking her legs and appeared to be struggling to get free. When the security guard ordered the male to release the female, he turned around and lunged at the guard with fists raised. The guard pepper sprayed the male. A physical struggle ensued, with the security guard being joined by other guards and using a baton to bring the male to the ground. The male student was charged with disorderly conduct and later pled guilty to disturbing the peace. The crowd that viewed the incident became incited and many viewed the guard's actions as being racially motivated. Civil rights and students' organizations demanded an investigation by the university. The investigation panel eventually concluded that the security guard had overreacted and used unnecessary force, but had not exhibited any overt racial bias. The university was also faulted for not providing sufficient training to its security guards. Although the guard had initially been told that he would not lose his job and was even still in line for a promotion, he was terminated. He sued for wrongful termination. What should the court decide? Why (*Lloyd v. Drake University,* 686 N.W.2d 225 [Iowa 2004])

5. An employee of a large retailer complained to his employer that monetary credits were being issued to customers without receipt of proper docu-

mentation. In his view, this increased the chances that the company would overpay credits to customers who did not return goods. He also claimed that money was knowingly being withheld from contract customers through a practice of under-issuing credits. This arguably raised the risk of inaccurate accounting, with company revenues being overstated and customers not getting full refunds. Lastly, he claimed that a practice of canceling and reissuing pick-up orders could permit couriers to overbill the company, reducing its profits. After a series of meetings in which the employee's contentions were discussed, the employee was terminated. When he was told of the termination, the manager stated that the employee was "looking for perfection in an imperfect process" and that he was disruptive. Company documents listed the reason for termination as "inability to perform job." Supervisors testified that they had found the employee to be difficult to deal with because he was confrontational, held strong views, and asked too many questions. Was the employee wrongfully terminated for whistleblowing? Why or why not? (*Day v. Staples,* 555 F.3d 42 [1st Cir. 2009])

6. Largely due to concern over the effect of smoking on its health insurance costs, an employer prohibits its employees from using tobacco products at any time and conducts random tests for nicotine. An employee was hired contingent on successful completion of a nicotine screening. The employee was a smoker, although he was attempting to break the habit and often chewed nicotine gum to quell his desire for cigarettes. He was allowed to start on the job but was terminated when his nicotine test came back positive. At the time of the termination, he was in a probationary period and not yet a participant in the company's health plan. Massachusetts, the state in which the employee worked, does not have a state law prohibiting discrimination against users of tobacco products. On what other grounds might legal action be taken against this employer? Would the employee likely succeed? (*Rodrigues v. EG Systems,* 639 F. Supp. 2d 131 [D. Mass. 2009])

7. The activities director for a nursing home requested and received FMLA leave to have a child. She was temporarily replaced by another employee, whom some of the residents seemed to favor. Shortly after the start of the leave, an

investigation was begun into the activities director handling of a checking account that contained residents' funds. Dates and check numbers had not been recorded for every entry, and it was ultimately determined that there was a discrepancy of about $70. While she was still on leave, the nursing home asked the activities director to attend two conferences. She went to the first conference but declined to go to the second, citing her nursing infant. The director of the nursing home became angry and asked, "How is that going to change in two weeks when you come back?" Shortly before her return, she was told by another employee that the nursing home was going to give her "a hard time" when she got back and that she should look for another job. On her first day back from leave, the activities director was terminated for "misappropriation or mishandling" of patient funds. The activities director sued. What should the court decide? Why? (*Kohls v. Beverly Enterprises*, 259 F.3d 799 [7th Cir. 2001])

8. The manager of a hair salon was terminated after informing her employer that she would be unable to return to work after a medical leave. The manager had been experiencing knee problems and learned that she would need surgery to remove a growth from her knee. When she told the area manager about this, the area manager blew up and told the manager that the store was too busy to allow her to take time off for surgery. The manager attempted to have the surgery rescheduled, but her surgeon told her that the condition needed immediate attention. On hearing this, the area manager told the store manager that she was being "selfish" and repeatedly yelled at her over the phone. The leave lasted longer than expected due to complications. By the time the store manager had exhausted her twelve weeks of leave, her doctor determined that she would be able to perform only seated work. Formerly, the store manager had spent about 90 percent of her time cutting hair. The employer terminated the manager for exhausting her FMLA leave and not providing a medical clearance to return to work. The letter from her doctor regarding medical restrictions was received by the employer five days after the manager had been terminated for exhausting her leave and not providing a medical clearance form allowing her to return to work. The former

manager sued. What should the court decide? Why? (*Bryson v. Regis Hairstylists*, 498 F.3d 561 [6th Cir. 2007])

9. An employee was hired as general manager of a new assisted-living facility. For several months, she received positive feedback on her progress. At a meeting, two supervisors inquired about her child-rearing plans. She admitted that she planned to have children and was fired two weeks later. She was replaced by a 60-year-old woman. Her supervisor's manual included a policy on progressive discipline that was generally adhered to. However, she also received and signed a disclaimer that stated in part: "I understand that [neither] the policies and procedures of the facility, nor the Handbook … are intended to constitute a contractual agreement…. I understand that my employment is 'at will.' … " What should the court decide? Why? (*Kuest v. Regent Assisted Living, Inc.*, 43 P.3d 23 [Wash. App. 2002])

10. A school principal strongly believed that conversion of his public school to charter school status was needed to raise the performance of students on standardized tests. Leading a conversion to charter school status was not among the principal's enumerated job duties. However, the principal stated that he "would be remiss in his duties as the leader of [the school] if he did not explore any and all possibilities to improve the quality of education." After the faculty voted and rejected the idea, the principal continued to push for a revised plan and proposed to meet with faculty about this new plan. The school superintendent got wind of the principal's continuing efforts and expressed his displeasure. The principal cancelled his proposed meeting but was terminated shortly thereafter. Only four days before the termination, the principal had received a rating of "high quality performance" from the deputy superintendent. The former principal sued. What should the court decide? Why? (*D'Angelo v. School Board of Polk County, Fla.*, 497 F.3d 1203 [11th Cir. 2007])

11. An African American bank clerk had worked at her job for twenty-six years when she was fired. At the time of her termination, she was working reduced hours due to a serious wrist injury. A customer had come to the clerk to remove a $34 charge that had mistakenly been made against her account. The customer was correct about the

mistake, which had not been made by the clerk. However, in completing a form to document the change, the clerk accidentally put the name of her coworker--whom she was talking to at the time on the form as the "originating bank representative." When a copy of the form came back to the coworker, she reported it to her supervisor, who initiated an investigation. The investigation led to termination of the clerk on the grounds that her inadvertent use of her coworker's name was "falsification of bank records." The clerk would not have profited in any way from using her coworker's name on the form. She had never been disciplined before. A number of bank employees had been fired by this bank for similar offenses in the past. However, two employees were not fired after they failed to adequately check a signature card, thereby allowing an imposter to access a dead customer's

safe deposit box, There was also evidence that a number of employees, including white employees, had made inaccurate statements on time cards and not been terminated. The former clerk sued. What should the court decide? Why? (*Scott v. FirstMerit Corp.,* 167 Fed. Appx. 480 [6th Cir. 2006])

12. After reading this chapter, what are your thoughts about Mr. Casias, the employee terminated for his use of medical marijuana? What types of wrongful termination claims best fit his case? Would he be likely to prevail on any of these claims? Why or why not?

13. Does the employment at will with exceptions standard provide sufficient protection for employees? Would it be better if all employers were required to meet a just cause/due process standard for terminations? Why or why not?

CHAPTER 19

Downsizing and Post-Termination Issues

This final chapter considers a number of legal issues related to the ending of employment relationships. In contrast to Chapter 18's focus on the termination of individuals, this chapter deals with the legal implications of downsizing, including provision of prior notice to employees, selection of employees for downsizing, the use of early retirement incentives, and eligibility for unemployment insurance. Employers have shown increased interest in constraining the behavior of former employees after they leave employment through the execution of waivers of legal claims and a variety of restrictive covenants that limit former employees' ability to become competitors or take advantage of information acquired on the job. At a time of serious economic and financial crises, the topics discussed in this chapter may become all too relevant to employees and employers alike.

Downsizing

Downsizing is not a legal term. Instead, it is a euphemism used to describe the involuntary termination of numerous employees who have done nothing to deserve that fate. **Downsizing** (or RIF—reduction in force) is used in this chapter to refer to terminations that affect numerous employees and that are based on employers' decisions to operate with fewer staff or to cease operation entirely.

THE CHANGING WORKPLACE

Downsizing as a Fact of Contemporary Working Life

People who work for a living have always been subject to job loss and employment insecurity. But there is now a pervasive sense of threat, undergirded by the very real experiences over the past several decades of millions of "downsized" workers. One reason that things seem different now is that job loss reaches white collar professionals and managers to a much greater extent than earlier. And unlike previous times when workers would be laid off during downturns in the business cycle, but with the prospect of eventual recall, contemporary job losses are often characterized by employers as permanent. Decisions to shed jobs are made not only in the face of financial exigencies and cyclical downturns, but also as part of a relentless process of maximizing shareholder return, pushing the envelope on productivity, outsourcing, offshoring, and "restructuring." As one author has put it, America's workers have become "disposable."[1]

Downsizing first found a name in the 1980's, became infamous by the 1990's, and continues into the present — with no end in sight. It is a rare day when the business sections of newspapers do not contain reports of companies shedding hundreds or thousands of jobs, along with the workers who held them. For example, Whirlpool recently announced that it would be closing its refrigerator plant in Fort Smith, Arkansas.[2] Some of the thousand or so jobs at this plant will be relocated to other plants in the U.S. and to Mexico. The company attributes the move to sluggish consumer demand in the U.S. The closing will occur despite the presence of what the company itself says "is a great work force" at the unionized Fort Smith plant. The town has lost about a third of its manufacturing jobs since the late 1990's. In addition to the thousand jobs lost at the Whirlpool plant, the closing is expected to lead to some six hundred additional job losses at smaller suppliers in the area. The future for the Whirlpool workers, many of whom were nearing retirement and whose average age is 53, is uncertain at best.

Anecdotal accounts of downsizing are abundant; more systematic data on the extent of downsizing are harder to come by. The Bureau of Labor Statistics tracks the number of "mass layoff actions" (firms that experience at least fifty initial unemployment insurance claims filed within a five-week period) on a monthly basis. With this imperfect measure, the BLS counted at least 14,000 mass layoff actions each year between 1996 and 2010, with the largest numbers occurring in 2001 (21,467), 2008 (21,137) and 2009 (28,030). These layoff actions affected well over a million workers each year and over two million in some years.[3] Not all unemployment is the result of downsizing (some people lose their job due to terminations for individual reasons, because seasonal work or temporary projects have been completed, and so forth), but unemployment has remained at stubbornly high levels for the past several years. In October 2011, the unemployment rate stood at 9.0 percent, a figure that represents some 13.9 million unemployed persons.[4] Sobering as these unemployment numbers are, they do not reflect the millions of workers who are under-employed in part-time or low-level jobs, or who have become discouraged and withdrawn from an active pursuit of work.

While some victims of downsizing are able to pick up the pieces and find comparable alternative employment, many others find it difficult to replace lost income, benefits, and self-esteem. When the Manchester Tool Company in New Franklin, Ohio closed its doors, nearly one hundred employees lost their jobs.[5] A year later, less than fifteen percent of those employees held steady jobs elsewhere. The closing was especially wrenching for the plant's older workers who "appear paralyzed, struggling with their self-confidence as they consider their bleak odds of finding work."[6] Even when downsized employees find new employment, the price is often a substantial reduction in pay. The effect of downsizing on pay can persist for decades, in part because downsized employees who start anew elsewhere are often laid off again by their new employers.[7] Sometimes downsizing literally kills employees. Shortly after the announcement of the closing of a steel mill in Lackawanna, New York, several young, relatively healthy employees died of heart attacks. While the precise cause of death in these cases is difficult to pin down, epidemiological studies find a clear association between job loss and heightened rates of heart attacks, strokes, chronic illnesses, and mortality. A study of high seniority male workers in Pennsylvania during the 1980's found that death rates increased by fifty to one hundred percent following a job loss.[8]

Whether the turmoil associated with downsizing will subside at some point and the economy will be better off as a result of taking this bitter medicine remains to be seen. Uchitelle is skeptical that downsizing will eventually redound to the benefit of all:

> [T]he promised payoff is not on the horizon. The layoffs continue unabated. Some are inevitable as American companies adjust to the growing competition from abroad. But there has been no return to the old stability.... What started as a legitimate response to America's declining hegemony has become an unending, debilitating condition.[9]

There is evidence that even on the narrower score of helping individual companies be more profitable, downsizing frequently does not produce better financial results for firms.[10] As Uchitelle points out, we have gone from a nation that seriously debated full employment legislation in the 1970s that would have committed the government to provide jobs as an employer of last resort to one where downsizing is pervasive and seemingly accepted as a necessary fact of life.[11]

---

[1]Louis Uchitelle. *The Disposable American: Layoffs and Their Consequences*. New York: Alfred A. Knopf (2006).

[2]James R. Hagerty. "As Whirlpool Exits, Job Hunts Begin—Fort Smith, Ark. Shows Grit Amid Loss." *The Wall Street Journal* (November 18, 2011), B1.

[3]U.S. Bureau of Labor Statistics. "Mass Layoffs in December 2010 and Annual Totals for 2010." *Bureau of Labor Statistics News* (January 27, 2011), 3.

[4]U.S. Bureau of Labor Statistics. "Employment Situation Summary." *Economic News Release* (November 4, 2011).

[5]Michael Luo. "Nearly a Year After Plant Closed, Many are Struggling to Recover." *New York Times* (February 10, 2009), A1.

[6]Luo, at A1.

[7]Michael Luo. "Years After Layoffs, Many Still Struggle to Match Old Salaries." *New York Times* (August 4, 2009), A1.

[8]Michael Luo. "For Workers at Closing Plant, Ordeal Included Heart Attacks." *New York Times* (February 25, 2010), A1.

[9]Uchitelle, ix.

[10]Wayne F. Cascio. "Strategies for Responsible Restructuring." *Academy of Management Executive* 19, 4 (2005), 40–41.

[11]Uchitelle, 124–26.

The Decision to Downsize

Employers regularly decide to go out of business, close facilities, relocate, subcontract, outsource, reduce staffing to save money, redirect resources to other uses, adopt new business strategies, restructure their organizations, sell business units, and merge with or acquire other companies. These business decisions typically result in many employees losing their jobs (although employment opportunities might thereby be opened up or made more secure for other individuals). The law provides employees with very few options for challenging employment-threatening business decisions. Thus, in ruling against the plaintiffs in a case involving an employer who closed two plants at which the vast majority of workers were over 40 and replaced them with two new plants in other states in which an equally wide majority of the workers were under 40, the court observed:

> *The ADEA was not intended to protect older workers from the often harsh realities of common business decisions and the hardships associated with corporate reorganizations, downsizing, plant closings and relocations. Unlike law and social policy in many European countries, the laws of the United States do not prohibit or seriously discourage these plant closings and relocation activities and the attendant dislocation, unemployment and new employment.*[1]

Challenges to downsizing decisions derive primarily from the National Labor Relations Act (NLRA). The NLRA affects employment-threatening business decisions in two ways. First, downsizing might lead to unfair labor practice (ULP) charges if it is deemed to interfere with the exercise of employees' NLRA rights or used to discriminate against employees based on their union activity. Second, the employer might have a legal obligation to bargain with union representatives over the decision to downsize.

In a case involving the shutdown of a textile plant by a company that owned a number of textile plants, the Supreme Court observed that "when an employer closes his entire business, even if the liquidation is motivated by vindictiveness toward the union, such action is not an unfair labor practice."[2] But because the employer in question operated multiple plants, this was only a partial closing. The Court concluded that "a partial closing is a ULP … if motivated by a purpose to chill unionism in any of the remaining plants of the single employer and if the employer may reasonably have foreseen that

---

[1]*Allen v. Diebold, Inc.*, 33 F.3d 674, 677 (6th Cir. 1994).

[2]*Textile Workers Union v. Darlington Mfg. Co.*, 380 U.S. 263, 273–74 (1965).

such closing will likely have that effect."[3] It was ultimately decided that the plant closing was motivated by antiunion animus and that a chilling effect on other employees at other plants was reasonably foreseeable.[4] Remedies for violations included back pay and opportunities to transfer to other facilities, but not compelled reopening of the closed facility. *Thus, although employers can always choose to go out of business entirely, they must not selectively close facilities for the purpose of inhibiting unionization at their remaining facilities.*

Relocation of work from one facility to another can also violate the NLRA if motivated by hostility toward unions. Following a representation election, an employer transferred part of its operation to another plant and terminated the employment of six employees who had been assigned to operate those machines.[5] The court upheld the National Labor Relations Board's (NLRB) decision that the employer had committed an unfair labor practice (ULP). Evidence of discrimination included the facts that the six discharged employees were known union supporters, the company had threatened employees with a plant closing or job loss throughout the organizing campaign, the owner had vowed to "take care" of the fired employees, and the company offered false and contradictory reasons for the transfer of work. Because the plant where the work was originally performed still existed in this case, the Board ordered that the employer return the operation that had been transferred.

Boeing's decision in 2009 to construct a second assembly line at a nonunion facility in South Carolina and to assemble Boeing 787 Dreamliners there was challenged by the union that represents its employees in Washington State.[6] The General Counsel of the NLRB issued a complaint against the company. The complaint alleged that Boeing violated the NLRA by making coercive statements and threats to its employees for engaging in protected activities and by retaliating against them for past strike activity and to chill future strike activity. As evidence of the discriminatory motive behind the work relocation decision, the NLRB pointed to statements like the following, made by a senior company official in a newspaper interview:

> *The overriding factor (in transferring the line) was not the business climate. And it was not the wages we're paying today. It was that we cannot afford to have a work stoppage, you know, every three years.*[7]

The ULP charges were dropped after Boeing and the International Association of Machinists negotiated a new labor agreement that included commitments to build a new line of 737s in Washington State.[8] Although this politically-charged case was ended through negotiation rather than NLRB or court decisions, it is a clear illustration of how labor law–for better or worse—can be used to challenge business decisions that would otherwise be beyond the reach of the law.

The second way in which labor law is relevant to downsizing decisions is that in unionized workplaces, these decisions are sometimes mandatory topics of bargaining. If

---

[3]*Darlington,* at 275.

[4]*Darlington Mfg. Co.,* 165 N.L.R.B. 1074 (1967), *enforced,* 397 F.2d 760 (4th Cir. 1968), *cert. denied,* 393 U.S. 1023 (1968).

[5]*NLRB v. Taylor Machine Products, Inc.,* 136 F.3d 507 (6th Cir. 1998).

[6]Steven Greenhouse. "Union Issue May Upend Boeing Plan." *New York Times* (April 21, 2011), B1.

[7]U.S. National Labor Relations Board. "Boeing Complaint Background." Viewed September 20, 2011 (http://www.nlrb.gov/).

[8]Lawrence E. Dubé. "NLRB's Controversial Boeing Case Closed; Lafe Solomon Praises 'Win-Win' Settlement." *Daily Labor Report* 237 (December 9, 2011), AA–1.

a downsizing decision is a mandatory topic of bargaining, the employer has a legal obligation to bargain in good faith with the union prior to taking any action. Business decisions that involve a change in the scope or direction of a business are comparable to decisions to enter or leave a line of business and are not mandatory topics of bargaining. Thus, a company that provided maintenance and housekeeping services under contract with a nursing home did not violate the NLRA when it terminated the contract (due to dissatisfaction with the low fees paid by the home) and laid off the employees who had performed this work without first negotiating with their union.[9] On the other hand, subcontracting and outsourcing, in which employers continue to produce the same things by substituting the services of the employees of another company for the work of their own employees, are generally mandatory topics of bargaining. The same is true for the relocation of work from one facility owned by an employer to a different facility owned by that employer, particularly if labor cost differentials that might be affected by negotiations played a part in the decision.[10] A company that manufactures brass buttons violated the NLRA when it subcontracted its die-cutting work to other firms.[11] Even though the company already subcontracted the vast majority of this work and the contract firms used a superior technology, the company failed to bargain in good faith when it unilaterally implemented further subcontracting. The decision did not amount to the kind of fundamental shift in the nature or direction of the business that lies outside of the collective bargaining process; brass buttons were still being manufactured for sale and the only thing that had changed was that all, rather than most, of the die-cutting was being done outside the firm. A failure to bargain in good faith charge was rejected by the NLRB in the Boeing case because even though work relocation decisions of that type are usually mandatory topics, the Board concluded that the union had previously waived its right to bargain on the issue.[12] *To the extent that downsizing decisions are mandatory topics of bargaining, unionized employers must negotiate in good faith before finalizing such decisions. Regardless of whether employers are legally required to negotiate over the decisions themselves, employers are obligated to negotiate with unions over the effects of downsizing decisions on employees (e.g., transfer rights, retraining, severance pay, and extended benefits).*

The duty to bargain often survives the takeover of one company by another. *Successor employers must bargain with unions that represent employees at acquired companies, although they are generally not bound by the terms of existing labor agreements.* Whether an employer is a "successor" or simply a different firm depends on the degree of continuity between the new operation and the prior operation, including the number of former employees of the acquired firm hired; the extent of similarity in operations, products, and customers; and the length of time between when the old operation ceased and the new one began. In one case, a firm was found to be a successor obligated to bargain even though the original business was closed for seven months before the new operation started and the former employees were rehired through newspaper ads rather than the employment records of the acquired firm.[13] The outsourcing or **privatization** of public services often raises questions about whether the private companies taking over functions previously performed by public employees are successor employers with bargaining obligations. When a private transportation company took over from a school district responsibility for providing bus transportation for some of the district's students,

---

[9]*First National Maintenance Corp. v. NLRB,* 452 U.S. 666 (1981).

[10]*Dubuque Packing Co. v. NLRB,* 1 F.3d 24 (D.C. Cir. 1993), *cert. denied,* 511 U.S. 1138 (1994).

[11]*O.G.S. Technologies,* 356 NLRB No. 92 (2011).

[12]"Boeing Complaint Background."

[13]*Fall River Dyeing & Finishing Corp. v. NLRB,* 482 U.S. 27 (1987).

the private company was a successor employer that was required to bargain with the union that represented the drivers and mechanics when they were public employees.[14] Relevant facts included that the contract required the private company to offer incentives to encourage existing employees to apply for jobs, the majority of the drivers and mechanics were, in fact, former employees of the district, the company purchased the school district's buses and leased one of its maintenance facilities, the same routes were maintained, the district's route planning software continued to be used by the private company, and the contractor was required to comply with the district's administrative directives. It did not matter that the employees were now covered by the NLRA rather than state law or that the privatization was for only part of the district's transportation operations.

Informing Employees Prior to Downsizing—WARN Act

Although employers usually have a free hand in deciding to downsize, the implementation of downsizing decisions is sometimes affected by the **Worker Adjustment and Retraining Notification (WARN) Act**.[15] *Employers covered by the WARN Act are prohibited from ordering plant closings or mass layoffs until the end of a sixty-day period that follows the provision of written notice to affected employees (or, if the employees are unionized, to union representatives) and to state and local government officials.* **Affected employees** are those who are reasonably expected to suffer **employment loss** stemming from a plant closing or mass layoff, including termination (other than a quit, discharge for cause, or retirement), a layoff lasting more than six months, or a greater than 50 percent reduction in work hours during each month of any six-month period. Other measures that might be used by struggling employers—including cuts in pay or benefits, short-term layoffs (less than six months), and limited (less than 50 percent) reductions in work hours—do not bring the WARN Act's notification requirements into play.

Clippings

A former computer programmer for Lehman Brothers has sued the firm under the WARN Act. The suit was brought on behalf of himself and about a thousand other employees of the investment bank who lost their jobs without notice on or within 30 days of September 9, 2008. The firm filed for bankruptcy under Chapter 11 of the bankruptcy code on September 15, 2008 and its investment banking and trading businesses were sold to Barclays. The employees allege that Lehman Brothers violated the WARN Act by conducting a mass layoff without the necessary prior notification. The damages sought include salary, commissions, bonuses, accrued holiday and vacation pay, 401(k) contributions, and health insurance coverage for the 60 calendar days following the terminations. In light of the firm's bankruptcy filing, the prospects for recovery of these damages are murky at best.

"Fired Lehman Worker Files WARN Act Suit on Behalf of About 1,000 Former Employees." *Daily Labor Report* 219 (November 13, 2008), A-13.

---

[14]*Dean Transportation v. NLRB*, 551 F.3d 1055 (D.C. Cir. 2009).
[15]29 U.S.C.S. §§ 2101–2109 (2011).

Only relatively large employers are covered by the WARN Act. Specifically, employers are covered if they have 100 or more full-time employees or have 100 or more full- and part-time employees working in the aggregate at least 4000 hours per week (excluding overtime hours). The usual problems of counting employees to determine statutory coverage are even more acute under the WARN Act because downward fluctuation in employment levels is inherent in the circumstances under which the act is applied. The relevant point in time for determining coverage is the date that the first notice of an impending closing or mass layoff is required to be given (i.e., sixty days prior to the downsizing).

The meanings of the terms *plant closing and mass layoff* are central to the act and not self-evident. Under the WARN Act, a **plant closing** is a permanent or temporary shutdown of a single site of employment when that shutdown results in employment loss during any thirty-day period for at least fifty full-time employees. A **mass layoff** is a reduction in force that is not caused by a plant closing, but that results in employment loss at a single work site during any thirty-day period for at least 500 full-time employees (regardless of the percentage of total employees) or at least 50 full-time employees (when these comprise at least 33 percent of total employment at the work site). (Note that this definition of mass layoff under the WARN Act is quite different from the definition used by the Bureau of Labor Statistics for statistical purposes.)

But wait! It gets more complicated still. In the messy real world, closings and layoffs do not necessarily occur at single points in time. The WARN Act provides that when there are employment losses for two or more groups of employees at a single employment site (e.g., several "waves" of layoffs)—and none of these groups are individually large enough to meet the numerical standards for plant closings or mass layoffs, but they do so in the aggregate—the employment losses over any ninety-day period can be combined to establish that a plant closing or mass layoff has occurred (unless the employer can show that the employment losses stemmed from separate and distinct causes). A downward spiral of financial problems that eventually ends in the closure of a facility is a single cause. Thus, a hospital that began laying off employees due to funding problems several months before it decided to close its doors was liable for failing to give notice dating back to sixty days before the very first employee was laid off.[16]

Multiple notifications might be required under the WARN Act. In one case, an employer gave notice of a mass layoff but then decided to permanently close the plant. The employer notified the union that the mass layoff was being converted to a permanent shutdown, but it did so on the same day that it closed the plant. The court concluded that although the employees were already laid off, the prior notification was not sufficient because they had incurred the new employment loss of a termination. Thus, the employer had failed to provide the required sixty-day notice of a plant closing.[17] An employment loss does not occur if, prior to a plant closing or mass layoff, the employer offers to transfer the employee to another work site within a reasonable commuting distance and with no more than a six-month break in employment or the employer offers a transfer to another work site regardless of the distance, no more than a six-month break in employment, and the employee accepts within thirty days. Thus, the WARN Act contains an incentive for employers to offer downsized employees continued employment through transfer to other facilities (i.e., such employees cannot

---

[16]*Hollowell v. Orleans Regional Hospital*, 217 F.3d 379 (5ᵗʰ Cir. 2000).

[17]*Graphic Communications International Union, Local 31-N v. Quebecor Printing Corp.*, 252 F.3d 296 (4ᵗʰ Cir. 2001).

be plaintiffs in WARN Act cases, and the offer of transfers might affect whether notification is even required). An employer avoided liability under the WARN Act after closing a plant without notice by informing employees that they would receive their pay and benefits for the next sixty days unless they accepted jobs with a successor company that was planning to operate the plant on a greatly reduced scale. Some of the employees who took positions with the successor company sued to receive the full sixty days' pay and benefits. The court ruled that because the original employer had continued to pay them despite their no longer performing work, they had not suffered employment loss.[18]

Collins v. Gee West Seattle LLC
631 F.3d 1001 (9th Cir. 2011)

OPINION BY CIRCUIT JUDGE SMITH:

In this case of first impression, we must determine the meaning of the term "voluntary departure" under the Worker Adjustment and Retraining Notification ("WARN") Act. We hold that, if an employee leaves a job because the business is closing, that employee has not "voluntarily departed" within the meaning of the WARN Act. Rather, that employee has suffered an "employment loss." We reverse and remand.

* * * In January of 2007, Gee West Seattle LLC ("Gee West") purchased and began operating several automobile franchises in Seattle, Washington. Due to a number of financial losses, however, Gee West commenced efforts to sell the business in July of 2007. On September 26, 2007, Gee West informed its employees … via written memo that although it was "actively pursuing" the sale of the business it would "be closing its doors at the end of business on Sunday October 7, 2007." In the event a buyer was not found before October 7, 2007, Gee West would terminate all employees except designated Accounting and Business Office employees. Employees were further notified that "[n]otice could not be given sooner because Gee West was actively seeking business to keep the business running," as well as "seeking potential purchasers, and attempting to sell inventory, and [it was] concerned that potential purchasers would not have made a purchase, had [its] workforce been seeking alternate employment."

Prior to the September 26, 2007 announcement, Gee West had employed approximately 150 employ-ees. Following the September 26, 2007, announcement, however, employees began to stop reporting to work. By October 5, 2007, only 30 employees reported at the various Gee West facilities.

Gee West ceased business on October 5, 2007, rather than October 7, 2007, because too few employees remained to maintain operations. Gee West reopened on October 6, 2007, for inspection by a potential purchaser, but the sale did not go through and the business was permanently closed. Documents created after the filing of this case by Saundra Godin, Gee West's Human Resources Director, show that every employee (who was terminated after September 26, 2007) left because the "business closed."

* * * The WARN Act requires that: "An employer shall not order a plant closing or mass layoff until the end of a 60-day period after the employer serves written notice of such an order (1) … to each affected employee." An "affected employee" is one who "may reasonably be expected to experience an employment loss as a consequence of a plant closing …" The 60-days' notice requirement, however, applies only "if the shutdown results in an employment loss at the single site of employment during any 30-day period for 50 or more employees …." "[T]he term 'employment loss' means (A) an employment termination, other than a discharge for cause, voluntary departure, or retirement …."

* * * Employees filed this lawsuit … claiming Gee West violated the WARN Act by not giving 60-days' notice before closing its doors. * * * The [district] court concluded that the roughly 120 employees, who left

---

[18]*Long v. Dunlop Sports Group Americas*, 506 F.3d 299 (4th Cir. 2007).

between September 26, 2007, and the final closure on October 5, 2007, did not suffer an "employment loss" because they "voluntarily departed" within the meaning of the WARN Act. The court reasoned that, since "voluntary" means "done or undertaken of one's own free will," the "pre-closure departure of the 120 employees ... is not any less 'voluntary' for having possibly been motivated by the belief that they would be unemployed in the near future." Accordingly, the district court held that "an employee who leaves of their own free will prior to the closure of a business (absent allegations of constructive discharge) 'voluntarily departed' for purposes of the WARN Act and has not suffered an 'employment loss' as defined by that statute."

* * * Having ruled that the Employees, who left Gee West between September 26 and October 5, 2007, had "voluntarily departed," the district court concluded that there was no cognizable WARN Act claim. Because fewer than 50 employees suffered an "employment loss" as a result of the business closure, no notice needed to be given. Employees now appeal. * * *

On appeal, Employees argue ... that ... the district court erred by interpreting the term "voluntary departure" to include an employee's departure from a job because the business was closing .... * * *

We begin our analysis with the statute's plain language. Under the Act, "[a]n employer shall not order a plant closing or mass layoff until the end of a 60-day period after the employer serves written notice of such an order ... to each affected employee." An "affected employee" is one who "may reasonably be expected to experience an employment loss as a consequence of a plant closing ...." It is undisputed that Gee West is an "employer" and that Employees are "affected employees" under the Act. Therefore, unless a statutory exception applied, Gee West was required to give written notice 60 days before shutting down its plant to every employee that "reasonably expected" to be terminated—i.e., all 150 employees still working with Gee West 60 days before the plant closure. Having failed to do so, Gee West committed a facial violation of the WARN Act.

However, Gee West argues that notice is not required, focusing entirely on the statutory term "employment loss." "[T]he term 'employment loss' means (A) an employment termination, other than a discharge for cause, voluntary departure, or retirement ...." Seizing upon the dictionary definition of

the term "voluntary," Gee West argues that, because all but 30 employees left their jobs of their own free will prior to October 7, 2007, Gee West's closing did not qualify as a "plant closing" under the WARN Act. This argument, however, flips the basic structure of the WARN Act on its head. Instead of placing the onus on the employer to give 60-days' notice before closing a plant, Gee West's reading of the Act would measure an employer's liability based solely on the number of employees remaining at the plant at the time of its closure, even though employees departed because of the plant closure. Such an interpretation is inconsistent with the basic structure of the WARN Act and frustrates its purposes. We reject Gee West's argument.

"Employment loss" is relevant to two distinct issues under the WARN Act. First, it defines those affected employees to whom 60-days' notice must be given .... "Affected employees" are all those who "may reasonably be expected to experience an employment loss as a consequence of a plant closing." Therefore, the affected employees must be determined prospectively in order for the employer to give proper notice. Second, a plant closing occurs "if the shutdown results in an employment loss at the single site ... for 50 or more employees." In this case, the relevant inquiry is not the expected employment loss, but the actual employment loss. However, as the Department of Labor noted, because employers must determine at least 60 days in advance whether notice must be given, employers must accurately determine how many employees will lose employment.

* * * As the DOL suggests, the starting point for determining whether there is an actual or reasonably expected employment loss (as a consequence of a plant closing) is to determine how many positions will be eliminated by the closing. In the case of Gee West, this would be all 150 employees, except for selected Accounting and Business Office staff. The Act, however, also excludes those who retire, are discharged for cause, or voluntarily depart from the definition of those experiencing employment loss. Thus, those whom the employer reasonably expects to retire, to discharge for cause, or to voluntarily depart before the closure are not affected employees under the Act, as they cannot "reasonably be expected to experience an employment loss." Gee West does not dispute that Employees are affected employees and thus reasonably expected to experience an employment loss.

Similarly, those employees who actually retire, are discharged, or leave for reasons unrelated to the shutdown do not count as "employment loss" when determining that there has been a plant closing. However, unless there is some evidence of imminent departure for reasons other than the shutdown, it is unreasonable to conclude that employees voluntarily departed after receiving notice of the upcoming closure. For example, Gee West argues that 150 affected employees reasonably expected loss of employment, and those employees' positions were eliminated, but that only 30 employees actually experienced employment loss. Gee West claims that all other employees voluntarily departed after notice was given. This argument would allow an employer to escape responsibility for failing to give proper notice simply because its employees subsequently leave the business due to its imminent closure. The unexpected and urgent need to find new employment is precisely the type of pressure that … Congress was attempting to eliminate by creating the WARN Act. Employees' departure because of a business closing, therefore, is generally not voluntary, but a consequence of the shutdown and must be considered a loss of employment when determining whether a plant closure has occurred. Gee West's argument that only 30 employees lost employment as a consequence of the plant closing is thus not credible. Indeed, Gee West's records note that all employees who were terminated after Sept. 26, 2007, left as a consequence of the business closing.

* * * An examination of the basic purposes of the WARN Act further confirms this understanding. We have previously clarified that the WARN Act "is a wage workers' equivalent of business interruption insurance. It protects a worker from being told on payday that the plant is closing that afternoon and his stream of income is shut off, though he has to buy groceries for his family that weekend and make a mortgage payment the next week." Therefore, "it makes perfect sense to require the company to pay the worker for 60 work days," in order for the worker's "stream of income [to] continue[ ] to flow for 60 days after he knows the plant will shut down, so he has two months to look for a new job, perhaps in a new town if the plant shutdown decimated employment in his town." * * * [W]hile Congress meant for the Act to "compensate for actual lost earnings" resulting from an Employer's violation of the Act, Congress also intended to give terminated employees time to readjust

without immediately searching for a new job or being pressured "to mitigate damages by taking any job offered."

Gee West disputes our understanding of the purpose of the WARN Act. It argues: "The employees' reasons for abandoning their jobs are immaterial. Some may have left Gee West early because they found alternative employment. The WARN Act was certainly not intended to provide [Employees] with double income, and that is why the Act excludes voluntary departures from its coverage." We have expressly refuted such an interpretation of the WARN Act. In *Las Vegas Sands*, we held that damages under the WARN Act are not offset by wages earned by another employer during the statutory time period. Removing from the Act's protection those employees that, as a result of deficient notice, had to quit early to find a job (the very thing the Act presumes they will do) is entirely inconsistent with the Act's goals.

Employers, such as Gee West, who are trying to keep a business afloat and whose futures are uncertain have other protections under the Act, and need not resort to a broad definition of voluntary departure to avoid liability. Struggling businesses face difficult issues such as whether to give notice at all, since closure is not certain, and whether giving notice will hasten the business decline or impair efforts for a sale. Recognizing these difficulties and the public policy interest in giving employees such notice as is practicable, Congress provided that an employer who is actively seeking capital or business in order to avoid or postpone a shutdown may give only such notice "as is practicable" if giving 60-days' notice would "preclude[ ] the employer from obtaining the needed capital or business. This provision of the WARN Act, otherwise known as the "faltering business" exception, explicitly provides for the situation confronted by Gee West without resort to a broad interpretation of voluntary departure. * * *

In sum, we hold that an employee departing a business because that business was closing, has not "voluntarily departed" within the meaning of the Act. To hold otherwise would be inconsistent with the Act's general structure and its overall purpose. It would also render the "faltering business" exception superfluous. We decline to adopt this holding. Further, because there was at least some evidence in the record that

Employees left their jobs because the business was closing, summary judgment is inappropriate. We reverse and remand. * * *

CASE QUESTIONS

1. What was the legal issue in this case? What did the appeals court decide?
2. Why, despite the fact that these employees left employment prior to the actual closure of the business, does the court conclude that they were affected employees who suffered employment loss? Why would the contrary conclusion be "inconsistent with the basic structure of the WARN Act and frustrate[] its purposes?"
3. What if employees faced with possible job loss in a downsizing accept severance packages? Would they no longer be affected employees because of voluntary departure or would they still be affected employees who left their jobs due to an imminent mass layoff? Why do you say that? (See *Ellis v. DHL Express*, 633 F.3d 522 (7th Cir. 2011), *cert. denied*, 2011 U.S. LEXIS 6619).
4. The court leaves open the possibility that the "faltering business" exception to the WARN Act's notification requirements might apply in this case. Would the employer likely prevail on these grounds? Why or why not?
5. Do you agree with the decision in this case? Why or why not?

In *Collins v. Gee West Seattle LLC,* the court must decide whether the employees of a company that closed were affected employees entitled to advance notification under the WARN Act, even though most of them had already stopped reporting to work prior to the closure.

The WARN Act contains some rather large loopholes. Employers are excused for not providing the full sixty-day prior notice when a closure or layoff is due to a natural disaster; when a capital infusion or new business is being sought, which, if obtained, would avoid or postpone a closure, and the employer has a good faith belief that giving notice would make it impossible to obtain the needed capital or business; and when the closure or layoff is the result of business circumstances not readily foreseeable at the time when notice should have been given. Under these circumstances, the employer is required to provide as much notice as possible and to explain in the notice why the full sixty-day prior notice requirement was not met. Likewise, if a layoff is originally thought to last less than six months but extends longer, the employer is liable for failure to provide required notice unless the extension is caused by business circumstances not reasonably foreseeable at the time of the initial layoff and notice is given as soon as it becomes apparent that the layoff will extend beyond six months. The closure of facilities or operations understood to be temporary in nature and layoffs that result from strikes or lockouts do not require any prior notice.

JUST THE FACTS

In 2001, when the financial practices and overstated earnings of Enron were attracting the intense scrutiny of federal investigators, Arthur Andersen served as the firm's auditor and consultant. In the weeks leading up to issuance of a subpoena to produce Enron-related documents, Andersen employees destroyed thousands of the documents sought by the Securities and Exchange Commission (SEC). When this conduct was revealed in November 2001, it led to rampant media speculation about Andersen's continuing viability as a firm. During the first two months of 2002,

Andersen attempted to negotiate with the SEC and Department of Justice (DOJ) to head off possible charges. On March 1, 2002, Andersen was informed that the DOJ would seek an indictment of the company. On March 7, 2002, at the same time as top managers attempted to reassure employees in an e-mail that matters were being worked out, the DOJ filed a sealed indictment charging Andersen with obstruction of an SEC investigation. On March 14, 2002, the indictment was unsealed and became public knowledge. Clients immediately began to defect and the firm lost $300 million in business over the next two weeks. On April 8, notices of termination were issued to 560 employees. The employees remained on the payroll for between two and five weeks longer. Under the circumstances, did Andersen meet its WARN Act obligations? Why or why not?

Roquet v. Arthur Andersen, 398 F.3d 585 (7th Cir. 2005), *cert. denied*, 126 S. Ct. 375 (2005).

For their trouble, plaintiffs in WARN Act cases are entitled to receive back pay for the number of days that they were deprived of timely notice, up to a maximum of sixty days. Courts have differed on whether eligibility for back pay is based on calendar days or only days on which work would have been performed.[19] Employers are also liable for health insurance premiums and pension payments for the period of the WARN Act violation, but not for the likes of holiday and vacation pay.

Selecting Employees for Downsizing

Short of the wholesale closure of a business unit, decisions must be made as to which employees will be selected for termination. The main legal requirement in this regard is that the means of selecting individuals for downsizing must not be discriminatory. A particular concern in this context is age discrimination.

Determining whether a discharge is actually part of a **reduction in force (RIF)** is not always straightforward. In a case that raised this issue, the court outlined the relevant considerations for determining whether a RIF has occurred:

> *A work force reduction situation occurs when business considerations cause an employer to eliminate one or more positions within the company. An employee is not eliminated as part of a work force reduction when he or she is replaced after his or her discharge. However, a person is not replaced when another employee is assigned to perform the plaintiff's duties in addition to other duties, or when the work is redistributed among other existing employees already performing related work.*[20]

Thus, when a 56-year-old manager was terminated in what the company claimed was a RIF but an employee 24 years younger was hired the day after (and at the same salary) to perform the same managerial duties, it was easily concluded that the company's RIF justification was pretext.[21] Likewise, when an existing employee was changed from part-time to full-time status with fundamentally different responsibilities to cover the duties that had been performed by a terminated employee, a court concluded that this was equivalent to hiring a new employee as a replacement.[22] In contrast, a downsized bindery

---

[19]*United Mine Workers of America, International Union v. Eighty-Four Mining Co.*, 2005 U.S. App. LEXIS 25039 (3d Cir.).

[20]*Godfredson v. Hess & Clark, Inc.*, 173 F.3d 365, 372 (6th Cir. 1999).

[21]*Miller v. Eby Reality Group*, 396 F.3d 1105 (10th Cir. 2005).

[22]*Tinker v. Sears, Roebuck & Co.*, 127 F.3d 519, 522 (6th Cir. 1997).

worker could not show that another employee was hired or reassigned to perform her duties where her former duties were assumed by another (younger) employee in addition to his other functions.[23]

Determining whether a termination is part of a RIF matters because, if it is, that fact necessitates a modification of the approach typically used in discriminatory discharge cases. If downsizing is seized upon as an opportunity to rid organizations of older employees, the ADEA is violated. But ferreting out discrimination in this context is problematic. When employers determine, however wisely or foolishly, that jobs have to be cut, courts are loath to question this decision. Thus, "when a company exercises its business judgment in deciding to reduce its work force, 'it need not provide evidence of financial distress to make it a legitimate RIF.'"[24]

ELEMENTS OF A CLAIM

Discriminatory Discharge in a RIF (Age)

The plaintiff must establish a prima facie case by showing the following:

1. The downsized employee was age 40 or over.
2. He was selected for termination from a larger group of candidates.
3. He was performing at a level at least substantially equivalent to the lowest level among the group of employees retained.
4. The group of employees retained included one or more substantially younger employees who were not performing any better than the terminated employee.

OR

1. The downsized employee was age 40 or over.
2. He was performing his job to his employer's reasonable expectations.
3. He was terminated (or suffered another adverse employment action such as failure to transfer or rehire).
4. Other similarly situated employees (i.e., those with comparable positions, skills, and qualifications) who were substantially younger than him were treated more favorably or
5. There is additional direct, circumstantial, or statistical evidence indicating that the plaintiff would not have been discharged "but for" his age.

If a prima facie case is established, the employer must articulate the lawful reason(s) for selecting the employee for termination.

The plaintiff has the opportunity to show that the stated reasons are pretext and that it is more likely that the decision was based on the employee's age.

© Cengage Learning 2013.

No one deserves to be downsized. In downsizing cases, it is usually not helpful to ask whether the discharged employee was meeting her employer's legitimate performance

---

[23]*Schoonmaker v. Spartan Graphics Leasing*, 595 F.3d 261, 267 (6th Cir. 2010).

[24]*Regel v. K-Mart Corp.*, 190 F.3d 876 (8th Cir. 1999).

expectations at the time of discharge, as is typically done in other discriminatory discharge cases. Further, because positions disappear during genuine reductions in force, it is not useful to ask whether the employer sought to fill the vacated position or did so with someone whose protected class characteristics differ from the plaintiff's. As one court put it, "[t]he question in this context is not why members of the group were discharged or whether they were meeting performance expectations, but whether the particular employees were selected for inclusion on the list for discharge because of their age."[25] While employers are free to downsize, they must be prepared to explain why particular individuals were selected for downsizing; citing a reduction in force by itself is not sufficient to defeat a discrimination claim.[26]

Courts accept the general legitimacy of downsizing and the likelihood that many of those who are downsized will be over 40 simply because of the large proportion of the workforce comprised of this age group. A relatively heavy burden is placed on plaintiffs terminated in a RIF to establish a prima facie case of disparate treatment based on age.[27] The first approach (see Elements of a Claim) to defining a prima facie case is tailored to the (typical) situation where an employer claims that performance was a factor in selecting employees for downsizing. This approach asks whether any inference of age discrimination can be drawn from a comparison of the ages and relative performance levels of employees terminated with those retained. The second approach is more general and can be used to analyze situations where, for example, some employees are given the option to transfer and others are not.

In *Wittenburg v. American Express*, an employer's selection process for downsizing is scrutinized, but ultimately upheld.

Wittenburg v. American Express
464 F.3d 831 (8th Cir. 2006), *cert. denied*, 127 S. Ct. 2936 (2007)

OPINION BY CIRCUIT JUDGE SMITH:

Bonnie Wittenburg, a former Equity Research Analyst for American Express Financial Advisors, Inc.'s ("AEFA") Equity Investment Department ("EID"), brought this employment discrimination suit against AEFA, asserting … age discrimination in AEFA's termination of her employment. AEFA filed a motion for summary judgment, which the district court granted. We affirm.

* * * In November 1998, AEFA hired Wittenburg, then age 46, to work in its Minneapolis office as an Equity Research Analyst in the Technology Sector of the EID. * * * Wittenburg worked hard, displayed "excellent investment skills," and provided "first class service" to the portfolio managers. In fact, Wittenburg was named "Analyst of the Year" in 2000 because of her "outstanding efforts and achievements."

In Fall 2001, AEFA hired Ted Truscott as its Chief Investment Officer ("CIO") to manage all investment activity at AEFA. * * * In February 2002, Truscott initiated a two-year project to redesign the EID. The redesign project involved the addition of three portfolio managers hired from a competitor, the creation of a new satellite office in Boston, and the merger or movement of certain funds to AEFA's satellite offices in San Diego, Boston, and New Jersey. In discussing AEFA's

---

[25]*Mitchell v. Data General Corp.*, 12 F.3d 1310, 1315 (4th Cir. 1993).

[26]*Diaz v. Eagle Produce*, 521 F.3d 1201, 1211–1212 (9th Cir. 2008).

[27]*Johnson v. Franklin Farmers Cooperative*, 378 Fed. Appx. 505, 509-10 (6th Cir. 2010).

hiring of the three new portfolio managers, Truscott stated that AEFA planned on hiring more managers in Boston because AEFA "needed to be competitive as the best fund families out there. We will hire talent where we feel we have gaps. That said, we are not averse to hiring younger portfolio managers or analysts and growing them."

As part of the February 2002 redesign plan, AEFA included a reduction-in-force ("RIF"), which, according to Truscott, was necessary and "related to the transfer of investment portfolios to the newly formed Boston office." The February 2002 RIF involved only portfolio managers. One of the portfolio managers terminated in the RIF was Al Henderson, age 62. According to Henderson, Dan Rivera, Head of the Equities Department and a decisionmaker in the February 2002 RIF, told him that he was fired because AEFA wanted to retain "those that were younger" because younger employees have "more years of service ahead of them."

The second RIF occurred in June 2002 and was, according to Truscott, "related to the transfer of portfolios to the then being established San Diego office." This RIF primarily impacted portfolio managers; however, three analyst positions in Minneapolis were also eliminated. As part of the redesign process, a team ... [of managers] created a talent review of the approximately 25 people in the department. The review ... indicated whether the analyst was a "keep," "maybe keep," "maybe," "maybe drop," or "drop." These ratings were generated to educate the leaders about the individuals working in the department and to identify employees in the department that might be affected by the reorganization.

In late 2002, the EID held its ratings alignment meeting.... The group first discussed Mahowald's proposed ratings for each of the analysts, including Wittenburg. The proposed ratings were subject to change based on the group's discussion. Mahowald's proposed rating for Wittenburg was G3/L3, but after the ratings alignment meeting, her 2002 rating was lowered to a G4/L3. The other Technology Sector analysts' ratings in 2002 were: G3/L3 for David Friedrichsen (age 40), G3/L1 for Kurt Lauber (age 35), and G3/L1 for Dean Ramos (age 39).

Wittenburg's low rating in 2002 was mainly because of her poor performance on funds and negative input she received from portfolio managers. * * * Wittenburg complained about her 2002 rating to Mahowald. At that time, she asserted that her G4 rating was too low based on "Starmine" data for 2002. Starmine rated Wittenburg's 2002 performance highly, awarding her four stars out of a maximum of five stars. Wittenburg, however, acknowledged that Mahowald did not have access to the Starmine information on her 2002 performance when he gave her the G4 rating. Mahowald agreed with Wittenburg about what the "Starmine" data showed, but he disagreed that the data should have impacted her performance rating, considering AEFA does not use the Starmine data for evaluating performance. * * *

In September 2003, Truscott informed Mahowald that a third RIF would occur. * * * [It was] determined that AEFA only needed to retain one Technology Sector analyst based on business need; therefore, three of the four Technology Sector analyst positions would be eliminated. To implement the RIF, AEFA used the multiple incumbent process. Consistent with that process, the performance ratings of analysts for 2002 and, in the event of a tie, 2001, were used in determining which analysts within each sector to terminate. Like all other analysts, Wittenburg's 2002 ratings were used.

With regard to the Technology Sector, AEFA terminated Wittenburg, age 51, in the third RIF, along with Friedrichsen, age 41, and Lauber, age 36. Only Ramos, age 40, was retained. * * * Ultimately, of the 7 analysts selected for job elimination, 4 were 40 years or older.... AEFA retained 51-year-old Sandy Hollenhorst, who was hired by Mahowald in 2001.

AEFA notified Wittenburg of her position elimination on November 18, 2003.... * * * After her termination, Wittenburg sought a position as a portfolio manager at AEFA but was not hired. She subsequently brought suit against AEFA, asserting claims of age discrimination under the Age Discrimination in Employment Act (ADEA).... * * *

First, Wittenburg relies on the following statements of AEFA personnel to support her age discrimination claim: (1) Truscott's statement that AEFA is "not averse to hiring younger portfolio managers or analysts and growing them;" (2) Forker's 2002 notes indicating that the analyst department would "maybe add a junior person;" and (3) Rivera's comment during the February 2002 RIF that AEFA wanted to retain "those that were younger" because they have "more years of service ahead of them."

A plaintiff must establish "some causal relationship" to show "the significance of [decisionmakers'] noncontemporaneous statements, or statements made by persons other than the relevant decision-maker, to the resolution of the ultimate issue of intentional discrimination." Therefore, we consider factors such as (1) whether the statements were made by employees who took part in the decision or influenced the decision to terminate the plaintiff; (2) the time gap between when the statements were made and the date of termination; and (3) "whether the statement itself" is "an exhibition of discriminatory animus" or merely an "opinion that such animus might exist."

Truscott, a decision-maker, made a general statement regarding the company's willingness to hire younger workers. Such a generalized statement does not evince a discriminatory policy or practice, nor does it tend to establish that age was the basis for Wittenburg's termination over a year later. * * * Likewise, Forker's reference to "junior person" in her notes does not show discriminatory intent. Wittenburg has failed to present evidence that Forker equated "junior person" to a "younger person" or how such a notation relates to her termination in the 2003 RIF. Additionally, Wittenburg admits that Rivera was only a decisionmaker in the initial phase of the department downsizing, not in the 2003 RIF. Rivera's comment could be characterized as a non-contemporaneous, non-decisionmaker's opinion about company retention policy during a prior RIF. Taken together, these comments by AEFA personnel fall short of establishing pretext in AEFA's stated nondiscriminatory purpose given for her termination.

Second, Wittenburg points out that AEFA "got rid" of the eight oldest analysts in the department by the end of the "two-year makeover plan" and gave four of the five oldest analysts low G4 or L4 ratings in 2002, thereby setting them up for termination in the 2003 RIF. Wittenburg, however, ignores evidence that several members of the protected class survived the RIFs. Out of 31 analysts affected by the 2002 and 2003 RIFs, 17 were 40 years old or older. Of those 17 analysts, 6 were terminated, 4 resigned, and 7 survived the RIFs. In comparison, of the 14 analysts in the non-protected class, 4 were terminated, 2 resigned, 2 were transferred to the hedge fund, and 6 survived the RIFs. Also, of the 20 analysts evaluated, Steve Schroll, age 46, and Paul Stocking, age 41, both members of the protected class, ranked 1st and 2nd, respectively, in the

2002 analyst rankings. In addition, the two analysts terminated with Wittenburg from the Technology Sector were both younger than she—Friedrichsen, age 41, and Lauber, age 36. Furthermore, Hollenhorst, who was the same age as Wittenburg in 2003 (age 51), was not terminated during the 2003 RIF.

Third, Wittenburg argues that Mahowald demonstrated age discrimination by rating Wittenburg a "maybe drop" during the June 2002 RIF, while ranking younger employees with lower scores in the "keep" category. Wittenburg, however, survived this first round of layoffs. * * * Furthermore, Wittenburg does not challenge AEFA's contention that these performance ratings were not used in the 2003 RIF.

Fourth, Wittenburg challenges AEFA's explanation for the RIFs, noting that Truscott stated that the RIFs were for cost-cutting, while AEFA represented to the district court that the RIFs were done to improve performance funds and not for cost-cutting. Truscott consistently testified, however, that the reason for the RIF was to redesign the EID, moving analysts [sic] positions from the Minneapolis office to the satellite offices. * * * A company need not provide evidence of financial distress to make an RIF "legitimate." * * *

Fifth, Wittenburg asserts that AEFA's reliance on her 2002 "G4/L3" rating to justify her termination is pretextual because (1) Mahowald conducted the performance evaluation knowing that there could be another RIF within the department in 2003 and that his performance ratings would determine which analysts would be eliminated; (2) Mahowald failed to present Wittenburg with a written review of her rating; (3) she received a high rating from Starmine based on the same performance data that AEFA used; (4) inaccuracies appear in the 2002 performance evaluation; (5) other similarly situated employees outside of her protected class received more favorable ratings; and (6) AEFA used a single year's performance evaluation to justify her termination.

Wittenburg relies on an email that Dewald sent to Mahowald in April 2002 to prove that Mahowald knew that another RIF could occur in 2003. However, the email does not establish that fact. Dewald said that "Option 2 may become a mute [sic] point 18 months from now," indicating a lack of certainty. * * * Regarding Mahowald's failure to present Wittenburg with a written review of her rating, no analyst—either within the protected class or outside the protected class—received written reviews in 2002. In addition, Mahowald met separately with each analyst to orally deliver his 2002 year-end performance reviews.

Wittenburg's high Starmine rating is also insufficient to prove pretext. Wittenburg admits that Mahowald did not have access to her 2002 Starmine rating when he gave her the G3 rating, which was changed at the ratings alignment meeting to a G4. In addition, Wittenburg admits that AEFA never used Starmine data for evaluating performance.

As to the inaccuracies in her 2002 performance evaluation, Wittenburg points to an error by the hedge fund managers stating that she had recommended the purchase of a certain stock for several months when, in fact, she had the stock rated neutral for nearly the entire year. Wittenburg, however, does not allege that Mahowald knew of this "erroneous assumption" when he analyzed the portfolio manager feedback, which indicated below average results for Wittenburg. Also, although Wittenburg argues that the "L" rating is subjective, "the presence of subjectivity in employee evaluations is itself not a grounds for challenging those evaluations as discriminatory." Instead, Wittenburg must present "affirmative evidence that [AEFA] manipulated the rating system" to discriminate against her on an impermissible basis. Wittenburg attempts to meet this burden by arguing that she received an L3 rating despite being the only analyst to complete Mahowald's special project for 2002. However, Mahowald explained that although Wittenburg was the only analyst to complete the special project, her ratings on the stocks did not help portfolio managers make money and consequently was not a positive consideration in her rating. Mahowald also stated that her L3 rating was a direct result of the negative feedback portfolio managers gave Wittenburg.

Wittenburg next argues that Mahowald intentionally rated her lower in 2002 as a pretext for age discrimination. Wittenburg contends that similarly situated employees outside of her protected class were treated more favorably in terms of their L ratings. Specifically, she argues that Mahowald elevated the L ratings of Ramos, Lauber, and Steve Roorda by crediting them for completing a special "private placement" project that she was not assigned. Mahowald, however, explained that these analysts only received the special project because the private placements were "done in that analyst's area of expertise, [meaning that] they logically had extra work to do to research and recommend and otherwise monitor that investment." Furthermore, Wittenburg overlooks that, in 2002, Roorda, age 45, fell within the protected age group.

She also challenges her 2002 ratings based on AEFA's reliance only on the 2002 performance evaluations in deciding which analysts to terminate in the 2003 RIF. We have noted, however, that "there is nothing inherently discriminatory in an employer choosing to rely on recent performance data more heavily than past performance in deciding which employees to terminate in a RIF," as this is a business judgment properly left to the employer's discretion. Truscott explained that AEFA measures analysts' performance in the "short run" because "many consumers look at one-year performance and make their decisions on this" and because "the track record at American Express had been so terrible that we needed to see how we were doing on a one year basis."

Finally, Wittenburg argues that pretext is also shown by conflict in AEFA's statements and its hiring actions. According to Wittenburg, AEFA claimed it needed only one Technology Sector analyst but then immediately assigned significant Technology-Sector stock coverage to Industrial Sector analysts Roorda, age 45, and Larry Alberts, age 49, and advertised for analysts to fill two vacancies two months after the 2003 RIF. However, "employers often distribute a discharged employee's duties to other employees performing related work for legitimate reasons." Furthermore, Roorda and Alberts are actually in the same protected class as Wittenburg. However, because "the ADEA prohibits discrimination on the basis of age and not class membership," we look to whether the replacement is "substantially younger" than the plaintiff. * * * We conclude that Roorda and Alberts are not "substantially younger" than Wittenburg, as the largest disparity between Wittenburg and Roorda is six years. As to AEFA advertising to fill two vacancies two months after the RIF, the two vacancies arose from among the ten surviving analyst positions.

Therefore, AEFA did not create two new analyst positions after terminating Wittenburg. * * *

Accordingly, we affirm the judgment of the district court.

CASE QUESTIONS

1. What was the legal issue in this case? What did the court decide?
2. Why don't the statements made by various managers provide convincing evidence of discriminatory motive?
3. What is the evidence regarding the effect of the RIF on older workers? That the performance ratings were manipulated to favor retention of younger workers?
4. Were the employer's subsequent actions in redistributing duties and advertising for analysts consistent with the claim that the employee was terminated in a genuine RIF? Why or why not?
5. What things did the employer do in carrying out this RIF that helped it prevail in this case?

A university was found to have willfully violated the ADEA when its oldest employees were terminated, while substantially younger employees were hired or had their contracts extended to perform the duties of some of the discharged employees.[28] The university had developed its criteria for selection decisions made in the RIF *after* the individuals slated for downsizing had already been identified, and it failed to use up-to-date information about employee performance and qualifications. Higher skill requirements were placed upon the terminated workers than upon their replacements (e.g., older workers were criticized for lack of computer skills while the same deficit was overlooked in younger workers). Worse yet, there was evidence that a decision maker spoke of getting around the "legal hurdle" of the ADEA. Shifting or after-the-fact explanations for decisions about who to downsize are especially likely to attract judicial notice. One of the decision makers in a downsizing in which the oldest office employees were terminated said that the decision was made by rating each of the office staff on flexibility, sense of urgency, initiative, multitasking abilities, accuracy, and attitude, and terminating the three lowest scored employees. This procedure, based on undefined, subjective criteria that were not consistently applied (one of the three lowest rated employees was retained) was bad enough. But after the lawsuit was filed, the employer produced an "Overview Matrix" which purported to explain the terminations and offered explanations that differed from the original scoring. Noting the discrepancy in explanations and the failure to identify specific decision makers who reached the judgments described in the "Overview Matrix," the court denied summary judgment to the employer.[29]

In the university case mentioned above, one of the downsized employees was described as having skills suited to the "pre-electronic era."[30] The directors also used terms such as *vision* and *agility* to describe the characteristics they were looking for and saw older employees as lacking in those attributes. Language of this sort is often a telling indicator of age bias. Termination of a school administrator because she allegedly lacked "21st Century skills," when the school superintendent had made repeated comments linking age and proficiency in computer use, was sufficient evidence of discriminatory motive to warrant a trial.[31] Testimony from managers that "more tenured employees" who had "been around a while" had a harder time adapting to the store's new business model, in addition to evidence that the plaintiff was regularly referred to by managers as

---

[28] *EEOC v. Board of Regents of the University of Wisconsin*, 288 F.3d 296 (7th Cir. 2002).

[29] *Paup v. Gear Products*, 327 Fed. Appx. 100 (10th Cir. 2009).

[30] *Board of Regents*, at 303.

[31] *Marlow v. Chesterfield County School Board*, 749 F. Supp. 2d 417 (E.D. Va. 2010).

"Grandma," created "a convincing mosaic that her age was a determinative factor in a corporate culture hostile to older workers.[32]

In contrast, an employer was able to successfully defend its termination of a marketing director during a RIF. The company decided to close down a pet food business that it had started a few years earlier but that had lost over $10 million. Of the eighteen employees terminated, ten were under 40 years of age. The 59-year-old plaintiff's claim failed because although he was the oldest person terminated, more than half were under 40; it was uncontroverted that the business he had spent the majority of his time on had sustained a large loss; and there was, in fact, a genuine reduction in force based on an objective plan to restructure the company.[33] In another case, a 58-year-old quality assurance manager was terminated in a reduction in force. He had only recently moved from a plant-level job to a newly created corporate position. The court placed great emphasis on the fact that when selected for the job, he was told that he would have to travel regularly, be very energetic in pushing the company's new quality assurance initiative, and produce results in short order. His boss came to the conclusion that he was not sufficiently energetic and committed to change and placed his name on the list of people to be downsized. Although the court acknowledged that the boss's criticisms hinted at stereotypical views of older employees as slow moving and resistant to change, his expectations were made clear at the outset and were not met. The court also observed that insofar as the boss had only recently hired the employee into the new position, this created a strong inference that something other than age accounted for the termination.[34] Likewise, the termination of a 55 year-old employee in a downsizing because he had an "obsolete skill set" did not violate the ADEA.[35] While an employer cannot simply assume that older workers' skills are outmoded, changes in this employer's business meant that the type of sales experience possessed by the employee was no longer as relevant.

In another instructive case, an employer was upheld when it terminated two older retail store employees during a RIF. After it was determined that the store would have to eliminate two full-time positions, a plan was developed to select for termination the two least senior employees in "nonskilled" positions. The rationale was that this would save training costs and have the least detrimental effect on store operations. The ages and identities of the employees selected for termination were not known until after the selection procedure was applied. In ruling for the employer, the court observed that this was a genuine RIF; management, in consultation with the regional human resources director, had developed an objective selection procedure not based on age; alternative procedures were considered but were not feasible; and the employer adhered to its stated procedure.[36] Likewise, a 65-year-old physician terminated in a RIF at his hospital was unable to show age discrimination because over 300 other employees, both younger and older, were also terminated.[37] A comment made by the new hospital administrator about "getting rid of the old guard" was not credited as evidence of discrimination because the statement referred to elimination of an area of the hospital other than the one in which the plaintiff worked. The court also criticized the plaintiff's efforts to compare himself to younger employees in other positions who

---

[32]*McDonald v. Best Buy,* 2008 U.S. Dist. LEXIS 78524 (C.D. Ill.).

[33]*Godfredson,* at 374.

[34]*Mitchell,* at 1317–18.

[35]*Marlino v. MCI Communications Services,* 574 F.3d 447 (7th Cir. 2009).

[36]*Regel,* at 880.

[37]*Tubergen v. St. Vincent Hospital & Health Care Center,* 517 F.3d 470 (7th Cir. 2008).

were not similarly situated and rejected his claim that he was treated less advantageously than younger workers in being given consideration for reemployment because he never applied for any of the new positions.

JUST THE FACTS

A 52-year-old employee with thirty-four years on the job was terminated by Boeing during a RIF. Under the "Redeployment Selection Process (RSP)" used by the company, the supervisor compared the performance of employees on nine criteria, rating them on each criterion with a 1–5 scale. The 52-year-old was given a cumulative score of 17, while a 36-year-old coworker was scored 39. The younger coworker was retained. In a regular performance appraisal conducted earlier that year by the same supervisor, the older worker was described as "doing a great job." Complaints about the older worker's performance in her filing duties that had been mentioned previously but had never adversely affected her performance ratings were highlighted in the RSP. There was also evidence that the supervisor unilaterally decided to eliminate from the final scores the one criterion on which the older worker had received a perfect score. The older worker sued, challenging her termination in this RIF.

See, *Cotter v. Boeing*, 2007 U.S. Dist. LEXIS 45995 (E.D. Pa.).

While most challenges to downsizing allege disparate treatment, adverse impact claims are also possible. One basic consideration in these cases is that statistical evidence has to demonstrate adverse impact on the entire protected class (all employees 40 and over), and not just some part of it (e.g., employees over 55 years of age).[38] The use of early retirement incentives by downsizing employers can complicate the statistical analysis needed to establish a prima facie case of adverse impact. In a case challenging a downsizing by the Federal Deposit Insurance Corporation (FDIC), the court ruled that older employees who had accepted buyouts had to be omitted from the analysis because, at least under the facts of this particular case, those employees had voluntarily accepted buyouts and thus did not suffer adverse employment actions.[39] Once this group of older workers was excluded, the data no longer showed adverse impact against the FDIC's older workers.

In adverse impact claims brought under the ADEA, employers have the burden of showing that the challenged downsizing decisions were based on one or more reasonable factor other than age (RFOA).[40] Whether employers can lawfully base downsizing decisions on employee's salary levels is murky. Since salary is related to length of service and older workers, on average, are likely to have higher seniority, decisions to weed out higher-paid employees tend to disadvantage older workers. Salary level can thus be viewed as a "neutral" selection criterion that results in the disproportionate selection of older employees for downsizing. If so, its use in downsizing decisions would not necessarily be illegal, but would need to be defended by the employer as a reasonable factor other than age. An employer's burden under the ADEA to defend challenged practices as reasonable factors other than age is lighter than the "job-related and consistent with business necessity" showing required under Title VII. Courts might very well view the desire to lower costs as "reasonable," with

---

[38]*Lowe v. Commack Union Free School District*, 886 F.2d 1364 (2d Cir. 1989), cert. denied, 494 U.S. 1026 (1990).

[39]*Aliotta v. Bair*, 2010 U.S. App. LEXIS 16763 (D.C. Cir.).

[40]*Meacham v. Knolls Atomic Power Laboratory*, 128 S. Ct. 2395 (2008).

the only question being whether employers would be required to demonstrate any particular level of financial distress. The availability of alternative downsizing criteria that would have less detrimental effect on older workers would not have to be considered.

RIFs frequently present questions of whether downsized employees will be allowed to transfer to other workplaces, change positions, consult, or be rehired. In general, *it makes both practical and legal sense to offer experienced employees the opportunity to retain employment.* Employers are not required to offer downsized employees the opportunity to transfer or otherwise retain employment; "[b]ut when internal job placement services are benefits of employment which are provided to younger employees, an employer must provide roughly the same benefits to ADEA-protected employees, and when an employer responds to a RIF by transferring employees to available positions, it may not refuse to transfer older employees based on their age."[41] A 53-year-old employee who was terminated in a reduction in force was unable to prove that his employer violated the ADEA when it transferred other younger employees. The court described the shortcomings of his case as follows:

> [A] showing of discrimination requires more—much more than simply identifying employees who obtained jobs around the same time that the plaintiff was looking for a position. A valid comparison would have entailed showing that these employees also encountered a RIF, that they obtained positions for which Radue [the plaintiff] was qualified, and that the supervisors in charge also knew that Radue was looking for such positions. Without this, there's no basis for inferring that the other employees were similarly situated.[42]

Practical Considerations What are some feasible alternatives to downsizing? If downsizing must occur, what criteria should be used to select those individuals who will be downsized?

In contrast, a woman who was not rehired for a related job after she was terminated from her position as an insurance adjuster during a reduction in force was allowed to go to trial on her age discrimination claim. Although the company president stated that displaced employees "should have preference" for new jobs and would be given training, the woman received only a cursory interview and a younger employee who had never worked for the company was hired. In addition to throwing doubt on the employer's stated reasons for not rehiring her, the woman was able to show that the interviewer wrote down her age and that the ages of other applicants were circled or underlined on resumes and other documents.[43] Similarly, and just a few months after he was downsized, a 56-year-old employee saw an advertisement from his former employer for a position that was very much like his previous one. The advertisement listed four specific qualifications, all of which were possessed by the former employee. He applied for the job, but a much younger employee who did not possess all the stated qualifications was hired. The court rejected the company's contention that it was free to conclude that the hired employee was a "better fit" despite the failure to meet its own qualifications.[44]

What conclusions can be drawn regarding how employers should go about conducting reductions in force? Much of the advice that applies to any termination applies equally here, particularly the need for documentation of the reasons for termination, sound performance appraisals, and careful review of termination decisions. More specific to the RIF context, *employers should have clear, objective criteria for deciding who to downsize. These criteria must not include age and should be applied consistently before the fact of termination. Decisions should not be based on vague criteria related to stereotypical views of older workers, such as potential for growth, acceptance of change, and vision. Statements made to and about downsized older employees should not include code*

[41]*Radue*, at 615.
[42]*Radue*, at 619.
[43]*Corneveaux v. CUNA Mutual Insurance Group*, 76 F.3d 1498 (10th Cir. 1996).
[44]*Carberry v. Monarch Marking Systems, Inc.*, 30 Fed. Appx. 389 (6th Cir. 2002).

words suggesting bias against older employees. If all (or a disproportionate percentage) of people initially selected for downsizing are older employees, this should prompt a review of selection procedures and decisions. If a RIF is needed, hiring new, younger employees or substantially changing the duties of existing employees to absorb the duties of terminated employees should generally be avoided.

Early Retirement Incentives

The ADEA generally prohibits mandatory retirement. One important exception is for persons who have held "bona fide executive or high policy-making positions" for the two years immediately preceding retirement, who reach 65 years of age, and who will receive an annual retirement benefit of at least $44,000 per year. A chief patent attorney for a pharmaceutical company who was forced to retire at age 65 did not fit within this exception.[45] While the attorney might have qualified earlier in his career, another attorney had already been hired and assumed most of the attorney's higher-level duties. Thus, in the last year of his employment, he had no ultimate hiring or firing authority, no control over his cost center, was no longer closely involved with patent preparation, no longer met with research scientists, and had very few and only superficial contacts with executives. The explicit or implicit mandatory retirement policies of law firms are increasingly being challenged, with a key question being whether the partners forced to step down are true partners or employees covered by the ADEA.[46] *With just a few exceptions, employers must not force employees to retire when they reach a specified age.* However, as an alternative to terminations, downsizing employers often attempt to increase attrition by offering inducements for employees to voluntarily leave employment.

Clippings

The EEOC has settled an age discrimination suit brought against AT&T and three of its subsidiaries. The EEOC alleged that the companies violated the ADEA by denying former employees who had accepted early retirement incentives the opportunity to be rehired. Attaching a ban on re-employment to the receipt of early retirement incentives has an adverse impact on older workers, since they are the ones who are offered these deals. While the employers did not admit to wrongdoing, they agreed to make policy changes and to give "priority status" in selection to qualified plaintiffs who had been denied re-employment.

"EEOC, AT&T Settle Suit Alleging Age Bias in Company's Bar on Rehiring of Retirees." *Daily Labor Report* 207 (October 26, 2011), A-1.

Under the Older Workers Benefit Protection Act, it is legal for employers to offer **early retirement incentives** to entice workers to leave their jobs sooner than they otherwise might have, even though the minimum age or service requirements might exclude younger employees. However, *early retirement incentives cannot be extended to one age group (e.g., employees between 52 and 56 years of age) but denied to older employees.* A school district's early retirement incentive violated the ADEA when it provided for payment of health insurance premiums until age 65 and then provided a lump sum payment only for employees who retired after age 65. The incentive treated employees between 55

---

[45]*Raymond v. Boehringer Ingelheim Pharmaceuticals,* 653 F. Supp. 2d 151 (D. Conn. 2009).

[46]Nelson D. Schwartz. "Easing out the Gray-Haired. Or Not." *New York Times* (May 28, 2011), B1.

and 65 equally, but by defining "early" retirement in terms of age and denying the benefit to employees who retire after age 65, the plan was discriminatory.[47] Nor, as the case against AT&T demonstrates (see "Clippings"), should employers deny reemployment opportunities on the basis of prior receipt of an early retirement incentive. Allstate Insurance found itself in a similar predicament when its policy of not rehiring employee-agents for a year after termination or until any severance benefits had been exhausted, whichever was longer, was challenged as discriminatory against older workers.[48]

Employees mulling over when to retire obviously have an abiding interest in learning of their employer's intent to offer retirement incentives. Who wants to retire and learn shortly thereafter that if he had remained on the job a few months longer, he would have been in line for an enhanced retirement package? On the other hand, employers might prefer not to divulge the existence of early retirement programs until they are a certainty and would rather not provide incentives to employees who are going to leave anyhow. A number of courts have held that as an aspect of the fiduciary responsibility of employers under ERISA to manage benefit plans in the interest of beneficiaries, *employees must be informed regarding the status of early retirement incentive plans that are under "serious consideration."*[49] Plans are under **serious consideration** when there is a specific proposal, the proposal is being discussed for purposes of implementation, and members of senior management with the authority to implement the plan are engaged in the discussion. Employers can (and should) gather information about plan options and engage in discussions at all levels of management without triggering the duty to disclose that an early retirement offer is being considered. However, *once the plan solidifies to the point that it is sufficiently concrete to be considered as a proposal, the discussion shifts from strategy to implementation, and high-level managers become involved in reviewing and approving a specific plan, employees must be informed.*

Employers that offer early retirement incentives typically want assurance that employees who accept these benefits will not subsequently sue for age discrimination. The Older Workers Benefit Protection Act permits waivers of rights or claims under the ADEA, but it establishes stringent conditions for such waivers.[50] Some of these conditions were outlined in Chapter 18, including a knowing and voluntary waiver, extra benefits beyond those that would normally be available, waivers that are in plain language, waivers that explicitly refer to the ADEA and advise consultation with an attorney, waivers that do not pertain to any claims arising after the date of execution, a sufficient amount of time to consider offers, and seven days to reconsider acceptance. *In the case of group early retirement offers, employees must be given at least forty-five days to consider the offers. Additionally, employees must be informed in writing regarding the class, unit, or group of employees covered by the early retirement incentive offer; any eligibility factors for the program; the time limits applicable to the program; the job titles and ages of all individuals eligible or selected for the program; and the ages of all individuals in the same group who are not eligible or selected for the program.*

Courts strictly apply the conditions for a valid waiver of ADEA rights. A "General Release and Covenant Not to Sue" entered into by an employee terminated in a RIF and his employer, IBM, was deemed not enforceable because it lacked the requisite clarity.[51] The language confused the purpose of the release of claims (to establish that a right or claim has

---

[47] *Jankovitz v. Des Moines Independent Community*, 421 F.3d 649 (8th Cir. 2005).

[48] Janet Cecelia Walthall. "EEOC, Allstate Insurance Settle Age Bias Suit for $4.5 Million." *Daily Labor Report* 175 (September 14, 2009), A-13.

[49] *McAuley v. IBM*, 165 F.3d 1038 (6th Cir. 1999), *cert. denied*, 527 U.S. 1066 (1999).

[50] P.L. No. 101-433, 104 Stat. 978 (1990), Sect. 201.

[51] *Thomforde v. IBM*, 406 F.3d 500 (8th Cir. 2005).

been relinquished) and the covenant not to sue (an agreement not to enforce any right or claim via a lawsuit). In contrast, a waiver and release of claims signed by an employee who was terminated at age 62 and received a severance package of 20 weeks' pay barred a subsequent age discrimination claim based on the termination.[52] The waiver stated in part that

> *Employee, in exchange for the payments and other consideration embodied in this Agreement, waives, releases and forever discharges the Company ... from all claims, causes of action, [or] lawsuits ... which Employee may now or hereafter have against the Company from the beginning of time through the date of this Agreement, including but not limited to: (i) any claim or cause of action arising under Title VII of the Civil Rights Act of 1964, as amended, the Age Discrimination in Employment Act (the "ADEA"), ... and any other common law, federal, state or local law prohibiting discrimination or limiting an employer's right to terminate employees .... **Nothing in this Agreement shall limit or restrict Manager's [sic] right under the ADEA to challenge the validity of this Agreement in a court of law. This waiver and release does not apply to any claim that may arise under the ADEA after the date that Employee signs this Agreement.**[53]*

Although the language in this agreement is not exactly the stuff of everyday conversation, the court found that it clearly informed the employee that any ADEA claims based on employer actions taken up to the date of the agreement were being waived and released, and it did so in language understandable to employees. The absence of even one of the required elements is sufficient to invalidate a waiver. An otherwise acceptable waiver was not upheld because it was executed in the context of a RIF and the employer failed to provide details regarding the precise group of employees targeted for downsizing.[54] Although this might seem like nit-picking, such information is critical to employees understanding whether they might have age discrimination cases—and hence understanding the true nature of any waiver of their rights.

Effects of Bankruptcy on Employee Rights

Financially struggling companies often file for bankruptcy. Such companies are likely to owe wages to their employees; have obligations under benefit programs; and in unionized workplaces, have contractual obligations to employees under labor agreements. Employees are not considered secured creditors. However, when employers file for bankruptcy under Chapter 11 and continue to operate as they reorganize, the wages and benefits earned following the bankruptcy filing by those employees who are retained have a high priority claim on the company's resources. These payments are treated as administrative expenses necessary to maintain the viability of the enterprise. Employees have a weaker claim for wages and benefits earned prior to petitions for bankruptcy. These claims have lower priority and are limited to amounts earned within ninety days before the filing of the bankruptcy petition.

Nonunion employers are generally free to cancel expected raises or bonuses, cut wages, or reduce benefits as means of lowering costs. What about unionized employers? They can approach union representatives and attempt to convince them to agree to needed concessions. However, failing at that, unionized employers cannot unilaterally alter the terms of labor agreements or conveniently ignore them. *Nor does filing for bankruptcy necessarily absolve an employer of its obligations under a labor agreement.* The Bankruptcy Code contains a set of procedures that must be followed before

---

[52]*Ridinger v. Dow Jones & Co.*, 651 F.3d 309 (2d Cir. 2011).

[53]*Ridinger*, at 311.

[54]*Kruchowksi v. The Weyerhaeuser Co.*, 446 F.3d 1090 (10th Cir. 2006).

bankrupt firms can alter or circumvent labor agreements.[55] *Firms must present union representatives with proposals based on the most complete and reliable information available, provide the union with all relevant supporting information, and bargain in good faith.* If the union rejects the proposals without good cause, the court may permit the employer to make the desired changes. However, the proposed changes must be truly necessary to allow the company to reorganize (not merely a "wish list"), they must treat employees and other parties equitably (employees should not bear the full brunt of cost cutting), and they usually cannot be implemented until the court has approved them. The unionized musicians of the Colorado Springs Symphony Orchestra were given first priority for payment because the symphony had stopped paying them after it filed for bankruptcy, but before any change in their labor agreement had been approved by the court.[56] The court also held that the musicians—by remaining ready and willing to resume playing—were performing post-bankruptcy petition services necessary to preserve the bankrupt estate. "[T]he mass exodus of the Orchestra's most important assets would have hastened the organization's collapse."[57]

Post-Termination Issues

Legal issues do not necessarily end with the termination of employment. For one thing, employees who lose their jobs often file for unemployment insurance and former employers sometimes contest those filings. Former employers might also seek to enforce *noncompetition agreements* and other forms of *restrictive covenants* aimed at limiting the ability of former employees to use knowledge or trade secrets obtained through employment to compete against them.

Unemployment Insurance

Employees who involuntarily become unemployed and are able to work, available for work, and actively looking for it are eligible to receive unemployment insurance. **Unemployment insurance** is intended to partially replace lost earnings during periods of unemployment for people who have demonstrated an attachment to the workforce. Unemployment insurance is provided for through a combination of federal law, principally the Federal Unemployment Tax Act (FUTA)[58] and state unemployment insurance laws. Federal law governs the funding of unemployment benefits and sets out broad parameters for coverage, whereas state laws contain the details of coverage and benefit levels.

Eligibility Criteria and Benefits The requirement of **involuntary unemployment** raises many questions. Employees who are laid off or terminated based on business considerations during downsizings are eligible for unemployment insurance. However, if an employee is discharged for misconduct, she might be disqualified. The misconduct usually must be serious and intentional to disqualify an employee from the receipt of unemployment benefits following termination; employer dissatisfaction with performance is generally not enough. However, a court found that an employee's failure to comply with her employer's rule that all workplace injuries be reported during the same shift was intentional misconduct that disqualified the employee from receiving unemployment insurance.[59]

---

[55] 11 U.S.C.S. § 1113 (2011).

[56] *Peters v. Pikes Peak Musicians Association*, 462 F.3d 1265 (10th Cir. 2006).

[57] Peters, at 1273.

[58] 26 U.S.C.S. §§ 3301-3311 (2011).

[59] *Schmidgall v. FilmTec Corp.*, 644 N.W. 2d 801 (Minn. 2002).

JUST THE FACTS

On July 4, 2010, a Dillard's store in Indiana held a barbecue for its employees. There were leftovers. The manager in charge said that he wanted the unused hot dogs and hamburgers to be placed in a break room freezer so that they could be used for a planned Labor Day barbecue. The next day, a Dillard's employee ate two of the left-over hotdogs which apparently had been placed in the break room refrigerator rather than the freezer. The manager reviewed a surveillance video and identified the employee as the "suspected hotdog thief." The manager confronted the employee and he admitted to eating the hot dogs. It was not clear whether the employee had heard the manager's order to have the food placed in the freezer for future use, although the manager believed that he did. The employee was presented with the option of signing a statement admitting guilt or "spending the night in jail." The employee signed the statement and was promptly terminated for theft of company property. He filed for unemployment insurance and his claim was contested. Is this employee eligible for unemployment insurance? Why or why not?

See, *Koewler v. Review Board of the Indiana Department of Workforce Development*, 951 N.E.2d 272 (Ind. App. Ct. 2011)

Employees who quit their jobs are not usually eligible for benefits, but there are exceptions to this rule. If a quit is actually a constructive discharge, it is not voluntary. Courts consider whether a reasonable person would have felt compelled to quit under the circumstances, such as harassment[60] or extreme verbal abuse by a boss. Employees who leave their jobs due to health hazards might still receive benefits, particularly if they can show that the health problems caused were serious and that their employer was apprised of the situation but did not eliminate the problem. For example, a painter was eligible for unemployment insurance when she quit her job after repeatedly suffering chest pains and headaches due to sensitivity to the type of paint being used. The employee had informed her supervisors, and the company had actually purchased safety equipment for her, but for reasons that are not entirely clear, she was not allowed to use the equipment.[61] However, several city government employees who quit their jobs in response to what they saw as inadequate protection against workplace violence were not eligible for unemployment insurance.[62] Although an altercation had occurred in city hall and police protection that had been provided was removed about a month later, the court decided that the plaintiffs had voluntarily resigned because they had not personally been targets of the violence, the city had allowed them to work at home for three days after the incident, police protection was provided for a meaningful period of time, and the violent employee was not expected to return. Employees who go on strike are not eligible for unemployment insurance for all, or at least part, of the time they are on strike. However, courts

---

[60]*Munro Holding v. Cook*, 695 N.W. 2d 379 (Minn. App. 2005).

[61]*Pahl-Jones v. ASI Sign Systems*, 2002 Minn. App. LEXIS 4.

[62]*Adkins v. Gatson*, 2005 W. Va. LEXIS 131.

have sometimes found striking employees to be eligible for unemployment insurance when their employer made repeated statements that the employees had been permanently replaced and no longer had jobs.[63] In an unsuccessful strike at Northwest Airlines, during which the carrier ended up unilaterally imposing a 25 percent wage cut, the court determined that a pay cut of this magnitude amounted to a constructive lockout.[64] Since the employees were deemed not to be voluntarily on strike, they were eligible for unemployment insurance.

To receive unemployment benefits, the involuntarily unemployed also have to demonstrate an attachment to the workforce, both prior to and following their loss of employment. Most states establish eligibility for unemployment insurance by examining the claimant's work history over a specified period of time (the **base period**) prior to the job loss (usually the first four out of the five quarters preceding the claim for benefits). Only individuals who meet minimum earnings and hours of work standards during this base period are eligible. Part-time employees or those who have irregular work histories are often unable to meet these criteria and are denied benefits. Unemployed persons also must show that they are "able" to work, in the sense that they possess the requisite physical and mental abilities.

Availability for work raises more questions. The unemployed must be willing to seek and accept "**suitable employment**." In general terms, suitable employment is work that does not endanger the health or safety of the employee, work for which the individual has the requisite training and experience, and work that is within a reasonable distance of the individual's residence or last place of employment. Unemployed persons who place excessive restrictions on the types of jobs they will accept or the circumstances (e.g., hours, schedule, location) under which they will work may be deemed unavailable for work and denied benefits. However, unemployed persons are not generally expected to accept employment that is substantially lower-paying and less skilled than their usual work. Individuals who refuse to take jobs that are vacant due to a strike are usually still eligible for unemployment benefits. An employee might also reject employment for religious reasons. For example, the Supreme Court found that the constitutional rights of an employee were violated when he was denied unemployment insurance because he turned down a job that would have required working on Sunday.[65]

Unemployment benefits generally last up to twenty-six weeks (assuming suitable employment is not located before then). During periods of high unemployment, benefits are usually extended for additional weeks. In many cases, employees exhaust their unemployment benefits before finding new jobs. In most states, unemployment insurance is limited to about 50 percent of weekly earnings. However, because maximum benefit levels are also specified, the actual earnings replacement rate is more like 33 percent.[66] Unemployment benefits might also be reduced by severance pay received. In most years since the 1980s, less than 40 percent of unemployed workers have received unemployment insurance benefits.[67] While low-paid and part-time workers are more likely to be

---

[63]*Titan Tire Corp. v. Employment Appeal Board*, 641 N.W. 2d 752 (Iowa 2002).

[64]*AMFA Members v. Northwest Airlines*, 2006 Minn. App. Unpub. LEXIS 1031, review denied, 2006 Minn. LEXIS 730.

[65]*Frazee v. Illinois Department of Employment Security*, 489 U.S. 829 (1989).

[66]Christopher J. O'Leary. "U.S. Unemployment Insurance: Progress and Prospects." *Employment Research* (W.E. Upjohn Institute, July 2000), 3.

[67]U.S. Government Accountability Office. *Unemployment Insurance: Receipt of Benefits Has Declined, with Continued Disparities for Low-Wage and Part-Time Workers.* GAO-07-1243T (September 19, 2007), 4.

unemployed, these workers are also less likely to receive unemployment benefits when out of work than are higher-paid full-time workers.[68]

Clippings

A bad economy with rampant downsizing means that many unemployed persons will file unemployment insurance claims. Although these benefits are not paid directly by employers, more former employees receiving unemployment compensation translates to higher unemployment taxes for their former employers. On behalf of a lengthy list of corporate clients, Talx Corporation processes more than thirty percent of all unemployment claims in the U.S. While the firm says that it merely follows the wishes of its clients, its marketing materials promise cost savings and improved winning percentages for employers contesting unemployment claims. The firm has come to the attention of authorities in numerous states for failing to respond to requests for information in a timely fashion, providing inaccurate information, delaying the processing of claims, and appealing large numbers of cases on questionable grounds. As New Hampshire legal aid lawyer Jonathan P. Baird put it, "It's sort of a war of attrition. If you appeal a certain percentage of cases, there are going to be those workers who give up."

Jason DeParle. "Contesting Jobless Claims Becomes a Boom Industry." *New York Times* (April 4, 2010), A1.

Insurance Claims   Unemployment insurance payments are provided through state agencies. Employers do not have a direct role in administering these benefits. However, employers are required to supply information regarding their former employees' length of employment and the reasons for their job loss. An administrative appeals process can be invoked by both former employees and employers, occasionally resulting in court cases. Unemployment insurance taxes are experience-rated. Employers who have less stable employment and produce more claims pay more taxes. *Employers should not routinely contest unemployment insurance claims. Solid grounds for contesting claims include evidence that the former employee voluntarily quit, was terminated for serious misconduct, is receiving other payments (e.g., workers' compensation), or committed fraud. The former employee's statement to the state agency regarding the circumstances of his termination should be examined for accuracy. Employers must provide clear statements of the reasons for terminations and supporting evidence to state agencies that decide unemployment insurance claims.*

Restrictive Covenants

Restrictive covenants is an umbrella term that refers to a wide variety of contractual agreements that aim to protect employer interests by limiting the ability of former employees to do such things as going to work for competitors, disclosing trade secrets or other sensitive information, soliciting clients or former coworkers to do business with or join other firms, and making disparaging comments about their former employers. The increasing use of restrictive covenants to constrain the activities of former employees raises important legal and public policy questions.

---

[68]GAO, at 5, 12.

> ### *Clippings*
>
> So, how do they make Thomas' English muffins, with all of those butter-pooling nooks and crannies? The answer is a closely guarded trade secret, known to only seven people. One of those people is Chris Botticella, a former vice president for Bimbo Bakeries USA, which purchased the Thomas' brand in 2009. Mr. Botticella left the company in January 2010. It was believed by coworkers that he was retiring, but instead, he had accepted a position with Bimbo's rival, Hostess Brands. Hostess had been trying unsuccessfully to learn the secret of Thomas' muffins for years. Mr. Botticella actually accepted the position with Hostess in October 2009, but he wanted to remain with Bimbo Bakeries until the end of the year to obtain his year-end bonus. Shortly before leaving, he downloaded numerous files containing confidential information and copied them to a flash drive. Bimbo Bakeries obtained an injunction prohibiting Mr. Botticella from working for Hostess. An appeals court upheld the injunction and Hostess withdrew its offer of employment, leaving Mr. Botticella unemployed and with plenty of time to hone his muffin-making skills.
>
> William Neuman. "A Man with Muffin Secrets, But no Job to go with Them." *New York Times* (August 7, 2010), A1.

Noncompetition agreements are contracts that restrict the ability of former employees (or former owners or partners) to form or join businesses that compete with their former employers for specified periods of time following employment. Given the importance of information and client relationships as sources of competitive advantage, employers are increasingly turning to noncompetition agreements ("noncompetes") to rein in their former employees. And these agreements are no longer limited to executives and high-tech workers. As David L. Lee, a Chicago employment lawyer put it, "More and more employers seem to be using non-competes with pretty much everybody." The number of such agreements in use is unknown, but disputes over them are becoming more common, as indicated by an 81 percent increase in the number of court decisions involving noncompetes over the last decade (including a 37 percent increase from 2004 to 2006 alone).[69] Noncompetes and other restrictive covenants are now frequently among the stacks of papers that employees are required to sign on their first day of employment, as well as among the requirements for receiving severance pay when employment is terminated.

But the fact that restrictive covenants are now widely-used does not mean, as *Proudfoot Consulting v. Gordon* shows, that they are easily enforced.

Courts consider a number of factors when deciding whether to enforce noncompetition agreements (by issuing injunctions against former employees or awarding damages for breach of contract), and their willingness to do so varies considerably across states. California's courts have been especially prone to invalidating noncompetition agreements.[70] As with any other contracts, restrictive covenants must be supported by consideration. For newly hired employees, being allowed to commence employment appears to be sufficient. But to impose noncompetition agreements on existing

---

[69]Barbara Rose. "Non-compete clause tying hands of employees." (February 25, 2008) *chicagotribune.com*.

[70]*Edwards II v. Arthur Andersen*, 44 Cal. 4th 937 (2008).

Proudfoot Consulting v. Gordon
576 F.3d 1223 (11ᵗʰ Cir. 2009)

OPINION BY DISTRICT JUDGE TRAGER:

This case arises out of an employment agreement ("Agreement") between appellant Derrick Gordon ("Gordon" or "appellant") and appellee Proudfoot Consulting Company ("Proudfoot" or "Proudfoot North America" or "appellee") that contains a number of restrictive covenants. The Agreement prevents Gordon, for six months after his employment with Proudfoot ends, from working for a direct competitor or client of Proudfoot, contacting Proudfoot's clients and soliciting Proudfoot's employees. The Agreement also bars Gordon from using or disclosing Proudfoot's confidential information and from retaining Proudfoot materials after his employment ends. After Gordon left Proudfoot in June 2006 to work for the Highland Group ("Highland"), a direct competitor, Proudfoot brought suit to enforce the restrictive covenants.

Following a bench trial, the district court held that all of those restrictions ("Restrictive Covenants") were enforceable under Florida law. * * * On appeal, * * * we conclude that the injunction was not improper. However, we reverse the damages award. Proudfoot failed to establish that Gordon's solicitation of Bombardier for Highland resulted in Proudfoot's loss of the project that was the basis of the damages award.

Proudfoot North America is a management consulting firm that provides consulting services to improve clients' work processes by eliminating redundancies, streamlining processes and implementing systems of management. Proudfoot North America, which is headquartered in West Palm Beach, Florida and has offices in Atlanta and New York, operates and markets its services in the United States and Canada and has clients located in both countries. Management Consulting Group ("Proudfoot Global"), a publicly-traded company based in the United Kingdom, is the parent company of a number of Proudfoot affiliates across the globe, including an affiliate in Europe ("Proudfoot Europe") as well as Proudfoot North America.

Gordon worked at Proudfoot North America from March 1999 through May 2006 [as a Senior Process Consultant, Project Manager, and for the last year, Project Director]. * * * On April 18, 2006, Gordon was offered a position by Highland, an operational management consulting firm that competes directly with Proudfoot. After Gordon tendered his resignation from Proudfoot on May 1, 2006, Proudfoot CEO Luiz Carvalho ("Carvalho") met with Gordon. At this meeting, Gordon lied to Carvalho about the offer that he had received, stating that the offer was from a private equity firm and never mentioning Highland. After Carvalho offered Gordon the position of Vice President of Business Delivery for Proudfoot Europe, Gordon accepted that position and withdrew his resignation. Vice President of Business Delivery is a critical position that has ultimate responsibility for all aspects of delivering services to clients and for defining strategy for each client account. While in this position, Gordon's office was located in London. On June 12, 2006, Gordon again notified Proudfoot that he was resigning. This time he did not withdraw his resignation, which was voluntary and became effective on June 23, 2006. Gordon never informed Proudfoot that he was leaving to work for Highland.

During his tenure at Proudfoot North America, Gordon worked on many client projects in the United States and on a client project in Mexico. … [D]uring Gordon's tenure at Proudfoot North America, his "territory" included the United States and Canada. At Proudfoot, Gordon had access to, and received, information in various forms about specific Proudfoot clients and projects, as well as about Proudfoot's operations generally. Gordon received hard copies of a number of Proudfoot materials, including training manuals and videos from the numerous training sessions he attended, a list of Proudfoot Europe's employees, business cards of Proudfoot clients for whom he had worked, and a Proudfoot employee newsletter. Gordon retained these materials after leaving Proudfoot, but insisted that he did so unintentionally.

While at Proudfoot, Gordon also had access to * * * information about Proudfoot's clients, including pricing information. Moreover, during his tenure as Vice President of Business Delivery for Proudfoot Europe, Gordon conducted high-level reviews of the company's client projects in Europe and received information about those projects. In addition, Gordon also had access to information about Proudfoot's operations. At trial, he admitted, generally, that he had "access to confidential information about Proudfoot's business." Moreover, the district court concluded that Gordon was exposed to Proudfoot's "methodology for [providing] operational management consulting services" as well as to Proudfoot's "products and offerings and tools." In addition, during his tenure at Proudfoot, Gordon accessed and downloaded information from the Knowledge Management database, a project database that contains information about all of Proudfoot's client projects, from around the world, dating back to the 1980s and other information about Proudfoot's business operations. * * *

On June 26, 2006, Gordon started working at Highland. Highland, whose headquarters are located in the United States, does business and maintains offices in North America and Europe. At Highland, Gordon served as a Project Manager responsible for day-to-day delivery and execution of client projects and the direct supervision of process consultants. Gordon was promoted to Director of Operations in June 2007. At Highland, Gordon worked on projects for different clients; one of those clients was Bombardier, who was also a client of Proudfoot Europe. In September 2006, Highland assigned Gordon to a project for Bombardier called "Bombardier Interiors." In February 2007, eight months after leaving Proudfoot, Gordon helped solicit a different Bombardier project for Highland called "Bombardier Logistics." Gordon was the Project Manager for that project until his promotion in June 2007. * * *

The Agreement Gordon signed with Proudfoot contains four Restrictive Covenants. Three of the Restrictive Covenants are found in a "Noncompetition and Nonsolicitation" clause, which restricts Gordon from engaging in certain activities for six months after his employment with Proudfoot ends ("six-month restrictive period"). First, the non-compete provision prevents Gordon from "[s]erv[ing] as an employee ... or consultant for ... any business which is a Direct Competitor" ("competitor non-compete covenant" or "competitor non-compete clause"). "Direct Competitor" is defined as "any person or entity engaged in the business of providing professional services to advise clients as to the design and installation of systems and processes to improve the productivity and efficiency of their business operations." Second, the non-compete provision also prevents Gordon from "[s]erv[ing] as an employee ... or consultant for ... any business which is ... a Client" ("client non-compete covenant" or "client non-compete clause"). "Client" is defined as "a person or organization, which at any time within the three years preceding the date of termination of Employee's employment

has received a proposal or bid from [Proudfoot], or has received any services from [Proudfoot]...." Third, under a non-solicitation provision, Gordon is prohibited from "contact[ing] any client of [Proudfoot]" or soliciting any Proudfoot employees ("non-solicitation covenant" or "non-solicitation clause"). The Agreement also provides that the six-month restrictive period "shall be tolled during any period in which Employee is in violation of this Noncompetition and Nonsolicitation provision."

In addition, fourth, the Agreement also includes a clause concerning confidential information ("confidential information clause") that is distinct from the Noncompetition and Nonsolicitation clause. The confidential information clause defines what constitutes confidential information and requires Gordon to return all Proudfoot documents and materials to the company upon the termination of his employment. Unlike the six-month time limit of the other three covenants described above, this clause prevents Gordon from disclosing or using this information "at all times after the termination of [his] employment."

On August 23, 2006, Proudfoot filed suit against Gordon in Florida Circuit Court seeking injunctive relief and alleging breach of contract. * * * On April 15, 2008, the district court * * * entered a final judgment awarding Proudfoot $ 1,659,000 in damages and enjoining Gordon, for six months, from: (1) working in North America or Europe for Highland or any other direct competitor; (2) contacting any client of Proudfoot; and (3) soliciting any Proudfoot employees. Gordon was also enjoined from possessing, using or disclosing any confidential information of Proudfoot and was directed to return any such information in his possession to Proudfoot. The portion of the injunction preventing Gordon from using or disclosing Proudfoot's confidential information did not include a time limitation. On appeal, Gordon challenges the district court's grant of the injunction and the damages award. * * *

In 1996, Florida adopted [a state law], which "contains a comprehensive framework for analyzing, evaluating and enforcing restrictive covenants contained in employment contracts." For a restrictive covenant to be valid, "[t]he person seeking enforcement of [the] restrictive covenant shall plead and prove the existence of one or more legitimate business interests justifying the restrictive covenant." [T]he statute enumerates a non-exhaustive list of "legitimate business interest[s]." Among these are: (1) "[v]aluable confidential business or professional information that otherwise does not qualify as trade secrets"; (2) "[s]ubstantial relationships with specific prospective or existing customers, patients, or clients"; and (3) "[e]xtraordinary or specialized training."

In addition, to be enforceable, restrictive covenants must be reasonable with regard to time, area and line of business. Once an employer establishes a prima facie case that the contractually specified restraint is "reasonably necessary to protect the legitimate business interest[s] … justifying the restriction," the burden of proof shifts to the employee to show that "the contractually specified restraint is overbroad, overlong, or otherwise not reasonably necessary to protect the established legitimate business interest[s]." If the court finds that the "contractually specified restraint is overbroad, overlong, or otherwise not reasonably necessary to protect the legitimate business interest[s]," the court is required to "modify the restraint and grant only the relief reasonably necessary to protect such interest or interests." * * *

The district court found that Proudfoot established three legitimate business interests, a prerequisite under the statute for any form of relief. These interests are: (1) Gordon's receipt of the information outlined earlier, which the district court found was valuable and confidential; (2) Proudfoot's substantial relationships with specific prospective and existing customers; and (3) the extraordinary and specialized training provided to Gordon. * * * [T]he district court found that the Agreement provided "in plain fashion, that the covered area is North America and any other territory to which Gordon is assigned during his employment." That finding was erroneous as the competitor non-compete clause in the Agreement contains no such explicit geographic limitation. However, Gordon concedes that because the competitor non-compete covenant did not include a geographic limitation, it was permissible for the district court to supply a reasonable geographic scope. Here, the district court found that, even if the Agreement were silent, North America and Europe would be a reasonable geographic area because Proudfoot conducts its operations in that territory and Gordon was assigned to that territory.

Once the district court determined that the Restrictive Covenants were enforceable and defined the geographic scope of the competitor non-compete clause, the district court concluded that Gordon breached all four Restrictive Covenants. The district court found that Gordon's employment by Highland breached the competitor non-compete covenant. The district court

also found that Gordon's solicitation of Bombardier and his work on projects for Bombardier violated both the non-solicitation clause and the client non-compete covenant. Finally, the district court determined that Gordon's retention of Proudfoot materials after his employment ended breached the confidential information clause, which required Gordon to return these materials to Proudfoot. * * * The district court concluded that Gordon's breach of the competitor non-compete covenant, based on his employment with Highland, tolled the six-month restrictive period from the time he began working for Highland in June 2006 through the date of the district court's judgment. * * *

In attacking the injunction and damages award, Gordon argues that the competitor non-compete clause should not have been enforced because the training he received did not rise to the level of a legitimate business interest and because he did not intentionally retain any confidential Proudfoot materials. Gordon also contends that, even if the competitor non-compete covenant were enforceable, his work for Highland in Canada should not have been considered a violation of that covenant because Canada should not have been included in the geographic scope of that covenant. Finally, Gordon asserts that even if he breached the competitor non-compete clause, that breach should have been disregarded because it was not intentional. * * *

The district court found that all three of Proudfoot's legitimate business interests – confidential information, training and client relationships – justified the competitor non-compete clause. Although Gordon argues that Proudfoot failed to establish a legitimate business interest in his training, it is unnecessary to address that challenge because Proudfoot was only required to establish one legitimate business interest to justify the non-compete covenant and we conclude that the district court did not err in finding this covenant was justified by, and reasonably necessary to protect, Proudfoot's legitimate business interest in its confidential information.

The district court found that, while at Proudfoot, Gordon received information about Proudfoot's clients and business operations, including training materials, pricing information, information about Proudfoot's methodology for providing operational management consulting services and information about Proudfoot's products, offerings and tools. The district court concluded that this information constituted "valuable confidential business information" and that "the confidentiality of that … information is at risk so long as [Gordon] is employed by Proudfoot's direct competitor." ... [T]he district court reasoned that "when an employee has access to confidential business information crucial to the success of an employer's business, that employer has a strong interest in enforcing a covenant not to compete."

Gordon does not dispute that he received valuable confidential information during his tenure at Proudfoot. His only argument related to Proudfoot's confidential information is that he did not intentionally breach the confidentiality clause's restriction against the retention of Proudfoot materials because he unknowingly kept certain Proudfoot materials after leaving Proudfoot and never used or disclosed those materials while working at Highland. Gordon mistakenly assumes that Proudfoot's interest in its confidential information would only have justified the enforcement of the competitor non-compete covenant if Proudfoot could establish that he breached the confidential information clause by improperly retaining and using Proudfoot materials. Gordon, however, ignores the fact that the information that he received was clearly not limited to the physical materials he retained. Gordon admitted that he had access to confidential information about Proudfoot's business, including pricing information. In addition, Gordon was exposed to Proudfoot's methodology for providing operational management consulting services as well as to Proudfoot's products, offerings and tools. * * * Even if it is assumed that Gordon's accidental retention of Proudfoot materials should not be considered a material breach of the confidential information clause, the district court's conclusion that Gordon's employment with Highland endangered the information that he received at Proudfoot ... provides a basis to enforce the competitor non-compete covenant. * * *

Gordon asserts that Canada should have been excluded from the geographic scope of the competitor non-compete covenant and that, if excluded, there would be no breach of the competitor non-compete covenant. * * * [D]uring the first six months of his tenure at Highland, he worked exclusively in Canada. * * * [I]f a restriction preventing Gordon from working for a direct competitor anywhere in the United States was reasonably necessary to protect the confidential information Gordon received, a point that Gordon does not contest, it is unclear why that information would not be equally relevant to the Canadian market. Even if Gordon never accessed confidential information about specific Canadian clients, Gordon points to no evidence

showing that the confidential information he did receive was only relevant to the United States and could not be used by a competitor to compete unfairly against Proudfoot in the Canadian market. As such, we cannot say that the district court clearly erred in including Canada in the geographic scope of the competitor non-compete covenant. * * *

Gordon also argues that because he had a good-faith reasonable belief that his work for Highland in Canada did not violate the Agreement, the district court should not have relied on his breach of the competitor non-compete covenant in granting the injunction and tolling the six-month restrictive period. * * * [W]e are not persuaded that, in a case governed by Florida law, injunctive relief [would be refused] if an employee reasonably believed that his conduct did not violate the restrictive covenants at issue. * * * [Florida law] states that "[t]he violation of an enforceable restrictive covenant creates a presumption of irreparable injury to the person seeking enforcement of a restrictive covenant." Nothing in the statute suggests that intentional breach is a precondition to relief, and no Florida state court decisions under this statute have required plaintiffs to prove intentional breach in order to benefit from the statutory presumption of irreparable injury. * * * Even assuming that intent would, in some circumstances, be relevant under Florida law and that Gordon's belief was reasonable, we fail to see why such a belief should have prevented the district court from using Gordon's breach as a basis to toll the six-month restrictive period and to enjoin prospectively Gordon from working for Highland. The fact that Gordon may have reasonably erred in determining the scope of the competitor non-compete covenant does not grant him a license to work for a competitor in violation of the Agreement.

The district court's damages award is overturned because there was no showing that Gordon's breach caused the claimed damage. The $ 1,659,000 damages award against Gordon was based on Gordon's contact with Bombardier in February 2007, which led to Highland obtaining the "Bombardier Logistics" project. * * *

During the first half of 2006, Proudfoot was first introduced to, and began its sales process with, Bombardier. * * * Proudfoot submitted a proposal or bid to Bombardier in late May or early June 2006 while Gordon was still employed by Proudfoot. After its proposal was accepted, Proudfoot conducted a business review for Bombardier starting in mid-June 2006. After the business review ended, Bombardier hired Proudfoot to conduct a productivity-related project for Bombardier that included work focusing on lead times, productivity gains and procurement. * * * Gordon did not work on Proudfoot's project for Bombardier.

While at Highland, Gordon worked on two projects for Bombardier in Canada. In September 2006, Gordon was assigned to a project for Bombardier called "Bombardier Interiors," which had begun prior to Gordon joining Highland. In February 2007, Gordon was personally involved in the "design and discovery" phase of a second project for Bombardier called "Bombardier Logistics." During the "design and discovery" phase, Highland would do an initial analysis for a client in the hopes of convincing the client to hire Highland for an implementation project. Gordon attended all the formally scheduled meetings with Bombardier and all of the meetings where Highland made presentations to Bombardier about the proposed project. At these meetings, Gordon explained the benefits of the proposed project to Bombardier. Bombardier elected to hire Highland for the proposed project, which ultimately generated $ 2,600,000 in revenue for Highland. * * *

Proudfoot may seek damages for any breaches of the enforceable restrictive covenants in the Agreement, but "[a]n award of damages for breach of contract is intended to place the injured party in the position he or she would have been in had the breach not occurred." As one court has explained:

To recover damages for lost profits in a breach of contract action, a party must prove a breach of contract, that the party actually sustained a loss as a proximate result of that breach, that the loss was or should have been within the reasonable contemplation of the parties, and that the loss alleged was not remote, contingent, or conjectural and the damages were reasonably certain.

Thus, Proudfoot bears the burden to prove both that it sustained a loss and that "its lost profits were a direct result of" Gordon's breaches of the client non-compete covenant and non-solicitation clause.

* * * One of the reasons why injunctions are a favored remedy for breaches of restrictive covenants is that it is "inherently difficult" to determine "what damage actually is caused by the employee's breach of [of a restrictive covenant]." The district court erred, as a matter of law, in awarding Proudfoot damages for Gordon's solicitation of Bombardier because the district court never found that absent Gordon's breach, Proudfoot would have obtained the Bombardier Logistics project. Moreover, even if the district court had made such a finding, neither the underlying facts found by the district court nor any evidence in the record could support such a conclusion. The fact that Highland's "profits are inextricably linked to Gordon's breach of the Restrictive Covenants" is irrelevant absent a finding that Gordon's solicitation of Bombardier caused Proudfoot to lose business. Damages for breach of a noncompete are intended to make the prior employer whole, not to punish employees. * * *

Although Gordon has failed to establish that the injunction was inappropriate, we reverse the damages award. Proudfoot did not establish that it would have obtained the Bombardier Logistics project were it not for Gordon's breach; accordingly, Proudfoot has failed to establish that it suffered any financial loss.

CASE QUESTIONS

1. What were the legal issues in this case? What did the court decide?
2. What did the restrictive covenants that were at the center of this case say? What is the significance of the "tolling" provision incorporated into the agreement?
3. Why were these restrictive covenants enforceable against the former employee?
4. Why did the appeals court reject the lower court's ruling regarding damages? How should damages be decided in a case like this?
5. How well did either party handle this situation? How might the situation have been handled differently by both parties?

employees, some additional benefit beyond continuation of employment is likely needed.[71] Courts regularly state that noncompetition agreements are disfavored as restraints on trade, and they will be enforced only if former employers can bear the burden of showing that the restraint is no greater than necessary to protect legitimate business interests. The employer's need for the agreement is balanced against its detrimental

---

[71]*Powerhouse Productions v. Scott*, 260 S.W.3d 693 (Tex. Ct. App. 2008).

Practical Considerations Should employers use noncompetition agreements or other restrictive covenants? If so, under what circumstances? What should an employer do if someone that the employer wants to hire is a party to a restrictive covenant with a previous employer?

effect on the former employee's ability to earn a living and its effect on the public.[72] Valid employer interests in this context include the protection of trade secrets and other confidential information, protection of customer relationships, and possibly protection of employers' investments in training employees. The simple desire to be shielded from business competition is not sufficient to justify a restrictive covenant. Agreements are more likely to be deemed overly broad and not enforceable the longer they remain in effect, the wider the geographic area to which they apply, and the more numerous the activities that are restricted. Noncompetition agreements are enforceable only if the firms that former employees join are genuine competitors. A court refused to enforce a restrictive covenant when a former executive of May Department Stores took an executive position with Victoria's Secret Stores.[73] The different target markets, mix of products, and marketing strategies of the two companies demonstrated that they were not truly competitors even though both sold intimate apparel.

Employers whose former employees take actions deemed to violate restrictive covenants frequently seek court orders to stop the former employees from competing against them. One of the criteria for issuing an injunction is that there will be "irreparable harm" to the former employer if the former employee's work with a competitor does not cease immediately. If employers are not vigilant in policing violations of these agreements and wait too long before taking legal action, injunctive relief may be denied. For example, in a case where the employer had laid off the employee and then waited several months after learning of his competing activities before seeking an injunction, a court refused to find that there was the type of irreparable harm that would justify granting an injunction.[74] Noncompetition agreements also present interesting questions for the new (or prospective) employers. It is not uncommon for an employer that wants to hire an employee bound by a noncompete to negotiate a settlement with the former employer. As one employment lawyer has put it, "Noncompetition agreements are really an invitation to bargain between two employers about what is important."[75] The new employer might also file a court action seeking a declaratory judgment stating that the former employee is, in fact, not violating any enforceable contract. New employers sometimes find themselves in the awkward position of attacking agreements that new employees had entered into with their former employers, while at the same time wanting to execute their own noncompetition agreements with the new employees and not send the message to their other employees that these agreements would be readily voided if they jumped ship.[76] Thus, *employers should use noncompetition agreements only if important business interests are at stake. These agreements should be crafted to be no broader than necessary to protect those important business interests. Employers with these agreements need to be vigilant in enforcing them. Both former and new employers have a variety of options and will generally find it advantageous to negotiate.*

Nonsolicitation agreements are another variety of restrictive covenant. They sometimes are packaged with noncompetition agreements and other times appear as stand-alone agreements. Some courts give employers more leeway in using nonsolicitation agreements because they impose a less total restriction on the former employee's actions

---

[72]*Modern Environments v. Stinnett*, 561 S.E. 2d 694, 695 (Va. 2002).

[73]*Victoria's Secret Stores v. May Department Stores*, 157 S.W.3d 256 (Mo. Ct. App. 2004).

[74]*Static Control Components v. Future Graphics*, 2007 U.S. Dist. LEXIS 36474 (M.D.N.C.).

[75]Michael R. Triplett. "Challenging Noncompetition Pacts Creates Special Burdens for Old, New Employers." *Daily Labor Report* 53 (March 20, 2006), C-2.

[76]Triplett.

and ability to earn a living.[77] Nonsolicitation agreements restrict former employees from approaching their former employers' customers, clients, or employees. These agreements are more likely to be upheld where the client relationship is long-standing, the former employee's knowledge of the client rests solely on her work with the former employer, and—again—the restrictions are not overly broad. The Idaho Supreme Court refused to enforce a nonsolicitation agreement against an engineer who changed firms because the agreement barred him from "providing any services to [his former employer's] clients, current, past and potential, without regard to whether [the employee] had any contact with these clients."[78] California law enforces agreements preventing former employees from soliciting clients of a former employer only if doing so is necessary to protect trade secrets. A pension fund investment consulting firm was unsuccessful in obtaining a court order stopping former employees from soliciting clients to take their business to a new firm started by the former employees. The consulting firm argued that knowledge of the particular investment strategies of clients was a type of trade secret, but the court concluded:

> [I]t is not unusual for clients to follow consultants when they switch firms.... These kinds of relationships, rather than any special knowledge of the client's investment information or strategy, are the key to competition. But under California law, these kind of personal and professional relationships, developed over time, are not considered a "trade secret" the exploitation of which would prevent an employee from soliciting a former employer's clients.[79]

However, the court did order the former employees to refrain from using or recreating the former employer's custom-designed computer programs, which were trade secrets; disparaging the former employer; and soliciting their former coworkers to quit and come to work with them.

JUST THE FACTS

A publishing company prints and distributes a magazine called *Local Life* in Johnson County, Texas. On May 1, 2008, the company hired William Cobb to sell advertising for *Local Life* as an independent contractor. The parties signed a "Contractor Agreement" containing a noncompete clause in which Cobb promised that, upon termination of his contractual engagement with Caye Publishing, he would not work for a competing third party or start another publication for a term of one year. Cobb resigned on September 23, 2009. In early November 2009, he published and distributed a magazine titled *Who What Where* in the cities of Aledo and Weatherford, which are located in nearby Parker County. Caye Publishing then sued Cobb for breach of contract, misappropriation of trade secrets, and tortious interference with contract. Should the court grant an injunction preventing Cobb from starting a new publication or publishing his existing magazine? Why or why not?

See, *Cobb v. Caye Publishing Group,* 322 S.W.3d 780 (Tex. App. 2010).

---

[77]*Freiburger v. J-U-B Engineers*, 111 P. 3d 100, 105 (Idaho 2005) (noting that some courts use different standards, but choosing to apply the same "no more restrictive than necessary" standard to all types of restrictive covenants).

[78]*Freiburger*, at 106.

[79]*Rogerscasey, Inc. v. Nankof*, 2002 U.S. Dist. LEXIS 7165 (S.D.N.Y.), at 5–6, *affirmed*, 50 Fed. Appx. 461 (2d Cir. 2002).

Noncompetition agreements often specifically refer to trade secrets and confidential information, but even in the absence of such agreements, courts have traditionally recognized a duty of employees under common law not to divulge such information. **Trade secret** refers to information (including formulas, programs, devices, methods, and processes) that has actual or potential economic value because it is not generally known to others, and the owner makes reasonable efforts to keep this information secret.[80] The definition of trade secrets used in most states is expansive and not limited to inventions or purely technical matters. Lists of customers can be trade secrets, but the lists cannot be readily compiled through other means, and employers must exert efforts to maintain their secrecy. In a case involving a pension analyst who memorized information about clients before going out and starting his own competing firm, the court ruled that trade secrets include information that is memorized; they are not limited to information recorded and stored on paper, in computer files, or on any other particular medium.[81] An employer will not be able to successfully justify restraints on former employees to protect trade secrets when the employer has not previously taken sufficient steps to maintain the secrecy of the information.[82] *Employers that want to ensure that trade secrets and other confidential information will not be divulged or used by former employees must make reasonable efforts to preserve the confidentiality of that information.*

A Concluding Thought

Terminated employees will commence the search for new work, and their former employers will seek to fill at least some of the vacated positions. This discussion brings us full circle in our tour of legal issues in employment. You should now have a better idea of how to meet both the spirit and the letter of the law—and to keep your employer's name out of any future editions of this book.

Key Terms

downsizing, p. 679
privatization, p. 683
Worker Adjustment and Retraining
   Notification (WARN) Act, p. 684
affected employees, p. 684
employment loss, p. 684
plant closing, p. 685

mass layoff, p. 685
reduction in force (RIF), p. 690
early retirement incentives, p. 700
serious consideration, p. 701
unemployment insurance, p. 703
involuntary unemployment, p. 703
base period, p. 705

availability for work, p. 705
suitable employment, p. 705
restrictive covenants, p. 706
noncompetition agreement, p. 707
nonsolicitation agreement, p. 713
trade secret, p. 715

Chapter Summary

Employers are generally free to go out of business, close facilities, eliminate positions, and reduce the number of people they employ. The primary legal constraint on downsizing decisions is the National Labor Relations Act (NLRA). Employers violate the NLRA when they close facilities or parts of their business if the decision is motivated by a desire to discourage unionization at the employer's remaining facilities and it is reasonably foreseen that the closing would have that effect. Likewise, the relocation of work from one facility to another in an attempt to defeat unionization also violates the NLRA. Many downsizing decisions are

---

[80]*Rogerscasey*, at 4 (citing California law, which incorporates, as have most states, the Uniform Trade Secrets Act).

[81]*Al Minor & Associates v. Martin*, 117 Ohio St. 3d 58 (2008).

[82]*Omega Optical v. Chroma Technology Corp.*, 800 A. 2d 1064 (Vt. 2002).

mandatory topics of bargaining that unionized employers must bargain over in good faith before implementing. Unionized employers are also required to bargain over the effects of such decisions on employees.

The Worker Adjustment and Retraining Notification (WARN) Act prohibits large employers from ordering plant closings and mass layoffs until the end of a sixty-day period following the provision of written notice to affected employees or their union representatives. Employees are affected if they are reasonably expected to suffer employment loss stemming from a plant closing or mass layoff. *Employment loss, plant closing,* and *mass layoff* all have specific definitions under the WARN Act. Less than full notification can be provided when a plant closing or mass layoff is due to a natural disaster, when efforts to obtain a capital infusion or new business would be compromised by notification, or when business circumstances are not readily foreseen. Employees whose rights under the WARN Act are violated are entitled to back pay and benefits for the period of time they were deprived of timely notice, up to a maximum of sixty days.

Antidiscrimination laws prohibit employers from selecting individuals for termination based on their protected class characteristics. Age discrimination is commonly alleged in downsizing or reduction-in-force (RIF) cases. In a true RIF, terminated employees are not replaced. However, allocation of an employee's responsibilities to existing employees who perform the duties in addition to their own duties is not replacement. Terminations in the course of downsizing are analyzed differently, and a somewhat heavier burden is placed on plaintiffs in establishing a prima facie case than with other discriminatory discharges. Early retirement offers can be used to reduce employment levels. However,

any waivers of ADEA rights associated with acceptance of these offers must meet the requirements of the Older Workers Benefit Protection Act. Under the Employee Retirement Income Security Act (ERISA), employers have a fiduciary duty to inform employees about upcoming early retirement offers when those plans are under serious consideration.

The Federal Unemployment Tax Act (FUTA) and state unemployment insurance laws combine to govern the provision of unemployment benefits to persons who are involuntarily unemployed, able to work, available for work, and actively seeking suitable employment. Employees who quit their jobs or are fired for serious misconduct generally are not eligible for unemployment insurance. Individuals must demonstrate attachment to the workforce both before and after applying for benefits. Minimum earnings and work duration requirements during a base period prior to applying for benefits must be met to be eligible for benefits. To remain eligible, individuals must be willing to seek and accept suitable employment. Benefits can be received for up to twenty-six weeks, and this period is sometimes extended when unemployment is high.

Knowledge, customer relationships, and other key sources of competitive advantage reside within employees and can leave with them when they depart to take other employment or to pursue business opportunities. Noncompetition agreements are increasingly being used to address this reality, but such agreements are not always enforced. The key issue is whether the agreements are viewed as overly broad and restrictive. Even without any explicit agreements, common law aids employers that want to protect trade secrets and other confidential information from being divulged or otherwise misappropriated by former employees.

Practical Advice Summary

- Employers must not selectively close facilities for the purpose of inhibiting unionization at other sites or relocate work based on antiunion motives.
- Before implementing many downsizing decisions, unionized employers must
  - Bargain in good faith over the decisions themselves (particularly subcontracting, outsourcing, and other decisions that involve the relocation rather than elimination of work).

  - Bargain in good faith over the effects of downsizing on represented employees including consideration of severance pay and transfer rights.
- Successor employers must bargain with unions that represent employees at acquired companies, although they are generally not bound by the terms of existing labor agreements.
- Large employers must not order plant closings or mass layoffs.

— Until written notice is provided to union representatives (individual employees in non-union workplaces) and certain government officials.

— For at least sixty days thereafter.

- Employers must not select employees for downsizing based on their protected class characteristics, including age.
- Employers terminating employees in the context of downsizing or a reduction in force should
   — Have clear, objective criteria for deciding whom to downsize.
   — Have these criteria in place before downsizing decisions are made.
   — Apply downsizing selection criteria in a consistent manner.
   — Not base downsizing decisions on stereotypical beliefs about older workers (e.g., unable to change).
   — Not include code words suggesting bias against older workers in communications about the reasons individuals were selected for downsizing.
   — Review selection procedures and decisions if a disproportionate (relative to the age composition of the pre-RIF workforce) percentage of people selected for downsizing are employees over 40 years of age.
   — Not hire additional younger employees or substantially change the duties of existing employees to absorb the duties of terminated employees.
   — Whenever possible, offer employees faced with downsizing the opportunity to transfer or otherwise retain their employment.
- With very few exceptions, employers cannot require that employees retire upon reaching some specified age.
- Employers can establish a minimum age and other criteria to define eligibility for early retirement offers, but cannot make such offers available to younger employees while excluding older ones.
- To be valid, waivers of ADEA rights by employees accepting group early retirement offers must meet the general conditions for ADEA waivers. Additionally, employees must be given
   — At least forty-five days to consider the offer.
   — Information in writing regarding the group of employees covered by the program.

— Eligibility factors and time limits for decisions.

— The job titles and ages of all employees eligible or selected for the program.

— The job titles and ages of employees in the same group who are not eligible or selected for the program.

- Employees must be informed regarding the status of early retirement offers that have not yet been finalized but are under "serious consideration," which occurs when
   — There is a concrete proposal under consideration.
   — Implementation of the proposal is being discussed.
   — High-level managers are involved in reviewing and approving the proposal.
- After filing for bankruptcy, unionized employers
   — Cannot unilaterally alter or ignore the terms of labor agreements.
   — Must bargain over any changes to existing labor agreements.
   — Must receive bankruptcy court approval before instituting changes in terms and conditions of employment if negotiations fail to produce agreement.
- Employers should not routinely contest unemployment insurance claims. Solid grounds for contesting claims (or continuation of benefits) include evidence that the former employee
   — Voluntarily quit.
   — Was discharged for serious misconduct.
   — Is receiving other payments.
   — Has committed fraud.
- Employers should examine the accuracy of statements provided by former employees to state unemployment insurance agencies explaining the circumstances of their job loss.
- Noncompetition agreements should be
   — Used only if important business interests are at stake.
   — Crafted to be no broader than necessary to protect those interests.
   — Signed before employment begins or with additional consideration provided.
- Employers that want to ensure that trade secrets and other confidential information will not be divulged or used by former employees must make reasonable efforts to preserve the confidentiality of that information.

Chapter Questions

1. A wholesale grocery warehouse and distributor terminated two hundred employees in a mass layoff. The company had been experiencing financial problems for many months. Its largest customer was United Supermarkets, which accounted for about forty percent of its orders and which had been a customer for more than thirty years. On January 8, 2004, United notified the wholesaler that it would be placing more orders with alternative suppliers due to a problem that the wholesaler was having in filling United's orders in a timely fashion, but that it hoped to continue to do business with the wholesaler. On January 15, 2004, United informed that wholesaler that it would no longer be United's primary supplier. Discussions with the wholesaler's bank and business consultants on January 20, 2004 led to a decision to lay employees off. Employees received notice in their January 22, 2004 paychecks. The terminations occurred days later. Did the employer violate the WARN Act? Why or why not? (*Gross v. Hale-Halsell Co.*, 554 F.3d 870 (10th Cir. 2009))

2. Nine employees were part of a mass layoff that included all of a lumber plant's 130 unionized employees. The layoff began on September 26, 2006. In October 2006, the nine employees were briefly called back to work. They worked for less than a week and then were laid off again on October 17, 2006. The employees were eventually recalled to work on April 16, 2007. Would these nine employees be "affected employees" entitled to WARN Act remedies? Why or why not? (*United Steel, Paper & Forestry, Rubber, Manufacturing, Energy, Allied Industrial and Service Workers International Union v. Ainsworth Engineered (USA)*, 2008 U.S. Dist. LEXIS 91541 (D. Minn.))

3. A salesperson in his fifties had a profitable account taken away from him and turned over to a 33-year-old salesperson. The supervisor who made this decision told the employee that he was "too old" to work on the account because most of the buyers were young people who liked to mountain bike. At sales meetings, the supervisor referred to the employee as "the old man" and asked other attendees whether "the old guy" could make it up the stairs. The company ran into financial problems and terminated

sixty-seven employees over a two-year period. Another twenty-four employees who voluntarily left during this period were not replaced. The company never had any formal plan for the execution of a RIF. The salesperson was terminated during this two-year period at age 57. He was given no reason for his termination, although the company now says that it was part of the RIF. The salesperson was told by another employee that the employee had heard his supervisor tell another manager that he needed to "set up a younger sales force." The salesperson sued. What should the court decide? Why? (*Blair v. Henry Filters*, 505 F.3d 517 (6th Cir. 2007))

4. A 59-year-old employee was terminated after thirty-five years on the job. The company cited financial problems as the reason for the termination. Two other sales employees, a 57-year-old and a 48-year-old, were also terminated. The 59-year-old's duties were absorbed by a 41-year-old existing employee. For several months prior to his termination, the 59-year-old was repeatedly asked about his retirement plans by company managers. The 59-year-old sued for age discrimination. What should the court decide? Why? (*Goodpaster v. Materials Handling Equipment Corp.*, 2010 U.S. Dist. LEXIS 114474 (N.D. Ind.))

5. Wachovia Securities announced in October 2008 that it was being purchased by Wells Fargo. Brokers were told that those who remained with the company after the sale would receive a "meaningful" retention bonus to be paid in January 2009. Although no precise figure was mentioned, brokers who remained with the firm assumed that Wachovia would follow industry practice and base the retention bonuses on the previous year's commissions. If so, the bonuses would be in six-figures. Some of Wachovia's brokers subsequently declined job offers with competitors. In January 2009, Wachovia announced that the bonuses would be delayed. In February 2009, they announced that the bonuses would not be paid at all. A number of the brokers sued. What should the court decide? Why? (*Uphoff v. Wachovia Securities LLC*, 2009 U.S. Dist. LEXIS 116679 (S.D. Fla.).

6. A company wanted to reduce the size of its workforce through an early retirement offer. From past experience, the company realized that

employees were reluctant to accept such offers because they assumed that a more generous offer would be forthcoming in the future. The company addressed this matter in the Summary Plan Description (SPD) that it issued to employees for its early retirement program. The SPD stated that if any future early retirement plans were offered, "the benefits would not be as good as those contained in this plan." Four years later the company adopted another early retirement plan that had more generous benefits than the previous plan. A group of employees who left under the earlier plan sued. What should the court decide? Why? (*McCall v. Burlington Northern/Santa Fe Co.*, 237 F.3d 506 (5th Cir. 2000), *cert. denied*, 122 S. Ct. 57 (2001))

7. A 55-year-old vice president learned that his business unit was being eliminated. The company gave him and other employees the option of accepting an "enhanced" severance package. However, to obtain the more generous severance pay, the vice president had to sign a release waiving legal claims stemming from his employment or the termination of his employment. The vice president continued working in a temporary capacity for almost a year after he signed the separation agreement and waiver of legal claims. Although statements were made to the effect that the company would try to find another permanent position for him, nothing materialized and the vice president ceased to do any work for the company. The former vice president sued, alleging age discrimination in the company's failure to rehire him for a permanent position. The company maintains that he waived his right to take legal action by having signed the separation agreement and waiver. Is the waiver of legal claims valid in this case? Why or why not? (*Kellogg Co. v. Sabhlok*, 471 F.3d 629 (6th Cir. 2006))

8. An employee was hired to drive a car used to transport patients to and from hospitals and nursing homes. In his first three and a half months on the job, the employee had four accidents with the employer's vehicle. Each of the accidents involved striking stationary objects, and none occurred while patients were being transported or caused serious damage. The employee was fired after the fourth accident, and the state agency denied unemployment insurance. What should the court decide? Why? (*Pesce v. Board of Review*, 515 N.E.2d 849 (Ill. App. 1987))

9. An employee of a financial information services company located in New York performed her work by "telecommuting" from Florida. The employee had a home office in her residence, was provided with a second telephone line and computer equipment by her employer, and was given access to the company's mainframe computer located in New York. The employee was required to be available during normal business hours, and she maintained daily contact with her supervisor in New York. At some point, the employer decided to end the telecommuting arrangement. The employee was offered employment at the New York office, which she declined. She initially filed for unemployment insurance in Florida. The employer contested this claim on the grounds that she had voluntarily left her job. Subsequently, she was informed that she might be eligible for unemployment insurance (with higher weekly payments) in New York. Her claim for benefits in New York was again contested by the employer, this time on the grounds that she had not been employed in New York. What should the court decide regarding her eligibility for unemployment benefits and from which state any benefits should come? Why? (*Allen v. Commissioner of Labor*, 794 N.E. 2d 18 (Ct. App. N.Y. 2003))

10. A senior executive for Estee Lauder, based in New York, had worldwide responsibility for one of its brands and North American responsibility for another. He resigned to take a position in California with a competitor of Estee Lauder. When the executive was originally hired, he had signed a noncompetition agreement. The agreement barred him from working for a competitor anywhere in the world for a twelve-month period after leaving employment. The executive sought to obtain an order from a California court finding that the agreement was not enforceable under California law. Estee Lauder maintained that the agreement was enforceable and that New York law applied. Which state's law is the relevant law in this case? Should the appropriate court enforce this agreement? Explain. (*Estee Lauder v. Batra*, 430 F. Supp.2d 158 (S.D.N.Y. 2006))

11. A mechanical engineer held the position of product manager for a company that manufactures home medical products, including wheelchairs and wheelchair controllers. In this capacity, she developed marketing strategies and

was privy to company financial and pricing data. When she was promoted to product manager, she signed confidentiality and noncompetition agreements. Under the terms of these agreements, she was required for three years following termination of her employment to keep confidential any information related to the medical products company's business and to refrain from working for a competitor anywhere in the United States. The noncompete included a reimbursement clause under which the company promised to pay the employee her existing salary if she was unable to find other work because of the restrictive covenant. The mechanical engineer left the company in July 2003 and subsequently formed a consulting company. Her company provided consulting services to another company that was in the final stages of developing and testing a new type of wheelchair controller. Was the engineer in violation of enforceable confidentiality and noncompetition agreements? Why or why not? (*Jacono v. Invacare*, 2006 Ohio 1596 (8th App. Dist.))

12. Business Designs, Inc. (BDI) uses "digital thermal resin transfer imaging" in its specialty of producing signs and decals advertising car washes for service stations. The founder of the company spent a number of months developing the product. As business grew, he hired two employees who assisted with all phases of the work. The two employees became dissatisfied and joined a former employer who was starting a new company. The employees had not been required by BDI to sign noncompetition agreements, and the company did not have a formal confidentiality policy. The new company used the same imaging process. Within a week, the company was able to ship full sign packages to numerous former customers of BDI. BDI sued the former employees. What should the court decide? Why? (*Business Designs, Inc. v. Midnational Graphics*, 2002 Iowa App. LEXIS 524)

13. What do you think about the increasing use of restrictive covenants? Should employers who attempt to enforce these agreements against employees who have been fired have to show that the terminations were for cause? Why or why not?

14. Is downsizing a sensible business strategy? Should employees be entitled to greater legal protection from downsizing? If so, what form should this protection take?

Glossary

A

Abatement period The amount of time that the employer has to correct the problems.

Abuse of discretion A standard used to determine if plan administrators abused their discretion by making decisions in an arbitrary and capricious manner.

ADA Amendments Act (ADAA) A law amending the definition of disability under the ADA.

Administrative employee An employee whose work is not directly related to production.

Adverse action The requirement that employers obtain the consent of employees or applicants before seeking to obtain credit reports and provisions for prior and concurrent notice when denying an employment opportunity.

Adverse employment action Harassment that does not directly alter a person's employment status, but makes it more difficult to perform well and stay on the job.

Adverse impact The disproportionate limitation or denial of employment opportunity for some protected class group that results from the use of a "neutral" requirement or practice that cannot be adequately justified.

Affected employees Employees who are reasonably expected to suffer employment loss stemming from a plant closing or mass layoff, including termination (other than a quit, discharge for cause, or retirement), a layoff lasting more than six months, or a greater than 50 percent reduction in work hours during each month of any six-month period.

Affirmative action Those actions appropriate to overcome the effects of past or present practices, policies, or other barriers to equal employment opportunity.

Affirmative defense A means by which employers can avoid vicarious liability by establishing that they exercised reasonable care to prevent and correct any harassment or a plaintiff unreasonably failed to take advantage of any preventive or corrective opportunities provided by the employer or to avoid harm otherwise.

After-acquired evidence Evidence showing that there is another consequence to employee falsifications and omissions during the hiring process.

Alternative dispute resolution Alternatives to going to court for resolving disputes.

Americans with Disabilities Act (ADA) A law that protects "qualified individuals" from discrimination "on the basis of disability."

Appeals court Circuit courts that accept the facts of cases as given and focus on whether the lower courts properly applied the law in deciding cases.

Appeals procedures A procedure for appealing adverse benefit determinations.

Applicant flow data Compares the protected class composition of an applicant pool to that of the group of people who pass the test and are successful (or at least till in the running) in obtaining an employment opportunity.

Applicant   Any person who indicates an interest in being considered for an employment opportunity.

Apprenticeship programs   Programs that typically combine classroom instruction with work under the guidance of experienced coworkers.

Appropriate bargaining unit   The group of employees for which representation is being sought.

Appropriation of a name or likeness   A type of privacy tort. It occurs when an individual's name or likeness is used by others without consent and for their own commercial or other ends.

Arbitration   An alternative dispute resolution (ADR) procedure in which a neutral third party (the arbitrator) functions more like a private judge. Arbitrators hear disputes and render decisions that are almost always final and binding on the parties.

Arising out of employment   Refers to the underlying causation of the injury or illness. These phrases are deceptively simple.

Arrest   The act of being "picked up" by the police and taken to the police station with the intent of being charged with crimes.

Assumption of risk   A traditional common law defense to negligence claims.

Authenticity   Also referred to as genuineness, it is one of the three general grounds for establishing BFOQs.

Authorization cards   The evidence that an election is warranted. They serve as the decisive indicators of employee preference.

B

Background check   Checks used to verify information provided by candidates and to determine whether any disqualifying factors exist.

Banding   A process where test scores are treated as estimates of tested-for characteristics (e.g., verbal ability, intelligence).

Base period   Period considered for establishing eligibility for unemployment insurance. This is done by examining the claimant's work history over a specified period of time prior to the job loss (usually the first four out of the five quarters preceding the claim for benefits).

"Because of sex"   Harassment where the victim is harassed in sex-specific and derogatory terms clearly motivated by general hostility to the presence of people of the same sex in the workplace; or in a mixed-sex or, in a mixed-sex workplace, disparate treatment of people based on their sex.

Binding past practice   Exists when a practice is clear, it has been consistently engaged in over a substantial period of time, and the practice existed with the knowledge and at least tacit consent of both the union and the employer.

Bona fide occupational qualification (BFOQ)

Breach of contract   A failure to live up to binding promises, regardless of intent.

Burden of proof   The plaintiff's obligation to show, generally by a "preponderance (the majority) of the evidence," that his rights were violated.

C

Card-check procedure   Entails obtaining the employer's agreement to recognize the union if a majority of employees sign authorization cards.

Cash-balance plans   Defined benefit pension plans that also include some features of defined contribution plans.

Certificate of creditable coverage   Documentation of prior coverage under a group health plan.

Chain of custody   The parties who handle the samples for drug testing.

Circumstantial evidence   Evidence that hints at the possibility of discrimination, but by itself is not sufficient to compel that conclusion.

Citations   Indicate the nature of the violations, the OSHA standard(s) violated, the monetary penalties associated with the violations, and the amount of time that the employer has to correct the problems (the abatement period).

Civil service laws   Laws which are intended to ensure that merit, and not political patronage, guides employment decisions. Besides specifying job classification, testing, hiring, and promotion procedures for public employment, civil service laws usually incorporate processes for review of disciplinary decisions.

Civil Service Reform Act (CSRA) The act that governs collective bargaining by federal government employees.

Class-action lawsuits Lawsuits where numerous plaintiffs join forces in claiming that their rights were violated in essentially the same manner by their employer.

Collective bargaining The institution which recognizes the value of employees banding together to deal with their employers and the fact that the desires of employees and employers sometimes clash.

Common law test A widely used method for determining employee status.

Common law The law that claims to remedy harm to people caused by other people or companies.

Comp time The practice of paying for overtime work with compensatory time off rather than overtime pay.

Comparative evidence Evidence hinting that the employer is shown to have treated the plaintiff worse than another employee under the same circumstances, with the only difference being that the other employee was of a different race or sex.

Comparator A person of the opposite sex who is in the same workplace and receives a higher rate of pay for performing the same type of work as the plaintiff.

Compelling governmental interest A very important public purpose.

Compensable factor The requirements of a job.

Compensable time Time spent in the principal work duties of an employee, during work hours or during time off and not punctuated with breaks, periods of waiting or downtime and other activities.

Compensatory damages Remedies awarded for a wide range of damages beyond loss of wages, including pain and suffering.

Complaint procedure A procedure identifying a set of actors to whom harassment complaints can be made.

Concerted activity Any effort by employees to join together for "mutual aid or protection."

Conciliation A settlement agreement.

Conditional offer of employment An offer of employment that is "conditional" upon satisfactory results from the medical exam.

Confirmatory tests More sophisticated tests used when initial screening tests come back positive.

Consent decree Affirmative action arising out of legal proceedings, imposed as a part of a judicially approved settlement between parties.

Consent Any request for a reference accompanied by a written "release of information" form that is signed by the former employee and that grants permission to communicate information about the employee.

Consolidated Omnibus Budget Reconciliation Act (COBRA) An act that requires that employers who have group health insurance plans and at least twenty employees offer continuation coverage to employees (and other beneficiaries if there is family coverage) who experience qualifying events that would otherwise cause the loss of their health insurance.

Constitution The most basic source of law addressing the relationships between different levels of government (e.g., states and the federal government) and between governments and their citizens.

Constructive discharge A resignation that occurs when an employee is presented with the stark option of resigning or being immediately terminated.

Consumer credit report Any written, oral, or other communication of any information by a consumer reporting agency bearing on a consumer's credit worthiness, credit standing, credit capacity, character, general reputation, personal characteristics, or mode of living which is expected to be used or collected in whole or part for the purpose of serving as a factor in establishing the consumer's eligibility for employment purposes.

Consumer reporting agency Any entity that regularly gathers or evaluates information on consumers to furnish reports to third parties.

Content validation A primary strategy for validating employment tests that require the performance of the same behaviors and skills as the job in question.

Contingent (nonstandard) work A term used to contrast full-time, year-round employment with a single employer that is expected to continue indefinitely, with looser (i.e., more flexible or less secure, depending on where you sit) relationships that exist only as long as some particular project or piece of work needs to be done.

Continuous leave   Leave taken all in one block with no work occurring between the beginning and end of leave.

Contributory negligence   A traditional common law defense to negligence claims.

Controls   Standards that will effectively make particular operations safer for employees.

Convictions   The stronger evidence of lack of fitness following either a trial or a guilty plea.

Cost-benefit analysis   Analysis in which the costs to employers of complying with a standard are compared to the economic value of the expected improvement in worker health.

Covenant of good faith and fair dealing   A type of wrongful discharge claim. It pertains to terminations that are undertaken in bad faith and that have the effect of denying employees the benefits of their contractual employment relationship.

Criterion validation   A primary strategy for validating employment tests that refers to a measure of job performance.

Cutoff score   A specified score below which scores are deemed as "failing" and disqualify candidates from further consideration.

D

Davis-Bacon Act   An act for construction contracts.

Decertification elections   Provision given by NLRA, in which employees decide whether they want to continue to have union representation.

Defamation   False statements that reflect badly on a person, communicated to others, which results in damage to the person's reputation.

Defined benefit plans   A plan that promises a specific pension benefit upon retirement.

Defined contribution plans   Plans in which employers establish and define what their own contributions, if any, will be but make no promises regarding the eventual payout to employees.

Direct evidence   Verbal or written statements that unequivocally express a discriminatory motive.

Direct threat   A current, specific risk to safety or health of an employee, coworkers, and customers, arising from the employee's disability, judged on the basis of objective medical evidence.

Disability   A physical or mental impairment that substantially limits the performance of one or more major life activities.

Disclaimers   Written statements incorporated into employee handbooks, employment applications, or other important documents that "disclaim" or deny that any statements in those documents create contractual rights binding on the employer.

Discrimination   The limitation or denial of employment opportunity based on or related to the protected class characteristics of persons.

Discriminatory effects   The focus in adverse impact cases where plaintiffs must show, usually through statistics, that some employment requirement or practice affects one protected class group more detrimentally than others.

Discriminatory intent   The key element of disparate treatment in which the decision maker based a decision, in whole or part, on a protected class characteristic of the affected employee.

Disparate treatment   The unequal treatment based on one or more protected class characteristics that results in the limitation or denial of employment opportunity.

District court   A trial court whose role is to establish the facts of the case and to reach a decision about the merits of the employee's claim.

Diversity   A concept asserting that human and cultural differences should be valued.

Dodd-Frank Wall Street Reform and Consumer Protection Act   An act enacted in 2010 in response to the banking crisis that led to the failure of numerous banks and investment firms, consolidation of others, and a controversial "bail-out" of large financial institutions. It tries to strengthen oversight of the financial industry and incorporates several different whistleblower provisions.

Domestic partner benefits   Benefits made available to employees' domestic partners.

"Don't ask, don't tell" policy   A policy stating that gay and lesbian service members be discreet and not talk about or openly engage in homosexual behavior and the military refrain from engaging in fishing expeditions to ferret out gays and lesbians in the ranks.

Downsizing A euphemism used to describe the involuntary termination of numerous employees who have done nothing to deserve that fate.

Drug testing Tests that require employees or job candidates to provide urine, blood, saliva, or hair samples that are sent to laboratories and tested for substances indicating use of illegal drugs.

Drug-Free Workplace Act (DFWA) A state law which requires that covered employers develop and communicate policies prohibiting drug use, possession, sale, or distribution in the workplace; inform employees about the dangers of drug abuse and options available for drug counseling and treatment; establish penalties for drug abuse violations; and report to the funding agency any convictions relating to drug use or sale in the workplace.

Due process *See* Just cause.

Duties test The examination of the nature of an individual's duties and responsibilities.

E

Early retirement incentives Offer given by employers to entice workers to leave their jobs sooner than they otherwise might have. The minimum age or service requirements might exclude younger employees from early retirement incentives.

Economic realities test An approach used by courts to distinguish between employees and independent contractors, particularly in Fair Labor Standards Act (wage and hour) cases.

Economic strikes Strikes undertaken to place pressure on an employer to offer more satisfactory terms and conditions of employment Undertaken to pressure employers to meet employee negotiation demands.

Effort The amount of physical and mental exertion required by a job.

Electronic Communications Privacy Act (ECPA) The act that has been used to challenge employer incursions on the privacy of electronic communications. Employers (and others) are prohibited from intentionally intercepting (through the use of electronic, mechanical, or other devices) wire, oral, or electronic communications and from disclosing such information. The intentional, unauthorized accessing and disclosure of stored electronic communications are also prohibited.

Employee Free Choice Act (EFCA) A requirement that employers recognize unions chosen through a card-check procedure.

Employee Polygraph Protection Act (EPPA) A law which states that private sector employers must not request or require that applicants submit to polygraphs or other mechanical or electrical truth-determining devices (including voice stress analyzers).

Employee Retirement Income Security Act (ERISA) The principal federal law regulating benefit plans.

Employee An individual employed by an employer.

Employer The party legally responsible for the actions of its employees.

Employment at will with exceptions A legal regime under which employees bear the burden of showing that their termination was for an "illegal cause" prohibited by law. But if they fail to do so, the default rule is employment at will; the termination is legal regardless of how dubious the reasons or circumstances.

Employment at will The doctrine which holds that in the absence of a contract promising employment for a specified duration, the employment relationship can be severed at any time and for any reason not specifically prohibited by law.

Employment loss An employment termination, other than a discharge for cause, voluntary departure, or retirement. It stems from a plant closing or mass layoff, including termination (other than a quit, discharge for cause, or retirement), a layoff lasting more than six months, or a greater than 50 percent reduction in work hours during each month of any six-month period.

Enforcement procedure A wide variety of procedures that exist for bringing and resolving claims related to violations of employment laws.

English-only rules A rule curtailing the use of other languages in the workplace.

Equal Pay Act (EPA) An act that is targeted specifically at pay discrimination based on sex.

Equitable tolling A doctrine stating that if employees are unaware of their rights because they were actively misled by their employer or the employer failed to meet its legal obligation to post information in the workplace, a court might excuse an untimely filing.

Ergonomics   Study that deals with the fit between the physical demands of jobs and the physical abilities of people.

Escalator principle   A principle stating that employers must attempt to place individuals returning from military service into the positions, including promotions, they likely would have attained absent the service.

Essential functions   Tasks that are central to why a job exists.

Establishment clause   A clause in the First Amendment prohibiting governmental entities from sponsoring or supporting religion.

Exclusive remedy   Workers' compensation for injuries and illnesses that arise out of and in the course of employment.

Exclusive representative. Status of the union   It means that unionized employers must generally refrain from dealing with individual employees regarding their wages, hours, terms, and conditions of employment.

Executive employee   An employee who manages other employees.

Executive Order 11246   A legal provision that requires companies with contracts worth at least $10,000 to have a nondiscrimination clause included in their and their subcontractor's contracts, and abide by its terms.

Executive order   Orders that affect the employment practices of government agencies and companies that have contracts to provide goods and services to the government.

Exempt employee   An employee for whom employers do not have to follow FLSA requirements.

Exercising legal rights   An instance in which public policy wrongful discharge claims are recognized. If employees are terminated for exercising legal rights they can approach court.

Experience rating   Ratings under which employers that have worse records of injuries and claims pay more, providing a financial incentive to invest in safety.

F

Facially discriminatory policy   Employers that base employment decisions, including hiring and promotion, on protected class characteristics, and argue that it is necessary to limit a particular type of employment to people with specific protected class characteristics.

Factor other than sex   Any factor other than sex that an employer in an Equal Pay Act case can use to justify the differential in pay.

Failure to reasonably accommodate   A major type of discrimination in which an employer discriminates when it fails to be flexible in meeting the needs of disabled employees and those whose religious beliefs and practices come into conflict with workplace requirements.

Fair Credit Reporting Act (FCRA)   The major federal law regulating the gathering, sharing, and use of information by employers and consumer reporting agencies.

Fair Labor Standards Act (FLSA)   The principal federal statute regulating wages and hours.

False Claims Act   An act which applies to individuals who come forth with information about a knowingly false or fraudulent claim made against the federal government. The law allows the Department of Justice to join in suits to recover the amounts lost through fraud or individuals to sue on behalf of the government.

False imprisonment   An unlawful restraint upon one's freedom of locomotion or the deprivation of liberty of another without [her] consent

Family and Medical Leave Act (FMLA)   The principal federal law governing the provision of leave to employees for parental and medical reasons.

Federal Labor Relations Authority (FLRA)   The authority that oversees collective bargaining by federal government employees.

Fellow servant rule   A traditional common law defense to negligence claims.

Felony   More serious crimes for which imprisonment of more than a year in a state or federal prison may be imposed.

Fiduciary duties   A number of important responsibilities held by the people or entities that control and manage benefit plans.

Fiduciary   Anyone who exercises discretionary authority or control over the administration of a benefit plan or its funds.

First Amendment A legal protection against wrongful discharge. Under first amendment substantive constitutional rights–freedom of religion, speech, association–can be invoked when a termination or other discipline is used to suppress those rights.

Fit Implies that the candidate has the knowledge, skills, abilities, and other characteristics (e.g., motivation) to perform a particular job well.

Forced distribution method A method which requires that predetermined percentages of employees be placed into particular performance categories.

Foreseeability The ability to anticipate harm before the fact.

Four-fifths rule An EEOC guideline stating how different test outcomes must be to conclude that discriminatory effects (or "disproportionate selection") are occurring.

Fourth Amendment An amendment of the U.S. Constitution protecting public employees against unreasonable searches or seizures.

Fraud A false representation of a material fact made to another person.

Free exercise clause A clause in the First Amendment protecting the "free exercise" of religion from infringement by the government.

G

General duty clause Clause in the OSH Act that places basic responsibility for workplace safety with employers and can be invoked for enforcement purposes in the absence of specific standards.

Genetic Information Nondiscrimination Act Laws that extend broad protection against discrimination on the basis of genetic information in both health insurance and employment to all employees covered by Title VII of the Civil Rights Act.

Genetic monitoring Monitoring genetic information for adverse health effects due to occupational exposures.

Genetic screening Genetic information that can identify individuals who have diseases that are not yet manifest, who are genetically disposed toward developing conditions in the future, or who are at greater risk of having children with inherited conditions.

Genetic tests Tests aimed at assessing the predisposition of persons to developing medical conditions or passing them on to offspring.

Glass ceilings Artificial barriers based on attitudinal or organizational bias that prevent qualified individuals from advancing in their organization into upper management positions.

Goal Objective or target reasonably attainable through a good faith effort.

Good faith bargaining The obligation to "confer in good faith with respect to wages, hours, and other terms and conditions of employment," the "mutual obligation of the employer and the representative of the employees to meet at reasonable times," and the "execution of a written contract incorporating any agreement reached."

Good faith effort A sincere effort.

Grandfathered Plans that existed prior to enactment of the PPACA and no significant changes resulting in reduced benefits or increased cost to plan beneficiaries were made to the plans.

Grievance arbitration Arbitration in which the arbitrator decides disputes regarding the interpretation and enforcement of an existing labor agreement.

H

H-1B dependent employer Employers who must certify that they have not and will not lay off any Americans in the same job category during the ninety days before and after filing a petition. They must also attempt to recruit U.S. workers and attest that the qualifications of H-1B hires are better than those of any American applicants.

H-1B visa Visas granted to persons in "specialty occupations" that require a bachelor's or higher degree in that field.

H-2 visa Visas granted for foreign nationals who come to the United States to perform work on a temporary or seasonal basis.

Harassment policy A legally adequate policy prohibiting harassment.

Harassment that results in tangible employment action A sexual advance or demand for sexual favors that can be "traded" for some employment outcome.

Harassment   A form of disparate treatment where the victim of harassment is subjected to inferior working conditions because of her sex, race, or other protected class characteristic.

Health Insurance Portability and Accountability Act (HIPAA)   An act that restricts but does not eliminate the use of preexisting condition exclusions by health plans.

Hierarchy of controls   Controls which run from measures that might eliminate a hazard entirely, to engineering controls that do not eliminate hazards but automatically provide protection from them, to administrative measures that limit the extent of exposure, to training and warnings that teach employees about how to protect themselves from hazards, to personal protective equipment that is worn by employees and provides the last line of defense between the hazard and the worker.

Honesty tests   Paper-and-pencil tests used by employers to determine the integrity of job candidates.

Hostile environment   An environment resulting from a wide range of verbal conduct, including insults, epithets, tasteless jokes, profanity, and requests for sexual favors; physical conduct, including touching, exposure, staring, stalking, sexual assault, and rape; and displays of images, including pictures, posters, e-mails, web sites, and pornography.

I

Identification of problem areas   The requirement that makes the self-analysis more dynamic by examining flows into and out of positions and the organization. It attempts to get at the question of why an employer's workforce looks the way it does.

Illegal alien   Non-citizens who are not eligible to work in the United States.

Immigration Reform and Control Act (IRCA)   The protection against discrimination that applies only to citizens and legal immigrants. It has two main requirements. First, all employers are prohibited from knowingly hiring or retaining on the job unauthorized aliens. Second, employers with four or more employees are prohibited from discriminating in hiring or termination decisions on the basis of national origin and citizenship.

Impasse   A bargain reached when negotiations over one or more mandatory topics have become deadlocked and both parties are warranted in assuming that further negotiation would be futile.

Implied contract   Written or oral statements by employers—and their entire course of conduct in dealing with employees—give rise to enforceable contractual rights. This is an implied contract. This includes the employer's informal policies, past practice, industry customs, and treatment of the individual employee.

In the course of employment   Refers to the time, place, and setting in which it occurs.

Independent contractor   A person doing work who is in business for herself and not dependent on a particular employer to engage in this line of work.

Inspections   Conducted to enforce standards. OSHA tries to determine whether employers are complying with the law through conducting inspections.

Integrated enterprise   Organizational entities presented as separate that might be deemed parts of a single.

Intentional infliction of emotional distress   A variety of common law tort claim that is often raised in conjunction with privacy claims. Plaintiffs must show: (i) intent to harm, (ii) behavior that is so outrageous, shocking, or atrocious as to be beyond the bounds of what is tolerable in a civilized society, and (iii) severe emotional harm or distress.

Intentional interference with a contractual relationship   A contract-related claim for which tort damages are available. Occurs when intentional, improper interference causes a third party to breach or not enter into a contractual relationship (the latter is sometimes referred to as "interference with prospective business advantage") with the plaintiff.

Interactive process   A process aimed at involving disabled employees in identifying an appropriate and mutually agreeable accommodation.

Intermittent leave   Periods of leave mixed with periods of work.

Internet applicant   An individual who expresses interest in employment via the Internet or other electronic data technology.

Intrusion upon seclusion   A type of privacy tort. It occurs when the solitude or private affairs of an individual are intentionally intruded upon and the nature of the intrusion is such that it would be highly offensive to a reasonable person.

Investigation   A warning, not by words but by action.

Investigative report Any written, oral or other communication similar to a consumer credit report but based on personal interviews with friends, neighbors, or other associates.

Involuntary unemployment Employees who are laid off or terminated based on business considerations during downsizings.

J

Job analysis A validation study in which the tasks of a job and the knowledge, skills, abilities, and other characteristics needed to perform the job are detailed.

Job evaluation A systematic process for rating jobs in terms of certain compensable factors.

Job group analysis A set of job groups combining individual job titles in a contractor's workforce.

Job-related and consistent with business necessity A reasonable factor used by an employer to justify discriminatory selection of people.

Joint employers Employers who share in the liability for violation of an employee's rights.

Jury System Improvements Act A law that protects persons who serve on federal juries from discharge, intimidation, or coercion by their employers.

Just cause Legal provisions under which employers bear the burden of proving that terminations were carried out properly and were based on good reasons. The default rule is that if an employer cannot adequately defend a challenged termination, that termination is wrongful and the employee is entitled to reinstatement, back wages, or other remedies.

K

Key employee Salaried employees who are among the top 10 percent of a company's employees (i.e., those within a seventy-five-mile radius of the employee's workplace) in pay.

Knowledge The fact that the employer was aware, or should have been if proper screening procedures had been followed, that the person hired was unfit.

L

L-1 visa A visa designed to allow multinational companies to temporarily transfer staff from foreign facilities or subsidiaries to operations in the United States.

Labor agreements Contracts specifying the wages and many other terms and conditions of employment for the employees they represent.

Labor organization Any organization or employee representation committee or plan, in which employees participate and which exists for the purpose, in whole or in part, of dealing with employers concerning grievances, labor disputes, wages, rates of pay, hours of employment, or conditions of work.

Labor trafficking The recruitment, harboring, transportation, provision, or obtaining of a person for the purpose of obtaining his or her labor or services, through the use of force, fraud, or coercion and that subjects the person to involuntary servitude, peonage, debt bondage, or slavery.

Labor unions Organizations of employees that represent employees in their dealings with employers.

Legal alien Non-citizens who are eligible to work in the United States.

Legal compliance strategy Knowledge of employment law that help recognize, analyze, and deal effectively with the many employment law issues that one is likely to encounter.

Liberty interest Exercised to maintain employee's good name. Employees who successfully assert a liberty interest are entitled to due process in the form of an opportunity to establish the falsity of the charges brought against them.

Lilly Ledbetter Fair Pay Act of 2009 An act which established that each discriminatorily low paycheck is a separate violation that starts the limitations period anew.

Limitations period The length of time that an aggrieved person has, to come forward with a complaint.

Liquidated damages Remedies awarded for serious, intentional violations in amounts up to twice the actual damages incurred.

Living wage Levels of hourly pay in excess of federal and state minimums.

Lockout An employer's choice to withhold from employees the opportunity to work despite their willingness to remain on the job and continue negotiating.

M

Major life activities   Activities that include caring for oneself, performing manual tasks, seeing, hearing, eating, sleeping, walking, standing, sitting, reaching, lifting, bending, speaking, breathing, learning, reading, concentrating, thinking, communicating, interacting with others, and working. Additionally, the term includes the operation of "major bodily functions."

Malice   An intent to harm a person's reputation.

Malicious prosecution   Prosecution that occurs when criminal proceedings are initiated against an innocent party, the party initiating criminal proceedings does so without probable cause, the criminal proceedings terminate in favor of the accused party, and the accusing party was motivated by malice.

Mandatory topics   Issues that, if raised by either party, must be negotiated over. Disagreement over a mandatory topic is a sufficient reason for failing to reach agreement in negotiations.

Mass layoff   A reduction in force that is not caused by a plant closing, but that results in employment loss at a single work site during any thirty-day period for at least 500 full-time employees (regardless of the percentage of total employees) or at least 50 full-time employees (when these comprise at least 33 percent of total employment at the work site).

Material Safety Data Sheet (MSDS)

Materially adverse action   A materially adverse harmful act which must be severe enough that it would likely have "dissuaded a reasonable worker from making or supporting a charge of discrimination.

Matter of public concern   Political or social matters that concern the larger community.

McNamara-O'Hara Service Contract Act   An act to do with contracts for many different types of services.

Mediation   An alternative dispute resolution (ADR) procedure in which a neutral third party (the mediator) facilitates negotiations between the disputing parties to help them reach an agreement but does not have the authority to decide the dispute or impose a settlement.

Mediators   Neutral third parties who, by entering negotiations and exerting control over the bargaining process, help unions and employers reach their own negotiated settlements.

Medical examination   Any procedure or test that seeks information about an individual's impairments or health.

Medical inquiry   Questions about disabilities, medical and psychological conditions, medical histories, medications taken, and workers' compensation claims filed.

Medical review officer   Individual who interprets the results and communicate them to the department.

Mental Health Parity and Addiction Equity Act   An act which requires that employers with fifty or more employees that choose to cover mental health and substance abuse treatment at all must do so at the same level and under the same terms as medical and surgical treatments.

Migrant and Seasonal Agricultural Worker Protection Act (MSPA)   An act that covers most seasonal agricultural employees and farmworkers with basic but important provisions.

Mine Safety and Health Act   Enacted in recognition of the particular hazards involved with mining. This law is enforced by the Mine Safety and Health Administration.

Minimum wage   The minimum wage required to be paid by the employers for each hour of work in a workweek. Under the FLSA, employers must pay employees at a rate no less than the minimum wage of $7.25/hr for each hour worked during a workweek.

Misdemeanors   Less serious criminal offenses for which fines and/or imprisonment of up to one year, usually in a county facility, may be imposed.

Mixed motives   The underlying premise that employment decisions are made both for discriminatory and lawful reasons.

Montana Wrongful Discharge from Employment Act (WDEA)   The act which effectively eliminated employment at will in Montana. It replaced a patchwork of common law wrongful discharge claims with a statutory framework that more clearly spelled out the rights of employees, but also limited the liability of employers for wrongful discharge and offered incentives to use alternative dispute-resolution procedures.

Musculoskeletal disorders (MSDs)   Repetitive stress injuries or cumulative trauma disorders.

N

Narrowly tailored   An affirmative action plan that causes minimum harm to the interests of nonpreferred persons while serving an important public purpose.

National Institute of Occupational Safety and Health (NIOSH)   The agency that provides scientific and technical advice to OSHA.

National Labor Relations Act (NLRA)   The principal federal law concerning self-organization and collective bargaining by private sector employees.

National Mediation Board (NMB)   The agency that administers RLA.

Negligence standard   A provision of law under which an employer is liable for the harassment of an employee by coworkers and third parties if it can be established that the employer knew or should have known about the harassment and failed to take prompt and appropriate action to stop the harassment.

Negligence   The legal concept based on the idea that people sometimes have a duty to other people to exercise reasonable care in carrying out certain activities.

Negligent hiring   Extends the liability of employers for harm caused by their employees beyond actions undertaken within the scope of employment (the subject of respondeat superior claims) to harmful actions that lie outside the scope of employment, but for which the careless hiring of an unfit employee set the stage.

Negligent misrepresentation   An intent to falsify or reckless disregard for the truth.

Negligent training   Training that occurs when there is a duty to others (in this case to provide adequate training), when that duty is breached (no training or clearly inadequate training is provided), when there is harm to one or more parties, and when breach of the duty to train is the proximate cause of harm.

Nepotism   Favoritism toward family members and other relatives.

Neutral message   The wording of want ads and other types of job announcements that do not express or imply a preference for some protected class group over another.

Neutral requirement   A practice that refers to anything other than protected class characteristics used as grounds for making employment decisions.

Neutrality agreements   Agreements in which employers pledge to remain neutral and not oppose unionization.

No solicitation agreement   A variety of restrictive covenant. They sometimes are packaged with noncompetition agreements and other times appear as standalone agreements.

Noncompetition agreement   Contracts that restrict the ability of former employees (or former owners or partners) to form or join businesses that compete with their former employers for specified periods of time following employment.

Nondiscrimination clause   A clause stating that no discrimination be allowed against any employee or applicant for employment in any form during the performance of the contract and suitable notices be provided by the contracting officer in conspicuous places, setting forth the provisions of this nondiscrimination clause.

Nonexempt employee   An employee entitled to the protections of the FLSA.

O

Occupational Safety and Health Act (OSH Act)   The principal federal law requiring private sector employers to keep their workplaces free from hazards that threaten the safety and health of employees.

Occupational Safety and Health Administration (OSHA)   The agency that has overall responsibility for administering and enforcing the OSH Act. OSHA establishes safety standards, conducts inspections of workplaces, and provides information to employers and employees about workplace safety and health issues. Occupational Safety and Health Review Commission (OSHRC). Independent from OSHA, it hears appeals of its enforcement actions.

Office of Federal Contract Compliance Programs (OFCCP)   An organization responsible for monitoring compliance with E.O. 11246 and other laws requiring affirmative action by contractors.

Older Workers Benefit Protection Act   An act permitting employers to provide less extensive coverage for older workers so long as the amount spent to provide benefits to older workers is at least equal to the amount spent providing those benefits to other workers.

Omnibus Transportation Employee Testing Act
The federal law that requires drug (and alcohol) testing of employees in transportation-related occupations, including airline, railroad, trucking, and public transport workers.

Opportunity wage   The permitted wage of $4.25/hr to employees under 20 years of age for their first ninety calendar days on the job.

Opposition   Resisting or speaking out against discrimination apart from participating in formal enforcement procedures.

Oppressive child labor   An FLSA requirement that minors (14–15 years of age) can be employed in certain service or retail occupations, subject to restrictions on their hours of work.

Ordinary course of business   The term that refers to uses that are routine, for legitimate business purposes, and about which employees are notified.

Organizational display   An organizational chart that depicts the organizational structure of a company, including the units within it and the relationship of each unit to other units in the organization.

Organizational profile   An organizational display or a workforce analysis portraying the staffing patterns in an organization.

Overly broad publication   The conveying of information about former employees to people other than those who have a legitimate need for that information.

Overtime   A pay at least one and one-half times an employee's regular rate of pay for each hour worked in excess of forty in a workweek.

P

Participation   Involvement in the enforcement of an antidiscrimination law, such as by filing a charge, bringing a lawsuit, giving testimony, and assisting in the investigation of a discrimination charge.

Partner   Individuals who personify the business and function as principals rather than agents.

Patient Protection and Affordable Care Act (PPACA)   A law intended to ensure that most Americans will have adequate health insurance coverage.

Pattern or practice (of discrimination)   A disparate treatment case where the plaintiffs marshal statistical data showing the systematic effects of an employer's discrimination and evidence of intentional discrimination against individuals in the larger affected group.

Pay docking rule   An approach of the DOL to determine whether employees are paid on a salary basis.

Pay secrecy policies   A policy that discourages employees from sharing information about their pay.

Payroll method   The method under which an employee is counted for each full week between when she is hired and when she leaves employment, regardless of the number of hours the employee worked during those weeks.

Pension Benefit Guaranty Corporation (PBGC)   A corporation that intervenes when the employer is unable to meet its obligations to retirees.

Pension plans   Plans designed to provide retirement income to employees or to otherwise defer income until after employment ends.

Pension Protection Act of 2006   An act having the key objective of placing defined benefit plans on firmer financial footing.

Performance appraisals   Appraisals that provide welcome recognition of accomplishments and needed feedback on how to improve performance.

Performance criteria   Criteria for evaluating employee performance that include work quality and quantity, attendance and punctuality, judgment, ability to work with others in a team, and leadership.

Performance improvement programs   Programs under which an employee is given outcomes that must be attained over some specified—usually short—period of time, with specified negative consequences ensuing if the desired performance is not forthcoming.

Performing a public duty   An instance in which public policy wrongful discharge claims are recognized. The duty in these cases is something that is not strictly required by law, but it is clearly an action undertaken in the public interest.

Period of incapacity   Period other than the actual period of hospitalization when a person is unable to work, attend school, or engage in other regular daily activities due to a serious health condition.

Permissible exposure limit (PEL)   The maximum allowable level of exposure to a hazard.

Permissive topics   All nonmandatory topics that are not illegal to incorporate into a labor agreement.

Physical/mental impairment   A physical or mental disability substantially limiting an individual in the performance of one or more major life activities.

Placement in a false light   A type of privacy tort. Occurs when characteristics, conduct, or beliefs are falsely attributed to an individual; this false information is broadly publicized; the person publicizing the information knew or should have known that it was false; and being placed in this false light would be highly offensive to a reasonable person.

Plaintiff   The employee who is suing.

Plant closing   A permanent or temporary shutdown of a single site of employment when that shutdown results in employment loss during any thirty-day period for at least fifty full-time employees.

Polygraph   A test that measures changes in physiological responses, including respiration, blood pressure, and perspiration (galvanic skin response).

Preemployment inquiry   Questions on application forms, during interviews, or in the course of informal chatting with job candidates divulging information about employees.

Preemption   Superseding.

Preexisting condition exclusion   An aspect of health insurance plans that denies coverage for a specified period of time for the treatment of conditions that existed before an individual enrolled in a health plan.

Preference   A discrimination or bias.

Pregnancy Discrimination Act (PDA)   A law which states that discrimination based on pregnancy, childbirth, or related medical conditions is sex discrimination and violates Title VII.

Presumption of prudence   A practice which companies that offer their own stock as an investment option when the documents of the defined contribution plan call for that will generally be deemed to have acted prudently, even if there are problems with the stock.

Pretext   The underlying premise that employment decisions are made either for discriminatory or lawful reasons.

Prevailing wage   The average wage paid to a class of employees in the relevant geographic area as determined by the DOL.

Prima facie case of failure to reasonably accommodate religion   A case where it can be shown that the employer was informed of a sincere religious belief or practice that conflicted with an employment requirement, and the employee or applicant has suffered an adverse employment outcome due to adhering to the religious belief or practice.

Prima facie case of pay discrimination   A case established when there is one or more persons of the opposite sex working in the same establishment who receives a higher rate of pay although performing work substantially equal to that performed by the plaintiff.

Privacy torts. Kinds of privacy invasions   Under common law, four different types of privacy torts are recognized in most states: intrusion upon seclusion, public disclosure of private facts, placement in a false light, and appropriation of a name or likeness.

Privacy   One of the three general grounds for establishing BFOQs that primarily relates to requirements for employees of a particular sex.

Private sector   The companies or enterprises where the employer is a corporation.

Privatization   The outsourcing of public services to private companies.

Professional employee   An employee whose duties are original and creative.

Progressive discipline   Entails making a genuine effort to correct undesirable behavior, not just going through the motions and creating a paper trail before terminating an employee.

Promissory estoppel   A contract related claim occasionally raised in discharge cases. Key elements of promissory estoppel are reasonable and detrimental reliance on a clear promise.

Property interest   The existence of employment policies, and express or implied contracts as defined by state laws.

Protected class   The characteristics of people, such as race, sex, and age, which are considered impermissible grounds for making employment decisions.

Proximity   The connection between events as they actually unfolded.

Public disclosure of private facts   A type of privacy tort. It occurs when private facts about a person that are of no legitimate concern to the public are broadly disclosed to others in a manner that would be highly offensive to a reasonable person.

Public policy exception to employment at will   Common law claims under which employers are liable in tort for wrongful discharge when they terminate employees for taking actions that public policy requires or commends.

Public safety   One of the three general grounds for establishing BFOQs which refer to protecting the safety of others.

Public sector   The companies or enterprises where the employer is a government agency.

Punitive damages   A remedy available in employment cases intended to punish the employer in cases of serious, intentional violations and to create an example to affect the behavior of others.

Q

Qualified privilege   An immunity from liability that is conditional rather than absolute.

Qualified   One having the skill, education, experience, and other job-related requirements for the job held or sought and able, with or without reasonable accommodation, to perform the essential functions of that job without posing a "direct threat" (that cannot be eliminated by reasonable accommodation) to one's own or others health and safety.

Qualifying event   Circumstances under which eligible employees are entitled to take FMLA leave.

R

Race norming   The prohibition that employers cannot establish separate minimum standards based on protected class or obscure the existence of different standards by altering scores (e.g., by creating separate percentile scores for whites and persons of color).

Railway Labor Act (RLA)   A federal labor law that governs collective bargaining in the highly unionized railroad and airline industries.

Random drug testing   A testing methodology in which a specified percentage of the workforce is selected for periodic drug testing without prior notice and absent individualized suspicion of drug use.

Rational relationship standard   A standard of constitutional scrutiny. Any state government action must bear a rational relationship to the legitimate state objectives and interest. Under the rational relationship standard, a court presumes that the classification is constitutional and the plaintiff bears the burden of demonstrating that the classification at issue bears no legitimate purpose.

Reasonable accommodation   The extra flexibility and support to which qualified individuals with disabilities are entitled.

Reasonable action   Identification of goals for improvement in the utilization of women and minorities and making of timetables for achieving these goals.

Reasonable basis   Basis for concluding that action is appropriate.

Reasonable expectation of privacy   A key concept in workplace privacy law. Although tied most directly to privacy claims based on the Constitution, this concept is also relevant to invasion of privacy claims brought on other grounds.

Reckless disregard for the truth   Displaying an intent to falsify.

Record of disability   A record of an erroneous diagnosis of disability.

Recruitment   One or more ways in which an employer communicates information about the availability of an employment opportunity and persons interested in pursuing the opportunity make their interest known to the employer.

Reduced leave schedule   A type of intermittent leave during which an employee's normal daily or weekly hours of work are reduced.

Reduction in force (RIF)   *See* Downsizing.

Refusal to commit an illegal act   An instance in which the public policy exception to employment at will is recognized. Under this employees can approach court if they are terminated for refusing to commit an illegal act.

Regarded as being disabled An actual or perceived physical or mental impairment whether or not the impairment substantially limits or is perceived to substantially limit, a major life activity.

Regular rate of pay The premium at which overtime hours of work must be compensated.

Regulation A principle, rule, or law created by administrative agencies, that are put in place only after an elaborate set of requirements for public comment and review has been followed.

Rehabilitation Act A law that covers federal government agencies and federal contractors.

Relevant labor market The protected class composition of people who are qualified for the type of work in question and reside within a reasonable recruitment area.

Religion A term defined as all aspects of religious observance and practice, as well as belief, unless an employer demonstrates that he is unable to reasonably accommodate to an employee's or prospective employee's religious observance or practice without undue hardship on the conduct of the employer's business.

Religious advocacy Employees conveying their religious beliefs to others in the workplace with the aim to interest coworkers or customers in a particular religion.

Religious harassment The unwelcome, pervasive religious communications of an employee that form a hostile environment for others.

Religious organization exemption An exemption that absolves churches of any liability for discriminating on the basis of religion.

Remedy Compensation that the employee is entitled to receive if the legal action against her employer is successful.

Representation elections Secret ballot elections held under the supervision of the NLRB and generally in the workplace during work time.

Respondeat superior The common law doctrine that makes employers directly liable for harm to others that occurs when employees act within the scope of their employment.

Responsibility Accountability for outcomes, supervisory duties, and involvement in important decisions.

Restoration To bring back to the same position held before leave commenced or to an equivalent position with the same pay, benefits, and other terms and conditions of employment.

Restrictive covenants An umbrella term that refers to a wide variety of contractual agreements that aim to protect employer interests by limiting the ability of former employees to do such things as going to work for competitors, disclosing trade secrets, or other sensitive information, soliciting clients or former coworkers to do business with or join other firms, and making disparaging comments about their former employers.

Retaliation One major type of discrimination that occurs when an employee who asserts her rights under the law is subjected to a materially adverse action for doing so.

Reverse discrimination Use of affirmative action by an employer where protected class characteristics are taken into account in making employment decisions that other employees find discriminatory.

Right to know The idea that employees have a right to receive information about the dangerous chemicals that they encounter on the job so that they can take steps to protect themselves.

Right to sue letter A letter issued to the employee alleging discrimination.

Right-of-control The hiring party has the authority to control where, when, and how the work gets done, even if that party chooses not to fully exercise its authority or to delegate certain decisions to the person doing the work.

Right-to-work laws Laws passed by the states making it illegal to incorporate union security provisions into labor agreements.

S

Safety standards Standards created by OSHA about which employers must become aware of and comply with all standards that apply to their operations.

Salary basis test Test to determine whether employees are genuinely paid on a salary basis.

Salary A pre-specified sum that an employee is paid for discharging the responsibilities associated with a position.

Same-sex harassment   Harassment where harassers choose to harass people of the same sex.

Sarbanes-Oxley Act (SOX Act)   An act intended to encourage the reporting of financial wrongdoing by protecting employees of publicly traded companies (as well as officers, contractors, subcontractors, and agents of such companies) who disclose information, assist in investigations, file charges, testify, or otherwise assist in proceedings related to fraud against shareholders of publicly traded companies. However, plaintiffs have established a track record of mostly futility in pressing Sarbanes-Oxley whistleblower claims.

Scope of employment   Actions performed by employees relating to the kind of work that they were hired to perform; taking place substantially within the workplace during work hours; and serving, at least partially, the interests of the employer.

Selection rate   The percentage of applicants who pass the test and are hired or continue to be considered for employment.

Self-analysis.   A reasonable basis for concluding that one's own action is appropriate, and reasonable.

Serious consideration   A situation when there is a concrete proposal under consideration, implementation of the proposal is being discussed and high-level managers are involved in reviewing and approving the proposal.

Serious health condition   A medical condition that involves inpatient care in a hospital (or similar medical facility) or continuing treatment by a health care provider.

"Severe or pervasive"   Pertains to the degree of harm posed by particular acts and the frequency and regularity of harassment.

Sex-plus.   Cases that most often involve differential requirements based on sex.

Sex-stereotyping   Differential appearance standards for men and women.

Similarly situated   Refers to how strictly comparable the situations of employees must be.

Skill   What one needs to know and be able to do to perform a job.

Social movement   An organized effort to create needed changes in workplaces and society.

Soft skills   Motivational, interpersonal, and communication skills.

Standards of performance

Stare decisis   The desire for consistency and stability in the law; a Latin phrase that means "let the decision stand."

Statute   The laws enacted by legislatures.

Strict scrutiny   The most stringent form of judicial review of government actions.

Strikes   The most highly publicized and dramatic manifestation of labor relations. Employees withhold their labor, refusing to resume work until their employer agrees to more favorable terms and conditions of employment or refrains from engaging in ULPs.

Subjective criteria   The standards and means of assessing candidates that are not uniform and clearly specified. They rely heavily on intuition and "gut" feelings, rather than systematic observation and measurement.

Subordinate bias theory   A recent Supreme Court ruling which underscores that employers should closely review employment decisions and recommendations made by lower-level managers.

Substantially limited   A term indicating that not all impairments will constitute disabilities and an impairment need not completely prevent or even "significantly restrict" the performance of a major life activity to be a disability.

Suitable employment   Work that does not endanger the health or safety of the employee, work for which the individual has the requisite training and experience, and work that is within a reasonable distance of the individual's residence or last place of employment.

Summary judgment   A judgment without a full trial where the court determines that even if the allegations of the plaintiff are accepted as true, they are not sufficient to support a legal claim.

Summary Plan Descriptions (SPDs)   Important documents that accurately inform employees about their rights and obligations.

Supervisors   Individuals who have the authority, in the interest of the employer, to make personnel decisions (e.g., hire, discharge, discipline, and promote), to responsibly direct other employees, to settle their grievances, or to effectively recommend such actions.

Sweatshop Firms that pay very low wages for long hours of work, provide unsafe conditions, and staunchly oppose unionization.

T

Temporary worker A variety of contingent worker.

Tenure Guarantee of job which is typically conferred following a relatively lengthy probationary period and a formal assessment of past and likely future performance.

The National Labor Relations Board (NLRB) The agency that administers the NLRA, including holding elections to determine whether employees desire union representation and determining whether unfair labor practices (ULPs) have been committed.

The Privacy Act The act that regulates the handling of personnel records by agencies of the federal government. The act defines record broadly to include "any item, collection, or grouping of information about an individual that is maintained by an agency."

Tipped employee Employees who customarily and regularly receive at least $30 per month in tips.

Tort The civil wrongs that harm people.

Trade secret The information (including formulas, programs, devices, methods, and processes) that has actual or potential economic value because it is not generally known to others, and the owner makes reasonable efforts to keep this information secret.

Training and development programs Programs that can make employees more productive and help them get ahead in their careers.

Training contracts Agreements entered into either prior to employment or before the receipt of some special training that require employees to either stay with the employer that provided training for a specified period of time following receipt of the training or be liable for repayment of training costs.

U

U.S. Supreme Court The highest court in the United States to which appeals court decisions can be appealed to.

Unconscionable A term used in contract law when the process of contract formation essentially involves a "take-it-or-leave-it" offer of an agreement drafted by a more powerful party (a "contract of adhesion") and when the contents of the agreement unreasonably favor the more powerful party.

Underutilization A lower percentage of women or persons of color in a particular job group than would be expected based on their availability.

Undue hardship Accommodations that are unduly costly, extensive, substantial, or disruptive or that would require fundamental alteration of the nature or operation of the business.

Unemployment insurance The insurance that intends to partially replace lost earnings during periods of unemployment for people who have demonstrated an attachment to the workforce.

Unfair labor practice strikes Strikes undertaken in response to employer ULPs (e.g., refusal to bargain in good faith) for the purpose of pressuring employers to comply with the law.

Unfair labor practices (ULPs) Certain actions of employers and unions prohibited by NLRA to protect employees' rights to self-organization and give collective bargaining a chance to work.

Uniformed Services Employment and Reemployment Rights Act (USERRA) An act detailing the extensive legal requirements surrounding military service.

Union security provisions Clauses that require all employees in a bargaining unit to pay union initiation fees and dues (or equivalent amounts) within a specified period of time (not less than thirty days after hire) under penalty of discharge by the employer.

Unwelcome Unsolicited, unprovoked, offensive, and unwanted harassing conduct faced by a person.

V

Validation study The evidence needed to establish the validity (and hence job-relatedness) of a scored employment test.

Validity Refers to whether the test actually measures what it purports to measure.

Vesting The acquiring of a nonforfeitable right to receive a pension by an employee covered under a pension plan, after a specified number of years of service.

Vicarious liability   Legal responsibility for damages for occurrence of harassment unconditionally placed with the employing organization, despite the organizations' best efforts at prevention.

Visa classification   The various classifications of permits that will permit foreign nationals to work in the country.

Visa   A document that will permit foreign nationals to work in the country.

Volunteer   An individual who performs hours of service for a public agency for civic, charitable, or humanitarian reasons, without promise, expectation or receipt of compensation for services rendered.

W

Welfare plans   Any benefit plans covered by ERISA that are not pension plans.

Whistleblower Protection Act (WPA)   An act which prohibits taking or failing to take a personnel action because an employee or applicant has disclosed information that is reasonably believed to show (1) a violation of a law, rule, or regulation or (2) gross mismanagement, gross waste of funds, abuse of authority, or a substantial and specific danger to public health or safety.

Whistleblowing   An instance in which public policy wrongful discharge claims are recognized. Whistleblowers report activities engaged in by employers or their agents that are illegal or otherwise injurious to the public.

White-collar exemption   Exemptions for executive, administrative, and professional employees.

Word-of-mouth recruiting   An essentially costless method of recruitment where employers depend on current employees to spread the word about jobs to their friends, family members, and other associates.

Worker Adjustment and Retraining Notification (WARN) Act   An act which prohibits employers from ordering plant closings or mass layoffs until the end of a sixty-day period that follows the provision of written notice to affected employees (or, if the employees are unionized, to union representatives) and to state and local government officials.

Workers' Compensation   The exclusive remedy for injuries and illnesses that arise out of and in the course of employment. Employees who are hurt on the job generally file workers' compensation claims and accept the meaningful, but comparatively limited, remedies.

Workforce analysis   A list of individual job titles for each department or other organizational unit in order of pay level.

Working conditions   "Hazards" (how dangerous the job is in terms of physical hazards) and "surroundings" (e.g., elements such as fumes, outside work in cold weather).

Workplace bullying   Repeated interpersonal mistreatment that is sufficiently severe as to harm a targeted person's health or economic status.

Workplace safety programs   Programs which help instill a safety culture in an organization, making safety a central concern that is closely monitored, discussed, rewarded, and continuously improved.

Workweek   The basic unit of time for determining compliance with the FLSA's minimum wage and overtime requirements.

Case Index

Note: Boldfaced cases and page references indicate decisions reported in the text.

Subject Index